THE
ISLAND OF FORMOSA
PAST AND PRESENT.

HISTORY, PEOPLE, RESOURCES, AND COMMERCIAL PROSPECTS.

TEA, CAMPHOR, SUGAR, GOLD, COAL, SULPHUR, ECONOMICAL
PLANTS, AND OTHER PRODUCTIONS.

BY

JAMES W. DAVIDSON, F.R.G.S.
CONSUL OF THE UNITED STATES FOR FORMOSA.

WITH TWO NEW MAPS, FRONTISPIECE IN COLOUR, ONE HUNDRED AND SIXTY-EIGHT
ILLUSTRATIONS FROM PHOTOGRAPHS, AND COLOURED REPRODUCTIONS
OF TWO CHINESE POSTERS.

MACMILLAN & Co.
LONDON AND NEW YORK.

———

KELLY & WALSH, Ld.
YOKOHAMA, SHANGHAI, HONGKONG, AND SINGAPORE.

———

1903.

"Japan Gazette" Press,
Yokohama.

NITAKAYAMA (MOUNT MORRISON) 13.880 FT.

THE HIGHEST PEAK IN THE EMPIRE OF JAPAN.

TO

THE MEMORY OF

MY FATHER.

ERRATA.

PREFACE.

A few words may not be out of place in explanation of the circumstances that brought me to Formosa and resulted in the preparation of this work.

On the return voyage from the Peary Arctic Expedition, I learned from a member of the Relief Party, of the outbreak of war between Japan and China, and, long before reaching American shores, I had decided to arrange, if possible, to visit the scene of hostilities. Soon after my arrival, I was fortunate in obtaining support from a newspaper syndicate, and in December, 1894, proceeded to Japan. March, 1895, found me in Formosa, watching the Chinese military preparations to oppose the then expected Japanese invasion.

To my surprise, I then learned that there was no book in the English language which dealt with the island in anything like an exhaustive manner. What works did exist, however valuable in their way, were more or less limited in scope, and none of them appeared to touch upon the resources, trade, or industrial affairs of the island. This, together with the exceptionally fortunate position in which I found myself, as war correspondent with the Japanese army, for doing justice to that very important epoch in Formosan history which includes the occupation of the island by the Japanese (1895) and the consequent termination of the Chinese regime, induced me to undertake the work. It will be seen that, throughout the book, I have consistently adopted the historic point of view in the treatment of all subjects, my opinion being that far more vivid ideas may be obtained of a land and its people by following the country through its trials and tribulations, its prosperity and success, than by merely describing it from a survey of present conditions.

Having decided to write the book, my first task was to collect as large a library of reference books, manuscripts, and papers as was procurable. The chief present-day works to which grateful recognition is due are :—

" *Missionary Success in Formosa*," an excellent work by that well-known authority, the Rev. William Campbell, F.R.G.S. This book deals with episodes relating to missionary work including that undertaken during the Dutch occupation.

" *The Japanese Expedition to Formosa* " (1874), a very complete and valuable treatise, kindly placed at my disposal by its author, the late Mr. E. H. House.

"*Journal of a Blockaded Resident in North Formosa,*" an interesting account of the French operations in the island in 1884, by Mr. John Dodd.

"*Geschichta der Insel Formosa,*" by Professor Reiss, perhaps the most scholarly essay yet published on the history of the island.

"*Ile Formose,*" a French work by the late M. C. Imbault-Huart, covering much historical ground.

"*Reports of the Imperial Chinese Maritime Customs,*" issued annually, and presenting a valuable account of the most prominent events in Formosan history, occurring between 1866 and 1896, together with a vast fund of commercial information.

I had also at my disposal the original works of Valentyn, Coyett, and other Dutch writers, the archives of the Spanish Mission, and many ancient Japanese and Chinese writings, as well as various other contributions to the history of the island, of which I made free use.

Mr. Y. Ino contributed a comprehensive account of the Formosan savages; Dr. W. Wykeham Myers, M.B., presented me with an excellent paper on the sugar industry; and Mr. de la Touche with a valuable report on the ornithology of the island, which appears in the appendix. To those kind friends I would express my sincere and hearty thanks.

With the above exceptions, the book is the result of personal research, extending over a period of eight years; and I believe that, in these pages, the student will find much which is new to him. Regarding the industrial chapters, I wish to state that I have received much assistance, always most willingly granted, from Japanese officials who have placed valuable reports at my disposal, and also from up country residents in the camphor districts, as well as in the coal and gold fields, who have most hospitably entertained me at various times and have very courteously given me such information as I desired. Foremost among these friends I must mention Mr. S. Miyoshi, an officer of the Formosan Government, to whom I am under great obligations for his unremitting kindness.

I also beg to acknowledge my indebtedness to Mr. Ernest A. Griffiths of the British Consulate, Anping, for much useful assistance; to the late Marquis Saigo for two valuable old photographs, and to Mr. Y. Ino, Dr. Y. Okada, Dr. A. Norris Wilkinson, M.R.C.S., Mr. T. G. Gowland, Mr. G. Greiner, and other friends for help in securing suitable illustrations.

The labour of constructing a map of Formosa proved somewhat difficult, owing to the absence of any comprehensive one in English or any accurate Japanese map. Every available map was referred to, conflicting points were investigated, and a new draft was made as nearly correct as was possible in the absence of any authoritative topographical surveys. Accuracy is not claimed, and, indeed, is impossible until the completion of the government surveys. To the various Japanese explorers in the savage district, whose names will be found on my map, I am indebted for much material never before published, without which the representation of that practically unknown region must have been far more incomplete. I would, above all, express my gratitude to Mr. T. Obanawa for the first outline drawing taken from the latest military surveys, which formed the ground-work of my map. It should be noted that all names are given according to both Japanese and Chinese pronunciation.

Unfortunately the book had to be written in Formosa itself, whereas it was necessarily printed elsewhere, thus rendering it impossible for me personally to revise the proofs. Errors have crept in, though, I trust, not of such a nature as to obscure the text, and, owing to the absence of any authoritative system of romanizing Formosan names, it has been difficult to ensure absolute uniformity of spelling. For any such shortcomings I can only crave the reader's indulgence.

J.W.D.

Taihoku, Formosa, January 25th, 1903.

NOTE ON NOMENCLATURE AND PRONUNCIATION.

The Japanese have, with few exceptions, retained the Chinese written nomenclature, but as they in most cases give the characters a different pronunciation, each place seems to have two names. In the historical sections, dealing as they do with events which occurred prior to the Japanese occupation, the Chinese names are used, but often with the Japanese pronunciation in brackets. It later chapters describing the island under Japanese rule, and in the map, the Japanese name is given first, and the Chinese in brackets, with the exception of a few well known names such as *Kelung*, *Takow*, etc., and some English names of islands in the Pescadores.

The Japanese, as well as the Chinese names, as far as possible, are spelled according to the *Romaji* system.

a is pronounced like *a* in *father*.

e ,,	,,	,, *ey* ,,	*they.*
i ,,	,,	,, *ee* ,,	*meet.*
o ,,	,,	,, *o* ,,	*so.*
u ,,	,,	,, *u* ,,	*rule.*
ai ,,	,,	,, *ai* ,,	*aisle.*
au ,,	,,	,, *ow* ,,	*cow.*
ei ,,	,,	,, *ei* ,,	*eight.*

CONTENTS.

ILLUSTRATIONS, MAPS, AND DIAGRAMS.

CHAPTER I.

FORMOSA'S FIRST KNOWN VISITORS.

FORMOSA : Its area—Location—Geography—Its earliest history—Formosa known as the Loochoos—The arrival of the Lonkius—Invasion by the Malays—The earliest known Chinese visitors—Formosans raid China-coast villages—Chinese nomenclature—Chinese expedition of 1368—Wan-San-ho visits the island—The pirate Liu Ta-kien and his pursuers run to Formosa—Pescadores garrisoned by Chinese—The first known Japanese visitors — The Hachiman pirates make their headquarters at Kelung—Japanese and Chinese pirates occupy Taiwan—The Chinese coast suffers—The Chinese Emperor forbids intercourse with Japanese—Futile attempts to occupy Formosa—Arrival of the Hakkas—The island prosperous—The seventeenth century.

CHINESE geographers inform us that once upon a time some fierce dragons which had dwelt for ages at Woo-hoo-mun (five-tiger gate), the entrance to Foochow, bestirred themselves into activity and for a day's frolic glided out unseen through the depths of the ocean. Arriving in the vicinity of the present island of Formosa, they became extraordinarily playful, and after ploughing through the earth itself they made their ascent, throwing up the bluff at Kelung head, and then writhed their way towards the south and with violent contortions heaved up a regular series of hills and mountains until at last, with a flap of their formidable tails, they threw up the three cliffs which now mark the extreme south of the island. Whether it was the custom of these remarkable beasts to sport for the benefit of mankind I am not sufficiently versed in Chinese legendary lore to say, but, at all events, that was the result attained in the instance referred to.

According to the latest maps, Formosa has an area of about 15,000 square miles, which is half the size of Scotland, or a trifle larger than the American states of Vermont and Connecticut taken together. The length of Formosa, in the sense of the longest straight line from the northern to the southern end, is 264 miles, but by any practicable roads, the distance from one end of the island to the other is about 350 miles. Its greatest width is about 80 miles. Lying to the east of South China, it is separated from the mainland by the Formosa Channel, which at its southern entrance between South-west Cape and Breaker Point is 245 miles wide, narrowing at the northern end to 62 miles.

To the southward lie the Philippine Islands, of which Cape Engaño in the north is 225 miles from the southern extremity of Formosa, while Manila, the capital of the group, lies 390 miles farther away. To the northeast lies the Loochoo group, stepping stones toward Japan, with Kagoshima, the southernmost island of Japan proper, 660 miles distant from Kelung, North Formosa. To the west about a hundred miles distant is the mainland of China with the Pescadores Islands in between, though only some twenty-five miles from the Formosan shore. To the east lies the boundless Pacific, practically uninterrupted until the Hawaiian Islands are reached 4,700 miles away. Through nearly its entire length the island is intersected by a range of lofty mountains, while parallel ranges, receding in height as they lie towards the west coast, give to the traveller who approaches the west side of Formosa on a bright day a beautiful view of four, and, in some points, five or six separate lines of waving colour, distinct yet harmonious, rising higher and higher until the main ridge with its great elevations, capped by Mounts Sylvia and Morrison with their respective heights of over eleven and twelve thousand feet, finds an ending in a background still one shade lighter, the encircling sky.

The mountainous district is almost wholly confined to the eastern half, and continues to the eastern shore itself, where cliffs with an estimated height of six thousand feet present a perpendicular face to the sea. These are the highest sea-coast cliffs known, I believe, in the world. In the midst of these rugged scenes, we find that the descendants of the oldest of Formosa's known inhabitants, the savage aborigines, have their homes. In the western half, the slope, intersected by numerous valleys, extends towards the sea, to be finally lost in the large undulating plain over which the Dutch, the Chinese, and now the Japanese flags have successively floated.

Of all the dominions which, previous to the late Japanese war, acknowledged the authority of China, no corresponding portion of area can be compared with Formosa in interest and future importance ; and this equally, whether we consider the variety and richness of its soil ; the stores of its mineral wealth ; its scenery, grand and picturesque ; or the character of its aboriginal inhabitants—tribes of savages as wild and untamed as can be found in all Asia, and sufficiently unknown and unaccounted for to please the most enthusiastic ethnologist.

Before dealing with the history of Formosa, it is necessary to state that it has been most conclusively proved by several eminent scholars that the island of Formosa was for many centuries known to the Chinese as a part of the Loochoo group, and was variously designated both in historical writings and in maps as " Great Loochoo," " Lesser Loochoo," etc.[1]

To gain an insight into the history of Formosa, the arrival of its savage inhabitants and their origin, the first Chinese visitors, etc., is a task beset

---

[1]. M. L'Hervey Le Saint Denys, a distinguished French scholar, was the first to advance this theory. Later Mr. C. Imbault-Huart in his splendid book " L' Ile Formosa," and Prof. Ludwig Riess in his learned paper " Geschichta der insel Formosa," published by the German Asiatic Society, throw much additional light on the subject.

with difficulties. The Chinese historians, to whom we must look for these ancient annals, give but brief mention of what was to them a foreign land, and this, combined with the fact that they confused Formosa with the Loo-choo islands, renders even these scanty materials vague and unsatisfactory.

A learned authority[1] speaks of the arrival in Formosa of emigrants from the north-east at a period several centuries before Christ. These people, known as Lonkius, held sway in the island and were visited by Chinese up to the second half of the 6th century, when bands of uncivilized Malays swept up from the south and brought the whole west coast of the island under their control, and the Lonkius who survived the conquest retreated into the mountains. The Chinese, who had been familiar with the natives before their overthrow, were surprised on visiting the island at a later date (about the year 605), to find it inhabited by strangers, with whom they could not converse. Later, a second expedition was despatched to the island, and the commander now, believing the new occupants to be Malays, had provided himself with natives from different southern Malayan islands, with the result that at least one of them was able to make himself understood by the Formosans. The object of the expedition, as stated by an eminent Chinese historian, Ma Touan-lin, was to compel the new arrivals, to whatever race they might belong, to recognise the Emperor and pay tribute as willing subjects. To this the Formosa Malays would not agree. Consequently the commander attacked them, burnt their villages, and then returned to the mainland.[2]

Unable to enforce submission, it was quite natural that the "Son of Heaven" should not deign to consider the island of Formosa worthy of attention, its inhabitants having chosen to remain outside the pale of celestial civilization. At all events, Chinese history speaks of no further official intercourse with the island for several centuries. That the Chinese traders whose interest had been aroused by former expeditions should likewise have avoided the island, the sight of which could scarcely have been missed by trading vessels traversing the China seas, is unlikely, and it is probable that not only did they carry on a bartering traffic with the natives but that small numbers of them established themselves in the island.

The Malays there do not appear to have shown the skill in ship build-ing which natives of some of the southern Malayan islands exhibited, still, that they were not entirely ignorant of navigation, the annals of Loochoo bear witness. Towards the end of the 12th century several hundred Formosans suddenly appeared in some of the small seacoast villages of Fokien Pro-vince, robbing and pillaging the houses. They seemed specially intent upon securing iron, and from such houses as they were able to enter they carried off the iron rings from the doors. Upon the approach of a cavalier in armour

1. Prof. Ludwig Riess.

2. The dates of these two expeditions are variously given. The first expedition is stated in some accounts to have taken place in the year 605 and the second expedition in 606, while other accounts give the date of the first expedition as 606 and the second as 611. There is a greater discrepancy as to the accomplishments of the two expeditions. While one account states that the last mentioned returned to China with several thousand prisoners, a second account states that the sole trophy of the expedition was a single garment worn by the natives.

the Formosans endeavored to possess themselves of his metal garments. So much did they value the iron points of their spears that after throwing the weapon at the enemy they pulled it back by the aid of a line a hundred feet long which was attached to it. When eventually dispersed by the Chinese the Formosans fled to the shore and, catching up their bamboo rafts, they ran quickly into the water and soon disappeared from the coast not to return again.

The next mention of Formosa is found in the annals of the Ming dynasty, where it is stated that previous to the 16th century the name Kiloung had been applied only to a port in the north of the island, further-more that the ancient name of the port had been Pe-kiang (North Bay).[1]

Previous to the close of the Yuan dynasty in 1368, during a period when the Chinese were much engrossed in warlike preparations with a view to the conquest of Japan and the Loochoos, an expedition was despatched to the Loochooan kingdom. It was the intention of the officer in command, Admiral Yang-tsiang, to sail from north China, but a certain literate, a native of Fokien Province, presented a memorial to the effect that the principal island of the Loochoo group could be more conveniently reached by taking a route from South China, which would also have the advantage of permitting a visit to the Pescadores. His suggestions were convincing to the officers concerned and, after promoting the literate in rank, they induced him to join the expedition as adviser. The expedition set sail and, as had been planned by the adviser, the Pescadores were visited, but upon continu-ing the journey the island of Formosa appeared in sight and the commander being convinced that it was not the kingdom of Loochoo, the desired destina-tion of the expedition, the unfortunate adviser had his head cut off as the penalty of his presumption.

Although unfortunate for the literate the expedition was of great value in clearing up the mystery which had surrounded Formosa and the Loochoos for centuries. It was now discovered that the islands were separate and apart, that the principal island of the Loochoos lay many *li* to the north east, while Formosa, so far as the natives of the kingdom of Loochoo were concerned, was a foreign land.

No further attempts were made to visit the principal Loochoos, *via* Formosa, and although the latter island was known to the Chinese for some time as Little Loochoo[2] which seemed more appropriate now that the principal Loochoos, in which they were chiefly interested were known to be a distinct group, it was not again confused with the main group lying to the north east.

Chinese authorities see fit however, to commence the history of For-mosa from the year 1430, which was the date of the visit to the island by

---

1. These statements which are pointed out by Klaproth, an early writer on China, and referred to by the author of "Ile Formose," are conclusive evidence that Formosa was known to the Chinese previous to 1430, which Chinese historians give as the date of the first visit to Formosa.

2. As a reminder of this blunder Little Loochoo remains to day in Formosa, being the name applied to a small island lying close to the southwest shore of Formosa and sometimes known to foreigners as Lambay island.

the eunuch Wan-San-ho, an officer of the Chinese court. It has not been discovered whether the historians were ignorant of the error into which their people had fallen, and in which they stupidly remained for centuries, or whether they considered that, inasmuch as the island had been long confused with the Loochoos, historical truth would be likewise confusing, so that an authentic history could not safely date back previous to a period at which evidence could be obtained that the material dealt with referred to Formosa alone.

At all events, Chinese historians record that during the Ming dynasty, in the year 1430, Wan-San-ho, while returning from Siam, was driven by storm to this island, landing at a place on the south-west coast, later known as Taiwan. The natives, although uncouth and untamed, treated the stranger with kindness, and furnished the means by which he was enabled to return to the mainland. On his return to China he reported his discovery to the Imperial Court and described the island as a magnificent land occupied by a strange and barbarous race. He furthermore displayed herbs and other plants valuable for their medicial properties which he had obtained while in the island.[1] This seemed to arouse an interest among the officials, and the island was for some time the subject of considerable discussion, although years passed by, and no Emperor seemed sufficiently impressed to endeavour to include it in his own dominions.

More than a century passes by before Chinese historians again refer to Formosa, although, according to Japanese history, both Chinese and Japanese pirates made occasional visits to the island during this interval.

Chinese historians inform us that in 1564 a Chinese Admiral, Yu Ta-yeou, cruising in the east China seas encountered a Chinese pirate chief, named Lin Ta-kien, who was in command of a large force, including Japanese, who were then occupying the Pescadores. Upon the approach of the Imperial fleet the bold pirate did not wait to be attacked, but with full sail charged straight for the intruders and assailed them briskly. Yu Ta-yeou met the attack without confusion and returned the fire with much effect. After five hours of fighting, on the approach of night, the enemy set sail for the Pescadores. But the admiral made such haste to follow that he was able to secure a position commanding the entrance before daylight. When the pirate arrived he found his pathway blocked, and with his numbers greatly diminished by the previous day's combat, he believed himself too weak to successfully attack, so sailed to Formosa, landing at a place near the present village of Anping. Yu Ta-yeou followed him even there, but owing to low water and ignorance of the port, decided not to risk his vessels in any further attempt at capture, so returned to the Pescadores, where he made prisoners of the pirate's followers stationed there.

The admiral left a sufficient garrison to protect the newly-acquired possessions, and sailing back to China reported his exploits to the higher officials. The Imperial Court received his tidings with great satisfaction and at once appointed a mandarin of letters as governor. Colonists were attracted to the

---

1. It is stated that certain of these plants introduced by Wan-San-ho are still in use in China for medical purposes.

new territory and a regular trade to the Pescadores was for the first time instituted. The pirate, although freed from outside interference, could not see much of value in the uncultivated island of Formosa with its barbarous inhabitants, and, no doubt smarting under defeat, was led to seek an outlet for his anger ; for he slew every native he laid hands on, and then, caulking his vessel with the blood of the poor victims, he set sail and retired to Canton where he died a miserable death, richly deserved.

Of the two peoples, the Japanese and the Chinese, the former were undoubtedly the most energetic in obtaining a foothold on the island. About the close of the Ashikaga dynasty (1336-1443) in Japan, a large portion of the Empire was a scene of constant combat, and especially in the districts of Satsuma, Hizen, Higo, Chikuzen, Chikugo, Nagato, Iwami, Iyo, Izumi, and Kii, where the fighting was more continual, great numbers who had been deprived of their property were forced to desert their native land. Of these the sea attracted a large number, to whom, half pirates, half traders, the China waters afforded a lucrative field of adventure.

• The most formidable of these rovers were united under a banner bearing the characters Hachiman (God of War). When trade was slack, the China coast villages were sacked and then burned, and vessels were captured and plundered, until the approach of these colours struck terror into the hearts of all beholders. Such exploits brought them numerous enemies, and, after several years of unchecked license, the combined opposition of Chinese officials and merchants compelled the Japanese to seek some resort of greater safety than the high seas and China coast. This brought them to the Pescadores, and in the sixteenth century to Formosa, which, considering that it was an unclaimed land and inhabited by a feeble race of savages, was most suited to their requirements. The band of rovers, with the warlike retainers of the Daimyos Murakami and Kono as leaders, were most active in the north of the island, making the port of Kelung their headquarters. They combined piracy with legitimate trade, resorting to the former when opportunities for the latter were not at hand. Whilst confining their efforts principally to the China seas, these bold adventurers had on several occasions reached far to the south, even to Siam. The gains from their raids were as a rule brought to Kelung, their headquarters, and thence the crafty rovers sailed to the northward as legitimate traders, to dispose of their cargoes of silk, porcelain, spices, drugs, and other eastern products so easily gained.

But the Japanese had not the monopoly of this method of trade. Chinese pirates were likewise engaged in it, and occupied South Formosa in the vicinity of Taiwan as their headquarters, while the Portuguese, Spanish, and Dutch, who later appeared in the eastern seas, adopted the same tactics whenever it suited their convenience to do so.

Piratical raids on the China coast were now so numerous that hardly a village on the coast of Fokien and bordering provinces escaped. Legitimate trade was threatened with extinction, and even the warships of the Empire could not avail against the fierce rovers. Eventually the Emperor despatched messengers to Japan, and strong representations were made to the government as to the damages inflicted by Japanese pirates. What steps the island government took to comply with the demands of its big neighbor we are not informed. It is quite likely that the home authorities were just as unable to control their adventurous countrymen as the Chinese were to punish them for their misdeeds. At all events, the Japanese continued to raid the China seas, and the Chinese Emperor at length forbade his subjects to hold any intercourse with any Japanese, and furthermore ordered that every Japanese caught in China and every Chinese returning from Japan should be speedily decapitated.

This condition of affairs continued during the 16th century, but the traders and pirates were but little affected, while Formosa profited by the situation.

The location of Formosa and its political condition could scarcely have been more favorable to both Chinese and Japanese as a link between the two nations now estranged. It was, as it were, a neutral port open to the vessels of all countries, where trade could be conducted without fear of official disturbance or the imposition of tribute or taxes. Formosa thus became the commercial clearing-house between Japan, China, and the neighboring southern countries.

The growth of the trade and the large profits obtainable later attracted to the field a better class of merchants, who gave more attention to legitimate business than to the raiding and destroying of villages. In 1592 merchants of Nagasaki, Kyōto, and Sakai, having received special permission from the Shogun to engage in foreign commerce, fitted out vessels and sought their fortunes in the southern seas. They made their headquarters in Formosa at the town of Taiwan, and thence carried on a regular trade with Japan, China, Macao, Annan, Siam, Luzon (Philippines), and Java.

The authorities in Japan were no doubt aware that the European nations now interested in the eastern seas would not long permit Formosa to continue an unclaimed land, and that consequently it behoved Japan to strengthen her position in the island. The first attempt to secure Formosa as a tributary possession was made at the completion of the subjugation of the Loochoos by troops from the Japanese province of Satsuma, when officers were sent to Formosa to reorganize the Japanese settlements there, and to place them on a more secure footing. This mission was unsuccessful.

Six years later, Iyeyasu, the first shogun of the Tokugawa dynasty, despatched the governor of Nagasaki, Murayama by name and a Christian, to conquer the island of Formosa by force of arms. He landed with a force of three or four thousand men. History does not record his exploits in the island. The Chinese had now flocked thither in considerable numbers, and against them and the large savage population, perhaps, the Japanese commander despaired of success with the small force at his disposal. At all events, he returned to Japan, where not only he himself but his whole family paid the penalty of death for his failure.[1]

So far as the traders resident in Taiwan were concerned, both Chinese and Japanese appear to have lived side by side without any exhibition of hostility towards each other. No doubt the bond of mutual benefit to be derived from

---

1. This record is from the Jesuits. Japanese accounts refer to the expedition as merely the exploits of an officer interested in trade and who had received permission to engage himself thus, the same as many private individuals before him, but do not state that he was in any way acting for the Japanese Government.

their trading transactions was the principal factor in fostering the friendship between these two peoples who, as a class, generally displayed much aversion to each other. While the Japanese in Formosa carried on the most lucrative and extensive trade the Chinese were more numerous. The Chinese pirates who resorted to the island as a safe retreat, were as a rule divided into bands, and, according to the scanty historical material which we have at hand, established a rough form of government over their settlements. So admirable was the organization that the different bands lived together without discord and chose their leaders by vote, while a supreme chief was appointed to look after the interests of the combined bands whenever anything arose of common concern. The strongest of them was a powerful band under the leadership of one Gan Shi-sai (Sen Shi-chi). Their exploits brought large returns, and by combining legitimate trade with piratical raids they eventually attained a position so formidable that smaller bands combined with them for their own protection, and thus nearly the whole of the China and Formosa trade was brought under their control. In 1621 Gan Shi-sai died, and was succeeded by Ching Chi-lung, a famous character, and the father of Koxinga, whose exploits occupy a prominent place in after chapters of this history.

Meanwhile more Chinese had been flocking to the island in considerable numbers desiring to reap benefit from the richness of the soil rather than from marauding expeditions. The first of this class to take refuge in the island were the Hakkas. In China they were considered as outcasts, in fact the name signifies "stranger"; and, although industrious, they were driven about from place to place and, like the Jews, possessed no land they could call their own. To the other classes of mainland Chinese, with their exaggerated views of ancestral worship, the Hakkas were but little better than barbarians and were considered fit subjects for persecution. From a life of misery and oppression on the mainland the wanderers sought peace in Formosa. To them the island was indeed an El Dorado, and emigration increased so rapidly that in a century it was estimated that one-third of the Hakkas of Kwangtung province, where they were most thickly gathered, had emigrated to Formosa. Once having established close communication with the natives, they eventually became indispensable to both traders and islanders, and by sheer energy attained a position of much importance.

CHAPTER II.

FORMOSA UNDER THE DUTCH.

1514-1655.

IT is now necessary to take a step backward and review the exploits of the three great maritime powers, Portugal, Spain, and Holland, which of all European nations were the first to appear in the China seas.

The Portuguese, the pioneers in commerce and discovery in the East, made their first expedition to China in 1514. In 1517 a fleet arrived under the command of Andrade, who was sent as ambassador to China on behalf of his sovereign, Emanuel I. The strangers were well received, and were establishing a trade when the mission was suddenly brought to a close by the Chinese, who had become irritated at the violent disposition of a brother of Andrade, the commander. For some years after, the Portuguese were allowed to anchor only at islands off the coast, and in 1557 permission was granted to them to land and erect storehouses upon an island nearer the mouth of the Canton River, to which the name Macao was given by the settlers.

The Portuguese have been commonly described as the first Europeans to establish themselves in Formosa, and some late accounts of the island speak of a Portuguese settlement in Kelung in 1590. This is evidently an error, and no doubt arose from the fact that the Portuguese gave to the island the name it now bears: "Formosa." Portuguese accounts recording their adventures in the Far East contain no mention of any Portuguese settlement in Formosa, and careful researches fail to discover any material that could be construed as evidence of such. However we do learn that Portuguese sailing down the west coast of the island were struck with its beauty and gave it the name of "Ilha Formosa," (Beautiful Isle). A Dutch navigating officer named Linschotten, employed by the Portuguese, so recorded the island in his charts, and eventually the name of Formosa, so euphonious and yet appropriate, replaced all others in European literature.

The Spanish, jealous of the success of the Portuguese, made vigorous endeavors to rival them in the East. Expeditions were successfully undertaken to the Philippines, and in 1571 Manila was founded and measures taken to make it the trade depot of the Far East.

In 1595, a Dutch fleet under the command of Cornelius Houtman arrived in Java and found but little difficulty in establishing commercial relations on a firm basis. The sudden interest in Oriental trade thus aroused in Holland resulted, in 1602, in the organization of the Dutch East India Company, and hand in hand with England, united by the bond of Protestantism against their Catholic enemies—the Spanish and Portuguese, the two nations strove for success in eastern waters. Friction between the two, however, soon arose, and the Dutch pushed on alone into Chinese waters to dispute the monopoly of commerce then held by the Portuguese in Macao and the Spanish in the Philippines. The first Dutch expedition in 1601 was a failure, the high Chinese functionaries of the southern province having received orders that no more "barbarians" should be allowed to enter the Empire, and the Portuguese, who had much to gain, had pictured the strangers in the darkest colors to the Chinese. It was then that the Dutch East India Company arrived upon the scene determined to drive the intriguing Portuguese from Macao. In 1603 the first attack was made, but beyond destroying a few of the enemy's galleons, nothing was gained, and the Dutch were forced to retire. The next year an embassy was sent to open negotiations with the Imperial Court. At the same time Admiral Van Warwijk sailed for Macao, but encountering a typhoon very common in those waters, was obliged to run for shelter to the Pescadores then but little known. It was not entirely an ill wind, however, for the knowledge gained during the occupation of the group eventually led to the possession of Formosa.

From the Pescadores the admiral communicated with the Fokien authorities in hopes of obtaining some commercial privileges, but the answer was that $30,000 must first be paid for the favor of an interview. This proposition was naturally rejected, and the Dutch fleet having been surrounded by fifty Chinese war junks, further negotiations became impossible and the admiral returned to India with his fleet.

In 1607 a new attempt by Matelief likewise resulted in failure through the impossibility of obtaining supplies.

From 1607 to 1622 no attempt was made by the Dutch to obtain a position in China, although during this period they continued to harass the Spanish and to quarrel with the English. In the latter year Cornelius Reyersz arrived in the China seas in command of a fleet of six vessels with 2,000 soldiers, to attack the Portuguese at Macao. Appearing before the town he bombarded Fort Saint François for five days, and encountered but little difficulty in landing 800 men, who captured an entrenchment and advanced to the city walls. Here the Portuguese defended the place so stoutly that the Dutch, unable to gain an entrance, had nothing left them but to return to their ships with a loss of 136 killed, 124 wounded, and 40 prisoners. The Chinese now complained that this was equivalent to an attack upon themselves, inasmuch as the Portuguese were their recognized tenants. They consequently became more obstinate than ever in their refusal to grant the long sought trading privileges. The Dutch in turn accused the Chinese of aiding and abetting the Portuguese, and of showing partiality in granting them exclusive commercial rights. Frustrated in their designs on Macao, the Dutch sailed to the Pescadores, well known to them through the visit of Admiral Warwijk, with the intention of compelling the Chinese to grant them full liberty of trade.

No opposition was encountered from the force at the Pescadores ; in fact the natives were panic-stricken, as in accordance with an ancient prophecy red-headed men were destined to become their masters, and they believed that at last the fatal day had arrived.

The first work of the Dutch was to build a fort, in the construction of which hundreds of Chinese, including the crews of many junks which had been captured, were condemned to labor. Of 1,500 workmen thus employed it is related that 1,300 died in the process of building "for they seldom had more than half a pound of rice for a day's allowance," and were literally starved to death. The Dutch pleaded in vindication the cruel usage received by their countrymen who had been imprisoned by the Chinese. Furthermore, batches of natives were sent to Batavia to be sold as slaves, and the awful fact is recorded that not more than half of them reached their destination alive, the others having either been thrown overboard upon the appearance of sickness or having died on the way.

Valentyn, who acted as historian for the Dutch, says that after having built the fort, the Dutch despatched several vessels of their numerous fleet to the mainland of China and resolved to force the Chinese into trade. Several villages on the coast were ravaged, and many cruelties committed, actions which were characterized by the frank historian as a disgrace to Christianity.

An envoy was now despatched by the Dutch to Amoy where he was received by the authorities with great pomp, but when the dignitaries ordered him to knock his head upon the ground "so that the bystanders might hear the cracking of his skull" he refused compliance with this customary indignity, and after fruitless negotiations returned to his superiors. The admiral now resolved to repair to Foochow. The high authorities received him with the greatest honor. No doubt they were apprehensive of the danger of having such formidable neighbors as the Dutch so close at hand, and furthermore a petition had been presented to them by the Amoy merchants complaining that the Dutch by their constant attacks on vessels trading with the Spanish, had completely destroyed the lucrative trade formerly carried on between Amoy and Manila.[1] The officials were consequently inclined to turn a willing ear to the Dutch proposals. At length after much discussion, towards the close of the year 1623 an agreement was reached by which the Dutch were to remove to Formosa, the Chinese were to supply them with as much merchandise as they desired, and furthermore five junks laden with silk and other goods, and accompanied by a Chinese official were to be despatched to Batavia. Just as the conclusion of the difficulty which had existed between the Dutch and Chinese for years was about to be happily reached, an incident occurred which placed all again in jeopardy. Two sampans loaded with inflammables suddenly appeared among the Dutch vessels at anchor in the Chinchoo river, and two of the latter were set on fire, one being totally consumed, while the three others sailed down the river, destroying every junk they met on the way and returned to the Pescadores. The Chinese appeared on the scene shortly after and presented an ultimatum to the Dutch. If the foreigners would remove to Taiwan, freedom of commerce would be granted them. If not the Chinese would declare war against them. As a demonstration 150 war junks with 4,000 men arrived off the Pescadores and blockaded Peiho (Panghoo) island and preparations were made for obstructing the entrance by sinking vessels in the channel. The Dutch now confined to one barren island found themselves lacking in supplies. At length a new commander, Sonck by name, arrived from Batavia with orders to acquiesce in the demands of the Chinese and to occupy Formosa. A formal cession of the island was now made, which, considering that the Chinese had no right to it and never claimed any, was probably not a heart-rending task for them.

Preparations were now made to abandon the Pescadores, and Dutch and Chinese worked alike in tearing down the fort, the twenty guns and much of the material being taken on board the Dutch ships to be transported to Formosa.[2]

Previous to this in 1620 a Dutch ship was wrecked in the vicinity of Taiwan. The commander of the vessel, no doubt with the intention of turning the mishaps which had befallen him to some advantage, sought permission from the Japanese to erect a very small establishment to be used as a sort of depot for the Dutch who were trading with Japan. To assure the colonists that he had no design to deprive them of any large extent of territory, he stated that a piece of land not larger than that which could be measured with the skin of an ox would be sufficient. Pleased with the modesty of his request

---

1. This important trade employed 30 to 40 Chinese junks running constantly between Amoy and Manila. Silk, porcelain, and other products were carried amounting to a million and a half dollars in gold annually. At that period there were more than fourteen thousand Spanish in Mexico who were dependent upon the raw silk of China to weave the celebrated fabrics so much in vogue at that time. The Spanish vessels carried this merchandise from Manila to Mexico. So extensive was the intercourse with China that 20,000 Chinese had located in Manila. By destroying this trade as well as the Portuguese commerce in Macao the Dutch had hopes of driving out their rivals and obtaining this trade for themselves.

2. Some traces of the old fortification still remain in the Pescadores, and the Chinese speak of a mysterious sunken castle which with its walls and turrets still intact can be seen beneath the waves on favorable days. The tale is probably a superstitious fancy.

permission was granted, whereupon the wily Dutchman with an old trick in mind proceeded to cut the ox-skin in very long narrow strips and after fastening them together produced a line of sufficient length to surround a vast plot of ground while the Japanese were struck dumb with astonishment.

The Dutch with their possessions departed in August, 1624, from the Pescadores and after a day's journey appeared in the vicinity of the settlement of Taiwan. No opposition was made to their large force and they consequently were enabled to take possession of the port without delay. Their first task was to place themselves on an amicable basis with the former inhabitants. The Chinese in the island then numbered about twenty-five thousand and their headmen ordinarily the pirate chiefs, were induced to be friendly by the promise of 30,000 deer skins to be delivered annually. The Japanese who, although few in number, consisted of large merchants with considerable capital at stake, seemed to have been satisfied with the assurance that their trade would not be disturbed.

The Dutch now found that the situation in Formosa was above their highest anticipations. Although the entrance to the harbour at high water was only thirteen feet deep, still for the trading vessels of those days it was sufficient. Besides there was the possibility of creating a considerable trade in such articles as the island itself produced and the still greater advantage of being independent of outside sources for food supplies. Still in those early days trade depended not upon the quality of the goods but upon the military force to control the markets. The Dutch consequently valued the island chiefly on account of its strategical position. From Formosa the Spanish commerce between Manila and China, and the Portuguese commerce between Macao and Japan could by constant attacks be made so precarious that much of it would be thrown into the hands of the Dutch, while the latter's dealings with China and Japan would be subject to no interruptions.

The first measure of the new government was to strengthen the defences of the island. A temporary fort was at once thrown up on a raised sand bank at the entrance of the harbour of Taiwan. But as this structure was of little value it was replaced four years later by Fort Zelandia (Zealand), a very large and substantial structure. Besides this a small stone redoubt known as Utrecht constructed on a hill "a pistol shot's distance" from its elevation commanded Fort Zelandia. A second and smaller work called Fort Provintia was built at a subsequent date near the mouth of Formosa river not far distant from Fort Zelandia. Both these structures were erected on the highest elevations in the vicinity, which enabled signals to be exchanged between them.[1]

The Dutch with much foresight at once sought friendly relations with the savage tribes. Perhaps with the knowledge that the Chinese were treacherous

---

1. Fort Zelandia consisted of a central stronghold, built on a small hill, partly artificial, in the form of a bastioned fort on a square each side of which extended about sixty yards. This was strengthened, at about one hundred yards distance on the northern side, by a wall following the course of the shore and meeting the fort at its western and northern angles, its own angle being also protected by a kind of bastion. The walls were of great thickness, though hollow in the centre. They were built of small bricks specially brought from Batavia, and were extensively loopholed.

The ruins of both forts still remain. Fort Zelandia within the confines of Anping village and Fort Provintia within the city walls of Tainanfu.

and unsympathetic but little pains were taken to win them over as loyal subjects of Holland.

The territory surrounding the port was owned by the Sakkam tribe, and the Dutch by fair and just treatment were soon enabled to win their affection. Ground was secured from the tribe near the mouth of the Formosa river from Fort Zelandia at a distance of about a mile, and here around Port Provintia the town of Sakkam was erected.

From the Sakkam tribe the Dutch gradually extended their jurisdiction always observing a kind and considerate policy over these wild children whose friendship was so essential to the company's success.

With the Chinese and Japanese the Dutch were not considerate, and, regardless of their promises, they no sooner felt their position secure than they began to lay plans for restricting the trade of these two peoples. The first offensive measure of the new government was to lay a duty upon sugar and rice, two staple articles which even at that early time were exported in considerable quantities. The Chinese settlers paid this without murmuring; but the Japanese, who were more extensively interested in foreign trade, refused to submit to these exactions, justly protesting that they as the earlier settlers of Formosa should be exempt from taxation, and moreover that the Dutch had promised them freedom from offensive interference. This gave rise to bitter hatred on both sides and as the matter was referred to Japan and placed before the Court of Yedo, the whole Japanese commerce enjoyed by the Dutch was placed in peril.

Still the Dutch, nothing daunted, rushed along at a headlong pace intent only on obtaining the maximum of financial gains in the shortest time possible. Trade had now reached a very flourishing state and the port of Taiwan bore the appearance of great commercial activity. Chinese junks from many ports in China unloading cargoes of silk and other native merchandise; Japanese ships loading European manufactures, spices, cotton stuffs, and various Indian products, and completing their cargoes with rice, sugar, and raw silk for such vessels as were destined for Japan; Dutch vessels loading or unloading for or from China, Japan, and Batavia, these added to several warships and numerous small craft made up a picture, the like of which could not be seen in the whole East.

The Dutch not only traded with the Chinese and Japanese in Formosa but also sent their own ships to China and Japan to deal directly. Peter Nuits, the Dutch Governor in his report on trade stated that silver was sent by junks from Taiwan to the mainland city of Amoy, sometimes to be remitted to their agents who resided there, sometimes to be given to the merchants who were to provide merchandise for the markets of Japan, India, and Europe. This could only be done with the connivance of the Governor of Foochow, and was very advantageous, for goods could thus be obtained so as to allow a greater profit than those delivered at Taiwan by the Chinese compradores.

Also, when the time arrived for the departure from Taiwan of the Dutch ships for Japan or Batavia, if their cargoes were not complete, they were sent across to China by stealth, where they were filled up with goods which were brought on board in great quantities and at a cheaper rate than they could be bought at Taiwan, the difference in the price of silk alone being some eight or ten taels per picul. If time allowed these vessels returned to Taiwan; otherwise, they were sent direct to their destinations.

The principal exports were raw silk and sugar to Japan, the amount of the latter being as much as 80,000 piculs in one year; silk piece goods, porcelain, and gold to Batavia; while paper, spices, amber, tin, lead, and cotton were imported to Formosa, and with the addition of Formosan products such as rice, sugar, rattans, deerskins, deer-horns, and drugs were exported to China.

In 1627, five cargoes of raw silk valued at 621,855 guilders ($240,000 U.S. gold) were sent to Japan, and two cargoes of silk piece goods valued at 559,493 guilders ($224,900 gold) were sent to Batavia and Holland. The whole Chinese trade amounted to about one million dollars (gold) a year, which generally meant one hundred per cent profit. The expenses of the colony were about 214,000 guilders ($85,944 gold). After all accounts had been settled there remained for the Batavian Government 85,000 guilders ($34,165 gold). The employees of the company were poorly paid, and were accordingly obliged to engage in trade to recompense themselves for their labors.

These advantages attracted in 1626 the envy of the Spaniards, who founded a colony on the north coast at Kelung, as will be described in length in later pages. The Dutch had as yet extended their jurisdiction only a few miles from Taiwan (Sakkam) and the Spanish were permitted to occupy the north in peace and quietude for the time being.

The Dutch, who appear to have thoroughly mastered the difficult problem of governing savages, fully appreciated the advantages that would accrue from the conversion of the natives to Christianity and the influence that could be gained by kindly and generous treatment of the subject race.

These natives seemed to be superior to Chinese, and the Dutch owed much of their tranquillity to them. They then occupied all of Formosa, the Chinese not having sufficient strength to force them from their lands as they did in later days. They were of good morals, and their miserable huts, which were grouped about to form villages, were never far from a temple where they might worship, The work was done by the women, the men employing themselves in hunting stags. Their laws of wedlock were most curious, a married man not residing permanently with his wife until he was fifty years old, and it was a great disgrace should a woman give birth to a child before her thirty-seventh year.

There was but little government among them, although each village generally had its chief, and whole districts were often engaged in bloody feuds. The aged were highly esteemed and possessed great power over the youth. Those who had proved themselves brave in battle were given the

highest rank that could be bestowed.   Burial of the dead was not practised ;
the corpse was fried at a fire, and after having been wrapped in cloth was
preserved in a small building hung with curtains.

The religion of the savages resembled somewhat the bacchanalia of the
Greeks.   The principal idols in Formosa were the goddess Takarupada and
her male consort Tamagisangak, and a demon called Sariafay.   To these
they offered the heads of pigs and stags, and their worship was attended with
the most licentious ceremonies.

Protestant missionaries such as we have at the present day were at that
time unknown, but the Dutch company, not moved by the love of morality alone,
were so convinced of the advantages to be gained that they did not hesitate
to engage ministers at home and to bring them out to labor among the
savages.   Among these, Georgius Candidius, the first in the field, arrived in the
island in 1627 and at once engaged himself in learning the language.   After
obtaining a thorough knowledge of it, he entered upon his work with zeal
and was very successful.   Most of the villages around Fort Zelandia were
christianized, and in each of them school-masters were placed to instruct
both old and young in the leading doctrines of the Scriptures.

The discontent aroused among the Japanese at the obstructions placed
in the way of their trade in Formosa, and the injustice with which they had
been treated by the Dutch, grew until it resulted in a coup d'état almost
unparallelled in history whether for the magnitude of the risks involved or
for the amount of success obtained.

There lived at Nagasaki a bold adventurer named Hamada Yahei, who
had been incited against the Dutch by the tales of a district officer named
Sueji Heijo who some time previously, having received government permission to engage in trade, sent ships destined for Foochow.   On the journey the
Pescadores were touched where the Dutch then in possession interfered with
the trader to such an extent that he was forced to abandon his journey and
return to Japan.   Yahei was entrusted with an expedition bent upon avenging
the wrongs of his countrymen.   His younger brother Kozaimon and his son
Shinzo accompanied him.   Upon leaving Nagasaki many Chinese took the
opportunity of taking passage with him, so that he mustered nearly five
hundred men altogether.

One day towards the end of April 1628, the expedition appeared in the
harbor of Taiwan and on its mission becoming known there was some consternation among the Dutch, not that the Japanese would injure them if it
came to a fight, but that trade would suffer should hostilities commence.

The difficulty is most clearly expressed in a letter sent by Governor
Nuits to the Governor-General at Batavia, in which it is stated that the
vessel under Yahei had arrived with 470 Japanese on board, and as the
mission had been reported as a hostile one by a Chinese passenger it was
necessary that the Dutch should take some measures to protect themselves
as well as to punish the Japanese for their impertinence.

The chief, Yahei, had sent a letter to the governor asking for permission
to trade, but the latter in answer reprimanded him for his impoliteness and

suggested that it was the custom to call and make personal application. This had the desired effect, and Yahei presented himself at the governor's official residence. He was there informed that as it was customary to search Dutch ships in Japan and seize all weapons and ammunition to be held until the departure of the ships, the governor had determined to do likewise, and therefore Yahei must deliver up all weapons and ammunition, which would be kept in custody by the Dutch and returned to the Japanese on the day of their intended departure. Yahei would not agree to this, so he was held a prisoner in the House, while in pursuance of the governor's orders an officer with soldiers was sent aboard the Japanese ship to disarm it. Swords, spears, bows, and arrows, 15 guns with ammunition, and all the oars were secured and carried ashore. The governor then inquired of Yahei why he had brought so many arms, adding that it could be not for trade, but hostile purposes, and that they were always prepared to defend their colony and had many soldiers and warships; so that they were not afraid of any foemen. Moreover the Japanese were now helpless, as all weapons and ammunition had been taken from them. Yahei replied that he had not brought the arms to attack the Dutch but to protect himself against the pirates on the high seas. To this the governor rejoined that at Taiwan there was no fear of pirates and that his property would be returned to him on his departure.

Yahei made an unsuccessful attempt to recover the arms. Later he signified his desire to go to China and asked that seven or eight Chinese junks might be sold or loaned to him that he might secure certain goods that had been left in China the preceding year. Although the governor did not like the request, he felt obliged to grant it rather than show his hostility so strongly as to injure Dutch trade in Japan. But Chinese sailors refused to join the vessels, on the ground that their presence would so anger the Chinese authorities that punishment would be inflicted upon their families. Consequently the permission was withdrawn. Further ground of complaint was given by the discovery on board of some deer skins, the export of which had been forbidden. But as only a few were found no formal notice was taken of the offence, although the governor signified his intention of detaining Yahei until further instructions were received from Batavia as to the disposal of the case. Yahei, however, was not to be thus daunted. The capture and imprisonment of the governor in his own capital by this adventurous trader and his six companions is quite a remarkable tale, and the journal of a Dutch military officer affords a reliable account of it.

June 29th, 1628.

" Yahei and other Japanese wishing to return to Japan sought permission from the governor but were refused. They were politely informed of his decision, but after some discussion Yahei suddenly showed great signs of anger, and springing like a wild cat caught Governor Nuits and with the aid of his companions bound him hand and foot. He was warned against calling out with the threat that if he made any noise his head would be struck off. A Dutch officer in the next room made his escape and gave the alarm calling out that if the soldiers were not sent quickly to the rescue their Chief would be killed. Many Dutch at once surrounded the house, but the Japanese rushing out made such a fierce attack upon them, killing and wounding several, that they fled. At the beginning of the disturbance another officer and I hearing the disturbance tried to pass out of the gate but were prevented by the Japanese. At last my companion jumped out of the window and escaped, I following his example. The Japanese captured and killed two servants of the governor. The soldiers were now gathered together, and three or four of the big guns were turned on the Japanese but inflicted greater damage on our own people. At this time I secretly communicated with our governor and could not refrain from weeping at his plight. He told me to stop the firing at once otherwise his life would be in danger. The Japanese also informed me that if I did not stop the firing they would present me with our chief's head. I at once ordered our soldiers to cease firing, and on this the Japanese showed themselves inclined to settle the case peacefully. There is a report that the Japanese with the aid of native Formosans and Chinese intend to attack our fort to-morrow night. If that is so I cannot obey the governor's orders, and at a consultation of our officers we decided to send a messenger to the Japanese asking them to release the governor. If they do not comply we shall attack them and rescue him by force, and if we cannot save our beloved officer and his son, we will fight until there is not one Japanese left alive. It was thought best however to report this decision to our chief before putting it into execution, so we made known to him our plans. He replied that he believed a peaceful settlement would be arrived at and begged us to wait until to-morrow before sending the message to the Japanese.

A polite message was sent to the Japanese this morning asking for the release of the governor, and if this was refused it was determined to back up the demand with an armed force. An answer was received to the effect that the case would be settled peacefully, and requesting us to wait until the afternoon when they, the Japanese would send a report. The report arrived and our chief informed us that the affair would be peacefully settled and that he would be released providing he gave his son and five other hostages as a proof of sincerity."

Delay followed, during which the Dutch were sorely tempted to commence hostilities against the Japanese, but the council, wishing to preserve the life of their chief as well as peace, refrained from fighting, and on the evening of July 2nd the council received from Governor Nuits a letter mentioning the conditions under which the Japanese would release him. They were as follows:—

1. The Chief's son, one officer (Muysart) and three Dutchmen were to be delivered up to the Japanese as hostages and taken to Japan. Five Japanese, including Heijo's cousin, would likewise be left with the Dutch and they might be taken in a Dutch ship to Japan to be exchanged for the six Dutch hostages.

2. The eleven Sakkam people and two Chinese interpreters captured and imprisoned by the Dutch during the trouble were to be released and such of their property as had been confiscated should be restored.

3. Appropriate presents were to be made to Yahei by the Dutch officers in Formosa.

4. Before the Japanese should depart from the port the Dutch ships should bring ashore all their oars.

5. The Japanese had remaining in China 20,000 catties of silk and when an attempt was made to secure it by Yahei and his party the Dutch prevented them. Therefore as the property had now no doubt been captured by pirates the Dutch were to indemnify them for this loss. Furthermore, the Japanese several years before had been deprived of 1,500 catties of silk which the first Dutch Governor had confiscated owing to the non payment of port taxes. This must be returned to them.

The council after giving the subject due consideration came to the conclusion that they would agree to articles 1, 2, and 3, but that they could not accept article 4, and must request that article 5 should also be withdrawn. As the Japanese stated that the loss of the silk was caused by Dutch interference, it would be better to consent to this and to refer the case to the authorities in Japan, who might be induced to return the property. The same to apply to the silk confiscated by the Dutch.

Having noted their decision as stated above the council prepared a document in the proper form, which having been sealed and signed by seventeen Dutch officers was transmitted to the Japanese, who formally accepted it.

On the 4th the hostages were exchanged and on the 5th, 12,053 catties of the silk promised was handed over, and the balance delivered in money at the rate of $14.10 per hundred catties. The other condition having also been fulfilled, the governor after seven days' imprisonment was released, and the Japanese announced their intention of returning to their native country at once. At this time the Dutch factory still remained in Hirado, Japan, but the Formosa Governor upon his release advised all the Dutch to gather at.

Nagasaki where he believed the inhabitants "were more peaceful and expenses would be lighter."

The Japanese not contented under Dutch rule now withdrew from Formosa, but the Chinese increased with great rapidity until all the districts around the Dutch factories were occupied by these people, and the capitation tax yielded 200,000 guilders annually. For a time this latter class submitted to the various taxations without murmuring, but eventually, dissatisfied with the rule of the foreigners, they attempted to better their condition by rising in rebellion, in hopes that their superiority in number would avail against the superior arms of the Dutch. In this they were disappointed, for the foreigners, gathering about them nearly 2,000 native Christians, attacked the rebels with great force, so that the slaughter was very heavy among them, especially as the natives took this opportunity to obtain revenge for the many years of cruelty they had endured at the hands of the Chinese.

Now with the Japanese difficulty disposed of, it behoved the Dutch to apply their trade monopoly doctrine to the Spanish who were comfortably settled in the north of the island. There was to be no argument, no lengthy consular reports in which each side proclaimed the superior quality and the cheapness of their own goods, but an appeal to arms; for the Dutch were determined that eastern traders should deal with them or not deal at all.

The Spanish along with the Portuguese had been driven by the Dutch from participation in Japanese trade, and the former wishing for some station where they could renew and protect their trade had decided on a site in the north of Formosa, without any intention of disturbing the Dutch who were occupying the south of the island.

The expedition was organized in Manila at the close of the governorship of Fernando de Silva and consisted of three companies of infantry under the command of Don Antonio Carreño de Valdes and a provincial prelate, Fr. Bartolome Martinez, as director of the expedition with five Dominican friars as assistants. A dozen Chinese boats and two Spanish galleons were prepared to carry the party.

On the 8th of February, 1626, this expedition set sail, and after delaying in a northern harbour of the Philippines for three months awaiting a change of monsoon, the expedition continued on its way, reaching the northern coast of Formosa early in May. On the 10th they landed the troops on the shores of a bay which they called Port Santiago, but finding that the situation was not well protected in all seasons, the provincial prelate gave orders to reconnoitre the northern coast in hopes of obtaining a more secure location. At last a position was discovered with a harbor which they considered magnificent and protected from all winds. To this place they gave the name of Santissima Trinidad but it was none other than the port of Kelung, long known to the Chinese by that name and occupied by Japanese pirates only some twenty years before.

The first task in those days was to erect forts, and the Spanish accordingly set to work to build a strong structure to serve as a place of security against all comers. At the entrance of the bay stood an island which formed the key to the harbor. On this was erected a strong fort, and on a hill 300 feet above the sea level was raised a second fortification. Over this was flown their beloved banner of Castile, and now satisfied[1] with his labours the prelate returned to Manila with the majority of the expedition.

The natives, who, at the first boom of the cannon had fled in great terror to the hills, were now induced by the good friars to return. A small chapel dedicated to All Saints had been erected, and untiring labors were made to convert the natives to Christianity. The first converts were two young men the sons of a Chinese who had long been a resident of the port, and who had married a native woman. The friars rejoiced at this, the first recognition of the true God in their colony and celebrated the occasion with great pomp. During the ceremony of the sacrament a salute was fired, the troops were paraded, and the function was carried out with a solemn pageantry the like of which had not been seen in the island, and which must have impressed the natives. From this time, deserved success attended the efforts of the friars, until in 1627 the converts were so numerous that in the provincial chapter of 1627 the new territory was declared a Vicariate, and Father Francisco Mola, assisted by four friars, was despatched to the island to take charge.

After the establishment of the colony at San Salvador on a permanent basis the Spanish forces proceeded in 1629 to occupy Tamsui, which even at this early period was frequented by many Chinese merchants, who came from Fokien to barter with the Formosa natives. The natives here, as at Kelung, fled at the sight of the Spanish. It seems, however, that either they or the Chinese had erected some sort of fortification, as Spanish accounts state that a fort was captured and upon its ruins the victors built a substantial fort to which the name San Domingo was given. A church was next built, which was dedicated with great pomp to the Lady of the Rosary, while the natives, who had now recovered from their fright, assisted in making a road from the fort to the top of the hill upon which the church stood.

Peter Nuits the Dutch Governor of Formosa, reported these facts to his home authorities and exposed in an interesting report the injury that the Spaniards were doing to Dutch trade and the necessity of sending an expedition to drive them away.

" We ought to render ourselves masters of Kelang (Kelung) for the following reasons :

1. From this place the enemy can always equip vessels to attack ours which are trading with Chinchoo, and it is almost impossible to protect our ships. If one vessel is taken by the company the loss will be greater than the whole expense of fitting out an expedition to capture Ke-lang.

2. If the Spanish remain, on account of the large capital at their disposal they will be a source of embarrassment and inquietude to us and will also attract to their colony a large share of merchandise.

3. If they are once firmly established, it is to be feared that they may incite the natives and the Chinese to revolt against us. This would be a great misfortune, for without the amity of the latter we should not be able to hold our own, unless we greatly reinforced our garrison and fleet, which would considerably augment our expense and seriously diminish our profits.

4. Kelung once reduced, we should have an opportunity of employing greater capital, since the merchandise which would otherwise go to the Spanish would then come to us and at the same time the Chinese would have to lower their prices."

---

1. Although their general situation is known, no definite traces now remain of these forts on what is at present known as Palm Island, at the entrance of Kelung harbor, and the Spanish descriptions are not sufficiently detailed to enable the writer, in spite of careful research, to identify the ruins that are found with the forts alluded to. Chang Ching, the son of Koxinga, not having a sufficient garrison to defend them, saw fit at a later period, to destroy these strongholds, fearing that the Tartars might turn them against himself.

The Dutch authorities in Batavia do not seem to have been impressed with the importance of these suggestions, for no expeditions were authorized. Consequently for twelve years the new colony enjoyed perfect tranquillity. It was only in 1641 when the Spanish severed their ties with the Portuguese that the Dutch decided to dispose of their dangerous neighbor. Accordingly a squadron of three vessels was despatched to North Formosa to deliver an ultimatum to the Spanish Commander. It is an unique despatch worthy of reproduction here.

To Gonsalo Portilio,
Governor of the Spanish fortress
In the Island of Kelung
SIR,
I have the honor to communicate to you that I have received the command of a considerable naval and military force with the view of making me master by civil means or otherwise of the fortress Santissima Trinidad in the isle of Ke-lung of which your Excellency is the Governor.
In accordance with the usages of Christian nations to make known their intentions before commencing hostilities, I now summon your Excellency to surrender. If your Excellency is disposed to lend an ear to the terms of capitulation which we offer and to make delivery to me of the fortress of Santissima Trinidad and other citadels, your Excellency and your troops will be treated in good faith according to the usages and customs of war, but if your Excellency feigns to be deaf to this command there will be no other remedy than recourse to arms. I hope that your Excellency will give careful consideration to the contents of this letter and avoid the useless effusion of blood, and I trust that without delay and in a few words you will make known to me your intentions.

May God protect your Excellency many years.
The Friend of your Excellency,
PAULUS TRADENIUS.
Fort Zelandia, August 26th, 1641.

This letter, which for frankness and energy contrasts singularly with most of the communications of like purport in our days, the Spanish Governor answered in a courteous and formal manner as follows :—

"To the Governor of Taiwan.

Sir; I have duly received your communication of August 26th, and in response I have the honor to point out to you that as becomes a good Christian who respects the oath he has made before his king, I cannot and I will not surrender the forts demanded by your Excellency, as I and my garrison have determined to defend them. I am accustomed to find myself before great armies, and I have engaged in numerous battles in Flanders as well as other countries, and so I beg of you not to take the trouble of writing me further letters of like tenor. May each one defend himself as best he can. We are Spanish Christians and God in whom we trust is our protector.

May the Lord have mercy on you.
Written in our principal fortress San Salvador the 6th of September 1641.
(signed) GONSALO PORTILIS."

On receipt of this answer the Dutch sent an expedition against Kelung and Tamsui which on its arrival met with such strong opposition from the Spanish that the assailants were forced to retire after an ineffectual cannonade and a useless disembarkation of troops.

After the departure of the Dutch the Spanish Father Bartolome Martinez[1] and the governor of the fort which had so ably repulsed the Dutch

---

1. The death of Father Martinez was a great loss to the colony. After a distinguished career in Spain he was despatched to Manila where he became interested in the Chinese and decided to establish a Dominican mission in China. His first labors on the Chinese mainland were in Macao, but meeting with much opposition from the Portuguese, he at last retired to the convent of Binondo in Manila, applying himself to the study of the Chinese language. Becoming proficient in the tongue, he joined his countrymen in Formosa and was of such assistance to them in the administration of the colony and possessed so much influence with the natives that he was elevated to the rank of Vicar. Thenceforward he dedicated himself to the conversion of the natives of Formosa. Previous to his death and during the fighting with the Dutch he exhibited a daring spirit, occupying without hesitation the most dangerous localities and encouraging his subordinates to the defence of their country and their God.

embarked in a small boat propelled by both sail and oar for fort San Salvador. But the boat was capsized and in spite of all efforts to save them three persons were drowned including the venerable father.

The Spanish authorities at Manila, with very poor policy, now recalled three out of the four companies in Formosa for a campaign against the Mindanao Moors. The Dutch were of course not slow to take advantage of this ill-advised step and made preparations for a second expedition. Upon learning of this, which could hardly have been a surprise to the commander of the Spanish colony, he at once called for supplies and reinforcements, and the Manila Governor with a shrewdness quite on a par with the former recall of the troops, sent a few provisions, a little ammunition and a *reinforcement of eight Spanish soldiers*.

On the 3rd of August 1642, eighteen months after the first attack, the Dutch appeared off Tamsui with a comparatively powerful squadron of four frigates, a large cutter, nine small vessels, besides several transports, under the command of Hendric Harouse.

The invaders at once landed. The Spanish commander had sent only 12 Spanish soldiers, 8 Indians of Luzon, and 40 native archers to oppose the Dutch disembarkation, and this force was, of course quite inadequate. The Dutch having thus gained the beach and the unprotected suburbs of Tamsui, laid seige to Fort Domingo. The Spanish, regardless of their small force, held out gallantly, defending their position night and day without rest.

The Dutch at last succeeded in mounting artillery on an elevation commanding the fortress and were thus enabled to inflict great damage on the fort, the defenders of which after six days of determined but futile opposition surrendered on the feast day of Saint Bartolome, the 24th of August, 1642. Kelung fell in a similar manner, and with its capture the Dutch became the undisputed masters of Formosa. The victors captured forty pieces of large artillery, a large quantity of ammunition, and twenty-five thousand dollars in silver, and merchandise valued at more than one million dollars, the property of merchants established there. So great was the joy at their victory that the Dutch celebrated it for eight days. The Spanish garrison, five Dominican missionaries, and one Franciscan were carried as prisoners of war to Taiwan and thence to Batavia, where the governor treated them with courtesy and kindness, and eventually granted them unconditional pardon and permission to return to Manila at their pleasure. The ex-governor of the defunct colony, fearing that the loss of their Formosa colony would be visited on his head, remained behind, and the rest of the party selecting Father Juan de los Angelos as their temporary commander departed from Batavia, arriving in Manila June 29th, 1643.

The loss of these admirably situated posts of commerce was keenly felt by the Spanish colony in Manila, and there were even suggestions, never carried into effect, that a strong expedition should be sent to recover them from the Dutch.

The Dutch followed up their victory by appearing with their squadron off Manila. The Spanish were greatly alarmed, and feared that the attack on Tamsui and Kelung might be the prelude to an expedition to drive them from the Philippines. The enemy landed a force in hopes of inciting the natives to rebel, but according to Spanish accounts were not successful, owing to the attachment of the natives to the Catholic religion. It does not appear that the Dutch had any real intention of attacking the colony, but were there only to intercept Spanish transports and galleons ; for after having watched the coast for some time and given battle to the Spanish squadron, they set sail and disappeared. This discouraged the Spanish from making any attempt to recover their possessions in North Formosa, and no farther efforts were made by them to interfere with the trade of which Formosa was the principal mart.

Freed from all competitors the Dutch now enlarged their domains and established factories at both Kelung and Tamsui, erecting in the latter place a substantial brick and stone fort of such solidity that, with a sufficient garrison, it would be absolutely impregnable against any engines of war that those early days could produce.[1] A clergyman was also stationed in Tamsui to look after the spiritual welfare of the natives.

From Kelung the Dutch rapidly spread their authority throughout the beautiful Kapsulan plain lying to the southward of Kelung, nestling between the high mountains of the interior and the rough rock-bound coast of the Pacific. In 1648 the Dutch could count 47 villages under their control in this fertile plain. To the south, Dutch rule had extended to the most remote settlement of importance, the village of Liangkiau.

At the height of their prosperity about the year 1650 the villages under Dutch jurisdiction numbered 293 and were spread over forty-five clañs, and had even reached the east side of the island, 37 of them being located in the vicinity of Pilam near the south-east coast. For administrative purposes they had divided their territory into seven districts, five lying to the east or north of Sakkam (Tainanfu), one on the south coast, and the other on the south-east coast. Of these the most important were Sakkam, Favorlan, Matau, and Soulang.

The company received considerable revenue from taxes, and it does not appear that much was paid out for the benefit of the island.

Tribute was collected from China, though for the first few years the amount received scarcely exceeded three thousand *reals* per year. Immigration fostered by disturbances in Fokien province brought many families to the island, and by the middle of the century this tax totalled nearly forty thousand *reals*. It was estimated that the new arrivals numbered

---

1. This most interesting relic of Formosan history.—"The Old Dutch fort" with its walls of nearly eight feet of masonry and lime still commands the port of Tamsui, as firm and solid and as imposing as when built two hundred and fifty years ago. That it has not lost one iota in strength and is still formidable the French bombardment of 1884 clearly proved, for during that engagement the fort was struck hard and true, but the shells did no damage and scarcely left a mark on the noble structure. It is a most impressive monument of longevity and as such was selected as the most fitting place to celebrate the 60th year of the reign of Her Majesty Queen Victoria on April 23rd, 1897. The fort is at present occupied as the office of the British Consulate.

some twenty-five thousand families. Deer hunting was a profitable occupation, not only to the hunters but to the Dutch, who received one *real* per month as license money from each hunter. Other taxes were numerous, even the unfortunate fishermen being obliged to give to the government a portion of their catch. Out of this considerable revenue the natives received but little in return, and that only with the idea of obtaining additional gains for the company. Finding that agriculture was not progressing as they wished and learning that the absence of domesticated animals for draft purposes was a serious drawback, the company advanced the minister Gravius during the middle of the century 4,000 *reals* with which he purchased 121 oxen for distribution among the natives.

The military force in the island consisted of about one thousand well armed men, one third of whom were employed as a garrison at Fort Zelandia. Still it must be apparent to the reader that the Dutch success with the natives was not altogether due to this military force.

True it is that the form of administration allowed the savage clans much liberty as to their own form of government; their native customs were not generally disturbed, and they chose their own village elders. As to the latter the Dutch had encouraged this method of obtaining headmen for the villages, and rarely expressed dissatisfaction with the peoples' choice. They recognized the elder officially; with much ceremony investing him with a silver-headed staff, ornamented with the company's coat of arms, as insignia of authority.

To preserve their influence with the elders the latter were all assembled once a year at a grand ceremonial feast[1] held at Sakkam. On this occasion new appointments were confirmed, orders given for the succeeding year, presents lavishly bestowed on the most worthy of the elders, and the participants returned to their respective districts.

The real success with the natives, however, was due neither to the military force nor the system of civil government, although of course these were important factors, but to the individual character of the missionaries, who labored with the natives, not for the sake of trade, but to save souls. The government fully appreciated this and vested them with much authority.

As the missionaries were much concerned with the government, and as the success attained during the short period of their labors has never been equalled in any land peopled by so called barbarians, I may be excused for reviewing their labor rather minutely.[2]

As previously stated Candidius, a Protestant divine, was the first missionary engaged. Upon arriving in the island and looking over the field he

---

1. The Dutch called this a land-dag (diet) and took special care to explain laws enacted by the government and to admonish the delegates to give a kind reception to the Chinese merchants and hunters who might come to their respective places.

2. In the succeeding pages of this chapter I have supplemented my information, gathered from various sources inaccessible to the general reader by quoting freely from the first volume of the valuable work of the Rev. William Campbell, which embodies much information compiled from official reports regarding labors of the Dutch clergy in Formosa.

Missionary Success in Formosa, by Rev. Wm. Campbell of the English Presbyterian Mission, Tainanfu. In two volumes, published by Trübner & Co., 57, Ludgate Hill, London.

expressed his belief that both the disposition and the circumstances of the natives were favorable for their conversion to Christianity. " With good capacities, they were ignorant of letters ; their superstitions rested only on tradition, on customs to which they were strongly attached and which had been almost totally changed within the last sixty years, and no obstacles were to be apprehended from the government." Candidius applied himself with zeal to the work, and in a manner so effective that during the first sixteen months of his stay, part of which had been occupied in studying the language, he instructed 120 of the natives in the Christian religion. Two years later Robertus Junius arrived in Formosa to join in the work. Candidius returned to his native land, but in 1633 accepted a second appointment and was located in Sakkam with his colleague Junius.

In the year 1635, Candidius and Junius had by their zealous labors so far progressed that about 700 natives of Formosa had been baptized by them, and the next year the opportunities for propagating the gospel in Formosa were so favorable that the two divines communicated with the authorities at Batavia, begging that new laborers might be sent to so promising a field, and stating that employment might be found even for ten or twenty clergymen.

Accordingly, two ministers were despatched from home the next year, one of them, Lindeborn by name, was accompanied by his wife. They had sailed via Japan, where Mrs. Lindeborn, the first European lady to appear in that country, created much wonder among the Japanese.

Junius in 1636 established the first school in Formosa, commencing with a class of 70 boys, whom he taught to write their mother tongue in roman letters. The government were interested in the work, and furnished the students with rice and clothes. The natives took advantage of the opportunity to such an extent that three years later the schools had been increased to five, and 485 boys were receiving government aid.

New recruits for the missionary forces continued to arrive from the home land, and the number of converts increased rapidly. Candidius returned to Europe and Junius became his successor, taking the lead of his colleagues in the amount of work accomplished. As to his success the following extract—the original orthography of which is preserved—from a pamphlet published in London in 1650 will enlighten us.

" OF THE CONVERSION OF FIVE THOUSAN . NINE HUNDRED EAST INDIANS IN THE ISLE OF FORMOSA.

"And whereas the *Gentiles* or *Heathen* are first to be instructed and Preached unto, that they may beleeve, before they should be baptized ; This Reverend M. *Junius* tooke great paines dayly, in first instructing them in the grounds of Religion, Catechizing them, to bring them to beleeve : So that of persons grown up in that isle of *Formosa* FIVE THOUSAND and NINE HUNDRED, of both Sexes, gave up their Names to Christ ; and professing their faith, and giving fit answers to questions propounded out of the Word of God, were baptized by him ; (of which number of persons so dipt in water, the infants of persons in Covenant are not reckoned, and to such persons in (*Soulangh*) and *Sinckan*, and elsewhere being instructed well in the Doctrine of the *Lords Supper*, was that Ordinance of Christ also administered with much reverence, joy, and edification.

" And because the instructing of persons to Reade and to Write, tends much to further, not onely Civill and Poli ical good, but also Spirituall ; herein also M. *Junius* tooke much paines, in furthering of both, instructing some to Teach others, and in Visiting and Ordering the Schollers.

" And besides a few *Dutch* men, that were Teachers of others ; in the *Six Townes* before said, of the *Heathenish* natives that he gained to Christ, about *Fiftie* of them he so instructed and fitted for this worke, that excelled in Godliness, Knowledge, Industrie, Dexteritie and Sedulitie ; that before his departure thence, they had taught *six hundred* schollers to Reade and to Write ; and that instructed, as well the elder as younger persons, in the Rudiments of Christian Faith."

It was a strange sight in Asia in those early days to see hundreds educated in the use of the Latin alphabet and flocking to a Christian church on Sundays and living in accordance with the teachings of Christianity. But such was common in Formosa in several of the districts in which the missionaries had especially exerted themselves. "To our surprise, we daily see young people not only marrying according to Christian rites but going together into the fields, and, not only bringing children into the world, but even living together; while formerly they would have rather died than live thus."

The material part of the life in Formosa in which the missionaries were concerned is well illustrated in the following extract from a letter written by Rev. Robert Junius to the Governor-General, Antonius van Diemen, and dated at Tayouan, 23rd of October, 1649.

"Although the inhabitants of Dovale annoyed us very much in the late hunting expeditions, and drove away many Chinese who had hunting licenses; still, 1941 *reals* have been received from that source. The expenses—as Your Excellency will see from the specifications - have amounted only to 627 *reals*, so that the surplus is 1314 *reals*; to which sum my account (according to Your Excellency's orders), has been debited."

"The season has again commenced in which the Chinese begin to hunt, and several have already applied for licenses, but I am of opinion (and have spoken to the governor about it, who I wish could also agree with me) that it would be better not to grant any hunting licenses for this year, for the following reasons: 1st. Because the Company has still, if I am rightly informed, several thousands of skins here which, from a lack of vessels, they have not been able to ship to Japan. 2nd. Because the deer have decreased considerably in numbers in nearly all the hunting fields, by the continual hunting which is resumed every year; and if the hunting were now prohibited the deer would again multiply very fast, and this would greatly please the inhabitants in whose fields the Chinese hunt every year. 3rd. For the very important reason that, if we allow the Chinese to hunt, our influence and reputation will greatly suffer thereby, as the inhabitants of Dovale and (it is to be feared) of Vovorollang will be constantly coming out of their villages to chase away, to rob, and to murder the hunters; and all this we shall not be able to prevent, seeing that these people usually hunt at a great distance from Tayouan.

"Many Chinese who were too poor to pay for their licenses requested me to advance them the money; promising that, after the hunt, they would sell me the skins—large and small—at 10 *reals* a hundred; and the late governor permitted us to do so, on condition that we held ourselves responsible for whatever loss might be sustained by the Chinese running away or becoming insolvent. He was the more inclined to grant this, as there would thus be brought to us all the skins they were in the practice of having secretly transported to China; but he stipulated that we should ourselves advance the money spent in preliminary expenses, and approved of the whole arrangement for this particular reason, that, if the accounts were settled by us, he would be able to see what profit the licenses yielded, and would thus find a way for defraying in future the expenses required for the support of the clergymen in Formosa, etc.

"The Chinese are very desirous of borrowing money from us, as otherwise they must borrow it from their countrymen, who show no mercy in their dealings with each other, and who charge from 4 to 5 *per cent.* for monthly interest. If the hunting licenses, therefore, are sold again this year as in former years, we shall advance the money on the terms I previously mentioned, and endeavor to arrange that the quarter which they pay over and above the *real* is not paid in *cash* as they have done hitherto, but in skins.

"The hunting will thus produce every year from 500 to 1,000 *reals*, making an annual increase from. Formosa of 4,000; which we doubt not will greatly please Your Excellency. The Chinese who live in the villages, however, are very poor, and may not be able to pay a quarter of a *real* per month. If Your Excellency had allowed the 1,000 *reals* of the collection to remain in our hands, they would have given very willingly; and if they continue to pay a quarter of a *real* monthly, they will certainly try to recoup themselves by cheating the poorer class of our aboriginal people, whom they daily defraud, and who, on that account, can never better their condition."

In 1657 the Dutch decided to establish a college, with the object of educating young natives to become suitable and capable clergymen. It was located at Mattau. The reasons for selecting this situation are recorded in the minute book of the church of Tayouan as follows:—

"In the first place, the village of Mattau, like Mesopotamia itself, is situated in the midst of the rivers, so that many a deserter or runaway will, as it were, be caught in his wicked purpose to escape. For it is much to be feared, especially in the beginning, that after these young natives have been separated for some time from their parents and relatives, they will desire (contrary to what is right and proper in this case) to revisit them, and thus run off again in the face of our wish and consent; whereas, if the seminary were erected in Mattau, the rapid current and the great depth of the rivers—more particularly in the time of the monsoon, would effectually prevent them from doing so.

"Add this also, that Mattau is situated nearer to the hunting-fields than either Soulang or Sinkang, thus making it easier to obtain fresh deer flesh; and although the abundance and variety of fish may not be greater than in Soulang, yet supplies can be more easily obtained, inasmuch as Mattau has a greater number of fisheries than any other place."

"The applicants, whose age ranged from ten to fourteen, were to possess a good character, good memories, and quickness of apprehension ; it being also desirable that they should know by heart the Prayers and the Catechism, be very adept in learning the Dutch language, and well acquainted with reading and writing, having already proved themselves to be among the most willing to receive this training ; while a preference should be shown for orphans and such as are miserably poor.

"The order, manner, and time of instruction should be as follows :—

"*First :* As a general rule, the young inmates shall be instructed in the Formosan language in the morning, and in the Dutch language in the afternoon.

"*Secondly :* The time given to instruction in the morning shall be 4 glasses, beginning at sunrise ; that is, from 6 till 8—two glasses to be allowed (*i.e.* 1 hour) for breakfast—and then, again, for four glasses, *i.e.* from 9 till 11.

"*Thirdly :* The time given to instruction during the afternoon shall be four glasses ; that is, from 3 till 5.

"*Fourthly :* Till the young people become better acquainted with the Dutch language the Sub-Director shall employ the Formosan language in giving early morning instruction in the Catechism — zealously endeavoring then to implant in the hearts of his pupils the right understanding thereof. The same task shall devolve upon the Regent from 10 till 11 in the forenoon, and every morning, from 9 till 10, the young people shall be diligently exercised in reading and writing—Thursday, however, being considered a holiday, when the scholars shall be at liberty to play and amuse themselves, or be permitted to go out.

"*Fifthly :* In the afternoon the Dutch language is to be taught, and the book called *The Door or Port to Language* be employed for that purpose ; a work written by Comenius, and containing some familiar phrases in the Dutch and Formosan languages.

"*Lastly :* The Consistory desires to have the following Rules adopted :—

"1. That the Sub-Director shall see to have all the young people up in the morning before sunrise ; that they properly dress, wash, and comb themselves ; and, thereafter, that morning prayers be read, all present reverently kneeling.

"2 That before and after the usual lessons prayers shall be said or read.

"3. That at meal-times, that is, at breakfast, at dinner-time (12 o'clock), and at supper (6 o'clock)— a blessing shall first be asked, and afterwards thanks be returned.

"4. That while dinner and supper are being partaken of, a chapter from the Bible shall be read aloud.

"5. That the young people shall take it by turns to read a chapter during dinner and supper, and the prayers appointed before and after meals, and before and after instruction.

"6. That no young person shall be allowed to leave the seminary without the special permission of the Director.

"7. That the Sub-Director shall not be allowed to give more than a blow with the ferule by way of punishment in cases of misbehavior.

"8. That the young people who remain out longer than the time appointed shall be punished as the Director thinks fit.

"That every day two Monitors shall be appointed, whose duty it will be, in rotation, to mark those who speak any other language than Dutch during college-time, or who do not behave properly ; and report such delinquencies to the Sub-Director.

"10. That the Sub-Director shall take especial care that the clothes of the children are kept neat and clean, that the building itself be properly cleansed in all its parts, and that attention be given to all such things as may tend to the advantage and weal of the place.

"The Consistory also leaves it to the Governor and Council to appoint a certain number of slaves to attend to the more servile duties, to prepare the food of the young people, to see to their clothing, and to do such other work as may be required for domestic purposes."

The Dutch missionaries took extremely drastic methods in their effort to force the natives to give up their sins. They declared idolatry a crime and subject to a punishment unmerciful in its severity. The lengths to which their zeal carried them is indicated by a letter of the Governor and Council of Formosa to the Governor-General and Councillors of India, an extract of which reads as follows :—

     *   *   *   *   *   *   *   *   *   *

TAYOUAN, 2 MARCH, 1658.

"Considering the manifold complaints, and our own daily observation, that the Formosans living on this plain, and especially those amongst them who are less instructed, in the face of our repeated and serious admonitions, persistently continue to practice the sins of idolatry, adultery, fornication, and sometimes even of incest ; considering, too, that many of them offend in this way because they are so ignorant of the laws of God and man that it seems difficult to punish them according to their deserts, we have unanimously resolved to issue the accompanying proclamation.

"Before arriving at this decision, we all agreed to consult the Consistory about the matter, and their opinion is that the proclamation in no way deviates from the righteous law of God. It was also remembered by us that there are many weak Christians here who are exceedingly deficient in knowledge; that, indeed, the greater portion of the people are still benighted heathen.

"Let it, therefore, be borne in mind that this, our proclamation, is intended for all, but more particularly for those who have received daily instruction in the principles of true religion and sound morals; and that in addressing the people of every class, we only conform to the custom of our beloved native land, whose inhabitants, by the grace of God, are gifted with a far higher degree of knowledge and understanding than the inhabitants of this place.

"Thus, in keeping with what has just been stated, we now declare that idolatry in the first degree shall be punishable with public whipping and banishment; that those who are guilty of incest shall be severely whipped in public, and condemned to wear chains during a space of six years; while the less heinous sins enumerated in this proclamation shall be proportionately punished according to circumstances, by the decision of the judge. And in order that none may pretend ignorance of the matter, this our proclamation shall be translated into all the dialects of the island, and affixed in public to churches and schools; arrangements being also made for having it read in public once a month; that all the people may, as far as lies in our power, be taught to cease from the practice of those vile things which have been referred to."

* * * * * * * * * *

It was natural that these simple islanders should resent the disgrace, punishment, and forced desertion of their old religion contemplated by their Dutch masters ; for that old religion was doubtless as dear to them as the new religion was to their oppressors.

It seems that the Supreme Council to the Governor-General and Councillors of India did not indorse such rigorous methods, for two years later a letter was sent to the Governor and Council of Formosa from which the following is an extract:—

AMSTERDAM, April 16th, 1660.

"Honorable, equitable, wise, and very discreet Gentlemen,

"We are also in receipt of a missive from Governor Coyett and his Council, dated 2nd of March, 1658. From it we see that, in order to intimidate and prevent the Formosans from committing idolatry—to which they seem much addicted, notwithstanding the most serious admonition and censure—proclamations and ordinances have been issued by the said Governor and Council, with the approval and consent of the Consistory; in which documents, persons committing idolatry are threatened with the severest punishment, such as public whipping and banishment.

"Now, as we can in no way believe that these are the appropriate means whereby poor benighted people will be led to forsake idolatry, and be brought to the saving knowledge of the truth, we are quite averse to their being employed; and this the more so, from our conviction that such means would only cause them to show still greater aversion to our rule, and lead them at last to the adoption of even desperate measures.

"Our conviction is, that if we cannot influence the inhabitants by precept and instruction, they are much less likely to be influenced by severe punishments of this kind; and as we are of opinion that Christians ought in no case to resort to such measures, it has greatly surprised us that the consistory should have given consent to their adoption in the present case. Thus, although the object be to Christianize the nations, we cannot refrain from declaring that these methods sorely displeased us, because they may be considered harsh and cruel, and because they are contrary to the spirit and character of the Dutch nation. We confidently expect, therefore, that the punishments proclaimed will be considered mitigated—that, while the ordinance itself may not be publicly retracted, it will not be put into execution."

This appeared not only to the Dutch missionaries but to many modern divines,[1] as an expression from the Dutch governors in India that they did not desire the conversion of Formosans to be placed to the fore as a government measure, lest it should give offence to the Japanese whose commerce they wished to preserve and by whom Christianity was at that time heavily persecuted. If this condemnation of the Dutch governors is based wholly on their refusal to approve of the rather extreme measures taken by the Dutch missionaries to propagate the Christian religion among the Formosans and

---

"1. The work was progressing favorably, churches and schools were multiplying, the intermarriages of the colonists and natives were bringing them into closer relationship with each other, and many thousands of the islanders had been baptised, when the Dutch governors in India fearful of offending the Japanese who were then persecuting the Christians in Japan—in which the Dutch helped them to their lasting disgrace—restricted these benevolent labors, and discouraged the further conversion of the natives. Williams' Middle Kingdom, Vol. II, Page 434."

which stands in such marked contrast to the peaceful methods of the missionaries of our day, it would seem that such criticism smacks strongly of bigotry and illiberality. It may be that the Dutch Company did by later measures restrict the Christian work among the natives to an extent that would cause just indignation in the hearts of all sincere teachers of the Bible ; but Dutch Formosan history does not give any evidence of their having done so.

Whatever stand the Dutch Company were prepared to take in pointing out to the natives the paths of honesty, morality, and generosity, we have abundant evidence that the officials were not inclined to take the same route themselves. Regardless of the fact that their position in Formosa was a comfortable one, that their trade was profitable, and that they virtually controlled the foreign commerce of Japan, they were still envious of their neighbors and ready to again harass their Portuguese rivals as they had at intervals for half a century in the past.

Although the Chinese government had permitted Chinese junks to communicate freely with Formosa and no difficulty was found in obtaining as much merchandise as the company desired, still the Dutch ships were not expected to enter a China port to trade although they occasionally did so with the connivance of the Fokien governor. Their China trade, however, was small compared with that of their rivals, and it was decided at the first opportunity to strengthen their commercial relations with the Empire if possible.

As soon as it became evident that the Manchus were in the ascendency the government of Batavia considered it a time favorable for their purposes and accordingly despatched a deputation aboard a richly freighted ship with one Schedel as envoy to petition for direct trade. They arrived at Canton in January 1653, but except in the case of the cargo brought with them the Portuguese were successful as of old in preventing any further trade, even after the authorities has been presented by the Dutch with costly presents, and the governor had given his formal permission for a factory to be built.

There was nothing now left for the envoy but to return. Having been advised that an embassy to Pekin might bring forth good results, the Company, in 1655, appointed Goyer and Keyzer as its envoys, who in due time appeared at the capital. The success of this venture has been recorded as follows :—

"The narrative of this embassy by Nieuwhof, the steward of the mission, made Europeans better acquainted with the country than they had before been—almost the only practical benefit it produced, for as a mercantile speculation it proved nearly a total loss. Their presents were received and others were given in return ; they prostrated themselves not only before the Emperor in person, but made the 'Kotow' to his name, his letters, and his throne, doing everything in the way of humiliation and homage likely to please the new rulers. The only privilege their subserviency obtained was permission to send an embassy once in eight years, at which time they might come in four ships to trade."[1]

Still Formosa remained to the Dutch as a profitable possession, and would perhaps have been theirs to this day had not the Company with extraordinary short-sightedness been so engrossed in making the maximum of profits for the moment, that they refused to expend the money necessary to make themselves secure against Chinese invasion.

---

1. Williams' "Middle Kingdom," Vol. II, Page 431.

CHAPTER III.

FORMOSA UNDER THE DUTCH.
1644-1661.

DURING the whole period of the Dutch occupation of Formosa, China was visited with numerous calamities, not only from wars waged by foreign invaders, but the greater civil war which, gradually sweeping down with in-creasing force, overwhelmed the capital itself; and the invading Tartars, the ancestors of the present rulers of China, in 1644 drove the Mings from the throne, causing their own chief to be recognized as Emperor of China by most of the northern provinces. At the close of the following year, twelve of the fifteen provinces had submitted to the usurper. Formosa gained many thousands of inhabitants by this long war, for the Chinese were flying to other countries to escape the troubles in their own.

Among the daring spirits which those turbulent days produced was Chêng Chi-lung (Tei Shi-ryo), also known to foreigners as Iquan, who, as previously related, had succeeded to the command of a band of pirates who had their headquarters in Formosa. This man was born in a small village on the seashore in the Fokien province.[1] His early life was a struggle with poverty, for his trade was that of a tailor, and people thought more of their lives during his time than they did of fine robes. He later emigrated to Macao where he served the Portuguese, and having received much Christian teaching while there, he was converted and baptized by the name of Nicholas. Not destined to remain long on the tailor's bench, he sought greater opportunities by becoming a petty trader, and while thus engaged journeyed to Japan. This seemed the turning point in his eventful career, for success crowned his efforts from that time onward. He made his home at Hirado in the dominion of the *Daimyō* Ōmura, near the present city of Nagasaki, and there married a Japanese woman of the Tagawa family, to whom, in the year 1624, was born a son named Chêng Kung (Tei-seiko), later known as Koxinga, who lived to become one of the most extraordinary characters that ever appeared in China. His father, from a petty trader, grew by foreign trade to be the richest merchant in China, and afterwards at his own expense fitted out a fleet to oppose the Tartars. His success gradually drew around him a vast number of Chinese vessels till he became commander of as great a fleet as ever appeared in the China seas, and eventually attained, by his political intrigues, vast undertakings, and piratical raids, such great wealth that even the Chinese Emperor could not compete with him. His fleet of 3000 sail gave him command of the seas, and none dared oppose him.

Five years after the birth of Chêng Kung (Koxinga) his father, at the request of the Chinese Minister of War, removed to China, having been appointed commander-in-chief of the troops opposing the Tartars. Soon after his departure, his wife, who remained in Japan, gave birth to a second son, who was named Shichizaemon. This son did not develope the love for adventure and renown which made his elder brother so famous, but remained quietly in Japan all his life.[2]

The mother and Tei-seiko now left Japan to join the father at Nanking, which was then the capital of China.

Here the son at the age of fifteen was placed in the Imperial University, where he was known by his school-mates as a heroic person rather than a scholar.

Upon reaching the age of twenty-two, accompanied by his father, Tei-seiko was presented to the Chinese Emperor who, pleased with the young man's appearance as well no doubt as desirous of granting a favor to the father, conferred upon him the great honor of bearing the name Koxinga,—the honorable gentleman who bears the same family name as the Emperor. He was then appointed commander of the Central Body Guard and was ennobled

1. In the small fishing village of Shih-tsing, near Anhai in the Chinchoo prefecture, the ancestral temple of the Chêng family still exists, and we are told that some twenty years ago there was to be seen there a portrait of Koxinga, dressed as a literary graduate. Koxinga's father was born in a small hovel of the village, and it is claimed that Koxinga's body, which was removed from Formosa, is buried on a mountain near by. Many relatives of the family reside in the vicinity.

2. The descendants of Shichizaemon served the government for many years as interpreters of Chinese, and there reside to this day in Nagasaki certain Japanese who point with pride to him as their ancestor.

as a count. This was at the beginning of the Tartar invasion, and soon after, the emperor, unable to hold the capital, was driven out, and travelled as a wanderer to Foochow.

Koxinga's father continued loyally to oppose the Tartars, at least in outer appearance, although it is claimed by some historians that at the same time he aided the Tartars by furnishing them such intelligence as he thought would be for his own advantage. At all events, after the Tartars had made frequent overtures to both father and son the father alone weakened, and either suffered the Tartars to come into the three provinces, the only territory they had not already captured, or after useless fighting, surrendered to them.[1] Whether from fear or confidence, the Tartars made him king of Pingan in South China, and loaded him with fine presents. It looks as though it was fear which actuated them, for we learn that having decoyed him out of the city and away from the haven where his fleet was anchored they seized and carried him to Peking, where he was made prisoner and loaded with chains.

The son, now more determined than ever, betook himself to flight. The mother wished to join him, but before she could leave her palace, it was suddenly surrounded by Tartars, and rather than surrender, the brave woman committed suicide. It was then that Koxinga, who, although the recipient of military honors, had served as a civil officer, visited the Temple of Confucius, and casting his scholastic garments into a fire, with much prayer and lamentation resolved to spend the rest of his days in armed opposition to the Tartar invaders. There were many stout loyalists with him, who, in a similar manner, pledged their allegiance to Koxinga and his cause, so that he was possessed of ninety learned men at once who were suitable for responsible offices under his command.

About this time the Emperor of the Ming dynasty died at Foo-chow and was buried without the pomp and ceremony to which his rank entitled him. Soon after, Koxinga and his followers in two large war vessels went to Namoa (on the coast near Amoy), where he assembled several thousand soldiers under his standard. He styled himself "Count Koxinga, Commander-in-Chief," and established his headquarters on the island of Koro (Kulangsu) which is separated from Amoy by a narrow strait. This district still recognized the old dynasty, and several parties of Tartars who attempted to fortify themselves within its borders were attacked by Koxinga and in every instance were defeated and driven thence. But the first of many great victories was the defeat of a strong force at Tonan, which was considered so creditable an accomplishment that the rank of Duke was bestowed upon him. He also soon drove the Portuguese from Amoy and occupied that quarter with his troops. These successes brought to his standard pirates from all over the China seas, and his power was fast becoming as formidable as that of his father before him.

Such a menace to the Tartar government brought from them splendid offers of reward, if he would surrender, but these only increased his resolution.

---

1. Historical accounts greatly differ on this point.

He was soon able to point to seventy-two military stations which he had established in different parts of the provinces, and he threatened the capital itself. The Tartars, now greatly angered at the young commander's obstinacy, took revenge on the father for the doings of the son by throwing him into a vile dungeon and adding fifteen chains to those that were already laid upon him. But Koxinga was not to be stayed. Regardless of this, and planning the complete extirpation of the Tartars, he implored aid from the Japanese *Shōguns*, for with their assistance he believed success would be assured.

Not succeeding in this, Koxinga planned to move on to the capital, Nanking, alone. With this end in view, he reorganized his naval force, but while on his way with an expedition to Chekiang Province, a great storm arose and many of his ships were sunk, drowning eight thousand of his soldiers, amongst them his own son. Although in despair at this calamity, it did not delay him long, for his ships were soon repaired, and we find him the next year with a new expedition ascending the Yang-tse-kiang river to attack Nanking. His force, Chinese history informs us, consisted of fifty thousand cavalry and seventy thousand infantry. Of the latter, ten thousand were known as the "iron men," they being encased in heavy armour decorated witd red spots like the leopard, and were always placed in the front rank that they might cut off the feet of the Tartar[1] horses.

Koxinga, though opposed along the way, advanced steadily, gaining villages day by day, but having reached the city of Ching Kiang, a more serious obstacle was met with, in a fort built in the river. It is described as consisting of timbers covered with earth, surrounded with walls built in some places so high that they stood thirty feet above the water, and mounted upon them were guns and cross bows. The fortification was ten miles long, and horses could with safety travel over the whole surface.

Among the forces sent to oppose Koxinga at this point, were many Tartar generals who had become renowned for their achievements while battling against the armies of the old dynasty. But the young commander was equal to them all, and after a five days' struggle, during which time he lost not a single boat, the Tartars retreated towards the capital. Koxinga was now able to advance and secured several important stations. The Tartars, thoroughly alarmed, called for numerous reinforcements, which were speedily sent them, there being among the number large bands of warriors in iron armour which, it is said, glistened brilliantly in the sun. These haughty warriors sent this word to Koxinga and his men in a contemptuous manner, "Pirates are unworthy of our swords," but when they appeared in gorgeous battle array to fight with the "pirates," Koxinga fought so well that after three days the Tartars found that they were no match for him and retreated with great haste.

---

1. Ricci the missionary who was an eyewitness states "Never before or since was a more powerful and mighty fleet seen in the waters of this empire than that of Koxinga numbering more than 3,000 junks, which he had ordered to rendezvous in the bays and rivers round Amoy. The sight of them inspired one with awe. This squadron did not include the various fleets he had scattered along the neighboring coasts.—*China Review.*

The young commander then divided his forces into five divisions, carrying colors of red, white, black, blue, and yellow. One division was armed with Japanese muskets, another with large spears, while there were corps of trumpeters, bearers of fire signals, color-bearers who bore flags representing centipedes, etc., etc. All the forces were well drilled and disciplined, and the cavalry charges of the well mounted Tartars caused no confusion in the ranks.

At last, in the year 1658, the capital, Nanking, was reached and the retreating Tartars sought safety behind its walls.

Plans were now formed for the attack upon the city and the positions told off to the different divisions, but discontent and dissension arose among his officers, causing great confusion and resulting in defeat just as victory was within his grasp. Stricken with grief he was obliged to return to Amoy, and with demoralization among his troops his fond hopes were doomed to disappointment.

The Tartars took advantage of Koxinga's discomfiture and soon appeared off Amoy with a powerful squadron containing, according to Riccio, some eight hundred large junks. Although Koxinga, so great had been his losses, was only able to muster some four hundred junks he determined to attack his enemies. The battle that ensued was both on land and water. Koxinga commanded the naval force and gained the victory, until finally the Tartar commander, learning of the total defeat of his land force which had attempted the capture of the fortress of Kokia, at once put out to sea and refused further combat. This was on June 17th, 1660, and Riccio, the missionary, states that so great was the loss that for many weeks after, putrid corpses and tangled wreckage strewed the shores of Amoy and Quemoy.

When the news of this crushing defeat reached Peking, the Emperor, despairing of conquering Koxinga by ordinary military methods, decided to force him to submission by cutting off his supplies. The Chinese inland had yielded to the Tartars, and in token of submission had shaved their heads. All these people living within four leagues of the sea, from Canton to Nanking, were by imperial decree commanded to retire inland and to submit to having all their dwellings and fields destroyed. Regardless of the supplications and tears of the many millions of inhabitants, the order was carried into force, and to prevent the villages from being rebuilt, forts were erected at a distance of every three miles each being garrisoned with 100 men, who put to death all the unfortunate beings whom they happened to find in this belt with its twelve mile radius. The Chinese were crowded into the interior and their distress was indescribable, while Koxinga now deprived of provisions was subject to great inconvenience and forced to resort to worse piracy than ever.

Koxinga now found himself in such a perilous position that he began to look about for safer quarters. In this state of affairs the large and fertile island of Formosa attracted his attention, and he commenced secret preparations with the hope of gaining the beautiful isle for his own.

The attack on Zelandia by Koxinga.

The Dutch possessions in Kelung in 1664.

(From engravings in "Verwaerloosde Formosa" 1675 Amsterdam.)

The extensive preparations for war made by Koxinga at Amoy and Quemoy made it very evident to the Dutch that the "Beautiful Isle" was the goal in view. That Koxinga had held secret correspondence with the Formosan Chinese the Dutch were well aware of, and consequently they strengthened the garrison of Fort Zelandia and increased their vigilance over the Chinese population. New arrivals from the mainland were closely inspected and on the least suspicion, the unfortunate emigrant was thrown into prison and cruelly tortured in hopes of gaining information as to Koxinga's plans.

Previous to this, in 1657, the Dutch had been somewhat alarmed as to Koxinga's intentions, and messengers had been sent to Amoy to deliver to the young chief several valuable presents and to inquire if he had warlike designs against the company. The messenger was kindly treated and returned to Formosa with the assurance that there was no truth in the rumor. To quiet the fears of the company Koxinga endeavored to strengthen the commercial ties between himself and them. In 1658-9, junks to a number never before seen in the port of Taiwan arrived from Amoy, and exports rose to a height never before equalled.

On the return of Koxinga from his futile expedition against Nanking the Formosan Governor, Coyett, made an earnest request for help from Batavia. Accordingly, in 1660, twelve ships with large reinforcements were despatched from Batavia, with orders that, if the alarm in Formosa proved groundless, the fleet should proceed against Macao. The garrison at Taiwan now consisted of 1,500 men, a force which the admiral thought invincible against any number of Chinese troops. A decisive answer was now demanded of Koxinga to the question whether he was for peace or war, to which the artful chief replied by letter that he had not the least thought of war against the company.

Regardless of this he continued to increase his forces in Amoy, and the governor's suspicions were not allayed. Admiral Vander Laan, however, was of a different opinion. To him the fears of the governor and council seemed without reason. The admiral had received orders from Batavia to remain in Formosa if necessary, but if it were found that his presence was not required he was to proceed and attack Macao. The latter course appeared to the admiral more likely to bring him greater renown, and after a quarrel with the Formosan governor and his associates he left the island, and after a futile attack on Macao sailed for Batavia, leaving only three ships and one yacht to protect Taiwan.

Upon arriving the admiral accused the governor of unreasonable apprehension, and the council, wearied with the expenses and with the false alarms of the governor for several years, suspended him from office and ordered him to Batavia to defend himself. Hermanus Clenk, his successor, sailed for Formosa in June 1661. Meanwhile we find Koxinga in Amoy maturing his plans which had for long been in preparation.

In 1661 Koxinga sent a message to Japan soliciting aid from the Shogun, ostensibly to battle with the Tartars. Ten years before he had received some assistance from the same source in the shape of supplies : tin, copper, and an apparatus for constructing armor, but on the present occasion the Japanese refused even to consider his request. Among Koxinga's followers there was a great diversity of opinion as to the advisability of attacking the Dutch. Some feared the Dutch were too strongly fortified to be driven out, while others were confident that by skilful generalship the island could be occupied. even though the soldiers of Koxinga were comparatively poorly armed and though the Dutch warships were vastly superior to their own.

At this stage of affairs, a Chinese who had formerly been employed by the Dutch as interpreter arrived on the scene and having obtained an interview with Koxinga, laid before the chief a minute description of that portion of the island occupied by the foreigners with a carefully drawn map to illustrate the topography, and expressed himself as confident that Koxinga could drive out the present occupants.

The chief then discussed the question fully, and fearing that his plans would become prematurely public, he confined the interpreter to a single room. Spies were then despatched to Formosa who, on returning, confirmed the interpreter's assertions in every particular. Koxinga now assembled his officers and announced to them that he had determined upon the expedition against the Dutch and ordered his followers to make immediate preparations accordingly. At this time the Dutch fleet which Coyett had desired to remain at Formosa had just departed from Taiwan disgusted with the thought that the Formosan governor had been frightened by baseless rumors and intending to report accordingly to the council at Batavia. But in accordance with Governor Coyett's fears, no sooner had the fleet departed than Koxinga sailed from Amoy. Koxinga did not mean to burn his bridges behind him, and accordingly left a large force strongly fortified on the borders of his territory, his son Chêng Ching (Teikei) now twenty years old, being in command of Amoy.

The Formosan expedition consisted of 25,000 of his best troops in a great number of war junks, with Koxinga as commander-in-chief and 26 generals as assistants. Arriving at the Pescadores he there completed his plans, gathering information as to the best means of attack, and on a favorable day he sailed with all his forces. In the vicinity of the island soundings were made and observations taken as to the current.

Running to the north of the port of Taiwan the vessels were brought in close to shore, soundings giving but ten feet of water. Sails were then lowered and the vessels proceeded slowly to the south skirting the coast, until they reached a favorable spot, about four miles to the north of Zelandia, and there with much firing of guns and beating of drums the force landed without difficulty, while thousands of their countrymen who flocked to the scene tendered them every assistance.

Only four Dutch ships were in the harbor at the time and the direction of the wind was such that they could not leave their anchorage to battle with Koxinga. Meanwhile, in two hours' time, several thousands of Chinese had been landed. Numerous junks cleared for action were at once stationed between Fort Zelandia and Fort Provintia which stood on opposite sides of the harbor, while Koxinga with a large force occupied a position which would enable him to cut off land communication between the two forts.

Captain Pedel, the commander of the Dutch naval force, decided that as he was unable to oppose the invaders by sea, his men would be profitably employed on shore, and accordingly marched with 240 men in hopes of dislodging the enemy, and preventing the further landing of men. Then occurred the first engagement. By the time the Dutch troops came up 4,000 Chinese had already occupied the place; but confident that the enemy would not stand fire, the Dutch immediately attacked them. Instead of giving way, the Chinese returned the fire with musketry and arrows, and the Dutch, finding they were also being attacked on the flank, threw down their arms and fled, leaving the captain and 118 men dead on the field. One half only of their company reached the fort alive. A second party of 200 men under the command of Captain Aeldorp likewise advanced against the enemy, but returned without accomplishing any good or suffering much loss.

At the time the European settlers numbered about 600 and the garrison about 2,200 men.

The Dutch do not appear to have made the most of the force at their disposal.

Equally ineffective seemed the four Dutch ships, for although they did make an attack on the Chinese junks and destroy several, one of their own squadron was burnt by Chinese fire boats and the rest escaped from the harbor, two to return, while the third sailed for Batavia, not reaching her destination until after some fifty days owing to the south monsoon. No further opposition was for the time encountered. The remainder of Koxinga's men were safely landed and in a few hours had cut off all communication between the forts and the open country. The Chinese were now securely placed, and earthworks had been erected overlooking the plain.

Koxinga's soldiers were armed with several different kinds of weapons, but the greatest dependence was put on the cross-bows, the arrows for which were carried on the backs of the men; other corps were armed with cimiters and targets, two-handed swords three to four feet long, and pikes with iron pointed heads. The army also included two companies of blacks provided with muskets, in the use of which they were very proficient.

Koxinga possessed no cavalry, but supplied their want to a certain extent with fleet runners who were protected by shields besides light armor. So swift and courageous were these warriors that it is said they dared charge even into the very arms of the enemy regardless of their number, and their fierce attacks gained them the cognomen of " mad dogs " from the Dutch.

Koxinga's position now being secure, he sent messengers to the two Dutch forts, summoning the garrisons to surrender, threatening to put all to fire and sword if they refused, adding: "This island was the dominion of my father and should descend to none other than myself. Foreigners must go."

After a consultation it was agreed to send deputies to Koxinga, offering to surrender Fort Provintia, thus permitting the Dutch to concentrate their forces at Zelandia.   These deputies went to his camp, then consisting of about 12,000 men, who were besieging Fort Provintia.

The Dutchmen were conducted into a spacious tent where they awaited the leisure of Koxinga, who at the time was employed in combing his long black shining hair of which he was very proud. " This done, they were introduced into his tent, all hung with blue; he himself was seated in an elbow chair behind a four square table; round about him attended all the chief commanders, clad in long robes, without arms, and in great silence with most awful countenances."

Koxinga listened quietly to their offer, but in answer replied that Formosa had always belonged to China, and now that the Chinese wanted it the foreigners must quit the island immediately. If this was not acceptable let them hoist the red flag. Next morning Fort Provintia surrendered with all its garrison and arms and the red flag of defiance waved over Fort Zelandia.

To better defend themselves against the enemy all the men capable of bearing arms were assembled at the remaining fort, and the city was set on fire.

The intention was to deprive the Chinese of shelter in the vicinity of the fort, but although the fire was partially effectual, the Chinese were still able to preserve many of the buildings. Koxinga then ordered his artillery to advance and with twenty-eight cannon to storm the fort; but so strong was the fire from the Dutch that the streets were filled with the slain, and the besieged, making a successful charge, were able to spike the enemies' guns.

Koxinga seeing that his attack on the formidable Zelandia would not succeed in driving out the Dutch, instituted a close blockade, knowing that hunger and want must come at last.

Still annoyed at the obstinacy of his foes he vented his rage on the open country, inflicting much suffering upon such foreigners and their sympathizers as he could lay his hands on. It was useless for the Dutch to strengthen their position, as this led to the blockade being made more effective, while the foreigners scattered through the country were subject to greater suffering and even death.

The ministers, school-masters, and prisoners were especially singled out for punishment, it having been proclaimed that they had been secretly encouraging the native Christians to rise and kill the Chinese living among them. Some were crucified by the Chinese on the crosses erected in the very villages where they had been pursuing their gracious work, while all were subjected to great indignities.

The following extracts translated from the day-journal of Fort Zelandia tell the pathetic tale in their own words.[1]

Tuesday, 17th May, 1661.—Several inhabitants, as well as their elders, dwelling in the mountains and plains, yea, more or less all the people of the south, have surrendered to Koxinga; each of the elders having received as gifts a light-colored silk robe, a cap surmounted with a gilt knob, and a pair of Chinese boots. These fellows now speak with much disdain of the true Christian faith, which we have endeavored to plant in their hearts, and are delighted that they have been exempted from attending the schools. Everywhere they have destroyed the books and utensils, and have again introduced the abominable usages and customs of heathenism. On the report being spread that Koxinga had arrived,

---

1. Translation as appearing in *Missionary Success in Formosa*, Rev. William Campbell. The reader will find many interesting translations regarding the siege in the first volume of this valuable work, of which a portion of the remainder of this chapter is an extract.

they murdered one of our Dutch people; and, after having struck off the head, they danced around it with great joy and merriment, just as they formerly did with their vanquished enemies. All this a certain Stephen Yansz had himself been witness of in the south.

* * * * * * * * * *

"In the army, it was reported that Soulang had been taken and the inhabitants carried away; and that the clergymen, Hambroek and Winshem, without the one knowing the fate of the other, had fled to Baklaan.

" *Tuesday 24th May.*—At five or half-past five in the afternoon a flag of truce was displayed by the enemy, and the Rev. A. Hambroek, accompanied by one Ossewayer, a Chinese Mandarin named Sangae, and the interpreters Joucko and Ouhincko,—the three first on horseback, the others on foot—were seen approaching from the ' Pine Apples ' to the foot of the redoubt.

"When these persons were asked what the object of their coming was, they replied that they were the bearers of a letter from Koxinga.

"Thereupon, it was agreed that Mr. Hambroek alone, or in company with Ossewayer, should be allowed to enter the Castle, and that the Ensign Claermont should be sent to politely inform the Mandarin that, while the contents of Koxinga's letter were being taken into consideration, and an answer was being prepared, we requested him to remain with the interpreters before the fortress, either in a house or wherever else he chose. To this request the Mandarin complied, Ossewayer accompanying him.

"On Mr. Hambroek entering the Castle, he handed to the Governor the letter which Koxinga had charged him to deliver.

"The Governor then called all the members of the Council together, and, in their presence, he opened and read the letter. It contained the following, as may be seen from the annexed :—

"Translation of a letter written by Pompoan to Mr. Frederick Coyett, Governor in Tayouan.

' The Teybingh-Sjautoo-Teysiang-kon, Kok-Seng sends this letter to Governor Coyett, in Tayouan.

' You Dutch people, a few hundreds in number, how can you carry on war against us, who are so powerful by our numbers ? Really, it is as if you were bereft of your senses, and that you had no understanding.

' I, Pompoan, say that it is the will of God that all should live and remain preserved, without perishing. I am, therefore, well inclined that men should remain alive; for which reason I have sent you so many letters. You people ought well to consider how very important a matter it is that the lives of your wives and children should be spared and all your possessions preserved.

' I now send you my Mandarin, named Sangae, also the Rev. Mr. Hambroek and the interpreters Ouhincko and Joucko, with salutations to the Governor; offering him, at the same time, peace, on the conditions which will now be mentioned. I beg you duly to consider what I say.

' *First*, If you surrender the fortress before my cannons have made their effect felt on its walls then I shall treat you in the same way as I treated the Commander of the Fort Provintia, named Valentyn ; that is, I will spare your lives, and if any one has anything to ask or desire, I will grant it as I granted it to him. I speak the truth, and will not deceive you.

' *Secondly*, If, even after my cannon have battered your walls, the Governor and some others, great as well as small, shall hoist the white flag on the Fort and come out to me, saying, Peace! then I shall immediately issue the order, " Cease firing, it is enough !" so that you may feel confident in my word. And when afterwards, your commanders great and small (*sic*), come to be accompanied by their wives and children, I shall give immediate command to bring all my cannon on board my ships, on being convinced that you people seriously wish to have peace.

' By this command, the Governor and his people will see that I desire peace, and they will, therefore, have every reason to trust me.

' *Another word* :—After peace has been concluded, your soldiers will require immediately to leave the Fortress, that my soldiers may enter, with the object of taking care of it and of all the houses within its walls. I shall maintain such a degree of order that not the " tiniest blade of grass or even a hair of your possessions" shall be hurt. I will also give permission for some slaves, male and female, to remain within the houses to take care of the things ; and further, every person who wishes to live in his own house at Sakam[1] or Tayouan will be allowed to leave the place and to take his money and possessions with him.

' *One word more* :—It is the usage of the Chinese to grant everything that has been asked of them ; but the fortress we cannot leave to you, as we attach very great importance to it. All that you people desire, you can get, with the exception of two days interval to carry away your possessions, as the inhabitants of Sakam had ; this being withheld because you people have delayed so long to come to a decision, whereas the people of Sakam surrendered before they felt the effect of my cannons. After waiting such a long time, therefore, you folk shall not have one hour's delay given you; for after my cannons have made a breach in your walls, you will have to quit instantly.

' *Finally*, I know it is the duty of the Dutch, who have come such a long way for the carrying on of trade, to endeavor to keep their fortress, and this even pleases me ; as I do not see anything like a fault or crime in such an endeavor, so that you have no cause of fear for having acted thus.

---

1. Sakkam.

'If I speak a word, if I promise anything, the whole world may trust me and be certain that I shall keep my word, as formerly. I have no wish to deceive anyone. Every Dutchman in your fortress may take note of this letter; for the contents from beginning to end are founded on truth and verity. Matters are now come to such a pass that we can either spare or take your lives; therefore, you must quickly decide, and if you take a long time for consideration, it is the same as if you wished to lose your lives.

'Mr. Coyett has on a former time declared that he did not understand Chinese writing, and many a letter have I written him without his having understood them. I now send you this letter by the interpreters Ouhincko and Soucko, who have read and translated it to the former Deputy-Governor, Valentyn, in order that he might have it properly written out in Dutch. May you folk now take it quite to heart.

'*Indited* in the fifteenth year, and on the 26th of the fourth month.'"

"On the margin was written :—Translated to the very best of my abilities, 24th May, 1661.—J. Valentyn.

"The Council then resolved to send the following letter in reply :—

'Frederick Coyett, Governor and Director of the Castles and people in the Island of Formosa sends this letter to Mr. Koxinga, encamped with his army at Bockenburgh on this place.

'TAYOUAN, 25th May, 1661.

'Last night, at sunset, we duly received your letter through the medium of the mandarin, Sangae, and of Rev. A. Hambroek, accompanied by Ossewayer.

'We have perfectly well understood its contents; but we cannot give you any other answer than the one we already wrote to you on the 10th instant; namely, that we are under obligation, for the honor of our omnipotent and true God—confiding completely in His aid and assistance—and for the welfare of our country and the Directors of the Dutch India Company, to continue to defend the Castle, even at the danger and peril of our own lives.

'It was our desire to send you this answer last night; inasmuch, however, as during that evening on which Sangae arrived, your troops in the town Zelandia were actively engaged under our eyes in throwing up works against us, and as Sangae refused to prevent their doing so, saying he was not authorised to interfere, we were prevented from executing our good intention, for the simple reason that we were busily occupied in throwing up works in our own defense. The soldiers under you can tell what answer we returned to the cannons directed against our place, and by this we abide.

'FREDERICK COYETT.'

"In the meantime, Mr. Hambroek gave us some account of the vicissitudes of our countrymen living in the north, having been one of them. He informed us that, as soon as the coming and arrival of the enemy had been announced, they all met at Soulang, but the bad feeling of the villagers and the vicinity of the enemy made it advisable to retire to Mattau, and latterly to Dorko. As it was considered dangerous to remain there, and as the want of provisions was beginning to be felt, they proceeded further north, to Tilosen.

"Meanwhile, the love and good will of the inhabitants had gradually decreased, which was owing to their having received a letter from the Governor of Fort Provintia, written by command of Koxinga; in which letter it was stated that, if they submitted to the authority of Koxinga, he would grant them the same terms as he had granted the garrison of that place. These terms, the inhabitants (except a few living to the north of the Zant river, probably, with the intention of proceeding later on to Kelang[1] and Tamsuy[2]), had jointly considered it to be best and most advantageous for them to accept, seeing that they all, and especially their wives and children, were now in a very lamentable state, and that there prevailed among the soldiers near them a spirit of discord and insubordination. One hundred and sixteen persons—among whom were four clergymen and five judicial officers—had joined the Dutch inhabitants in the neighborhood of Fort Provintia, all of them suffering from want of provisions, the enemy, also, being in very much the same condition.

"Eleven persons of some rank or other had left Provintia on command of Koxinga, who ordered them to appear before him at Bockenburgh. Fifteen had been ordered to come, but only eleven appeared, as Koxinga permitted four of them to remain beside the property at Provintia, thus giving heed to their representation that, if they were all to leave the place to appear before him, the people might create many disturbances and riots. When Mr. Hambroek left, these four persons were still residing there.

"Before Mr. Hambroek and the other Dutch persons retired to the north, on the report that Koxinga was about to come to this island with some inimical design, the Mattau people left on 27th April for the mountains, to punish the rebellious Duke-e-duckians, and returned with three heads which they had struck off. According to the former heathenish custom when celebrating a triumph, they began to dance round these heads and to perform other ridiculous antics; whereupon Mr. Hambroek forbade them. but they were insolent enough openly to contradict and disobey him when thus reproved for acting in their old way.

---

1. Kelung.
2. Tamsui.

"The chattels of the judicatory officials and of the clergymen—which they left behind them when fleeing from the respective villages, and which were found by the enemy later on—had been sealed, and were now guarded by the Chinese whom Koxinga had appointed for this service. Mr. Bocx and the Rev. Mr. Leonardus had received a part of their possessions through the written medium of the secretary of the mandarin to whose charge the fortress of Provintia is intrusted. Mr. Hambroek has also received a promise that his possessions will be restored to him. He further told us that, in consequence of the reiterated requests addressed to him, Koxinga had granted their petition by allowing them to act freely even in matters pertaining to religion.

"Wednesday, 25th May.—It having meanwhile become four o'clock in the afternoon, the friends who arrived yesterday, namely, Mr. Hambroek and Mr. Ossewayer, took their leave; bearing with them the letter which we had written yesterday to the mandarin Koxinga.

"Mr. Hambroek came into the castle, being forced to leave his wife and children behind him as hostages, which sufficiently proved that, if he failed in his negotiations, he had nothing but death to expect from the chieftain. Yet he was so far from persuading the garrison to surrender that he encouraged them to a brave defence by hopes of relief, assuring them that Koxinga had lost many of his best men and ships and begun to be weary of the siege. When he had ended, the council of war left it to his choice to stay with them or return to the camp, where he could expect nothing but present death. Everyone entreated him to stay. He had two daughters within the castle, who hung about his neck, overwhelmed with grief and tears to see their father ready to go where he knew he must be sacrificed by the merciless enemy. But he represented to them that, having left his wife and other children in the camp as hostages, nothing but death could attend them if he returned not; so unlocking himself from his daughters' arms, and exhorting every one to a resolute defence, he returned to the camp, telling them at parting that he hoped he might prove serviceable to his poor fellow prisoners.

*   *   *   *   *   *   *

"These friends greatly rejoiced (as we ourselves do) at our bravery, and the victory which, by the blessing of God, we had thus far achieved, hoping that after obtaining some more victories, we might be speedily delivered. May the Almighty and good God grant that, to their and our joy, these hopes may be realized; and may He deliver us out of the hands of our enemy and into the welfare of the Company!

"Koxinga received his (Hambroek's) answer sternly; then causing it to be rumored about that the prisoners excited the Formosans (Aborigines) to rebel against him, he ordered all the Dutch male prisoners to be slain; this was accordingly done, some being beheaded, others killed in a more barbarous manner, to the number of 500, their bodies stripped quite naked and buried 50 and 60 in a hole; nor were the women and children spared, many of them likewise being slain, though some of the best were preserved for the use of the commanders, and then sold to the common soldiers. Happy was she that fell to the lot of an unmarried man, being thereby freed from vexations by the Chinese women, who are very jealous of their husbands. Among the slain were Messrs. Hambroek, Mus, and Winshem, clergymen, and many schoolmasters, who were all beheaded.

"Saturday, 13th August.—Last night we captured two boys and a Chinese, and in the morning we interrogated one of them—with the Chinaman—who confessed as follows:—

"That Mr. Hambroek had been his master . . . . . . that Van Druyvendal and a schoolmaster, named Frans van der Voorn with three other Dutchmen had been brought as prisoners from Sinkang; that the two first named had been crucified at Sakam—the others having been liberated—and that Mr. Hambroek, assisted by the interpreter Maurits, had procured Koxinga's permission to offer up a prayer for them. After hanging for three days, they were carried—still alive on the crosses—to Sinkang, and here the crosses were again planted in the ground till the sufferers died, the place of their execution being just before the house of the Governor. At that time our married Dutch people were still residing there, and two of Druyvendal's sons were in the house of a mandarin at Tilosen; while his wife with her two children were living in Dinkang.

"Tuesday, 16th August.—This morning at the break of day, a certain soldier named Hendrik Robberts came swimming to the "Pine Apples," and afterwards to the redoubt. Having been carried into this place, he gave us the following account:—

"Last month, that is, in July, the interpreter Druyvendal and a young schoolmaster had each been fastened to a cross by having nails driven through their hands and the calves of their legs, and another nail driven into their backs. In this sad condition they were exhibited to public sight before the house of the Governor, and our own people had guarded these victims with bare swords. At the end of three or four days they expired, after meat and drink had been withheld from them all that time. The reason of their execution is said to be that they were guilty of having incited the inhabitants against the Chinese; but to their last breath they denied that they had ever done so.

"Saturday, 27th August.—In the morning at dawn Pierre Megriet, a certain Dutchman coming from Sinkang, entered this place. He reports that, after the surrender of the Fortress Provintia, he remained there 18 days in company with several disabled persons; and that those who enjoyed good health had immediately been sent to the villages in the North and South, among them being the schoolmaster, de Heems, and Ian Lambertsz. Afterwards, fourteen of the sick and disabled were carried to Sinkang, that they might there be taken care of; but before they arrived seven of his companions had already perished.

*   *   *   *   *   *   *   *   *   *

"The Chinese had stored much gunpowder and *paddy* in the Church at Sinkang.

"The inhabitants loudly lament about the injustice the Chinese are committing in taking away from them their very best lands, their rice, their cattle, and their wagons. They had to bear this in silence, and even to appear contented. The elders amongst them went about in Chinese robes of great value.

"Our people, the Dutch, not regarding the prohibition of the Chinese, would often repair to the village in the hope of being able to pick up a stray article of food wherewith to fill their hungry bellies, but they were very often interfered with and were thus made to suffer great want.

"He had also seen with his own eyes two of our countrymen—although he did not know their names—crucified at Sakam; that is, their hands, after having been crossed over the heads, were fixed with a nail to the cross, another nail was driven through the calves of their legs and another through their arms. In this way these poor creatures suffered torments till after the lapse of three days they died. But that was not sufficient, as it seemed; for those barbarous heathens carried them to Sinkang where they died and where they were buried, the latter being more than might well have been expected. The Chinese soldiers left the inhabitants perfectly unmolested, but the peasants often foully abused them. The Chinese forced all inhabitants who had adopted Dutch (Christian) names to take other names according to the desire of their parents or friends. Severe punishments were threatened if this command was not obeyed.

"Forty-two of our countrymen who were on board the vessel *Urck* had been all—except the purser and his servant—taken to Sinkang with ropes around their necks, one of them having on no other clothing save a pair of trousers, and another only a shirt. The Chinese mandarin commanded fourteen of these poor creatures to be beheaded by the Sinkang people, who were obliged to do so. The chiefs of the villages killed most of them. Five more, namely, the purser called Stephen, the dreamer, his servant, the surgeon, the mate, and another person, were carried to Sinkang. We do not know what the subsequent fate of the others was, but we trust they have been sent to the South.

"When he was taken by *sampan* to Sinkang, the Deputy-Governor with his family and servant, the clergyman Leonardus with his family, the schoolmaster Jonas, all the surgeons of the villages, as also the surveyors, Philip May and Joannes Bronner, with their families had been left behind in Sakam, while the schoolmaster Ossewayer had received permission to dwell without hindrance in the house of his wife's mother. The Rev. A. Winshem with his wife and the schoolmaster, Samuel, were also living at Sinkang; and when he left they were dwelling all together under the roof of the mandarin who had taken up his abode in the house of the judiciary office.

"*Monday, 24th October, 1661.*—We examined, a second time, the two black boys who escaped from the town on the 13th of this month and one of them still persists in declaring that many of the Dutch people—among them the Rev. Mr. Hambroek and Ian Hammersen—had been decapitated in Sinkang, and that many others had died of privation.

"He declares, also, that he saw Ossewayer and some of the soldiers beheaded, that the vessel *Urck* had been cast ashore and the crew killed in Sinkang, that all the remaining Dutch people had been killed in the villages; while the schoolmasters, Jonas, Ananias, and Philip May, only, were still living at Sakam, the Governor, the Rev. Mr. Leonardus, and Bronner, having been carried to China."

A few days after his appointment by the Batavian Council, Clenk arrived off Taiwan, when, instead of the prosperous and peaceful colony over which he expected soon to rule, he saw to his dismay hundreds of Chinese soldiers, a red flag floating over the principal fort, and the harbor filled with formidable-looking Chinese craft, where formerly anchored many junks with their rich merchandise, which had made the company's fortune.

Aware that Fort Provintia had been surrendered and that Fort Zelandia was beleaguered by thousands of Chinese troops, Clenk, who, though a weak and vacillating character, apparently possessed a keen sense of humor, though he could not manage to land his own soldiers and showed no anxiety to get within shooting distance of shore himself, had sufficient nerve to send ashore a document condemning poor Coyett for his groundless fears as to Chinese invasion, recalling him to Batavia without loss of time, and ordering him to hand over his seal of office to his newly-appointed successor (Clenk) who now presented himself to accept it. This remarkable humorist now sailed away and was not seen again in Taiwan.

Clenk then sailed to Japan and later returned to Batavia, giving a wide berth to the land over which he had been appointed to rule.

The Dutch, yearning to aid their suffering countrymen, despatched a large junk full of provisions, which, sharing the run of misfortunes that befell the Dutch during this period, encountered a storm when within sight of Taiwan and was driven to the southwards, eventually bringing up at Batavia.

Two days after Clenk's first departure from Batavia as the new governor of Formosa, the ship *Maria*, which, the reader will remember, fled from Taiwan upon the first arrival of Koxinga and had a long passage owing to the south monsoon, arrived in Batavia. The Dutch authorities now obtained full information as to the Formosa difficulties, and furthermore a despatch was received from Coyett begging for reinforcements and supplies; 1,500 soldiers, 20,000 fuses, 400 tons of rice, 500 casks of salt meat, 40 casks of Spanish wine, and 200 bottles of arrack were itemized as necessary. The governor of Batavia now bestirred himself and fitted out ten vessels with 300 soldiers to be sent to the rescue. A certain Jacob Caeuw was placed in command, although he is described as being unfamiliar with both navigation and war and further discredited as being unable to speak except through his nose. In spite of all this, Commander Caeuw on appearing in Formosan waters prepared for action. Unfortunately the proverbial gale turned him from his purpose just as he, according to his own report, was preparing to inflict a telling blow on the enemy. A month later he returned, but Koxinga had now so strengthened his positions that it would have been folly to have attempted to dislodge him with the small number of troops at Caeuw's disposal. Indeed Fortune seemed to keep all her frowns for the Dutch and all her smiles for the Chinese general, who stumbled on a Dutch warehouse in which were 200,000 bags of rice and 1,000 pigs, just as he was becoming seriously inconvenienced for lack of supplies for his enormous force. Caeuw now ordered three of his ships to take the offensive against the Chinese fleet.

But fate seemed against the Dutch in all they undertook. Two of the vessels ran on a sand-bank, thus falling an easy prey to the Chinese; the larger one was destroyed by a single shot which struck the powder magazine. All except one officer and five seamen, however, saved their lives by swimming. The third ship with its crew of 118 men was also captured by the enemy. Still with all his success Koxinga was unable to make an impression upon the solid Fort Zelandia, and furthermore, owing to the short range of his guns, he could not prevent small boats from the Dutch fleet communicating with the fort. Still the besieged did not gain much by this, inasmuch as Koxinga had command of the plain, and his army, which with local levies now numbered nearly a hundred thousand men, could not have been dislodged by a force many times larger than the Dutch garrison. As the outlook was not bright and supplies not over-abundant, the women and children and other noncombatants were placed in charge of Commander Caeuw to be carried to Batavia when he should see fit.

Extract from the "Day Journal" of Caeuw, commander of the fleet and reinforcements.

"*21st October, 1661.*—This afternoon, two little black boys deserted the town and made their appearance at the Castle. One of them was a slave of the sub-factor Michiel Baly, and the other was free born, but had been serving as a slave in the house of the mandarin Beepontok, Governor of the town. They told us as a fact—they themselves having been witnesses thereof—that Koxinga, enraged because his troops were daily diminishing in number, and especially because so many of his men had been killed and wounded on the 16th of last month, when our vessels appeared before the batteries of the enemy, first fed and regaled, and then beheaded, all the Dutch soldiers in his power; not only those who surrendered themselves after the capture of Fort Provintia, but those also who were scattered throughout the country at the various stations. The clergymen Hambroek, Mus, and Winshem; the former secretary of the Court of Justice; Ossewayer, former judicatory officer in Soulang; Gillis Bocx and several inhabitants of Sakam, having been previously regaled in the same way, were afterwards beheaded; but the clergyman Leonardus, and the former unworthy Deputy-Governor of Provintia with his wife and five children, had been sent to China. The half-sister of Mr. Leonardus' wife, a girl of sixteen and the offspring of a Quinan father and a Japanese mother, was married to a Tartar mandarin, and was now living at Sakam, where she had not only adopted the Chinese manner of dress, but had also bandaged her feet. The daughter of the Rev. A. Hambroek, a very sweet and pleasing maiden, Koxinga took to be one of his concubines, and she had, consequently, been placed in his harem. All the remaining Dutch women were kept under guard in Castle Provintia.

"It afterwards appeared, when these boys were put to torture (sic), that they had been sent to spy out the Castle. They persisted, however, in declaring that they had spoken the truth.

*   *   *   *   *   *   *   *   *   *

"*20th November.*—The catechist, Daniel Hendrickx, whose name has been often mentioned' accompanied this expedition to the south, as his great knowledge of the Formosa language and his familiar intercourse with the natives, rendered his services very valuable.

"On reaching the island of Pangsuy, he ventured—perhaps with overweening confidence in himself—too far away from the others, and was suddenly surrounded by a great number of armed natives, who, after killing him, carried away in triumph his head, arms, legs, and other members, even his entrails, leaving the mutilated trunk behind."

*   *   *   *   *   *   *   *   *   *

Subsequently Koxinga relaxed hostilities for a short period, no doubt feeling that time would gain him the fort without the sacrifice of many of his men. The spirits of the Dutch rose accordingly, as they trusted that the Batavian Government would send reinforcements in numbers sufficient to enable the Fort Zelandia garrison to oppose Koxinga on somewhat more equal terms.

Meanwhile the viceroy of Fokien had proposed that if the Dutch fleet would assist him in expelling the remnants of Koxinga's force from Amoy and its vicinity, he in turn would aid the Dutch in Formosa to the full extent of his power. The Dutch governor consented to this, and five ships were accordingly despatched to the viceroy's aid, but three were lost in a storm and the other two returned to Batavia where Caeuw, the commander, was severely censured and heavily fined for having left the China seas without even paying his respects to the viceroy, who was daily waiting his arrival at Foochow in accordance with the promises made by the Formosa authorities.

Koxinga was naturally pleased at this, while the besieged garrison grew so disheartened that they despaired of holding out much longer. Koxinga, now impatient at the long delay, prepared for decisive action. Opportunely a deserter from the Dutch offered to take service under Koxinga's banner. His assistance was availed of and having thus obtained information as to where best to press the attack the Chinese assailed the fort from three near batteries. The Dutch opposed them bravely, but nevertheless they succeeded in making a breach, and gaining one of the redoubts they caused great annoyance to the Dutch and made ready for a general assault.

On this the besieged began to deliberate and the majority of the council decided that further opposition was hopeless. Governor Coyett yielded his opinion as to the advisability of surrendering, and in a message to Koxinga

THE DUTCH SURRENDER TO KOXINGA.

(FROM AN ENGRAVING IN "VERWAERLOOSDE FORMOSA" 1675 AMSTERDAM.)

declared that he would hand over the fort, and the following conditions were eventually agreed upon :

1. All hostilities to cease and be forgotten by both sides.

2. Zelandia and its outworks, artillery, war materials, merchandise, treasure, and other state property to be given up to Koxinga.

3. Rice, bread, wine, arrack, meat, oil, vinegar, ropes, canvas, tar, anchors, gunpowder, bullets, and fuses may be taken by the Dutch ships now in harbor.

4. All private movable property may be taken to the ships after inspection.

5. Twenty-eight of the councillors may each take two hundred rix-dollars, and twenty other civilians may take altogether one thousand rix-dollars.

6. The Dutch soldiers may retire with loaded rifles, flying banners, burning lint, and may embark to the accompaniment of beating drums.

7. The names and particulars regarding all Chinese debtors or lease-holders shall be extracted from the company's books and be handed over to Koxinga.

8. All papers and books belonging to the government may be taken to Batavia.

9. All prisoners to be returned within eight or ten days and those in China as soon as possible. All those not imprisoned shall be allowed to go to the company's ships in safety.

10. Koxinga will return the four ships' boats which he had captured.

11. Koxinga will provide sufficient boats to take the Dutch and their goods off to the ships.

12. All vegetables, cattle and other beasts, and such like shall be supplied to the Dutch at proper prices.

13. While the Dutch remain no Chinese soldiers will be allowed to enter the castle (Zelandia) or go further than they now are.

14. As soon as the agreement is signed two out of the Councillors from each side shall be exchanged as hostages.

15. Those watchmen who guard the godowns shall stay two or three days after the Dutch civilians and soldiers have been taken to the ships. They will then be taken on board together with the hostages.

16. Koxinga will give the military mandarin, Moor Ongkun, and Pimpan Jamooje, political councillor, as hostages, and the Dutch will send Jan Oitzens Van Waveren, second officer in the government, and St. David Harthouwer as hostages, both parties to remain until all the conditions of this agreement have been faithfully executed.

17. Chinese prisoners will be exchanged for Dutch prisoners.

18. Misunderstadings or anything else arising of great importance shall be settled by mutual agreement.

The Dutch could scarcely have expected more of Koxinga considering their own actions when playing the role of conquerors a few years before. Koxinga permitted the Dutch to take with them their own personal property and embark under their own flag for Batavia,—a great contrast to the treatment the poor Chinese in the Pescadores received at the hands of the Dutch when the islands were first occupied by them. The Dutch artillery, stores, merchandise, and other property falling into the hands of Koxinga was valued at $8,000,000.

The events of the siege are concisely reviewed in the following quaint but pathetic letter written by Rev. Joannes Kruyf to Rev. Baldaeus, Ceylon.

"Dated at NEGAPATAM, 13th of October, 1662.

*   *   *   *   *   *   *   *

"To give you a particular account of the late miserable state of the Isle of *Formosa* is both beyond the compass of a letter and my present strength; and though I tremble at the very thoughts of it, yet will I mention the chiefest transactions: The first assault of the furious *Chineses* was made against the Castle of *Saccam*, whereabouts, after they had cut some of our soldiers in pieces, they took my eldest son and my wife's brother, who tho' very young, had one of his arms cut off.

"The next day our ship, called the *Hector*, being engaged with a vast number of the *Chinese Jones*[1], was blown up, and in her some of our best soldiers, among whom was also my father-in-law, *Thomas Pedel*. The fort of Saccam being, after a defense of a few days, forced to surrender for want of fresh water and other necessaries, the minister, officers, schoolmasters. soldiers, and in general, all the inhabitants of the flat country, were forced to make the best terms they could for themselves. The Squadron of Ships commanded by Mr. *Kauw* (after it had for a small time rejoiced our drooping spirits) being dispersed by tempests, and the ship the *Urck* forced upon the sands and taken by the enemy, the same was neither seen nor heard of in five or six weeks after.

"To be short, the country being overrun by the *Chineses*, our soldiers everywhere routed, *Koukeren* laid in ashes in sight of our fort; such of our countrymen as had not secured themselves by a timely flight, fell into the hands of the merciless enemies, who sacrificed the Reverend Mr. *Hambroek* with his son, and divers others in Tiloceu, to their fury: As also Mr. Peter Mus, Minister of Favorlang, and Mr. Arnold Winsheim, Minister of Sinkan, who had their heads cut off, and their wives with many others carried into slavery. By this, there being great want of necessaries in the Fortress, the soldiers died daily of the bloody flux, scurvy, and dropsy: So that in nine months time, having lost above 1600 men, both by famine and the sword, we were forced (for the preservation of our lives) to capitulate.

"Who can without tears remember the unexpected destruction and ruin of so many families, and of near thirty ministers, partly in their lives, partly in their fortunes (among whom I had my share, having lost all I had gathered in fifteen years' time), the loss and dishonor of the Company, with unspeakable miseries . . . . All which we ought to look upon as the effects of God's just indignation, on account of our manifold sins."

Poor Coyett and the members of his Formosan Council, who appear to have been painstaking and conscientious, after all their suffering and anxiety during their last year in Formosa were on their arrival at Batavia imprisoned and their possessions confiscated, while Coyett was banished for life to one of the Banda islands.

One cannot review the trying labors of the governor and his little band of faithful followers in Formosa without being filled with indignation against the arrogant Dutch authorities who, ignorant of the conditions existing in the island and no doubt hoping to hide their own incompetence, thus made scapegoats of the unfortunate Formosan officers. Had these conceited grandees condescended to act on the suggestions of a petty colonial officer, the island of Formosa might have remained a Dutch possession to the present day.

That great injustice had been done to Coyett was at length recognized, and the Prince of Orange recalled him from banishment to spend his few

---

1. Junks.

remaining years in his native land a free man. This, however, was but a scanty reward for the services rendered to his country.

Thus, in the year 1662, after thirty years' continuance, Dutch authority in Formosa ceased; for, although Kelung was recaptured by Admiral Bort in 1664, it was again abandoned in May, 1668, as no longer profitable,[1] and the Dutch territorial possessions in the China seas ended.

NOTE.—The following is a list of the Dutch clergymen who served in Formosa, with (so far as is recorded, the period of their arrival in the island, and the date of their departure or death.

	from	till			from	till
Georgius Candidius	1627	1631	Joannes Cruyf		1649	1662
Robertus Junius	1629	1641	Rutger Tesschemaker		1651	
Georgius Candidius	1633	1637	Joannes Ludgens		1651	
Assuerus Hoogeteyn	1636	1637*	Guilielmus Brakel		1652	
Joannes Linbeborn	1637	1639	Gilbertus Happartius		1653	
Gerardus Leeuwius	1637	1639*	Joannes Bakker		1653	All deceased before 1665 or about that time.
Joannes Schotanus	1638	1639	Abrahamus Dapper		1654	
Joannes Bavius	1640	1647*	Robertus Sassenius		1654	
Robertus Junius	1641	1643	Marcus Masius		1655	1661
N. Mirkinius	1641	—	Petrus Mus		1655	1662†
Simon van Breen	1643	1647	Joannes Campius		1655	1662†
Joannes Happartus	1644	1646	Hermannus Buschhof		1655	1657
Daniel Gravius	1647	1651	Arnoldus a Winsem		1655	1662†
Jacobus Vertrecht	1647	1651	Joannes de Leonardis		1656	1662
Antonius Hambroek	1648	1661†	Jacobus Ampzingius		1656	1662†
Gilbertus Happartius	1649	1652	Guilielmus Vinderus		1657	1659*

* Deceased in Fomosa this year.   † Beheaded by the Koxinga party.

But little is left now in the island to mark the Dutch occupation. The splendid fort at Tamsui, the ruins of the two forts in the south, and a few traces of other works are the only remains.

Of the thirty years' labor of the missionaries all signs seem swept away. No evidence of their Christian teachings are to be found to-day even among such tribes as the Dutch were most successful with, and whose converted members could be counted by thousands. Yet it is certain that radical changes for the better have been made in the customs of the savages of the plains, though to what extent these improvements are due to Dutch teachings and to what extent to outside conditions, as for instance the large immigration of Chinese, of course no one can say. Upon the arrival of the Dutch in Formosa, the savages occupying the plains were addicted to head-hunting just as the hill savages of the island are at present. To understand the horror of this practice the reader must remember that it was not resorted to as a matter of revenge or necessarily of hatred. While superstition is mingled with it to a great extent, and the severed head is looked upon as a sort of fetich, the custom is no doubt most highly valued for the opportunity it allows the warlike buck to exhibit his prowess and thus to gain power and influence in the tribe. He who has taken a head is exalted above those who have not, and of course the more heads are taken the greater is the reputation of the slayer, who becomes a fanatic and a murderer for no other reason than this. The Dutch were successful in inducing most of the natives resident in the plains to do away with this horrible custom, and although some of them were later forced into the hills by the incoming Chinese, neither those that remained nor their descendants returned to that most barbarous of practices head-hunting.

Furthermore, we learn that upon the arrival of the Dutch they found other strange customs in vogue among the natives; for example, men and women would not labor together; a husband did not live permanently with his wife until his 50th year, and it was a great disgrace for her to bring forth a child before she was 37 years old. When a woman of younger years was discovered with child, a priestess was called who kneaded the body of the mother until the unborn child was killed, thus causing abortion and inflicting upon the mother the most extreme torture. Candidius writes of one woman who had had sixteen children killed in this way.

---

1. It is interesting in connection with the above event to note that there exists on Palm Island near Kelung a cave accessible to travellers at the present day which contains cut in the solid rock walls the names of several persons over dates which run back to the period of the Dutch occupation. The inscriptions so far as they can be deciphered are as follows:—

1664
JACOB SCHENCK
1664-1667
JACOB BOSCH
NICOLAWS GROS
anno christi
1667

C. K. HANS HENRICK
Rotenporg
1667
JAN DANNES
1668

†
H. I. S.
K. B.
1667

Burial rites were also very offensive, the corpse being grilled over a fire before interment.

The missionary Junius states in a letter, written in 1644, referring to one of the Dutch townships, "We now daily see young people there not only marrying according to Christian rites, but going together into the fields, and, not only bringing children into the world, but even living together; while formerly they would rather have died than lived thus." So far as is known, the old customs have never again been practised since the departure of the Dutch.

If these reforms, as well as the abolition of head-hunting among the savages of the plain, were the result—and it is pleasant and not unreasonable to believe that they were—of the labor of the Dutch missionaries, these good men have been abundantly rewarded for their work extending over the third of a century, during which, at the risk of many hardships, even of death itself, they taught the natives about the true God.

As to the work of Dutch schools all traces have likewise disappeared. Considering the number of natives who were taught the Dutch language we might reasonably expect to find some Dutch words incorporated in their present speech. Ethnology teaches us that peoples associating with each other even for a short period are quick to enlarge their vocabulary by adopting useful words, the equivalents of which their own language does not possess. But the present case seems an exception, for though the Dutch introduced much that was new to the Formosans, and to describe which the native tongue possessed no terms, no Dutch words exist in the savage dialects as spoken in the island to-day, at least so far as is shown by the vocabularies which have as yet been compiled. Interesting relics have, however, been handed down to us in the shape of land contracts, etc., in the native language, but written in roman characters as taught by the Dutch. Some of these documents are dated as late as 1801, which shows that the natives appreciated the value of roman characters and used them among themselves for some hundred and fifty years after the departure of the Dutch.[1]

---

1. Rev. Wm. Campbell of the English Presbyterian mission, Tainanfu, has given us much exact information as to the scope of the labors of the Dutch missionaries. Besides his work "*Missionary Success in the Island of Formosa*" previously referred to, he has produced two books which will be of great interest to linguists and students, and of possible value to missionaries who may engage in work among the savages. The first publication issued, "*St. Matthew in Formosan*" consists of the gospel of St. Matthew in Formosan (Sinkang dialect) with corresponding versions in Dutch and English, edited from Gravius's edition of 1661. The second publication, besides a scholarly preface, consists of the Articles of Christian Instruction in Favorlang—Formosan, Dutch and English, from Vertrecht's manuscript of 1650, with Psalmanazar's pretended Dialogue between a Japanese and a Formosan, and Happart's Favorlang Vocabulary.

Both "*St. Matthew in Formosan*" and "*The Articles in Formosan*" are published by Kegan Paul, Trench, Trübner & Co., Ld., London.

CHAPTER IV.

FORMOSA THE KINGDOM OF KOXINGA.

1662 - 1683.

Koxinga establishes his court—Koxinga's tour of inspection—The advance of agriculture —Designs on the Philippines—Mission of Riccio—Massacre of Chinese in Manila—Illness and death of Koxinga—The character of Koxinga—Chêng Ching his son succeeds—Overtures from the Tartars—Chêng Ching arrives in Formosa—His administration—A Dutch expedition appears—Dutch and Tartars combined attack Chêng Ching—The Dutch embassy—Humiliating performances —Manufacture of sugar and salt introduced—Schools established—Riccio visits Formosa—Commercial envoy to Philippines—Life of Riccio—English factory in Formosa—Revolt on mainland—Chêng Ching to the front—Defeat of Fokien King—Death of Chêng Ching—Chêng Ko-tsang—Chêng Ko-shwang, the third king—Mainland possessions lost—Imperialists occupy Pescadores—Boy king surrenders—Formosan independence ended—Life of Riccio.

Now in undisputed possession, Koxinga constituted himself sovereign of the island, assumed a princely style, and established his palace and court at Zelandia,[1] which then took the name of Anping-Chin (the City of Peace). The capital of the island was fixed at the neighboring village of Sakkam, to which was given the name of Ch'eng-tien-fou (Shô-ten-fu) and which was later known as Taiwanfu.

Chinese laws, customs, and forms of government were introduced, and all traces of the Dutch administration were obliterated. Some Dutch people remained unwilling residents in the island, however—women, children, and priests, whom Koxinga detained as prisoners.

The new ruler appears to have been as eminently fitted for diplomacy as he had been for the life of a rover of the seas. He placed his son Chêng Ching (Teikei)[2] in command of his possessions at Amoy and the vicinity, and appointed able officers over his departments in Formosa and the Pescadores.

---

1. The present village of Anping.

2. This young man appears to have been as heavily burdened with names as his eminent grandfather. Chang Ching, Ching-Keng-mai, Chêng Ching, Cheng King, Tcheng King, are but a few of the appellations bestowed upon him by foreign writers of to-day.

With Formosa, the Pescadores, and Amoy in his power Koxinga had supreme control of the China seas. Still he devoted his time to the welfare of the island and refrained from attacking his Tartar enemies on the mainland until his position was well established in Formosa. After having appointed one of his trusted subjects as governor of Taiwan district, Koxinga started on a tour of inspection in order to see with his own eyes the extent and condition of his new domain. A body-guard of 300 artillerymen, 300 shield-bearers, and 300 archers accompanied the first king of Formosa when he travelled in state.

From Taiwan the expedition proceeded northwards. Sinkang, Bacca⁻luang, Soulang, and Mattau were successively visited, and Koxinga never failed to treat the inhabitants with kindness and consideration, and further won their good-will by distributing tobacco and clothes among them. So pleased were the natives with this unusual treatment that they spread the news far and wide of the goodness of the new ruler, and their kinsmen warmly welcomed him whenever he appeared among them. It is recorded that Koxinga noted with interest the ingenious construction of the bamboo houses of the savages and furthermore observed in the savage districts much fertile land that he might appropriate on some future day should his people require it. Koxinga and his party proceeded even to Tamsui and other ports of the far north, and the long stretches of fertile land still uncultivated impressed him more than anything else that he saw.

At the close of his journey he called together his officers, both civil and military, and addressed them as follows: "In order to establish our rule over this island, we must have food for our subjects. With insufficient food in a house even a family, in spite of the ties which bind them together, finds it difficult to live happily. So in this island, notwithstanding the patriotic spirit of our subjects we cannot hope for tranquillity unless we can provide them with the necessaries of life. Again with very few of our subjects engaged in agriculture we are not provided with the most necessary of all munitions of war,—abundant food to support us while fighting the enemy. Hence our soldiers, whose occupation is to guard us against our foes, should prepare for battle by engaging during times of peace in agriculture."

Accordingly plots of land were distributed among the soldiers, who were forced to spend much of their time in these fields of peace, "to our great benefit, for having no idle moments they will have but little time for trouble."

No efforts were spared to encourage agriculture and other peaceful pursuits. Proclamations were published throughout the island that service in the fields was obligatory. Inducements were held out to Chinese to settle in the island, and to agriculturalists very liberal treatment was accorded. To parties of emigrants who combined together and established farming settlements, all the land which they could cultivate was given. They were free from taxation for three years, after which a land tax was imposed. But if the farmers were able to pay the tax or a portion of it previous to the expiration of the three years a reduction was made in the future assessment,

They had, however, to submit to military training and to join the army should necessity arise.

With such wise laws providing alike for the prosperity and defence of the island, it was not strange that Chinese from the mainland should flock to the banner of the new ruler in great numbers, and that the island should assume a new aspect. Settlements sprang up along the coast, and the new arrivals lost no time in breaking the soil over wide districts, pleased to have their labors under such generous protection as that given by Koxinga.

Contented with the result of his administration and emboldened by the sight of his numerous warriors daily increasing in number and efficiency, and the wide stretching fields producing an abundance of supplies, Koxinga began to think of enlarging his possessions.

With such an aim in view it was not strange that the rich cluster of islands known as the Philippines, the most northern of which lay but a few hours sail to the south of his domain, should prove most tempting to him.

Koxinga, as shrewd as he was bold, had formed the acquaintance of an Italian Dominican missionary named Vittorio Riccio, who had been in charge of a mission in Amoy, and whom he treated with the greatest kindness and eventually made a mandarin. With his thoughts intent on the Philippines, Koxinga skilfully turned Riccio's friendship to good account by sending him to Manila in 1662 as ambassador to the Spanish governor. The purport of the despatches he bore was that the governor should pay tribute to Koxinga, or his colony would be attacked. A European friar converted into an ambassador for a Chinese pirate was something of a novelty. At all events, the reception accorded him left nothing to be desired; for as he rode through the streets in full uniform, troops were drawn up and saluted him as he passed. Chinese were then living at the capital in considerable numbers, and as they were known to have received at the same time letters from Formosa the Spanish authorities at once accused them of conniving at rebellion. They were a power to be recognized, however, and consequently the Spanish made their preparations secretly, and to insure success went even so far as to demolish outlying forts, so that the majority of the troops might be assembled at Manila. In this way 8,000 infantry and 100 cavalry were ready for the fray, and after having raised fortifications, constructed redoubts for the treasury funds, and secured their armament, the Spaniards incited the Chinese to rebel so that a pretext might be afforded for their massacre.

"Two junk masters were seized, and the Chinese population was menaced; whereupon they prepared to defend themselves, and then opened the campaign for which the government was secretly longing, by killing a Spaniard in the market place. Suddenly an artillery fire was opened on the Parian, and many of the peaceful Chinese traders in their terror hanged themselves; many were drowned in the attempt to reach their canoes in order to get away to sea; some few did safely arrive in Formosa and joined Keuseng's (Koxinga's) camp, whilst others took to the mountains. Eight or nine thousand Chinese remained quiet, but ready for any emergency, when they were suddenly attacked by Spaniards and natives. The confusion was general, and as the Chinese seemed to be gaining ground the governor sent the Ambassador Riccio and a certain Fray José de Madrid to parley with them. The Chinese accepted the terms offered by Riccio, who returned to the governor leaving Fray José with the rebels; but when Riccio went back with a general pardon and a promise to restore the two junk masters, he found that the malcontents had beheaded the priest. A general carnage of the Mongols followed and Juan de la Concepcion says in his historical work on the Philippines that the original intention of the Spaniards was to kill every Chinaman, but that they desisted in view of the inconvenience which would have ensued from the want of tradesmen and mechanics. Therefore they made a virtue of necessity and graciously pardoned in the name of His Catholic Majesty all who laid down their arms."[1]

Koxinga, on hearing of the event from returning Chinese who were fortunate enough to escape in boats, lost no time in organising a large expedition with which he hoped to wreak full vengeance on the Spanish. The Spanish forces in Manila were not superior in strength to those that the Dutch had possessed in Formosa, and it is not unlikely that Koxinga would have had like success, had he landed his party in the Philippines. But while energetically engaged in the work of preparation he was attacked by a dangerous illness which put an end to his ambitious plans.

On May 1st, 1662, Koxinga was suffering from a severe cold. Nevertheless he ascended the stairs to the upper balcony of his palace and there with a glass searched the seas towards the Pescadores looking for the arrival of some vessels expected. Eight days later he again ascended the stairs and as before made careful observations with his glass. With the help of his faithful aides he then descended to his study. His cold had now developed into a disease, of what nature Chinese history does not acquaint us, and Koxinga was much weakened by its ravages. Here he changed his dress for his ceremonial robes, and then with much solemnity he took up the sacred testament of the first Ming Emperor and bowing reverently before it, sat down with the precious document in his hands. His grief now overpowered him, and looking towards his courtiers he cried, "How can I meet my Emperor in Heaven with my mission unfulfilled?" Then bowing forward and covering his face with his hands the defender of the Mings breathed his last.

His death at the early age of thirty-nine cast a deep gloom over the island, and the grand funeral which followed was attended by thousands of weeping mourners.

Koxinga was perhaps the most remarkable character that modern history exhibits in the Orient. Of all the band of adventurous rovers that sailed the China seas there was none to compare in courage, enterprise, and ability with this young chief. Born in Japan of a Japanese mother and a Chinese father, we may believe he inherited courage and soldierly ability from the former and craft and diplomacy from the latter. At all events he possessed these attributes to a high degree, and was as successful in one as in the

---

1. Foreman's " Philippine Islands."

other. Holding one of the highest military commands in China at the age of twenty-two and dying while still under forty, his greatest exploits were accomplished during that period of life when others are ordinarily engaged in study and in preparation for the great deeds they hope to accomplish when they have arrived at perfect maturity. That his abilities were great is attested by his followers,—a motley congregation, for all those who were oppressed or discontented found shelter under his banner, and it is a strong proof of his powers that thousands of men twice and even thrice his age were content to obey the authoritative commands of a youth who was not always gentle in his infliction of discipline.

Koxinga was not a vulgar pirate. He did not war for personal profit. The cause of his ancestors was ever present with him, and his possessions in both China and Formosa were a welcome refuge to all Ming loyalists, while his life's work was to restore the lost empire. But he was even more than a mere warrior: he was a man of iron will, of terrible fiery earnestness. The death penalty which he inflicted upon an offending soldier he sought to inflict also upon his own son for his misdeeds. And yet he was not cruel; at least not so as compared with those Europeans who at the same period were from time to time engaged in warlike exploits. The Crusades, the persecution of the Huguenots, the Spanish campaigns in the Netherlands, the conquests of Mexico and Peru, and even the Dutch in the Pescadores exhibit deeds of cruelty which exceed anything laid to the charge of Koxinga. Still it has pleased most modern writers to describe him as an atrociously cruel and dastardly pirate. It would appear that they have either judged him by the standard expected to-day, which is unjust, or from the descriptions of him given by the Dutch, no safe authority inasmuch as the latter were naturally prejudiced observers. Koxinga came to Formosa as a declared foe of the Dutch, and for months carried on a life and death struggle with them. European history of the period teaches us that it was not the custom of commanders to treat avowed friends of the enemy with kindness. And Koxinga was no exception. Five Dutch clergymen were killed by his followers with or without his direct orders. Koxinga was not opposed to the teachings of Christianity *per se*, as the writings of Riccio show, and if in obedience to direct commands from the chief, the unfortunate missionaries were executed, their fate was due rather to their nationality than their occupation. The same principle applies to the native Christians referred to above, who were slain rather as traitors than as Christians. Against this we have the fact that the Dutch, numbering about one thousand, were allowed to depart in their own vessels, and that, contrary to all usages of war even in our own times, they were permitted to carry their private property with them. About one hundred prisoners were reserved as hostages. Surely there was no cruelty in that. And the same Dutch who complain of the extreme barbarity of Koxinga record in their own annals the murder of 1,300 out of 1,500 Chinese sailors who were forced by the Dutch to labor in the Pescadores and were literally starved to death; and also the fact that hundreds of innocent natives were shipped in chains to foreign lands where, if they survived the cruel journey, they were sold into slavery. When we contrast Koxinga's conduct towards the Dutch with that of the Dutch and the Spanish towards the Chinese our sympathies are all for the former. His mission demanding tribute of the Spaniards in Manila is evidence that he gave himself but little trouble respecting the justice of his undertakings, but neither did the European governments at that period.

In whatever light we view him, it appears that he was not inferior to the European commanders of his time, and he was so far superior to such commanders in the Orient that his conduct, compared with theirs, entitles him to the admiration of unbiassed critics.

In his private life he was frugal and modest in his wants. He was proud of the authority vested in him, but does not appear to have used that authority tyrannically; otherwise he could not have secured and preserved the willing loyalty that his immediate followers yielded him. He trained his subjects in various industries, and enforced agricultural labor on his officers and men. Even his own family were not exempt. His wives and their female companions were forced to weave and spin, and the products of their toil were placed on the market along with those of more humble hands.

Possessed of an immense amount of energy, determination, and natural ability, Koxinga with his own hands carved out a kingdom for himself and provided a safe refuge for all loyal followers of the Ming dynasty, against which the haughty Emperor of China, with his boasted nine countries, could not prevail. Truly this was the work of no ordinary man!

When the report of Koxinga's death reached Amoy, there was much sorrow among his faithful subjects there. The mainland followers of the dead ruler proclaimed Chêng Ching, his eldest son, the second King of Formosa, and his formal acceptance of this high dignity was celebrated with great ceremony. Meanwhile, in Formosa, the brother of Koxinga had been placed on the throne in the belief that Koxinga, who had quarrelled with Chêng Ching had intended that his son should not be his successor.

Chêng Ching, although generous and kind-hearted, appears to have thought more of pleasure than of warfare or diplomacy, and devoted his younger days wholly to a very extensive sowing of wild oats.

To his father—a courageous warrior who had dedicated his life to the punishment of his Tartar enemies,—this son appeared as a worthless scamp who gave but little thought to his father's cause, and much to the foibles of life. A strict disciplinarian, Koxinga was prepared to punish him for his misdeeds as he would have punished the lowest soldier in his army.

Chêng Ching had married a quiet, homely woman, but not finding her to his taste he spent his time with concubines. Furthermore, the young prince fell in love with a woman who had formerly been nurse to his youngest brother. Upon her he showered attentions, neglecting his true wife as well as the duties of his office. Koxinga was greatly enraged at the misconduct of his son, and upon the birth of a child to the young couple, according to Formosan reports, he sent a messenger across from the island with orders to kill the son, the

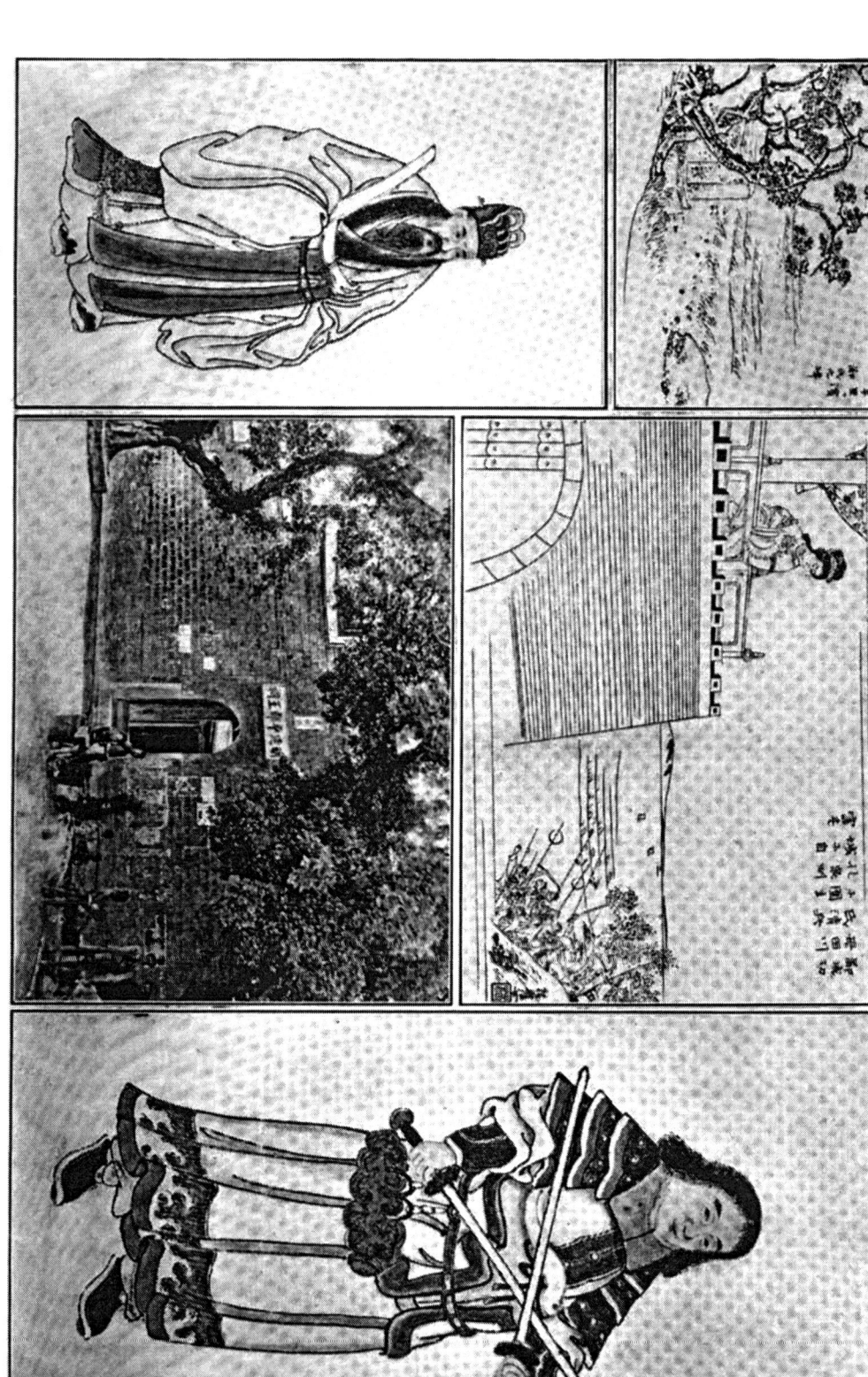

Monument to Koxinga erected near
Hirado, Japan at the Place of His Birth.

Koxinga's Mother in Her Tsen-chu Castle,
attacked by Tartars (From an Old Print.)

Koxinga.
(From a Chinese Scroll.)

mistress, and the newly-born babe. The illegitimate child was accordingly disposed of, but the messenger returned without having accomplished the rest of his mission. Koxinga, still determined that his unworthy son should not survive him, sent a second and third messenger to Amoy, but both fell into the hands of Chêng Ching, and the relentless parent was thus balked in his severe designs.

With the death of Koxinga the Tartar government bestirred themselves, believing that the opportunity for disposing of the last adherent of the Ming dynasty was at hand. Overtures were accordingly made to Chêng Ching, who was not unwilling to consider them, although he determined not to yield if the imperial authorities should insist on his shaving his head; a humiliating token of submission. Reports reached Chêng Ching that a strong force was preparing to march against him, while the Dutch had again appeared in the China seas, apparently with the intention of recovering their lost territory.

The Tartar government again sent a messenger to Chêng Ching informing him that, as the Imperial Government lacked suitable officers, they would gladly grant him position and wealth if he would surrender, shave his head, and grow a queue.

Chêng Ching treated the messenger with great kindness and announced his willingness to accept the conditions, but begged that the high authorities be informed that he did not like the idea of shaving his head. The messenger, highly elated at the apparent success of his mission, returned and reported so favorably to his superiors that all warlike preparations against Chêng Ching were discontinued. The shrewd young prince, pleased with the success of his ruse, for such it was, was enabled to gather his followers about him and complete the extensive preparations necessary for his removal to Formosa. He left a strong garrison of trusty subjects in Amoy and with the rest of his force he departed, stopping first at the Pescadores, where he reconstructed the local government and placed a loyal officer in command. He sent an officer to Formosa to announce that he was about to come to the island to take up the reins of government.

This created some little consternation among the authorities in Formosa, who had, as mentioned above, proclaimed the brother of Koxinga as ruler of the new Kingdom of Formosa.

A message was accordingly sent to Chêng Ching informing him that while his father's officers recognized that it was customary for the son to succeed the father, in the present instance he had by his misbehavior forfeited all his rights; that his father's death had been hastened by his unfilial conduct; and that the brother of Koxinga was a loyal and generous man whom all respected and was, therefore, fitted to govern the island.

Chêng Ching now believed he was justified in gaining his rights by force, inasmuch as he had given his father's officers the opportunity of admitting him peaceably, and they had refused. Accordingly his forces sailed from the Pescadores and landed in Formosa,

Their disembarkation was strongly opposed, but they fought so fiercely that they were not only able to hold their ground, but succeeded in killing the hostile general in command. One of Chêng Ching's officers, availing himself of a momentary lull in the fighting, advanced towards the Formosans and cried in a loud voice: "Here is Chêng Ching. The commander of your forces lies dead. Let us all join the standard of the true son of our late beloved King!" Many of the island officers, moved by this appeal, left their ranks and joined the forces of Chêng Ching, by whom they were very kindly treated.

Koxinga's brother was then invited to visit his nephew's camp. This man, who appears to have been a truly generous character, accepted the invitation, and on meeting Chêng Ching embraced him affectionately and declared that their separation was due to mischievous plotting on the part of certain ambitious officers who had hoped to ensure the permanency of their own positions by so acting. In consequence of this declaration on the part of the uncle the leaders of the other party were executed, and all opposition to Chêng Ching was at an end.

Chêng Ching was now declared the rightful successor of Koxinga to the throne of Formosa, and established his court at Zelandia as his father had done.

Chêng Ching devoted himself to strengthening the fortifications of the island, and when this had been accomplished to his satisfaction, he placed trusted officers in command and then departed for Amoy to look after his possessions there. Arriving at his destination he found that the imperial government had been endeavoring to undermine his influence during his absence. The young ruler took strict measures to restore his authority, and executed all who had listened to the honeyed promises of the Tartars.

Previously to this the council at Batavia had, in 1662, equipped twelve vessels, which they placed under the command of Admiral Bort with orders to again attempt the restoration of Dutch influence in Formosa. Arriving in the China seas the fleet eventually anchored at the mouth of the River Min, where deputies from the governor came aboard and induced the admiral to send two of his officers to arrange with the Chinese concerning combined operations against Koxinga's followers. The negotiations, however, resulted in no advantage to the Dutch, and Bort, rather than return without having fired a gun, commenced a series of attacks on the fleet and garrisons of Koxinga, burning and destroying them in a piratical manner, which was alike ineffectual either in weakening Koxinga's position in Formosa or forcing the Chinese into trade.

Bort returned to Batavia with his fleet in 1663, and was again despatched the same year with a stronger force, consisting of 16 ships, 1,386 sailors, and 1,234 soldiers, with orders to make reprisals on both Tartars and Ming Chinese, if necessary to recover Formosa. The governor of Fokien received Admiral Bort favorably and agreed to co-operate with him in driving the Ming Chinese from Amoy and Formosa.

Chêng Ching as the successor of Koxinga was now in Amoy, as previously stated. Aware that the Tartars and Dutch were about to attack him he made active preparations to strengthen his position in Amoy. Upon the arrival of his opponents, he strongly defended his position, but after several skirmishes in which he was defeated, he despaired of victory and together with his family retired to Formosa. Amoy now fell into the hands of the Tartars and the subjection of the whole province to Manchu rule was thus effected.

As a reward to the Dutch for their assistance in winning for the Tartars a district which years of diplomacy and war had failed to give them, the latter now proceeded to fulfil their promises of aiding their foreign allies to recover Formosa by lending them *two junks*; a piece of news which is said to have made the Formosan king laugh when it was reported to him.

Chêng Ching now sent word to the Dutch that there were residing in the island the widow of Jacobus Valentyn (a former magistrate in the Dutch service), the clergyman Leonardus and his wife, and many other Dutch prisoners, about a hundred in all. He offered to release them and furthermore to permit the Dutch to trade in Formosa, for which purpose a place of residence would be given them, either at Tamsui on the north coast, or on the island of Kelung in its vicinity. He urged the foreigners to believe in his sincerity and no longer to trust to the false promises of the Tartars. If only for the sake of their suffering countrymen one would have thought that the Dutch would have agreed to Chêng Ching's generous proposals. But it was not so. They continued to confide in the Tartars. After useless delay, the whole fleet sailed for Formosa, where the commander spent a considerable time in fruitless negotiations. While on this expedition Bort recaptured Kelung, as previously mentioned, left Captain de Bitter with 200 men in charge, and then returned to Batavia. Kelung did not prove a profitable possession, and it was consequently abandoned five years later.

The Dutch Council, chagrined at these results, fitted out no more expeditions, preferring to adopt the less expensive plan of sending an embassy to communicate with the Celestial Empire and again petition for trade and permission to erect factories on the mainland. The embassy reached Foochow in 1664, and Peking a year later. "The same succession of prostrations before an empty throne, followed by state banquets, and accompanied by the presentation and conferring of presents, characterized the reception of this embassy as it had all its predecessors. It ended with a similar farce, alike pleasing to the haughty court which received it, and unworthy the Christian nation which gave it; and the only result of this grand expedition was a sealed letter, of the contents of which they were wholly ignorant, but which did not, in fact, grant any of the privileges they so anxiously solicited. They had, by their performance of the act of prostration, caused their nation to be enrolled among the tributaries of the Grand Khan, and then were dismissed as loyal subjects should be, at the will of their liege lord, with what he chose to give them. It was a fitting end to a career begun in rapine and aggression toward the Chinese, who had never provoked them." [1]

---

1. " Williams—*The Middle Kingdom*"—page 438 Vol. II.

Chêng Ching now gave his attention to promoting the prosperity of Formosa, which he divided into prefectures, and established a good administration over all. A worthy governor was placed in charge of the Pescadores, the defences of the island were greatly strengthened, and the garrisons largely increased to prevent invasion.

Chêng Ching showed his loyalty to his father's cause by erecting a palace, which was placed at the service of the princes of the Ming dynasty. Like his father, he encouraged agriculture by presenting large tracts of uncultivated land to arriving immigrants and inducing his soldiers to employ their idle days by working in the fields. He planted sugar cane and introduced the manufacture of sugar. He studied the method of producing salt from sea water and induced his subjects to manufacture this necessary commodity.

With the responsibilities thrown upon him as ruler of his father's domains, Chêng Ching seems to have banished all thoughts of those reckless pleasures which marked his early career and to have devoted himself to the welfare of his people and his land. Although still a young man, so much ability did he exhibit that within a few years he had fostered such a diversity of industries that the inhabitants could live in comfort, and were independent of any foreign productions. In honor of his eminent father the young king erected, in 1666, a splendid temple, built substantially that it might last for ages.

Having provided for his subjects' material wants, Chêng Ching now took measures to afford them educational benefits. By his orders schools were established and maintained by every district. Examinations were held once every three years, and such scholars as reached a certain standard were admitted to a high school, from which, should they be so fortunate as to graduate, they were appointed officers of the government and given rank and position. Thus were laid the foundations of the educational system of the island.

He invited two men of ability to serve as advisers, and with their help he was enabled to attend closely to all details of administration. Tax regulations were introduced, and wine and shipping were subjected to a light impost which, with the addition of the land tax, formed the only financial burdens his subjects were asked to support.

In 1665, the Christian missionary Riccio again visited the island, and though some of the members of the court were opposed to his presence, Chêng Ching presented him with fine clothes, received him in the palace, and bade him go where he liked so long as he did not create discord.

With the Manchu government now in control of the mainland, communication with Formosa was forbidden, thus causing much inconvenience both to the island and to Amoy, for the inhabitants were mutually related to each other. But eventually Chêng Ching with the assistance of the Amoy residents carried on a secret communication, trading vessels departing from Amoy at night arrived safely in Formosa, and commerce was revived to a considerable extent. It is said that women who had been kidnapped for the purpose often formed an important part of these cargoes.

Again the Tartars endeavored to persuade Chêng Ching to shave his head and renounce his allegiance to the Imperial Government, promising that he should be recognized as hereditary governor of the island.   Although the messenger was treated kindly the young king refused the offer and declared that, like his father, he would rather lose his life than sacrifice one hair of his head.

Chêng Ching feeling that some share of foreign commerce was necessary for the prosperity of an independent state, sent the Italian Dominican Riccio to the Philippines, to arrange a commercial treaty and re-establish friendly relations which had been broken off years before by his father. Siam, Japan, and other countries were invited to join in the Formosan trade. As to the success obtained by these negotiations we are not informed ; but the English East India Company saw fit to avail themselves of the young king's generosity, and during the latter half of the seventeenth century had an emporium established in the island.

To the researches of Rev. William Campbell we are indebted for an interesting historical episode which quaintly informs us of the acceptance of Chêng Ching's offer by the English.   It is a letter addressed to the " King of Tywan," its opening sentences running thus :

" Charles, by the grace of God, King of England, Scotland, France, and Ireland ; having most graciously licensed severall of his Merchants to trade into all the habitable partes of the World, amongst whom Sir Wm. Thompson, with some other Merchants, are, by the said most gracious King, authorized Governors of the Merchants to trade into these Eastern parts.   Now for the directing and overseeing their Affaires at Bantam and partes adjacent, they have appointed mee (Henry Dacres), Agent.   The said Henry Dacres, therefore, on behalf of the said Sir Wm. Thompson, Governor, sends greeteing unto your most Excellent Majesty ; and having seen your most gracious Letter directed to all Merchants in Generall, inviting them to trade into the partes under your Majestie's Jurisdictions, has, without delay, sent this small Ship and Sloope with Mr. Ellis Crispe, Capt., to acquaint us with the Merchandize desireable to bee Imported, and of Merchandize proper for us to Exporte, and when wee shall bee acquainted therewith by him, and have the permission of Friendship and Affection of your Majesty (which wee moste humbly desire) wee shall requeste the said Sir Wm. Thompson's leave to solicite your Majesty ; and because we would have your Majesty know that wee are Englishmen, and a distinct Nation from Hollanders (some people of which Nation about ten years since were driven out of your Land by his Majesty your Renowned Father), we have sent on this our Shipp Capt. Sooke, with eight other Chinamen, who have for long time traded and been acquainted with us and our Nation."

A long table of conditions for the settlement of the factory follows, while other letters which our authority inspected reported a favorable commencement having been made.   As to particulars of this establishment, however, we are not informed, though it does not appear to have resulted in much advantage if we may judge by the following peremptory command from the Court of Directors to the Company's representatives at Bantam, under date of February 28th, 1682 :—

" As to the Trade of Tywan, we hereby expressly require you, that if you have made no better earnings of it before this comes to your hands, you do order our Factors to desert the Place, and bring off what they can with them.   To which purpose we have written a menacing Letter to the King, and probably may send a Ship to be with you in March or April next, to go down to Tywan to fetch off our Servants ; and after that to use some forcible means for our satisfaction of the debt he owes us."

Trouble again occurred on the mainland, and in 1673 the provinces of Kwang-tung and Fokien revolted against the Manchu Emperor Kang-he.

Chêng Ching, always ready to inflict a wound on the Tartars, resolved to join the king of Fokien. Accordingly he fitted out an expedition and landed near Amoy, encamping at Chinchoo. Jealousy arose between the two high commanders, and it is said that the king of Fokien refused to acknowledge Chêng Ching as a sovereign prince. At all events the Formosan king seems to have turned his forces against the Fokien chief with the result that the latter's power was so far destroyed that upon the appearance of the Imperial army he was forced to submit to the emperor and receive the tonsure. The surrendered soldiers were now combined with the Imperial army and this large force marched against Chêng Ching, who retreated to Amoy.

In 1679 we find Chêng Ching again on the offensive, laying siege with 20,000 men to the principal strongholds of the Imperialists in Chowchoo and Chinchoo. The garrisons could not be reduced, however, and in a few months a large army of Imperialists approached Chêng Ching's forces from three directions, compelling the Formosan king to retire to Haiching (Kaicho) near Amoy. Here he erected strong fortifications with walls and trenches and prepared to offer a stout resistance to the Imperial troops. A high official was despatched to command the Tartar expedition against Chêng Ching. After numerous battles the Amoy fortifications were at length captured and the Formosan king returned to Formosa, never again to attempt the restoration of the Ming dynasty in China.

Chêng Ching with his kingdom in a prosperous condition and having abandoned warlike expeditions against the Tartars, devoted his last days to teaching Chêng Ko-tsang (Teikokuzo), an illegitimate son of whom he was very fond, the duties of the high office which at his father's death would descend to him.

In 1682 Chêng Ching died at the age of 39 respected and honored by all his subjects, a powerful enemy of the Tartars for nineteen years, having begun his career, which included many battles great and small, by his father's side when but a lad.

Chêng Ko-tsang, who, although young in years, had developed into a character greatly resembling his grandfather Koxinga, was the son selected by Chêng Ching to be his successor. But scarcely had the father breathed his last when the young heir was made the subject of an infamous plot to deprive him of his rights. Chêng Ching's mother declared that the throne should not go to Chêng Ko-tsang, claiming that the youth was not a true son of the dead king, but the child of other parents, who in infancy had been presented to the king by his favorite concubine as his own son. Several influential officers were induced to accept this explanation, and Chêng Ko-tsang was secretly strangled in his palace at the instigation of the so-called true sons and their grandmother.

Chêng Ko-shwang (Teikokuso), the eldest of the surviving sons, aged twelve years, now came to the throne and entered upon a troublesome career.

In the next year the Tartar governor of Fokien intrigued against the young king and used his influence with the loyalists to betray him. The plot was, however, discovered and the ringleader was punished with death.

A few months later a successful attack was made by the Tartar army on Tung-sang, the only spot then held by the Formosans on the mainland. Flushed with this success, the governor with a fleet of ships now attacked the garrison at the Pescadores and after a short engagement occupied this most important position.

These victories were a hard blow to the young ruler, who considered the Pescadores as the entrance to his kingdom. He accordingly proposed to his officers that they should retire from Formosa and occupy Luzon island to the south. Some preparations were actually made, and maps and a complete description of the new land obtained, but his subjects generally gave evidence of so much opposition to the plan that the boy king was obliged to abandon it.

It was now suggested by one of the officers that the island should be surrendered to the Peking government while there was yet time to hope for mercy. A message was accordingly sent to the Imperial commander at the Pescadores offering to hand over the island, shave their heads, and become subjects of the emperor, but asking that the officers should be left in command of the island holding themselves subject to Imperial orders. The Imperialists rejected this offer and sent back an intimation to the young king that now that Formosa was already practically conquered it was too late to send in proposals of conditional surrender.

Several islands near Formosa were now captured by the Imperialists. The Fokien governor proclaimed a general amnesty to all who would submit to the emperor, and this promise had the desired effect both of inducing many Formosan emigrants to return to China, and of weakening the enemy upon the island.

The young king now sent a letter of unconditional surrender to the Pescadores commandant who forwarded it to Peking. The following is an extract from it: "When kneeling at the feet of Your Majesty, I look upon China's greatness which has existed in unbroken brilliancy for ages, I cannot do otherwise than acknowledge that it is the will of Heaven which has vested you with supreme power to govern the nine countries." An Imperial officer, Wu Chi-cho (Gokeishaku), was sent from Peking to take over the island. The boy king welcomed him cordially, and on July 19th, 1683, with much ceremony delivered to him the official records, etc., and by proclamation notified the people of Formosa of the conditions of surrender. Chêng Ko-shwang now shaved his head in accordance with Manchu customs, and directed his former followers to do the same.

Thus for thirty-eight years after the fall of its last emperor the old Ming dynasty was recognized in Formosa, and the brave warrior Koxinga may well have turned over in his grave and hurled bitter reproaches on his weak, defenceless grandson.

Chêng Ko-shwang was now ordered to visit Peking. This was but little to the young ex-king's liking, and in order to avoid it if possible he forwarded his seals of office to Peking and petitioned that as he was not accustomed to the harsh northern winds, he might be excused from making the long journey to the capital and be instead permitted to reside at Fokien, the home of his ancestors. The emperor was obdurate, however, and the boy was obliged to obey the authoritative command. To the credit of the Peking government and no doubt to the surprise of Chêng Ko-shwang, instead of punishment he was the recipient of kind treatment from the Imperial authorities, and the hereditary title of Hai-ching kung or "Sea-quelling Duke" was bestowed upon him,—a title which his descendants still bear.

Thus ended the rule of the Koxinga family, and the "Beautiful Isle" now became a Chinese possession.

NOTE.—The Italian Dominican friar, Vittorio Riccio, referred to above, was so much concerned with the history of Formosa that we consider a few lines in reference to his interesting career not out of place here.

Riccio was born in Florence. In 1648 he arrived in the Philippines, where he ministered to the spiritual wants of the Chinese until 1655, when he was sent to China. He was then ordered to Amoy where he erected a church and made many converts. The good father here noted the cruel Chinese custom of throwing away sick and deformed infants to meet a cruel death. He accordingly opened his house to these waifs and by publishing throughout the settlement his desire to care for this class, many lives were saved.

Chêng Ching, the wild, debauched son of Koxinga, gave Riccio much trouble, and did not hesitate even to send soldiers to assault him, who robbed him of all his possessions. Koxinga, however, had won the regard of the friar on account of the kind and generous treatment which the latter received at the hands of this great chief. Koxinga was now on his famous expedition against Nanking. But eventually defeated, he returned to Amoy where, in June, 1660, he fought a desperate battle both by land and sea against the Tartars, who had followed up their successes to this point. Father Riccio, much concerned, was repeating the rosary with his converts, imploring the aid of Heaven for the success of Koxinga "who had shown himself so favorable to Christians." The prayers of the Father were answered and his champion was victorious. Then followed the events leading up to the occupation of Formosa by Koxinga and the departure of the Dutch. Riccio was now, much against his will, obliged to enter the service of the Formosan ruler, by whom he was sent to Manila as ambassador. He accordingly visited the Philippine capital, but was naturally unsuccessful in obtaining submission to Koxinga, which was the object of his mission. It speaks well for Riccio that instead of remaining in Manila, where his safety was assured, he returned to China to deliver the answer to Koxinga. Forced by storm into Amoy he was immediately placed under arrest, but through the assistance of an influential Christian native he was released after eight days' confinement. Although Koxinga was now dead, several of his lieutenants were intent upon carrying out the hostile plans against Manila which their late chief had formulated. But the wise Father Riccio succeeded in persuading them that the greater advantages of commerce with the Philippines could not be obtained if hostilities were commenced. Wrath against the Spanish gave way to interest, and eventually Chêng Ching decided to avail himself of the suggestions of Riccio and accordingly despatched him again to the Philippines, but this time on the peaceful mission of inviting commercial intercourse. After fifteen days' journey Father Riccio arrived in Manila, where he was very warmly received and his mission brought to a successful termination. He now embarked on his return trip to China, but upon arriving at Amoy he found the Tartars in possession. He was very cruelly treated and even his life was threatened by these people, who regarded him as a friend of the Ming Chinese. There occurred about this time a great inundation at Amoy in which at least ten thousand people perished. Riccio saved himself by tearing his clothing in strips and with these binding together a number of timbers found in a temple where he had taken refuge, and thus constructed a raft upon which he kept himself afloat, although he nearly perished from hunger, having been three days without food. Towards the end of 1664 all foreign missionaries in China were subject to great persecution and were later ordered to Peking. Father Riccio fearing that, as he was the known friend of Koxinga, he would be treated very severely, escaped to Foochow, where he remained in hiding until he had an opportunity of fleeing to Formosa. From Formosa he returned, in 1666, to Manila where, instead of finding the home he expected, he was imprisoned on suspicion of disloyalty and later was banished to the then desolate province of Laguna. His innocence was later established and he was permitted to return to Manila. His virtues then received due reward and he filled many high posts, including that of the vicar of the Formosan mission and of meridional China. He wrote several famous religious works, and the history of his life now remains in manuscript in the archives of the Dominican Order at Manila. In 1685, after a long and severe sickness, Riccio died respected and honored by all who knew him.

CHAPTER V.

FORMOSA A CHINESE POSSESSION.

1683-1800.

Formosa becomes a prefecture of Fokien—Taiwan adopted as name—Administrative
Divisions—Rebellion of 1701—A miracle maker—Liu Chow chosen leader—The
Imperial camp attacked—Rebels defeated—Liu Chow executed—Luchow the
Chinese statesman—18th century prosperity—Character of population—Three
divisions of inhabitants—Hakkas and Puntis—Chinese officials in Formosa—
Universal corruption—Jesuit map makers visit the island—Little Loochoo
island—Government of Aborigines—Cruel treatment by interpreters—Passport
Regulations—Viceroy of Fokien—Camphor monopoly—Death penalty for cutting
trees—Two hundred Chinese decapitated—Rebellion of 1722—Choo Yihkwei as
duck feeder—Government troops—Prices for rebel heads—Capital captured by
rebels—Choo Yihkwei as Emperor—Rebels defeated—A scene of misery—New
prefecture: Changwha and division Tamsui—Luchow describes and prescribes
for Formosan troubles—Rebellion of 1731—Rebellion of 1770—Hong Chau its
leader—Rebels defeated—Count Benyowsky—Great storm of 1782—Great
rebellion of Tetifui secret society—Quarrel with rival society—Slaughter of
Imperialists—Changwha and Kagi captured—New era introduced—Fang-shan
added to rebel victories—Extensive Imperial force arrives from China—A high
commissioner's success—Victory by Imperialists—Rebellion put down—Capture
of the leader—The emperor expresses dissatisfaction with Formosan officials—
M. de Grammont's letter—Rebellion of 1795—Clever strategy—Defeat—Close
of 18th century.

FORMOSA, from its position, fertility, promising state of cultivation, and large population, was the most important acquisition of territory added to the Chinese Empire by the Tartar dynasty. The greatest value of Formosa lay in the fact that, compared with other semi-tropical lands of like fertility, it could on account of its climate lay the soil under heavier contributions.

Upon coming under the domination of the Tartar government in 1683, the island was at once constituted a "*fu*" or prefecture of Fokien province, and thus became an integral part of the Chinese Empire. The name of Taiwan, which at first was only applied to the small island where the Dutch were established, later designated the whole island, and the town of Sakkam, which had considerably increased during the reigns of Koxinga and his descendants, was declared the capital under the name of Taiwanfu.

Taiwan was divided into three "*hien*" or districts, known as Choolo, Taiwan, and Fangshan, under civil magistrates, and one "*ting*" or maritime division, Panghoo (Pescadores) under a marine magistrate. These magistrates submitted themselves to the Taiwanfu or prefect, who in turn was under the authority of the censor of Taiwan, afterwards known as the Taotai, who was the highest authority in Taiwan, and was to make a circuit of the departments once annually.

This latter officer was responsible to the governor of Fokien, although it is stated that he had the right to communicate directly with the Peking government. The garrison was composed of 8,000 men at the beginning, but was gradually increased to 14,000 and commanded by a general with the title of "*tsungping*", who was responsible to the commander of the Manchu garrison at Foochow as well as to the admiral and the governor-general of Fokien.

Appreciating the fact that the followers of Koxinga had not been taught to love the Tartars, the mandarins quite wisely permitted the first few years following Imperial occupation to drift by without the adoption of any extreme means of enforcing distasteful government measures upon the inhabitants, who were known to be rather independent in their views. To this, no doubt, were due the few years of peace which, with one exception, marked the close of the seventeenth century.

In 1696 there was an attempt to incite rebellion, but it failed owing to the shrewdness of a district officer. Fangshan (Hozan) in the south was the seat of this plot, the particulars of which are as follows: A certain Imperial officer, Chin Tsu (Chinsu) by name, had appropriated to his own use a large quantity of government rice which had been placed in his keeping. The deficit having been discovered and Chin Tsu subjected to official questioning, the guilty officer was at a loss what to do. At this stage he consulted his brother-in-law Oo Chu (Go Kyu) who appears to have been of a rebellious turn of mind, and having been joined by a third person, named Tsu Yu-lon (Shu Yu-ryu) of like character, the officer was advised by both not to make good the missing rice, but to declare that this, as well as the remaining stores, was the property of the people, and that the government had no rightful claim upon it. The three persons above mentioned then laid plans for rebellion. To further strengthen their position an attempt was made to induce Lin Shin (Linsei) the district officer to join. This officer allowed his petitioners to believe he acquiesced in their designs, and after having thoroughly learnt the plans of the rebellion, he sent exact information to the government office, whereupon the offenders were secretly captured and all killed with the exception of Tsu Yu-lon, who escaped. Thus what threatened to be a formidable rebellion was nipped in the bud.

More serious, however, was the affair which occurred six years later. In the year 1701, in the district of Kagi, a certain country rough named Liu Chow (Ryu Kya-ku) who prided himself upon the extensive influence he possessed among a class of people of his own character and upon the terror which by his mere presence he could inspire in the peaceful Chinese, gathered his friends together and with solemn ceremony, sealed by the drinking of blood, induced them all to swear allegiance to his banner against the Imperial government. Some time passed and Liu Chow, still in the midst of preparations, was unable to keep the ardor of his followers at fever heat. There were expressions of discontent, and the influence of the chief appeared to have waned considerably. It was now evident that nothing short of a miracle would raise the prestige of the leader sufficiently to place him in possession of an adequate force. Liu Chow appreciated this and was not unwilling to attempt the seemingly impossible task. Accordingly a bright flame appeared over the house of the ambitious chief for many nights, and first the village and then the country people for miles around came to look at this strange phenomenon and to meditate as to its meaning. Liu Chow who had daily nursed the miracle with abundant supplies of camphor evidenced no special interest in the affair, disclaimed all knowledge of it, and when questioned as to its possible presence being an expression of favor from Heaven, was politic enough to disagree with his interviewers. The light continued to appear and at length the wise men decided that it was a divine manifestation and that their leader had been thus declared to them. Accordingly a large concourse approached the house of Liu Chow. Upon entering a brilliant light flashed out from an apparently empty incense dish, thus guiding their footsteps aright. This was sufficient; the Heaven-favored man was implored to become their leader. Further manifestations of supernatural approval appeared in the back yard, where from a dark hole in the earth were vomited swords and spears. The people dared not approach too close to the sacred hole, and the smith and workmen who were installed at the bottom by the miracle maker, were taxed to the utmost to produce sufficient heaven-made swords to satisfy the many mystified sightseers who gathered around.

Liu Chow accepted the high office and with a large force marched towards the north with drums beating and gongs sounding, to conquer the island. The government camp at Mokongwei (Bokobi) was first attacked. It was easily captured and was burned to the ground, the people's houses having first been looted. The savages from the hills followed in the wake of the rebels and murdered many who had so far escaped. Having destroyed much property, Liu Chow now retired to Chisuishi (Kyu-suikei) in the Kagi district, where he planned fresh enterprises.

An Imperial general at this period set out with his forces to put down the rebels. A few days later reinforcements were sent him from Taiwan, and with this augmented force Liu Chow was attacked. The rebels could make no effective opposition and the camp was destroyed, the leader, however, escaping to a distant mountain. While the ambitious plans of the bold rebel were thus frustrated, he made the country feel his rage, and every night raided neighboring settlements, murdering and pillaging all whom he could lay hands on. His career although exciting was not long, for in 1702 he and his two sons were captured and dragged to Taiwanfu, where they were executed, while his wife and other members of the family were banished from the island.

This rebellion taught the Imperial government that the island required more attention than they had at first been inclined to bestow upon it, and that with constant insurrections it might prove to be as great an incubus as it had been when governed by their dreaded enemy Koxinga.

According to the best account at hand, that of Luchow, the famous Chinese statesman, there were, about the middle of the 18th century, nearly two millions of Chinese[1] in Formosa engaged in the cultivation of sugar and rice, and about four hundred vessels were plying continually between the island and the Chinese coast. When we consider that a great part of the sugar consumed in the northern provinces of China was produced in the island, and that the rice upon which millions of people in Fokien at that time depended almost entirely for their support, was derived from the same source, we may fairly conclude that our author did not exaggerate its commercial activity. Many parts of the opposite shore in Fokien were so barren that without the aid of the oil cakes from Formosa, which were used as a fertilizer on the sandy hills, even the sweet potato could not have been produced.

It was these considerations which attracted so large a number of settlers and also tended to make the island an abode for a race of outlaws—thieves, swindlers, and murderers—who had been forced to fly from their country. When once they reached Formosa, they retired to the distant hills and there lived out of reach of the avenging arm of justice.

The inhabitants of the island at this time consisted of three distinct classes, viz.: the civilized aborigines, the non-civilized aborigines, and the Chinese. The first consisted of those of the aborigines who had not only submitted to the Chinese, but had adopted many of their customs and had advanced toward what the Chinese considered as civilization. Among these were the natives who had been taught by the Dutch, but who, once deprived of their instructors, had soon forgotten them and their teachings, although the Jesuit Du Halde, who wrote seventy years after the Dutch occupation, notes that there were many who understood the Dutch language and could read and write it, and many who had preserved some relics, chiefly Dutch books, in their houses. This class was not numerically large in those early days, although there was not a very broad line between them and the other aborigines of the plains who had been forced to acknowledge the authority of the Chinese and yet retained their primitive customs. In later years, however, these natives of the plains gradually adopted the customs of the Chinese, until eventually nearly all were recognized as civilized aborigines. The second class consisted of the unsubdued and independent tribes and villagers who, with the savages of the plains, had originally occupied the whole island, but who were too proud and too brave to bow before the hordes of incoming Chinese, preferring rather to be driven if necessary into the very

1. From the fact that the present Chinese population of the island is only about two and a half millions and that immigration has always been very brisk, the large population given by Luchow would seem to be overrated.

heart of the mountains where they might live undisturbed. This they were eventually forced to do, and became known as the "hill barbarians."

The Chinese were divided into two classes, the Hakkas and the Puntis, the latter including, besides the Fokienese, the few other emigrants from different provinces, which made up together the whole Chinese population of the island. The Hakkas we have described in a previous chapter. The Puntis comprise those Chinese who consider themselves born natives of their respective home provinces. Broadly this class includes all Chinese except the Hakkas. Philologically the word "Punti" denotes a native or original indweller of the soil, whilst "Hakka" signifies a stranger, or, as we might phrase it, an immigrant from afar. Feuds between these two classes, constant on the mainland, were often repeated in Formosa. Inasmuch as they were both indisputably of the same blood, the origin and reasons of their demonstrations of enmity—Oriental duplicates of Celt and Saxon feuds—appear passing strange, and have not been satisfactorily explained.

The Hakkas, an energetic hardworking race, courageous and cruel by nature, and notably hostile to any form of government, occupied as a rule the border districts and were thus in constant contact with the savages. The Fokienese differed from them not only in language but somewhat in appearance, and from the frequent quarrels that broke out between them we are led to believe they differed also in politics. Sometimes starting only in a quarrel between families, disputes often reached such a pitch and the fighting was so determined and disastrous, that it was necessary for the Imperial troops to step in to enforce peace.

The large numbers of Chinese who had come from Amoy and neighboring villages were distinguished for their perseverance and economy. Many of this class had been in the island before the Dutch occupation, and their numbers had increased greatly during the Tartar invasion of the mainland and the numerous civil wars. They occupied at first but a few scattered spots on the west coast, but as their numbers increased they gradually spread towards the interior, driving the savages before them. The aborigines made a stout resistance, but by force of arms, or by that equally effective weapon, intoxicating spirits, their lands were gradually taken from them, the denuded victims fleeing to the mountains, in whose friendly jungles peace and refuge could be found. Quite naturally, this entailed, not only on the individual but on the whole Chinese race, the undying hatred of the entire savage population. By the Dutch these wild children were not considered of a fierce warlike disposition, but on the contrary were looked upon as peaceful and good tempered. We are thus led to believe that the extreme antipathy with which the savages regarded the Chinese,—a condition which has continued until the present day, and will last, we believe, as long as the two races come in contact,—was due to the misdeeds of the celestial race, and that but little blame should be attached to the savages.

It was not an easy task to govern such a wild and turbulent population. Evidence was not wanting that besides their clan fights and the constant warfare with the savages, the inhabitants were not averse to extending their field of operations so as to include the mandarins should those dignitaries conduct themselves in an unsatisfactory manner. The officials, with full knowledge of the delicacy of their position, took extensive measures to enforce their authority and provide against rebellion. Some 10,000 Manchu troops, many of them mounted, were distributed throughout the plains to give the alarm should there appear the least sign of a rising against the government.

The high Imperial authorities likewise thought it necessary to have a keen eye on their subordinates in the island, and the better to keep the latter in hand they were allowed only three years' service, which did not permit of a close acquaintance with the inhabitants and so lessened the risk of their joining with the masses in rebellion. While this system no doubt afforded the government some protection against disloyal officials, it worked great harm in encouraging these men to make hay while the sun shone, and the Formosan inhabitants were accordingly squeezed sufficiently during the three years to permit the retiring officer to live the rest of his days in luxury. A separate official class, consisting of interpreters who acted as middle men between the Manchus and the Hakkas, savages, and southern Chinese, were given permanent positions and were responsible for a large share of the constant troubles between the authorities and the people. To such an extent did misrule and abuse exist that the inhabitants looked back with great regret to the days of the Koxinga rule when peace and justice reigned.

To obtain a better knowledge of the island, the Chinese despatched the Jesuits De Mailla, Regis, and Hinderer, to Formosa. These men, during the years 1714-5 travelled from the extreme north to the south and constructed a map of the whole island.[1] De Mailla, who in his writings gives much valuable matter regarding the savages and the methods of governing them early adopted by the Imperial authorities, affords us the following information.

Although the aborigines of the plain had submitted to the Chinese they still retained much of their old form of government.

Each village chose three or four men of seniority and good character, who thus became possessed of full power with the authorities to adjust all disputes and determine punishment for all crimes, and should a person express dissatisfaction or refuse to obey the dictates of these judges, he was at once driven from the settlement by the villagers and not allowed to return; furthermore no other village of the same tribe would receive him. Tribute was paid to the Chinese in grain, and to appraise this a Chinese low official was placed in each village, who was expected, besides this duty, to be familiar with the language of the people and to act as interpreter when his superiors visited the district. These officers were in a position to have done much good for the poor aborigines, whom, however, they cheated and robbed without pity. Petty sovereigns, they ruled in each village supreme, being feared by the natives and also by the mandarins on account of the power they had of causing evil. But the mandarins were also disliked because of their constant demands,

---

1. It is interesting here to note that the small island to the southwest coast of Formosa, known as Lamai to the natives, was placed on the map by the Jesuit surveyors under the name of Little Loochoo. In the English admiralty charts, however, this appellation is discarded and Lambay adopted instead.

and their haughty aud tyrannical demeanor resulted in much discontent, often driving the more oppressed into rebellion.

Under the Dutch rule these natives had proven very tractable. The allotted number of stag hides were delivered to the Company's factories without any show of hostility ; in fact the aborigines behaved in every respect as loyal subjects. But they were not then ruled with a rod of iron ; a school teacher who taught them the rudiments of Christianity was their master, and he attached them to himself by moral rather than by physical suasion. Thus it happened that, during the war between the Chinese and the Dutch, many of these people remained loyal friends to the latter, and not a few were cruelly put to death for having expressed their sympathy with the Dutch.

It was not only the savages who suffered at the hands of the mandarins. Realizing that once beyond the borders of official rule, the Chinese themselves would pay little attention to their demands, the mandarins took care to despoil them while they had them in hand. The system of requiring passports from all arrivals gave great opportunity for such extortions. Right in theory, it was worthless in practice. With the intention of avoiding the further influx of bad characters, regulations were issued by the government requiring every new colonist to be provided with a passport, to be granted only when his neighbors gave ample testimony to his good citizenship and industry. This regulation, however, was frequently evaded by the officers in Fokien, who were only too ready to give troublesome people good characters in order to get rid of them, while those who deserved the privilege were subject to squeezes according to the applicants' wealth before the desired permission could be obtained. The many hundred thousand emigrants from Fokien, Kwantung, and Chinkiang found to their cost that the obtaining of the passport on the mainland was the smallest part of their troubles. On landing in Formosa they were pounced upon by the mandarins, and a fee was demanded so large that very commonly the poor settlers had no other means of paying it than to pledge to the officers a certain portion of their gains until the whole demand should be discharged. Thus on their arrival many of the emigrants found themselves, in a manner, slaves to the mandarins, and to these extortioners much of their hard earnings reverted.

A traveller who visited the island in those early days says :—" Though they are industrious, yet the emigrants have deservedly a reputation for insubordination and lawlesssness. They associate much in clans, and clannish attachments and feuds are cherished among them ; but they are very fond of intercourse with foreigners. Many of them are unmarried or have left their families in China, to whom they hope to return after amassing a little property."

While the people were thus more difficult to govern, the mandarins were more unfit to administer. On the one hand the people were there to enjoy greater freedom from the grinding rule of magistrates, and on the other the mandarins were there to proceed with more open and extreme extortion than in China itself, since complaint was difficult and relief more so. It was not a combination that worked well, and through new acts of oppression on the one side and greater evasion and resistance on the other, no part of the Chinese Empire was so frequently disturbed by rebellion as Formosa. Even the Viceroy in Fokien made no attempt to exert any control over the actions of his subordinates in the island. According to Imperial regulations this high official was expected to visit Formosa once a year, but in reality he very rarely trusted his valued person to the troublesome Formosa Channel. Nor was his visit desired by the island inhabitants, for the local mandarins, who were obliged to make him a costly present on his appearance, squeezed the people just so much the more to make good this extraordinary expenditure. Freed from responsibility, the Formosan officers conducted themselves as best suited their own interests, and their interests were emphatically opposed to those of the people. Arbitrary measures and heavy extortions eventually led the colonists to combine that they might defy the official demands.

Early in the 18th century, the forests were declared government property, and the cutting down and sale of trees a government monopoly. Camphor was thus included, and the penalty for cutting down a tree was death. In the year 1720, upwards of two hundred persons were decapitated. This was more than the inhabitants could bear, and a heavy earthquake was taken by the discontented people as a sign that they should overthrow the hated government.

There lived at that time a colonist, from Changchow-fu, called Choo Yihkwei, a worthless character, who, detested by the inhabitants of the village where he lived, left the place and became a police runner. Soon afterwards he lost his situation, and, having no land to cultivate, sought a livelihood by feeding ducks. According to their custom, these feathered creatures marched out daily in regular rows, like files of soldiers, and returned in the evening in the same manner. This circumstance appears to have suggested to our hero his first idea of military tactics, and he was not slow to improve the occasion. Having met some of the outlaws, he prepared a sumptuous dinner, and for that purpose killed his ducks. From that moment he became a desperado. Choo Yihkwei now availed himself of the popular feeling against the Manchu officials, and declared his life dedicated to the people's cause. To his immediate associates he adroitly proposed that their enterprise should be carried on under the semblance of patriotism on behalf of the fallen Ming dynasty, of which he was a clansman, his surname being Choo. All assented, an oath was duly administered, and every conspirator bound himself to press new recruits into the service, so that their number soon increased to several hundreds.

The government now saw fit to send some troops against them. The valiant commander, as every other Chinese hero must do, reported a victory, though the rebels escaped to the mountains. To make sure, however, of their extirpation, a reward of three taels for every head of the malcontents of the rank and file, and five taels for those of the chiefs was promised to the aborigines of the mountains. This offer was too tempting for these savages to resist, yet, finding it difficult to catch the marauders, they decapitated some innocent people and burnt their houses. Having done this, they presented to the authorities the heads of their victims. Such a proceeding, under the sanction of government, gave rise to confusion and misery; the people detested their rulers and naturally favored the cause of the insurgents.

Under these deplorable conditions, fresh troops, commanded by a brave general, marched in pursuit of the outlaws. Although victory upon victory[1] was obtained according to the account of Luchow, the rebel army, like a hydra, grew stronger and stronger the more it was beaten, until it had made its strength felt from Fangshan in the south to Tamsui in the north. Notwithstanding all these defeats, the rebels determined on more extensive operations, even to the capture of the capital itself with the public treasury, while diplomatically they did not lose sight of the fact that their success depended upon keeping on good terms with the people. War was accordingly waged only against the government, and all their enterprises centred on one point, namely, its entire overthrow.

While the noble imperial troops were revelling in victories and enjoying the satisfaction of having destroyed the lawless band—one report of a formidable engagement stating that several tens (*sic*) of rebels were actually annihilated—the insurgents had increased their influence through the three prefectures, killing the officers, until at last, by a clever strategical movement, they threw the Imperialists off the scent and entered Taiwanfu, the capital, taking possession of all public documents, the treasury, and much gunpowder and many fire-arms.

Having gained this important victory, the rebels declared the Chinese imperial government at an end, and with much pomp and solemnity performed the ceremony of crowning Choo Yihkwei emperor, changing the era to that of Yong-ho (Eiwa). Thus the once humble duck-feeder was elevated to the throne, being, in the pride of his heart and the hearts of his followers, a mighty potentate. The Chinese officers, civil, military, and naval, fled aboard forty vessels to the Pescadores, and later to Amoy, where they arrived safely with the exception of two officers, who, unable to bear the disgrace of their cowardice, committed suicide on the way. The situation could not now be disguised, and accordingly a humble note was addressed to the governor, who, in turn, wrote to the Emperor, promising that in two months the rebels should be extirpated.

Thus within one hundred years the Formosans for the fourth time were subjected to an entire change of masters.

While terrible forces were collecting on the shores of China, Choo Yihkwei most resolutely maintained his imperial rights, and treated his subjects, as he formerly had his ducks, with due consideration. Plunder was forbidden and property as well as lives protected. If any one of his soldiers failed to pay sufficient regard to his injunctions, the culprit was beheaded

1. When we here speak of battles, the reader must not suppose there were engagements like those of Gettysburg and Waterloo; for though there were more encounters within two years than during the wars of Napoleon, yet the Chinese fought with hard words, the chief weapons of their warfare, which they flung at each other with great violence, and being firm believers in the adage—" But he who is in battle slain will never live to fight again," accordingly retreated with great ease and promptitude.

then and there. Such discipline naturally had its effect, and the whole populace was inspired with confidence in its new master.

At length the new Chinese army, consisting of 22,000 soldiers and 15 high officials, embarked at Amoy. The commander having called a council of war, their future proceedings were discussed, and it was unanimously agreed that since the number of rebels amounted to 39,000 men, it would be folly to kill them all. Therefore, it would be best to slay only the chiefs, and to grant life to the heedless multitude. Moreover, every rebel who surrendered of his own accord was to be allowed to return home unmolested. This was certainly a wise plan, but in order to slay the chiefs it was necessary that they, like the rabbit who figures in the famous receipt for rabbit pie, should be first captured; and herein was the difficulty.

Arriving in Formosa the greater part of the army landed at Tamsui, and the first exploit of the Imperialists was the burning of the rebel fleet, which was anchored at Lokiang (Rokko). Then a fort was taken by storm, which, however, was afterwards discovered to have contained no garrison. The subsequent events were one continued series of victories over the disheartened rebels, who often did not wait for the attack but fled at the mere appearance of the conquering Imperialists. The assault of these soldiers was, according to our author's account, simply overwhelming. The fire of their matchlocks and batteries, " shaking the very earth, spread terror into the rebel ranks."

Our authority goes on to say :

" In consequence of this signal success, a report of victory was sent to the continent, and all looked for the great rewards which the Imperial munificence would assign to them. When lo ! to their utter astonishment, there arrives an Imperial rescript, in which His Majesty assigns, as the cause of the rebellion, either the extreme want of his loyal subjects, or the extortion of unprincipled officers ; and decrees, that to massacre a misguided people would be cruel and wicked, because they were his children; and, therefore, he commands the governor of Fokien to soothe and quiet the rebels, not to kill them. On the arrival of the civilians sent to soothe the people, affairs took a most wonderful turn. Nine-tenths of the rebels surrendered, and even Choo Yihkwei's immediate associates, after a hard fought battle, fell into the hands of these compassionate officers. In almost all similar events, the celestial terrors were slighted ; but when the extreme mercy of the Emperor was made known, the people were touched to the very heart, and of their own accord became obedient."

Whether silver balls were found more effective in this warfare than leaden ones, we are not told by our author; but the sudden and almost entire submission makes us rather suspect this was the case. Notwithstanding all this, the remaining rebels were still stubborn, and baffled all the efforts of the victorious army. There were many skirmishes which led to no satisfactory results, and only emboldened the rebels to persevere in their resistance.

The person of Choo Yihkwei was, however, eventually secured, the headmen of the village in which he had sought refuge having handed the fallen emperor over to the military commanders. The mercy held out to the people was not bestowed upon the exalted Choo Yihkwei, who was placed in a bamboo cage and carried to Peking, where he was crucified.

Epidemic diseases now began to break out among the soldiers, and great numbers found their graves in the island.

With the Imperialists in possession of the plains, great anxiety was caused to a large number of the rebels who, with an excess of enthusiasm, had cut off their queues, thus advertising their disloyalty whenever they appeared. These hasty braves now found it necessary to keep in hiding, and the savage districts offered the most secure retreats. To drive these fugitives from the hills, the aborigines received orders not to harbor any rebels; and though these inoffensive people, while overawed by the presence of the military, did not dare enter into a league with the outlaws, yet when they were freed from such restraint they were very slow in the execution of the orders of the government against a class whom they feared even more than they did the officials.

The Emperor Kanghe had in the meanwhile died, but his successor immediately took vigorous measures for subjugating the country. He ordered that all the disposable forces of Fokien should remain in the island as a garrison, that the civil appointments should be increased, and that a censor should constantly reside in the island to watch over the behavior of the officers. The grand scheme, which was to suppress the prevailing rebellious spirit, was the reformation of the people, that they might see the advantages and learn the duty of passive obedience; the savages of the mountains were to be tamed, and then changed into men. To insure the future peace of the island, a line of fortresses was to be erected, and no efforts were to be neglected to render the people virtuous. The execution of these and many more commissions was entrusted to an Imperial envoy; and it is on record that he, in conjunction with the local authorities, obeyed the Imperial commands to the best of his ability. After the exhibition of this paternal kindness, we hear nothing more about the rebellion. The fire was extinguished, but unfortunately the embers were still smouldering, and a few years afterwards the flame again appeared, to give new anxiety to his Imperial Majesty.

The island had now become a scene of the utmost misery and wretchedness. The country had been laid waste, and pestilential diseases had swept away great multitudes. The rich and fertile land, long given up to war and bloodshed, now found its fields deserted and industry paralyzed. Furthermore, at this same period (1723), a terrific storm swept down upon the island. Giant waves rolled over the coast districts destroying vessels both large and small, drowning thousands, and leaving scarcely a building uninjured in the settlements near the coast.

After the terrible insurrection of 1722, it was found that the district of Choolo was too large to be conveniently administered by a single magistrate, and the northern portion was detached to become a new prefecture, named Changwha, while the north part of the island was formed into a *ting* or division, Tamsui, and was placed under the authority of a marine magistrate.

Chinese officialdom was naturally much disturbed by the Formosan rebellions. The authorities of the Flowery Kingdom welcomed additions to their standard that they might add to their wealth and influence. But Formosa had so far threatened to consume more of the Imperial treasure than could be disgorged from the island by the combined efforts of mandarins for years. It was consequently a subject of much thought among the literati. Chief among these was Luchow, and, as much of his advice shows evidence of careful thought, as well as of a fine knowledge of the conditions existing in the island, we give it space here.

He tells us that the aborigines were of a stupid disposition and were often misled by the Chinese merchants, who did not scruple to rob them of their property. To remedy this evil Luchow states that the good people ought to be exhorted to be content with their rightful property, and that the soldiers who were apparently not over-honest should be warned not to trouble the people in any way. The authorities, while not ceasing their own vigilance in detecting any sign of rebellioh, should lessen the chances of possible failure by rewarding informants who exposed parties engaged in questionable intercourse with the savages.

To secure submission from the savages these people should be given one month in which to surrender, and in case of their obstinacy, measures should be taken to capture them, for which purpose natives under the control of the government should be utilized, and in order to strike terror into the hearts of the hillmen, the jungles and border forests should be set on fire, thus smoking out the inmates. Furthermore they should be prevented from tilling the ground and all supplies cut off, which would reduce them to starvation and consequently to obedience. Salt, a most necessary article of food to them, and iron, without which they could not make useful weapons, should not be allowed to come into their possession. The Chinese should equip themselves with good shields, spears with large shafts, and above all with firearms in lieu of bows and arrows, for the mere noise of the former created great consternation in the savage ranks. Finally, better forts than those of wood and bamboo should be erected. Our author further states that the Chinese soldiers were insufficiently paid, and were thus tempted into lawless act ons to better their condition, and that they were neither properly rewarded for bravery nor sufficiently punished for cowardice. To assist the regulars in time of war he proposed that a militia be organized, the members to serve only during times of emergency. A like experiment had been made by a former military commander, but as only 600 cash (some 30 cents gold) per month, and sufficient rice to keep the men from starving was given them, our author attributed the failure to this scanty pay.

Whether any of the above suggestions were adopted history does not inform us. At all events, the natives continued their attacks on the Chinese settlements, and respected the high rank of the son of Heaven as little as they had done in days of yore. Luchow then expressed himself as persuaded that strict methods only would avail. By constructing a strong line of military posts along the frontier and inducing the people to settle in these districts and gradually encroach upon the savage domains, thus only could the savage invasions

Formosan Mineral Districts.

Gold Mines at Zuiho (Suihong) The Centre of the Northern Gold District.

A Valley near Taichu (North Central Formosa) abounding in Petroleum Oil Springs.

be prevented. In order to curb the power of the hillmen, intercourse between tribes ought to be restricted as much as possible. Much care should be taken lest Japanese or Dutch landing on the east coast might shelter themselves amongst them, "a thing above all others to be avoided." It appears that in former times certain merchants obtained from the government the monopoly of trade with the natives. There were also interpreters appointed to transact business with them. It has, however, been discovered that these persons cheated the innocent hillmen, thus oftimes causing the latter to raise a disturbance. These unscrupulous parties should be kept under strict surveillance, and no occasion given the savages to complain of injustice. As to the colonists of Formosa, our author calls them a bad set, who were accustomed to trifle with the laws, and the first step to be taken should be to teach them to respect and obey the prohibitions of government. More-over, the inhabitants, stirred up by designing attorneys, delighted in litigation. To abolish this evil, it was essential that justice should be executed impartially, that illegitimate gifts of money to the public courts should be done away with, and that mischievous demagogues should be seized. Colonists before being permitted to land should be able to prove that they had friends who would give them employment, thus insuring that they should not become burdens on society. The colonists, being debauched and given over to drunkenness, thus often running into debt, should be forced by law to give up these dissolute habits. Marriageable women, who frequently passed the age of thirty without husbands, should be prevailed upon to enter the blissful state of matrimony at twenty-five. Furthermore, the women, instead of spending their days in idle gossip, should employ themselves in rearing silk worms and planting hemp, to enable them to provide materials for the apparel of their families. Much difficulty existed in regard to shipping. The custom officers should be kept under careful observation, that they did not demand fees to which they were not entitled, whereby the people were induced to import prohibited articles that they might indemnify themselves. Luchow, realizing that the promotion of education was a prominent factor in teaching obedience, recommended that free schools should be widely distributed, and that high rewards should be held out to successful literary candidates. (This advice was not long neglected, and numerous schools were soon established). As most of the rebellions had had their rise in the cupidity of the officers, our author advised that legal exactions should be as few and as light as possible, and that there should be a reduction of the land tax. At the same time he suggested that the ravages upon the defenceless people occurred on account of the small pay which the officers received. On this account there should be clearings of new lands, the proceeds of which should be devoted to increasing the emoluments of the Imperial servants in the island.

The viceroy of Fokien, to whom the peace of Formosa meant much, since the funds for the island were drawn from his province, and worse still, the Peking authorities might disgrace him for his misgovernment of Formosa, was especially active, and believing that the government could not establish control over the whole island, he confined himself exclusively to the western plains. He gave no heed to the uuruly clans who were engaged in constant warfare on the savage border. The camphor monopoly still existed, but all were allowed perfect freedom in the cutting down of trees, though no steps were taken to protect the laborers against the savages. The Hakkas and Pepohoans were constantly at loggerheads with each other, and the custom of head-hunting progressed as freely as the most bloodthirsty savage could wish.

Regardless of the comprehensive plans of the authorities and the advice of the literati, the rebellion of the Chinese settlers against the government continued for more than a hundred years with but brief interruption, while warfare with the savages was a yearly occurrence, as sure to happen as the summer typhoons.

In 1731, after a brief breathing spell, the Chinese again took up the cudgels against their paternal government. The Imperial troops were at this time busy warring in the north with the savages. Accordingly one Woo Fuh-sing (Go Fukusei), a resident of Fangshan (Hozan), considering the time opportune, gathered together a few malcontents, who exerted themselves in again disturbing the Manchu dragon. Early in the year, they attacked and destroyed by fire the government camp in the neighborhood. The governor of Taiwan now marched in person against the rebels, and succeeded in inflicting a total defeat upon them, although not without considerable loss, including three high officials on his side. A few days later Woo Fuh-sing and some thirty of his companions were captured and executed.

Of the numerous engagements with the savages, which had continued with greater or lesser severity from the days of the first arrival of the Chinese authorities, we refer but to one,[1] for while there are others of importance, they were affairs confined to the savage district, and can, therefore, be more appropriately dealt with in a separate chapter devoted to the aborigines.

It was in the year 1731, when the savages of Taikasei (Taikosei), a turbulent tribe who had lavishly indulged in murdering Chinese and burning their property, surrounded and attacked the northern taotai and his party, who were traveling through the north on a tour of inspection. The official and his followers made a stout fight, and succeeded in escaping to the walled city of Changwha. Thence the taotai despatched a detail of regulars to annihilate the offenders. The savages were not only unwilling to be exterminated but further had the audacity to continue to oppose the regulars until the very walls of Changwha were reached, when the survivors of the Imperial forces withdrew into the city, to report to their superiors the insolence of the barbarians. Some ten tribes had now combined, and with this force Changwha was surrounded, and all outside intercourse cut off. The Chinese inhabitants of the city were greatly disturbed, for fear that the savages should gain entrance and kill them all. Consequently large numbers tried to escape, only to fall into the hands of the enemy, who were soon enabled to count among their possessions several thousands of Chinese heads. As soon as news of this mortifying defeat

---

1. The incident here given is novel, inasmuch as it records a combat in which the savages threw aside their usual methods of warfare, and marched across the plains in large numbers to attack one of the principal cities.

reached the governor-general, that official at once deprived the taotai of office, and sent a reinforcement against the enemy.   The savages were apparently satisfied with what they had already gained, and realizing that they could not oppose the superior numbers which were being sent against them, they retired to their mountain fastnesses.   The Imperial troops, however, followed them up, and crossing the border, killed several thousands.   The savages now fled to a stronghold at the top of a precipitous mountain, where they prepared to defend themselves.   After considerable difficulty, the Imperialists at length discovered a route by which they could gain the summit, and although the savages opposed them stoutly, and rolled huge rocks over the mountain side, which came crashing down amongst them, the mighty warriors of the emperor, according to Chinese report, did not hesitate or waver, but steadily advanced until they gained the heights and slaughtered the savages there.

After this important disturbance, trouble with the savages and fights among the different native clans kept the troops busy until 1770, when the government was again made the target of the discontented.

Hong Chau (Okyo), a resident of Fangshan (Hozan) district, had engaged so extensively in warlike deeds of a doubtful character, that he was looked upon with considerable terror by the inhabitants.   At this period robbers, who were present in large numbers, devoted themselves to stealing oxen.   Without these useful beasts, cultivation would be greatly endangered.   Consequently the people were in a dilemma how best to guard against such depredations.   Eventually the services of Hong Chau were engaged at the price of five bushels of millet per year for every animal protected.   This arrangement was for a time satisfactory; for, as the most formidable rogue of the district, he commanded obedience from the lesser lights.   However, one man was bold enough to engage in a dispute with Hong Chau.   Just what was in question we are not told, but at all events the decision was against the bold cow protector, who was so greatly angered in consequence, that he went so far as to defy the law by capturing his opponent, and revenging himself by tearing off the unfortunate man's nose and ears.   The government was then appealed to, and the arrest of Hong Chau was ordered.   This was considered by the bold rogue to be another insult, and he accordingly prepared to treat the authorities as he had their informant.   He gathered his followers about him, raised the standard of rebellion, and attacked the nearest military camp, massacring the officers and men.   The district governor immediately sent a force against him, but although some of his lieutenants were captured, Hong Chau escaped, it is said, to the savage districts.   He evaded seizure for some time, and at length the government, annoyed at the district officer's incompetence, deprived him of his office.

As though the raids by the settlers were not enough to sufficiently disturb the luxurious dreams of the emperor, a foreign adventurer, the Count de Benyowsky, of whom we shall speak at length in the following chapter, visited in 1771 the eastern coast, and threatened for a while to become a formidable opponent of the Imperial government.

Besides the calamity of war, Nature seemed to have inimical designs on the island, for in 1782 occurred a storm and inundation for which Formosan history has no parallel.

The official report of the storm states that in May (an unusual month for typhoons), a wind, rain, and swell of the sea together, for twelve hours, threatened to overwhelm the island. When the storm ceased, the public buildings, granaries, barracks, and salt warehouses were found totally destroyed, and most of the private houses also were in ruins. Of twenty-seven ships of war, twelve had disappeared leaving not a piece of wreckage behind, and twelve more were wrecked; of other ships about two hundred were lost. Without the harbour, a great number of barks and small vessels disappeared during the fearful gale, which to the people seemed a visitation of the gods in punishment for their many sins. The emperor directed that all houses thrown down should be rebuilt at his expense (i.e., from the public treasury), and that provisions should be supplied to the people. "I should feel much pain," said he, "if any of my children were to be neglected." Subterranean convulsions, it is very probable, added to this calamity.

This event was followed, four years later, by the most important and bloody rebellion which Formosa had yet witnessed, and its suppression by indiscriminate denunciation and cruel punishment was an exhibition of severity, the like of which the island had never seen. Chinese official accounts afford us the only detailed descriptions that are to be procured, but from such references to it as were made by foreign writers at that time, we are led to believe that, in the Chinese accounts, the magnitude of the affair is considerably underrated. M. de Grammont states in a letter of March 1789, "the troubles in Formosa are ended at last, but at the cost of a shameful and expensive war to China. She has lost at least a hundred thousand men, destroyed by disease or the swords of the rebels; and she has expended two millions of taels."

This rebellion was the natural outcome of the over-abundant impetuosity of the inhabitants. Besides the thousands of malcontents who were always awaiting an opportunity to strike a blow at the Tartar government, there abounded district clans and societies so hostile towards each other that not infrequently they were engaged in open combat. Prominent among these opposing factions were those inhabitants of the island who had immigrated from the mainland districts of Tsweng-choo (Senshu), and Chang-choo (Shoshu). The Imperial officials found these unsympathetic parties difficult to govern, for if they rendered a judgment in favour of one, the other side was sure to be thrown into a paroxysm of rage.

In 1782 representatives of the two clans, residing in a village of Changwha Prefecture, met together for one of their gambling contests. During the play everything progressed as smoothly as could be wished, but the division of the stakes at the close was a very delicate operation, in which the losing side frequently endeavored to evade their obligations by killing their opponents. Much loss of life was not unusual in these affrays, and at length they became so serious that on one occasion Imperial officers interfered and executed a certain Chang-choo native, who was head gambler and chief murderer in turn. Every member of the clan was now a fierce enemy of the government, while the Tsweng-choo people became enthusiastic friends of the authorities. The combats between the two clans now grew more frequent and bloody than ever, and other districts in the island were drawn into the quarrel.

At this period Lin Shoan-wen (Lin So-bun), a native of Chang-choo, and an ambitious soul, saw in the island a promising field for his purposes. Accordingly in 1784 he arrived in the new land, and at once devoted himself to gaining converts to a secret society known as the Tei ti fui (Ten Shigai) of which he was the self-appointed head. As a result of his exertions, the society flourished, and the Chang-choo people, recognizing in it an opportunity to further injure their rivals and attack the government, joined it in large numbers. The Tsweng-choo people likewise joined the government volunteers in order to assist in inflicting punishment on their rivals.

The island was divided by the secret society into two districts, the north and the south ; Lin Shoan-wen and Choan Tah-tien (So Dai-den) being the respective chiefs. To the northern division was attached an influential Chinese named Yang Koan-shung (Yokokun), who, together with certain of his relatives, was engaged in unceasing quarrels with another branch of the same family. His chief opponent was his brother-in-law Yang Mah-si (Yo Ma-sei) who to spite Yang Koan-shung organized a second and rival society known as Laikongfui (Raikokwai). With these two societies in full blast, the Imperial authorities became somewhat alarmed. Accordingly a local leader o Kagi and his son were arrested, but the son escaped by bribing the guards, and gathering his followers about him, he attacked Tauromun (Torokumon), a village near Yunlin, destroyed it with fire, and killed among others a government officer. A civil officer of Taiwan advanced with a military force to the camp of the rioters, and arrested some fifty or sixty of the culprits. This officer believed that the two secret societies were organized to further the quarrel of the two brothers-in-law, who were prominent members of the opposing clans previously referred to, and to put an end to the feud, he confiscated all the property belonging to the father, which appeared to be a prominent cause of irritation between the two families. Besides this, he arrested thirty-eight men, including three leaders who were specially troublesome. However, the governor of Changwha was not satisfied with what he considered the lenient policy of the Taiwan officer, and accordingly seized several members of the society, executed them all, and burned one of their villages. The society made capital of this, and pointed out to their neighbors the unmerciful way in which their government treated them. By this means the society received a great accession of strength, till, believing themselves sufficiently strong, they broke out into open rebellion and killed Imperialists whenever they were able. Lin Shoan-wen now came to the front, and led his men against Changwha, which was guarded by only eighty Imperial soldiers, captured it, and killed the local governor. A neighboring government camp likewise fell into the hands of the insurgents. The rebels were guilty of the slaughter of some two thousand men, women, and children, including thirty officers. This created considerable alarm among the authorities, and owing to their own gross maladministration, both civil and military, there was no available military force at hand to crush the rebellion.

With Changwha and much of the surrounding territory in their possession, the rebels considered the time ripe for administrative organization. With this in view, Lin Shoan-wen was declared ruler of the new domain, the era was changed to that of Shuntien (Junten), and civil officers were appointed to the different posts. When the details of government were completed, a great feast was held, which Lin Shoan-wen attended, robed in garments of great splendor (it was privately said that these had been stolen by the noble chief from the Imperial officers whom he had captured) and conducted himself with all the dignity that a mighty sovereign should possess. The rebel forces now added Kagi to their possessions, murdering the officers, and plundering the people as they advanced. To the northwards towards Tamsui a second division of rebels was despatched, which succeeded in capturing Teck-cham (Hsinchiku). However a force of 13,000 men, including drafts made from the inhabitants by the local Imperial officers of the district, advanced on the city which they succeeded in re-occupying.

Imperial troops now arrived from China, and landing at Tamsui, were able to keep the northern part clear of rebels.

The insurgents in the south now attacked Fangshan, capturing the city and driving the Imperialists out of the district. The governor of Taiwan at once gathered together a force of 900 volunteers, 1000 soldiers, and 1000 of the plain savages, and with this army was able to hold the capital against a fierce attack of the rebels. When the news reached the mainland that, with the exception of Taiwanfu and the extreme north, the whole island was in the hands of the rebels, the consternation among the officials was great; and a fleet, and the most renowned military officers were despatched to suppress the rebellion. The Imperial forces reached the island early in 1787, some landing at Lokiang, and some at Anping. One column 3,000 strong, aided by a naval squadron, attacked Fangshan, and after a sixteen days' engagement defeated the rebels, and restored the district to Imperial rule. Success likewise attended the regulars in the north, and Kagi was recaptured. The weather, however, was unceasingly bad, and large numbers of the troops died of disease, while the rebels succeeded in surrounding the city and cutting off all outside communication. Thus besieged, the Imperialists were subjected to great privations, and were so straitened for supplies that for a considerable period they were obliged to exist on oil cakes as their only food.

A close watch was kept on the city walls, and if any of the unfortunate inhabitants came out to forage, they rarely escaped with their lives. Later an Imperial force succeeded in reaching Kagi, but only temporary relief could be given, and the situation soon relapsed into its former condition. The year passed, and the rebels still held the larger portion of the island. The emperor now despatched from Peking a civil officer of high rank, to settle the difficulties. This dignitary landed in Lokiang at the end of October, with 9,000 men and 120 officers. The new arrivals advanced against the insurgents, defeating them first at Paquasoan (Hakkeizan), and again at a village near Kagi, from which the insurgents fled in such haste, that according to a Chinese report, "Their shadows were left behind;" and after desultory fighting for several days, the Imperialists secured possession of Kagi city and vicinity.

Imperial troops now advanced against the insurgents simultaneously from Kagi and Taiwan. Both forces were favored with uninterrupted victory, while the terror-stricken rebels fled before them like frightened deer. Eventually after many months of fighting, the rebels were driven from the settled districts, and there remained but one place over which they held control. This was the stronghold of Talichau (Tairizai), a formidable position protected by a high wall and fortifications. The Imperialists after a vigorous and lengthy engagement captured this place also. Among the prisoners was the rebel prefect of Changwha who, having formerly been an Imperial officer, now received but little mercy from the authorities ; 160 guns large and small, 230 spears, several thousand bushels of rice, and 800 cows, comprised the principal booty secured by the Imperialists at the close of this engagement. The energetic commander of the regulars now advanced well along the savage border, establishing fortifications where they were most needed.

Thus after nine months of constant battling, in which popular account asserts money formed not a small portion of the munitions of war, the rebellious population was induced to settle down for the moment in peace. Lin Shoan-wen had escaped to the hills, taking refuge in the savage district. The hillmen do not appear to have been especially friendly, for they handed the rebel chieftain's mother and father over to the Imperial commander. Lin Shoan-wen now fled into the Polisia district, where he pleaded with his friends to protect him. But their fidelity to their former leader had now faded away, and they replied to his prayers by seizing the hunted man, and handing him over to the military, who satisfied old grudges by " cutting him into a thousand pieces." The victorious Imperial officers were now greatly lauded, while the Emperor evidenced his pleasure by bestowing increased rank and numerous decorations on them.

The island now remained quiet, the settlers working off their surplus energy by fighting either with one another, or with the savages, until in (795) the unrest of the population again found vent.

Chien Chu-choan (Chin Shu-zen) was a former member of the secret society which was responsible for the previous rebellion. He lived at Fangshan, where he was nominally engaged as a sugar merchant. He later removed to Changwha and gathered many of the old society together again. Having collected a force of some four hundred men, who swore fealty to him, he decided on a bold stroke. He engaged numerous vessels, which he despatched with skeleton crews to Lokiang, he himself meanwhile marching by land against the city. On arriving late in the evening, signals were exchanged between the land forces and the decoy ships, and preparations were made for a night attack. Suddenly numerous lights flashed up on board each junk, giving the craft the appearance of being crowded with soldiers, while Chien Chu-choan advanced on the city spreading out his scanty force, with the view of deceiving the enemy as to his real strength. The savage clamors of the assailants added terror to the illusion. The Lokiang garrison, aroused from their slumbers, took but one look at the seemingly enormous forces approaching both by land and sea, and then fled from the city horror-stricken.

This victory gave great courage to other members of the society in Changwha, and upon a pre-arranged date Chien Chu-choan advanced from Lokiang, and joined the Changwha rebels in an attack on Paquasoan (Hakkeizan). The rebel force was small, but an accidental explosion of gunpowder in the Imperialist fort, killed several officers and men, and the fortification, as well as Changwha, fell into the hands of the insurgents. The success of the new party was not lasting, however, for after a few days of prosperity they were so badly defeated while attacking a neighboring village, that half of the survivors fled to the hills for refuge. Chien Chu-choan was eventually captured and executed, thus closing the last rebellion of the 18th century.

CHAPTER VI.

FORMOSA VISITED BY BENYOWSKY.

1771.

Events on the east coast—The life of Count de Benyowsky—The count lands on the east coast—Attacked by natives—Subsequent slaughter—Licentiousness incites natives to second attack—The count secures the assistance of a Spaniard—Third attack by the natives—The slaughter of 1,156 natives in return—Treaty with a friendly tribe—Accompanies them as an ally in battle—Defeat of the Chinese —Returns loaded with presents—Officers advise establishing a colony—The count refuses and embarks for Macao—Endeavors to interest foreign nations in establishing colony—Brilliant promises.

It is now necessary to digress from the chronological order of the previous chapters and to go back to the year 1779. At this period, the reader will recollect the Tartar masters of Formosa were busily engaged in curbing the spirit of rebellion ever present among the people, many of whose ancestors were the followers of Koxinga. Interesting events were at the same time occurring in the eastern districts,—events which, if they had been fully known, would have caused no little anxiety to the Imperial authorities, who had already had much trouble with the inflammable inhabitants of the western districts, and would have dreaded to have their influence still further weakened by the appearance of another enemy in a land already teeming with foes.

We are about to relate the adventures of Count de Benyowsky. Fortunately for the historian, this interesting nobleman leaves us abundant descriptions of his exploits in his memoirs, written originally in French, but later translated into English. Detailed reviews of the English version have been compiled, and to the most complete of these the present chapter is indebted.[1]

This remarkable adventurer, whatever other qualities he may have lacked, will hardly be denied the possession of great bravery, enterprise, and ambition. By birth a Hungarian nobleman, he served several years as an officer in the Austrian army, visited Holland and England in pursuit of nautical information, and then went to Poland, where he joined the confederacy against the Russians, becoming a commander of cavalry and quarter-master-

---

1. As contained in a collection of papers on Formosa, compiled by Gideon Nye, Jr.

general. He was subsequently taken prisoner, and in 1770 was banished to Kamtschatka, being then twenty-nine years of age. Here, in conjunction with several other exiles, he conceived the project of seizing a vessel and escaping from Kamtschatka, bearing away with him the Russian governor's daughter, Aphanasia, who had been so fascinated by the noble captive that she determined to share his fortunes, though aware that his wife was then alive in Europe. In 1771 he effected his escape in company with ninety-six other persons, touched at Japan, the Loo-choo group, Formosa, Macao, and at length, in a French ship, reached France. The French government, desirous of profiting by his talents, commissioned him to found a colony in Madagascar, which he did, persevering for three years amidst no ordinary difficulties. But the desire of the French ministry to reduce the island under their authority not coinciding with the count's wish and the treaties which he had made with the native chiefs, in which he had recognized their independence, he resigned his commission—at least so he himself avers. Upon this he was chosen king by the friendly chiefs, and left the island with authority to negotiate a commercial treaty and if possible to enter into an alliance with some European government. He applied to the British ministry in 1783, as it would appear, without success; but he received aid from private parties in London and from a commercial house in Baltimore, U.S.A. Leaving his wife in America in 1784, he set out again for Madagascar, where he commenced hostilities against the French, and was killed in battle in 1786. His widow died at her estate near Betzko in Hungary, December 4th, 1825.

With this account of the man the reviewer turns to his book, and opens it at the point of the count's arrival on the eastern shore of Formosa. From reading Anson's voyages the company of returning exiles had become desirous of adding Formosa to their other discoveries and, accordingly, on the 26th of August, 1771, they made the eastern shore in latitude 23° 22' N.

They anchored in fourteen fathoms and sent two boats ashore with sixteen men, who returned in a few hours with three of their number wounded and with five native prisoners. The report of the officer was that they found the harbor good, the soundings from eight to three fathoms; that on landing they saw a fire and a few islanders to whom they signified their desire for food. They were accordingly conducted to a village, where they were fed with roasted pork, boiled rice, limes, and oranges. The natives appeared quiet; but observing several parties of armed men assembling, the officer had judged it prudent to withdraw, lest they should seek a quarrel. After making them presents of some knives, he began to return; but before reaching the shore, he was assailed with a flight of arrows which wounded two of his men; this was returned with a discharge of musketry, which prostrated six natives and checked the remainder. They rallied, however, and attacked the party again as it was about to embark in the boats, but were driven away at length with the loss of sixty slain, besides the five prisoners.

Upon this inauspicious commencement, the count would have quitted the place, but his associates insisted on entering the harbor and taking vengeance, as if enough had not been inflicted already. On the next day, therefore, he brought the vessel up within one hundred fathoms of the shore, and ordered twenty-eight of his men to land. They were immediately met by unarmed natives bearing branches of trees, and prostrating themselves at their feet. This submission pacified the enraged party, who immediately laid aside their caution with their anger, and entered the village; but having indulged in some licentiousness, the natives again fell upon them and drove them, some entirely naked, from the village. Benyowsky himself was obliged to go and meet them with a reinforcement, when they again drove the natives from their village, killed two hundred persons, and finally set the village on fire.

Satisfied with what they had seen, the adventurers weighed anchor, and with a light wind and northward current, coasted the island, proceeding towards the north. The count observed that the current caused the vessel always to follow the windings of the shore, gliding inward as an indentation was met, only to swing seawards as the opposite bank was neared. The nature of the current kept the vessel always at the same distance from the coast and removed any apprehension of its being thrown on the land by the force of the current, even though there might not be wind enough to make the helm effective. After coasting a short distance in this manner, they were piloted by two native boats into a beautiful harbor with three fathoms of water. This he named Port Maurice; but we find nothing more definite as to its position, the count having left us in doubt on that point not, perhaps, without design. Numerous boats immediately appeared, bringing supplies of poultry, hogs, rice, and fruits. Soon after, another party arrived with a European at its head. He declared himself a Spaniard from Manila, from whence he had fled seven or eight years before, having unfortunately killed a Dominican whom he had detected in criminal intercourse with his wife. He had formerly been captain of the port of Cavite at Manila; his name was Don Hieronimo Pacheco. To secure the aid of this man as interpreter and friend, Benyowsky gave him valuable presents and promises of more if he found him faithful during his stay at the place. But as if the adventurers were doomed never to be long out of trouble, the next morning, while a party of them were obtaining water, they were attacked by the natives.

The watering place, it appears, was at a distance from the anchorage, and though Don Hieronimo warned them to beware of the natives of that district, who were hostile to his tribe, the party suffered themselves to be surprised, and three of them were slain. Don Hieronimo and his friends resolved to avenge the death of the three. Since Benyowsky's associates also demanded vengeance for the death of their comrades, their leader reluctantly consented, and "in order that his men might not expose their lives to no purpose" he led them himself. But when he was once engaged he proceeded with no lenient hand. He first killed all the prisoners he had taken; then he attacked all the boats that were approaching, not knowing whether they sought peace or war, and hanged the men. Forty-two of his party left the ship and, with two hundred under Don Hieronimo, proceeded a short distance inland in search of their remaining enemies. They met the hostile tribe and drove them towards a steep hill, where the guns of the ship being brought to bear upon them on one side, and the Spaniard and the count pressing them on another, the poor savages in despair threw themselves prostrate on the earth. Benyowsky now declared that he would fire on his own party if they continued the massacre longer. Upon this the slaughter ceased, but not until eleven hundred and fifty-six, as afterwards counted, were slain; among whom were many women who were armed in the same manner as the men and who died fighting for their homes. Six hundred and forty captives were taken, all of whom were handed over to the Spaniard and his friendly natives.

The day after this bloody affair, the count requested permission to " establish a camp " on shore, to which his friends readily agreed, and themselves prepared huts for the reception of their foreign allies. When these were finished, Benyowsky removed on shore with the wounded and the women of his party. Here he was introduced to the family of Don Hieronimo and many other friends, from whom he learned that Huapo, one of the independent chiefs of the country, had heard of the chastisement which he had inflicted on his enemies, and was coming to thank him. He was also told that his visitor could muster as many as 20,000 or 25,000 armed men ; that his residence was about thirty miles inland; that he was much annoyed by Chinese on the west; and that his central territories were civilized, but that the eastern coast, excepting of course Huapo's division, was possessed by savages. During the day, an officer arrived from the chief to announce his approach and make preparations for his coming. The count received him with much respect, and managed to secure his friendship. After hearing his history the officer requested him to delay his departure till the arrival of the chief, by whom he had been sent with troops to protect the count from danger. Benyowsky returned suitable thanks, but did not fail to remark that the kind precaution was quite superfluous, and that he needed no aid in his own defence. The dress of this officer is minutely described by the count: "He wore a long close garment fitted to the body and reaching from head to foot, Chinese half-boots, a white shirt, a black vest, and a red outer garment with buttons of coral set in gold. His bonnet of straw was exceedingly pointed and the upper extremity ornamented with horse-hair dyed red. His arms were a sabre, a lance, a bow and quiver, with twenty-five arrows. His troops were naked, with the exception of a piece of blue cloth around the middle; and their arms were bows and spears." The interval until the coming of Huapo was spent in dining with the officer, and in exhibitions of gunnery. Meanwhile "the islanders had become so familiar as to leave their daughters in our camp."

The arrival of the prince is described as follows : " First came six horsemen, with a kind of standard ; these were followed by a troop of infantry with pikes; after them came thirty or forty horsemen and another body of infantry with bows; a troop armed with clubs and hatchets came next; and the last of all came the prince attended by twelve or fifteen officers mounted on small but beautiful horses. The rest of the troops came without any regular order. On their arrival at our camp every one lodged where he could, and there was no guard set." The prince immediately made the count welcome to the island and thanked him for the effectual manner in which he had

humbled the hostile tribe.   He proceeded further to state his opinion that the
count must be the stranger predicted by their diviners, who was to break the
Chinese yoke from the neck of the Formosans; he, therefore, offered to aid
him to the full extent of his power in carrying out his design of liberating the
island.   " This beginning," says Benyowsky, " and the representation of Don
Hieronimo that I was in fact a great prince, insensibly led me to play a new
part, as though I had visited Formosa for the purpose of satisfying myself
concerning the position of the Chinese and of fulfilling the wishes of the
inhabitants by delivering them from the power of that treacherous people."
The count was, indeed, no stickler for the right, whenever he could gain his
ends by playing a new or a double part.

At another visit, the chief entered more into the details of his plans, and
left no reason to doubt that vanity induced him to declare war upon the
Chinese.   As the count already · cherished the idea of returning later on and
founding a colony on the island, he foresaw that the friendship of a native
chief would be very serviceable, not merely on the ground of present safety
but also by rendering the proposal of a colony more reasonable in the eyes of
some European power.   He resolved, therefore, to secure by all means the
friendship of Huapo.   For this purpose he showed him the ship, gave him an
exhibition of fireworks, and upon retiring, the chief gave in return his belt and
sabre, as a token that he would share with him the power of the army.   The
count also prepared presents for the chief, consisting of two pieces of cannon,
thirty good muskets, six barrels of gunpowder, two hundred iron balls, besides
fifty Japanese sabres, probably a part of the spoil from a Japanese junk which
our adventurers had previously captured.

The count improved the interval before the next visit in questioning Don
Hieronimo and in deciding upon the terms of acceptance of the proposals
which the Formosan prince had made.   The more important proposals were
as follows: That the count should leave some of his people on the island
until his return; that he should procure for the prince armed vessels and
captains to command them; that he should aid him in expelling the Chinese,
on condition of receiving at once the proprietorship of the department of
Hwangsin, and when completely successful, that of his whole territory; that
he, the count, should assist him in his present expedition against one of the
neighboring chieftains, in consideration of the payment of a certain sum of
money and other advantages; and, lastly, that they should enter into a
permanent treaty of friendship.

To all these propositions, except the first, the count assented, and
stated the cost of procuring the required supplies of men and shipping.   They
then prepared to ratify the agreement of perpetual friendship, by means of
ceremonies very similar to those which are observed in several islands of ·
the Eastern Archipelago when a savage chief would assure a guest of his
friendship: " We approached a small fire, upon which we threw several
pieces of wood.   A censer was then given to me and another to him.   These
were filled with lighted wood, upon which we threw incense, and turning
towards the east, we made several fumigations.   After this ceremony the
general read the proposals and my answers, and whenever he paused, we

turned towards the east and repeated the fumigation. At the end of the reading the prince pronounced imprecations and maledictions upon him who should break the treaty of friendship between us, and Don Hieronimo directed me to do the same, and afterwards interpreted my words. After this we threw our fire on the ground and thrust our sabres in the earth up to the hilts.

" Assistants immediately brought a quantity of large stones, with which they covered our arms ; and the prince then embraced me and declared that he acknowledged me as as his brother." When these ceremonies were ended, the count was dressed in a complete suit, after the fashion of the country, and was received with every demonstration of joy. Accompanied by the chiefs, he rode through the camp and received the submission of all the officers, which was signified by each touching with his left hand the stirrup of the count.

" After having determined to assist the chief in his expedition," says the memoirs, "I thought proper to make some inquiries on the subject." A very commendable mode of procedure, certainly, for all adventurers who do not mean to be turned from their purpose by any disclosures of the right and the wrong which a subsequent inquiry might evolve. What he learned was as follows, to quote his own words : " Hapuasingo, a native chief allied and tributary to the Chinese, had demanded that Huapo should punish with death several of his subjects on account of certain private quarrels ; but that Huapo, instead of acceding to the request, made an unsuccessful war against Hapuasingo, and was compelled to pay him a considerable sum as an indemnity ; that the Chinese governor, under the pretence of obtaining further reimbursement for his expenses, had in conjunction with Hapuasingo seized one of his finest districts ; that his enemy's capital was not more than a day and a half's march distant ; that his army did not exceed 6,000 men while the Chinese were about 1,000 with fifty muskets." Benyowsky promised to maintain the quarrel of his friend, and required sixty horses for the transport of forty-eight of his company, with four *parteraroes* and ammunition.

On the third of September, the combined army set forward to meet the enemy, moving only in the morning and evening to avoid the extreme heat of noonday. At regular intervals they were refreshed with supplies of rice, fruits, and brandy,[1] while their horses were limited to the healthier article, rice. When they drew near the seat of war, the deserted villages and fields told that the enemy had taken the alarm. Within six hours' march of the enemy's capital, the count halted for the army of Huapo, which was one day's march in the rear, to come up. But small parties of the enemy having appeared and engaged in skirmishes, Benyowsky pitched a sort of camp, and fixed his small cannon for its defence.

Presently the whole army of ten or twelve thousand at least approached him and attacked his camp. Twice he drove them back with great loss, and pursued them the second time until night. At this time Huapo arrived, and it was resolved to attack the enemy in their turn the next morning. The count divided his own little force into three parts and attached one part to

1. Probably " Samshu " (Chinese Wine).

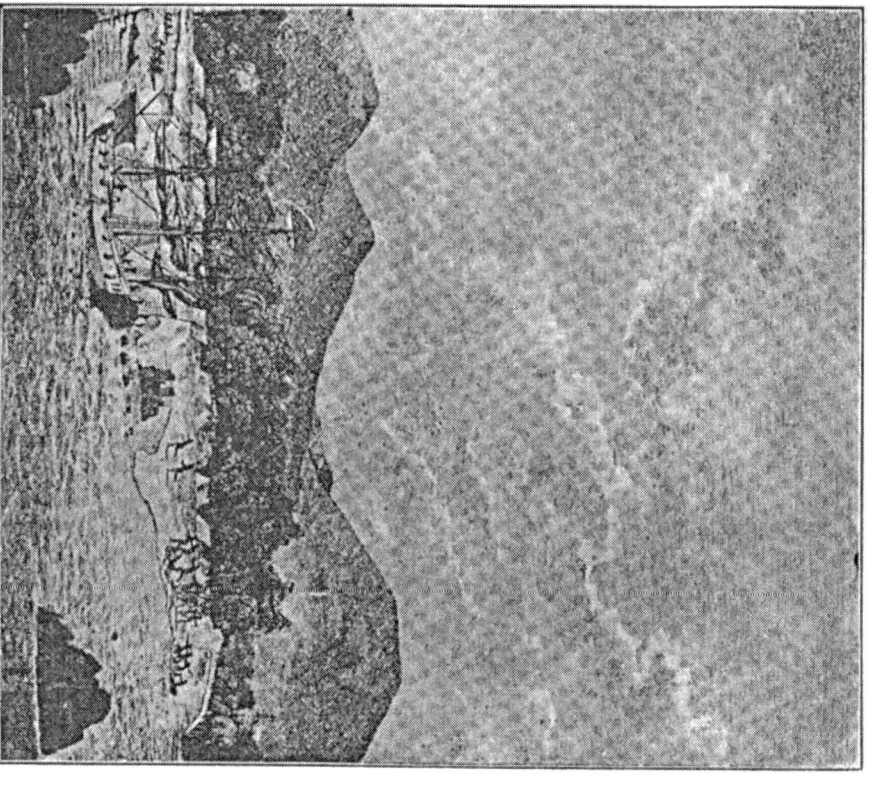

COUNT DE BENYOWSKI ARRIVES ON THE EAST COAST OF FORMOSA 1771.

(FROM AN ENGRAVING IN "MEMOIRS AND TRAVELS OF MAURITIUS
AUGUSTUS, COUNT DE BENYOWSKY" 1790 LONDON.)

CHINESE PUTTING THE DUTCH AND NATIVES TO TORTURE.

(FROM AN ENGRAVING IN "VERWAERLOOSDE FORMOSA" 1675 AMSTERDAM)

each division of his allies.   But the noise of the musketry and cannon alone, after the experience of the preceding day, was enough to put the enemy to flight.   The result was a great slaughter.   When Huapo was sought for in order to receive his prisoners, it was found that, like a prudent man, he had quite withdrawn from the scene of danger, preferring to be a spectator rather than an actor.   To him the count delivered the captive chief, on condition that the prisoner should suffer no personal injury.

The battle appeared decisive and, all warlike operations being over, the count announced his intention to return and embark immediately.   The chiefs and the general overwhelmed him with protestations of friendship, and did not forget the more solid expression of their gratitude.   The presents of the prince consisted of some fine pearls, eight hundred pounds of silver, and twelve pounds of gold.   For his private use, the count received a box containing one hundred pieces of gold which together weighed thirteen pounds and a quarter ; and the general was charged to attend him with one hundred and twenty horsemen and to provide subsistance.   The count left with the chief the *parteraroes*, whose usefulness he had seen so fully tested, and one of his companions to teach their use as well as to learn the native language, until the return of the count to Formosa.   On the way back to the coast, they passed through a pleasant, well-cultivated country, watered with fine streams and very populous, as appeared from the frequency of the villages.

When he arrived on the coast, the count distributed the whole of his presents among his associates, officers, and women, reserving nothing for himself.   This act of generosity gave him unbounded influence over his companions, but no more than was necessary, as immediately appeared.

His confidential officers came in a body and endeavored to persuade him to accept the territory that had been ceded to him and, resting from his wanderings, to fix his residence on this friendly island.   " If we exiles reach Europe," said they, " what shall await us there in the land which has cast us out of its bosom ?   Here we can live safely and happily under your command, and we are enough to found a European colony."   Indeed, they argued the point so well that we almost wonder they did not succeed ; but it appears that the count, from his past experience, had some suspicion that the morals and habits of his followers would be little security against insubordination and crimes, which might prevent him from ever seeing his family again, and from securing some governmental patronage.   Hence he would not yield to their entreaties, and at length prevailed on them to accompany him.   Accordingly, they left the harbor on the 12th of September, and, sailing around the northern headland of the island, steered for Macao.

In conclusion we would say that we have quoted from this curious book, rather because it speaks of a subject otherwise quite unknown than because it is of undoubted veracity in all its statements.   It is extremely doubtful whether the aborigines were in possession of horses.   Travellers on the east coast, at least, have not met with roads made by the aborigines which struck them as suitable for cavalry, nor have they known of the Formosan savage who possessed either gold or silver, especially the latter, in large quantity, or even pearls, although some rubies have been seen. But as the author was no doubt inclined to give a favorable aspect to his proposed enterprise of colonizing the island, the gold, silver, and pearls were probably included as a relish to his description.

In Europe, however, Benyowsky's scheme was considered to be rather a visionary one. This was no doubt due to the fact that the rewards promised were greater than any careful statesman would be inclined to believe possible. To the country which would support him the count promised to pay an annual tax, to assist his patron in time of war with soldiers and sailors from the island, and furthermore he guaranteed to return all funds invested with interest within three years.

CHAPTER VII.

FORMOSA UNDER CHINESE RULE.

1800 - 1862.

*First half of nineteenth century—Lawlessness of inhabitants—Formosa's early commerce
—Political divisions—Number of towns and villages under Imperial control—
Formosan troubles repeat themselves—Adventures of pirate Tsah Ken—He visits
Formosa and is driven thence—Changchoo and Tswengchoo people in combat—
Thousands killed—T'sah Ken visits Fangshan—Natives incited to rebel—Fang-
shan captured—Taiwanfu attacked—Imperial troops arrive—Rebels defeated—
In 1808 pirate Tsu Pun visits Formosa—Headquarters at Suao—Imperial
officer purchases savages' assistance—The pirates dispersed—Clan fights 1809
and 1811—Rebellion of 1824—Clan fight 1826—Serious conflict between Hakkas
and Fokienese—The capital Taiwanfu captured—Mutual extermination—Peace
restored—Clan fights 1834, 1844, 1852, and 1853—The Taiping rebellion excites
Formosans—Rebellion 1852—Chief magistrate killed—Fangshan captured—
Rebels defeated—In 1853, 1856, futile attempts at rebellion—In 1856 rebels
obtain temporary success—Changwha captured—Southern and eastern kings
proclaimed—Rebels defeated and leaders executed—Rebellion in Tamsui—Taotai
killed—Inhabitants oppose likin—Mandarins yield—Immigration increases—
New tings: Taifang, Lokiang, and Komalan established—Early Chinese
description of Taiwan, Fangshan, Kagi, Changwha, Tamsui, Pescadores—
Chinese officers in Formosa—Their duties and their emoluments—The military.*

In spite of the advance of officialdom in Formosa the first half of the
nineteenth century was not a peaceful period. The Chinese inhabitants
obtained, not only in China, but among students of Oriental affairs throughout
the world, the reputation of being a fierce and turbulent population, and
even the emperor frequently referred to them as his "troublesome children."

The island had now attained considerable commercial importance. The
shipments of grain to China greatly increased year by year. With Formosa to
supply the most necessary food products, the coast districts on the mainland
were enabled to support a larger population, and accordingly multiplied in
proportion to the increase of productions. To such an extent did this reach,
that during the early half of the present century Formosa was familiarly

known as " The granary of China." [1] If wars broke out, or violent storms prevented the shipment of rice, a scarcity immediately ensued, and great distress was felt, the result being an increase of piracy by the Chinese, who had no scruples in resorting to crime in order to stave off destitution.

Some little trade was also carried on with the natives. In districts where the authorities had control, certain merchants were given the monopoly of this trade. There were also linguists appointed to transact business. This was not satisfactory, however, except to the traders themselves, for the natives were so cheated and imposed upon that disturbances often arose.

Some idea of the exports in those early days may be formed from the following report published in 1833 : [2]

"The quantity of rice exported to Fuhkeen (Fokien) and Chekean (Chikiang) is very considerable and employs more than three hundred junks. At Teentsin (Tientsin) alone, there arrive annually more than twenty junks loaded with sugar. The export of camphor is likewise by no means small (shipped principally to Canton). The owners of the plantations are generally Amoy men, whose families live in their native country. The capital they employ is great; the trade profitable. Oil cake is also one of the important exports, being used as a fertilizer on the opposite coast of Fokien where the sandy hills were converted into tracts capable of cultivation."

For administrative purposes the island had been divided into four *hiens*, or prefectures, under civil magistrates, and two *tings*, or seaboard divisions, including the Pescadores, under marine magistrates. The *hiens* from south to north consecutively and the number of settlements in each at this period were: Fangshan *hien*, consisting of one town, 8 Chinese villages, 73 uncivilized, and 8 civilized native villages ; Kagi *hien* of one town, 4 Chinese villages, 22 uncivilized and 8 civilized native villages : Changwha *hien* of one town, 16 villages ; and Tamsui *ting* with one town, 132 farms, and 70 native villages.

The Chinese authorities had shown neither ability nor desire to extend their island domains much beyond the borders laid down by the Koxinga family. As yet they had made no claim whatsoever to the vast interior occupied by the aborigines, and never interfered with the internal affairs of the savages. Nevertheless, the nineteenth century found the Chinese authorities engaged in constant war, either with their own people or with the savages, while in later years different foreign nations were added to their foes.

As with everything else in China, these disputes repeated themselves year after year. The accounts of nearly every engagement tell us that by ill treatment the Chinese incurred the hatred of the savages, and a band of avengers would sweep down from the hills, attack a small Chinese settlement, and flee back to their friendly jungles with the dripping heads of their Chinese victims. If the attack were serious, or if an Imperial officer lost his head, the Imperial troops would be despatched into the savage territory where they would slaughter the first unfortunates that they fell in with, regardless whether they had been implicated in the attack or not.

As to the troubles with their own countrymen, the mandarins by their rapacity incited the people to rebel, or the lawless mobs would seek to advance their personal interests ; and fighting would be the result. The Imperial troops

---

1. "China" in this instance must have referred to the maritime provinces and not to the interior of the vast empire.

2. Canton Register. May 18th, 1833.

disorganized and ill-equipped were harassed by guerilla tactics until the rebels gained sufficient strength to advance *en masse* and crush them by force of numbers (in two instances the capital itself was captured). The high authorities, now thoroughly alarmed lest the report of their negligence should reach Peking, would exert themselves to the utmost. Reinforcements would be poured into the island, while the rebels, ofttimes weakened by disputes among themselves, were unable to resist, and were reduced to submission either by force or bribes. And then when all was over, a magniloquent report bristling with the glorious deeds and splendid victories of the Imperial troops would be sent to Peking, resulting in an Imperial decree declaring pardon and forgiveness to the rebels and higher rank and numerous decorations to the Imperial officers.

We now lay before the reader an account of the most important of the disturbances which marked the nineteeth century.

From the year 1800, a pirate named Tsah Ken (Sai Ken), a native of Tswengchoo (Senshu), who cruised along the China seacoast attacking junks and trading ships, had frequently visited Formosa, which he considered a safe retreat in time of need. Well acquainted with the island, he endeavored to advance his own interests by inducing the discontented classes to rebel. In 1805, Tsah Ken landed at Tamsui and communicated with the banditti living in the mountains, but was soon driven out by the Imperial troops. The turbulent classes now took advantage of the confusion to rob and pillage the district. The village headmen raised volunteer forces of Changchoo men and opposed the banditti, and furthermore, when the pirate attempted to land at Lokiang (Rokko) they marched on that city, no doubt enjoying such an opportunity of striking a blow at their old enemies, the Tswengchoo clan, who occupied the place. Arriving at Lokiang, the Changchoo people met with an unfriendly reception, which eventually led to a serious combat in which many were killed on both sides and much property was destroyed. Tsah Ken, the pirate, took advantage of this to pillage several districts. The feud between the two clans now spread into the surrounding districts, and all the Chang choo men joined to crush their opponents. The Tswengchoo people throughout the country were accordingly attacked, and, except at Lokiang, great numbers were massacred, and thousands who escaped from their homes were literally driven into the sea to meet death by drowning. At length, after great damage had been inflicted, the two clans became reconciled and for the time settled down again in peace.

Meanwhile, Tsah Ken had interested himself in South Formosa, and joined forces with the insurgents of Fangshan district (Hozanken), leading them in an attack on Fangshan city (Hozan) and Tangkang (Toko). Although the Imperialists stoutly defended their positions, the insurgents were successful, and the two cities fell into their hands. Thus encouraged, the rebels attacked Anping and laid siege to Taiwanfu, while the pirate watched operations on board his junk at a safe distance from the city. Having effectually stirred up the population, Tsah Ken seems to have been content, and accordingly departed from the island, although he returned later to reconnoitre the position.

A force of a thousand regulars was now hurried across from China and landed at Lokiang. They then advanced towards the south, strengthening themselves with large numbers of volunteers collected along the way. Upon reaching Anping, the rebels, frightened at the sight of the formidable force sent against them, retired, the Imperialists clearing the district and later recovering Fangshan. The rebels now retreated to Tohah-hun (Toshien), whence they again fled in several directions,—some to the savage territory and some to the sea, where they made their escape in junks. The Imperialists had now restored communications, and quiet again reigned in the island. Four years later the pirate Tsah Ken met a richly deserved fate, being drowned at sea.

In 1808, a second pirate, Tsu Pun (Shifun), a native of Canton, made several visits to the coast from Lokiang to Tamsui. One night a high Imperial officer arriving off one of the northern ports discovered one of Tsu Pun's ships in the harbor. The officer at once attacked the craft, which ran out and eventually anchored at Suao (So-ō) on the north east coast where the pirate intended to fix his headquarters. Tsu Pun now plotted to rid the district of Imperialists, and for that purpose sought the assistance of a Chinese interpreter who had close relations with the savages. The prefect of Taiwan, hearing of this, came to Banka where he equipped a force, with which he crossed the mountains and marched to Gowi (Goi) a village near Gilan. Placing himself in communication with the savages he presented them with a large quantity of cloth and 1,000 dollars, in return for which they were induced not only to repudiate their promises to the pirate but to join in an attack against him. The interpreter, who had not acquiesced in Tsu Pun's designs, now led the savages, and with the assistance of an Imperial squadron they were able to drive away the enemy, whose party was last seen fleeing eastward aboard 16 junks.

In 1809 we find the clans again in combat with each other; and in 1811 another rebellion broke out, which was brought to an early close by the execution of the two leaders, one of whom had formerly been a fortune-teller.

In 1824 a native of Fangshan district, with his followers, rebelled, but a number of villagers formed a volunteer corps and captured the leader and others implicated, thus putting an end to the disturbance.

In 1826, more clan fighting, originating this time in a dispute as to the ownership of a pig. It eventually reached considerable proportions, involving a large district, and resulting in much loss of life and property. Rebellious parties now thought this a favorable opportunity, and having induced a tribe of savages to assist them, the village of Tionkan (Chuko) was attacked and captured. The government now sent a detail of regulars, who recovered the village and drove the rebels into the mountains.

A more serious affair, resulting in the loss of the capital, broke out in 1830 and continued at intervals until 1833. It had its start in a land dispute between villagers, Hakkas and Fokienese being the parties concerned. One of the villages complained to the authorities and presented them with gifts. The case was, therefore, officially dealt with in favor of the donors. This brought down upon the heads of the officials the wrath of the losing party, who, with all their clan and thousands of sympathizers, immediately broke out into open rebellion. The insurgents first appeared about fifteen miles from the capital, Taiwanfu, and twenty or thirty officers with nearly two thousand men were killed at the first outburst. The news soon spread and there was a general rising throughout the island, large numbers of Imperial troops being killed, and many forced to seek shelter in the mountains. While troops were being levied and despatched from the four south-eastern provinces of China, the different parties among the insurgents were engaged in mutual extermination.

One clan, with 30,000 men, seized the capital, driving the Imperialists from the city and repeatedly defeating them whenever they appeared, until at last the remaining regulars were obliged to seek refuge in the north.

A fleet and a renowned military officer were despatched to suppress the rebellion; commissioners were sent from Peking for the same purpose, and woe be to such officers in China if they do not win success by some means or other! The army landed in different parts of the island, but the fleet sailed direct for the capital. Fortunately for the Imperial navy, just as the fleet was anchoring in the harbor, the occupants of the city were marching against a hostile clan who had attacked them. The capital was thus easily recovered, and in eight or nine months, whether by force or by money (if report be true not much less by the latter than by the former), the insurrection throughout the island was checked, and the announcement was made that " Now all is quiet again and the mind of His Majesty is filled with consolation."

From the " *Peking Gazette* " it appears that the emperor acknowledged that the rebellion had originated in the oppression and maladministration of the officials. The general then in command of the army was accordingly dismissed from service. Through the carelessness of this officer the 20,000 troops stationed in the island had been practically annihilated by being permitted to mix with the people in trade, etc. Hence, upon the breaking out of the rebellion the officers were helpless and in a deplorable plight. The governor of Fokien would naturally have received the larger portion of the blame, but fortunately for him he had in the meantime died ; for, " Had he been alive," says His Majesty, " I would have inflicted such a death upon him as would have been a warning to all careless governors.

" Publish this At Home and Abroad."

In 1834 there was serious clan fighting in Fang-shan ; in 1844, the Changchoo and Tswengchoo people were again at war ; in 1852 four districts were similarly engaged, and in 1853 a serious conflict between opposing clans occurred at Tieng-lieck (Chureki).

The Taiping rebellion on the mainland had its counterpart in Formosa, but was limited to numerous small parties who appear to have been too jealous of each other to join hands and thus stand considerable chance of success.

In 1852, a resident of Fang-shan district, who had been employed as a servant at the district office, joined a band of would-be insurgents. The chief of Taiwan district was at this time temporarily residing in the vicinity, and he was accordingly made the first object of attack. In this the insurgents were

successful, and, after having defeated the attendants, they killed the high
official. The insurgents now advanced against the walled city of Fangshan,·
while at the same time northern rebels attacked Kagi city. The local government was now in rather a dangerous position. The Taiping rebellion was
spreading through the mainland empire and not a man could be spared.
Fortunately for the empire, however, the turbulent Formosans do not seem
to have understood that the golden opportunity to drive out the Imperialists,
perhaps for ever, had arrived. Accordingly, with a small force of some
4,000, many of whom were volunteers, the government was able to recover
the two positions held by the insurgents.

In 1853, a " professional rebel," who had probably served his apprentice-
ship with the Taipings, came from the mainland with his followers to the
island, but, owing to some miscalculation, fell immediately into the hands of
the authorities, who put an abrupt end to his career.

The same year (1853) in Kagi, and the next year in Kagi and Fangshan,
there were futile attempts at rebellion.

Again, a few years later, towards the close of the Taiping rebellion on
the mainland, a popular outburst of opposition against the cruel measures
the authorities were adopting with the intention of preventing the possibility
of an outbreak, threw the north into rebellion. Chinese official accounts
speak of the troubles as clan fights, in which the mandarins were engaged, not
in defending themselves, but in quelling the belligerents. The most reliable
authorities, however, describe the warfare as directed against the government.
and furthermore that one of the highest officials of Tamsui was killed, while
Tamsui village (Hobe) was plundered. Though the rebels were but a rough
unarmed mob, they held the Imperial troops at bay for fifteen days, and when
peace and order were again restored, the Tamsui ting was dismissed from
his position as incapable of keeping the " Emperor's little children quiet." [1]

An attempt made in 1861 to thrust upon the people the burden of a
$2\frac{1}{2}$ $^o/_o$ *likin* tax on every marketable commodity, resulted in a general riot.
The Chinese closed their shops, refused to engage in trade, and the mandarins
were pelted and mobbed at every opportunity. The mandarins, as usual
under such circumstances, had to give in, and assure the people that they
would, at least for the time, stop the offensive measure. It was very evident
that, however much they might yield to a local tax, the colonists would not
endure one which was to be applied, as it was officially stated, to the suppression of the rebellion on the mainland, with which they were not immediately
concerned.

The next year (1862) the cloud of discontent that had been for months
gathering over the district of Chang wha (Shoka) at last burst into torrents
of bloodshed and rapine. A family dispute took place between two clansmen
which eventually involved thousands of their respective adherents, and led
them to resort to arms. Before the quarrel reached its crisis, however, an
influential neighbor, Taiwan-Sang by name, interposed, and arranged terms of
peace between the contending parties. But that the warlike spirit which had

1. Reports of this rising are much at variance.

so long been cultivated, and the numerous arms and ammunition that had been collected, might be of some use, the erstwhile enemies swore eternal union under the leadership of Taiwan-Sang and declared their intention of attacking the government, demanding a change of officials, and more honest and considerate treatment in the future.

When the news of the pending insurrection reached Taiwanfu the commander-in-chief of the Formosan forces made preparations to march against the offenders, but was overruled by the taotai, who thought to bring about a peaceful settlement, by himself visiting the scene, and inquiring into the people's grievances. With this object in view the taotai started on his mission, first having sent word to the Tamsui ting to join him at Changwha with 500 soldiers. The taotai reached Changwha, and after having summoned the leaders of the rebel party to an interview, promised the people that their complaints should be attended to, bestowed upon Taiwan-Sang, their chief, a blue button, and furthermore promised to secure an official position for him, if he would disband and quiet the dissatisfied section. While both representatives were congratulating themselves on the advantageous solution of the difficulty, the Tamsui ting, who appears to have been of a haughty, excitable nature, came in upon them, and upon learning of the settlement arrived at, broke out into a torrent of abuse against the taotai, accused him of cowardice, and declared that the bestowal of position upon a rebel would only incite other unscrupulous people to rise for the purpose of obtaining similar advantages. The ting then seized upon one of the leaders, decapitated him, and had the nephew of Taiwan-Sang bound and placed in the keeping of some of the people present. The boy's guardians, however, proved to be his kinsmen and permitted him to escape and carry information to the headquarters of the rebellious society. The Tamsui ting now sallied forth from the city with his braves, but the alarm having spread, he was soon surrounded by an infuriated mob. The official, finding progress in his chair impossible, got out and commenced to run from the scene, but seeing that his corpulency would not admit of much more than a waddle, he consented to the suggestion of his chief attendant, and mounted his back. This servant, like the majority of the ting's followers, sympathized with the rebels, besides having private grudges against his superior, so after having carried his master a short distance, he permitted one of the braves to thrust a spear in the ting's back, and, as he fell crying for help, the chief attendant settled up old accounts by deliberately carving off the unfortunate officer's head. Thus rid of their chief, the braves joined the rebel party, and rushed back to occupy Changwha, carrying with them the dripping head of the mandarin, which they finally posted on one of the gates of the city.

One of the Imperial officers, disliked for his exactions, saw the wild mob approaching, and rather than fall into their hands, he killed himself in despair on the city wall. The citizens opened the gates and bid the rebels welcome. Upon gaining the city, a rush was made on the military officers' quarters, where the taotai, and the former Changwha magistrate who had fled thither for refuge, were found. These two officers they secured in separate rooms, and treated with moderate kindness, placing food and drink before them,

The taotai complained of faintness, and to restore him an opium pipe and some tea were given him. Unable to bear the humiliation of his capture and no doubt fearful as to his future, the taotai mixed up a little opium with the tea and tossed off the poison, thus inviting death. The other mandarin, who had given satisfaction to the people during his term of office, was released by the rebels, not, however, before they had deprived him of his queue and moustache.

Having thus cleared the place of officials the rebels seem to have forgotten that they were originally organized for the purpose of demanding a change of officers and better government, and now declared their intention to separate the island from Imperial rule, and govern it themselves. Formosa was accordingly divided into two kingdoms, and the two rebel leaders were proclaimed as the southern and eastern kings, respectively. Expeditions were sent against Kagi, Lokiang, and Yunlin by the new rulers, who dyed their banners in the blood of their victims as they advanced, but as to their actual successes, accounts vary. That many lives were lost, including an Imperial general is, however, certain.

Imperial troops now arrived from the mainland under the command of an admiral and a general, and by advancing upon the rebels from the south and north simultaneously, the new arrivals were able, after many months of labor, to defeat the rebels at every point, and to restore the Imperial rule. The two would-be kings later fell into the victors' hands, one to be crucified, and the other beheaded.

The Tswengchoo and Changchoo people, who had been so actively engaged in exterminating each other in preceding years, appear from this time onward to have bequeathed their warlike proclivities to the Hakkas and Fokienese, for the clan fights which followed were principally between these two factions, although not infrequently they joined hands to slaughter the poor Pepohoans. It has been estimated that thirty thousand lives were lost in these combats during the sixties.

It would be wearisome to the reader, and occupy too much space, to detail all these. Suffice it to say that although these engagements do not appear to have resulted in great loss of life, a petty warfare was constantly going on. If it ceased in one part of the island, it broke out in another, and the only respite, if any, was during the few weeks of harvest time, when the opposing parties were wise enough to lay aside the weapons of war for those of peace.

Still such constant troubles do not appear to have affected immigration, and the number of arrivals increased year by year, for though the island had a reputation for official tyranny and disorder, it was also well-known for its prosperity, and immigrants were willing to put up with the one to obtain the other.

The western, southern, and northern parts were now thickly settled, and for administrative purposes two new ting:—Taifang and Lokiang—were added, to be followed in later years by a third, Kamolan ting.

In a Chinese work entitled " *Statistics of Taiwan* " published under the auspices of the government, there is a unique account of the condition of the Chinese portion of the island early in the present century, an extract from which is given below. Mr. Swinhoe[1] whose translation is taken, expresses his opinion that "the general puff which the island received was no doubt given to attract a larger flow of emigrants."

" The district of Taiwan is a land of luxuriant vegetation, broad and level, and very fertile. The western and northern portions offer large tracts of champaign country, highly capable of cultivation. Hundreds of families of our people are already engaged there in husbandry, associated with the natives of the land. The colonists are from different parts of the empire, no village claiming one surname (as in China), and no two men of the same heart. The aborigines are addicted to spirituous liquors, and are blood-thirsty. They wear no caps, shoes, or clothes; and have no marriage or burial rites. Merchants and travellers resort to the colonies in numbers, and merchandise flows its endless round. Rice grows in excessive quantities and is plentifully exported to China. The farmers have therefore no need of granaries to store away their grain.

" Taiwan hien." The land of this district is of no extent, and is poor through long cultivation. It yields only one crop in the year. The colonists are fond of ornaments and fine clothes. The five grains abound, and there is no lack of the necessaries of life. The men engage themselves in husbandry, but the women, instead of spinning, waste their time in embroidery. The people are compassionate and hospitable, regarding as their relations all who suffer from sickness or want. (Another early author describes the city of Taiwan as ranking among cities of the first class in China in the variety and richness of its merchandise and in population.)

" Fangshan (Phœnix hill) hien comprises large tracts of level and waste lands, abounding in bamboos, fruit bearing, and other trees. There is here well watered ground, suitable for the plantation of early rice. This the colonists have begun to turn to good account. Merchants have water carriage for their goods, and broad roads enable them to use transport carts drawn by oxen. Beyond the jurisdiction of this department in a southerly direction, natives from the Canton province have settled and mix indiscriminately with the aborigines. These settlers are a riotous set, fond of litigation and fighting, and reckless of life.

" Kagi hien was formerly known as Choo-lo hien, from its native name. The soil in this department is very rich, and grain when sown is left to nature to bring it to maturity, not needing the labor or attention of men. The colonists here also are fond of abusing and fighting one another. They are jealous and outvie each other in dress and ornaments; and in marriage ceremonies they take into consideration dowries, which last is a bad custom. Their good qualities, however, counterbalance the evil, for families live under the same roof to the number often of several generations. Disputes between neighbors are frequently settled by a friendly word. They share willingly with their friends anything they possess on the promise of repayment at a future day. Benighted travellers can gain admission and hospitality at the first door they apply at, and few will refuse them shelter.

" Changwha (manifest change) hien. This department has been but recently established and people eager to enter a new field flocked thither in multitudes. They soon formed roads and thoroughfares and villages worthy of admiration; to the marts of which there are few commodities that do not find their way, but they rule at rather high prices. The habits of the colonists are similar to those of the citizens of the capital.

" Tamsui (Fresh water) Ting comprises two subdivisions, Tamsui and Choo-tsin (Bamboo dyke). The villages here daily increase in size, and the smoke of the cottage fire thickens. There are numerous settlers on the Tamsui river; their habits are honest and economical, and few fights or lawsuits occur. Grain and other produce of the soil are cheap; but cloths, silks, furniture, and all imported goods are several times dearer than at the capital.

" Pang-hoo-ting (Pescadores) comprises a cluster of islands in the midst of the ocean, the soil of which is not adapted for rice or corn. It produces sesamum, sorghum, and vetches. The inhabitants build their houses of mud and straw, and depend upon fishing for subsistance. They boil the sea into salt, and distil spirits out of sorghum; they catch fish, crustacea, and mollusca, for food, and dry them for exportation. Cloth, silk, yellow peas, and millet are imported thither from Taiwan."

Until comparatively modern times the viceroy of Fokien governed Formosa as a *fu*, or prefecture. This high functionary, finding the order that he should visit Formosa yearly very irksome, succeeded in getting the time extended to once in three years. He, however, was as lax in obeying this new order as he had been in the former case. Still, when once he did arrive, the local officials were under the necessity of providing presents proportionate in value to the time that had elapsed since his excellency's

---

1. Swinhoe's " Notes on Formosa."

last visitation. Should they neglect this pious duty they were liable to removal for the most trifling offence. To meet the emergency, the people of the island were correspondingly squeezed, and as our authority states "thus at the expense of all classes the exalted servant of the Emperor walked the path of duty and returned, unlike most other travellers, with a well filled purse."

The Taiwan taotai, the chief authority and highest magistrate, resided at Taiwanfu, and had to make a circuit of the department once a year, and we may believe he emulated the viceroy in these tours, to the terror of the minor officials, who no doubt dreaded his visits as much as he himself did those of the viceroy. The next civil functionary was the Taiwan *fu*, or prefect; then the Taiwan *hien* or district magistrate, and lastly the Haifang ting, or marine prefect. The chief military and naval authority was the *chintai* who was at once commodore of the fleet, and commander-in-chief of the land forces. He also resided at the capital.

To Mr. Swinhoe, British consular representative in Formosa during the old order of things, we are indebted for the following particulars regarding salaries emoluments, etc. :—

'The salaries paid to the officials were but of nominal value and the funds for this purpose were deducted from the land rents and grain taxes. The taotai for instance only received 1,600 taels (at that time about £600) per annum; but his emoluments were large, those drawn from taxes on camphor especially. The yearly income he is said to have made out of that, which was then the most important trade of the island, was of almost fabulous amount.

'The chi-fu or prefect, besides court-fees, lined his pockets from the immense salt-monopoly of the island, which he ruled uncontrolled. He had salt-offices, or Yen-kwan, at every place of any importance, and the toll was enforced with great rigor. These offices had regular and constant couriers running between them and the capital. Foreign manufactured salt was not permitted to be imported, and vessels had been made to discharge their cargoes of it overboard before gaining admission into the ports.

'The Hiens or district magistrates held the Petty Assizes and adjudicated in all cases of secondary importance. In these courts, by legal fees, and a process of intimidation, they generally managed to make pecuniary matters go smoothly for their own interests.

'The tings warmed their nests by the exaction of exorbitant port dues, all of which were set against the current expenses of their office. They were empowered to lay hands on so many private vessels a year, for the purpose of conveying rice to the imperial garner. These junks were paid a nominal freight, and often detained idle for months. Thus the junk-men were but too glad to escape by payment of a moderate squeeze. The system led to an embargo being laid on all vessels that refused to pay the toll or escape-money, and as use makes custom, the Chinese from that time on regarded this exaction of the mandarins simply as K'ow-fei, or port charges, although the official conveying of rice had a few years later practically ceased.

'The military offices were not behind in the contest, and although the officers were known to pay as high as 2,000 taels for their positions, they still made them lucrative. At all ports they had their military port dues amounting to about one third of the civil port dues. The sum for native junks varied according to their cargoes, but was usually twenty to thirty dollars.

'On foreign vessels at any port in Formosa not open to trade, the exactions were usually made at fifty taels per mast, whether the vessel came in with full cargo or ballast. At Tamsui, on the opening of the port to foreigners, these exactions were done away with as regards foreign vessels.

'Great fear was always entertained of the rebelling of the Formosans, and to provide against this, soldiers required for service in Formosa were not enlisted from the island, but brought over from the mainland. In former years, they were relieved yearly, subsequently once in three years, but eventually it became too often a life service, the bones only of the exiled soldier being returned for burial to his native land at last, when his relations came forward with the means to pay the transportation. The military affairs were in a great state of corruption, too many officers in command leaving their posts defenceless, and putting in their pockets the money intended for their men.'

The above is a picture of everyday and commonplace officialdom in China. Nevertheless, it sometimes comes as a considerable shock to those unfortunates who have had their lives or property endangered by the existence of the pernicious system. The foreign community at Hobe experienced a vivid illustration of this in the early days of the port.

One evening, to the alarm and surprise of all, it was announced that some disaffected villagers a few miles away were about to sweep down upon them, plundering the people, and murdering the mandarins. The authorities fell into a paroxysm of fear, and had the gongs beaten to assemble the troops. The foreigners were least anxious, as the garrison was believed to number seven hundred men, and that number they thought could give sufficient protection. But after beating the gongs all the afternoon only one hundred men were mustered. Then came the disheartening disclosure that although the names of seven hundred men were on the books, and although full pay was drawn for that number, the noble representatives of the Empire had pocketed the balance, believing that if they were willing to run the risk of having but a one-seventh force to protect them, surely they should be well paid for it. Shrewd reasoning (for them) of course !

CHAPTER VIII.

FOREIGN INTERCOURSE AND MASSACRE OF BRITISH SUBJECTS.

1801-1847.

WE must now again depart from chronological order, and return to the days following Count Benyowsky's expedition, in order to resume the record of foreign intercourse with the island.

So far as is known, the eighteenth century passed away without the visits of any foreigners to the island, with the single exception of the great French traveller La Perouse in 1787.

Nature seemed determined that none should succeed the Dutch in Taiwan, for during the century which elapsed between the departure of the Hollanders and the period now under review, she did her best to hide all traces of the harbor of Taiwan, which in earlier days had sheltered many vessels, Japanese, Chinese, and Dutch. This excellent anchorage with 13 or 14 feet of water at low tide during the days of the Dutch, suffered a marvellous change, having almost totally disappeared, and leaving but a shallow river discharging itself over a dangerous and surf beaten bar.

There is no record of any foreign vessel attempting an entrance since the expulsion of the Dutch in 1662. Towards the close of the century large vessels could not approach within a mile of the shore, and the largest Chinese junks were obliged to anchor outside, and to land and receive cargoes in lighters.

After the Dutch, the first recorded attempt on the part of foreigners to trade was in 1824, when the ship *Jamesina* visited Formosa, and cruised along the coast from one end to the other. She steered first for Taiwanfu, but in consequence of sands which lie outside, could not get within three miles of the shore, which was so low that only the tops of the trees and highest houses could be seen from aboard. About sunrise, the high mountains in the interior were generally seen, but during the day they were always obscured. Those on board were "readily supplied here with water and provisions at moderate prices, and many little articles of manufacture peculiar to the island were brought off."

Being unable to sell any of her cargo, the *Jamesina* "ran to the southward, as far as 22° 20' N. without being able to find any good harbor or roadstead." She then returned to Taiwanfu, procured a pilot, and proceeded to the northward, visiting Lokiang in lat. 24, and then continued her course to a village about forty miles further. These places are reported as mere roadsteads.

The *Merope* also visited Formosa in July of the same year. Being driven off Taiwanfu in a heavy gale, she ran to the northward, and, when the gale moderated, found herself off the town now called Hobe, and in the harbor of Tamsui. Being in need of repairs, the natives recommended her proceeding to Kelung, also in the north of the island, which was "found to be a most excellent and secure harbor, perfectly landlocked, but rather difficult of entrance, owing to a rapid tide of five or six knots sweeping past its mouth." A survey of this harbor was made by the commander and officers of the *Merope.*

In 1827, the *Dhaulle* called at the same ports as had been visited by the *Jamesina* and *Merope.* She also rounded the north eastern point of the island, proceeding down the eastern coast about thirty miles to the mouth of a small river, upon whose bank was a Chinese village. She then proceeded to the southernmost part of the island.

In 1832, the western coast was visited by the ship *Lord Amherst,* but no regular foreign trade was established with the island until some twenty years later.

In 1842, after the close of England's war with China, the whole civilized world learned with horror of the massacre of one hundred and ninety-seven British subjects, put to death by Chinese officials, and of eighty-three who perished through ill treatment and starvation.

This mournful fate befel the crews of the ships *Nerbudda* and *Ann* which were wrecked on the Formosan coast. The first was a transport, and as soon as she struck the rocks, all the Europeans, including the ship's officers, accompanied by two Manila men and three Hindoos, left in the ship's boats, leaving two hundred and forty British Indian natives to their fate. The wreck had occurred not far from Kelung. The natives, all British subjects, remained by the ship five days after they were thus abandoned, and then as the vessel had drifted off the reef and was lying in the comparatively smooth water of Kelung Bay, they attempted to reach the shore on such crude rafts as they could construct on board. In this they were very unfortunate, for some were drowned in the surf, others were killed by Chinese who came down to strip them as they reached the shore, and the rest were seized, confined, heavily ironed under circumstances of great cruelty, in small parties, and in separate prisons, and left there, with scarcely any clothing and a very small allowance of food, for about eleven months, during which time, many after great suffering died from the privations. At the expiration of this period, the survivors, with two exceptions, were carried to Taiwanfu, the capital of the island, where they were again imprisoned.

The brig *Ann* was wrecked during the following March to the southwest of Tamsui, also in the north of the island. Of the fifty-seven souls on board, fourteen were Europeans and Americans, five Chinese, thirty-four British Indians, and four Portuguese and Malays. The brig was driven about midnight, by the violence of the wind and sea, so high on shore that when the tide ebbed she was left dry, and about daylight the fifty-seven men quitted her and got on board a Chinese junk, in hopes of being able to put to sea. This could not be effected, however, owing to the violence of the gale, and as a host of armed Chinese soldiers had now surrounded them, they surrendered without having fired a single gun or made other show of resistance. They were instantly stripped stark naked, dragged some distance without a particle of covering, and exposed to a cutting north-east winter wind. Two men died from cold, and several others dropped from the same cause combined with fatigue, and were carried on in baskets to the capital, some hundred miles from the scene of the wreck. Here, like the *Nerbudda* men who had preceded them, they were separated into small parties, covered with irons, and put into filthy prisons, where they were subjected to such barbarous treatment and given so little food that several, unable to survive such suffering, met with a cruel death.

On August 13th, 1842, all the survivors, with the exception of ten persons who, it is surmised, were considered to be principal men of their classes and were to be sent to Peking for execution, were carried to a wide plain just outside the capital, where irons were put upon them and they were placed upon their knees. Mr. Newman, a seacunnie on board the *Ann*, describes the preparations and his own narrow escape as follows :

" On being taken out of his sedan to have his hands shackled behind his back, he saw two of the prisoners with their irons off and refusing to have them put on. They had both been drinking and were making a great noise, crying out to him that they were all to have their heads cut off. He advised them to submit quietly, but they still refusing, he first wrenched off his own and then put them (the soldiers) into theirs (the irons), to the great pleasure of the soldiers, but when the soldiers wished to replace his, he declined. As they were on the point of securing him, he accidentally saw the chief officer seated close to them. Going before him he threw himself on his head and commenced singing a few Chinese words which he had frequently heard repeated in a temple. The officer was so pleased with this procedure, that he turned round to the soldiers, and ordered them to carry him back to the city."[1]

All the rest of the unfortunate men, one hundred and ninety-seven in number, who knew not for what purpose they had been brought out from

_____
1. Chinese Repository, Vol. XII., p. 248.

their vile prisons, were placed at short distances from each other on their knees, their feet in irons, and their hands manacled behind their backs. Thus in fearful suspense they waited for the executioners who went around and with a heavy two-handed sword coolly proceeded with their awful work.

When the heads of all had been severed, they were stuck up in cages on the seashore for exhibition to the populace. The bodies were afterwards thrown together into one common grave.

The wickedness of this awful deed impressed even some of the Chinese themselves, and not a few believed a violent storm which followed to be a demonstration of Heaven's displeasure. One of the Chinese in later years described the event to a foreigner as follows:—[1]

"Oh! yes. I remember that day well, and a black day it was for Formosa. They began the work about 9 a.m. and finished about noon. All the authorities and thousands of spectators were present; but before they had finished, the sky darkened, thunder and lightning with a tremendous storm of wind and rain set in, the rain lasting three days, all the watercourses and the country flooded, houses, men, and cattle swept away, the number of the people drowned being estimated at from 1,000 to 2,000. Ah! that was a judgment from Heaven for beheading the foreigners; but it was done in revenge for your soldiers taking Amoy."

A gallant young man, Robert Gully by name, who had honorably distinguished himself at the taking of Ningpo was among the murdered. He had been previously engaged in commercial pursuits, and had embarked on board the *Ann* to revisit friends in Macao, intending later to return to Peking, when the vessel was wrecked on the Formosan coast.

A journal was kept by Mr. Gully to within three days of his death, and another by Captain Denham of the *Ann*, one of the prisoners saved to be sent to Peking. Both vividly describe the experiences of the unfortunate captives.

The following extracts have been made from this journal,[2] in which the reader will find interesting particulars regarding the actions of the Chinese concerned in the crime, and descriptions of the country as it then appeared:

"*March 14th.* Shortly after breakfast we heard a noise outside, and saw spears and flags. Our guards told us we were going away. One of them called Mr. Roope aside, and took him up a ladder where he sung out to me for assistance. Captain Denham and myself went up to him and found the soldier trying to persuade Mr. Roope to go up stairs, and made motions for us not to go out to the mandarins. We went up to a small clean room, where the man wanted us to remain, but thinking it was only for the purpose of plunder that he wished to keep us, we determined to go with the rest. Perhaps the fellow had heard of our offer to the junkman and really meant well, but it was difficult to judge. We were then all taken before three mandarins, tickets put round our necks, and we marched under a strong escort of soldiers to a small walled town, inland about three miles. The walls were of round stone and chunam. We passed from one end of the town to the other, where we were seated under the walls close to a mandarin's office for about half an hour, I suppose for the people to have a good look at us. We were then taken into the mandarin's premises and divided into two parties, the soldiers having previously told us we were going to be beheaded, which I should have believed, if they had not overdone the thing by beginning to sharpen their swords on the stones. We were put into two cells about eight feet by seven each, in each of which were stowed twenty-five of us and three jailers or guards, the weather extremely cold, nothing to lay our heads on, and nothing but a sprinkling of straw to keep us from the damp bricks. The land on each side of the road was cultivated and rice

---

1 Reported by W. Maxwell to a Hongkong journal.

2. Journal kept by Mr. Gully and Capt. Denham, during a captivity in China in the year 1842. Chapman and Hall, London, 1844.

growing, the fields were very small, and only divided by a low round embankment about one foot high. The villages appeared to be pretty, from their being surrounded by bamboo. Here, for the first time I saw a wheeled cart, but we had before noticed the marks of wheels on our first march. It was a very clumsy affair, drawn by a bullock. It was passing across the ploughed ground, for no reason that I could see, except that there was no other road. The wheels were composed of two solid pieces of wood joined together in the centre, with a hole which merely slipped on to the axle-tree and was confined by a linchpin. The cart was of bamboo. The wheels made very curious gyrations in their passage through the mud. In the villages we were stared at by everybody, women and all. The women were unaccountably plain, even for Chinese women, both here and through all parts of the island I have seen, but they have a very pretty fashion of wearing natural flowers in their hair. On our road we passed several parties employed carrying the brig's guns in the same direction that we were travelling. Altogether, I think under other circumstances I should have enjoyed this trip much, but my feet were so painful with the sores of our former march that I could not. As it was, it was a great relief after the crowded granary, and I think did me good.

"15th. Nothing of any moment occurred except that we were joined by the gunner and sea-cunnies, missing up to this time. They had been much better treated than ourselves, and had clothes given to them, though rather of a fantastic nature. The treatment may, perhaps, be partly attributed to their thinking the gunner to be some great man from his having a mermaid marked on his arm, in the way common among sea-faring people. They partly labored under this mistake up to this present meeting. Both this day and the 16th, we were crowded by visitors who were a great nuisance. The government people who came, all told the same lie,—that we were going to be sent away in a junk. One fellow took the trouble to draw me on one side to explain it more clearly. If we ever placed reliance in their words, we were undeceived on the evening of the 17th, for we were then all taken before mandarins, ticketed, a fresh name given to each, and ornamented with handcuffs, we were placed in chairs and conveyed out of the town. We passed outside, and for some miles over a country tolerably cultivated. We were told in the villages we passed through that we were going to have our heads taken off. During the passage my bearers capsized my chair three times, which was occasioned by the slippery state of the footpath. I enjoyed this much more than the bearers, who got a good blowing up from the soldiers by whom we were attended, every time it happened. At last they persuaded the men who had charge of the key of my handcuff to allow me to walk, which I agreed to do as long as the road continued soft. (The man with the key attended me all the way to Taiwanfu). I was glad enough to take advantage of the permission to walk. I particularly observed that the soldiers in many instances carried a very superior kind of matchlock to any I had seen in China before, and they were cut outside, six square, and as well as the bore were quite smooth and bright. Some again were wretched-looking beings with rusty spears, shields, and old caps, without any stiffening in the borders. These I conjectured were the militia, the others regulars. A short time after, I observed wheat growing, but the crops were only small and poor in comparison to those common in England. This was the case throughout the whole journey to this town, and I dare say the Chinese understand as little about growing wheat or barley as our farmers know about rice. We soon came to a very barren description of country, interesting to geologists only. Immense plains stretching inland as far as we could see, composed of round stones, the same as we call 'boulders' in Yorkshire, with hills or mountains formed of the same, no vegetation being visible except now and then a green spot on the very tops of the hills, the first of which was some miles from the sea. Up to the time of our wreck, I had always imagined the shore of Formosa to be very bold, from having seen these hills often while at sea. The land, between them and the sea, is so very low and without trees that it must be very deceiving to any one at sea, and I doubt very much if the channel, as laid down in the chart, is not too wide. During this, our first trip in sedans, we were shown many little roadside public houses, where we were taught how to spend our mace by the man who had charge of each. These houses, together with every building we passed, were formed of the before-mentioned boulders and mud, with, in many instances, a large wide-spreading tree or trees with seats close to them. The country had a most wild and heavy aspect, more so than any I ever saw, and I began to think Formosa a sad misnomer. The scattered houses were few and far between and the people appeared a more wretched ill-clothed race than I ever saw in China before. This day's march, altogether in a southerly direction, was about twenty-five miles; we crossed several streams running to the westward, all of which were evidently smaller than at some other seasons of the year. We also passed several small towns not walled, or if so, the walls were only of mud, but all had gates, one a brick one, the other bamboo. We suffered all sorts of abuse and indignities in passing through these, as well as all the others throughout the journey; but women did not join in this, although they showed the usual curiosity of the sex. We arrived at our halting-place, a large town with high walls made of brick, about dusk; for some time previous to getting there, the country was a continued paddy swamp interspersed with small hamlets, surrounded with bamboo, which grows here larger than I ever saw in other places. I have noticed it full sixty feet high. I found, on minute inspection, that the axle-trees of the wheeled carts turned with the wheels. The bazaar of this town appeared well furnished with fish. We observed the mast heads of several junks a short distance to the westward, and these were the only signs of the sea that met our eye until we got close to Taiwanfu."

Mr. Gully throughout his journey in Formosa saw a great many graves "precisely like our own," and but very few with the usual Chinese-shaped tombstones. He complains much, and evidently with good cause, of cruel treatment. He says :

"Our jailer I believe to be the most wicked brute that ever was created. We were in a den so small that not one of us could stretch our legs at night, being coiled up like dogs. During the time I had the piles, I did not sleep for nights together. Ten of us, viz., the five sea cunnies, two Manila men, the gunner, Mr. Partridge, and myself, with a bucket in a wretched hovel only eleven feet six inches by seven feet six, and for the two months and more we were confined in it, and never allowed out but once a day to wash, and at first this was not allowed, and when it was, for upwards of a month only one or two could wash every morning, unless they washed in the water used by the others, the villain of a jailer being too lazy to furnish more than a few pints every morning."

All sorts of provisions, especially vegetables and fruits, seem to have been plentiful, but the supply for the prisoners was often small enough. The mangoes were good, and were sold among the people at the rate of 1,500 and 2,000 for a dollar. He found this fruit wholesome, and ate it, rind and all, to cure the dysentery. He also took opium for the same purpose, and thus notices its effects: "in a quarter of an hour it began to make me feel quite happy, in an hour quite sick, and laid me on my back the whole day." He often also complains of the nightmare, bad sleep, etc. He thus describes his residence :

"*July 25th.* Up as usual. Fine morning, but s'ept badly. Nightmare all night. I have just thought that in case this should survive us, it may be interesting to know the furniture of our abode. The cell is all but as large as the opposite one from which we were removed, but we have three advantages over our opposite neighbors, viz. 1. There are only three of us. 2. The window has only single bars. 3. We have air-holes in the roof. To sleep on, we have five hard-wood planks about eight feet long by fourteen inches wide and two thick. A bamboo is slung nearly the length of the place, on which in the daytime we hang our mats, two in number, for sleeping on. Besides these I now see two towels hanging from it, one made from part of an old pair of cotton drawers, and the other of grass cloth given me by Zu Quang Loon. Ditto belonging to Mr. Partridge, and a bundle of papers, sketches, etc, tied up by a string. On the east wall are remains of a picture of Chin Hoe, damaged by the rain. The window faces the west. On one side of it is hanging my pipe, given me by the captain's party. On the other is a small looking-glass given me by one of the jailers, a number of pencils and four monghoons. Our pillows of pieces of bamboo, with a quanny-mat for keeping the afternoon's sun out of the place, and a chequer-board are on the planks. On the north wall are hanging our washing-tub, which cost us fifty cash, a broom for sweeping the planks, a basket containing some hooks, etc., belonging to the former occupants; a basket containing our chop-sticks and spoons of bamboo, the gunner's towel and a stick for carrying a lantern. In this wall is a small recess containing a clay lamp and stand, a few bamboo sticks and two iron wires for cleaning pipes, three papers of tobacco and some waste paper. In the corner two sticks have been driven into the wall, on which rest the logbooks and some papers. Below that is a small shelf, on which are placed several cups, and broken saucers, and paints, two chow-chow cups (I broke the third a week ago), given us by Jack, a small earthenware kettle for boiling tea-water and brewing samshu when we can get it, given us by Aticoa. Below the shelf is suspended a hollow piece of bamboo holding our fire-pan, and below a small fire place, likewise a present from Aticoa, a cooking pot bought by ourselves, another containing charcoal (the pot given by Jack) several old straw shoes, and pieces of bamboo for smoking out the mosquitoes. On the south side are pendant, 1st the Bank, a string of cash about eighty or ninety, a small basket containing a few opium pills and our stock of tea, my hat which cost thirty cash; have covered it with oiled paper. I am sitting on a bamboo stool which belongs to the former occupiers of the place my foot resting on another given Mr. Partridge by the towka (I suppose the head jailer). Opposite is the door, behind it the bucket ; on my left is the window, on the sill of which are two combs, one of which I bought for thirteen cash a few days after my arrival at this town, being money I had saved from the mace per day allowed us during the journey. My fan is sticking in the window, and I am writing with this book resting on a board painted red, with black characters on it, and two green eyes above looking at them. I think this is all. No, I have forgotten to mention that on the south wall hang my long ell trousers given me by Kitchil, lascar, my grass cloth ones, given me by the lotier, and a pair of wooden socks given me by Francis, and from the same string hangs Mr. Roope's log. If you can call anything in this list a luxury, you must recollect that we have only had it lately ; for two months we had nothing, and were annoyed by myriads of fleas, bugs, lice, ants, mosquitoes, and centipedes, without a possibility of getting rid of them, except by death or a miracle. I have on my back now the only shirt (and a woollen one, too) I have had for nearly five months, and half a pair of cotton drawers are on my legs. I omitted to mention, on the north wall is my calendar. Every morning I scratch with the head of a rusty nail, the day of the month. We have also a third wooden stool lent to us by Aticoa. Employed we are, but the days are awfully tedious, and I am at a loss for something to pass away the time, and feel the want of books."

We have space for no more extracts ; these, however, are enough, and they show fairly and fully the manner in which the prisoners passed their days and nights, and show us also somewhat of their sufferings.

When the news of the outrage reached the British world, excitement was aroused to fever heat, and many advocated instant retaliation on the Chinese authorities concerned. Great Britain's Plenipotentiary in China, Sir Henry Pottinger, at once took the case up, and in December, 1842, arrived at Amoy and had an interview with J'liang, Governor of Fokien and Chekiang.

The following proclamations issued by His Excellency illustrate well his own opinions regarding the outrage:

"Sir Henry Pottinger, Bart, her Britannic Majesty's Plenipotentiary in China, has, on his arrival at Amoy, learned, with extreme horror and astonishment, that many more than a hundred subjects of her Britannic Majesty, who were wrecked in the ship *Nerbudda* and brig *Ann*, in the months of September, 1841, and March, 1842, on the coast of the island of Formosa, have been recently put to death by the Chinese authorities on that island, who allege they perpetrated this cold-blooded act in obedience to the imperial commands.

"Had the unhappy people who have suffered on this occasion even been prisoners of war, taken whilst fighting with arms in their hands, their massacre (which is aggravated by a lapse of time of nearly a year) would have been a most flagrant violation of the acknowledged and well-understood rules and feelings which distinguish warfare amongst civilized nations, and contrast it with the sanguinary and inhuman practices and ideas of mere savages; but when her Majesty's Plenipotentiary calls to mind that the unfortunate individuals on whom this foul deed has been committed, were inoffensive camp followers and seamen, who neither were armed nor had any means of defending themselves or of molesting others, and who were specially entitled, as distressed and shipwrecked men, both by the laws and usages of China, to kindness and protection, the Plenipotentiary has no language by which he can sufficiently proclaim the sentiments of abhorrence and detestation with which he views this lamentable affair, the recollection of which will remain as a stain and disgrace in the annals of the Chinese empire.

"Her Britannic Majesty's Plenipotentiary has already obtained positive official proof, that the commands issued by the Emperor for putting to death her Britannic Majesty's subjects were drawn from his Imperial Majesty by the gross and merciless misrepresentations of the local authorities on Formosa, who, with the object of personal aggrandizement, basely and falsely reported to the Cabinet at Peking, that both the ship *Nerbudda*, and subsequently the brig *Ann*, had gone to that island with hostile intention, an assertion not more lying and false, than manifestly absurd, since neither of those vessels were ships of war, or had, when wrecked, any troops or other fighting men on board of them. Her Britannic Majesty's Plenipotentiary now intends to respectfully, though firmly, submit the real facts of this dreadful affair to the special notice of the Emperor, through the imperial commissioners and ministers, and demand, in the name of his sovereign, the Queen of Great Britain, that the local authorities on the island of Formosa, whose false and pitiless misrepresentations have led to the horrid event which has called for this proclamation, shall be degraded and (condignly) punished; and, further that their property shall be confiscated, and its amount paid over to the officers of the British Government, to be applied to the relief and support of the families of the innocent men who have been put to death on false and foul accusation. Without this just atonement, Her Britannic Majesty's Plenipotentiary is not prepared to say that the event which has occurred, and which it becomes the Plenipotentiary's unwilling duty to report to Her Majesty's Government, will not be the cause of a further serious misunderstanding, or that it may not even lead to a renewal of hostilities between the two empires, which would be greatly to be deplored, as involving this country and its people in fresh misery and evil for the crimes of a few shameless and unworthy miscreants in power, who have, from base motives, imposed on their own sovereign. Her Britannic Majesty's Plenipotentiary, however, trusts that the emperor will, in his wisdom, see the justice as well as policy of making the retribution which is herein pointed out; which is due both to England and China, which will avert further calamity. That all persons may know the real state of the case, this proclamation is published in the English and Chinese languages for general information.

God save the Queen.

"Dated on board the steam frigate Queen, at Amoy, on the 23rd day of November, 1842, corresponding with the Chinese date, 21st of the 10th month in the 22nd year of Taukwang.

(Signed)   HENRY POTTINGER *H. M. Plenipotentiary*."

Sir Henry Pottinger now demanded that the Chinese officers concerned in the outrage be degraded and punished, and their property confiscated for the use of the families of the sufferers. Iliang, the governor-general, examined into the facts himself, and expressed to the English envoy his regrets at what had taken place. As has often happened, however, the Chinese authorities were able to smooth over the affair by degrading and banishing the Formosan commandant and intendant. Thus did China escape the consequences of a crime of such magnitude that, had it been committed by any other nation, it would at once have been taken as a *casus belli*, and full and complete retribution exacted.[1]

---

1. The prisoners were confined some in the prefectural prison and some in the district granary. W. Maxwell thus describes in the columns of a Hongkong journal, a visit to these buildings some fifteen years after the event above referred to:

"The granary consisted of a number of small houses forming a square, many of them entirely ruined, and we wandered for some time amongst the rubbish and dilapidated houses, scanning with eager eyes the walls for writing. We had just about given it up, when, entering a house in repair at one of the corners of the square, we noticed a caricature done in pencil on the wall, then near to it a few letters of a word which we could not decipher. Looking further along the wall, judge of our joy at seeing an almanack and particulars distinctly traced in pencil on the wall, in a very good business hand with the following inscription :

"The undermentioned were brought to this prison from the head military mandarin's house after being heavily ironed. on the 10th day of August :—F. Denham, Master, G. Roope, 1st mate, D. Partridge, 3rd do., S. Coen, Gunner, J. Seadore, Seacunnie, Jurnaul, Lascar, belonging to late brig *Ann*. She was lost on the island on March 10th, 1842, at midnight near Tamsui ; also Syrang and Burra Tindal of the Nerbuddha transport wrecked about September 1841———Frank Denham."

On another part of the wall of the same room was written Agosto 10——20 and on the wall opposite D. Partridge, dates commencing August 10th and continuing to August 22nd at which time most likely the prisoners were sent to Amoy where four of them eventually arrived.

In another room was found a calendar with particulars under it, exactly the same as the one noticed above, written also by Frank Denham; but with Chinese pen instead of a pencil. He had evidently been separated from the others ; the Chinese say because, from some marks of anchors, etc., punctured on his arms they considered him a head-man.

CHAPTER IX.

WRECKS AND OUTRAGES ON NAVIGATORS.

1848-1867.

Era of atrocity—Savage tribes of Formosa—Outrages on navigators—Loss of ships "Kelpie" and "Sarah Trottman"—Wreck of "Larpent"—Massacre of twenty-seven of the crew—Survivors sold into slavery—Berries, an Englishman, bought for six dollars—Their escape—Search for captive foreigners—Harry Parkes visits Formosa—U.S.S. "Macedonian" in the north—Loss of "High Flyer" and "Coquette"—Sailors of Prussian transport attacked—Prussian landing party inflicts punishment—Wreck of the "Rover"—The captain, Mrs. Hunt, and the crew murdered—H.B.M.'s. S. "Cormorant"—Futile attempt at reprisals—First visit of Le Gendre—Defeat of American naval expedition—Death of Lieutenant McKenzie—Le Gendre's second visit—Meeting with savages—Friendly agreement—Duplicity of Chinese—Renewal of barbarities—Chinese indifference.

The history of the third quarter of the present century covers a period filled with important events. It tells of attacks by the savages on ship-wrecked foreigners, and of armed parties being landed under Prussian and American officers to punish the offenders. It tells of the opening of Formosan ports to foreign residence and the renewal of that trade which had been interrupted for nearly two centuries. It tells of troubles with the mandarins and the occupation of Anping by British troops. The period closes with the first Japanese expedition, the punishment of the savages, and the temporary occupation of South Formosa by Japan.

The period under review is a continued tale of depredations and atrocities on the part of the Formosans and of the sufferings of those foreigners who were unfortunate enough to be cast on those inhospitable shores. That the reader may have a clear understanding of these events and of the subsequent ones which led to the first Japanese expedition, which put an end to these troubles, the subject has been treated in the following chapters continuously, without regard to other events, such as the opening of the island to foreign trade, etc., which, although they occurred at periods previous to the Japanese expedition, were still in no way concerned with our present subject, and can, therefore, be treated to better advantage in a later section of this book.

Whatever may have been the nature of the savages in the central and northern districts, the tribes who occupied the south of Formosa were extremely cruel and bloodthirsty. Foreigners gave the place a wide berth when they could, but the island was near the course taken by the numerous sailing ships running along the China coast and from central China to the United States, and, unfortunately, shipwrecks were frequent.

The wild seas surging around the island coasts are extraordinarily violent, and many a ship-wrecked crew reached land only to meet with a torturing death, more cruel, more brutal than even the sea would inflict ; for the Formosans were as little regardful of mercy as they were appreciative of the power of civilized governments. And the Chinese who shared the island with them, if not openly as bold in making an attack, looked on with a certain complacence, and no doubt often hid their own crimes by falsely accusing the savages.

Until the Japanese expedition in 1874, civilized governments did little to discourage such inhuman treatment of their subjects. The usual feeble protestations of the foreign authorities, the occasional flying visit of a warship, must have created amusement rather than terror, while the polite Chinese officials, with their craft and deceit, were as little efficient in satisfying the demands of justice and humanity then as they have been since.

That men of our own race were, during the last half of the present century, actually bought and sold as slaves is hard to realize, especially when we consider that Formosa was in the direct track of eastern navigation, and that foreign powers were possessed of sufficient naval forces in neighboring waters to have taught the Formosans to respect the life and liberty of unoffending foreigners.

Prominent among the events which directed attention to Formosa was the melancholy fate of the passengers and crew of the clipper ship *Kelpie*, which sailed from Hongkong for Shanghai in October, 1848, and was never afterwards heard of. It was believed, however, that she was wrecked on the Formosan coast. There were also reports that her passengers, including an American, Mr. Thomas Nye, and an Englishman, Mr. Thomas Smith, and her crew were in the island living in a state of slavery.

The next year the ship *Sarah Trottman*, with a cargo of tea, was lost off the southern coast, and a few months later (1850) the ship *Larpent* was likewise wrecked.

The next year three of the survivors of the *Larpent*, all Englishmen, who had been held in captivity, succeeded in putting off in a boat which, although fired at from the shore, managed to reach the British gunboat *Antelope* off the south end of Formosa. They were received on board, but, little to occidental credit, the native boatmen, instead of receiving their promised reward were driven away from the ship. The rescued men were carried to Shanghai when their depositions were taken by Mr. Alcock, the English consul, and the following account shows the fiendish atrocity of the savages and the state of slavery in which they sometimes held their victims when their thirst for blood had been satisfied :

"The *Larpent*, belonging to Mr. Thomas Ripley, left Liverpool for Shanghai on the 18th May, [1850,] in command of Captain Gilson. On the 12th September (116 days out), at about 5 p.m., she was off Botel Tobago, a small island sixty miles east from the south end of Formosa, when she was put about and stood across to Formosa with a northeast wind. The ship held on this tack until 20 minutes past 9 p.m., when she struck on the mainland of Formosa stem on, so close to land that the men could have got on shore from the flying jib-boom. When she struck she was going at the rate of four or five knots. The fourth mate, Mr. Bland, had the watch at the time; and he afterwards informed the men in the boat that he went aft to tell the captain there was land ahead. From the survivors, who were in their hammocks, we learn that they were awakened by the striking of the ship, and on rushing on deck found everything in confusion. The watch ran to the braces, and backed the foreyard which sent her right off. It was, however, soon seen that she had experienced great damage, and was making water fast, and the crew was sent to the pumps. She had at this time run a mile and a half from the shore; the water, however, gained so fast on them that, leaving the pumps, they commenced getting the boats out. The first got out was the jolly boat, but she was immediately stove alongside. The launch and starboard quarter-boat (a life-boat) were afterwards got out, and into them were put provisions, a few cutlasses, and some powder, but no shot. The crew got into the boats about 2.30 a.m., the captain, first mate, and six men in the life-boat; the second, third, and fourth mates, and twenty men in the launch. There was no sea, and they lay off to see the ship go down, which she did about 3.30 a.m. by Captain Gilson's watch. At daybreak both boats made for the shore, and all hands landed. Shortly afterwards four of the inhabitants came down to the beach; they were not Chinese, but belonged to one of the aboriginal tribes. They tried to pilfer but were driven away with the cutlasses. The captain, fearing hostility on the part of the natives, ordered the boats to be launched, and they then stood down the coast together until about 3 p.m., when the people in the launch hailed the captain, and told him they could go no further, as the boat was making a great deal of water, and that it required eight men to bail her. He replied that they must do the best they could, that if they liked they might try and reach a Spanish settlement that lay eighty or ninety miles to the westward, or Hongkong. They told him they could not venture in the state the boat was in. He then promised to stay by them until the boat was repaired; night came on and the launch hove to, having, according to the mate's calculation, run about ninety-four miles; next morning the life-boat was not visible. The launch was then rowed ashore, and the crew landed near Sugar-loaf Point, where they hauled the boat up, and set about repairing her and cooking provisions; while thus engaged they were fired upon with matchlocks from a neighboring wood. Several were killed and wounded, nine took to the water, who were pursued by the natives in catamarans. The second mate, Mr. Griffiths, not being a good swimmer, made back for the land, but was attacked and his head cut off. Alexander Berries and George Harrison kept together, and escaped to a rock, where they remained two days without food or water. William Blake (carpenter) and James Hill (apprentice) escaped together in another direction. The two first, driven by hunger, landed and shortly afterwards encountered about fifty of the natives, who at first presented their matchlocks at them, but did not fire. Two women then gave them clothes to wrap round their loins, as they were naked, and an old man took them to his house. Three days afterwards, George Harrison escaped on a catamaran to a Chinese sampan lying off the coast, but the men in her put him to death.

" Berries remained with his protector about four months, when a Chinaman who lived about five miles off bought him for six dollars. With this man, whose name was Kenah, he remained until he was taken on board the *Antelope*. While with this man, Berries learned that Blake and Hill had escaped to some Chinese village, and that some time after, they were sent eight miles into the interior, where Berries saw them while going with his master to a village called San Sianah. The master of Berries was willing to give him his liberty; but as the other men's master would not part with them, they agreed to run with Berries to San Sianah, where they were hospitably received by the mandarin. Their master's wife followed to reclaim them, and the mandarin paid her $14, the ransom she asked. Shortly afterwards, the *Antelope* was off the coast, when the mandarin sent his son and four men in a boat to put them on board. Berries during his captivity made four or five attempts to get on board English ships, and once nearly succeeded in reaching the *Flying Dutchman*, but the wind getting up prevented him.

" Armstrong and Hill learned that the master in the life-boat had put into the village where they were first captured, for the purpose of obtaining water, but none of them have ever heard of him since. None of the three men state that they saw all their comrades murdered, but they are the only survivors of the crew of the launch, as during their residence they picked up a sufficient knowledge of the language to understand what the natives said, and they never mentioned that there were any more saved."

Soon after this information had been given, H.B.M.'s S. *Salamander* was ordered to visit the scene of the wreck, to make investigations as to the whereabouts of the twenty-seven men still missing, and to reward those who had befriended the three already rescued. For this purpose a subscription of $865 had been raised among the residents of Shanghai.

(Sir) Harry S. Parkes also visited the island in 1851, for the purpose of gaining information regarding the *Larpent's* crew. He was apparently satisfied that most of the Chinese of Formosa could not be depended upon to assist in the release of captive foreigners, for in a private letter he expressed the opinion that as to the possibility of foreigners being retained prisoners in the island, there was the fact—to set against the assurances everywhere made that such was not the case—of Berries, Blake, and Hill, the survivors of the *Larpent's* crew, having been so detained there upwards of nine months, with the knowledge, as it turned out, of the beforesaid Le Wanchang (a man of considerable influence) who, in reply to the surprise expressed at his not having endeavored to effect their release, sought to shelter himself under what was bare pretext, namely, that the masters (captors) of the shipwrecked men had declined to give them up, on account of the general desire that they should be detained until they had acquired sufficient knowledge of the language to enable them to distinguish the tribe who committed the massacre, and the other tribes and settlers who resided in the same vicinity, fearing that the men when restored to liberty might return with an armed force, as they frequently threatened to do, and revenge themselves indiscriminately on all the people living at the south end of the island.

Americans immediately interested addressed the United States Legation, pointing out that after the testimony of the three of the *Larpent's* crew who had been held in slavery, it was not unreasonable to think that other Europeans and Americans might still be held captive, and that the subject should be investigated, both through the Chinese authorities, and directly by officials of the United States. Application was accordingly made to the commanding officer of the American squadron on the East India station, to despatch one of the vessels under his command to Formosa. While on the point of sending a vessel, the report of H.B.M.'s S. *Salamander* was furnished, and this, with some other considerations, led to a postponement of the matter; in the meantime, the American chargé d'affaires in China despatched, no doubt with the best of intentions, a Chinese to Formosa to make inquiries. The man returned with a very voluminous report, which seemed to satisfy, at least for the time, the American authorities. Why, it is difficult to see, for the visit of a few days at one of the Chinese settlements on the southwest coast of the island, could scarcely be very productive of a knowledge of affairs occurring across the mountains, in savage territory that had never been penetrated by the Chinese, and which was occupied by tribes, whose only association with the Chinese was on the battle-field, and then as enemies.

Still more incomprehensible was the conduct of Captain Abbot of the U.S.S. *Macedonian*, who, in 1854, was ordered from the Perry expedition to visit Formosa in search of captive foreigners. In the *American Expedition to Japan* we find the following:—

" As to our supposed shipwrecked and captive countrymen, Captain Abbot made the most diligent investigation (in Kelung), through the *medium of his Chinese steward*, but could gain no intelligence; although his inquiries were made, not only of the mandarins or officials in and about Kelung, but also of all classes of the people. The report from all was uniform; they declared that they neither knew nor had heard of any shipwreck of any American or European vessel on any part of the island; nor had they ever known or ever heard of the existence of the crew, or any part thereof, of any such vessel anywhere in Formosa, and Captain Abbot became quite convinced that, in this particular, they told the truth, and reported to the commodore accordingly, that he had 'no belief that any of our missing countrymen are alive on the island of Formosa.'"

When we consider that the wrecks occurred a distance of nearly two hundred and fifty miles from Kelung, which is a port in the north, that the north and extreme south were absolutely without communication at that time, and also the relations in which the inhabitants of the different portions of the island stood toward each other, it is clear that a person might have remained for years in hopeless and degrading slavery, without such a fact becoming known beyond the immediate neighborhood. If *the Chinese steward* above mentioned had been successful in extorting the desired knowledge under such conditions, it would have been little short of a miracle, and it seems to us that Captain Abbot's conduct amounted to criminal negligence.

The year after the visit of the *Macedonian*, a fine large ship, the *High Flyer*, a New York clipper, was lost on the south coast. She was commanded by Captain G. B. Waterman, whose wife, Mr. Chas. Spencer Compton, and three hundred or more Chinese, were passengers on board. The American clipper, *Coquette*, belonging to Messrs. Russell & Co., also carrying passengers, was lost about the same time.

In addition to the long catalogue of authenticated instances of barbarism, there was such general and well-founded suspicion concerning the fate of several ships that had disappeared in the neighborhood that the mercantile community had come to look upon the passage of this part of the coast of Formosa as, in certain respects, the most hazardous in the Eastern seas. The ferocious character attributed to the inhabitants may be understood by the fact that they were usually designated " The Cannibals," although it was not known that the term had anything more than a figurative application. " It was used as a comprehensive description of a people who, bound together by the defensive and offensive ties of piracy and outlawry, regarded all strangers as their enemies; repelled the approaches of their nearest partially civilized neighbors, the Chinese; acknowledged the authority of only their own wild natures, and demonstrated their resolution to resist all influences from abroad by the unsparing and merciless destruction of the helpless sufferers who were forced from time to time to seek shelter at their hands."[1]

In 1858 the British government despatched the warship *Inflexible* to Formosa. The island was circumnavigated and a close search of the coast made in the hopes of discovering ship-wrecked foreigners; Mr. Swinhoe, who was later British consul, accompanied this expedition as interpreter. Prussia was the first state to take measures to punish the natives for their

1. " *The Japanese Expedition to Formosa* " by E. H. House.

misdeeds. In 1860, the transport *Elbe* of the Prussian expedition to East Asia visited the south of Formosa, and a small party of sailors was landed. Without any apparent provocation the savages immediately opened fire on them, and the party was obliged to return to the ship. The Prussian commander now ordered the savage village to be destroyed. Accordingly a small armed force was placed on shore, and although the savages were possessed of fire-arms and at first evidenced a determination to defend themselves, a few volleys from the new breach-loading rifles[1] of the Prussians were sufficient to send them scampering out of range, not, however, until several had been killed, including the chief.

Although English vessels, as well as those of Flensburg and Altona, and others, which were frequently off the Formosan coast, were occasionally molested by the savages, American ships were by far the greatest sufferers. The most atrocious case was probably that of the American bark *Rover*. This is memorable, not alone for the distressing circumstances connected with it, but also because it led to a condition of affairs which affected various countries more or less directly, and a certain connection can be traced between it and the decision reached by the Japanese government to despatch an expedition to Formosa a few years later.

On the 9th of March, 1867, the *Rover* departed from the Chinese port of Swatow for Newchwang in the north. On the way thither the ship encountered a severe gale, which drove her close to the south of Formosa, where she struck, it is supposed, upon the Vele Rete rocks. Badly damaged, the vessel soon sank, the captain, named Hunt, his wife, and the crew making their escape in boats. With some difficulty they reached a point on the south-eastern shore of the island, where they landed, but which unfortunately proved to be territory occupied by the Koalut tribe. Their presence was soon detected by the savages who, without one qualm of conscience, swept down upon the little unarmed party already weakened and exhausted, and brutally murdered every one of them except a single Chinese sailor, who had hidden himself on the first appearance of the assailants. This man, the sole survivor, was successful in escaping from the district, and later reached Takow, the western port, where he related the circumstances. Thence the information reached Taiwanfu, whence it was communicated by the British consul to his Minister in Peking, who conveyed it to Mr. Burlingame, the American Minister, and he at once occupied himself in devising measures of redress.

With chivalrous promptitude Captain Broad of the British navy, who was then stationed at Taiwanfu, at once started in the gunboat *Cormorant* to the scene of the slaughter, in hopes of succoring any survivors who might be found. On the 26th of March he reached the Koalut country and commenced his explorations. His errand of mercy was unsuccessful, however, being brought to a sudden close by an attack made on him by the savages. Not being prepared for a land engagement, he was obliged to withdraw to

---

1. It is interesting to note that this was the first use in actual warfare of the new "Zündnadel" rifle, which had at this period just been introduced by the Prussians, and the principle of which was later adopted by several other governments.

his ship with one of his men wounded. Having no other method of obtaining redress, Captain Broad shelled the savages and drove them out of the jungle where they were hidden. He then returned to Takow.

In the month of April, 1867, General C. W. Le Gendre, the United States consul at Amoy, endeavored by every practicable means to place himself in communication with the chiefs of the marauding tribes in hopes of obtaining from them promises of good behavior for the future, but the Koaluts exhibited much hostility and even refused to allow the consul to land. The Chinese officials on the western coast were then interviewed, but evidenced little interest in the outrage, and furthermore disclaimed any direct authority over the people of the savage districts, declaring their inability to interfere. The Peking government, however, after having been pressed by the American minister, who affirmed that China was responsible for the deeds of the Formosans, did express a willingness to inflict chastisement. After three months' delay and a good deal of red tapeism in Washington, orders were given to Admiral Bell to conduct an expedition into the savage territory and enforce attention to the demands of civilization. It is humiliating to an American to admit that after all the needless delay, which contrasts so unfavorably with the promptness of the English captain of the *Cormorant*, the expedition was a rank failure. Had any of the Americans survived the first attack, it was quite evident that the savages would have found ample time to dispose of them in three months, and it is greatly to be deplored that months should have been spent in official dilly-dallying when lives were to be saved. The expedition consisted of the two ships *Hartford* and *Wyoming*, and a force of one hundred and eighty-one officers, sailors, and marines, under command of Flag-Captain Belknap,[1] was landed on the 19th of June.

The Americans experienced immense difficulties in forcing a way through the thick jungle; the intense heat rendered it almost impossible to conduct operations in the middle of the day, and many of the party were attacked by sunstroke. The savages, who had taken up a position in the jungle behind rocks and other places invisible to the Americans, kept up a heavy fire whenever their foes appeared. Lieutenant-Commander A. S. McKenzie was shot dead while gallantly leading a charge up a hill, and finally, after a desperate engagement, the force was compelled to withdraw in some confusion to the ships, and soon departed from the island. Admiral Bell and others of the American officers stated in their reports on the expedition, that they were confident that the only effective method of rendering the region permanently safe would be to drive the aborigines from the shores and place the coast in possession of some powerful ally. The Chinese were urged to undertake that task, inasmuch as the island nominally belonged to them. But past events had already given proof, and more vivid evidence was forthcoming later, that the task was beyond both their inclination and their power.

After this ineffectual attempt to bring the Koaluts to reason, a second visit was made, in September, 1867, by General Le Gendre, in company with a considerable Chinese force.

---

1. Afterwards Admiral Belknap, in command of the U.S. China and Japan squadron.

The steamship *Volunteer*, in the Amoy viceroy's service, was placed at the disposal of the consul, and on the 4th of September, 1867, accompanied by a French gentleman, Mr. Joseph Bernare, he sailed for Formosa.

On arriving at Taiwanfu, the civil officers gave him a most flattering welcome. There had gathered to greet him the Taotai, the Chintai, or general commanding the forces of the island, and his second in command, all red buttons of the second grade, with the prefect and the sub-prefects. General Le Gendre immediately announced the object of his visit and informed the officials that he had come to witness in person all of the details of the expedition which the viceroy had promised should be despatched. The effect of this declaration was soon noticeable, " first in the faces, and then in the language, of the officials."

The expedition, which an hour before they had announced as ready to move at once, was, now that they found it was to be accompanied by one who would see that it was carried out, to be subject to countless delays ; besides, " there would be also danger to the person of the consul, and they could but decline such a responsibility." However, Le Gendre was not without experience of Chinese duplicity and was consequently not to be so easily balked. He insisted upon the immediate fulfilment of the promise, and informed the generals that he would relieve them of any responsibility for his personal safety. They were assured that he had not come to Taiwanfu merely to hear what they had to say ; but, without regard to fatigue, to judge for himself as to the measures taken to execute the orders of the viceroy. It was evident that the Chinese officials had hoped they might elude the order of their superior on the mainland, which was so onerous to the purse of the intendant, and that the difficulty could be removed by means of a comedy played at a distance and among themselves, without any troublesome witnesses, in which a few heads of savages sent to Foochow with great display would be an easy and less expensive denouement.

The chronicle of this adventurous trip of General Le Gendre to territory totally unknown, and not only surrounded by mystery, but at that time clouded with unusual gloom and terror, forms an interesting and valuable report. Not only does it describe well the savage districts through which he travelled, but it acquaints the reader with the difficulties encountered in holding intercourse with the Chinese mandarins. Its greatest interest, however, is in its uniqueness. A foreigner, unaided, negotiates a treaty of peace with the chief of a band of wild savages, head-hunters, and in a few short interviews converts them from blood-thirsty murderers seeking the life of shipwrecked mariners, into merciful servants, who, at least so far as the chief Tokitok and his immediate tribesmen were concerned, from that time forward gave shelter and assistance to the unfortunates cast upon their shores. Le Gendre was unable to negotiate with other tribes in the south, and Tokitok's authority, while supposed to exist, was in reality too weak to insure obedience to his wishes. The plucky American's expedition is described in his report to the United States minister at Peking, the important parts of which are herewith reproduced :—

" On the morning of the 10th we left Taiwanfu, occupying the center of the column. The prefect had most liberally provided transportation for myself, Mr. Bernare, the interpreter, and one or two servants, as well as for our luggage and provisions. Finally, an escort of honor of eight men preceded me, and were to remain with me during my stay in Formosa. Leaving Taiwanfu, we followed a very narrow road, yet practicable for chairs carried by skilled bearers. The second day we reached Pitou, (Pithau) a large town of 70,000 inhabitants. Here there was a review of the troops by General Lew. But there being no appearance of an advance, I called on the general for an explanation. His excuse was that on leaving Taiwanfu he had been furnished by the intendant with only the insufficient sum of $5,000. But he promised to make up the deficiency himself in case the other delayed much longer. He begged me to believe that he was most anxious to execute the orders of the viceroy, and s id that I should hold the intendant, and not him, responsible for any delay. Thus I had to note once more the wisdom of the viceroy in intrusting the command of the expedition to a man of such ability, and so ambitious of distinction. I believe that he thoroughly understood that day that the orders of the viceroy had to be executed under my eyes, and with all possible celerity. He agreed to leave in any event on the 14th.

"On the morning of the 14th, the intendant had not been heard from. We left, however, advancing towards Long Kong by a narrow road, crossing on our way four streams, on light bamboo rafts. Long Kong is a small port difficult of access, but secure for junks. The main products are sugar and rice. At this town Chinese authority practically ceases. Here, however, taxes are paid more or less regularly.

"We spent the night in a sugar mill, and left at daylight for Pangliau, which we reached the same night. Pangliau extends along the shore at the summit of an arc of a circle, forming a bay, and is, therefore, too open to be secure. The products are rice and peanuts. Women pound the rice and till the fields, while the men are entirely taken up with fishing. To the east, at a cannon shot from the sea, rise abruptly from the valley, high mountains, the exclusive domain of the savage aborigines, who receive from the Chinese (or half-caste) population a certain share of their crops, as a royalty for the lands they have rented to them forever. There for the first time we notice that none leave the village without being armed.

"We were still far from our destination and at the foot of the high hills occupied by the savages. There were no roads, but only hunters' paths, and these never yet traversed either by Chinese or Europeans. Nor, on account of the monsoon, was it practicable to reach the southern bay by sea, and we were, therefore, by force of circumstances condemned to a rest, the end of which no one could foresee. Fortunately, on the next day the general received 8,000 taels from the intendant, and he was most anxious to advance. I thought the circumstances favorable to hazard my advice, a thing which until then I had declined to do, being anxious to avoid taking any part in the management of the expedition. I intimated that it would not be impossible to cut a road over the mountains. We had to do it at intervals over a line some forty or fifty miles long, and, if there was no interference on the part of the aborigines with whom we were not at war, the work might be accomplished in four or five days. The general seized my idea at once, perceiving how he could thus be extricated from his difficult position. Moreover, the result of opening such a way would be to establish a connection between the northern and southern parts of the island. Such communication, prompt and sure, would withdraw the aborigines from their isolation and open the way for the establishment of Chinese rule over them. The Bootan (Botan) tribes, whose territory we were to pass through, made no opposition and the work commenced.

"A fortunate diversion in our monotonous stay at Pangliau occurred in the arrival of two young Englishmen, Messrs. Pickering and Holmes. The former I had met six months before during my visit in the United States steamship Ashuelot. Knowing him to be versed in the various dialects of the aborigines, I had begged him, in the name of humanity, to proceed to the south point, with a view to rescue if possible the Rover's crew, and he had promised to make the attempt. He had accompanied Admiral Bell in his expedition to the southern bay. They were now returning from the southern bay where they had gone for the purpose of recovering the remains of the lamented Mrs. Hunt, and of rescuing eight Bashee islanders who had been cast on the south-east shore and who, after losing two of their number by the hands of the savages, had been reduced to slavery. They had expended all their funds furnished by the British consul, Mr. Carrol, from the moneys appropriated to this humane object by his government ($250), and were reduced to their last resources. Having done the best I cou'd for the poor Bashees, I sent them to General Lew, who supplied them and gave them a guide to Takao (Takow). At my request he ordered the money advanced by Mr. Carrol to be refunded to him.

"As to Mr. Pickering, who had succeeded, both in the rescue of the Bashees and in recovering the remains of Mrs. Hunt, I did not hesitate to accept his kind offer to remain with me. From his knowledge of the island and people, he was enabled to render me valuable service.

"The road across the mountains being finished, we left Pangliau at noon on the 22nd. The same day, having crossed without opposition a high range of hills, we came to Chi-tong-kiau, a half-caste mixed village on the sea shore. We went again across another range, arriving at dark at Tong kau (Tang-kang), where we spent the night. We had gone half of our way without meeting other difficulties than such as arose from the nature of the localities. All concurred in predicting opposition from the savages on the next day, but nothing of the kind occurred, thanks probably to the care the general had taken to occupy the doubtful passes by detachments of his troops; and the same evening we reached Liang-kiau safely.

"Liang-kiau is situated at the far point of the curve forming the bay of that name. The port is not secure, for on the evening of our arrival we saw the wrecks of four junks. There are about 1,500 inhabitants, mostly engaged in the culture of peanuts, rice, sweet potatoes, a little sugar cane, and also in fishing; some, however, trade with the aborigines.

"To this place General Lew had sent an officer in advance, to prepare the population and explain the object of the expedition. Following the sea towards the south for one-half hour, Tautiau is reached. It is another small port where the Chinese authority is but little respected. There the anchorage for junks is excellent, at the mouth of a small river, and there in fact was the rendezvous of the flotilla, carrying the heavy artillery and munitions of our small corps of operations. On the left, in the plain near the mountains, at one hour from Tautiau, lies Poliac, a village settled by a race of Hakkas from Kwang-tung province, crossed with the aborigines. They consider themselves to be the subjects of Tooke-tok, (Tokitok) the chief of the eighteen tribes of the aborigines occupying the southern end of the island, as well as of the Emperor of China. Poliac is the entrepot of the aborigines. There they find gunpowder and shot; there are manufactured their guns, excellent arms, much superior to those used by the Chinese soldiers.

"Further yet, coming back to the sea, that is to say, to the right, at five hours' march from Tautiau and Poliac, and in the heart itself of the mountains, nearly at the center of the southern bay, may be found the half-caste village To-su-pong, where no Chinese ruler had ever penetrated. China ends there. The space bounded by a line going east and south from Poliac to the eastern and southern shore of the island is occupied by the Hwan tribes, eighteen in all, numbering 955 warriors and 1,300 women and children, and forming a confederation under Tooke-tok of the Telassok tribe. Among them the most prominent are Bootan, Hwan, Ca-che-li, Cu-su-coot, Pat-ye-ow, Cheu-a-kiak, Duk-se-ah, Ba-ah, Bomg-hoot, Sa-bo-ou, Pe-po, Kow-laug, Ling-miano, Koo-luts (Koa-luts.)

"General Lew had an excellent base of operations at Liang-kiau, having the sea on the right and holding the new line of communication with Tai-wan-fu. He had Tautiau in his hands; a few pieces of artillery and a small force enabled him to hold Poliac, and his army could advance by a good wide road in the direction of the point, and fall on the Koo-luts from the summit of their mountains, and drive them into the sea without possible escape. For this operation it is well that he did not require a large force of regulars; for of the 1,000 men promised, only 500 had been furnished, and these, although armed with good European rifles, were inadequate to the task before them. On my remarking this to the general, he informed me that he had enrolled 1,500 of the country militia, who had been trained in the school of adventure in their fights with the savages. I could not but fear that men called away at the time of the rice harvest would not have much ardor in their work. And there was the risk that when they came to action they might, after all, be better affected towards the savages, from whose friendship they could derive gain, than towards the Chinese authority, that could only make promises. Whatever might have been the case, it is certain that these considerations had an effect on future operations.

"Before reaching Liang-kiau, and while preparing for his advance, General Lew had issued a proclamation announcing the object of his mission, viz., the destruction of the Koo-luts for the murder of the crew of the American bark *Rover*, thus rectifying the first proclamation, in which the *Rover*, in consequence of written information received from Mr. Carrol, the British Consul at Takao, was qualified as a British bark. This proclamation, backed by the unprecedented military display, had deeply impressed the half-caste population, and the fact had also extended to the savages. So that the latter, doubtless in consequence of the terror inspired by the presence of the troops, and also being solicited thereto by their Chinese friends who feared the consequences of war, sent on the day of our arrival at Liang-kiau, a Chinese and half-caste deputation to convey the assurance of their regret and deep repentance for the murder of the *Rover's* crew, and to promise in their names that the like should never occur again, if the general would only agree to make peace. For this, the Chinese professed their willingness to become sureties. This disposition on their part having been announced to me by Mr. Pickering, previously to being communicated to me by Lew, I frankly said to him that I considered it quite in accordance with the generous policy of the United States to sacrifice a vain revenge (which might be hereafter used as a pretext for retaliation) to the incomparable advantage we would gain in securing ourselves against the recurrence of crimes such as we had come to punish; still, that I did not wish to force upon them a solution which might be contrary to their instructions, and consequently I would decline lending my hand to it, unless they were quite disposed to accept it. Having received the assurance that such was the case, after many prolonged interviews I demanded the following:

"First. I must see Tooke-tok and the chiefs of the eighteen tribes, in order to receive in person their regrets and assurance for the future.

"Second. The Chinese authorities must furnish me with the bond of the Chinese and half-castes from Liang-kiau to To-su-pong.

"Third. They must require of the savages the refunding of the expenses incurred by Mr. Pickering in recovering the body of Mrs. Hunt, and new efforts were to be made towards recovering any effects of Captain Hunt in the hands of the savages.

"Fourth. A fortified observatory must be erected at the southern bay, as a guarantee of Imperial protection at a place where it has hitherto been wanting.

"We agreed to act on this basis, and the delegates of the savages undertook to arrange the contemplated interview at Poliac within three days. Yet the day preceding the proposed interview with the chiefs, before taking the responsibility of promising to forgive and forget, I thought it prudent to obtain in writing from the viceroy's agents the acquiescence they had so willingly given verbally, and I wrote them a note to that effect, asking for a speedy reply. Ill-served, I doubt not, by my interpreter, who had agreed to hand the letter to the generals and explain it, I saw the day passing away, but no answer. Yet Tooke-tok, the eighteen chiefs, and a numerous escort had arrived the same evening at Poliac, and sent me word that I was expected on the morrow. On the other hand, the delay of the generals in answering my note caused me to suspect some evil design on their part, and made it my duty to be all the more cautious before passing my word to Tooke-tok. I, therefore, notified them that I would not meet Tooke-tok before receiving their answer, and such delay would probably ruin everything. It was in vain; they gave me many specious excuses, but no answer.

"The next morning I requested Mr. Pickering to see Tooke-tok and explain to him the reason I could not come. He found him in Poliac, attended by six hundred warriors. Yet the desired answer from the generals had not been received, and, the day advancing, Tooke-tok, unable to find proper quarters at Poliac, or perhaps suspecting treachery on the part of the Chinese, or else tired of waiting, concluded to leave. General Lew, who by that time had come to the conclusion to answer my note, was visibly troubled at the disappearance of Tooke-tok, and begged of me to let him arrange another interview with the chief. I consented, and three days afterwards was informed that Tooke-tok would meet us at the volcano, some four miles from the east coast of the island, i.e., in the midst of the savage territory. We left on the morning of the 10th of October, without other escort than Mr. Bernare, Mr. Pickering, three interpreters and one guide, and reached our destination at noon. I found Tooke-tok surrounded by a number of chiefs and some two hundred savages of both sexes. We sat on the ground without ceremony, in the center of the group. We were unarmed, they had their guns between their knees. All knew what had prevented me from meeting them before, so without preamble I began by asking what could have led them to murder our countrymen. Tooke-tok hastened to reply that a long time ago white people had all but exterminated the Koolut tribe, leaving only three who survived, to hand down to their posterity the desire for revenge. Having no ships to pursue foreigners they had taken their revenge as best they could. I observed that in this way many innocent victims must have been killed. 'I know it' said he, 'and am an enemy to the practice, and, therefore, sought to join you at Poliac to express my regrets.' I then asked him what he intended doing in the future. His answer was 'If you come to make war, we shall resist you, of course, and I cannot answer for the consequences; if on the contrary, you desire peace, it shall be so forever.' I told him I had come as a friend, and on hearing it he put his gun aside.

"I added that we were not unwilling to forget the past, but that in the future, far from murdering the unfortunate castaways, he should promise to care for them and hand them over to the Chinese at Liang-kiau. He promised to do so. I added that in case a crew was sent ashore for water, or anything else, they should not be molested. This point he agreed to, and we settled upon a red flag (at the chief's request) as a sign through which ships would make known to him or his tribes a desire to land a party for friendly purposes, under the contract we had entered into that day.

"I then hazarded the question of the fort. I wished it to be erected at the center of the bay, where the unfortunate Lieutenant McKenzie met his fate. But Tooke-tok refused; it would bring misfortune on his tribe. 'Every one in his own place,' said he; 'if you place Chinese in our midst, their bad faith will cause our people to rise in anger. Build your fort among the half-castes; they will not object to it, and it will satisfy us.' I assented to this request, when, rising, he addressed me, saying: "We have said enough, let us depart, and not spoil such a friendly interview by words that would make us enemies." All my efforts to retain him failed. The interview lasted three quarters of an hour.

"Tooke-tok is a man of fifty; his address is easy and his language most harmonious; his physiognomy is sympathetic, showing great strength of mind and indomitable energy; he is of sanguine temperament, not of a high stature, even small, but square shouldered and well built; his hair, which is grey, is shaved on the fore part of his head, in Chinese fashion, and he wears a small queue twelve or fifteen inches long. But his costume is peculiar to his race, and distinct in all respects from the Chinese.

"The same day, instead of returning to Liang-kiau, we went to the left, across the territory of the savages and of the Ling-hwan, directing our steps to the southwest part of the island, called To-su-pong, where I decided to locate the fort. This location is on a promontory, one mile distant from a small half-caste village also called To-su-pong. From it can be seen every part of the bay; we could distinctly see the roads followed by the expedition of Admiral Bell, and boldly projecting was the fatal rock, a gloomy mass of trachyte, near which fell McKenzie. Full of thought about this painful spot, we set out to return to Liang-kiau, to hurry on the erection of the fort and the writing of the bond to be given by the Chinese and half-caste population.

"The establishment of a fort had often been the object of a serious controversy between General Lew and myself; not that he would systematically oppose it; he had, on the contrary, acknowledged its advantages to the Chinese; but because of an obscure point in the viceroy's instructions he did not feel authorized to erect it before he conferred with the Foochow or Peking authorities. I could scarcely subordinate my departure to such delay, and yet I wanted the fort. I wanted it because of its asserting the Chinese authority where it had so long been denied; for I considered that it would command respect from the Kooluts in case they should happen to lose sight of their promises; finally, and chiefly, because it would become a secure refuge for the too numerous victims of these stormy seas. In short, I insisted, and we agreed at last that a temporary fort should be erected at a point selected by me, and that in it they should place two guns, a small force of regulars, and one hundred militia. This provisional arrangement was to be converted into a more permanent one, as soon as the more explicit orders that I was asked to solicit should reach Taiwanfu. I declared myself satisfied; for I did not imagine that the viceroy would break his word with me; and should he, I could then appeal with confidence to the instructions of your excellency.

"I must here render full justice to the loyalty of the general. In two days he had erected a circular enclosure, formed of trunks of palm trees and sand bags, which I visited in company with the generals. I did not exactly see one hundred men in the fort, but I concluded to shut my eyes to this deficiency. As a compensation, doubtless, there were three guns instead of only two, as promised. Over it the Chinese flag waves.

"We were about coming to the conclusion. The general had handed me a spy glass and nautical instruments belonging to the *Rover.* I had the body of Mrs. Hunt, as Mr. Pickering had left to bear to Tooke-tok a red flag I sent him. I had only to consign to a regular writing with the Chinese authorities the results of the expedition. These documents established a joint responsibility in this humane duty between the savages and the Chinese from Liang-kiau Bay to the fort of To-su-pong. It is the morale of the whole expedition.

"This brings us down to the 15th of October. I then thought of returning. I did not then know to how many annoyances (not to say humiliations) I should be subjected during this closing part of my mission. The steamship *Volunteer,* from the time I had left with the two generals, had gone to Takao. Later, when I saw we were really on our way to the south, I requested (by letter) the officer commanding to proceed to Liang-kiau. The answer was that the viceroy had ordered the steamer to remain at Takao; but on the 11th of October I received a despatch to the effect that he had waited long enough, and that I must fix the day of my return to Amoy. I did not answer the communication, but on the morning of the 16th, I sent my interpreter to Takao to say to him that my mission in Formosa having come to a close, I wished him to proceed to Tan-tiau and save me, after a hard trip of nearly two months, the fatigue of a long journey to Takao; and I said that I would take upon myself all responsibility.

"I remained four days in To-su-pong after the withdrawal of the Chinese troops. On the 20th, the British gunboat *Banterer* arrived, on her way back to Amoy from the Bashee Islands. I met the commanding officer and the British consul at Takao on the beach. At their request, I furnished them with the main points of my mission, and its results. I refused their kind offer of a passage to Takao, and returned to Liang-kiau. There I found Mr. Pickering just returned from a visit to Tooke-tok, from whom he had received a most cordial reception. The Chinese had not been so fortunate. They had sent a deputation to him to secure for their countrymen the protection promised to foreigners. The chief answered that he had done nothing, and would do nothing with the Chinese officials. The deputies insisted, stating that the chief was merely to treat of matters of mutual importance. Said Tooke-tok, 'If it is simply to talk I can send my daughters,' and at once he begged Mr. Pickering to escort them to Liang-kiau, begging him to see them safe back to their friends at Poliac. Those two girls appeared without fear before the Chinese officials. Refusing to kneel before them, they boldly said that their father had treated with the foreigners because he respected their courage. He had seen them fearlessly ascending the mountains under fire (alluding to the bold charge under Lieutenant McKenzie); they had met him on his own territory to treat of peace, and their intentions were clear; but it was different with the Chinese officers, and he desired to have nothing to do with them. Having delivered this message, they refused to say more and returned to Poliac with Mr. Pickering. Trifling as it may seem, this circumstance, together with the intrigues of the interpreter, had a great deal to do with General Lew's change of manner towards us. We had given him no cause whatever for irritation.

"On the morning of the 21st we made our parting visits to the generals, which they returned the next day. In the afternoon we received a note from the interpreter, stating that he had failed to induce the officer to bring the *Volunteer* to Liang-kiau, and that we must be at Takao on the 25th, the day fixed for his departure.

"We could not well leave the same evening by land, the general having but two chairs for us. We concluded to go by sea in a junk offered us by him. The wind was fair, yet we made no progress, as we kept continually tacking about, and in the morning we returned to Tan-tiau. It was with great difficulty we could obtain even two chairs, so that there was no conveyance for Mr. Pickering and our servants. Then, as we could not return with the army, we needed an escort. Mr. Bernare, who saw Lew on this occasion, was instructed to accept without discussion any transportation that might be offered. But when he heard that the military escort was refused, he observed to the general that I was suffering from an old wound in the eye and could not be troubled by these dispositions, so different from my expectations. His answer was, he regretted it, but it was all he could do. Having directed Mr. Pickering to proceed on foot and detain the *Volunteer* until our arrival, I started with the generals the next day. We advanced rapidly, and at noon were at Longkong, where we received no hospitality. At 3 p.m. we were at Chi-tong-kiau, and could have reached Pang-liau the same evening. Suddenly our coolies halted, leaving us in the middle of the street, and disappeared. Having waited an hour, we were informed by one of our servants that the general intended to stay there that night. I sent Mr. Bernare to him, who was told that the coolies were tired and that he could not force them to go on. In vain did Mr. Bernare observe that the coolies would go on if the Chinese authorities would only permit them to do so. We were at their mercy.

"Fortunately we found a small junk loaded with wood. I hired it, paying partly in advance, but we had to wait an hour while she was unloading. While this was going on, we noticed an officer in disguise ordering the owner of the junk not to take us. The man hesitated; but having received from me the promise of protection, he concluded to take us on. The next day at 11 a.m. we were at Long-kong, and the wind having changed, we went ashore and made our way on foot to Takao, where we arrived in the middle of the night.

"On the 25th, as we had been notified, we were on board the *Volunteer.* But now that we were on board, the commander refused to leave, and I had to give him a peremptory order to start the next morning. During the day Mr. Carrol sent me a note stating that he was expecting important despatches from Taiwanfu, and had requested the *Volunteer* to be delayed one day, believing that I would have no objection. I called on him to say that I was, to my great regret, compelled to leave at once.

"Having left at last with a favorable wind, suddenly, without a word of warning, we put back to Taiwanfu. What could I say or do but submit? The next morning the wind had fallen, the sea was as a lake, yet we remained at anchor. At length we set out, but only in a short time to put in at the

Pescadores. In short, having left Takao on the morning of the 26th, we reached Amoy at 5 p.m. of the 30th. Two months before we had made the trip in 18 hours.

"Before closing this, I beg to be allowed to mention here the names of two gentlemen of high social standing, who, without possible hope of reward, have not hesitated to freely lend me their aid in the accomplishment of a mission which has proved laborious to me, while for them it has been full of danger and privation. They are Mr. Joseph Bernare, of Canton, and Mr. Pickering, of Taiwanfu. Mr. Pickering was by the side of Lieutenant McKenzie when shot by the savages on the 7th of June last.

"I have the honor to be, sir, very truly, your obedient servant,

CHAS. W. LE GENDRE,
United States Consul.

His Excellency Anson Burlingame,
United States Minister at Peking."

For a period of several years following the visit of General Le Gendre, the better disposed of the savage population proved their sincerity by extending a helping hand to foreign castaways and reporting their presence to the nearest Chinese station. But after all, the territory which Tokitok controlled was of very uncertain extent, and while he kept his own immediate tribesmen in order, he frequently found difficulty in curbing the savage spirit which existed among his neighbors. In fact, it was no unusual thing for many of the eighteen tribes to deny his assumed right entirely, when it is so pleased them, and some of them, especially the Botans, withdrew themselves altogether from the confederation and refused to recognize the authority of any chief but their own.

Many outrages committed by other savages living further north brought misery to the crew of several foreign ships, while the Chinese still looked on with indifference, not heeding the calls for redress made by the foreign authorities.

CHAPTER X.

THE JAPANESE EXPEDITION OF 1874.

*Slaughter of Loochooans—Commission to Japan—Claims on China—The expedition
decided upon—Secret preparations—Expedition organized—American assistants
—Unexpected interference of Mr. Bingham—Sailing of first transport " Yuko
Maru "—Opposition of representatives—Arrival of transport at Amoy—New
obstacles—Opinions of United States officials—The transport anchored off
Formosa—Liangkiau bay—Interview with native villagers—An inspecting
party lands—General aspect of locality—Appearance of natives—Chewing of
betel nut—A native banquet—The village of Sialiao—Native homes—Landing
of troops and stores—Deficiencies of military system—Camp established
—Native laborers—Impracticable workers—Difficulties with the natives—
H.B.M.'s S. " Hornet."*

MR. E. H. HOUSE accompanied the Japanese expedition as war
correspondent for the New York *Herald*. On his return to Japan he drew
up a complete and careful account, not only of the incidents of the expedition occurring in Formosa, but of the diplomatic transactions which
passed between the governments of Japan and China as a result of it. I
have examined other reports, but as the information they contained was
also included in the former work, I have, with the kind permission of the
author, Mr. House, constructed from his narrative the following chapters
relating to the " First Formosa Expedition."

A large fishing and trading vessel belonging to one of the islands of
the Miyako group of the Loochoos was wrecked on the southern coast of
Formosa in the month of December, 1871. The disaster occurring in
proximity to the territory of the Botan tribe of savages, fifty-four of the
crew were murdered. A few survivors were eventually able to return to
their homes, and through them the news of the crime was made known to
the highest authorities with whom they were acquainted.

The Loochooans are a mild and quiet people, and as their previous relations with other lands had been of the most peaceful nature, the unexpected
attack caused quite a panic among them. Since the early part of the seventeenth century, the islanders had been subjects of the daimyo of Satsuma,
and it was not unnatural that the Loochooan officials should now apply to

Japan for relief. But great were the changes then taking place in the empire, for the whole political system was under revision. Since the once powerful Satsuma was now bereft of authority, they proposed to send a commission directly to Tokyo, not only to press the demand for protection, but also to settle other no less important questions which the restoration had brought forth.

In the summer of 1872 the commission was sent, and on its arrival in Japan met with a warm welcome. The request and claims were satisfactorily arranged, and it was agreed that Japan should undertake to afford full and sufficient protection to the inhabitants of Loochoo and all its dependencies. It was agreed further that their territory was henceforth to be considered as belonging properly to the Japanese Empire.

It now behoved the Japanese to take prompt action regarding the atrocities committed by the Formosans. As the Chinese held sway over the western part of the island, there was ground for the belief that they would also claim jurisdiction over the wild tribes who inhabited the eastern and southern districts. But when the matter was placed before the Peking authorities, the Japanese were given to understand plainly that the Chinese government would in no way assume responsibility for depredations committed beyond the boundaries occupied by their own people. They were consequently not disposed to inflict punishment for past offences, nor would they agree to prevent them in the future. On receiving this reply, the Japanese decided to take the matter into their own hands, and preparations for an expedition against the savages were accordingly commenced.

The plans and organization were carefully concealed by the government, chiefly to avoid such criticism and unasked for counsel from the representatives of foreign governments as might tend to embarrass their efforts ; for at that day foreign officials seemed to look upon Japan as their ward, and as dependent upon them for instructions, thus oftimes harassing and hampering the Japanese in their most praiseworthy efforts. As the expedition was one which would benefit not only Japan, but also the whole maritime world, no doubt was felt but that it would be in time universally commended. Its success meant alleviation from the attacks which had given the southern coast of Formosa a name for atrocity and depredation without a parallel in the Orient.

General Le Gendre, who was considered the best authority on affairs relating to the savage territory of Formosa, was secured to act as adviser, and as it was decided to engage other Americans for certain responsible positions, Lieutenant Commander Douglas Cassel, of the United States Navy, was offered the rank of Commodore in the Japanese service, and Lieutenant James R. Wasson, formerly of the United States Engineers, was appointed a colonel in the Japanese army.

The expedition was now organized with Okuma Shigenobu, of the Imperial Council, as chief commander, General Le Gendre as his associate, General Saigo of the War Department, as commissioner and commander of the forces, and Lieutenant Commander Cassel, United States Navy, and Lieutenant Wasson, United States Engineers, as foreign assistants.

The Japanese, not having a sufficient number of vessels for the conveyance of troops and munitions of war, secured others, among them the British steamship *Yorkshire*, and the Pacific Mail steamship *New York*, the size of the latter making her of the greatest importance, not only to the convenience of the Japanese, but even to the success of the expedition. That she might not be permitted to fulfill her contract was a question that no one thought of for a moment. Mr. Bingham, the American minister, was evidently friendly, for from the first day of his arrival in Japan, he had shown his regard for the Japanese, and was, moreover, well known for his views that Japan should have the right of independent action, unmolested by foreign interference of any description.

The sailing of the first ships of the expedition from Shinagawa, during the second week in April, 1874, gave rise to numerous rumors, which, circulating in Yokohama, caused no little excitement. On this occasion, the majority of the foreign residents and the press of the city were not backward in attacking the government, and much misrepresentation and fiction was put forth. Then came an unlooked-for difficulty. The American minister had been early informed of the plans of the expedition and apparently concurred in them, but to the great surprise of all and to the consternation of those interested, he now came forward with a protest against the employment of any Americans, except on condition that Japan should first obtain the written consent of China to the expedition. He had also sent secret orders to the agent of the Pacific Mail Steamship Company to delay or altogether prevent the departure of the *New York*. This last impediment was indeed a real calamity, for at that late day the loss could not be replaced; and, to make matters worse, the agent had been instructed to give no clue to the reasons for thus breaking his contract; hence the mystery in which the whole affair was shrouded left the officials no means to discover whether it was intended to prevent the voyage entirely, or only to check it for a while.

Fortunately the officials were not to be turned from their earnest convictions, and the Americans associated with them were agreed that nothing less than the most peremptory orders from their government would induce them to withdraw.

The loss to the Japanese of the *New York* necessitated the chartering of a small steamer totally inadequate for the work intended, but the best that could be secured. The troops were crowded aboard this craft already overloaded with stores, and it is certain that the safe arrival of the vessel at Amoy was due only to the very favorable weather with which their journey was blessed. After the departure of this vessel, all haste was made in securing other transports. The foreign representatives and the Yokohama press were most active in trying to persuade the world that Japan, in sending an expedition to punish the savages, was committing an act of war against China, and it was thought best, under these circumstances, for General Le Gendre to abandon his purpose of accompanying the mission, and to return to Tokyo and use his efforts in counteracting these injurious impressions.

A week after her departure from Nagasaki, on the 3rd of May, the

Yuko Maru duly arrived at Amoy, where it was found that outside diplo-matic influence had again thrown grave obstacles in the way of the expedi-tion. In compliance with the instructions of his consul, the English agent of the Japanese there, Mr. P. Manson, had abandoned them, while a pilot named Patterson, who had expressed a desire to act as pilot and interpreter to the expedition, had also been warned by the consul that if he joined the party he would get two years' imprisonment. It was freely asserted by a portion of the community that Japan was in the act of waging war against China, and efforts were made to annoy all persons connected with the expedition—the Americans alone lending their approval to the course taken by the Japanese.

The officers of the United States steamship *Monocacy* were, of course, familiar with what Americans had undergone at the hands of the Formosan aborigines, and their sympathies were unconcealed. Owing to the hostility met with in the settlement, the original intention of obtaining horses and cattle at Amoy was relinquished, some flat-bottomed shallow Chinese boats wherewith to effect a landing in Formosa were purchased, and a Chinaman, the proud possessor of the adopted name of Johnson—a naturalized Ame-rican citizen of high intelligence and with good knowledge of Formosan ways and customs—was secured as interpreter. On the 5th of August, two days after her arrival there, the transport left Amoy on the last stage of her journey. The Formosa strait was crossed in the night, and at nine o'clock the next evening the ship was anchored in Liangkiau Bay.

Liangkiau Bay, which had been selected as a landing place, is a mere indentation in the coast entirely open to the west and north winds. It is situated in latitude 22° 6' N. and longitude 120° 42' W. Two small rivers empty into the bay. For a few miles the shore line is low and sandy, but rises in lofty bluffs to the north and south. Even near the coast the ground is extremely irregular, and the whole valley, which is of limited extent, is closely encircled by mountains some thousands of feet in height.

It was the earnest intention of Japan, and strict orders to this effect had been issued, to settle the difficulty by peaceful methods if possible, and to use arms only as a last resort. In accordance with this purpose, the interpreter, Johnson, was sent ashore to seek certain natives of some standing in the district and induce them to come on board the ship for a conference. He was successful, and returned with the sons and near relatives of the "headman" of the village of Sialiao, who had served General Le Gendre as guides upon the occasion of his visit in 1872. Lieut.-Commander Cassel received them at once and had a most interesting conversation with one Miya, the oldest of their number.

The information to be conveyed to these men had been preconcerted in Tokyo, and was imparted as follows:

They were told that the government of Japan had determined to send an expedition to aboriginal Formosa, to punish the Botans for the murder of Japanese subjects in December, 1871; that the sovereign of that empire was at first greatly incensed with the people of the Liangkiau valley for not having undertaken to chastise the offenders in the same

Commander-in-chief Saigo and his staff. (1874).

Tokitok. Isa.
S.Midzuno. (Marquis) Saigo.

Savage visitors at Commander-in-chief Saigo's headquarters. (1874).

manner as, in conformity with the agreement entered into with the United States consul in 1867, they would have dealt with them if they had molested Americans; that later investigations had shown that the Sialiao people had really not been indifferent to the fate of the shipwrecked Loochooans, but had aided General Le Gendre in his inquiries concerning their fate, in return for which orders had been given to protect them from all annoyances that they might apprehend in consequence of the presence of a foreign force; that twenty thousand soldiers were ready to start for Formosa at the shortest notice, should they ever be needed, but that, if trustworthy assurance of the co-operation of the Sialiao communities and the tribes of Tokitok could be obtained, only the advance body, a few thousand in number, would be brought. The native deputation, through Miya, promptly answered that they were ready to afford all the assistance in their power, and to give the troops every facility for landing and encamping; though they could not speak for the savage tribes, in regard to which they had no new intelligence to give, except that of the recent death of Tokitok and the succession of his eldest son. These subjects having been disposed of for the moment, an offer was made to engage the services of Miya and one of his companions, as a medium of communication between the Japanese and their own people at the outset, and, subsequently, the inhabitants of Southern Formosa in general. The proposal was readily accepted, and the interview terminated as satisfactorily as could be desired.

Before returning to the shore, Miya and his companions were informed that the Japanese officials intended landing, for the purpose of picking out a suitable place for establishing an encampment for the arriving force, which was expected to number about three thousand men.

The next morning a few of the higher Japanese officials, with the American attachés, went on shore with this purpose in view. It had not been the intention to land on any territory over which the Chinese claimed jurisdiction, if objections should be made by the proper authorities, and Lieut.-Commander Cassel had received orders from Tokyo, in case such objection were offered, to abandon the position and proceed to a point some distance further south. Here again, if after inquiry he met with a similar result, he was again to seek a more southern point. But at the last spot designated, which would be outside of Chinese jurisdiction, he was ordered to effect a landing in spite of resistance and by the use of such force as might be necessary. Fortunately, however, the little party met with no opposition, the plans were carried out, and the landing was effected at the point first indicated.

That a favorable view of the surrounding territory might be secured and a suitable camping ground thus be selected, they ascended a small hill some three hundred feet in height, located near the shore. The pathway ran through fields of barley and sweet potatoes, and in approaching the hill two or three small hamlets were touched. The best of the dwellings to be seen were mud huts with coarsely-thatched roofs. Sage brush, clusters of low palm-trees and of the pandanus, so thick as to form an almost impassable jungle, were scattered about the surrounding plain, which, with the exception of a few roughly-cultivated tracts, seemed sterile and sandy.

The winding footpath twining its way through tangled jungle afforded a superb position for ambuscades, which would prove unapproachable for any force not perfectly familiar with the country. Warfare in accordance with the methods usually at the command of modern invading armies could scarcely be successful. The passage on the hill side was annoying and wearisome. The path was narrow and abrupt, through irregular gullies and over sharp and broken masses of coralloid rock, and the heat was excessive. From the top of the hill, the entire Sialiao, or Liangkiau valley, which appeared to be about fifteen square miles in extent, was visible. It was surrounded by a range of mountains averaging perhaps two thousand feet in height.

The dress of the natives is described as being similar to that worn by the Amoy Chinese—the better classes wearing a loose jacket and wide breeches reaching a little below the knee, while about their heads light turbans were twisted. Their only ornaments were red cords wound about their long queues, with here and there a bright coin braided in, and rude silver bracelets about the wrists. The costume of the lower classes shrank to a mere waist and loin-cloth of the most abbreviated form consistent with decency. The women were clad almost identically like the "head men," and nearly all of them wore on each wrist a silver bracelet. Their hair was braided into long tails and wound about with white cords. In some cases it received additional adornment by the insertion of artificial flowers. Occasionally heavy gold rings and glittering trinkets were added to the person.

Children were plentiful, apparently "too numerous for the supply of raiment on hand," for the majority of them were naked. Few of the women were naturally disagreeable in appearance, and would have been pleasing but for the disgusting dribble of betel-nut juice constantly disfiguring their countenances.

While the natives of neither sex were specially talkative, their mouths were always active, the chewing of the betel-nut furnishing occupation. "Their cheeks were distended, to an extent which the most inordinate chewer of tobacco could not rival, by masses of red pulp, from which streams of stained saliva overflowed the gums, discoloring the whole interior of the mouth with an unwholesome pinkish hue. The nuts were sometimes so large as to protrude between the teeth, producing an effect half ghastly, half grotesque, and shedding ruddy rivulets upon the cheeks and chin." All in all, men, women, and children had a sort of openness of countenance and independence of bearing, which was doubtless attributable to their freedom from oppressive authority and their self-reliant habits of life.

The settlement of Sialiao consisted of about a dozen houses, the outward appearance of which was far superior to what one would expect to find in such a place. Of one story, they were neatly built of fine red brick and cemented stone. The roofs were of compact tiles and the spaces underneath the eaves were decorated with simple bas-reliefs. The interiors were substantial and tolerably clean, in fact, in every way superior to the quarters of the Chinese in the coast cities.   They were generally double, two structures of equal size, perhaps twenty-five feet square, standing one behind the other, partially separated by a courtyard of nearly the same dimensions.   On each side of this courtyard were narrow passages connecting the two buildings, while in the rear were outhouses for cooking, etc.   The floors of most of the main buildings, and of the yards, were paved with large square bricks or stones. There were arm chairs that would not discredit a New England farm house. Tables were abundant, but less elaborate in form and ornamentation.   The beds were like shelves set in recesses of the wall, although occasionally one was seen of stately build.   While the political authority of China was not in any way recognized in these villages, its influence prevailed in many ways, notably in the rude attempts at Chinese art to be found in the panels in the walls.   Most prominent of all the interior display was the stand of weapons to be found in every household.   Old matchlock muskets in the usual condition of such instruments, short swords in queer wooden scabbards, which were so constructed as to cover only one side of the blade, the other lying exposed ; bows and iron-pointed arrows, and variously fashioned spears and lances.   Pigs and chickens occupied the enclosed spaces about the houses in great numbers, while the streets were in possession of droves of water buffaloes, drab-colored beasts with large retreating horns, the points of which were usually carried on a line with their noses.   These beasts are most useful to the natives, who employ them as draught animals.

The landing of the troops commenced at once and in a rather disorderly manner.   The Japanese at this time had adopted in part the foreign military system, and the result was great confusion in many matters which we consider essential to success in arms.   The old idea seemed to prevail to a considerable extent, that the soldier belongs to a superior class and should not be subjected to menial labors, even when it came to work in the field. Consequently, a hundred soldiers might be seen accompanied by an equal number of coolies to do the work of building shelters, cooking, and a good part of the digging of trenches.

The manual of arms, tactics, and manœuvring seems to have been about all of the foreign system adopted.   The commissariat, the quarter-master's department, in fact all branches of transportation, were conducted in accordance with the old Japanese system.

Fortunately, the natives in the vicinity of the point selected for landing, if not friendly, were at least not positively hostile, and the landing was consequently a mere matter of transfer.   The confusion and carelessness, the numerous awkward incidents of the disembarkation, would have placed them at the mercy of the natives on shore, and no doubt have resulted in a repulse at the outset, had the natives developed into an enemy and opposed the Japanese, as the " Hartford " expedition had been opposed before them.

The camp was fixed in a little plain lying between two rivers, and it was the original intention to defend the inland extremity by an elaborate entrenchment.   The sides which were partially protected by the streams were to be strengthened by other earthworks reaching to the sea.   The entire space thus marked for enclosure was a little over forty acres.   It included a considerable stretch of sandy beach, and a poorly-cultivated field of sweet potatoes, which latter seemed to be the sole agricultural achievement of a wretched little village of a dozen mud hovels, which also lay within the camp ground. The piece of land in question was occupied with the clear consent of the owner, who agreed to turn it over temporarily for a reasonable consideration. The tents were pitched about noon and a line of sentries established. Although the marines commenced their duties with willing activity, the work of trench-digging was seemingly distasteful, and as the number of troops was really too small to accomplish much in this direction, it was decided to engage all the natives who wished to work, at the rate of thirty cents per day. To the Western reader that sum will appear small indeed, but to the Liangkiau resident it was an amount magnificent and totally unprecedented. Furthermore, notice was given to the visiting headmen who came to assure the Japanese of their good will, that as many of their people as they chose to send would be employed on the same terms. About one hundred applied at once and were set to work.

Now that the camp was established, the soldiers found themselves surrounded by few of the comforts that they had been formerly accustomed to. The heat was extreme and of that enfeebling quality which most rapidly breeds disease, while the wind brought but little relief. On the evening of the second day, the light of an enormous fire burning at a distance, apparently five or six miles to the south of Liangkiau, attracted the attention of all. For an hour or so it blazed up quite rapidly and then faded as quickly away. It was thought by many to be a signal of warning among the savage tribes. It was later found to have been their work, but the object was to clear away the trees and shrubbery from the possible approaches which could not be barricaded, and would now expose an advancing party to an unobstructed fire from the sheltered hill tops.

About four hundred natives came in the next morning and applied for employment. A motley crowd they were, not half of them capable of doing effective work. About one third were women, some with infants strapped to their backs. At least a quarter of the remainder were too old and infirm for any kind of toil, and in one case a blind man was actually seen with a useless pickaxe in his hands, led about by a child and encumbering the progress of the work whenever he attempted to take part in it. The Japanese officers were not inclined to discriminate and all were set to the task. After two hours in which these allies kept fairly busy, they withdrew for "chow" and rest. From then on, nothing was heard from them until two in the afternoon when they returned to send in a message to the effect that, according to their ideas of wage and labor, thirty cents a day was insufficient. Very little more work was attempted, and even that came to a complete standstill at five o'clock, when a general cry for payment arose. Then followed a scene of indescribable confusion, wild cries, and insane gesticulations from the natives, met by the vain efforts of the Japanese to explain matters and pacify their new friends. In their determination to get more, the fact that they had agreed to work for thirty cents a day had nothing to do with the case. The clamor and excitement lasted for quite an hour, and the bald-headed agitator of the day before seemed to be the prime leader in the tumult.

Eventually the Japanese came to the conclusion that it was useless to hope for any practical assistance from these people, and, though not half a day's work had been done, those who had worked or pretended to work were called together and given their full day's wage. Our author expresses himself "surprised at the complete calmness of the Japanese in dealing with them, the indifference they showed to the frequent menaces, and their obvious determination not be roused to irritation by any display of violence."

A day or so later, the "excitables" of the surrounding villages sent an embassy to deliver the message that, after a solemn conference, they wished to announce that fifty cents a day would be the least accepted for a day's work by the people of Liangkiau. Johnson, the interpreter, explained "that the prodigality of many of the subordinate officers in their various transactions, had given rise to the most extravagant and insatiable expectations."

Evidence of this was soon forthcoming. The owner of the potato patch, the reader will remember, had agreed to turn it over to the Japanese for a reasonable compensation. He now sent word that his interpretation of a reasonable compensation was four thousand dollars, a sum the like of which had probably never been seen or heard of throughout the whole valley. The occupants of some of the mud huts in the village had agreed to rent them for a reasonable sum. They likewise now informed the Japanese that six hundred dollars was their price. There was some delay in the transmission of their message, which came near leading to an undesired conflict. The houses were to be occupied as storehouses, and coolies had been notified to proceed to them with the luggage. Upon arriving at the village, they were met by the inhabitants, who had armed themselves with spears and swords, which they brandished about the unsuspecting coolies, driving them out of the single village street and afterwards barricading it against all comers. On going to the spot the officers found the natives formed in battle array, some with guns in their hands, saucy, defiant, and overflowing with mock heroics. They were quieted, if not satisfied, however, on being assured by the Japanese that their property should not be molested and the previous bargain would be considered null and void. The field laborers were also notified that their services would be dispensed with, whereupon they joined in the general disturbance and bore themselves as though fresh insults had been heaped upon them. This necessitated the abandonment of all work on the fortifications, the number of soldiers being barely sufficient for a safe camp guard, while the services of all the coolies were required in moving the supplies and similar duties.

While the construction of the camp was in progress, the *Hornet*, a British gunboat, steamed into the bay, and a party of officers landed to take observations.

Accompanying them was H.B.M.'s consul for Formosa, who came to gather information regarding the course of events in the south. The *Hornet* remained over night and sailed the next morning.

CHAPTER XI.

THE JAPANESE EXPEDITION, MAY, 1874.

Suspicions aroused—Arrival of army and nary officers—New camp selected—New difficulties with the natives—Unauthorized tours of exploration—Conference with savage chief—Appearance of aborigines—Friendly relations established—Confidence in General Le Gendre—A feast prepared—Presentation of gifts—Straggling and the penalty—Satsuma soldier decapitated—Boat's crew of frigate "Nishin" attacked—Violent storm—Assault on reconnoitring party—Another unauthorized excursion—Japanese force attacks—Futile pursuit of the savages—First regular engagement—Skirmish of the Stone Gate—Six Japanese and sixteen aborigines killed—Arrival of General Saigo—Fresh stores and reinforcements—Visit of two Chinese men-of-war—A friendly mission—Letter from viceroy of Fokien — Announcement of Chinese claim to savage territory—National salutations—Unjust accusations in Japan—Protest of Mr. Bingham—Okuma, followed by Okubo, investigates in Formosa—Incidents of encounters—Questionable discipline—A warlike interpreter—Second conference with Isa and other chiefs.

REPORTS were brought to headquarters on the morning of the 9th (May) that the plain in every direction had been traversed by little bands of armed hillmen who made no concealment of their hostility. That there was no general good feeling to be depended upon in any part of the country was evident. Even the inhabitants of the valley a short distance from camp looked daggers whenever any of the expedition passed by. Their suspicions were thoroughly aroused, and this was not strange considering their point of view. All the efforts of the Japanese to put them at ease had from the first resulted in failure.

On the 10th of May the forces were increased by the arrival of Admiral Akamatsu, the senior naval officer of the expedition, and General Tani, the next in military rank to General Saigo. These gentlemen were now the officers of highest rank in the expedition, Generals Saigo and Le Gendre being still detained in Japan, owing to the confusion caused by the various obstructions previously described. A large transport, which arrived soon after, brought two hundred soldiers, a fresh force of laborers, and abundant supplies, while a third transport on the 16th brought additional troops and stores. Lumber having arrived, the laborers were soon at work erecting " shanties," which being tied together without injury to the wood itself, could be torn down at will and used for other purposes, if necessary.

The heat by day was excessive, though the nights were cool. Already prostration and illness from these changes in temperature were felt among the men. As the old camp was in danger of being flooded if heavy rains should fall, a new camping place was, on the 11th, selected upon a hillside which rose from a small inlet just below the point forming the southern boundary of Liangkiau Bay. However, upon the arrival of a party at the intended site to prepare for occupation, they were met by about sixty natives who refused to allow the work to proceed, claiming that the graves of their ancestors would be disturbed. The Japanese soldiers gave way and the matter was referred to headquarters. The officials again placed themselves in communication with the headmen of that particular district, and for the second time—it being thought clearly settled in the morning—assured them that there would be no desecration of burial places, but that on the contrary each grave would be surrounded by a bamboo fence. They were also warned that there was a limit to endurance, and that these repeated acts of ill will might perhaps tire out the patience of the officers who were earnestly endeavoring to treat them with kindness and consideration.

A great deal of trouble and annoyance was caused by the private and unauthorized tours of exploration which parties of Japanese volunteer attachés and others were constantly indulging in, when not under the direct eye of their officers. Partly in consequence of this and partly for other reasons, it was thought expedient to send a messenger to the headquarters of those chiefs of the eighteen tribes who were supposed to hold the greater part of the authority and influence formerly possessed by Tokitok, and to invite them to an interview for the purpose of declaring to them the pacific designs of the Japanese so far as they were concerned and securing if possible their co-operation and good will.

Miya, the friend and ally, acted as messenger, but the chiefs showed no inclination to come down to the valley, though they agreed to meet the Japanese at one of the hill villages. This the deputation, consisting of seven officers, were obliged to accept, and after a fatiguing climb, with constant exposure to the burning sun, since there was no shelter, save low growths of thick pine on the mountain sides, they eventually reached their destination, a little village, which was found to resemble those on the coast.

The principal chief among those gathered to meet the Japanese, was Isa, who was not only at the head of an influential tribe but was also invested with certain authority as guardian to Tokitok's son and successor, who was also one of the party. Our author describes the meeting as follows :—

" The party was led to one of the best cottages, in the principal room of which a man was standing alone, who did not wait to be accosted, but immediately withdrew. This was afterward found to be the chief Isa. Up to the moment of his sudden exit, there had not been a single indication that the village was occupied by any besides the regular denizens; but as he stepped forth, a body of about forty wild looking men came into view as suddenly as if they had been called up by magic. It was impossible to imagine where or how they had been concealed. The fabled call of Roderich Dhu could not have been more startling in its effects than the silent summons of this savage warrior. His followers gathered compactly about the door of the house, and, although there was probably no intention of the sort, it seemed for a moment as if they wished to give substantial proof of their mastery of the situation and to show the strangers the helplessness of the position into which they had allowed themselves to be led.

" This did not last long. Isa presently returned, accompanied by the younger son of Tokitok, a fine-looking lad of about eighteen years of age, and by other chiefs. In the conversation that followed, Isa took the sole control on the part of the natives, rarely consulting at all with his associates. His manner, as well as that of his companions, appeared to indicate that his was the most potent voice in the affairs of those Southern tribes that still remained in confederation. The personal appearance of this leader was striking. He is tall and muscular and considerably above the European average in stature and physical development. His complexion is dark, and the expression of his countenance is vigorous, resolute, and intrepid. At times it assumed an air of extreme ferocity, and it was easy to see that if he were moved to sudden wrath his features would at once fall into that demoniac distortion with the power of assuming which everybody in the region seemed to be gifted. His eyes are remarkable and quite exceptional. They are almost colorless,—that is to say, there is hardly a distinction between the dull bluish white of the corners and the pupils. This, however, was afterward discovered to be the effect of a peculiar malady from which they suffer, and, as a consequence, they were not often lighted up; but occasionally a gleam came into them as fierce and vicious as that of any wild beast. And this, so far as we could then judge, was when he was at his best—attending a friendly conference and exercising a species of rough hospitality. There were reasons, at a later date, for modifying this estimate of his character. In dress he was like the average Chinaman of this district, excepting that his garments were of somewhat better quality, and were slightly embroidered. His arms—matchlock, spear, bow and arrows, and sword—were in good condition and polished to the highest degree. His general demeanor was very serious, and by an uninitiated observer would not have been regarded as particularly pacific. He sat almost all the while in a rigid position, hardly moving his head one side or the other, which immobility, again, though not then clearly comprehended, was undoubtedly due to his impaired eyesight. When he spoke, he delivered his sentences with great rapidity, and in a harsh guttural tone, which had apparently as little of the music of amity in it as the growling of a tiger. But his words were not discourteous and all his intention seemed to be to show a willingness to hold pleasant relations with the new comers. Like all the inhabitants of Southern Formosa he chewed betel-nuts constantly, with the juice of which his teeth and lips were darkly stained. He was also marked with a disfiguring species of ornamentation which is peculiar to the tribes of the Eastern coast; the lobes of his ears were abnormally distended by the insertion, in large bored holes, of heavy plates of silver. None of his companions were without these fantastic decorations, although some wore shells or pieces of crystal, instead of metallic substances.

" The interview was not very long, and although the colloquy was necessarily slow, requiring a triple translation each way—from Japanese into English, thence into Chinese and again into the savage dialect, with the same process reversed in replies—there was little occasion for extensive discussion. The mere forms of meeting and recognition, and the interchange of a few reassuring words were about all that was really required. Isa manifested some curiosity as to the ultimate purposes of the Japanese, and was told that he would undoubtedly receive full information as soon as Generals Saigo and Le Gendre should arrive, but that the designs of the expedition were not likely to affect him or his subjects, or any well-disposed tribes. The name of General Le Gendre appeared to possess a singular charm over these people. Attention was called to the fact that the Japanese party had put faith in the integrity of the natives by coming among them unattended by a guard, and the hope expressed that the chiefs would return the confidence by visiting the encampment, without followers, as they might choose. To this Isa demurred, whereupon it was furthermore suggested that any of the foreigners would willingly go to the interior and remain there as a hostage during the term of such a visit. Still the mountain leader would not respond, but when he was asked if he would come after General Le Gendre's arrival, he readily answered in the affirmative. Alluding to the circumstance that the Japanese had travelled in a strange region without an escort, he offered to send a detachment of his own men back to the camp with them, but this, naturally, was declined. After about an hour of conversation, it was announced that a pig had been killed, and a feast was ready. The anxiety of preparation for this inevitable solemnity, I ought to have mentioned, was the reason given, earlier in the day, for not coming out to meet the visitors at a distance from the village. The pig, with its accessories, was disposed of, tea and sam-shu were drunk, and the assemblage broke up, a little after three o'clock, with formal expressions of courteous satisfaction on all sides. Just before leaving, the American gentlemen exhibited the capacities of the Winchester and other rifles which they carried, to the interest and astonishment of the natives, whose fire-arms are yet of the most primitive class; and at the suggestion of the Japanese officers, the present of a Snider was made to each of the chiefs.[1] These were accepted with assurances that they would be treasured as memorials but also with modest doubts as to the ability of the recipients to make effective use of weapons so far superior to those of their customary experience. The excursionists returned to their camp at six o'clock in the evening."

In spite of warnings and serious admonitions, parties of irresponsible Japanese would persist in wandering about through regions too remote from camp to allow them to return to it or to enable them to receive help in case of attack. On the afternoon of the 17th, a body of one hundred men were

---

1. In November, 1895, while the guest of Rear Admiral Tsunoda, then on a tour of inspection, I passed down the east coast and among other landings, a visit to Liang-kiau in the south was made and a meeting held with several chiefs, the eldest of whom produced one of these same Sniders that Mr. House speaks about, in splendid condition, and after fondly relating its history, proudly called attention to the faithfulness with which the savages had lived up to the promises made to the Japanese in 1874.

sent a distance of two miles, on a reconnoiting trip. When keeping together and not making too intimate an acquaintance with the jungle they were not in much danger, but half a dozen of them being possessed, for what reason it is difficult to say, with the desire of visiting a village near by, the roofs of which could be seen through the underbrush, separated from the rest. They went, remained a while, and saw nothing that struck them as suspicious, but on returning they were fired upon by natives hid in the thicket. One man, a sergeant of a Satsuma regiment, was shot dead, while another man was wounded in the neck. The number and location of their hidden enemy being unknown, the survivors ran back to the reconnoiting party, which advanced with all possible haste to the spot. They found their companion headless, the body stripped, and his weapons taken away. Although no trace of the enemy could be found, the result of all after inquiries upon the subject pointed to the members of the Botan tribe, which had slaughtered the Miyako Shima fishermen in 1871, and the Japanese were now on the ground for the purpose of punishing this same tribe. Posts of observation were known to exist on every hill-top, and it was a very simple matter for one of the savage sentries to report every movement of the strangers and to waylay them by side paths, with which, of course, the aborigines were familiar. This severe lesson, however, was not effective in inducing reckless Japanese to restrain their curiosity and leave exploration to such parties as were ordered to engage in it.

It was decided not to take any steps on the offensive until the arrival of Admiral Akamatsu, who had started in the *Nishin* the day previous for a short trip to the east coast. He returned on the 19th, and reported an attack made on the frigate's boats by savages. There was consequently some talk of a combined military and naval attack on a large scale; but the matter immediately in hand required first attention, and the penalty for the assault on the *Nishin's* crew was consequently postponed.

Outside work of all kinds was delayed for a few days by a violent storm such as only Formosa can produce, lasting half the week, and converting the camp-ground into a lake of no trifling depth. Everything moveable, including clothes and other valuables, was washed away and never seen again. For forty-eight hours no food could be cooked. Lines of sentinels at night could not be maintained, the camp being guarded only by isolated pickets, stationed upon pieces of ground that were not too deeply submerged. It was finally found necessary to shift quarters as quickly as possible to a sand ridge bordering the beach.

In the midst of the storm the little British gunboat *Hornet* returned, to remain in the neighborhood a considerable time, as was stated.

The savages were now becoming fully aroused, and the engagement, our author's account of which follows, will give the reader an idea of the difficulties met with in combating the Formosan savages on their own ground:

"On the 21st of May, a detachment of twelve men was sent out to examine the locality where the Satsuma soldier had been killed four days before. Their instructions were to visit the village at which they had previously halted, to inquire into the circumstances, and to ascertain beyond a doubt to which tribe the unknown enemies belonged. It was recognized that the murdered man had been roaming in places where he should not have been, and that the assailants were perhaps not bound to know that his errand was innocent; but, on the other hand, apart from the fact that the Japanese were in no case disposed to look upon his death with indifference, he had gone nowhere near the established limits of the Liangkiao district, and the actual intrusion, as well as aggression, had been on the side of the savages. It was understood that this scouting party was not to expose itself to danger, and was to confine itself to gathering such information as could be obtained without serious risk; but the restless spirit of the men was, as usual, entirely beyond reasonable control. They found the place to which they had been sent entirely deserted, and thought proper to push forward to the next settlement, a couple of miles beyond. When they were about four miles from the camp they were suddenly confronted by a body of not less than fifty natives, who fired upon them, severely wounding two of their number. They returned the fire, and killed one of the enemy, whose corpse was afterward found by the coast villagers, half-concealed in the jungle, after which they retreated hastily to the shore. The alarm being given, the entire Japanese force not on guard duty, about two hundred and fifty altogether, turned out and marched rapidly to the scene of the encounter. They reached it about half-past five o'clock in the afternoon and were greeted by an irregular volley from the bushes, which they could only return at random. They advanced, however, at a double-quick, the troops in the rear showing the greatest impatience, and making every endeavor, even at the expense of order, to press forward to the front. But their alacrity was not equal to the speed of the natives, who, from their familiarity with the country, were enabled to retreat without injury, sending a few scattered and ineffectual discharges behind them. As it was growing dark, the Japanese abandoned the pursuit for the night, and divided their force; one half bivouacking near the foot of the mountains, to receive the enemy in case _they should attempt to renew the contest, and the other returning to the camp.

"At the last village in the valley, several suspicious circumstances were observed. The inhabitants were in a state of unusual trepidation, and their matchlocks were not only seen lying about in disorder, but, on examination, were found to be black and begrimed, as if they had been recently used; whereas it is the habit of these people to keep their arms in the cleanest possible condition. Hearing this, the Japanese officers determined to send out a force especially to disarm these villagers, and to post notices warning them that if they assisted or sheltered the Botans, who were by this time known to be the active antagonists, they would be treated as enemies. Thus far, every incident of a hostile character had occurred in a region over which the savages exercised no legitimate control, and which lay entirely within the possession of the inhabitants of the Liangkiao valley, with all of whom the Japanese had established friendly, or at least perfectly pacific, relations. The provocation had been wholly on the part of the mountaineers. There had been no intention even to approach them, for a considerable time to come, and it was clearly laid down that relations were to be established with them by peaceable means, if possible. The punishment for the outrages of 1871 was to be left to their own rulers, provided they would undertake the task, and was not to be enforced by the Japanese except in the event of an absolute refusal or defiance from the Botan chiefs. But now it seemed needful to prepare for meeting these repeated assaults in some effective way. It was determined not to withdraw the outposts—an action which might have been regarded as an indication of weakness--but to re-inforce them sufficiently to enable them to hold their ground, at the same time authorizing no forward movement that should render a contest inevitable. This condition of inactivity, however, it was easier to decree than to ensure.

"On the morning of the 22nd, two companies, led by Colonel Sakuma, who had already won distinction in the Saga contests,[1] went out to the support of those who had been left behind the night before, and to perform those duties, mentioned above, which concerned the suspected villagers and which did not necessarily involve a conflict on this occasion. But curiosity, or some stronger motive, induced them to push forward to the mountain path, near which the savages had been lost sight of. Here, half way through a narrow and precipitous pass, the enemy again rose upon them, and the first genuine engagement ensued.[2] The mountaineers were at first estimated to have been two hundred and fifty in number, but this was subsequently found to be a great exaggeration. They were about seventy. But they had enormous advantages of position, which I had afterward the opportunity of examining on all sides, and which I shall endeavor to describe more particularly in another chapter. Although one hundred and fifty Japanese had marched to the spot, the difficulties of the situation were such that not more than thirty could be actively employed. There was no road, and the fighting was actually done in the middle of a river which runs through the rocky gateway by which the Botan country could be approached from this direction. The savages were posted behind masses of stone which they had selected beforehand, and the Japanese assumed such stations as they could best find at the moment. The exchange of shots lasted a little over an hour, at the end of which time the natives all ran away, at least such as were able--leaving not one to be seen in any direction. They took their wounded with them, but sixteen dead bodies were left behind, the heads of most of which were cut off and brought back into camp. Six Japanese were killed, one of whom was an officer; and nearly a score were wounded, most of them very slightly.

"War against the aborigines was now fairly in progress. These events had brought about a necessity for immediate action, and, although the only direct engagement that had taken place was of a comparatively trifling character, it was essential that it should be followed, as speedily as might be, by operations upon a broader scale. It was unquestionable that the imprudence of a few individuals, moving without responsibility, had tended to precipitate hostilities; but it was also evident, from the promptness of the natives to take advantage of these acts of carelessness or indiscretion, that they were determined upon a conflict, and that no amount of caution could have long averted one."

While the battle of "Stone Gate" was in progress, several large ships entered the bay. Two were transports, and General Saigo, the commander-

---

1. Saga, in Kyushu, was the scene of the insurrection in the early part of 1874.
2. Later known as the engagement of the "Stone Gate."

in-chief, with his staff and fifteen hundred soldiers and laborers, landed from one, while the other was heavily loaded with supplies, besides fighting men. A Chinese frigate and gunboat followed soon after and excited much curiosity ; for since the opposition of the foreign ministers had been made known, there was great uncertainty felt as to the course of action the Chinese might adopt.

There was, accordingly, a feeling of much relief when it was found that the ships came on a friendly mission, as the officers expressed it, with the special intention of assuring the natives thereabouts, both by personal visits to the chiefs and proclamations to the masses, that the Japanese were engaged in a good work, and that aid should be extended to them whenever possible. They were also bearers of a letter to General Saigo, evidently not so friendly in spirit. It thus appeared that the Chinese authorities were naturally not unfriendly to the task undertaken by the Japanese, and that the foreign representatives, in their assumption that the Japanese were declaring war against China, were worrying themselves over an affair, in which the country most concerned saw but little cause for anxiety. The Chinese messengers were loud in their protestations of kindly feelings, and stated that they had been authorized to convey the true sentiments of cordial friendship entertained by the viceroy of Fokien and his court. According to these messengers, the government of China had never felt the least objection to the Japanese expedition.

Although the foreign representatives had been unceasing in their hostility to the Japanese, it was evident that as yet their opposition had had no influence with any except a few of the highest Chinese officials, and that these had not deemed it necessary to notify the other officials of the rôle that they were to play. Mr. Williams, United States chargé at Peking, writing on the 29th of May, said that the authorities at the Chinese capital did not at that time consider the action of the Japanese in visiting Formosa to be warlike. Mr. Henderson, the United States consul at Amoy, wrote June 1st and 3rd that the Chinese had not hitherto " pretended to claim that part of the island where the savages reside, or in any manner to be responsible for their conduct," and that he had been so informed by " a high officer in the Chinese service."

The first inkling the Japanese had that the promptings of the foreign advisers had already produced the seeds of opposition, was the contents of the letter brought to General Saigo. This letter purported to be merely an answer to the despatch from General Saigo, which was delivered by Fuku-shima Kunari to Li Wo Nen, the viceroy of Fokien, notifying him of the departure of the expedition for Formosa, as the result of the conference between Soyejima Tancomi and the members of the Tsung-li-yamen in the spring of 1873 ; conveying anew the desire of the Japanese government to maintain the most-cordial relations with that of China, and asking that he, the viceroy, would use his efforts to prevent both his own subjects and foreigners from giving aid to the savages or supplying them with arms and ammunition or other materials of war. The viceroy's letter now stated that China claimed authority over that part of the island,

and expressed the wish that the Japanese general should withdraw his troops. Under any circumstances this communication was a subject to be settled by diplomatic agencies, and a commanding officer could not allow it to affect the course of his operations, even were he so inclined. General Saigo had been ordered to investigate the circumstances of the original murders, to enforce retribution, and to take measures to prevent the recurrence of massacres by the natives. The Chinese officers present furthermore proposed a joint expedition, Japan to accept a Chinese force to aid in punishing the Botans. But even had their aid been desirable from a military or diplomatic point of view, it would have been decidedly unwise to have joined hands with a people who were so intensely and, one might add, so justly hated by the savages.

After the Chinese officers had carried out their intention of representing the expedition in a friendly light to the people of Liangkiau—which, inasmuch as the people of that quarter refused to recognize Chinese authority, was received with the utmost indifference—the warship departed.

The Japanese in Formosa derived much satisfaction from the visit of these officials. It now appeared that, regardless of the reports of certain foreign ministers, China was inclined to look upon the expedition as a justifiable one.

This was the condition of affairs in May ; but a month later, no doubt encouraged by the support that was given them by (Sir) Harry Parkes and others of the diplomatic corps in Japan, all was changed, the Chinese assuming an attitude which they could not long maintain and from which they were eventually forced to retire. Mr. Bingham, the United States minister had always been a true friend of the Japanese, always heartily opposed to the system of oppressive interference which was exercised by many of his colleagues, and at every opportunity, both in private and in official communications, he had been found supporting the Japanese in all their actions deserving of consideration. In the Formosa affair alone he had deviated from his usual path and expressed himself as heartily displeased with the Japanese. The steamship New York was held back at his instigation, and he was constant in his opposition to the Americans who had joined the expedition, and now protested that their early departure aboard the Yuko Maru from Nagasaki had been in violation of his instructions. But as he had issued no peremptory orders as minister of the United States that they should not go, they did not see fit to comply with his private wishes. It was, however, taken in a more serious sense by certain members of the Japanese government, with the result that Okuma Shigenobu was directed to fully investigate the matter at Nagasaki, and later Okubo Toshimichi, a member of the Imperial Council, was sent from Tōkyō to further examine into the affair and settle decisively all questions as to the propriety of the successive methods adopted in the organization and workings of the expedition. The conclusion was arrived at that the engagements of the American officers in no way conflicted with the public law of nations—a conclusion that was later confirmed by the opinion of the State Department at Washington. As to the expedition, Okubo stated that he was convinced that every reasonable precaution had been taken to preserve the good faith and credit of the government. With regard to General Le Gendre, the only question raised was as to the place where his services could be best utilized. In consideration of the difficulties which were now thrown upon them, it was decided that the capital would be the best place for him to remain.

The presence of the commander-in-chief now in Formosa rendered it desirable that the whole subject should be reviewed and a plan of action in dealing with the savages be determined upon.

The Japanese at the time of this expedition had apparently not entirely done away with the barbarous custom of decapitating dead bodies, which had been a regular accompaniment of Japanese warfare in all former times. Our author says it existed to no great extent, and probably would not have been begun at all had not the Botans been so free with their knives, which incited some Japanese, principally Satsuma men, to retaliate in kind. This retaliation led, however, to the identification of the son of the chief of the Botans, whose head was one of several which were carried from the battle-field. Evidence of the disabling of the chief Alok himself was also present. He had been fatally wounded, and among the weapons picked up after the encounter his gun was found.

General Saigo expressed strong disapproval of the mutilation of the dead, and gave orders that it should not occur again. He approved the decision that had been agreed upon several days before, that the first two attacks, in which one soldier was killed and two wounded, should be passed over for the present ; but that the third had been upon too extensive a scale. The Formosans were watching closely to see what action the Japanese took, and to hesitate then would be to give confidence to the savages, who, in their own minds, would be convinced that the Japanese remained on the defensive because they were afraid. This might result in an aggressive combination of many tribes, an event which the Japanese naturally desired to avoid. At this time it should be noted, only the Botans and their closest neighbors were known to be in alliance against the Japanese.

The discipline of some of the members of the force seems to have been decidedly doubtful, and control over them was exercised rather by the personal influence of the general than by the application of any strict rules. These men seemed to be semi-independent adventurers, seekers after martial fame, who were determined to be at the front at every opportunity, and if opportunities did not occur in the regular course of events, to make them. Valor they had in abundance, but in discretion and tact they were sadly lacking. An illustration of how much authority some of these volunteers assumed is furnished in the performance of a young interpreter, which came under the observation of our author.

"He was a native of Hizen, the province in which the last Japanese rebellion occurred, and many of his friends and family were concerned in that ill-advised outbreak. Some of them committed suicide, and he himself fell under suspicion, and was closely watched in Tōkyō, for a time. Knowing this, and longing for an opportunity to prove his fidelity to the Government, he asked for and received an appointment as one of the translators for this expedition. He felt confident, although his functions were those of a non-combatant, that he could find, or make, an occasion for giving some sign of personal devotion. A day or two after his arrival, he began to lay plans for private enterprises, one or two of which he carried into effect, somewhat to the annoyance of his superiors. It was he who led off a party of explorers on the 12th, and he also, after the murder of the Satsuma man, on the 17th, went inland on his own account, to look into the affair. At last the forward movement of the 22nd gave him his chance. He started off with his rifle and plenty of ammunition, forgetting his hat and coat in his eagerness to get to the front. Being observed, and asked what he was about, he replied that he guessed he was out deer-hunting—a bit of pleasantry suggested by experiences in Yezo, where he had long resided. That was the last seen of him until he came into camp at nightfall bringing three heads with him. I regret to say that he had cut them off himself. I suppose it would not be fair to regret that he had killed their owners, the work of destruction being a foregone conclusion, and he having so much more to gain—at least from his point of view—than any of his associates, by taking a prominent part in the day's work."

When the rattling of musketry was heard in camp at the commencement of the engagement of the twenty-second, the inhabitants of the villages in the Liang-kiau valley expressed their desire to join in the fighting against the Botans, and appeared on the scene with their rude weapons ready for instant combat. There seemed to be no doubt that the Botans were not only the enemy of strangers, but of their own neighbors as well, and there was no lack of friendly advances from many quarters, as soon as the news of the defeat of Alok had spread abroad.

The camping place proved not unhealthy, for although the intense heat still continued, most of the Japanese who were prostrated by it at first, were soon in good health, and all but one of the wounded eventually recovered. The Japanese soldier, compared with his European compeer of that time, surely lived in luxury. He was relieved from the fatiguing labors of the field and even of the light task of preparing his rations. His food, of the best to be procured and in profuse quantities, was brought to his tent, and beer and spirits were added if he needed them. When off duty, he lounged about in loose cotton robes and straw slippers freely provided for him, and if he was not happy, he should have been. Nine-tenths of the troops were young men from twenty to twenty-five years of age. Quarrels were unheard of, and the serenity at all times, except when in chase of the enemy, was uninterrupted. The national love of personal cleanliness was easily gratified by the nearness of the sea and the rivers, in which the men could dip a dozen times a day. The anxiety for cleanliness about the camp evidently did not exist to any great extent, and sanitary laws, if there were any, were wofully disregarded. Masses of refuse and foul matter were allowed to collect about the tents, from which danger might have been apprehended, but the occupants remained unconcerned. It was not the future but the present that engaged their attention, and this was spent in slumber, social sports, and athletic contests on the sands near the camp.

The Japanese authorities were desirous of meeting the chief Isa that they might make known to him their intentions concerning the hostile tribes. The chief at first appeared apprehensive lest his party should be mistaken for the enemy by out-posts of Japanese, but upon being assured that the soldiers would be withdrawn from the place of rendezvous, he made known his consent. Having made the journey and arrived at Miya's house in Sialiao, the place selected, he and his companions were immediately joined by the two Generals Saigo and Tani, Admiral Akamatsu, the American officers, and a few others. The chief won the respect of all by his demeanor. For the first time in his life, he was confronting strangers, who, instead of recognizing his supremacy, were prepared to dispute it if necessary. His position was one that would have caused agitation to many a man whether diplomat or soldier ; but the savage was tranquil, composed, and dignified.

The absence of Le Gendre was very severely felt, for he alone by past experience was familiar with the organization, power, and location of the tribes. However, information already gained convinced the Japanese officers that the strength of the savages had been greatly over-estimated, and that the hundreds and thousands of usual accounts could more correctly be regarded as tens. In fact, the word tribe, as commonly used when speaking of the savages, gives an erroneous impression, for a so-called tribe, as the term is used in Formosa, practically means the occupants of a single village, and in the south it is unusual to find any village of more than a couple of hundred inhabitants. There was also reason to believe that the entire number of Tokitok's former followers would not exceed three thousand persons, while the able-bodied fighting men would be very few. That the chief could not successfully oppose the Japanese with this small force must have been very evident to him, and left but one path for the proud savage to choose: he must submit to the Japanese demands. This would not be a difficult task, nor a humiliating one.

"On the part of the Japanese, it was desired that Isa should signify his friendliness by promising not to harbor or protect the Botans in any manner, and to hold as prisoners any fugitives that might escape into his territory; by allowing the Japanese free circulation among his villages, and such intercourse with his people as might become necessary during their expeditions to the interior; by sternly admonishing the Koalut and other tribes that had shown signs of animosity, of the danger they were incurring, and by making such arrangements in the settlements along the coast as would enable ships to anchor unmolested, and their crews to go on shore for water or provisions. These were the only demands presented, and the chief was repeatedly assured that whatever force the Japanese might bring to Formosa, and however powerful they might prove themselves against their enemies, they would ask nothing of their allies but these few and necessary evidences of a friendly disposition. On the other hand, the Japanese proposed to guarantee immunity to the people for whose good behavior Isa would answer by issuing papers of protection to their 'head men,' and by sending them flags with certain inscriptions, the display of which would prevent all aggressions from the soldiers. In response, Isa readily agreed to the several requests, in a manner that implied a sense of their moderation, and in one or two instances went voluntarily far beyond the requirements in his offers of co-operation. He said, for example, that everything having now been made clear to him, he would sanction the free admission of the soldiers and sailors wherever they needed to go; that he did not believe the Koalut or any other tribes would hereafter oppose them, but if they did, he would himself come into the camp, guide the Japanese to the treacherous region, and assist them in punishing the breach of faith to the extent of utter extermination, if it must be. He objected, however, to visits from the inhabitants of the villages of the west coast, saying that he could not have any dealings with them, and that their presence would lead to endless quarrels. He was, in return, assured that there was no intention of forcing these or any other unwelcome intruders upon him, and that there would certainly be no interference in any of their local disagreements. With regard to the Botans, he signified an entire willingness to see them all extirpated, together with their unruly neighbors, the Kusukuts. It appeared to be established beyond a doubt that these two tribes were actually of the eighteen over which Tokitok had been supposed to rule, and that they did at one time form part of the confederation; for, in accepting the offer of the flags, Isa said that he should require only sixteen, that being the number of villages now within his influence;—the other two he left to the Japanese.

"The conference lasted about two hours. During the whole of it, the native chiefs, of whom there were four besides the leader and spokesman, sat upon one line of benches, while the principal Japanese and American officers occupied another line, opposite to and parallel with them. The interpreter Johnson, who was a treasure of intelligence and acuteness, stood at one end, nearest to the speakers. All that was said in English was translated by him into Chinese, which language, it now appeared, was understood by Isa, though he could not use it. He nodded at the end of each sentence, to signify his comprehension of the meaning, and gave his answers in the strange rapid guttural accents of his own speech. It seems to be a language the sounds of which are produced almost entirely by the throat and tongue, hardly requiring any movement of the lips. While he was talking most emphatically, the muscles of his mouth were motionless, and it was often a question, in the partial obscurity, whether he or one of his companions was speaking. Whatever he said was put into Chinese by one or another of his attendants, and thence into English by Johnson. His associates took very little part in the discussion. One of them showed considerable confusion when the recent misbehavior of the Koaluts was spoken of, and it turned out that he, though not the actual head of that tribe, was a sort of responsible agent for two or three villages, of which Koalut was one. He endeavored to excuse the discharge of the fire arms at the time of the *Nishin's* visit, and, I believe, declared that the Japanese had mistaken the shooting of birds, by some boys, for a hostile attack. It was not thought desirable to examine into the question at this particular time. One request Isa had to make on his side. He stated that the settlement belonging to his people which lay nearest to the scene of the recent skirmish had been entered by soldiers and coast inhabitants, and some of the houses destroyed, in consequence of which the people had fled to the mountains. He wished the troops to be particularly notified that the village in question was not a fair object of attack. It was explained to him that this, as well as certain adjoining places, had been suspected of giving aid to the Botans; but that if he would be answerable for them, and it should be found they had been unjustly treated, they should not only be protected but should receive ample compensation.

"All matters of business having been adjusted, the chiefs were now notified that General Saigo had some presents to offer them, which were duly brought in and distributed. They consisted of two superb Japanese swords, packages of silk, woollen and cotton cloths, and a variety of what we should call 'fancy goods.' They were not received with much warmth, but that was rather to be attributed to awkwardness, I imagine, than to indifference. In return they handed over their gifts of dressed skins and live chickens, mentioning that the cattle were waiting outside and would be delivered in the morning. A few tubs of Japanese 'sake' were added to the endowments of the aborigines, half a dozen cups of Chinese 'Samshu' were handed around, and the meeting ended a little after midnight."

CHAPTER XII.

THE JAPANESE EXPEDITION OF 1874.
JUNE—JULY.

Projected march—Estimated strength of savage tribes—U.S.S. "Monocacy" appears—Movement towards the interior—Laborious progress—Costume of a war correspondent—Arrival at Stone Gate—Details of the engagement of Stone Gate—Singular discovery of graves of the murdered Loochooans—Mountain climbing—Native barricades—An Amiya village—Capture and destruction of Botan and Kusukut—Results of the expedition—Third conference with savage tribes—Power of the Gatlings as explained by Johnson—Voyage to the east coast—Reception by the savages—New camp established—Japanese explorations—Second visit from Chinese officials—Personnel of the party—Yanagiwara the Japanese envoy to Peking—First suggestion of remonstrance from China—Conference in Shanghai—Violation of Chinese pledges—Interviews between General Saigo and Commissioner Pan Wi—Chinese visits to the interior—Final conference—Local Chinese view of affairs — Consternation among Chinese generally—Chinese garrisons strengthened—Military improvements—View of the inhabitants of the north—Japanese at Khelai—Chinese expedition to Suao—Panic among Amoy Chinese—Action of United States officers—The viceroy's letter.

IT was now time to devise plans for active operations, with the design of driving the hostile savages from their strongholds, occupying the principal posts, and keeping open the avenues of communication. While it had been found that the number of savages to be conquered was much less than had been expected, difficulties of travel in the interior were far greater than had been anticipated. The opportunities of foreigners for personal observation had been so limited, and their information, such as it was, not now being available the march was to the expedition a trip into an unknown territory.

The headmen of the Liangkiau valley had given estimates which placed the number of effective men of the whole eighteen tribes at 2,360.[1]   Of all

1. Botan	.. ..	250	Pakolut ..	.. ..	155
Sawali	.. ..	240	Siapuli	.. ..	142
Kusukut	.. ..	190	Osuantao..	.. ..	130
Mantsui	.. ..	175	Loput	.. ..	126
Kuchilai	.. ..	165	Chinakai ..	.. ..	120
Patingi	.. ..	160	Lingluan ..	.. ..	114
Peiqu	.. ..	86	Baya	.. ..	90
Koatan	.. ..	60	Tuilasok ..	.. ..	74
Koalut	.. ..	50	Chiksia ..	.. ..	63

these tribes only two were known to be openly in arms against the Japanese, —the Botans and Koaluts, but a few other villages were thought to be in sympathy with them, though they had not so far expressed any hostile intentions. If the information was correct, there were at the outside not more than 375 or 400 men to be overcome. Thirty had already been killed or had died from wounds. The number seemed insignificant enough, but the real strength of the enemy was in the formation of the country, affording, as it did, natural barriers which for foreigners were extremely difficult of penetration. Of their absolute inaccessibility the savages were themselves convinced.

It was first of all necessary to gain some knowledge of the roads and passes, and the general topography of the savage districts. If any successful engagements should take place with hostile natives, so much the better, but it was not expected that any opposition would be met with. To accomplish this survey, it was arranged that three columns should be sent out with instructions to concentrate in the heart of the hostile territory. The departure was commenced on the first of June, having been delayed on account of heavy rains, which fell on the 24th May; the roads being in some places almost impassable, and the rivers were so swollen that it was extremely dangerous to ford them.

These storms, which were of frequent occurrence, came with great suddenness, raging with fury for two or three hours, and then giving way in the day time to an intolerable heat lasting for an hour, which was then followed by a fresh deluge. At night it was the same, except that the alternations of heat were omitted.

On May 29th, the U.S.S. *Monocacy* had appeared in the harbor in the morning, but, owing to the very unfavorable weather, left without being able to communicate with shore, in fact she was at one time in considerable danger. Her visit was intended as one of observation, and the United States consul at Amoy was on board as a passenger.

The first detachment of troops, five hundred in number, was sent to Hongkong, a settlement some six miles north of headquarters, which was still in the territory independent of China, the practical authority of the empire extending then only as far south as Pangliau, some twenty-five miles distant. The next day, three hundred men started eastward for the scene of the "Stone Gate" skirmish of May 22nd, and the third column, numbering four hundred men, marched to the south-east towards Chiksia.[1]

---

1. The general purposes of these combined movements were stated as follows: "The headquarters of the hostile tribes were known to be Botan and Kusukut. A few tributary settlements in their neighborhood were believed to be held by their men, and it was tolerably well ascertained that the northern roads, as far as Ninai, were in their possession. The duty assigned to the Hongkong force, under General Tani, was to proceed to Ninai, starting before sunrise on the 2nd, and to descend as rapidly as possible to Botan. The Chiksia column, under Admiral Akamatsu, was to move upon Kusukut. The central body, which was led by General Saigo, was to pass over the difficult road from the "Stone Gate" to either Kusukut or Botan, as might be desirable. This road, which is, in fact, nothing but the roughest kind of mountain-pass, was known to be not only full of natural impediments, but also to have been artificially obstructed by the enemy; circumstances which account for the greater length of time allowed for the troops to reach their destination."

For various reasons, the foreign officers accompanied the central body under command of General Saigo. Our author also chose that route that he might examine with closeness the scene of the conflict of May 22nd, which he had known by observation from only one side. That the march was not without considerable hardship is evident. The sun was at its fiercest, and the streams to be forded, although some were not passed without difficulty, were most gladly welcomed. The advantage of a campaign in savage territory was that it at least permitted a disregard of personal appearance, and our author, who found that a suit of thin "pajamas" a straw hat, an umbrella, and a pair of straw sandals was the proper uniform for a journalist in the tropics, mentions that he was humorously congratulated by an officer on being able to go to war in a sleeping dress.

The Japanese soldiers wore close fitting leg-coverings from the knee to the ankle, and soft thick sandals, both familiar articles of Japanese dress, while extra sandals were carried suspended from the waists. Leather shoes were entirely unsuitable for such a march. With the alternate swelling and shrinking from soaking and sudden drying, leather shoes became extremely painful to the wearer, while the sharp stones of the hills tore them to rags long before the completion of the journey.

As the expedition drew near to the circle of hills inland, the country was found to be of much richer verdure than on the coast and along the Liang-kiau valley, which for the greater part was destitute of trees. As they slowly ascended, patches of shrubbery and clusters of willows by the side of the rivers were seen, but such views were not frequent, as a rule the country still preserving a rugged and barren appearance. It was not until reaching the neighborhood of the "Stone Gate" that abundant foliage was seen. Here the trees on the hills showed a luxuriant growth.

They passed through the gate about noon, and the opportunity was taken to gain a closer view of the locality which was the scene of the memorable little engagement now familiarly known as the "Battle of Stone Gate." It was a brilliant affair for the Japanese, only some forty of whom were actually engaged, and was the single opportunity of distinguishing themselves they had during the expedition. The savages needed no second lesson, and were willing to bow in submission to the conquerors from that time forward. Mr. House describes the engagement as follows :—

"The situation held by the Botans appears as nearly impregnable as any stronghold possibly can be. The sides of the "Stone Gate" are two rocky acclivities which rise at sharp angles, and often perpendicularly, to a height of nearly five hundred feet on one side and four hundred and fifty on the other. The distance between them, at the base, is about thirty feet, which is entirely filled by a rapid stream that dashes in foam over rough rocks through the greater length of the pass, and is waist deep at its only fordable point. Except under pressure of the most desperate necessity, no one would ever dream of attempting to scale these heights; and in fact no earthly power could accomplish such a task if any attempt, however feeble, were made to defend them. The crag on the right hand pillar is topped by sharp spires not unlike the needles of the Chamouni valley in form—though of course much smaller—and certainly as forbidding in their defiance to intruders. But over this barrier a score of Japanese marines did actually pass, with the view of assailing the savages from above.

"Before the action really began, a few shots were fired at the advancing line from a rude fortification that had been thrown up just within the right side of the gate—that is, to the left of the besiegers. Whether this was intended only as an outpost, or not, I cannot say, but it was hurriedly abandoned on the approach of three of the unattached volunteers of whom I have spoken, who took possession of it and remained there for some time, quite unconscious that the enemy were lying concealed behind rocks and trees within a few yards of them. It did not suit the purposes of the Botans to destroy them, which they might easily have done, their plan being to lie in wait for a greater number of victims. In course of time, some twenty-five other Japanese came into the pass,—carelessly and without precaution, as is their injudicious custom—and began looking about for the ford. When they were all exposed, and for the moment defenceless, they were fired upon from a distance of certainly not more than forty feet, and in some cases less. By this first discharge two or three of the Japanese were killed, and more than half of them were wounded. They immediately sought such concealment as they could find among the rocks which are scattered over the bed of the river. The Botans held a tolerably regular line of boulders, which creates a sort of fall or rapid just above the ford; and thus, for several minutes, the opposing forces silently confronted each other. As nearly as I could learn, by close inquiry from natives and others, there were about seventy savages present. Of course the strength of their position gave them advantages equivalent to an infinitely greater superiority of numbers.

"After the few inactive moments of which I have spoken, other Japanese began to enter the pass and establish themselves, and, at the same time, some of the wounded endeavored to retire. This was the signal for a second discharge from the Botans. But, in rising to fire, they partially uncovered their bodies, which was at once taken advantage of by the Japanese, who threw in an effective volley, under cover of which some succeeded in shifting their position to points a little nearer the enemy. This manœuvre was several times repeated, a soldier rising purposely, in case of need, to draw the fire of the defenders. By these means all the Japanese gradually worked themselves closer, but the progress was so slow and the number of the wounded increased to such an extent that the officer in command, Colonel Sakuma, ordered the bugles to sound a recall. Nobody could misconstrue such a command, coming from Sakuma, his reputation for bravery in action having been long ago established, but as the greatest of English sailors was once blind to a signal for retreat, so these ardent pioneers were deaf to this unwelcome strain. Not to put too fine a point upon it, I suppose I must admit that they disobeyed orders; but I have not learned that anybody has since greatly blamed them for it. I afterward heard one of these contumacious warriors, when called upon to give his reason for not returning, say that it would have been more dangerous to go back than to advance, and that mere prudence would have kept him where he was. He was reminded, however, that he had been seen to leave his place, rejoin the main body, and then return to the fighting ground; to which he answered, with some embarrassment, that it was true, but he had been compelled to do as he did, as he had a wounded comrade who had been shot, just beside him, in the arm and the stomach, to assist to the rear.

"Thus irregularly, and with no directions except those suggested by their own minds to the participators, the contest went on for nearly an hour, the Japanese steadily, though very slowly, getting nearer their opponents. It might be supposed that a sudden rush would have put an end to the business, as indeed it would have done on dry land, in anything like a fair field. But here the soldiers were up to their waists in a stream the current of which was so powerful that they could only with great effort force their way against it. The best and only thing they could do was to watch their opportunity and creep from behind one rock to another. At length, Colonel Sakuma conceived the idea that a small body of riflemen might ascend the cliff, to his left, and assist in dislodging the savages by firing upon them from that commanding height. About twenty marines started upon this errand, and, after a severe struggle, reached the summit. Their task was undoubtedly the most laborious of the day. It was not only difficult, but dangerous as well, for no previous attempt had ever been made to effect a passage, and the whole acclivity was in its primitive condition of unbroken irregularity. From the bottom, many parts of it looked like sections of smooth and polished stone, affording no hold for feet or hands. As they worked their way upward, the scaling party seemed to be clinging and crawling by the aid of some insect-like property of adhesion, and not by human efforts; and the possibility of their accomplishing the work was often doubted by those who watched them. At last, after many disappearances in chasms and crevices, or behind concealing masses of rock, they sprang upon the topmost ledge with gestures of triumph and shouts that, though only faintly heard, were vigorously echoed in the valley. By this time the Botans were closely pressed from below. Some of the attacking party had approached so near them that their boulders no longer afforded them a secure protection. One or two had already turned and fled when the marines appeared over their heads. That sight decided the matter. They broke in a body, and made for the river-banks, leaving sixteen of their number dead behind them. Of those who escaped, fourteen were mortally wounded—among them, as has previously been stated, the leader of the Botan tribe. Of the number of less severely wounded we never had any account. Our own casualties were six killed and thirty wounded, all but one of the latter of whom recovered."

From Stone Gate and beyond, the course of the river, which was believed to be that which flows into Liangkiau Bay, north of Sialiao, runs for nearly a mile through a narrow plain. About half way there, the expedition turned from the river to the left, and began an abrupt ascent. In passing through one of the several deserted villages belonging to the half castes or people of Chinese descent, in the plain below, the remarkable discovery was made of the actual graves of the murdered Loochooans whose deaths the expedition was there to avenge. It was a striking coincidence that there, upon the threshold of the Botan country, the troops should be reminded of the cause of their coming. The inscriptions on boards erected above the graves

Liangkiau Natives
in Chinese dress.

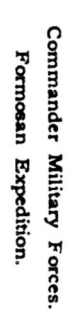

SAIGO

Commander Military Forces.
Formosan Expedition.

The Battle of Stone Gate. Fought May 22nd, 1874.

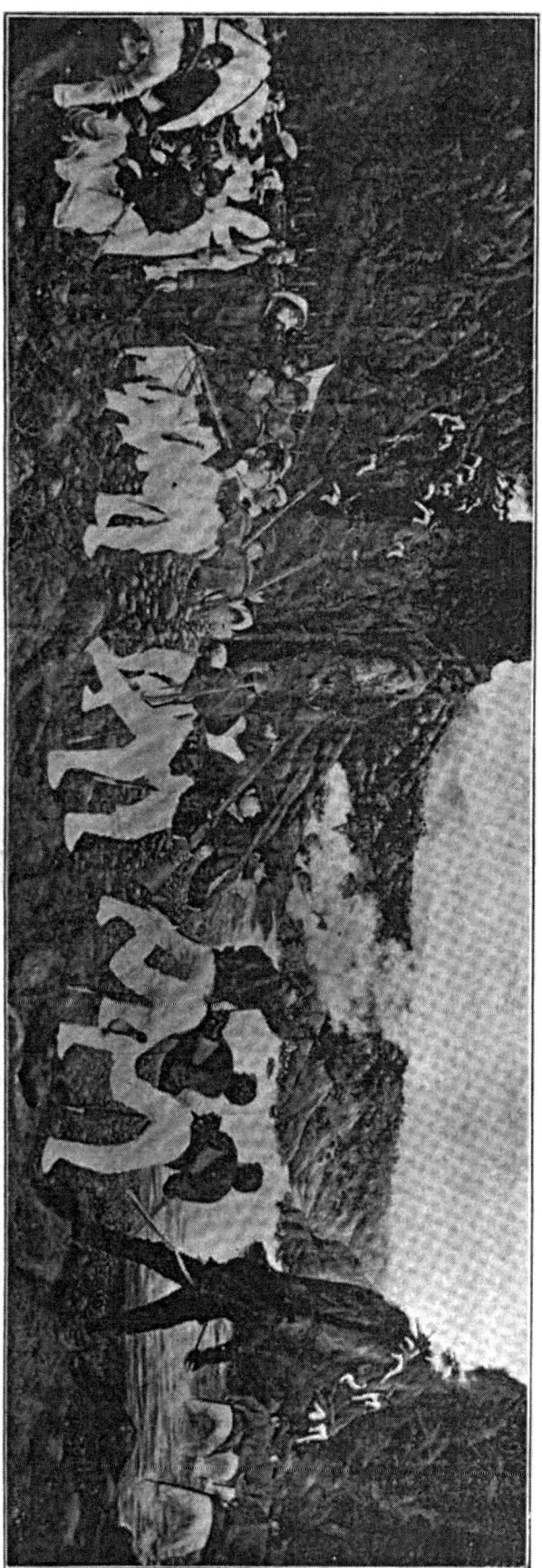

The Japanese Expedition (1874) against the Botan Savages.

were explicit, and after inquiry made it clear that the men were really buried there.   Regarding their deaths the Liangkiau people had reported that the wrecked party were mistaken by the Botans, into whose hands they had fallen, for Chinese, and in hopes of a reward, they were brought by them across to the nearest Chinese speaking village.   The Chinese of course did not recognize them, and although told that, unless a hundred dollars were paid for them, they would be killed on the spot, did nothing to save them, but on the contrary, according to some reports, expressed themselves as ready to join in the slaughter, and did so.

Proceeding, the march became hourly more difficult, until less than a mile an hour could be done.   Numerous mountain streams were forded and steep hill sides scaled, until at last the troops reached the highest elevation of a lofty ridge, beyond and below which could be seen a deep · valley.   Upon entering the valley, however, rapid progress was still impossible, owing to the numerous barricades made by the savages by means of felled trees and interlaced boughs.   These obstructions increased, until by night-fall the party was confronted by a maze of barricades, in which the largest trees yet seen in the island were thrown across the pathways in such tangled profusion, that to pierce through them was practically impossible. It required perhaps half an hour to clamber over one, and there were always more beyond, causing such delay that all hope of reaching Botan that day was abandoned, and the order was given to encamp that night where they were.   The soldiers, worn out by the day's exhausting march, were soon asleep in the open, regardless of the painful positions in which they were obliged to lie, caused by the sharp stakes and twisted boughs that were everywhere about.   Little did these tired, hungry men then know that only a quarter of a mile ahead was a village with water and food in abundance and with comparatively luxurious sleeping quarters.   General Saigo, a man of powerful frame, and less sensitive to fatigue than many others, had with a few companions pushed on and reached this favored spot believing that the others would follow.   General Saigo, however, was evidently not wholly insensible to the hardships of the situation, for it is said that his hunger was so great, that he slily dug potatoes from the field with his own hands and devoured them raw on the spot.

Early next morning the troops arrived at the village, which was found to be a place of little importance, lying about seven miles from the western and two miles from the eastern coast, and containing only a dozen houses, all built in the same way—eight posts set in the ground, straw plaited over and between them, and a fragile upper frame supporting a thatched roof. This village, it was later learned, was called Amiya after the people who inhabited it.   This tribe, which is scattered in various parts of the south, is looked upon as an inferior one, and is allowed to exist solely because of its weakness, which is taken advantage of by its stronger neighbors, who force its members to perform menial services.

Botan was soon discovered, not far distant, and a few shots were fired from the thicket as the soldiers approached, slightly wounding two or three of the party. A volley was fired in return which silenced the assailants. The place was then burned and the troops encamped in the vicinity.

The column commanded by Admiral Akamatsu had reached Kusukut, its destination, on the afternoon of the 22nd, but on attempting to enter, it was received by a sudden fire from an ambuscade. Three Japanese were killed and two wounded. The savages were speedily driven from their position, the houses of Kusukut destroyed, aad a camp pitched not far distant. Early the next morning the column started with the view of joining General Saigo, but owing to difficult roads and the ignorance of the guides, they travelled all night only to find themselves close to " Stone Gate " in the morning. Hence, however, it was an easy matter to follow the course of the central party, and the column arrived at Amiya about noon.

Nothing having been heard of the Hongkong party under command of General Tani, which was to have left for the interior before daylight on the 2nd, small squads were sent by various northern pathways to gain news of it if possible, and also to burn all deserted villages identified with the interests of the enemy. The latter task was completed, but no information was obtained regarding the missing column. In consequence of this, another night was spent at Amiya, and on the morning of the 4th, the missing column arrived, having been delayed owing to the bad condition of the roads.

It was now decided that as all the villages of the offending savages had been destroyed, the main body should return to Sialiao to prepare for further operations on the east coast, leaving sufficient men to guard and keep open the communications in the captured districts.

On the return trip, our author was the subject of an act of noble heartedness, which is so worthy of being recorded that I quote it here : " The last two or three miles were as bitter as any I ever passed over, but I was happily stimulated, at the most depressing point, by a charming little trait of kindness and good feeling. Several wounded soldiers were carried by me in litters, most of them lying at full length, and speechless. One, however, was sitting upright, his injuries being such as to make that position the least painful to him. His arm was shattered and the flesh of his breast was torn away. Seeing that I was limping along with an extremely awkward gait, he stopped his carriers, and asked what was the matter. I told him that my feet had been bruised and cut, whereupon he insisted that I should throw away my useless shoes, and take his cloth socks and sandals. ' You see,' he said 'I have no use for them now.' This was from a man who, while suffering from two dreadful wounds, spoke in the brightest tone, and smiled as cheerfully when he spoke, as if he had lain on a bed of roses. For a few moments, certainly as long as he was in sight, I strode erect and forgot that I had ever felt a smart."

The kind treatment extended to the Americans of the party, was considered by them to be such as was not often found in close alliance with the rigors of rough campaigning, and was often commented upon by them.

Upon returning to the headquarters camp, the troops rested and refreshed themselves. It was evident that no further general movement would be necessary for some time to come.   The heat, although much greater than in any part of Japan, was, owing to the cool nights, such as could be tolerated without excessive discomfort.   Much had been accomplished in a few weeks which, it had been thought, would require months ; and that even then the Japanese would be unsuccessful, was the opinion of the Chinese officers who were visitors the month before.   Their own government, they said, had some time before undertaken the subjugation of the savages, in a war which lasted over a dozen years, and had then to abandon the enterprise as hopeless.   It was true that the Botans believed themselves invincible, and were generally so regarded by their neighbors.   Yet scarcely thirty days had elapsed ere the Japanese were in supreme control.

A third conference was held with the headmen of the friendly tribes, with a view to establishing ports on the east coast.   Flags were distributed as had been previously promised, to be used as symbols of friendliness, and thus guard against unwelcome visitations.   The recipients were Isa of Sawali, Kalutoi of Mantsui, Sinjo of Pakolut, Lulin of Laput, Pinali of Linguan, Minat of Tuilasok, and a representative of the Koalut chief.   It was finally agreed, but not without some hesitation on the part of the chief, that the Japanese should occupy temporarily a piece of land on the east coast as an additional point of departure against the tribes.   Offers of payment were made by the Japanese, but declined by the savages.   After considerable persuasion they were induced to go to the camp, not far distant, and to visit the general's tent.   There they were evidently not at their ease, and stayed only long enough to receive a few gifts of colored cloth and pictures, and to catch a glimpse of the Gatling guns, which they begged might not be fired.   Their extreme anxiety over this matter was better understood, when it was later discovered that the interpreter Johnson had represented Gatlings as being endowed with the extraordinary power of projecting missiles across the island, over and even through the mountains, at the pleasure of the operators.

On the 11th of June, after a passage lasting from ten in the morning until three in the afternoon, the frigate *Nishin* under the command of Admiral Akamatsu, assisted by Major Fukushima, passed the bay in which the *Rover* tragedy had occurred, and reached a small indentation previously selected as a landing place, which, although affording but slight protection from gales, was one of the very few points on the east coast where landings could be made.   Even on their arrival, when the sea was comparatively calm, it was with considerable difficulty that fifty marines and some others were landed.   Three chiefs, with their followers were at hand to welcome the Japanese, and three of the flags given the day before were seen among them. A blazing fire had been built by them, with what design no one could conjecture.   The savages apparently expected the new comers to sit down, and were somewhat concerned at their unwillingness to subject themselves to any heat besides that which the mid-day summer sun was already supplying.   The savages were in much better humor than they had before been, and seemed to be at ease.   During the afternoon numbers of aborigines and natives of Chinese descent came in from various directions.   They were all heavily armed, but prompt in their protestations of friendship, which were expressed by placing the hand upon the breast to signify, it is said, that the heart is good. Among the arrivals was the Koalut chief himself, who now near his native domain was devoid of fear. He was a small man with a wreath of flowers tastefully woven into his hair, and is represented as having an effeminate face and large mild eyes; yet this man was the leader of the most bloodthirsty tribe, except the Botans, in the south. Another of the visitors was noticeable for a most extensive decoration composed of leaves and twigs, while another, the son of a chief, was embellished with a pheasant's plume of great length. While thus prettily dressed with the simple adornments of nature, they were disfigured by bored ears, and lips stained with betel-nut juice. A feast was prepared by the chiefs, consisting of rice and eggs and sweet potato samshu, which liquor when heated, was passed around with persistent and, to the foreign guests present, oppressive hospitality. It was very evident that with the natives the samshu was the powerful part of the feast, and it was not long before its effect became noticeable, in the increasing jollification, and the affectionate tenderness which the natives were showing towards each other.

Even Isa himself, who had during the afternoon conducted himself with unbending dignity, began to make jokes, and several times "distorted his face in what was intended to be a smile." When accompanying the foreigners to their boats, he kicked about the sand involuntarily, and pretended he had done it out of pure gaiety. When last seen by our author, "He was trying to walk through a fishing net that hung in his way, but of which he was as oblivious, for the moment, as of the ancient feuds of his race." It was an extraordinary affair, this demonstration of thorough good feeling, on a shore which had never before been approached by strangers without exciting hostility, and in a spot which only twenty days previously had witnessed a murderous attack on the part of the inhabitants, against the very guests of to-day.

The following day the camp was pitched, the process being scrutinized, apparently with interest, by an English gunboat that had followed the *Nishin* the day before.

On the 14th, General Tani with the latest reports was conveyed to Nagasaki, on board a small transport which also carried many invalids. Two days later Admiral Akamatsu and Major Fukushima sailed in the *Nishin* for China, bearers of despatches to the Japanese minister at Peking.

The ground first occupied between the two rivers of Liang-kiau valley having been found inconvenient, unhealthy, and generally unsuitable, a new encampment was made to the south of Sialiao, on a level plot of ground some twenty acres in extent, slightly elevated above the sea, and open to the breezes at all times. A healthy, airy site.

There was but little to interest the participants of camp life. Once a week or so, a company coming in from the mountains, and another departing to take its place. An arriving steamer at rare intervals, bringing newspapers and letters from Japan. And occasionally, they gathered together to hear the narratives of Japanese explorers who had returned from various parts of the interior, whither they had been sent to gather information. Major Fukushima had already travelled extensively through the Chinese districts; but the later observers went exclusively among the savages. From these latter reports, it appeared that the different tribes were alike ignorant of all but the rudest methods of cultivating their small fields of rice, tobacco, and potatoes. Of the same wild and barbarous nature, they were also alike in their hatred for the Chinese, whose skulls formed prominent displays in all villages, as a result of the frequent head-hunting expeditions. The occasional visits of friendly headmen from the interior also afforded some relaxation. Invitations to visit their native homes were numerous, but failed to afford a lasting pleasure.

Relief from the excessive monotony of the situation came in the unexpected arrival, on the 21st of June, of two Chinese ships of war from the north, which anchored in the usual place in Liang-liau Bay, about two miles distant. On board were, according to a message sent ashore, "Certain officials of high rank, who had been commissioned by the government of Peking especially to confer with the Japanese representatives in Formosa with a view to the adjustment of all questions concerning the present condition of affairs, and to establish satisfactory arrangements for the future."

They landed early the next morning, and were escorted by Japanese troops, looking unusually picturesque, half of them being clad in the old national war costume, and the other half in the modern military garb, to the village of Chasiang, a mile north of the old camp, where quarters had been obtained for them. Every consideration and respect was shown them by the Japanese, and to such an extent that it was commented upon by the foreign attachés accompanying the visitors.

The party consisted of an officer named Pan Wi, who indirectly represented the central government; Ya Hen Lin, the taotai or governor of Chinese Formosa; an assistant of the latter, and Messrs. Giquel and de Segonzac, two French gentlemen long connected with the administration of the Foochow arsenal, and high in the confidence of the Chinese authorities.

A conference was at once granted, General Saigo representing the Japanese. Arriving at the old headquarters, after a few formal salutations, the conversation was opened with the announcement that the principal Chinese delegate, Shen Pao Chen, was detained by sickness at Taiwan-fu, and so could not be present. Inquiries were then made by Pan, asking if a copy of the report of certain interviews, held at Shanghai between himself and Yanagiwara, the Japanese minister to Peking, had been received, and he was informed by General Saigo that they had not.

It is here necessary to state that the Japanese official in question who was a skilled attaché of the Foreign Office, Tōkyō, had received his appointment without reference to the question in hand, and, having been delayed in leaving Tōkyō owing to the manifestations of foreign interference, did not reach Shanghai until the 29th of May. He carried credentials which had been prepared as early as the 8th of April, the chief purport of which was to again assure the Tsung Li Yamen of the friendliness of Japan. While Yanagiwara was on his way, the first word of formal warning that the Chinese government might be moved to take a suspicious view of the Japanese proceedings was sent in a despatch from Peking to Tokyo. This document, while admitting that the subject had been previously discussed at the time of the visit of Soyezima in 1873, put forth the pretence that the Yamen had never supposed that it was intended to send an armed force to Formosa. To attempt to deal with the hostile savages without an armed force to fall back on, must have appeared as preposterous to the Chinese, as the statement did to both foreigners and Japanese.

Upon the arrival at Shanghai of Yanagiwara, he was visited by Pan Wi, then on his way to Formosa. The interview which resulted seems to have been encouraged by the Japanese envoy, principally with the idea of ascertaining the views of the Chinese government, for the Chinese official seems to have gained nothing except the advice to abandon the trip to Formosa, for although General Saigo's powers in the internal management of Formosa were full and unrestricted, he had no authority to adjust disputes that might arise between the two governments. This information evidently did not discourage the Chinese Commission, for as stated above, they arrived in Formosa for the purpose of securing an interview with Saigo.

Pan Wi having put his question in regard to the report of the Shanghai meeting, and received his answer from General Saigo, the interview continued as follows :—

" He (Pan Wi) proceeded to express his regret that a notification had not been sent to China in regard to the intention of the Japanese to visit Formosa, and punish the offending savages. If such warning had been given in time, the Chinese government would have supplied a force to accompany the Japanese, and assist in the operations—but the work having now been completed, it was too late for China to attempt to participate. Saigo answered that word had certainly been sent to declare and explain the purposes of his government, and, furthermore, that Soyezima, the Japanese ambassador, had requested the whole subject to be examined, at the time of his visit, one year ago. The Chinese commissioner said it was quite true that a messenger had recently passed through China with letters from the Japanese authorities, but that the bad condition of the roads between Foochow and Peking had made it impossible for him to deliver his news in time. Saigo remarked that it was a mistake to suppose that the work was entirely done, and that he expected to be obliged to remain yet some time, to execute all the instructions of his government and secure guarantees for the future safety of his countrymen; to which the commissioner replied that he understood and respected that view of the affair, and did not dispute the general's right to entertain it. He entirely comprehended the purposes of the Japanese and admitted the propriety of their fulfilment; but, inasmuch as the whole of Formosa, with all its inhabitants, savages and others, belonged to China, it became the duty of the Chinese authorities, also, to inquire as to who had been the assailants in the slaughter of the Loochooans, in 1871, and to discover, in a more general way, who among the population were well-behaved and who were criminals; this was one of the most important parts of the service with which he was charged. The taotai of Taiwan then observed that he had heard it was the intention of the Japanese to attack the aboriginal settlement of Pilam, on the eastern coast, and he wished to inquire if this was true. The question, for some reason, was not answered,—possibly because the fact of Japan having no cause whatever of complaint against Pilam rendered it unworthy of a serious reply. The commissioner next produced his own record of the interview, before alluded to, between Pan and Yanagiwara, which Saigo read and found to contain, on the part of the Japanese minister, a repetition of the frequently declared object of his government,—namely, to destroy or sufficiently punish the Botan murderers, by means of an expedition which should furthermore take effective measures to prevent the recurrence of such outrages. This document having been read, the Commissioner said he would like to know what plan the general had decided upon, if any, for the prevention of future misdeeds. In response, Saigo stated that he undoubtedly had a plan which seemed to him suitable and sufficient, but he did not think it desirable to reveal it, especially as his operations were still in progress. The savage tribes were not yet completely brought to terms, and his troops were scattered in various parts of Southern Formosa, and it seemed to him altogether inexpedient to communicate the details of his plan. The commissioner said that he had come to Formosa by the direction of his government, to superintend the settlement of the affairs of the entire disturbed district, in co-operation with the Japanese commander; and asked if the latter had nothing to disclose, with a view to mutually carrying out this design. Saigo answered that he also came under very distinct directions from his government, but that they related solely to the punishment of the savages and the security of life for the future, and did not contemplate any co-operation with Chinese officials; that on his arrival he found that the Chinese-speaking people of the region were in no way under the control of China, and that the savages were utterly wild and lawless, beyond the control of everybody, and requiring to be dealt with by a vigorous hand. This he had done by himself, and he had now no scheme of co-operation to propose, nor could he accept or submit to any. The commissioner—counselled, I think, by the foreign gentlemen beside him, though I must not be positive on this point—continued to press his proposal for repeated conferences and combined action, but Saigo steadily declined, particularly as these suggestions were always accompanied by declarations that the legitimate sway of China extended over all Formosa and its people—a position which the Japanese general was not disposed to admit, conceiving that the question had already been debated and adjusted by Soyezima in Peking, and that, under any circumstances, it was not necessary for him to discuss it here. In fact, he remarked that if the commissioner desired to continue discussions based on that theory, he thought it would be more appropriately done through the Japanese envoy to the Chinese court—that it was more correctly a subject of negotiation between the two nations than between individual commissioners at a distant point."

This concluded the official part of the meeting, but arrangements were made for a second interview on the 24th for the presentation of certain points held in reserve by the Chinese.

The Chinese were evidently disposed to make up for lost time in attempting to establish friendly relations with the natives, for the next day was spent in sending communications to the independent coast villages and messengers with presents, etc., to those savage tribes, with, of course, the exception of the Botans and Kusukuts, who, as a result of the exertions of the Japanese, could now be visited with safety.

The last and most important conference between the Japanese general and the commissioner began on the afternoon of June 24th and was continued through the 25th. Our author reviews it as follows:

"The results arrived at promised a speedy termination of the active operations of the Japanese. Although the refusals of Saigo to assume the responsibility of absolute decision were as positive as ever, he nevertheless found it possible to promise that the Chinese proposals should be forwarded, with favorable endorsements, to his government, and to indicate his personal satisfaction with their general tenor. There would have been slight occasion for subsequent proceedings, if the course of the Chinese officials had been sustained by those who sent them, and the conditions which they expressed themselves ready and empowered to fulfill had been faithfully and promptly executed by their superiors. It is hardly desirable to follow minutely the course of a conversation which extended over so many hours, and in which many points were introduced, at times, which proved to be irrelevant to the final settlement. Each party conducted his side of the discussion in the way that best suited his individual or national character. The Chinese officer was circumspect, deliberate, wary, and highly polished in tone and expression. General Saigo was frank and straightforward, and, though always courteous in manner of speech, was, I presume, far too abrupt in his declarations of determined conviction to suit the circuitous smoothness of Chinese statecraft. A single instance will show the vast difference in the methods of treating the questions at issue adopted by the two men. The topic of the future control of the savages was under consideration. China's representative declared the readiness of his government to give pledges that they would maintain a sufficient force to keep perfect order in future. The general replied to the effect that he did not doubt that pledges would be given, but was by no means assured that they would be adhered to with fidelity. On being asked why, he intimated that the whole course of the Chinese, in the Formosa business, had been one of duplicity; that they perfectly well knew the Japanese causes of complaint two years ago, and now pretended ignorance of them up to a late period; that they had disclaimed jurisdiction over the savage territory until within a few weeks, and now announced that they had always assumed it; that it had been open to them at any time since 1871 to punish the Botans, by themselves, for the massacre of the Japanese subjects, whereas they now affected great regret at not having been invited to accompany the expedition for chastising them, and that, all things considered, he did not believe they would keep the savages in subjection, even if they promised to. Whereupon Pau Wi flew into a rage, prudently directing his ire, however, not toward the general, but against the interpreter, whom he accused of falsely translating what Saigo had said; averring that it was impossible that the Japanese commander could have used such language, and directing him to report to his master exactly the rebuke he had received. But it is not at all in Saigo's nature to accept a proposal for this sort of evasion, so he stated that his interpreter was not at all responsible, and repeated his conviction; but added, when the commissioner gave indications of irrepressible wrath, that if this particular subject was disagreeable, it could be abandoned for a while, and resumed at another time. Episodes like this were certainly not frequent, but their occasional occurrence served to show that the Japanese officer would not agree to any terms of settlement that should not strictly bind the Chinese to the complete fulfilment of all their obligations. This detail is anticipatory. From the beginning, the sole desire of the commissioner, Pau, seemed to be to establish the right of his government to jurisdiction over the whole of the soil of Formosa. Equally from the beginning, the Japanese general pointed out how repeatedly that claim had been waived. At the same time, he did not hesitate to assure the Chinese official that the Japanese had no purpose of attempting to wrest from China even an imaginary possession. His design was, as it had always been, to inflict a necessary punishment, and establish a state of security for the future. Gradually, the idea was brought forward, on the other side, that the difficulty might be arranged by China's assuming the task of preserving peace throughout the disturbed region hereafter. Then arose the amusing little break in the discussion which I have described above. In course of time the suggestion arose and gained favor that the Chinese might give substantial guarantees of their intentions. This grew out of an intimation, on the part of the Japanese, that, if all this region had really been under China's control, then Japan had been doing the work that China ought to have done but had neglected, at an expenditure which should properly have fallen upon the other party. Although merely an incidental observation, not intended as especially pertinent, this was, I think, somewhat eagerly seized upon. Suppose that the Peking government would undertake to reimburse the Japanese for their outlay,—would that meet any of the questions in dispute? It seemed to be agreed on all sides that this would at least stand as strong evidence of good faith. And so, after many divergencies and variations of slight import, it was ultimately agreed, on the evening of June 25th, that the active operations of the Japanese should be suspended, pending a reference of terms of settlement, for final consideration, to the respective governments. These terms were to be substantially as follows :

'The Chinese authorities to reimburse the Japanese for the cost of their expedition.

The Chinese to guarantee such occupation of the savage territory of Formosa as should prevent the recurrence of outrages upon strangers.

'These conditions effected, the Japanese forces to be withdrawn.'

The Chinese commissioner expressed not the slightest doubt of the willingness of his government to subscribe to this agreement, and gave it to be understood that he was acting with full authority in offering it, and that the reference to Peking was solely a matter of formality. It was, therefore, reasonable to believe that the occupation of Southern Formosa would terminate in a very short time, and that the duties of the Japanese, in that island, were virtually ended. They were, in fact, required to do nothing until the time of their departure, which took place in December, and which might have taken place much earlier but for the bad faith exhibited by the Peking government."

From the arrival until the departure of the visitors no opportunity was lost of showing them all the formal courtesy and respect the occasion admitted. On the 26th of June they took leave, but were obliged to travel overland to Takow, forty miles distant, before embarking, as their ships had been forced to leave Liangkiau Bay owing to a violent storm the day before.

From other writings we are informed that, at least by the Chinese throughout the island and even in certain of the coast ports of the mainland, the Japanese expedition was considered to be but a preparation for a general attack on China. Even the same Chinese envoy who had lately been sent to confer with General Saigo, but was excused on account of illness, considered the necessity of strengthening the defences of the island so immediate that he personally remained in Formosa to superintend the work, and M. Giquel, of the Foochow arsenal, who, it will be remembered, accompanied the acting commissioner on his visit to the Japanese camp, was placed as assistant. The object seems to have been not to prepare for offensive operations but simply to oppose the Japanese, should they attempt to advance northward.

Mud forts were erected at many different stations along the western sea-board. Every important garrison from Tamsui, in the north, to Pithau and Takow, in the south, received additional reinforcements,[1] and special efforts were made to strengthen the defences of the old city of Taiwanfu.[2]

1 The total number of Chinese troops landed in the south of Formosa during the period between the 25th August and the 17th November, amounted to 10,970. "Imperial Chinese Maritime Customs Reports—Takow, 1874."

2. Campbell's "Missionary Success in Formosa."

Especially in Taiwanfu and Takow were remarks about the Japanese a never-ceasing topic of conversation, and junk after junk departed loaded with Chinese seeking passage to China, where it was thought greater safety awaited them.

Before the arrival of the expedition, Japanese visitors had been very numerous, and now that troops had followed, it was thought that every spot previously visited by the Japanese spies, as they were now considered to be, would soon be occupied by Japanese forces. A state of considerable excitement was the not unnatural result, and that this excitement was not confined to the lower classes is evident from the energy which was aroused among the officials.

To give the Chinese a base of operations, should the Japanese attempt a flank movement through the savage territory, sub-prefect Yuen was entrusted with the construction of a road to extend from a place near the village of Ch'ihshan, twenty-five miles inland and to the east of Takow, across the summit of Kunlun mountain to Pilam on the east coast.

The route was important also from the fact that on the Kunlun mountain was the point from which savage tracks converged to different points of importance, such as Hongkong village and the Botan territory, in the south, and Suao and Changwha villages, in the north. The undertaking was commenced with 500 workmen protected by 500 soldiers, and as the work advanced three different camps of Cantonese troops were established in support of it. However, owing to the unusually wet summer, but little progress was made, so that by the end of September the road had only reached the summit of Kunlun mountain.

From this point the original plan was abandoned, and an old path by a different route, formerly used by Chinese travellers, was improved, and used for a great part of the distance. This, combined with that which they had already built, gave them, by the end of November, direct communication with Pilam. It must be remembered that what is usually called in Formosa a Chinese road, is, in reality, but a foot-path by which pedestrians can proceed, but utterly impassable for cavalry or artillery. In the present case beasts of burden and even sedan-chairs could not be utilized, and furthermore it was entirely unavailable during the wet season, as a river-bed formed a portion of it.[1]

In the north of the island during the early days of the expedition, the Chinese officials were not without considerable anxiety. But as time passed and no bad news was received, they felt somewhat easier, believing that the Japanese expedition must have had the countenance of the Peking government. Consequently the Japanese ships, bound to and from Liangkiau, that put into Kelung for coal were supplied without hesitation, flying as they did the ensign of a friendly power.

The reconnoitring parties which, towards the end of June, reached far toward the north on the east coast, and eventually emerged at Khelai, a place north of the settlement usually marked on the maps as Chockeday,

---

1. Campbell's " Missionary Success in Formosa "

created a fresh scare in official circles. The position being strategically one of importance, the inference was that the Japanese were meditating a second landing either in the neighborhood or perhaps at Suao, the well-known east coast harbor forty miles to the north.

As a result Suao was at once garrisoned and strict enquiries instituted as to the strangers' doings while at Khelai. By this time, however, the Japanese were through with their work and away, their departure, being reported to the Chinese officials as due to the wrecking of their steamer, a sea-going cargo boat, and the outbreak of fever among them. Chinese settlers, who for years past had been trading with the savages in the vicinity of Khelai, gave the information that the Japanese on their arrival had taken great pains to ingratiate themselves with all the inhabitants, whether aborigines or Chinese. Presents of dollars, foreign clothing, cloth, bangles, fans, rings, etc., were lavishly given. Permission was sought to erect a number of straw huts. Plans of the locality were drawn, many trips made into the neighboring hills, and what appeared strangest of all to the informants, over one hundred samples of soil were collected, packed, and carried away. In consequence of an outbreak of fever, the camp was struck, and the Japanese retired. In proof of these assertions, the informants produced presents which they had received, besides handing over to the Komalan-ting a quantity of effects, including a national ensign left behind by the Japanese.[1]

About the middle of July, a claim was made on the Chinese officials of the island by a Japanese merchant at Suao Bay, for the alleged robbery of his property while trading there. The Chinese, now effectually aroused, were not inclined to give any more excuses for the Japanese to settle Formosan difficulties themselves; so they at once despatched Taotai Hia with a force of five hundred men and some light artillery to Suao. With the rumors then current among Chinese, their anxiety lest the Japanese should land at Suao is not to be wondered at. For, once established there, it would have been an easy matter to combine with the powerful factions of the Changwha district, then in almost open rebellion against the Chinese officials, and, together, notwithstanding the small Japanese force, the island would in all probability have fallen an easy capture.

The claim of the Japanese trader settled, a victory gained over a savage tribe in the vicinity, and work commenced on a road from Changwha across the mountains to Suao Bay were the results of Taotai Hia's expedition.[2]

On the mainland, the greatest anxiety was felt at Amoy, the principal China port engaged in trade with Formosa. In fact, it resulted in a partial panic among the lower, if not the higher, classes, shared to some extent by the local authorities. At any rate, no official attempt appears to have been made towards arresting it. Many of the populace fled into the interior, and numbers of merchants suspended their business in anticipation of the necessity for sudden flight.

That Americans were assisting in the Japanese expedition was to the Chinese officials a matter of great importance, and it would seem that as a

1 and 2: Imperial Chinese Maritime Customs reports—Tamsui, 1874.

result of their protestations, the United States consul was led to interfere. Even the viceroy of Fokien had become so impressed with the trend of events that he had directly addressed Consul Henderson on the matter, such direct transmission being quite without precedent. The translation of this rather unique document, omitting a few opening lines of courteous greeting, is herewith given:—

"Now we have investigated this Formosan business, as well as the statements of the taotai of Formosa and the captain of the *Yang-wa*, to the effect that this expedition to the savages of Formosa has been planned by the former American consul at Amoy, Le Gendre; also one Cassel, and many others assisting. We have also examined and found that Formosa has long belonged to China, and the savages are certainly under Chinese jurisdiction, and other nations have nothing to do with them. On this occasion Japan has sent soldiers to punish the savages without previous consultation with the Foreign Office, and the Japanese commander-in-chief, without awaiting a communication from me, on his own motion took soldiers and formed a camp at Liang-kiau, in entire violation both of International Law and the treaty between China and Japan. We twice sent communications to the commander-in-chief, requiring him to take back his soldiers, and twice sent communications to the Board of Trade to be presented to your honorable self, to be examined and acted on ; all of which are on file. We have received your despatch, in which you show your desire to carry out treaty obligations, and, in settling matters, to preserve lasting peace and friendship, as well as your purpose to perform your duties ; for all which we desire to express our hearty thanks. We have appointed Shen, second in the Board of Trade, and formerly acting prefect of Fuchow, to go to Amoy, and also have sent a communication to Li, admiral at Amoy, telling him to await the coming of Shen, and then with him to have a consultation with the U. S. consul, and together concert some plan of action. And in accordance with the provisions of Art. I. of the Treaty of the 1st year of Hienfung (1858), that the two countries shall mutually assist in preserving friendly relations, we ask your honorable self to request the commander to take his soldiers back to Japan. And if in the vessels that have gone to Formosa there are American citizens aiding the Japanese, we ask you to punish those that are acting improperly, whether on land or sea, in accordance with the 11th article of the Treaty and the laws of your country. From the time when your honorable self arrived in China, you have always managed affairs in strict accordance with right, so that the streets are full of praises of yourself by rulers and people, and ourselves are truly thankful. Now that there are affairs in Formosa, over which you are consul, you can show your friendly feelings by acting in accordance with the treaty, and by taking measures in connection with Admiral Li and Prefect Shen. Thus can you show friendly feeling. We have sent a communication to Admiral Li, and also one to Prefect Shen ordering him to go to Amoy and arrange the whole affair with you, for which purpose we give them full powers. And we request you to act with these two, not only as officials but as friends. Hoping thus, with best regards, etc., etc., etc."

The interview which followed still further showed the great anxiety of the Chinese. They appeared to be under the delusion that were the Americans withdrawn the whole project would fall through. Especially were they concerned regarding the connection of General Le Gendre, who, as a former United States consul, still appeared to them to be in some way an agent of the government. Not satisfied with the assurances that notifications had already been sent by the consul to the Americans in Formosa, it was at their solicitation that duplicates were sent by a small Chinese gunboat, which they were only too anxious to offer for the purpose.

This boat arrived in Liangkiau harbor on the afternoon of July 1st. A messenger landed, who announced himself as deputy marshal of the U.S. consul at Amoy.

The communication from the consul, which he delivered to the Americans, warned them against participating in any hostile action against the Chinese government. It is believed the Americans addressed considered it sufficient to send in response, a brief statement explaining the actual condition of affairs, that there was no intention of assisting in warlike operations, and promising to withdraw in the event of war with China. The consul had also drawn up and had printed a circular, which, as there were only three Americans on the expedition, seemed an extravagant waste of printer's ink, warning all citizens of the United States to " at once withdraw from the Japanese armed expedition now operating in the island of Formosa, and hereafter to avoid any connection with that enterprise, under penalty of arrest and trial for violation of the laws of neutrality. That the three American citizens thus addressed did not obey was, considering the misapprehensions under which it was evident the instructions had been issued, a credit to them as well as fortunate for the consul, whose superiors in Washington saw fit to severely condemn his unjustifiable interference.

After frequent protests that they were not responsible for the conduct of the savages, these not being under Chinese jurisdiction, the Chinese now came forward with the assumption that the whole island and people of Formosa were under Chinese authority. That this was an after-thought was sufficiently clear. Specially remarkable was the assertion of the viceroy of Fokien in his letter to the consul—"the savages are certainly under Chinese jurisdiction"—when it is noted that in a letter from the Fokien authorities in 1867 in answer to the demand for reparation made by the United States consul in regard to the *Rover* massacre, it was stated : "But as in the *Rover* case the Americans were not murdered in Chinese territory or in Chinese seas, but in a region occupied by the savages, relief cannot be asked for them under the treaty. The savage territory does not come within the limits of our jurisdiction." * * * * "We believe those savages to be wild animals with whom any one would disdain to contend." Again, as late as May, 1874, the Chinese admiral at Amoy, in consultation with the United States consul, reiterated the statement that the Chinese government admitted no responsibility for the deeds of the savages in Formosa.

CHAPTER XIII.

THE JAPANESE EXPEDITION OF 1874.
JULY—NOVEMBER.

Public feeling throughout Japan—Mission of General Le Gendre to Fokien—His arrest and release—Formal disapproval declared by United States officers—Okubo sent on special mission to Peking—Frequent conferences—Chinese declarations—Unsatisfactory progress—Valuable assistance rendered by Mr. Wade, British minister—An ultimatum—Okubo's last word—Message from Prince Kung—The agreements signed—Chinese destruction of Japanese works in Formosa—The effect in Japan—Affairs in Formosa—Serious outbreak of fever—Proclamations presented to savages—Evacuation by Japanese—Chinese authorities take command—An attempt to exert authority over savages fails—Chinese military expedition enters savage territory—They are surrounded, routed, and two hundred and fifty killed and mutilated by savages—Savages not again disturbed—Japan justly commended—The ocean highway secure.

In Japan, with the knowledge of a serious dispute existing with China, the inhabitants were in a high state of patriotic excitement. China had insulted them and China should be immediately dealt with severely. There was no doubt that the masses were ready for instant combat, but fortunately the officials were able to restrain the people and promote the better interests of the country by a peaceful solution of the difficulty.

An intended measure in the interest of peace was the despatch of General Le Gendre to the south of China. He left Japan towards the end of July, and was to proceed to Fokien and there enter into negotiations with the viceroy. This was not suffered to be, however, for upon arriving at Amoy, through which it was necessary for him to pass, he was forcibly arrested by the United States marshal of the Amoy consulate, who had called in the assistance of officers and marines from the U.S.S. *Yantic*. He was then sent to Shanghai, but here he was immediately released. It was then too late to fulfill his mission to Foochow, and he consequently made no attempt to return south. It is not necessary to speak further of this second interference in the affairs of the Japanese, inasmuch as the action of every official connected with this arbitrary and illegal exercise of consular authority was at once repudiated, and the strongest disapproval, short of actual dismissal from public service, was expressed by the United States government at Washington.

A few days after the departure of General Le Gendre, Okubo Toshimitsu, an eminent minister, who was well worthy of the implicit confidence placed in him by the Japanese, was sent upon a special mission to China with full powers to act in the name of the emperor. At Tientsin he was joined by General Le Gendre, and the party reached Peking on the 10th of September.

Meanwhile the Japanese minister, Yanagiwara, had been a witness of repeated acts of Chinese duplicity. The report of the negotiations held between General Saigo and Pan Wi has been related in a former chapter. Yet Commissioner Shen, early in June, had caused to be sent to the Chinese government a statement that he had himself arranged affairs with the savages, and that Saigo had declared his readiness to return to Japan with his troops "at the first command of his government." This was communicated to Yanagiwara, by the taotai at Shanghai, on the 8th of July. Arriving later in Peking, the minister found that despatches from the late Chinese visitors to Formosa were on several occasions produced for his inspection as evidence that the affair was already settled, and that nothing remained but for the Japanese to withdraw their troops.

The arrival of Okubo soon put a stop to this perpetual chicanery, and, at his instigation, negotiations for an immediate and final settlement were begun at once.

After thoroughly reviewing the subject, Okubo stated his own view to the Tsung-li Yamen and concluded by submitting, on the 14th of September, two propositions, namely: That although China claimed jurisdiction over the savages, she had taken no steps to govern or reform them, and that, if the alleged power of control existed and failed to be exercised, it was not possible for China to escape the accusation of virtually encouraging the natives in their barbarous acts towards shipwrecked people.

On the 16th, a second conference was held: the Chinese, equal to any occasion, answered the above propositions by boldly asserting that China had "improved the manners" of the savage aborigines, "organized their communities," "educated those who had good and intelligent dispositions," and "actually established government over them." It was admitted, however, that their "policy was to civilize them, not by hasty and precipitate measures, but gradually and steadily." Regarding the maltreatment of castaways, they stated that if foreign ships were wrecked and the sailors injured, if the ministers of those nations demanded satisfaction, "minutely setting forth the circumstances attending each event," China "would examine into such affairs and would never neglect them." "Consequently," it was added, "if your government had written minutely about the present matter, our Yamen would have taken the proper measures to examine into and settle it. Then our Yamen would have established proper laws over the savages, and would have instructed them to protect foreigners in the future." Such assumptions require no further comment.

On the discussion continuing on the 19th, Okubo could but express dissatisfaction with the replies as given. As to the appliance of International Law to the question, their attention having been called to it, the Chinese stated that as such codes had but lately been compiled by Europeans, and " there being no mention of China in them," they " intended to negotiate without adopting any of the opinions therein contained."

It is not necessary to describe in detail the declarations which followed, except to refer to one statement which appears specially significant. " As to the evidence concerning aboriginal Formosa," said the Chinese officer, " we fear there may be some obscure points in it ; but henceforward, we will extend our laws and administration over the territory of the savages, restrain their wicked and violent actions, and take such measures as will preserve forever the friendly relations between the two countries. If, on the contrary, you will not consent to entrust our government with the management of the present affair, we shall then have nothing more to say."

Respecting the evidence spoken of, the Japanese commissioner replied that none whatever had been produced, and that until some substantial proof of the Chinese position had been offered, he should continue to dispute it. Speaking from another point he said :—" Now that communication is established between the Eastern and Western worlds, safety and protection must be accorded to the navigators of all nations. Formosa is a very important island in the direct highway of commerce, but its people are like pirates in their practices."

Meetings between the representatives continued at intervals through the month of September with no satisfactory result, the Chinese confining themselves to reassertions of their previous statements, and Okubo refusing to accept them. The ignorance of the Chinese on questions of international law became so apparent, it is said, that on one of these occasions Okubo presented to the Yamen a condensed translation of the code. On the 5th of October affairs had reached such an unsatisfactory state that the Chinese became almost menacing in their tone, and, even intimated to the commissioner that it would be well for him to return home at once while he could do so with safety. To this Okubo stated : " If you hold that further discussions are impossible, and will not answer my questions, our conferences shall end to-day, and the object of my mission (the desire of maintaining the friendly relations between the two governments) shall be arrested here." The meeting then terminated by Okubo announcing his intention of returning to Japan at once. He was afterwards led to reconsider this determination by the courteously expressed desire of the Yamen officials that the negotiations should continue. Furthermore it was requested that the unpleasant observations that had passed should not be included in the record of the transactions. This proposition to amend the record Okubo declined, stating that he himself could make no alterations in the transactions, but that such might be rectified by after correspondence.

Soon after the arrival of Okubo, the British envoy, Mr. Wade, who was in close touch with the Chinese authorities, expressed his desire to learn from the Japanese the precise nature of their functions and the progress they were making. Okubo declined to give this information, stating that the Chinese refused to acknowledge the correctness of the statements made by Soyezima, former ambassador to Peking, as to the denial by the Tsung-li Yamen of Chinese authority over the savages of Formosa. As long as this was not conceded and the question of veracity between the two governments remained unsettled, the negotiations could not be such as would justify their being revealed. Apparently Mr. Wade appreciated the propriety of the Japanese view of the situation, for he thenceforward confined himself to getting information from Chinese sources. It does not appear that the actions of the British minister were at any time the result of a feeling of hostility towards Japan, and although he on one occasion expressed his intention of telegraphing to England for armed support, it seems that this was with the special desire of protecting English commerce, which then amounted to many millions of dollars a year. That he was desirous of acting as arbitrator was evident, but while the Chinese were not averse to accepting his assistance, the Japanese commissioner declined from the first.

On the 10th of October, an ultimatum was transmitted by Okubo, allowing but five days for further negotiations, when at the conclusion of this period, if a definite answer was not given, the meetings must come to an end. A message having been later received to the effect that, as the emperor was absent from the capital, an extension of the time was desired, Okubo readily consented to an additional delay.

On the 15th an answer was received by Okubo which showed a decided inclination to bring the matter to a speedy end.

At an another meeting, on the 18th, at Okubo's apartments, the Chinese, while wishing to avoid a discussion of the question as to their right to south Formosa, expressed their willingness to recognize their negligence and offer a sum of money in compensation for the slaughtered Loochooans. A step backward was taken on the next day, however, when the Yamen notified Okubo that a difficulty had arisen, the special points of which were that, while willing to pay an indemnity for losses sustained by Japan, they could not consent to give a written declaration to that effect, neither could they deliver the amount until after the Japanese troops had been withdrawn. They furthermore objected to stating the precise sum of the indemnity, but said it should be left to the discretion of their government.

These conditions did not satisfy the Japanese commissioner in the least. As the Chinese had already once repudiated their oral declarations, he was not inclined to give them another chance, and as he informed them : "If I should rely upon your words at the present moment, and afterwards there should be found in them some points unsatisfactory to our government, we must again charge you with a wrong, and some great difficulty might arise. I therefore want some trustworthy written proofs." On the 24th, the offer was renewed and again rejected. On the 25th, what was expected to be the final letter was sent by Okubo containing the following expressions of opinion :

" Now I am quite hopeless and am about to leave. The notice given to you of an intention to punish the aboriginal tribes was set at naught by your Tsung-li Yamen, and when we sent a commissioner with troops to take vengeance upon the tribes that had murdered our shipwrecked people, and to remove the evils which threatened the navigators of those seas, you afforded us no encouragement in our difficult and dangerous task, but affected to be very proud of your mercy in not 'shooting an arrow at us.'   Under these circumstances, our philanthropic action, to our lasting regret, has been designated by you by the bad name of a hostile deed, while our undertaking to punish the savages arose only from the necessity of protecting our own people.   Henceforth, inside and back of the mountains, we shall continue to clear land, protecting those tribes which submit to us, and punishing those who oppose us, and shall complete our plan of action without permitting any molestation on the part of your country. Finally, I have to say that, as the present case cannot be decided by arguments, each country must go its own way and exercise its own rights of sovereignty.   I do not wish to hear any further explanations and arguments you may have to offer.   I am in haste to depart, and cannot go to your Tsung-li Yamen to take leave of you."

Of all public men in Japan of that day, Okubo was the most conspicuous for qualities of forbearance and toleration.   That he should have been forced to express himself in so peremptory a tone was, at least to those who were acquainted with his character, sufficient proof that leniency and gentleness had been carried to their extreme limit, and that every honorable means of conciliation, on his part, had been exhausted.

Preparations were made for leaving Peking without delay, and during the afternoon General Le Gendre and a part of the suite set out on their journey to Tientsin.   Upon being informed of this and that the withdrawal of the entire mission was imminent, Prince Kung went in haste to the residence of the British minister, Mr. Wade, and requested him to take a message to Okubo which might have the effect of detaining the party. The visit was made at once and Mr. Wade informed the Japanese commissioner that he was empowered to declare that there would now be no objection made against Okubo's resolution to obtain written evidence of consent to the terms proposed, that the payment of one hundred thousand taels should be made immediately "as relief to the sufferers" (meaning the families of those who had been slaughtered in 1871, and the survivors) and four hundred thousand taels "as indemnity for the various expenses of the expedition," after the troops had been withdrawn.

Now convinced that at last a sincere effort at settlement would be made, Okubo deferred his departure, went the same day to Mr. Wade's residence, and there stated that the amount of money to be paid being a matter of secondary importance, five hundred thousand taels would be received subject to the conditions that the Formosan expedition be publicly recognized as just and rightful and the money paid before the withdrawal of the troops.   Acting again as willing messenger, Mr. Wade conveyed this decision to the Chinese authorities.   Whether he used his influence or not to induce the Chinese to accept the terms is not known.   With the Japanese official, however, he never attempted to exert the slightest influence.

On the 27th, Mr. Wade rendered most valuable service, inasmuch as he guaranteed that the draft of the articles of agreement which had been prepared by the Yamen, should not be subject to any alterations.

The terms having now been pronounced satisfactory by Okubo, the document was on the 31st of October duly signed and sealed at the Office of the Tsung li Yamen. [1]

The following are the contents of the several papers, given in as literal a translation as is compatible with presentation in the usual English form.

"AGREEMENT.

"[PREAMBLE.] Whereas, Okubo, High Commissioner Plenipotentiary of Japan, Sangi, Councillor of State and Secretary of the Interior Department [on the one part], and [names of Prince Kung and nine other Chinese officials] of the Tsung li Yamen of China [on the other part], having discussed the subject of Articles of Agreement and fixed the manner of their settlement; and it having been understood that the subjects of every nation must be duly protected from injury; that therefore every nation may take efficient measures for the security of its subjects; that if anything [injurious] happen within the limits of any state, that state should undertake the duty of reparation; that the aborigines of Formosa formerly committed outrages upon subjects of Japan; that Japan sent troops for the sole purpose of inflicting punishment on these aborigines, and that the troops are to be withdrawn, China assuming the responsibility of measures for the future; therefore, the following Articles have been drawn up and agreed upon;

ARTICLE I.

"The present enterprise of Japan is a just and rightful proceeding, to protect her own subjects, and China does not designate it as a wrong action.

ARTICLE II.

"A sum of money shall be given by China for relief to the families of the shipwrecked [Japanese] subjects that were maltreated. Japan has constructed roads and built houses, &c., in that place. China, wishing to have the use of these for herself, agrees to make payment for them. The amount is determined by a special document.

ARTICLE III.

"All the official correspondence hitherto exchanged between the two states shall be returned [mutually] and be annulled, to prevent any future misunderstanding. As to the savages, China engages to establish authority, and promises that navigators shall be protected from injury by them.

CONTRACT.

"With regard to the question of Formosa, Mr. Wade, H. B. M.'s Minister, having spoken on the subject to the two parties, they, the said Commissioners of the two nations, have arranged for settlement thus:—

"I.—China agrees that she shall pay the sum of one hundred thousand taels, for relief to the families of the subjects of Japan who were murdered.

"II.—China wishes that, after Japan shall have withdrawn her troops, all the roads that have been repaired and all the houses that have been built, etc., shall be retained for her use; at the same time consenting to pay the sum of four hundred thousand taels by way of recompense; and it is agreed that Japan shall withdraw all her troops, and China shall pay the whole amount without fail, by the 20th day of December, the seventh year of Meiji, with Japan, or on the 22nd day of the eleventh moon, the thirteenth year of Tung Chi, with China; but, in the event of Japan not withdrawing her troops, China shall not pay the amount.

"This settlement having been concluded, each party has taken one copy of the contract as voucher."

Our author explains that the "special document" referred to in Article II. was made a separate subject of consideration chiefly because grave doubts existed as to the Chinese fulfilment of an agreement which would involve the complete surrender of their strongest points of objection. It was thought desirable by the Japanese commissioner that the name of Mr. Wade, who had already (Oct. 27th) given a personal pledge that the terms of settlement should not be altered, should appear in testimony of his knowledge of China's submission in respect to the questions which had been disputed with so much persistency. It was consequently introduced in the subjoined contract as given above.

With regard to certain peculiarities of phraseology in these documents, it is also explained that the acceptance of the sums of money ostensibly as "relief" or "consolation," and as payment for improvements that were to

---

1. The valuable assistance rendered by Mr. Wade was much appreciated by the Japanese, and gained the emperor's personal thanks.

be diverted to the use of China, was in consequence of repeated and urgent representations that the dignity of that nation would thereby be saved from a rude shock. Okubo had naturally at first spoken only of "indemnity ;" but the Chinese were almost piteous in their appeals to be spared the humiliation that they fancied would be implied by the use of that word. Never once during the discussions, did Okubo show himself unreasonably obdurate, and he was frequently ready to waive points of mere nominal formality, so long as the vital requirements of his duty were not assailed. On the 21st of October he had written, in regard to the expenditures, as follows :—"Your country must be responsible, but, to save appearances, you wish that 'consolation money' shall be paid to our ill-treated countrymen by the special grace of your emperor." And, on the 23d : "Your proposal that the compensation should take the name of 'consolation' was at first unsatisfactory, but, considering the circumstances of your country, it has now been consented to." The Yamen, unfortunately for themselves, were not altogether content to let the matter stand thus, and subsequently conceived the idea of suggesting that the larger share of the payment should be understood as having reference to the roads and other works commenced or completed by the Japanese in Formosa. This was also acceded to.

It will be remembered that the Yamen had requested that the larger part of the indemnity should be given to the Japanese in payment for the houses built, roads constructed, and other improvements made in South Formosa. And now, this point gained, we find how baseless were these representations, when our author tells us that, after the departure of General Saigo, "suddenly forgetful of her anxiety to save appearances, China ordered the immediate destruction of every vestige of Japanese occupation, so that the laborious structure of deceptive artifice fell to pieces by her own action. If she did not want the houses and other improvements, then the money could be regarded as nothing but a direct indemnity—small in amount but sufficient to establish the principle ; and that she did not want them, she proved by obliterating all traces of their existence as soon as she could lay hands on them."[1]

The details of the settlement were wired from Shanghai to Tōkyō by Okubo on November 7th, and the news was at once transmitted to the various departments. The peaceful termination of the difficulty was welcome news to the Japanese at home. With the exception of the lower classes none were attracted by the prospect of actual war, although the nation was prepared in case hostilities could not be averted by honorable means. Large contributions offered by the people of every rank, from the

---

1. "During the night incendiarism on the part of the villagers who had had their queues cut off for looting laid waste the greater portion of the Japanese camp, so that out of the one hundred large wooden huts that composed it, only thirty remained intact." Imperial Chinese Maritime Customs Reports—Takow 1874.

This is the Chinese explanation of the affair, and while it may be true that a portion of the camp was destroyed by angry villagers, it appears odd that such extensive damage could have been done the first night after the departure of the Japanese and while the place was occupied by Chinese soldiers, unless the latter had either given their consent or had made no attempts to check it. As it is, this only speaks of a portion of the camp. Visitors to the same spot a few months later found that every trace of the Japanese occupation had been carefully removed.

Imperial Family to the peasantry, had been placed at the disposal of the government. Great numbers of citizens had enrolled themselves and offered their services as volunteers. Large accumulations of war material, the establishment of formidable armaments at the points nearest the Chinese coast, were all a part of the desire of the nation to be well prepared for war should it come.

The success obtained by Saigo was not more complete than the victory of Okubo. None doubted the bravery of the Japanese in war, but many were disinclined to believe that diplomatically the younger nation could prove itself a match for the cunning and smartness of a government whose only marked achievements have been the development of political stratagem.

Okubo, after visiting Formosa to personally acquaint General Saigo with the result, returned to Japan, reaching Tōkyō towards the end of November, where he was received with numerous manifestations of approval by the masses and unusual favor by the Imperial House.

In Formosa, after the visit of the Chinese delegates in June, no incidents of importance occurred to vary the unceasing monotony of camp life. Acknowledgment of submission had before the end of July been received from all the southern hostile tribes. There is nothing left to record except unfortunately the very serious outbreak of Formosan fever which brought death to more than five hundred Japanese soldiers and coolies. After the first serious outbreak of the disease, which occurred in August, it spread with such rapidity that, for the last few weeks of the occupation, the deaths averaged thirteen per day, and it is stated as a fact that General Saigo and one subordinate officer alone, out of the several thousand there assembled, escaped entirely untouched by the disease. During this period it had been necessary to bring successive reinforcements from Japan to take the place of those on the sick list. The American attachés suffered with the rest, Mr. Cassel's illness being of such severity that for some time grave doubts were entertained as to his recovery. Mr. Wasson left the island before the malady had assumed its worst form and was among the first to recover.

The required compensation was paid by China before the 1st of December, and General Saigo having previously (17th of November) been formally presented with orders by a special messenger of rank, took leave of Formosa with his whole force on the 3rd of December, more than two weeks before the stipulated time. Before departing he issued two proclamations. To the friendly aborigines the first was presented and read as follows.

"Our intention in coming here has already been announced to you; and you have well understood our motives and offered the best assistance that lay in your power. All the wild savages trembled and bowed before our arms. After this, we continued to occupy the land because of the opposition which was made to our acts by the Chinese government; but now, the negotiations between the two nations being brought to a conclusion, we have ceded all the land to China, according to its wish. We well know and deeply acknowledge the good and affectionate filial feeling you have shown towards us; and we heartily recommend you to henceforth attach yourselves to the Chinese officials as you have loved us, and to nobly obey their laws without making any opposition." [1]

1. That the Japanese commander did not exaggerate in referring to the affectionate regard existing between the savages and the Japanese of the expedition, I am assured. Rev. Wm. Campbell in his publication "*The Articles in Formosan*" in referring to the probable policy the Japanese will adopt in dealing with the savages now that the island has become a possession of Japan, says:—"So far as mere government measures are concerned a change will doubtless be made in the old Chinese policy of doing little more than attempting to exterminate the aborigines; because the Japanese are shrewd enough to know

The second proclamation was to the tribes that had united in hostility against the Japanese.

"A few years ago, the Botans committed an unpardonable crime in murdering some of our Loochooan subjects, and I, Yorimichi, respectfully obeying an Imperial order, came and chastised you. But as you repented of your evil deeds and asked for mercy, I forgave you, thinking you would wish for a peaceful and long life under our Imperial and benign government. But now, arrangements with China having been concluded, our empire has complied with the wishes of that nation, and we shall presently leave the place. Henceforth you must nobly obey, without making any opposition."

The embarkation[1] of the troops was a memorable event for the inhabitants of Liangkiau valley, who were present in great numbers and were joined by an unusual gathering of aborigines.

The savages had been apparently treated with consideration by all, and with extraordinary kindness by the officers, of the expedition, for they were visibly affected upon the departure, and when the general and his staff finally moved towards the boats, they clung to them; seizing their hands and clothing, and had to be detached by gentle force.[1]

On the 7th of December, the commander-in-chief landed at Nagasaki, and ten days later arrived in Tōkyō, where he was received with much honor and distinction.

During the following January an address was sent to the emperor by Okuma Shigenobu preparatory to the closing of the department which had been created to meet the requirements of the Formosa expedition. It read as follows :—

"In the first month of the past year Shigenobu and others, in accordance with the confidential instructions they had received, laid before Your Majesty a project for the chastisement of the savages. In April the Formosa Department was established and Shigenobu was appointed its chief, to superintend all business belonging to it. In May the commander-in-chief Saigo Yorimichi departed to the land of the

---

1. "About 8 a.m. on the 2nd December, the Prefect Chow arrived in the Japanese camp accompanied by a Formosan military regiment and 200 regular infantry as a body-guard. This cortege having no pretensions to military splendor, found its way to headquarters, where the prefect was received by General Saigo, a small body of Japanese infantry dressed, armed, drilled and disciplined in the French style, being drawn up in column and facing the Chinese troops,—also drawn up in military array.

"The general offered to hand over the outposts of the camp still held by the Japanese infantry, and on the prefect declining his offer, the general gave orders for his remaining guards to be withdrawn. These joined the infantry column, headed by General Saigo and his staff, and the whole body marched off with the greatest precision towards the seashore, to be then and there embarked on the vessels awaiting them. A few of the Japanese soldiers still remaining engaged in packing their belongings into carts, a body of marines came up for their protection; and indeed the fine military bearing of these men had quite an imposing effect, as with drums beating and bugles sounding they marched up to headquarters and took possession of the compound.

"The marines quitted the camp early in the afternoon, to keep guard over the considerable quantity of material that remained on the beach awaiting shipment. Of this all that the Japanese wished to take with them was shipped during the early part of the night; the remainder was set fire to by the sailors of the Japanese corvette, who were the last to leave the shore.

"A salute of twenty-one guns was fired by the Chinese corvette *Yang-wu* on the embarkation of General Saigo on board the transport, a compliment that was immediately returned by the Japanese corvette with the same number of guns.

"By 9 o'clock on the morning of the 3rd of December, the corvette *Yang-wu* was in solitary possession of Liang-kiau Bay, which had been for some time previously, one may say, thronged with war vessels and transports; and thus was amicably settled the Japanese Invasion of Formosa, which had at one time threatened to be so serious an affair."

Imperial Chinese Maritime Customs Reports—Takow, 1874.

---

that something of a parental attitude towards them will not only bring the practice of head-hunting to an end, and thus gain six thousand square miles of very valuable land, but strengthen their own hands by the creation of many loyal and most useful fellow subjects. In view of all this, it is impossible to forget the Japanese expedition to Formosa of 1874. The punitive nature of that expedition will be remembered, but the self restraint with which the members of it acted is less generally known. Bunkiet, second son of Tokitok, once told the writer that the native tribes were very sorry when the time came for the Japanese soldiers to leave, and it is quite possible the name of General Saigo continues to be mentioned with feelings of respect in the villages east from Liang-kiau. May a like firm, yet generous, course be followed in the present much larger undertaking."— Preface pages VIII and IX.

savages at the head of a force, exterminated the wicked, pardoned the submissive, aud remained there a long time encamped.   During the same month the Minister Plenipotentiary Yanagiwara Sakimitsu was despatched to China, and iu August the High Commissiouer Plenipotentiary Okubo Toshimichi also was sent to that country.   Toshimichi and the others worked diligently aud devotedly iu the discharge of the important trust committed to them.   In October a convention was exchanged with the said country, and iu November Toshimichi and the rest reported the fulfilment of their mission.   In December Yorimichi returned iu triumph.   From the institution of the Commission up to this date a period of eight mouths had elapsed.   Hereupon the wrongs of the sufferers were for the first time redressed, the position of a subject 'hau' for the first time cleared up, security restored to the mariners of all couutries for the first time, aud the dignity aud iufluence of the State consequently vindicated.

"After our troops had started and were on their way, foreign public servauts remoustrated.   The Chinese Governmeut hastily despatched au Euvoy, sent letters and mauifested a wide differeuce of opiuion.   Some persous not comprehending the views of the Governmeut, began to doubt whether it was justified in the course which it was taking.   Others discussed the want of funds, and rumor became so noisy that the State was agaiu imperilled.

"Shigeuobu and the others nevertheless accepted the respousibility, but day and night they were so busily employed that they feared lest their strength might be unequal to the task.   Fortunately, the wise resolutiou of His Majesty never wavered, aud the councils of the Governmeut became still more resolute.   Great military preparations were made, and the mind of the people, both iu the towns and iu the country, learnt to recognize the Imperial purpose.   Some desired to cast away their lives and to die for the national cause, others offered to coutribute towards the aimy expenditure.   The civil aud military officers uuited all their efforts, and the great work of chastisiug the savages became au accomplished fact.   We have nothing to be ashamed of before foreign nations coucerniug this measure, and its glory will not pale before the deeds done in ancient times.

"If, while public rumor was clamorous, we had hesitated or drawn back, the injuries doue to the sufferers would uot have been redressed, the position of a depeudeut 'han' would uot have been cleared up, the mariuers of the world would never have knowu security, and a land of marauders would have been established for ever.   Had such been the result, we should uot ouly have beeu disgraced in the eyes of the world, but it would have been a sigu that the dignity aud iufluence of the State were about to fall prostrate.   Consequently important interests were involved iu the chastisement of the savages.

"I humbly pray that His Majesty will eagerly carry ou the work aud carefully pouder, that by reflectiug ou the past he may be euabled to thiuk out the policy of the future so as to exalt his wise work to the highest piunacle and glory, and that he will uot stop with the chastisement of the savages."

The Tsung Li Yamen did not deem it of sufficient importance to acquaint their Emperor regarding the peaceful settlement arrived at, and had they done so His Majesty would have been filled with wonder, for it is asserted that no word of the entire transaction was ever allowed to reach the throne, and that the Emperor died early in 1875 without a suspicion of the danger that had once threatened his dominions.

During the first months of 1875, the Chinese made a few vigorous efforts to assume authority over the savages of the south.   They made flying visits here and there, but prudently avoided any approach to the interior.   Shen-Pao-Chen, profiting by his late experiences, submitted a memorial to the Throne recommending that henceforward Formosa should be governed by a system commensurate with its position and requirements, and that the viceroy of Fokien should be removed to this more important locality.   In accordance with this design, a small body of soldiers was sent down to Hongkong, the small village to the north of Liangkiau Bay, in which locality they were believed to be safe from savage intrusion.   They were soon to be undeceived, however, for in January, a couple of Chinese, while travelling along the roads to the south of the village, were waylaid and murdered in the usual way.

To retaliate on the savages, an expedition was arranged and the garrison of 500 men marched into the mountain fastness of the Sai-tao (Lion's head) tribe, to seize the village from which it was supposed the offenders had come.

They were able to reach the place without opposition, promptly burning it to the ground, while the occupants, old men, women, and children, were immediately put to death.   Believing they had accomplished all that was necessary they turned back towards Hongkong, but before proceeding far a detached column of three hundred men was most furiously attacked by the savages, who rose up on all sides throwing the soldiers into great confusion, although, it is said, their leader behaved with coolness and courage. The savages were not particular as to weapons ; firearms, spears, arrows, and rocks hurled down from the heights above, were all used with effectiveness against the enemy. At last with a fearful rush, savages, armed with swords and knives, closed in about the terror-stricken Chinese, with the result that about two hundred and fifty headless bodies were left rotting in the savage jungle, only about fifty men returning to report the deplorable ending of the first attempt to extend Chinese rule over the inhabitants of south aboriginal Formosa.[1]

From the day of the departure of the Japanese, up to the present, there has been no act of hostility towards foreigners on the part of the South Formosa savages. In fact, on several occasions foreign parties have travelled in their territory and met with no mishap. Towards the Chinese there has continued to exist the hatred which no influence can eradicate. The two have been at war from the days of the earliest history, when a Chinese pirate driven by storm landed in Formosa and, after killing all the natives whom he met with, painted his ship with their blood : and although actual war may be prevented by outside influence, the traditional hatred will find some means of expression as long as the two classes come in contact.

Japan did good work in ridding the Pacific Ocean of a scourge which had threatened the safety of mariners for more than a score of years, and she should receive abundant credit for it.

Even those who, at the time of the expedition, believed Japan had some ulterior design, must now agree with the testimony of a certain foreign employé of the Chinese government[2] who was in the best possible position to understand the situation and who says :—

"Whatever had been the original purpose of the Japanese in fitting up an expedition of so costly a nature, it is impossible to shut one's eyes to the fact that their action has resulted hitherto in unmixed good, the interests of the island alone considered. The punishment of the Bhootans (Botans) can only be looked upon as a necessary piece of severity which, will, in the long run, have consequences beneficial to humanity in general.[3]"

1. As to the number killed in this engagement several versions exist, by one of which the Chinese loss is placed at only ninety, including the chief officer. But I think we may safely take the statement of the Commissioner of Customs of Takow who, in the Imperial Maritime Customs reports for 1875, states in his version, which he says is a " resume of the actual facts," that out of " the body of 300 " Chinese, " The commander and most of his men were killed, only about fifty returning to tell the sad tale."

2. Mr. Henry Edgar, acting Commissioner of the Chinese Maritime Customs. Stationed at Takow, South Formosa at the time of the Japanese expedition.

3. After all expenditures had been paid the total cost of the expedition was found to be 3,618,050 yen. The troops sent aggregated 3,658 men carried in thirteen transports.

It is of special interest at this time in reviewing the different papers relating to the Japanese expedition to note the high rank to which many of the Japanese who participated in the expedition have risen. Most noticeable are the following : —

Admiral Marquis Saigo, the present Minister of the Navy, then a major-general.

Admiral Count Kabayama, former Minister of the Home Department, then a major in the army.

Rear-Admiral Tsunoda, ex-Chief of the Navy Staff of Formosa, then a navy lieutenant.

Rear-Admiral Tanaka and Rear-Admiral Kodama, former prefects in Formosa, then navy lieutenants.

Mr. S. Mizuno, first Chief of the Civil Department of the Formosan Government, and Mr. Sugimura, attachés to the expedition.

CHAPTER XIV.

FORMOSA OPENED TO FOREIGN TRADE.

1850—1868.

British occupation of Formosa suggested—Parker, Perry, and Harris recommend American occupation—Early foreign traders—The opium clippers—Formosa opened by America and Russia—Confirmed by English and French treaties—The first consulate—Robert Swinhoe—Trade in the early "Sixties"—First foreign firms and their representatives—Opening of customs—Early residents—Early trading vessels—Formosan pirates—Formosan wrecks—The "Kwang Foong" and "Soberana" cases—Experiences of John Keley while a captive of pirates—Chinese on the east coast—First steam-engine introduced—Foreigners assist the Pepohoans—Private attempt to establish a colony—The Talamo affair—The British government interferes—Great earthquake of 1867—Difficulties with the Chinese—Mr. Rainbow attacked—A merchant force enforces order—English naval force frequently landed—Unceasing troubles with officials—Attempt to collect illegal mast dues—A crisis (1868) in the south—Roman Catholic chapel destroyed—Christians persecuted—Mr. Hardie murderously assaulted—Taotai's insolence—$500 offered for a foreigner's head—Mr. Pickering attacked—A missionary accused of murder—Ambuscades erected and troops gathered to oppose British Consul Gibson—Amoy taotai arrives—Consul Gibson decides to seize Fort Zelandia and Anping—English naval force landed—Anping shelled—Lieut. Gurdon storms the town—A daring enterprise—Engagement with Chinese troops —Mandarins comply with consuls' demands—English force withdrawn—Satisfactory conclusion—Unjust condemnation—Troubles in the north—Messrs. Kerr and Bird attacked by Banka natives—Rescued by Loochoxans—The American war-vessel "Aroostook" and English gunboat "Janus" arrive—Peace and order restored.

In the five preceding chapters we have dealt, in chronological order, with events occurring in that portion of Formosa known as the "savage territory." We must now carry the reader back to the middle of the century, to continue with that portion of the history in which foreigners and Chinese were concerned, and which we last recorded in chapter VIII, concluding with the account of the massacre of one hundred and ninety-seven British subjects.

The latter half of the present century embraces a period of great commercial activity, when the leading countries of Europe and America were reaching beyond their native shores, and searching the world to obtain a foothold, wherever trade prospects were promising. With the invention of the steamship, distant lands were brought in closer touch, and the Orient with its riches attracted large numbers. In 1842, Hongkong was taken by the British; in 1854, Commodore Perry forced Japan to unlock her treasures; and in 1859, France obtained entrance to Cochin China.

Although Formosa was nominally possessed by China, it was well known that, over the larger half, that nation claimed no jurisdiction, and that even in the Chinese districts the authority of the emperor was weak and dubious. This, combined with the well known productiveness and the wonderful tales of the island's hidden riches which occasional travellers had placed before an eager world, drew the eyes of Europe and America to the " Beautiful Isle."

The British were the first in modern days to suggest the occupation of Formosa. It was during the period following the withdrawal of the British East India Company from China, when the English, now freetraders, were on the lookout for a position where British trade might be conducted without the interference and oppression of the Chinese mandarins. First in 1833, and afterwards in later years, Formosa was frequently suggested by the British in China as a convenient and desirable acquisition. In fact, towards the close of the " thirties " the choice lay between Chusan, Ningpo, and Formosa ; and Hongkong, which was ultimately occupied, was but rarely referred to.

With the opening of trade in Hongkong the number of foreign ships in Eastern waters greatly increased. America shared largely in the China trade, and her swift clippers were familiar visitors. With uncharted coasts and frequent typhoons many a good ship came to the East only to find a grave. Of all the Orient, Formosa was most feared ; the large number of wrecks occurring on its shores and the blood-curdling massacres of the crews, or the life of slavery to which the captives were reduced, if they fell into the hands of the savages, placed the island prominently before the world, and humanity demanded that the cruel outrages should cease.

As Americans were the chief victims in these disasters, the attention of the Washington authorities was called to the advisability of occupying a portion of the island ; nd thus rendering assistance to the shipping world in general, as well as securing to the United States a naval station in the Orient and an *entrepôt* for American goods.

Mr. Gideon Nye, an American merchant well known in China, was the first to broach the subject to the United States authorities. He had been for sometime endeavoring to induce the government to search for his missing brother, who, having been a passenger on board the clipper ship *Kelpie*, which was thought to have been lost on the Formosan coast, was believed to be existing among the savages of the island in a state of slavery. It was principally, no doubt, with the idea of preventing a repetition of these disasters, that

Mr. Nye with the assistance of Dr. Peter Parker, then U.S. commissioner to China, endeavored to induce the U.S. government to take possession of a portion of the island then occupied by the savages. Commodore Perry was also favorable to the suggestion, and some of his officers made a trip to the island, and a complete report was drawn up in which the commodore strongly advocated its occupation. In a letter to Dr. Parker, Mr. Nye in 1853 writes : " Formosa's eastern shore and southern point, with the contiguous Island, Botel Tobago-Xima, in the direct route of commerce between China and California and Japan, and between Shanghai and Canton, should be protected by the United States of America ; and I will willingly assist in its colonization, if I receive the assurance of the government of the United States ·that I should therein be recognized and protected.

"I am quite aware of the willingness of some other persons to aid in this under a similar assurance ; and I am quite clear that at this time a commencement might be made without objection from any power."

Mr. Townsend Harris, the first American envoy to Japan, was greatly struck with the benefit to be derived by America as well as by all other countries having commercial interests in this part of the world, if the island of Formosa, in part or in whole, was secured to America. To interest the government in this proposal he applied himself diligently to the task of collecting material from many sources, from which he was able to draw up a paper of considerable length on the island's past and present, its resources, etc., which was presented to the Secretary of State with the suggestion that the territory be purchased.

What would have been the result of these recommendations under ordinary conditions we cannot say. · Scarcely was the question laid before the United States government when the existence of the American Union was threatened by civil war, and all citizens of the Republic were called to arms.

Thus while the U.S. government was disinclined to consider propositions for adding to her domains when even her own integrity was in jeopardy, other governments eagerly scanned the voluminous reports of Parker, Perry, and Harris, and applied to themselves the advice of the three Americans. France and Germany were specially interested, and both looked wistfully towards this eastern jewel. But with matters of great importance at home these governments were obliged for the time to give up all plans of eastern colonization, and, with the exception of the merchants who had an eye on the island's commercial possibilities, Formosa appears to have eventually dropped out of view of European nations and remained unthought of for a number of years.

As the foreign commerce of China developed, and American and English vessels frequented the China seas, an occasional schooner called at a Formosan port in hopes of picking •up some profitable trade; or more often, a fast clipper darted across the channel with a store of opium to be disposed of at a large profit. Takow and Tamsui were important ports for this traffic, and at the close of the "fifties" an Irish American, commonly known as Mooney, had settled in the harbor of the former port, aboard a hulk which he had placed there as a receiving ship for the opium brought at intervals by his swift clippers.

The large opium merchants, whose headquarters were generally at Hongkong, had receiving ships, heavily armed and manned by full crews, usually of Manila men, at each of the four treaty ports on the China coast, so that the inhabitants could purchase the drug.

The clippers ran up and down the coast carrying to the receiving ships the amount of opium required, and returning with the silver or other commodities obtained in return. They were engaged in an adventurous enterprise, exposed to numerous dangers, and requiring courageous skippers and daring crews to pull them through safely. The vessels were usually from one to two hundred tons burden, strongly built, splendidly outfitted, and on lines that admitted of great speed, some of them having been built by the famous yacht builder, White of Cowes. They were, for their size, heavily armed, commonly mounting from six to ten guns. A well equipped craft carried, perhaps, three or four guns (on the largest clippers eighteen pounders) on each side; a large gun, even up to a sixty-eight pounder, on the largest vessels, amid ships, and very often another gun on the forecastle. The necessity of such an armament in comparatively modern days arose from the existence of numerous Chinese pirates, who, in their fast lorchas, did not shrink from attempting the capture of a rich prize like an opium clipper, whether on the outward trip with opium or on the return voyage with silver. The clippers were also commonly provided with long heavy oars some forty feet in length, which, if the ships were threatened by pirates in calm weather or in the near vicinity of land, could be run out of the ports and manned by five or six men each, moving the ships some three or four knots an hour, if conditions were not unfavorable.

Trade was usually conducted on board the receiving ship, or, if no permanent vessel existed, on board the clippers themselves as they arrived. Chinese shroffs looked after the sale of the drug and the care of the treasure.

Precious metals in any shape were accepted, but silver was principally used. It came sometimes in sycee bars, sometimes in blocks eight or nine inches in length, and not a little in broken vases, decorations from temples and even personal ornaments, while the larger quantity was in Spanish or Mexican dollars, the principal trading coin of the East.

The beginning of the commercial career of the island may be dated from 1858, when the two Hongkong firms, Jardine Matheson & Co. and Dent & Co., first engaged in the Formosan trade. True it was not until 1860 that they had representatives actually established in the island as general merchants; still in 1858-9 they both handled a large quantity of Formosan camphor, which was obtained as prearranged from the mandarins who had a monopoly of the trade.

The first step in opening the island to foreign trade was taken by the diplomatic representatives of America and Russia, Mr. Reid and Count Putiatine, who in 1858 were successful in inducing the Chinese government to declare Taiwan open to foreign residence and trade. Subsequently other ports were opened by the English and French treaties ratified in 1860, at the close of the war with China,[1] France obtaining the opening of Tamsui in the north,[2] to which Kelung was added in 1861 with the consent of the Imperial authorities as a dependent port of Tamsui; the British obtaining, three years later, the recognition of Takow as a dependent port of Taiwan. Though Taiwan was thus nominally opened in 1858, yet it was not until 1865 that local provisions had been made and the place was actually opened to foreign residence. Robert Swinhoe, the first consular representative to visit Formosa, was in December, 1860, nominated by the British government as vice-consul at Taiwan, and Geo. C. P. Braune as assistant. In July, 1861, Mr. Swinhoe arrived at Takow, having been conveyed from Amoy aboard the British gunboat *Cockchafer*. He and his staff travelled overland from Takow to Taiwanfu, and on arriving at the capital they were installed by the authorities in the Fungshin temple outside the city walls, close to the canal.

The neighborhood of the temple, however, proved to be an unruly one, and the foreigners were pestered by crowds of people who were not always polite in satisfying their curiosity. Mr. Swinhoe was obliged to ask assistance from the mandarins to disperse the mobs, who were becoming very disagreeable. But to the dismay of the consul, an officer returned with the information that the mandarins were quite unable to drive away the crowds. In fact, but a week had elapsed since the people were in open riot against the authorities, who had attempted to impose likin to raise funds for the mainland military expenses.

Under these conditions it was apparent to Mr. Swinhoe that quarters inside the wall would be more pleasant, and he accordingly accepted an invitation to spend his first night at a well-to-do Chinese merchant's house within the walls. Later he secured a comfortable residence within the city, and remained there during the rest of his stay in Taiwanfu.

With the disappearance of the commodious harbor of the Dutch, Taiwanfu lost its importance as a port. In 1860, the produce exported from the city consisted mainly of sugar and rice. The imports were opium and a small quantity of shirtings. Takow to the south was now springing into prominence. It possessed a harbor sufficient for those days; it was nearer the sugar district; goods could be easily transported to and from the capital; Messrs. Jardine Matheson & Co., had stationed the hulk *Pathfinder* there and Messrs. Dent & Co., the *Ternate*, both of which were used as receiving ships. Mr. Swinhoe found Taiwanfu very unhealthy, three out of seven of

1. Art XI —In addition to the cities and towns of Canton, Amoy, Foochow, Ningpo, and Shanghai, opened by the Treaty of Nanking, it is agreed that British subjects may frequent the cities and ports of Newchwang, Tangchow (Chefoo), *Taiwan*, Chao-chow (Swatow), and Kiung-chow (Hainan)

Treaty of Tientsin, 1858. (Great Britain and China.
(Ratified in 1860.)

2. Art. VI. - Experience having demonstrated that the opening of new ports to foreign commerce is one of the necessities of the age, it has been agreed that the ports of Kiung-chow and Chao-chow in the province of Kwangtung, *Taiwan* and *Tamsui* in the *island of Formosa* (province of Foh Kien), Tang-chow in the province of Shangtung, and Nanking in the province of Kiangsu, shall enjoy the same privileges as Canton, Shanghai, Ningpo, Amoy, and Foochow.

Treaty of Tientsin, 1858. France and China.
(Ratified in 1860.)

his servants died, and towards the end of the year he was obliged to cross to Amoy to recuperate from an attack of fever.

Ultimately it was decided that Tamsui offered greater commercial possibilities and that the consulate at Taiwanfu was for the time unnecessary. Accordingly, Mr. Swinhoe transferred his office to Hobe, the port of Tamsui district, arriving there in the middle of December (1861) on the British gunboat *Handy*.[1]

Mr. Swinhoe was unable to obtain quarters on shore until a year later; so for the time he established his office and residence aboard Jardine Matheson & Co's receiving ship *Adventure*, which had arrived but a few months before to participate in the trade of the newly opened port.

At this time, there were no foreigners resident on shore in any part of the island, and at Tamsui the only foreign subjects were the master and crew of the *Adventure*, who were under British protection. The fast little clippers, Dent & Co's *Wild Wave*, a brigantine of 159 tons, and Jardine Matheson & Co's *Vindex* of about the same size, were regularly appointed to look after the Formosan trade of the two companies. They were well armed against pirates, each vessel carrying seven guns besides large crews, the *Wild Wave* having a force of forty Malays. These little clippers darted into Tamsui and Takow with opium and out again with currency and native produce.

Contrary to general belief, Formosan tea was regularly exported to China previous to the arrival of foreigners in the island. Mr. Swinhoe states in 1861 that it was much imported by Chinese dealers at Amoy and Foochow to mix with the better class of teas. Furthermore, Mr. Swinhoe was the first to call the attention of foreigners to these teas, he having sent samples to three different tea-tasters for inspection the same year.[2]

The exports in 1861 consisted of rice, indigo, sugar bark, ground nut cakes, camphor, coal, grass cloth fibre (ramie), wood, rattans, tea, pickled vegetables, pulse, barley, wheat, and sulphur.

In 1862, Dent & Co. and Jardine, Matheson & Co. were both regularly established at Hobe, with agents residing there, and also kept Chinese establishments with shroffs at Banka, which was at that time the most important city in the north. P. F. da Silva was the agent of the former, and the latter managed its business through Chinese agents, with an Englishman, Captain William Morrison, who travelled between Tamsui and Takow, to keep a surveillance over both. Early the next year an Englishman, Churlton C. Rainbow, arrived in Tamsui and took charge of Messrs. Dent & Co.'s business as resident agent, and in 1864 both firms had residences for their agents and godowns on shore. Although the treaty port was at Hobe, the trade of the north was found to be all conducted at Banka (a city adjoining

---

1. CONSULAR NOTIFICATION.—Owing to the greater advantages offered by the harbor of Tamsui above all others in the island of Formosa, the undersigned has removed his establishment thither from Taiwanfu, and Tamsui therefore will henceforth be recognized as the Consular Port opened to British trade in Formosa.

The limits of the harbor are defined by the bar at the mouth of the river to seaward and the gorge some four miles up the river to landward.

2. See chapter on tea.

Twatutia on the north, and some eleven miles from the port.) Consequently, the English acting-consul at Tamsui succeeded in gaining permission from the Chinese authorities to extend the boundaries of the treaty port of Tamsui so as to include Banka.[1]

The Imperial Chinese Maritime Customs opened at Tamsui in 1863. The first commissioner (acting) was Mr. Howell, an Englishman, and his successor was Mr. Schenck, nephew of Admiral Schenck, U. S. N.

Vessels trading with Takow were obliged to proceed to either Amoy, Foochow, or Tamsui to have their cargoes assessed before they could go to Takow to discharge, two tidewaiters being established at the latter port to guard against smuggling. In a similar manner, vessels leaving Takow were obliged to make use of one of the before-mentioned ports before they were allowed to proceed to their several destinations.

This great hindrance to shipping was, however, but of short duration; for on the 5th of May, 1864, Mr. William Maxwell opened the customs at Takow, as first commissioner, and established his office on board the opium receiving hulk *Pathfinder*, previously referred to. A branch office of the customs was opened at Anping at the close of the year to start work from the 1st of January, 1865. Mr. W. A. Pickering, who became in later days a prominent character, then a tide-waiter, was placed in charge.

In the south, trade now appears to have improved, and was soon double that of Tamsui. The two pioneer firms had built godowns and acquired property in both Takow and Taiwanfu, and quite a large foreign population, including the representatives of two new firms, had gathered there.[2]

1. NOTIFICATION.—This is to give notice to all whom it may concern that the limits of this port are extended up the river to include the town of Banka.

British Consulate   (Signed) Geo. C. P. Braune, officiating Consul
Tamsui, Formosa, 7th July, 1862.

(Published in the North China Herald 6th Sept. 1862.

2. The foreign firms already established in Takow in 1864 were as follows :—

Jardine, Matheson & Co.)
Dent & Co.   } British.
MacPhail & Co.   )
Lessler & Co. (afterwards Lessler & Hagen), German.

The foreign residents in Takow and Taiwanfu at the end of 1864 were as follows :—

At Takow :—
Robert Swinhoe, H.B.M.'s Consul.
William Maxwell, Commissioner of Customs.   )
Brodie A. Clarke, Assistant in Customs. |
William G. Merrick, Tide Surveyor, Customs. |
George Gue, Tide Waiter, Customs.   } British.
George D. Henry, Tide Waiter, Customs. |
James W. MacPhail, Partner in MacPhail & Co. |
Robert R. Rothwell, Clerk in MacPhail & Co.   )
M. L. Lessler of Lessler & Co., German.
P. F. da Silva, Agent, Dent & Co. } Portuguese.
Mrs. Silva.   }

At Taiwanfu :—
Neil MacPhail, Partner in MacPhail & Co.   )
Alexander Morrison, Agent, Jardine, Matheson & Co. |
William Alexander Pickering, Tide Waiter in Customs (Anping). } British.
John William Mingort, Clerk in MacPhail & Co.   )

In 1865, a second German firm started at Takow: Kielmann and Alisch. Dr. James L. Maxwell, a Scotch Medical Missionary, arrived the same year. Other changes and additions in 1865 were the arrival

Consequently Vice-Consul Swinhoe,[1] who had encountered considerable difficulty in communicating with the Chinese officials at Taiwanfu, re-established his consular office in the south; this time at Takow, where he hoisted his flag on board the opium receiving hulk *Ternate*, belonging to Messrs. Dent & Co., (remaining there until 1866 when he removed to a residence on shore). Mr. Braune was left in charge of the consular office in the north, which was continued as an agency of the south, and in 1865 a British consular office was opened at Taiwanfu, under the charge of Mr. Thomas Watters (Assistant).

Of the trade in South Formosa the chief article of import was opium, practically the only import in which foreigners were interested. Exports consisted of brown sugars, from Takow, and white from Taiwanfu, turmeric (chiefly to the northern parts of China for food, dye, and medicine), lungars and ground nuts, and sesame oils. Rice was exported from Takow in large quantities until 1865, when the Chinese government prohibited its export, except to Amoy and Foochow under pass—which pass was difficult to obtain. Although this prohibition was removed two years later, it was again imposed in 1869. In Takow and Taiwanfu, in 1866, the value of imports was $1,608,789 and of exports $1,158,778.

At Tamsui and Kelung there was less commercial activity. Until 1866

1. No other foreigner during either the past or present has succeeded in associating his name so firmly with Formosa as the late Robert Swinhoe, F.R.G.S., F.Z.S. Although in Formosa but a few years, so thoroughly possessed was he of that important faculty to the scientist—great powers of observation—that he was enabled to gather much general information about the island, while his contributions on scientific subjects and his discoveries among the birds and beasts of Formosa will carry his name down to posterity. It is not inappropriate, therefore, to devote a few lines to his career.—Mr. Robert Swinhoe, the British Foreign Office List informs us, was educated at King's College, London, and matriculated at London University in 1853. He was appointed Supernumerary Interpreter at Hongkong in 1854, transferred to Amoy the following year, and a year later was appointed second assistant at the same port and at Shanghai. He was attached to Lord Elgin's special mission to China (1856) and at its conclusion returned to Amoy, where he was later appointed Interpreter. In 1858 he accompanied H.M.S. *Inflexible* as Interpreter on an expedition to Formosa in search of certain Europeans who were believed to be existing in a state of slavery at the sulphur mines on that island. He accompanied the expedition of 1860 to North China acting first as interpreter to General Napier and later to the Commander-in-Chief, Sir Hope Grant, and received a medal for this service. He was appointed Vice-Consul at Taiwan, Formosa, Dec. 22nd, 1860. He sent an exhibit of Formosan produce to the Great International Exhibition of 1862, and obtained honourable mention and a medal in return. He was made a corresponding member of the Royal Zoological Society of London, of the North China Branch of the Asiatic Society and of the Asiatic Society of Bengal. He was appointed Life Fellow of the Royal Zoological Society of London in 1862 ; Fellow of the Royal Geographical Society and corresponding member of the Ethnological Society in 1863 ; towards the close of the same year he was elected an Honorary Fellow of King's College, London. He was promoted to be Consul at Taiwan in 1865 and placed in charge of the Amoy Consulate 1866, and of the Ningpo Consulate the next year, where he remained until 1875, when he closed his consular career and retired on a pension. He was soon after elected fellow of the Royal Society of London. His death occurred on the 28th of October, 1877.

of a new custom's assistant, Henry James Fisher, and the establishment at Takow of Brodie A. Clarke as a mercantile agent.

In 1866 Dr. Patrick Manson, M.D., arrived. Dent & Co. closed their agency in Takow this year, and P. F. da Silva was taken into partnership in the firm of Lessler and Hagen. Elles & Co. opened at Takow with G. Remedios in temporary charge, W. H. Taylor arriving at the end of the year and assuming charge as first agent. A. W. Bain arrived as assistant in the firm of Elles & Co. at the end of the same year.

In 1867 Tait & Co. under J. C. Masson, and Boyd & Co. under Robert Craig started business in South Formosa. MacPhail & Co. suspended business during this year. Rev. Hugh Ritchie of the Presbyterian Church Mission arrived during this year and joined Dr. Manson of the same mission.

In 1869 Brown & Co. commenced business in the south, and Robert J. Hastings arrived as tide-waiter in the Customs.

Of these pioneers but two remain in the island at present (1897) : A. W. Bain, now at the head of Bain & Co., and Robert J. Hastings, now at the head of Wright & Co.

British subjects numbered only nine, against fourteen in the south,[1] but there were three new mercantile arrivals.   Mr. John Dodd, who established himself in Tamsui in 1864, Mr. James Milisch, a citizen of Hamburg, who started the firm of Milisch and Co. in 1865, and the Americans Field and Hastis who about this time started in the coal and camphor business at Kelung, associating with them (Dr.) Yung Wing, a Chinese who later attained a high position in official circles, and was eventually naturalized as an American citizen.   1867 saw a considerable increase, and by the end of the year there were ten British subjects resident in Tamsui and three in Kelung, four Americans in Tamsui and three in Kelung, and five continental Europeans in Tamsui, twenty-five in all.   The value of exports from the two northern ports in 1866 was $379,321 and of imports $1,058,682.

Previous to the establishment of a foreign consulate in Formosa, the island's camphor trade had been exclusively in the hands of two or three of the wealthiest foreign firms, who employed schooners to collect it as fast as native agents stationed at the chief ports along the coast had purchased it. These large firms found this trade extremely lucrative, but upon the establishment of the foreign inspectorate, it was declared that the whole coast was not open to foreign trade.   Thus limited to the treaty ports, Tamsui and Kelung, it appeared that business was not so profitable, and the firms withdrew their vessels.   Chinese who had been formerly hampered by lack of capital were now not slow to avail themselves of this lucrative trade, and by a judicious distribution of gifts, as well as by promises of certain sums to be paid regularly to the officials, they succeeded in obtaining the exclusive right of dealing in camphor, which right, however, was again lost in 1868, when the monopoly was abolished after considerable foreign pressure had been brought to bear.[2]

With an increase in the trade came a corresponding improvement in shipping facilities.   Captain Thomas Sullivan, master of the *Wild Wave*, Captain Roper, master of the *Vindex*, and Captain Alexander Morrison, agent of Jardine Matheson & Co., were the pioneer skippers of Formosa. True, occasional tramp schooners, often of Hamburg or Danish origin, visited the Formosan ports, but none of them were so identified with the earlier trade as were the *Wild Wave* and *Vindex*.

For several years the only arrivals were schooners, brigs, and small barques of from 100 to 250 or 300 tons.   Sailing ships up to about 600 tons occasionally arrived at Kelung, and steamers at extremely rare intervals entered the same harbor.   The first steamer to identify herself with the Formosan trade was the *Union*—204 tons—commanded by Captain Wilson.   This vessel was owned by Dent & Co. and made her first

---

1. British subjects residing at Tamsui in 1866 :—

William Gregory, Acting British Consul.	John Dodd, Agent, Dent & Co.
John William Howell, Customs Agent.	John Barry, Gunner in Dent & Co.'s hong.
George F. Hume, Tide Surveyor, Customs.	Robert Rimmer.
Charles Powell, Tide Waiter, Customs.	Richard Hicks.
Richard Goodridge, Tide Waiter, Customs.	

Neil McPhail and Alexander Morrison, entered as residents of Taiwanfu, spent a portion of their time in Tamsui.

2. See chapter on Camphor.

trip in 1863. Among the other craft most familiar to the pioneers were the schooners *Dodo*, the *Salamander*—106 tons—Captain Roper, *Pearl*—85 tons—Captain Ebert, and the *Eliza Mary*, which first arrived in 1866 under command of Captain Hoole. The *Pearl* made frequent trips between South Formosa and the mainland ports until June, 1866, when she was lost with her cargo and all on board save one, while on a voyage from Takow to Amoy laden with rice and general produce. The *Eliza Mary* made numerous trips between Amoy and South Formosan ports with opium and general cargo. She continued to run on this line until the middle of 1870, when she was wrecked at Takow, Captain Beattie being her master at that time. A year previous to her loss (Captain) Hermann Vosteen[1] first arrived in Takow aboard her as boatswain. The *Rubicon*, of 204 tons, also a well-known schooner on the Formosan coasts, ran until 1871, when she was wrecked on the Pescadores.[2]

Among the visiting steamers previous to 1870 were the *Yuen-tsze-fu* of 315 tons, Captain Storks, the *Vulcan* of 130 tons, Captain Randall, and the *Elfin* of 174 tons, Captain Thomas. The last named was the first to visit Japan with Formosan produce. In December, 1864, this vessel arrived from Yokohama with a general cargo, and was despatched to Yokohama in the following month also with a general cargo. The S. S. *Island Queen*, a paddle-wheel steamer of 120 tons under Captain Burkett, made occasional trips from Foochow in 1865, and was the first and last side-wheeler to appear in the South Formosan ports. She was afterwards sold to the Chinese government, was renamed the *Hai-tong Yuen*, and was destroyed at the bombardment of Foochow by the French in 1884. The *Taiwan* of 217 tons, Captain Roper, was the first regular liner from Hongkong viâ Swatow and Amoy to Takow, Anping (Taiwanfu), and Tamsui. She was not a success, however, and was soon withdrawn. The steamers *Douglas*, *Kwangtung*, and *Yesso* were all well known in the north Formosan ports. The latter vessel was built at New York in 1864 with labor at $7.50 a day. She was brought out for Dent & Co. by a Captain Dearborn, and was then bought by Douglas Lapraik and his associates. She bore the name of *Yesso* for some time until it was discovered that the Chinese characters were those used to represent the heavenly deity, a discovery which somewhat shocked the more religious of her patrons, and the characters were thereupon changed.

Life both on land and sea was not without hardship and danger in those days. On shore the natives frequently gave exhibitions of their hostility to foreigners, and on the unlighted, and, we may say uncharted, coasts of the island, numerous pirates hovered. These, if they could not capture the speedy foreign craft on the open seas, frequently joined with the natives on shore in pillaging any vessels that were unfortunate enough to be wrecked.

1. Capt. Vosteen remained in South Formosa and became a well-known pilot. He continued to be engaged in shipping matters in Takow and Anping until the late occupation of the island by the Japanese.

2. The whistle of the steamer soon proved to be the death knell of the little clippers, at least so far as Formosan trade was concerned. The *Wild Wave* was sold to the Japanese and lost with all hands on board on her first trip to the Loochoos. The proud little *Vindex* was degraded to the rank of a junk, and now converted into a lorcha is carrying poles from Foochow to Shanghai. The *Salamander* was sold to the Portuguese at Macao.

So numerous were the pirates in south Formosa that they frequently defied the mandarins. They formed a village known as Koksikong, five miles to the north of Taiwanfu, then the capital, and there they gathered in large numbers, varying their exploits on the sea by preying upon the inhabitants of the surrounding country. The fishermen of Anping appear to have been their constant victims, and towards the end of 1866 a party of pirates landed at Anping, plundered, ravished, and rioted for three days, and then returned unmolested to their stronghold. And this with the capital and largest city but two miles distant. In the north the pirates had their headquarters at a large village called Pe-sua-tun, lying just behind Paksa Point, a promontory on the coast between Tamsui and Teckcham, (Shinchiku), where frequent wrecks occurred.

Formosa was indeed notorious for wrecks, and escape from the pirates and other wreckers was quite exceptional for any vessel that happened to be cast on the coast out of sight of the principal ports. Upwards of one hundred and fifty foreign vessels were wrecked and lost on or near the Formosan coast (occupied by Chinese) between 1850 and 1869, and out of this number over thirty were plundered and many burned by the pirates, wreckers, and villagers, while the known loss of life is over a thousand. Instances of these cruel attacks may be learned from the list of wrecks. The most noticeable of these outrages (wrecks occurring after 1870 are treated in the following chapter) were the cases of the foreign vessels *Eena, Moon Keen Kele, Kossuth, Martha and Emily, Soberana, Lucky Star, Abeona, Kwang Foong* and *Mabe*.[1]

1. The following list refers to the important wrecks occurring on or near the Formosan coast between 1850 and 1869. The author regrets that this list is not complete. The facts that there was no record kept of wrecks previous to 1861 and that many vessels were surmised to have been lost on the Formosan or adjacent islands regarding which no definite information was ever received render it necessarily imperfect. Even in later years wrecks were not always recorded; the material for this list together with that contained in the following chapters, was obtained only after extensive research in many different quarters With the exception of British vessels, the later lists of which are believed to be complete, it is likely that there are some omissions. For wrecks from 1870 to 1885 see concluding pages of Chapter XV. For wrecks in subsequent years see Chapter XVII.

Of the wrecks previous to 1850, we have but little information. Foreigners were not resident in the island at that time and the Chinese, of course, kept no records. Among the most prominent of the disasters was the wreck of the British brig *Ann*, which was lost in March, 1842, on the northwest coast of Formosa, and the British ship *Nerbudda* in September, likewise on the west Formosan coast. Out of fifty-seven souls belonging to the former and two hundred and forty belonging to the latter there were but twelve survivors, the others having been either put to death by the officers of the Chinese government in Formosa, killed by the plunderers, or perishing through ill-treatment and starvation (See Chapter VIII). In 1849 the ship *Sarah Trottman* with a cargo of teas was lost off the southern coast of Formosa. The English opium clipper *Kelpie* was also thought to have been lost on the Formosan coast about this time.

Wrecks on coasts of Formosa and adjacent islands :—1850-1869 :

1850———The British ship *Larpent* was wrecked on the south Formosa coast. Out of her crew of thirty, there were but three survivors, the others having been either killed by the savages or drowned while trying to escape. The three survivors were kept in slavery in the island for some time, but eventually reached China (See Chapter IX.)

1855———The New York clipper *High Flyer* was lost with all on board on the south Formosa coast. She was commanded by Captain G. B. Waterman, whose wife as well as Mrs. Charles Spencer Compton and three hundred or more Chinese, were passengers on board.

————The American clipper *Coquette* disappeared during this year, and is believed to have been lost on the Formosan Coast. She had a large number of passengers on board.

1857 ———The vessel *Vixen* was wrecked during a typhoon on the Formosan coast.

1859 ———The British ship *Eena* was wrecked near Tamsui. Plundered by soldiers and natives.

1861———The American brig *Moon Keen Kele* wrecked and plundered near Pa-te-chui.

————December—The Siamese vessel *Kossuth* grounded near Kok-si-kong, whence she might have been got off had not the natives from shore (Chinese) come on in large numbers and, after plundering and

The two most dreaded districts on the west side of the island were the dangerous shores in the vicinity of Koksikong in the south, and Lamkan and Paksa Point near the village of Pe-sua-tun in the north. The usual cruel methods of the residents of these two piratical villages may be understood from the two instances below.

In a violent typhoon on the 29th of September, 1866, the British barque *Kwang Foong* was driven ashore at Koksikong. Soon after striking, considerable confusion was observed on shore, and but a short time elapsed before a crowd of 300 Chinese, armed with long knives, came on board and commenced to plunder. Not only was the ship stripped, but the clothes of all on board were torn from them, and they were driven from the ship. On shore, naked and helpless, they were obliged to agree to pay one of the pirates $600 for showing them the way to Taiwanfu (a few miles distant). The crew reached the capital, but in a pitiable condition, having travelled for two days under a scorching sun. They were quite naked save for a few pieces of old mats which they had picked up along the way, and their feet and legs were severely cut by the oyster shells over which they had walked when wading through the shallows and creeks. The mandarins either did not desire, or were powerless, to punish or control these fierce pirates of Kok-si-kong.

The wreck of the Spanish barque *Soberana*, December 31st, 1863, at Lamkan, North Formosa (Captain Olano's protest. Spanish Consular Reports, Amoy). "It grew dark with fresh breeze, rather dense mist, and some rain, thus preventing us from seeing about us, and so it continued until 2 o'clock, when the vessel gave a strong jerk forward. The order was immediately given to luff her, but it was of wrecking her, set her on fire. The captain and crew finding it useless to resist such large numbers of armed men deserted the vessel and went to Tainan.

1862—February—The Singapore registered vessel *Uncle Tom* was wrecked at the entrance of Tamsui harbor. The vessel sank leaving only above the water the tips of the masts, to which a few of the unhappy victims were clinging and calling for assistance. The sea raged so high that every attempt to put off a boat proved futile, and out of forty souls only three were saved. These managed to reach shore by availing themselves of pieces of broken timber.

1862.—November. The English vessel *Martha and Emily* went aground on the N. W. Formosa coast. She was in no great danger and could have been floated had not one of the Chinese would-be plunderers shot the captain dead. This so terrified the crew that they deserted the ship, which was then immediately plundered.

1863.————. The Hamburg vessel *Esther* was wrecked on the Formosa coast.

————December. The Spanish bark *Soberana* was wrecked at Lamkan and plundered by the Chinese (See main text).

————. The American vessel *Lucky Star* was wrecked on the west coast of Formosa. The captain, his wife and crew were very harshly treated by the Chinese and released only on the payment of a considerable ransom by the foreign agent in charge of the Customs.

1864.————. The vessel *Talamo* was wrecked on the Formosa coast.

————. The Hamburg brig *Herer* was wrecked on the Formosan coast.

————. The vessel *Mathilde* was wrecked on the Formosan coast.

————March. The British brig *Susan Douglas* while on a voyage from Hongkong to Ningpo was wrecked on the island of Samasana off S. E. coast Formosa. The captain and crew were kindly treated and supported over a month by the natives, the captain then obtaining passage to Takow aboard a junk. The others, with the exception of one Hawaiian who died in the island, were rescued by the British gunboat *Bustard*. (Lieut Tucker.)

1864—April.—The British ship *Netherby* with a cargo of tea grounded on a rock to the north of the Pescadores. She was immediately boarded by piratical villagers who plundered whatever they could lay hands on. In this instance, however, good resulted from evil, for the removal of so much cargo lightened the ship considerably, and a strong north breeze springing up she stood out to sea and proceeded on her voyage without loss of life and with but little damage to the ship.

————September—The British barque *Truro* was wrecked near Lokiang W. coast, Formosa. The vessel was looted by the natives, even the crew being stripped and plundered.

1865—September—The Hanoverian brig *Amphitrite* was wrecked 30 miles north of Taiwanfu, W. coast Formosa.

October—The barque *Ibrona* was wrecked on the sand bank near Goche, W. coast Formosa. The boat was at once surrounded by natives. The master Wm. Murray endeavored to keep them off, and

no avail, and we found that we were tight on the rocks, and that it was impossible to get the vessel off. Owing to the heavy sea breaking over her she suffered greatly; still as we were near the shore we hoped to be able to save something in the morning. We were intending to disma-t her, but shortly discovered that the water in the hold had risen to 8 feet, and consequently we got the boats in readiness so as to save our-selves and the ship's documents. At day-break we saw that we were close on to the island of Formosa, and notwithstanding that between the vessel and land the sea broke fearfully, we were forced to lower our boats in order to convey a rope ashore, and then see if we could save anything out of the cargo. But, at the moment the rope was being conveyed, a heavy sea upset the boat and shattered it to pieces, the boat's crew being saved with great difficulty. We lowered a second boat with similar results. We then endeavoured to float life preservers with a line attached, but were alike unsuccessful in this. We now threw out a water cask which, to our great joy, reached the shore; but scarcely had it touched before the natives on shore cut the ropes and bore away the cask. We then threw out a large hencoop which also reached the shore, and our Chinese passengers crying out to their countrymen on land, the latter this time made fast the rope, to our intense relief. But in less than five minutes, upwards of a hundred Chinese appeared, and utilizing our line came on board, armed with big knives. They then searched us taking away whatever we had, whilst others entered the cabin and commenced plundering our provisions and the cargo, which they were taking out through the hatchway leading from the cabin. The ship's papers and other documents, chronometers, etc., we had placed in a junk which was then alongside, but the Chinese discovered it, and tearing off the cover, they threw the books and papers into the sea and carried away the instruments On board it was general plunder, and on shore there were upwards of 2,000 men. At this point the Chinese commanded us to go on shore, and as we were leaving they stripped us one by one leaving us with only our shirts and drawers and some in a state of absolute nudity. Finally they conducted us to a house, minus three of the men for whom they demanded $300 ransom; and not having money on our persons, we of course could not comply, but the owner of the house said that if we would grant him a document ordering the Spanish consul at Amoy to pay the amount, he would advance the money, which he did, or pretended to do, and the three men were brought forward, and the document was given in return. On the 24th of January we all assembled together and were sent to Tamsui, at which place we presented ourselves to the British consul, who gave us clothes and lodging while a vessel was prepared to send us to Amoy. Signed by the Captain, First and Second Mate, and three of the crew, 19th January, 1863."

The coasting trade was rendered hazardous and subjected to great in-conveniences by this tendency to piracy which manifested itself among certain classes of natives. On one occasion, a foreign vessel was kept lying six weeks in Kelung, waiting for a cargo of rice which had been bought on the east coast, on account of a fleet of piratical junks which hovered off

though a few soldiers appeared on the second day they made but little effort to protect the vessel; on the evening of the third day having run out of ammunition the master was overpowered and the soldiers were the first to turn to and commence plundering. By daylight next morning the boat had been stripped and was then set on fire. The master, his wife, and the crew escaped over land and eventually reached Tamsui.

November—The Hamburg brig *Hoffnung* was wrecked a little to the north of Anping, W. coast of Formosa. Vessel looted and crew stripped and plundered by the natives.

December—The British schooner *Julia Ann* was wrecked 15 miles south of Takow, W. coast Formosa.

1866.—June. The British schooner *Pearl* bound from Takow to Amoy was lost with all on board except one.

——June. The British ship *T. F. Boyd* was wrecked on the Pescadores. Ship and crew stripped and plundered by the natives.

—— July. The ship *Fairlight* was wrecked on one of the Miyakojima group, N. E. of Formosa. A young American, John Gibney, and 197 Chinese were drowned. It appears that the Loochoo people who inhabit the islands behaved with their usual nobleness on this occasion. They brought in wrecked property that had floated ashore, fed the sufferers, declined remuneration, and actually sent a large quantity of rice and a couple of bullocks on board the *Prince Kung*, which took the wrecked people away.

——July. The British ship *Mabe* was wrecked at Lamkan, N. W. coast of Formosa. Crew all saved, but the vessel plundered and then burned by the natives.

——September. The German brig *Eduard* wrecked at Anping during a typhoon.

——September. The Dutch vessel *Pielides*, wrecked at Koksikong, W. coast Formosa, during typhoon and plundered by the natives.

——September. The British barque *Kwang Foong* wrecked at Koksikong during typhoon and plundered by the natives, the crew being stripped of their clothing. (See main text).

——November. The barque *Bintang Ammum* was wrecked at the entrance of Tamsui harbor. Abandoned by master and crew. Purchased by Dodd & Co. Natives plundered the wreckage on shore, and English naval force landed, burned a few houses occupied by plunderers, and recovered a portion of the stolen property.

1867.—March. The American barque *Rover* was wrecked on the Vele Rete Rocks, S. of Formosa. Captain Hunt, his wife, and crew made their way in boats to the south coast of Formosa but were all, with the exception of one Chinese, cruelly murdered by the Botan savages (See Chapter IX.)

——October. The British ship *Philomela* was wrecked near Lakiang, W. coast of Formosa. Crew arrived at Taiwanfu destitute.

1869.—October. The British schooner *Flying Buck* was stranded north of entrance to Takow harbor. (Unless otherwise mentioned the vessels given above were total wrecks.)

the eastern point of the island; and the vessel finally left port with only about half her intended cargo. On another occasion a number of piratical lorchas, which cruised for some days off the north point, caused a suspension of communication by sea between Tamsui and Kelung. The British gunboat *Flamer* came in contact with the pirates on several occasions. She figures in the following account in which an American describes his own personal experiences while a captive of the pirates and the methods by which these rogues carried on their traffic. (United States Consular Reports.)

"I cleared in the lugger *Rockway*, bearing the American flag[1] on the 4th of March, 1865, from Ningpo, bound for Foochow in ballast. On the morning of the 10th of March at about 1 a.m., it being very thick and dark, blowing hard from the N.E., I came to an anchor off Chiatouan island to the northward of Sanpan pass; a good many wood junks were also at anchor there, apparently bound for Ningpo. There were also two Canton lorchas lying astern of them. At daylight, while preparing to weigh, I observed that the decks of the lorchas in question were crowded with armed men (with matchlocks and spears) also that they were making ready to fire their big guns. They then hailed me in pigeon English to come on board, but I told them that my sampan being broken I could not. Each lorcha then sent a boat, and one also came from the shore, boarded me, and took possession of my vessel, my crew consisting of one European (a passenger) besides myself and 18 Ningpo men, these immediately going down into the hold.

"They enquired whether I had any cargo or money, and on my replying in the negative, they took me forcibly on board one of their own lorchas, they then locked me up in company with the other European (a passenger) Henry Lee or Leetch, an Austrian, in a sort of quarter-galley from which I could see a little of what went on, through a crack about 9 inches square. We were shut up there for about four days. On the fourth day, they were attacked by several mandarin gunboats, of which I counted nine, (through the chink) but after an engagement these were beaten off. This occurred while the lorchas were under weigh. We then ran to the northward and came to, so far as I could make out, Tak-sen Bay near Wan-chew. Remaining there some days and then leaving by night we ran southward to Meichew Sound and there captured two junks laden with charcoal, after which we put into port, sold the charcoal, and turned the junks' crew adrift again. We also took two junks laden with hard coal, and then proceeded to Chin-chew Bay, where we fell in with a Canton lorcha bound for Hongkong with a cargo of salt.

"The pirates hailed her in Chinese, which was answered. They then chased her towards a city called Tong-Boo (to the southward of Meichew Sound) and on her anchoring ran alongside, boarded and took her, cutting her cable and, hoisting her foresail, took her out to sea, and forced her crew into their service by taking out half her hands and distributing them in their own vessels, and replacing them with men of themselves. I may state that always while at sea, they let us out, and everywhere except in any close harbor when we were kept locked up. Shortly after this we fell in with a Foochow lorcha laden with sugar and sugar-candy, with a mandarin, some women, and soldiers on board. They boarded and took her, killing the mandarin and all on board except one woman and child. They sold her cargo at Meichew Sound and broke her up there. They then proceeded to the coast of Formosa, and anchored in a port, which from the description, must I think have been Kelung, remaining there three days. (A European boat boarded us here, but with only Chinamen on board). They then ran to the southward looking for a convenient and safe spot I imagine to lay in, and got into a small river, but whereabouts on the coast, I do not know except that it must have been to the southward of Tamsui; after we had laid there about twenty days, as near as I could guess, a gunboat bearing the British flag made her appearance. (I was then immediately with my companion shut up as before) she remained off the river two days firing at the pirate at long range, sinking one of the lorchas and wounding and killing some of her crew.[1] No one was killed on board the vessel I was in, but the shot and shell came very close, splashing all over the vessel, some water even coming through the chink. A portion of a shell took a piece out of our mast. The crews of the pirates hauled the lorchas quite close in shore, in a foot or so of water, and hoisting several guns from the hold erected a battery on shore. The reason that the junk sank was that a portion of a shell went right through her bows under water; while this was going on there were people on board from the shore, who appeared to me to be mandarin soldiers who were assisting.

"On the gunboat leaving they immediately weighed and got outside without taking anything out of the sunken lorcha except her crew, and proceeding to the mainland anchored at Nanguan, staying there a day went to Pi-ki-san, an island to the northward and eastward of Wanchew where there were anchored several other pirate junks. They here repaired damages, got in provisions and ammunition and sent their wounded to be treated ashore. Soon after we again put to sea taking two wood junks. After beating off a mandarin convoy, they returned to Pi-ki-san; here they were attacked by eighteen or nineteen mandarin gun-boats, which, however, did them little or no damage and after some firing disappeared. They then started again leaving their prize in charge of the other vessels. The same kind of proceedings went on until we got into Leishau Bay, where I made my escape, under the following circumstances. At about eight o'clock at night while the crew were smoking opium and gambling, my fellow-prisoner said to me, that the sampan was down and hauled close up under the stern, and as the night was very thick and dark we might escape, we then got into the sampan and with the help of a small paddle managed to reach the shore, and pushed the boat well out to the sea and let her drift so that she might not lead to our discovery. We sat on the rocks all night and in the morning

1. British Gunboat *Flamer*, Lieutenant Eaton Commander. The port referred to was Aulan.

making our way across the mountain got to the town of San-Sah. We went to the mandarin station to the great astonishment of the inmates, who could not conceive where we came from. However by signs we succeeded in making them understand, also that we were desirous of going south (to Foochow) where we arrived on the 28th of August, after having been captives to the pirates since the 10th of March. I did not know what month it was, but fancied it must be October, or November. We were treated properly by the pirates, let loose and made to work at sea but confined when we might be likely to escape. I don't know what became either of my vessel or her crew, but I do not think the latter were killed. I was owner of the vessel *Rockway*. I asked them why they kept us prisoners and they said that if they did not, a gun boat (foreign) would be sent after them, and that as I traded at Ningpo, while I was there they would be unable to come near that port. They always endeavored to evade steamers, and on sight of one prepared for action, but they did not the least care for sailing vessels. The junk I was on board had twelve guns on deck, and her hold was filled with captured goods of all kinds, with numbers of guns and small arms and ammunition. On deck she had four 16 pounders, one 18 pounder, and the remainder were 12 pounders. I think the other was armed about the same, but the captured lorcha was armed with 9 pounders taken from the others The principal people spoke a little pigeon English. Some of them told me they had been pirates thirty years, some of them having their headquarters in Formosa. They were well stationed as boarders, and fought well, and had apparently not much fear of death. They had some watches and clocks on board, but more for sale than use. They had good telescopes and opera-glasses which they used. They endeavored generally to get in close under the land and send the watchers on the hills to look out, and on any trading vessels being seen they used to run out and chase them. They had on board a shroff for whom they expected to get a large ransom at or near Ningpo. The shroff of the *Rockway* got away three months ago, I found out the fact, separately from me and my companion. I forgot to mention that at Chi-atow an English paddle-wheel steamer fired a few shot at the lorcha which was returned. (Signed) John Keley, Master of the *Rockway.*

In 1854 Chinese settlers began reaching down the north-east coast. Barter trade on the east coast in the vicinity of Suao Bay was commenced in 1854, when a settlement now known as Suao was established on that bay. In 1858, 1862, and 1864, attempts were made by the Chinese to occupy the fertile valley to the south, but they were each time eventually driven out by the savages. Shortly after the second of these attempts, the village, which was enclosed by a wall of earth surrounded by a ditch, was surprised in the dead of night by savages, and about four hundred of the Chinese killed. An enterprising Chinese, however, undaunted by these experiences, established himself on a small bay, known as Tang-o, five miles south of Suao, erected there a saw-mill, and engaged in cutting timber for the Kelung market. He also set up some camphor stills, the locality being very favorable from the abundance of camphor trees in the vicinity. This was more than the savages were willing to put up with, however, and after numerous brawls the manufacture of camphor in that district was discontinued. From this time on, repeated attempts were made by the Chinese to reach further towards the south. A few years later their persistency was rewarded by the establishment of a small settlement, then known as Sin-cheng, close to the Pacific coast and forty-five miles or so to the south of Suao. The settlers did little in the way of cultivating the soil, maintaining themselves by bartering salt, gunpowder, foreign and native clothes, needles, beads, thread, and such like, for firewood, dye roots, fruits, hemp cloth, deer sinews, horns, skins, etc.

The Chinese officials gave no assistance to these enterprising pioneers, nor was such assistance desired, for even when the mandarins did consider that they could profitably exert their authority, the colonists refused to recognize their right to do so. So determined were the people in this respect that the fertile Kapsulan plain with its large and prosperous villages for many years refused to submit to official rule, and even in late days there were many settlements which, though they submitted to a nominal rule, refused to contribute to official expenditure, and the authorities usually met with defeat if they endeavored to enforce payment.

East Coast Views.

High Cliffs of East Coast (After Guillemard.)

Karenko Village.

Suao Village.
Karenko Beach.
Savages at Pinam pulling in Boats.

The Chinese officers noted, however, the success of the saw-mill and the utility of the product for government works. This induced them to take a step utterly at variance with usual Chinese conservatism. They erected, in 1867, a steam saw-mill at Suao, notable as one of the first instances of the adoption of steam power by the officials of the empire, uninstigated by foreigners. The bulk of the timber obtained was used in the construction of the government docks at Foochow. With this innovation, Suao at once sprang into prominence, and a number of foreign vessels entered the bay. A few foreigners settled there, and the port had at one time every promise of becoming a flourishing city.

At this period there was organized at Suao an expedition which, for uniqueness, as well as humanity, of purpose deserves a page in history. The Chinese had cruelly driven the natives known as Pepohoans from their fertile lands, and not content with this, had taken from them whatever little property the fugitives had afterwards amassed by dint of hard and patient labor. These poor people were thus deprived of nearly every means of subsistence. Upon the arrival of the Chinese at Suao, the Pepohoans were located there in considerable numbers. They were not long allowed to live in peace, however, and were soon in a deplorable state. The foreigners at the port were much impressed with the condition of these peaceful natives, and, with the intention of assisting them, it was decided that a tract of fertile land south of Suao, then unoccupied except by roving head-hunters, should be secured, and the Pepohoans placed in possession of it. In 1868 the first party, consisting of Pepohoans under the command of a foreigner, met with such local opposition that it was deemed best to wait until the following year when an attempt on a larger scale could be made. During this interval, the plan, which was first undoubtedly inspired by purely philanthropic motives, appears to have assumed a commercial aspect ;—two foreigners being ambitious to secure exclusively for themselves the possession and government of the proposed colony. It would not be just to them, however, to neglect to state that the success of the original scheme, for the sake of the Pepohoans alone, necessitated that the enterprise should be conducted on a sound commercial basis ; and men of business in Formosa, notwithstanding their sympathy for the Pepohoans, were not inclined to give up their time and money without some prospect of at least a return sufficient to meet their expenses.

The leader of this expedition was an Englishman named Horn. No other foreigner had, at this time, seen so much of the Formosan savages ; in fact it was Horn that recovered the body of Mrs. Hunt, who, with her husband and the crew of the American vessel *Rover*, were massacred by the savages of south Formosa as recorded in a previous chapter. James Milisch, a citizen of Hamburg, and a mercantile resident of Tamsui, was the financial backer. Horn had allied himself to the Pepohoans by marrying, according to their rites, one of their own people, a beautiful girl who had much influence among them. The two leaders received the support and assistance of a cosmopolitan assembly such as the Far East frequently exhibits: two Scotchmen, one American, one German, one Spanish Mexican, one Goa Portuguese, and a large force of Pepohoans. The desired piece of land was secured without opposition other than from the savages who lived on the distant hills. It was some twenty miles south-west of Suao and was about a five hours' journey by sea. A place called Talamo marked its northern limits, and here was erected a fort consisting of a square walled stockaded enclosure with projecting corner towers for defence and enclosing a number of grass huts. Here the Pepohoans, men and women, together with the few Chinese who happened to be there on business, were sheltered. In the rear were grown sweet and European potatoes, and tobacco. The possession extended to Lamo which marked the end of the valley. A broad road was constructed between the two points.

Horn occupied as residence, a little, solitary, newly built house on the top of a rock surrounded by branches of the river. He was frequently molested by the head-hunting savages, who would sweep down from the hills in the dead of night and attack the colony. On one occasion he received a severe spear thrust in the foot and other slight wounds.

The Pepohoans who settled there were required to cultivate the land, and were provided with implements and food. The Chinese, other than traders, were not desired, and if they appeared in the neighborhood, the savages of the surrounding hills usually attended to them. Upon the first arrival of Horn, he buried the bones of some forty headless Chinese who had disputed possession with the savages. However, some Chinese were temporarily permitted to engage in cutting rattans and dye root and were protected by Horn and his Pepohoan braves. To recompense Horn and his partner, a tax of 15°/₀ was levied on all productions of the colony. Nor was this exorbitant, as was later proved.

As this venture was in territory over which the Chinese government neither had nor claimed to have jurisdiction, the particular tribe of savages who were the former occupants had consented to the occupation and had been compensated. But the Chinese officials were not pleased to have their ill-treatment of the Pepohoans made an excuse for an asylum being established by foreigners, and accordingly they represented to the English government that a portion of the emperor's dominions had been seized by English pirates who refused to submit to Imperial rule or to pay taxes. After many months had passed, and much money and time had been expended, without the least hint of a possible objection being made by the British government, the good officials, as English officials are wont to do, listened to the Chinese reports, pictured a force of English adventurers driving crowds of peaceful innocent Chinese with their wives and children by fire and sword from their homes and fields, and then sent orders to China that Horn should be ordered out of the district and that the Chinese authorities should be placed in possession. Poor Horn was thus dispossessed without any compensation, and he and James Milisch, who had invested much money in the place, were obliged to declare themselves insolvent soon after. The poor Pepohoans with their families, were immediately driven out by the Chinese authorities; and without homes, without friends, hated by the Chinese and the mandarins alike, their plight was so sad as to make one feel even happy to think that the Chinese who followed were speedily driven from the place, and that quite an addition was soon after made to the rows of skulls which graced the residences of several savages. Horn was visited by an English gun-boat and given but a short time to get together his private possessions. He promised to comply with the demand. It was during the stormy season when the seas that sweep the north-east coast of Formosa are extraordinarily wild and rough. Horn, however, kept his word. He waited for safe weather until the last day of his limit had expired, and then departed with some thirty of his most intimate Pepohoan friends, whom he did not desert even at the last, aboard a small schooner, his only means of transport. It was his intention to sail to Suao, but his vessel could not beat up against a fierce northern gale, and was driven to the south of the island, where it was wrecked, and the few grief stricken Pepohoans who survived brought to the foreigners in the south the news of the death of some twenty persons, among whom they counted their white friend and protector Horn.[1]

This period was marked by an earthquake the most severe ever experienced in the island since the first days of the Dutch. That greater damage was not done was owing to the limited area in which it was most severe, the scanty population, and the unpretentiousness of the buildings. It occurred on the 18th of December 1867, and the vicinity of the town of Kelung sustained the greatest damage, although the shock was felt generally through the island, but most severely in the north. Foreigners in the Custom service reported that at Kelung some fifteen shocks were felt during the day, but that it was the first movements that did the damage. In fifteen seconds after the first perceptible shock the damage was done and the town of Kelung was in ruins. The force of the earthquake may be judged when it is noted that the water of Kelung harbor ran out, leaving the bottom of the bay exposed. Fortunately there were no foreign vessels present, but the Chinese junks which were there, large and small, were in one second left dry on the bottom and in another caught by the huge returning wave to be either swamped or dashed into the town with fearful speed, to work havoc among the few remaining houses left near the shore. Multitudes of fish were thrown upon the shore and promptly gathered by the populace. The earth opened in places and closed again. A large gorge was formed by the splitting of a mountain side through which now runs a stream of hot water from a volcanic pit abounding with sulphurous springs and geysers. Many other physical changes were noted, including the deepening by a few feet of the anchorage at Kelung. The loss of life was never known; it is extremely doubtful if there was any count made, but probably several hundreds perished. A calamity of this sort is doubly felt among a Chinese population, for there are none to give a helping hand in relieving the misery. The present case was

1. While a guest of Admiral Tsunoda in 1895 we walked about the hills to the south of Suao on the north-east coast, and the writer was greatly astonished to meet, near a small village there, a young woman of handsome features, fair complexion, and light hair; the face and form of a Caucasian but otherwise a savage. Her dress was that of the native Pepohoans and ragged and dirty. Two small children of darker hue but hair decidedly light in color followed her about, while her companions appeared to be pure Pepohoans. On returning from this trip the writer made some inquiries and obtained information which leads him to believe that this woman was the daughter of Horn.

no exception. A foreign official at Tamsui states in his description of the disaster: "The apathy of the populace was astonishing; they watched the rescue of the wounded with apparently the greatest merriment."

While the opening of Formosan ports to foreign trade had been secured by treaty, yet treaties were not always respected, and the recognition of the rights and privileges embodied in them was not gained without a vigorous struggle. When we consider the undisguised antipathy which, during the early days, was displayed against the foreign residents, those engaged in mercantile pursuits especially, the officially instigated attacks, the intrigue and trickery which the British consular official, oft times unprotected, had to contend with, we shall willingly give due credit to those plucky pioneers who stuck so manfully to their posts in those stormy days.

In the earlier days, the foreigners who visited the coast were inclined to take the law into their own hands. Captain Roper, master of the schooner *Vindex*, on one occasion obtained the release of one of his Chinese who had been imprisoned at Aulan by clearing for action and threatening to fire on the town; Captain Enscoe of the schooner *Madge* refused, while at Kelung, to permit his vessel to be searched by the Customs officials. He warned the party off and when they appeared regardless of his threat, he opened fire on them and they speedily retired; Captain Sullivan of the *Wild Wave* endeavored to chastise some yamen runners while personally appearing before a Chinese official to make a complaint regarding some commercial transaction. On this occasion, however, the yamen runners were too much for the gallant skipper. They literally jumped on him, and it was with difficulty that he was rescued and removed to his boat. Such attempts at obtaining justice were not encouraged after the establishment of consulates, and the merchants who followed the old "sea traders" were sensible men of business and not inclined to break the laws either of their own country or of China.

The lower classes of Hobe Chinese were an unruly set, and caused the foreigners frequent trouble. On this account, the presence of a gunboat was necessary during the construction of the first foreign house (Dent & Co.'s) in 1862. On one occasion, during the same year, Mr. Rainbow, agent of Dent & Co., was attacked by the coolies, and his house, in which he had taken refuge, was besieged by the truculent natives and bombarded with stones. Captain Roper, of the steamer *Vindex*, then landed a force of armed lascars and dispersed the crowd. Upon appealing to the officials, the foreigners were informed by the former that they were unable to punish the offenders. The next day some fifty armed lascars were landed from British ships, and this force, led by the British consul, marched through the streets of Hobe and to the house of the headman of the turbulent coolies, with the intention of seizing him; but he had evidently been forewarned and had made good his escape. The Chinese throughout the village became very amicable upon catching sight of the armed lascars and showed no further signs of hostility. The self-declared helpless officials now gave evidence that their weakness was not so marked after all, and the reported leaders in the outbreak were promptly brought to justice.

In 1865, a British naval force was landed and adopted similar tactics. It seems that a certain fortification known as the "White Fort" was a prominent sea mark for incoming vessels. But owing to a rapid growth of bushes that had sprung up in front of it, its use as a mark was greatly impaired. The Chinese authorities were requested to clear away the bushes, and a petty military official with a few men was deputed by the authorities to perform the task. Expecting trouble from the villagers, this officer requested the presence of some of the foreigners. Accordingly an English lieutenant, the custom's agent, the British consul, and a gunboat's cutter with five men in charge of a man-of-war's-man, Farrington by name, proceeded to the spot. The work planned had scarcely been commenced before some two or three hundred Chinese armed with spears appeared, seized the military officer above mentioned, and then commenced to stone the foreigners. The naval officer advised an immediate retreat to the boats, which advice was acted upon, but before the beach was reached, Farrington received a severe cut on the head. The villagers fortunately did not follow up the retreating foreigners, and the party escaped without further injury. The next day the British gunboat steamed near the place, a strong armed party went ashore, cut down the bushes, and then marched through the streets of the village, whereupon the people exhibited all the signs of undying affection, and, so far as appearances went, there was not a man who would ever think of lifting a hand against the foreign visitors. It seems that the opposition to the removal of the bushes was the work of the pilots, who had incited their village friends to oppose the measure, fearing that, if the sea marks were made clear, the foreign vessels would dispense with their services as guides.

In the month of December, 1866, naval forces were twice actively engaged on shore. The first case was at Kelung where a lieutenant's Chinese servant was seized by village rowdies and confined on shore with the object of extorting money from him. The lieutenant landed a small force, recovered his servant, and pulled down the house wherein he had been confined. The second landing occurred in Tamsui. A Dutch barque, the *Bintang Anam*, had stranded on the sands of the harbor, and Mr. John Dodd, a British merchant, had purchased the wreck from the master. The neighboring villagers, however, succeeded in plundering much of the wreckage as it came ashore; on some occasions even using force to wrest it from such Chinese as Mr. Dodd had authorized to collect it. Application was made to the officials, but without success, and the commander of the British gunboat *Havoc* landed a force, secured the return of much of the stolen property, and burned two houses to punish the natives. On another occasion, the following year, coolies in Kelung interfered with the conveyance of the luggage of a party of Europeans. A collision ensued, during which one of the Europeans was knocked down with a stone. The party had to retreat leaving the luggage in the hands of the coolies.

The mandarins watched with concern the increasing prosperity of the foreigners, and endeavored by every means possible to check foreign trade. Business was accordingly carried on under great disadvantages. The local officials had strongly opposed the establishment of the Customs service in charge of foreigners, depriving them as it did of the many and varied squeezes which they had before imposed at their pleasure. Mast dues were a common form of extortion which had always been enforced on junks and foreign vessels, and it was a great disappointment to the officials to find that, after the establishment of the Customs, foreign ships would be exempt from these dues. They consequently endeavored to avenge the loss of the $40 mast dues by placing every possible obstacle in the way of foreign trade. A favorite method was to occasionally declare an embargo, contrary to the provisions of the treaty, upon the export of rice, thus depriving foreign ships of cargo which they expected. Frequent friction resulted between the British consul and the commissioner of customs—the latter, acting as he did under instructions, refusing to grant an export permit to foreigners shipping rice. In 1866, on Mr. White, the commissioner, refusing to grant an export permit to Messrs. MacPhail & Co. to ship rice from Taiwanfu to Amoy in their schooner *Pearl*, the British acting consul, Mr. Watters, disposed of the difficulty, and himself gave permission to the ship to leave without the usual customs clearance, on the owners giving the guarantee required by the treaty. The *Pearl* left Takow on the 9th June, but was lost on her way to Amoy with all her cargo and all hands except one.

Mr. Watters was not superstitious, however, and continued to enforce treaty rights, repeating the action he had taken in the case of the *Pearl* whenever necessity arose. An American schooner, the *Teenlee*, was the next vessel similarly despatched. Meanwhile Chinese vessels were almost daily exporting rice without any opposition. In September of the same year a pass was obtained, not, however, without considerable difficulty, by Messrs. MacPhail & Co. and they exported under it a considerable quantity of rice to Amoy.

The difficulties between the local government and the few foreign residents, which had commenced from the first year of the establishment of the Customs, became more numerous and irritating towards the close of the "Sixties." No doubt the aristocracy of the larger Formosan cities, with courage gained by the thought of the distance between them and the mainland, as well as from the knowledge that the appalling attacks on foreigners in bygone years had remained unpunished, thought the island a fitting place to give abundant evidence of their well known hatred for the foreign devil.

During the year 1868, however, a crisis was reached in the series of outrages, which made it plain that either the foreigners must forsake Formosa one and all, or some more effective method than the mere presentation of written and oral protests must be introduced. That the Chinese hoped that the foreigners would be forced to adopt the former plan, seems evident; for the persecution was apparently prearranged, commencing as it did simultaneously in the north and south of the island. In the south, which we will deal with first, British Consular Reports[1] inform us that the more vexatious of the difficulties began in April of that year, when six thousand dollars worth of camphor, the property of Ellis & Co., was seized at Goché, regardless of

1. British Blue Book 1869 (China No. 3.)

the fact that the camphor was bought consistently with the terms of the treaty, which expressly stipulated that camphor was one of the articles of legal trade.

The United States gunboat *Aroostook* was then fortunately visiting the southern portion of Formosa, and General Le Gendre, United States consul at Amoy, who was on board, joined Mr. Jamieson, the acting British consul at Takow, in a visit to the taotai at his yamen in Taiwanfu to remonstrate with him on the action of his subordinates in the north. There was not much gained by this, the taotai claiming all camphor in the island, and denying the right of any one to trade in it without his special permission. He, however, came to a distinct agreement with the two consuls that the camphor in question should be returned or a money indemnity paid instead. The difficulties which followed are graphically described by Mr. Dond Matheson[1] in a narrative of the Formosan troubles which he placed before the Earl of Clarendon with the hope of inducing that high official to modify his decision of inflicting severe punishment upon Mr Gibson, acting-consul, for the measures adopted by that officer in disposing of the Formosan troubles.

In the following narrative of the difficulties previous to the landing of the naval force, Mr. Matheson's account is taken as the authority:— Liang Taotai, following the policy of his predecessors who had succeeded in expelling the Protestant missionaries from Taiwanfu, refused to ratify a purchase made by the Roman Catholics within the capital city's walls, or to take any notice of an attack made upon their premises— an outrage no doubt instigated by the same officials from whom they were now seeking redress. "They allowed and encouraged most infamous reports, regarding the proceedings of both Catholic and Protestant missionaries and their converts, to spread unchecked throughout the whole south of Formosa, until the underlings of the various yamens, seeing that the popular mind was sufficiently excited, were able, without fear, to lead parties to the destruction of all the chapels within their reach."

In the beginning of April, a Roman Catholic chapel at Koe-kan was sacked and burnt, the Protestant chapel at Pitow, the district city, was also sacked and destroyed. On the same day, in the streets of Pitow, the yamen underlings brutally assaulted a Protestant catechist who barely succeeded in escaping their knives, and who upon reaching the district mandarin's yamen was coolly shut up in prison by that official and was not released for seven weeks. "On the 24th of April, another Protestant catechist was set upon in a village only five miles from the consulate at Takow, and was murdered in open day and in the public street, his body cut in pieces, and his heart eaten by some of the bolder of his murderers at the north gate of the old city, close by. In Pitow, the houses of the adherents of the Protestant Church were broken into and sacked, the women driven out to the streets and the males of the party compelled to flee for their lives to Takow. The Roman Catholics in Taiwanfu were, in the beginning of May,

---

1. Mr. Dond Matheson, of the firm of Messrs. Jardine Matheson & Co., and at that time one of the Committee for Foreign Missions of the English Presbyterian Church.

once more outraged, their premises again destroyed, and one of their number bambooed and imprisoned by the district magistrate of Taiwanfu. The remonstrances of Mr. Acting-Consul Jamieson were utterly without avail, nor was a visit of that gentleman, accompanied by Lieutenant-Commander Keppel and a party of men from Her Majesty's gun-boat *Janus*, to the district magistrate of Pitow, of any farther value in securing the release of the imprisoned Protestant catechist."

At the end of June, Mr. Hardie, the agent for Messrs. Tait and Co. at Taiwanfu, was suddenly and without warning murderously assaulted by one of the official servants of the Likin office, while traveling from Takow to Taiwanfu. The man had, unheard by Mr. Hardie, stepped up quietly behind him and with full strength had stabbed him in the side of the chest with a knife. It fortunately impinged on a rib, and Mr. Hardie escaped most miraculously, with but some loss of blood and a severe pleurisy which followed. The would-be murderer was accompanied by another rough of the same stamp, and it was with great difficulty that Mr. Hardie defended himself from a repetition of the attack, which might easily have been fatal. British interests were at this time in the hands of John Gibson, acting-consul, and, at his urgent instigation, the officials did make a show of punishing the offender, but in a manner that was so palpably a sham that the witnessing crowd laughed, and Consul Gibson, who was present, left in disgust, after declaring to the officer in charge that he considered it an additional insult. On the departure in July of the former acting-consul, Mr. Jamieson, Mr. Gibson had taken charge, but although the Chinese officials were formally notified, the taotai refused to recognize Mr. Gibson as acting-consul, and it was not until the arrival of Lord Charles Scott with H.M.S. *Icarus* that the taotai would humble himself to acknowledge the consular officer.

On the 30th of July, the Protestant chapel at Pitow, while in process of rebuilding, was again attacked by the Pitow soldiery, the new materials carried off, and the remainder of the building destroyed. Mr. Gibson had counselled the rebuilding of the chapel in hopes that the officials having so often been complained to, might themselves think best to act differently in the future. It was but another vain hope; for only a short time elapsed before the building was again destroyed.

In August, Goche was again the seat of a disturbance of which Mr. Pickering, of the firm of Messrs. Ellis and Co., was the intended victim. As the taotai had refused to grant passports to foreigners for any place outside of Takow and Taiwan, Mr. Pickering, possessed of only the consular passport, had started out for Goche to inquire after the camphor which, in spite of the taotai's promise, had not been forthcoming. Upon hearing of the foreigner's departure, Taotai Liang issued a proclamation offering a reward of $500 for Mr. Pickering's head, and gave orders that he should be killed. To carry this order into effect, the ting of Lokang with a few soldiers made an attack on the lodging place of Mr. Pickering, but the latter, being a man of daring and resolution, stood his ground firmly, and with the free use of fire-arms routed his assailants. He then with great difficulty made his way to the seashore, where he boarded a small boat which, encountering a storm, was, after a very dangerous voyage, driven to Tamsui in the north of the island.

On the 29th of August, Lord Charles Scott and the acting-consul had an interview with the taotai, during which the latter behaved in a most insulting manner and, finally becoming enraged, struck Mr. Gibson sharply over the hands with his fan, and then withdrew. After waiting some time for his return the officials left. It would seem that such an affront should have been sufficient cause to have broken off relations with this insolent dignitary, but negotiations were continued in writing and finally resulted in eliciting from him a despatch complying with the acting-consul's conditions, accompanied by the usual promise that justice should be done. But it proved to be but the " old old story " for not only were none of the wrongs righted, but new threats were made against the merchants; and a demand that their goods which were still in the hongs should pay likin, although they had already paid custom dues. To add to these peculiar proceedings, mast dues were asked for the ships besides the customs dues, and to revenge themselves against one hong which had been more obnoxious than others, an attempt to ruin it was made by placing a double likin on all goods proceeding from that hong into Chinese hands.

On the 2nd of September, the British consul, who had reasons for believing that the promises the taotai had made a month before to Lord Charles Scott had not since received a thought, informed the Pitow magistrate in whose district most of the criminal cases had occurred, that on a certain day he would pay him a visit at his yamen, accompanied by the Lieut. commander of the *Bustard*. He received for answer an injunction not to come to Pitow; for, as the taotai had not given any orders regarding criminals, the magistrate had nothing to discuss with him, and moreover the people would be much enraged if he came. This despatch was abundant evidence that but little faith was to be placed in any statement, written or oral, that the taotai might make. Mr. Gibson, much dissatisfied with the attempt to bar him from visiting the city of Pitow, only eight miles from the consulate, wrote back insisting that the magistrate should receive him on the day fixed. The next day brought a return despatch from Pitow stating that a large collection of human bones, including three skulls and other bones evidently fresh, had been found the afternoon before under the ruins of the Protestant chapel; and that they showed clearly enough that Dr. Maxwell, the Protestant missionary physician, and his assistants had been guilty of the hideous crime of murder and that they had concealed their act by secreting the bones of their victims. This impossible charge was followed by a demand that the consul should seize Dr. Maxwell and have him tried, and that a certain Chinese protestant should be sent to Pitow to be punished as such an atrocious crime deserved. The consul answered promptly that he would come the next day bringing Dr. Maxwell and the Chinese protestant to Pitow to be tried before a joint court. The magistrate now effectually foiled, took the only course left open to avoid exposure of his sham plot, refused to see the consul under any conditions, and moreover warned him that if he persisted he would find his way barred by force. Under these circumstances, it would have been unwise to attempt the visit, and it was afterwards found that the yamen had collected a considerable armed force at Pitow and erected three strong ambuscades on the road over which the consul and his party would have had to pass. The consul's complaints to Taiwanfu of this outrageous conduct on the part of the taotai and his subordinates resulted in an insolent and derisive answer.

This state of affairs continued until the end of October, when two events occurred which made future relations with the taotai unendurable. " First came a despatch to the consul from the taotai stating that he had referred the mercantile questions in dispute to the viceroy and had been answered that he, the taotai, had erred only in too much leniency toward the foreigners, and that it behoved him to act more strictly in the future." A few days later the house of Elles and Co.'s compradore was sacked, and money and property carried off to the value of several thousand dollars. Not content with this, a mandarin and soldiers were sent down to Takow to seize the compradore who, it was believed, had escaped to that port.

At this juncture, H.M.S. *Algerine* arrived, followed a day or two later by a Chinese gunboat, bringing over the Amoy taotai, who had been detailed by the vice-regal government at Foochow to come to Formosa and settle the questions in dispute. After a week's delay in Taiwanfu, the official, accompanied by the Taiwanfu taotai, appeared in Takow, where a conference with Mr. Gibson was held in the presence of the commanders of the *Algerine* and *Bustard* and Dr. Maxwell, Dr. Manson, the agents of Messrs. Elles and Co., and Messrs. Tait and Co. As it appeared that the taotai was without any definite power to remove any of the offending officers, it would have been folly to discuss the matter with him. As to the numerous complaints, he said that he had discovered that " the Formosan difficulties were of no importance ; that in a day or two he would start back to Amoy," and when the consul informed him that this would not be satisfactory unless he suspended Taotai Liang's commission " he laughed off the whole affair." Finding that Tseng, the Amoy taotai, had no inclination to do justice for the past or even to discourage a repetition of misdeeds in the future, the consul now took a step which instantly altered the whole situation. In the consul's account of the position he states : " If Commissioner Tseng withdrew from the island in a state of dudgeon, I could only apply material force to the local officials ; and I at once foresaw that when material force had been successfully applied, I should be still in this predicament, either, first of raising a native rebellion in the island ; or second, of having nobody with whom to settle our embarrassments ; but perhaps both."

On the 20th of November, the consul started from Takow with the *Algerine* and *Bustard* for Anping with the determination of taking military possession of the Fort of Zelandia, and the ramparts of the village of Anping, "not only as a material guarantee in the shape of a reprisal, but as a basis for action, Anping being the key to the capital of Taiwan."

Upon arriving at their destination the next day, Lieutenant Gurdon, the senior naval officer, who approved of the plan, landed a force of marines and the boats' crews of the two vessels. A reconnoitring party took military possession of the fort and the ramparts of the village without opposition. The doors of the magazines of the fort were found locked, while the soldiers and their commandant had all departed. The civil government was not interfered with, it being the intention to allow the native merchants to trade as usual and to protect the foreign customs house. Proclamations were issued enjoining the people to proceed with their occupations as usual, and another set of proclamations were transmitted to Taiwanfu, warning the people that if they molested the British consulate or the foreign houses, the city should be bombarded. As Lieutenant Gurdon considered that it would not be prudent with his small force to occupy Fort Zelandia, on account of its ruined condition, and as the fort was within range of the gunboat's guns, the landing force was re-embarked and a proclamation was published to the effect that the village of Anping and Fort Zelandia were held by British forces and that no other military or naval forces would be allowed to enter it.

The consul returned on the 22nd to Takow on board the gunboat *Bustard* and the next day informed Tseng, in a despatch, of the proceedings at Anping. This had an immediate effect, the taotai claiming an interview at once. This was granted, and after a great deal of argument, Tseng practically acceded to all demands; the removal of the taotai of Taiwan, of the district magistrate of Pitow, and of the ting of Lokang, to be effected by the Amoy taotai taking his steamer to Foochow, and there obtaining immediate dismissal of the offenders by the viceroy.

Meanwhile Lieutenant Gurdon at Anping had boarded a man-of-war lorcha that was lying inside the bar, and informed her captain that he must move her outside before six o'clock that night, or she would be taken possession of. He then proceeded on shore and visited the heptai (Chinese military commander) informing him that he must leave the town within a space of twenty-four hours, in default of which he would be taken prisoner. In the afternoon, the lorcha not having moved, boats were sent manned and armed, which took possession of her and she was moved outside, anchored close to the gunboat, and her crew sent ashore with the exception of the captain and two men who were detained on board.

A deputation of merchants from Taiwanfu arrived during the afternoon and went on board the gunboat with a request to the commander that the heptai might be allowed to remain in Anping. In answer they were informed that unless they would deposit the sum of 35,000 dollars with the naval officer as a guarantee that Consul Gibson's conditions with the Amoy taotai were carried out, orders would not allow of their request being granted. One of the terms of the settlement arrived at with the Amoy taotai was that the British gunboat should hold military possession of Anping until offending Chinese officers had been removed. This decision was apparently satisfactory to all, excepting the Taiwan authorities, who, having been ignored in the decision, determined to retake their seaport, which was now held by the single gunboat *Algerine*. It is not quite certain but that these officials thought they were assisting the Amoy taotai in this action, but it is shrewdly suspected they were stung at the thought of the single gunboat with its handful of men. On the 25th, therefore, the Taiwan authorities sent down 500 men to reoccupy the place, which they did and began at once to erect fortifications and mount guns. Lieutenant Gurdon upon being informed of this, immediately sent a letter to the heptai stating that unless he sent the troops out of the town and ceased mounting guns on the fortifications within an hour of the receipt of the despatch, the gunboat would open fire on the town. Word was also sent to the inhabitants ordering them to abandon the town as it would be fired upon at 3 p.m. No answer having been received, at four o'clock a slow fire was commenced from the pivot gun with shot and shell at 2,000 yards, confining the fire as much as possible to the batteries that were being armed, and ceasing, after over an hour's firing. Early in the evening the lieutenant received a despatch from the consul at Takow informing him of the agreements arrived at and that the British forces were to continue to occupy Anping until the agreement was ratified by the vice-regal government of Fokien. The extreme importance of the position was apparent ; for if the authorities should succeed that night in putting Anping in a state of defence, the small British force at hand could be easily defied and the negotiations which had now reached a successful issue would be worse than useless. With this in view, Lieutenant Gurdon determined to storm the town of Anping the same night. The night attack which followed was, for the commander and his company— twenty-five in all—as brilliant an exploit as the East records. The description of this daring and successful engagement is given by Lieutenant Gurdon in his official report as follows:

" At 10.30 p.m. I left the ship in the gig and the cutter, the gig containing one officer and eleven men, and the cutter one officer and thirteen men, making a total of two officers and twenty-three men. I landed on the beach about two miles below the town through a heavy surf, in which, notwithstanding every precaution, the gig was swamped and sunk. After forming on the beach I advanced on the town, feeling my way with great caution, throwing out skirmishers and taking advantage of every inequality of the ground to conceal my advance ; when I got within 800 yards of the fortifications, seeing that the enemy was on the alert, I took advantage of a steep bank, making the men lie down behind it, and determined to wait until the moon had gone down.

" At 2.40 a.m., the moon having gone down, I advanced again, and succeeded in penetrating into the heart of the town without being discovered. I then managed to obtain a guide, and made for the Heptai's Yamen. On breaking into the Heptai's Yamen we discovered a guard-room full of soldiers, in number about fifty, who immediately barricaded the door, and extinguished the lights ; however, port-fires being at hand, they were immediately lighted, the door was burst in, when, notwithstanding all my personal endeavors and those of an interpreter I had with me who assured them their lives would be spared, and they themselves allowed to go free if they laid down their arms, they would not, and reluctantly, in self-defence, I was obliged to give the order to fire. The Chinese soldiers succeeded in breaking down a door in their rear, and escaped ; suffering, however, a serious loss of eleven killed and about six wounded.

" I then marched to the Custom-house, halting there till daylight before I advanced further, posting sentries on Fort Zelandia commanding the town, and also in the neighboring streets. I managed to write a despatch here, informing the British Consul at Takow of what had taken place, and requested him to proceed to Anping in Her Majesty's ship *Bustard* which I ordered up to reinforce me immediately. This despatch I succeeded in getting conveyed to the consul by offering a heavy bribe to a native courier.

" Directly it was daylight I concentrated my men, and advanced to take possession of the line facing towards Taiwan-foo. I had only just reached the lines when I observed a large body of the enemy advancing to the attack, led on by a mandarin carrying a yellow flag. I immediately lined the embankment, and opened a heavy fire on the enemy, who stood and returned the fire for about five minutes, when they broke and fled towards Taiwan-foo, sustaining a loss, as I have since ascertained, of six killed and about ten wounded I posted sentries and established guards round the entrenchments, barricading the gate leading to Taiwan-foo, and withdrawing the planks of it.

" During the afternoon a deputation of the chief merchants of Taiwan-foo arrived, informing me that they had been sent by Liang Taotai, of Taiwan, and requesting to know what my terms were, as they were empowered by Liang to grant any demand I preferred. I informed them that I required a sum of 40,000 dollars to be paid over to me before noon the next day, as a guarantee that all Mr. Gibson's demands were fulfilled, the sum in question not to be returned until his agreement was ratified by the vice-regal Government of Fukien. In case this demand of mine was not complied with, I informed the deputation that I should advance on Taiwan-foo. During the night I was informed that my demand of a guarantee of 40,000 dollars would be complied with, they being guaranteed to arrive at my head-quarters not later than 4 p.m. that day, viz., the 27th instant. At daybreak on Friday morning Her Majesty's gunboat *Bustard* arrived with Mr. Gibson, the consul, on board, and about 10 a.m. Lieutenant Johnson and thirteen men from her landed to reinforce me.

"During the day I employed the force in destroying all stores of arms that I could discover, blowing up the magazine in Fort Zelandia to prevent any accident happening from the large quantity of powder stored there, and which was stowed in a very dangerous and careless manner. The 40,000 dollars arrived at head-quarters from Taiwan-foo about 4 o'clock, and were sent off to Her Majesty's gun-vessel *Algerine* for safe custody, I giving a receipt and guarantee to the persons bringing it that it would be restored on the fulfillment of Mr. Gibson's demands by the vice-regal Government of Fukien. On Sunday, the 29th instant, at about 11 a.m., Tseng, Taotai of Amoy, arrived for a conference, and was received with all due honors.

"The consul requested me as senior naval officer to make any demands that I required from the Chinese authorities, when I requested from them, before Her Majesty's forces under my command reembarked, the payment of the sum of 10,000 dollars, to be applied as follows: the sum of 5,000 dollars for repayment to the British Government of any expense incurred by them in the present expedition, also the further sum of 5,000 dollars, to be paid to me as ransom for all guns and other Government stores remaining in the town of Anping, the sum in question to be distributed as prize-money to the officers and men under my command. This demand was complied with, when I on my part agreed to return the sum of 40,000 dollars deposited as a guarantee with me, to restore the man-of-war lorcha, taken by Her Majesty's ship under my command, and to embark the forces under my command, at that time in possession of Anping; these promises being conditional on Tseng Taotai fulfilling the following requests:—that he should send Mr. Gibson a despatch guaranteeing the dismissal of Liang Taotai and other officials implicated in the late disturbances in Formosa; that Tseng Taotai should guarantee that no Chinese military force should attempt to occupy Anping until the ratification by the vice-regal Government of Fukien of the British Consul's requests; the town of Anping in the meantime being held by us from a gunboat; that all indemnity money demanded by Mr. Gibson should be paid immediately, and delinquents concerned in the late outrages brought to trial and punished forthwith. These requests were all complied with, the taotai of Amoy returning to Taiwan-fu about 2 p.m.

"On Tuesday, the 1st of December, the Tsien of Taiwan-fu arrived with the sum of 10,000 dollars, the indemnity required by me before the embarkation of Her Majesty's forces under my command, for which I gave him a receipt, and handed over to him in return the 40,000 dollars in my possession as a guarantee for the fulfilment of the consul's demands. The man-of-war lorcha had been returned to the Chinese officials on the previous day. An arrangement was also made with the Tsien to receive over civil possession of the town from me at 10 o'clock the following morning, Her Majesty's forces under my command embarking immediately after the ceremony. At noon on Wednesday, the 2nd instant, the Tsien of Taiwan-fu arrived, and was received with all due honors at the main guard, where I handed over officially to him the Civil Government of Anping; Her Majesty's forces then marched down to their boats, and embarked without delay, after having held Anping since Thursday, 26th of November."

Anping when captured had mounted on its fortifications forty-one guns, and there were in store ready for mounting no less than 101. The above mentioned guns varied in size, but the greater number consisted of 18 and 12-pounders. About 4,000 stand of arms, consisting of gingalls, matchlocks, including some of British make marked "B. & Co.," bows and arrows, swords and spears were destroyed, besides the magazines of the fort blown up by the captors.

As the acceptance of $40,000 guarantee money was considered unwise, inasmuch as the Chinese might think that the expedition was in quest of money rather than of justice, the consul advised Lieutenant Gurdon to return it, which was done.

The whole affair was a great surprise to the Chinese mandarins. They had been so accustomed to violating treaties and crawling out from under the wreckage unhurt, that to encounter such a sudden and unceasing display of determination threw them into a great state of consternation. Disputes that had remained unsettled for months were now brought to a close in almost as many hours.

The following were the substantial results obtained by Consul Gibson:—

The camphor monopoly was abolished and proclamations issued declaring the right of foreigners and their employés to go and buy freely.

Passports were to be issued by the taotai on application, to merchants and others to travel for business or pleasure within the island of Taiwan.

An indemnity of $6,000 was paid Elles and Co. for the loss of camphor.

An indemnity of $1,167 was paid to the Protestant Mission for loss of property.

A payment was made of all claims of Elles & Co.'s compradore for loss of property.

Liang taotai, the district magistrate of Pitou, and the ting of Lokang were all removed, and the various criminals connected with the several outrages were punished to the satisfaction of the consul.

Proclamations were issued acknowledging the injustice of the slanders hitherto circulated against Christianity and Christians, and protecting them thoroughly against a renewal of such.

The right of residence and of work to missionaries in the island was declared.

Proclamations were issued calling for joint courts in dealing with mixed cases.

The consul, with patient determination and admirable foresight, had with the aid of the gallant naval force won a victory that would seem worthy of great commendation. It is much to be regretted that the Earl of Clarendon strongly disapproved of Mr. Gibson's proceedings, and in a despatch to Sir Rutherford Alcock, then British minister in Peking, he so severely condemned the consul that it could not have been otherwise than extremely humiliating to this servant of the public who had conscientiously labored as best he could for the restoration of peace and order in the island, and who, if guilty (and it was generally believed in the East that he was not) could only be accused of having acted with excessive zeal and determination. Whether the circumstances demanded such condemnation or not, this is not the place to discuss, but it must be noted that Consul Gibson accomplished much good for the island, thereby benefiting every foreigner residing there since.

The Chinese were taught to respect foreigners, and instead of Formosa being known, as it had been for years, as a place where the lives of aliens were in constant peril, it soon obtained a safe reputation, and though there was an occasional outburst against the foreigners, especially in the north, the mandarins were generally prompt to give satisfaction. Influential friends, including Mr. Dond Matheson, wrote strongly in the vice-consul's behalf, but H.I.H. Prince Kung had also written and given the Chinese side of the affair with, it would appear, telling effect. Mr. Gibson was dismissed and died soon after, it is said, of a broken heart.

While the clouds were gathering over the south, Tamsui in the north was in the midst of a storm. The hatred towards foreigners, which since the opening of the port had been gradually increasing, had now with sympathetic encouragement from the mandarins assumed such proportions that Acting-

Vice-Consul Holt wrote in a despatch to Peking dated Oct. 14th, 1868, that " the situation was so serious that he might be driven at any moment to haul down his flag. Remonstrances, expostulations, despatches, letters, messages, and visits have alike failed in insuring common justice; and our very lives are threatened by people whose recent course of action has been so atrocious as to prove that the will is not wanting to murder us." Events that had occurred gave evidence too vivid, that this was the case.[1]

As yet, although they had the right, no foreigners were established up river from Tamsui, and the Chinese were determined that they should not be.

Messrs. Dodd & Co. were the first firm to make the attempt, and it was this that caused the trouble in the north. As the first step, a hong in Banka known as the Lok Tow hong was leased from Mansoon, widow of a former camphor merchant named Laktow, and bargain money fifty dollars was paid down. The widow had had a little property left her at her husband's death, and having no influential family or powerful clan to help her, she was most unmercifully squeezed by the Banka mandarins for imaginary fees said to have been due them for camphor shipped to Hongkong during the lifetime of her husband. Owing to the opposition of these same mandarins who had sealed up the door of the hong in question, and the fear of the poor widow that she would be squeezed still more, Messrs. Dodd & Co. found great difficulty in obtaining possession of their newly leased property. As a British firm, they accordingly addressed the acting vice-consul on the subject, who in turn addressed the haekwan, (an expectant taotai and the highest officer at that time in the district) remonstrating against the obstacles thrown in the way of Messrs. Dodd & Co., and demanding that the property should be handed over to them. The consul after a short delay received an answer from the mandarin stating that the seals had been removed and that Messrs. Dodd & Co. were at liberty to enter into possession of the property.

Messrs. Dodd & Co. having been informed of this permission, gave orders to their compradore to take possession. On attempting to carry these orders into effect the employé of the firm was immediately turned out by followers of a hostile clan, known as the Huang-hsing clan, who resided in the locality. Upon hearing of this, Mr. Crawford D. Kerr, manager of the firm, accompanied by Mr. S. Godfrey Bird, a member of the same firm, forwarded a card and letter with which the consul had provided them to the Tamsui ting's yamen. An answer was returned stating that the Tamsui ting was absent at Teckcham, and that the persons left in charge of the civil police refused to do anything unless they received a squeeze, and the squeeze not being forthcoming they accordingly did not act.

Not believing that the Chinese would oppose entrance to the hong if made by the foreigners representing the firm holding the lease, the two gentlemen above mentioned visited the property. Arriving at the gate of the court yard of the hong, Mr. Kerr forced open a small wicket which was fastened with a nail and with which the gate had been barred,

---

1. British Blue Book No. 6—1869—China.

when, without a word of warning, and without the slightest provocation, a mob of some five hundred coolies swarmed out from the adjoining houses and other places of concealment. The two gentlemen attempted immediate flight, but before they had gained many steps they were assailed in the most violent manner with guns, knives, spears, and stones by the ferocious ruffians, who had now caught up with them. Mr. Bird was struck down by a stone and beaten and stabbed with spears and muskets. Mr. Kerr was also struck down to the ground by a large stone, which inflicted a severe wound. Fortunately the whole affair took place but some fifty yards from the precincts of the Tamsui ting's yamen, and it was towards this that the two foreigners were struggling. But with no weapons of defence it was a difficult task and they were frequently struck down with bamboos and spears. One of the mob attempted, while Mr. Bird lay on the ground, to dash out his brains with a large stone which the ruffian had lifted above his head with both hands, but in throwing it he fortunately missed his aim. Mr. Kerr was knocked into a vile cesspool by a severe blow in the face from a musket butt. They managed, however, half dead, and covered with blood and mud, to crawl to the yamen where, instead of the assistance they required, the underlings endeavored to force them back into the hands of the mob, although in their weakened condition from loss of blood this would have meant certain death. Fortunately a number of shipwrecked Loochooan sailors, detained in the yamen as prisoners, were present, and they gave the two wounded men kind attention, frequently lifting them from the ground, bathing their cuts and wounds, and washing away the blood and mud. Without the assistance of these kind hearted Loochooans it is doubtful whether the two foreigners would have escaped alive. After a considerable lapse of time the mandarins of the yamen, no doubt beginning to appreciate the seriousness of the attack, allowed an escort to guard the chairs in which the wounded and almost unconscious men were carried to the river where their boats were waiting to take them back to Tamsui. The property which they had carried to the hong itself was seized by the hostile mob who furthermore, unopposed by the Tamsui ting or by any other authority, cut loop holes in the walls of the neighboring Chinese buildings, through which they could insert firearms, and raised a subscription equal to fifty per cent of the income of the hostile faction "in order to frighten the English and drive them from the port." They also threatened to attack the other foreign hong and swore that they would die rather than fail. All up-river business in which the foreigners were concerned now necessarily came to a standstill.

The position had become so perilous not only to business interests but to the very lives of the small foreign colony itself that Mr. Holt, having no other means of communication, despatched a small boat across the dangerous Formosa Channel to Foochow to ask for immediate assistance.

On the 15th, the Tamsui ting who had heard that armed assistance had been requisitioned, hurried up from Teckcham to exercise a little of the old fashioned diplomacy, hoping to smooth things over by a few mild words and new promises. After several anxious days of waiting the United States gunboat *Aroostook*, with General Le Gendre on board, arrived to look after American interests and the British gunboat *Janus* followed a few hours later.

The good old " gunboat policy " at once resulted in the demands made by the consular officer being granted. In this case, the Chinese authorities wisely sought, and allowed themselves to be guided by, the advice of the American Consul-General, Le Gendre, who brought the dispute to a speedy and satisfactory close without resort to any other exhibition of force than the mere presence of the two gunboats. The points gained may be summed up as follows: The offending servants at the Tamsui ting's yamen who had ignored the consul's card and letter were punished with dismissal ; four of the principal ringleaders in the attack on the two foreigners were kept in cangues and exposed for one month in front of the yamen ; proclamations were issued by the Tamsui ting, one of which was cut in stone and put up in one of the public streets, instructing the people to be on friendly terms with the foreigners ; all property destroyed or stolen was made good ; and the hostile clan was fined 1,000 dollars for the attack. While it would appear that one month's punishment was extremely light for the ringleaders of the mob who were bent on murder, still it must be remembered that Chinese were the offenders, and it was, as it unfortunately is at present, quite the custom for America and England to treat the Chinese with the greatest leniency, not to say partiality.

Taking this into consideration, the year 1868 may be said to have ended in a very satisfactory settlement of disputes long standing in the north and south ; in the restoration of peace and justice ; and in laying the foundation of the prosperity and comparative tranquillity which was now to follow.

CHAPTER XV.

FOREIGN INTERCOURSE AND EVENTS OF THE PERIOD,
1870-1884.

THE year 1870 was a precarious one for all foreigners. For during this year arose a question of great importance to the island and to foreign trade. Sir Rutherford Alcock, the British minister at Peking, annoyed at the constant difficulties which his nationals were encountering in Formosa, recommended to the Earl of Clarendon, Secretary of State for Foreign Affairs, that all consular establishments should be withdrawn from Formosa and that the island should be closed to British trade. That this would have effectually shut out all foreign commerce is certain. No other nation had consular representatives in the island; and with the exception of the British, the foreign trade was at that time so small that it is unlikely that any other consulates would have been established.

Naturally and very fortunately this proposal met with marked opposition from the British merchants in Formosa. From the south a memorial was presented to the Earl of Clarendon protesting against the abandonment of Formosa and stating that in the year 1869, "the year in which as a consequence of the successful operations of the late Vice-Consul Gibson in putting an end, for a time at least, to the reign of terror which had so long prevailed, a freer intercourse between British merchants and Chinese merchants was obtained, there was an instant revulsion from the intense commercial depression of 1868 and a very large increase in the general trade returns." *

In the north the increase in the foreign trade of 1870 over that of 1869 was very marked. The export of camphor had greatly increased, while that of tea had doubled. With these evidences of prosperity before them the British Foreign Office could not claim that British trade was on the decline, and it would have been cowardly to have admitted that the constant troubles with the Chinese and mandarins had frightened them out of the island. Consequently, the proposition of Sir Rutherford Alcock was not favored in England: while the constantly increasing trade and the rapidly lessening difficulties between foreigners and Chinese which marked the following years gave abundant evidence of the wisdom of such a decision.

Just as a reminder of the old days and as evidence that the hatred for foreigners had not yet been entirely eradicated, we have one more attack on foreigners to relate, which, with the exception of a few disturbances against the missionaries, probably more in opposition to the religion than to the foreigners themselves, was the last open riot against foreigners in the island.

Towards the close of 1872, the members of a certain powerful clan residing in Banka began to exhibit considerable opposition to such Chinese as had accepted foreign employment. Eventually they sought vent for their rage by attacking the hong of Messrs. Boyd & Co. Mr. Laidlaw, the firm's agent, was able, however, to get the doors of the building firmly secured and barricaded, and upon the attack commencing he was in a position to defend himself and his employés, whom he had armed, at least for the time. After having attempted to beat in the front door with large stones, the mob turned their attention to the rear of the hong which they likewise found securely closed. They then proceeded to plunder and destroy everything they could lay their hands on. The townspeople had now appeared in large numbers armed with spears and knives, and it became extremely doubtful if the single foreigner and his few armed Chinese could long hold the mob at bay. Fortunately, the news of the attack had been conveyed to the two other foreign firms, and Mr. Cass and Mr. Darling of Messrs. Elles & Co. and Brown & Co. respectively, started at once to give assistance to their friend. They were armed with a fowling piece and a revolver. Arriving on the scene they found that the movements of the rioters were directed by two persons who had mounted the roofs of the neighboring buildings and were beating gongs for the purpose of summoning the natives to close their shops and join in the attack. Messrs. Cass and Darling accordingly made for the rear of the hong, and the crowd, probably under the impression that more foreigners were coming, allowed them to reach the door. With their weapons they managed for awhile to prevent the rioters from coming to close quarters, but were all the while assailed by showers of stones, and began to feel their strength failing. In this predicament they were advised by a friendly Cantonese who had accompanied them to climb up on the roof and thus gain entrance to the hong. There appeared no other choice, and accordingly Mr. Cass mounted the roof, but as Mr. Darling was about to climb up, he observed a man charging at him at full speed with a spear. Without hesitation Mr. Darling raised his gun and fired ; but at the same time he received two sword thrusts from other quarters. He then managed to gain the roof, bleeding profusely from two bad wounds. As they were about to proceed, Mr. Cass unfortunately broke partly through and was immediately attacked from below by Chinese with their spears. The Cantonese, seeing his master's dangerous position, at once possessed himself of the revolver and fired all six chambers at the mob below, while Mr. Darling also fired a shot. This gave Mr. Cass time to extricate himself and eventually enter the hong. A force of well armed Chinese from the Elles hong now arrived and were able to disperse the mob, who luckily possessed no fire-arms and were, therefore, at a disadvantage.

On the news of the attack reaching Tamsui, the British acting-consul applied to a Chinese gunboat in the harbor for assistance, but the commander refused to despatch a force, and the consul was obliged to take matters into his own hands. He, therefore, collected a volunteer force consisting of ten foreigners, principally from an English steamer then in port, and with this small number he immediately started up river to the scene of the trouble.

This prompt action prevented further disturbances, and the consul promptly sought the mandarins with a demand for the punishment of the culprits. As a result it was decided that the rioters should pay $800 to repair the damage done the hong and $1,000 compensation to the wounded Englishman, while as a warning to others that foreigners were not to be interfered with, the two leaders should be placed in cangues and exhibited in the principal street.[1] Notwithstanding that the mandarins had consented to all, they neglected to carry the last item into effect. Upon the consul protesting against this, the authorities informed him that the money they could easily pay, but that the punishment of the two leaders they could not inflict as the two Chinese were headmen of a clan more powerful than themselves. Upon learning this the consul informed the officers of the arrival of a British gunboat which would remain at Tamsui until the two culprits appeared before him as had been agreed. This had its effect, and only one day elapsed before the two would-be murderers were brought before the consul, when it was observed that they were wearing the collars prescribed, which were a becoming addition to their regular costume.

Rev. William Campbell tells of a narrow escape which he had in 1875 at Tiam-a-khau, a market town just south of Kagi. The people of this village

1. The cangue consists of a frame of wood some three feet square and weighing ordinarily about 25 lbs. The frame is divided into two parts to admit of being placed over the criminal's head. It contains an opening for the neck and sometimes for the hands. After being closed it might be likened to a huge wooden collar extending straight from the neck.

appear to have belonged to a clan the local head of which was one Gow-chi-ko, a turbulent, lawless character much feared by the authorities. His large residence was just outside the village, and all the houses adjoining were surrounded with strong bamboo stockades, while many armed men were always at hand to defend it either against an attack by the officials or the people.

Gow-chi-ko was much opposed to the work of the missionaries and especially to the rebuilding of a chapel in a neighboring village. Finding that the Christian work was progressing in spite of his protests, he endeavored to put a stop to it by other methods. Accordingly, at his instigation, an armed body attacked a Christian house in the village. A woman was cruelly speared, several men wounded, and the place plundered. Rev. W. Campbell upon hearing of the outrage at once visited the village to investigate. He intended to spend the night there and occupied a house near his chapel. About midnight he was startled at hearing people rushing through the fence which surrounded his chapel grounds and at observing the glare of lights moving about the house. The thrilling experiences of that night Rev. W. Campbell relates as follows :—[1]

"I jumped up to find that my bedroom was already on fire, and on looking out through the bamboo bars which served as a window, I could see a crowd of ferocious looking ruffians setting fire to the chapel and to the roof of our own house. One could take in the position at a glance. It was Gow-chi-ko's men out on one of their terrible raids. They seemed like demons as, with blackened faces and long knives in their hands, they darted about under the bright glare of the burning chapel. I called out for assistance, but learned afterwards that the preacher and his wife with some brethren who were sleeping in an adjoining hut, had made their escape.

"Supposing they would hardly dare to attack a foreigner, I attempted to get out by the door of the mid-room, but was immediately driven back by the spears which were levelled at me, and which for a moment I warded off with the Chinese blanket held over my arm. I shouted out that the British consul would have them punished if they persisted, but their knives and spears were again brandished in front of me and struck frequently into the little blanket. On retreating into the preacher's room, I was at once pursued by ten or a dozen of these cowards, who were evidently afraid to follow one singly into the smaller apartment. They kept poking their spears in at the door, and then commenced to break down the thin partition on my left. While standing here at the foot of the small bed one of the spears was thrust through the lathing and passed within an inch of my body.

"The place now began to fill with smoke, the dry grass roofing being on fire all round, and the chapel itself enveloped in flames. My own little bedroom was crumbling to ashes, and continually the heated air in the blazing bamboos would become expanded and burst like the report of so many pistols. At this moment those in the midroom retreated to the outside, when I tried hard again to follow them away from the burning house, the heat and smoke of which had now become almost insupportable. The sight which met my eyes at the door was certainly alarming. There was nothing but fire and smoke all over the chapel, and there seemed something almost fiendish in the determination of that crowd as they stood back awaiting my exit with uplifted knives and spears. I once more rushed inside, and badly injured my hands and bare feet in trying to break a way of escape out from the back, and while thus engaged, some one smashed the bars of the window-opening in front and cast in a burning torch, which began to set the loose straw of the bed on fire.

"I quite gave it up at this point, committed myself to God, and for the last time dashed out, expecting nothing but to be cast upon those awful spears. To my surprise, the whole party was seen to be quickly moving away to the right. The wind had somewhat risen, and they could no longer endure the smoke from the burning chapel behind, nor the flames which were beginning to lick over the house before which they had been standing. Having no other clothing about me save my sleeping-shirt, I sprang out from the door, climbed over an earth embankment on the left, then got severely scratched in tearing through a thick, prickly fence higher up, and ended by tumbling down into a ditch, where I lay for a minute or two half unconscious, and trembling on account of the intense coldness of the night.

"On lifting my head above the tall grass here, I could see several torches spread over fields on the other side, as if search were being made for those who had just escaped. Without raising myself, therefore, I crept slowly along, got up into a hillside somewhat further off; and lay concealed there till a retreat was sounded and the whole gang ran off in the direction of Tiam-a-kau."

With these disturbances, to which might be added some few attacks made during later years on some of the chapels in the south and Rev. Dr.

---

1. Missionary Success in Formosa. By Rev. W. Campbell, Vol. II., Trubner & Co., London.

MacKay's chapels in the north and the killing of some native Christians, no further troubles in which foreigners were concerned are to be recorded. True the seaside villagers continued for several years to plunder wrecked vessels whenever they had the opportunity. However, that did not necessarily imply hostility to the foreigners but merely a robber's longing for other people's possessions. The fact that Chinese junks were similarly treated if they fell into the wreckers' hands is evidence of this. From this period on, foreigners were well treated by the Chinese of the island. Merchants met with no opposition from traders and others, travellers throughout the Chinese districts were as a rule received with civility, and even the Chinese mandarins began to find that it was to their advantage to respect treaty rights. Of course there were commercial difficulties, there were robber bands to be avoided, and there were lawless districts through which it was not always safe to travel. Still it can not be said, taking the Chinese inhabitants of the island as a whole, that the feeling exhibited towards foreigners was all hostile. In fact in many districts the natives were very friendly.

The early seventies saw much increase in trade both in the north and south. Although Chinese had been exporting Formosan teas for some years, no foreigner entered that trade until 1867, when Mr. John Dodd made a shipment of 2,030 piculs (269,990 lbs.) In 1869, the export by foreigners had doubled, in 1870 it had doubled again, and in 1872 it had again increased nearly two-fold when 19,513 piculs (2,597,229 lbs.) were shipped. There was also a marked increase in the export of camphor. In 1872 there were five British firms established in the north of the island, at Twatutia.

A fortnightly steam service between the mainland and Formosa was inaugurated in the autumn of 1871, and the *Hailoong* (the sea dragon), a small steamer 150 feet long and 277 tons register, under the command of Captain John Farrow, was put on the run. She was the pioneer boat of the regular line then instituted, which was later known as the Douglas Steamship Company. The course was Hongkong, Swatow, Tamsui, and Taiwan, with Amoy as the junction point. As the arrivals and departures of 1872 had more than doubled those of 1869 and 1870, and the export of tea had increased four-fold during this period, it was believed that a regular line was needed and would be supported. The *Hailoong* in a few years proved to be too light to handle the increasing business and she was supplemented by the S.S. *Formosa* of about 500 tons register, once a crack ship of the P. & O. Co. [1]

---

1. From this small start the line rapidly increased in wealth and importance, and was later organized as the Douglas Steamship Co. From the early days with the little *Hailoong* until the present with four steamers specially suited for the work, the service has not ceased, and so prominent a part has this line played in the history of the island's commerce that a few notes regarding its career will not be out of place here.

Although the two vessels *Hailoong* and *Formosa* were both running, it was found necessary in 1875 to add still further to the company's carrying capacity, and the S.S. *Taiwan* of 500 tons was placed on the line. This vessel had been originally built for Russel Sturgis & Co. of Manila and was run for some time under the name of *Leonor*. She was sunk, however, in the great typhoon of 1874 close to the praya wall in Hongkong harbor and directly in front of the offices of Douglas Lapraik & Co. The Douglas Company then purchased the boat, raised and repaired her, and she was named the *Taiwan* and placed on the Formosan line. She was lost Feb. 14th, 1882, on the Pescadores. The *Albay* now replaced the *Taiwan*. She had also been purchased from Russel Sturgis & Co., and she had likewise been wrecked in the great typhoon, having been literally thrown on top of the *Leonor* and against the

The junk trade was also much improved, and in the early "seventies" there were three large fleets engaged. The junks proceeded during the southwest monsoon to every important port on the adjacent mainland and even as far north as the Gulf of Liaotung. The three fleets were divided as follows:—The *Hsiakiao* line consisting of those junks trading to Amoy and adjacent ports, the *Siaopeh* (the small northern line) of those trading to Shanghai, Ningpo, etc., and the *Tapeh* (the great northern line) of those trading to the Shantung coast, Tientsin, Kinchau, etc. The interests of these three lines were looked after in the different ports by a merchant who was appointed once a year and who held a position somewhat resembling a Lloyd's agent. This merchant possessed as insignia of office an incense urn, and was, therefore ,generally known as the *Lu chu*, or keeper of the incense urn.

Among the events of this period should be recorded the great typhoon of August 9th, 1871, which destroyed four foreign vessels in the north of Formosa. In the harbor of Kelung, the British vessel *Westward Ho* and the French barque *Adele* were both lost, and that lives were saved was due entirely to the brave efforts of two Formosan residents, John Dodd and another Englishman named Margary, who was then attached to the British consulate, and who was later killed by the savages in Yunnan. It was at the wreck of the French barque *Adele* that lives were specially endangered. The British gunboat *Elk* was in harbor, but was unable to render assistance, but Dodd swam off alone to the stranded vessel though he was several times dashed back on shore. He eventually succeeded, however, in reaching the ship and, thrown up by a high wave which dashed over the vessel, he managed to grasp the rigging. The night was so dark that the French had not observed the brave efforts made for their rescue until he was actually on board the ship. Dodd was now given a rope, and with this he plunged into the wild sea and swam to shore, where he joined the rope to a shore line which had been already prepared by helpers on land. As soon as the line was secure, Dodd and Margary plunged in and, going hand over hand, reached the vessel and saved the crew. All were got safely on shore, although the vessel had broken in two from the violence of the storm. It was a wild black night and the tempest was the greatest that had ever been witnessed by the oldest inhabitant. The French government sought to reward Mr. Dodd for his brave exploit and offered him the Legion of Honor, but the British government, for some reason unknown, did not permit him to accept this well deserved token, but itself conferred upon him the Albert Medal of the First Class.

---

praya wall. The *Albay* ran until 1885 when she was lost just outside Swatow. In 1884 the *Thales*, 820 tons, which had been formerly used as a British transport carrying troops to Abyssinia, was secured by the company and placed on the Southern line which has Anping as its terminus. The *Fokien* of 500 tons was now built by the company and placed on the regular line where she ran until 1895, when she was sold to the Chinese government. Shortly after the addition of the *Fokien* to the fleet a new vessel was built and named the *Hailoong* after the pioneer boat on the line. In 1895 the *Haimun* was built under the superintendence of Mr. Francis Ashton, who had designed her with the Formosan requirements in view. In this he was very successful; for although the boat is of light draft and only of 633 tons register, yet she has a carrying capacity of 20,000 half chests of tea. Thus from a single steamer in 1871 with a capacity of 7,000 half chests, the Douglas Company have in 1897 three comfortable steamships with a combined capacity of 54,000 half chests, on the line to Tamsui, and one steamer, the *Thales*, on the Anping line.

Much excitement was naturally aroused throughout the island over the Japanese expedition in 1874, which has been described in previous chapters.

In 1873, Count Kabayama, then a captain in the army, and Mr. Mizuno landed in Taiwanfu from a Japanese ship, and travelled overland to Tamsui and thence on to Suao. There were some half-dozen different Japanese visitors in the island that year, and being clad in European costume they were looked upon with considerable curiosity by the natives. It was first thought that they were merchants come to take stock of the resources of the island, but the events of the next year proved that they were the advance agents of the expedition which followed.[1]

The Japanese expedition acted as a great stimulant on the mandarins concerned with Formosa. Although some two hundred years had passed since the Chinese had obtained possession of the island from the Koxinga family, they had improved but little on the old chieftain's defences. No foreign power had before questioned their possession of the island, which to the Chinese mind was sufficient evidence that none ever would. But they had now had a rude awakening and were prepared to make such changes as appeared necessary to hold the barbarians at bay.

The greatest evils appeared to be, first, the absence of the chief administrative officer, who resided in Foochow; Formosa being but a province of Fokien. Second, the unsuitable division of the island into administrative districts. Third, the non-existence of proper land communications; and fourth, the miserable condition of the so-called Formosan army.

As an example of the bad arrangement of the administrative divisions in the island, it may be noted that, previous to 1875, the whole district south of Taiwanfu bounded on the east by the savage territory and on the west by the sea, some 400 square miles, formed one district known as Fangshan. To govern this expanse of country there was a magistrate with 500 of the usual quality of Chinese braves. Under these circumstances the Chinese of the district were naturally inclined to put up with only about as much official control as they thought was really good for them. The rule of the magistrates was therefore limited to the more quiet and industrious of the inhabitants who sought official aid in settling the more serious of their civil disputes. Criminal cases were disposed of by the villagers themselves who lynched the offenders. These villagers also reserved the right of carrying on the barter trade with the savages. A trader who encroached upon what they considered a personal right was liable to be put down as a criminal and to receive criminal's punishment as above. The Hakkas were even less favorably inclined towards the officials, and many of the large villages would not permit an official to enter on any pretext. These communities were well armed and their settlements strongly fortified.

The eastern half of the southern part of the island, although nominally under the rule of the sub-prefect residing at Taiwanfu, was practically independent of his authority. True there were some interpreters attached to the office, and border officers with a visionary militia, who were expected to keep peace in the district.

---

1. See chapters X, XI, XII, and XIII for narrative of the Japanese Expedition.

Even the influence and authority that had once existed, had now been practically lost. We are told of a village, Siehmali (Sha-mari), about five miles east of Hengchun, inhabited by savages who during the reign of Kienlung (1736—1796) shaved their heads, and became loyal subjects of the emperor. But this did not appear to be of special importance to the Chinese, who extended no encouragement to the converted savages, and furthermore took no interest whatsoever in the village or its occupants. In 1875 the savages had partially readopted their native dress and paid but little attention to the growth of queues. To a visitor it appeared that they had the vices of both races with none of the virtues of either, and they are described as "lazy, debauched, and drunken," while much of their property had fallen into the hands of the Hakka immigrants. Our authority adds: "From the above it is easily to be conceived that the general public in 1874 was rather inclined to the fallacy that the Chinese government had no claim to these parts of the island."[1]

Shen Pao-chen (Chin Hotei), the Imperial commissioner who had been sent to take charge of the island and arrange defences to prevent the occupation of the Chinese districts by the Japanese, was impressed with the necessity of introducing great reforms, and accordingly set to work with much vigor. Fang shan district was divided in two, the division point being marked by a river running inland not far north of the sea-coast village of Pangliau. The portion to the north retained the old name, while the territory to the south became Hengchun district. As a seat for the magistrate of this new district, a wall was erected around one of the villages and a new town founded there. On the south-east coast a new district was also established which included the territory east of Fang-shan district, north of Heng-chun district, and south of Suao district. The new district town was established at Pilam (Pinan), and the sub-prefect, who formerly resided at Taiwanfu, now took up his residence at this place. A road had been constructed from the west coast, and Pilam could be thus reached from Takow in four days. It was also accessible by sea, although a landing could only be made in calm weather, and vessels were unable to remain there longer than a few hours at a time, as the great depth of water afforded no anchorage.

While the commissioner did but little in constructing new roads he improved some of the old paths, especially those crossing the central mountain ranges in south Formosa, thus facilitating communication with the east coast. He also constructed one military road as described in the account of the Japanese expedition. For improvement in the defences, the commissioner erected a fort about a mile to the south of Anping, to obtain building materials for which a large portion of the venerable old Dutch fort Zelandia had been destroyed. The fort was planned and built under the superintendence of the French engineer, M. Berthault, and was completed in 1876. It was said that the designer somewhat followed in outline some of the fortifications which form the outer belt of the defences of Paris. The armament consisted of 18 ton

1. Chinese Maritime Customs Reports. Takow, 1875.

guns. On the lower part of Saracen Head at Takow a new fort, which in design was a Chinese modification of a European plan, was also erected. The armament consisted of six rifled guns not of sufficient size to be of much service in coast defence. Another smaller fort was erected in such a position as to command the entrance to the harbor.

Among the events of the next few years, the introduction of foreign appliances by the officials was the most notable. Coal mining in the island had been strictly prohibited for many years for fear that operations might disturb the genial influence of the geomantic properties of the districts. The Kelung people, however, were willing to take the chances, and had continued to secretly mine coal and export considerable quantities of it, seemingly without inciting the dragon to work vengeance on the neighborhood. Upon learning this, the governor-general of Fokien decided to withdraw the prohibition, and in order that the Foochow arsenal with which he was concerned might obtain cheaper coal he was even prepared now to encourage mining operations. In 1870 at his instigation a commissioner visited the coal districts and reported favorably on the introduction of foreign machinery. M. Dupont, a French engineer in the employ of the Foochow arsenal, was the first foreigner to survey the coal districts, he having completed this task in 1868, and his report was in 1871 resuscitated and placed before the governor-general. The matter after some discussion was dropped, however, and nothing more was heard of coal mines until 1874, when Shen-Pao-chen, the Imperial commissioner to the island, visited the coal districts and after conferring with the Peking authorities definitely announced that modern machinery would be introduced at once. Mr. Tyzack, a mining engineer, was placed in charge of the work, and by the end of 1877 a mine fully equipped with machinery was in operation.[1]

Petroleum oil had been known for many years to exist in different parts of the island, and among the innovations introduced during this period the purchasing of machinery to be utilized in this industry should be included. In 1877, two American experts arrived provided with the necessary appliances, and work was commenced early in the next year, but numerous difficulties arose, and after having sunk two wells and produced some 400 piculs of oil, the work was abandoned the same fall.[2]

The third improvement during 1877 utilizing foreign appliances was the construction of the first telegraph line in Formosa. The line was laid from Takow to Taiwanfu and Anping, a distance of some thirty miles, and was opened to the public in November. The scale of charges was very moderate— twenty words for $1.00, and the line gained favor with the Chinese at once.

Not only in the introduction of foreign machinery did the authorities show themselves specially enlightened and energetic, but in furthering native enterprises as well. An immigration bureau was organized and large numbers of coolies from the overcrowded districts in Swatow and vicinity were brought to the island, and given grants of land in the sparsely settled districts between Takow and the extreme south of the island. The scheme was a successful one, and though many of the new arrivals suffered from

1. and 2. See Chapter on the Minerals of Formosa.

fever and some were killed by the savages, the proportion was small, and but a few years elapsed before many of the formerly uncultivated districts were bringing forth large yields to the benefit of all concerned. A later attempt, however, when 1,000 Cantonese were brought over and located on the east coast was not so successful, the majority of them dying of fever.

The political changes during this period were of much importance to the north. Ever since the first foreign mercantile arrivals at the port of Hobe they had suffered great inconvenience from the absence of any government. The port was under the control of the Tamsui ting (marine magistrate); but as this official resided at Teckcham some miles to the south, Hobe, as well as the whole north, was practically without official control. In 1877, Tamsui was converted into a district under a magistrate, and the name of Tamsui ting was abolished. From this time on, it possessed a regularly constituted government, which was of inestimable value to the port, and made possible the great industrial development which in time transformed Tamsui into the most important commercial centre of the whole island.

Other changes of value to the north occurred in 1878, when Kelung was formed into a ting, or sub-prefecture, and Komalun ting the large rice producing place commonly called Kapsulan, became a district known as Gilan hsien. The same year Teckcham ting was converted into a district and became known as Hsinchu hsien.

The three newly formed hsiens or districts now constituted a new fu or prefecture styled Taipeh fu, and the new capital, Taipeh, was marked out on a tract of land adjoining Banka to the north-east and then unoccupied save for agricultural purposes. The acting-prefect removed from Teckcham to Banka, which he occupied temporarily in May 1879, and work was commenced upon the construction of Taipeh at once.

As soon as the new city was marked out, a prohibition was issued against the planting of rice within the city limits, and after the portion of land desired for official purposes had been decided upon, the remaining portions were divided into lots and offered to purchasers for building purposes at a nominal figure. So rapidly was the work pushed forward that, before the end of the year (1879), the north, south, east, and west gates were approaching completion, the Examination Hall accommodating 10,000 students was entirely completed, and the Confucian Temple and the Prefect's Yamen were in course of construction. A year or so later the various buildings had been practically completed. The wealthy men of the district were called upon to meet the cost of all these improvements. The first expenditures were for the prefect's yamen, $28,000, and a smaller yamen $6,000, the examination hall $34,000, and the Confucian temple and other shrines $50,000. Besides this, the construction of the gates and funds for the erection of the city wall, streets, etc., would require a large sum. While all wealthy Chinese were forced to contribute, the larger portion of the funds came from one man—a Chinese locally known as Lim pan ban, who owned a large portion of the lands in the north of the island, and who was naturally a very handy man whenever the officials wanted money. It is stated that he furnished as much as half a million dollars during the construction of the city. Besides the above sources of income, a special tax had been imposed which was called " *Chingfu-chu*" and was to form a fund for city improvements. The impost, which was entirely exclusive of the regular likin taxes, was as follows: Opium $11 per chest, tea 10 and 20 cents a chest according to quality, and miscellaneous goods $2.40 per picul.

Work was not commenced on the city wall for several years, as the ground, having been formerly a rice field, was too soft to bear the weight of the heavy structure. Bamboos were, however, planted all along the prospective line of the wall with the idea that, when they grew up in some three or four years, the ground would be sufficiently strong and solid to bear the heavy wall of brick and stone.

The first prefect of north Formosa was Hiang Tao. He appears, however, to have been rather a weak character, inasmuch as the Tamsui sub-prefect whom he was expected to supersede continued to hold the post as the chief official and was so considered by the people. Hiang Tao died early in 1878, less than a year after receiving his appointment. His successor Lin Tachuan was of a different stamp and at once introduced a definite change in the administration. The first move was to transfer the presumptuous sub-prefect to Lokiang to take charge of that city. The new prefect was very popular, but, like his predecessor, his rule was short. Only three months from the date of his arrival he was taken suddenly ill and died.

Civil examinations were first held in the new city in 1879, and two years later military examinations were held for the first time since Formosa had become a possession of China.

There were two war scares during this period. In 1877, relations between the Spanish government and the Chinese authorities in Formosa were somewhat strained owing to a controversy that had been going on for some time in regard to the Spanish vessel *Soberana*, which was wrecked and plundered by the Formosan natives in the year 1863, as described in the previous chapter. It seems that after fourteen years of fruitless negotiation, the Spanish at last determined to obtain justice even though it required an armed expedition to exact it. The Chinese understand requests of the latter type, and upon the appearance of the Spanish admiral, promptly granted the compensation demanded. The sum obtained—$18,000—was sent to Madrid and divided among the survivors and the families of those who suffered by the loss of the *Soberana*.[1]

Even after the controversy had been thus disposed of, the Chinese were in a state of panic. During this period, a Spanish vessel appeared at Kelung and created great consternation among the officials there, it being believed that she was but in the advance of a Spanish fleet which was about to shell the town. It was later discovered, however, that the vessel referred to had simply put into Kelung for the purpose of coaling, after which she sailed away; and neither she nor any other Spanish vessel, I

---

1. On the 27th of May, 1879, the Spanish consul-general at Amoy published a notification requesting all persons entitled to a part of the sum of 18,000 Spanish Dollars, paid to the Spanish Government by the Chinese Government as compensation for the pillage of the Spanish vessel *Soberana* wrecked off the coast of Formosa in 1863, to present themselves, or their attorneys, to the Spanish Foreign Office at Madrid, before the 19th of August, 1879.

believe, has touched at Formosa since.   The scare was thorough, however, and far reaching.   Troops were brought in from the mainland, and the defences of the island were improved to some extent.

The second shock to the tender sensibilities of the authorities, who, since the first Japanese expedition, were easily thrown into spasms upon the appearance of a foreign flag whose presence they were unable to account for, was in 1880, when it was fancied that Russia was about to declare war against China.   The appearance of numerous Russian warships seemed to confirm the impression, and measures were at once taken to strengthen the defences and prepare for the coming war.   Orders were given to Chinese men-of-war to survey the North Formosa Channel and to keep a watch on the Russians.   In the island four new fortifications were erected between Tai-wanfu and Taipehfu, and a modern fortress was built at Kelung costing the government a large amount of money.[1]   This latter structure was a source of great pride to the Chinese, and its five modern Krupp guns were thought to be quite sufficient to demolish the Russians or any one else that dared to put in an appearance.   At Takow the authorities placed in position, in the two forts which had been built on either side of the harbor, four 7 inch 6½ ton and two 6 inch 80 cwt. muzzle loading rifled Armstrong guns which had been purchased the previous year.   But the dreaded Russians, like the Spanish, disappeared from the channel one day never to return, and Formosa breathed freely again.

Although no reference has been made to warfare with the savages in the last two chapters, the reader must not suppose that during this period peaceful relations existed.   Indeed, it may be taken as an established fact that from the first year of Chinese occupation, warfare with the savages never ceased.   The severity of the fighting was, of course, dependent upon the number of soldiers who presented themselves for slaughter and on the movements of the colonists.   It would be impossible to record all the actions. In 1875, as related in a former chapter, 250 Chinese soldiers were killed in one engagement in the south.   In 1877, the heavy fighting seems to have been transferred to the east coast.   Gunboats were continually engaged in carrying troops from Kelung, and after months of hard battling, the true details of which were never made known, the savages in that particular district were for the time subdued, and General Sūn, the victorious commander, was rewarded with a yellow jacket.

Those hardy Chinese, the Hakkas, also gave trouble to the soldiers on the east coast this same year.   It seems that the braves had appropriated some rice from the shopkeepers for no other reason than that they were unable to agree as to the price.   This naturally resulted in a quarrel, and, where Hakkas are concerned, a quarrel is not far from a fight.   After several severe engagements, General Sūn himself was obliged to march with reinforcements to save his quarrelsome braves from total extinction.   The

1. This structure was erected on the sand near the beach on the S. E. side of the harbor. Great difficulty was found in laying a substantial foundation even at a considerable depth. It was ultimately necessary to drive piles and large numbers of teak beams, and cross pieces were used in forming the foundation. The stone and cement superstructure was of great weight.   It was destroyed by the French in 1884, but the ruins can still be seen at Kelung.

Chinese officials never felt much love for the Hakkas, and the brave general endeavored to remove all likelihood of future trouble in this particular district by killing some 500 people, practically the whole settle-ment, it is reported.

The last of the "seventies" and the first half of the "eighties" wit-nessed many coast improvements. The local officers of this period, who had shown themselves enterprising and enlightened, appreciated the require-ments of navigation. The taotai of Taiwan applied himself to the task of constructing a good harbor in the south. Takow is situated on the edge of a lagoon, the entrance to which is through a chasm seventy yards wide, unfortunately impassable except to small vessels drawing less than six feet, owing to a troublesome bar. It was the intention of the taotai to dredge the bar and to build a breakwater to the south of the entrance. The matter was taken up earnestly during 1878 and 1879; plans were made and estimates prepared, when unfortunately the taotai died. His successor appears to have been less progressive, and the subject was dropped. Much was done, however, in establishing lights,—the result of the repre-sentations of Customs officials. In 1882, a harbor light at Anping, in 1883, a light-house at South Cape, and a harbor light on Saracen Head were established.

There was a slight increase over the last period reviewed in the number of wrecks occurring on or near the Formosan coast, but there was a per-ceptible decrease in the number of ships plundered. During the present period (1870-1885), there were only some half dozen cases of plundering out of some thirty or more wrecks. The sea-coast Chinese of Formosa appear in rather a bad light when their conduct is contrasted with the truly noble treatment and hospitality which the Loochooan islanders invariably extended to foreigners wrecked on their shores. What greater evidence of benevo-lence, charity, and gentleness can there be than the kindly conduct of the natives of one of the most southerly of the Loochooan group only a few miles distant from north Formosa, who not only cared for the crew of a wrecked foreign vessel but furnished them gratis with the means of returning to the mainland? And this was not exceptional. There is not an instance where the same kindly spirit was not exhibited. The following incident is well worthy of a permanent record :—

Early in August, 1873, the German schooner *R. J. Robertson* was wrecked on one of the Miyakojima group. The vessel and its cargo of tea was a total loss and there was also some loss of life. The natives treated the survivors with much kindness, providing them with clothes, food, and shelter, laboring greatly to save something for them from the wreck, and refusing to accept any compensation whatsoever. After the vessel had been totally destroyed by the waves, the headmen of the island presented the wrecked foreigners with a junk by which they could return to "their native land." The following document was then drawn up and placed in their possession, and they em-barked with the good wishes of all the inhabitants, who appeared at the place of departure to bid them farewell :—

" The officer in charge of Kung-ku island, a dependency of the Loochoos, issues a passport to enable certain persons to return to their native land.

" Whereas on the 17th day of the 6th moon of the 12th year of Tung-chih, a foreign vessel drifted to this island and became a wreck, her captain stating that prior to her breaking up, she had encountered a gale of wind, and that of her company only eight persons escaped on shore ; and whereas the captain has made application for assistance and asks the loan of a junk wherein to return home, therefore, inasmuch as he and his party are greatly to be commiserated, he is presented with a junk—the returning of which is not looked for—also with provisions and water for the voyage.   Hence this passport issued by way of safeguard to the foreign captain.

" Dated this 24th day of the Intercalary 6th moon."

Among the unfortunate mariners cast upon the Formosan shores were sixteen savages who arrived at Kelung in May, 1874, aboard three canoes with outriggers.   The Chinese thought that they came from some part of the East Formosan coast, while the foreigners were at first of opinion that they were from the Bashee islands, not far from the south of Formosa.   The men were in a very weak and famished condition, one of them dying-from sheer exhaustion about a week after his arrival.   They were well cared for at the Custom house and gradually improved in health, although at first they were unable to retain solids on their stomachs.   The story of their adventures was now learned, and greatly to the surprise of the foreigners, it was found that they were from the Pellew islands, and that they had journeyed the enormous distance of 1,600 miles.   They had been carried away from their fishing grounds during a heavy gale, and had drifted about the ocean for sixty days, when they eventually reached Formosa.   It speaks well for the strength of their craft as well as their own powers of endurance that they should have held out so long.   As soon as their health permitted, they were sent to Hongkong, whence they obtained passage to the Caroline islands and ultimately to their home.

A lamentable loss of life was associated with one of the foreign wrecks during this period.   Towards the end of June, 1874, the British steamer *Laptek* struck an unknown rock to the north of Formosa, and to save the vessel from sinking, the captain ran her ashore in Ma-sou Bay, where she ultimately became a total loss.   The Chinese gunboat *Fusing*, then at anchor there, promptly answered the call for assistance, and brought off all passengers and light packages.   H.B.M.S. *Kestrel* eventually afforded protection, and considerable cargo, mostly sugar, was saved.   Messrs Dodd & Co., Lloyd's agents, then took charge of the wreck and dismantled her in the interests of the underwriters.   While this work was going on, Lieutenant Gardiner and six men of the *Kestrel* were placed on board to prevent smuggling, and Mr. Greig, of Messrs. Dodd & Co., was also on board representing Lloyds.   On the night of July 17th, just as salving operations were completed, a terrific typhoon broke over the north of the island, during the height of which Lieutenant Gardiner, Mr. Greig, and seven others lost their lives while endeavoring to reach shore by swimming, the boats having previously broken up.   Although a most careful search was instituted, only one of the bodies was ever recovered, and that was so fearfully mangled, having been partially eaten by sharks, that it was unrecognizable. It was believed that the others had been washed out to sea and devoured by sharks. A monument to their memory was erected, and now stands near the beach at Kelung.[1]

The dangerous coast of Formosa, and the reputation the natives had as plunderers made the island a favorite resort for unscrupulous shipmasters or owners who desired to lose their ships, in hopes either of obtaining insurance or a large indemnity from the Chinese government. That this was attempted at least once we have very good evidence. In 1878, an American ship ran into Kwalian Bay at the extreme south of Formosa. This caused much surprise among the natives, as the bay is rarely visited. The crew did not appear to be very amicably inclined, and when natives appeared in their boats, the sailors threatened to shoot them if they came near. The village mandarins were likewise warned off. At sunset, a second vessel appeared and anchored at some distance from the first arrival. Then a small boat, carrying apparently all the crew, put off from the first ship and hastened towards the other vessel. Immediately afterwards a loud explosion was heard, and it was found that the deserted ship had been blown up. The scene in this little melodrama now changes to Takow. Three large men-of-war are in port. Officers and blue jackets, mandarins, with their long robes, and military attendants in bright uniforms are moving about on shore, an uncommon scene for the quiet little port. A naval court of inquiry has called forth all this unusual display. An American ship, the *Forest Belle*, has been wrecked at South Cape, and a valuable cargo has been plundered by the natives. The captain and crew have escaped, and the former now appears to demand heavy compensation from the Chinese government for the outrage. The last act is now before us, and, as with all well regulated dramas, justice must be obtained, virtue rewarded, and the villain exposed. In this particular instance a good missionary saves the situation. He appears very unexpectedly, announces to the great dismay of the villainous captain that he has just returned from a trip to the aforesaid South Cape district, and that he is aware of the true facts of the so-called "wreck and plundering by the natives." Arrest follows and, as the curtain falls, the American captain is being led off to prison, while numerous mandarins break out in a chorus of huzzas.

Wrecks on coasts of Formosa and adjacent islands 1870—1885 continued from page 180 Chapter XIV. For subsequent wrecks see Chapter XVII. Unless otherwise mentioned the vessels here named were total losses.

1870—November. The French brigantine *Clarisse* was wrecked off the Pescadores and the crew plundered.

————November. The British barque *Virgilia* was wrecked N.E. of Formosa.

————————. Old Formosan trader *Eliza Mary* was wrecked at Takow.

---

1. " In the Midst of Life we are in Death."
Sacred to the Memory of

LIEUTENANT CHARLES GARDINER R N., JAMES GREIG, Esq., Merchant, *John Westmoreland* leading stoker, *John Scarff* 2nd Cap. F. Castle, *Robert B. Mingo* able seaman, and *George Osborne, Henry Thiggins* and *Hubert Simmons* stokers.

H.M.S. " KESTREL "

Who were drowned at the wreck of the S.S. *Laptek* off Formosa during a typhoon on the 17th and 18th of July, 1874.

——————————. The British brig *Escape* was wrecked at Paksa Point, N.W. coast of Formosa. Plundered and burned by the natives.

1871————————. The schooner *Rubicon* was wrecked on the Pescadores.

——————February. The British ship *Westborn* was wrecked on the Pescadores.

——————July. The British ship *Loudoun Castle* was wrecked on S.W. coast of Formosa. The mate and 12 men reached Takow in an open boat. Captain and rest of the crew (10 men) were captured by savages, but subsequently eight escaped and the remaining three were released.

——————October. The British vessel *Westward Ho* was wrecked in Kelung harbor on the 9th, during typhoon. Two lives lost.

——————October. The French vessel *Adèle* was wrecked in Kelung harbor on the 9th, during typhoon.

——————October. The British vessel *Anne* was wrecked in Kelung harbor on the 9th, during typhoon.

——————October. The British barque *Loch Nair* was wrecked at the entrance of Tamsui harbor on the 10th, during typhoon.

1872—March. The British vessel *Polar Star* was wrecked two miles south of Namkan, N. W. coast Formosa, and in spite of the presence of soldiers the vessel was stripped by the natives.

——————July. The Norwegian schooner *Daphne*, a well known Formosa trader, departed from Amoy for Takow, S. W. Formosa, and was never heard of afterwards. It is surmised that she either foundered in the turbulent Formosa Channel or was wrecked on some part of the dangerous eastern coasts of the island and there destroyed.

——————September. The British brig *Spartan* was wrecked on W. coast of Formosa 60 miles N. of Anping. The crew and vessel were plundered by the natives.

1873—July. The German schooner *R. J. Robertson* was totally wrecked on one of the Southern Loochoo Islands. The captain, his wife, and six of the crew were the survivors. They were very kindly treated by the natives, and after staying in the island for some time were presented with a junk and provisions, by which means they were enabled to reach Kelung. (See main text.)

1874 - June. The British steamship *Laptck* was wrecked at Masou Bay on the N. E. coast of Formosa, eight miles from Kelung. There was no loss of life in the wreck itself; but to prevent plundering Lieutenant Gardiner and a party of men from H.M.S. *Kestrel* were placed on board together with a Mr. Greig, agent for Lloyds, and while they were there a terrific typhoon arose, and in endeavoring to swim ashore Mr. Greig, Lieut. Gardiner, and six men of the *Kestrel* were drowned. (See main text.)

——————July. The ship *Oliphant* was wrecked off Kelung.

——————August. The British barque *Caroline Hutchings* stranded a little to the north of Takow.

——————————. The German barque *Hydra* was wrecked on one of the Miyakojima group N. E. of Kelung. The crew reached Kelung in safety aboard a boat which they had constructed themselves from the wreckage.

1875.—January. The German schooner *Progress* was wrecked on the North Rock, Pescadores, and four lives lost.

——————October. The British brigantine *Alexandra* was wrecked near Tockcham, N. W. coast Formosa.

——————October. The British schooner *Lochbulig* drifted on to the S. W. Point of Lambay Island, S. W. Formosa, and was wrecked and partially plundered by the natives.

——————————. The British barque *England* was wrecked at Taan, W. coast of Formosa, 80 miles south of Tamsui.

1876.—May. The German barque *Sudan* wrecked on S. W. Cape, Formosa.

——————June. A big typhoon raged along the Formosa Coast on the 10th of this month and many native and some foreign craft were destroyed.

——————June. German barque *Traviata* was wrecked at Takow during above mentioned typhoon.

——————June. The Danish barque *Fyen* was wrecked at Takow during above mentioned typhoon.

——————June. The German barque *Wilhelm* was wrecked at Tainanfu during above mentioned typhoon.

——————June. Danish schooner *Auguste Reimers* was wrecked at Tainanfu during above mentioned typhoon.

——————November. The American barque *Milo* was wrecked off the coast of Formosa.

1877——July. The Chinese gunboat *Fuhsing* was lost on the Formosa coast during typhoon.

——————December. The British barque *Novelty* was wrecked on a rock between Capes Pitow and Samtiao about 12 miles from Kelung when on a passage from Kelung to Shanghai.

1878————————. The American ship *Forest Belle* was blown up by her captain at South Cape, Formosa. An attempt was then made to obtain compensation from the Chinese government, the master claiming that the ship had been plundered and destroyed by the natives. His plot was exposed, however, and he was imprisoned.

1879—February. The British steamer *Taiwan* was lost on the Pescadores.

——————October. The French vessel *Antoinette* was wrecked on the Pescadores.

1880—January. The British barque *Pamenio* was wrecked on East Coast near Steep Island. Her position at first was not so dangerous, inasmuch as she had been driven over a sand bank into deep water and was there anchored in comparative safety. Unfortunately the occurrence happened during the prevalence of the N.E. monsoon, and thus her chances of getting out were small; for during the monsoon there is always more or less swell rolling in. H B.M. S. *Lapwing* endeavored to get her out but failed. Ultimately she was towed partly over the bank by a Chinese government steamer and was there left; it being impossible to move her any further. Rough weather setting in, she became a total wreck.

1881—January. The British three-masted schooner *Chingtoo* was wrecked at the entrance of Takow harbor.

———August. The Danish barque *Flensburg* was wrecked on Table Island, Pescadores.

1882———. The British barque *Cuba* was wrecked at Kelung.

—————————. The S. S. *Hailoong* stranded at Paksa Point. The wreckers came down in thousands, and the cargo, principally teakwood, was carried inland. Thus lightened the vessel floated off.

———October. The German brig *August* was wrecked on the Pescadores.

1883—January. The Norwegian barque *Henrick Ibsen* was wrecked at the Pescadores on Pehoe Island while on a voyage from Amoy to Taiwan.

———August. The American barque *Spartan* on her way to Honolulu found herself becalmed off north Formosa. A boat was lowered and four of the crew including the captain's son made for the island. When last seen, the boat was nearing the island, but was never heard of again. Search parties w re sent all about the north of the island without finding any trace of the missing ones. Inasmuch as the boat departed during a perfect calm and the shore was near at hand, this disappearance was a great and unexplained mystery.

1884—September. The British barque *Beta* struck on a shoal on the west coast near Lokiang. She was plundered and destroyed by the natives and the crew were taken off by the British gunboat *Fly* and carried to Takow.

1885—August. The British barque *M. A. Dixon* lying in the roadstead drifted on to Saracen Head, Takow, and was wrecked.

———September. The German schooner *Nicoline* was stranded near Lokiang. The vessel was then attacked, but the natives were beaten off. Subsequently the ship floated off and got away.

CHAPTER XVI.

THE FRENCH CAMPAIGN IN FORMOSA.

1884 - 1885.

Franco-Chinese War—The Formosan campaign—The "Volta" visits Kelung—Consternation among officials—Formosan defences strengthened—Admiral Lespes demands the surrender of Kelung—Chinese refuse and a bombardment results—Kelung captured—Liu Ming-chuan orders the government collieries to be destroyed—Foreigners leave Twatutia—Skirmishes at Kelung—Customs reopened—Tamsui harbor closed with torpedoes—British gunboat "Cockchafer" in harbor—Dangerous position of foreigners on shore—Heavy cannonading—Results nil—French victories in vicinity of Kelung—Liu Ming-chuan retreats and is imprisoned by the turbulent Banka populace—Second bombardment of Tamsui—French troops land—Chinese make strong opposition—A severe contest—The French defeated and retreat to their boats—The Mission Hospital and care of Chinese wounded—French heads on exhibition—The Chinese strengthen their position—Hakkas as warriors—Curious cases of wounded—Chinese power of endurance—Blockade of Formosa declared—Notification of Admiral Courbet—A Chinese traitor—Chinese defeated at Liangka—Hardships for the foreign community—Christmas at Tamsui—French foraging parties—French forces increased at Kelung—Chinese fort near Kelung attacked without success—Second attack succeeds—Attack on Fort Bamboo—A creditable engagement—Bravery of a Chinese officer—Heavy losses—Chinese alarmed—Fortifications erected to protect Taipeh—Troops and munitions arrive notwithstanding blockade—Condition of affairs in the south—Defences strengthened—Takow harbor closed—Takow fort fires on French—Large number of junks sunk by French—Running the blockade—High prices at Tamsui—Pescadores bombarded - French in possession—The blockade raised—Foreigners return to Twatutia—A new phase in warfare—Many Chinese destroyed by tampering with unexploded shells—Treaty between China and France signed—Great joy among French at Kelung—French losses—Admiral Courbet at the Pescadores—His great disappointment—His death—The Tamsui engagement as given in the "Peking Gazette"—Rewards to the Chinese warriors.

AFTER a rest of some twenty years, disturbed only by internal rebellion and warfare with the savages, which was so perpetual that it ceased to be of interest to the outside world, Formosa again became the scene of war with a foreign nation. It was at the close of the Franco-Chinese war of reprisals in 1884, that Formosa, while taking no part in the main controversy itself was seized as a material guarantee for the payment of an indemnity which France had imposed upon the Chinese government. The campaign was unique in that the foreign forces were not always the victors and that France, one of the greatest military powers in the world, was forced to admit that the actual results of the campaign frequently failed to correspond with the carefully laid plans, that the anticipated victories, in at least two instances, were victories for the Chinese, that the commissariat arrangements proved entirely inadequate, and that altogether, from a military standpoint, the war was a failure and made a profound impression as such throughout the world. It is, however, necessary, in justice to the French, to explain that the failures were not due to lack of bravery or skill on the part of the forces actually engaged, but to the mistaken judgment of the French authorities, who were so convinced of the feebleness of China as well as so over confident of their own strength that they endeavored to carry on warfare, under the name of reprisals, with a small force and insufficient funds ; not deigning to ask the French Parliament to authorize a declaration of war.

The struggle in Formosa was a severe one ; and the expenses incurred and the large loss of life made the attempted seizure so costly that the French, who had anticipated instantaneous victory, must have been completely astounded.

Of all the material at hand descriptive of the campaign in Formosa, the letters of Mr. John Dodd, which appeared in the Hongkong *Daily Press* and were afterwards published in book form,[1] present the most interesting narrative. The following account is largely taken from Mr. Dodd's narrative which, however, has been revised by a gentleman who served in the French army during the Formosa campaign and who has been able to supplement Mr. Dodd's account in many places, and to correct some few statements wherein he believed the author had been misinformed.

In the " Beautiful Isle " the war of 1884 on the mainland was not regarded with perfect equanimity ; and the Chinese mandarins, without knowing why, were fearful that they might be involved in the troubles. A little episode occurred in June which served to increase the anxiety. It was the visit of the French cruiser *Volta*, under command of Captain Fournier, to Kelung. To obtain supplies of coal was apparently the only object, and as the Chinese were a trifle slow in effecting its delivery, the gallant captain gave the officials notice that unless the desired commodity was forthcoming at once he would open fire on the forts. The Chinese respond to this style of requests much more readily than to those made in the customary way, and the result was that the supplies were soon on board, and the *Volta*

---

1. Journal of a Blockaded Resident in North Formosa During the Franco-Chinese War, 1884-5. Hongkong *Daily Press* Office.

Ruins of a Chinese **Fort at Kelung**, destroyed by the French.

Kelung Harbor.

Kelung Village looking seawards.

Pictured Rocks on **Palm Island, Kelung.**

A Street in Japanese, **Kelung.**

steamed away towards the north.   Such an officer as her commander would seem marked for a career, and sure enough he appeared later on the scene as a diplomat and treaty maker.

Thanks to the Russian scare the defences of the island had been improved somewhat, and a hundred feet or so from the beach on the east side of Kelung stood a fort which had been erected at that time.   This structure was over 300 feet in length and mounted five Krupp guns of 1881 model.   The Chinese thought it quite impregnable; under its protection, the whole country was safe; and should the outer barbarians ever venture to appear before it, their ships or armies would be immediately destroyed.

Preparations were now made throughout the island to strengthen the defences.   Liu Ming-chuan, who had been appointed at Peking, arrived in Formosa July 16th as Imperial commissioner to look after the military preparations and to take command of the island.   His arrival was duly acknowledged with a salute from the Chinese soldiers, which, however, unduly excited the commander of the French gunboat *Parseval*, it being thought that the Chinese were about to commence operations.   The excited officer ordered the decks cleared for action, but fortunately for the foreigners on shore, the mistake was discovered before any harm had been done.

On the 22nd of July, the corvette *Villars* arrived at Kelung and anchored in the inner harbor, and shortly after the little *Parseval* left for parts unknown.   This arrival of a large ship created almost a panic. The few foreign residents were becoming rather anxious and the Chinese shopkeepers talked of clearing out.   About this time the German steamer *Welle* arrived with a cargo of ammunition, torpedoes, telegraph wire, etc; but the French commander refused to allow the material to be landed. The Chinese made preparations for discharging; but fearing a collision with the *Villars*, they ordered the *Welle* to Tamsui, where, on her arrival, Chinese transport *No. 13* and a few junks took over all her cargo.

The Chinese were now actively engaged in massing troops at Kelung, and preparations for war appeared to be the order of the day.   The little foreign settlement at Tamsui was not unnaturally concerned, and the arrival of the British gunboat *Cockchafer* was warmly welcomed.

On the 4th of August, the French ironclad *La Galissonière*, bearing the flag of Admiral Lespes, and the gunboat *Lutin* arrived at Kelung, making three French men-of-war in port.   The admiral lost no time in sending an officer at once to demand the surrender of the forts guarding the harbor, and declaring that if this demand was not complied with, he would open fire on the forts at 8 a.m., the following morning.   The Chinese refused to hand over the place, and accordingly, the three men-of-war commenced operations precisely at 8 a.m., on the 5th.   A heavy cannonade took place, the French gunners firing with excellent precision, an eyewitness stating that not a shot missed its mark.   The sheltered position of the *Villars* enabled her to rake the large fort, while the mitrailleuses fixed in the tops poured a storm of bullets into every weak spot of the fortifications, until the "great fort" was soon reduced to a mass of ruins.   The range was about a thousand yards and the fort was manned by several hundred Chinese. Two other fortifications, small and of little importance, were easily destroyed, and the *Lutin* made good practice at an old fort on the opposite side of the bay where were stationed a number of soldiers. No casualties were reported on board the men-of-war, but the *La Galissonière* had three holes put into her just above the water line. The Chinese loss was variously stated from 50 to over 200, the latter figure being given by a Chinese in the government service. After the bombardment, a body of marines landed, planted the French colors on the ruins of the fort, and proceeded to take possession of Kelung city.

With an acuteness and decision not always characteristic of his race, Liu Ming-chuan, upon hearing of the bombardment, at once ordered the machinery and works at the Kelung coal mines to be destroyed, the pits flooded, and the stock of coal on hand—some 15,000 tons set fire to. This was with the intention of depriving the French ships of a well supplied coaling station, and the orders were carried out the same day as received.

Kelung residents had, previous to the bombardment, taken refuge on board the German schooner *Johann Carl*, whence they were removed by the launch *Alice* to the gunboat *Cockchafer* which arrived on the scene soon after. They were brought to Tamsui, with the exception of Messrs. Brownlow and Grant, of the Customs service, who remained at their posts for the time.

The foreign residents of Twatutia who lived ten miles up the river, out of reach of the gunboat's protection, went on the eve of the bombardment down the river to Hobe (Tamsui), as it was decided that Twatutia, a kind of junction point for Chinese soldiers on their way either to Kelung or Tamsui, was unsafe. The wealthy inhabitants had already departed in numbers for the mainland, and foreign hongs were left each to the tender mercies of five soldiers to protect them against robbers.

Liu Ming-chuan after the bombardment hurried over to Kelung to take command of the troops. The next few days were marked by a few skirmishes on shore of but little importance. During an engagement on shore, out of 120 marines the French lost one man killed, six wounded, and one wounded man whom the Chinese had taken prisoner died on the road as the captors were bringing him to Taipeh-fu. The French as a precaution against recapture destroyed with dynamite the Krupp guns in the large fort. Meanwhile, two more French men-of-war had arrived, making five in all.

British Consul Frater on the 11th, having received advices from the French admiral, issued a circular stating that foreigners residing in Kelung did so at their own risk. The Customs were, however, reopened a few days later with Mr. Brownlow in charge, and it appeared that neither the French nor the Chinese were interfering with the trade.

Ships could purchase such coal as was in port; but the great difficulty in getting coolies to load it virtually put a stop to the traffic.

At Tamsui, the entrance of the river had been closed by laying down six torpedoes in the shape of a semi-circle on the inside of the bar. The Douglas steamers *Fokien* and *Hailoong* running to the port, as well as the German steamer *Welle*, were, whenever necessary, piloted over the torpedoes by the Chinese who had laid them down. The mandarins engaged in planting the guns that had been brought to the island by the latter steamer.

Trade was resumed during the middle of the month at Twatutia, it being regarded for the time as safe, and the country thereabouts had quieted down to such an extent that a good deal of tea was brought in. Life for the foreigners was very much cramped. They were prohibited from making trips into the country; and even in the settlement, with religious processions, crackers, and gongs going at all times of day, and the watchmen making a great noise with bamboos all night, rest was well nigh impossible except to the Chinese guards told off to protect foreign hongs, who after disappearing all day, except at meal times, "return at night, and instead of guarding the property, turn in early and sleep as soundly as Rip van Winkle did till morning."

Under the impression that the French would attempt to enter the Tamsui river, ballast boats and junks loaded with stones were sunk at the entrance. A number of Hakka hillmen were added to the government force. They were armed with their own matchlocks, which in their ignorance they preferred to foreign rifles. Much was expected of them, as the life of warfare they had led on the savage border had trained them to be good shots and handy with their knives.

By the end of August the French had succeeded in holding the shore line at Kelung, but were unable to advance beyond it; and as Chinese soldiers had for some days been erecting earthworks and digging entrenchments on the hills on the east side of the bay overlooking the shipping, the French sent word ashore for the Europeans to come on board the *Bayard*, as they intended opening fire on the earthworks which were now just visible.[1] The firing was not successful either that day or the next, the nature of the country being in favor of the Chinese; and for many days the shelling was a regular event, the Chinese not apparently suffering much damage themselves, or being able to inflict any upon the French. This condition of affairs continued through September, the French having gained only the summits of the near hills surrounding the harbor.

General Liu Ming-chuan left Kelung on the 9th to visit Tamsui and Taipehfu. On his arrival at the latter place he was met at the wharf by some 200 soldiers, 5 buglers, and 2 or 3 drummers. The march up the street with the soldiers in front, the band next, and the general in the rear in his chair, made an imposing parade. His presence is also said to have had a

---

1. The following notification was sent to the foreigners on shore : —
(Copy.)—Messieurs the Agent of Customs and Representatives MM. Dodd and Lapraik & Co.
   I have the honour to inform the gentlemen of the Custom House, and the Representants of MM. Dodd and Lapraik & Co. that it is possible at every moment I may open the fire against the Chinese working in the mountains at new entrenchments near in direction of the houses of the concession between the both houses.

Le Cde. de *Bayard*,
(Sd.)   G. M. PASSAYON.

most stimulating effect on the soldiers on guard in the foreign hongs. All appeared in full force with uniforms and rifles, although for several days the muster in one hong had produced only one soldier and a boy in a soldier's coat.

On the 11th, the British gunboat *Merlin* arrived: but departed at night after communicating with the *Cockchafer*. The celebrated traveller, Mr. A. R. Colquhoun, was on board and made a flying trip up river to Twatutia.

The *Cockchafer* was piloted through the obstructions, and took up her anchorage in the river. On the 24th, the French warship *Chateau Renaud* arrived off Tamsui and overhauled the *Welle* and *Hailoong*, which arrived the next day. On the 26th, the *Vipère*, described as "a snaky looking craft," joined the *Chateau Renaud*. The second day after her arrival she overhauled the *Fokien* and gave chase to the British steamer *Waverly*, which was supposed to have had soldiers and war materials on board. After a shot had been fired across her bow she was boarded by a prize crew from the *Vipère*, and when last seen from Formosan shores she was steaming towards Foochow.

The French fleet under Admiral Courbet arrived off the port of Hobe, October 1st, and gave notice that the forts would be bombarded the next day. The Twatutia residents, realizing the danger of their position up river, left for the port the same day, after having communicated with the consul. Treasure, opium, tea, etc., were taken along with them, and the Chinese compradores and a few soldiers were left in charge of the hongs and such property as remained, principally furniture.

The foreigners were now all gathered together at Tamsui. It was but a little community at the best, and their conduct during the trying ordeal through which they passed speaks much for their bravery and tact. The two ladies could not have displayed greater heroism, and one cannot but feel, after reading the account of the bombardment, that their escape from all injury was marvellous. When it is remembered that the Chinese were fighting Europeans and that past history has given plentiful evidence that ignorant Chinese soldiers are not very discriminating as to just who are their enemy and who are not, so long as they belong to the outer barbarians and are somewhat similar in appearance, we cannot but acknowledge that the foreign residents were placed in a most dangerous position.[1]

---

1. The foreign residents in North Formosa at this time, who were witnesses of the bombardment and subjected to the subsequent blockade, were as follows:—

A. Frater, Consul
Mrs. Frater } British Consulate.
P. W. Peterson, Constable
E. Farrago
C. S. Taylor
W. Brennan
W. G. Harling
R. McGregor
H. T. Wavell. } I. M. Chinese Customs
H. H. Moutell
J. G. Freeth
G. H. Himmell and Messrs.
Brownlow and Grant
who were first in charge at Kelung but later removed to Tamsui.

Grant Scott, of Boyd & Co.
John Dodd, E. P. W. Skrimshire, and A. E. Hubbard, of Dodd & Co
W. Christy of Douglas Lapraik & Co.
C. H. Best of Tait & Co.
Rev. G. L. Mackay, D.D., Rev. J. Jamieson and Mrs. Jamieson, of the Canadian Mission.
C. H. Johansen, M.D., Foreign Community Doctor.
Albert Sutliffe, American Correspondent, arrived just before blockade commenced but after the bombardment and landed at Hobe.

The following account of the bombardment and subsequent blockade as given by Mr. Dodd will be found a correct narrative of the events, although we believe that the modest author has lessened the dangers and privations to which the foreign community were subjected:

"Much to our astonishment, the Chinese opened fire on the French ships at about twenty minutes to seven a.m., and the French returned the fire within a couple of minutes, every ship engaging the small battery and the new earth battery thrown up within the last two months, erected on a spur of the hill running down to the pilot village. This earth battery is mounted with four or five Krupp guns.

"It was the general opinion here, held by both Chinese and foreigners, that the French would demolish both batteries in about half an hour, would land marines and sailors, and find Tamsui in their possession in the course of a few hours. Before giving an account of the bombardment it will be as well to give you a sketch of the entrance of the river, the position of the batteries, and ships of war. At the south entrance there is a long sandy beach running for some distance across the river; further to the south is the Lohan group of hills called the South Hills, highest point 1,700 feet or so. No fighting took place on that side of the river, so that no further reference is necessary.

"As you pass over the bar, you notice, on the north side of the river, the flat beach and the black beacon, and a little further on the White Fort, and on the spur in the rear thereof the earth battery. From the seaward it would be rather difficult to make the latter out. At the back of the fort are downs where are encamped several bodies of men under tents. The encampments are generally on the slope of the hills or in some hollow place, out of sight of the French shipping, and in the rear rises the Tatun group of hills called the North Hills, height 2,800 feet at the extinct crater, 3,600 at highest point of the range. A little further on, past the White Fort, you come to the Customs beacon, then the pilot village. From this place there is a road made by foreigners which leads to Hobe. Following this road for half a mile or less, you come to the Customs offices, in rear of which and perched upon a bluff is the old Dutch Fort, now the British consular offices. On the side of the Red Fort (as it is called) is the new consulate dwelling-house. Following the lower road, past the Customs offices and passing through a small collection of mud shanties, and under the shade of some fine specimens of banian trees, you arrive at Messrs. D. Lapraik and Co.'s premises, which place was the appointed rendezvous.

"On the heights, in rear of Messrs. D. Lapraik & Co.'s and on a level with the consulate, are the commissioner's house and the assistants' quarters, the residence of two missionaries and their families, also the Girls School, lately built, and the Oxford College erected two or three years ago. Every home flew the English flag. Following the road past Messrs. D. Lapraik & Co.'s house, you come to Messrs. Tait & Co.'s premises, and in rear of the Haikwan and military mandarin's quarters are the doctor's house, flying the German flag, and the hospital, flying the English flag: then comes the town, which runs along the side of the river and up the slope of the bluff in rear of the main street. At the end of the town, situated on an eminence, two sides of which slope down to the river side, just a mile distant from the other European houses, are Messrs. Dodd & Co.'s bungalow and godowns called Piatow.

"All the inmates of the various houses were thinking of getting up, or were just up, and were perhaps pondering over in their minds the curious fact that they were soon to be spectators of a bombardment. Outside the bar were to be seen the *Triomphante* under the lee of the spur on which the earth battery is situated; some distance from her and plainly visible from Piatow was the *Galissonière*; next came the *Duguay Trouin*. The raky looking *Vipère* was somewhere near the *Triomphante* at the commencement of the action, perhaps close in shore, making four vessels in all. We do not believe any notification was given to the Chinese authorities about the intended bombardment; so they commenced the ball themselves with a discharge of two guns, one of the shots passing over the *Triomphante*. Within a couple of minutes, as has been previously stated, the four ships went at it hammer and tongs as fast as ever they could. The noise was something tremendous. Every house shook, windows rattled, and plaster fell from ceilings. Even at Piatow, quite three miles from the men-of-war, if not four, the concussion was felt as described. I may here mention that the gunboat *Cockchafer*, Captain Boteler, had taken up her position opposite Messrs. D. Lapraik & Co.'s house (the rendezvous) and had placed there 10 sailors to protect the properties and lives of those on shore. Messrs. Dodd & Co. not being able to remove all properties in the shape of tea, etc., to the godowns at the rendezvous, on account of short notice, and Piatow being in an isolated position, they applied through the consul for protection, and Capt. Boteler had the goodness to send on shore a corporal's guard of marines, eight men in all. Out of a complement of 61 men, there were told off for shore work 18 men.

"At first the shot and shell seemed to be directed towards the White Fort and earth battery, and the encampments on the slope of the downs; but before long the air became alive with them, and between half-past 7 and 9 o'clock there was not a place on the north shore or on the river from the White Fort to Piatow that could be called safe. Between these hours especially the firing from all the ships at once was really appalling; there was scarcely a moment between the shots at any time, and every now and then broadsides from the *Galissonière* and *Triomphante* were simply deafening. It would not have mattered so much if the fire had been directed at the forts and soldiers in the neighborhood, but after the first half hour or so shot and shell were heard whizzing through the air, and seen bursting in the neighborhood of foreign houses, some of them dropping close to the gunboat. As soon as the fire was opened the ladies on the hill left their houses and made their way to the rendezvous. It was a very dangerous walk, for shells were falling, bursting sometimes on the grass, at other times ricochetting right off where they struck, *i.e.* to the right looking in the direction of the passage taken by the projectiles. It is perfectly wonderful that the ladies were not hit by one of them.

" On arriving at the ' rendezvous ' the fire from the *Triomphante*, lying under the spur of Earth Battery Hill, seemed to be crosswise to the fi e of the other two vessels. Many of the shots and shells were thrown over the spur, some of them, perhaps striking the top, ricochetted dangerously close to foreign houses; finally one struck the back angle of the wall of the Red Fort and buried itself in the grass not 50 yards from the consul's drawing room : another shell or part of a shell went clean through the roof of Mr. Jamieson's house; and another went through the roof of the Girls School; and many shots fell in Dr. Mackay's garden. Whilst this was going on, the rendezvous and the gunboat opposite were in very hot quarters. Several shells burst in the river between the two, and one fellow ricochetted from the hills at the back and struck the back of Lapraik & Co.'s house. In the meantime the hills in the neighborhood of Piatow, where a few peasants shewed themselves, came under the fire of the heavy guns of the *Galissonière* or *Triomphante*, bursting here, there, and everywhere; the booming of the guns and the whistling and whirring of shot and shell in the air was anything but pleasant, and as many of them at the distance of nearly four miles came whistling close to us, some falling to the right and others to the left and in front, we thought for a long time that our house had been taken for a fort in the distance. Several shots fell not a hundred yards from the flagstaff, and some nearly went into the cargo boats at the end of the wharf.

" At about 8 a.m., we thought we would go in the gig and call on the gunboat to see what was going on there and at the rendezvous. Just as our gig approached the gunboat we saw several shots drop near the Customs offices; one during the day went through the commissioner's private office.

" On running alongside the gunboat, part of a shell fell close to Lapraik & Co.'s jetty, while as we were going up the side of the vessel, a shot or part of a shell fell close to her starboard bow, and before we had been half an hour on board part of a shell dropped right under her bows.

" We left for Piatow again in the gig and saw from the water shell after shell bursting on the sides of the hills in rear of the town and close to Piatow, dropping sometimes not far from groups of peasants who thought it safer to be there than in the town. Many of them could be seen at different times during the day picking up shot and parts of shell. They said they could be sold to the blacksmiths. A case was reported that some men, who were anxious to see the inside of an unexploded shell, met their death in the attempt to satisfy their curiosity.

" On arriving at Piatow we noticed the gunboat dropping up the river with the tide, slowly. Captain Boteler, thinking the ladies in the rendezvous would be safer a mile or so up the river, took them on board, but it looked for sometime as if they had jumped from the frying pan into the fire. Shot and parts of shells seemed to be dropping all round her. The ladies were at first on the bridge, but suddenly a shot dropped into the water within a few yards from them, which caused a retreat below. Slowly the gunboat proceeded, and it really appeared as if the French gunners were taking pot shots at her, though of course that is out of the question. Every minute a piece of shell or a shot fell in the exact place occupied by her a minute before, and so it went on until she arrived at Piatow. For a time the shots fell short, but suddenly they came nearer, and she was compelled to go further up, outside the limits of the usual anchorage of the river. Here for a time they were out of danger, but as the tide fell, in an hour or so afterwards, she had to move back again some 400 or 500 yards, and as she would then be within range of the shots, it was deemed advisable to land the ladies at Piatow.

" After 10 o'clock the fire slackened every now and then, and it was supposed that the White Fort had been destroyed and the gunners at the earth battery had found it too hot for them, for they did not, we believe, fire after 10 a.m. The earth battery seemed to be as safe a place as any, the men were under good natural cover and had a pit to jump into after loading. If any one shewed himself above the fort for a second the ships poured in a deadly fire. Very little destruction of life, however, took place amongst the soldiers. It is difficult to find out the exact number killed, but we do not believe that during the 13 hours' bombardment twenty soldiers in all were killed and wounded.

" Eight of the wounded were taken by their comrades to the Mission Hospital and were attended to by Dr. Johansen, of Tamsui, and Dr. Browne, of the *Cockchafer*. Some were only slightly wounded, others very severely. The soldiers who brought the wounded to the hospital, as well as those to be met with in the streets during the bombardment and since have been friendly disposed towards the foreign residents, not showing animus towards the barbarians on shore at all, which is wonderful to be recorded. . . . .

" The peculiar sound made by the shot and shells when passing overhead will never be forgotten by Tamsuiites. After about four hours of this kind of thing, the most timid felt more or less accustomed to the constant danger we were in. It was now about noon, the first gun having been fired at 20 minutes to 7. It seemed like an age and as if the sun had stood still. Even at this period of the day people began to remark how slow old time was travelling, notwithstanding the number of the events that were being crowded into every ten minutes. Shot and shell were flying around Piatow, dropping in the same place almost, time after time. There seemed to be no doubt at times that the gunners were determined to hit the house or the Chinese transport anchored under the lee of the hill on which the bungalow was situated. Then again the poor gunboat came in for like attentions, and on the adjacent hillside quite close, shell after shell burst, affording much employment to men and boys, who made collections which became of marketable value later on.

" At 1 p.m. we sat down to tiffin, and although the big guns of the *Galissonière* especially and of the dangerous *Triomphante*, were belching forth huge projectiles, it was astonishing at tiffin time to find how callous every one seemed to be, and how brave and lively the two ladies were who graced our table. They had been driven from their houses, had run the gauntlet all the way to the rendezvous, then from the rendezvous to the *Cockchafer*; had been under fire for nearly three hours in what was considered the safest place of refuge, seeing shell and other projectiles dropping all round, and finding it so dangerous they had taken refuge again on shore to find that even there there was no safety. In the afternoon the Frenchmen still continued to fire independently, and often broadsides were indulged in, the shot flying all over the country in places where there was no enemy to be seen within a mile or two. What excuse they can give for this apparently reckless sort of warfare, deponent knoweth not, but there must have been something wrong somewhere. Just about this time a live shell entered the roof of a house close by, right at the end of the town, and we saw the whole house suddenly collapse, and a cloud of dust rise high up in the air.

"Under the ruins, it is said, were found the bodies of an old man, an old woman, and a child. Between 3 and 4 p.m. the ladies left Piatow, as the fire then was not so continuous. As we were walking along the jetty to the boat a shell dropped about 30 yards from us and buried itself in the mud. It did not explode, so we had it dug out and found it was a 60 to 70 lb. projectile. This led to a search all round, and several were found close by.

"Later on in the day Chinese hawking shot and shells about, asking $2 first of all ; finally big shot or shell about 70 lbs. in weight fetched 60 cents. Nearly every foreigner has a collection picked up on and around his premises. At 4 p.m. firing from the four men-of-war almost ceased, but they gave us occasional shots right up to 8 p.m., the bombardment having lasted some 13 hours. After the morning's work, the *Vipère* changed her position to the south of the *Duguay-Trouin*, and being a small craft capable perhaps of finding her way in, her movements were watched carefully. She had her foretopmast struck, and certain people said that they could see an opening in her side. The general idea was that she was crippled and had left her first position in consequence."

It was estimated that the four ships engaged in the bombardment of Tamsui must have fired, on the 2nd inst., at least 1,000 rounds ; indeed it was believed that 2,000 would be nearer the mark, and our author adds : "if you put each shot down at an average of £5, the satisfaction of killing and wounding twenty men was dearly purchased."

Early in October the French had a victorious engagement in the vicinity of Kelung, and Liu Ming-chuan, with a thousand soldiers, fled to Banka, a suburb of Taipehfu. The inhabitants of this city—some 40,000—who were considered the most turbulent lot in the north killed some few soldiers, seized Liu Ming-chuan, and took him to a temple where he was made a sort of prisoner, it having been rumored about that he had an idea of taking the treasury, money, and stores, and making for Teckcham, a walled town some thirty miles south of Tamsui.

For the next few days the French men-of-war engaged in irregular firing, most of the projectiles finding their way to parts of the hills unoccupied by the enemy, but nothing else of importance occurred.

The Japanese sloop *Amagi*, Captain H. Togo, came to watch operations, and an occasional English man-of-war also made short visits to the scene.

Although it was observed that the 7th of October was apparently "washing day" on the French vessels, unmistakable preparations were in progress, indicating that a descent on Tamsui was in view. Several men-of-war had anchored as close inshore as they could get, and the admiral had temporarily moved his flag from the *Galissonière*.

"At about 8 a.m. the next morning the 'early bird,' with binoculars adjusted, had observed various signs of extra activity amongst the shipping, and before an hour had slipped away, and just as we were sitting down to a 9 o'clock breakfast, the booming of cannon, from every ship, carried our recollections back at once to the 2nd instant, and one and all decided that the French, after a long five days' comparative rest, had determined to succeed in not only forcing a landing but in carrying the place by storm. Dark looking transports were in view, and we foreigners on shore, who had been kept in suspense so long, now thought that the day had arrived when the whole strength of the French would be put forth, and that before evening we should see Tamsui taken, and the hordes of Chinese soldiers, encamped all over the place, driven past the limits of the port.

"The French commenced firing with their heavy guns, and if the cannonading was not quite as heavy as on the 2nd inst., it was certainly as dangerous to foreign houses and to foreigners. No one at first knew for certain what was the object of the French, for neither the Earth Battery nor the White Fort returned a shot. The fire from the *Vipère* and *Galissonière* seemed to be chiefly in the direction of the White Fort and in the neighborhood of the Earth Battery, and it is supposed that the idea was to clear the way for troops landing to the north of them, who, if successful, would soon be in possession of the battery and wire connected with the torpedoes, when, if exploded satisfactorily, the *Vipère* might find a safe course across the bar and into port. Her guns would then be in a position to play on General Sûn the Chinese Commander's headquarters and on various encampments, hitherto safe from the fire of ships stationed outside the bar.

"French troops landed on the beach to the north of the Black Beacon, when they were soon under the lee of the downs, and out of the sight of foreigners on the top of the Red Fort, on the top of Piatow House, and other high lookouts. Gun after gun poured out of the sides of the *Galissonière* and *Vipère*, and the muffled sound of distant guns was heard, fired probably by French ships stationed to the north of the port. At half-past nine o'clock a sound like that of heavy musketry fire could be heard, but it was, we believe, the noise of machine guns covering the landing party, and from its regularity differed from volleys of musketry or the irregular fire of skirmishers advancing. Some very heavy fighting was apparently going on on the downs, and we were expecting at any moment to see the Chinese flying before the French. At ten o'clock the fire from the ships became hot in the neighborhood of the Red Fort. Captain Boteler, the British consul, the commissioner of Customs and others had taken up their quarters early within this relic of old Dutch brickwork, the walls of which are seven to eight feet thick, of solid masonry and hard as the bricks themselves. A few shells came over the fort, others fell in the vicinity of the 'Girls' Schools,' knocking up clouds of dust.

"At 11 a.m. the *Vipère* had rigged up either a cannon or a machine gun at her foretop, and was blazing away furiously, from her decks as well as from the tops.

"Amidst the rattle of machine guns and the constant heavy booming and often clattering sound from the well-recognised big guns of the *Galissonière*, we became alive once more to the fact that 'War' was going on in a most unmistakable fashion. Shells were exploding all round the foreign settlement, and again it might be said that no foreign building was safe. To illustrate this assertion we have only to state that the Red Fort (consulate) was struck hard and true, rather low, however, but the shell made no impression on the firm and solid masonry, and then flew back into the prison yard, demolishing the cook-house completely, the ordinary occupants of which were fortunately absent. Without doubt this was a "bad shot," if the Frenchmen were not aiming that way. The gentlemen in the fort felt that although surrounded by brick walls of an extraordinary depth they were nevertheless in a perilous position, and this idea was borne out by the repeated shot and shell which continued to fall all round the fort, much to the consternation of foreigners inside who had gone there especially to watch the landing, and the meeting of French and Chinese troops.

"From Piatow we could see shell after shell bursting close to the Girls' School, which was unfortunately not very far from some tents occupied by soldiers. Many of the shot made sad havoc in villages situated under clumps of trees on the hills, where no soldiers were visible, and at noon a still shell came in the middle of the Hûbei market place, knocking the walls of a temple down and sending a brick against a poor old woman's leg, smashing it at the ankle. The "sick boy man" of the *Cockchafer* bandaged her leg temporarily, but Dr. Browne could not give attention to this case as he had already gone to the hospital to attend to wounded Chinese soldiers, who were being brought in about this time one after the other. Thundering roars of distant cannonading to the north came resounding over the downs, and the smarter report of guns from the *Galissonière* continued in quick succession; and although the circle of danger was more circumscribed than on the 2nd instant, there was a fair sprinkling of shots in parts occupied by foreigners. In addition to the "hot time" experienced at the Red Fort (Consulate) and in the neighborhood of the missionary houses—where fragments of shells seemed to congregate especially, leaving their marks in close proximity to dwellings—there was at this period an uncertainty about the safety of foreigners generally, which must have taxed the brain of the timid as well as the brave more or less! A blue jacket was despatched from the Red Fort to the missionary houses, and a shell burst close to him on his way thereto.

"Another shot struck the garden wall of the Customs assistants' residences and left its mark. An enormous shot fell in the mud opposite Messrs. D. Lapraik & Co.'s godowns, and another planted itself in their tennis lawn. An erratic still shell fell in the compound close to the hospital, and another right in the road close to the compradore "Assoon's" store, and far away up the river close to Piatow shells might be seen bursting too close for our safety, two of them following each other rapidly, clearing out a lot of peasants, who were watching from the heights close by a spectacle only to be surpassed by that of the 2nd inst. Whilst all this was passing, men's minds were undergoing a variety of exercise; the good and true qualities of some rose to the surface, and the eccentric and curious traits of others were developed to an absurd degree. For the most part, however, it must be admitted by all that demoralisation was not observable, but on the contrary, every one, from naval officers on board the *Cockchafer* to the latest arrival in these parts, kept cool and collected (although there might have been here and there a slight fluttering about the hearts of some) . . . .

"The arrival of wounded men at the mission hospital corroborated certain vague reports about the landing of French troops, which had been flying round for some time. It at length became known that the French had landed a force of some 500 to 800 men, variously estimated by different authorities; that on landing they had used machine guns placed in the bows of the boats; and that on effecting a landing they had proceeded inland at a very rapid pace. This could be seen by foreign eyes, but on approaching the ascent leading towards the downs--Chinese soldiers say--the French found themselves in the neighborhood of some paddy fields, and that suddenly from two sides from the hills overlooking the same, Chinese soldiers, who were ensconced in the cover, opened fire, and fighting became at once sharp and decisive. The skirmishers sent out in advance probably were at a disadvantage, not knowing the country, but it mattered not, the whole party advancing inland were soon engaged in a sharp contest, and judging from the number of Chinese wounded brought into Hobe, the French riflemen must have used the occasion to some purpose.

Without entering into further details, we will only state that the fire from the ships almost ceased after 2 p.m., and that afterwards what was considered by those who heard it a very sharp musketry engagement did take place, ending in a retreat towards the boats which landed the French troops.

On the beach opposite the boats, the reserves stationed there poured in volley after volley on the enemy, wounding and killing in all not less than 200 Chinese soldiers. They were seen in front of the boats to be in perfect order and to pour volleys in the direction of their enemies, till finally the boats shoved off and the day's operations ended.

"In the course of the afternoon some 120 Chinese soldiers, nearly all northern men, were brought into the mission hospital, where they were attended to by Dr. Johansen, of Tamsui, and Dr. Browne, of the *Cockchafer*. On calling at the hospital at about 5 p.m., the same day, I found that about 120 had been brought in, fifty had been bandaged up and their wounds dressed, and that 70 men were *hors de combat*, many of them badly wounded, some in three and a few actually in five places. What a scene it was,—one that I shall certainly not forget. The mission building has one large room at the entrance and several others adjoining and in rear of the big room. Each wounded man was brought in on two planks, carried by two comrades who had brought them carefully for a mile or two. On arrival every attention was paid them by the doctors and attendants, but very soon the rooms became overcrowded, and the slightly wounded were attended to and packed off. Then the severe cases were looked into, and after temporarily dressing the wounds, administering morphine to those in great pain, &c., the doctors left the patients in charge of their friends, who stood by them and attended to their calls for water and tea during the whole night.

"A most unmistakable scene in the market place occurred. Some six heads of Frenchmen, heads of the true French type were exhibited, much to the disgust of foreigners. A few visited the place where they were stuck up, and were glad to leave it—not only on account of the disgusting and barbarous character of the scene, but because the surrounding crowd shewed signs of turbulence. At the camp also were eight other Frenchmen's heads, a sight which might have satisfied a savage or a Hill-man, but hardly consistent with the comparatively enlightened tastes, one would think, of Chinese soldiers even of to-day. It is not known how many of the French were killed and wounded; fourteen left their bodies on shore, and no doubt several wounded were taken back to the ships. (Chinese accounts state that twenty were killed and large numbers wounded.)

"In the evening Captain Boteler and Consul Frater called on General Sūn, remonstrating with him on the subject of cutting heads off, and allowing them to be exhibited. Consul Frater wrote him a despatch on the subject strongly deprecating such practices, and we understand that the general promised it should not occur again, and orders were at once given to bury the heads. It is difficult for a general even situated as Sūn is—having to command troops like the Hillmen, who are the veriest savages in the treatment of their enemies—to prevent such barbarities . . . .

"It is said the Chinese buried the dead bodies of the Frenchmen after the engagement on 8th instant by order of General Sūn. The Chinese are in possession of a machine gun taken or found on the beach.

"All the Frenchmen capsized out of the boat were picked up and saved. Notwithstanding the first and second bombardments and the fire from the vessels, almost every day between the 2nd and 8th inst. very little damage has been done to either the earthwork or the miserable little fort called the "White Fort." The latter is almost on a level with the sandy beach, and is faced with sand bags, running some 15 feet or more in front. You could see the huge shot from the *Galissonière's* guns strike the sand bags without doing any damage to the ricketty little stone fort in the rear.

"Many of the wounded gunners brought into hospital during the bombardment of the 2nd instant were almost blinded with sand, and particles of sand had been driven deep into their skins, which must have been very painful. The shot from the machine guns fell like hail around the fort at times and you could see distinctly the commotion in the water and on the sands in front, hot enough to drive away any enemy, and yet behind the sand bags there was safety, excepting of course against those ugly customers, shells, which are bursting here, there, and everywhere. It is said that the Frenchmen who landed on the 8th instant carried each 100 rounds, and when they were expended they had to retire. The Hillmen, on hands and feet, followed them right up to the beach in true savage style. The *Vipère* is back again close to the *Galissonière*."

"The houses near the consulate having been proved to be unsafe, two lady missionaries and their husbands and children, the consul, the commissioner of Customs and five or six other gentlemen removed and took up quarters in the house of Messrs. D. Lapraik & Co., with a guard of ten blue jackets and an officer. At Messrs. Dodd & Co.'s, Piatow, were two ladies and several gentlemen with a guard of five marines of the *Cockchafer*, while the Custom officers lived principally in boats."

The few days following this failure to land troops were not marked by anything unusual. The French ships were obliged to battle with the elements for some days, a strong north-easter proving more formidable than the Chinese forts, and driving three out of the five ships to mainland ports for shelter. Meanwhile, the Chinese on shore were more active than ever in making grand preparations for the *Francy Man* should he visit them on shore again. The guns of the White Fort were removed and placed in a newly erected earthwork overlooking the place where the French had landed on the 8th.

Liu Ming-chuan with some 6,000 men was stationed at Taipehfu in the Banka plain, while the forces at Hobe were daily strengthened, until, in the middle of October, there were assembled about 6,000 men in the neighborhood. Among these were new levies of Hakka hillmen. They were considered by the foreigners to be a dangerous lot to have in the neighborhood, and as they did not speak the same language as the general and other officers, it was feared that misunderstandings might arise with serious results. The other soldiers present were principally northern men, and were said to be well armed. The Hakkas, although armed with their primitive matchlocks, were considered to be brave men and were hardened to the privations of warfare. Their matchlocks are described as long-barrelled guns, fixed into semi-circular shaped stocks, with pans for priming powder, and armlets made of rattan, worn around the right wrist and containing pieces of bark-cord, which, when lighted, would keep alight for hours, if necessary. When in action the Hakka pours a charge of powder down the muzzle ; on top of that are dropped two or three slug shot or long pieces of iron, without wadding. The trigger is made to receive the lighted piece of bark, and when powder covers the priming pan and all is ready, the trigger is pulled and if,—if the weather is dry, off goes the gun. The ordinary method of handling these weapons is to place the lower end of the butt against the right breast, high enough to enable the curved end to rest against the cheek, and the eye to look down the large barrel, upon which there are ordinarily no sights. This method is sometimes varied by discharging the guns from the hip, and it is quite customary for the Hakka to lie flat on his back, place the muzzle between his toes, and, raising his head sufficiently to sight along the barrel, to take deliberate aim and fire. He is able to make good practice ; while his presence, especially when surrounded by rank grass, is decidedly difficult to determine.

Rev. Dr. Mackay's Tamsui Mission Hospital, with Dr. Johansen in charge, which had rendered such great services to the Chinese wounded and had no doubt been the means of saving many lives, was visited on the 19th by General Sūn, who thanked the doctor in charge as well as Dr. Browne of the *Cockchafer* (who had given valuable assistance) for their attentions to the sick and wounded. The patients then numbered only a dozen, a good many of the wounded having left, fearing that the French might land again and kill them ; others, seeing their wounds healing nicely, went away into the town. One man who had been shot through the left shoulder, in the region of the collar bone, after a week or ten days' treatment suddenly shouldered his rifle and left for the front, preferring life with his comrades to being confined in the hospital. It was supposed that the bullet had pierced the upper part of his lungs. Another instance occurred seven days after the French landing, when a Chinese walked into the hospital with his skull wounded and the brain visible. Several others, shot through the thighs and arms, bones being splintered in many pieces, bore their pain most heroically. Soon after the engagement, when there were seventy men in the hospital, some being badly wounded with as many as three shots apiece, there was scarcely a groan to be heard. One of the wounded came to the hospital after having had a bullet in his calf for nine or ten days. Dr. Browne extracted the bullet, and off the man went back to the front. Many other instances like the foregoing might be recorded, all of which indicated that the Chinese could recover in a few days from wounds, which, if not actually fatal, would have laid foreign soldiers up for months.

No further attempt was made to land, and on October 22nd the foreign community was surprised to receive a circular issued by Consul Frater, to which was attached a "*Notification de Blocus*" issued by Admiral Courbet, dated Kelung, 20th October, declaring a blockade of the coast of Formosa.[1]

Instead of being lessened, the dangers to the foreign community were now enhanced, and all trade was at a standstill, which meant a great loss for the merchants. Much inconvenience was already being felt owing to several persons running short of supplies, and there was not a little anxiety as to how they would get along if the blockade was a protracted one. The short notice scarcely permitted of their arranging their affairs and clearing out, and with the Chinese hordes on one side making it unsafe to retreat up river and with French guns on the other, their position was not unlike that of the proverbial " rat in the trap."

The Chinese were quite unable to comprehend that the blockade was a serious matter; for, during the afternoon, a fleet of Chinese coasting boats prepared to clear out. They sailed past the Pilot Village and White Fort, and had just rounded the black beacon, when suddenly the *Duquay Trouin*, which had been left on guard, opened fire, one shot falling ahead, one near, and a third appearing to fall right among them. With a great desire to proceed and the wind against them on their return to harbor, the "gallant Tai Kongs" were undecided. The ugly rattle of a Hotchkiss in the tops, however, soon put an end to their indecision, and the brave coasters put about and returned to port, safe and sound, with an exact and clear understanding of the word "*blocus*." The hope of some of the junkmen that night would enable them to slip out without detection was dispelled by the appearance of a strong search light, which, sweeping all around the ship, made escape impossible.

1. M. Le Contre Amiral Lespés.

No. 513.
NOTIFICATION DE BLOCUS.

Nous soussigné Vice-Amiral Courbet, Commandant en chef les Forces Navales Françaises dans l'extreme Orient.

Vu l'état de représailles existant entre la France et la Chine, agissant en vertu des pouvoirs qui nous appartiennent.

Declarons:

Qu'à partir du 23 Octobre, 1884, la côte et les ports de Formose compris entre le Cap Sud (Latitude 21° 50' Nord, Longitude 118° 32' Est) et la pointe Dôme (Latitude 24° 30' Nord, Longitude 119° 35' Est) en passant par l'Ouest et le Nord, seront tenus en état de blocus effectif par les Forces Navales placées sous notre commandement et que les bâtiments amis ou neutres auront un delai de trois jours pour achever leur chargement et quitter les lieux bloqués.

Il sera procédé contre tout bâtiment qui tenterait de voiler le dit blocus conprimément aux Lois Internationales et aux traités en vigueur avec les Puissances neutres.

A bord du Cuirassé le *Bayard*,
Rade du Kelung, le 20 Octobre, 1884.

(Signed)   S. COURBET.

A few days later a report got into circulation that some Chinese and a certain foreigner had been in communication with the French. This disagreeable rumor arose from a discovery made on the day of the French landing, when two Chinese who were arrested under rather suspicious circumstances were said to have been found in possession of a foreign letter, money, and bills, and also French flags with certain round patches of different colors on them. It was supposed that the flags were to be used by the Chinese traitors as signals or guides to the French troops should they land again. After the men had been imprisoned and tortured, they implicated a Hobe Chinese named Tan Akoon, whose family quarters were situated near the beach, opposite to which were anchored one or two French men-of war, and close to the road which led over the first downs. Akoon had, some fifteen years before, been dismissed from foreign employ, and had been since employed as a yamen runner and interpreter. For some days previously he had been calling at the foreign hongs reporting that the mandarins had sufficient evidence to prove that the master of the hong was in league with the French, and subsequently he gave out that the compradores and others were mixed up in the affair. These false reports for the time created considerable excitement. Akoon was seized in Twatutia, where he was tortured, and then brought down river to Hobe and decapitated. His head was placed on a pole and exhibited in front of General Sūn's quarters as a warning to others.

On November 2nd, a Chinese force was defeated by the French in the region of Liang-ko overlooking the Kelung rapids, the Chinese reporting a loss of two hundred and stating that machine-guns, mounted on wooden supports, perched on elevated spots, effected the most damage. The French loss was reported as twenty dead.

December followed with but little to relieve the monotony. The foreign community, not having received any outside supplies for some months, were now obliged to put themselves on half and three-quarter allowances, besides laying aside something, that their Christmas dinner might not lose by the blockade. The French allowed mails and stores to be landed for the personal use of the consul and the officers and crew of the *Cockchafer*, but refused to allow anything of like nature to be delivered to the foreign community. This they, of course, had a right to do, but it does seem that they might have acted with a little more generosity under the circumstances, especially as they were using Hongkong for all purposes as a naval supply depot. However, Christmas day was celebrated by the whole Tamsui community with a dinner, in which "huge pieces of beef, lordly turkeys, and fatted capons, home made puddings, pies and cakes" played a leading part. A regatta which had been planned for the day had to be postponed on account of the weather; it took place on the 29th of December, however; the programme including numerous boat races with foreign and native boats, and finishing up with a greased pole with a pig at the top, and the distribution of prizes amounting to $150.

During the month no fighting of importance transpired. The Chinese killed a few Frenchmen who were out foraging for bullocks, and the French destroyed one village where a party of their men had been attacked. The friends of the French officer who was killed during the landing having communicated their desire to recover the body, General Liu Ming-chuan, with that manliness and generosity which characterized his later days, offered Taels 200 ($150 gold) to any one who would find and produce the body of the dead officer. As a result the head was discovered some days afterwards, but the body could not be identified, it having been buried with others on the downs.

The French no doubt found great difficulty in advancing into the country. The nature of the place was most favorable to the Chinese, the vicinity of Kelung being hilly and full of cover, and the only roads being narrow pathways. Chinese soldiers were scattered about without regard to rank all over the hills, behind rifle pits, or hidden in thick covers, and even up trees, it was said. French soldiers advancing were exposed to the fire of these unseen riflemen, some of whom were adepts at savage warfare. They moved through the long grass, now erect, now on all fours, suddenly raised themselves just high enough to take aim and fire, then lay down again, and crawled away like snakes from the tell-tale smoke, so that they made but poor targets for even the best of the French riflemen.

The new year, 1885, brought but little consolation to the blockaded residents, and the French were still persistent in their refusal to allow stores or mails to reach the community. The junk communication, however, between certain parts of Formosa and the mainland was never more regular than during the days of the blockade, making it easy for the Chinese to get their mails in the old fashioned way, while the foreign merchants who trusted their mails to the government postal authorities had to go without them. But it was the monotony of the situation that was felt worst of all. The long days of suspense. Would it last one month or a year?

The new year was marked by considerable activity on the part of the French in amassing troops at Kelung. On the 21st of January, the transport *Canton*, belonging to the Compagnie Nationale, arrived at Kelung, having sailed from Algeria December 3rd. She brought 971 men,—16 having deserted and 13 died on the way. The French troops on their arrival were quartered in Chinese houses and temples; and, as the weather was bitterly cold, all wooden portions of the houses were torn down for firewood. In one house, while obtaining fuel in this way, $1,500 was discovered and turned over to the commandant. With no suitable quarters and an almost daily downpour of rain, the soldiers were very miserable indeed.

The French force at Kelung consisted of

Legion Etranger	971
Batallion Afrique	900
Marine Infantry	350
Blue Jackets	800

The land expedition was under the command of General Duchesne, known to the French as the conqueror of Madagascar. The new arrivals did not have much to do in the shape of fighting until February 7th. On that day the first attack was made on a Chinese fort which lay to the north-east of the Custom house and on the second range of hills. The French force consisted of 800 men from the "Legion Etranger." Two 13 centimetre field guns were planted on the first range of hills and two 7 centimetre mountain guns were taken with the troops. The Chinese force amounted to some 3,000 men. The attack was made about four o'clock in the morning, but the Chinese position was too strong, and the French withdrew without much loss. Four days later, the engagement was renewed, the French making a blind attack with 60 men; while 600 men surprised the Chinese by coming in by an unexpected route. The Chinese fled over the hills leaving, 20 dead behind them. The French loss was 7, of whom 2 were killed and 5 wounded. Four Krupp guns of 7 centimetres were captured, and many Mauser rifles. A force was left in possession of the fort, which was well located and commanded a large district.

On the 3rd of March, preparations were made to attack a fort known to the French as Fort Bamboo, on account of the bamboo stockade that surrounded it. This was on a curiously shaped hill with almost perpendicular sides and a flat top, at the back of a village known as Wan Wan. It was a most commanding position, and its capture by the French with the small force at their command was most creditable. The French brought 330 men to the attack, and the pathway was so steep that they were forced to use storming ladders. In gaining this pathway and reaching the fortifications, the French were for two miles under fire, but so determined was the charge that the Chinese weakened and finally retreated. The tale is told by a member of the French expedition ; and a young Chinese officer, an Anhui man, is credited with exceptional bravery. After the Chinese had fled from the field this officer returned with a small squad, which he led without a sign of fear against the French now greatly outnumbering his little band. This gallant charge in the open field was an exhibition of such rare bravery for the Chinese that the French officer in command was much affected and ordered that the enemy should not be fired upon if it could be helped. But, regardless of their inferiority in numbers, the Chinese officer and his men did not falter, and it became necessary for the protection of the French troops to give the order to fire a volley to frighten the enemy from the field. As soon as the smoke had cleared away, the French were surprised to find this officer again leading his men to the front. Again did the French fire, and again did the Chinese appear to retreat ; but, with an evident determination to conquer or die on the field, the Anhui man again returned for the third time, with scarcely a corporal's guard remaining. With much regret the French officer gave the order to fire, and the brave little band, lacking only in wisdom, met death to a man.

The Chinese loss was estimated by the French at 1,500 in all. The French loss was 180 men, of whom nearly a hundred were killed on the field. The Chinese were principally armed with Mausers and had mounted in their fortifications four guns, three of them being 7 centimetre Krupps.

Chinese accounts say the French carried the fort by storm and then turned their attention to the encampments, and that the Chinese force numbered over 3,500 men.

This defeat greatly alarmed the mandarins in the north, and, undoubtedly, if the French had followed up their success, they would not have found much difficulty in reaching the capital. Their delay was taken full advantage of by the Chinese, and extensive work was carried on in erecting fortifications round about Taipehfu and Hobe. For quite a long time, at least 2,000 men were employed at this work in the neighborhood of Kantao. At Hobe military work had been carried on for several weeks without interruption, except one day in February when the *Villars* steamed close to shore and discharged a few shells at the working party, without apparently doing them any damage. In spite of the blockade, numbers of soldiers and quantities of munitions of war were landed at Pilam (Pinam) on the south-east coast. The men crossed to Takow and thence overland to Taipehfu. In March it was estimated that there were not less than 30,000 Chinese troops gathered in the north.

In the southern part of Formosa, Chinese Customs reports speak of preparations made to oppose the French should they make an attack there. Soon after the first arrival of the French in the north, troops were collected at Takow and vicinity, where there was a fort on "Saracen's Head," in which four 6½ ton, M.L. Armstrongs had been mounted in 1879; besides this, two nine-inch American rifled guns were placed behind earthworks on the northern end of the Head. During September, many natives, apprehensive of danger, left for the mainland, and the families of foreigners were also sent across the channel. In October, an attempt was made to block the harbor. Junks loaded with stones were sunk in the entrance, only to be broken up, and the stones scattered far and wide by the tidal current; so that within 48 hours after the work of filling up had been effected the original depth of 25 feet was got. These efforts were twice repeated, but on both occasions with similar results. A French man-of-war appeared off Anping on the 15th of October, and two days later another arrived off Takow.

The authorities, now somewhat alarmed, ordered the light on Saracen's Head to be discontinued. On the 23rd, the British man-of-war *Champion* brought the first news of the blockade to the south, and informed the surprised residents that three days would be allowed for vessels to leave. Accordingly, the British S.S. *Pingon*, the only vessel in port, departed on the 26th. On the 25th, the Chinese opened fire from Saracen's Head fort at the French gunboat *Lutin*. She did not reply, and after five shots the firing ceased. This was the only time that this fort had occasion to take action. On the 2nd of November, the Chinese revenue steamer *Feiho* was captured outside Anping by the French, and on the 26th, Anping light was extinguished by order of the authorities. During the last days of November the work of closing the harbor was again attempted.

On the 1st of December, the South Cape light was extinguished. From the 15th of December onward, French ships appeared outside Takow and Anping. Prices of imports at once rose greatly, opium reaching as much as $1,000 a chest; so that junks were induced by the high freights to take the chances of encountering a French man-of-war. Early in January, however, a radical change in the conduct of the French fleet took place; several men-of-war appeared on the scene, proceeding to take vigorous action against all Chinese craft then in the vicinity of the treaty-ports, burning and sinking every vessel that came in sight, although they had previously raised the blockade for three weeks, without, however, notifying the same to any one. On the 7th, the French ships again reappeared and notified south Formosa residents that a "*new*" blockade of the coast from Taika river to the South Cape would be commenced that day. The sinking, burning, and destroying of junks was kept up throughout the month, and the coast was soon cleared of sails during daylight, but many still managed to run in safety during the night, when apparently no effort was made to stop them. The amount of destruction during the first day after the return of the French, and before the junks from the mainland had been apprised of the renewal of the blockade was very great, the coast being strewn with wreckage all along. Vessel after vessel ran straight into the arms of the French, and all met the same fate. From Amoy alone eight junks arrived off Anping, of which seven were sunk; only one, running the gauntlet, escaped into port, to the intense chagrin of the blockaders. The value of property destroyed on this occasion was reckoned at $100,000. As the state of affairs became known at the Pescadores and on the mainland, junkmen grew more cautious, and either waited for better times or ran across at night to Pa-te-chui, a place north of Anping, or on to Takow.

There are several small Chinese ports to the north of Taiwanfu, higher up than Kok-si-kon, in the direction of Pa-te-chui, where junks can run in; and during the campaign, favored by the strong north-east gales, and the shoal water preventing French gunboats from following them, a safe haven was frequently made. Many of the junk-anchorages on the west coast are formed by outlying longitudinal sand banks, inside of which light draft boats can sail at flood-tide; the inlets, however, become perfectly dry at low tide. These sand harbors run inland a long way from the sea; but, even supposing there had been water enough, the navigation was quite unknown to the foreigners and, therefore, naturally the French did not attempt to enter them.

A great number of junks in the north of the island also fell into the hands of the French. As a rule, the crews were taken to Kelung, where they were set to work at road-making. It is said that the opium captured out of junks was sold by the French at Kelung to Chinese buyers. If this be true the transaction must have proved rather profitable, as valuable cargoes of the drug were undoubtedly carried by most of the blockade-running junks.

On the 16th of March, the British gunboat *Swift* arrived at Tamsui, and a circular was sent round stating that the *Swift* would take away anyone desirous of leaving. But as only some few hours' notice was given, the Tamsui residents did not feel that they could prepare for their departure in so short a time; besides, the majority, who had property in north Formosa, were loath to leave it to the protection of the Chinese only. The *Cockchafer* had also been ordered back to Kelung; but as the Chinese had been actively engaged for several weeks laying down split bamboo baskets of a circular shape, full of large stones, right across the narrowest part of the entrance of the river, the channel was so entirely blocked that even cargo boats and gigs were obliged to enter by certain narrow courses close inshore. It was thought that the Chinese authorities would remove obstacles sufficiently to make a channel for the *Cockchafer* to go through, but as they were disinclined to do this, the gunboat had to remain, notwithstanding the rather serious complications between Great Britain and Russia, which had led to the summary withdrawal of all other British men-of-war from Formosa.

Early in March the Tamsui residents were, by the kindness of Admiral Lespes, given an unexpected treat. This officer allowed a mail from the *Swift* to be landed, the first for many weeks. No stores, however, arrived, and the blockade had naturally caused a great rise in the prices of such goods as were to be procured in Formosa. Fortunately for the Tamsui residents, an enterprising Chinese storekeeper managed to get across some flour, for which he found a ready market at $4 per bag. Potatoes were in demand at $7.20 per picul; kerosine oil, usually sold for $2, brought $5, and other necessaries, including native produce, sold at an advance of from 30 to 100 per cent. The poorer classes of Chinese suffered much privation, and Chinese New Year passed off with less noise and fewer presents than usual.

The Chinese commander-in-chief, General Sūn, who seems to have been a man of great activity, completed, in early April, a stone and bamboo bridge across the river at Tamsui from Sand Point to a spit running out into the river on the further side of Pilot Village.

On the 3rd of April, the *Duguay Trouin* got up steam early in the morning and fired several shots to the north, one of which killed two Chinese soldiers near the earth battery, completely knocking the head off one of them. To the blockaded foreigners this seemed the beginning of another bombardment, but in reality it proved to be the last shot fired by the French in their operations against Formosa. On the 28th of March, five French ships—two ironclads, two cruisers, and a troop-ship—rendezvoused off Anping, and proceeding on the 31st to the Pescadores, bombarded and took those islands, after an almost bloodless engagement with the forts. The casualty-list showed only 3 killed and 7 wounded. On April 1st, the French flag was hoisted at Makung, and the *Bayard*, with Admiral Courbet on board, fired a salute of 21 guns, declaring the Pescadores a French possession under the old name of "Fisherman Island." After the bombardment, which, it is interesting to note, is reported as having been heard in Takow some 65 miles distant, the south of Formosa was free from blockading ships. The German schooner *Faugh Balaugh* put in at Takow seeking freight; but her rates were so high that no one seemed willing to ship, and eventually she went away empty.

The S.S. *Pingon*, which had now become a Chinese transport, was captured on the 11th off South Cape by a French cruiser. There is some evidence tending to show that this was the result of an arrangement between the mandarin in charge of the ship and the French naval authorities, who are said to have paid the traitor handsomely.

April 5th was a glorious day for the blockaded residents in Formosa and worthy of being remembered by them. The event is thus described:

"Yesterday afternoon a merchant vessel was seen steaming towards the port; as she approached the shipping, she was discovered to be the *Hailoong*. What could be the meaning of the *Hailoong* coming to Tamsui? Pigs must have declined, or advanced in price, or something must have happened! The eagle eyes of our harbor master are on her; he adjusts a long telescope. Steady, he says the flags are speaking. What do they say? what? can it really be so? Yes; no! yes! There is no doubt about it—the signal is, is,—(oh! it is too much of a good thing)—oh dear! hold me up! gently now! Say it again! 'The blockade is raised!' Shouts of gladness rent the air. Come on board the *Cockchafer*; let us see what the signal man says there. Ho! signal man, what say you? Tom Bowling replied, avast there! Splice the main brace! Yo ho, lads, ho! By the soul of Nelson, I swear the signal runs:—'The blockade is raised!' Hurrah! hip, hip, hurrah! Pipe all hands and let us be merry! Everyone echoed let's be merry to the tune of 'God save our Gracious Queen!' The feeling of happiness has not been experienced by any of us for many weary months. We now know what the word really means. No end of main braces were spliced. The *Hailoong* was brought to in the usual way (a shot across her bows). She was ordered to anchor to the south of the corvette. A boat was seen to board her, and before you could say 'Rule Britannia' she was off again, steaming southward. The news must have been unknown even to the French, and it was thought that the *Hailoong* had been referred to Admiral Courbet, supposed to be at Makung."

In the south, the news that the blockade had been raised was brought on the 15th by the British S. S. *Amatista*, which arrived from Amoy with a notification from Admiral Courbet. Accordingly, on April 27th, the Saracen Head light was relit, the next day the Anping light was also shown, and on the 1st of May the South Cape light resumed operations. There was little need for labor in removing the obstruction in the river, the strong tides having washed so much of it away that by the end of April there was a depth in the shallowest part of 11 feet 6 inches at low water. An address of thanks for the protection given to foreigners during the blockade, signed by all the foreigners was, in May, presented to the taotai, Liu Ao, through the British consul.

In the north, although the French admiral had given official notification of the removal of the blockade, and the French ships had departed from Hobe, the Chinese soldiers were still kept at work on fortifications, and the authorities were loath to remove the harbor obstructions, fearing that the departure of the French was but a ruse to catch the Chinese napping. On the 19th, the British steamships *Namoa* and *Hailoong* arrived, but were not allowed to enter. A passage, however, was made for the *Cockchafer*, which departed on the 21st after nine months' stay in the Tamsui river. The French still occupied Kelung and its immediate vicinity, reserving the right to search vessels of any nationality, and to seize rice and all contraband of war.

The Twatutia residents returned to their up river quarters, and preparations were made for the opening of the tea-export trade, the season for which was now just commencing. New tea came pouring into the town from the country, together with a considerable quantity of old leaf from the year before, which had been stored until the blockade should be raised. Trade, however, was still destined to be much hindered ; for lead, which is necessary for lining the tea chests, was a contraband of war, and thus none could be landed. Chinese packers were consequently buying up leaden " joss " candlesticks, and fishermen were said to be even parting with the " sinkers " attached to their nets, for the same purpose. Packers were now anxious to secure lead, gladly paying $20 per picul for what had cost $6 the previous year. An attempt was made to smuggle lead across as specie stowed in treasure boxes, but this being discovered by the Custom authorities the consignees were fined. Importers then endeavored to buy it in boxes said to contain tin plates. Upon examination the boxes were found to contain about two tin plates only, the remainder of their contents being lead. This state of affairs continued until June 5th, when a notification was issued by the English consul that all restrictions as to cargoes had been removed.

The month of May passed very quietly for all concerned. Occasional rows occurred between French foraging parties and Chinese. But it is not known that any resulted seriously, with the exception of the case of two Frenchmen, who, while out foraging for fowls, became pressing in their attentions to certain Chinese tea-picking damsels, with the result that one of them was killed and the other had to run for his life. A French party was immediately sent to the locality, some ten men and women were carried away as hostages, and, according to some accounts, cruelly treated. Numerous tales were circulated regarding the terrible things done by the French, but there was no evidence to prove any of the charges made.[1]

A new phase of warfare was brought to light during the French operations in Formosa. It should be instructive to commanding officers to note that nearly as many Chinese were killed by tampering with the unexploded shells found on shore after the bombardment, as the French were able to slay in many of their engagements. One case—perhaps the most striking—was that of an inquisitive Chinese who deliberately sat astride a shell and proceeded to attack it with a hammer. It is needless to say his researches were soon greeted with success, and the explosion which followed not only deprived the poor ignorant fellow of his life but worked havoc on the surrounding landscape. Another inquirer tried to unscrew the end of an unexploded shell, with the same result. One explosion of like nature caused the death of four Chinese, and several other casualties from this cause occurred with fatal results. In the Pescadores also, the loss of life was considerable, there being no less than five explosions, the result of tampering with unexploded shells, and more than twenty persons lost their lives. The majority of these accidents were the result of hurling large stones against

---

1. In connection with this capture the French were accused of great misconduct, it being said that maids were outraged and men cruelly treated and eventually shot. Mr. Dodd does not refer to any such actions on the part of the French, and the author places but little confidence in such reports, originally put forward as they were by Chinese, who would quite naturally represent their enemies in the worst possible light. Tales, some of them circulated by foreigners, were numerous regarding the atrocities committed by the French, but no foreigner witnessed the acts described, and the reports, coming as they did from the Chinese, should not have been trusted.

the shells. In a house occupied as a torpedo-station at Hobe the "expert" in charge, with a desire, no doubt, to obtain the favor of his particular "joss" for the torpedoes in his possession, was so profuse in the burning of joss paper that some of it, coming in contact with the torpedo fuses, caused an explosion leading to the destruction of several houses. Thus, without assistance from outsiders, the Chinese inflicted quite as much damage on themselves with munitions of war as they did on the enemy.

On the 9th of June, the treaty, article IX of which stipulated that Formosa and the Pescadores islands should be evacuated, was definitely signed, and a few days later the news reached Formosa.

When this was published in the military quarters at Kelung the joy of the French troops knew no bounds. It would be hard to select a more uncomfortable camping-ground in the whole inhabited East than Kelung with its two hundred days of rain. To the local unhealthiness, the little cemetery, under a frowning cliff, owes much of its crowded state. Seven hundred men were buried there, only one hundred and twenty of whom were killed on the field of battle; a hundred and fifty died of wounds; all the others succumbing to the climate. Loss of life from cholera and fever was likewise very severe in the Pescadores; three cemeteries, each crowded with graves, give sad evidence of this.

On June 21st, General Duchesne and his remaining troops, after a sad farewell to their dead comrades left behind them, departed from Kelung. Thus, after an occupation of Formosa for more than nine months, French operations in the island came to an end.

Admiral Courbet's death in the Pescadores was another deplorable event of a campaign in which so much was sacrificed and so little gained. It is said that the admiral, who had in the name of France taken possession of the Pescadores, was much impressed with the advantages of the harbor of Makung,—a port easy of access to vessels of the largest tonnage and sheltered from all winds, with a location so central that, if utilised as a naval station, it could be made second to none in the East. In order to carry out his plans the admiral applied to his government for the necessary funds and material. His representations met with favor, and the material was actually despatched, having reached as far as Singapore, when the order was reversed, and the island abandoned. Admiral Courbet had not been idle, however, having completed surveys, constructed two small jetties, made improvements in the several arrangements of defence, and established a considerable commissariat depot. Furthermore, and not of less importance, the admiral had succeeded in winning the hearts of the simple Chinese natives. Strict orders were enforced preventing the French soldiers from disturbing the people. The islanders respected and admired the kind-hearted admiral, and it is said that at his death no small portion of his mourners were Chinese, and that their grief was genuine. It was a sore disappointment to the gallant admiral to think that all advantages must be given up. The illustrious officer used all his power and influence to induce his government to reconsider their decision and retain the Pescadores, an acquisition of such palpable political and strategical importance to its possessor. All, however, was of no avail, and on June 9th the treaty which provided for the evacuation of Formosa and the Pescadores was finally signed. Two days later, saddened and discouraged, it is said, with the turn of events, Admiral Courbet breathed his last on board the *Bayard*. To their chief's memory, and that of the officers and men who had lost their lives on the field of honour, a monument was erected, and now stands, a conspicuous object on the principal island of the Pescadores group.

ENGAGEMENT BETWEEN FRENCH AND CHINESE TROOPS AT TAMSUI. MEMORIAL FROM LIU MING-CHUAN, PUBLISHED IN MANUSCRIPT "PEKING GAZETTE" OF NOVEMBER 11TH, 1884.

"His Majesty's Slave Liu Ming-chuan, Director of Affairs in Formosa, who holds the brevet of Provincial Governor, humbly submits the following report, showing how the enemy's troops were landed and attacked at Hobe (Tamsui), when our troops fought a sanguinary battle and gained a victory.

"The Memorialist has already reported to His Majesty the details of attack by different divisions of the French fleet upon Hobe, and of the energetic resistance that was offered by detachments of the Chinese troops selected as reinforcements for that place.

"On the 4th of October, the French fleet was reinforced by three vessels, making a total of eight in all, and these opened fire from their heavy guns against the Hobe forts, the cannonade being kept up on successive days. So unintermittent and fierce was this fire that our troops were unable to maintain their ground, and Sun K'ai-hua, Chang Kao-yuan, and Liu Chao yuan had no resource but to conceal their troops in the woods which skirted the shore, where the men remained on the alert, passing the nights in the open air, afraid to take any rest whatsoever. At 5 a. m. on the 8th, the enemy's ships suddenly dispersed, and Sun K'ai hua, feeling assured from certain indications that a force would be landed, directed Kung Chan-ao, the officer in charge of the right wing of the *Cho Sheng* regiment, to conceal himself in a place known as Chia Chang, or "dummy creek," Li Ting-ming, who commanded the central division of the same regiment, having orders to lie in ambush in a place called Yü-ch'ê K'ou, while Fan Hui yi, officer in command of the rear division, was directed to hold himself in the rear. Chang Kao-yuan and Liu-Chao-yuan ensconced themselves with two battalions, each from different regiments, behind the hill at the back of the large fort in order to prevent the enemy from circumventing our forces, and a battalion of the hillmen enrolled by Li T'ung-en, under Chang Li-ch'eng, were concealed in a gully in the hill on the northern road

"These arrangements had just been completed when a lateral fire was opened by the enemy's ships. which discharged no less than several hundred rounds from their heavy guns, filling the sky with smoke and flame, the shell falling round like hail. While this fire was going on, about a thousand of the enemy's troops were embarked in launches and foreign boats and landed at three points on the shore, from whence they made a straight rush for the fort, their bearing being fierce in the extreme.

"As soon as Sun K'ai-hua saw that the enemy were pressing close upon him, he stopped their advance at different points with the aid of Li Ting-ming and Fan Hui-yi, Chang Kao-yuan and others advancing to the attack from the northern road. The enemy's men were armed with weapons of precision and fought with all their might, the struggle lasting without intermission from 7 a.m. till noon. Time after time were they driven back, but they advanced again and again. Our men engaged them fiercely at close quarters, Chang-Li-ch'eng attacking them on the flank, while Sun K'ai-hua assailed them boldly in the front and killed a standard bearer, capturing the flag which he carried. The zeal of our men was increased when they witnessed the capture of the flag, and a simultaneous rush was made from every side upon the enemy, twenty-five of whom were beheaded, amongst them being two officers, exclusive of about three hundred killed by musketry fire. The enemy, being unable to hold their own, finally broke and fled, our men pursuing them to the sea shore, where some seventy or more were drowned in the struggle to get to the boats. The enemy's ships while endeavoring to cover this retreat with their guns struck one of their own steam-launches, and a Gatling gun which had been left behind was captured by our men.

"The two divisions under the command of Sun K'ai-hua were the foremost to carry out his plans, and bore the brunt of the fight for a longer period than any others; they had consequently the largest number of casualties, three lieutenants being killed and over a hundred privates. All the other battalions also suffered loss.

"The above particulars of the victory were reported to the Memorialist by Sun K'ai-hua, and he would draw attention to the fierce attack made by the enemy's troops on this occasion upon the port of Hobe, when they landed their men with a fixed determination to gain the day, the intensity of their resolve to fight to the death being evidenced by the fact that their boats stood out to sea as soon as the men had been landed, in order to cut off their retreat. After the destruction of the fort our men had no guns to protect them, and had to rely solely on their own muscle in the deadly struggle that took place. Though shot and shell rained down upon them, their courage never failed them, nor did they once flinch, and in spite of the odds against them they managed to behead the standard-bearer and frustrate the fierce intentions of the foe, therein assuredly displaying energy of no ordinary kind."

The memorialist then proceeds to mention certain of the most deserving officers, naming the form of reward which he suggests should be bestowed on each. Sun K'ai-hua heads the list, his name being followed by that of the commanders of the battalions who led the van of the fight. (The above is a good example of the trustworthiness of Chinese reports. According to the memorial 326 of the French troops were killed besides seventy or more drowned, more than 390 in all. The true loss was only between 14 and 20 and the memorialist was well aware of it).

DECREE ANNOUNCING CHINESE VICTORY AT TAMSUI; PUBLISHED NOVEMBER 6TH, 1884.

"Liu Ming-chuan reports that the French forces having made an assault on Hobe, the Imperial troops gave them battle, and gained a victory under circumstances which he describes.

"The French fleet being stationed at Taipei, Hobe, and other places, the French troops made a vigorous attack upon the 8th of October, and landed. Sûu K'ai-hua, Provincial Commander-in-Chief, advanced by different routes to attack them with the forces under his command, Chang Kao-yuan, Provincial Commander-in-Chief, and others, also leading their divisions against the enemy.[1] The French troops were repulsed, and again advanced several times, but our troops engaged them at close quarters, Sûu K'ai-hua making a direct advance upon them with his men, and beheading the officer bearing the standard, which he captured, besides killing about 300 of the enemy. Being unable to hold their own, the enemy fled in confusion and were defeated, numbers of those who retreated to the sea shore being drowned in the struggle to get to the boats.

"It is naturally fitting that rewards of an exceptionally liberal character should be bestowed upon those officers who specially distinguished themselves upon the occasion. The bravery, loyalty, and martial prowess displayed by Sûu K'ai-hua, Acting Commander-in-Chief of land forces in Fokien, whose name is recorded for a substantive appointment to this rank and who holds the position of Brigadier-General of the Chang-chou Division, are especially deserving of commendation, he having placed himself in the van of battle; and as a special Act of Grace We hereby command that he be invested with the hereditary title of *Ch'i-tu-yu*, or noble of the 7th grade. Also that the following articles be bestowed upon him :—

1 Feather-tube of white jade.
1 Thumb-ring of white jade.
1 Dagger with a handle of white jade.
1 Flint and steel.
1 Pair of large pouches.
2 Small pouches.

"Liu Ming-chuan represents that Chang Kao-yuan, Provincial Commander-in-Chief, has already been recommended for rewards in the Kelung affair, and that Brigadier-General Liu Chao-yu being his, the Memorialist's, great-nephew, he does not apply for rewards for either of these officers. As they have both, however, distinguished themselves in battle they should naturally receive marks of special favour as well as the rest, and We hereby command that a white jade feather-tube, a white jade thumb-ring, a dagger with a handle of white jade, a flint and steel, and a pair of large pouches be bestowed respectively on Chang Kao-yuan and Liu Chao-yu. Chang Kao-yuan will further be committed to the Board for the determination of the most liberal forms of reward, and Liu Chao-yu will have the brevet of Provincial Commander in-Chief bestowed upon him."

Here follows a long list of rewards bestowed upon various officers, one of whom obtains the distinction of the Yellow Riding Jacket, while two are to have their names recorded for appointment to the post of Brigadier-General upon a vacancy occurring. Others receive the title of *baturu* in addition to the bestowal of brevet rank, while others, again, are to be honored with the decoration of the peacock's feather.

The Decree concludes with the announcement that Her Majesty the Empress Dowager has ordered the sum of Tls. 10,000 from the Privy Purse to be bestowed upon the soldiery who displayed bravery during the action, and calls upon Liu Ming-chuan to continue rigorously to resist the insults of the foe.

1. The officer was wounded and carried to the rear, and on his way was attacked and beheaded with the two sailors who carried him. Sûu was on the point of retreating, but Colonel Li advanced and won. French loss only fourteen killed on the ground.—*Author*.

CHAPTER XVII.

PROGRESSIVE FORMOSA: A PROVINCE OF CHINA.

1886—1894.

Liu Ming-chuan recommends administrative changes—Formosa becomes an independent province—Liu Ming-chuan, Formosa's first governor—Administrative reorganization—Capital established at Taipeh—Old Taiwanfu becomes Tainanfu—New Taiwanfu—Confusing nomenclature—New official posts—Innovations bring additional taxation—New burdens strongly condemned by southern populace— Liu Ming-chuan imprisoned by infuriated natives—Camphor monopoly again declared—Consular protests result successfully—Unjust taxation in north—The island's defences strengthened—Taipehfu reconstructed—Electricity introduced— Telegraph lines and cables laid—Kelung in prospective as a great shipping port —Railway construction commenced—Kelung-Taipeh line—Engineers encounter numerous obstacles—Chinese superintendents susceptible to bribes—Difficulties of construction on Kelung line—Harbor work at Kelung—Twatutia and southern line—Peking officials discourage harbor and railway work—Kelung's prospects blighted—A trip on the railway—The rolling stock—Passengers, and novel methods of collecting fares—Chinese freight agents—Savage warfare on the increase— Governor Liu's pacification policy—Increased head-hunting—Savages on the offensive—Ling Chiau-tong's expedition—Heavy losses—Governor Liu's nephew and followers killed at Gilan—Liu personally takes the field—Unsatisfactory results —Liu reports victories to Peking—Liu retires from office—A sketch of his life— The Tokoham savage war—Numerous engagements—Mutilation of the dead— Cannibalism practised by Chinese—Chinese rebels in Yunlin and vicinity— Changwha attacked—Shao Yu-lien, Liu's successor, retires, and Tang-ching-sung becomes acting-governor. Wrecks during period 1886-1894.

PREVIOUS to the French war, Formosa was but a prefecture of Fokien province, dependent upon the officials of the latter in all matters, and constituting, as one authority describes it, "a sort of place of banishment to which subordinate officials, who must be provided with places but were unfitted for responsible administrative work, might be relegated." But during the later period, from the time of the arrival of Liu Ming-chuan, this deplorable condition of affairs was much improved upon. The temporary occupation of the south of the island by the Japanese in 1874 called attention at once to the great need of reform in the method of governing the island, and the attack by the French ten years later furnished the Imperial authorities with strong evidence that the value of the island from a strategical standpoint caused it to be coveted by ambitious powers, and that it could only be preserved as a possession of China by making radical changes in its political and military government.

During the French war, Liu Ming-chuan had been placed in sole command, responsible only to the central authorities. Under his superintendence, Formosa had been carried safely through the war, and it was now apparent that the exigencies of the times required that the island should be made an independent province, and that officials of high rank and undoubted ability should be henceforth placed in charge of it. Therefore, in 1887, the island was declared by Imperial decree an independent province, and the Imperial Commissioner Liu Ming-chuan was appointed the first governor. The new province was made subject to the general control of the governor-general, formerly of Fokien-Chekiang, but now of Fokien-Chekiang-Formosa. The Customs service, which had formerly been under the superintendence of the Tartar general of Foochow, was, from the first of December, 1887, placed under the local governor.

A thorough reorganization and redivisioning of the island was now necessitated. In former days, Formosa comprised one complete prefecture, four districts, and three sub-prefectures. Now the island became a province with four prefectures (Taipeh, Taiwan, Tainan, and Taitung), eleven districts, and three sub-prefectures.[1]

As a result of these changes and additions, the seat of government (which had been formerly at the old town of Taiwan-fu in the south, which city had been in turn the capital of the Dutch, Koxinga, and the Chinese,) was now removed temporarily to the new city of Taipeh, which had been lately in course of construction. Consequently the big southern city no longer remained the capital of the island, and was therefore not entitled to bear the name Taiwan (Formosa), but became instead, merely the capital or fu of the single prefecture Tainan. It was, therefore, renamed Tainan-fu.

1. THE ISLAND AS DIVIDED WHILE A PROVINCE OF THE CHINESE EMPIRE.

Circuit.	Prefectures.	Districts.	Sub-Prefectures.
Taiwan (Formosa)	Taipeh (Taihoku)	Tamsui Gilan. Hsiu-chu (Shinchiku).c	Kelung.
	Taiwan (Taichu) a	Taiwan (Taichu). Changwha (Shoka).. Yunliu (Unriu). Miaoli (Byoritsu).	Puli (Holisha).
	Tainan b..	Anping Kagi. Fangsha (Hozan). Hengchun (Koshun).	Panghu (Boko).d
	Taitung (Taito), a department at south-east end of island.		

　　　　a. Near Changwha.
　　　　b. The old city of Taiwan.
　　　　c. Formerly Teckcham.
　　　　d. The Pescadores.

In connection with this, it is necessary to go further and explain that it was the intention of the government to build a new capital city in the centre of the island near Changwha. Accordingly, the new city was laid out and the construction of official yamens commenced. The name of the new city became Taiwan-fu, or the capital city of Taiwan (Formosa), and it was also to be the seat of a new prefecture called Taiwan. These alterations resulted in much after confusion as to names. The maps, previous to the French war, show Taiwan-fu near the south-west coast, some two miles from Anping. Subsequent maps show it in the north-central part of the island, many miles from the coast. The reason of this has now been explained, and it will be necessary for the reader to bear in mind that, in the following pages, the old southern city is spoken of as TAINAN-FU and the new central city as TAIWAN-FU.

The alterations in the administration of the province likewise necessitated great changes in official positions in the island, and many new offices were formed.[1]

While the reorganization of the administration of the island was a great boon in many ways, it brought with it not only increased taxes to provide for the legitimate expenses of the new and greatly enlarged system, but also heavy extortions to satisfy the hoards of mandarins and their hangers-on who were now brought into office. The Chinese of Formosa were, therefore, inclined to look upon the changes as rather a mixed blessing. While Formosa was a prefecture of Fokien, taxes were only imposed on tea, camphor, and opium. Additional funds for the government were obtained from taxes on land and salt, while the Fokien government made an annual grant to the island of some $660,000 (Mexican). The return received from the above sources was not, however, sufficient to provide for the expenses of the new administration, introducing as it did improved defences, railways, and other expensive innovations. Accordingly, in May, 1886, the system of charging likin on native produce shipped outwards was instituted. Imports, with the exception of opium, which had been paying from $150 to $180 a chest for some years, were exempt. As tea and camphor had been previously taxed, and as these were the principal products of the north, the natives of the north had little to complain of; but in the central and southern districts, where sugar was placed at a considerable disadvantage by the new taxation, opposition to the likin was very marked both from Chinese and foreigners. In fact so much hostility was aroused towards the new Governor, Liu Ming-chuan, whom the Chinese looked upon as responsible for the impost, that His Excellency avoided travelling in the dissatisfied districts, and

---

1. The following official positions were established upon Formosa becoming a province :

CIVIL.	MILITARY.	
Governor and Commander-in-Chief stationed at Taipeh.	Chen-tai (Brigadier) stationed at Tainan.	
Lieutenant-Governor and Treasurer stationed at Taipeh.	Chen-tai (Brigadier) „ „	{ Pang-hu (Pescadores.)
Prefect stationed at Taipeh.		(at Hobe(Tamsui),
Prefect stationed at Taiwan.	Tung-ling (General of " braves ") stationed	{ at Kelung, and
Taotai and Acting Judge stationed at Tainan.		{ at points on the
Prefect stationed at Tainau.		(savage border.

on one occasion, upon visiting the big southern city of Tainanfu, he was actually imprisoned in his own yamen by the hostile populace, and upon gaining his freedom and returning to the north he never ventured in the south again. His popularity with the natives in the north also was not uninterrupted; for a short time after the taxation fiasco in the south, it was declared that foreign imports leaving a treaty port for other ports on the coast were liable to likin charges. This affected the natives in the north and resulted in immediate opposition so intense that the governor thought it wise to withdraw the offensive measure, at least for the time. After the first heat of anger had cooled down, the tax was revived, this time to remain. That the natives permitted this was good evidence that the Formosan populace had been brought under better control than in former years. One can scarcely imagine a more unjust method of raising revenue than this. Governor Liu had discriminated against his own kin who were so unfortunate as to live in any place in the island other than at the treaty ports, and made the poor struggling peasants in the country pay a heavy tax, from which the residents in the treaty ports, who were generally more wealthy, were entirely exempt. Camphor now again (November, 1887) became a government monopoly, merchants desiring to deal in the drug being obliged to purchase through the government offices. In spite of this, the demand for camphor was so slight during 1889, and the market price so low, that but little revenue was obtained. In 1890, however, a large demand for camphor arose, and the price of the drug went up twofold, so that the government was enabled to dispose of its camphor at $30 (silver) a picul (133 lbs.), a profit of $18, which brought in $116,694 revenue for the year. The re-establishment of the monopoly, which the reader will recollect was abolished as the result of consular protest in 1869, was plainly an infringement on treaty rights, and it was abolished in 1891, when an excise tax payable monthly on each still, commonly known as the "camphor stove tax," was substituted as a means of revenue. To this was also added a likin tax payable when the drug was transported to the port of shipment.

Having thus disposed of the financial question—always a disagreeable subject in China—it is a pleasure to refer to the reforms instituted and the great improvements made throughout the island with the intention of furthering its industrial development. Liu Ming-chuan, whatever else may be said against him, must be acknowledged to have been an intelligent, liberal-minded, progressive person, with none of the conceit and bigotry characteristic of the usual Chinese officials. Among the innovations introduced at his initiative may be counted many from foreign lands; and, from a backward, half savage prefecture, Formosa became known as the most progressive province of the whole empire. No sooner had peace been restored than the work of improvement was commenced. The strengthening of the island's defences was prominent in Liu's mind, and the construction of modern forts of the best designs, to be provided with heavy modern guns, Armstrongs and Krupps, was at once begun.

The temporary capital of the new province was placed at Taipehfu. No sooner had this been decided upon than the city began to assume a new appearance, reflecting the energetic spirit of the governor. In 1885, the work of reconstruction commenced. A substantial wall was built to surround the city, streets were rearranged and paved with stone. A capacious yamen was constructed and the streets lit with electricity; this, we believe, being the first instance of the official adoption of electricity in any part of the empire. It was later found, however, that the system was too expensive, and, with the exception of the yamen, which continued to be thus illuminated, the lights were withdrawn. Outside of the city and in Twatutia several streets were paved, and in 1888 Governor Liu introduced jinrikishas, the new roads having been constructed with this in view, by laying down in each street some two or three sets of parallel tracks constructed of long slabs of stone a foot wide, placed end to end. In between these tracks the streets were paved with cobble stones. That the jinrikishas might be well established the governor ran them at his own expense for some time, and then turned them over to the coolies.

Equal attention was given by this phenomenal Chinese official to inland communication. A cable steamer, the *Feicheu*, was purchased; and, in October, 1887, the laying of a cable from Anping to Dome Bay in the Pescadores was completed. While this was of little importance to the commercial world, there being scarcely any trade between Formosa and the Pescadores, it was of great value from a political standpoint, the strategical importance of the islands demanding that they should be in communication with the capital. Of greater interest to those having business in the island was the construction of the line between Tainanfu and Taipehfu, which was completed in March, 1888. This, together with the line previously constructed between Takow and Tainanfu, united the north and south. Of still greater benefit, both commercially and politically, was the construction of a cable line from Tamsui to Sharp Peak at the mouth of the Min river in Fokien, also completed in 1888, thus joining Formosa to the world's telegraphic system. The service in Formosa was placed under the superintendence of Emanuel Hansen, a Danish expert.

If the reader is acquainted with affairs in China and has noted the extremely conservative tendencies of the mandarins and "feng shui" worshipping literati, he will no doubt observe with some surprise the progressive spirit exhibited by Liu Ming-chuan. Although no railway had yet been constructed by officials in the whole Empire of China, Governor Liu decided that Formosa should have one. Aware that one of the great obstacles to the commercial development of the island was the lack of harbors, Governor Liu's attention was devoted to the forming of some practicable plan which might lessen these disadvantages. Kelung was the only harbor in the island available for the largest ships, and it was the governor's idea that, by improving the harbor and constructing a railway from north to south, he could convert Kelung into the shipping port, to the great advantage of commerce and peace; for it was anticipated that, with the railway to afford rapid transport, the inhabitants of Formosa could be better controlled. To obtain Imperial sanction to the undertaking, Governor Liu represented to the authorities that, if the capital was removed into the interior as they had recommended, it would be necessary, as there were no roads, to construct a railway from the new capital to one of the coast ports, preferably Kelung in the north. This proposition met with some opposition in Peking, but eventually Imperial approbation was obtained.

Early in March, 1887, the work was commenced, and to quiet anti-foreign critics the governor himself gave evidence of his interest in the enterprise by accompanying a German engineer, Mr. Becker, and personally supervising the marking out of the first four miles. The headquarters of the railway were established at Twatutia and the work was commenced at that point. This city stands in a plain which extends some seven miles towards Kelung, is nearly level, and consists of rice fields traversed by numerous irrigation streams. Consequently, the first few miles presented no difficulties other than the construction of many small bridges and culverts. Foreign engineers were employed to peg out the line, and soldiers were distributed along the route as fast as the work was ready ; the task of directing the labor being assigned to the officers in command. A 3 feet 6 inch gauge was adopted and 36 lb. steel rails used. The maximum gradient was 1 in 30 and curves of 5 chains minimum radius were permitted.

As there is much talk of railway construction in China at the present day, the details of the Formosan work here given may prove of interest and value. The foreigners worked under great disadvantages. They were without authority over the soldier laborers and their officers. The line as surveyed by them was frequently diverted, and the pegs which they had placed were often pulled up by the soldiers to be utilized as firewood. A level road bed and a minimum of curves was not recognized by the workmen as of much necessity : they gave the preference to their own eye rather than to the instruments, and were altogether inclined to go forward with the road much as if they were constructing a Chinese footpath through the savage district. Furthermore, the Chinese superintendents were very easily bribed. For a small compensation they would introduce alarming curves to avoid some grave in which the payee was interested. The course of the line was also dependent upon the amounts paid by the owners of rice fields. It is stated that the Chinese in charge frequently diverted the line out of its intended direction towards the property or grave of some rich farmer with the intention of inducing that individual to come forward with liberal bribes, whereupon the line would, according to their assertion, be changed. All this naturally annoyed the foreign engineers, and frequent complaints were made by them to the governor. But as that official had no other method of redress than through his generals, the bad work continued, as the officers were inclined to support their own officials and themselves rather than the foreigners. So intolerable was this that there were as many as five changes made in the head engineer. Owing to these obstructions, the line progressed so slowly that, in the spring of 1889, only eleven miles, commencing at Twatutia, had been completed. Regular traffic was then opened over this section.

From this point, the construction became more complicated, owing to the hills towards Kelung, and progress was correspondingly slower. If the

Chinese officials had been able to do bad work on the plains they were doubly able to make a mess of it in the hills. The first encounter was with a low spur which could have been tunnelled through easily, but through which the Chinese preferred to make a 60 feet cutting and then to bring the road up with embankments on each side. The cutting was accordingly commenced ; but, as the material handled was clay which softened under rain, it was alternately dug out by hand and filled in by nature, while the upper part became a quagmire. The engineers now advised that another route around the spur should be adopted or that a covered way should be erected as fast as the work through the cutting progressed, and that means should be taken to draw off the water. These plans were all rejected, however, and the Chinese continued to dig out as before. Sickness now broke out among the soldier navvies and eventually reached such proportions that native laborers had to be employed ; and, as they still made no satisfactory progress, the work had to be abandoned and the plan of an alternate route accepted, as had been formerly proposed by the engineers. Proceeding with the line, a hundred-foot iron bridge was constructed, another cutting, two embankments, four small bridges, and the line was brought up to the range of hills surrounding Kelung. Similar difficulties were encountered here as at the first hill. The engineers demanded that the principal hill should be tunnelled, and the Chinese declared in favor of a cutting. It was necessary to make a cutting on the side of the ridge for some distance, and the Chinese executed the work in their usual careless way. No drainage measures were taken, and as a result two extensive earth slips necessitated greatly increased labor. Work was now commenced on the tunnel. The Chinese refused, on the score of expense, to timber the sides and use props according to the plans of the engineers. On one occasion the roof fell, in and whenever rain occurred, much labor was required in clearing away the stuff brought down by the water. The climax was reached when the ends of the tunnel approached each other and it was discovered, to the dismay of the engineers, that the general in command had fixed the level of the heading at one end 14 feet higher than at the other. From the tunnel to Kelung was but a little over a mile, and here, perhaps, where, owing to the heavy grades, the best work was required, the worst on the whole road was done. The Chinese totally disregarded the survey laid out by the engineer, and as no foreigner was present to superintend the work, it was executed with such sharp curves and steep grades that it would have been impossible for any train to negotiate it. Upon an engineer inspecting the work, this fact was made known to the governor, and the line had to be altered. As it was the governor's desire, for economical reasons, to utilize as much of the old line as possible, only the most necessary changes were made. The line when completed was consequently at this section very imperfect and troublesome.[1]

In October, 1891, the road was completed to Kelung, and regular train-service was commenced on the 20 miles to Twatutia, the engines being driven by English engineers. The road terminated at a newly constructed

---

1. The Japanese have entirely reconstructed this portion of the line. New tunnels have replaced the heavy grades, the sharp curves have all been taken out, and the whole road now represents none of the extraordinary features for which the old one was famous.

wharf touching the harbor. Although well located, there was only some three feet of water off the wharf, and dredging was necessary before it could be of service. A dredger was accordingly purchased and for some three years was at work in the neighborhood of the terminus. It was a small machine and poorly cared for. As effective results were not obtained, its use was finally discontinued.

From Twatutia the line runs to the south. The first work of construction was to bridge the Tamsui river. The river had to be crossed at Twatutia, where it is about a quarter of a mile wide, although during the freshets it attains to much greater width. An iron bridge was on that account proposed by the engineers as the most serviceable. But the expense of this discredited it in the eyes of the Chinese directors, and accordingly a wooden bridge was erected (1889) by a Cantonese contractor. At the north end an iron swinging span centered in a masonry pier was erected, giving a clear passage of 23 feet. This was worked by hand and was opened at intervals every day to permit junks and large river boats to pass through. The bridge was 1,498 feet long, divided into 46 spans besides the draw.[1]

From the bridge the line ran over nearly level ground for some seven miles. It then ascended to a tableland on a maximum gradient of 1 in 30. The work progressed very slowly, and the line contained many unnecessary curves and heavy grades. In 1891, the line was opened for 20 miles southward, and by the end of 1893 it had been completed for the 20 additional miles to Hsin chu (Teck cham) when regular train-service was instituted over the whole 60 miles. Among the several foreigners who had been employed during the work of construction, W. Watson, C.E., held the position of chief engineer and H. Mitchell as locomotive superintendent, while H. C. Matheson, C.E., who had arrived in the island to fill the position of superintendent of the coal mines, became in 1887 consulting engineer of the railway.

Although the railway had been surveyed to the south of the island terminating at Takow and some of the material from the abortive Woosung railway was shipped to the south, no portion of the line south of Hsin-chu was constructed. It seems that the progressive schemes of Governor Liu were not looked upon with favor in Peking. The high officials, perhaps not without reason, feared that if Kelung were converted into a fine harbor with wharfs, docks, and godowns, and with steam communication with the interior and extensive coal mines at hand, it would be a temptation too strong for ambitious countries on the lookout for coaling stations to withstand. Accordingly, nothing more was done at Kelung, so that instead of its becoming the great shipping port which had been anticipated, even the old trade dropped off year by year. The railway became a mere passenger line, the service not being sufficiently reliable to be entrusted with freight. The government collieries were now closed, and frequently months elapsed without the appearance of a single foreign vessel. A big white building of the usual style of foreign architecture was the ghostly remnant of the last foreign firm long since gone. As time went on, matters grew worse and

1. This bridge, after having been subject to considerable repairs in 1895, was totally destroyed by a freshet and gale in August, 1897.

worse, until, in 1894, two Custom House officers, the only foreigners in Kelung, wearily spent their days in enforced idleness, watching for the smoke of a foreign steamer. Kelung was dead! It might have dropped off the island completely without causing the least inconvenience to any one save the pitiably poverty-stricken natives who lived in their squalid huts in the tumble-down village.[1]

1. The author had the privilege of travelling on the Formosa railway on several occasions early in 1895, and can personally vouch for its wonderful properties. The manner of running the railway was no less novel. The assistance of foreigners had long since been dispensed with, and the road and stock were now entirely in the hands of Chinese. Upon entering the railway station at Twatutia, my attention was at once attracted to the locomotive which was to carry us to our destination. Never in my experience had I seen one in like condition. The brass work had turned to a dirty black, the iron work to a speckled brown, and, like a wounded warrior, it was bandaged from head to foot. Still with all its blemishes it held steam, and a grimy Chinese was shoveling in coal at a fearful rate, that there might be no deficiency. Fearful of the consequences, but unshaken in my resolve to ride to Kelung, I entered an affair which resembled a stock car fitted with seats. The so-called passenger coach was of the short type familiar to travellers in Europe, and was divided into two compartments, or rather had one small section, seating four, reserved at one end but opening into the main compartment. A long seat running along each side, accommodated passengers, and in the centre, also parallel with the car, ran a sort of elevated baggage stand apparently intended for small baggage. A door and a small platform were at each end. No attempt at decoration was visible, although the small first class section had a poor apology for cushions. Having provided myself with a first class ticket, which created considerable astonishment, I took a seat in the small compartment, and was soon joined by a greasy railway guard and a conductor whose only claim to respectability was a very unsanitary silk-jacket which had long since lost its beauty. Upon my arrival being proclaimed throughout the car, other unsavory individuals gave me their company, and to my chagrin I observed that they were permitted to avail themselves of this privilege though possessed of only second class tickets. The car was now fast filling up with all sorts of animal freight. A crate of chickens, two large round baskets with three young pigs in each, innumerable pairs of chickens and ducks, a quarter of pork, baskets of vegetables, and all sorts and varieties of boxes, bundles, and other goods. There seemed to be no rule as to what should be carried in the coaches, and in the present instance it was difficult to tell which had been given the preference—live stock, freight, or human beings. We now got under way and whizzed along the richly cultivated plain stretching Kelung-wards from Twatutia. For the first few miles all went smoothly, and then we commenced to negotiate the mountain passes; at least so it would seem to one inattentive to the passing landscape. But to my surprise I found we were still on the level plain and that the curves and grades could not be attributed to any irregularity in the earth's surface. Still they were there, and away we went swinging around at a high rate of speed with the passengers clutching on to the seats and windows, and in a few moments swinging back into line again. On looking out of the rear coach the track appeared something like a pair of gigantic cork-screws flattened out. But now the conductor awakened to his duties and commenced the collection of fares. But few were provided with tickets, the others desiring to pay, or as it proved, not to pay, on the train. I had already been treated to much that was novel in railroad management; but I think the collecting of fares was the greatest revelation. The conductor first went through and collected tickets and fares from such as were willing to deliver or pay the equivalent in full, and then started after the delinquents. They comprised a large proportion and appeared greatly opposed to adding their mite to the collection. Still our conductor was obdurate and stuck to each one until he got something out of him. The passengers commonly produced a small string of cash which they handed to the conductor who made a rough estimate of their value, ordinarily to find a great shortage. He then demanded the balance due and the wrangling commenced. At it they went at the top of their voices until the passenger by dealing out a few cash at a time had paid somewhere near the amount, or by greater vocal power had worn out the conductor. It is quite safe to say that not a single individual of this class paid the full amount nominally known as the fare. But regardless of this labor, the conductor was no doubt pleased; it permitted him to abstract his "squeeze" which would not have been possible had all provided themselves with tickets. Having disposed of this, the conductor next tackled the destitutes; at least such they were according to their own distressing tales. Three or four of these refused absolutely to produce anything, and the wrangling recommenced. The conductor now searched the clothes of the offenders, and to me it appeared that affairs were coming to a crisis. But I was wrong. From a gesticulating, raving madman whom it appeared nothing but blood would satisfy, the conductor instantly assumed a most perfect composure, as though his work had been one round of pleasure, and then seizing a chicken from one of the delinquents, a sort of combination pillow and small trunk from a second, and a roll of filthy clothing from a third, he returned to my small compartment, tranquil and apparently satisfied. Whether or not the stuff was redeemed on the arrival of the train at Kelung I cannot say.

One more feature may strike the reader as novel. The Chinese in charge of the stations along the line actually worked in opposition to one another. They conducted the business on the principle of personal enhancement, and only paid in as much of the funds collected as they thought necessary to enable them to retain their positions. Especially was this observable in the shipment of camphor. A foreign camphor merchant informed me that, previous to the delivery of the camphor at the station, it was common to send word to the agents at some two or three of the different neighboring stations and to set them bidding against each other for its shipment from their station. It was then delivered to the lowest bidder and by him forwarded to its destination, while the lucky agent pocketed a generous share

Although the period under review was one of comparative progress in many ways, no advance was made in gaining control over the savages. In fact there was greater bloodshed during these few years than there had been for a considerable period before. Liu Ming-chuan had very ambitious ideas as to civilizing savages. At the close of the Franco-Chinese war in 1886, he announced that it was his intention to subdue the various tribes and open their territory to Chinese trade. But not only did he not succeed in this, but, on his departure from the island, affairs were worse than they had been for years, and places that had formerly been in the occupation of Chinese settlers were then abandoned and desolate, especially in the central section of the island. In 1886, the headmen of the aborigines of the plains and a few others of the more peaceful tribes accepted the invitation of Governor Liu and visited him at Changwha, where they were very kindly treated, and eventually consented to some sort of an agreement by which the border savages were to cease killing Chinese and furthermore were to engage in agricultural work, Liu promising to pay monthly a dollar's worth of rice to each laborer. Just and reasonable as this plan would appear to one unacquainted with the savages, it was the reverse of successful when put into operation. For with the wilder hill-tribes this act of their fellow savages was considered equivalent to entering the ranks of the enemy, and they consequently lost no opportunity of giving evidence of their disapproval. The unfortunate savages of the plains and border districts were now placed between two fires, on one side they dared not refuse allegiance to Liu, and on the other the hill savages were murdering members of their band at every opportunity.

In the previous year, 1885, warfare had been continual; the savages had adopted a specially aggressive attitude, even coming out of the hills and attacking the plain villages; and the Chinese had revenged themselves by firing the forests on the border, thus compelling the savages to withdraw. Naturally this rendered camphor manufacture quite out of the question, and in truth the export for this year was only three piculs. The existence of the camphor trade demanded some strict measures on the part of the military, and in 1886, the famous Ling Chiau-tong marched 1,500 of his soldiers against the tribes to the south-east of Tokoham and inland from Changwha. Although the campaign that ensued was but little more than mere skirmishing, yet in two months the Chinese losses were 500, and no advantage whatsoever had been gained by them. Perhaps the greatest service the expedition rendered was to concentrate the attention of the savages on the west, thus permitting a large Chinese force to approach the savage border on the east coast near Gilan without attracting too much attention. In 1887, a general and 400 soldiers were killed, and additional forces were sent to Gilan, hostilities on the west side being for the time abandoned. On the east, fighting of greater or less severity continued for many months, resulting in the death of Lau, a nephew of Liu Ming-chuan.

of the charges. There was absolutely no uniformity in rates, and this system naturally became so un-satisfactory and unreliable that but little freight was entrusted to the tender mercies of the employés of the Formosan Imperial Railway. If the Chinese intend to dispense with the assistance of foreigners in their railways now in course of construction, no improvement over the above can be expected, and it is doubtful, unless some decided improvement in the officials is made, if they will ever become large carriers of any except government freight.

It seems that Lau entered the savage district to the south of Gilan with 180 Chinese soldiers. About a thousand savages surrounded them during the night and killed the whole party with the exception of some two or three soldiers who escaped and carried the shocking news to the governor. This was a severe blow to Liu.

If the governor's policy was not a success, its failure could not be attributed to lack of energy on his part. In 1886, Liu had even taken the field himself, and for several months had suffered the privations of a soldier in the far from comfortable, we might even say unsafe, border districts. But little good resulted, and Liu's "forward policy" had to be abandoned. True, however, to the traditions of his class he permitted no rumor of failure to reach the authorities in Peking. On the contrary, he officially declared (and his declaration was published in the Peking Gazette) that, as a result of his labors, 478 villages with an aggregate population of 88,000 savages had submitted to Imperial rule. Just exactly where the governor found them all is not stated. Even had he included the already conquered and peaceful Pepohoans, who had not been engaged in the warfare described, and could not, therefore, be rightly counted as new subjects, the 478 villages must have stretched his powers of imagination to the utmost.

In the spring of 1891, the Chinese camphor men and the savages near Tokoham (Taikokan) engaged in several lively combats, in which the Chinese soldiers were eventually involved and which resulted in trouble of a more serious nature than even some of the previous affairs. Governor Liu, however, withdrew from the island on account of ill health during the month of June[1] and left the exciting savage problem in the hands of his successor.

On several occasions the savages had swooped down upon the little Chinese villages, killing a dozen or so of the peasants and flying back

1. Soon after the departure of Liu Ming-chuan from Formosa, he responded to the calls of the emperor, and, despite failing eyesight, occupied himself with official duties at Peking, where he was attached to the staff of Prince Kung. Important military commands were offered him by the throne during the war with Japan ; but owing to his ill health these were refused, and eventually he obtained Imperial permission to retire into private life, in which he remained until his death.

Liu Ming-chuan was a man of wide reputation. The Taiping rebellion some forty years prior to his death afforded him the first opportunity of showing his metal. By organizing volunteer bands he protected his native province, Anhui, against the insurgents so successfully as to attract the attention of Li Hung-chang, who at once availed himself of Liu's services. At the commencement of the Franco-Chinese campaign Liu Ming-chuan was sent to Formosa, at that time one of the most important positions.

He filled his office very creditably. The French were unable to advance further than Kelung, and he inflicted on them at least one severe defeat. But it was at the close of the hostilities that his ability was shown most conspicuously. He entirely reconstructed the official organization of Formosa—a great task in itself—and introduced various foreign improvements, until the island in a few years became known as by far the most progressive province of China. Liu as governor made mistakes, but the evil resulting was slight compared to the great good he accomplished. He was capable, liberal minded, and progressive ; friendly to foreigners, and a great believer in foreign institutions. He died in 1896, and in an Imperial decree his demise is thus recorded :

"A few years ago we regretfully permitted him to retire into private life owing to serious maladies contracted while serving his country. Recently, we were anticipating the pleasure of receiving him again into our councils, to rely upon his advice and to shower upon him further marks of our respect and admiration of his high qualities, when the sad news of his lamented death now reaches us, which we receive with great regret. As a last token of our appreciation of Liu Ming-chuan's loyal services to the dynasty, we hereby command that he be granted the posthumous title of Senior Guardian of the Heir Apparent and let his funeral obsequies be conducted on lines usually granted to the rank of a Governor. Special memorial temples are further ordered to be built in the provinces where he has served, and let his martial deeds be recorded in the dynastic history. Any 'black marks' against Liu's name in Boards are also hereby ordered to be erased, and let the said Boards further report to us what pecuniary grants should be made to the deceased officer's family." Here follows a list of honors conferred upon his sons.

to their forest homes with the heads. The savage raids becoming more frequent, the governor sent a force under a general to punish the savage village, Ma-su, which, besides its collection of peasants' heads, was the proud possessor of the heads of eight Chinese soldiers. In this the officer was successful; but after destroying the village the general became ambitious, and with the intention of controlling the aborigines, he distributed detachments in many villages along the savage border. This was more to the liking of the savages, and on several occasions they were successful in burning the outposts and killing many of the men comprising these small garrisons. The soldiers of two large garrisons and 1000 local braves under the command of Lin Wei-yuan were then marched out to Tokoham to inflict heavy punishment on the troublesome barbarians. But scarcely had the large force entered the savage district before a still larger body of savages had surrounded them and cut off their supplies and, more serious still, their line of retreat. Upon learning of this predicament, reinforcements were immediately sent and the army extricated from its alarming position. Towards the end of the year the savages were called upon to surrender, but to no purpose; and in an engagement which took place soon after, there was considerable loss of life on each side, including two high military officers, and two equally high civil officers wounded among the Chinese. While some slight success was eventually obtained by the Chinese, who were able to burn three villages, still at the close of the year nothing had been gained, and the Formosan governor memorialized the throne for more troops. The next year neither side was much inclined to aggression, and consequently the troubles gradually quieted down, although they were far from being settled. In 1892-3, especially during the autumn when it assumed a more active phase, warfare was almost continual. In 1894, new outbreaks and turbulence of a severe nature were reported, and up to the actual occupation of the island by the Japanese, scarcely a month elapsed without finding the Chinese braves engaged with the savages at some point along the disputed border. Nor did the north have a monopoly of the savage troubles. Engagements between savages and Chinese were also frequent in the south, and in 1892 it was found necessary to send a force of 1,200 men into one of the southern districts.

One horrible feature of the campaign against the savages was the sale by the Chinese in open market of savage flesh. Impossible as it may seem that a race with such high pretensions to civilization and religion should be guilty of such barbarity, yet such is the truth. After killing a savage, the head was commonly severed from the body and exhibited to those who were not on hand to witness the prior display of slaughter and mutilation. The body was then either divided among its captors and eaten, or sold to wealthy Chinese and even to high officials, who disposed of it in a like manner. The kidney, liver, heart, and soles of the feet were considered the most desirable portions, and were ordinarily cut up into very small pieces, boiled, and eaten somewhat in the form of soup. The flesh and bones were boiled, and the former made into a sort of jelly. The Chinese profess to believe, in accordance with an old superstition, that the eating of savage flesh will give them strength and courage. To some this may appear as a partial excuse for this horrible custom; but even that falls through, if one stops to think that superstitious beliefs are at the bottom of cannibalism as practised by the most savage tribes of the world. During the outbreak of 1891, savage flesh was brought in—in baskets—the same as pork, and sold like pork in the open markets of Tokoham before the eyes of all, foreigners included; some of the flesh was even sent to Amoy to be placed on sale there. It was frequently on sale in the small Chinese villages near the border, and often before the very eyes of peaceful groups of savages who happened to be at the place. The savages, bad as they may be, are not cannibals, and though the victim's head is severed from the body, it is carried away as a certificate of the warrior's prowess, and the body remains untouched where it falls. Although the subject is dealt with at length in a subsequent chapter, it may be well to state here that the Chinese ordinarily deserved all the punishment they received from the savages. Their treatment of these children of the forest was always cruel in the extreme. Contracts were made which were never intended to be fulfilled, and all the deceitful tricks that cunning Chinese could contrive to deprive them, not only of property but even of life, were played upon the ignorant savages.

Some years had now elapsed without any serious popular outbreak against the officials. The authorities, therefore, considered the spirit of the people sufficiently humbled to permit of the imposition of new burdens upon them. A tax on rice fields was much favored by the officials as it would produce the greatest revenue, and believing the time opportune an attempt was made to put this tax in force during the year 1887.

Exactions to which the rich were alone subjected gave the masses but little concern; but when a tax was proposed which would decrease directly the earnings of all, the people were up in arms in an instant. In many of the more peaceful districts, opposition took the form of large demonstrations in which village leaders harangued their followers and numerous petitions were framed to be presented to the local officers. In the border districts, however, where many are armed to protect themselves from the savages, the disapproval was expressed in a more practical manner. One night, thousands arose and seizing Yunlin and other villages in the vicinity, marched on, gathering recruits along the way, and attacked the big inland walled city of Changwha (Shoka). New fortifications had been erected on the hill Hakkezan (Paquasoan) overlooking the city, and the government forces made such a stout defence that the rebels were unable to effect an entrance and were obliged to content themselves with capturing the neighboring villages. Eventually a large number of troops was assembled at Changwha, and, after a few weeks of skirmishing, peace was again established, while the authorities made some trifling concessions, with great show, as evidence of their beneficence.

Upon the retirement of Liu Ming-chuan in June, 1891, Shao Yu-lien became governor of the island and took over the seals of office on the 25th of the following November. Although the new incumbent appeared to be enterprising and liberal-minded, he took no steps to carry out the progressive plans of Liu Ming-chuan, with the exception of some minor improvements, the construction of a powder-mill, etc.

Shao held office as governor until October 21, 1894, when he gave over charge of the island to Treasurer Tang Ching-sung, who became acting-governor and was the last officer under the Chinese regime to hold this position. His career does not end here, however, for Tang plays a leading part in the chapters yet to come.

NOTE.—The wrecks during the period 1886—1895 were few in number, but the loss of life was very great. Out of nine vessels there were over six hundred lives lost.

1886—January 26th. The German barque *Guaymas* went on shore about 7 miles south of Saracen Head and became a total wreck.

. ———June 5th. The German three masted schooner *Wilhelm Meyer* was wrecked in the Takow inner harbor.

———September 11th. The German schooner *Niederhof*, lying in the roadstead of Anping, broke from her moorings during a south-west gale and went on shore about 2½ miles north of the harbor; a total wreck.

1887—September 15th. The governor of Formosa's S.S. *Wayling (Waverly)* struck on a reef to the north of Round Island, Pescadores, and became a total wreck. The captain and three officers, who were foreigners, and three hundred and sixty-six Chinese were drowned.

1888—October 12th. The governor of Formosa's S.S. *Wayling* (No. 2) struck on a reef to the N.W. of the Pescadores and became a total wreck. Loss of life large—number not known.

1889———The British ship *Anglo Indian* was wrecked between Namkam and Paksa Point. No sooner did the vessel strike than it was attacked and plundered by the Chinese villagers. A portion of the crew were stripped of all their clothes and driven inland, and fourteen others, while attempting to escape, were drowned at sea.

During the years 1890 and 1891, there were no foreign ships wrecked on the Formosa coast. This is notable as being the first period of even a year's duration, for fifty years, without a wreck on the Formosan or Pescadores coast.

1892—During the 9th, 10th, and 11th of October a fearful typhoon raged in the Formosan channel, destroying many native craft and two foreign steamers as given below.

———October 9th. The Norwegian steamer *Normand*, a vessel of 2,400 tons loaded with coal, was caught in the typhoon, and on the evening of the 9th carried on the rocks off the Pescadores, and was soon a total wreck. Upon striking, a number of the crew went up in the rigging and hung there for two hours. The mast at length broke and precipitated them into the sea. Two of the number by clinging to the wreckage were washed ashore the next day at Pachau Island about 18 miles distant from the scene of the wreck. The Chinese treated them very kindly, and eventually they were picked up by the small Anping steamer *Sin Taiwan* which had come out with Consuls Merz and Warren, Dr. Myers, and Mr. Hastings, to search for survivors of the *Bokhara*. Although it was thought that others from the doomed vessel might be found alive on some of the numerous islands of the group, this proved a vain hope. The officers and crew numbered twenty-six.—Twenty-four were lost. All Norwegians. The position where the vessel was lost was afterwards ascertained to be off or on the Tortoise Rock, two and a half miles S. W. of Sand Island.

———October 11th. The English steamship *Bokhara*, an old but powerful vessel of the P. and O. Company, departed from Shanghai on the 8th of October for Europe viá Hongkong with the homeward mails. On the 10th, upon entering the Formosa Channel, the *Bokhara* encountered a mountainous sea, and on the 11th, she struck the full force of the typhoon. In the course of the day the vessel became unmanageable, all life boats and everything movable was washed overboard, and the smoking room smashed in by the heavy seas which swept over her. At 9.45 p m. the gravest mishap which had so far befallen the unfortunate vessel occurred. Three huge seas sweeping over her smashed the after skylights, the stoke hole doors, and put out the fires. Then it was recognised that the ship was entirely helpless and there was nothing to do but await the end. That was not long delayed, for at half past eleven, at what seemed the very height of the terrible storm, the *Bokhara* struck the rocks with a terrible crash, a great sea swept over the deck, and within two minutes the doomed ship had disappeared; and with the exception of a few on deck every soul on board sank with her. Out of one hundred and forty-eight persons there were but twenty-three survivors. Among the passengers lost were the members of the Hongkong Cricket Club who were returning from Shanghai. The wreck was one of the most distressing that had ever occurred in Eastern Seas.

1894———November. The American barque *Mary. L. Stone* was wrecked near Steep Island, N. E. coast of Formosa. There was no loss of life, but the vessel and her cargo became a total loss.

CHAPTER XVIII

THE JAPANESE OCCUPATION OF THE PESCADORES AND WAR PREPARATIONS IN FORMOSA.

1894 - 1895.

Japanese occupation of Formosa mooted—The writer's journey to the island—Crossing the Formosan channel—An adventurous journey—Arrival at Tamsui—Geographical remarks on the north—Nomenclature causes much confusion—Rumors of arrival of Japanese forces—Chinese tales—Thousands of Chinese seek safety on mainland—News of the armistice—The writer interviews the governor—Rewards for Japanese heads—The governor's explanation—The writer obtains permission to accompany Chinese forces—The island's military forces—Schedule of war prizes —French overtures to Pescadores commander—Liu Yung fu suspicious—Formosa offered to England—Japanese attack the Pescadores—The strategical value of Pescadores long recognized—The campaign in the islands—The Japanese victorious—News of defeat causes panic among Formosan Chinese—Vigorous efforts to strengthen the island's defences—Chinese soldiers—The system of enlisting— Anxiety among foreigners—Riotous soldiers—Serious loss of life—Chinese officials without authority—German blue jackets landed to afford protection—Position critical—British gunboat " Redbreast" arrives—Governor Tang warns foreigners and declares his people beyond control—English marines landed. U.S.S. " Concord" pays flying visit—Rows and riots of daily occurrence—Turbulent condition in country—Cantonese soldiers possess themselves of Pat-li-hun village— Disturbances in Kapsulan district—Enforced military contributions—Doubtful honors—An improvised gunboat—Shore life of the foreign guards.

DURING the summer of 1894, war broke out between the empires of Japan and China. The following spring, hostilities were discontinued.

Some months before the signing of the Treaty of Peace between the two nations, the island of Formosa came into the range of possibilities as a future possession of Japan. The Eastern press, usually alert, had on this subject but little to say. And so well had the Japanese succeeded in keeping secret their designs that, even up to the departure of the transports for the Pescadores, the newspapers were filled with matter pertaining to the march on Peking, with scarcely a reference to Formosa. The well known American journalist, the late Col. John Cockerill, of the *New York Herald*, however, from the moment of his arrival in Japan was of opinion that Formosa and the Pescadores were prizes that the Japanese intended to obtain either by direct conquest or cession by treaty. So convinced of this was he that, in the middle of February, while the other correspondents in the empire were preparing for the march on Peking, he proposed that the present author (who had come to the East as war correspondent for a number of American journals) should at once start for Formosa. From this time onward, therefore, the events narrated come under my own personal observation.

It was at that time impossible to get definite information as to the island or the Pescadores; there were no books in the English language obtainable; and to the English speaking people in the East generally, Formosa was a land of tea, camphor, savages, and fever. No more definite information could be obtained. It was Colonel Cockerill's suggestion that the trip should be made as quickly and quietly as possible, and that I should be at work on the ground before the arrival of the Japanese. With this in view I left Japan at the end of February, 1895, via China ports, the only route then open, and after a delay of eight days in Shanghai I arrived on March 21st, 1895, at Amoy, which is directly across the channel from Formosa.

I found Amoy in a considerable state of excitement over rumors which, as later ascertained, were due to a Reuter telegram to the effect that the Japanese fleet had established a blockade of North Formosa. The result of this was that the comfortable Douglas steamship *Formosa*, leaving the day before for Tamsui, had refused to carry Chinese passengers, and the owner of the *Peking*, a very small steamer indeed for ocean traffic, had decided to profit by the *Formosa's* fears and carry over the passengers and cargo that had been left behind, the captain having instructions to steam back to Amoy in case the boat was not allowed to land; extra supplies of coal, distributed all about the deck in bags for this emergency, being provided. Fortunately arriving just in time, I engaged the only passenger cabin in the boat, and after a four hours' stay in Amoy, the little craft, loaded down to the water's edge and with 170 Chinese packed in between the rails on the lower deck, got under way, with a stiff wind ahead and the prospect of a rough sea outside. After three hours' steaming, the wind increased and we were soon battling with a heavy north-east gale. The lower deck was but a few feet above the water line, and the miserable Chinese crowded together there were constantly submerged, their piteous howling and frightened cries rising above the roar of the storm. With no protection, every wave threatening to sweep them overboard, it ultimately became a matter of life and death, and the captain changed his course and eventually headed the *Peking* in towards the Chinese coast which we had left but a short time before. Here we found a satisfactory harbor at Lioloo Bay.

By three o'clock next morning the storm had abated, and we again entered the channel. After breakfast, passage tickets were collected from the Chinese. It was to me, a "new hand" in China, a very interesting operation, and the captain's method of securing the required fare, from a quartette of celestials who were, according to their own testimony, in absolute poverty, was as novel as it was effective. At his orders they were brought upon the upper deck forward, and there secured by tying their queues to an awning spar where they were left to bewail the meanness of the "foreign dog" who had the effrontery to demand passage money from them. After a few bad lurches of the steamer, one of the four paupers found somewhere up his sleeve the required $3, and was released. In a few moments another one signified his willingness to produce, and was allowed to go to his companions, from whom he took up a collection of something over $1.50, which was accepted for his passage. A few more plunges of the steamer, which threatened to scalp the two remaining, brought from one a silver chop dollar and a string of two or three hundred "cash," which although great in bulk had a value of only twenty or thirty cents, and he was given his liberty. The remaining vagabond producing nothing but howls, the captain finally relented, and he re- turned to his friends with the satisfied smile of one who has played and won.

The captain, a kind-hearted man and a careful seaman, I believe, had a Chinese crew and two foreign officers: an engineer dark enough to be a Lascar and a mate who did the best he could, but who seemed to know very little about the use of charts, and furthermore was at a great disadvan- tage from being deaf. The result was that the captain found but little opportunity for rest while at sea. The engineer, who had apparently arrived on board at Amoy in a sober condition, had immediately proceeded to get drunk, and by the time we were under way was full seas over. This did not tend to make a disagreeable journey any more pleasant for me, and after learning of an incident which might have resulted fatally to all on board, I began to consider my safe arrival at Tamsui very doubtful. It was after the heavy gale had forced us to turn back towards the China coast. Every one aboard was on the alert, with the possible exception of the foreign engineer. The little craft was so battered about by the storm that I was unable to keep in my narrow bunk and was forced to take up quarters on the floor. Every wave splashed up against the cabin door and threatened to break it in, although my cabin was adjoining the pilot house above the upper deck. With but a partition between, I could hear the captain's commands above the roar of the storm. To give orders to the deaf mate it was necessary to send a Chinese boy to bring him to the side of the captain, who then shouted in the mate's ear until he signified that he understood. After plunging along in the darkness, we neared the China coast, when suddenly, to the great alarm of the captain, he saw rising before him what appeared to be a rocky cliff. He grasped the handle of the engine-room telegraph, ringing vigorously to reverse, but there was no answer. Again he rang and again no answer. Now thoroughly alarmed, he ran to the ventilator leading down to the engine room, shouted loudly, blew his whistle shrilly, and still there was no answer, while the rugged cliff ahead seemed almost upon us. It appeared even now too late to avert a catastrophe ; but, leaving the pilot house, the captain ran below down into the engine-room, and there lay the engineer in a drunken sleep before the engines. One can imagine the emotions of the captain, who with his own hands reversed the engines, and, awakening the Chinese assistant, placed him in charge. We were to be spared, however, for the fancied rocks proved to be but a bank of heavy fog through which we were soon passing.

After three days battlirg with the gale, we arrived at ten o'clock on the morning of March 23rd off the island, and in sight of our destination. The storm had subsided as suddenly as it had risen three days before. The rushing waves of yesterday had quieted down into a gentle ripple, and after our cold, wet, miserable journey, the bright warm sun bathing the whole scene with radiance was welcome to me no less than to the shivering, half-drowned Chinese down below. As we neared the shore, a broad river sparkling in the sunlight stretched on ahead until lost in a chaos of Chinese shipping, junks, cargo boats, lumber rafts, and sampans—with the high masts and shining funnel of a foreign steamer standing out proudly above them all. To the right and left rose high hills of uninterrupted verdure. Further back to-wards the interior, were other ranges ever increasing in height, and varying from the rich green of the foot hills to the delicate blue of the last range, the summits of which were lost in soft, grey clouds. If the Portuguese made their first visit on a day like this, I can well understand their enthusiasm and foin with them in the exclamation of joy—" Ilha Formosa," " Ilha Formosa " —with which they greeted their first view of this garden spot.

After passing over a troublesome bar, which admits no steamers draw-ing more than some 13 feet, we dropped anchor in the quiet waters of the river in front of the Chinese Custom House on the north bank. Above us on a hill two hundred feet high dotted with magnificent building sites, could be seen the old Dutch fort,—to all appearance as strong and formidable as on the day when it was built, nearly two hundred and fifty years ago. Near by stood a red brick building, the residence of the British consul. Further on were missionary schools, and, not far from them, residences occupied by mission-aries and Custom House officers. Along the bank on the north side of the river were numerous small structures and mud shanties, with one large foreign building occupied as a shipping office for the Douglas line of steamers. This was all that could be seen of the village of Hobé, or Tamsui, as it is usually known. Still through this unpretentious little port the chief trade of the island is conducted. In addition to the ordinary activity of the place, squads of soldiers in their picturesque uniforms were seen here and there, moving ammunition, unearthing old guns, etc., while on the north side on a spur stretching towards the sea could be seen a large body of troops erecting earthworks and improving the defences of a fort. On the southern hills, distant about a mile and a half, were just visible the earthworks of a newly erected battery. This was my introduction to Formosa.

Before proceeding further, let us take a look at the map. We note that the extreme north of the island forms a large promontory with Hobe (Tamsui) on the west and Kelung on the east, there being only about 5′

difference in latitude between the two places.   By sea the distance is about thirty miles, but by railway via Twatutia (Daitotei), to Kelung which is the usual passenger route, the distance is about thirty-three miles.   At Hobe from the west side of the promontory extends inland, in a south-easterly direction, the Tamsui river, and upon it, ten miles from its mouth, is situated the walled city of Taipeh-fu, (Taihoku), the capital of the island.   Adjoining this to the south and west is the old city of Banka, and to the north the settlement of Twatutia (Daitotei), where the foreigners live and where the majority of Chinese tea merchants have their quarters.   All these are some-times referred to under the common name of Tamsui.   In reality, with the exception of Hobe, they are but suburbs of Taipeh (Taihoku), the capital.

The term Tamsui was formerly used in a most liberal way; it might mean the harbour, the river, the villages of Hobe, Twatutia, and Banka, or the whole northern district.   At present, the Japanese confine the word to the name of a river, and a port at the mouth of this river.   With the advent of the Japanese, the nomenclature became very confusing, for one more name or, more correctly speaking, a new pronunciation, was added to every namable place and thing in the island.   The name still remained the same so far as meaning was concerned, but the Japanese pronunciation of the Chinese characters was given, and the two frequently sounded about as much alike as Paris and Sonderhausen.   Thus, a man might give as his place of residence, Daitotei, Twatutia, Taihoku, Taipeh or Taipehfu, and still refer to the same place.   Of late there has been, fortunately, a tendency to use only the Japanese pronunciation, and foreign merchants residing at the capital or its foreign suburb now usually give their mail address as Taihoku or Daitotei.   These names are not yet, however, recorded internationally as telegraphic addresses.[1]   As the island is now a Japanese possession, the Chinese names should be permitted to fall into disuse.   This will simplify the nomenclature problem greatly, as fortunately there is scarcely any variation in the Roman spelling of the Japanese pronunciations.   The Roman spelling of the Chinese pronunciation is frequently given in as many as six or more different ways by as many so called authorities.   Tamsui, Tamshuy, Tamshui, Tamsoui, Tansui, are all one, likewise Changwha, Changhwa, Changhoa, Chamhue, Chanhua, Tchanghoua, to which now is added the Japanese pronunciation Shoka.   Hobé struggles along with nine different spellings all the way from Kobi, the English spelling of the Japanese pronunciation, to Hou-ouei.

I found business much disturbed in the north of the island, the uncer-tainty of the situation being the principal cause.   The situation gave full play to the Chinese love of prevarication, and descriptions of furious battles with the Japanese were in vogue long before these sturdy warriors had even left Japan.   Day after day, the same reports, were disseminated, sometimes brought to you confidentially, as though the matter was a great secret, and again published broadcast, frequently with proclamations on the walls, but

1. The following Formosan towns are recorded internationally as telegraphic addresses:—Akoten, Auping, Bioritsu, Changwha, Giran, Hokuto, Horio, Horisha, Hozan, Kagee, Kelung, Koro, Koshun, Pescadores, Makong, Rokuko, Singchoi, Shinyeisho, Soo, Taichu, Taikakan, Taiko, Tainan, Taipeh, Taito, Takow, Tamsui, Toshiyen, and Toroku.

always equally false and always just as improbable, if one gave them but a moment's thought. Still, the Chinese with childlike confidence believed in them implicitly and would cast them aside only when a new report came to replace them. The fact that the old ones had been again and again proven false was no obstacle to sincere belief in the new ones.

So things continued day after day, the timid being incited to pack up and seek safety on the mainland. Many wealthy Chinese were the first to leave, with such treasure as they could carry. Movable property was stored away in such quarters as appeared to offer some security, and the poorer people sought safety for their valuables by burying them in the ground. As time progressed, even the shopkeepers disposed of their stocks and closed their shops. All day long the streets were filled with carriers; and river boats, loaded down with the miscellaneous truck of a Chinese household and crowned with the whole family on top, found their way slowly down to the port. To these little family parties, except, perhaps, to the laughing babies, there was nothing amusing or interesting in this hurried departure from a land which they had selected as their home. Besides, China meant harder work and less pay, and for some, perhaps, it meant starvation. It was not that they feared Japanese rule as they understood it; but the air was filled with mystery and uncertainty. Weeks of anxious expectation of something about to happen, some dreadful calamity coming to overwhelm them, had been too great a strain to support. The mandarins did not help them in any way; for with obscure proclamations about horrible black dwarfs who would carry away the women, kill the children, and reduce the men to slavery, they excited consternation among the wealthy and drove the poor into the army with the hope of keeping the foe at bay.

Such was the condition of affairs in early April. The telegraphic news of the attack on Li Hung-chang, followed by the declaration of an armistice for twenty-one days, was good news, and relieved the anxiety of the people for the time. However, later details to the effect that the armistice did not include Formosa was a great shock to the whole populace. It was quite reasonable to believe that if the Japanese had demanded the insertion of this condition it was not without some purpose, and as to this there could be but one explanation: the seizure of Formosa by force. To the common people it but added to the mystery and made it still more difficult to comprehend why Formosa, which had taken no part in the northern difficulties, should be the coming scene of so much trouble and disturbance.

With the news of the armistice came orders from Peking to defend the island. That the majority of the higher officials at the capital had much confidence in the ability of the Formosan forces successfully to oppose the Japanese, I cannot believe. It was done purely with the hope of shifting the burden of war on to the shoulders of the islanders, and getting the Japanese troops away from their position in such alarming proximity to the capital, thus relieving the northern officials of responsibility and danger. But others, together with the great mass of southern officials, who had had no personal experience of the Japanese as warriors, were firm in their belief that the Formosans could defeat the enemy if they were but given the chance.

The failure of the northern Chinese troops was not fully appreciated in Formosa; consequently, the Peking officials did not find it difficult to establish among the Formosan authorities a highly exalted idea of their own prowess. Profuse praise and flattery; frequent reference to the invulnerable defences of the harbors; the formation of the island, in itself a natural fortress; the renowned bravery and warlike reputation of the inhabitants whose ancestors had defeated the Dutch and whose present people had defeated the French, was sufficient. To the Formosans the total annihilation of the Japanese if they should but appear seemed assured.

Now that Formosa was soon to be the seat of war I made preparations to witness, if possible, the struggle from the Chinese side. With this in view, a fellow-countryman of mine, standing high in the Chinese Customs service, had the kindness to arrange that I should be received by the governor and commander-in-chief of the military forces of the island, Tang Ching-sung. The time was fixed; and with two sedan chairs and four bearers, quite a novelty to me, we were carried through the streets, past the big gate of the entrance of the walled city of Taipeh and finally into the governor's compound. Outside the governor's yamen, rather an ordinary specimen of the usual style of Chinese official architecture, we were stopped by a messenger who informed us that I was to be received formally as befitting a foreigner who had come so great a distance to associate himself with the Chinese in this war. Then the heavy outside gate, simultaneously with three sets of heavy doors, all in line, swung open automatically, to all appearance, and the first sight of Chinese officialdom greeted my eyes. To the rear could be seen the governor with his attendants grouped about him, and lined up on each side in unbroken rank were files of brilliantly uniformed Chinese soldiers with shining spears and bright colored banners. The large archways, the fantastic carving of the pillars, the brilliant ornamentation and weird designs on every side, were all new to me and interesting in the extreme. We were carried to the entrance of the governor's reception-room where His Excellency greeted us. The decorations of this chamber, which differed but little from that part of the building through which we had just passed, had added to them numerous odd looking scrolls, on which drawings of landscapes made up of mountain scenery, falling waters, and pavilions shaded by fantastically shaped trees, were hanging on the high walls. Wood carvings adorned the cornices of the rooms and bordered the doorways, while standing out in vivid contrast to these were numerous panels covered with bright red, on which were inscribed in black characters the valued words of Chinese sages.

I found the governor a pleasant looking man, apparently about sixty years of age. After the usual small talk had been exchanged, I exhibited to him at his request some photographs taken at Port Arthur. They were principally scenes from the battlefield, depicting Chinese dead in the streets, mutilated bodies of Japanese, and decapitated heads with the eyes, noses, and mouths gouged out with spears. The governor was apparently much interested and showed no displeasure at the remark that the offering of a reward for Japanese heads in Formosa was encouraging just such mutilation of the Japanese dead as had incited the latter at Port Arthur to take full revenge. His Excellency, on a later occasion, explained the situation fully, and not without some reason from a Chinese point of view. "It is impossible for me to do otherwise," said he, "it has been the custom for generations, and the soldiers expect it, and would not fight if this inducement was not held out. My people do not think they should enter such hazardous employment without good pay, and as we cannot afford to pay every soldier high wages, we make it up by rewards for special work done." As to the severing of heads from the enemy's dead, "yes, that is unfortunate," he said; "but it is the only method we have of proving that our men have really killed the man for whom they seek reward. They cannot bring the body, but the head they can easily carry. The last schedule of rewards was for the Japanese when dead, but you will notice in my present proclamation, 150 taels (1 tael about 75 cents U.S. currency) are offered for the capture of a private soldier alive, and only 100 taels when dead; for a Japanese general 600 taels when alive, and only 500 taels when dead. I do this to encourage my men to capture them alive, hoping in this way to avoid useless slaughter." [1]

The prime object of my visit was attained, credentials being secured granting me permission to join the officials of any force and to enter any of the fortifications during the campaign. In a few days my credentials reached me. They were drawn up on a large sheet, were elaborately written in three colours, red, blue, and black, covered with big seals, and resembled at a distance a brightly colored poster. Thus armed I was ready for the fray.

The governor claimed to possess a force of 80,000 men, consisting principally of Swatow, Hunan, and Canton men, besides native levies. Aside from the Cantonese, who were considered the best fighters on the mainland, much dependence was placed on a native general with his army of Hakkas; that hardy race who trade with the savages of the mountains and who have been gradually clearing the jungles and driving the aborigines farther and farther into the interior. Accustomed to mountain warfare and with experience such as only guerilla fighting can teach, they defeated the French in Tamsui in 1884, when armed with the crudest of matchlocks; so that with this experience and well equipped as they now were, they were considered competent to give considerable trouble to the Japanese. The infantry were armed with new single and repeating Mausers, Lee, and modern repeating Winchester carbines. Their pay was six taels ($4.50 gold) a month, and I was informed that they were at that time paid promptly and fully. Out of this sum the soldiers had to provide their own food.

---

1. The following schedule was published in the vicinity of the camps and in out-of-the-way places, by the governor's orders :

70,000 taels; for the capture of a big man-of-war.	600 taels; besides other rewards according to circumstances; for the seizure of a Japanese general.
4,600 taels; for the capture of a small cruiser.	
400 taels; for the sinking of a ship's boat.	150 taels; for the seizure of a Japanese soldier.
800 taels; for the sinking of a boat carrying soldiers.	500 taels; besides other rewards; for killing a Japanese general.
	500 taels; for killing a Japanese officer.
600 taels; for seizure of a Japanese officer.	100 taels; for killing a Japanese soldier.

During the early part of April, it was generally believed among the officials that the Japanese were preparing for an expedition to the south, and that the Pescadores would, no doubt, be the first place of attack. Scarcely had this news been received when a rather interesting little episode occurred at the Pescadores. About a fortnight or three weeks prior to the actual arrival of the Japanese fleet, two French war-ships suddenly appeared in Makung harbor, and the senior officer at once began showering hospitalities and attentions on the Chinese commandant stationed there. This official, who, besides being of a decidedly festive nature, was undoubtedly living in constant dread of a Japanese attack, cordially reciprocated and accepted the overtures made to him by the Frenchman. Before long the intercourse assumed practical shape and, if the telegrams sent by the Pescadores commandant to General Liu Yung-fu who was in command of the troops of south Formosa may be accepted as reliable evidence of what was going on, it would appear that the French senior officer made constant and urgent appeals to the commandant to hand over the islands to French custody and permit the French flag to be hoisted on all the forts. According to the commandant's reports, the French officer assured him that the occupation would only be temporary and carried out in the interests of friendship to the Chinese government, and that retrocession would be at once made as soon as the troubles then going on between Japan and China were settled. Liu Yung-fu, who never seemed to have forgiven the French for what they did to him when commanding the Chinese troops in Annam, was furious at the bare suggestion, and from the very first asserted that only some treacherous motive could possibly underlie anything done by the French. He wired most positive orders to the commandant to pay no attention whatever to any overtures of the sort; but, on the contrary, to look on all such as being prompted by hostile and self-interested motives. He further ordered, in the event of any more French ships appearing with officers inclined to interfere, that the forts should open fire upon them.

This act of the French was, no doubt, incited by the report that China had offered to cede the island of Formosa to England. If such proved to be the case, France wished to be in a position to look after her own interests, and the Pescadores would have served her purposes admirably. That Formosa was actually offered to England by China and that Lord Rosebery and Lord Kimberley twice declined to entertain the offer in any way, has been practically confirmed. In just what manner and through what channels these offers were made has not been officially stated; but a popular account says that, while China was in the last throes of defeat, the possibility of Japan seizing Formosa and the Pescadores and from these important strategical points carrying on war with the mainland induced China to propose this solution. Formosa in England's possession would be saved from the enemy; and no doubt, with the queer ideas in vogue at the Chinese Foreign Office, it was hoped that when all had quieted down England might be induced to return the island. No doubt they were prepared to offer some mainland concession in return for this valuable assistance. The island was then offered without any conditions, and tempting as the proposal was, Lord Kimberley, then Foreign Secretary, believed that to accede to the transfer would probably result in the partitioning of China; and that Russia, France, and Germany would demand their share; entailing an operation which, although perhaps desired by some, was fraught with such danger to all that none cared either to begin it themselves or to recognize the right of others to do so.

The news of the bombardment of the Pescadores reached Taipeh through Chinese sources, and consequently had been much garbled on the way. The first news was to the effect that the Japanese fleet had appeared off the entrance to Makung, whereupon the Chinese opened fire, sinking two of the Japanese warships. The others then fled, leaving the Chinese victorious. According to the Formosan governor-general's schedule of prizes, this entitled the officers of the fort which had been successful, to ten thousand taels per warship. Accordingly, the amount was drawn from the Pescadores treasury and distributed among the officers, and the governor was notified to that effect. A few days later there was apparently some mistake; for the commander of the forces at the Pescadores, a poor old man, lame and nearly blind, and, it was said, some seventy-five years of age, was brought up as a prisoner from one of the southern ports of the island, whither he had fled from the Pescadores. He was in a sorry plight, and it was rumored that he would be sent before the Board of Punishments as a penalty for his timidity in fleeing before the enemy. Besides this, he was held responsible for the twenty thousand taels which had been appropriated as the reward for the destruction of the two Japanese men-of-war. No doubt the possession of this sum appeared to the officers concerned of greater importance than the mere sinking of the two warships, which was a matter of such small moment and could be accomplished at their leisure during the day. In the heat of the battle they evidently forgot their obligations, for they fled without firing a single effective shot.

The strategical value of the Pescadores has long been recognized. The Dutch, Koxinga, the Manchus, and the French had all in turn occupied it prior to a descent on Formosa. Lying in the fairway between the Chinese mainland and Formosa and with a harbor unequalled by any in the latter island, it may be considered as the key of Formosa. When the Imperial forces occupied the Pescadores during the close of the seventeenth century, Koxinga's grandson is said to have given up all hope of opposing them; for, as he notified his followers, "the enemy have entered the gateway." In later years, the Chinese had erected forts with large modern guns, and it was believed that the defences were practically impregnable. The Japanese likewise appreciated the necessity of occupying the Pescadores, if action in the south, either on the mainland or on the Formosan coast, was anticipated.

On March 20th, after a five days' trip from Saseho naval station, the expedition, consisting of the fleet and transports, arrived off the Pescadores and anchored near Pachau island to the south of the principal islands of the group. Bad weather on the 21st and 22nd prevented an immediate attack on the forts; but on the 23rd, the storm having abated, the ships got underway, and at 9.30 a.m., upon the first flying squadron drawing near Hau-chiau, the fleet subjected the Kon-peh-tai fort to a heavy bombardment, to which the Chinese replied for nearly an hour before they were silenced. During the afternoon, the disembarkation of the troops commenced. By the aid of steam pinnaces each towing several cutters, the troops, consisting of the first, second, third, and fourth companies of the first regiment of reserves under the command of Colonel Hishijima, were all landed in less than two hours. The landing of the troops brought the Kon-peh-tai fort into action again, but without inflicting much damage on the Japanese. The troops on shore engaged in a skirmish with some 300 Chinese soldiers, afterwards reinforced by 150 more, near a commanding knoll which both forces were desirous of occupying. After a few volleys from the Japanese, answered by an irregular fire from the Chinese, the latter eventually fled, leaving the position in the hands of the Japanese. Staff-quarters were then established in the village of Chien-shan. At 2.30 on the morning of the 24th, the troops advanced with the intention of taking Kon-peh-tai fort and Makung (Mako) with a temporary company of mountain artillery under Captain Arai and the naval contingent with quick firing guns under Naval Lieutenant Tajima in the van. The night was very dark and the only available route was so frequently cut up with ditches running in every direction that progress was laboriously slow ; only some two miles being made after three hours of painful tramping. By about 4 a.m., the Japanese force had all reached the rallying ground, and thirty minutes later, led by the 2nd battalion of the first regiment of reserves, were advancing towards the fort. The 5th company, under the command of Captain Kinoshita, formed the advance guard, and a detachment of this company, under command of Lieutenant Ishii, were the first to engage the Chinese forces, 200 of whom had taken up a position outside the fort and appeared to dispute the advance of the Japanese. The engagement was very brief, the Chinese flying before the small number of determined Japanese. Meanwhile, the temporary battery of mountain artillery had been shelling the fort from a position too far distant to do much damage to the stronghold, but in a manner sufficiently effective to frighten out the garrison, who left in such haste that, thirty minutes after the first gun had been fired, the Japanese were in possession. Thus was the principal port captured in the Pescadores. The naval contingent were also enabled to participate in the engagement, and with their two quick-firing guns did much execution. The 4th company of the 1st regiment of reserves and the naval contingent captured the village, after only a slight skirmish with the enemy. The place had been held by a garrison 500 strong. With the 2nd company of the 1st regiment of reserves leading the van, the Japanese forces now reassembled and advanced on the capital and principal city of the islands, Makung. No opposition was encountered on the way, with the exception of some ineffective firing from the Yui-wang island fort ; and upon reaching the city, the 1st company stormed the Chinese infantry encampment, being followed soon after by the 2nd company, which dashed through the gateway with the intention of dividing into three sections and attacking the enemy from different sides. But to their amazement, their plans were found unnecessary, the garrison, with the exception of some thirty who did make a slight show of resistance, having fled. Some shots were fired at a few stragglers, and at 11.50 a.m. the occupation of the city was complete. Another engagement the same day resulted in the capture of the fort in the Yuan-ching peninsula by Commander Tanji with a naval force ; about 500 of the enemy surrendering without making any resistance whatever. Two days later (March 26th), blue jackets occupied the Yui-wang island forts and found the place empty, the garrison having fled. Soon after the Japanese entered, a native presented himself, apparently on a very important mission, which proved to be the delivery of a letter stating that the Chinese commander and garrison wished to inform the Japanese that they surrendered the fort. Thus fell the key to Southern China. The Chinese prisoners, with the exception of eight officers, were given their liberty. The spoils of the little campaign were considerable, including 18 cannon, 2,663 rifles, over a million rounds of ammunition, 797 casks, and 3,173 bags of powder, a thousand bags of rice, etc., etc. Rear-Admiral Tanaka occupied the post of first governor of the group, and a government office and military post offices were at once erected. Although the loss of life on the battle-field had been practically nil, a fearful epidemic of cholera, not unlike that which had carried off so many of the French in the same islands ten years before, broke out, and upwards of 1,500 Japanese died in a few days.

The news of the utter defeat of the Chinese at the Pescadores eventually became known and threw the whole of Formosa into a panic, so that the Douglas and one smaller line of steamers could not make trips fast enough to carry all the people that wished to get away. Tramp-steamers engaged in the trade both in the north and south, and the unusual sight of departing junks loaded down with men, women, and children was of daily occurrence.

For some time previous, reports had been in vogue that the Formosan officials intended to desert the island. The governor had denied this, and endeavored to instill confidence among the frightened masses by a proclamation[1] which afforded considerable satisfaction to the soldiers and people who were most concerned with the governor's movements ; the former fearing that the treasure would escape them, and the latter that, in the absence of the chief officials, the whole place would be turned over to the soldiers and coolies.[1]

The Formosan officers were now spurred on to greater efforts. Two steamers, formerly known as the *Cass* and *Smith*, but now renamed *Arthur* and *Martha*, and several other steamers were actively engaged in transporting troops and munitions of war to the island, and every effort was made to increase the number of native levies. No doubt the numerous proclamations which warned the people of the horrible suffering that

1. " I, the Governor of Formosa, Taug, hereby proclaim that since the sixth moon of the past year, I have enlisted and drilled over one hundred corps of able-bodied soldiers from different provinces of the mainland and over 80,000 native volunteers, having spared neither pains nor money in the purchase of all improved implements of warfare, making this island impregnable against all possible attack. With the patriotism which you, citizens of Formosa, have recently manifested to my great satisfaction, in so freely subscribing to the Government loan from the people, and I, the Governor, with a mother of over eighty years of age, and my whole family by my side, hereby publicly dedicate even to death, the best of my strength and ability to the defence of the welfare of our people. Therefore, I hereby enjoin upon you, citizens of Formosa, that you continue to follow your daily vocations undisturbed, resting assured that you having made all possible preparations, Heaven will undoubtedly grant you triumphant victory over the enemy, as a reward for your patriotism.
" Issued this twenty-first year of Kwangsui, 2nd moon."

The Pescadores Islands.

The Dreary Treeless Flats of the Pescadores.
Inside the Walls of Makung (Mako), the Capital of the Pescadores.
Inside a Pescadores Fort erected by the Chinese.

would befall them should the Japanese once get the upper hand, induced many of those who had not the means of crossing to the mainland to enlist. All the bad characters of Formosa—and the island has always had its share of these—recognized in the military service abundant opportunities to carry on their old trade, and were consequently the first to enlist. Nearly all the unemployed, loafers and even beggars, had braced up sufficiently to join the gallant defenders. There was no requirement other than the strength necessary to walk up to the numerous enlisting stands which were located in all frequented places, and to be able to hold a gun after having been declared a soldier. I watched the operation on several occasions. The enlisting booth usually consisted of a table with three chairs, with a so-called military officer in the centre and a clerk on each side. The officer would first harangue the crowd, no doubt dwelling on the glorious life of a soldier, the steady pay and light work, the gorgeous uniform, the possibilities of large reward, etc., and now and then throwing in an occasional witty remark would bring forth loud laughter from the crowd, reminding one strongly of a street medicine seller. Occasional listeners who appeared specially affected by the warrior orator's eloquence would from time to time step to the front, not without a slight show of embarrassment, however, much as though they were about to purchase a drug, the efficacy of which they were not quite so sure of as the seller seemed to be, and as if they were a little apprehensive of the jeers of the crowd. Upon presenting themselves at the table, the applicants were asked a few questions by one of the officials, and were then presented with a small wooden check, after which they went to the back of the stand to be later taken off to the various garrisons.

For the first few weeks the troops appeared to be well commanded and were so closely confined to the forts and camps that, unless moving in a body under orders of their commander, they were rarely seen in the streets. I am convinced that it was the governor's intention to enforce good order among his men, so far as he was able. But towards the middle of April, it became more and more evident that the soldiers, who had greatly increased in numbers, were determined to have a row now and then in spite of their superiors. In the foreign settlements in the north, the position occasioned no little uneasiness, and it was thought best to send the women and children to the mainland. At Twatutia in the interior, no help could be expected from a man-of-war, and with thousands of undisciplined soldiers about them, it was not at all improbable that, if general rioting commenced, the possessions of the foreigners would appear sufficiently attractive to be early attacked. Accordingly, the foreign merchants took every measure to protect their lives and properties. Rifles were collected in considerable numbers and placed within easy reach, extra watchmen were engaged, and one of the largest hongs in the settlement brought in several sturdy Manila men as armed sentries, they forming a great contrast to the sleepy Chinese watchmen, who were more concerned in protecting themselves by getting away at the right moment, than in defending the property of their employers. Furthermore, two small guns were mounted on a launch belonging to Messrs. Lapraik, Cass & Co., in order to protect treasure when transported up and down the river. As time went on, the position became more and more alarming. The soldiers were beginning to exhibit signs of turbulence, and large numbers of new levies arrived from Canton—the scum and refuse of that city. The Chinese merchants were greatly disturbed, dreading now their own country's troops as much as they did those of the enemy. The feeling of insecurity increased day by day, and on April 24th it was intensified by a row, during which the soldiers clearly showed that they would not put up with much interference on the part of their officers. The English and German consuls had made urgent appeals to their respective ministers as to the need of foreign guards to protect the foreign settlement. The German admiral dealt with the matter promptly, and to the extreme satisfaction of the foreign community, twenty-five stalwart sons of the fatherland, under command of Navy Lieutenant Timme, were landed from the German flagship *Irene* and arrived at Twatutia just as the soldiers were engaging in a little riot within the city.

The first knowledge of the trouble reached the foreign business houses at noon. It was but a hurried notice that the soldiers in the city were attacking the governor's yamen. In a few moments, the streets in the immediate vicinity of the foreign houses became a scene of panic not easily forgotten. Chinese were running about in all directions, all possessed with the common idea that the long feared moment had at last arrived, and that their homes, possessions, wives, and daughters were at length to be given up to pillage at the hands of the hordes of uncontrolled soldiers. The details of the affair as subsequently told are as follows:—The soldiery had been holding the movements of the governor and all the higher officials under the very strictest scrutiny for some time past, boldly announcing their intention to allow none of these to leave the place alive, if they attempted flight from the island. At a little before noon on the morning of the 22nd, it became apparent to a body of discharged troops and roughs in the city that a much hated colonel was about to leave the governor's yamen with the evident intention of proceeding to the port and quitting the island. A few days prior to this, the governor had sent his mother to Canton, and her luggage was now being forwarded, when the soldiers who were carrying it through the streets were stopped by others and the luggage examined, apparently under the impression that it was the property of the colonel in question. This resulted in a fight between the baggage carriers and the interfering soldiers, and finally the participants rushed back to the governor's yamen. Naturally this created a good deal of excitement, and a big crowd of natives gathered outside. The colonel above referred to, who was in command of these troops, was specially disliked by his men owing to his having appropriated the 800 taels which had been given him by the governor's mother to be distributed among the soldiers on her departure. He now appeared on the scene to inquire into the disturbance. The unpopular officer could scarcely have anticipated his reception, however; and, it is said, that upon becoming aware of the situation, he availed himself of his strategical knowledge and took up a position under a table, from which hastily improvised fortification he endeavored to communicate with the enemy. In this engagement his foes were his own men and he was greatly outnumbered. The unfortunate man was dragged forth and literally sliced into pieces.   About the same time one of the governor's secretaries who, believing the yamen was about to be looted, was attempting to run away with some valuables, received a volley, six bullets taking effect.   By this time a great hubbub was going on outside, and the governor's soldiers, no doubt fearing some opposition from that quarter, commenced to fire on the crowd.   After about two hundred rounds had been fired, the governor made his appearance and succeeded in quieting his brave defenders, but not until eighteen unarmed inhabitants of the city had been cruelly killed, two severely hurt, and twenty more or less wounded.   The wounded were taken to the hospital, but the Chinese doctor in charge had barricaded the doors and refused for some time to take them in. This little affair brought home very forcibly to the foreign residents the real danger to which they were exposed.   Public placards had been distributed all round the place, informing the people that the governor had been endeavoring, through the medium of foreign hongs, to send out of the island the money that ought legitimately to be used as payment of the troops. The governor himself, thus libelled in no measured terms, was quite unable to take any steps to stop the circulation of these statements, his authority at the time scarcely extending more than fifty paces outside his own yamen door.   The other officers in the capital were likewise without authority, and it is said that the district magistrate gave up $200, upon his life being threatened.   The soldiers at the forts in Hobe declared that they would fire on any vessel, English or otherwise, suspected of taking treasure away from the island, and furthermore that they would kill the governor-general should he attempt to escape.   Some of the troops were known to be two months or so in arrears of pay, and so great was their enmity against the officials that the foreigners were quite convinced that the soldiers would carry out their threats to the letter.

A British gunboat, the *Redbreast*, a stanch little craft of 805 tons, under the command of Lieutenant Stuart, had arrived in Hobe and taken anchorage in the river.   She could thus afford efficient protection to the British consulate and the one British firm established there, but could be of little use to the Twatutia residents ten miles up river.

During the last days of April, the situation became so alarming that the governor called a meeting of the consuls and informed them that he had lost all control over his people, soldiers and others, and unless Foreign Powers intervened, or sufficient foreign protection was provided, as soon as it was officially known that the treaty ceding Formosa to Japan had been ratified, Formosa would be thrown into a state of anarchy and rebellion.   Furthermore, that he was unable to protect the lives and interests of the foreigners on the island.   Later events proved that in this he told the truth.

On April 26th, H.M.S. *Spartan* arrived, followed by the battleship *Centurion* with the British admiral on board.   This officer made a trip up the river to Twatutia, and after a few hours' visit, he came to the conclusion that the situation warranted outside protection, and thirty marines, under the command of Captain W. Shubrick, were accordingly landed from the *Spartan* for duty at Twatutia.   The *Redbreast* was joined a few days later by the

German gunboat *Wolf,* evidence that the energetic German admiral intended to do his share in protecting the settlements, regardless of the fact that his nationals were greatly in the minority. The U.S.S. *Concord* was, at the request of General Kemper, United States consul at Amoy, despatched from Nagasaki, and arrived off Tamsui on the 2nd of May. Considerable amusement was caused to the foreign officers over an order which had been given by a Tamsui mandarin to the Customs, to the effect that the United States ship should not be allowed across the bar, as the vessel was filled with armed Japanese troops. It seemed that three Japanese stewards armed with nothing more formidable than bread knives had been the cause of this report. Commander Craig spent a few hours on shore and then steamed away on the morning of the 4th, scarcely giving the situation the attention it deserved.

During the early half of May the atmosphere was thick with rows and riots. Scarcely a day passed without news of some disturbance in the northern district. Fortunately these were confined to the Chinese, although rumors were current of attacks planned against the foreign community, causing some little anxiety; for the Chinese sometimes tell the truth, and it is not always safe to cast aside all their tales. Frequently a row occurred close at hand, in which the soldiers were usually the offenders and the villagers the victims. As an example, on May 7th, while writing in my room, I was suddenly startled by hearing several rifle reports. On running out into the street, a strange sight met my eyes. The Chinese were rushing about greatly excited, chattering as only Chinese can, workmen were running here and there carrying tea boxes in different stages of construction, girls who had been picking tea were wobbling down side streets as fast as their little deformed feet would admit, and merchants were bringing in their wares from the front of the shops and closing doors and windows in great haste. Running up the street and crossing over to where the firing was going on, I joined a crowd of jabbering natives enraged at ten or twelve Cantonese soldiers who were firing into the upper story of a house, the top rooms of which had been converted into a gambling chamber. Quite a crowd had now gathered; and the soldiers, apparently not desirous of spectators, fired a shot. The bullet whistled by unpleasantly near, inducing the crowd, including myself, to retire with more haste than dignity. The trouble originated in the gambling room. A dispute had arisen, ending in one of the players, a Cantonese soldier, raking in the "pot" and trying to escape. He was soon caught, however, and the money taken from his person in no gentle manner. Upon being released, he reported the affair to his comrades, fifteen or twenty soldiers visited the house, and the row commenced in dead earnest. In the course of it several were wounded, two severely; one dying during the night. Soon after, the Cantonese, who had been the cause of the trouble, was seized by order of the authorities and taken into the city for trial, but his comrades again came to his rescue, and after a short scrimmage, in which a boy was killed and several persons were wounded, his release was effected.

Nor were these troubles confined to the cities; banditti roamed the country, and mobs of soldiers occasionally swooped down on the villages, having everything their own way while there. The village of Pat-lihun near Hobe was subjected to one of these unwelcome visits. On this occasion, a large number of Cantonese soldiers encamped near made a raid on the town, driving every male inhabitant out of the place and then coolly substituting themselves as husbands, lords, and masters. A body of the grief-stricken men, so unexpectedly and unwillingly divorced, immediately visited the capital to impress upon the governor that marriage under such conditions was very evidently a failure and to beg that a force should be sent to drive out the invaders. This did not result satisfactorily, and after a few days of family life, the Cantonese left of their own accord, and the villagers returned to their homes and families, not, however, with any great increase of affection for their countrymen who had partaken of their hospitality unasked.

The Kap-su-lan district also suffered much from soldiers and bandits, and the Gilan magistrate was kept busy decapitating undesirables. To the south, nearly all travel between Tainan and Taipeh came to a standstill, two Chinese merchants transporting treasure up country were relieved of ten thousand dollars, and the whole country was so given up to anarchy that, notwithstanding all the horrors of Japanese rule as portrayed by the Chinese mandarins, the majority of the merchants and the more intelligent of the Chinese farmers were, without doubt, secretly wishing for the coming of the invaders. The condition of affairs could not be worse, and the people had hopes that it might be better.

With all the anxiety that the situation must have given them, the local officials sought consolation by making all the money possible. Considerable sums were received from the mainland, and money was filched right and left from the wealthy inhabitants of the island. It was said that the expenses incurred in keeping up the regular army exceeded $750,000 (silver) a month. Taking this as correct, the amounts demanded monthly from different sources, under the pretence that they were required for military purposes, must have exceeded that sum several times. The militia and volunteer brigades, which formed the largest share of the island forces, were armed and equipped principally from the mainland, but received no pay except when engaged in active service. The organization of these different native bands was, as a rule, the work of some rich man or group of rich men, whose motive was the hope of obtaining personal protection. One well-known Chinese, who owns large property throughout the island, was absolutely forced by the mandarins to contribute one million dollars, in return for which he was declared commander-in-chief of the Formosan citizen soldiers, an inconvenient honor which he would no doubt have paid liberally to have avoided had he dared.

Besides the fifty-five foreign guards at Twatutia, Messrs. Lapraik, Cass & Co. had very generously placed a large steam launch at the service of the foreign community. It was handed over to the officers of the British gunboat *Redbreast*, who equipped it with two machine guns and put a gunner—Mr. Bowden—and several blue jackets on board to man it. The little craft was then made spick and span, painted white, and rechristened the *Patrol*.

Her special duty was to lie about the river at Twatutia and carry the foreign residents down to the port when the situation became too dangerous for them to remain at Twatutia.[1]

1. The British marines at the settlements consisted of six gunners of the marine artillery and nineteen privates of the marine infantry, besides three non-commissioned officers and a bugler. They were under the command of a cool-headed, experienced officer, Captain Shubrick. Life on shore even in Formosa was a great treat for both officers and men, and I was told that shore rations were also welcome, being usually superior to any on board ship. No rations are issued to landing parties by the British government, but as we understand it, one shilling and six pence a day is allowed each man to cover this item, and a local compradore furnished them with three really big meals at a figure a little less than this. Each man also receives from the British government six pence per day as a field allowance, commonly called "Hard lines money."

The foreign residents kept the men, both English and German, provided with refreshments and tobacco and gave them a sing-song at the Twatutia club, which was note-worthy as the largest gathering of foreigners ever held in Twatutia.

The German guard numbered three petty officers and twenty-two men, all blue jackets. They were young men and had only been one year in the service. Their commander, Naval Lieutenant Timme, was a fine looking young officer full of energy, and ready with his men for any emergency. It was almost amusing to watch little squads of four or five of the Germans marching about with their eyes wide open, eager for a legitimate opportunity to show their mettle. I have not the least doubt that the whole fifty-five men, both English and German, would gladly have marched against ten times their number of armed men, and I am sure they would have given a good account of themselves if they had had the chance.

CHAPTER XIX.

THE RISE OF THE FORMOSAN REPUBLIC.

1895.

China sues for peace—The Shimonoseki conferences—Japan demands the cession of Formosa—Viceroy Li Hung-chang and Count Ito discuss the question—A report of the third, fourth, and fifth conferences—The Treaty ratified and Formosa ceded to Japan—A Formosan deputation visits Peking and protests against the cession—Formosan Republic planned—Its mainland supporters—The people unconcerned—Tcheng Kitong arrives in Formosa—A proclamation of rebellion—A good omen—The Declaration of Independence—The self-appointed President—The Powers officially notified—The new government—Half-hearted republicans desert—The career of Lim Pan Bang and his escape from Formosa—The first day of the Republic—The populace but little interested—The Republican flag—Five Japanese men-of-war appear at Tamsui—A damper on the Republican celebration—The Customs refuse recognition—A Japanese launch explores the harbor—The situation exciting at Taipehfu—A savage head exhibited—Foreign military instructors engaged—Billy Waters as Minister of War—The defences strengthened—Troops and munitions arrive from China—French assistance sought—Officers from French cruiser interview President Tang—The defences of Formosa—Campaign difficulties—Kelung splendidly fortified—The Hobe defences—Military curios—The republican army—The government arsenal and powder mill—Jing-galls—Formosan soldiers well armed—Chinese military drill—Target practice—Uniform and equipment—The volunteers—Army trumpeters—Military camps—Life of a soldier—Sick and well housed together—Official pageants.

WITH the Japanese ever victorious, and Peking within easy reach, we find China, which but a few months before was boasting of its prowess, now humbled before the victor and suing for peace. The negotiations were characterized by the usual Chinese shilly-shallying, and several so-called peace commissioners were sent, apparently for no other reason than to beat around the bush and obtain an inkling as to the probable designs of the victors. But the Japanese, who were not without experience of Chinese official methods, promptly sent all uncredited wanderers back to their homes, without giving them even the satisfaction of an interview. Meanwhile the

Japanese army advanced, and the young emperor of China, not relishing a hasty exit out of the back door of his capital, now provided the necessary credentials, and Li Hung-chang and his son Li Ching-fong were sent as plenipotentiaries to Japan. Among the tasks committed to Viceroy Li Hung-chang and his associate was the preservation, if possible, of the island of Formosa to the celestial empire. It was a battle of diplomacy in which past-masters were engaged, and in this case with the Chinese on the defensive.

The negotiations took place at Shimonoseki, Japan, and the first meeting with Count Ito and Viscount Mutsu,[1] the Japanese plenipotentiaries, was on March 20th. The report of the conferences was published by an English journal, the *Peking and Tientsin Times,* and the discussions between the Chinese and Japanese plenipotentiaries as given in this journal are said to be correct. Such portions as refer to Formosa are herewith reproduced :—

The subject of ceding Formosa to Japan was not discussed until the third conference. Then Count Ito remarked in a casual sort of way, " Our forces have now gone to Formosa ; I don't know what sort of people they are in the island." "Colonists from Kwangtung," said the Viceroy, "and very turbulent they are." Count Ito: "Some savages are still left?" The Viceroy: "The savages occupy three-tenths, the colonists the remainder. To continue the subject, since the Minister has introduced the Formosan question, I presume the wish to occupy it accounts for the unwillingness to grant an armistice. It will not be very palatable to Great Britain, and when I spoke of the possibilities of clashing with the interests of other Powers, I had this in my mind. What if we lose it?" Count Ito: "An injury to China is not an injury to Great Britain." The Viceroy: "Formosa and Hongkong are very near each other." Count Ito: "War between two Powers does no injury to a third." The Viceroy: "Great Britain is said to be unwilling that any other Power should occupy Formosa." Count Ito: "If China were to present Formosa to any Power, I fancy it would be received smilingly enough." The Viceroy: "Formosa having been ranked among the provinces cannot be given to any Power." Then the Viceroy told a story of a conversation with Okubo, who passed through Tientsin on his way to Peking, after sending an expedition to Formosa, and who agreed that the murder of some Japanese traders by a few irresponsible savages was not worth quarrelling about.

The subject of Formosa was again brought up towards the close of the fourth conference, held on the 10th of April, by the Viceroy stating that he could not give up Formosa. "In that case, I must take it," said the Count. "The French found it too hard a nut to crack," said the Viceroy, "besides which we want to be friends." "Indemnity and the cession of territory are like debts," said the Count; "after the debts are paid, we shall naturally be friends." "You press your debtors too hard," said the Viceroy; and he went on to point out that Formosa was full of malaria, and the people had to use opium as a prophylactic. "We intend to prohibit the use of opium," said the Count. "I respect you for it," said the Viceroy; and then he indulged in the old misrepresentation, that Great Britain forces opium into China, against the government's will. "It will be necessary to find some means of prohibiting your people." said the Count, "and the importation will soon stop." The Viceroy then rose to take leave of Count Ito; while they were shaking hands, he asked once more for a reduction of the indemnity; Count Ito smiled but shook his head, saying "Impossible;" and the sitting was at an end.

During the fifth conference held on April 15th, the cession of Formosa was again referred to. With both Liaotung Peninsula and Formosa in view, Viceroy Li complained that the territory Japan asked for was too large, and had great possibilities; but Count Ito said that whatever resources existed in the new territory had to be developed, and could not be regarded as a set-off to the indemnity. Besides as any wealth that might accrue would be spent in the territory, there would be no surplus. "Let us turn to Formosa," said the Viceroy, "which the Chinese have not exploited well. It has coal mines, gold mines, and kerosene oil wells. If I had been Governor, I should have opened all these." "Again there is the expense of development," said the Count. "The greater the expenditure," said the Viceroy, "the greater the return. Since in the future the gain will be so solid, what can stand in the way of a slight reduction? In that case it would be easier for China to borrow the requisite amount. When I was in Peking, some foreigners were ready to lend twenty millions sterling on the security of Formosa. After I reached Japan every one heard that Japan was bent upon obtaining possession of the island, and so that affair can no longer be mentioned. So much having been offered with the island as a pledge, naturally it could have been sold for much more." Count Ito refused to be talked over, though the Viceroy begged again and again for only a little concession in either money or territory.

The discussion now passed to the question of the position of Chinese landholders in territory ceded to Japan, and the Viceroy asked that absentee proprietors might be confirmed in the possession of their property as securely as Japanese subjects. Count Ito pointed out that this was difficult, as aliens cannot possess real property in Japan. The Viceroy said that he referred to land which had been handed down from father to son for generations, but Count Ito explained that " if Japan allows Chinese to own real property in the interior, then Foreign Powers will certainly avail themselves of the most favored nation

1. Now Marquis Ito and the late Count Mutsu.

clause to put obstacles in our way." The Viceroy went on to warn Count Ito that Japan might expect a good deal of trouble in Formosa. "It is not an uncommon thing," he said, "for the people of Formosa to rise and murder their officials. When that happens it will not be imputed to us." "You recall your officials and withdraw your troops," said Count Ito, "and we will be responsible for the rest." Then a long discussion took place as to the time within which Formosa was to be handed over, the Viceroy proposing that the cession should be completed in six months after the exchange of ratifications. Count Ito would not hear of six months, and proposed that officials be sent to effect the transfer immediately after the exchange of ratifications. He pointed out to the Viceroy a special section dealing with Formosa, which was substantially as follows: "All fortifications, rifles, and guns, with public buildings, etc., are to be handed over to the control of the military authorities of Japan. The soldiers shall be permitted to take all their baggage and private effects to some place indicated by the Japanese officials, and the Chinese soldiers shall be directed to remain in that place till their withdrawal . . . . And by a certain fixed date the Chinese government shall have withdrawn them all. The expenses of removal shall be borne by China. After the troops have been withdrawn the officials of Japan shall return their rifles, and then civil officers shall be sent to assume control Official residences and property shall be handed over to them. The remaining details shall be settled by the military officials of both Powers." *The Viceroy*: "That all relates to matters connected with the transfer, which I have no authority to determine." This seems to have taken Count Ito rather aback. "The Grand Secretary," he asked, "has authority to change the date, and this matter is of equal importance with the rest of the treaty, why has he not authority?" "All these are details," said the Viceroy, "to be discussed after the exchange of ratifications; the treaty only cedes Formosa to Japan, and until the exchange of the ratifications Formosa is Chinese territory." *Count Ito*: "I might send troops to Formosa at once by virtue of the armistice; Formosa is not included in that." *The Viceroy*: "Let Formosa be omitted from the treaty until you have taken it." After some more discussion as to the date of the transfer, Count Ito had a clause drawn up to the effect that within a month after the exchange of ratifications the two countries should send High Commissioners to arrange the transfer. *The Viceroy*: "Within a month is pressing us too hard. The Premier and I are too far from Formosa to really appreciate all the conditions involved. The best way would be for the Chinese government to direct the Governor of Formosa to come to an understanding with the High Commissioners sent by Japan to Formosa as to the regulations and details of transfer. When ratifications have been once exchanged, and the two countries have fairly entered upon cordial relations, then any matter can be discussed." *Count Ito*: "A month is enough." *The Viceroy*: "Everything is in a state of confusion. Two months would allow things to become comparatively settled. Why be in such a hurry about Formosa when it is actually in your mouth?" *Count Ito*: "We have not swallowed it yet, and we are very hungry." *The Viceroy*: "Two hundred millions are enough to appease your appetite for a time. After the exchange of ratifications it will be necessary to memorialise the Throne to send commissioners, and a month is too little." *Count Ito*: "It may be put thus: 'A rescript shall be obtained within a month, etc." *The Viceroy*: "One may not say 'obtained.'" Then Count Ito wanted to know if these commissioners could be sent within a month. "Yes," said the Viceroy, "but as to the transfer of the island, that depends on the Governor." Count Ito replied that it must be clearly stated that the transfer was to be completed in two months; and at last after bandying the matter for some time to and fro the clause as it appears in the treaty was agreed to: "Each of the two governments shall, immediately upon the exchange of the ratifications of the present Act, send one or more Commissioners to Formosa to effect a final transfer of that province, and within the space of two months after the exchange of the ratifications of this Act, such transfer shall be completed." And after all there is good reason to believe that, but for the firmness of Mr. Foster, the American adviser, the Chinese would have tried to evade this clause of the treaty.

The fifth conference was the last, Count Ito declaring that the demands of Japan both for indemnity and the cession of territory being final they were no longer open to discussion. The treaty was accordingly signed on the 17th, three days before the expiry of the armistice, and ratified at Chefoo, China, on the 8th May, 1895.

No doubt the higher officials of the island were informed of the signing of the treaty at Shimonoseki soon after it occurred; but to the people in general nothing was known further than that the cession of the island to Japan was very probable. To protest against this, a commission, consisting of a number of prominent residents backed by all the censors, board secretaries, and *hanlins* hailing from Formosa and Fokien province, visited Peking and presented a number of memorials to the emperor, praying that the island should not be ceded to Japan; and that if China were really unable to hold it, it would be far better to present it to England.

Although the deputation made out that they had received but little satisfaction from the central government, it is now well known that the very plans of the republic were actually formed within the walls of the capital city.

The principal supporters were found, however, among the higher officers of the middle provinces, who, having taken no active part in the war, still believed in the superiority of their own braves, and were thus easily persuaded to furnish the funds for this monstrous act of duplicity, to which the whole history of warfare shows scarcely a parallel. Furthermore, their connection with the movement was characterized by a display of ignorance and conceit to an extent that could be found in no other country than China. It was a remarkable movement. Not that the Chinese officials would have any conscientious scruples in endeavoring to evade the conditions of a treaty already ratified by their emperor, but that one would scarcely expect Chinese officials to take such a course as the present in attaining their object. Chinese literati in connection with a republic and independence are almost inconceivable.

Just previous to the declaration of independence by the literati of Formosa, a memorial consisting of sixteen characters was telegraphed to the emperor at Peking by the provincial government of the island. It ran as follows : " The literati and people of Formosa are determined to resist sub- jection to Japan. Hence they have declared themselves an independent Island Republic, at the same time recognizing the suzerainty of the Sacred Tsing dynasty."

Whether the organization of the republic was initiated by Acting-Governor Tang and his associates or by the officials on the mainland is unknown ; but that the latter furnished the instructions is conclusively proved. That it was not a movement of the people, as the above telegram would imply, there is not a doubt. They knew nothing of it, and the republic as organized was the work of the officials from first to last. This should be borne in mind. The reports sent to the mainland regarding the " will of the people," " the people united to serve the Imperial Government," " the election of the republican officers by the people," etc., etc., were simply canards circulated by the officials to win sympathy and support. True the people were sometimes notified by proclamations as to what was going on ; but in not a single in- stance did the authorities consult with the people or even allow them an interview that they might express their wishes. The people were incited to oppose the Japanese, but were not inclined to endorse any other movement of the officials. It is doubtful if a thousand men in the island ever knew what the word " republic" meant.

Many of my readers are perhaps familiar with the exploits of General Tcheng Ki-tong, a Chinese officer, who, while military attaché at the Chinese embassy at Paris, was found guilty of embezzling public money and com- municating certain letters to the press. This discovery led to his recall; but, as such offences lie easy on the heads of Chinese officials, it was not long before the degraded general was again in close touch with the higher lights of the empire. With the idea of holding Formosa by declaring the island a republic, arose the urgent need of some official well versed in international law and republican forms of government. Tcheng Ki-tong was exactly the man for the place, and after a conference at Peking and a few days in Tien- tsin and Shanghai, the newly deputed official arrived in Formosa to occupy nominally the position of Minister of Foreign Affairs, but in reality to organize the new republic in accordance with foreign usages, so as to gain recognition from foreign powers, and to act as the adviser of the newly elected president.

The movement in the island was first made known to the people by the publication of the following proclamation on the walls of the city :—

"China has been grossly insulted by the Japanese dwarfs, and we cannot be other than their enemies. Therefore, we, the literati and all the populace, must join together and oppose the barbarians if they dare to land. If any one sympathizes with the dwarfs let them be seized and killed at once."

(Signed)   "All the populace of Formosa."

It was not at first believed that the above proclamation was issued with the governor's sanction ; but later it was found that, though none bore the official seal of his approval, they were scattered broadcast without his interference or disavowal. About this time, Tcheng Ki-tong arrived on the scene with apparently definite orders, and the affair, which had until now been carried on in a half-hearted irregular manner, began to assume definite shape.

To the natives of the island, the opposition to the Japanese, in spite of the fact that the emperor had nominally ceded the island, appeared in no other light than an act of loyalty to their sovereign. Still with the mild ideas of patriotism that exist in the Chinese mind, there were great numbers, in fact the majority of the middle classes, who wavered between two opinions. That it took but little to influence them to join one side or the other is evidenced by the attention that was given to outside omens. A Chinese account runs as follows : "Owing to the long drought in the island for the past two months, it was feared that the crops would bring in a poor harvest, and the agricultural portion of the Taipeh prefecture began asking one another whether this was a sign of Heaven's disapproval of their determination to resist the Japanese. In consequence of this, many became half-hearted in their manifestation of loyalty to China ; but when, on the 22nd of May, a splendid rainfall began to pour down and lasted long enough to ensure a bountiful harvest, the sentiment immediately turned the other way, and this was taken to mark the full approval of Heaven to resist the Japanese occupation to the death. Every one who possessed any weapon then began at once to sharpen his sword or bayonet for the coming struggle. A couple of days afterwards the independence of the New Republic was declared."

On the 23rd of May, the new government was announced as organized, and the declaration, of which a translation follows, was widely published :—

Official Declaration of Independence of the Republic of Formosa.

The Japanese have affronted China by annexing our territory of Formosa, and the supplications of us, the People of Formosa, at the portals of the Throne have been made in vain. We now learn that the Japanese slaves are about to arrive.

If we suffer this, the land of our hearths and homes will become the land of savages and barbarians, but if we do not suffer it, our condition of comparative weakness will certainly not endure long. Frequent conferences have been held with the Foreign Powers, who all aver that the People of Formosa must establish their independence before the Powers will assist them.

Now therefore we, the People of Formosa, are irrevocably resolved to die before we will serve the enemy. And we have in Council determined to convert the whole island of Formosa into a Republican State, and that the administration of all our State affairs shall be organized and carried on by the deliberations and decisions of Officers publicly elected by us the People. But as in this enterprise there is needed, as well for the resistance of Japanese aggression as for the organization of the new administration, a man to have chief control, in whom authority shall centre, and by whom the peace of our homesteads shall be assured,—therefore, in view of the respect and admiration in which we have long held the Governor and Commander-in-Chief, Tang Ching Sung, we have in Council determined to raise him to the position of President of the Republic.

An official seal has been cut, and on the second day of fifth moon, at the *ssu* hour, [9 a.m. May 25th], it will be publicly presented with all respect by the notables and people of the whole of Formosa. At early dawn on that day, all of us, notables and people, farmers and merchants, artizans and tradesmen, must assemble at the Tuan Fang Meeting House, that we may in grave and solemn manner inaugurate this undertaking.

Let there be neither delay nor mistake.

A Declaration of the whole of Formosa.

[Seal in red as follows] An announcement by the whole of Formosa.

The seal cut for the self-appointed President of Formosa bore the words "Great Seal of the President of Formosa." But to show that he was still loyal to the Emperor of China, President Tang later adopted the following heading: "President of the Republic of Formosa and Ex-Acting Governor of Formosa" in all his official communications and proclamations.

To the various viceroys and governors of the Chinese empire, President Tang sent this despatch:

TRANSLATION.—"Japanese having demanded the cession of Formosa by China, this has been resisted by the people of the island. We repeatedly memorialized His Majesty to reconsider this portion of the Treaty with Japan, but were as often repulsed by the Throne. In their loyalty to the dynasty the people of Formosa have sworn to oppose the Japanese to the death. Having received His Majesty's commands to return to the mainland, and while everything was in a critical condition, the people and gentry (*sic*) suddenly presented me with a seal and various insignia of rank appointing me President of the new Formosan Republic, the above words being cut in the seal; also the new flag of the Republic being a blue ground and yellow border, I was compelled to consent to act as President of the Republic for the time being, pending a second choice by election of the people, at the same time recognizing the suzerainty of the Emperor of China and standing in the relation of a tributary state to China. We are also consulting upon appealing for outside aid and a thorough reorganization of the state. I had no alternative but to accept the election of the people in the midst of the general confusion; while on the other hand I take the opportunity of telegraphing the above to my colleagues and the various Powers of Europe and America. As to our ability to stand long against the enemy it is difficult at present to prognosticate, but I earnestly hope that you will take pity upon us and aid us where you may. (signed) Tang Ching-sung."

The first business of the new government was to notify the Powers, with the intention of obtaining the recognition of the new republic. The intimations were sent by telegrams on the 23rd. Of course, it was pure folly to expect that this republic, established after the territory had been ceded to Japan, would be recognized by the Powers. Had the movement been a few months earlier, the position would have been different. Still even then, with the knowledge that open support was being extended to the island from China, the deception would have been so evident that it is extremely doubtful if the Powers, with the very possible exception of Russia, France, and Germany, would have given their assistance in furthering the subterfuge.

Arrangements had been made to house the new government in the old yamens at Taipehfu. The Parliament House was installed in the yamens formerly used as headquarters of the Defence Board, the Navy Department in the old Military Secretariat, while the President occupied his palatial Government House as of old. The Cabinet consisted of Ministers for War, the Navy, Home Affairs, and Foreign Affairs. They were installed in the large yamens which formed the old Provincial Treasury.

The military officers serving under Imperial Commission at the time of the Declaration of Independence were General Liu Yung-fu, Commander of the Chinese forces in the south, Chiu Hung-chu, an expectant Under-Secretary of the Board of War and a scion of one of the oldest and most influential

Formosa Republic (Tainan) one dollar
Government note, one fourth natural size.

Formosa Republic (Tainan) ten cent
postage stamp, natural size.

Tang Ching Sung, ex-Acting Governor and
first President of the Formcsa Republic.

The Black Flag chief Lu Yung Fu, President
of the Formosa Republic organized at Tainan.

families in Formosa, commander of the forces in the central districts, and Admiral Yang, naval commander of the Chinese army in the north.

Upon the declaration of independence, notice was given that, in order to dispense with half-hearted republicans, any official or private individual would be permitted to leave within the space of three days, after which no departures would be permitted unless on government business. This permission was immediately taken advantage of, either from fright or keen intelligence, by some one hundred and fifty persons of different ranks and conditions, including Ku, the provincial treasurer, and Yang, the Fokien admiral,—the latter taking passage on a Chinese gunboat which had been lying in Kelung harbor for some time. Only five or six of the "deserters," for so these people were styled, were military officers of any importance, the others being civil officials from Kelung, Tamsui, and Taipeh, with their families.

Chief among the refugees was the famous millionaire of the island, Lim Pan Bang, (Liu Wei yuan) the wealthiest landed proprietor in Formosa.[1]

On the first day of the organization of the republic, Lim was residing in his comfortable residence in Twatutia. On the next morning, he was gone. No one had observed his departure, not even his own body-guard, who, had they been aware of his intended flight, would have certainly frustrated it. Formosan body-guards were of that peculiar type that they protected their own interests much more than those of their masters. People who pretend to know say that the dignified celestial made his escape to the port of Hobe, clad in the rags of a common coolie. A foreign steamship had just arrived, and within an hour she departed specially chartered. The next morning, the Senior Commissioner of the Imperial Stud was landed at Amoy, having turned his back on the republican government and his millions of property in the "Beautiful Isle."

The first day of the new republic was greeted with a drizzling rain. The mass of the Chinese were unable to appreciate the seriousness of their position ; in fact the Declaration of Independence appeared to them to be of but little more importance than any other piece of official business. I expected that the memorable day would find the streets filled with holiday makers arrayed in their best clothes, the houses gay with flags, and the day noisy with fire crackers. It was not so; for all jogged along as usual. The pretty tea-girls (and Formosa has some pretty girls), were picking tea with no addition to their old time coquettishness, the tea-box makers and painters

---

1. The history of Lim Pan Bang would be very interesting could reliable details be obtained. According to Chinese reports, a remote ancestor of his was once one of the crew of a Chinese junk. On one of the voyages, the crew mutinied, and, after disposing of the master, they landed in Formosa with rich spoils. Lim's ancestor then settled down in the island permanently, and by careful investment of his ill-gotten gains, was soon on the road to fortune. It is also commonly believed that this same adventurer rendered such valuable service to Koxinga that he was considered by the pirate king as one of his most trusted officers. Generation after generation the fortune of the family steadily increased. As the island developed so did they enlarge their property, until the estates of the present Lim reached from north to south and were valued at many millions. The Chinese officials, however, were not to go without their share, and frequent contributions were demanded. In return he was decorated and given the rank of Senior Commissioner of the Imperial Stud. Furthermore, the honorary position of Second or Assistant Governor was bestowed upon him, no doubt much to his regret; for while he had but little to say in the affairs of government, he had much to do in furnishing funds for the proper maintenance of his position and the keep of the large number of soldiers committed to his charge.

were working away in their usual busy style. Not a new flag or a fire-cracker in the settlement. At the president's yamen, however, the court was crowded with enthusiasts, the whole square was brilliant with new flags, including two large banners which bore the characters, "The President of the Republic of Formosa"; while above them all, floated the new flag of the nation; a blue background with the centre decorated by a hungry looking yellow tiger possessing a tail of greater length than is customarily allotted to a real tiger. The people, principally officials and their friends, fired off crackers and chattered and buzzed away with the idea, no doubt, of mutual encouragement; for the lack of enthusiasm with which the towns-people regarded the affair must have been rather disheartening to the leaders. It was somewhat amusing to note how many of the Chinese mer-chants condemned the movement wholly, because the ex-governor had introduced it during the busy season. As one local tea merchant informed me: "My talkee that new fashion blong velly good, but just now my too muchee pidgin, no have got time."

While those gathered about the Government House were still celebrat-ing the glorious occasion, a messenger arrived with the news of the arrival of five Japanese men-of-war off the port. The effect of this was at once visible; the crackers now became limited to an occasional explosion of a stray misfire by a Chinese small boy, the crowd began to melt away, while the officials withdrew to formulate some plan of action. They were beginning to realize that, in declaring the "Beautiful Isle" independent, there was something else to do besides hoisting new flags and firing off crackers. With that great love for publishing proclamations which I believe is charact-eristic of all Chinese officials, it was thought that a proclamation would effectively dispose of the present difficulty. Accordingly, the people were informed that the Japanese had arrived and that it behoved loyal citizens of the state to rise one and all, and drive the hated dwarfs from the island, and to punish anyone found sympathizing with them. Down at the port the tiger flag was hoisted over the big fort and saluted with twenty-one guns, all in plain view of two Japanese men-of-war lying off the harbor. Mr. H. B. Morse, Acting Commissioner of Customs, was ordered to fly the new tiger flag over the Custom House; but he refused, stating that he was collecting customs for the Imperial Government of China only, and not for the Republic of Formosa. No attempt to force him to comply was made, but he was informed that the president intended that the duties collected should go into the treasury of the new government, and that Chinese would soon be placed in the positions then occupied by foreigners.

The Japanese men-of-war outside, no doubt, surmised what was going on, and with the intention of making a closer investigation, the *Naniwa* and *Takachiho* steamed in quite close to the port and within easy range of the guns at the fort. Three other vessels flying the Japanese flag remained well outside. A steam launch then put off from the *Naniwa* and, about 10 a.m., steamed boldly across the bar right up the river for about a mile to where the British gunboat *Redbreast* was lying. There some inquiries were made of Lieutenant Edwards, the officer then on duty, as to the condition of affairs on shore, and after the visitors had made some remarks to the effect that the two Japanese men-of-war had come on in advance of Admiral Kabayama's party who were to follow in a few days to take over possession of the island, the plucky little crew swung around and steamed out again to the *Naniwa*, but not without taking soundings along the way. On shore, but a few rods distant, a Chinese officer, followed by a number of soldiers, was running to and fro in a great state of excitement, trying to induce some one to go out and capture the saucy marines who were actually surveying the whole harbor right before his eyes. I believe that, as the launch was about to cross the bar, some two or three rifle shots were fired at her from a sand spit near the mouth of the river, but without creating any alarm on board.

At the capital, Taipehfu, on the morning of May 25th, the new silver seal of the republic was carried through the streets, followed by a big parade in which the officials and soldiers participated, there being, however, a noticeable absence of townspeople and merchants. The situation now became exciting in the extreme; although the attention of the villagers was somewhat diverted by the arrival of a party of Chinese with the head of a savage who had been killed in the camphor districts. The gory relic was carried about the streets of Taipehfu by three soldiers in uniform, followed by a howling laughing rabble of Chinese. The people along the way all dropped their work and lined the road, apparently obtaining much satisfaction in viewing the mutilated head. After being exhibited about the streets, the trophy was taken to the second government yamen, where a number of fiends had the extreme pleasure of spitting upon it, jabbing it with sticks, and engaging in other highly enlightened practices. The three soldiers were paid $20 for their part in the performance, and they took the next morning's train for the south, no doubt to win equal fame and fortune in the southern towns.

Before the declaration of independence, three foreigners had been engaged as military instructors, two receiving a salary of one hundred and fifty dollars, and one, Mr. Billy Waters, as chief artillery instructor, receiving three hundred dollars a month. Mr. Waters, miner, bar keeper, pugilist, etc., after many ups and downs in life, at last, with the birth of the republic, rode on the flood-tide of fortune. From artillery instructor to Minister of War is quite a jump, but Mr. Waters, who informed me that he was at one time the "champion pugilist of the state of Montana," was equal to it and did not fail to make the most of his opportunities. His first mission was to Nanking viâ Shanghai, whither he went to conduct business of state with Viceroy Chang Chih-tung. He returned to Shanghai bringing munitions of war and a considerable amount of treasure with which to carry on the struggle. At Shanghai he was in constant communication with the local officials and taotai, and was attended by two high deputies of the viceroy of Nanking.

Active preparations were now made to strengthen the defences and increase the forces of the new republic. The different headmen throughout the country were forced to contribute large numbers of native troops, and several steamers were busily engaged in bringing troops and munitions of war from the mainland. The steamships *Martha* and *Arthur*, under the

German flag, had been chartered by the Formosan republic, and were for some weeks kept plying between Formosa and the mainland, carrying troops and ammunition. Soon after the establishment of the republic, the owner, Count Butler, wired definite instructions to Shanghai that neither vessel was to be permitted to carry munitions of war. Other owners were not so scrupulous, however, and several chartered vessels, under the flags of European nations, carried on the transportation of war material without molestation. It would appear that the Customs treated the new republic very leniently, in clearing vessels with troops and ammunition for a country then nominally in rebellion against the emperor. Without the least pretence at secrecy, ships carrying undoubted contraband of war departed for ports in Formosa after the cession of the island and the establishment af the republic. The principal shipments were made from Canton, Foochow, and Shanghai; and, had a repetition of the *Kowshing* affair occurred, the Japanese could scarcely have been blamed.

The Viceroy Chang Chih-tung was, so far as is known, the principal patron of the new republic. Besides furnishing arms and ammunition, he sent much treasure to the island, and during the days of confusion just prior to the arrival of the Japanese, a foreign firm was approached by the agents of the viceroy with the request that they should aid in the transport of $200,000 to the president of Formosa.

Although very boastful of their own strength, the new government began to look around for foreign assistance. With the knowledge that the French press was agitating for intervention to prevent the Japanese occupation of Formosa and the Pescadores, the new president had hopes that the great European republic might extend its sympathies and help to its poor little sister in the far East. Certain overtures were made to the French, and it was extensively rumored about, not only in the island but in the foreign journals on the mainland, that the whole French fleet would soon appear in Formosan waters. At last the day was definitely stated, and, sure enough, the French arrived; not, however, with their fleet, but with one small cruiser, *Beautemps Beaupré*. Two of the officers went up to the capital and had an interview with His Excellency Tang. Just what transpired was kept secret, but General Tcheng Ki-tong informed me a few days later: "We are very hopeful." Still it was extremely unlikely that France would be induced to interfere at that late hour, and certainly no naval officer would hold out false hopes of encouragement. Thrown now on their own resources, the officers of the republic exerted themselves even more than before to strengthen their position from a military point of view.

In summing up the defences of Formosa, it is well to divide the island into two parts, north and south. Although geographically not far apart, the conditions of each are so entirely different that, in planning a campaign, they would need to be handled as separate problems. The monsoons which blow strongly at certain seasons on the Formosan coast are responsible for this. That portion of the year which would be desirable for a prolonged campaign in the north would, owing to the monsoon, be entirely unsuitable in the south, and vice versa. In the north there are only two harbors open to sea-going steam vessels, Hobe (Tamsui) and Kelung. The former affords a safe anchorage in the Tamsui river to vessels drawing less than thirteen feet. Kelung has a large harbor open to vessels of any size and can be used with more or less safety all the year round, but is usually troublesome during the north-east monsoon. The harbors on the eastern side are practically non-existent, with the exception of Suao Bay. Those on the western coast are mere roadsteads with sand banks and shoals, some of which, however, can be negotiated by Chinese junks and steam launches. The local military authorities had confined themselves to the erection of modern fortifications at Kelung and Hobe. The Chinese are great sticklers for old customs; and as the French had bombarded Kelung and attempted to land troops at Tamsui, they thought it followed as a matter-of-course that the Japanese would attempt the same. It must be admitted that Kelung was admirably prepared to meet almost any fleet that was likely to be sent against it. The harbor with its narrow entrance is surrounded by high hills and bluffs, several of which were crowned with splendid fortifications mounting heavy modern guns, including one twelve-inch, one ten-inch, two eight-inch, and two six-inch Armstrongs. Scattered about were also a number of small batteries for close range firing containing some thirty or forty small Krupp guns of six and a half centimetres, and several machine guns from the arsenal at Nanking. So impregnable did this position appear that a certain foreign resident of Kelung was absolutely convinced to the last that if the Japanese were to appear, their defeat was inevitable. Well equipped troops to the number of 20,000 men, inclusive of local levies, guarded this district, which also comprised the villages of the surrounding territory and coast line south for some twenty miles.

At Hobe (Tamsui), the "great fort" on the northern side of the river, the principal protector of the port, contained one twelve-inch, and one ten-inch Armstrong's, and two eight-inch Krupp's. Several batteries had been newly erected in the vicinity of the port and on both sides of the river. About three miles up the river and on the south bank, a long trench had been constructed along the mountain side, defended by one eight-inch and one six-inch Armstrong. Long lines of newly built trenches and ramparts, connected in such a way that troops might be marched between different points of strategical value without coming in sight of the enemy, surrounded the village of Hobe to the seaward. Upon these were mounted most interesting old curios in the shape of guns. The display in its way was really magnificent. There were Spanish guns, Dutch guns, and representative guns of apparently every imperial dynasty in China since guns had been invented. They were of all sizes, from little fellows of three feet to monsters of from ten to fifteen feet in length, but all were in one uniform condition of rust and rottenness. The soldiers could be seen nearly every day prospecting around for these old cannon, which had lain so long on the ground that the majority of them were buried from sight. Upon one being found, there was as much joy expressed as we might expect from the discovery of one of Captain Kidd's treasure chests; the assistants were called, the old weapons were exhumed, the mud scraped off them, and they were carried away by a crowd of soldier-coolies to the fortifications.

There they were mounted on parapets so small that there was scarcely room for the gun carriages, and made of such soft, newly thrown up earth that the discharge of the guns could not but have rendered great service to the enemy, inasmuch as it would have inflicted terrible slaughter on the gunners standing by and the infantry lying low in the trench behind. So apparent was this that it is impossible to believe that any Chinese who had ever witnessed the discharge of any fire-arm would have consented to act as gunner or to be within a hundred yards of such weapons when fired. Incomprehensible as it may seem, some of these cannon were absolutely without any carriage whatsoever, being mounted by partially covering them with earth, but leaving both ends exposed. Perhaps the Chinese idea was that the moral effect of a long line of frowning muzzles would be sufficient to frighten away the Japanese and that it would never be necessary to fire a shot. Whether this was so or not, the village people seemed to be much impressed with the formidable nature of these instruments, and greeted the approach of a fresh one with a chorus of "Ai-yas."

Twenty camps, containing ten thousand soldiers in all, were stationed at Hobe and scattered along the river a dozen miles to Twatutia. According to the president's reports, there were, including native volunteers, fully one hundred and fifty thousand men under his command in the island. With a liberal discount for exaggeration, there were no doubt altogether from north to south about half this number, say seventy-five thousand men. Two thirds of the troops, according to the official report, were on duty in the northern half of the island. Counting the in-country volunteers, the Hakkas armed by the president, the regular army from the mainland, it is safe to say that the number in the north reached some fifty thousand men.

The government arsenal at the capital with its thorough equipment of modern machinery, including a complete rolling mill, had been manufacturing ammunition for four years, so that there was an abundance on hand even for a protracted siege.[1]

The powder mill had also been kept running full time, turning out explosives which, I was informed, were of fair quality. Altogether in the arsenal, powder mill, and rifle repair shops, some 800 men had been daily at work for a considerable period. They would not have been Chinese if, even in their foreign built establishments, they had not added something to show that they were still loyal to that "Olo custom," and in the new arsenal, mingled with modern Krupps and Gatling guns, were to be seen a number of those most ridiculous of weapons—the old Chinese jing-galls.[2]

------

1. The full working capacity of the arsenal was some three hundred 8, 10, and 12 inch and six hundred 6 and 7 inch chilled shells, besides 1,000 small shells for field guns and 500,000 rifle cartridges, per month.

2. Jing-galls are of various lengths, but those used in Formosa averaged about nine feet, and had bores of about an inch in diameter, now varying considerably with the amount of rust that had been allowed to accumulate in them. Their mechanism was decidedly simple; in fact that was one of their chief defects. One kind consisted simply of a long barrel with a matchlock mounted on a wooden tripod with a sort of stock, presumably to be placed against the shoulder of the marksman. There were a large number of breech-loaders with half of the circumference of a portion of the barrel at the butt end cut off lengthways, so that a permanent cartridge, made apparently of cast iron and provided with a handle, might be inserted and shoved well into the barrel; after which a piece of bar-iron placed between its head and the butt of the barrel provided against the cartridge being thrown out when the weapon was discharged.

It should be noted that, whatever was the equipment of the army on the mainland, the troops in Formosa were generally well, and some of them splendidly, armed. Several thousand were provided with late model 44 calibre Winchester repeating carbines, weapons which will compare favorably in cost with any military rifle in use in Europe ; and which are considered unsurpassed for all-round work, especially guerilla warfare, which the Formosa-Chinese troops were expected to adopt. Other rifles, some of which were magazine, were the comparatively modern Mauser, Lee, Remington, Spencer, Peabody, and Martini-Henry. These were divided among the different corps so that all soldiers of one camp were possessed of the same kind of rifle and had an abundance of proper ammunition for the same. It can safely be said that the regular troops of Formosa were well-armed, well-uniformed, and that many were well-drilled in a sort of semi-European style. I witnessed their drill on several occasions, and, while there was much that reminded one of a pantomime at home, still the men were in picturesque uniforms all of similar design ; they stood straight and well in line ; generally in single rank, and seemed familiar with the use of their weapons. Their various movements appear to have been directed by drum signals. Formed in one long rank with the officers in mandarin dress, the roll of a small drum prepared them for the movement required, which was executed immediately after a low "boo—oom" from the big drum ; the latter on one occasion being an affair about six feet in diameter, and requiring two men to carry it. Banners and colors were in great number and variety, and seemed to be limited by no general regulations, but selected at the pleasure of the commander. The best organized troops had first a large flag with characters denoting the division, then followed a smaller flag denoting the corps or camp of 500 men, the company flag to each hundred men, and lastly one small banner to every squad of ten soldiers ; although, to do them justice, we must state that usually the squad color-bearers also carried arms. Of target practice there was very little. When any did take place, it was usually on a range of small area and provided with a trench running the entire distance from the marksman to the target. The reason of this I could never learn. It was the custom on certain occasions for high Chinese dignitaries to attend and sit in state to the rear of the marksmen. Near the target, but protected from wild shots, was placed a drummer who pounded vigorously whenever the target was struck, no very difficult task considering the size of the targets and the close range. Still it was possible to miss ; and if common gossip is to be believed, a small compensation, varying with the degree of excellence the marksman wished to attain, was sufficient to induce the drummer to entirely overlook the target and record as bull's eyes any shots which fell scattered about the surrounding landscape. Furthermore, it was quite possible by similar means to insult the drummer to such an extent that

---

The charge was ignited usually by a match-lock arrangement, although some rude attempts had been made to provide the weapons with a hammer for the use of percussion caps. They were absolutely of no practical use, and no better example of the conceited ignorance and incompetency of the Chinese officials could be found than the fact that even the high officials of the Board of War at Peking declared that, after due examination, the Chinese jing-galls were found to be of superior carrying power to the modern weapons bought in foreign countries ; and thereupon 200,000 of these worthless playthings were ordered to be manufactured for distribution throughout the empire, and this after 112,874 pieces had been already made for the use of seven provinces.

he would quite lose his head, and while certain persons were shooting, neglect to drum at all, thus making it possible for any one to play a joke on his best enemy if he desired and had the all necessary funds.

The ordinary soldier was dressed in a large sleeved Chinese jacket of some attractive color, trimmed with a wide border of a darker shade. This jacket was generally made specially prominent by large stiff circular pieces of cloth, usually of white, light red, or yellow, eight or ten inches in diameter, and sewn one in front and one behind, on the centre of the jacket. This bull's-eye, for such it might be termed considering that it covered the heart, bore, in Chinese characters, the division, corps, company, and number of the wearer. It was perhaps the most striking part of the whole costume, especially when appearing on the darker shades of uniform. It is no exaggeration to say that the bull's-eye would identify the Chinese as a soldier long before the uniform could be made out. And that it was placed over the most vital parts of the body is still more incomprehensible, affording, as it did, a most splendid target for the enemy. No doubt the reader has often seen in street shooting-galleries brightly colored figures representing men in different positions with targets of vividly contrasting colors on their breasts. No description I could give would afford a more correct idea than this of the Chinese soldier, who thus accommodatingly furnished his foe with such splendid directions as to the best place to aim at. The jacket was the principal part of the uniform and the only one in which regularity could be found throughout a camp, with the possible exception of the head covering, which in some cases was an ordinary straw hat covered with paper and brightly painted, and in others a native woven straw peak-shaped thing, the brim of which was turned slightly outward. A waistcoat, an affair fastened around the neck and body by strings, and furnished with a row of pockets, took the place of a cartridge belt. Trousers, with the exception of those worn by the body guards of certain high officials, were non-uniform, and of all colors; but owing to the custom of lower class Chinese of wearing merely knee-breeches, these garments were so short that not enough of them could be seen to mar the uniformity of the corps. No attempt at any other leg covering or footgear was generally made. Common straw sandals were often worn, and occasionally a pair of Chinese shoes. Certain of the lower officers were provided with extremely wide brimmed straw hats, trimmed with black and supporting tassels. Their garments were entirely distinct from the soldiers' uniforms, and were ordinarily but the usual garb worn by mandarins, except that some were made of materials perhaps more bright, and embroidered with gay designs, so as to make their appearance more dashing and impressive. This was left, however, entirely to the officers' own desires, there being no regulation or system respecting the uniform to be worn by this class.

As to equipment, besides the rifle, the troops were provided with knives and sheaths of home manufacture, some of them very long and with exteriors quite dazzling in appearance. The blade, however, when drawn exposed a blunt edge which would be of but little use in combat. A pistol, usually an ancient relic of the old horse-pistol type, single-fire percussion caps, and loading with a rammer. A large number, however, were provided with a modern

"American revolver made in Belgium" according to the inscription on the barrel. They were self-cocking, automatic ejecting, and provided with all modern improvements, except as to the material of which they were constructed. Apparently cast-iron lightly nickled, they were such weak affairs that it would have been positively dangerous to fire them off. Other baggage, which will be described later, was permitted by most commanders to be carried *ad libitum*, and it cannot be said that the Chinese did not take advantage of the permission.

The native volunteers were armed and equipped in a more miscellaneous way. It would require too much space to describe the varieties of arms with which they were provided:—from old blunderbusses that no one dared to use to modern rifles which often, from lack of proper ammunition, no one could use. The old fashioned Chinese pikes and spears had lost none of their popularity, and there were but few bodies of troops that did not include a corps of these sword-bearers, just to help out appearances. Trumpeters gayly uniformed were in abundance, and in times of safety marched at the head of the column blowing long deep blasts with brass horns, five and a half feet in length. This inspiriting music, which was so freely discoursed before the battle, was notably absent during the presence of the enemy.

As a rule, the soldiers were quartered in camps consisting of 500 men each. Low mud shells, scarcely sufficient to keep out the rain, comprised the barracks, and in them troops were crowded like cattle; while, surrounding all, was a mud wall upon which an occasional sentry stood guard. No attempt was made to provide separate buildings for hospital use, although numbers of the northern troops were dying off like flies. The sick and well were all housed together, and the former received no special favors. Perhaps a soldier friend brought the regular rations to his dying comrade and burned joss sticks in his behalf. The officers gave no heed until death brought relief, when the body was ordered out to be buried by friends, if there were any; if not, to be thrown into a trench with the rest who had passed before. The pay of a soldier varied from one to three taels of silver per month, including rations, or five and six taels when soldiers were expected to procure their own food.

Most interesting were the frequent processions which accompanied high Chinese officials when out on a short journey. They were pageants worthy of reproduction on comic opera stages of the west:—A corps of trumpeters, followed by little boys fantastically dressed and with very high-peaked hats, beating gongs and cymbals, others with drums, a squad of spear bearers, an attendant or so on horseback, and finally the richly decorated chair with its numerous bearers surrounded by the body-guards well armed and gorgeously uniformed, having, in addition to jackets similar in shape to those of the common soldiers, leg shields consisting of pieces of cloth attractively embroidered, hanging down from the hip to below the knee and hiding the leg as seen from the side.

CHAPTER XX.

THE JAPANESE OCCUPATION OF NORTH FORMOSA.

1895.

Mixed Brigade, Imperial Body Guard, Prince Kitashirakawa commander, arrives at Samtiao point—Landing operations—March on Kelung—Difficult travel—Engagement at Kinchu chang—Lord Li arrives off Samtiao—Formal transfer of Formosa effected—The transfer negotiations in detail—The author joins Chinese forces in Kelung—Chinese soldiers' baggage—The military train to Kelung—Officers in name only—Chinese discipline—Arrival at Kelung—Exhibition of Japanese heads—A day of confusion—Chinese forces at Kelung—Commander Chung wounded—The return journey to Taipeh—Panic stricken civilians—Women and children abandoned—A scene of despair—Japanese troops approach Kelung—The Japanese navy and Chinese forts in combat—Colonel Kojima's land forces enter Kelung—An opportune rainstorm—The west side fort offers strong resistance—East-side castle and Palm Island forts fall easy captures—Chinese attack Chinese—Kelung occupied—Interesting hospital cases among wounded Chinese—A midnight visit to the president—Escape of republican officials—Chaos at the capital—The treasury looted—Flight of President Tang—Government buildings burned down—At the mercy of uncontrolled soldiery—Rifle fire unceasing—Soldiers quarrelling over the spoils—Looting of the arsenal—War munitions at a discount—Krupp mountain-guns for $2.—A million-dollar robbery—Telegraphing under difficulties—Taipehfu on fire—Powder mill destroyed—Powder magazine explodes—A hundred killed—Ghastly scenes—Chinese apathy—Foreigners in Taipeh—Trip to the Japanese camp—Japanese troops to the relief—The Japanese in possession—Affairs at Hobe—Hungry soldiers—German steamer " Arthur " attacked—Consternation among officials—An odd cash bargain—Battery opens fire on S.S. " Arthur "—German gunboat " Iltis " to the rescue—Foreigners at Hobe—Powder magazine explodes—Ex-President Tang at Nanking—Official sale of women and children—Japanese arrive, and occupation of north Formosa effected—Refugee Chinese braves—Narrow escape of the S.S. " Ningpo "—Japanese headquarters established at Taipeh.

To the first mixed brigade of the Imperial Body Guard, under command of the Imperial Prince, Kitashirakawa, fell the honor of being the foremost troops to enter the newly acquired territory. They were despatched from Port Arthur aboard fourteen transports on the 22nd of May, and on the 26th, the vessels dropped anchor in the port of Nakakusuki, Chujo Bay, in the Loochoo group of islands, north east of Formosa. Here they effected a junction with Admiral Viscount Kabayama, the newly appointed governor-general. Next evening the transports left, and at 9 a.m. on the 29th, the ships assembled some five miles to the south of Agincourt Island close to the N. E. coast of Formosa, where orders were received for the troops to land at a roadstead near Samtiao point (Samshokaku). Prior to this, official information had been received to the effect that the tiger flag was flying over the forts at Tamsui, that a republic had been declared, and that vigorous preparations were being made on every side to oppose the occupation of the island by the Japanese.

The transports, escorted by the *Matsushima* and *Naniwa*, anchored in Samtiao roadstead at 1 p.m. At 2 p.m. the first boat-load of infantry was safely landed. It was then ebb-tide and, moreover, a strong western gale swept in upon the shore, rendering the task of landing one of great difficulty and danger. Owing to sandy shoals, the soldiers were often obliged to jump from the boats into water up to their waists, and then wade ashore. The work continued during the afternoon and all night, the natives on shore rendering valuable assistance. A Chinese force, consisting, according to native reports, of 500 men, made its appearance during the first afternoon and engaged the Japanese infantry then on shore. The assailants were soon driven off, leaving behind them four dead, a number of Martini-Henry rifles, and their uniforms which they had discarded as they retreated. The next day, the 30th of May, four of the delayed transports arrived; all the forces, about 12,000 strong, were landed; and by the afternoon of the 31st, horses, supplies, reserve munitions, etc., were practically all ashore, and the Imperial Prince consequently gave orders to advance towards Kelung early the next day.

The troops encountered exceedingly bad roads; narrow and rugged, winding over mountains and through dense woods. H.I.H. Prince Kitashirakawa and his staff had to dismount and walk for the greater part of the distance. The mountain and machine guns were dismantled and carried by the soldiers, and there were not a few ugly falls in consequence. The first village reached was Chish-wang-ting, a small place among the mountains. The streets were placarded with official proclamations exhorting the people to take up arms and resist the invading *Wojen*, and stating that Russia, France, and Germany were sending warships to protect the Formosan people. On June 1st, the head of the column left the village. The advance guard consisted of the second regiment, a company of engineers and medical staff corps, the whole under command of Major General Kawamura. That night they bivouacked on a mountain called Santiau-tahling. Heavy showers aggravated the hardships of camp life, and the roads were the worst yet encountered. The intention was to descend at daybreak on the Chinese stronghold at Kinchu-chang (Kinkosho), where a battery had been firing at Japanese scouting parties during the preceding day. Meanwhile, Major Sunaga, commander of the 2nd battalion of the 2nd regiment, had a slight skirmish with a small Chinese force which soon retreated.

At 5 a.m., the advance guard was divided into two columns, one following the coast line, the other advancing to engage the enemy's artillery. The Japanese troops were forced to proceed over the narrow pathways in single file, occasionally exchanging shots with Chinese outposts. The village of Kinchu-chang was soon surrounded, and the first real combat commenced. The mud walls of the houses protected the enemy, and after a hard fight, during which Chinese and Japanese losses were about equal, the enemy retreated to the north-west. Another ineffectual effort was made to oppose the Japanese advance, and the braves, as they eventually retreated, were exposed to the Japanese fire and shot down in considerable numbers, including General Chung, commander of the Kelung troops, who was wounded by a shot which entered the sedan chair in which he was being carried to the rear. By half-past eight, the district had been cleared of all Chinese. The main republican force had advanced that morning from Kelung and was said to number eight or nine hundred. They were armed with Martini-Henrys, their markmanship was good, and they had made an obstinate resistance, their loss during the engagement being about one hundred killed ; while on the Japanese side, Captains Ono and Utsuki and Lieutenant Sato were killed and thirteen privates wounded, some seriously. Although the Japanese were now in complete possession of the approaches to Kelung, a sharp lookout was kept on the Chinese. Presently some two hundred of the enemy approached, but after a little firing, during which thirty Chinese were killed, they retreated towards Kelung. The Japanese captured two cannon, fifty-seven rifles, and a large quantity of ammunition.

Although the Japanese had now for three days had their forces on shore, the final transfer of Formosa was yet to take place. Lord Li Ching-fang, the adopted son of Li Hung-chang, had been deputed as Imperial Commissioner to hand over the island. Li did not regard this as a desirable task, quite understanding that the further he and his illustrious father kept away from the new-born republic the better for them both. Li Hung-chang had accordingly memorialized the throne in respect of the unsuitability of the appointment, and also of his own inability to be present, on account of sickness. The anti-Li faction, however, was too strong, and his excuses were not accepted. Lord Li then applied to the Shanghai Taotai for a force of one hundred foreign-drilled men as a body-guard, but he was likewise unsuccessful even in this. Li Ching-fang, now greatly disturbed, made overtures to the Japanese that they should first suppress the rebellion before he formally handed over the island. Without taking into consideration this rather curious request, the Japanese appreciated the embarrassing position in which Li Ching-fang was placed, and granted him permission to make the formal transfer on board a Japanese man-of-war. Highly pleased with this concession, Lord Li and his secretaries left on the last day of May, aboard the *Kung-yi*, viâ the Pescadores, and arrived off Samtiao Point (N.E. coast of Formosa), where an interview was held with Governor-General Kabayama then aboard the *Yokohama-maru*, and after lengthy negotiations, on the second and third of June, the transfer of the island was formally effected. A detailed account of the negotiations was published, of which the following is a translation as given by the *Japan Mail*:

When the *Kungyi* arrived off Tamsui, she was met by a Japanese man-of-war which delivered a letter from Admiral Kabayama requesting Lord Li to meet him in a bay close to Samtiao Point some twelve miles E.S.E. of Keluug. The *Kungyi* proceeded under escort of the man-of-war till another man-of-war was met, when the first one returned to her station. Samtiao Point Bay was reached on Saturday afternoon.

The next morning, June 2nd, Lord Li went on board the *Yokohama-maru* to confer with Governor General Kabayama as to the transfer of Formosa. This was the first meeting. The conference was attended on the Japanese side by Governor-General Kabayama, Minister Mizuno, Secretary Shimamura, and Interpreters Nire and Okubo, and on the Chinese side by Lord Li Ching-fang, and two Secretaries. At the commencement of the meeting, in reply to an inquiry by Viscount Kabayama, Lord Li said that, after returning to China from Shimonoseki, he had fallen sick and was undergoing medical treatment at a hospital in Shanghai, when he received the commands of his Sovereign to proceed to Formosa as Commissioner for its transfer: that he had no alternative but to obey the Imperial order despite his indisposition; and that he had been chosen for the post probably on account of his connection with the peace negotiations, as well as because he had once represented his country in Tōkyō. Viscount Kabayama then praised the services rendered to China by the Viceroy Li and Lord Li at Shimonoseki and subsequently, and assured Lord Li that his appointment as Commissioner was especially fortunate. He further stated that, as he had intended to arrive in Formosa by May the 25th, he had instructed Secretary Shimamura and other officials to proceed thither before him by the warships *Naniwa Kan* and *Takachiho Kan*. Arriving at Tamsui, these officials had attempted to go ashore to give early notice of Viscount Kabayama's arrival to the local authorities, but they had not been able to do so because the steam launch of the *Takachiho Kan*, in which they were proceeding toward the shore, was repeatedly fired at from a fort on the right bank of the river. The Governor-General was, consequently, obliged to change his course in the direction of Kelung. For the purpose of meeting the Chinese commissioner at Taipeh-fu, he had caused his escort to land at Santiao chue, but they, too, had been attacked by the insurgents. Under these circumstances, continued Viscount Kabayama, it became necessary to employ, for the suppression of the insurrection, troops that had originally been despatched for the purpose of maintaining order and tranquillity after the transfer of the island. Finally, he inquired what were Lord Li's ideas about the manner of effecting the transfer. In reply, the Chinese Commissioner stated that the inhabitants of Formosa, holding himself and his father responsible for the cession of the island, had conceived sentiments of hatred against them; that he would certainly be killed should he go ashore; that he would, therefore, request the Japanese Commissioner to effect the transfer of the island without landing; and that, concerning the resistance of the inhabitants of Formosa to the order of the Chinese Government, he understood that his father had sent telegraphic notice to Count Ito. The Governor-General replied that he had received from Count Ito a telegram respecting the notice alluded to by Lord Li; that it was not necessary to effect the ceremony of transfer on land; and that he would endeavor to consult the convenience of the Chinese Commissioner in every way possible. This assurance was received by Lord Li with evident satisfaction. The conversation then turned upon the telegraphic correspondence that had taken place between the Viceroy Li and Count Ito. Lord Li said afterwards that, the inhabitants having risen in insurrection, it was impossible for him to effect the transfer in a proper manner; and appealed for the assistance of the Governor-General, confessing that, without the latter's kind consideration, he should be unable to discharge the duties of his mission. The Governor-General remarked that, according to the stipulations of the Shimonoseki Treaty, it would seem necessary to draw up a catalogue of the forts, fortifications, and all other Government property, but that, under existing circumstances, it being impossible to go through such formalities, the only feasible course appeared to be that the transfer should be made *en bloc*, omitting all specification of details. He asked the Chinese Commissioner's ideas about the method of procedure and place of effecting the transfer. Lord Li answered, that since he was unable to stay long in Formosa on account of sickness, he desired to accomplish the purpose of his mission as quickly as possible; that, Formosa having b en ceded to Japan by Treaty, the sovereignty over the island had already passed into her hands; and that the transfer was a mere formality. He then asked permission to continue the conversation in his personal capacity, and begged leave to lay before the Governor-General a private memorandum on the subject of the transfer, which, should there be no objection on the part of Viscount Kabayama, might at once be recognized as an official document. To this proposal Viscount Kabayama replied that, much as he desired to expedite the conduct of business, he could not agree to hold a private conversation at a meeting of the Commissioners of the two countries. But as he had received special instructions from Count Ito, he expressed himself willing to endeavor, within the limit of those instructions, to suit the convenience of the Chinese Commissioner; and he consequently proposed to send Minister Mizuno and Secretary Shimamura to the latter's ship to confer with his secretaries. This proposal having been gladly consented to by the Chinese Commissioner, the time of conference between these officials was fixed at 2 p.m. on that day. Lord Li then referred to a story that he had learned from the Captain of a Japanese warship at Tamsui, to the effect that some Chinese officials having with difficulty escaped from forcible detention by the populace, had fled to Foo-chow; and drew the attention of Viscount Kabayama to the desperate and wicked character of the people of Formosa. The Governor-General, in reply, referred to the bravery and good discipline of the Imperial Guards, and bade the Chinese Commissioner be at ease as to the suppression of the insurrection. After conversing about the geography of the island and the customs and manners of the inhabitants, Lord Li observed that the dominions of Japan and China having come into closer proximity, the friendship between the two countries ought to be more intimate than formerly. He also thought it exceedingly fortunate that Viscount Kabayama had been appointed the first Governor-General of the island. After a correspondingly courteous reply from the Governor-General, the conference came to a close. It was then 10.45 a.m.

At 11.20 a.m. the same day, Viscount Kabayama paid a visit to Lord Li on board the *Kung-yi* accompanied by Major Matsukawa, Commander Takikawa, and Interpreters Nire and Okubo. At this meeting there were present on the Chinese side the same officials as on the occasion of the first conference. The Governor-General remarked that he should send his subordinate officials to the Chinese ship, as promised, at 2 p.m., and hoped that a satisfactory result might ensue from their consultation with the officials under the Chinese Commissioner. Lord Li once more alluded to his inability to stay any length of time on account of ill-health, and added that the sovereignty of the island having already passed into the hands of Japan, he hoped to effect as quickly as possible the object of his mission, which, after all, had no concern with anything but the mere formality of transfer. The Governor-General concurred entirely with the Chinese Commissioner as to the advisability of a speedy completion of the transfer, but wished to say a few words on a matter of some importance. He had hitherto believed that the resistance offered to the Japanese troops on their landing a few days previously had been the act of insurgents only, but he had just been surprised to find, from a notification discovered in a barrack at Sieti, that the Chinese officials had issued instructions to the inhabitants and troops under them to attack and drive away the Japanese. He had already reported the matter to the Government at home. At this announcement, Lord Li seemed to be considerably embarrassed. He, however, did all in his power to explain away the unpleasant revelation. He stated that he had heard of the establishment of a republic only since his arrival there; that the insurgents had by force prevented the civil and military officials from obeying the Imperial command recalling them; that under these circumstances, the notification in question was presumably the result of coercion; that he himself would in all probability be subjected to such coercion, should he go ashore; that the notification and the seal attached to it might altogether be a forgery; and that, under any circumstances, the Government at Peking had nothing to do with the matter. The Governor-General then passed on to the subject of the suppression of the insurrection, and observed that the insurgents could not be regarded in the light of legitimate belligerents; that the object of the Japanese Government being on the one hand, to purge the island of such as might offer resistance to its arms, and, on the other, to treat all good citizens with consideration and clemency, he had no doubt that the people, appreciating the just and righteous conduct of the Japanese Government, would soon be glad to place themselves under its administration. Lord Li seemed to admit the truth of these observations. He extolled the ability of the Governor-General and said that the inhabitants of Formosa were to be congratulated on possessing such a ruler. He also begged that, upon the complete restoration of order and tranquillity in the island, the Governor-General would let the people understand that Formosa had become Japanese territory in consequence of the Peace Treaty, and would otherwise endeavor to remove the feeling of resentment against the Li family. The Governor-General assured him most emphatically that he should spare no pains to eradicate any sentiment of umbrage from the minds of the islanders. Lord Li thanked Viscount Kabayama, bowing his head several times, and the Governor-General promised to supply him with a convoy on his return voyage to China. The convoy was, however, declined afterwards by Lord Li. This conference terminated at 11.45 a.m.

In fulfilment of the Governor-General's promise, Minister Mizuno and Secretary Shimamura waited upon the Chinese Commissioner on board the *Kung-yi* at 2 p.m. Minister Mizuno asked for the production of the memorandum alluded to by Lord Li in his conversation with Viscount Kabayama, and the document was at once shown to him. It was in the form of a note describing very fully the state of things then existing in Formosa. Minister Mizuno observed that the condition of affairs in the island was of course well-known to the Governor-General; but should such a note be officially addressed to him, it would be tantamount to a recognition by the Commissioners of the two countries of the outbreak of an insurrection and the establishment of a republic. The Governor-General would then demand the suppression of the insurrection by China before the transfer of the island; whereas the Chinese Commissioner would not be able to agree to such a demand. Minister Mizuno, consequently, advised the withdrawal of the note. Lord Li acknowledged the justice of these observations, and complied with Mr. Mizuno's advice. Minister Mizuno then presented to the Chinese Commissioner a draft memorandum on the whole. Referring to the catalogue of government property in the different parts of the island, he expressed himself entirely unable to draw it up, as he had never been in Formosa, and he therefore desired to effect the transfer on the basis of any catalogue compiled by the Japanese Commissioner, who doubtless knew more about the island than he. Mr. Mizuno accepted the offer, and proceeded to arrange with the Chinese Commissioner about the manner of enumerating the Government property, the names of the islands, and so forth. Minister Mizuno then demanded the transfer of the submarine telegraph between Tamsui and Foochow, since that line had been constructed for the benefit of the island. Lord Li replied that the question of the cable was beyond the scope of his mission; moreover he did not even know whether the cable belonged to the Government or to a private company. It was finally arranged to include the line in the catalogue with a note that the matter should be settled on a future occasion between the Governments of the two empires. In the course of the above conversation, Lord Li remarked in a laughing way that, China having given to Japan a whole province, it mattered little to her whether or not she retained a telegraphic cable. At this stage of the conference, Mr. Ma entered the room and remained until the end of the meeting. It was decided that the matters arranged at the conference be set down in a duplicate note in Japanese and Chinese. At 4 p.m. Messrs. Mizuno and Shimamura left the ship.

At nine o'clock that evening, Secretary Shimamura waited upon Lord Li on board the *Kung-yi*, with a note bearing the signature and seal of Viscount Kabayama, which document then received the signature and seal of Lord Li. This completed the transfer of Formosa. After conveying his thanks to the Governor-General for the speedy completion of the ceremony, the Chinese Commissioner left for the north by the *Kung-yi* at thirty minutes past midnight, on June 3rd.

On June 1st, after having learned of the Japanese landing, I presented my credentials to a military mandarin and was placed in the officers' car attached to a military train carrying Chinese troops from Taipehfu to Kelung. I had scarcely taken my seat when a distant hum of voices increased to a perfect babel, and several hundred Chinese troopers swarmed down upon us, filling the station, the side tracks, and the train. The men possessed such a quantity of baggage and of such a character as to lead one to suppose that they were determined to have "all the comforts of home" on the battle field. Rifles, bayonets, pistols, two handed swords, knives of all sizes and conditions, cartridge belts most of them containing 80 rounds of ammunition, a blanket, and a bowl for rations, comprised an equipment which might be expected; but to this were added fans, umbrellas, lanterns, dishes, pots, small baskets containing pipes and tobacco, pictures, tin cans, pieces of rope, pieces of iron, big boxes, small boxes, straw mats, pieces of boards tied together, and bundles as big as bushel baskets containing I know not what—all carried helter-skelter without order or method. It was simply a mass of unwashed individuals, excited faces, red uniforms, boxes, bundles, loud clamors, and, to say the truth, strong odors. They were running backwards and forwards from the platform to the open cars, trying to get all their baggage safely stowed before the train should start. They were constantly running into each other in their haste, dropping bundles, and quarreling about space, until I, in my ignorance of how little angry talk counts with the race, thought a free fight inevitable. After a short time the noise subsided to a certain extent, the troops had arranged themselves in a number of open cars, produced their pipes, and settled down with a certain show of comfort. Unfortunately it commenced to rain, which stirred them all up again, and the din was renewed. The military officers and myself were in a closed carriage with vacant seats at one end. There was at once a rush made for this compartment by many times more men than could be accommodated. It mattered little to them that the car was reserved for the use of the officers. They did not intend to ride in an open car in the rain if they could help it. In they came, regardless of the protests of their nominal superiors, shouting and jabbering, until the noise was deafening. The vocal contest was finally ended by a plucky petty officer, who grabbed the chief intruder, a big fellow with bundles hanging all over him, turned him quickly around, and proceeded to kick him and his followers out of the car. It was not exactly our system of enforcing military discipline, but it was effective and we had no further trouble. The soldiers then returned to the flat cars to quarrel with their companions who had taken their places during their absence, until finally we got under way. After having zigzagged along for about half the distance, we stopped for water and then proceeded running around the numerous curves at a reckless speed. Within a few miles of Kelung our heavy train entered a steep grade. Our speed decreased as we ascended, until, just as we were about to reach the summit, we came to a dead standstill. We then backed down again to the level and, after a stop of a few moments, ran up at full speed. We gained a few feet on our previous record, but did not get over the ascent. The railway attendants then requested the soldiers to get out of the cars, but not one budged ; they only chattered and remained where they were, enjoying the whole situation immensely. There was nothing to be done but to run back about two miles, where we remained stationary for some half hour, while steam was being coaxed up to rather a dangerous pressure, I fear, and then rushing forward at an alarming speed, we negotiated the hill and dashed down the other side into the village of Kelung.[1] Here the soldiers poured out and scattered down the roadway with their many possessions carried Chinese fashion; their guns as shoulder poles with the bundles balanced at each end. The station was crowded with excited men, women, and children, with all their valuables about them, who filled the cars as soon as the soldiers had left them. Six train loads of people had been carried away, and as many loads of soldiers brought into Kelung during the day.

In the harbor, sanpans and junks were transporting families, who sought safer refuge, into the country, the children brimming over with happiness, laughing and singing, considering it all a holiday ; but the anxious faces of the parents giving evidence of different thoughts.

The town of Kelung itself was almost deserted, shops and markets closed, and such few villagers as were seen were hastening away to safer quarters. The soldiers were devoting much attention to three Japanese heads which had been brought in the night before with great bravado, and for which 300 taels reward had been paid. Later they were packed in saw-dust and sent to Taipeh-fu, where they were stuck on bamboos together with a blood-stained jacket and cartridge pouch belonging to a Japanese private, and placed in front of the president's yamen in the presence of a large and admiring audience.

Arriving at the Custom House in charge of Mr. Dulberg, I at once sent my credentials to General Chung. In answer he informed me that the following day, a force of 2,000 men would advance to the front, and that I could join them. A new proclamation was published during the day, stating that 30,000 taels would be divided among the soldiers, if they succeeded in driving the Japanese back to the coast.

The 2nd of June was a day of great confusion and excitement in Kelung. The Japanese were drawing near, and the retreating Chinese were pouring in all day. Many had already dropped their bright colored jackets, and some had turned them inside out. They all looked tired and worn out, and were glad to seek even such a temporary refuge as Kelung. Trains bringing troops continued to arrive from Taipeh nearly every hour. After alighting, the men wandered about all over the place, paying but little attention to their officers. There were now altogether some twelve thousand troops in and about Kelung, and with their numerous gay banners and their brightly colored uniforms the effect was very picturesque. Later in the afternoon, General

---

1. This heavy grade, in which on ordinary occasions passengers were frequently obliged to leave the coaches and even in an emergency to assist in pushing the cars, has been avoided by the Japanese, who have constructed a long tunnel through the range formerly ascended.

Chung was brought back wounded. He had gone out with a small party of about 300 guards to reconnoitre and lay out a plan of campaign for the morrow, but the long-range shooting of the Japanese, so terrifying to the Chinese, brought him down with a shot through his leg as previously described, before he even knew he was in their vicinity. During the day, three Chinese were beheaded, who were found to have rendered assistance to the enemy and were wearing, attached to their clothes, a tag bearing characters written by Japanese. One of the heads was placed on a long bamboo pole and swung over the railroad track, the other two were taken to Taipeh fu, tied up by their queues, and left on short poles to grace the western gate.

I lost the opportunity of witnessing the next day's fight in consequence of the wounding of Commander Chung, who requested me not to attempt to go out, as the officers were losing all control over their men. One had only to note the wild disorder of the soldiers, quarrelling among themselves, killing their officers, robbing and looting at every opportunity, to know that a foreigner would have had but little chance among them. And to make matters worse, my interpreter and boy had run away to Taipeh-fu. Unacquainted as I was with their language, it became necessary to give up all plans of accompanying the Chinese troops, and to return to Taipeh. At the station there was a perfect panic. The place was strewn with guns and ammunition boxes, spears, banners, broken furniture, Chinese boxes, etc.; and hundreds of villagers, women with children in their arms, were begging places in the cars, while the men were pulling and crowding them back to make room for themselves. Even among the men it was a fight for places, and the weakest were forced off the cars to add their angry yells to the cries of the women and children. I believe not a woman or a child secured entrance, and as the train literally plowed through the hundreds that surrounded it, a cry of despair arose that was heartrending in the extreme. Several Japanese men-of-war had been seen well out from the harbor, and with the Chinese soldiers straggling in from all directions, it was believed by the terror-stricken non-combatants that they were caught in a trap, out of which the departing train offered the last chance of escape. During the night the last preparations to oppose the Japanese were made, the forts were crowded with soldiers, entrenchments on the surrounding hills were all occupied, and the last of the native families had followed the departing train to Taipeh, surprised that they were not attacked on the way.

The direct attack upon Kelung was entrusted to the 2nd battalion of the 1st regiment and a company of engineers under the command of Colonel Kojima.[1] The attacking column was on the move at early morning (June 3rd). Some skirmishes of little importance now took place, the Chinese retreating towards Kelung. After advancing a short distance, they came to a junction point from which three roads diverged. Here the column took the wrong road and eventually emerged on the summit of a mountain some four

---

1. The protection of the right flank of the advancing column was assigned to Major Sugawa with half a battalion, while the task of covering the left fell to the lot of the 7th company of the 2nd regiment. The reserve consisted of the 1st brigade (minus 8 companies), a battalion of engineers, and the medical corps.

or five thousand metres to the south of Kelung. A rest was now taken, and as the position was a good one, it was decided to establish headquarters there temporarily. About this time, the Japanese fleet off the coast opened fire against the forts overlooking the harbor.

The military attack was not, however, commenced at once; about two hours being spent in waiting for the arrival of the bulk of the attacking column and reconnoitering the surrounding district. From the position now occupied by the main column, the city of Kelung could be seen below. One slope ran down towards the right and another towards the left, and a single road led down between the two to the city. On the slope to the right stood a high watch-tower, while to the seaward of that was a large fort built to oppose the enemy on sea or shore. To the south of the city were several batteries along the summit of a hill pierced with a railway tunnel, while across the harbor crowning a high hill were the Chinese colors floating over a fort and battery erected there. The bright banners and gayly uniformed Chinese troops could be seen here and there; and with the knowledge that modern guns of large calibre were mounted in the different forts, it appeared that the day's fight would be a memorable one. The navy was the first to commence active operations. Since early morning, the Japanese squadron, led by the flagship *Matsushima* with Admiral Arichi in command, had been cruising off Kelung. Later in the day, steam pinnaces had carefully reconnoitered the enemy's position, and returning had reported that many Chinese soldiers in white uniforms were crossing the small channel to Palm Island and occupying the fort there. The Japanese troops were now seen to be approaching, and to draw off the attention of the various forts, the fleet fired blank cartridges for some time. The forts did not answer, and at 9.13 a.m. the squadron ceased firing. The *Oshima* now arrived, making five vessels altogether, the others being the *Matsushima, Naniwa, Takachiho,* and *Chiyoda.* At this time one of the pinnaces brought the information that Chinese, estimated at 1,000 and carrying a large amount of supplies, were approaching Palm Island, and that upon sighting the launch, the Chinese had fired upon it. The *Takachiho* now approached the Palm Island fort and fired. This fort as well as the west side fort answered with several rounds. Upon perceiving this, the men-of-war all formed in line of battle, and at about 10.30 o'clock, by taking a circular course, the vessels approached one by one to a position some 6,000 metres distant and bombarded the fort, firing some fifty rounds altogether. Palm Island fort with its fine modern guns (one 12-inch Armstrong, two 10-inch and two 7-inch Krupps) made but little effort to defend itself, and after firing some 12 rounds ceased altogether. One of the other forts with two 7-inch guns fired 6 rounds. The shells of one fort invariably went over the Japanese warships, while those from the other as invariably fell short.

At noon, Colonel Kojima with the bulk of the column began to march down into the valley in the direction of Kelung. Under ordinary circumstances this would have exposed him to a strong fire, but fortunately it began to rain so heavily that the onward movement was quite concealed. On arriving at the entrance of the town, however, their presence was greeted with a heavy fire from the surprised soldiers.   The Japanese returned the fire with good will, and, a second column supporting them from the heights above, the Chinese soon fell back, retreating into the village, and eventually out along the railway track towards Taipehfu, leaving Kelung in the possession of the column of 500 men.   Meanwhile, the fort garrisons still remained to be dealt with.   The west side fort, armed with two 7-inch Krupps, as well as smaller guns, was found the most difficult place to capture. Its very high elevation, commanding a position with steep slopes on all sides, made it impossible for the Japanese infantry to effect any damage upon it. Even a mountain-gun had little or no effect, there being no position from which shells could be thrown into the fort.   After a several hours' engagement, some six hundred of the garrison seemed about to retreat, and the rapidity of the fire from the fort greatly lessened.   The Japanese took advantage of this pause, and a squad of nineteen privates was able to gain entrance to the fort from the rear and was soon followed by a company.   The rest of the Chinese garrison immediately fled, and the Japanese flag was raised over the fort.   Meanwhile, the castle fort near the Custom House with three 7-inch Krupps and four Krupp field pieces had fallen an easy capture, the troops marching in singing their national song.   Palm Island fort with its mammoth guns had given up with scarcely a struggle.   The garrison from the east side fort, with two 7-inch Krupps and one 7-inch Armstrong, had also evacuated it without returning the Japanese fire.   From Chinese sources it would appear that prior to the capture of the village, the Cantonese troops occupying a battery on the hill over the old railway tunnel, made the best fight, but oddly enough it was against their own countrymen instead of the Japanese. It seems that, as the deserting Chinese soldiers from the various Kelung camps attempted to run away by the road passing the encampment, the only road then open, the Cantonese shot and cut them down, killing and wounding about fifty, and driving the others back.   The Japanese loss during the engagement was three men killed, one officer and twenty-five men wounded; and the Chinese had about two hundred and fifty men killed. Considering the great strength of the forts, and the large force of 12,000 well equipped Chinese, the Japanese, with forces strikingly inferior in number and unprovided with field artillery, had reason to feel proud of their day's work.

Unfortunately an accidental explosion of Chinese gunpowder occurred in a temple after the city had been occupied, causing considerable loss of life.

To the little foreign community at Twatutia, 20 miles from Kelung, the early days of June were days of anxiety, while the Chinese were almost panic-stricken.   The news of the Japanese victory at Kelung was known on the afternoon of the day of the capture, the republican officials making no attempt to deny it.   Towards evening, the wounded began coming into Twatutia.   They were provided with a space on the side walk in front of the Chinese hospital, where they received but scant attention from the Chinese doctor in charge.[1]

---

1. Some interesting cases were seen among the Chinese wounded, illustrating the wonderful penetrating power of the .315 (8 millimetres) calibre bullets which were here used by the Japanese for the first time in warfare.   One Chinese had been shot in the back, the bullet passing through the right lung, then through the arm which must at the time have been close to his body.   The wound

During the next day, June 4th, considerable confusion prevailed. Petty officials with their families were going down river, many shops were closed, and the streets were comparatively empty. During the evening, it was rumored about the city that the president and Ex-Governor Tang, with his trusty friend and adviser General Tcheng, intended deserting their beloved republic and joining their monarchic friends on the mainland, where, if there was not political freedom, there was at least freedom from Japanese men with guns, and that was something to think of. All were much interested in ascertaining the truth of this report, inasmuch as the flight of the officials meant a regime of anarchy; and to satisfy ourselves on the point, a foreign friend and myself started about midnight for the city. It was a black night and drizzling rain was falling. The shop-doors were closed, and with the exception of a passing soldier, no one could be seen. Arriving at the city wall, we found the gates closed and a heavy guard of soldiers on duty there. Still even in times like this, there are ways and means, and the showing of a silver dollar between the doors was sufficient to induce one of the guard to unbar and unbolt the big affair and bid us enter. The rain had now increased to a heavy shower, and with the exception of an occasional flash of lightning, all was pitch darkness, while the silence of the streets through which we passed was very depressing. Reaching the president's yamen we found a big guard outside the gates with loaded rifles, ready to prevent the entrance of any one who had no business there, and equally ready to prevent any one leaving who they thought was better there. We had a little difficulty in satisfying the guards that we really had important business with the president, and, if I remember rightly, a dollar or two was used here as a helper. Even then, the big heavy gate was swung open just wide enough to allow us to squeeze through and then hastily closed, and the big heavy beams again placed across and all made secure. Inside the great building was a scene that I shall never forget. All was in darkness, except here and there a flickering torch, lighting up the grotesque decoration of the place, the wierd faces of the grinning Chinese sages painted on the doors, and showing the apartments stripped of all valuables, as though flight was in view. Even the soldiers were very quiet, listening attentively to every sound, but not without evidences of extreme anxiety; for the Japanese were expected at any time, and the tales of the fighting at Kelung were not encouraging. Soldiers dripping with rain, bearing messages to the president, were constantly arriving, probably from different outposts. Their rifles were ready for instant use, and I was quite alarmed to see several of them carried in the most reckless manner, loaded, and with the hammer at full cock. General Tcheng Ki-tong was called upon, but he had nothing to say about any intended departure either of himself or the president; in fact, he declared, nothing was further from their

in the back was a small red spot looking as though the skin had simply been scratched off, on the chest was a wound somewhat larger, while the arm contained a hole large enough to put one's finger in, and the bones were badly shattered. Another case was that of a man who had been shot near the elbow joint; the bullet, passing along in the arm through the wrist and finally striking the small bones of the hand, had literally torn it to pieces. The aperture at the elbow resembled a small round burn with the skin off, and no opening could be seen, while the arm, so far as outside appearances went, was uninjured.

thoughts. We then departed, accompanied by two Chinese officials who wished to escape from the city without attracting attention, and who begged to be permitted to pass as our servants. At the railway station, we found numerous soldiers watching the president's special car to provide against any attempt being made by His Excellency to escape by rail.

At 2 a.m. on the 5th of June, the yellow Republican Tiger gathered in his long tail, and laid down and died for lack of nourishment. The president had made an unexpected exit, the minister of Foreign Affairs had urgent business elsewhere, the eight members of parliament, who had been drawing the princely salary of fifty cents per day, had gone down river to Hobe to escape with their families to the mainland; and all that was left of the treasure was being fought for by a crowd of murderous fiends, who were making night hideous with their yells. Thus the ten-day republic was fast fading away. It seems that the president had divided fifty thousand dollars among his own body-guard as release money, that he might leave his yamen. The news of this soon spread, and when other soldiers called to demand their share of the spoils, they found the ex-governor not at home. Thus foiled, they took the next best means of giving vent to their rage by firing the president's big yamen. This magnificent structure, built partially of wood, was all ablaze in a moment, and the flames shooting high in the air could be seen for miles around. The first flame marked the last hour of peace and order, and but a few moments intervened before the yells of the rioters and the cries of their victims, with the occasional sharp report of a rifle, rose above the crackling and the roaring of the fire. All now realized that they were at the mercy of the thousands of Chinese soldiers and the town's rabble. Although it was still dark, all were on the alert, and a low hum of voices could be heard from the hundreds of peaceful though terrified Chinese who were anxiously waiting the coming of daylight. The rifle reports now became more frequent, while the pattering of feet and the hum of excited voices added to the tumult.

No one seemed to know exactly how or when the president got away. The German blue-jackets saw some guards approach the river with two or three mandarins, and depart on a steam launch during the night. The president was probably one of them, but even if he left disguised, it was marvellous that he should escape the Chinese soldiers who were watching his every move. The looting of the treasury was attended with considerable loss of life. Greedy soldiers, anxious to carry as much as possible, ran away with dollars wrapped up in cloths, and dropped them along the way. It did not take long to remove the several hundred thousand dollars that the officials had been forced to leave, but woe to the Chinese who was found by the crowd with more than his share of the silver. Fifty feet from the foreign club there lay, during the day and night, the body of one looter who was actually kicked to death; the silver, of which he had too great a quantity to conceal, having been taken from him. A second body was lying on the side walk not far distant, with its throat cut, and the rats were at the corpse before it ceased to breathe. The scene at the yamen where the treasure was, must have been one of great excitement. The money was all in silver, and its great weight was a guarantee that no one of the fighting looters would obtain a very large sum. The result was that hundreds flew to the scene and were enriched ; and, according to popular report, after the yamen had been stripped, the crowd devoted themselves to searching the streets to pick up the silver that had been dropped on the way.

At ten in the morning a friend and I walked to the president's yamen, which was still smoking with the conflagration of the earlier morn. We found hundreds of robbers overrunning the place and carrying away everything they could lay hands on ;—chairs, cushions, bed clothes, mats, boxes, lamps, lanterns, trunks, mirrors, mandarins' clothes, flags, foreign pictures and frames, curtains, broken clocks, pieces of crockery, stools, benches, Chinese couches, doors, pieces of richly carved wood-work, in fact everything of value which had remained untouched by the fire. Long processions of Chinese carrying away the loot and returning Chinese running back for more could be seen all day in long unbroken lines in every street leading to the city. Not far distant we found a half hogshead of samshu [1] in the centre of an admiring crowd who had been drinking one another's health to such an extent that several were obliged to hold on to the big barrel with both hands in order to preserve their equilibrium. They were quite good tempered, proposed that we should join them in one for the president, and ladled the spirits out in any quantity to every man, woman, and child, who came flocking from far and wide, bringing pails, pots, and cans to hold the stuff. So freely was it handed out that the ground round about was muddy with the waste.

Returning to Twatutia, we found that the arsenal had been broken into, and long lines of robbers were filling the streets in its vicinity. Bars of lead, copper-ingots, copper slabs, zinc, tin, brass, big and small pipes, big sheets of steel requiring sometimes five men or more to carry them, boxes of nails, screws, long steel and sheet iron bars, pieces of machinery, parts of guns, machine guns, mountain guns, even field guns, enormous quantities of cartridges and gun shells, in fact simply everything that was, or could in a short time be rendered, movable, were being hurried away. From the oil-house came tins and buckets of oil, chemicals, including sulphuric acid, a tin of which breaking in the street created considerable excitement among coolies who walked into it bare-footed and then indulged in the wildest display of Chinese language I had yet heard. The looters never hesitated at grabbing anything in the arsenal; but, after having carried it several blocks and becoming weary of the weight, they would usually stop and examine it, as though there might be after all a doubt of its value, and then rush down upon the first well-to-do looking person passing by, with an offer to sell for $25, $50, or whatever fanciful price they thought the object might bring. Once refused they were perfectly willing to drop down from dollars to cents; and in some cases, a string of cash would be sufficient to purchase an article which might cost to replace several hundred dollars. However, copper, tin, spelter, brass plates, etc., found ready purchasers among the less scrupulous of Chinese merchants, who bought great quantities at about one-tenth or twentieth of their real value. A brand new Gatling gun went begging for a few dollars, splendid

1. An intoxicating liquor brewed from rice.

little Krupp breech-loading mountain guns could be obtained for two dollars or so, scarcely more than the coolie hire.[1]

The several thousand Chinese soldiers, now engaged in a more profitable profession, were willing to dispose of their rifles for a few cents, and large numbers of old muskets were thrown into the rice fields outside the city as worthless. Brand new Winchester repeating carbines could be purchased for a dollar or less, and it is absolutely no exaggeration to say that cases of cartridges and ammunition were lying about the streets practically *ad libitum*, and could be had by any one who cared to carry them away. One firm offered 75 cents for new rifles and secured more than 600 at that price. The rifles were immediately sent down river and despatched to Amoy. A great deal of the plunder was sent across the river, and there were probably not a hundred houses in the district that did not contain some of it. So bold did the looters become that they actually endeavored to remove the telegraph instruments from under the hands of Mr. Hansen, the foreign expert employed by the government, who on this occasion had very pluckily stepped in after the Chinese connected with the place had fled, and continued the service for the accommodation of the foreigners. In order to get my press telegrams off and at the urgent request of Mr. Hansen, I spent several hours, revolver and carbine in hand, commanding the doorway. On my departure a German guard was placed at the entrance, and the place was not again molested.

During the evening it was discovered that the powder mill was burning, and that the city of Taipehfu, which had now been deserted, was again on fire. It was feared by the foreign community that the powder magazine might catch fire, and as it was thought to contain a large store of powder, the explosion of which might result seriously for the foreign houses, a number of the residents stayed up the greater part of the night. At last, at approaching daylight, worn out by the excitement of the day before, the last man on watch retired ; and while he was enjoying his first wink the long feared explosion came off, just when it was least expected.

At about 6 a.m., came a huge boom, followed by a roar like the beating of a hundred temple drums, every vibration of which seemed to cause a similar vibration in the houses, which shuddered and rocked back and forth as during an earthquake, while a huge pillar of dense black smoke arose to a great height in the air. The Chinese about the streets were panic stricken, the men chattering wildly, the women wailing and praying, and the children crying. That the barbarians had at last arrived and were employing some terrible implement to kill them all was the universal idea. The magazine was, perhaps, a mile and a half from the city, and great quantities of explosives were stored there, the bulk of which was fortunately packed in boxes or canisters. Going out to the scene about half an hour after the

---

1. After the day's work of the looters, a foreigner who had been originally connected with the arsenal informed me that 150 tons of best selected English ingots and Japan copper slabs, 20 tons of tin, 100 tons of spelter, besides an enormous quantity of copper and iron pipes, brass sheeting, etc., had been carried off ; that including the injured machinery it would require some $500,000 to make good the loss. This, together with the large amount of loot taken from the different yamens and not including the silver obtained from the treasury, would easily reach, if not considerably exceed in value, one million dollars.

explosion, I found the ruins still smoking, while unexploded powder was lying about everywhere in big piles, with here and there, a little stack of boxes containing powder, dynamite, or fuses. The paddy fields surrounding the ruins of the building contained great quantities of earth and debris; and plastered with dirt, or partially covered with the mud and muck, could be seen dead and wounded bodies of Chinese, some so disfigured that the only semblance to human beings was the quivering flesh of a mangled trunk, a besmeared limb, or the hair attached to a head just protruding from the mud. It was a ghastly picture, the wailing and crying of wives and mothers in the surrounding houses adding to the fearfulness of the scene. With characteristic apathy, Chinese were standing by, much amused, and laughing at the groans and writhings of the wounded. One poor unfortunate was sitting upright in the paddy field, now covered with water, moaning with agony and imploring the passers-by to assist him, but his movements, awkward from pain and weakness were entirely too much for the crowd. They laughed and chuckled, considering it the best of fun, and left their countryman to die without a helping hand. Our attention was called to a wounded man who had fallen, in rather a remarkable position, about two hundred feet from the ruins. He was lying with his feet in the paddy field, his body resting in nearly an upright position against the bank of the roadway which was four or five feet above the field, and his head, with all the back of it blown off, was bent at nearly right angles and rested on the pathway, with the eyes open and the face turned upwards towards the blazing Formosa sun. He was breathing, and moved his lips as if to speak, and that the poor fellow was too near death to articulate amused the crowd so greatly that they laughed most heartily. This was more than we could stand, and by taking two celestials bodily and forcing them to assist us, the body was removed from its unnatural position and placed on the pathway out of the glaring sun. The groans of the dying man became weaker and weaker. At last came a quiver of the limbs, and then the funniest part of the whole exhibition to the Chinese audience took place in a convulsive kick, as the poor wretch breathed his last. The Chinese have many good traits, no doubt, but when it comes to a matter of pity for suffering humanity, they are but little above the beasts. Certainly not less than a hundred persons lost their lives. What caused the explosion will never be exactly known; perhaps the looters in their haste threw the explosives about or were smoking the ordinary Chinese pipe and blowing out the fire and ashes, thus igniting some of the loose powder. Fortunately for the safety of foreign houses, a great portion of the stock had been carried away before the explosion occurred. While returning, we were somewhat shocked to observe a smiling robber following us closely with six paper boxes of dynamite. Observing our alarm, the Chinese loosened his hold and the packages were just dropping when my friend caught them. We silently deposited the load under water in the neighboring rice-field and took the first path towards home, undesirous of encountering any more companions similarly loaded.

Firing, at the rate of twenty or thirty shots a minute, was heard all the morning. Although much of it was the result of the Chinese love of noise, in numerous cases, especially in Banka and outside of the city, the constant fire day and night was to keep out the robbers who were looting right and left. Several women and children were slain; and, as for the men, they were too numerous to attract any attention, and were lying about the hot streets dead and dying, while the river carried many a bloated body out to sea.

Now that affairs were every hour growing more serious, the Chinese merchants prepared a petition to the Japanese, requesting them to come on to Taipeh with all haste, that the dangerous class of Chinese might be driven away and the indiscriminate burning and looting of property might cease. The Chinese, whilst they were praying for the Japanese to come, were naturally not a little averse to putting their signatures to a paper inviting them, for the reason that should the mandarins return and be victorious (and to the Chinese this seemed possible) the signers would be promptly beheaded as spies and traitors. Meanwhile, their property was in the greatest danger, and in some cases had been already burnt. Murder was a constant occurrence, and Twatutia was in imminent danger of being destroyed by fire. The capital city had been fired, the arsenal had been stripped, the saw-mill and timber-yard had not a movable object remaining, the powder-mill was burnt, the magazine exploded, and, frenzied by their success and encouraged by lack of opposition, the looters were looking about for more plunder. Nothing now remained but the private property of foreigners and Chinese; and the report was freely circulated that the houses of the former would be attacked. If the assault came off on not too large a scale, the lives of the foreign community could probably have been all saved, so admirable were the plans of the English and German guards. Property, at least the larger part of it, however, would, if the mob were at all determined, fall an easy capture. At all events, it was an exciting and dangerous experience, such as few have passed through and emerged from unharmed.[1]

To afford protection to the foreign houses was the task set before the English and German guards, fifty-five men in all, and the little launch gunboat *Patrol* with her machine gun and a small armed crew. The designs of the two commanders were that, in case of a serious attack, the hong of Messrs. Jardine, Matheson & Co., and the German consulate at the extreme south end of the street should be vacated, and the foreign occupants assemble at Messrs. Tait & Co's large hong, which, owing to its situation

1. The residences of the foreign community of Twatutia, with two exceptions, were either on or near the bund of the Tamsui river. At the time we write of, the hong of Jardine, Matheson & Co., which was represented by Mr. C. H. Best and Mr. M. Woodley, was the last foreign building to the north, surrounded by a nest of Chinese shanties, and in the most dangerous situation of all. The next building towards the south and up river was occupied by Dr. C. Merz, the German consul. In the next block was the Twatutia foreign Club, and at the north end of the third block the hongs of Boyd & Co. represented by Messrs. A. F. Gardiner and G. M. T. Thomson, and Tait & Co. represented by Messrs. R. H. Bruce and E. H. Low. Two streets back of the Foreign Club was the hong of Brown & Co. with no representative, and two blocks to the south was the hong of Lapraik, Cass & Co. represented by Messrs. Francis Cass, Francis Ashton, and B. N. Jenkins; while Captain Shubrick, commander of the English marines was there as a guest. On one street forward was the office of Reuter, Brockelmann & Co. and the residence of their representative, Mr. R. N. Ohly, where, thanks to his kind hospitality, I was at this time residing. In the next block to the south resided Mr. E. Hansen, electrical engineer. Back from the river one block was the hong of A. Butler & Co. and the residence of Mr. J. B. Siebenman, while several blocks to the south back from the river and near the Arsenal was the residence of Count A. Butler, where Lieutenant Timme, in command of the German marines, was staying as a guest.

would afford the best rendezvous. The foreign guards would then undertake to protect the two blocks of houses in between. Should, however, the attack be too strong for the small force, the hong of Messrs. Lapraik, Cass & Co. was likewise to be deserted and the efforts of the guards confined to the two houses facing the bund. Here the last stand was to be made, and should the hongs be then strongly attacked from the rear, which would probably be the first move attempted by the rioters, the foreign guards and all the residents were to seek refuge on the armed launch *Patrol*, and protected by its machine gun, as well as by the guards, would be carried down river to Hobe. Some loss of life would no doubt result, however, should matters come to this pass.

It was very unfortunate that such a state of affairs should exist while the Japanese were only ten miles away and would, if notified, have probably come on with a few hundred men, which would have been sufficient to quell all trouble in the city at once. It was resolved that it would be best for all concerned if the Japanese were notified. To do that promptly there was only one way. It was decided that a small party should make the journey and notify the Japanese. Mr. Ohly, Mr. Thomson, and myself volunteered to make the trip. We left about noon, heavily armed and accompanied by an armed Malay, a Chinese coolie, and a Chinese flag-bearer, and took the route following the railroad track. We found the people along the way perfectly peaceful, the majority of houses had small white flags raised; and, if it had not been for the constant firing on every side, one might have thought it was an ordinary trip during peaceful days. Nothing of interest occurred on the outward journey other than meeting occasional little parties of looters, one of whom carried in his hand a gold chain and gold cross evidently stolen from a Christian. The first sight of the Japanese we had was just before reaching Sui-teng-ka, (Suihenkiaku), about 10 miles from Taipehfu. We were there stopped by a sentry, and were much surprised to hear the private soldier speak to us in perfect English, "To what port are you going, gentlemen?" We explained our business, and were soon passing through the camp to the commander's headquarters. After having had weeks of Chinese rabble, the manly appearance of these soldiers was a most refreshing sight. They had advanced on that day 500 strong from Kelung, regardless of the 20,000 Chinese troops they believed were in Taipeh to oppose them. Headquarters had been established in a pretty little Chinese joss-house, and all about the camp had been made neat, spick, and span. We were received very cordially and with expressions of confidence. At our suggestion, it was decided to move the whole camp on to Taipeh at once. We joined the officers at their evening mess, consisting of rice, dried fish, and a bowl of vegetables, and after a pleasant hour's visit we were on our way back; 500 soldiers marching briskly along with us, regardless of the ten miles journey they had just completed, and willing to face another ten miles without the least appearance of discontent. They were a merry set every one of them. A full moon made night radiant, and the troops moving in one unbroken line along the zigzag railway track resembled a giant snake. And no snake could have created greater terror among the Chinese on the hills about us, who ran back into the interior, shrieking and howling as though their last hour had come. So terror-stricken was one poor old man that he ran towards the troops, and falling at the knees of the commander, yelled and cried like a madman. It was with difficulty that he was made to release his hold and return to his home in the darkness of a bamboo grove. The beating of gongs, the wailing of women who were hurrying away with their children, the wild shouting of the men as they ran from house to house warning the inmates to flee, made up a scene that I shall not soon forget. But the Japanese marched steadily onward, and no doubt it remains to this day a mystery among the simple minded Chinese who witnessed that night's quiet entry, how it was that the Japanese did not kill them all when they had such an excellent opportunity ; for these people fully realized that if the situation had been reversed, the Japanese would have been utterly exterminated. Out of consideration for the inhabitants of the city, the commander decided not to enter during the night ; for the Chinese in their present condition of nervousness would have been thrown into a state of great alarm. However, if there appeared any sign of fire or rioting, he determined to take in his men at once.

We were advised to remain with the troops ; but, believing that the successful termination of our mission would be welcome news to both foreigners and Chinese, we decided to return, and started at once for the city only some two miles distant. We were just entering the outskirts about 2 a.m., and were congratulating ourselves upon having met with no mishap, when six shots were fired at us at close range ; but thanks to the darkness and the ordinarily poor aim of the Chinese, we escaped with only a slight shock to our nerves. But it was all a mistake, so we were told with many apologies : the Chinese who fired at us were guarding the street from armed robbers, and they took us for such ; but when we informed them that we had been to fetch the Japanese they were most enthusiastically happy. The report of the arrival of the Japanese circulated throughout the city during the few hours following our return ; and, although a Chinese courier went about the streets beating a gong and crying at the top of his voice ; " Do not despair, have courage, for the great one-eyed Lim will come to-morrow from the south with twenty thousand fierce braves and drive the cowardly invaders back into the sea, whence they came," his tidings were received with but little confidence, and the Chinese soldiers and other rabble cleared out at once. The Japanese marched in at daylight (June 7th) without meeting with any opposition, and were welcomed by all peaceful citizens.[1]

While we were having our little amusement up river, the foreigners down at Hobe were not without protection ; though, had it not been for the German gunboat *Iltis*, they would have had more than their share of trouble. The steamship *Arthur*, formerly the *Cass*, with Chinese officials and others aboard, arrived at Hobe from Shanghai on the 1st of June. On the morning of the 4th, the incoming Chinese soldiers retreating from Kelung made things in Hobe look a little serious. The *Arthur* had remained at anchor in the

1. H.I.M. the Emperor of Japan was graciously pleased to express his satisfaction with the efforts of our little party by conferring on each of us the Imperial Order of the Rising Sun, with the decoration and brevet that accompanies this honor.

river; and during the morning, the Chinese paymaster of the forces went on board, carrying with him $45,000 which was intended for, and properly belonged to, the troops,—an action not calculated to promote kindly feelings among the poor starving wretches on shore. In the afternoon, the soldiers, realizing that, without food or money, they were being deserted in a strange land, commenced to fire on passengers going off to the *Arthur*,—people who were fleeing from the country with what valuables they could hastily collect. The latter were thus forced to turn back towards land; and, as their boats touched the shore, they were overrun by the hungry rabble and everything of value appropriated.

During the evening, Captain Jenssen, in command of the *Arthur*, came ashore, called on Acting-Commissioner Morse of the Customs, then started to return to his ship, but was fired upon by the soldiers, forced to turn back, and was taken prisoner by the Chinese about nine o'clock. The Chinese still continued to fire on the ship, and the report that President Tang was on board quite naturally enraged them all the more. As the *Arthur* was inside the harbor and perhaps half a mile up the river, she was practically in the power of the Chinese, who could use the big guns of the forts and sink her if they desired. Word had already been sent aboard that, if she attempted leaving, the torpedo mines would be exploded, and if that failed, they would send her to the bottom with the big guns. As the tide turned and the *Arthur* could not leave on account of low water, the captain was released. All night an intermittent fire was continued; and the native boats on the river continued to receive attention, and were forced to run ashore, and submit to being plundered.

A futile attempt was made the next day to get the vessel out, but such a continuous shower of bullets poured down upon the bridge and forecastle-head that it was impossible to work the windlass. In the afternoon, there was more firing from shore, so Captain Jenssen signalled the German gun-boat *Iltis*, which was some 600 yards away, that he was in need of help. The commander sent word that he advised Captain Jenssen and his officers to leave the ship. This they could not do in safety, owing to the armed soldiers who would undoubtedly fire upon them. Captain Jenssen, however, succeeded in persuading his passengers to give up their arms, 500 of which, lacking a safe repository, were thrown overboard as soon as secured.

On the morning of the 5th, the soldiers were still firing on the ship. Meanwhile, an armed body went on board, demanded money, and extorted $10,000 from the frightened officials; while later, two other gangs, following the same tactics, secured $35,000 between them, dividing the amount among the soldiers as far as it would go. A Customs deputy was also taken from the ship and held in his own yamen for ransom, but he escaped by a back door and arrived at a foreigner's house for protection with his clothes torn to rags. Early in the evening, word was sent from the commander of the big fort that the men were beyond his control, and that they threatened to turn the 45 ton gun on the vessel and sink her, if any attempt was made to leave; and just to show that such a thing was possible, pot shots were taken with smaller guns at sampans and cargo boats near the bar, thus cutting

, off all shore communication with the steamers *Formosa* and *Bygdo*, both lying outside.   The special grievance among the men at the fort and different batteries was that they had had no hand in the spoils.   When the commander of the fort was asked what could be done, he said that he possessed no authority over his men, but hinted that he believed the soldiers would give up the guns for $5,000, adding that, if that amount was not given them and delivered before morning, the *Arthur* would be sunk with all on board.   Two foreigners, Mr. Nightingale, of the Chinese Customs, and Mr. Waters, very bravely went to the fort late at night to open negotiations. Mr. Morse, acting-commissioner of Customs, succeeded in collecting the amount, and at four o'clock in the morning, the money had been paid into the hands of the soldiers concerned, and the four breech-blocks of the big modern guns had been placed in the possession of Mr. Morse.

Although the *Arthur* seemed to bear the brunt of the excitement, it cannot be said that the foreigners on shore were without their share. [1] Their premises were overrun by the rabble, and it required much tact to avoid arousing the rioters to hostile action.   The sight of the gunboat *Redbreast*, anchored about a mile away, and the *Iltis*, close at hand, no doubt tended to promote good behavior.   The English consul was provided with an armed guard from the *Redbreast*.

On the morning of the 6th, although the big fort had been effectually disposed of, the soldiers were making more trouble than ever, and considerable shooting had been going on in the streets of the village.   At 7 p.m., while the crew of the *Arthur* were about to weigh anchor and get away, a shell from the south shore, where there was a field battery of 9 pounders, came crashing on board, going through the upper deck on the port side, passing through the body of the captain of the ex-president's guard, and fetching up against the steel bulkhead without exploding.

Another shell hit the upper deck, and exploding killed six men instantly. Other shells came uncomfortably near, but no further damage was done. Altogether nearly fifty Chinese on board had been wounded—some fatally. As soon as the first shell was fired, Commander Ingenohl, of the *Iltis*, gave the command to clear for action, and soon after the signal from the *Arthur*, " Help, I am attacked." had been read, the first shot was fired. This exploded just below the battery; but now, having found the range, which was about 2,800 metres, the return shot from the Chinese battery, which did not hit either vessel, was answered with a second shell, which exploded in the battery, killing, it was afterwards ascertained, 13 men.   In five minutes, a third shell was fired; but the Chinese, who like fighting only when they have it all their own way, had already deserted the battery.   At 8.30, the

1. The foreigners on shore were Mr. L. C. Hopkins, H.B.M.s Consul, Mr. Robert Touzalin, in charge of the hong of Messrs. Lapraik, Cass & Co, Doctor Anglar, the community physician, and the following Customs officials:—Mr. H. B. Morse, Acting Commissioner, Mr. J. D. de la Touche and Mr. Larsen, assistants, Mr. Dülberg, Mr. Muller, Mr. Nightingale, Mr. Sheridan, Mr. Heinrichs, Mr. Schneider, Mr. Schwarzer, and Mr. Cantwell.
    On the 7th, several hundreds of refugee soldiers had literally taken charge of Messrs Lapraik, Cass & Co.s godowns.   Mr. Touzalin, the firm's representative, succeeded in persuading the men to deliver up to him their arms, and large stores of weapons and ammunition were secured by him and placed under lock and key.

Arthur steamed out unmolested with her 2,000 soldiers and many officials of the republic on board.[1]

Just about noon, as affairs were quieting down, and but a few hours after the explosion of the big powder magazine up river, the Chinese created a new excitement by endeavoring to combine business with pleasure, by indulging in a social smoke during the looting of a powder magazine. Result, six dead, besides a considerable but unknown number who found a grave underneath the mass of earth and stone which came crashing down upon them. At noon, two Japanese ships arrived off the port, and the firing which had been heard from every side ceased instantly. H. B. M. S. *Rainbow* arrived on the 7th, and H. G. M. flag-ship *Irene* on the 8th. Both saluted the Japanese admiral.

On June 8th, eighteen weary cavalrymen came into Hobe from Taipeh-fu, having led their horses most of the way, owing to the non-existence of proper roads ; and the occupation of Hobe by the Japanese was effected. The next day, more Japanese troops and several civil officials arrived, and the first task undertaken was the forwarding of the Chinese soldiers to Amoy. These unfortunates were in a deplorable state, and so alarmed were they lest they might be left behind that considerable force was required to keep them back while any fire-arms that they possessed were being taken away, and precautions made that the steamers should not be overloaded. Both from Kelung and Hobe, shipments were carried on for several days. A few deaths occurred, seemingly from weakness combined with an extreme nervous shock. The writer saw two instances of this. In one case, the man was standing on the wharf, waiting to cross the gangway. He made several unsuccessful attempts to push into line, his thin ghastly yellow face plainly indicating want of nourishment combined with deprivation· of opium. Without a sound from his lips, he fell dead where he stood, the body rolling over once, and falling with a splash off the wharf into the water. The other poor wretches with sickly grins on their faces shoved up further, availed themselves of the space just vacated, and the embarkation continued as before. The other case occurred just as the S. S. *Formosa* had cleared the wharf and was about to put to sea. A soldier appeared in a sampan with a ticket in his hand, frantically urging on the sampan man to reach the vessel before it was too late. The Chinese on board were shouting to him to make haste, and already the screw had commenced to turn. After much splashing and vigorous rowing, the sampan gained the

1. Tang Ching sung, Ex-Treasurer, Ex-Acting Governor, and Ex-President of the Formosan Republic, finally arrived at Nanking after his escape from Tamsui. He evidently thought it unwise to go on to Peking, not that he would be declared a rebel, but that he might be called on to explain the whereabouts of the large amount of government money that remained in Formosa. It is said that after his arrival at Nanking he fell upon his face before the viceroy, and refused to stir until pardon was granted for his failure to keep the Japanese out of the island.

The refugees brought over from Formosa to China included many women and children, those destined for Foochow being taken care of by the mandarins at Pagoda anchorage. Those who were so fortunate as to have homes were despatched to them. However, there were many p or women without friends or relatives; and these, according to the report of a reputable foreign journal published at Foochow, were sold at about $8.00 apiece, the child or children, if there were any, being thrown in. Buyers, it was understood, were not allowed to pick out the handsome and younger women; and that none of the more unmarketable of the poor creatures should be left in the hands of the government, the faces of all were covered up while the selection was being made.

12 inch Gun in Tamsui Fort.

An Entrenched Hill on the Tamsui River.

View from the north of Hobe showing old Dutch Fort on left and Customs Jetty on right.

Looking westward from Hobe Village.

Hobe village and port of Tamsui.

side, and the soldier stepped out of the boat. He was now safe aboard; visions of home, family, and native land no doubt flitted through his mind; he ascended a few steps of the ladder, and then, just as the hands of his countrymen were out-stretched to assist him on deck—the hoisting of the gangway had already commenced—he fell over backwards, dead, with the passage ticket still clinched tightly in his hand.

What were the total Chinese losses in battle, by disease, and in rows and riots, no one knows. There is nothing upon which to base an estimate. The losses by disease in the garrisons were very large, but no number can be given.[1]

As an indication of what the losses were, it is well to note that, out of 1,500 men enlisted at Ningpo and brought to Formosa, only 100 returned to the mainland. The survivors reported that the greater number died of disease, a hundred or so were killed at Kelung by the Japanese, and some deserted or left their comrades to join the southern troops in the centre of of the island.

With the knowledge that Liu Yung-fu, the Black Flag Chief, was holding out in the south, large numbers of the Chinese troops retreated in that direction. Reports coming in from the country told of much suffering among the smaller bands of soldier refugees. The Chinese in-country residents had been frequently raided during the earlier part of the season by these same braves, and were now, on the latter's downfall, prepared to retaliate. They refused to furnish food to the weary wanderers, and by the application of guerilla tactics, did much killing and robbing. Furthermore, the art of diplomacy was sometimes brought to bear, as the following incident will show:—A body of Cantonese soldiers stopped for food and rest in a little village not many miles from Taipeh. The villagers willingly provided them with food at fair prices, but when the soldiers were about to leave, the village elder stepped forward, informed them that the Japanese had occupied several of the larger cities, and suggested that they should leave their weapons and ammunition behind them; for if the Japanese caught them armed, they would certainly be all killed. This seemed like good advice, so the soldiers agreed, and after relieving themselves of their weapons, they were about to start on their journey. But no sooner had the last soldier laid down his rifle than the accommodating villagers grabbed up the weapons and poured a deadly fire on the now disarmed "braves." Many were killed, and all were robbed of everything they possessed, even to their clothes.

To go back to the Capital, Taipehfu, we find, on the morning of June 7th, the Japanese in possession.[2] The city inside the wall had been

---

1. Those soldiers who died were not replaced, although their names were continued on the list; and it was not at all unusual for little garrisons, quite away from the dangers of inspection, to have the male children of the soldiers put down on the roll. This can be better understood when it is pointed out that the military mandarin drew full pay for a certain number of soldiers, and while the pay roll bore the correct number of names, a roll call would show a far less number of men. In case a high Chinese official passed that way, coolies were engaged for the day, clothed in the gaudy uniform, and guns placed in their hands, - the ranks were full, the mandarin smiled and passed on—the old rogue knew that he did the same on a larger scale—and on his departure the coolies were discharged, while the regulars returned to their opium pipes and fantau.

2. The Japanese occupation of the north of the island, of course, put a stop to the further arrival of troops and munitions in the northern districts. However, one vessel had a very narrow escape from running plump into the arms of the Japanese at Tamsui. It was the steamer *Ning-po* which the Kwang-

practically deserted by all respectable Chinese, and no opposition outside having been met with, an advance squad of six Japanese were quite surprised at being fired on as they advanced towards the city wall. Their surprise, however, was but small compared with that felt by the few armed robbers who later found that they had tackled a force five hundred strong.

When the Japanese troops reached the city gates, they found them all closed and barricaded, so that it became necessary to use a ladder, which, by the way, was handed over by an old man from the inside, to scale the wall and thus gain entrance to the capital. It might be interesting to state that Captain Yamada, a staff officer of the Imperial Body Guard, was the first Japanese to enter, he having climbed up over the backs of several of his soldiers, who formed themselves into what is sometimes called a " human ladder." The Chinese were very quick to produce white flags, some of which bore a crude attempt at a red circle in imitation of the national flag of Japan. In the native city of Banka were many large banners with inscriptions calculated to please the victors, such as :—" Loyal subjects of Japan," " We are all of one nation," " We welcome you as friends," etc.

A yamen in the vicinity of the ex-president's premises was occupied as the military quarters. Coolies were at once employed in cleaning the streets and gutters and removing the muck and garbage to the river. Upon the arrival of some of the higher officials, Taipeh was selected as headquarters for the Imperial Body Guard and chief seat of the Japanese civil administration in the island.[1] On June 17th, the ceremony of the inauguration of the administration of the island was celebrated. H.I.H. Prince Kitashirakawa, Admiral Count Kabayama, and other high Japanese officials were present, and all the consuls, together with the leading Chinese and European residents, comprised the foreign guests. An enjoyable entertainment was given, and much pleasure was afforded by the presence of the large band from the Japanese flagship, which gave the first band concert ever heard in the island.

1. As soon as the occupation of Taipehfu was completed, the following proclamation in English and Chinese was posted about the city :—

PROCLAMATION.

His Majesty the Emperor of Japan, having acquired by cession from His Majesty the Emperor of China, under the Treaty of Peace concluded at Shimonoseki, on the 17th day of the 4th month of the 28th year of Meiji, the full and perpetual sovereignty of the Island of Taiwan and the Islands appertaining or belonging thereto, and the Islands composing the Pescadores Group, that is to say, all Islands lying between the 119th and 120th degrees of Longitude east from Greenwich and the 23rd and 24th degrees of North Latitude, together with all fortifications, arsenals, and public property on said Islands.

Now therefore, I, Admiral Viscount Kabayama Sukenori, His Imperial Japanese Majesty's Governor of Taiwan, the Pescadores, and their dependencies, have by Command and in the Name of His Majesty the Emperor of Japan, taken possession of the ceded Islands aforesaid, and as His Imperial Japanese Majesty's Governor of Taiwan, the Pescadores, and their dependencies, I have assumed the administration and government thereof.

All inhabitants of [the ceded territory peacefully pursuing their ordinary and lawful vocations will receive full and constant protection.

tung officials had loaded with arms and ammunition, and despatched for Tamsui. She had just passed Hongkong when the officials, to their great consternation, received news of the occupation of Tamsui by the Japanese. The mandarins naturally lost no time, and by availing themselves of two fast launches they were able to overhaul the Ning-po when about 90 miles from Hongkong. She accordingly returned to Canton on the 10th of June, and her cargo was discharged by special arrangement into private godowns. Soldiers had also been engaged and assembled at Canton, but, on receiving news of the Japanese occupation, they were disbanded and presented with a dollar and a half each to return to their houses.

As it was originally believed that the pacification of Formosa by the Japanese would be accomplished without much trouble, Count Kabayama's staff was organized exclusively on a civil basis.   However, now that it had been discovered that extensive preparations had been made to oppose the Japanese, it became necessary to change it to a military one.   The Governor-General, Admiral Count Kabayama, assumed the command of the Imperial troops in the island.   The administration was divided into four general divisions, i.e., the Governor-General's Office, the Military Bureau in charge of Major-General Oshima, the Naval Bureau in charge of Rear-Admiral Tsunoda, and the Civil Bureau in charge of Mr. S. Mizuno.[1]

For the first few weeks all went as merry as one could wish.   The Imperial Body Guards were as a rule polite to foreigners, and as kind to, and considerate of, the Chinese as one could expect.   Nothing occurred to mar the general satisfaction that Formosa had come under the dominion of Japan.   Business, which had been at a complete standstill for several days, revived with a rush the very day the troops arrived.   The feeling of confidence seemed to exist in the neighboring country districts also, for deputations arrived to express the friendliness of their respective villages and to announce their desire that troops should be sent at once, that the people might be placed under the protection of the Japanese government. The speedy occupation of the whole island now seemed assured; but, as later chapters will show, this was not the easy task it was at first supposed to be.

1. The Governor-General's Office comprised two divisions; the Staff Department and the Aide-de-Camp Department.   The Military Bureau was subdivided into the Director's Office, the Artillery Department, the Engineering Department, the Gendarmerie Department, the Paymaster's Department, the Cash Department, the Provisions Department, the Medical Department, the Judicial Department, the Telegraph Department, and the Post Office Department.   The divisions and personnel of the Civil Affairs Bureau was as follows: —

Agricultural and Industrial Department	B. Hashiguchi.
Financial Department	B. Hashiguchi (Acting).
Educational Department	S. Izawa.
Home Department	B. Maki.
Foreign Department	H. Shimamura.

Rear-Admiral Tanaka was the first prefect of Taipeh, and S. Nomura the first commissioner of Customs.

CHAPTER XXI.

THE JAPANESE OCCUPATION OF MID FORMOSA.

1895.

The expedition against Teckcham—Personal experiences—Aggravating coolies—A deserted village—Numerous skirmishes—The Japanese machine gun—The occupation of Teckcham—City a soldier's camp—Chinese ideas of gratitude—New methods of insurance—Our force weakened—Insurgents surround Teckcham—Trouble along line communication—An improvised fortress—Characteristics of the Japanese soldier—Japanese commissariat—Japanese armament—The Murata repeating rifle—Chinese soldiers—The white flag defiled—A trip to Kelung—A Chinese drug store—The southern expedition abandoned—Fighting outside Taipeh—Chinese again attack Teckcham—Annihilation of a Japanese convoy—Brave conduct—Suicide of six soldiers—A squadron of cavalry exterminated—A struggle for life—Large force takes the field—Niulango and Longtampo captured—The attack on Tokoham—White flags shelter insurgents—Stringent measures—Large expedition formed—Capture of Sankakeng—A pitiful scene—Operations conducted by Matsubara, Yamane, and Naito columns—Niulanwa and Sinpu occupied—Headquarters removed to Teckcham—The north central districts—Insurgents strongly fortified—Kiukianna and Juharin occupied—Main expedition formed—The fortified hill of Chapisoan (Senpitsusan) captured—Tiongkong (Chuku) and Taufan occupied—Peep on the Chinese side—Aulang occupied—A skirmish near Maoli—Obstinate resistance at Chenkansoan—Maoli, Taiko, and Koloton occupied—Treacherous use of white flag—A hard fight—Bravery of two soldiers—Taiwanfu occupied—Plans for capture of big inland city of Changwha (Shoka) and its fortifications—A memorable engagement—Skilful strategy—A decoy camp—Night attack—Panic-stricken braves—A surprised garrison—An army amok—The fall of Changwha—Heavy loss of life—Skirmishes in neighborhood—Capture of Tarimu—Changwha a fever pit—Putrifying bodies poison the air—An army incapacitated—Chinese laborers in fortune—Imperial approbation—Preparations for southern expedition—A deplorable change—The Japanese coolie in Formosa—Undesirable individuals—Disease in the island—Savages accompany a Japanese force—First meeting with savages—A Formosan gale.

THE first duty of the Japanese administration was to plan a campaign against the rebels throughout Formosa, who now had their headquarters at Tainanfu in the south of the island, the capital of the republic. The famous pirate and Black Flag Chief, Liu Yung-fu, had declared himself the president "elected by the people," and commander-in-chief of the troops in the island. Even the village garrisons but a few miles from the Japanese capital of Taipeh, who were formerly under the command of President Tang, now reported to Liu Yung-fu far away in the south. Under these circumstances, the Formosan republic cannot be said to have ceased when the Japanese captured Taipeh in the north. It was merely reorganized and the seat of government transferred to the south. It was now quite evident to the Japanese that the subjugation of the island was a task that could only be accomplished by a considerable army thoroughly equipped on a war basis.

The first expedition was to be to the south towards Teckcham (Hsinchu), a walled city forty miles from Taipeh. A company had been previously despatched on a reconnoitering expedition, and had proceeded, not however without considerable difficulty, nearly as far south as Teckcham. Here the Chinese troops were encountered in such large numbers that it was impossible to push on further. This party brought to Taipeh the information that, according to Chinese reports, the enemy's forces in Teckcham aggregated about 2,000. It was also ascertained that a general with five battalions of infantry, which had been collected at Changwha (Shoka), was hourly expected. Hereupon, a detachment, consisting of a battalion of the 2nd regiment, two companies of engineers and artillery, and a troop of cavalry, assembled outside the north gate of Taipeh, and took up the march for the south.

I had obtained permission from the Imperial Prince to accompany the expedition,[1] and as it was quite likely that it might be necessary to do without horses, owing to the possible non-existence of roads, I decided, rather than risk the long marches under the burning Formosan sun, to avail myself of a Chinese chair with four carriers, which had been offered me by the commander. As Japanese interpreter, Mr. Kurushima, a young volunteer soldier of the Imperial Body Guards, was detailed for my service. He had been educated in an English school, could speak and write English fluently, and proved himself to be an exceptionally bright and reliable young man.

Our first march of sixteen miles was a pretty stiff one for troops unaccustomed to the heat of a Formosan sun, and dressed as they were in the winter uniform, with headgear affording absolutely no protection against the sun. We made our first camp at Toahong (Toshien). Nothing had occurred of importance. We had followed the railway track, and the road lay between well cultivated rice fields, and among hills covered with bamboo groves. Even the railway had not escaped the looters: the telegraph poles, wooden

1. Thanks to the United States minister in Tōkyō, I was not unknown to the military staff, and consequently found it not a difficult task to obtain credentials temporarily, awaiting the more authoritative documents from the Military Department in Tōkyō. June 15th, I was invited to meet the Imperial Prince Kitashirakawa, and I received the necessary military passports from his hands, and was informed that I should have the same conveniences given me in Formosa, as had been afforded the war correspondents in the north, and I would be attached to the Imperial Body Guards until peace had been established.

bridges, and even the wooden ties had been torn up from beneath the rails and removed. We slept that night in a Chinese temple. By forcibly ejecting a lot of little josses who were occupying the only stand in the place, we obtained a satisfactory dining table, and as soon as we had disposed of the army rations, a small mosquito-net was rigged up, the table doing duty as a bed, while the wierd old idols looked down on us from all sides, frowning more than ever at the intrusion.

The next morning at five, we were on our way again, following the railway, and, as on the day before, we found the Chinese peaceably at work. Each house had out its little white flag. The natives were not interfered with in any way, and in turn the Chinese made no trouble for the Japanese. We encamped that night at Tiongliek (Chureki), after a march of twelve miles. A military telegraph had been constructed thus far by the telegraph corps accompanying the reconnoitering party, which had advanced to this point a few days before. The inhabitants of the town and district were found to be chiefly Hakkas; that hardy race of Chinese whose customs and manners differ much from other Chinese, and whose women with their unbound feet, their graceful gait, and their hair-dress somewhat resembling that of Japanese women, are fresh and not bad-looking.

The next morning about 5, we heard sharp firing outside. It was a skirmish between a party of mounted scouts and a detachment of the enemy. We were up and along with but little delay, and the cavalry, now supported by a company of infantry, was sufficient to induce the Chinese to retire to a stronger position on the top of the surrounding hills. The detachment was here divided into three columns, one to proceed along the railway track and the two others along the table-lands leading up to the hills on the right and left. At a short distance from a small village, in which a considerable amount of arms and ammunition had been found, a detachment of the enemy appeared on the brow of a hill in front and opened fire on our main column. To obtain a better view of the enemy, my companion and I joined the advance guard; but upon our coming out in the clearing, and proceeding a few rods, the firing was so heavy from the Chinese just ahead of us, that the members of our little band scattered, and my companion and I lay down flat and embraced the railway embankment most affectionately, while eleven bullets with a most disagreeable plunk, went into the mud of the big ditch at our feet. The main column, about 1,000 metres from the enemy, did not reply, but sat down to noon mess. Meanwhile, the artillery had planted a battery of mountain pieces, and after firing a few well aimed shells we were again advancing along the plateau, the enemy retreating to a high line of hills stretching from right to left, a splendid position, and with the railway passing through the only apparent break. The Chinese commenced a brisk fire upon the approaching cavalry and infantry, now closing in about them, and then with Chinese braggadocio began advancing down from the hills towards us. Several detachments were sent out to the east and west, and the artillery, again brought into play, sent such a hot fire of shells among the Chinese that they were soon retreating like sheep. It was a hot day and my chair coolies were a great source of annoyance. During the morning we had progressed but a short distance, when several rifle reports were heard. This seemed to amuse my chair coolies, until suddenly, in close succession, two bullets whizzed through the air a rod or so off and well above us. My chair was dropped like a shot, and a movement to the rear was executed by those five coolies with a speed equalled only by that of the missile which had alarmed them. My interpreter drove them to the front again, but I saw it was useless to depend further on the chair, and decided to tramp it for the rest of the day. A few hours later, several staff-officers were resting in a shady grove. A bench was brought forward by an orderly for one of the higher officers, who invited me to share it with him. I accepted, and later we both rose to greet an officer just arriving, and then returned to the bench. But to my companion's merriment and my dismay, I found that one of my coolies, whom we had dubbed "mandarin," had taken possession of our bench and was busily engaged in searching for the enemy which infested his person. This was the first of the many incidents which convinced me that my coolie was a thorough republican. He recognized no class or distinction ; the humblest Japanese coolie and the Imperial Prince were alike to him. While in charge of the baggage it was invariably his custom, when stopping, to place the load with its long pole across the roadway, to sit down in the middle of a narrow pathway, and complacently watch half a hundred soldiers, a troop of cavalry, or perhaps a battery of artillery turn from the road to pass him. Two white tags floating above each little pile of baggage marked it as the property of the American correspondent, and as such it was respected. The chair coolies collectively were even worse. They never took a parallel path to the one on which the troops were marching, and they thought nothing of setting down the chair in such a position as to throw a whole file of soldiers into confusion. They would charge through a troop of cavalry or a battery of artillery ; would, without compunction, plant the chair and themselves down in front of the regimental commander, blocking his sight during some important manœuvre, and would everlastingly get their big chair in the way when given the slightest opportunity. Politeness, pleadings, threats, kicks, were of no avail.

The army marched into the village of Tokohao where camp No. 3 was established. The village was totally deserted, the shops being left wide open, exposing the shelves filled with goods, as though waiting a customer. There was no confusion, and the village must have been deserted on very short notice, inasmuch as no attempt had been made to close doors or store away valuables. Some of these shops were specially enticing ; but I must state that, although the soldiers were roaming about the streets, I did not see one enter a shop ; and in the morning, as I walked through the village, all seemed to be intact.

Before retiring, we learned of severe fighting that had occurred on the seashore, between a detachment of about sixty of our troops (infantry) and a considerable force of Chinese, who had sought refuge in a very substantial stone building provided with loop holes, through which the Chinese were able to fire on their opponents without danger to themselves. After an engagement of several hours, during which the Japanese met with some loss, a portion of the wall was blown up with gunpowder, the brave fellows volunteering for this task being nearly all wounded in accomplishing it, one fatally.

At 3 am. the next morning, we were up, and an hour later, on our way ascending the tableland that lay before us. The Chinese forces were down in the low lands ahead, and commenced firing at 5.30. We advanced to the brow of the elevation, the mountain and machine guns were brought into position, and the hills resounded with firing such as the interior of Formosa had not heard before. Some very good work was done by the mountain-gun battery, and the Chinese were soon on the retreat, running along the narrow pathways of the rice fields, crossing a river, and ascending a hill beyond. This offered a splendid opportunity for marksmanship, and many a retreating brave went down with a bullet in his back.

On this day, there were several opportunities for my coolies to add to their reputation. They all appeared now in splendid array. Silk coats, rings on their fingers, new pipes, embroidered tobacco pouches ; and " Mandarin " strutted proudly about with a fur cap and silk trousers. My chair I found converted into a receptacle for stolen goods. In other words, my coolies had spent the day in looting. I threw the stuff into a neighboring patch of undergrowth and hurried them along. What the Japanese thought of it all I don't know. There must have been much anger smothered on several occasions, on account of those wretches. During the afternoon " Mandarin " again imposed himself upon the official circle, first by requesting the loan of the colonel's field glasses that he might note the enemy's movements, and secondly by waiting without any evidence of impatience until an orderly had carefully arranged the colonel's blanket and then occupying it himself. I was called to the scene and found " Mandarin " employing himself in removing scales from a number of offensive sores on his leg ; and, I regret to say, he did not always throw them clear of the blanket. Words utterly failed me, and I so far disregarded the usual methods of enforcing military discipline as to attempt a kick ; but " Mandarin " with much agility evaded this, and then left us with low mumbled expressions of disgust, to give his attention for the next half hour to the intricacies of a machine-gun.

We now commenced the march on Teckcham, four Japanese correspondents and myself accompanying the machine-gun battery, which was taking a route well to the left of the main column. I could not but admire the cheerfulness with which the fellows in charge of this battery plodded along. They had great loads to carry under any circumstances, but in the middle of summer, under a Formosan sun, and dressed in heavy winter garments, their task appeared almost heroic.[1]

1. The Japanese machine-gun is manufactured in Osaka, and is similar to the Maxim gun so far that the recoil is utilized in providing power for loading and ejecting the cartridges. It is ·443 calibre and can be fired up to 600 shots a minute. This weapon was used for the first time in warfare in Formosa. It was not found satisfactory, however, and it is reported that this particular type will be abandoned. The chief difficulty in Formosa, so far as I was able to observe, was that the cartridges frequently jammed, and it was often necessary to either abandon its use or to stop in the middle of an engagement and take the weapon to pieces to extract the unruly cartridge, which refused to come out any other way. Each

Through the field, uphill and downhill, fording the river, with our clothes alternately soaking wet and drying in the burning sun, we proceeded until, meeting a company of infantry marching with all haste that they might be the first to attack the walls of the distant capital, we joined them, leaving the machine-gun battery to follow more slowly.   About 11.30 a.m. we caught the first glimpse of the towers of the city, and the inspiring sight hastened all; for each company was ambitious to be the first to plant the national flag upon the walls.   The apparent danger to a small force of men in attacking a walled city, which might contain several thousand soldiers and have hidden mines around it, did not worry our small detachment in the least.   They marched on with quickened steps, although much exhausted by the heat and fatigue of the seven hours' work they had already performed, exposed to the glare of a blazing sun, and then breaking into a run, they hastened along, shouting, cheering, and with faces beaming with enthusiasm.   The Chinese had constructed a moat, but the Japanese plunged into it from the banks, holding their guns and ammunition above their heads, and were clambering over the opposite bank, almost as quickly as if they had a bridge.   I, however, crossed on a trembling bamboo ladder which had been thrown across for my use, and was thus able to keep up with the head of the company without having to take a mud bath.   We anticipated a good fight in Teckcham as the Japanese had surrounded the place on three sides, and the Chinese uniformed troops had been plainly seen to enter the city.   On reaching the heavy gates, we found them barricaded from within.   Ladders, which we had carried with us, were placed against the walls, and a stream of Japanese were climbing up and sending shot after shot at the Chinese soldiers who were occasionally seen as they darted here and there among the houses.   As evidence that the Chinese were surprised at the suddenness of the attack, old jing-galls and numerous antediluvian cannon mounted on the wall were found loaded but unfired.   A small force of modern soldiers could have held the city for several days; but the Chinese made no attempt, although preparations for a prolonged siege were seen on every hand.   The wall had been strengthened and in some places rebuilt, and was defended by cannon of all sizes and conditions; while the big gates were closed with a mass of rocks and sand, reaching half way up the gate way.   The city was filled with Chinese soldiers.   We knew that; for their bright uniforms had been seen but a few moments before.   Now came a sudden stage transformation scene.   From furious soldiers in battle array to peaceful smiling merchants and smirking coolies would be quite a feat for European soldiers; but the Chinese accomplished it in the ten minutes' interval between the time when the first Japanese soldier scaled the wall and when the Japanese were in complete possession.   It was an irritating position.   Had the Chinese force, which greatly outnumbered ours, made any attempt at defence and later surrendered, they would have won the respect of every Japanese in our party.   It is difficult for a civilian

gun was mounted on a light carriage which was pulled by Japanese soldiers, who were also loaded with their carbines and soldier's kits.   The ammunition for a day's use was in wooden cases carried on the backs of soldiers.   Eighty pounds was the usual allowance to each soldier, who had besides his regular kit of over sixteen pounds.

to realize the sickening disgust of a soldier who, after plodding along in the heat, day after day, to attack the enemy, finds his opponents discarding all warlike equipments, and coming forward smirking and disclaiming all knowledge of the enemy. Rifles and ammunition, uniforms, spears, and other equipments were strewn about the streets ; and from their quantity it appeared that the Chinese soldiers must have numbered at least a thousand. That many of them were still present the houses crowded with men gave evidence, but unfortunately there was no means of ascertaining who were soldiers, and the Japanese made no attempt to do so. The victors behaved splendidly. No shops were broken into, no one was molested, and in an hour or so the gates were opened, sentries posted, and communication with the outside freely permitted. At first the people, crowded into the houses, would not come out, but after a few doors had been forced open by the Japanese, they gradually came forth, and busied themselves in hoisting white flags over the doorways, and in freely offering tea and cakes to all who passed. But as the Japanese still showed no signs of ill will, the Chinese quickly changed their ideas of the situation, and in a very short time the tea and cakes were withdrawn, the merchants opened their stores, and, instead of giving away their wares, doubled their prices ; the beggars crawled out of their hiding places, all seemingly possessed with the idea that the Japanese were there for their special benefit, and that any extortion was perfectly proper. Now was a Japanese guilty of some slight breach of etiquette, the same wretches who were but a few hours ago wailing and crying in the dust, shouted and chattered away as though they intended to eat up the guilty fellow on the spot.

It was necessary to obtain some assistants among the Chinese, especially as the Japanese interpreters understood only the Peking dialect, which is entirely unknown to most of the Formosan Chinese. A bright looking native, formerly a petty Chinese official, was discovered who could speak the Peking dialect. He was at once engaged as assistant, and a tag denoting this fact was given him as a sort of passport. His new position, combined with his former power for evil, made him appear to the natives a very formidable character; and in true Chinese style he availed himself of that reputation to the utmost. Unable to squeeze their money according to the "olo custom" he devised new means quite as effective. Calling from shop to shop and from house to house, he told the occupants that for a small premium he could insure their buildings against harm from the Japanese, and allow their business to continue untrammeled; but if they did not produce the necessary fee, he would promptly hand their property over to the Japanese for destruction. A large sum of money was thus obtained, and to each contributor he gave a small flag bearing an inscription in Chinese, to the effect that the occupant was a good man, etc.; flags which could, of course, have been made by any one, and would have received equal consideration from the Japanese. Unfortunately for the enterprising official, he visited, during one of his tours, a store, the top floor of which was occupied by several Japanese correspondents. The storekeeper inquired of one of the correspondents as to whether the charge demanded was excessive or not, with the result that in a very few moments, the insurance company was placed under arrest, and the Japanese were more cautious in the selection of assistants.

News having reached us that the villagers had made an attack on small parties of Japanese coming in from Taipeh, a large portion of our infantry was at once despatched along the route to keep open communication with Taipeh. Chinese military officials apparently learned of this ; for the next morning (24th) a large force approached from the south and took up a position on the surrounding hills but a short distance from the city. The first attack was made on an outpost, which, re-inforced with but thirty men, bravely held their ground. Meanwhile, a battery of mountain guns was placed in position. The Chinese were now boldly marching down the hillside in good order, their gay uniforms and banners plainly visible. The first shell was fired from our side and exploded among them. They hesitated a moment, and then as the fire from two machine-guns was added to the battery, they suddenly turned tail, scattered in great confusion, and fled like frightened deer. Yet they outnumbered us probably ten to one. Another Chinese column on two occasions assembled, and was twice dispersed with ease, though our small force did not dare go far from the city, knowing that many Chinese soldiers were within the walls, who would doubtless rise against the Japanese if they were given the slightest opportunity. The expedition thus far had cost the Japanese a loss of eighteen men killed and wounded, while the Chinese had about one hundred killed.

With the intention of joining the expedition ordered to the south, I left Teckcham on the 27th of June to return to Taipeh. The insurgents had been making considerable trouble along the line, tearing down the military telegraph and making a strong attack on the commissariat station at Tiengliek. Our returning party consisted of one company of infantry. On the 28th, just before reaching Tiengliek, we encountered the enemy ; but as we were greatly outnumbered, and besides, had been ordered to hurry on to Taipeh, we hid in a bamboo grove until the Chinese disappeared over the hills. We then proceeded, and in a short time passed the ruins of a large mud-brick house which had been the scene of a brisk fight on the 25th. On that day, a strong body of insurgents had attacked a company of infantry posted there. The Chinese were dispersed, with the exception of a party which had taken possession of the above-mentioned house, which they had provided with loop holes, through which they fired on the Japanese with considerable effect, killing two and wounding four. The Japanese found that their bullets could not penetrate the thick walls, so after a futile siege for a while, they put a sudden end to the combat by setting fire to the roof. The Chinese were horror-stricken at this solution of the affair and attempted to escape, but some twelve or fifteen remained too long and found a grave under the smoking ruins. On reaching Tiengliek we were joined by a company which was waiting for a reinforcement of artillery. They had engaged in an unsuccessful skirmish during the morning, with a loss of one killed and three wounded, including a lieutenant. We remained in the village during the heat of the day : then we marched all night and reached Taipehfu at 8 a.m. the next morning, having passed on the way several companies of infantry and a battery of artillery despatched to aid the small force scattered between Tiengliek and Teckcham.

The trip had been one of much value and interest, and the Japanese had treated me with great kindness. I formed on this my first journey, many impressions which my later experiences did not lead me to change. First, that the Japanese were brave and courageous; that for quiet and soldierly discipline, for cheerfulness under adverse circumstances, for sturdiness and endurance, they were a superior body of men. Physically they were all small, but very noticeable was their evenness in height, weight, and strength. A military man familiar with the condition of roads such as existed in Formosa can readily understand that under a burning sun in summer, seven to eight miles a day would be a very good record.[1] Nevertheless the Japanese, in spite of their winter uniform and the fact that they were wholly unaccustomed to the semi-tropical climate of the island, having arrived but a few days before from cold Manchuria, made an average advance of more than thirteen miles a day; and on one day, one of the hottest I have experienced in the island, sixteen miles were marched. The military coolies, the ammunition carriers, kept their places in rank; and so equal were their powers of endurance that not a man fell out. The diet was one that gave great advantage to the Japanese as well as Chinese soldiers. Rice in the East can be easily obtained, is easily transported, and can be easily prepared. Large iron pans were carried by the commissariat corps but rarely used, as every village, even a group of farm houses, contained all the appliances necessary. Every soldier carried a small oblong basket holding about a quart of rice which was the ration for each meal. Vegetables, fish, and sometimes meat, were given in varying quantities as they could be obtained.

The brunt of the campaign in Formosa was borne by the infantry. While it is true that cavalry were utilized, still the absence of passable roads marred their usual effectiveness. The artillery was limited to mountain-gun batteries. Field-guns were brought to Kelung and later to Teckcham, but no occasion was found for their use. The Chinese have a great horror of all artillery, and had it not been for the difficulty of transport, this arm would have been found of the greatest value. It is interesting to note that the magazine rifle[2] and the machine-gun with which the Japanese troops in Formosa were provided were used for the first time in warfare during the Formosan campaign.

The Chinese troops equipped with good weapons or bad, without drill,

1. The French troops in Madagascar advanced at an average rate of not over four miles a day.

2. The Imperial Body Guard were armed with a ·315 calibre ten fire repeating rifle called the Murata, made at the arsenal in Tōkyō. While a very serviceable long range weapon, it seemed to have a weak spot in its repeating mechanism. The extra cartridges were contained in a second barrel, as is found in the Winchester rifle. This necessitates a long spring which has to be sufficiently strong to push up the last cartridge and yet not too strong to render the loading of the last two or three cartridges too difficult a task to be accomplished without taking the rifle down from the proper position of loading. On one or two occasions I noted that the spring did not bring out the cartridges, either because of a jam or too weak a spring; and again it was sometimes necessary to place the rifle in an unguarded position, and engage all the soldier's attention and no little strength, to force in the last two or three cartridges. However, this was very rare, and it was always to be used as a single fire weapon entirely independent of the magazine. The above defect is to be remedied, however, and preparations are now being made to arm the infantry with a new rifle, in which I believe the underfeed principle, similar to that of the magazine rifles, is to be adopted.

and unskilled in foreign tactics, protected by magnificent forts with big modern guns, or behind mudwalls with jing-gals, conducted themselves always with scarcely a redeeming feature. Their forces never advanced to make an attack unless they were confident that their position permitted of an easy retreat and that they greatly outnumbered their opponents. I know of hardly a single instance where, in the clearing, they have held their own against an approaching force, under anywhere near equal conditions. It is a usual manœuvre for the Chinese to draw themselves up in mighty splendor on some open plot of ground in full view of the enemy, and should the latter advance towards to them, to commence to fire off every available firearm, although they may be entirely out of range. This continues until the enemy has advanced sufficiently near to make his bullets felt in the Chinese ranks, and then there is a scatter and a scramble for a safer position, where their forces rally again to repeat the same tactics as before. The great *forte* of the Chinese in Formosa was guerrilla warfare and street fighting. Unarmed carriers, commissariat coolies, and scouts, small reconnoitering parties, were their special delight.

The greatest obstacle that the Japanese encountered was the smiling villagers who stood in their doorways, over which they had flown a white flag, watching the troops pass by. For these natives the Japanese had at first a kind word and a smile. But scarcely were the troops out of sight before guns were brought out through the same doorways and shots fired at the first unfortunate party whose numbers were sufficiently small to make it appear safe to the treacherous occupants. Troops now return and find the mutilated bodies of their companions in the streets; while at the doors and windows of the houses near, are the same grinning fiends and the same little white flag, an emblem of peace, still floating over their guilty heads. It is pleasant to sit in one's home and to think of mercy even to one's enemy, but it is quite a different thing in the miserable camp of a soldier. I was much struck with the extreme leniency of the commander of the southern expedition, who made no attempt to surround the insurgents, who always allowed a path open for the enemy to escape, who had his communications cut off again and again; his carriers, messengers, and scouts murdered and mutilated by villagers who had declared their loyalty and hoisted the white flag to protect them in their treachery. With this weak policy, the month of July found affairs rapidly growing worse. The large bodies of insurgents learned that they could harass the Japanese with comparative safety, and the villagers that killing under a white flag brought no punishment. To the majority of Chinese there appeared but one reason for such conduct. It was that the Japanese feared them. Then came the organization of new bands of insurgents inspired by the idea that the Japanese could be easily driven from the island. To the Chinese who were peacefully inclined, the position was most desperate; for, placed between two fires, first forced to serve the rebels and then the Japanese, to the sacrifice of property and sometimes of life, there was no peace or comfort. Proclamations purporting to have originated with the governor-general were scattered broadcast, stating that all must pay tribute to the Japanese, that not even the pig, dog, cat, goose, or chicken would be exempt from taxation; and that the Chinese should not close their doors against the Japanese, but give freely to the conquerors of all they had, even to the women, who should be placed at the disposal of the soldiers. These proclamations, which were believed unhesitatingly by all, quite naturally stirred the people up to a great pitch, and it was not surprising that attacks were constant even in such districts as the Japanese had nominally occupied.

After two days' stay in Taipehfu, procuring the necessary equipment for the trip to the south, I left on a special military train for Kelung, making a very quick trip. The locomotive and coaches were much cleaner than formerly, but plainly showed that they had not escaped the last days of the republic. Every removable attachment about the engines had been stolen, and on the arrival of the Japanese, with their limited facilities at hand, it was no trifling work to replace the missing parts. The engines were finally tinkered up, however, and were again pulling the rickety cars which had been reduced by the looters to mere unfurnished vans. On reaching Kelung, I was surprised to note how little there was left to remind one of the sleepy town of Chinese days ; the streets were bustling with life, and the sound of the hammer and saw was heard on every side. Five men-of-war and fourteen transports were in the harbor, where I had never seen more than one foreign vessel before. As I had not been definitely stationed on any particular transport, I occupied in Kelung village a portion of a pharmacy store, where a Chinese druggist dispensed foreign drugs. Upon first entering the building, I was amazed at the big stock carried. Shelves and shelves of foreign drugs, while on one side arose tier after tier of celebrated brands of ale and stout and English and German beer in quarts and pints. "Familiarity breeds contempt," however, and upon a closer inspection, I found the enormous supply of foreign drinkables dwindled down to one small bottle of inferior brandy, the others containing Chinese samshu nicely sealed and with the original foreign label intact. The majority of the drugs were equally illusory. Most of the jars and bottles were empty, and those that did contain a few medicines were arranged with a most fearful disregard for labels. Ammonia was produced from a bottle whose only inscription was "A Refreshing and Delicious Beverage—Royal Ginger Beer."

The next morning I received information that I was to join the transport *Sakura Maru*, and, arriving on board, I was made very comfortable by the officers in charge. All arrangements for our departure were about completed when, to our great surprise, we were notified by Major-General Yamane to return to Taipeh, as the expedition to the south of the island had been abandoned for the present. The original intention had been to proceed with the second brigade of the Imperial Body Guards and land somewhere in the vicinity of Anping, the port of the southern capital, where Liu-Yung-fu and his 10,000 Black Flags were stationed. The equipment necessary for a summer campaign in the south had not yet arrived, and the few days' delay was sufficient to carry us into the period of the south-west monsoon, which rendered it dangerous to attempt the landing of men and supplies before the end of September.

It would seem that an effort might have been made to complete preparations say ten days sooner, or, better still, to send a second expedition to the south simultaneously with the first expedition to the north. Had the Japanese been aware of the real strength of the Chinese forces, this would no doubt have been done, but the Black Flags had been represented by all as blood-spitting monsters who, under command of the fearful Pirate Chief, would give the Japanese the greatest trouble. As it was, the delay was most unfortunate for the foreign merchants of the south, who had for more than a month been placed under the rather capricious authority of Liu Yung-fu and his several thousand braves, and the latter threatened at any moment to overthrow their new republic and its officers and to engage in indiscriminate looting. Although the distance by land was less than 200 miles from Kelung, the expedition would meet with almost insurmountable difficulties if they attempted the trip overland. For at that time of year, the mountain streams had become unfordable surging rivers which would defy all efforts to bridge them hastily with the usual temporary military structures, and the pathways had been converted by July and August rains into streams of mud, rendering the moving of heavy ordnance and supplies specially difficult.

On the 10th of July, a few Japanese couriers were attacked a mile or so outside the capital city. The firing could be plainly heard in Taipeh, and the majority of the better class Chinese were thrown into a perfect frenzy of fear, believing that General Liu and his southern army had appeared and would slaughter them all, in punishment for their submission to the Japanese. Large numbers of Chinese had already crossed to the mainland; not on account of their dislike of the Japanese, but because they had no confidence that the latter could protect them. Reports of engagements by the dozen reached their ears every day, and in these reports the Chinese were always victorious.

On the 11th, a large body of the insurgents assembled in the vicinity of Teckcham and made a fourth attack on that city. They took up their position on the east hills, throwing up entrenchments which they mounted with jing-gals. The Japanese, by a skillful manœuvre, attacked the enemy from two sides and inflicted a defeat, in which about two hundred of the foes were killed and one hundred and ten taken prisoners, while the Japanese loss was but eleven.

The Japanese, so far as the usual field engagements were concerned, found so little difficulty in defeating the Chinese, that the true test of a soldier, the moral courage to meet without flinching the charge of an enemy known to be not inferior in bravery or strength, was not ascertained. But there were several engagements in Formosa where the Chinese, confiding in their numbers, made savage attacks on small parties of Japanese; and the conduct of the latter on several occasions throws light on their ability as warriors, and should assist the impartial critic in forming an opinion as to their military character. The following account, therefore, of the brave conduct of a little party of thirty-five Japanese soldiers in Formosa is of value. On the 11th of July, Sergeant Sakurai, with thirty-four infantry soldiers, left Taipeh in charge of a flotilla consisting of eighteen Chinese river-boats loaded with rice to be conveyed up the river to Tokoham, where the first battalion was stationed. The soldiers, after having completed a portion of their tedious journey, were taking a rest on shore, and at 6 a.m., when preparing for their morning meal, some fifteen or sixteen natives assembled on the right bank of the river, but were not apparently exhibiting any unusual interest in the strangers. Suddenly, however, one of the Chinese raised a peculiar cry, and a shower of bullets rained about the Japanese, who were thus taken entirely by surprise. Scarcely had they seized their muskets when a large number of insurgents came tearing out from an ambush on the left and joined in the firing. Desperately and yet without any show of panic the sergeant ordered his men into line. After a brisk exchange of fire with the insurgents, who had now increased to some five or six hundred men, Sergeant Sakurai, who had crossed with a few men to the left bank, ordered Corporal Ebashi to join him. The party was accordingly reassembled on one side of the river, and Sergeant Sakurai to encourage his men declared that, "so long as his eyes remained black," the enemy should not touch the provisions under his charge. The insurgents had now surrounded them, and for three hours, shoulder to shoulder, the thirty-five men defended themselves and their boats gallantly. Escape became now impossible ; and Sergeant Sakurai, standing proudly out among them, said in a voice that could be heard by all, "the insurgents are many and we are few. We cannot defeat them, but let us die fighting gallantly." His words were scarcely uttered, when he fell dead with a bullet in his breast. Other losses had now reduced their party to twenty-four, and as the insurgents were closing in about them, the Japanese fixed bayonets, and, after concentrating their fire on the weakest part of the circle, they made a bold charge through the line, losing several of their comrades while doing so. But the insurgents again surrounded them, and, fatigued and weakened from lack of food and water, the Japanese again closed up and made a second charge. Corporal Oi had on the first attack received a fatal wound, but had roughly bandaged it himself, and continued with his men. His strength, however, did not prove equal to his pluck, and, after having followed a few paces, he dropped down, and with his last breath cried out to his companions, "Comrades, pardon me that I go before you (Shokun, osaki ni gomen wo komuru) "To Japan, long life! (Teikoku banzai)." Then drawing his sword he thrust it into his throat and fell dead before the Chinese could reach him. The survivors were again successful in breaking through the line ; but with so great a loss that there were but eight privates and Corporal Ebashi remaining. The wounded and exhausted men now sat down to gain a moment's relief. The corporal then ordered the unwounded men to attempt to reach the neighboring underbrush, and, if possible, escape and carry the news of the loss of the boats to headquarters. The insurgents were now drawing near—so near in fact that they could reach the Japanese by throwing their spears. The five wounded men, at the proposal of the corporal that they should take their own lives rather than be made prisoners by the Chinese, prepared to obey this last command. Two of the men most severely wounded drew their bayonets and plunged them into each others' breasts. Two other privates followed the example of their comrades, and the third, Corporal Ebashi, no doubt gratified at the bravery of his men to the last, coolly placed his bayonet before him and died by *harakiri*. Having witnessed the death of the last of their companions, the other four men scattered, three reaching a neighboring hill; and one, a private named Tanaka, hid in the tall water grass near the river bank with only his head above water. Almost famished for want of food, and weakened with exhaustion, he stood for eight hours in the same position, until it seemed as though he could hardly bear it longer. Towards midnight, the sky darkened, heavy clouds appeared, accompanied by peals of thunder and flashes of lightning, which gave way to torrents of rain. Then leaving his place of concealment and keeping a sharp lookout for Chinese soldiers, he reached the river bank. The fires of the Chinese camps were visible, and stripping himself of his clothes, reserving but his jacket, cartridges, and gun, he waded into the stream and, by keeping scarcely more than his nostrils above water, sometimes sinking into pit holes over his depth, falling and plunging along, he passed for some three miles unseen, when his heart was made glad by the neighing of a horse; for he then knew that he had reached the Japanese camp in safety.

When the news of the almost utter annihilation of the convoy of provision-boats had been reported at Taipeh, it was decided to despatch a squadron of twenty-one cavalry to reconnoitre in the vicinity of Tokoham. The troopers left on the 15th of July, and after an uneventful march over a flat country where every house flew a white flag and women and children ran out to watch the men riding by, the party came to the vicinity of Pankiu. Reaching the village, they entered by the western gate and were surrounded by the inhabitants, who offered them tea and other refreshments. Over the gate floated a banner bearing the inscription "The townsmen of Pankiu offer profound submission to the authority of the Japanese." Notwithstanding this display, the Japanese were a little suspicious; for the natives seemed more profuse with their hospitality than usual. Consequently, they hurried on until they reached the magnificent residence of the multi-millionaire Lim, one of the wealthiest men in Formosa. An officer and two sergeants entered the grounds and made inquiries as to the probable whereabouts of the insurgents. No one could inform them, and they therefore proceeded along the river towards Tokoham. They had marched about four miles when they observed a party of some forty men and women engaged in picking tea; these showed no signs of hostility, and the cavalrymen continued on their way. They had advanced but a short distance when they came to a large area of rice fields traversed by narrow paths. In one of these they proceeded single file; but, on reaching the centre of the fields, they were startled by three rifle reports from a point some three hundred paces off. No one was injured, but the officer in command at once ordered his men to dismount and prepare for action. Their position was an unfortunate one, a hill on one side, and a river on the other; while they could only move through the rice-fields along the narrow pathways. The insurgents now bobbed up in all directions, and in a moment several Japanese had been shot down; the horses now plunged into the flooded fields, and as it was impossible to make any effectual stand under such conditions, the command was given to retreat and for each man to save himself if possible. They immediately scattered, charging here and there, with such haste and in so many directions that the insurgents, not anticipating the necessity of directing their attention to so wide an area, were unable to prevent a few from escaping. Sergeant Muramatsu, spurring his horse to its utmost speed, dashed literally into the arms of the enemy, who, afraid of the rushing beast, scattered to each side with terror, and the sergeant passed through unharmed, though he was made a target for countless bullets from the disgusted force behind, and from the houses, trees, and bushes along the way, everyone of which now seemed crowded with the enemy. Here he was joined by a companion who had likewise escaped from the field; but scarcely had he time to exchange a word before his comrade's horse was shot, and its rider, sword in hand, was fighting furiously, until he was struck to the earth. The peaceful tea-gatherers of an hour before were now loud shouting rebels,—even to the women, who joined in the fight. The sergeant escaped them all, however, and a few moments later dashed up to the village of Pankiu. He gained the southern gate and was about to enter when his faithful horse, which had carried him safely against enormous odds, fell down dead. The natives of the village now crowded around, and he was led to the residence of Lim, which he and his companions had visited but a few hours before. Here, to his happy surprise, he was received with kindness and was taken into the presence of two of his comrades who had also been brought there by the villagers. Lim's retainers then escorted the three cavalry men, the sole survivors of that day's fight for life, to the nearest camp of Japanese troops, whence they returned to Taipeh the next morning to report the sad fate of their comrades.

As it was now deemed necessary to put a regular force in the field, a large detachment, under the command of Major-General Yamane, was despatched from Taipeh, on the 12th of July, in a southerly direction towards Long-tampo (Sin-tan-ha). Simultaneously, a battalion under Major Bojo marched by the left bank of the Tokoham (Taikokan) river with orders to join the Yamane column at Long-tampo. Formosan villages are often surrounded by almost impenetrable groves of bamboo, while thick hedges of bamboo interwoven with numerous thorny plants enclose blocks of houses. Close to these hedges and almost hidden by them are the Chinese huts, ordinarily of mud and straw, which, being provided with numerous apertures, can be converted into small size fortresses, not easily taken without artillery or fire. Similarly protected was the village of Long-tampo, and the insurgents, anticipating a visit from the Japanese, had sufficient time to further strengthen their position by barricading all entrances and occupying the most suitable houses. The main body reached Long-tampo on the 14th at 7.30 a.m., and the infantry commenced the attack at once. No advantage was gained until they were replaced by the artillery, who shelled the houses with the mountain guns, inflicting great damage on the village and effectually clearing the pathways. The infantry were now able to enter, and took possession of the village at 4 p.m. Over a hundred insurgents were killed, and the Japanese casualties amounted to eleven.

Major-General Yamane's position being menaced by a strong party of insurgents at the neighboring village of Niulangho, he advanced two days later and made an attack on the place, destroying the Chinese barracks and defences and killing twenty of the enemy without loss to himself. Returning to Long-tampo, the general received word of the missing Bojo column which was to have joined him many days before. A private, disguised as a Chinese and accompanied by two faithful Chinese, had with difficulty passed through the rebel districts, and now brought the alarming news that the Bojo battalion was surrounded by a large force of insurgents, and was without supplies. A detachment under the personal command of Major-General Yamane started at once to the relief, and, encountering the insurgents near Tokoham (Tai-ko-kan) about 1 p.m., commenced an immediate attack. Artillery planted on the left bank of the Tokoham river opened the engagement, while two companies of infantry forded the river, climbed the opposite bank under heavy fire, and advanced boldly into the village, which they captured after several hours' combat with the insurgents, who fought stoutly from the houses. The Chinese loss was considerable.

The Bojo column, now released, was able to join its rescuers. It seems that the force had been attacked by the insurgents a few miles beyond Sankakeng (Sankakuyu). The country was mountainous and the roads bad. After advancing within a few miles of Tokoham the force bivouacked for the night, the insurgents meanwhile greatly increasing in number. Next morning the enemy had further added to their strength, and the battalion retired about 400 metres and took up a position in a valley surrounded by lofty hills. It was determined to make a stand here. The column could have cut its way through the insurgents and retreated; but this would have necessitated the abandonment of thirty wounded men, and so it was decided to continue on the defensive and await reinforcements.

It was thought that the defeat of the rebels in two of their principal resorts would teach them the futility of battling with the Japanese, and that they would return to peaceful occupations. But the attacks upon provision trains and scouting parties, within a few miles of Taipeh, continued so frequently that it became impossible to keep up communication with headquarters. Japanese civilians were butchered and their bodies horribly mutilated, small villages with numerous white flags being the greatest offenders. There was now no other course open but to give up the idea of a peaceful occupation of the island and to prepare for bitter war against the natives. Such might have been avoided had a larger force been introduced during the earlier days of the occupation. It was an error, however, on the side of leniency, and one that can, accordingly, be excused. After due deliberation, the command was given to burn the few villages along the lines of communication to Tokoham (Taikokan) and in from Teckcham (Hsinchu) occupied by insurgents in armed opposition to the Japanese. A final attempt was also to be made to rid the whole district of insurgents. Troops were despatched from three directions. The largest force, nearly 2,000 strong, under Major-General Yamane, advanced from Tokoham; Colonel Naito (now Major-General) with 1,000 men moved from Haisoankau

(Kaisanko), and the third force, some 600 men, from Taipeh. The common objective point was Sankakeng, where it was believed the insurgents were assembling a large force.

We will confine ourselves to the experiences of the main column,[1] which will give us a general idea of the operations and avoid much repetition. The main column, under the personal command of Major-General Yamane, advanced, on the morning of the 22nd, from Tokoham to the vicinity of a village about five miles from Sankakeng. Here they encountered and repulsed a body of some five or six hundred insurgents posted on an eminence, inflicting a loss on them of some thirty-five killed, and suffering themselves a loss of three wounded. Such houses in the vicinity as had harbored the insurgents were burnt to the ground. The enemy were found next morning (23rd) re-assembled on the high hills surrounding the Japanese position. The precipitous sides of the mountains, combined with the opposition of the insurgents, made the task one of considerable difficulty. But artillery fire, supported by an infantry charge, was at length too much for the Chinese, who retreated with a loss of forty. It was not an easy victory, however, the Japanese meeting with a loss of twenty-four, including two killed. On the evening of the 23rd, all the columns assembled in the vicinity of Sankakeng, as had been previously arranged. The next day, having cleared the district of insurgents, the main column returned to Tokoham and the other columns to their respective starting points. There is nothing of special interest to record regarding the above engagements, except that it was found that young women often acted as spies, and that it was impossible to prevent the enemy from obtaining information regarding the Japanese troops. At one of the villages a pitiful scene was witnessed,—a woman, wounded in the body yet tenderly embracing a little child also wounded, having been struck in the head with a fragment of a shell. The mother and child were placed under the care of a military surgeon, who dressed their wounds and provided them with nourishment. In several villages, clothes, note books, and articles of equipment, stripped from the bodies of Japanese who had unfortunately fallen into the hands of the enemy, were found.

There still remained some scattered bands of rebels, and some few villages were yet unsubdued to the south of Taipeh. To deal with these the Matsubara column left Taipeh on July 29th; the same day the Naito column left Haisoankan (Kaisanko); and on the 31st, the Yamane column again took the field. These three columns were engaged several days, during which Niulanwa, and Sinpu (Sinpo), the latter with considerable difficulty, were occupied, and a large district cleared of insurgents. Sinpu was a village of about four hundred brick houses, very neat in appearance, and seemingly

---

1. The main column was formed of two battalions of infantry, a company of artillery, a company of engineers, and a medical staff. The left flank was covered by a company of infantry, a squadron of horse, a section of artillery, and half a company of engineers, under the command of Captain Hayashi. A detachment under Captain Toda was detailed to maintain communication between Captain Hayashi's force and the commissariat station at Toahong (Toshi-en). Another company of infantry was left at Tokoham as a guard, and yet another company was posted between that place and Tiongliek (Chin-reki) to preserve communi ations.

the home of many well-to-do Chinese. In one house was discovered the salted head of a brave soldier who had been killed on the previous day, while attempting to open the city gate that his commander might enter.[1]—

Now that the Imperial Body Guard was to be principally engaged to the south of Teckcham (Hsinchu) H.I.H. Prince Kitashirakawa removed his headquarters from Taipeh to Teckcham on the 31st of July. The arrival of His Highness was quite an event for the Teckcham Chinese, and they turned out in large numbers at the station to welcome him.

Teckcham was now occupied with a large number of troops. The reader will no doubt remember that the place is a walled city of considerable commercial importance, and that it had been repeatedly attacked by the insurgents and gallantly defended by the Sakai battalion on each occasion. Even with the presence of the imperial princes and a large number of troops, the insurgents still held their ground on the hills to the south of the town. Some of the positions thus occupied were of great strategical importance; a small body of determined men so located being sufficient to hold in check a large army. The villages to the north towards Taipeh, which had given such endless trouble to scouting parties and provision trains, had now been cleared of armed insurgents; and the whole attention of the Japanese forces, with the exception of those engaged in garrison duty, could be turned towards the hordes of regular organized Chinese troops and volunteers in the central parts of the island which as yet remained unvisited by the Japanese.

The strongest of these positions were the hills known as Chapisoan

---

1. Details of the operations of the Matsubara, Naito, and Yamane columns are as follows :—
The Matsubara column left Taipeh on the 29th of July, reaching Toahong (Toshi-en) on the same day. The Naito column, which left Haisoankan (Kaisanko) also on the 29th, encountered about 400 insurgents on the same day and defeated them, inflicting a loss of 64 killed. The Japanese loss was 5 killed and wounded. The column bivouacked that night to the north-east of Toahong. On the 30th, the Matsubara column reached Tiongleck. The Naito column continued its westerly march without encountering the insurgents.
On the 31st, the Yamane column left Tokoham and moved towards Sinpu (Sinpo). A detachment was ordered to advance along the left bank of the Tokoham river, while the rest marched to Suntanpo, whence a small force was despatched in a northerly direction. The enemy had constructed defensive works along the plateau extending from the left bank of the Tokoham a little to the northwest of Si-si, as far as to the south of Yang-mei-leck. This was the first objective point of the column. As usual, the insurgents retreated after a little fighting. The Naito column had now repaired to Tiongleck to replace the Matsubara column which had advanced to attack the enemy's left flank. Forty of the insurgents had been killed during the day, while the Japanese loss was eleven killed and wounded. The headquarters of the division and the Naito column remained that night at Tiongleck. The Matsubara column attacked on the 1st of August a strong fort on the left flank of the enemy and took it at 1 p.m. The Yamane column the same day drove the enemy from Niu-lan-wa and advanced to Sinpu. On reaching the vicinity of the last mentioned village, one platoon of artillery and two companies of infantry were sent to reconnoitre the place. The enemy were encountered at the East Gate and easily defeated. The reconnoitering party at the East Gate now searched the neighboring houses, and all being apparently quiet in the village, the troops were about to enter, but found the gate closed. A private, named Nakamura, then brought a ladder and had just scaled the wall when a volley was fired by the insurgents and the plucky soldier fell back wounded. It now being evident that the village was determined to resist the Japanese, the detachment retired and bivouacked for the night at Sau-kap-tsu (Sangosui).
The next morning, the enemy was found occupying positions on hills to the south of Sinpu, and on others to the west of Sankaptsui. At 11 a.m. the enemy began firing from both inside and outside of Sinpu village. The Japanese artillery returned the fire with good effect. Meanwhile the Naito column had advanced and taken up a position just north of the village, from which they were able to work great havoc with their artillery. This combined attack was too much for the insurgents, who retreated in great confusion, suffering heavy loss from the Japanese infantry as they ran. The East Gate was now entered by the Japanese, and many Chinese soldiers were captured in the village. Some resistance was encountered from squads of soldiers who had barricaded themselves in the houses, resulting in some close range combats. An hour later, however, all was quiet and the city completely occupied. The Chinese had about 150 killed during the day, while the Japanese casualties amounted to 7.

(Senpitsu-san) lying to the north of Tiongkang (Chang kong).   Before marching on this stronghold, Major-General Yamane was ordered to leave Sinpu
and push on towards Peipo (Hokpu), thus driving out the last known remnant of the rebels to the east of Teckcham.   Accordingly, General Yamane's
detachment left Sinpu on the morning of the 6th of August, and advanced
on the right flank of the enemy.   Near Suibisho (Tsuibetsun), the insurgents
opened fire from an ambush, while a second party attacked from a newly
erected entrenchment.   The advance guard and one company were able to
deal effectually with the enemy, however, and the column proceeded with
but little delay until the village of Kiukianna (Kiukinrin) was reached.   This
was occupied without opposition.   At Leitansoan (Ritosan) communication
was opened by cavalry scouts with the right wing of the expedition.   Scouts
also brought in the information that the enemy had retired to Juharin village,
and joined by the garrison of that place, was making preparations for a
vigorous defence.   Delayed one day by a swollen river, the right column
crossed safely on the 7th; but on reaching Juharin, it was found that the
regulars had retired, leaving but a few armed villagers, who, after a trifling
engagement, gave way, and the town was occupied.   The current was found
too strong to bridge the river above mentioned, and it took several hours to
transport all the troops over, there being but a single boat for that purpose.
One company engaged a party of insurgents entrenched on the high hill of
Tsuishenlin, defeating the enemy at a cost of three men wounded.   The
column encamped near this point for the night.   All was now ready for the
attack on the main division of insurgents fortified in the hills stretching in a
westerly direction to the coast.   To cover the whole district from coast to
interior mountain ranges, required a large force distributed over a wide
area.   The army was accordingly divided into three bodies, the right and
left wings and reserves.[1]

On the 8th of August at dawn, the troops having arrived from Teckcham the day before, the attack was opened simultaneously by both right
and left wings.   For a while the Chinese answered the artillery of the Japanese with their own mountain-guns, splendidly located on the heights above.
Major Maeda then charged at the head of two companies of infantry,
and easily gained possession of a stronghold in the enemy's left wing, the 500
armed occupants having retreated, leaving five dead, besides two mountain
pieces, and a quantity of small arms and ammunition.   The forts here were
destroyed, and the barracks and other combustible works burnt down.   The
Japanese followed the retreating insurgents, until the latter got within range
of Senpitsusan.   Meanwhile, towards the east, General Yamane had steadily
advanced from Suisen-rei, driving the enemy before him, until now he had
reached a position to the east of the left flank and in communication with
them.   Before proceeding, it was found necessary to send the field-guns back

---

1. The right wing was commanded by Major General Kawamura, and consisted of two regiments
(minus two companies) of infantry, half a squadron of cavalry, mountain artillery, (six pieces), machine-
guns, and a company of engineers.   The left wing under Colonel Naito was composed of a regiment (minus
a battalion) of infantry, a squadron of cavalry, artillery, and medical corps.   A company of infantry and a
party with machine-guns were left at Teckcham (Hsinchu) under the command of Captain Sawasaki.   The
left wing was to be assisted by the Yamane detachment, which had advanced along the mountains to the
eastward, as stated above.

to Teckcham, as this ordnance was too heavy for the narrow roadways and single plank bridges.

On the 9th at 5.30 p.m. (Chapisoan) Senpitsusan was attacked. A large force was known to be occupying the position, and a strong defence was anticipated. The insurgents, however, only bluffed, and after causing the Japanese needless manœuvering, fled over the hills pell-mell, throwing aside their gorgeous uniforms as they ran. According to native reports, the Chinese forces consisted of 3,000 of General Liu Yung-fu's "invincible" republican troops, and 1,000 irregular volunteers. Generals Li-i-gi and Yang were in command, and the latter was reported killed during the engagement. The whole Chinese loss reached a total of about 200 for the two days. Japanese loss, one officer and two privates. The bulk of the division now pushed on and occupied the village of Tiongkang (Chuko), the Kawamura column taking quarters in a fort a short distance to the south of the above village. The Yamane detachment advanced to Taufun (Tofun), and the Naito detachment occupied a place midway between that village and Tiongkang. Two Japanese men-of-war had engaged in the operations for two days, and consequently many retreating Chinese, who had fled towards the coast to escape in boats, found this impossible, and turned southwards, temporarily occupying Taufun (Tofun). On the Chinese side, we find the villagers to the south much disturbed over the capture of Senpitsusan. On the 10th of August, at Maoli (Bioritsu), then but a few miles distant from the Japanese, the Chinese troops were gathered to the number of several thousand. The rank and file consisted mostly of Hakkas, but the leaders were from Hunan, Canton, and other districts on the mainland, and the majority spoke the mandarin dialect, having been officials under the old regime. A detachment of the (ever victorious) Black Flags, who, according to popular report, simply reveled in blood, had arrived from the south to cheer up the soldiers and to publish abroad the mighty words of the exalted Liu, the chief of the southern republic. The local levies and village elders seemed anything but anxious for the fray, but were forced to assist by the regular soldiers, on penalty of death. Already several Hakkas had been beheaded because they had expressed their unwillingness to oppose the Japanese. At Aulang (Koro) on the night of the 10th, eighty Chinese soldiers entered the town with great bravado to inspect the houses, to see that no Japanese soldiers were there concealed. A vigorous search was instituted in the closets, under the beds, and in the attics ; in fact everywhere the Japanese were not likely to be found. It may be mentioned that no search was made outside the city. Had there been one, it would have resulted in very uncomfortable success.

On the 11th, three Japanese scouts entered Aulang without meeting with any opposition. The villagers informed the new arrivals that they had no desire of resisting the Japanese, and would be very grateful if they would take quick possession of the place, as it was feared the insurgents would return. The Chinese troops were busy just to the south of the village looting and burning ; and there was no little consternation at Aulang lest the noble protectors of the republic should practise the same tactics there, as a punishment to the villagers for their lack of loyalty to the mandarins.

On August 10th, 11th, and 12th, a portion of the army was employed in securing communication with the headquarters staff at Teckcham and the transportation of munitions of war. The advance guard spent the time in making a careful reconnaissance of the whole district. This party, on the 11th, while in the vicinity of Maoli (Bioritsu), came into collision with the foe, and retired after a short skirmish, during which they killed twenty-four of the enemy without loss to themselves. On the 13th, large numbers of brilliantly uniformed troops with gaily colored banners were found occupying the hill Chenkansoan (Kaukansan), southwest of Aulang.

On the 13th, the advance guard attacked the insurgents at Chenkansoan hill. The elevation in itself formed a fortification easily defended, and the Chinese made an obstinate resistance, not surrendering until surrounded by the Japanese troops, who crawled up the base of the hill under cover of mountain-guns. Some fifty Chinese were shot down in the paddy fields, as they retreated, and the total loss was probably seventy-five or eighty, while the Japanese had one officer and seven men wounded and one man killed. The left detachment, after having defeated a small body of insurgents on the way, reached Loankuisoan on this day, and despatched a cavalry patrol to Aulang.

On the 14th, the army continued the march. The advance guard entered Maoli, (Bioritsu), a village of about a thousand houses, during the morning without opposition, not only the soldiers but nearly all the villagers having fled. This desertion was apparently prearranged, as much property had been carried away and doors closed and barricaded. From Chinese reports it was learned that, a few days before, extensive preparations had been made to oppose the Japanese ; but the trusted officer of Liu Yung-fu, who was in command of the Chinese forces, having obtained full information of the Japanese successes, decided that "discretion was the better part of valor," and retired with his forces to Chang-wha (Shoka) in good time.

A general attack on the strongly fortified inland city of Chang-wha (Shoka) was now planned for the 27th. Accordingly, early on the morning of the 24th, the detachment, under command of Major-General Yamane, left Taiko (Taika), reaching Koloton (Holoton) about 11.30 a.m. The Chinese were very quiet, and the troops encamped there for the night. The morning's march had been over extremely bad roads, and the engineering corps had been obliged to repair or construct bridges and roads in twenty-one different places.

On the 25th, the advance guard under command of Captain Shiga left Koloton. After having proceeded for a short distance, a report was received from the cavalry that the insurgents had fired upon them. After advancing a short distance, they encountered a few insurgents who soon retreated, and an hour later, in the vicinity of Tokabio, they were strongly opposed. The engineering corps was suddenly fired upon from numerous Chinese houses, while marching over a narrow pathway surrounded by flooded rice fields ;

but by throwing themselves down into the fields and following along the pathway which partially protected them they were able to extricate them-selves.   An infantry patrol, sent to search the houses, found the white flag flying from the doorways, and banners inscribed " good and loyal subjects of Japan " attached to some houses which smelled rather strongly of gunpowder. Inasmuch as no arms were found and the smiling subjects protested that " it was some body else," the patrol returned.   As the Japanese advanced, the buildings became more numerous and the firing from them more frequent.   Eventually all attempt at deception was abandoned, and the houses on all sides suddenly bristled with insurgents, who opened a vigorous fire on the Japanese, picking them off, as they marched in the clearing, with ease and but little danger.   These houses were the usual Chinese buildings with a court enclosed by thick walls, while surrounding all stood a high hedge formed of a thick tangled growth of bamboo and prickly plants, forming a stockade extremely difficult to penetrate.   Taking a position behind the mud walls hastily provided with loopholes, the Chinese could fire with effect, while the Japanese bullets were ineffective against the thick walls.   After several unsuccessful attempts had been made by the Japanese to force their way through the dense thickets, it was decided to set fire to the little fortresses, and orders to that effect were accordingly given to a patrol.   Even this was difficult, as in some places it was almost impossible to get close enough to the houses.   At one such stockade Meguro Chukichi, a private, after making his way through a bamboo hedge, started towards a house, but fell fatally wounded by well aimed shots from within its walls.   His comrades were about to start to the rescue ; they were struggling to make their way through the bamboo, when the wounded man, observing their efforts, shouted that they should all return ; that " it is needless for you to add your lives to mine which you can not save" ; and then plunging his bayonet into his body he died instantly.   Another private, Ikeda by name, a few hours later succeeded in piercing the bamboo and was about to set fire to the houses, when he likewise became a target for the enemy's rifles and fell dying to the ground.   After suffering consider-able loss, a united effort of the detachment resulted in clearing away the bamboos from a single group of houses.   A squad made a charge on the houses and succeeded in firing them, at the same time recovering the body of the brave Ikeda.   Although hit in some ten different places, he was still breathing and conscious.   His last words were that his comrade should take his rifle and avenge his death.   Fighting continued between the Japanese and the insurgents until nightfall, and as no advantage had been gained on either side, the Japanese detachment encamped for the night. The next morning (26th), the enemy were still holding out in their fort-like quarters ; and the Japanese, in the absence of artillery, decided to destroy the structures with gun-cotton.   Lieutenant Matsuyama, of the engineering corps, undertook this task with good effect.   In a short time the houses had been destroyed, passages cleared through the ambush, and the insurgents, now forced into the clearing, thought retreat safer than a man-to-man fight, and fled.   After the engagement two companies of infantry and one battery of artillery were ordered to reinforce the left column. It was now learned that the enemy were drawn up in a position to defend Taiwanfu. Spreading over a wide district, from three directions, the Japanese marched steadily forward, driving the enemy before them until Taiwanfu[1] (Tai Chu) and its suburb was reached and this important position occupied, the rebels having fled toward the south. The Chinese loss during the day is unknown ; but more than fifty dead bodies were found along the line of march. The Japanese loss was twelve, including one officer and five men killed.

An expeditionary force was now organized consisting of two columns[2] under the command of Major-General Yamane. This force was ordered to march to the Toa-to-kei (Taito-kei) river, which stretches east and west, and lies to the north of Changwha, whence they were to advance on the big inland city by the most convenient route. Accordingly, on the 26th, we find the Changwha expedition on the banks of the Taito-kei river, a considerable force on garrison duty at Taiwanfu, and the main army just departing from Gubatau (Giubato). If the reader will glance at the map, he will observe that the city of Changwha (Shoka) occupies a position a little north of the centre of the island and a few miles from the coast. It is an important city and a distributing point for a large district. Famous for its lawlessness, it had on several occasions rebelled against the Chinese government, and its inhabitants, it was prophesied, would not submit easily to Japanese occupation. Besides the warlike villagers, a large force of Chinese regulars was known to be stationed there ; and there was a splendidly situated fort. Without taking into consideration the reported fierceness of the inhabitants, the defences of the city were sufficient to induce the Japanese to make very careful preparation and to bring into practice the science of strategy, for which during the former engagements there had been but little need. The left column, on approaching Changwha, encountered the first opposition from an unknown number of insurgents quartered in houses and practising the same tactics as had so annoyed the advance guard on their march to Taiwanfu. Possessing no artillery, the column commander reported to headquarters, with the result that a detachment of artillery and infantry, under the command of Major Surisawa, was sent as reinforcements. The enemy were easily disposed of, and the left column was enabled to reach the river without delay, ready for the engagement which had long been anticipated.

Changwha, a walled city, is situated less than five miles from the sea, in a plain scarcely above its level. To the east lies a range of hills, the highest of which—Hakkezan (Paquasoan)—which dominated the whole plain, was crowned with a well erected fort protected by four 12-centimetre late model Krupp guns, besides a large number of the usual miscellaneous relics

---

1. Taiwanfu should not be confused with Tainanfu in the south, which, in old days, while the capital of the island, was known as Taiwanfu. Taiwanfu consists of a number of official yamens, while a partially constructed mud wall surrounded the area originally intended to be the new capital of the island. Outside of the intended city is a Chinese settlement, a little more filthy than the average.

2. The right column, under command of Major Miki, consisted of the 2nd battalion of the 1st infantry, the 1st squadron of cavalry, the 3rd battery of artillery, a platoon of engineers ; while the left column, under command of Colonel Nakaoka, consisted of the 1st and 2nd battalions of the 3rd regiment, the 1st section of cavalry, and one company of engineers.

of ancient warfare so beloved by the Chinese. To the north, about 3,000 metres distant, ran a mountain stream which, with the heavy rains usual at this time of year, had been converted into a surging river. It was on the opposite banks of this river that the Japanese and Chinese troops met on the 27th ; the Japanese to the north hidden by fields of sugar-cane, which cover the district; the Chinese to the south protected by earth-works of some importance, which they had erected on the river bank; while a few rods to the rear stood formidable breastworks. It had always been the custom to ford the river at one point where it was comparatively shallow, and it was at this spot that the Chinese had built their defences and gathered a large portion of their forces ; for, if it "blong olo custom" to cross at this place, the Japanese would, according to Chinese reasoning, certainly do the same. But the Japanese have a reputation for dropping old customs, and they did so in this case. The right wing, under command of Major-General Ogawa, remained at the camp to divert the Chinese with large camp fires, etc.; while the left wing, under command of Major-General Yamane, under the shadow of darkness, crossed the river with considerable difficulty at a previously discovered ford some. 1,500 metres off. The column was now divided into three detachments. The first detachment, under command of Major-General Yamane, made its way quietly along to obtain a position to attack the city of Chang-wha itself. The second detach-ment with a battery of mountain-guns crawled along through the sugar-cane to cross the lower hills and gain a position to the east of the lofty fort of Mount Hakkezan, while the third with great caution slowly and quietly advanced to the rear of the Chinese troops guarding the river, and between them and the city. The whole force arrived at their positions without a hitch, and with the enemy still watching the moving figures and the numerous camp fires of the Japanese across the river. It was one of the cleverest exhibitions of strategy displayed during the whole war. The right column crossed the river before daylight, leaving a detach-. ment at the camping grounds to keep up the camp fires ; and all were now in position ready for the attack. With the first rays of morning, the Chinese were on the alert, and opened fire with great bravado on the decoy troops left across the river. This was to the Japanese the signal for action. Scarcely had the smoke cleared away when the detachment which had occupied the position to the rear of the Chinese on the river bank was down on the insurgents with a rush. The Chinese, too surprised to make any defence, were terror-stricken. They jumped into the river, ran right and left, even on to the bayonets of their opponents. Simultaneously, the second detachment began to climb the hill at the back of the fort of Hakkezan. The surprised garrison poured a rifle fire upon them, but the detachment did not hesitate. On the contrary, bayonets were fixed and a determined charge made, until the fort was entered, and the Chinese deserting the big guns still loaded, were climbing over the walls and plunging down the hillside in full flight.

Many of the retreating insurgents had fled into the walled city of Chang-wha, apparently with the idea of fighting from the walls, where a large force was now assembled. But the Japanese in the fort above them had witnessed the whole scene and turned the insurgents' own guns down upon the city. The Chinese had not thought of this; but like a flash their danger became apparent; and from a position of calm defiance, they were thrown into a frenzy of terror, and with a wild rush they sought escape through the South Gate. But to their horrible dismay, they found the Japanese even there; and turning back into the city they ran shrieking and howling like an army amok, firing at anything that attracted their attention. Only a few shots had been fired by the Japanese from the fort; and the Japanese infantry then scaled the walls and poured down into the city in large numbers. Street fighting with the panic-stricken braves occupied an hour; but by 7 a.m. all was quiet. Detachments were at once detailed to pursue the retreating insurgents, who had gone towards Kagi to the south and Lokang (Rokko) to the west, where they hoped boats could be obtained to carry them to the south of the island.

That the Chinese were taken entirely by surprise was evidenced in the city. The houses were found in good order. Fires were blazing and the food still cooking in preparation for the morning meal; costly robes and valuables of many kinds were there undisturbed, the whole scene betraying a retreat unexpected and hastily executed. The Japanese captured the four 12-centimetre Krupp guns of the fort, 410 other guns of different sizes and models, in and about the city, besides several thousand rifles, several thousand stands of miscellaneous small arms, and ammunition; flags, and uniforms sufficient to fill a good sized godown. Several horses and a mule should also be added. In no engagement since the arrival of the Japanese had such quantities of miscellaneous war munitions been captured. Most of it was in the city, which had been converted practically into a military camp. The loss of life, as may be expected, was very large; three hundred and seventy dead bodies were found in and near the city, and two hundred and fifty in the fort, along the river, and in the surrounding roads. The Japanese loss was but seven, including one officer. Considering the strong position and the armament of Fort Hakkezan, and that the enemy numbered over five thousand well armed regulars, including a company of Black Flags, the Japanese surely had reason to be proud of their feat in striking so fatal a blow, practically without loss to themselves. They had now advanced nearly halfway through the island within twenty days from their departure from Teckcham (Hsinchiku).

Major-General Kawamura was now ordered to advance with his column to the seaport of Lokang (Rokko) and to occupy that city, while the 2nd battalion of the 4th regiment and one battalion of cavalry were to occupy Perto (Hokuto) to the south, and one battery of artillery with one company of infantry were to garrison Hakkezan. Headquarters were established at Changwha, and it was decided to cease all operations pending the arrival of the second division, which was to advance against General Liu from the extreme south of the island. There were, however, some few engagements in the neighborhood after the capture of Changwha. Tarimu (Talibu) and a few unimportant villages were occupied, the

Old Chinese Yamen at Shinchiku (Teckcham).
Seagoing Bamboo Rafts near Rokko (Lokiang).
Kagi City.

Street Scene at Rokko.
View near Taichu.
Shoka (Changwha) City.

Chinese loss during the few days of fighting being 130 killed, while the Japanese lost eight in killed and wounded.[1]

Changwha (Shoka) is located in what may quite properly be called a basin. On two sides are elevations sloping towards the city, and nowhere in the vicinity of Changwha can there be found a lower level. While the Chinese had erected many substantial and fine-looking edifices, no attempt at drainage had been made, and not only the urban sewerage, but that from the elevated areas around flowed into the city, forming vile pools about the place and remaining stagnant year after year. Fine airy structures had even been built about these foul ponds, which no doubt enhanced the value of the property surrounding them in Chinese estimation. The Japanese, however, found the steaming stench far from attractive. Before reaching the city, some seventy streams big and small had been forded; and with night and day work, irregular and insufficient provisions, owing to the difficulty of transporting supplies, and the blazing sun and hot, damp nights of interior Formosa, the troops were in an exhausted and weakened condition. It was intended that they should recuperate in Changwha, as, it was thought, healthy quarters would be found for them in the numerous yamens and temples. This was a vain hope as later events showed.

After the occupation, the first work was to bury the dead. This was necessarily a slow task, and a week elapsed before all were disposed of, many having been found concealed in the underbush and river; the offensive gases from the putrifying bodies poisoning the air. No doubt this, added to the general filthiness of the place, caused the mortality which followed. At all events, an outbreak of fever spread throughout the army like wild-fire. From the highest officer to the lowest coolie, all were incapacitated. Only the very serious cases were taken to the field hospital; yet within the first few days these numbered 824, of whom 82 died. Of the hospital corps of one chief and five doctors, three were incapacitated, thus leaving but two to look after the numerous invalids. Sixteen out of the forty-one trained

1. September 3rd, insurgents to the number of five or six hundred made an attack on Taishorin (Toapona), one of the small garrisoned villages to the south of Changwha. The number being rather large for the small Japanese force on hand, reinforcements were requested, and on their arrival the enemy was defeated and retired towards Yunliu (Unrin). The Chinese loss during the day was some sixty killed.

Also on the 3rd, one company of infantry attacked the insurgents who had retreated south from Taishorin towards Tarimu (Talibu) After considerable skirmishing, during which the enemy at one time occupied a commanding position on a cliff-like hill, the Japanese at sunset reached the vicinity of Tarimu. Here a large force of insurgents surrounded their opponents, while the latter were filing along a narrow pathway surrounded by rice fields. It was not a favorable position, and the Japanese were not a little relieved to be soon lost in the shadows of night. About 10 p.m., the company marched out of the fields and lay in ambush near the north gate of Tarimu. Scouts were sent out, who found that the entrance to the city was barricaded, that everyone was on the alert, and that sentinels were posted in numerous places; furthermore that a large force seemed to be collecting near the gate, no doubt with the intention of attacking the Japanese, whom they thought were close by. Hereupon, the Japanese quietly retired and marched towards Shitoko (Chitong Kang), the Chinese still beating drums and gongs. About 8.30 a.m. a company sent as reinforcements was met with and the whole detachment now proceeded to Shitoko. Having obtained supplies here, the force at 1 a.m. two days later advanced on Tarimu. Heavy rain was falling, which hid from the enemy the movements of the Japanese. Having obtained a position close to the north gate a sudden charge was made on the city. The Japanese scaled the walls and opened up a heavy fire. The gate was now opened; and the troops, pouring into the city with trumpets blowing, and firing volley after volley, threw the Chinese into great confusion, so sudden an attack not being expected, and a night engagement not affording them the opportunity of defending their city from the walls. At 5 o'clock, the last of the enemy had retired and the Japanese were in complete possession. On the 6th and 7th, occasional skirmishes with the enemy also occurred with but little loss on either side.

medical assistants were struck down, and four died. The Japanese dead were cremated and the ashes buried in graves marked with memorial boards. The Chinese bodies were at first buried in long trenches holding twenty or thirty each, but as other bodies were discovered corrupt and poisonous, they were piled together, a few at a time, covered with wood, and cremated. I arrived in the city a few days later ; and even then long lines of carriers were daily seen transporting the sick back towards Teckcham at the rate of about one hundred a day. The patients who were unable to walk were transported on stretchers, there being three Chinese carriers to each stretcher. Every squad of carriers had a non-commissioned officer in charge, and every ten stretchers one Japanese coolie as an attendant. In Changwha I had a pleasant visit with Major-General Yamane, who had been extremely kind to me throughout my travels with the Japanese. He was quartered in a comfortable, semi-official Chinese building and, after a long talk, the general called my special attention to the sickness, that scarcely a man in the whole division had escaped without at least a touch of the fever, and that, among the military officers, he was the only man who had not once asked for medical assistance. Indeed he looked happy and well. I never saw him again ; for the brave soldier died three days later, to the great grief of the whole division. Major-General Yamane was as good and generous as he was brave. At the first opportunity, I left Changwha and its death fumes, and on reaching the high plains my heart was overflowing with thankfulness that I had escaped. The health of Changwha soon improved, and there was no repetition of the scourge.

Lieut.-General Viscount Takashima had kindly telegraphed, notifying me, if I desired to join the Second Division which was soon to depart for the south, to return at once. I had obtained a large collection of Chinese war munitions, necessitating several extra carriers. These, together with the chair coolies for my companion and self, made our party twenty-five in number, and we found some difficulty in keeping all the coolies in order. On reaching the Taika river, we found it impassable, and were obliged to wait four days before a boat could be got across ; and yet the stream was only some fifty feet in width. Two Japanese coolies who attempted to swim it were both drowned. About thirty streams big and small were forded before we reached Teckcham. We found all peaceful to the north of Changwha. No guards were needed and the farmers were working as industriously as of old. The villagers all seemed contented and were making more money than they had ever thought of before. Between fifteen and twenty thousand Chinese coolies were engaged altogether ; and with the very liberal pay they were receiving, large numbers of farmers were deserting the less profitable agricultural work. The supply stations were located at distances some six or eight miles apart, and forty cents was fixed as the regular wage for carrying between each depot. Large numbers of women and children were engaged in the work, and it was a very usual sight to see a mother and daughter struggling along with one package swinging from a shoulder pole, two small boys with another package similarly carried, and the father singly with one, or, assisted by a grown-up son, with two. A family which, for a long day's hard work, might formerly have earned thirty or forty cents, now received $1.60. Such prices brought in many applicants, and not unfrequently I witnessed actual queue pulling fights between Chinese to obtain the work. Prices had risen in consequence, and I found it impossible to engage coolies to carry us half a day's journey for less than $1.20 per man. Reaching Teckcham we took the railway for the forty miles to Taipehfu, ending our two hundred and fifty mile journey on the 28th. At the capital there was much satisfaction expressed at the occupation of Changwha, although great grief was felt that disease had claimed so many victims. That the labors of the Imperial Body Guards had also attracted attention on the mainland was evidenced by a message of approbation which Their Majesties were pleased to send to Governor-General Kabayama.[1]

Returning to the capital, I found extensive preparations in progress for the southern expedition, and thousands of Japanese troops and military coolies were arriving from Japan to engage in it. It was not considered politic to depend entirely upon Chinese, although they had so far been found satisfactory; so Japanese coolies were brought into the island in numbers sufficient to completely equip the expedition. Japanese coolies accompanied the Imperial Body Guards when they first arrived in the island, and whether they were then more carefully selected or were under better control I do not know; at all events they made no trouble. Also the soldiers of the guards seemed to be polite and gentlemanly, quiet, and good humored, and many well educated young fellows were among the privates. I was with them on and off for three months, and the conduct of officers and privates was such that I became enthusiastic over their general good qualities. On my return from the south, I found a decided change for the worse. Scenes of violence, approaching to ruffianism, took place in the streets. First, there appeared to be a deplorable change in the character of the soldiers. One saw among the new arrivals many who were rough, uncouth, insolent, and disagreeable. They, of course, formed but a small part of the whole; yet they were sufficient in number to lower the reputation of the service to which they belonged. Chinese are adepts in acts of foolishness, and often give cause for much irritability; yet there was but little forbearance shown them on the part of some of the soldiers. My experience with the Japanese troops in the field leads me distinctly to disbelieve the tales of wholesale slaughter reported by the Chinese, which occasionally reached the columns of foreign journals. The troops were then marching in large numbers under the control of their officers, who were educated and enlightened men. There is no doubt that occasional excesses occurred; for

---

1. "We are highly pleased with the loyalty and valor displayed by the different corps under your command, which, in spite of heat and difficulties, have in so short a period succeeded in driving the insurgents out of Taiwanfu and Chang-wha, thus completing the subjugation of the northern part of the island. The lingering heat of summer being still intense, it is Our wish that every one of you should take good care of yourselves."

The Empress also caused the following message to be transmitted to the Governor-General:—

"Her Imperial Majesty the Empress has been exceedingly gratified to hear of the occupation of Taiwanfu and Chang-wha by the Guards under the command of the Governor-General. Her Majesty has been profoundly pleased with the loyalty and valor shown by the officers and men, on whose account she feels especially concerned as they are operating in so hot and unfavorable a climate." Translation as given in the *Japan Mail.*

soldiers, whatever be their nationality, are far from immaculate ; but the injury to Japanese reputation thus caused was small compared with that worked by the coolies, individual soldiers, and the lower class Japanese, in the thousand little acts of harshness and abuse towards the Chinese during the period of occupation. Much as I respect the Japanese people in general, I must admit that the coolie class, as I encountered them on the streets, in public places, etc., were inferior to the Chinese coolie of Formosa in general bearing, in cheerfulness, and in politeness to strangers. I say "*of For-mosa* ;" for I do not wish to convey the idea that the coolie, as seen in this island, was a representative of the large mass of laboring men in Japan : in fact, so striking was the difference that two English gentlemen, both of long experience with the Japanese of all classes, informed me that they could not have believed that there was material in Japan from which to draw such a class, had they not witnessed their ill-mannered conduct with their own eyes. The reader should also understand that the Chinese in Formosa have of late been very friendly to foreigners and are more liberal-minded than the mainland Chinese; in fact they show none of the hostility to strangers common in some districts of China. Therefore, it would not do to extend this comparison either to Japan or to China. On the part of the military administration, whose whole attention was directed towards the completion of the occupation of the island, but little attempt was made to curb the high spirits of the Japanese coolies. It is true that the poor fellows spent a good deal of their time in the various hospitals, and large numbers found a grave in the island, and we should perhaps take into consideration the arduous labor in which they were engaged in a country not their own; with but scanty food ; often forced to sleep in the open fields, and exposed to an intense heat to which they were not accustomed.[1] Again the Chinese often thought they were ill-treated when they were not. Military rule is in many ways unpleasant, but is the same in that respect all over the world. If the necessity should again arise for the Japanese coolies to be made use of in military operations, some provision should be made to place them under more strict control than they were under in the expedition in question. One can scarcely blame the better class of Japanese for not having come to the island during the early days of the occupation. Quarters were few and miserable, and disease was attacking large numbers. During the latter part of August, the three government hospitals in the north of Taipeh, Kelung, and Teckcham received nearly 2,000 patients, and deaths were occurring at an average rate of 18 per day.[2]

---

1. This condition of affairs existed only during the period occupied by the Japanese in quelling the republican forces.

2. Hospital cases during the last part of August :

Hospital Location.	Wounded.	Cholera.	Typhus.	Dysen-tery.	Beriberi.	Malaria.	Enteritis.	Miscella-neous.	Total.	Average for one day.
Kelung	22	3	9	25	443	106	180	182	979	3
Taipehfu	7	10	0	54	203	16	188	237	715	9
Teckcham (Hsinchu).	4	28	0	24	23	6	160	46	291	6
Total	33	41	9	103	669	128	537	465	1,985	18

New applications for admittance to the hospitals were made at the rate of about one hundred a day, and large numbers were sent to Kelung to be despatched by transport to Japan.

The reader should understand that the operations so far had been carried on only in the northern half of the island, west of the central mountain ranges. No attempt had been made to occupy or even visit the savage territory. There was also some doubt as to what the reception would be should the attempt be made. The first sight of the savages was obtained by the Japanese troops at Maoli. The hillsmen had sent word down that a party of them desired to visit the Japanese camp. Having obtained permission, three chiefs made their appearance a few days later and begged the acceptance of their assistance. The Japanese were then informed that, some time before, Liu Yung-fu had sent presents of liquor and other things to the tribesmen, with a request that they should co-operate in opposing the Japanese. The savages refused, and accordingly the messenger, Wu by name, who was accompanied by a squad of soldiers, made an attack upon them. This greatly incensed the hillsmen, and they were extremely anxious to join in the warfare against the Chinese insurgents. Regardless of the fact that their request was refused, a small party came down a few days later, fully armed and prepared to accompany the Japanese. Their entreaties were so pertinacious that the officer in command did grant them permission to go for a short time, and food and quarters were provided for them with the army. All went well for several days, when the uneasiness of the new recruits gave evidence of discontent. At last it could be borne no longer; the savages presented themselves before the commander of the detachment and plainly expressed themselves as disappointed; the Japanese had come to Formosa to kill Chinese, and regardless of the fact that the people were to be found all about them and that it was very plain they were unarmed, the Japanese had absolutely allowed thousands to escape them. Such conduct was entirely beyond their comprehension and they would return to their own tribe, whose warriors, although few in number, could show a larger collection of heads than the whole Japanese force put together. And just to show what they could do in that line, they killed a dozen peaceful Chinese living on the border a few days later, and carried off their heads to the mountain fastnesses.

The first regular meeting with the savages was held in August near Tokoham, when seven came down and held a "pow-wow" with the major of the Japanese garrison stationed there. On a later date Mr. Hashiguchi, chief of the Agricultural and Industrial Bureau, and Rear Admiral Tanaka, prefect of Taipeh, made the trip to Tokoham. Their party, escorted by about seventy-five Japanese soldiers, made their way to the savage border and were there met by a band consisting of some twenty-three savages, men, women, and children. Some conversation was held with them through an interpreter; and after receiving presents of knives, showy red handkerchiefs, red woollen cloth, etc., twelve returned with the Japanese to Tokoham, and a feast was given them there. After considerable persuasion, a savage and his wife, two boys, and a girl, consented to return with the Japanese to Taipeh and visit the governor-general. They remained several days in the capital, were loaded with presents, and returned to their mountain homes well pleased with their treatment.

So far the Japanese had encountered none of those fearful gales for which the Formosan coast is famous. In fact, the possibility of their occurrence had been scarcely taken into consideration. Early in September, however, North Formosa was visited by a terrible storm, and within a day the Tamsui river had risen twelve feet above its normal level. This was a great surprise to the Japanese, who lost a considerable amount of stores, and much damage was done to the transports in and about Kelung. Fortunately, the loss of life was small.

CHAPTER XXII.

THE JAPANESE OCCUPATION OF SOUTH FORMOSA.

1895.

Military preparations during Japan-China war—Black Flag Chief, Liu Yung-fu, as commander—His career—Liu as a disciplinarian—Takow powder-magazine explodes—An appalling scene—Liu refuses doubtful honors in North China—Capture of Pescadores—A panic-stricken Taotai—Chinese accounts of wonderful victories—An imaginary "ruse"—Anxiety among foreigners—British marines landed—Chinese gunboat lands war munitions—Chinese official methods—Liu orders foreigners out of Anping—British reinforcements landed—Liu withdraws demand—The Formosan Republic—Tainanfu declared the capital—Republican organization—Aid received from mainland officials—Currency and postal systems —Raising the wind—Savages join Liu—Japanese South Formosan force assembles in the north—Plan of campaign—Transports at the Pescadores— With General Nogi's southern expedition—The landing—A hard fight near Ka-tong-ka—Pontoon bridge construction—Skirmishes—Pithau occupied—The defences of Takow—A "ruse de guerre"—Takow bombarded by Japanese squadron—Occupied by blue-jackets—Imperial Body Guards Division advances from Changwha—Engagements at Chuwaka and Talibu—Chinese defences near Yunlin—A strong fight—Capture of Kagi—Fourth Brigade advances from Pa-te-chui—Scattered bands encountered—Feeble resistance—Engagement near Oyato, at Bau-kang-boi—Chinese suffer a loss of a thousand killed near Shaulan —Japanese forces approach Tainanfu—Retrospect—Japanese heads on exhibition —Liu's warlike spirit weakens—Abortive attempts at surrender—Foreigners visit Japanese at Kagi—The last squeeze—Wealthy Chinese flee to China— General Liu vanishes—Black Flags surrender—Arrival of Japanese—Occupation of Tainanfu completed—Warship Yayeyama pursues merchant steamer Thales—A breach of international law—Foreigners as guides—Nogi's forces arrive—Foreigners in the South—Campaign against republican forces ended— Japanese losses in Formosa—Hospital records—Death of Imperial Prince Kitashirakawa—Chinese losses—Rebel leaders favored in China—Chinese official duplicity—Numerous insurgents—Rebellion followed by brigandage— Hakka rebellion—Rebellion in the north—Mid-Formosa rebellion—Foreign settlement of Twatutia attacked—Formosan banditti—Their subjection difficult— Chinese interpreters and blackmail—A difficult problem and its solution.

IN the previous chapter, we dealt exclusively with affairs in the north of the island. The Japanese gave little or no attention to the south until possession of the whole north of the island had been obtained. However, events in the south during this period were no less interesting. While thrilling scenes like those witnessed in the north, during the three days previous to the arrival of the Japanese at Taipehfu, were not duplicated, still exciting events occurred at frequent intervals for a longer period, and the "Butterfly Republic," interesting and amusing as it was, existed in full splendor for several months.

The war between the two empires was quite as disturbing a factor in the south as it was in the north of the island, and the Chinese government recognized the necessity of giving that part of Formosa its full share of attention from a military point of view. Accordingly, the famous "Black Flag" pirate chief Liu Yung-fu[1] was appointed to the command of the military affairs in the south, and great hopes were entertained as to his ability to hold the island against all comers !

Liu, whatever may have been his other faults, was a strict disciplinarian, and his presence in Formosa was not especially welcome to several officials who had reason to fear an investigation into military affairs. Among these was the commander of the Takow forts—Wan by name—who rightly or wrongly had established for himself a somewhat unfavorable reputation both from a military and moral point of view. In consequence of this, Liu declined to accept the transfer of the forts until all arms, ammunition, and buildings had been inspected and found to minutely tally with official inventories. This demand created some consternation in the mind of the retiring commander, and much activity was displayed by him in ransacking the various magazines and casements in order to bring out everything that could pass muster as an arm or as ammunition.

This was all well enough in itself, but unfortunately while soldiers were engaged in the work, about a ton of native made powder exploded in one of the magazines. Just how it was ignited is unknown. The only survivor, however, reported that the soldiers were as usual smoking while moving about in the magazine. The various rooms in the forts were used indiscriminately as magazines and dwellings. Thus, in the Saracen's Head fort, where the explosion occurred, upwards of 35 tons of foreign pebble powder, which fortunately was not ignited, were stored in rooms adjoining

---

1. Liu Yung-fu was originally chief of a large band of pirates, rebels and free-booters, known as the "Black Flags," from their banners which were black. They had established themselves on the Tonkin frontier, and there carried on bold and daring deeds of outlawry. When the French commenced hostilities against China in 1884 the celestial empire was not averse to accepting the pirate's assistance; and, by carrying on guerilla warfare, he was able to greatly harass the enemy, although it has not been found that he accomplished any great feat of bravery ! Still, he was credited with courage and military ability, and when the war was ended it was necessary for the Chinese government to dispose of him in some way, for fear that he might be tempted to turn his much feared hand against the government. To destroy him and his followers was a task too huge to be even thought of, and to leave him on the frontier to continue his piratical raids might lead to a reopening of the war with France just closed. It was, therefore, decided to engage him in official employment. He was given a high military title and was permitted to take with him 1,100 picked men of his band, who, together with a portion of the Imperial troops of the Kwangtung province, were placed under his command. With the commencement of the Japan and China war, Liu was ordered by Imperial edict to go to the defence of Formosa, where he arrived towards the end of the year 1894.

those occupied night and day by officers and men, some of whom were at all times smoking opium or tobacco.

The scene on entering the fort just after the explosion was said to be appalling. Human fragments were met with everywhere, not only in the fort itself, but over the whole hill, and in the village on the spit at the back; while the smell of burning flesh was sickening in the extreme! It was estimated that about 100 lives were lost, but the exact number could never be ascertained, as the commandant did all he could to minimize the extent of the disaster. For some minutes after the explosion took place, both the village and lagoon were bombarded with showers of human and animal remains, amongst which latter, the heads of dogs and pigs figured largely. One man was blown high up in the air, falling through the roof of a house in the village below in the midst of a woman's gambling party, of course creating tremendous consternation. A big piece of masonry was projected for a distance of about a quarter of a mile, and falling on board a junk fatally crushed one of her crew.

The commandant, Wan, was made to pay all the damage to the houses, and restore the fort to its original condition before Liu Yung-fu would have anything to do with the place.

Liu Yung-fu, in a memorial to the throne, impeached several other military officers, with the result that out of eight complained of, four were beheaded and the others were dismissed from the service. Such strict measures naturally had their effect, ridding the army of a number of undesirable characters.

Affairs were now going badly in the north of the empire. The Japanese were gaining victory after victory, and it seemed quite probable that they might reach even Pekin itself. In this gloomy situation the Tsung-li Yamen despatched two decrees in succession, ordering Liu to leave Formosa and hasten up north to take command of the troops then fighting against the Japanese. Liu, however, possessed of a large amount of good-sense, was not inclined to take any part in the north unless he could carry with him soldiers in whose ability and skill he had confidence; and, as there was no promise of this, he stated in a long memorial opinions which were not very complimentary to Chinese officials in general, and refused absolutely to stir from the island. No further attempt was made to induce him to accept northern service and he remained in command of the South Formosa forces, as had been first arranged.

The capture of the Pescadores by the Japanese threw the southern officials of the island into a considerable panic. In so great a fright was the Taotai at Tainan upon receiving the news, that it was necessary to relieve him from his post. His character is amusingly exposed in a memorial which the acting-governor of Formosa, Tang Ching-sung, sent to the throne, stating that " the said Taotai upon the loss of the Pescadores to Japan, immediately became so panic-stricken that he suddenly presented memorialist a petition requesting to be allowed to retire temporarily from office, in order to enable him to return to his home on the mainland to repair the graves of his ancestors; following this he telegraphed immediately afterwards the news of his father's serious illness and his determination to resign, in order to go home at once to attend upon his parents. This thin veil to hid·· dastardly cowardice was immediately reported by memorialist to the throne, and on the 5th of April last his Majesty's edict was received cashiering the said Taotai of Tainanfu and dismissing him from service." His successor was an expectant prefect, Chu Ha-chun by name.

With the Japanese at the Pescadores an attack on the adjacent South Formosan coast was expected at any time. The Chinese took advantage of the probability of an engagement, and most wonderful tales, emanating from Takow and Anping, were circulated describing this event. The Chinese press in Shanghai published a detailed description, actually telegraphed from Tainan, of a Japanese attack on Takow, during which the Chinese won a glorious victory, sinking five of the enemy's ships and destroying a large number of soldiers. On another occasion it is described how the Japanese appeared, and after having been decoyed into close quarters the Chinese suddenly attacked them; "The Japanese fled for their lives, but in vain ; those who did not die by fire perished in the water, so that by mid-day their losses amounted to twenty men-of-war and 20,000 men, and quite a large number of the warships of other nationalities were unintentionally damaged in the conflagration that ensued."

Again most circumstantial details were given of another great disaster that had befallen Japanese ships in Formosa, affording us new evidence of the strict discipline of old Liu. According to this report, the son of the Black Flag chief had destroyed, off Takow, fourteen Japanese ships, and only four out of the whole fleet had escaped. Exacting old Liu, upon learning this, fell into a great rage and chastised his son, by giving him sixty blows with the bamboo, for permitting the four ships to get away. Another example of Chinese prowess was reported during the campaign, which is worthy of record among the memorial deeds of the war. Upon the approach of Japanese warships on a certain occasion, the Chinese fleet provided themselves with large numbers of empty wine-jars, to the mouths of which they fastened bladders realistically painted to represent the heads of Chinese. These they floated out towards the Japanese fleet. The Japanese, greatly alarmed at the boldness of the Chinese swimming towards them, fired at the daring marines with such rapidity and wildness that they exhausted all their ammunition, and the defenders were therefore enabled to sweep down on their assailants and capture the whole fleet.

Further evidence of the wonderful strategical ability of the Chinese is afforded us in the following report. The Chinese filled long bamboo tubes with wasps and set them afloat, whereupon the Japanese, who mistook them for torpedoes, captured a large number, and took them on board their several ships. Upon breaking into them for examination—an unusual custom I believe—thousands of the wasps were liberated and flew about in a great rage, stinging the Japanese right and left. So great was the pain thus inflicted that the Japanese for the time-being were placed *hors de combat*, and upon the appearance of the Chinese in battle array fell easy victims.

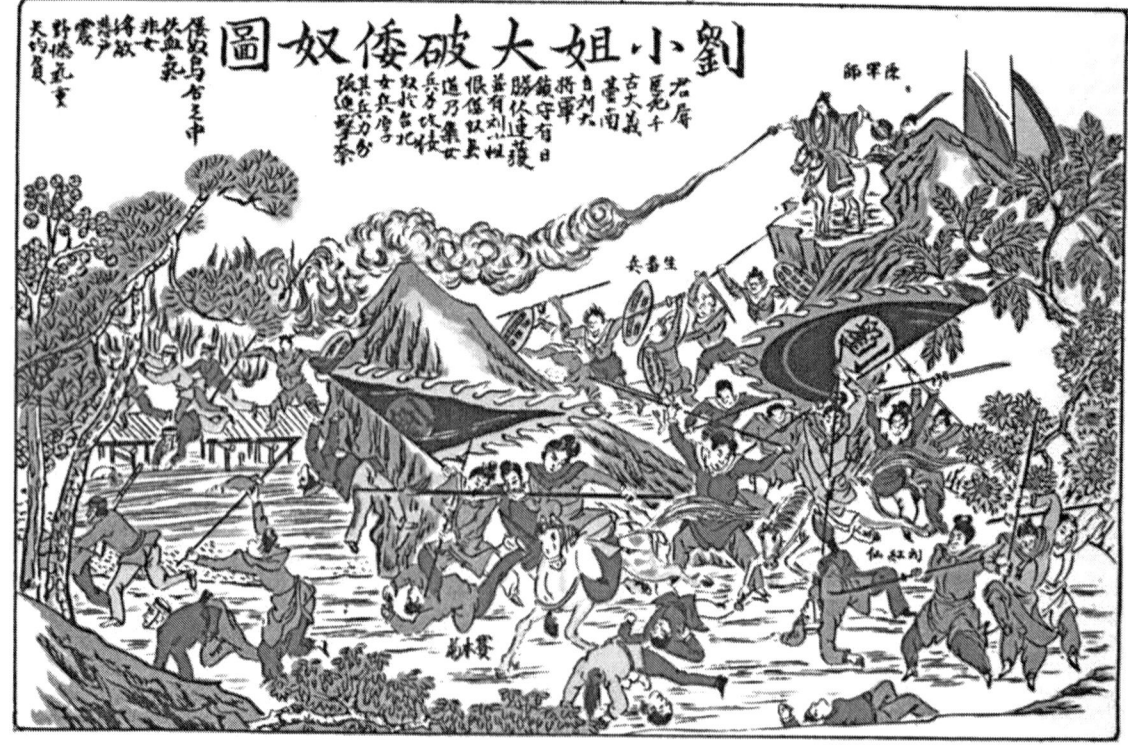

CHINESE POSTERS DESCRIBING EVENTS IN FORMOSA DURING THE
JAPANESE CAMPAIGN.

Two other oft-told tales were made the subjects of pictorial representation; one portraying the defeat of a party of Japanese infantry by Liu Yung-fu's daughters, who, aided by a few Formosan savages with their primitive weapons, were finding the task not a difficult one; and the other representing an impending execution of the then Governor-General, Count Kabayama, who, in the picture in question, is seen standing with other prisoners before Liu and several mandarins, while the executioner is near with his heavy sword awaiting the final word.

After the arrival of the Japanese at Taipehfu in the north of the island, the scene of Chinese victories was transferred to the inland districts. Here we are told a clever "ruse of war" was effected by a number of Black Flags, who disguising themselves as savage aborigines, visited a Japanese camp to ask protection for their tribe against the terrible "Black Flags." The Japanese were much moved and at once despatched "a few thousand men." The tricky guides led them to a narrow pass through the mountains. Here mines were exploded, and taking advantage of the confusion resulting, the Chinese troops poured out from their ambush and cut down the Japanese to a man.

The above tales, and countless others as improbable, were received with implicit confidence by the Chinese, and aroused much alarm among those who were under Japanese protection. Even foreigners gave occasional credence to the more probable of the reports, and one gentleman was so far deceived as to state in one of the Shanghai foreign journals that he had witnessed the destruction of a Japanese man-of-war during the fighting at Kelung.

Events in which foreigners were concerned may be said to date from the first days of May, 1895, when the situation assumed so serious an aspect that Admiral Fremantle, commander of the British naval force in China, landed a body of fifty marines at Anping for the protection of British lives and property. The place was over-run with Chinese military rabble; and if any opportunity arose, it was quite probable that indiscriminate looting and marauding would find much favor with them. The Japanese were at this time in occupation of the Pescadores, and although an occasional man-of-war was sighted off the coast, still no attempt was made to harass the Formosan authorities in any way. In fact on May 8th, for some unaccountable reason, the Japanese fleet permitted the Chinese gunboat *Chinghoi* to steam unmolested into Takow and land treasure and 5,000 rifles and ammunition for the Black Flags at the latter port. Fifty thousand rifles were, it is said, landed in Tamsui about the same time. If we note that the island was ceded by the Emperor of China on the 17th of April, we obtain an insight into Chinese official methods by observing, three weeks later, one of the emperor's ships still engaged in supporting a military force in active opposition to a nation with which His Majesty had signed a treaty of peace. In early June, the Japanese took possession of the northern capital, the Republic was transferred to the south of the island, and Liu Yung-fu was declared sole president.

While it has not transpired that Liu had any really hostile intentions against the foreign community, his bearing on several occasions was such as to cause some uneasiness. The action on the part of a Japanese gunboat, which, on the 13th of June, ran into the anchorage at Anping close to British men-of-war and merchant steamers, is said to have given rise, among the Chinese, to some resentment against the English. The land fort which opened fire[1] was under considerable disadvantage, being unable to direct a heavy fire against the Japanese warship without danger of injuring the English vessels. The foreigners were now accused of favoring the Japanese, and Liu appears to have become so excited over his fancied grievances that he eventually ordered the foreign community and the naval detachment to leave Anping, failing which he threatened to fire on H.B.M.S. *Spartan* then in the anchorage. The situation now became somewhat critical, and a special steamer, the *Wenchow*, was despatched to Amoy for reinforcements. The British cruiser *Rainbow* answered the call very promptly, bringing with her two officers and the marines who had been previously on guard at Twatutia. On her arrival, the Chinese claimed that she was a Japanese warship in disguise and that they were determined to fire upon her. So threatening did their attitude become that the *Rainbow* signalled to the merchant vessels to get up steam and proceed to sea. The two men-of-war had previously cleared for action, and their warlike appearance, together with an emphatic protest made by Consul Hurst on shore, led the Black Flag chief to abandon his hostile plans, at least for the time. Later on, a steam launch went out with a junk which, after taking some eighty marines and bluejackets aboard, conveyed them to shore, while the *Rainbow* and *Spartan*, with their guns run out, cruised up and down, in front of the forts, ready to take action if the Chinese fired on the junk, as they said they would. The shore guard now numbered 150. Several machine guns were also landed. On the 17th, the Norwegian steamer *Bygdo* took away to Amoy all the ladies and children of Anping and Tainanfu, and H.M.S. *Redbreast* arrived, also cleared for action, followed a few days later by H.M.S. *Plover*. All were now anxiously awaiting the arrival of the Japanese. Thousands of the natives were fleeing to the interior, and others taking passage to the mainland. From the latter Liu Yung-fu extorted a large portion of their treasure before they were permitted to leave.

With the large foreign force at hand, affairs went on quietly for some time, and the foreigners considered the safety of their position fairly assured. On July 1st, however, from a condition of comparative ease, the Anping community was thrown into a state of considerable consternation by receiving information that Admiral Buller had given instructions for the British forces, ashore and afloat, to be withdrawn, and was also urgently advising the withdrawal of the foreign community. The admiral's action was much criticized, and the English press, both in China and Japan, severely censured him. The reason given by the admiral for the apparent abandonment was that, owing to the impending south-west monsoon, it might be necessary at

---

1. Five shots from 28-ton guns were fired.

any time to run to the Pescadores for shelter, and that the naval guard on shore would then be left unsupported for an indefinite period. The guard was accordingly re-embarked on June 30th. The Chinese Customs staff also came to the conclusion that it was inadvisable to wait longer for the arrival of the Japanese, and accordingly the Custom House was closed on June 29th, and the staff withdrew.

To describe the organization of the Southern Republic, it is necessary to retrace our steps to the early days of June, when President Tang made his escape from Taipeh-fu, the northern capital. About this time, the taotai and the leading officials who had been stationed at Tainanfu, in compliance with orders from the Chinese emperor returned to the mainland, leaving an ex-mandarin, who had been serving as confidential adviser, to act as taotai, magistrate, and prefect. Ku-ku-ching su, commonly known as Khâ, Phoksia, and others of the *literati* to the number of about one hundred, asked Liu, who was then at Takow, to come to Tainanfu and protect the city. He consented and was installed in the Examination Hall, adopting the style of Assistant Commissioner. When Tang fled, however, the *literati* and others composing the so-called Parliament, elected Liu Yung fu to the presidency of the " Republic," which they determined should continue.

A " ways and means" committee was at once formed, and arrangements made for collecting the necessary funds from the people. This was done both by capitation tax and " voluntary " subscription. Besides the usual land and other taxes, a further and special war-tax was imposed to the extent of five per cent. of their possessions as fixed by official assessment. Besides this, Liu arranged to carry on the Foreign Customs, the proceeds from which went into his treasury. An executive council, elected from the " Parliament," and consisting of seven senators, sat in the city every afternoon. The chairman and vice-chairman of this body were Phok-siâ and Khâ respectively. Proclamations were issued setting forth that, as soon as the Japanese had been driven out of the island and peace fully established, railways were to be built, mines opened, and trade otherwise developed.

A silver republican seal had been made, which was now offered to Liu with much ceremony, while at the same time he was requested to assume the supreme direction. It was clearly agreed and announced that this step of forming an independent government in no way indicated a lapse from their allegiance to China ; on the contrary it was hoped that what they now did would tend to aid China in the hour of her need and helplessness, that the republic would be conducted in unison with the mother-government, both working side by side as "twin mountains." It was understood, too, that after peace had been established by the expulsion of the Japanese, the people of this island would once more put themselves under the rule of their old sovereign the Emperor of China.

As in the north, there can be no doubt but that Viceroy Chang Chi-tung, and even higher officials, secretly instigated and supported Liu, and through him the people, in carrying out this scheme. As a fact, every month Chang Chi-tung forwarded money, men, and arms in considerable quantity to Liu ;

indeed this support only ceased a month or six weeks before the occupation of the south by the Japanese, though, even then, the high supporters in Nanking and Foochow, at least verbally pledged themselves to redeem the paper-notes which Liu was obliged to issue as payment to his troops. The notes were really issued and supposed to be guaranteed by a foreign compradore, and their face values were $1, $5, and $10. Cash-notes, for face-values of 100, 500, and 1,000 copper cash each were on the point of being circulated when the extreme crisis arrived, which put an end to all such plans and calculations.

All government payments were for the last month or so made in these notes, proclamations being issued calling on the customs, hongs, and all the people to accept them as good and valuable tender. For some little time the notes were redeemed at par on presentation to the aforesaid foreign compradore; during the last week or two these redemptions were suspended, and thereupon bond notes, resembling the others in appearance, were issued, guaranteed by the wealthy people in the city. Another form of speculative note, mere "lottery tickets," were the outcome of a final and desperate attempt on the part of some of Liu's financiers "to raise the wind," the promise being to pay four times their face value " after the Japanese had been driven into the sea and peace restored!" It was truly wonderful how many fools there were who took the bait and bought tickets, some bearing as high a face value as $200.

President Liu also introduced a postal system, which was expected to help out the government's revenue, as well as to afford means of controlling the correspondence of the citizens. It appears that Liu had reason to suspect some persons of sending information through the post office (native), and so, in order to give him a pretext for *visé*, he decreed that no letters should leave the island unless they bore stamps issued by his government, and that all letters must pass through the customs before being sent on board steamers or other vessels for transmission to the mainland. It is said that he did actually, by this means, discover one or two treasonable communications.

Two issues of postage stamps, of three denominations each, were utilized, and according to official records, 9,300 letters passed through the post office during the time the first was in use, and some 8,000 of the second issue, and the stamps were *bonâ fide* used for postal purposes.[1]

---

1. The following details regarding the issue of postage stamps for the Formosan Republic may be of interest to philatalists.

The first or provisional issue, hurriedly got up, and printed with a native made die were as follows:—

Green=3 cents.	Violet=10 cents.	Red=5 cents.

The whole issue was only between 7,000 and 8,000 *sets*, certainly not more than 8,000, and then the die was destroyed.

These stamps were impressed on thin *Chinese* paper and were *not* perforated. Both with this issue and the following one the clearness of impression cannot be taken as any proof of genuineness, indeed very often they were indistinct and barely discernible, but for all that were sold and used.

Of this first issue the green were mostly used for postal purposes, and thus many sets of this issue were broken into.

According to the official records 9,300 letters passed through the post office during the time the first

It must be said in justice to Liu that he undoubtedly paid his troops in money so long as he had it, and clothed and fed them at government expense, and the Chinese generally spoke highly of Liu's personal integrity. It would appear that the strength of Liu's command, after Tang had bolted, including local levies, was not far short of 30,000 men. Of these only about 4,000 could be properly styled the original "Black Flags." The local levies, even the Hakkas, who were the most enthusiastic followers of Liu at first, decreased in number daily as the Japanese advanced towards Tainanfu, until in the end probably not more than 12,000 remained with the colours. At one time a band of savages from the south made a pretence of joining Liu. They were encamped in the city, and only received food in return for their services. Two died, whereupon the remainder decided that this was a bad omen, and so, taking the dead on their backs, the whole lot suddenly disappeared and were no more heard of. In the meantime they had got arms and ammunition from Liu, which they no doubt thought ample recompense for the trouble they had been put to.

Up to this time, the Japanese had occupied only the north and central districts. Having failed to despatch an expedition during the favorable season, and, later being prevented by the onset of the south-west monsoon, which would render the landing of troops in the south very hazardous, the Japanese did not commence the southern campaign until the month of October, to the considerable inconvenience of the foreign residents, who, uninformed of Japan's intentions, were kept in a state of anxious suspense for over five weary months.

The Japanese South Formosan expedition was to consist of the second (Sendai) division and the Imperial Body Guards, and of these two divisions there had arrived in the island prior to the opening of the campaign 25,826 men. The Imperial Guards, however, had been longest in Formosa and had lost several thousand men by sickness, thus reducing the total number of men ready for the field to about 20,000. Besides this, there were several thousand military coolies who had arrived from Japan for the transport service.[1] The above force was followed by 7,200 men of the Osaka fourth division of

---

1. There were about 800 Japanese coolies attached to each regiment, caring for provision and ammunition transport with the field forces. The second division employed 2,800 men provided with 800 hand carts in transport work in the field. There were, engaged in the rear in transport service between the army and different supply depots and as attendants in temporary hospitals, and in road and telegraph construction work, 3,870 men in all.

---

was in use. For obliterating stamps the postal mark used at first was a circle in which are the words "Taiwan Republic, Tainan" and in centre the date "September."

Second issue:—Blue (approaching in many cases to black)—3 cents. Red—5 cents, Violet—10 cents, but, half of this 10 cents issue were printed in black and in some cases in blue, the violet ink having run short. These stamps are more perfect in appearance as they are printed from a die obtained from Canton.

All the above second issue were on paper which had been rather roughly perforated, in fact looks as if it was done with a sewing-machine, and evidently before the stamps had been printed on their respective spaces, within which they are by no means regularly placed. A total issue of 18,000 sets of these were printed, of which about 8,000 odd stamps of various values have been used postally. The obliterating postmark that first came into use with this issue, consists of a larger circle than the first, round which are the words "Formosan Republic Taiwan," but dated in October. All the paper was ungummed. A final effort to replenish the depleted treasury was made by taxing each passenger flying from the island, and there were many thousands of these. The rate varied from two to four or six dollars according to the financial standing of the fugitives.

reserves, who did garrison duty as fast as the country was subdued by the field forces. They were pioneers, however, in the Kapsulan (Giran) district, and had their share of fighting with scattered bands of insurgents throughout the island. Lieut-General Viscount Takashima was appointed Vice-Governor-General of Formosa, and placed in command of the military. He arrived in the island in the middle of September and at once took charge.

The southern expedition, with the exception of the Imperial Body Guards, assembled at the Pescadores on the 3rd and 4th October, and was there divided into two armies. One, consisting of the fourth mixed brigade of the second division, under the command of H.I.H. Prince Fushimi, was ordered to land at Pa-te-chui (Ho-tei-shi) about 28 miles north of the Black Flag Chief's headquarters at Tainanfu. The other, consisting of the rest of the second division under the command of Lieutenant-General Baron Nogi, was directed to land at Pangliau (Borio), about 25 miles to the south of Takow. A third force, the Imperial Body Guards, which, in the previous chapter we brought down as far as the big inland city of Changwha, was to advance towards Tainanfu through the central districts. Thus, with Japanese warships playing their part at sea on the west, the savages creating an effectual barrier on the east, large forces marching from the north and south, it was very evident that the famous Liu and his equally famous Black Flags would be brought to bay, and their oft repeated boasts of bravery and superiority put to a test! Now let us see how it all turned out!

We will for convenience sake first follow the fortunes of the southern expedition under the command of Lieutenant-General Baron Nogi. I had the pleasure of being a member of that party, and Mr. Kashiwamura, formerly military attaché of the Japanese legation at Berlin, was detailed as my companion and kindly acted as interpreter.

At four p.m. on October 3rd, the *Kyōtō Maru* steamed out of Kelung harbor for the Pescadores with Lieutenant-General Baron Nogi and his staff, two companies of soldiers, and a few civil attachés, two or three Japanese correspondents, and myself on board. The trip was exceedingly pleasant, and we arrived at the Pescadores about 1.30 p.m. For the next four days, transports and men-of-war continued to arrive, until nearly 50 ships were assembled, including the I.J.S. *Sai-yen*, formerly the Chinese gunboat *Tsi-yen*.

Early on the morning of the 10th, the northern expedition, with General Takashima in command, departed from the Pescadores for the landing place at Pa-te chui (Ho-tei-shi) north of Anping. During the afternoon our expedition steamed out of harbour for Pang-liau (Borio), about 25 miles south of Takow, arriving near the landing place at daylight. The men-of-war that accompanied us at once landed marines, but no Chinese soldiers were seen, and the Japanese naval flag was soon flying from a neighboring mound. The soldiers from the transports were then landed, and in about two hours the whole fighting force of the expedition, consisting of 6,330 men, with 1,600 military coolies and 2,500 horses, was in readiness to take the field. A wharf had been quickly built, and the coolies were soon unloading the supplies from the transports with remarkable celerity and without mishap. Three steam launches, seventy-two Japanese sampans, and ten big cargo-boats were used for transporting men and stores from steamer to land.

The men-of-war cruised along the coast a short distance ahead of the army on shore, and the few scattered bands of the enemy that came in sight were quickly dispersed by an occasional shell from their guns. Two companies were sent at once to the south, where some Chinese soldiers were found, and after exchanging a few shots, the latter retreated in the direction of the small village of Ka-tong-ka (Ka-to-kiak).

Two companies of infantry were also sent along the beach road, but finding none of the enemy in that direction they marched towards Ka-tong-ka. On arriving near the village the next morning, they found it surrounded by a low stone wall loop-holed for rifle fire. Several cannon made the place quite a formidable stronghold, and, after the Japanese had surrounded the village, the stubborn resistance made by the Chinese showed that the latter intended to take full advantage of their position. A body of water, which nearly surrounded the village, greatly hindered the Japanese in attacking at close range, and the enemy were so well protected that it was only a waste of ammunition to fire from a distance. The Japanese made several futile charges with considerable loss of life before a battalion commander and one company succeeded in gaining an entrance through one of the gates, though not without loss, and set fire to some of the houses. A strong wind blowing in the right direction carried the flames quickly toward the Chinese, who were making a stout defence. Only one chance was now open to the enemy;—to come out into the open field and face the Japanese,—but this they did not care to do. With the crackling of the bamboo, the falling of houses, the awful roaring of the fire as it swept nearer and nearer to the horror stricken braves, who were now joined by others driven out of the houses in which they had sought shelter, the scene became one of intense excitement. The cries of the Chinese could be heard above the uproar, and the poor wretches crouched closer and closer to the stone wall, taking advantage of pits or trees and bushes already smouldering, to protect them from the stifling heat of the conflagration. At last they could bear it no longer, and, with a yell of terror, they threw themselves over the wall and made a mad rush for the scrub and jungle to the north. Many fell by the way, but the majority made good their escape.

This affair was a serious one for the Japanese, who lost 77 men (16 killed and 61 wounded) including three officers,—by far the greatest loss yet sustained by them in Formosa. Seventy bodies of Chinese were found, and probably a few others were consumed by the flames. Twelve cannon, several rifles, and some ammunition fell into the hands of the Japanese. The Chinese taking part in this engagement were not Black Flags, but were composed wholly of native levies.

One company of infantry was quartered near the village the night following, and in the afternoon of the next day a skirmish occurred with a few Chinese, who soon retreated with slight loss. Perhaps the most formidable enemy we met, and one which succeeded in creating much excitement and no little terror, was the Chinese water buffalo. Indeed, if General Liu had only mounted a troop of cavalry on these animals, he might have been victorious. The huge beast, upon being frightened, appears to go absolutely mad, and with head erect and angry snorting, charges straight through anything and everything. One ran "amok" into a temporary encampment, severely injuring an officer and forcing us all to make a lively scramble to avoid not only the wild beast but our own pack horses which threatened to stampede.

October 12th, in order to reach Tangkang (Toko) the main army crossed, on pontoon bridges, two rivers of considerable size. The Formosan bamboo catamaran, which consists of from eight to twelve bamboos placed side by side braced by cross-bars securely lashed, has such a shape and size that a number of them can easily be converted into a most satisfactory bridge by merely connecting them side by side, and protecting the bamboo by laying down a few boards and covering them with straw. Over two bridges thus constructed the whole army, including heavily laden pack-horses, passed in safety, and soon all were encamped at Tangkang. No opposition whatever was encountered in the city, the Chinese troops having deserted it long before our arrival. Tangkang is about seventeen miles south of Takow and has an estimated population of 12,000. It is a most flourishing city and exports large quantities of rice and sugar. The Chinese force formerly stationed here consisted of 1,000 men divided into two camps.

October 13th, a Chinese commandant sent an offer of unconditional surrender. General Nogi accepted it and waited, delaying his troops one day, but no Chinese appeared to lay down their arms.

October 14th, a squadron of cavalry reconnoitering to the north reached the big walled city of Pithau (Hozan), where they were agreeably surprised to see white flags of peace floating from the houses and a large white banner over the city gates. Upon attempting to enter, however, they found the gates closed, whereupon they scaled the wall and were greatly astonished at being greeted with a most vigorous fusillade. Upon this, they beat a hasty retreat, and were pursued for some distance by about 200 Chinese soldiers. On the same day a company of infantry defeated with but trifling loss a large force which had first surrounded them near Chakosui.

October 15th, one company of infantry was sent forward to reconnoitre Takow, but on approaching the city they were surprised to see the flag of the Japanese navy flying from the forts. They now started to return to the main army. After going a few miles eastward they came to a large walled city, the inhabitants of which resisted them. After some fighting, however, the Chinese retreated, and the assailants, entering the city triumphantly, were surprised to find they had captured Pithau (Hozan), the very place the main army was then preparing to attack.

October 16th—On this day the army advanced to Pithau establishing their camp for the night north of that city. We were all now in the highest spirits, for although the navy had deprived us of an engagement at Takow, we were drawing near Liu's headquarters and expected to lead in the attack on Tainanfu and Anping. How we also lost that opportunity the reader will soon learn.

We must, however, now go back a few days to describe the capture of Takow, one of the most important positions in the island ; the occupation of which was the principal object of the southern expedition. During the early days of the Formosan Republic, about 15,000 Chinese soldiers were stationed at Takow, four or five thousand of them being Liu Yung-fu's " redoubtable Black Flags " commanded by his adopted son ; but, as the Japanese were slowly and surely approaching, General Liu, Jr., seems to have felt it undesirable to oppose an attack on Takow, for we find him gradually withdrawing his troops, and on the day preceding the bombardment by the Japanese fleet, only about 500 Chinese soldiers remained to man the forts. It is said that a telegram was sent by General Liu at Anping ordering his son to hoist the white flag, not apparently with the idea of treating with the Japanese, but as a *ruse de guerre* to cover his men's retreat. On the 14th October, it is stated that another telegram was received from the same source ordering the commandant to haul down the white flag, and when the Japanese were in range to fire a few shots, and then retreat and reinforce the main body of troops at Tainan and Anping.

On the 12th October three Japanese men-of-war appeared off the fort, and H.M.S. *Tweed*, Lieut. Ward commanding, conveyed the British residents to a safe position outside, as it was expected that the attack would be made at once. However, on Lieut.-Commander Ward's boarding the Japanese Flagship (*Yoshino*) he was informed that no bombardment would take place that day, but the admiral requested that all foreign residents would leave Takow by 7 o'clock the next morning. Accordingly, H.M.S. *Tweed* embarked all the foreign residents, and proceeded, accompanied by the British tugboats *Sin Taiwan* and *Takow*, to a safe position to the northward of Ape's Hill.

At 7 a.m., true to time, the Japanese opened fire on the Takow forts at a range of about 6,000 yards. For the first half hour the forts responded, but after this their guns were silent, and it was evident that Liu's soldiers were carrying out their preconcerted plans—evacuating the forts and retreating inland. The forts fired twenty-four rounds, the best shot being from the 8-inch B. L. Armstrong guns in Apes' Hill fort, which struck the water about 500 yards from the *Naniwa Kan*. At 2 p.m. the Japanese fleet, consisting of seven ships, including the *Tsi-yuen* (the Armstrong cruiser captured from the Chinese) closed the beach to the southward of Saracen's Head, and at 2.15 p.m. twenty-five boats "manned and armed" were seen proceeding in a parallel line to the beach, steering for that portion immediately under Saracen's Head fort. At 2.30 the foremost boat's bows touched the beach, and five minutes later the Japanese sailors were in possession of the fort, without meeting any resistance whatever. the Japanese ensign being hoisted at the flagstaff. But now a greater task had to be performed, namely, the taking of Ape's Hill fort. With any other nation than the Chinese this would indeed have been difficult, but here, as before, there was no resistance, and the chrysanthemum flag was floating proudly from the fort flagstaff at 4 p.m. Takow was then in full possession of the Japanese, the loss of life amounting to four men on the Chinese side, two being killed in Ki-au village and two in Apes' Hill fort. It is hardly necessary to state that the casualties on the Japanese side were *nil*. The damage done to foreign property by the bombardment was infinitesimal, and a British naval officer stated that he was surprised to see so little destruction to the houses on shore, which he thought was due to the Japanese admiral's consideration in bombarding on such a bearing that the forts and houses were not in line. As soon as the Japanese flag was hoisted over Apes' Hill fort, the gun-boat *Tweed* proceeded into the inner harbor, and the foreign residents were once more installed in their houses. The Japanese warships actually engaged in the bombardment were the *Yoshino*, bearing the flag of Admiral Arichi, *Naniwa*, *Akitsushima*, *Tsi-yuen*, *Yaeyama*, *Hiyei*, and two transports, one of which (*Saikio Maru*) was placed at the disposal of the foreign residents. The forts were very little injured, notwithstanding that the Japanese fleet had kept up a heavy fire for seven hours. The very long range adopted by the Japanese accounted for this.

We must now leave the south of the island for the time and return to the northern and central districts to describe the advance of the Imperial Body Guards, and H.I.H. Prince Fushimi's expedition, which, the reader will recollect, had landed at Pa-te-chui (Hoteishi) to the northward of Anping.

The Imperial Body Guards had, as related in the previous chapter, established their headquarters at Changwha (Shoka) during September, and small detachments had occupied some of the neighboring villages. The unhealthiness of Changwha and the long enforced idleness of the troops caused them to welcome the order from headquarters to advance on Tainan. Originally 14,036 strong, their ranks had been so reduced by sickness that it is doubtful whether they were able to muster more than 7,000 men for this southern expedition.

Early on the morning of the 23rd October they moved out of Changwha. They marched in four columns :—the vanguard under Major-General Kawamura, the right column under Colonel Sakai, the left column under Colonel Naito (later promoted to Major-General), and the reserves under the immediate command of H.I.H. Prince Kitashirakawa.

On the 5th, the advance guard crossed the river near Pak-tau (Hokuto) and proceeded towards Chuwaka (Jusika) where they defeated seven or eight hundred Chinese, arriving by nightfall at Chitong-kang (Shitoko), where they encamped. On the 6th, the advance guard had an encounter near Talibu (Tarimu) with about 3,000 Chinese troops, resulting in the customary victory for the Japanese, by whom the village was occupied. The same day a detachment sent to the east defeated about 1,000 of the enemy, occupying a small village two miles and a half south-east of Chuwaka.

The first engagement in which strong opposition was encountered was in the vicinity of Yunlin (Unrin), which was reached on the morning of the

South Formosa Views.

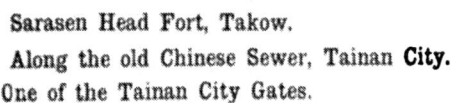

Sarasen Head Fort, Takow. Chinese City, Takow.
Along the old Chinese Sewer, Tainan **City.** A Chinese Garden, Tainan.
One of the Tainan City Gates. Along the route of the old Tainan Canal, now a roadway.

7th by the left column. The enemy had posted themselves at various strategical points on the left bank of a stream. They were easily dislodged from all places except a high entrenchment farthest up the stream, a strong position with both banks protected by impenetrable jungles of bamboo and well constructed palisades. To reach this fortification it was necessary to march for a considerable distance through a clearing below, which exposed the guards to the full fire of the enemy. However, by taking advantage of every irregularity in the ground, the Japanese were enabled to approach the eminence with but little loss, and once there they soon cut their way through the palisades and charged the enemy at the point of the bayonet. The Chinese garrison did not wait to test the enemy's steel, but fled from their stronghold along the road towards Toroku (Tau lak) leaving two hundred of their number dead in and about the stockade. Passing through Toko koe (Dokokai), Chi-tong-kang, and other villages, whence the Chinese regulars always promptly retreated without giving fight and leaving large amounts of ammunition, arms, etc., on the 9th the Guards approached Kagi (Chia-i), a large and important walled city, which, according to popular report, was garrisoned by ten thousand Chinese troops, regulars and volunteers included. Here the insurgents showed a strong disposition to fight. All the gates of the city were barricaded, and cannon and machine guns, mounted on the top of the wall, were worked with considerable skill. The plan was to attack from the north, east, and west, and after the three columns had arrived the engagement began. The walls were bombarded with mountain pieces for some time, and then the Japanese approached the three gates almost simultaneously. Bamboo ladders were planted against the walls, and, after a heavy fire, which drove the defenders back from their positions on the wall, a party of non-commissioned officers and men climbed over and poured volley after volley against the confused braves, now fleeing through the streets towards the south gate, which had been purposely left unguarded. The cavalry hurried the fleeing braves along for a few miles towards the south, and in a few hours from the beginning of the fight the neighborhood was freed from the enemy, and the flags of the "Rising Sun" replaced the "Black Flags" of Liu Yung-fu on the walls of the city. The opposing force is believed to have numbered about three thousand men, including six hundred Black Flags, who now fought the Japanese for the first time. The Chinese loss was over two hundred dead. The total loss of the Imperial Guards from Changwha to Kagi, including the casualties at the latter place, was fourteen killed and fifty-four wounded. The Guards were now ordered to remain at this point until H.I.H. Prince Fushimi's expedition was landed at Pa-te-chui.

The Fourth Brigade, consisting of 5,460 men and commanded by the Prince accompanied by Lieutenant-General Takashima, commander-in-chief of the Japanese forces in the island, departed from the Pescadores in nineteen transports on the morning of the 10th of October. The transports were accompanied by the three warships, the *Naniwa*, *Saiyen*, and *Kaimon*. After steaming for about two hours, the ships were met by a British man-of-war, which signalled to the *Naniwa* that she had brought an offer of

surrender from Liu Yung-fu The Japanese warship referred her to the
commander of the fleet at the Pescadores. At 10.50 a.m. the transports
reached their destination and the men-of-war opened operations by bombarding
the Chinese troops on the beach. A few hours later the Chinese retired, and
the landing of the troops commenced. Bluejackets were the first on shore,
and a portion of the 17th regiment were able to land during the day, the mixed
brigade under Prince Fushimi following. The anchorage is about three
miles from shore, and, with a strong wind blowing, the landing was extremely
difficult, the sampans taking seven or eight hours to make the trip.

Chinese troops were found occupying the village, but after a little
fighting they retreated, leaving the Japanese in possession. The natives
informed them that, a few days before, several thousand Chinese soldiers had
been sent to the village, but that most of them had retired early that
morning, only about eight hundred remaining to attack the landing parties.
Before the forces were on shore, it was observed that a portion of the village
was burning, but whether the conflagration owed its origin to shells from the
Japanese warships or was the work of the retreating Chinese is not
known. At all events it placed the Japanese under considerable inconvenience owing to the absence of roofed shelter.

Only the brigade staff, the fifth regiment, and two companies of
the seventeenth regiment were able to land during the day. An advance on
Kiam-tsui-kang (Yensuiko) and Ku-pa-to (Ki-bat-si) was made in three
columns, and then a bivouac was ordered for the night. During the 12th,
the mixed brigade were sent out against the scattered bands of the enemy
in the surrounding district, but with the exception of an engagement near
Kaw-wah-tau, the resistance was very feeble. Communication was opened
with the Guards Division by the arrival of two staff officers from Kia-tsui-
kang, which had previously been occupied by a detachment sent forward
from Kagi. On the 14th, orders were given by General Takashima to the
mixed brigade, that great care should be taken in thoroughly scouring the
district, that no Chinese soldiers should remain to harass any small parties
of Japanese passing through, or to endanger the lives or property of
peacefully inclined Chinese.

On the 15th, the van of the mixed brigade advanced to Kiu-sui-kei, and
the brigade staff to Kiam-tsui-kang. On that day the last of the supplies were
landed from the transports at Pa-te-chui. On the 16th, reinforcements were
sent to one company of the 17th regiment, which had been surrounded by
insurgents. An engagement took place resulting in the retreat of the Chinese
with a loss of sixty killed, while the Japanese lost nine killed and ten
wounded. On the 18th, information was received from native spies as to
the location of the mines and earthworks constructed north of Tainanfu
and that there were 10,000 troops distributed throughout the district.

On receiving information that some six thousand insurgents were
stationed near Ongo-ya-toi (Oyato), the commander of the mixed brigade
despatched the 5th regiment of infantry, one battery of artillery, and a troop of
cavalry to engage them. After a few hours fighting, in which three Japanese

were killed and fourteen wounded, including five officers, the enemy retreated, leaving eighty dead on the field. Two large cannon of ancient model were captured. On the same day the right column of the Guards' Division took Bau-kang-boi (Bokobi) without opposition, and proceeded to Tion-sha (Chu-sha). Here they encamped for the night. The right detachment of the mixed brigade met the enemy about four kilometres west of Toa-sua (Dai-sen-to), and fighting ensued. Later in the afternoon Ongo-ya-toi was occupied. The Chinese loss for the day was about four hundred killed ; the Japanese one captain wounded. One Krupp field-gun, one mountain gun, two bronze cannon, many rifles, and much ammunition were captured. The advance guard had been engaged most of the day. Near Moa-tau (Mato) two Japanese were killed, and in pursuing the enemy a force of about four thousand insurgents armed with repeating rifles was encountered to the south of the So-bung-go River. After a strong resistance from the Chinese forces, which were protected by earthworks, the Japanese were victorious, but suffered a loss of two killed and eleven wounded, while the Chinese loss was only thirty dead.

On the 19th, the right detachment surrounded 3,000 insurgents who had fortified the small village of Shau-lan (Shorio). The Chinese found escape impossible and a desperate conflict resulted, in which nearly 1,000 Chinese were killed, while the Japanese loss, killed and wounded, was thirty, including three officers.

The Chinese had laid mines along the regular routes, and caught two unsuspecting officers. Commodore Count Yoshii, adjutant to His Majesty, and Captain Ogawa, adjutant to the commander-in-chief, were following at a safe distance behind the troops, but had not noticed the detour that had been made to avoid the mines. Captain Ogawa was riding ahead when his horse struck a contact mine and a terrific explosion resulted. The officer was severely wounded and his horse killed instantly. Count Yoshii was wounded about the head, but not seriously. I was informed by this officer, that had the mine been properly constructed, they would have been certainly killed, but fortunately the explosives had been covered only with loose sand. At Shau-lan news reached the brigade of the occupation of Anping and Tainanfu, and both the Mixed Brigade and the Guards Division reached the southern capital without encountering further opposition.

Returning now to Tainanfu and Anping, we find great excitement prevailing during the early days of October. That the Japanese were soon to attack the south all were now aware. Great efforts were made to inspire the trembling braves with courage. Several Japanese heads had been brought into the city and exhibited, and later four cavalry horses, said to have been captured near Changwha (Shoka), together with a cavalry sabre and bugle ; and on a still later occasion the head of a Japanese petty officer, together with his uniform and sword, as well as thirty-four Japanese cavalry horses with saddles, were all placed before the astounded natives as evidence of the great victories the republican troops were winning in the central districts. This was all good enough while the Japanese were still in the north of the island, but when it became known that a big expedition had arrived at the Pescadores, even old Liu began to be uneasy, and, forgetting his warlike spirit, which he had so often boasted of, decided to propose surrender.

Liu's first efforts in this direction were made by a letter which the British consul took to the Pescadores and handed to the Japanese admiral.

The following terms of surrender were proposed by Liu :—

1.—The Japanese to pay up all arrears due to the soldiers.

2.—The Japanese to send him and his soldiers to Canton in their transports, and that the Shimonoseki Treaty be carried out as to all people having two years given them in which they should be at liberty to consider whether they would become Japanese subjects or not.

To these proposals the admiral replied that the fleet would be off Anping on the 12th at noon and would meet General Liu or his authorised delegates to discuss surrender of the island, and promising not to open fire without notice on the fort, unless the Chinese commenced the attack.

The flagship *Yoshino* appeared off the port at 7 a.m. on the 12th, but for some reason unknown did not come to anchor until 2.30 p.m., which gave Liu the opportunity of professing suspicions as to the *bonâ fide* intentions of the Japanese admiral. He therefore refused to go off and see him. On the day previous, Liu had requested Mr. Alliston, a visitor from Hongkong, and Mr. Harry Hastings, a resident of Anping, to take a letter for him to the Japanese troops at Kagi, containing a somewhat similar offer of surrender to that sent to the fleet, of which latter fact he also informed the general, begging that official to cease operations for the time. Messrs. Alliston and Hastings were escorted by twenty Black Flag soldiers. The latter, however, deserted when within about two miles of the Japanese lines. No difficulty was experienced in reaching the Japanese headquarters, but as the commander-in-chief was with the other division, no practical result could be arrived at, so the two foreigners returned empty-handed, though not without the full credit which such a plucky action undoubtedly deserved. Liu sent a deputation of two Chinamen to board the *Yoshino*. They called first on board H.M.S. *Pique* and were accompanied by H.B.M.'s consul to the flagship, where they presented a request that the admiral would give Liu a written guarantee of safety to and from the *Yoshino*. The admiral declined to parley further about the matter, as he considered that Liu had had assurances enough, and finally stated that the *Yoshino* would remain until 10 a.m. next day, when, if Liu did not appear in person or by deputy, the fleet would either open fire or heave anchor. Thereupon the deputation withdrew. At the stroke of 10, on the 13th, Liu having shown no inclination to keep his appointment, three of the ships got under way, leaving one behind. In the afternoon the Customs were asked to signal that the negotiators had left the shore. This signal was acknowledged by the Japanese ship, but again Liu failed to keep his word, for no deputation left the port.

That night Liu sent two deputies to the *Pique*, but every one had grown so disgusted at his vacillation that they refused to help any further in the matter, and the delegates returned to shore: On the 15th, the *Dante* with 1,800 passengers, and the *Thales* with about 1,400, left for Amoy, and from these passengers Liu levied $12,000. A compradore of a British firm had $8,000, which he was sending away, seized by Liu, who said the shipper had promised to contribute that amount to the war fund and had failed to do so. The Japanese despatch-boat *Saikio Maru* was fired on that day by the Anping forts, but received no injury. On the 17th, the report reached here that the Takow forts had sunk three Japanese ships. This was vouched for by Liu, who said he had it by special messenger—this was really two days after Takow had been occupied by the Japanese forces, naval and military. On the 18th, the British steamer *Thales* returned, and the first suspicions of a "bolt" on the part of Liu became assured by the news that he had arranged for a passage for his eight dogs by that steamer. On the morning of the 18th, General Liu successfully performed the "vanishing trick." The last known of Liu's movements was that on the night of the 18th, he went down to the Anping (large) fort on the pretext of inspecting it. He remained there that night, and next morning had disappeared, along with about 100 officers and his immediate body-guard. It was later discovered that he had escaped, disguised as a coolie, on board the S. S. *Thales*.

The news of Liu's departure spread like wild fire, and the soldiers began pouring into Anping settlement, where the only foreigners were Messrs. McCallum, Burton, and Alliston, the others being either in Takow, or on board the *Pique*, or in Amoy. In the city of Tainan-fu were Messrs. Ede, Fergusson, and Barclay, of the E. P. Mission. Messrs. McCallum, Burton, and Alliston persuaded the soldiers to lay down their arms, which were then stacked in the Customs opium-godown. This operation took nearly all day, between 6,000 and 8,000 rifles being eventually stowed away, together with several tons of small-arm ammunition. The men were placed in the compound, and on the night of the 20th, the forts and barracks were totally deserted, no soldiers in Anping or Tainan-fu being armed. Early on the morning of the 21st, Japanese marines and bluejackets from the Japanese men-of-war landed, and the occupation of Anping was thus completed. As soon as it was ascertained that Liu had escaped on the *Thales*, the Japanese warship *Yaeyama* started in pursuit. Catching up with the merchant ship some fifteen miles from Amoy, a party was sent on board to make a search. They discovered some seven suspects and demanded their surrender. The captain of the *Thales* quite rightly protested against the demand and the steamer, after a detention[1] of some ten hours,

---

1. The detention of the *Thales* was made an official matter, and H.B.M. minister demanded an explanation from the Japanese government regarding the conduct of a Japanese man-of-war in stopping a British vessel on the high seas and in boarding and searching her. The Japanese government promptly replied stating that they admitted "that the action of the man-of-war was contrary to the Law of Nations and that they greatly regretted the occurrence and were ready to make sufficient reparation for whatever damages the *Thales* had suffered through it." Vice-Admiral Arichi was removed from the command of the Formosan fleet soon after, it is believed, owing to this error for which he was alone responsible.

was allowed to proceed, two Japanese officers, however, accompanying her to watch the suspects. On her arrival at Amoy the English consul ordered the release of the suspects.

Lieutenant-General Nogi, whom we left at Pithau, advanced from that city on the 19th. On the 20th, at Ji-chang-hang (Nisoko), a village about seven miles south of Anping, the advance guard of cavalry were surrounded, but after some heavy fighting, in which the Chinese lost about 150 killed, the Japanese were victorious. At this village Messrs. Ferguson and Barclay, two well known missionaries connected with the English Presbyterian Mission, arrived. These gentlemen on behalf of the Chinese, had very philanthropically consented to undertake the perilous task of carrying a letter to the Japanese at Ji-chang-hang from the residents of Tainanfu, requesting the former to come at once to the city, and stating that they would meet with no opposition.[1] Upon the delivery of this letter, the Japanese advanced at once, arriving at the outskirts of Tainanfu at 7 a.m. and two hours later were in undisputed possession of every part of the city. (October 21st).

The northern expedition arrived in Tainanfu during the day, and the occupation of the island was completed.

Thus ended the first Formosan Republic![2]

The campaign now ended, the military coolies and the Imperial Guards, officers and men, were embarked on transports returning to Japan. The loss of life occasioned by General Liu's obstinacy had been large, not so much by battle, as from disease. Only about half of the Imperial Body Guards, who had been longest in the field, remained to return to their native land at the conclusion of hostilities! The others either died in Formosa or had been previously invalided to Japan.

The losses of the whole Japanese force, including military coolies and other regular attachés, during the Formosa campaign, from the date of landing in the north (May 26th) to the 15th of December, which includes the losses while subjugating some remaining bands of Chinese soldiers after the capture of Anping, were as follows :—[3]

Died in Formosa of disease	4,642
Sent to Japan for treatment	21,748
Remaining in hospitals in Formosa	5,246
Killed in battle (officers and soldiers)	164
Wounded (not fatally, officers and soldiers)	515

1. His Majesty, the Emperor of Japan conferred decorations on Messrs. Ferguson and Barclay as a token of appreciation of their valuable services.

2. The foreigners, who witnessed the Republic's dying struggles, were in Anping the British Consul R. W. Hurst, Mr. Allan W. Bain of Messrs. Bain & Co., Honorary Consul for the Netherlands, Mr. J. Poterson of Messrs. Julius Mannich & Co., Mr. A. Macgowan of Messrs. Tait & Co., Mr. B. N. Perkins of H.B.M.'s Consular service, and Messrs. Harry Hastings, Alliston, McCallum, and Burton, the two latter of the Republican Customs service, and several Parsee gentlemen. In Tainanfu the Reverends Ede, Ferguson, and Barclay. In Takow Dr. W. Wykeham Myers with his wife and daughters, who had bravely remained at their Formosan home throughout the campaign, Rev. Father Francisco Giner, and Captain Vosteen of the tug Sin Taiwan.

3. This number was divided as follows :—

	Killed in battle.	Wounded.
Imperial Body Guards	112	283
Second Division..	25	104
Fourth Mixed Brigade	27	128

Some idea of the hospital work may be obtained from the fact that from May 26th to November 15th, 38,798 applications were made at the various government hospitals for treatment. (In this number each applica- tion for treatment is counted. For instance one person may have applied a dozen different times and in that case 12 would be recorded). We thus find that Japanese troops were placed *hors de combat*, through disease or wounds, at the rate of some two hundred a day, and that the death rate averaged about 27 a day. The deaths not only included many officers but His Im- perial Highness Prince Kitashirakawa fell a victim to the terrible malarial fever of Formosa. One writer has called attention to the striking fact that Prince Kitashirakawa, landing with the Imperial Guards on the north- east of Formosa, commanded them throughout the whole of their advance southward, and that his corpse was put on board ship at Anping, the last objective point of the expedition. While the prince was on his way to Tainan, on the 18th October symptoms of malarial fever ap- peared, and his condition growing steadily worse he died at Tainan on the 28th. It appears that it is not in accordance with Japanese etiquette to announce the death of an Imperial Prince until the body has reached Tōkyō, so no ceremony or other display took place when the remains were sent off for shipment on board the *Saikio Maru* for transport to Japan. The body was enclosed in a very large Japanese coffin and carried to Anping by a troop of wrestlers who had, by special Imperial permission, accompanied the Guards Division. As soon as the body was safely deposited on board, the vessel, convoyed by H.J.M.S. *Yoshino*, left for Japan.[1]

The number of lives lost among the Chinese is difficult to ascertain. By taking the different engagements and counting the dead found on the field we obtain 6,760. This number, in my opinion, should be increased by a thousand ; for considerable numbers of wounded were carried away by the retreating Chinese, and many when wounded, crawled into the underbush, either to be later rescued by their friends or to die unknown. Others threw themselves into the streams, the bodies being carried out to sea ! I have witnessed several engagements in which the Chinese were fired at while in the thickets, or on the hills, where no opportunity was afforded for making a search to ascertain the number of killed. The figures given, therefore,

---

1. " The deceased Prince was only in his 49th year, having been born on the 1st of April, 1847. At the age of 23 he proceeded to Europe, and devoted seven years to study, most of which time he spent in Germany, acquiring not only a sound knowledge of military strategy and tactics, but also a good acquaintance with the German language. Of medium stature, he possessed a handsome and highly intelligent face, and was noted for the genial courtesy of his address. All scientific subjects and every- thing connected with intellectual development interested him keenly, and as the president of a number of various learned associations, he contributed materially to the cause of progress. He presided over the Second and Third Industrial Exhibitions, as well as over the Tokyo Geographical Society, the Japan Agricultural Society, and the Fine Arts Society, and in every case his zeal on behalf of those bodies helped sensibly to secure their success. Despite his scientific tastes, however, the Prince chose a military career, associating himself closely with the army and paying constant attention to his duties as a soldier. Passing through the various grades, he attained the rank of Lieut.-General and the command of the Fourth Division, from which he was transferred last year to the command of the Imperial Guards after the promotion of their previous commander, Field-Marshal H.I.H. Prince Komatsu, to be Director of the General Staff. He went to Formosa with the Guards, and took an active part in the whole campaign, sharing with his men hardships that probably undermined his constitution and invited the malady to which he fell a victim."—Extract from the *Japan Mail*.

include only those who have been found dead on the field after engagements. Adding this thousand we may estimate that the Chinese deaths were at the rate of about forty-five per day. Still, as in the case of the Japanese, it is not unlikely that disease carried off even a larger number. The mainland Chinese found soldier life in Formosa almost as unhealthy as did the Japanese.

Liu Yung-fu, after his escape from Formosa, went at once to Canton, where he was received with open arms. Tang Ching-sung, the northern president, and General Tcheng-ki-tong, who opposed the Japanese in the north, were likewise welcomed at Shanghai, and all were in high official favor. No further evidence is required to prove that the opposition in Formosa, the loss of over 12,000 men Japanese and Chinese, and many millions of dollars, is directly attributable to the duplicity of the Chinese government. In this trickery, for which modern history shows no parallel, China not only threw herself open to additional punishment from Japan, but she became liable for the total expense that the Japanese incurred in destroying the republic. Had any other nation attempted like treachery it would have been the signal for the immediate recommencement of hostilities. The Japanese, however, with a thorough understanding of China's means and methods, were perhaps not surprised at the turn matters had taken, and now that they had at last got rid of the Chinese regulars they were prepared to ignore both Liu and his official supporters. In this they showed good sense! No advantage would have been gained by taking revenge out of China, and the great task before them in Formosa required all their attention.

Although the Japanese were now in possession, the island contained thousands of turbulent fellows, who, either ignorant of the government's peaceful intentions, or confident that by opposing the Japanese they could eventually drive them away, or perhaps for both reasons, were encouraged to give great trouble, at frequent intervals. It would not be interesting to the general reader to relate in detail these numerous engagements, which differed from each other only in extent. Later, rebellion against the government practically ceased, but it was replaced by brigandage so extensive that travel in some districts, at certain times, became so dangerous that Japanese officials, off the more frequented routes, did not travel unless provided with a guard, and wealthy Chinese scarcely dared to leave the treaty ports.

The first difficulty occurred in November and December, 1895, and appears to have been with the Hakkas in the far south of the island. These people occupied, with the Pepohoans, the plainlands which extend from the base of the westernmost range of mountains up to the large river that enters the sea at Tangkang, about seventeen miles south of Takow. With the Pepohoans the Hakkas had always kept up a constant feud and they rarely met without fighting! The former people were on friendly terms with the Japanese, so that only the Hakkas had to be settled with. By damming up the Tangkang river the Hakkas had flooded a considerable portion of the plain. Here and there they had put rude fortifications, elevated above the surrounding water, with ready means to retreat to the rear, and eventually to the mountains, should the situation, at any time, call for abandonment. They were well armed, thanks to Liu, with Winchester rifles and had plenty of ammunition.

Later, these rebels were enabled to obtain large reinforcements, and it required a considerable force under Major-General Yamaguchi, with two months' hard work, before the Hakkas were subdued and South Formosa again quiet. Japanese loss in this expedition amounted to forty-eight (killed and wounded). Rebel loss about five hundred.

Scarcely had word reached the Capital of the defeat of the insurgents in the south, before rebels made their appearance in the north! On January 1st, 1896, rebels simultaneously attacked Gilan, Sui-hong (Zuiho) and several villages near Taipeh, the capital, which latter was also attacked. The Japanese were in each place limited to a mere handful of men, and so unexpected were the assaults that, in nearly every instance, with the exception of Gilan and Taipeh, they were successful. Upon news reaching Japan of this serious outbreak, reinforcements were at once despatched, and after a month's skirmishing, the rebels were driven into the hills and the north was again quiet. The rebellion had, however, cost the Japanese a loss of 128 killed and 58 wounded, this number unfortunately including many civilians, some of whom were teachers conducting a free school at Pachina. In some instances the Japanese were tortured to death, burned at the stake, and in almost every case where the Japanese had been captured such of the bodies as were recovered were found to be frightfully mutilated. The rebel loss, until their total suppression, was over 600.

During the summer months of 1896, the most serious rebellion of all broke out. Chip Chip Hokto, Yunlin, and other important inland villages were captured by the rebels and the Japanese driven from these districts. The latter then placed a considerable force in the field, and soon recovered their positions, destroying by fire thirty of the villages which had harbored insurgents either intentionally or otherwise. The Japanese were accused of much cruelty during the course of this trouble, but as the information came from Chinese sources it was difficult to ascertain the complete truth. However, that many innocent Chinese suffered there can be scarcely a doubt. This disturbance was a severe blow to the Japanese and a most deplorable affair for the Chinese, who suffered great hardships before its conclusion. In fact, so pitiful was the condition of the natives that several influential foreigners at Anping very philanthropically raised a relief fund to be distributed among the more needy, while their Japanese Majesties the Emperor and Empress granted $3,000, and the government $50,000, for the afflicted. From the commencement of the rebellion, until the country was pacified, the total Japanese loss was 247, of which number eighty were killed. The Chinese loss is unknown.

The above mentioned rebellion appears to have been the last important affair in which the natives were banded against the government for professedly political reasons. From that time on, the natives seem to have appreciated the futility of opposing the Japanese, and the more turbulent spirits among them, who were inclined to lead a life of excitement, devoted themselves to brigandage, intent upon bettering their financial condition, rather than " warring for home and country." Japanese no longer became the victims, unless they happened to be in the way of a successful raid, but natives, especially wealthy Chinese, often did! The Formosan banditti carry on their trade much on the same lines as members of their fraternity in the French possessions in South China. An armed party, generally of from fifty to a hundred, rush down from the mountains during the dead of night, seize such wealthy Chinese as are likely to pay a good ransom, and, in some cases, loot the village, afterwards returning to their mountain retreats, which are not uncommonly fortified. The bands are quite ready to fight when opposed by Japanese, but so sudden and unexpected are their raids that they rarely suffer much loss. During the month of January, 1897, a party of forty or fifty bandits entered the heart of Twatutia and carried away a twenty years old son of a wealthy Chinese, this seizure being made not more than three blocks from the nearest foreign residence and fifteen minutes walk from the barracks in the Capital. But, in the following May, the most daring assault of all was made. On this occasion, about seven hundred brigands, assisted by certain local Chinese, attacked Twatutia. Their arrival had been expected and small detachments of troops had been stationed on the various roads leading to the city. A large portion of the band had, however, succeeded in secretly entering the city on the previous night, and, it is said, availed themselves of a performance at a Chinese theatre, to assemble and complete their plans of attack. About 3 a.m. an outside party made its appearance very quietly to the east of the city, and suddenly attacked a small Japanese tax office. This alarmed the soldiers connected with the engineering corps occupying a building near by, who exchanged volley after volley with the attacking party for some time. The night was very dark, and it was impossible to distinguish their opponents, the flash of the rifles affording the only mark. Meanwhile, another party of Chinese had quietly found their way across the railway bridge into Twatutia, and joined the main body, who had, until then, remained in their hiding place at Twatutia. Now united, they sprang upon the frightened Chinese residents, and about one hour before daylight commenced a furious attack. Some Japanese buildings were in the vicinity and might have been attacked without much difficulty, but the banditti avoided them, confining themselves exclusively to breaking into houses occupied by rich Chinese merchants, one after another, along the principal street. Some fifteen or twenty houses were thus entered, chiefly by smashing in the heavy doors, and many valuables were secured. Rich silks, opium, money, etc., fell into the robbers' hands to the estimated value of fifty thousand dollars! The Japanese force now began to close in about them, and the banditti, after setting fire to a few of the Chinese houses, retreated as day was dawning, having suffered a loss of 124 killed, including Sen-sin, their leader, and 19 taken prisoners. The Japanese loss was three killed and seven wounded. About one hundred and fifty Mauser rifles were captured, and much of the stolen property recovered. This attack was a revelation to the Japanese,

Field Work of Japanese Infantry against Rebels.
Military Barracks at Taihoku.
A Band of Surrendered Rebels.

Military searching Houses in Disturbed District.
Military Storehouses at Ke-lung.
The Hut of a Famous Rebel Chief in the North Formosa Hills.

who were too confident of their strength. Immediately after this assault the police and gendarme forces were considerably increased.

The first and greatest task before the Japanese is the establishment of peace. Not peace for mainland Japanese and foreigners alone (the latter form a very insignificant part of the population), but peace for that great mass of natives who inhabit the island and who are now, with a few exceptions, naturalized Japanese subjects and have a right, as such, to demand the same protection and government assistance as is given to native born Japanese.

As for the savages they will no doubt prove less of a burden if left undisturbed in their mountain fastnesses. The savage problem is a minor one, and with the exception of the urgent need of some system to afford protection to camphor workers on the savage border, can well be left for future solution.

It is nonsense to say, as has been asserted, that the brigands have been goaded to their lawless life in order to keep themselves from starving, having been driven from their homes by the Japanese on former occasions. There never has, in the history of the island, been such a great demand for Chinese labor of all kinds, nor have there ever been in Formosa or in the whole of China such high wages ruling as at present. Chinese produce brings fully double its former price, and laborers demand and obtain more than double the wages paid under the Chinese regime.

After the easy victory gained by the Japanese forces over thousands of Chinese regulars during the late war, it may seem incomprehensible that in Formosa they have been unable to put down banditti. A word of explanation is necessary. The difficulty is not in fighting the rogues. That in itself would be an extremely easy task. It is in finding them. A village may be attacked at night ; by daylight the robbers have fled into the hills. A force starts in pursuit. But the robber does not wait for them to come and take him. He and his comrades quite naturally take to another hill, and when the Japanese force, advancing with great labor, over unknown paths, through jungle and stream, has reached the reported position, the place is empty, or the troops may meet a few humble peasants carrying implements of peace, working about the fields. There is no external evidence that the latter were the banditti of the night before, and yet they may very easily have been so. From a whooping, murdering rebel to a smiling peaceful agriculturist is for the Chinese an easy transition, and after the transformation the Japanese are absolutely helpless! There is nothing to be done. It may strike the reader that, by availing themselves of the assistance of Chinese, the Japanese would be able to obtain information as to the whereabouts of bad men. This will no doubt be the ultimate solution of the difficulty. But, so far, the Japanese have found it almost impossible to obtain Chinese informants in whose statements they can place trust. In fact, it is no exaggeration to say that innocent Chinese have lost their lives, that innocent people have been imprisoned, that property has been destroyed solely through the machinations of treacherous Chinese, who would not hesitate to cause the death of one of their own countrymen if a few paltry dollars were to be gained. It was unfortunately quite a common affair, soon after the arrival of the Japanese, for certain Chinese to demand black-mail of their wealthy countrymen and to report them as rebels if they did not produce. The Japanese have now learned that it is not safe to place confidence in Chinese, and while interpreters are still employed, but little dependence is placed in their reports. There are honest Chinese, there are liberal minded, kindly disposed Chinese who would have the interests of their people at heart. It can scarcely be said that the streets are crowded with them, still they exist, and the hope of the Japanese is that they may in time obtain the services of men of this class, who will not only assist in ridding the island of undesirable characters, but will give much aid in other matters of government. In fact it would seem that the happy administration of the island will be reached when Japanese and bright Chinese, educated in the methods of modern government, can work hand in hand.

NOTE.—Table of wrecks occurring on the coasts of Formosa and adjacent islands during the period 1895 to 1899.

1895 November 16th. The Japanese three-masted ship *Inaho Maru* of 400 tons burden, went to pieces during a strong wind this day, in the inner harbor of Kelung, having been stranded there by the unskillful navigation of her master, a few days before.

———December 21st. The Imperial Japanese Cruiser *Kohei*, during a gale, ran on an unknown rock near Hattan Island, S. E. of the Rover Group, and two hours later sank. Of the 160 souls on board, all reached shore by the aid of boats or rafts, with the exception of 37 who disappeared and were without doubt drowned. The cruiser was built at Fuchau by the Chinese Government, and was known as the torpedo catcher *Kwang-ping*. She was of 1,230 tons and was 236 ft. in length. The vessel was engaged in the battle of the Yalu and was surrendered to the Japanese at Weihaiwei.

———December 28th. The Japanese steamer *Hoshu Maru* of 714 tons was wrecked on a reef near one of the islands of the Loochoo group, N. E. by E. of Formosa. No lives were lost, but the vessel was a total loss.

1897—December 24th. The Japanese steamship *Nara Maru* of 2,519 tons, struck on a hidden rock near Okosho Island of the Pescadore group, and sunk with all on board almost immediately. The passengers and crew numbered 80 persons in all, and of this number only 7 succeeded in reaching shore.

1898—August 7th. At the height of a terrific typhoon, which wrought great havoc throughout the island, the Osaka Shosen Kwaisha's steamship *Enoshima Maru* of 1494 tons, lost both anchors and then tried to escape destruction by running for the open sea. The wind was too strong, however, and she was driven well upon the rocks a few feet from shore on the east side of the harbor. The vessel was totally destroyed but no lives were lost.

———August 31st. The American bark *Comet* of 673 tons burden, was wrecked near Aulang (Koro) N. W. coast of Formosa. The vessel was driven ashore during a typhoon while on a voyage from Amoy to Newchwang. After running ashore the deck-house was washed away, carrying the Chinese crew with it, but they were fortunately able to make effective use of it as a raft, and with the exception of one Chinese who was washed off and drowned, they were all picked up by the Douglas steamship *Hailoong* and carried to Amoy. The master, John C. Brodhurst and wife, the mate and Chinese steward, were lashed to the rigging of the *Comet*, where they remained for ten hours, suffering great hardship. They were at last sighted from shore, and the weather having moderated, a Chinese boat put out and rescued them. The vessel was a total loss.

———November 9th.—The Danish steamer *Activ* of 750 tons, while endeavoring to make Tamsui harbor, having arrived with a cargo of beans and general cargo from North China ports, ran ashore on the rocks to the south-west of the entrance. The vessel soon filled with water, causing the beans to swell, the pressure from this source eventually bursting the iron deck. The vessel was then deserted by the officers and crew who reached shore safely. The steamer was later sold at auction, but scarcely had the sale concluded before a strong wind arose, and that night the vessel slipped off into deep water and disappeared, to the great consternation of her Chinese purchasers.

The wrecks of steamships and foreign sailing vessels occurring on these coasts from the year 1850 to 1899, which we have recorded in Chapters XIV, XV, XVII, and XXII, total over a hundred vessels with a loss of life exceeding 2,000. Among the wrecks recorded, 46 were English, 17 German, and 15 American vessels.

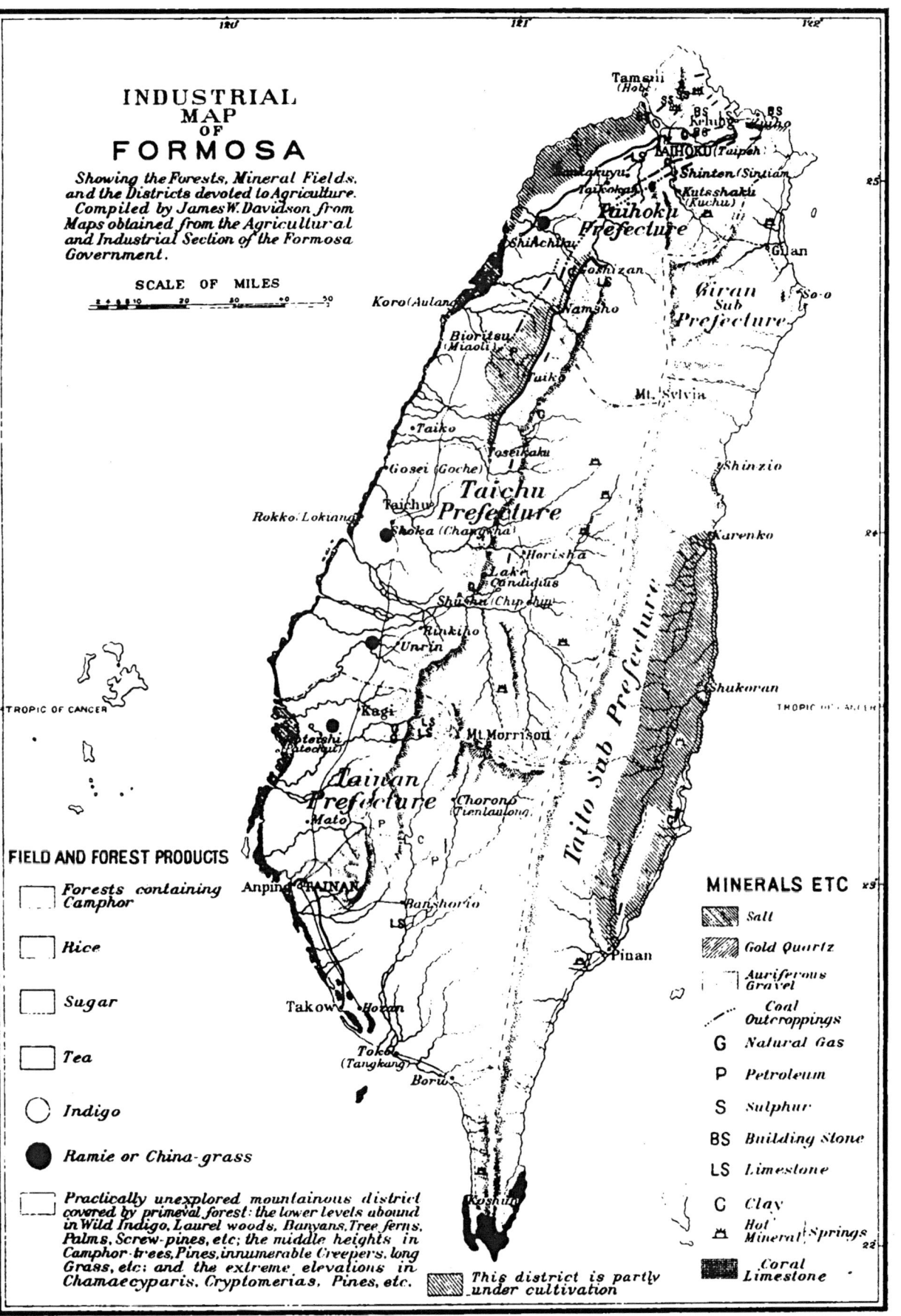

INDUSTRIAL MAP OF FORMOSA

Showing the Forests, Mineral Fields,
and the Districts devoted to Agriculture.
Compiled by James W. Davidson from
Maps obtained from the Agricultural
and Industrial Section of the Formosa
Government.

SCALE OF MILES

FIELD AND FOREST PRODUCTS

Forests containing Camphor

Rice

Sugar

Tea

Indigo

Ramie or China-grass

Practically unexplored mountainous district
covered by primeval forest: the lower levels abound
in Wild Indigo, Laurel woods, Banyans, Tree ferns,
Palms, Screw-pines, etc; the middle heights in
Camphor-trees, Pines, innumerable Creepers, long
Grass, etc; and the extreme elevations in
Chamaecyparis, Cryptomerias, Pines, etc.

This district is partly under cultivation

MINERALS ETC

Salt

Gold Quartz

Auriferous Gravel

Coal Outcroppings

G   Natural Gas

P   Petroleum

S   Sulphur

BS   Building Stone

LS   Limestone

C   Clay

Hot Mineral Springs

Coral Limestone

CHAPTER XXIII.

THE FORMOSAN TEA INDUSTRY.

Changes in world's Tea producing districts—World's producing districts compared—Statistics :—World's production—Tea, a possible new industry in various lands—History of Formosan Tea trade—Swinhoe the discoverer of Formosa Tea—His first Tea report—Early export to China—John Dodd ships Formosas—First export to foreign lands—Plants from China—Direct shipment to New York—Export 1867 to 1870—Amoy foreign merchants participate—Exciting season of 1872—Season 1873—Formosas at $10—Growth of trade 1874 to 1879—Disastrous season of 1880—Growers stimulated—Freight competition—Effect of French war on industry—Lead famine and novel methods of relief—Futile attempt to introduce Indian tea manufacturing system—The Japanese occupation—Government impost on Tea—Chinese tea packers—Adulteration—Attempted preventative measures —Twatutia tea merchants with official assistance prevent adulteration—Improper care of tea plant—Government regulations—History of cultivation—First cultivation—Plants from China—Formosan savages replaced by agriculturalists—Tea cultivation under difficulties—Payment for protection—Armed farmers—Immigration of skilled teamen—Rapid enlargement of area under cultivation—Tea in South Formosa—Twatutia centre of Tea district—Increase in production—Location of best tea districts—Tea in Kapsulan plain—Quality of different district Teas—Tea in the South—Local trade in sun-dried Tea—Preparation of virgin soil—Propagation of Tea plant—Transplantation—Drainage—Weeding—Plant at maturity—Absence of pruning and irrigation—Picking from bush—Picturesque scene—Indoor tea picking (cleaning)—Character of Formosa Oolong—Simple method of manufacture—Drying of green leaf—Manipulation of leaf—Up-country firing--Financial arrangements—Tea brokers—Negotiations with foreign buyers—Planters' knowledge of foreign markets—Shipments to Amoy—Tea picking girls in Twatutia—The social season—Earnings of tea pickers—Immorality—Firing establishments—Preparation of fuel—Method of firing—Packing—Primitive sheet lead factory—Tea boxes and their manufacture--A "lightning Artist"—Pouchong Tea industry—History of Pouchongs—Character of Pouchongs—Comparative export—Blossoms used for scenting—Process of manufacture—Packing—Transportation—Value Oolong export England and America—Foreign firms engaged—Shipments via Kelung—Fortune of Chinese Tea-planters—Curious disappearance of treasure—Foreigners as future planters—Sanitary conditions of tea districts—

*Cost of starting plantation—Working capital required—Receipts—Profits—
Chinese competition—Chinese plantations—Chinese advantage in labor—Chinese
food requirements—Difficulties for foreigners as planters—North Formosa
prosperity dependent on Tea—Tea as producer of wealth compared with other
products—Government support and assistance required - Statistics, Oolong Export
America and Europe, 1866-1898—Statistics, Pouchong Export, 1881-1898.*

In the face of the important proportions assumed by the Formosan Tea trade of to-day, it is interesting to read of the "possibilities" of that industry as it appeared to keen observers thirty-five years ago. "The tea grown on the Tamsui Hills is not of a superfine quality," states a writer in 1861, "but it is believed that it would readily find a market in Australia, the Cape, and Singapore. It rules at a price of ten dollars a picul (133 lbs.) and is much imported by Chinese dealers at Amoy and Foochow to mix with the better class of teas, and the mixed commodity is then sold to foreign merchants as Congous, Souchongs, etc."[1]

A third of a century, however, has wrought great changes in the Tea supply districts of the world. Amoy, once a great Tea mart of China, finds its own Tea trade rapidly disappearing, and is now practically dependent for its prosperity on the Formosan Tea districts, for owing to the present lack of suitable harbors in the island, the production goes almost wholly to Amoy for transhipment, as large steamers can safely load there throughout the year. Hankow, Foochow, and other Tea centres are also declining. In fact, regardless of the world's enormous consumption of Tea, largely as it is increasing, China has fallen, in a mere score of years, from the high position of virtually supplying all Europe and America with Tea, and finds her once vast export dwindling away. Japanese Teas have found much favor in America ; Indian and Ceylon Teas have met with a brilliant success in the United Kingdom and have gained an entrance into America and continental Europe—all at the expense of China.

The export of Formosa Teas, while yet comparatively small, has in this same twenty years increased from 8,000,000 pounds valued at $1,700,000 (Local currency) to 20,000,000 pounds valued at $7,000,000 ($3,500,000 U.S. Gold) and has to-day the highest *pro rata* value of any Tea produced in the world,[2] Still this rapid increase in production during the past should

1. "Treaty Ports of China and Japan," Published 1867. Hongkong.

2.   COMPARATIVE EXPORT FOR 35 YEARS.

	Formosa Teas (To America.)	Japan Teas (To America.)	Indian and Ceylon Teas (To United Kingdom.)	Total Export of China (Leaf) Tea.	Total.
1871	1,502,100 lbs.	17,258,000 lbs	15,351,600 lbs.	212,780,400 lbs.	246,882,100 lbs.
1876	6,487,800 „	17,608,000 „	29,001,700 „	214,524,800 „	267,122,300 „
1881	11,978,600 „	22,460,400 „	49,873,00 ι „	251,906,533 „	336,308,533 „
1886	13,798,000 „	26,502,000 „	87,167,000 „	247,440,400 „	374,907,400 „
1891	15,029,500 „	32,770,500 „	174,785,000 „	189,489,733 „	412,074,733 „
1896	19,327,500 „	52,748,500 „	215,405,000 „	151,413,467 „	428,882,467 „

This does not include comparatively small shipments of Formosa, Japan, and Java Tea to London.
The figures in the above table show that, during the period reviewed, the Formosan production increased thirteen fold, the Japanese three fold, the Indian and Ceylon fourteenfold, while the China production fell away about half. Meanwhile the world's consumption of (leaf) Tea doubled. The export of China brick Tea to Russia amounted to 76,949,200 lbs. during 1896.

not be taken as an indication of what the future has in store. The great mass of tea drinkers are desirous of a tea at lower prices than those demanded for the Formosan product. So that the market is at present limited, and the competition with other tea producing districts is becoming more keen year by year.

The tea plant is easily grown, given certain conditions of soil and climate, and several countries have clearly demonstrated that they can produce a marketable article, at an outlay which is not prohibitive. The Dutch East Indies are finding the cultivation of tea profitable, and are producing increasing quantities yearly ; in South America and South Africa, experimental gardens have resulted most satisfactorily ; Russia is taking a most active interest in the cultivation and has established government plantations in the Caucasus, and even in the United States experiments in tea growing are being made in several of the southern States. The great enterprise shown by Indian and Ceylon planters in introducing their product to new markets, combined with the possibilities of new producing districts, points to the likelihood of even more intense competition in the future, and although the probability is that China will be the heaviest loser, unless the Chinese government awakens to the perilous condition of their tea trade, still Japan and Formosa will also suffer, and to minimize this as much as possible the Japanese government should assist the industry in every way. In Formosa this could best be effected by the abolition of all imposts on Tea, improvements in means of communication, cheap railway freight for Tea, and the construction of a suitable harbor at Hobe (Tamsui.)

Robert Swinhoe may be called the discoverer of the Formosan Tea industry, and John Dodd the promoter. In the year 1861, a few years before the arrival of the latter personage, Consul Swinhoe writes in a report to the British government that Formosa Tea is shipped in considerable quantities to Chinese merchants on the mainland, that he has sent samples of the leaf to several Tea inspectors, and that they have reported that the "taste of the Tea is very fair, but the objection to it is owing to the coarse mode in which the leaves are prepared and packed." He then adds :—" As the hills, however, are no great distance from the harbor, this could be obviated by energetic speculators who might themselves visit the spot on which the article is grown and make their own arrangements."[1]

John Dodd, who had established himself in the island the year beforef made, in 1865, inquiries among the Tamsui farmers as to the possibilities o, the trade. The next year some purchases were made, some Tea plant slips were brought from Ankoi in the Amoy district, and loans were made to the farmers to induce them to increase the production. Kosing, a Chinese who had arrived from Amoy in the interests of Tait & Co., shipped a few packages in 1867, and John Dodd made a shipment to Macao, which brought good prices. Satisfied with the prospect he commenced Tea firing in

1. There is, however, evidence to show that this trade is of much earlier origin. Klaproth in his famous work on Asia refers to Formosan tea and states : " The Tea is green, not black. It is exported in great quantities to China, where it is used as a medicine. Generally the Chinese drink very little green tea."—Page 327, Klaproth, " *Memoires Relatifs à l'Asie* "—Paris, 1824.

Banka. Previous to 1867, the unfired leaf had been sent to Amoy in baskets to be fired there, but from 1868 onwards the total export was prepared for shipment direct to foreign lands, by skilled Chinese workmen brought from Amoy and Foochow.

Formosa Teas had now been examined in America, and in 1869 a trial shipment of 2131 piculs was made direct to New York in two sailing vessels. This is notable as the first, and up to the present day the last, direct shipment from Formosa to America. From an export of 2030 piculs in 1867 the trade increased to 10,540 in 1870, and prices rose from an average of $15 a picul to $30. Robert H. Bruce came to Tamsui this year and established the firm of Tait & Co. as exporters of Formosan Tea. The Amoy and Foochow merchants did not at first look upon Tamsui as a possible rival, but they were eventually forced to recognise the rapidly increasing trade, and the autumn of 1872 found, in North Formosa, the firms of Dodd & Co., Tait & Co., Elles & Co., Brown & Co., and Boyd & Co., established in the order given.

With the yet small production and the number of competing houses the season of 1872 was an exciting one. In previous years transactions had all turned out profitable, and so great was the eagerness of each firm to obtain as much of the production as possible, that insufficient attention was paid to quality. Choice Formosas realized in July and August $45-55, wonderful prices at that time! A few early shipments to America paid expenses, but on the news of heavy shipments of Oolong having been made from Amoy and Foochow, Tamsui Teas were refused with disastrous results, the losses being estimated as high as $375,000. This serious blow, occurring while the industry was in an embryo state, was very discouraging, and confidence in Tamsui as the coming tea district was rudely shaken. Prospects were now so gloomy that the firms showed no anxiety to enter the market during the spring of 1873. Meanwhile the Chinese growers were accumulating stock for which there was no demand. With total loss a not unlikely probability, prices rapidly declined. Towards the end of July a few purchases were made, but merchants in general were inclined to hold aloof. In August, however, prices had declined to a basis which seemed a guarantee against loss, and the foreign merchants commenced to buy, but with great caution. It was now that prices reached their lowest point, many clean wholesome teas bringing but $10.00 per picul (133 lbs) though a large portion of the stock was settled at from $11 to $15 a picul. But even at these phenominally low prices the demand was very limited, and by the end of the month choice Formosa Oolong practically went begging, none of the foreign firms caring for it at any price. Chinese speculators now stepped in and shipped the remaining stock to Foochow per junk, where it was worked up into scented Tea. In September news was received of the sale in America of the early shipments at a splendid profit. Prices now recovered fully 40%, and the autumn crop was eagerly taken up, thus partly recouping the Chinese growers, many of whom, during the summer months, had allowed their plantations to run wild, the prices ruling not covering the expense of packing.

While the Formosan Tea industry suffered in after years the vicissitudes common to so speculative a trade, still an extreme condition of affairs, such as existed in 1872 and 1873, was not repeated. The production increased rapidly, and while the prices demanded were generally higher each succeeding year, the operations were, on the whole, profitable to those engaged in the industry. The transactions were not marked with much interest until the year 1880, when the eagerness to enter the Formosan Tea trade somewhat resembled that exhibited in 1872, and justifies a brief description here.

This season opened with keen competition for the first Teas, and, though prices were at first fairly moderate, they soon rose to such a figure as to render the chances of profit to the buyer very doubtful. Nevertheless, Chinese continued buying during the spring and summer months, and, by the end of September, there was a stock in Amoy of 50,000 half chests, mostly held by the packers. In October the whole of the stock was suddenly bought up by the foreign firms. This led to fresh demands in the Formosa market, and the Chinese, anticipating a rise in prices, rushed into the trade most recklessly. Amoy native capitalists were prepared to furnish funds at from 15 to 18 per cent. interest, the only condition being that the Tea obtained should be consigned to them. The borrowers, as a rule men without capital, appreciating the fact that, so far as they were themselves concerned, there was nothing to lose, and perhaps something to gain, and further desirous to give the speculators no excuse for calling in the funds advanced, entered the market with absolute indifference to the prices demanded so long as they obtained the tea. Tea boys and shroffs availed themselves of the opportunity and started packing houses ; and even Tea firing men, who had been formerly content with their income of $6.00 a month, blossomed out into either brokers or packers ! In fact the Chinese, high and low, went quite mad over the prospect, and as a foreign merchant at the time declared : "the Tea business had a great fascination for cooks, whose souls you would think could never rise above an omelet." The growers, however, were alive to their own interests and raised their demands in accordance with the degree of anxiety shown to buy, until eventually so absurdly high were the prices, not only demanded but obtained, that there was but little prospect of a profit to the buyer. The crash came at last. The New York market showed no disposition to advance, and the Tea so eagerly purchased had now to be sold at a loss of from 20 to 30 per cent. Thirteen large Chinese packing houses closed their doors at once, and the multitude of petty merchants and brokers returned to more humble occupations. The Amoy capitalists were heavy losers, and the general bearing of the numerous victims during the winter months was decidedly expressive of the intention to steer clear of the Formosan tea business in the future !

If the merchants and brokers, however, lost money, the growers made it. Tea, which had cost them $12 to $16 per picul to produce, including the inland tax of $1.70 per picul, was sold at from $30 to $50 a picul. It was now their turn to be affected by the craze. With such a splendid result before them, they cleared off every hilly patch of land suitable for the cultivation of tea, even removing growing crops of rice, indigo, sugar, and hemp, and pushed on further toward the savage territory, thus laying the foundation for an increase in production as well as income. The losses on the season were slightly minimised by the low freight rates existing. The China Merchants S.S. Co. had extended their steamship service to Tamsui in competition with the Douglas line, and as a result brought down the freight charges between Tamsui and Amoy from 18 cents to 5 cents per half chest. At the close of the season the " China Merchants" steamer was withdrawn, and freight rates of 15 cents per half chest were established.

The next event of importance to the Formosa Tea industry was the attack on the north of the island made by the French forces in 1884 and 1885. On October 2nd of the former year, the port was declared blockaded, and from the 23rd of October all shipments were stopped. Although the bulk of the choice Teas had been shipped prior to this date, there were still some 25,000 half chests left in stock in Twatutia, and much unpacked Tea was in the hands of the growers. On April 16th, the blockade was raised, and Tea, both old and new, came pouring in from the country. But in the then general state of unrest the spring crop was very hastily and carelessly picked, mostly by unskilled labor, and the result was very inferior leaf. And then, although shipping was again permitted, lead was a contraband of war, and this metal was required to line the Tea boxes, without which the leaf could not be shipped to foreign markets. From thirty to forty thousand half chests of Tea were held in Twatutia for lack of lead. The price for the small stock of the metal on hand jumped from 6 to 20 yen per picul, and every pound which had been used for other and less urgent purposes was requisitioned for Tea. Chinese packers bought up leaden candlesticks and joss ornaments, and even the fishermen parted with the leaden weights attached to their nets. Chinese imported lead in treasure boxes declared as treasure, on which they had paid the heavy freight rates and insurance demanded for such a commodity. This was discovered by the Tamsui customs and stopped. Attempts were then made to get it through as tin, the lead being packed in boxes containing a few decoy plates of the former metal. This was likewise discovered. What other artifices were adopted by the wily Chinese and how successful they were is not known. On the 15th June (1885) news having been received of the restoration of peace between France and China, all restrictions imposed on the landing of munitions of war were removed, heavy importations of lead soon eased the situation, and the tea industry returned to its normal state. Towards the end of May the quality of leaf showed great improvement, and the season closed with a profit to the merchants in general. The native packers are said to have been specially fortunate, netting handsome profits on teas which they had shipped to Amoy for sale on that market.

Next of interest, in the history of the Formosa Tea trade, was the futile attempt to introduce the tea growing, firing, and packing system prevailing in

India. A Tea expert from Ceylon visited the island in 1890, the object and result of his visit being thus described in a Customs report.[1] " The proposal made was that the Government should grant a large tract of Crown land (say 1,000 acres) for the purpose, that the management should be under the joint control of the expert and an official deputy ; and that both Government and the promoters should share in the profit, if any. This plan had first been proposed for the black tea districts on the mainland ; having been negatived there, it was thought that a new province, with large tracts of unopened land, offered a more promising field. It was found, however, that, whatever had been the fortune of packers and shippers, the growers in this district were well satisfied with the prices received and the quantities disposed of by them ; and the boldness of the promoters of the plan, in trying to retrieve the fallen fortunes of China by coming to a district from which greater supplies were sent year by year at prices amply remunerating the producers, brought on the project a fate worse than its desert. Another reason given for the rejection of the proposals was the fear lest Formosa tea, being converted into Congou by the Indian method of preparation, and being thus brought to a level in competition with the mass of tea from the mainland of China, from India, and from Ceylon, would thereby lose the distinguished position it occupied as Oolong, and cease to command the high prices now obtained for it on the American market."

The acquisition of the island by the Japanese was the next event of importance. Although it was feared that the season of the Japanese arrival (1895) would be a very poor one, owing to military operations in the north, still it did not turn out so ; for the season's export slightly exceeded that of the previous year. As soon as the new administration was established in Formosa the Japanese announced that the people would be relieved from all taxation for one year. In 1897 taxes were imposed, including a tax on Tea. At present the impost is 2.40 yen ($1.20 U.S. Gold) per picul (133 pounds), which, with the addition of the Customs export tax of 1.10 yen, gives a total impost of 3.50 yen ($1.75 U.S. Gold) per picul. Although this is larger than the Japanese mainland tax, it is small compared with either the old tax in the island, which amounted to 6.35 yen ($3.17 U.S. Gold) or the present tax in the Amoy districts of China which is 6.85 yen ($3.42 U.S. Gold).

In the early days of the Formosa trade, the foreigners controlled almost exclusively the packing and firing, but afterwards Chinese gradually entered the field, and have absorbed the larger share of the business, although the foreign establishments still handle most of the choicer grades. The entry of the Chinese as packers was rather a calamity than otherwise, for in their hands, all sorts of malpractices arose. Their Tea was frequently adulterated, was badly picked, badly packed, and contained large quantities of dust, broken leaf and " lie Tea." These malpractices were so glaring that, at one time, it was greatly feared the favorable reputation which Formosa Oolong possessed would be lost. The Amoy Chamber of Commerce took

1 Tamsui Decennial Report, 1882 to 1892. Imperial Chinese Maritime Customs.

the matter up and issued regulations which, it was hoped, would lessen the evil, and, in later years, the foreign merchants in Formosa combined for the same purpose. The beneficial results, however, in both cases were very slight. Soon after the arrival of the Japanese, the local foreigners interested approached the authorities on the subject. The latter took the matter up at once, and regulations nearly identical with those proposed by the foreigners were put in force. It had been the custom for the more unscrupulous of the Chinese dealers to import inferior China leaf into the island, where it was mixed with genuine Formosa Tea and then exported as pure Formosa Oolong. The regulations now issued rendered such Tea liable to confiscation, imposed a fine on the dealer of double the value of the condemned Tea, half of which fine was to go to the informer. This resulted in an almost complete stoppage of the sale of spurious Formosas.

In 1898, the governor-general issued an ordinance, by the terms of which all those engaged in the Tea industry, either as planters, manufacturers, or dealers, are instructed to organize associations in their respective districts or towns, under the supervision of the government, with the object of preventing the manufacture and sale of adulterated Teas and of sustaining the high character of Formosas.

It is claimed by tea experts that the better grades of Formosa Oolong have of late years shown a tendency to fall off in quality. This is generally accounted for by the lack of care given the plants by the growers, the refusal to use fertilizers of any kind, and the careless methods of picking, the leaves being pulled off in bunches, whereas they should, of course, be carefully picked, one by one, so as to ensure the separation of the various grades. Owing to the non-use of fertilizers the highest quality of Tea is now only obtained from virgin soil, and of course the area of such is restricted year by year.

It would be of great advantage if the Japanese authorities, in connection with their efforts to prevent the export of impure Teas, could issue instructions as to the proper care of plants, and adopt some system of inspection to enforce obedience to such instructions. Now that Chinese teamen, by government orders, are to organize themselves into associations, the improvement might be effected through them without subjecting the planters to direct official surveillance.

So far we have studied the history of the industry from the merchants' point of view. The experiences of the pioneer planters are more interesting and no less important.

The date of the first cultivation of Tea in Formosa is difficult to ascertain. Tea has been found growing wild in the island but undoubtedly the first cultivated plants were originally brought from China. According to native accounts there were two plantations existing in the early fifties, one near Chim-hua (Shinko) and the other at Pena-be (Heirinbisho), both south-east of Taipeh. As the cultivation increased, the seeds, slips, and cuttings were obtained from these two gardens, and no more plants were brought over from China until 1865 and 1866 when, owing to the interest taken in the trade by John Dodd and other foreigners, large importations of the shrub were made for transplantation purposes. An obstacle arose, however, from the fact that the hilly ground, with a soil of light sandy loam most suitable for Tea culture, was principally in or adjoining the savage districts; and the untamed warriors of the forest were disinclined to give up their territory to their enemies the Chinese.

Formerly the savages in the extreme north were but rarely disturbed, and the boundaries of their districts remained the same year after year; but now, with the vision of ample profits from the Tea trade, the colonists made great progress in annexing the "hill barbarians'" land, and within ten years (1868 to 1878) the greater part of two ranges of hills, varying in elevation from 1,000 to 4,000 feet, lying to the east of Taipehfu, had been cleared of all heavy timber and forest trees, and the jungle with its savage occupants had been replaced by little plantations of Tea and other agricultural products. This was not accomplished without much dangerous toil, however, nor without considerable loss of life. It was customary for a Chinese headman to obtain a kind of charter from the authorities and then to assemble about him a force of some 300 or 400 men, who would drive back the aborigines, and reclaim by degrees the land, which would then be placed in the hands of the less warlike Tea farmers, who were constantly arriving from the mainland. The headman undertook to see that the aborigines did not return to plunder or kill, for which service he ordinarily received, after the third year, 2,000 out of every 10,000 Tea plants grown on the land which he had reclaimed and guarded. The Chinese had by this time fully recognized the promising future of the Formosa Tea trade, and numerous small capitalists had invested in plantations, while emigrants from Ankoi and other districts adjacent to Amoy had arrived in large numbers to profit by their knowledge of Tea culture. The Chinese, in their haste to plant the leaf, were not careful to remove all remnants of the forest, and numerous stumps of camphor and other trees were to be seen amidst the fields of Tea. Tea merchants were also attracted by the increased trade, and were willing to make cash advances to prospective growers, thus assisting in the laying out of plantations.

The district under cultivation continued to increase, and in 1877 almost every mountain slope on the hills visible from Twatutia (Daitotei) contained some Tea gardens. Further inland to the very borders of the savage land, and south to almost half the length of the island plantations were also to be found. Tea, however, from the southern gardens was found to be unsatisfactory in quality, and the later expansion of the industry was chiefly confined to the hills and plateaux of the north. Such energy brought the production in ten years from a few thousand to over eight million pounds.

From 1877 to 1887, the area placed under cultivation continued extending, from Twatutia as a centre, in all directions, and from over eight million the production increased to over sixteen million pounds. From 1887 to 1897, the new plantations were extended to the south and west rather than to the north and east, and from the quality of Tea already obtained from the new districts it is believed that the high grade leaf of the future will come from the plantations to the west and south-west of Twatutia. The increase for these ten years was not so marked as that of previous years ; but still a healthy increase, averaging nearly half a million pounds a year, is to be noted. The present annual production exceeds twenty million pounds. The industry is even yet in its infancy; and, with the vast extent of hills yet uncultivated and the satisfactory profits hitherto obtained by the planters, it seems not unreasonable, especially as the China Tea districts are gradually failing to produce a satisfactory Oolong, to anticipate a steadily increased production in the future.

At present the best Tea comes from Tsapgoahun (Jugofun) and the Paichi district in the vicinity of the town of Pankio. The gardens are all situated on the plateaux and hillsides, the more extensive ones covering an area of 15 to 17 acres, while those owned by the average small farmers extend over but two or three acres. The main centre of the production, however, is to the south and west, about twenty miles from Twatutia, where the soil is a reddish yellow sticky clay, most difficult to travel over in wet weather, but which produces large quantities of tea. The leaf is also widely grown in the Kelung district and extends even into the Kapsulan plain on the north-east of the island, while in the north-central districts, above the villages of Sui-teng ka (Suihenkiaku) and Sikkan (Shakko), the highlands are most thickly studded with tea plantations, though the quality of the leaf obtained from the latter districts is not generally of very high grade. Thoughout the north of the island the conditions for successful Tea culture, as laid down by specialists, are largely realized. A hot damp climate with a rainfall of not less than 80 to 100 inches per annum, absence of drought, and a soil of light sandy loam being best adapted for the purpose.

Soon after Tea became a profitable export from the north, the Chinese in the central and southern portions of the island made some attempt to grow it in their respective districts. It was generally believed that Tea would grow in any part of Formosa and that the hills to the rear of Tainanfu were specially valuable for that purpose. A number of plantations were established in the vicinity of Aulang (Koro) and Changwha (Shoka), but the product was found to be very inferior, and the planters soon wearied of the experiment. In 1878, several hundred plants were set out near Tainanfu, but the result was likewise so discouraging that no further attempt was made to grow the shrub for export in the south. There is, however, some internal trade in the south in sun-dried Tea, which the Hakkas, Pepohoans, and even the savages sometimes have for sale.

In preparing virgin soil in the hill districts, the long grass and shrubbery are first removed, the trees are then felled and the roots dug out, and frequently the whole patch of ground is burned over, fires that are sometimes seen at night with picturesque effect from Twatutia. The jungle being thus removed, a crop of indigo or sweet potatoes is planted, to be replaced, the following season, with young tea plants. There are two methods in vogue for propagating the leaf in Formosa. The first and most favored is by slips and cuttings. The best of these are obtained by bending down branches of the mother plant and covering them with earth. This is done in the early part of the year. In ten or twelve months the branch has taken root; it is then severed from the mother plant and is ready to be transplanted. The second method is by sowing ; but this is not much in favor.

In the newly cleared districts, the virgin soil is so fertile that no manure or fertilizer is required. The plants are placed in rows two or three feet apart, with a like distance between each plant. These rows are usually run at right angles to the slope of the hills, and in many cases form a dam, which, during heavy rains, is frequently filled with water or is washed away, leaving the Tea bush high above, with its denuded roots projecting down below. From this the reader may judge that but little attention is paid to drainage. Great care must be taken to keep the young plants clear of weeds and undergrowth, which, with the heat and moisture of Formosa, spring up very rapidly, and, if left untouched, would soon smother and destroy the tender shoots. After three years the plant has attained a height of two or three feet, and then being considered big and strong enough to yield a return for the labor spent upon it, is turned over to the tender mercies of the Tea pickers to be plucked of its foliage. From this time on, the plant does not obtain the attention from the cultivator it deserves, but fortunately the soil is so fertile that the result is not so serious as it would be in most of the Chinese Tea districts. Pruning and irrigation, both of which would be of great value, are very rarely resorted to, and frequently weeds are allowed to grow in gardens that are by no means abandoned. These carry on a struggle with the Tea plant which, if not choked out of existence, is oftimes so affected that the produce per bush is lessened in quantity as well as deteriorated in quality. In the well cared for gardens the weeds are kept down, and four times a year the ground between the rows is spaded. In the rainy season the roots are covered with earth, care being taken to loosen the soil, and make an air passage for the benefit of the leaves just about to sprout.

The picking of the spring, summer, autumn, and winter crops occurs for the most part during the months of April, June and July, August and September, and November respectively. Of the four crops the summer one is considered best, the autumn and spring ones take the second place, and the winter one the third; the last being so inferior that but little of it is shipped for foreign consumption. The work of picking is performed almost exclusively by women and children, who walk along between the rows, stooping down beside each bush and stripping it of its leaves, which latter are then placed in baskets strapped on the collectors' backs. A group of these Tea pickers, the girls attractively dressed in bright colors, laughing and chatting together and lacking the boorish appearance which often characterizes the rustic laborers in other climes, the dark green of the tea plants, and the hills gracefully sloping away towards the interior, forms in all a scene picturesque and engaging. Work under such conditions gives a brighter aspect to the usual dull agricultural life of the Chinese ; and the Tea pickers are to be envied by their more aristocratic city sisters who must suffer from *ennui* in their prison-like homes.

The pay for this labor varies according to the season, the leaves being stiffer and, therefore, more difficult to pick, in some seasons than in others. This remuneration runs from 2 to 4 cents (local currency) for about three catties, which will make about a ~~picul (133 lbs.)~~ of prepared leaf ; and a very rapid worker can, when the leaf is tender, pick from seven to ten catties a day, though the average picker earns but from 8 to 10 cents a day (4 to 5 cents gold). If the pickers wish to obtain midday food from the planter a few cents is deducted from the day's earnings. Besides the pickers who are engaged to pluck the leaves from the growing plant, indoor pickers are required who take out the twigs and leaf stalks from the Tea after it has been dried, and whose earnings are about the same as the outdoor Tea pickers. There are also male employés, such as cultivators at about 20 cents per day, food being provided by the planter. If cultivators are engaged by the year, their wage is about $30, or if for less than a half year from $4 to $5 a month.

Formosa Oolong is the pure article and free from all coloring matter. Compared with China and other Teas it has been subjected to the least amount of manipulation, and the process of manufacture is, therefore, very simple. The green leaves brought in by the pickers are spread out in the open air, in the sunshine if possible, and there stirred every five or seven minutes. In a short time the moisture in the leaf has evaporated slightly and there is some trace of fermentation.[1] The Tea is then removed into a well ventilated building and is there spread out in shallow circular bamboo trays 2½ feet in diameter, a few pounds to a tray, which are then placed in a bamboo frame, one above another, with a sufficient space between each to allow of a free circulation of air. Every ten minutes or so the leaves are stirred, which incites fermentation, although the process is not allowed to proceed far enough to place the leaf in the category of fermented teas, such

[handwritten margin note: "catty (1⅓ lbs.)"]

---

1. Mr. Hosie in an interesting consular report published by the British government on the trade and resources of Formosa, describes a crude tea preparing machine worked by foot power and used for softening the tea leaves. I have been unable to gain any information regarding this contrivance, but I can, at least, say that it is not in general use in the larger plantations. The machine is described by Mr. Hosie as follows : " Between the exposure in the open air and the firing, the leaf has to undergo a somewhat peculiar treatment, a process which I discovered accidentally, and which was unknown to the foreign tea merchants to whom I mentioned the matter. One day in September I was wandering at the base of the North Hill, near the port of Tamsui, on the lookout for a certain plant, when I suddenly found myself close to a farm house, and saw a man sitting on a high stool on the threshing floor turning rapidly with his feet what appeared to be a long cylindrical drum. On near inspection, I found that the machine was 8 feet long and 2 feet to 2½ feet in diameter, six sided, each side made of brown, coarse cloth let into a wooden frame work, that the axle ran right through the cylinder and rested on two wooden supports, one at each end. Between the support and the cylinder at one end were four treadles fixed in the axles. Working these with his feet the man caused the cylinder to revolve rapidly, each revolution being accompanied by a swishing noise inside the cylinder. On my expressing my desire for some enlightenment the man willingly unfastened one of the sides, which was the door of the cylinder, and laid it back on its hinges. Exposed to view were six bamboos, corresponding in number to the sides of the machine, fixed at equal intervals into the ends of the cylinder midway between the axle, to which they ran parallel, and the periphery of the " Cha-nung," or tea preparer, as the machine is called. At the bottom of the cylinder there was a heap of green tea leaves, which had been placed there after the necessary exposure on the threshing floor. As the machine revolves, these leaves are dashed against the bamboos, whereby their edges are rendered quite soft ; they are then removed and put into the iron firing-pans. It will be asked " Why are the edges of the leaves softened ?" The answer is easy. Were the leaves, after being picked and exposed for a short time, placed in the firing-pans, they would split up—the tea leaf is thick and brittle—and lose all semblance to the whole leaf which is so much desired. Such, at least, was the explanation given to me, and it appears to be very reasonable and natural."

Up-country Tea Manipulations.

Tea Plantation near San-kak-eng.
First Manipulation of Leaf.
First Fire Drying.

Tea Picking.
Second Manipulation.
Light Firing.

Ceylons

as China Congous or ~~Salous.~~ After two hours, the leaf is placed in big bamboo trays five feet in diameter, some forty pounds in each, and is stirred by attendants every ten minutes. After some two hours of this, the edge of the leaf begins to turn to a reddish brown and slightly to emit the odor characteristic of the prepared Tea. The leaves are now placed in metal pans, several pounds to each, over a wood fire, and subjected to considerable heat. After a few minutes, during which an attendant tosses and stirs the leaves, they attain the curled up and spongy appearance and smell desired. They are then placed in small trays resting on benches, on one end of which the operator sits, and for several moments rolls and twists the leaves. After another drying over the fire, the leaves are again placed in bamboo trays for a second rolling or twisting, and then, on the completion of this, are again dried over the fire. No set rule can be laid down for this drying process. The object is to remove sufficient moisture from the Tea to insure its standing transport and storage until placed in the hands of the exporters, and the amount of manipulation required to attain this is dependent upon the weather; hot sunny days, of course, greatly lessening the labor. Finally the Tea is subjected to a light firing over a charcoal fire, an operation which will be described later on. It is then packed in jute bags, holding some seventy pounds each, to be transported by boat, railway, or carrier, to Twatutia, the market of Formosa.

It is at this stage of the industry that the brokers, native merchants, and packers make their appearance. Although the final export is carried on through the foreign firms, there are usually numerous Chinese middlemen between the foreign merchant and the grower. Not infrequently the Chinese dealers and packers, who are sometimes men of capital, secure control over a certain amount of leaf by advancing money to the growers, who, when the season opens, turn the Tea over to them at a discount ordinarily of some ten per cent. less than the market price, and also allow for interest at a rate of about one per cent. a month. Again brokers and middlemen visit the plantations and make other financial arrangements, sometimes under orders from Twatutia packing-houses, and sometimes merely on speculation. In the latter case, samples are sent to the different Chinese and foreign firms in detail, and in case the Tea has been first secured by the native dealers and packers, samples representing the leaf as it comes from the planters or the prepared goods which have been given the final firing by the Twatutia native firing establishments are sent to the foreign firms, and if purchases are made the leaf is delivered at once. The brokers are generally sufficiently expert in Tea to avoid paying more than the Tea is worth. Unlike some of the Chinese Tea districts, which are often a great distance from the Tea marts, the furthest producing districts in Formosa are but two or three days' distant from Twatutia. The planters, consequently, are generally acquainted with the rise and fall of the market, and, though they are often stubborn in realizing that a decline has taken place, they exhibit great alacrity in demanding an advance when there is the least suspicion of an upward movement in the market. The broker's chances of a fortune, therefore, are not specially bright, but he usually insures himself a comfortable living from the squeeze obtained out of the very elaborate charges which purport to represent his actual expenditure. It is not unusual, when selling on commission, to charge the employer 14 to 15 yen per picul for expenses which probably do not really exceed half that sum. Sometimes, however, the broker, incredulous of the foreigner's reports as to a declining market, continues, for a time, to make purchases at the old prices and thus suffers considerable loss.

The stock in native hands, which is not disposed of to the foreign buyers in Formosa, is shipped to Amoy, a China port lying directly across the channel from North Formosa, where advances on it are made by the foreign firms there. Thus it comes about that there are two markets for Formosa Tea, and the proportion of the crop disposed of to foreign buyers in either market depends upon the variation of trade conditions from season to season. This is due to the fact that there is no suitable harbor in Formosa convenient to the tea districts, and that it is at present necessary to make Amoy the port of shipment. Should the Japanese government construct a thoroughly safe and convenient harbor in Formosa, preferably at Tamsui, it is possible that the market for the Tea would be eventually confined to the island. In 1898 one half of the total crop was settled in Amoy.[1]

But this is anticipating, and we must follow the leaf through the various channels before it is ready for the shipment to Amoy described above. Upon the arrival of the Tea at Twatutia from the country districts, the Japanese inland tax of 2.40 yen ($1.20 U. S. G.) per picul is paid. The goods are now delivered to the purchasers and placed in their godowns. Although partially cleared of coarse matter up-country, the Tea is not as yet considered clean. It is at this stage that the tea picking girls appear on the scene, and, sitting down in front of big bamboo trays, on which a quantity of Tea is placed, apply themselves to picking out by hand the twigs, stalks, and bad leaf.

To a stranger visiting Twatutia during the summer months, nothing is more striking than the crowds of girls, who at noon and night simply overrun the place. Fortunately the Tea picking period is looked upon by these coy damsels as the opening of the social season as it were, and a younger sister is brought out with considerable *éclat*, not unlike the début of a young lady attending her first social function at home. I say fortunately, for the slovenly and not always cleanly appearance which she exhibits in her own abode is quite the reverse of that shown when she blossoms out as a Tea picker. The best clothes are none too good, and her toilet is most carefully prepared. The coiffure is oftimes a work of art and is extensively decorated with the strongly scented blossoms of the magnolia, while, with her feet bound up in the very smallest compass, she is prepared to dazzle the community.

---

1. The settlements of Formosa tea in Amoy for six years are as follows :—

Season.	Settled in Amoy.	Season.	Settled in Amoy.
1893	70%	1896	60%
1894	52%	1897	48%
1895	51%	1898	50%

There are about one hundred and fifty Tea manufacturers big and small in Twatutia, besides the half dozen foreign establishments. The largest firms employ from one hundred to three hundred Tea picking girls during the busy months; but, if there is much tea on hand and it is desired to rush matters, the number of tea pickers, working in one establishment, may reach, for a few days, four or five hundred. On an average the total number daily employed in Twatutia exceeds some twelve thousand. Wages are paid each day according to the amount of work done; and, though 5 cents for 7 catties is the nominal rate, measurement is in favor of the employer and the average payment does not really exceed some 60 cents a picul. Even at this amount it is interesting to note that the earnings of these girls amount to nearly one hundred thousand dollars (local currency) a season.

The majority of the pickers are girls from 14 to 18 years of age, but old women and little children also form a considerable part of the corps. The hands and eyes of the young girls are the quickest; and a bright worker can earn in a single day (6 a.m. to 5 p.m.) as much as 15 cents, while the average picker can only secure from 9 to 10 cents. The Chinese tea men are very susceptible to a pretty face, and a possessor of one finds her work much lightened and her earnings often augmented. Several thousand Chinese leave their families in China every spring to work in the Tea establishments of North Formosa, and the circumstances under which young girls are sent from their homes each day to labor with strangers from the Chinese mainland, whose highest ambitions are to spend their idle moments in the opium dens and brothels of Banka, are not conducive to morality, although it would be perhaps incorrect to imply that the majority of the girls are not virtuous, or to assume that the percentage of those that fall is larger than it would be under similar conditions in some other countries.

The Tea which, up to this time, has been only very lightly fired, and is known to the dealers by the somewhat misleading term of "green leaf" must now be thoroughly fired to prepare it for the long voyage to America or Europe. The firing establishments in Twatutia, whether belonging to the Chinese or foreigners, consist of rooms holding from fifty to several hundred fire places. These fire places are simply circular holes two feet deep, two feet in diameter, and a foot apart, surrounded by, and the tops flush with, a low brick platform about a foot or eighteen inches high. Following the operations of firing, we find that the charcoal, which is the fuel used, after having been lighted, is allowed to burn until every particle of combustible matter has been consumed, the charcoal reaching a state of red heat. But before this result has been completely attained, the firing room has become a huge oven, the hundred fire places sending forth a flame and glow which tests one's powers of endurance to the utmost. The Chinese coolies, almost naked and with wet cloths about their heads, covering their mouths and nostrils, rush into the furnace, and with iron implements break up and agitate the burning mass, that the red heat may penetrate to the heart of every glowing coal. When the fires have ceased to emit smoke, they are banked with a layer of ashes to temper the heat, and in this way will remain alive for over a week without replenishing. A dozen or fifteen hours after the fuel has been first ignited, the fires are considered ready to receive the Tea. The receptacle used is a large basket some three feet in height, shaped like a dice box, with a bottom formed by a sieve placed a few inches below the centre, thus leaving open spaces at each end. The basket, having been put over the fire, some seven pounds of Tea are placed on the sieve and for the first two or three hours left practically untouched. By that time it is well heated, and firing-men pass from basket to basket turning over the contents. This is repeated about every hour, thus permitting the heat to diffuse equally throughout the Tea. Although as a rule 8 to 10 hours is sufficient firing, as with the drying of the freshly picked leaf in the country, no set rule can be laid down as to the time required. The object is generally only to evaporate every particle of moisture, and as soon as this is thought to have been accomplished the Tea is removed. In the earlier days of the trade, however, parcels of Formosa Tea destined for the English market were sometimes fired very heavily to give the liquor the very dark appearance much favored by consumers in Great Britain, and even at present some buyers prefer a Tea which has been more heavily fired than is really necessary for preservation.

While hot from the fires the Tea is packed in boxes containing an inner case of thin lead, which when soldered, becomes air-tight and prevents the contents from spoiling. The standard size of box is a half chest which holds about 40 pounds, although there are besides quarter chests and 10 lb. boxes. The lead is imported in pigs weighing upward of a hundred pounds each, and manufactured into very thin sheets in Twatutia by a very simple process. An iron pot and two pieces of tile constitute the whole apparatus required, and the rapidity with which plates of a very good quality are turned out is quite amazing. The labor is generally performed by two men, one of whom looks after the fire and trims the plates, and the other handles the tiles. A visitor to one of the establishments (if a room 12 feet square which not only contains the whole factory but is used as a living room for the workmen as well, should be honored by so pretentious a term), will find the chief workman standing beside a pot containing molten lead, and on the floor may be seen the two tiles, one on top of the other. Commencing operations the Chinese with one hand lifts one side of the top tile up slightly, and with the other hand dips a little of the molten metal out of the pot and with a dexterous movement dashes it in between the two tiles ; then, instantly dropping the upper one, and stepping upon it he applies sufficient pressure to force the melted lead to spread over the tiles. The metal hardens in a few seconds ; the upper tile is again lifted, the newly made plate thrown out, and the operation continued as before. These plates, after having been trimmed, are soldered together in the shape of a box.

For the Tea boxes, pine boards of the right thickness, and cut to about the proper length, arrive here from Amoy and Foochow and are knocked into boxes with but little alteration. Colored paper, bearing some printed adornment, is afterward pasted over them, or they are painted by a "lightning artist," who, dipping different parts of a brush in different pots, with this single implement dashes off a more or less complicated design in three or four colors in less time than it takes to write about it.

So far we have dealt only with the preparation of pure Oolong. There is, however, a growing industry in the manufacture of scented Tea or "Pouchong" (Pauchong) as it is commonly known. The term "Pouchong" means literally the kind in bags, referring to the small paper bags which are sometimes used in making up small packages of Tea. In Formosa, however, the term is applied almost exclusively to a scented Tea which is made entirely for Chinese consumption. A Chinese merchant named Go Fok-lu, in 1881, first introduced to Formosa the present method of manufacture. The demand for these Teas is rapidly increasing, and the production has for some years averaged 2½ to 3 million pounds, valued at upwards of 450,000 yen ($225,000 U. S. Gold), which is about 12 per cent. in quantity, and 6 per cent. in value, of the total production of Formosan Tea.[1] The handling of Pouchongs does not interfere with the Oolong trade for generally only the inferior and refuse Teas are utilized in the manufacture of Pouchongs. This relieves the market of the undesirable Teas which are not wanted by the Oolong trade. The native merchants are thus able to clean up their entire holdings without sacrifice. The greater part of the Formosa Pouchongs is exported, via Amoy and Hongkong, to Java and the Straits Settlements, and the remainder goes to Swatow, Saigon, Siam, Hawaii, and San Francisco.

While Oolong is the pure leaf without the addition of coloring or flavoring matter, Pouchong is the leaf artificially flavored with the scent of certain flowers, obtained by placing the leaf in direct contact with freshly picked blossoms, no chemical flavoring that can replace them having as yet been discovered. Tons of the strongly scented blossoms of the White Jasmine (*J. Officinale*), Jasmine (*J. Sambac*), *Oleacear* (*Olea fragrans*), and Gardenia (*Rubiacear*), known to the natives as Su eng, Boat-li, Ch'iu lan, and Ng-ki respectively, are gathered yearly to be used in the manufacture. In fact, such large quantities are required that the production of these flowers has become an industry in itself.[2] Scarcely an hour's walk from Twatutia (Daitotei) will bring one to large gardens filled with these fragrant plants. The prices of the blossoms vary with the demand, but generally range from 5 to 28 yen a picul according to the kind, the White Jasmine being the most expensive and the Gardenia the cheapest.

Several different processes are in use in the manufacture of Pouchong

1. The total Formosan Tea export for 1897 was 20,501,610 pounds, valued at 6,920,630 Yen ($3,460,315 U. S. Gold), and of that amount, 2,441,215 pounds, valued at 460,910 Yen ($230,455 U. S. Gold), was Pouchong Tea. In 1893 the export of Pouchong was 1,812,667 pounds. In 1894 it reached 2,290,266 pounds; and, high prices ruling, the production brought 760,930 Yen ($380,465 U. S. Gold) to the fortunate Formosan dealers. The export for 1898 amounted to 20,281 piculs (2,714,100 lbs.) valued at 526,733 Yen ($263,361 U. S. Gold). For later statistics of this trade see page 640, and footnote 2 on page 388.

2. While in Formosa only the four varieties above mentioned are at present used in the manufacture of scented Tea, in China the list is more extended and, according to Fortune, consists of the following:—

Rose; Plum; Orange; Jasminum Sambac; Ait; Jasminum paniculatum, Roxb; Aglaia odorata, Roxb; Osmanthus fragrans, Lour; Gardenia florida, L.

See page 26, vol. XXIV Transactions Asiatic Society of Japan. "A List of Plants from Formosa," by Henry.

Tea, but the general principle is the same. There are several grades, chiefly dependent on the kind and quantity of the flowers used. The proportion of blossoms to Tea runs from some 30 per cent. upwards, the largest quantity being required when the *Oleacear* flower is utilized, and in making one particular grade all four flowers are used together. The usual method of manufacture is as follows :—Tea, at this stage, the same as the Oolong exporters might be asked to buy, though of a lower quality, having been brought in from the country, is spread out on the floor of the building. The sweet smelling blossoms brought from the various gardens, freshly picked, after having been completely sprinkled with water, are now mixed with the Tea, and the mixture is then piled up to a height of 7 or 8 feet. The stuff is carefully covered with a cloth to prevent the escape of the flowery odor. After from 7 to 17 hours, according to the kind of flowers used and the season, the scent from the blossoms is found to have thoroughly permeated the Tea leaves, and the mixture is then turned over to the Tea picking girls who separate the now withered blossoms from the Tea leaf. In the case of the small *Oleacear* flower, however, the separation is usually done by the aid of a sieve. When this is completed, the Tea is put on the fire for seven hours, being subjected to about 180° Fah. of heat, after which the manufacture is considered complete. The Tea is packed in small, gaudily labeled paper bags, and these in turn in half-chests. .

The Formosa Tea, both pure Oolong and Pouchong, now packed and labeled, is ready for shipment. If the Tea is to be forwarded via Amoy which, just at present, is the favorite route, it is sent in cargo boats down river to Hobe (Tamsui), ten miles distant, where the Customs export duty of yen 1.60 per picul is collected. The steamers, which generally lie at a wharf, are loaded with ease and convenience, and in some eighteen hours after their departure from Hobe, Amoy is reached, and the Oolong for foreign consumption is there landed, receives its final matting, and is later transhipped aboard Pacific steamers to the western coast ports of America, or to London and New York via the Suez Canal route.[1]

The aromatic and pungent flavor of Formosa Oolong is highly appreciated in America ; but in England the demand is very slight, and the importation is almost exclusively used for mixing with other Teas to give flavor to the latter. We find consequently that of the total export nearly 90 per cent. goes to America and the remainder is shipped to Great Britain. The Chinese control the Pouchong trade, so that it may be said the foreign Tea houses are, with the exception of the few small shipments to London, exclusively engaged in supplying the American market. The value of this trade has in one year exceeded 7,000,000 yen ($3,500,000 U.S. Gold).[2] This trade is conducted almost wholly through six large firms, American and

1. Ordinarily the Tea with freight at 12c. per half chest can be laid down in Amoy godowns for about 16 to 17c. (silver) although opposition between rival steamship lines sometimes reduce freight rates to 10c. a half chest, making it possible to lay Tea down in Amoy for 14c. or so.

2. In 1893 the export of Formosan Teas reached 20,047,000 lbs. valued at 7,305,900 yen (3,652,950 U. S. Gold). Statistics are not available for 1902, but it is believed that this season will break all records in total crop as well as values. Figures obtained on December 1st, 1902, show that the total export for 1902 of all grades of Formosa will, doubtless, reach if not exceed 22,390,000 lbs., of which over 19,000,000 lbs., will be Oolongs, and the balance, something over 3,200,000 lbs., Pouchongs.

English. Of the above mentioned firms two have their head offices in Amoy with branches in Formosa. But little attempt has been made on the part of Japanese firms to enter the trade. The Formosan Trading Co., a Japanese organization, commenced business in 1896, and were small shippers for three seasons. A second Japanese firm is undertaking the manufacture of brick tea on a small scale, but it is not likely that there will ever be much rivalry in the Tea business between Japanese and foreign firms. As long as the trade remains as it is to-day—largely a commission and joint account business—American and English home firms will prefer to place their patronage, other things being equal, with established firms whose business ability has been proven.

The interest in direct shipments of Tea from Formosa to the United States is increasing, but as yet, aside from one or two experimental shipments, nothing has been done. A considerable quantity of Tea has, however, gone forward in Japanese bottoms from Kelung to Kobe, where it is transhipped to Pacific or Suez steamers. Some of this Tea received its final packing in Kobe and was invoiced from that port. Twatutia (Daitotei) the center of the Tea trade has communication with Tamsui port by river. The latter would therefore be the more convenient port of shipment. From this harbor the run across to Amoy is made by coasting steamers in 18 hours. Unfortunately, however, the harbor in its present state admits only vessels which draw less than 13 or 14 feet. Furthermore, its natural disadvantages are such that it would be very difficult to convert it into a good harbor for large shipping. Kelung is also unsatisfactory in its present state for, although it is accessible to large steamers, these cannot come in close to shore, and the difficulties in loading are sometimes considerable. With the harbor improvements now under way, Kelung will in a short time be freed from these disadvantages, and we may then expect to see it obtaining a large share of the trade.

One obstacle to shipment via Kelung, is in transporting the Tea from Twatutia to that port. The two places are connected by rail, but the rolling stock is at present insufficient for the handling of large quantities of Tea. From Tamsui it could be carried by boat round to Kelung, but with such difficulty that the sea route is entirely out of the question. The expense of shipment via Kelung to Japan is somewhat higher than via Tamsui to Amoy, although from Amoy to America, and Japan to America, freight rates are often the same.[1] The plans for Kelung harbor include dredging, the construction of piers and quays, the extension of the railway along the south-east side of the harbor, and lastly the construction of a breakwater.[2]

The dredging in the inner harbor will be completed in some two years and will provide as much space, so far as the needs of the merchant shipping are concerned, as will probably be required for many years. The extensive pier and quay work at present planned will doubtless consume several years before its entire completion ; though one small, temporary pier to

1. At present (1902) steamship freight between Kelung and Kobe is 15 sen a half chest, Kelung shipping expenses 2 sen, railway freight about 2 sen, giving a total cost of laying down Tea in Kobe from the Twatutia railway station of about 19 sen per half chest, (2 sen equals about 1 U. S. cent). For cost of shipment via Amoy see footnote on page 388.

2. See pages 623 and 638.

accommodate two large steamers is promised as early as May, 1903. In addition to good harbor facilities the willing and constant co-operation of the railway from Twatutia (Daitotei) to Kelung, a distance of 20 miles will be required. There is every reason to expect reasonable railway charges, and if the shipping companies place Kelung on an equality with other eastern ports as respects freight rates, direct shipment via Kelung will have much to recommend it. However, it must be taken into consideration that, owing to the higher cost of labor in Formosa, final matting and marking can be done more cheaply in Amoy; also, that the cities of Twatutia and Kelung are very unattractive as places of residence, and firms now established in Amoy would not remove to the island without the promise of very marked advantages. Still, the Formosan tea-firms are above all practical, and, regardless of vested interests in Amoy, they may be depended upon to patronize the route, which, all things considered, can handle the business on the most economical basis.

A few years, at the most, will decide this important question, and it is the writer's opinion that as the natural order of things must in time prevail, Kelung will come into its own, and Amoy which owes its existence as a commercial dependency of Formosa to the lack of proper harbor facilities in the island, will, with the change of conditions, cease to be an important port of transhipment for Formosan cargoes.[1]

The Japanese are naturally desirous of fostering the trade of the island, and it is quite possible that legislation may be introduced which will favor direct shipments from Formosa. It is to be hoped, however, that the government will content itself with so perfecting the harbor and railway facilities that the superior advantages of Kelung as a port of shipment will be sufficient attraction, and that no discrimination, will be shown in favor of any one route.

When, in July, 1899, the new treaties came in force and export duties were abolished in Japan proper, it was decided by the Formosan government that certain export imposts should be continued in Formosa, but that the trade with Japan should be given preferential treatment. Thus, the export duty on tea shipped via foreign ports was not only continued but was, in fact, unfortunately, increased from 1.10 yen a picul (133⅓ lbs.) to 1.60 yen, and reduced to 1.00 yen a picul when shipped to or via any port in Japan. The latter impost was designated as a " harbor tax."

Twatutia (Daitotei) has grown rapidly during the last six or seven years. A large number of new buildings have been erected and the foreigners are installed in commodious dwellings. Every season nearly seven millions of silver dollars are brought over from the mainland. A few hundred Chinese teamen, barefooted and dressed in common clothes, present themselves and exchange their Tea for the silver dollars. They return to the narrow confines of the Tea district and "presto" the silver disappears, and the following season the same ragged fellows reappear with the same poverty stricken appearance. The same mud, brick and straw huts remain up-country, the same crude farming implements are in use, and the same half starved dog rushes out to bark as you pass by. Perhaps an

1. For late developments in the subject of direct shipments see page 637.

extension of a Tea field may be noted or even a new rice field laid out ; but of prosperity, as we know it in the West, there is not a sign. What becomes of so much treasure is truly a mystery.

Under the new treaties with Japan, which have now come into force, it will be possible for foreigners to take up their residence in the country and to engage in trade on practically the same basis as the natives, except that land cannot be owned, although twenty year leases are possible. Under these conditions what are the chances for foreigners as Tea planters ?[1] I do not refer to the large foreign Tea firms. The owning or controlling of a plantation by them may be of indirect advantage in many ways, and the mere difference in values between the cost of cultivation and the ruling prices on the Twatutia market, so long as there is no special loss, may be a matter of secondary importance. But I refer chiefly to the outside investor, who desires to place his money in some profitable venture, or the ozone loving individual who wishes to engage in agricultural work and who would look forward to a life in the Formosa hills with pleasure, provided a comfortable income was to be obtained.

This subject might well be prefaced with the information that a good Tea producing district is usually an unhealthy one, the moisture and rain required being rather conducive to malarial fever. Still our planter might be provided with comfortable quarters and good food, and might spend a portion of his time in Twatutia, which though it has a bad reputation, does not appear to be specially unhealthy so far as foreigners are concerned. The question then resolves itself into one of profit and loss. To the writer it would appear that foreigners, and even Japanese, at least until the latter have greatly increased in number, will find it very difficult to compete with the Chinese in agricultural pursuits.[2] The only opportunity, therefore, would be for one who, having obtained new and fertile ground, could give such attentive care to the plants that the product would stand out clearly as superior to the average native grown Tea. But should he profit by the application of new means and methods, the neighboring native planters would eventually discover the cause of his success, and they might, the chances are they would, soon adopt a like system and probably undersell the foreigner in a few seasons, owing to their frugality and closeness in money matters.

It is difficult to form an estimate of the cost of production, an outsider, specially a foreigner, being obliged to pay for much that the Chinese planter would partially or wholly avoid. Some idea, however, of the capital required may be ascertained by the following estimate of the principal items :—

1. Several parties have made similar inquiries of the writer, as United States consular representative. The subject was dealt with in a consular report, a portion of which is reproduced in the present account.

2. Until the new order of things in Japan is made public and the exact privileges granted to foreigners are known, it cannot be definitely stated whether or not foreigners may engage in agriculture. But should a foreigner desire to control a tea plantation, there would doubtless be legal methods open by which he could do so, residence in the interior being allowed him.

For a plantation of 100,000 bushes.

25 acres of the most desirable land	...	...	...	...	...	...	800 00	Yen.
100,000 young Tea bushes, planted	...	...	...	...	...	...	1,600.00	,,
Cultivation and care of plants for three years ...	...	...	...	...	...	600.00	,,
Farming implements (native) and hut for cultivator ...	...	...	...	160.00	,,
Total...	...	...	...	...	...	...	...	...	3,160.00 Yen.

As regards the working expenses ; after studying the subject, on and off for nearly a month, I found it quite impossible to arrive at any satisfactory results. The Twatutia Chinese merchants know very little about in-country conditions, and inquiries made direct to the planters resulted in such a mass of conflicting statements—one man giving different figures at each interview on three different occasions—that I gave up in despair. Doubtless the simple rustics believed that the "barbarian" was planning to oust them all. If not, why should he be so inquisitive? The Agricultural Department of the Formosan government has published a table showing the working expense of an average plantation ; and as they have conducted an experimental Tea station, special opportunities have been afforded them for ascertaining the cost, though I am not quite sure that the figures given are correct in every instance. The government estimate is as follows:—

For a plantation of 100,000 bushes.

Cultivation	...	...	...	...	...	...	...	600.00 Yen.
Picking and manufacturing	...	...	...	...	...	...	1,750.00 ,,
Charcoal and fuel	...	...	...	...	...	...	338.00 ,,
Wear and tear of implements (cultivation and manufacture,)	...	...	100 00 ,,
Total...	...	...	...	...	...	...	...	2,788.00 Yen.

To which should be added

Transportation	...	...	...	...	...	...	120.00 ,,
Taxes ...	...	...	...	...	...	...	288 00 ,,
Interest on invested capital	...	...	...	...	...	316 00 ,,
Grand Total	...	...	...	...	...	...	...	3,512.00 Yen.

Receipts will depend upon the grade of Tea the planter succeeds in producing, as well as on the market prices ruling. The cost of picking and preparing is about the same for all grades of tea, so that the profit on the choicer kinds are often very large. A good plantation of 100,000 bushes will yield about 400 piculs of leaf, which when manufactured amounts to 120 piculs of clean prepared Tea. Assuming that the foreigner will strive to produce the highest grade of Tea and that he will personally dispose of his produce at Twatutia, without the aid of middlemen, he should average about 40 Yen a picul.

120 piculs @ 40 Yen ..	...	...	...	...	...	...	...	4,800.00 Yen.
Deduct working expenses ...	...	...	...	...	...	...	3,512 00 ,,
Net profit ...	...	...	...	...	...	...	...	1,283 00 Yen.

About 40% on invested capital.[1]

The above is on a basis of a 100,000 bush plantation, one ten times its size would represent a like increase in expenditure. With the foreigner

1. The Japanese yen here mentioned may be taken roughly as about the equivalent of the Mexican dollar and equal to about 50 cents United States Gold.

Tea Manipulation at Foreign Establishments.

Final Firing.

A Belle among the Picking Girls.

An Exporting Firm's Packing Shed.

Picking out Bad Leaves, etc.

Tea Tasting at Daitotei.

established in his new plantation, what would be his position financially as compared with his Chinese neighbors? A Chinese can live more economically than it would ever be possible for a self-respecting foreigner to do, and of course, as the former deals with his own countrymen, he requires no middlemen. A foreigner, if he lived on the plantation, would require a residence. A two storeyed structure would cost from 2,500 yen upwards. The Chinese planter would live in a wretched mud brick hut representing not more than a tenth of the outlay.

Chinese Tea plantations are often much smaller than the one above described. The largest, with the exception of those of a few millionaires like Lim of Pankio, who own big plantations which they rent out to growers on sharing terms, average about 10 to 15 acres, while the small gardens, forming the vast majority, are only from two to five acres in extent. The Chinese grower with the aid of the members of his family, the more numerous the better, performs all that is required in connection with the cultivation of the plant. After having obtained possession of the land either by purchase or lease, and having secured the necessary young plants, the Chinese grower, by avoiding the employment of outside labor, decreases his expenditure to almost half of that which the foreigner would be obliged to meet. After his plants have sufficiently matured to yield a return, should the planter find his labors too great for his family, the neighboring villagers and farmers combine to assist him. The planter has his little garden of sweet potatoes and other vegetables, perhaps a small rice field, besides pigs and chickens, which furnish food to the family. During the few days of picking and manufacture it may be necessary to call in outside labor; but the Chinese farmer would get more work out of his employés for less pay than the foreigner could ever expect to do. By these methods he reduces the amount of working capital to a minimum, and it is doubtful if the actual money outlay for production exceeds fifteen to twenty Mexican dollars a picul. But the foreigner could scarcely expect to be so successful. Were he perfectly familiar with the language of the country, he would be able to deal direct with his employés and exert a general supervision over his men, which would be a great advantage to him. Still he would require a native overseer, and it is likely that this individual would feather his nest at the foreigner's expense. If the foreigner was ignorant of the language, and consequently unable to carry on negotiations with Chinese, he would be obliged to employ a Chinese compradore and place himself almost entirely in this person's hands. Should his manager turn out to be honest, well and good; but apart from the integrity which this worthy would doubtless show in business affairs that were, or might be, eventually open to inspection, the chances are that by "ways that are dark and tricks that are vain" he would manage to turn a good share of the profits into his own coffers. Besides this, the foreigner's plantation would attract all the disreputable characters in the neighborhood, and a considerable quantity of Tea would be lost through robbery. Whether the foreigner could survive in competition with the Chinese under such conditions seems very doubtful. The Japanese planter would probably find himself in like difficulties, except that he would have the advantage over the European or American of lighter living expenses.

In closing, it may be well to devote a few lines to the important part Tea plays in the island's prosperity. First, it should be noted that the hills upon which the Tea flourishes would, were it not for this trade, probably be left waste or planted to sweet potatoes or some other crop of very little value. The industry, therefore, so far as land is concerned, is almost a clear gain, leaving as it does, the rich plains and valleys for the growth of rice, sugar, and other important products.

By glancing at the industrial map the reader will observe that the district under Tea cultivation is a comparatively small one in the north. Although occupying about one-sixth of the territory utilized by sugar, and only a fraction of that given up to rice, or the area covered with the vast camphor forests, the production brings to the island nearly five times the receipts obtained from sugar, over five times the receipts obtained from camphor, and more than one half of the total value of the whole export trade of Formosa.[1] Its importance to North Formosa may be judged by noting that, on an average, about 86 per cent. of the annual export receipts are obtained from Tea. It is not too much to say that the very existence of the port of Tamsui (Hobe) is dependent upon this industry. If the season is an unprofitable one to teamen, either growers or packers, a noticeable reduction occurs in the Chinese demand for piece goods and other foreign imports, and should the industry be ruined, as it has been in the neighboring districts of Amoy, the general trade of North Formosa would be almost nil, thousands thrown out of work, and the government revenue directly and indirectly cut down perhaps a million of dollars (the present direct taxes from Tea yield over half a million yen).[2] This the Japanese authorities should keep in mind, and regulations or imposts which would tend to hamper the Tea trade should be discouraged. So far the government has exhibited the right spirit. Regulations have been passed to prevent the adulteration of Formosa Tea, a fund has been provided for advertising the goods, and, although Chinese immigration is not generally permitted, easy methods have been devised by which Tea laborers may go back to China at the close of the Tea season and return to Tamsui in the spring. The government taxes now amount to about a tenth of the total value of the Tea export ; and with the lightly taxed Japanese and free Ceylon and Indian Teas in competition in American markets, it is to be hoped that, if any change is made, it will be to lighten the tax rather than to increase it.

---

1.   In 1897.   Yen.
Export of Sugar   1,494,041
    „   Camphor   1,339,435
    „   Tea   6,920,630
Total Export from Formosa   12,759,293
    „   „   Tamsui   8,315,766

(These sums may be reduced to U. S. gold dollars by dividing by two).

2. The government revenue for 1898, from the Tea manufacturing tax amounted to yen 406,711, and from the Customs export duty to yen 235,117 ; a total of yen 641,828.

FORMOSA OOLONG EXPORT TO AMERICA AND EUROPE AND TOTAL TEA EXPORT FROM COMMENCEMENT OF THE TRADE.

Season.	Export Formosa Oolong to the United States.	Export Formosa Oolong to Europe.	Season Average Price (Tamsui currency) per picul (133 lbs.)	Total Export of Formosa Tea (all kinds).[1]
1866	...	...	... ... $10	180,824 lbs.
1867	...	...	... ... $15	270,790 lbs.
1868	...	...	... ... $20	528,210 lbs.
1869	(285,200 lbs.) shipped direct from Formosa (to New York.)	...	{Choice ... ... $25 (a 28) {Fair ... ... $16 (a 20)	729,234 lbs.
1870	...	...	Choice ... ... $32 (a 35	1,405,348 lbs.
1871	...	...	(Choice ... ... $36 (a 40) {Fine ... ... $27 (a 32) (Good ... ... $38 (a 44)	1,982,410 lbs.
1872	2,032,220 lbs.	75,153 lbs.	Summer Teas : {Choice $45 (a 55) {Fine $38 (a 44)	2,601,801 lbs.
1873	1,261,361 lbs.	57,360 lbs.	(25 (a 30%, lower than Spring prices) 1872. During August good clean Teas could be purchased at $11 (a 15. Some even at 10 During Fall prices recovered fully 40%.	2,081,324 lbs.
1874	2,818,959 lbs.	283,742 lbs.	(May Medium to Choice $23 (a 45) June & July „ „ $36 (a 46 (Aug. to Dec. ., „ $12 50 (a 35)	3,338,846 lbs.
1875	4,896,345 lbs.	400,796 lbs.	(Lowest point ... ... Good $16) Highest point ... ... Choicest $40 (Medium and Fine ... ... $20 (a 36)	5,543,140 lbs.
1876	6,487,840 lbs.	1,102,369 lbs.	(Choice ... ... $44 (a 45) (Good $20	7,854,020 lbs.
1877	7,704,693 lbs.	608,884 lbs.	(Choice ... ... $33 (a 36) Fine ... ... $26 (a 32 (Good ... ... $17 (a 24)	9,230,754 lbs.
1878	8,152,168 lbs.	1 287,360 lbs.	(Choice ... ... $45 (a 55) Fine ... ... $30 (a 40 (Good ... ... $17 (a 25)	10,701,524 lbs.
1879	9,783,513 lbs.	1,056,034 lbs.	Third Crop : (Choice ... $55 (a 60) {Fine ... $45 (a 50 (Good ... $35 (a 36)	11,337,710 lbs.
1880	10,884,127 lbs.	636,295 lbs.	... ... $39.50	12,063,450 lbs.
1881	11,978,605 lbs.	614,151 lbs.	... ... $35.65	12,854,355 lbs.
1882	10,406,260 lbs.	752,473 lbs.	... ... $34.04	12,040,446 lbs.
1883	11,272,569 lbs.	1,018,481 lbs.	... ... $36.13	13,206,726 lbs.
1884	11,779,448 lbs.	726,293 lbs.	... ... $34.85	13,155,437 lbs.
1885	14,631,082 lbs.	931,270 lbs.	... ... $35.12	16,364,041 lbs.
1886	13,797,879 lbs.	920,470 lbs.	... ... $37.72	16,171,605 lbs.
1887	14,524,015 lbs.	1,199,950 lbs.	... ... $34.46	16,816,736 lbs.
1888	14,961,048 lbs.	947,514 lbs.	... ... $36.95	18,053,553 lbs.
1889	14,539,894 lbs.	1,007,646 lbs.	... ... $34.99	17,384,164 lbs.
1890	14,212,326 lbs.	975,264 lbs.	... ... $37.34	17,107,257 lbs.
1891	15,029,535 lbs.	746,229 lbs.	... ... $31.81	18,055,149 lbs.
1892	15,211,076 lbs.	735,368 lbs.	... ... $36.64	18,230,000 lbs.
1893	18,479,927 lbs.	744,981 lbs.	... ... $38.52	21,908,530 lbs.
1894	16,748,236 lbs.	754,444 lbs.	... ... $44.74	20,533,733 lbs.
1895	15,912,426 lbs.	784,891 lbs.	... ... $41.14	19,556,116 lbs.
1896	19,327,460 lbs.	572,257 lbs.	... ... $38.59	21,474,200 lbs.
1897	16,672,683 lbs.	685,651 lbs.	... ... $47.25	20,516,020 lbs.
1898	16,261,238 lbs.	688,318 lbs.	... ... $37.68	20,532,407 lbs.
1899	16,051,000 lbs. (estimated.)	489,347 lbs. (estimated.)	... ... $35 (a 36 (estimated.)	19,837,331 lbs.

1. The above total covers all grades and kinds of Tea exported for each calendar year as reported by the customs. The Japanese customs reports classify Tea in five divisions, and the 1898 figures for each are as follows :—

Tea, black (Oolong)	17,378,977 lbs.	Declared value Yen 5,696,841
Tea, black (Pouchong)	2,697,373 lbs.	„ „ Yen 526,733
Tea, bancha	199,766 lbs.	„ „ Yen 11,657
Tea, dust	200,564 lbs.	„ „ Yen 7,621
Tea, stalk	55.727 lbs.	„ .. Yen 3.244
Total	20,532,407 lbs.	Yen 6,246,096

FORMOSA POUCHONG EXPORT FROM COMMENCEMENT OF THE TRADE.

Season.	Total Export.	Average price Tamsui currency per picul (133 lbs.)	Season.	Total Export.	Average price Tamsui currency per picul (133 lbs.)
1881	40,666 lbs.	$ 26.25	1894	2,290,266 lbs.	...
1883	152,000 lbs.	$ 30.00	1895	2,700,000 lbs. (estimated)	...
1886	769,330 lbs.	$ 33.00	1896	2,279,900 lbs.	$ 26.00
1889	1,367,583 lbs.	...	1897	2,441,215 lbs.	$ 25 00
			1898	2,719,167 lbs.	$ 26.00
1893	1,966,833 lbs.	...	1899	2,911,636 lbs.	$ 26.16

The figures in both the above tables showing the export of Formosa Oolong to the United States and Europe, with the exception of the earlier years, are from the Amoy Chamber of Commerce returns, and are undoubtedly correct. The figures showing the total export including Pouchongs, etc., are from Chinese Customs Reports, the only available source for such returns, and for the last three years from the Japanese Customs Reports. The half chest of Oolong contains about 40 lbs. of Tea. Owing to the fact that, with the exception of the last few years, no separate entry was made in the Customs Reports which would show the export of Pouchong Tea, the table for the latter is incomplete. The fact that some Pouchongs are shipped direct and not landed at Amoy renders it impossible to obtain exact figures from the latter port, and again, as some small parcels not specified as Pouchongs when shipped from Formosa are later sold as such, the local customs figures are not wholly to be relied upon. But little more, therefore, can be claimed for figures in the Pouchong table than that they are approximately correct. Pouchong packages vary greatly in size, containing from 20 to 40 lbs. of Tea each.

CHAPTER XXIV.

THE CAMPHOR INDUSTRY.

The Camphor and savage questions inseparable—Formosan Forests—Price of Camphor in blood—Endless warfare—Camphor in the 16th century—First Formosan monopoly—Rebellion of 1722—Armed agriculturists occupy Camphor land—Nineteenth century traders—American firm secures Camphor monopoly—Taotai's agreement—Improvements at Takow—An American concession—Yearly export—English firms established—Monopolists defied—Foreign Governments interested—Le Gendre's Report—Increasing troubles with officials—Raid against foreigners—Camphor confiscated—$500 for a foreigner's head—British consul lands naval force at Anping—Monopoly abolished—Savages aggressive—Military forces in action—Governor's nephew and escort exterminated—Governor Liu takes the field—Tokoham campaign of 1891—Monopoly re-established—Stand taken by Formosan Government—Monopoly opposed by foreign representatives—Withdrawal of monopoly—Store tax introduced—Mandarins' private profit—Futile attempt to introduce Japanese stores—Speculator's unwise prophecy—Col. North's syndicate—Exciting speculation—Arrival of Japanese—Camphor industry of to-day—Location of Camphor forests—Soil—Manufacturing stations—Ports of shipment—A journey to the Camphor district—A Camphor station—Ascent of the mountains—Plant life in the hills—Rattan industry—Camphor forest—Home and life of Camphor tree described—Probable supply—Afforestation system required—Camphor trees in foreign lands—Industry in China—Value of tree apportionate to age—Cultivation of tree a questionable investment—Uses of tree apart from drug—Scientific cultivation—Record growth of Camphor trees in foreign lands—Tree-stripping—Savage district reclaimed by Camphor workers—Necessary requisites for Camphor manufacture—Camphor stills in operation—Probable effect of present monopoly—History of private ownership in Camphor district—Border life—Stockade life—Hakka pioneers—After-dinner contracts—Headhunting excursions—Border warfare—Victims of treachery—Savage prisoners—Camphor forest ownership—Armed artificers—Detailed description of construction of Chinese store—Distillers and their method of labor—From forest to still—Method of manufacture—Care of fire—Distillation—Financial arrangements—Arrival of Japanese and introduction of their stores—Detailed description of Japanese store—Operation of store in detail—Camphor

THE Camphor question is in reality the savage question, inasmuch as the success or failure of the industry is dependent upon the position occupied by the savages, and as, in a general account of either subject it would be quite difficult to separate them, I have included some material which may appear at first sight as more appropriate for the account of the Formosa savages given in a later chapter. It is only that phase of their life which has been exhibited in their contact with outsiders, who in this case prove to be Camphor workers or troops sent to protect the latter, that I make any pretence of recording here. I have also included such little information as can be obtained regarding other products of the forest besides Camphor.

Of all the products of Formosa none is of such interest as Camphor. The fact that it is snatched from the jungle over which the wild savage roams, and that it is not produced to any extent in any other part of the world, save Japan, accounts for this. It would be an inviting subject for the statistician, whose hobby is to study problems such as how many days consumption of matches placed end on end it would require to encircle the world, to figure out how many drops of human blood are represented in the few ounces of Camphor which the humane young lady purchases to keep her dainty garments free of moths, or how many lives are lost that some decrepid old gentleman may be cured of his rheumatic pains. The trees which produce this valuable article are unfortunately within the country of the aborigines or upon the immediate border of it. The methods of obtaining the drug adopted by the Chinese necessitates the destruction of the trees, which are never replaced : and while temporary permission is some- times granted by individual savages or their village headmen to work certain border districts, the aboriginal population as a whole naturally views with deep concern the gradual encroachment on their native soil : and, as a consequence, the border districts have, since the earliest days, been in a chronic state of disturbance. Every opportunity has been seized for the perpetration of outrages, and, sad to say, these outrages have not been on the part of savages alone, for the Chinese, on their side, seem never to have let slip any chance which presented itself of wreaking their vengeance on the unfortunate aborigines. The lives that during the last twenty-five years have been lost directly in consequence of this would sum up a very large number : while indirectly, for instance among soldiers sent into the savage districts to avenge the murder of some Camphor worker, and *vicé versâ*, among aborigines making a raid on Chinese peasants living near the border, there must have been a deplorable addition to the above mentioned loss of life. Statistics are not sufficiently complete to afford exact information, but the historical notes which follow will give some idea of the " butcher's bill."

Camphor is mentioned as an article of trade in the early history of Formosa, but whether it refers to the crystallized product of the tree, or simply to the wood which is used for building purposes, etc., is not clear.[1]

In the 16th century the Camphor forest extended down on to the plains, and along some of the plateaux, even to the west coast. At as comparatively late a date as 1868, Camphor trees were growing on the lower ranges of the hills north of Taipeh in the north, which are now given over to the cultivation of tea and other staples. The main supply, however, is now, as it always has been, in that vast district covering the mountain region stretching through the heart of the island from north to south.

Chinese historians tell us that, early in the 18th century, the government declared a monopoly in Formosa over Camphor and other products of the forest, the penalty for cutting down a single tree in contravention of the regulations being death. Under this rigorous law over two hundred people were decapitated in the one year 1720. This so enraged the colonists that two years later they broke out into a rebellion, during which many thousands lost their lives, and the capital of the island fell into the hands of Choo Yih-kwei, the rebel leader.[2] Although the government did not relinquish its

---

1. The early history of Camphor is wrapped in obscurity. While mention of the tree is found in several early records, there is not always evidence that the manufacture of the drug was practised. The first indisputable reference to the trade in the drug is made by Klaproth (Memoires Relatifs à l'Asie.—Paris 1824), who refers to the manufacture of Camphor as being one of the important industries of the island at the time of his visit in the early part of the present century. It is clear, however, that the crystallized product of the tree was known in very early days to the eastern nations, and that it was introduced into Europe by the Arabians. It has also been asserted that India was the first country to manufacture the drug, and 1,200 years ago a prince of that nation is said to have made a present of Camphor to the Chinese Emperor. At all events, the first intimate knowledge of the manufacture of the drug obtained by Europe, seems to have been got from India, and this land was the first customer for China's product, so that the known manufacture of Camphor in China dates back many centuries. Coreans were also acquainted with the drug, and it was they, who in later years, introduced the manufacture to Japan. Satsuma was the first province of Japan to profit by the instruction tendered by their neighbors, and some 180 years ago, sufficient Camphor was produced to place regular supplies in Nagasaki, where the drug was known as a special product of the above province. Later Kyushu, Shikoku, and other parts of Japan took up the manufacture. China, whether because she had exhausted the supply of available trees, or could not compete with Formosa and Japan, where trees were more plentiful, gradually withdrew from the industry, until at present the export of Chinese Camphor is practically nil.

2. See pages 70 to 73 Chapter V. for an account of this rebellion.

claims to a monopoly, the laws controlling the same were made more lenient, and, by the payment of certain royalties, work in the Camphor forests was permitted.

A boundary line established by the Formosan authorities in 1738, was expected to separate the savage regions, which the officials made no pretense of governing, from the Chinese district over which they nominally ruled. In 1788, a force of armed agriculturists, comprised of Pepohoans and other civilized aborigines, which had been formed by the authorities to aid in the subjection of Lim So-bun's rebel band, were given a large district of territory on the savage border, with permission to dispose of the Camphor growing within their respective boundaries, and afterwards to till the tree-denuded land so as to produce the necessary food-stuffs. For administrative purposes the concession was divided into six districts, and a tax was imposed. For some years the Pepohoans profited by their position and led a contented life ; but later on, their prosperity attracted the attention of unscrupulous Chinese, who stepped in, and by cunning and treachery gradually deprived the unfortunate pioneers of their possessions. From that period, (the beginning of the present century,) the Chinese, Hakkas chiefly, succeeded in controlling the manufacture. The savages have shown no disposition to engage in the industry themselves, work being regarded by them as quite on a level with small-pox, famine, and other plagues, while the more willing Pepohoans lost the opportunity from their own shiftlessness and general simplicity.

Upon the arrival of the first foreign traders, in the present century, the Chinese officials still claimed an exclusive monopoly of the Camphor industry. In 1855, an American, W. M. Robinet of Hongkong, the first foreigner in later days to engage in trade in Formosa, despatched a vessel, the American bark *Louisiana*, commanded by Captain Crosby, to Takow. The vessel returned with a profitable cargo, as did the *Santiago* which closely followed her. The success of these two voyages becoming known caused several other parties to take an interest in the trade.

Two American firms, Nye Bros. & Co. and Williams, Anthon & Co., contemplated starting at once permanent establishments, but were persuaded by Mr. Robinet to carry on business with him on joint account, and the new company at once bought the American bark *Science*, which was despatched, well armed and manned, to remain as a store ship, being commanded by Captain George A. Potter. At the same time the bark *Isabelita Hyne*, the ship *Architect*, and the schooner *Frolic* were sent over with funds to the amount of eighty thousand dollars and valuable presents for the authorities. An American, C. D. Williams, aboard the brig *Clarita*, accompanied the expedition, the first object of which was to inspect the various ports, select a site for an establishment, and enter into some agreement with the Formosan authorities. After calling on the officials at Taiwan (Tainan), he took passage in the *Frolic* and visited all the ports on the west coast as far to the north as Kelung. Mr. Williams' trip was successful, and he secured from the authorities an agreement giving his company the monopoly of all Camphor produced, and other trading privileges, as well as permission to form an establishment at Takow.[1] In consideration of these concessions, the Americans agreed that their vessels should pay one hundred dollars each voyage as tonnage dues, that they would protect Takow against pirates, and that, when necessary, they would furnish the authorities there with a ship to pursue the pirates, to be under the orders of the Chinese authorities and carry the Imperial flag during the time so employed. Captain M. Rooney was sent to Takow, and under his superintendence some improvements in shipping were introduced. A small channel which divided much of the water off the bar was filled up, and a signal station provided with a light was erected at the entrance to guide ships by day or night. On shore were constructed a granite storehouse capable of containing 1000 tons, two houses, and a wharf from which vessels could load. A considerable portion of the surrounding district was marked off, and over this small concession the American flag was flown. After an expenditure of the equivalent of $45,000 gold in these improvements, the Camphor promised was not forthcoming, and the first few vessels returned to the mainland with cargoes scarcely paying their expenses. Then the Americans, as merchants were wont to do in those early days, decided to force the authorities to carry out their agreement, and accordingly assembled their little fleet, making a naval demonstration before the astonished mandarins. On a visit to the *Science* being made by the prefect, the salute of three guns, with which it was customary to honor him, was withheld, and he was informed that forcible measures would be adopted if he did not act faithfully. The result was very satisfactory; as much Camphor was brought in as was wanted, with which and with other cargo, 78 vessels were in less than two years laden, bringing a large profit to the promoters. For coasting purposes a small schooner of 80 tons, the *Pearl*, was constructed and employed in collecting Camphor as fast as it was purchased by native agents stationed at the principal ports along the coast. Upwards of 10,000 piculs of Camphor were obtained yearly by the company at a cost of about $8.00 a picul, and sold at a very good price in Hongkong.

1. " Agreement entered into with the Taotai, or Intendant of Circuit in Formosa, about carrying on trade in the island.

" The Taotai grants the privilege of trading at Formosa to the owners of the ship *Science* on the following conditions:—

" The owners of the *Science* agree to protect the port of Takow against pirates with their ships; and whenever required by the Intendant or any other high officer, they will furnish a vessel to pursue pirates, which vessel, for the time being, shall be under charge of a Chinese Officer and carry his flag. They further agree to pay fifty dollars charges for each mast of every ship that loads for their account. The captain of the *Science* is to afford every facility and assistance to the authorities if it does not compromise his nationality.

" The Intendant, on his part, agrees to give the Captain of the *Science*, for the lawful trade to be carried on, every protection, and to see that all the Chinese merchants faithfully fulfil their contracts; and particularly the Camphor monopoly entered into with the Chinese contractors. He also grants to the Captain the privilege of building godowns to store goods, and permits him to place lights at the entrance of the Port on a flag-staff erected for such a purpose, and to station buoys on the bar. He will take measures that property of every kind shall be respected. Every hindrance is to be placed in the way of all other vessels attempting to trade in Formosa.

" It is also understood that, whenever there shall be a bad crop of rice and this grain become scarce, the Intendant's prohibition to export it shall be respected by the Captain of the *Science*; but

The successful operations of the American firm brought others into the field; and, after a vain attempt to interest the United States authorities in the island, the concession was sold to an English firm.

Upon the establishment of consular jurisdiction in the island (1861), two English firms, Jardine, Matheson & Co. and Dent & Co., shared the Camphor monopoly between them. Other foreign firms were, during the next two or three years, established in considerable numbers, the members of which strenuously opposed the monopoly as being an infraction of the treaty, discriminating as it did against individual enterprise.

There were, at this time, several settlers in the interior who possessed wealth and power enough to frequently defy the government authorities. It was common for them to sell Camphor to foreigners at Tamsui, and by providing the carriers with a large armed escort they were enabled to guarantee safe delivery at that port. This naturally resulted in frequent private wars, and on one such occasion, in 1863, about two thousand men were engaged on each side. Although the loss of life was small, it threw a large district into anarchy, and resulted in a considerable financial loss from the dislocation of trade.

On the ratification of the French and English treaties in 1860 and their subsequent enforcement, it was declared that the whole coast was not open to foreign trade, but only Tainan and Tamsui and its dependency Kelung. This was a blow to the foreign firms interested in the monopoly, as by visiting the west coast ports and thus getting nearer the field of production, they secured the Camphor at less expense and were better able to control the trade. The coasting vessels were withdrawn, and the foreigners concerned were obliged to confine their labors to the treaty ports. The monopolists purchased the Camphor from the producers at a very low figure and exported just enough to meet the demand at Hongkong without permitting the prices to fall; but now, with the additional expenses of transportation over-land, and the fact that the Camphor frequently got into other hands, the foreigners found it more difficult to pay the prices demanded by the government, while the consumers did not exhibit a willingness to meet the increased cost. A temporary lull in the trade resulted.

The Chinese compradores and others were not slow in availing themselves of the inactivity existing, and, though the contracts conceding to certain foreigners exclusive privileges had not been officially annulled, the Chinese above referred to practically rendered them nugatory by giving expensive presents to the mandarins, and obtaining thereby almost exclusive control of the trade! Every advantage and facility was afforded them by the officials, and every obstacle and hindrance placed in the way of foreigners trying to enter the market.

he shall be permitted to export all the rice which has already been contracted for,—within a month of the prohibition.

" It is further agreed that the Captain of the *Science* shall see that the crew of his ship, and also of other vessels coming to Formosa, shall not attempt to plunder or annoy the people, and shall be severely punished whenever they are found to do so.

Signed at Taiwan June, 27, 1855.

INTENDANT OF FORMOSA (L S.)
GEORGE A. POTTER (L.S.)

In 1865, there were at Takow the English firms of Jardine Matheson & Co., Dent & Co., and MacPhail & Co., at Tamsui and Kelung, the German firm James Milisch & Co., the American firm, Field, Hastus & Co., and the English merchant John Dodd, agent for Dent & Co. No little rivalry existed between these five firms in the Camphor trade. So much opposition, however, was shown them by the Chinese mandarins, who wished to corner all the profits connected with the industry, that affairs were very unsatisfactory, and so frequent were the resulting disturbances that the question came up before the English and American governments for solution. The stand taken by the foreigners was defined in a report by U.S. Consul Le Gendre to his government.

"If China had no treaties with foreign powers, in the present state of her relations with the Formosan tribes it could not be considered that the commercial and industrial liberties of the latter are interfered with by the collection of a tax on the products of the aborigines the instant the same pass their frontier. Therefore, there would be no legal grounds upon which to oppose the establishment of a government monopoly of the Camphor trade, within the limits of the island, under the immediate jurisdiction of the Chinese. But the privileges of the Empire, in this respect, have been singularly affected by the existing treaties. Heretofore, China could compel the foreign merchants, trading at the various ports, to deal exclusively with Chinese operators, called Hong merchants, who had been licensed by the native government for that purpose. The practice proved to be so injurious to the foreign trade that, in 1842, the British government took up the matter and made it a condition of peace to have it abolished. By Article V of the treaty of Nanking, of June, 1842, the Emperor of China agreed to permit British merchants residing at the treaty-ports to carry on their mercantile transactions with whatever persons they might choose to employ. The aborigines of Formosa are not excluded, and therefore the restrictions imposed upon our dealings with them by the monopoly heretofore existing could not be maintained, so long as the treaty remains in force."[1]

The Chinese, ever evasive, at first endeavored to overlook the question of the trade in the crystallized product as being petty and unworthy of their consideration, and produced for the inspection of the parties concerned a proclamation which declared that "in the mountains of every place the entire produce of timber is required for the navy, and no person shall be permitted to cut down the tree secretly. With regard to the article Camphor, in order to pay outlay for axes and saws and other implements, permission should be given to the (Government monopolist) foreman to erect sheds for its preparation, and he will be allowed to take and dispose of it as he pleases."[2]

1. Reports on Amoy and the Island of Formosa by C. W. Le Gendre, U.S. Consul at Amoy Government Printing Office, Washington, 1871.

2. *Proclamation on the Camphor monopoly issued by the Taotai of Formosa.* "By Imperial appointment, Military Intendant of Taiwan and the Pescadores with the power of Judge of Assizes, also Admiral, Director of the Board of Examination, and invested with the entire control of Military Affairs in Formosa.

Ting, Makes Proclamation. Whereas my office holds the vested right of establishing naval dockyards for the purpose of repairing and building vessels of war,

The timber required for such purpose from Foochow and Amoy I have already sent for, and now it is necessary that regarding that portion produced by this country I should give directions to foremen and linguists in each department that they may superintend its cutting down and conveyance to the naval dockyard. The two most important departments for the production of abundant naval timber are those of Tamsui and Komalan, (N. W. and N. E. Formosa).

Hence all the preceding Taotais have set separate foremen on the mountains of the said places to erect tents for the exercise of surveillance over the workmen and to make them shape the wood to the regulated lengths for conveyance to the sea ports, and after notifying to the managing office to carry it in boats for delivery to the dockyard for the requirements of the navy. This has long been the established rule. Now the former foreman of the Tamsui Department, *Kim Keshing*, yearly obstructed the delivery of the required cut timber and was by no means straightforward in his business. I, the present Taotai, having just taken over office, am desirous that the business of the dockyard be properly attended to, and will not suffer it again to be obstructed through remissness. I have therefore sent to deprive the said *Kim Keshing* of the (camphor) stamp accorded to him by the former Taotai *Hung*, and at the same time to confer it, of which deed this is the official notice, on *Kin Tai-chung* to invest him with the foremanship for the spring period, and the latter is expected to conform to its injunctions. The

The matter remained unsettled for some three years, and meanwhile rows and disturbances between the employés of the foreign firms and Chinese in the pay of the authorities resulted. Treachery and even murder were resorted to by the officials to keep the foreigners out of the trade.

During the year 1868, the conduct of the Chinese local officials became unbearable. In the north at Tamsui, during the early months of the year, several small lots of Camphor, which had been bought in the producing districts directly from the manufacturers by a foreign merchant, were conducted to Tamsui under the protection of an armed guard. This stirred up the monopolists, who resorted to a series of aggressive acts in the hope of rendering the trade so hazardous that foreigners would be induced to abandon it. With the assistance of hired agents, boats were stolen, boatmen in foreign employ were attacked and beaten, and employés of the foreigners were threatened with violence if they would not consent to desert their masters. Eventually an open conflict broke out, during which four or five natives were killed and several wounded. Some $6,000 worth of Camphor, the property of Elles & Company, was seized at Goche; but after pressure had been brought to bear by consular officials, the Chinese authorities agreed to restore it. However, upon Mr. Pickering, the firm's representative, attempting to visit Goche to inquire about the drug, which, notwithstanding the Taotai's promises, had not been restored, the Taotai issued a proclamation offering $500 for that gentleman's head. Subsequently, soldiers commanded by a military officer attacked him while in Lokiang (Rokko), and he was obliged to take refuge in a small boat, in which, after a dangerous journey, he reached Tamsui.

All business now came to a standstill, and attacks on foreigners, murders of Christians, destruction of foreign property, and other outrages became so alarming that Mr. Gibson, the British consul at Anping, was obliged to take a determined stand; British men-of-war were called to his assistance, a landing party took possession of Fort Zelandia, and after a skirmish, as described in a preceding chapter, drove the Chinese soldiers entirely out of the town. The effect of this exhibition of power was most

public are hereby informed that in the mountains of every place the entire produce of timber is claimed for the requirements of the naval dockyard, and no person shall be permitted to cut down trees secretly. With regard to the article Camphor, in order to pay outlay for axes and saws and other implements, permission should be given to the said foreman to erect sheds for its preparation, and he will be allowed to take and dispose of it as he pleases, as has been established by many precedents. Now I am informed that in the interior mountains certain persons are in the constant habit of secretly cutting down trees and stealthily preparing Camphor. Such malpractices are hereby strictly forbidden, and on the issue of this notice the public are enjoined respectfully to observe its restrictions, and assist in proclaiming its warnings that the law be not transgressed. And if any evil-disposed workman will not submit to be so restrained and in league with evil-disposed people secretly ascend the mountains and destroy the naval timber, and cut it up for secret use or secretly prepare therefrom Camphor for secret export with a view to personal profit, all such if taken in the act or convicted on evidence, shall be apprehended, and if they dare to make resistance information must at once be laid against them before the local authorities, who with the assistance of the military will seize the misdemeanants and deal with them severely and without leniency. The foreman is enjoined to be diligent in his duties and with regularity to cut down the timber, and report it for delivery without let or hindrance. Opposition will be punished. Respect this a special proclamation.

Reign Tungchih—2nd year, 9th moon, 25th day (6th November 1863).

salutary. Among other substantial results, the Camphor monopoly was abolished and a proclamation issued declaring the right of foreigners and their employés to go and buy freely; while an indemnity of $6,000 was paid to Elles & Co. for the loss of their Camphor.

The depressing effect which the monopoly had had on the Camphor trade became apparent at once when it was abolished. The export for the first six months following the date on which the monopoly was abolished amounted to 7,637 piculs against 1,313 piculs for the corresponding period in 1867. During the early part of the year, foreigners were obliged to pay to the monopolists $16 a picul for the drug, but immediately following the abrogation of the monopoly the price fell to $9, and for a short period even to $7.80. The enormous profits reaped by the monopolists, whose high prices were strangling the trade, were now open to free competition. At that period, however, the demand for Camphor was comparatively limited. Some found its way to India, where it was used in religious ceremonies, but the larger part was consumed in medicinal preparations, and the amount required for these purposes was not expected to vary much from year to year. Still it is not unreasonable to believe that the low price of the drug for the fifteen years following this period is responsible for its comparatively large consumption at present, inasmuch as its cheapness encouraged chemists to study more carefully its properties and to utilize it in several manufactures which are now firmly established, but which would probably not have been so, had the old or the present high rates prevailed.

Thus freed from government interference, several foreign firms engaged in the trade; the number of Chinese, principally Hakkas, employed in the manufacture on the border land of the savage territory increased greatly; and the aborigines were driven further and further into the interior, losing not only their lands but oftimes their lives. From an annual average in 1865-67 of 7,102 piculs the export increased to 14,240 piculs in 1868-70.

In 1875, the export decreased by half, owing to the extraordinary activity of savages, who were awakening to the fact that their lands on the west were fast falling into the hands of their enemies, the Chinese. Numerous savage raids were made on the Hakka woodsmen, and the necessary supply of Camphor chips was very difficult to obtain.

For the next five years the export improved somewhat, in 1880 amounting to 12,335 piculs. But from this year on, the trade fell away, until, in 1885, the export practically ceased, amounting to only 3 piculs (about 400 lbs.) for the year. Warfare between the Chinese and savages, which it is no exaggeration to say had existed in a greater or less degree from the first day of Chinese dominion in Formosa, reached this year to such a magnitude that it extended from the north of the island to the south, the border line being converted into one long battle-field, and the savages becoming so aggressive that they came out of the hills and attacked the plain villages; while the Chinese retaliated by firing large districts of forests, destroying the villages of the savages, and driving the inmates further into the interior.

Quite naturally the manufacture of Camphor came to a standstill. The next year large numbers of troops were employed against the savages : General Lin Chiau-tong marched 1,500 men against the tribes to the southeast of Tokoham (Taikokan) : a large force entered the east coast near Gilan ; and even Governor Liu himself for a few months took the field. In this year the Chinese losses were over 500, and during 1887 a general and 400 soldiers met their deaths on the east coast ; while later Lau, a nephew of the Governor Liu Ming-chuan, with his force consisting of 180 soldiers, was in the same district surrounded by the savages, and with the exception of one person, a young boy, totally annihilated, the savages escaping without the known loss of a single life.[1]

Though fighting did not by any means cease, it quieted down in some districts for the next few years, and it was not until the spring of 1891 that hostilities on a large scale broke out again. After a hundred or so of Camphor workers had been killed along the border, a large military force was again put in the field, a number of the villages near the savage territory were garrisoned, and later a large expedition marched against the savages near Tokoham. To describe the numerous troubles would be to repeat much that has been given in a former chapter ; and in leaving the subject it is sufficient to point out that up to the occupation of the island by the Japanese, scarcely a month elapsed without a combat between the savages and the Chinese braves.

From the year 1868, when the government monopoly was abolished, foreigners were permitted to buy Camphor in the interior and to transport the same to the coast, transit passes being issued for that purpose. But after the French war, the heavy expenditure connected with the campaign was made an excuse by the Chinese to again establish a Camphor monopoly. The stand taken by the governor of Formosa is thus described in the Custom Reports.[2] "The Camphor forests, reclaimed by warfare from the savages and brought under cultivation at government expense, are the property of the Crown, and that instead of utilizing the natural resources of such crown land under official administration they permit Chinese settlers (and traders) to do so. This can only

---

1. The details of this slaughter are as follows:—The Chinese were encamped for the night in the savage district, and with characteristic stupidity had no men detailed on outpost duty. Thus while wrapped in slumber to a man, doubtless confident that the morrow would bring them victory, they were quietly surrounded by the savages, who suddenly attacked them from all sides, with great noise, and cut them down one by one as they arose from their sleep. Not a shot was fired, and there was no opportunity for defence, even had the Chinese been prepared for a sudden attack, which appears doubtful. A young Chinese boy, a servant of Lau, the governor's nephew, escaped into the long grass and lay there hidden until the massacre was over and the savages had retired. He then reached the border districts, and later Taipeh, where the alarming tale was made known. Admiral Ting with several men-of-war was now ordered to the east coast, and Governor Liu decided to avenge the death of his nephew and party in person, and accordingly took command of a considerable force which was marched into the offending district. Quite a quantity of contact mines had been constructed in the Taipeh arsenal especially for use on this occasion, and having reached the scene of operations these mines were carefully buried along a leading pathway. An attack was then made on the savages, and following it the Chinese made as if to retire, and withdrew taking up a position some distance from the pathway where, nearest one of the largest mines, they had left a flag. The savages, believing the Chinese were weakening, rushed after them, and crossing the pathway, some thirty of their number were killed by the exploding mines. Not caring to cross arms in regular combat, Liu returned reporting a great victory, but in fact the engagement was a failure and the savages actually were able to push further out and to occupy land which at one time had been seized from them. Chinese government forces in that district were then withdrawn.

2. Dr. Hirth in the Tamsui Trade Report for 1891. Imperial Chinese Maritime Customs.

be done on conditions the framing of which rests with the government." The monopoly was farmed for a term of three years, the farmer agreeing to pay $12, the same to include Likin, and to deposit $5,000. While the monopoly was in the name of a compradore, it was in reality held by Lauts and Haesloop, then of Anping, who later transferred it to Reuter, Brockelmann & Co. of Hongkong, the price paid for Camphor increasing to $17½, and later to $20 a picul.

This was in direct opposition to the signed agreement of the authorities when abolishing the monopoly in 1869, and the foreign representatives quite naturally protested. The governor, however, strongly maintained that the rights of the government to the produce of the crown lands was indisputable, and that no restriction would be placed on foreigners buying from private dealers at places near the coast. Much trouble resulted, and Camphor purchased by foreigners was on a few occasions seized. As during the monopoly in early days, trade was much disturbed, the export for the years 1887 to 1889 averaging only about 4,000 piculs.

Fortunately for the Camphor trade, chemists brought before the world several useful inventions in which Camphor formed a useful ingredient ; celluloid, smokeless explosives, fireworks, etc. ; and in 1888 and 1889, it was thought that the demands for Camphor would be so great to supply these new wants that the market price rose about 100 per cent. At this point, Count A. Buttler of Tamsui made an offer to the Chinese authorities of $30 a picul which was accepted, and the trade passed into his hands and was held by him for nine months. Under the former rates, but little profit had accrued to the mandarins, but now about $18 clear gain was obtained. The distiller was, however, not much better off, the government allowing but $12 for the original cost and for local transportation. The protests by foreign representatives now became more pronounced, and the system of monopoly was abolished early in 1891. It was then announced that a tax of $18 on every picul produced would be imposed to defray the expenses of the military stationed on the savage border. This excessive tax met also with such opposition that it was replaced by a tax of $8 imposed on each stove, counting ten jars to a stove,[1] and likin of 57 cents a picul became payable when the Camphor was transported. An ordinance was also published at this time, prohibiting purchases in the producing districts, buyers being obliged to resort to one of four inland Camphor depots established by the government. This being an infringement on treaty rights was soon withdrawn. As in 1869, the abolition of the monopoly was marked by a great spurt in the amount of export, the figures reaching 18,881 piculs for the unrestricted trade of 1891, against 7,242 piculs for 1890. The stove tax remained in force until the arrival of the Japanese, and was a very imperfect and unjust method of taxation, and unsatisfactory to all responsible merchants.[2]

1. The distilling apparatus in use in Formosa is commonly called a stove.

2. The faults in the Camphor stove tax were many. It was difficult to keep a proper control over the stoves. Producers naturally did not wish to pay when the stoves were not working, and, frequently either from a scarcity of wood or water, lack of laborers, or from troubles with the savages, it was found

The mandarins profited largely by the trade, as the following figures will show: According to the amount produced by the average Chinese stove, it would require 16 jars to produce 125 catties of Camphor, which, with loss in weight and allowance for water, is considered to be about a picul in weight when shipped from the island. At the rate of taxation on a ten jar stove, this picul would be subject to a tax of $12.80, and, as the total output for 1892 was 17,540 piculs, the tax collected must have amounted to about $224,500, whereas only $95,000 was reported to Peking; while in 1893, it was about $426,000 collected against $160,000 reported.

A year prior to the war between Japan and China, some six or seven Japanese Camphor-men arrived on the island to establish the Japanese system of Camphor manufacture. They erected stoves near Taiko (Twao), but, owing to the indirect opposition of the Chinese, they were unable to make much progress. A few months after their arrival, some of the workmen died of fever, two or three literally starved to death owing to a flooded river which cut them off from all communication for a considerable period, and eventually the sole survivor gave up in despair, and left the island for Hongkong.

With the occupation of Formosa by the Japanese, and the reported hostilities of the natives toward them, it was thought that warfare in the interior would put a stop to the manufacture of Camphor, and that the commodity would accordingly become scarce, and the price correspondingly high. Furthermore, it was believed that a heavy tax would be placed on the drug by the victors, thus enhancing the value of Camphor held outside. This naturally attracted the attention of speculators, and a famous operator, Colonel North, organized in London a syndicate to purchase all the Camphor on offer, and in this way to obtain a corner on the drug. Crude Camphor of the Formosa grade was then bringing in London about $20 gold per cwt. News of the syndicate seems to have leaked out, however, and prices were put up on the buying brokers until $27 gold was reached; and then to the dismay of the syndicate, it was found that the Japanese operations in the island were not interfering with the export, and that there seemed no end to the supplies. Three members of the syndicate are said to have been so disgusted with the outlook that they threatened to unload

---

necessary to discontinue the distilling in certain stoves. If the owner desired to resume work with his stoves at some future date when conditions had become more favorable, a private arrangement was necessary, and this became the frequent cause of dishonest tricks on the part of the producer, and afforded abundant opportunity for the petty officers to squeeze. This system also induced hired distillers, whom it was difficult for the employer to watch, to sell the Camphor produced to unscrupulous traders who paid no taxes and were therefore able to offer a higher price for the drug, thus working great injustice to the real owner of the stoves who paid the taxes. The tax was unfair as it discriminated against certain distillers, and favored others. For instance, by taxing the stove instead of the production, the man with a poorly located stove yielding but a half picul of Camphor had to pay twice the sum proportionately paid by the owner whose stove yielded a picul, and four times the sum paid by the happy possessor of a stove yielding two piculs. The result was that producers with stoves of a low output were unable to maintain their laborers in an honest way, and were obliged either to pay heavy bribes to the officials or abandon their stoves and Camphor wood, which, under other circumstances, would not have been lost. Again the system encouraged a useless waste of trees; the distillers, being anxious to obtain heavy productions from their stoves to lessen their tax, selected only the lower portion of the tree and the roots which give the most Camphor, while the rest of the tree was allowed to rot, and frequently a whole tree after having been cut down was abandoned, if there was a suspicion that it would not yield high returns.

their shares; and, to avoid total collapse, the remaining members bought the discontented ones out. Camphor now reached the highest prices ever known. In October 1895, American refiners were bidding as high as $50 gold per cwt. without success, and refined Camphor was quoted in the New York market at 65 cents (gold) per pound in barrels and cases. In November, the price fell to 59 cents, and soon after the death of Colonel North, in May 1896, it dropped to 46 cents.

Formosa was naturally sympathetic with these movements. From $37 (Mexican) per picul in January 1895, Camphor rose to over $97 in October, but fell in early November to $65, recovering to $90 in December. From $90 in February of the next year, the price gradually declined, and in June, on the news of Colonel North's death, it fell suddenly to $36. It can be easily seen from these figures that 1895 and 1896 were very exciting years in the trade, and the chances of making fortunes and equally of losing them were most abundant. The manufacturers and local dealers, as a rule, profited greatly, and in direct contradiction to the prophecies of the speculators, the export for the island for the year 1895 exceeded 52,000 piculs (6,916,000 lbs.), the largest in the history of the trade.

This brings us down to the present occupation of the island by the Japanese, and we will now deal with the industry as it exists to-day. After years of destruction without replanting, the forests in which the Camphor trees are found are now limited to that vast tract of mountainous territory stretching from the far north to the south, and extending to the east coast of the island. The savages, helpless without the friendly protection of the woods, have retired with the disappearing forests, but have tenaciously stuck close to the border, and in most districts disputed inch by inch the advance of the Camphor workers. Although the trees are found throughout the mountainous district from north to south, they are most abundant in the north-central districts, and gradually decrease towards the south, few. trees of commercial value being found south of the 22nd parallel. The trees seem to grow best on moderate slopes at elevations not exceeding 4,000 feet, where the soil is well drained and consists of a rich vegetable mould and where the sun's rays can reach them.[1] Only glimpses have been caught of the vast interior districts, and but little is known as to the area of forests in which the Camphor tree is found; but, according to an estimate made by a Japanese expert, it is expected to reach over 1,500 square miles in extent.

Of the Camphor stations now existing, Tokoham (Taikokan), Lamshun (Namsho), Twao (Taiko), Tang-si-kak (Tosei kaku) are the most important in the north, and Chip Chip (Shushu), Polisha, and Linkipo in the centre. Camphor exists and has been worked in other places, but owing either to the difficulties of transportation or the too powerful opposition of the savages, the stoves have been abandoned, and with the exception of some small and unimportant stations, the manufacture is limited to the above mentioned

---

1. In some countries, where experiments have been made in the growing of the Camphor tree, sandy or loamy soil, provided it is well drained, has given very satisfactory results, the growth of the tree being very rapid.

places. Teckcham (Hsinchiku), Maoli (Bioritsu), and Goche, (Gosei) are important local markets, and much of the drug passes through these places to the ports of Tamsui and Kelung whence the Camphor is exported. Anping in the south, which at one time exported considerable Camphor, has been practically out of the trade for the last two years.[1] Takow, the other southern port, has shipped no Camphor since 1889.

That the reader may the better understand the Camphor industry I will ask him to follow me on an imaginary journey to the Camphor districts. There are no stations near the railway or along the main roads of travel, and it will be necessary for us to pierce the wild jungle and to travel over roads which no conveyance, not even the light mountain chair, can pass. We must, therefore, count on a rough tramp, fully compensated for, however, by the magnificence of the scenery and the uniqueness of a journey into the territory of the savage head-hunters.

Tokoham (Taikokan) is the nearest Camphor station to Taipeh-fu the cas pital, and can be easily reached in a day. However, the southern station offert greater inducements in splendid scenery, and it is to the important distric near Lamshun (Namsho) that I would take the reader. An interesting railway journey of 40 miles southward from Twatutia (Daitotei) brings us to Teckcham (Hsinchiku), where, unless we are in great haste, we spend the night. The next morning finds us spinning along on the little narrow-gauge railway, our toy passenger-car pushed by interesting Hakka coolies, men and girls. Tofun, 14 miles from Teckcham, is reached in two or more hours if the weather is favorable, and here we take our tiffin and secure our chair for the four hour trip straight towards the interior to Namsho, the border village. Leaving Tofun we cross a river, which has, for a short distance, a large stone dyke to prevent it overflowing in time of flood. As we proceed, the scenery changes. We leave the level tracts of cultivated land with its rice-fields, and gradually ascend into the foot-hills. Here, on the red sandy loam, we find numerous tea-gardens and some patches of ramie. Crossing over the first range of hills we enter a valley rather sparsely settled, and, having crossed it, find nestling at the foot of the mountains, our destination, the village of Namsho. It is a queer looking little settlement. A large number of small one-storeyed huts packed together with no trace of ornamentation, and every structure just like its neighbor. Quarters can be obtained here in a Japanese restaurant sufficient to shelter us for the night. We will do well to call on the Japanese chief of the local office and also perhaps on one or two of the principal Camphor merchants. I assume that we have provided ourselves with the necessary permission to cross the border, which is withheld only when the trip is considered especially dangerous. Doubtless the head of the police will provide us with one or

---

1. The cause of this stoppage of Anping exports was largely due to troubles and disputes with the officials in the Camphor districts and the fact that the disturbed condition of the country interfered with the transportation of both treasure and Camphor. Furthermore, during the Chinese regime steam launches were not allowed to engage in the coasting trade, and the Camphor from mid-Formosa ports was carried by junks. During the north-east monsoon, junks could not well make the trip to the north, and therefore during the winter months the drug was carried to Anping for export. Now steam launches are free of restriction and bring the Camphor to the northern ports at all times of the year.

more armed guards, and we may be so fortunate as to be accompanied by some Japanese engaged in the Camphor industry, who can intelligently describe to us the methods of manufacture.

We start early in the morning for our inland trip. Leaving the village and crossing a mountain stream, we come to a slightly elevated plot, on which stand several newly erected official buildings, which, when I visited the place, were occupied by the police inspector, the only Japanese officer stationed in the district. We see here the Chinese police or *kotei* as they are called by the Japanese. These hardy "sons of Han" are armed and uniformed, and, together with their Japanese companions, protect the district against savage raids, and also perform the usual duties of civil police in the village and neighborhood. A short distance from the river, situated in the centre of a beautiful grove of bamboo, we come to the roomy house built entirely of bamboo, occupied by Shi-ta-boi, a wealthy civilized savage chief. Although of like design, save for its size, to the structures possessed by his wild brethren in the interior, I was surprised, at the time of my visit in 1898, to find what a neat and well arranged affair it was. A mud-wall which surrounded the place and was provided with loop-holes for defensive purposes was well built, and the entire premises, so far as cleanliness was concerned, would have passed the most critical inspection. Inside the house was one large room with a sunken fire-place in the centre and mat beds raised a foot from the floor against the side walls. The furniture was very scanty, consisting only of a few Chinese benches. A gaudily colored foreign clock was the only ornament. On the occasion of my visit, the chief was absent, and the single servant present, a middle aged savage with the customary tattoo marks on the forehead and chin, moved about the place most languidly, not taking the least notice of his inquisitive guests. He did not understand a word of Chinese, and there being no one present conversant with the savage dialect we were obliged to satisfy our curiosity by personal observations, unaided by any explanations from this son of the forest. In accordance with all the traditions of his fellow savages in the hills, the door-way of the building was decorated with skulls. In this case monkey skulls were apparently considered about the nearest substitute for the human article, although I was informed that the chief has his own private collection of Chinese skulls, which, living, as he does, within Japanese jurisdiction, he dares not expose to the gaze of the multitude.

A short distance beyond, we commence our laborious ascent of the mountains. Our pathway is but a narrow trail, and we march along single file, our guard on the constant look-out, the forest growing more dense as we proceed. It is a dark wilderness we enter with no trace of habitations and a vegetation so dense that any side-excursions are quite out of the question, and even along the trail we must frequently brush aside the tall grasses which impede our progress. Such a mass of twisted and entwining plant life, impenetrable and shutting out the light and sun, it is difficult to comprehend without actually seeing it. Mother earth seems almost unnecessary; for the innumerable varieties of parasitical plants, drawing nourishment from the growths to which they are attached, are everywhere prominent. The rattan and other huge creepers, some as thick at root as a man's leg, wind erratically through the forest from tree to tree, binding all together in an endless chain, and affording support for countless plants, which hang down in graceful festoons. The rattan, wild in the forest, is far from recognizable as the smooth and shiny article which it appears when prepared for the foreign market. In the forest it is a dark-green climbing plant covered with sharp hooked thorns, growing sometimes to a length of 500 or more feet, and forming, where it is most plentiful, a natural barricade—which foot-soldiers would not care to charge. Here is the home of the Formosan head-hunter, and here he lies unseen and unheard, ready to pounce down on any unwary Chinese who may happen to pass by.

Rattan for export is obtained from this and like wild districts by a considerable number of Chinese, who are regularly engaged in this industry. The climber having been cut at the foot of the trunk, the workman pulls the long rope-like plant out, or, if this is not successful, advances knife in hand, and cuts away the clinging incumbrances, unwinding and disentangling the rattan as he proceeds. Not infrequently his movements are watched by the treacherous savages, and as he bends down at his labor he is shot or speared in the back. The rattan is used in the island in considerable quantities in lieu of rope, which for many purposes it excels. Suspension-bridges supported solely by rattan cables exist near the savage border. It is shipped to Hongkong and China where it is made up into furniture.[1]

At the lower levels few Camphor trees are seen; in fact so thick is the mass of tangled undergrowth and ferns that it is very difficult to tell what the jungle does contain. As we ascend, we find the mass of ferns, palms, and grasses gradually thinning, and an occasional giant tree makes its appearance, an outpost of the Camphor forest beyond us. The path now winds around the side of a cliff, the pathway scarcely wide enough to afford a foothold, while a single mis-step means a fall down the almost perpendicular precipice. The inexperienced among our party instinctively cling to the wall, while our Chinese guards, and even the coolies laden with Camphor, walk erect with not a trace of fear. Further on, we cross a deep ravine; a single fallen tree stretches across from bank to bank, and over this unsteady bridge our Chinese hill-men run with the agility of professional tight-rope walkers, though the timid tourist will, no doubt, elect to straddle it and help himself along with his hands. During the dry season it is usually possible to enter down into the ravine, and thus cross without testing such primitive bridges.

---

1. The export of rattan from Formosa, nearly all of it obtained from the savage districts, amounted, in 1897, to 1,488 piculs (198,700 lbs.) valued at 7,818 yen, and is shipped chiefly from Lokiang (Rokko), Keluug, Takow, and Anping, and finds a market in Hongkong and China. The price in Japan at present is 6 yen a picul, and as rattan brings only some 3 yen a picul in Formosa, a good export to Japan should be built up. The growth of rattan in Formosa is of great interest to botanists. The Malay Archipelago is the home of the rattan, in fact the name is undoubtedly derived from the Malay term " Ro-tang." Rattan is found in Formosa, Hainan, and the adjacent mainland, which has led some authorities to believe that it is a stranger in both islands, the plant being carried up from the Malayan Archipelago by the " Black Stream," which sweeps along the east coast with an average velocity of 30 to 40 miles a day (See Hosie's Consular Report, Commercial No. 11, published by British Government, 1893).

Now and then, as we come out on the clearing, the most magnificent mountain views appear before us. The nearest hills, clothed with dense forest, form a picturesque foreground for the dark blue masses of the high range beyond, and Mount Sylvia with its wave-like peaks, which were, during my first visit, covered with snow, makes in winter a superb crown. We continue to ascend higher and higher, and more numerous and larger become the trees. Now the pathway is so bad and the incline so steep, that we are frequently obliged to lay hold of the reeds and bushes along the path and pull ourselves up. Still there is an end to all things, even high hills, and after a last climb we see to our great relief a little clearing, with a few one-storey houses, a number of odd looking creations emitting a little smoke, which we later learn are the Camphor stoves; our destination, the Camphor station, *Shi-ju-pun*, has been reached, and our seven and a half miles' steady climb is at an end.

The Camphor laurel does not monopolise the forests in which it appears. It is, in fact, only one of several different varieties of trees which are found growing together. Camphor trees of various sizes are fairly numerous, but big trees, such as the Camphor worker most desires, are found only here and there, sometimes only a few rods, and again a third of a mile or more, apart. The Camphor tree attains an enormous height and girth in Formosa, and is properly the king of the forest. Trees are frequently seen with a circumference at base of twenty-five feet, a few reach even to thirty-six feet, and some have been observed in the island which required at least a forty foot line to reach around them. Nor are these measurements those of a knotted irregular body, for the Camphor tree is as straight and fine-formed a tree as one meets with, and as handsome a one as exists. Commercially the value of the material obtained from the felled tree places the Camphor laurel among the most valuable of trees. A tree forty feet in circumference would keep a single distilling stove supplied with material for several years, and would yield several thousand dollars worth of Camphor. Trees of average richness, measuring twenty feet around, which are often met with, would supply a stove for some two years, and, at the present price of Camphor, yield nearly two thousand yen worth of the drug. One tree near Tokoham (Taikokan), on land in which foreigners were interested, furnished chips for twenty Chinese stoves and yielded over $3,000 worth of Camphor, and that when the drug was bringing but $27 per picul. The trees, however, from which most of the Camphor is obtained, measure some twelve feet in circumference and yield something over fifty piculs of crystallized Camphor, at present valued at about fifteen hundred yen. Alarmist reports notwithstanding, the supply of Camphor trees in Formosa, assuming that the depletion of the forests continues at the same pace as at present, is still sufficient for the needs of the whole world for the next century. This, however, should not be taken as any excuse for the present wholesale destruction. The government would be very short-sighted if it did not introduce some system of afforestation by which trees destroyed would be replaced; for the future welfare of the island should be as much a matter of concern to the authorities as its present well-being. Furthermore, the difficulties of transportation increase as the Camphor seekers advance towards the interior, and it is necessary to guard against the drug reaching too high a price; lest scientists should be tempted to find some substitute, or other lands be induced to enter on the cultivation of Camphor.[1] Many of the hills on which the tree is found are not suitable for ordinary agricultural purposes, and these should be planted to Camphor. In other places it is a matter of doubt whether agricultural produce would not be of greater value, for it must be taken into consideration that, so far as we now know, from forty to fifty years are required before the tree reaches a sufficient size and richness in the drug to be of a value equal to the trees in the virgin forest, and that land devoted exclusively to Camphor would yield no income for that period.[2] A happy solution of this difficulty would be to plant in such situations as would permit of agricultural products being grown at the same place and time.

Apart from the drug, the tree yields a valuable wood for general purposes, ship-building, and cabinet work. Clothes boxes made of this wood are especially esteemed, owing to the Camphor scent being obnoxious to insects. Furthermore, the shade afforded by this evergreen would be specially useful for certain cultures,—e.g. coffee, cacao, vanilla, etc.

1. The high values reached and the increased demand for Camphor during the last ten years, has induced enterprising people in several countries to make investigations with the hope of introducing the Camphor industry into their own lands. Although the Camphor laurel is found wild in but a limited area in East Asia, it has been proven that it will grow readily in many parts of the earth and under various conditions of soil and temperature. In Italy, South-eastern France, California, South Carolina and Florida, Madagascar, Brazil, Egypt, Ceylon, the Canary Islands, and many other countries, it has been cultivated with most satisfactory results, and in experiments made, comparatively young trees in new lands have shown richness in the drug in some cases exceeding trees of like age in Eastern Asia. The Agricultural Department of the United States Government has taken an interest in the subject, and Florida and other Southern States may in future years become producing districts. The officials connected with the Government Gardens in Ceylon are actively carrying on investigations: several small plantations have already been set out, from which planters are being supplied with cuttings, while a still has been set up for experimental purposes. Even China, which of late years had practically ceased the manufacture of the drug, was stimulated into action by the high prices ruling during the Japan and China war, and the Chinese Customs " Trade Reports " show that during 1895, when prices reached their highest, China was able to export 1,756 piculs (233,548 lbs.), this being produced principally in the provinces of Chekiang, Kwangsi, and Fokien. The Camphor tree abounds in the central and southern provinces of China, and giants of the forest, 24 to 28 feet in circumference, are found in Kiangsi province.

2. It is quite possible that trees which are carefully cultivated on scientific principles will reach a growth and possess sufficient Camphor to yield a profitable return in a much less time than forty or fifty years. Under favorable conditions, the Camphor tree may repeat in a general way the history of the Cinchona tree in Ceylon. When the cultivation of the tree was first proposed, Ceylon capitalists looked unfavorably on the venture, for the history of the tree in its native environment made it appear that returns must be so long waited for; but in actual cultivation, the Ceylon planters soon narrowed down the period to a few years; and the product was of such a quality that Camphor cuttings planted in a government garden in Ceylon and carefully nursed have at the end of two years developed into vigorous trees, while leaves and twigs from these young growths have been found to be as rich in Camphor as the trunk of the tree. It is recorded that, in Italy a Camphor tree, in eight years from the planting of the seed, had attained a height of 90 feet and a circumference of over 3 feet; a tree planted in New Orleans in 1883 is now a sturdy fellow over 5 feet in circumference, although oddly, in comparison with the Italian tree mentioned, only some 40 feet in height. These two cases are undoubtedly exceptional, however, and an American botanical expert, Lyster H. Dewey, states as the result of experiments in America, that an average height of 30 feet, with a circumference of say 30 inches, may be expected in trees ten years from the seed. No attempt having been made to cultivate the Camphor trees in Formosa, no information can be given as to the probable rate of growth in this island. It is barely possible that, under some conditions, it may be found that Camphor can be obtained from the tree without cutting it down, as is at present done in Formosa and Japan. The tree might yearly be stripped of its leaves and twigs, and from them the drug be obtained. Leaves and twigs from trees in Florida less than 20 years of age have yielded about 1½ per cent. of the crystallized product.

Much as there is to be said against the old Chinese custom of destroying the tree without restriction and without replacing it, it must be admitted that the present occupation of the foot-hills by peaceful agricultural Chinese, the placing of the border line far in the interior in the north and west, the limitation of the scene of savage outrages to the main range of mountains, are due to the rapid advance of the Camphor workers and the destruction of the forest. Had it not been for the lucrative profits of the Camphor trade, or if the planting of new trees had been carried on from the first, the probability is that the Chinese would have shown no desire to risk their lives in the mountains, but would have settled down near the foot-hills, content with the yield from the plantations, while the savages would have roamed supreme over the virgin forest. And it may be some consolation to know that, even should the old system be allowed to continue, it will at least result in the eventual conquest of the whole island. So long, however, as the forests exist to shelter the savages, so long will they be able to preserve practically their independence; and unless the government is prepared to provide them with rations and supplies, as is done by the United States in their reservation system for the Indians, continual trouble is bound to result.

Given an abundance of trees, the next important requisite is water, without which the manufacture could not be carried on. Facilities of transport, and last, but not least, protection against the attacks of the savages, both those occupying the adjacent forest and those from afar who occasionally go considerable distances when a raid is planned, are equally to be considered.

Chinese and Japanese have now the control of the industry, foreigners being practically out of the business. The number of stoves in each district varies greatly,[1] the number in operation at any one time depending upon the price of the drug at that time. With the bringing into operation of the Camphor monopoly, and the correspondingly low prices paid by the government for the drug, certain districts, Bioritsu (Maoli) and Taichu chiefly, will suffer, and the number of stoves in each will undoubtedly be greatly lessened. Other small producing districts, such as Toroku (Taulak), Horisha (Polisia), and Gilan, will probably give up the manufacture altogether. Tokoham, owing to the low

1. The Camphor producing districts with the number of Camphor stoves (stills) in operation in January 1899 are as follows:—

Bioritsu (Maoli) district	1356 stoves.
Shinchiku (Teckcham) district	914 ,,
Taichu district	314 ,,
Saukakuyu (Saukakeng) district	241 ,,
Nanto (Namtau) district	191 ,,
Gilan district	23 ,,
Horisha (Polisia) district	13 ,,
Toroku (Taulak) district	5 ,,
Total	2057 ,,

In addition to the above, there are doubtless a number of stoves run secretly without government consent.

rates of transportation between it and Taipeh, will, under the monopoly, quite likely become the chief producing district in Formosa. In Tokoham, Japanese control most of the production, but in the other places mentioned they share it with Chinese, who, as a rule, have in each place the largest number of stoves.

It will now be necessary to take a step back into history to explain fully the procedure by which the Chinese obtained the right of cutting down the Camphor trees, and the reason of the frequent quarrels with the savages over the matter. A score or so of years ago, the inhabitants, chiefly Hakkas, living along the border were inclined to dispute the authority of the mandarins. Criminals from Canton were, in the early part of the century, banished to Formosa, and their descendants, together with other daring and oftimes unscrupulous fellows, who chose a life away from the uncertain pleasures of Chinese civilization, constituted a force sufficient to establish little settlements along the savage border, capable of protecting themselves not only from the savages but from extortion on the part of the authorities as well. Nearly every little settlement possessed a two-storeyed fort-like structure, to which the women and children could retire in case of trouble, and in the more dangerous districts the huts were surrounded with a strongly built stockade. John Dodd, the well-known pioneer of North Formosa, who was a frequent visitor to the Camphor districts in those early days, describes a night in the stockades as follows :—

"During the night, in such quarters there is not much sleep to be got. When the savages are on the war-path a good deal of powder is wasted, and shots are fired at intervals through the night to show that the inmates are awake and quite prepared for an attack. The life in a stockade--whether of stone or of the shanty type—is not a pleasant one, especially in the hot weather and at nights. Let alone the heat, either the mosquitoes worry your life out or the smoke from the mosquito fire almost suffocates you. Bundles of a dried fuzzy sort of shrub are lighted, which burns slowly throughout the night emitting dense fumes of smoke, which, if it does not asphyxiate the mosquitoes, certainly drives them into the open. To make matters worse the "cooeying" of savages in the woods, the yelping of pariah dogs, and a constant feeling that you are being or will be suffocated shortly, does not assist you to find repose. In the morning you get up feeling more like a baked owl than anything else, and with smarting eyes you hail the morn with delight."

It was these Hakka pioneers who produced the first Camphor in Formosa, and the methods they introduced were pretty well followed by the Chinese right down to the occupation of the island by the Japanese. The Formosa savages are very fond of roast pig and samshu,[1] a weakness which has resulted in the loss of a good deal of territory. The Hakkas by promising to give at certain seasons of the year a few pigs, a jar or so of samshu, some rice and salt, and such like articles, with perhaps a little gunpowder, found that the savages were willing to permit them to cut down the Camphor trees in a certain district. The agreements were usually entered into during the progress of a feast, at which the Hakkas had taken due care to see that their guests were "well charged" with drinkables. Once, however, firmly established in the new district and their position sufficiently strong, the settlers were inclined to forget all about their promises of pig and samshu ; but, unfortunately for the Hakkas, the poor savage had a very expressive way of showing his disapproval of such conduct. The wild man from some hidden spot on the hill-top patiently waited

1. An intoxicating drink made by the Chinese from rice.

until the settler left for the forest, and then speeding down with stealthy foot he sought a friendly clump of underbrush near the pathway along which he knew his man would pass. Here as quiet as death he watched until the unsuspecting Chinese passed ; then crouching he left his retreat, followed for a few steps, and then upright, with the full strength of his sinewy arm the spear was thrown. His victim falls to the ground severely wounded, the savage promptly finishes the deed with a long knife, and, severing the head from the body, throws it in the bag which he carries for the purpose, and disappears in the forest. Fighting now begins in dead earnest on both sides. The Hakkas, perhaps, band together, attack and burn a savage village, lives are lost on both sides, and, perhaps, prisoners are taken, who if they are of the female sex, or males who would prove useful as hostages, are not usually killed. After a considerable number of lives have been lost, a reconciliation meeting will be held, more roast pig and samshu puts the savages in good humor, new promises are made, and the savages return to their mountain homes, to break out again when some new act of treachery or unfaithfulness enrages them.

It sometimes occurred, however, that the border settlers were so strongly opposed by the savages, and that the latter exhibited so much determination not to part with their lands, that the Chinese adopted other methods of attaining their object. Some years before the arrival of the Japanese, a foreigner visited the Camphor district near San-kak-eng (San-ka-ku-yu), and upon entering the hut occupied by one of the leading dealers, he found two savages securely bound. Surprised at this, he made inquiries and was very coolly informed that they, the Chinese, had invited the savages down to confer with them, and that they were now negotiating with the prisoners for a plot of Camphor ground, but as their guests had refused to accede to the terms of the agreement as laid down by the Chinese, they had seized and bound them, and they would hold them prisoners until they acquiesced, which it was expected they would do. If they should prove too stubborn, the Chinese added, they would probably kill them.

Another instance occurred at Tai-ko-kan (Tokoham) in 1880. A Camphor merchant there instructed his interpreter to invite a number of savages down to a small settlement in the neighborhood, to a feast given in their honor. The guests arriving, roast pig and samshu were dealt out in generous quantities, and when the savages were in a state of intoxication, at a pre-arranged signal, numbers of armed Chinese rushed in and attacked them. This dastardly trick resulted in the capture of fifteen men, including some chiefs who had long been bitter enemies of the Chinese. The captors were very much pleased at the result of the *ruse* which afforded them an opportunity of making, as they termed it, an agreement. After much pleading on the part of the leading chief that his life might be spared, in return for which he would comply with their demand and let them have the Camphor desired, he was released on the arrival of his daughter and two sons, who were demanded by the Chinese as hostages to ensure the fulfilment of the so-called agreement. A few months later, a foreigner visiting the village saw the poor emaciated children, along with other prisoners, bound with chains running from their wrists and ankles to a long staff which they had to take about with them, and which, owing to their weakness, they found it difficult to carry. The chains were never removed and all were treated alike, young and old, sick and well, for the Chinese have absolutely no pity for the poor wretches they hold in bondage. The cases in which savages have been invited to feasts and killed or poisoned by the Chinese are very numerous. In fact, savages, even to this day, frequently refuse to drink from a cup handed them by the Chinese until the giver has first taken a draught of the liquor. Of course, it must be remembered that the savages rarely lost an opportunity of attacking the settlers, and the Chinese heads which they proudly exhibited in a row over the door-ways of their mountain homes were the most treasured of their possessions. In some cases, Chinese who understood that generous treatment of the savages was the best policy, were able to make more lasting arrangements, and as a rule avoided trouble.

The Chinese officials gave no great heed to the almost daily conflicts between the borderers and the savages. The murder of those who had been decoyed into the villages, the capture and holding as prisoners of any number of savages, was not thought to be a matter calling for official intervention. The willingness of the Chinese to pay the Camphor stove-tax was considered by the officials as giving them practically a right to the land on which the stoves were erected, and the terms of agreement with the savages were a matter of personal arrangement between the owners of the stoves and the wild men. Frequently the Chinese had no other title to show for his possessions than the official tax receipts, and these were generally accepted as evidence of ownership. Not infrequently, however, the manufacture was carried on secretly, and the officials were not notified at all ; and, even when the required notification was given the number of stoves was usually misrepresented.

A piece of land having been obtained, and having satisfied himself that the savages could be managed, the Chinese capitalist arranged for the construction of the stoves. Although various systems for financing the industry were in vogue, it was, and still remains, customary for the Camphor merchant to advance sufficient funds to a headman to pay for the cost of a stove, on the understanding that all Camphor produced by the same should be sold exclusively to him. The amount advanced was about $20 for the small Chinese stove; and about the same now suffices for the construction of the Chinese modified Japanese-style stove, which has entirely replaced the former. The actual cost varies with the locality.

Having now the land and the necessary capital, the headman sets to work to engage his workmen to construct the still. The men are all armed to the teeth, so as to be prepared for a surprise-attack on the part of the savages, who not infrequently make some demonstration or other before the work is over. The ground having been cleared, a rough shed is erected, and in this is constructed the apparatus for distilling, known as the stove, which will be described later on. The old Chinese stove was an interesting affair, but inferior to the Japanese model still; and the Chinese have been quick to recognize this.[1]

In running the stoves, the Chinese placed a headman in charge of the work of perhaps ten stoves, and this person received from 50 cents to a dollar for each picul (133 lbs.) produced. Besides, he arranged for the delivery of the Camphor to the merchant, paid compensation to the savages, and furnished supplies to the workers, all of which brought him something extra. As stated above, the merchant had advanced some $20 for the construction of each stove. To recover this sum the merchant takes the Camphor at from one to three dollars under the market price; or if larger sums, as working capital, have been advanced, three or four dollars under, until the debt has been paid off. The merchants have to take the risk of the stove being destroyed by savages, which occurs quite frequently; in fact a loss of one half on this account each year would not, to the larger merchants, be surprising. Upon the destruction of a stove the distillers are considered

---

1. The old Chinese stove has probably disappeared from the Camphor industry for ever. Still it served to manufacture more Camphor during the last century than any other appliance existing, and deserves the detailed description of its construction given herewith. A rough shed having been built, sufficiently large to cover the still, which if of the usual capacity of 10 jars, would measure say 7 by 10 feet, the ground enclosed is cleared of shrubbery and beaten down so as to afford a firm foundation. Four planks are now formed into a bottomless box-like frame 18 inches high. This frame is filled with earth which is stamped down hard and allowed to dry and form what might be called the foundation of the stove. Five round holes less than a foot apart are now cut out on each side of this base, each shaped so as to support a circular iron pan measuring some 15 inches across, resembling somewhat the ordinary Chinese rice cooking pot and intended to hold water. There is no chimney. The smoke is expected to find its way out through the single door of the furnace. After these have been placed in position each pan is covered with perforated boards projecting slightly over the edge of the pan, and provided with a wooden section which can be taken out when it is desired to clean the stove. After a little mud has been plastered on to hold the pan and boards tight, a retort for the Camphor chips, which is a cylinder made of wooden staves fastened with hoops, measuring some 20 inches high and from one foot diameter at the bottom decreasing to seven inches at the top, is placed over each pan and made firm by a liberal use of mud plaster. Two big planks are now placed lengthwise of the structure, reaching as high as the top of the retorts, and these are tied together by strips of wood connecting the two at each end. The space thus enclosed is packed full of earth pounded down hard. Now the whole structure is allowed to dry thoroughly, and a fire-hole extending to the opening under the pans is dug out. The earthenware jars in which the Camphor is collected, measuring some 17 inches in height by 14 inches in diameter, are now inverted over the holes formed by the top of the retort and the stove, or to speak more correctly, the still, is now completed. Before using the stove, however, it must be fire-dried and tested. This is done by building a roaring fire, which is kept up for two or three days, according to the state of the weather; the cracks in the earth, which will now appear, are filled up with a mixture of mud and ashes, and the stove is then ready for work. Bamboo pipes are laid to carry the water, only a very little flow being required; the necessary tools, baskets, tubs, etc., are procured, and distillation is commenced.

Ordinarily only one man or his family care for one stove. In the morning and afternoon the workman, carrying his axe, adze, and a basket, would make trips to the Camphor tree selected, and after three hours or so of labor, would return with some 60 catties (80 lbs.) of Camphor-wood chips, each some three or four inches in length. At the stove he breaks up the chips into smaller pieces with a wooden club, serrated on the side used, and then fills the retort, which holds about 9 or 10 catties (12 or 13 lbs.) with the same, and covers each top with the inverted jar. After each pan has been filled with water poured in at the top of the retort, a fire is lighted and allowed to burn slowly all night. The chips are now taken out, the bottom half being thrown away and the top half, together with a sufficient number of new chips, placed in each retort, the partly exhausted chips being placed on the bottom. The distiller continues thus changing the chips twice a day, refilling the pots, replenishing the fires, and making trips to the forest for fresh chips. During this time, the steam from the pan of boiling water passes through the perforated wood into the cylinders, heats and moistens the chips, and carries with it the fumes of Camphor, which, striking the comparatively cool walls of the inverted earthenware jar above, condenses there. After some ten days of this routine, the jars are removed, and the Camphor, which, upon being exposed to the air, quickly congeals and now resembles newly fallen snow, is detached from the inside of the jar by hand. The quantity obtained per jar varies with the skill of the laborer, ordinarily only about 4 catties (5½ lbs.) would be obtained, but if the fires are attended to with great care and the chips are rich in the drug, this amount may be increased to 6 or 7 catties. The jar is now returned to its place, and so the work continues, the fire not once being extinguished.

absolved from all debts connected with the same, they having no liabilities until money has been placed in their hands to erect new stoves. Furthermore, the Camphor workers were wont to sell the product secretly to outside parties, careful watching being required to see that this was not the rule rather than the exception.

Prior to the occupation of Formosa by the Japanese, some few experimental stoves after the Japanese design were erected in the island, but the new model was not adopted, the Chinese using exclusively the old style stove previously mentioned. After the arrival of the Japanese, however, th e Chinese made alterations in their stoves; the crystallization jar was done away with, the chip retort was enlarged, and a bamboo pipe arranged to carry the vapor back to a crystallization box similar to that used by the Japanese. Now the Chinese use either this model or the real Japanese stove exclusively.

In 1895, on the change in government, much interest was taken by Japanese merchants in the Camphor trade, and the representatives of several firms conmenced operations in the interior. They brought with them from Japan skilled laborers, and the work from the start was commenced on the principles of the industry as existing in Japan. The stoves or stills erected differed much from the old Chinese ones; and their superiority being evident, Chinese distillers quietly adopted them ; and as they, or the modification of them mentioned above, at present represent practically the only apparatus used in the manufacture of Camphor in the world, I describe them in detail here. The stove, invented by a Japanese named Toye, was first used about thirty-five years ago in Tosa province, Japan, and is considered a great improvement upon the old Chinese model which was used in Japan prior to the introduction of the new stove. Whereas with the old Chinese model in Formosa a number of pots or condensers, usually ten, comprised what was known as a stove, with the Japanese, as used at present, a single furnace with one crystallization box is called a stove or still.

In building the Japanese stove, it is customary to select a site with an elevation at the rear, on which to place the crystallization boxes, which should be well above the furnace. Such a plot having been cleared and teveled, a wall is constructed of earth and stone inclining inwards towards she top sufficiently to catch the edges of the water pan, and forming below a place measuring some two feet in height, which comprises the fire-place. In front is a small opening about 12 inches by 18 inches. As in the case of the Chinese stoves there is no chimney, this single door forming the only vent. In front and above the stove is built a shelf, on which chips can be placed to dry. On the pan, which measures some 2 feet 8 inches across, is placed a curved wooden rim projecting over the edge slightly, and strips of wood perforated are joined together and placed over the pan as a cover. On the wooden rim rests the wooden circular retort, ordinarily some 4 feet in height and 2 feet 7 inches in diameter at the bottom, decreasing to a little over a foot at the top, and in the best stoves built of Japanese fir, which is

Up-country Camphor Stills.

Old Model Chinese Camphor Still ("Stove")
"A" Fire-box. "B" Water-pan. "C" Chip-retort. "D" Crystallization Jar.

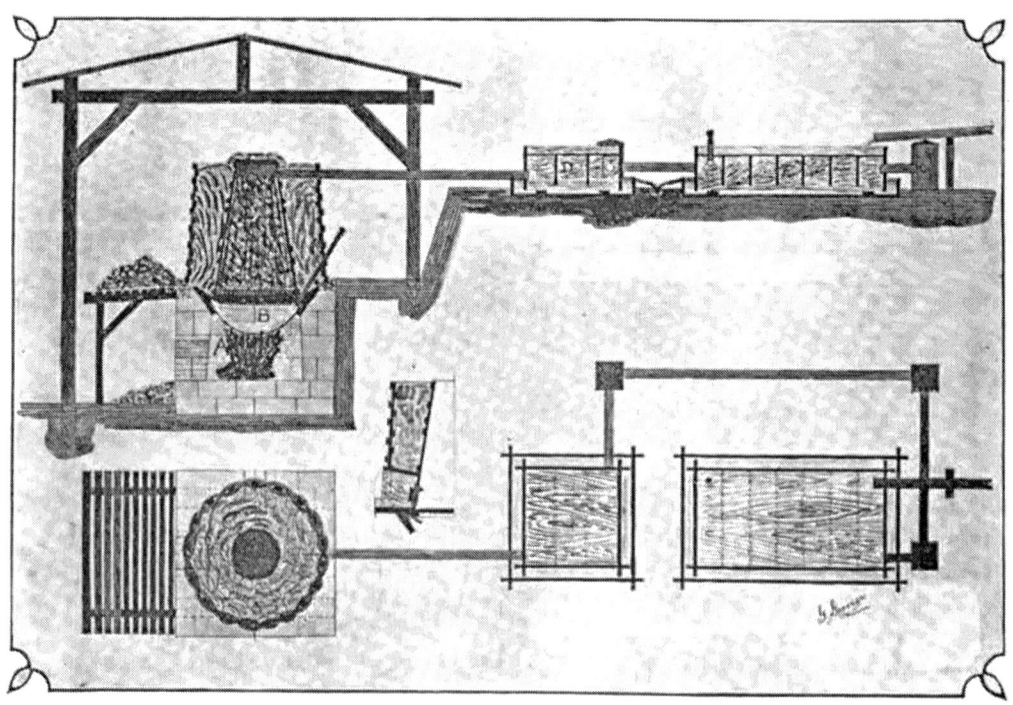

Present Model Japanese Still.
"A" Fire-box. "B" Water-pan. "C" Chip-retort. "D" Cooling-box.
"E" Crystallization-box.

considered a superior material for that purpose. On the upper part is a hole for a bamboo tube, and near the bottom is a small doorway, through which the used-up chips can be taken out. The retort is well plastered with clay or earth at all the joints, and around it is placed a large bamboo or rattan cylinder. The space between the two is tightly packed with earth, which not only keeps the steam from escaping, but lessens the danger of the retort bursting. To the rear and well above the stove, distant some 5 or 7 feet, are the crystallization and cooling boxes. While these vary in size and arrangement, in Formosa two are generally used. The smaller, which measures ordinarily 3 feet square by 1 ⅓ feet high, is merely a cooling receptacle. The larger measures 6 × 3 × 1 ⅓ feet, and is the crystallization box. In the latter, pieces of board, five to ten in number, are fixed crosswise, thus separating the box into as many sections as there are boards, plus one. In the boards, on what is the upper side when the box is in position, and at alternate ends of the same, are holes through which the Camphor vapor passes, it being thus forced to go the length of each board before finding egress into the next section, thus traversing a distance represented by the combined length of the partition boards used. Both the cooling and the crystallization box, when in position, rest face downwards, in slightly larger boxes forming reservoirs in which water is placed, until it reaches slightly above the mouths of the inverted boxes, thus shutting out all air. The sides of both the cooling and crystallization boxes project slightly above the tops, thus providing a place for water. A bamboo pipe, connected with some mountain stream or spring, delivers a steady flow, which keeps the box cool, and the overflow runs into the reservoir boxes below, keeping them filled. A steady inch flow of water is ample for all purposes. From the top of the retort above the furnace runs a bamboo pipe entering one side of the small cooling box, from the opposite side of which runs a second pipe which connects with the crystallization box. At the end of the box opposite to that which this pipe enters, is a small vent known as the testing tube, in which, during the progress of distillation, are inserted loosely a few reeds or blades of grass. When the stoves are working, the water in the reservoir boxes is warmed by the heat of the steam coming from the retort, and a pipe is run from one of them down to the water pan below, so that when the latter requires replenishing, it can be done with water already partially heated. In some of the Namsho stoves, the conducting pipe, after leaving the retort, runs once around the cooling and crystallization boxes before entering the former, the idea being that the vapor having travelled such a distance would lose much of its heat and condense more quickly. A rough shed has in the meantime been constructed, and after a few days, during which the stove is allowed to dry, the latter is ready for work.

To operate the stove, water is permitted to flow over the crystallization and cooling boxes into the reservoirs, and from one of the latter enough water is led through a bamboo pipe to the water-pan below to fill it. As soon as this has been accomplished, the fire is started. The retort, which holds ordinarily about 3 piculs, (399 lbs.), is now filled from the top with chips which are well packed in. The opening in the retort is closed with a tight-fitting cover cemented in with a mixture of mud and ashes, and the door at the bottom of the receptacle is likewise tightly sealed. The fire is kept burning fiercely until steam makes its appearance at the test hole in the crystallization box, whereupon the mouth of the furnace is closed sufficiently to temper the heat, and during the night a slow fire is continued. The next evening the door at the bottom of the retort is opened, the old chips are removed, and after the door has been cemented up again the top cover is taken off and fresh chips packed in, after which the top is closed again, and the distillation continues. Thus the chips are changed every 24 hours. As a rule the fire is replenished four times during the 24 hours, and the exhausted chips are commonly used for the fuel. Whenever fuel is added to the stove the pan is refilled with water, the amount used being about 28 gallons for the 24 hours. Hard water seems to give the best results. On the same principle as the old Chinese stove, the hot vapor from the pan passes through the chips in the retort, extracting from them certain resinous matter which is carried through the bamboo pipe to the cooling box, (thus lowering the temperature of the vapor), and thence on to the condensing or crystallization box. In the latter cooled by running water, the vapor passes through the various compartments, and the Camphor contained therein condenses on the sides and top of the box in the form of minute white crystals.

After some ten days of distillation the fire is extinguished, and for 24 hours the stove is allowed to cool off. The crystallization box is then simply turned up on one side, and the Camphor clinging to the boards is scraped off, that which has fallen into the water being skimmed off with a cloth scoop. It is placed in tubs, and looks for all the world like so much snow. The amount obtained varies greatly, being dependent upon the size of the stove, the richness of the chips, and the skill of the operator in controlling the fire. This last is a very difficult matter. No other contrivance than a few stones, or a piece of tin to close up the door of the furnace is utilized, and too much, or too little, fire will effect the result very seriously. The average will probably be found to amount to from 6½ to 7 catties (8 to 9 lbs.) for each day of distillation, although it has been known to run as high as 13 catties (17⅓ lbs.) It will thus be seen that the percentage of crude Camphor obtained, taking the retort as being filled once a day with 300 catties (400 lbs.), is about 2⅓. One stove in Namsho has been made to yield 5 per cent., probably the highest on record in Formosa. When the Camphor is placed in tubs provided with an outlet, there exudes a yellowish essential oil, known as Camphor oil. With the old Chinese stove but little of this was obtained, but by the Japanese it is claimed by Camphor makers at Namsho to run as high as 70 per cent. It has been to the merchants' advantage, however, to represent this amount as high as possible, as will be explained later, and according to government reports, the percentage of oil is expected to average about 50 per cent. From the oil there can, by certain processes, be extracted about 50 per cent. of Camphor; therefore figures showing the production of Formosa Camphor should have about 25 per cent added to them to represent the amount of Camphor which will be ultimately extracted from the oil. This is only approximate, however, as there would be considerable loss in weight during transportation, and some trifling quantities are disposed of directly for other uses than Camphor extraction. Furthermore, the percentage of yield of oil varies greatly with the quality of wood distilled, the construction and care of the stills, and specially the season, the yield of oil being greater in summer than in winter.[1] Formerly there was no plant in Formosa for treating the oil; but the Formosa government has now provided, in its Camphor establishment at Taihoku (Taipeh), an apparatus for this purpose.[2]

In comparing the two stoves and the system of working them, we find that the old Chinese model stove (of say ten condensers), would consume in a day about 200 catties (270 lbs.) of chips and yield about 4 catties (5⅓ lbs.) of Camphor, whereas a Japanese stove would consume 300 catties (400 lbs.) and yield about 6½ catties (8⅔ lbs.). The Japanese stove, however, yields double or treble the oil obtained with a Chinese stove, thus proving the

1. Experiments conducted by experts in Japan have given the following results:—

Camphor chips weighing 266 pounds yielded in summer 5.33 pounds of Camphor and 2.85 pints of oil, while in winter the same weights of chips distilled in the same apparatus yielded 6.66 pounds of Camphor and 1.11 pints of oil.

2. Prior to the arrival of the Japanese, Formosa Camphor oil was given but little attention in the island, the general opinion being that it was merely a refuse product of crystallized Camphor and of practically no value. Almost immediately following the occupation of Formosa by Japan, Japanese merchants who had arrived in the island, brought up such small quantities as could be obtained, and a market for the stuff was then established. In Osaka and Kobe exist factories for treating Camphor oil, and the Formosa article was accordingly forwarded to Japan. The crystallized product is obtained by subjecting the oil to repeated distillation until all the Camphor has been extracted. A quantity of crystallized Camphor equal to 50 per cent of the oil handled is obtained, and furthermore the residue amounting to about 33 %, is also a salable commodity. This residue takes the form of two oils known as "White" and "Red" or "Brown" oil and is used in Europe in various manufactures such as soap, paint, etc.

Owing to the confusion attending the establishment of the monopoly, as this book goes to press, definite figures as to the price of oil and Camphor cannot be obtained, but that some idea of the cost of manufacture and the probable proceeds may be gained, we will assume the Japan selling price of oil-camphor to be 95 yen a picul, and the cost of the oil laid down in Japan at 44 yen a picul, about this margin being necessary if the extracting is to be done at a profit.

Cost of Camphor Oil	.. 44.00	yen a picul
Coal	.. 1.82	
Miscellaneous Expenses	.. .56	
Wages	.. 1.80	
	————	
	48.18	yen
Proceeds from sale of 50 catties Camphor	.. 47.50	yen
,, ,, 18 catties Red Oil	.. 1.80	
,, ,, 15 catties White Oil	.. 1.60	
	————	
	50.90	yen

Waste during manufacture equals about 17 catties.

Taking the total production of Formosa Crude Camphor at 30,000 piculs, we obtain roughly the side products in the following quantities:

Total production Crude Camphor	.. 30,000	piculs.
Total upcountry production Crude Camphor Oil	.. 15,000	,,
Loss in weight during transportation, repacking, etc., and allowance for quantity consumed for outside purposes	.. 3,000	,,
Total Crude Camphor laid down in Japan for manufacture ..	.. 12,000	,,
Crude Camphor obtained (49 to 50%)	.. 6,000	,,
Red or Brown Oil (18%)	.. 2,160	,,
White Oil (15%)	.. 1,800	,,
Waste during manufacture (17%)	.. 2,010	,,

(1 Picul = 100 catties or 133 pounds.)

former superior in extracting power. Furthermore, the services of the distiller, (neither stove requiring more than one person) bring a larger yield with the Japanese stove, the cost of operating being therefore less per picul. The Japanese stove requires less fuel, although in Camphor making, fuel is not a question of importance, for after the fire is once started the exhausted chips obtained from the retort each day furnish a sufficiency. The first cost, however, of the best Japanese stove is some 20 per cent. higher. The Chinese stoves were very rudely constructed. The steam frequently leaked out through the retort, and it was quite common, in knocking a Chinese stove to pieces, to find recesses in the earth-walls filled with crystallized Camphor. While it may strike the reader that both Chinese and Japanese stills are very crude, it must be taken into consideration that, owing to the fact that stoves must be removed every few years, an expensive apparatus cannot be used, and moreover the steam carrying with it the Camphor fumes must not come in contact with metal. It is necessary, therefore, for most of the apparatus to be made of wood, although earthenware could likewise be used.

As for work in the forest, we find the Japanese and Chinese systems similar, although the adze-like tool used by the Chinese for cutting the tree is a little narrower and more curved, giving thicker chips. These chips consequently do not yield so readily to distillation. The tree is not first felled, but the workmen commence at once to cut the chips from the standing tree, and in this way soon cut away sufficient to cause the tree to fall. Sometimes, this point is reached sooner than anticipated, and occasionally results seriously. Within the space of a few months two Chinese workmen were thus killed in Namsho district. One man, either Japanese or Chinese, finds no great difficulty in cutting enough chips to keep a single stove supplied, besides looking after the distillation. As a rule the trees are within a mile of the stoves; and, as the workman usually brings in the chips as soon as he has obtained a picul (133 lbs.), the difficulty of transportation for a strong man is not much.

The Camphor tree of Formosa is said to be much richer in the drug than that of Japan. As a general rule, however, trees found growing in shaded valleys with a moist and heavy soil are not as productive as those found in a sunny clearing where the soil is poor. The latter conditions are more liable to produce wood strong and hard and rich in Camphor. Still this is not by any means an unfailing guide, for trees growing side by side, and alike in appearance and size will be found, one perhaps very rich in Camphor and the other practically barren; and the difficulty of it all is that there is no reliable test to ascertain which is which, without subjecting the chips to distillation; while, to add to the puzzle, a tree may yield more on one side than on the other.

One argument for government interference rests on the fact that the Camphor workers, anxious for the maximum of profits, utilize only the lower ten feet or so of a tree for distillation, as the branches and upper portions are not found to yield sufficient of the drug, and that they leave the rest of the forest monarch to rot, thus wasting vast quantities of wood which would yield considerable amounts of Camphor, and which, were it not that more tempting material was close at hand, would probably be used.[1]

It is while at work in the Camphor forests that the workmen are most frequently attacked by the "head-hunters," and if the persons killed are the sole protectors of the Camphor stove, as is very often the case, the savages do not cease their ravages until the stills are destroyed. In case of the murder of a workman, the capitalists ordinarily paid a certain sum, usually $10, to the family of the murdered man. In erecting stoves it is usual to place as many of them together as possible for purposes of defence, and it was customary to erect in some localities high scaffolding supporting small bamboo huts in which were stationed watchmen night and day, the expense being borne by all.

This constant trouble with the savages, and the dangers encountered while at work in the Camphor districts, is a very important factor in swelling the first cost of the drug. Admitting that the savages are atrociously barbarous, and that they are unreliable and treacherous, still, in the olden days, the Chinese practised so many cruel tricks on them that they were often justified in retaliating. They would, however, have been more deserving of sympathy had they been more discriminating in their selection of victims. Were the savages outraged or even offended in any particular district to an extent sufficient to incite them to murder, they killed the first unfortunate Chinese that they could reach, with absolute disregard as to whether he was the guilty party or not. The Chinese government appointed at many places along the border an officer called a "Bukungkiok," whose nominal duty it was to act as a protector of the savages and to control trade passing between savages and Chinese.

The Chinese officials were also anxious to provide against the destruction of the stoves, for such meant a loss in revenue, inasmuch as the government tax at that time was on the stove rather than the production. Occasionally an officer would appreciate the fact that honest treatment of the savages produced the most satisfactory results. The inherent instinct of the Chinese official to squeeze, however, generally proved too great a tempta-

---

1. Prof. Moriya, of the College of Agriculture in the Imperial University, who is perhaps the best authority on the Camphor manufacture in Japan, carried on experiments with the object of ascertaining the quantity of Camphor to be obtained from different parts of the tree. He worked with an improved apparatus of his own design and used wood which he declares would not have yielded over 2 per cent. if distilled by the ordinary model. The result was as follows :—

Twigs	2.21 per cent.
Branches	3.70 ,, ,,
Upper part of the stem	3.84 ,, ,,
Lower part of the stem	4.23 ,, ,,
Upper part of the stump	5.49 ,, ,,
Lower part of the stump	5.74 ,, ,,
Root	4.46 ,, ,,
Average	4.22 per cent.

Prof. Moriya obtained with his apparatus 10 to 15 per cent. of oil from the crude Camphor. His experiments have shown that a larger yield of oil is obtained from the upper than from the lower part of the tree, and furthermore that while the tree yields the most Camphor in winter it yields the most oil in summer.

tion, and the savages frequently suffered in consequence. As an example
of this, on one occasion, a few years ago, it was decided to open a new
district. On broaching the matter to the savages they agreed, promises
of a fair rental being previously held out. Prior to this, the savages
in this particular district had been controlled by a very humane and
just official who had gained their regard. But at the time I write of,
this officer had been replaced by a thorough rascal, from whose utter un-
scrupulousness they were soon to suffer. No sooner had the stoves been
erected, and the armed workmen gathered together, than the mandarin
began to persecute the hillmen. He pocketed the rents that rightly
belonged to them, and abstracted a "squeeze" whenever the savages
came down to trade. The aborigines were naturally much enraged at such
treatment, but they remained quiet, until small-pox broke out in the tribe,
and carried off a chief's wife and child. This crowning misfortune, which
they likewise attributed to the Chinese, was overpowering, and to appease
the gods, they started out on a head-hunting expedition. The Camphor
workmen, much alarmed by the hostility of the savages, deserted their stoves
and sought shelter in an adjoining village. On learning of this, the mandarin
exerted himself and eventually, by dint of numerous promises and much
feasting, succeeded in quieting the angry aborigines, and work was commenced once more. Not profiting by the lesson, however, the officer, as
soon as affairs were again running smoothly, renewed his nefarious practices,
in which he was ably assisted by numerous disreputable interpreters
who were continually clashing with each other to extort the largest
squeeze. Affairs were now in a state of chaos, and in hopes of inducing the savages to give up the destruction of stoves, a foreigner interested in the industry visited the district mentioned, and having the
confidence of the savages was able to persuade a party to come out and
meet him and talk the matter over. This greatly enraged a certain interpreter, who, for obvious reasons, desired to confine all intercourse with the
savages to himself, and who on learning of the proposed meeting, reported
to the Chinese official that the savages were planning a raid. Three hundred
Chinese troops were sent to the border, and as the seven savages were
leaving the forest on their way to the pre-arranged place of meeting, they
were suddenly attacked by the Chinese, two of them being killed and several
wounded. At first sight it appeared to the savages that the foreigner had
betrayed them, but later they learned the truth, and such vengeance was taken
by the tribe that about fifty Chinese were murdered, a thousand stoves destroyed, and the government deprived of taxes amounting to about $8,000.

It would not be correct to say that the interpreters were all cruel
rascals; in fact an occasional one, ordinarily the possessor of a savage wife,
took a true interest in the aborigines, and endeavored to obtain for them fair
treatment. Such conduct, however, did not always assist the schemes
of the Chinese officials. Nor were they always gentle in their methods
of showing their disapproval, as the following incident will show. An
interpreter, who was rightly regarded by the savages as a protector
of their interests, did not always concur with the plans of a local

general, who was largely interested in the Camphor district, and the latter decided to destroy the interpreter's influence with his forest friends, and thus obtain a larger degree of power for himself. He ordered the interpreter to bring the four leading chiefs of the tribe to his yamen that he might consult with them. Fearing treachery, the Chinese first refused to carry out the order, but eventually convinced that the mandarin meant no harm, he visited his friends, and by guaranteeing them perfect safety, was able to return with four chiefs. On reaching the yamen, to the intense dismay of the interpreter, the four confiding savages were at once beheaded. On learning of the murder, the tribe quite naturally thought that they had been tricked by the interpreter, and two of the latter's sons who were at work near the border were killed in revenge, while general head-hunting ensued for months. Tricks of this kind were very numerous, resulting in the total loss of confidence in the Chinese and the continuance of warfare with the savages.

With the arrival of the Japanese the conditions improved on the whole. There were no more Chinese mandarins to deceive the savages, who were now more sure of justice. However, the Japanese government, which had introduced a tax on production, was not so directly interested in the working of the stoves, and official protection was practically withdrawn in some districts, thus permitting the savages to murder without much danger of punishment. At present the government forces, distributed among the Camphor stations, are smaller in number than they ever were during the Chinese regime, and it cannot be said that the Savage Question has been by any means successfully solved. Chinese lives are lost so frequently that the matter is not given any attention ; and, unless a Japanese is the victim, retaliatory measures are but rarely adopted. Of course, all that is possible is done without the actual use of force by the civil authorities to induce the savages to be peaceful. Japanese are not allowed to enter their territory without official permission, Camphor-men are, wherever possible, forced to live up to their obligations, and the government generally endeavors, I believe, to act fairly and humanely. The Chinese are still regarded by the savages as their great enemies, and Japanese are comparatively rarely attacked. For instance, in Namsho district, which was visited by the writer, out of 38 persons killed only 3 were Japanese. The murder of one of these, a man about 42 years of age, was described to me as follows :

When last seen, the Japanese was at work alone in the forest reducing to chips the trunk of a tree. At the Camphor stove half a mile or so distant were two Japanese women and two sick men. One of the latter heard the report of a gun, but neither was able to go and investigate the cause. Other workmen in the neighborhood, however, heard the sound, and surmising at once that it was the work of savages, started off at a run through the forest towards the direction from which the sound had come. Chinese hillmen also joined in the search, and, being quicker footed, soon reached the place where the workman above mentioned was last seen. The Japanese now came up and called out their comrade's name, but obtained no answer. After some search, the stark-naked, headless body of their fellow workman was found. Tools, clothes, and all had been carried away by the savages. The party then ran further into the forest discharging their guns and hoping to get a shot at the murderer. In this they were not successful. After penetrating a short distance into the jungle they turned about and were returning slowly, when they heard from the summit of the adjacent hill the single report of a gun, a signal of defiance from the savage, that his pursuers might know that he had outstripped them and gained the protection of the dense interior jungle. The above attack occurred in January, and on the same day in February the headhunters came out again. Three Japanese were at work on a single fallen tree. One of the workmen whose position was a bit hidden by shrubbery thought he heard a suspicious noise. Although somewhat alarmed, there was no immediate repetition of the sound, and he was about to recommence work when again a noise was heard. He now saw a slight movement in the under brush near by, and on more careful observation discovered two crouching savages with pointed muskets taking aim at his two comrades. He secured his gun as quickly as possible to discharge it, but to his great horror it missed fire. Simultaneously he shouted to his companions at the top of his voice, and grabbing a loose piece of wood at hand, threw it with all his strength into the brush wherein the savages were concealed. This alarm from an unexpected quarter seems to have frightened the would-be murderers, for they dropped their weapons and fled through the forest, and although the Japanese started at once in pursuit the two head-hunters were not seen again.

In the year 1898, in the Goshizai district, three Japanese officers went with seven savages to visit the latters' village. On nearing their destination, the officers were attacked by a party of outside headhunters who were joined by the very savages accompanying the Japanese. One of the officers was able to escape and fled into the jungle, eventually reaching the village of Goshizai. The bodies of his two companions were later found, badly mutilated and headless. A military expedition was sent against the offending tribe to punish them for the outrage. The savages retired as the military advanced, and no opportunity occurred for a battle. The Japanese then burnt one of the villages and returned to the plains. This act had a very beneficial effect not only on the tribe punished, but also on the savages in the adjoining districts, and there has been a notable lessening of head-hunting raids in that particular territory ever since.

That the headhunting propensities of certain of the Formosa savages is a very serious matter is obvious when we note that, during the year 1898, savages attacked the Camphor workers and others 303 times, and that 635 persons were killed and wounded. During the single month of September, savages attacked on 45 different occasions, causing injury or death to 85 persons. In other words, this is one attack for every 16 hours, and a life or an injury to one person every 8 hours. This death roll is evidence that the Japanese have not yet solved the savage question.

Soon after the arrival of the Japanese, through, I believe, the advice of the former prefect, Mr. Hashiguchi, bu-kon-sho officer, the equivalent of the Chinese *Bu-kung-kiok* were established along the savage border, the duties of the incumbents being to control the savages within their districts. It was desired that these officers should devote their time to the study of the savages, learn their language, become familiar with their customs and super-stitions, and take an interest in them and their life, and so gain their regard and respect that they might be guided by the officer's advice, protected from outside persecution by him, and gradually led along the paths of civilization by peaceful methods rather than by force, although force was to be at hand should it be required. This admirable policy, which has given splendid re-sults in certain American Indian reservations, would, doubtless, have worked equally well here, had the government considered the matter of sufficient im-portance to make the office an important one with generous compensation so that it might be attractive to really efficient officials. Instead, the office was considered an inferior one, the chief official ranking but little higher than a clerk with a salary corresponding to his position.

The post was not at all an attractive one, and the officers, of varying ability, who were placed in charge, were shifted about, being changed in some places once or twice a year, and of course the value of the services of even a conscientious and capable official would, under such circumstances, be almost nil.

The savages are attracted by personality rather than system, and there-fore the scheme could only be successful when good officials were placed in positions for long terms, so that each savage might become familiar with the officers and follow them out of personal affection.

The officers in Formosa were also under great disadvantage in not having the police under their command, the result being that, when occasion arose for police assistance, a second authority entered the district clashing with the bu-kon-kok and causing confusion and dissatisfaction. This, com-bined with the unattractiveness of the position, owing to its low rank and small pay, entirely annulled the most valuable parts of the system, and towards the last the bu-kon-kok became an office of scarcely any value either to the savages or the Camphor workers who looked to it for protection. In 1898, the offices were abandoned, and the affairs of the savages were placed in the care of police officers in each district. At the present writing the police are still in charge, and the beneficial results from the employment of civil officers whose sole occupation was to care for, direct, control, and if necessary, punish these children of the forest, will probably not for the time be obtained.

It is thought by some Japanese authorities that the government is under no obligation to do anything for the savages, so long as the latter are beyond the pale of civilization, and pay no taxes. In Europe and America, however, savage tribes are now generally considered as the wards of the ruler who governs *de jure* the territory of which they occupy a part. America, for instance, which asks nothing more of the Indian than that he should be at peace with his neighbors, spends annually from eleven to four-teen million dollars gold in caring for two hundred and fifty thousand Indians.

Japan with a hundred thousand savages would surely be justified in spending a few thousand yen on them.

The Japanese merchants who arrived in the island to engage in the Camphor business soon after the occupation were under the impression, as were the old manufacturers, that the new government would give efficient protection to them. The Chinese authorities in the old days generally considered the payment of a considerable sum in Camphor taxes a claim for the services of a few soldiers in keeping order. In many districts troops were stationed, and in others some payment to the savages on condition of their keeping the peace was made. The mandarins were not by any means always successful in this; but still, ineffective as their savage system was, they recognized the right of the manufacturer to some protection. The Japanese government introduced temporarily a different policy, that of practical non-interference with savage affairs. It was not wise to follow in the footsteps of the Chinese who officially announced to Peking that the aborigines were not men but wild animals, and should be treated as such, and who, by their clumsy interference, had reduced the export of Camphor one year to only three piculs; and the Japanese, being totally ignorant of the savages and their ways, apparently thought it best not to declare any policy of control until the authorities were more familiar with the situation. Thus, the protection of the Camphor workers was practically left in the hands of the manufacturers. A border village was given its quota of police, some ten or twelve in number, and perhaps some uniformed Chinese police known as Ke-tei; but these are more to keep the villagers in order than to protect the Camphor workers from attack.

The manufacturers employ Japanese, Chinese, and even the civilized aborigines to protect their workmen, one single firm paying in 1898 as much as twelve hundred yen a month on this account. These armed guards are known as Ai-tei, and receive from $15 to $20 a month wages. At some places where the savages are specially aggressive a considerable force is required. For instance in Twao (Tai-ko) the manufacturers are obliged to support about a hundred armed men. In Tokoham, owing to the assurances made to the savages by the authorities to the effect that Chinese would not generally be employed as guards, Japanese are for the time utilized. As the wages of Japanese in Formosa are very high, and as Tokoham district is a notoriously dangerous one, requiring the services of many guards, the expense of protection is very high, and the manufacturers are much handicapped by it.

The Japanese government has made no clear declaration regarding the status of the savage, but in an ordinance relating to the control of the forests it is written: "All forests and prairie lands for which no title deed or other positive evidence of ownership exists is hereby declared government property." No person is permitted to purchase or otherwise obtain land from the savages or to occupy land nominally held by the savages, without the consent of the Governor-General, who may grant a concession if he sees fit."

The so-called savage territory, within the boundaries of which the wild natives are independent, is over 5,000 square miles in extent; and when we note that barely 100,000 savages are scattered over this large reserve, while the rest of the inhabitants of the island, over two millions in number, are limited to an area scarcely twice as large, it is very obvious that the savage district is not supporting its full quota of population.

Still, in all justice to our wild friends, it must be taken into consideration that their territory, consisting exclusively of mountain land, is not capable of supporting as large a number of persons as an equal area of the fertile plains of Western Formosa, and furthermore that their method of living, hunting being their chief occupation, requires a large and unpopulated district. What the government will eventually accept as constituting "positive evidence of ownership" and whether they will or not recognize tribal interests at all remains to be seen. It may be that the villages and surrounding cleared land showing traces of agricultural work will in time to come be admitted as the property of the savages, and the wild forest unused, save as an occasional hunting ground, will be held as government land. Hitherto, however, the authorities have in come cases recognized the right of the savages to receive gifts and money as the nominal rent of Camphor lands, although they have demanded that parties claiming rights based on agreements with the savages, shall obtain the government's recognition before operations are commenced. In some places, however, at Lamshun (Nam-sho) for instance, the civilized aborigines who own valuable Camphor lands, their right to which was recognized by the Chinese authorities, have likewise been recognized by the Japanese government as the undisputed proprietors of the same.

The Japanese manufacturers brought with them Japanese laborers from Japan to work in the Camphor districts. The Komatsu Company for instance started with about 200 Japanese laborers, but this number was, in a year or so, reduced to 30. In Namsho district four were killed by the savages while collecting Camphor chips, and thirty died of malarial fever and kak-ke (beri beri). This great mortality naturally discouraged many Japanese from taking work in the Camphor districts, and they found other situations more congenial. The Japanese companies, therefore, gradually introduced Chinese laborers, and now the latter are employed in greater numbers than the Japanese.

The Japanese laborers were not paid regular wages, but received ordinarily 14 yen for every picul of Camphor produced, and 7 yen a picul for oil. If the market price was high, increased pay was sometimes given. As one laborer has entire charge of a stove the work is very hard. The man goes to the forest, reduces the portion of the tree he desires to chips, and returns to attend to the stove and manufacture the Camphor. Even at night the fire must be replenished, and the laborer has to depend upon veritable "cat naps" for sleep. A representative of the merchant usually takes delivery of the Camphor at the stove. While the laborer is obtaining the wood, he cannot distil, so in reality he finds he only has some 20 or 22 days for actual manufacture. The merchant furnishes him with the stove, tools, and a home. The average earning of a Japanese Camphor worker is between 25 and 30 yen a month, although some specially successful distillers have made as much as 40 yen. The Chinese are employed on a totally different basis. Money is advanced to them by the Japanese companies for the construction of a stove, the loan being returned in monthly instalments of say 5 yen; and the Camphor is sold to the merchants at a price usually 2 yen below the market rate, until the debt is paid off. Sometimes the Japanese construct the stove and the Chinese pay a rental, say 3 yen a month, besides, in some districts, say 3 yen as land rent to the savage chief, and other small charges, amounting in all to some 10 yen. The Chinese agree to sell all the Camphor to the merchant who owns the stove at the market price ruling in the hill. Upon delivery of the Camphor to the merchant, the 10 yen mentioned is deducted and the balance handed over to the Chinese distiller. Although a Japanese distiller is more skillful in his work and can obtain a larger amount of Camphor than the Chinese laborer, the latter is now preferred by several Japanese merchants, inasmuch as the Chinese generally has his family with him, the wife and children frequently assisting in the work, and if the laborer falls ill, some relative usually appears to carry on the work until the man is well again. If a Japanese falls ill it means interruption of the work for the time, and results in confusion, and often in financial loss. Over 600 Japanese are now engaged in the various branches of the industry, 400 of them being Camphor distillers. It might be mentioned that the labor system in vogue in the Camphor districts is quite opposed to the fundamental principles of all industrial organization. To obtain full value from the toil of the Camphor workers there should be a better division of labor than there is. When it is noted that a steady, continuous heat for some ten days is required to get the best results, it can be easily seen how great the loss must be from improper firing, owing to the stove being attended to by one person who must also cut from the tree and bring in the chips, thus leaving the stove at times without an attendant. One man could quite easily attend to the firing of two stoves, and one man could easily supply two stoves with chips.

After the Camphor has been collected at the stoves and most of the oil drained off, coolies carry it down in sacks or bamboo baskets lined with large leaves, and the oil in old kerosene tins, to the nearest market, where it is examined. The Chinese merchants store the Camphor in big vats, and sometimes cover the stuff with water, (in which it is not soluble), to prevent evaporation. Formerly the Chinese frequently took the drug direct from the water and packed it wet, believing that the gain in weight thus obtained would be to their advantage, but it was in fact quite the reverse, as exporters would, if they found the least trace of water, make such a heavy reduction for it that it usually yielded a profit to them rather than to the country merchants. The Camphor destined for shipment via Hongkong was formerly packed in wooden boxes lined with lead, this covering preventing, to a considerable extent, the evaporation of the drug. These boxes held about 138 lbs. of Camphor. Japanese merchants shipped almost entirely to Japan;

the Camphor being packed in tubs, and the oil in old kerosene oil tins. From the country districts it was brought by railway or boat to Keelung or Tamsui, from which ports it was exported.

The loss in weight during transportation was very large. As the hill-men invariably dipped the bag or bucket into water to add to its weight, the in-country merchants took from the producers twenty catties extra of Camphor for each picul to make up for this and for loss on account of evaporation. The total loss from mountain to Hongkong was often 30%, and from Hongkong to Europe about 5%. The merchants, before accepting the Camphor, made a careful search for adulteration, which was very common with the Chinese-produced Camphor. Chief among the stuffs used for adulteration, is a material known by the Chinese as Chai Yen, consisting of a certain sea-weed product dissolved in water and boiled until it becomes of the consistency of soft paste. The stuff is then carefully mixed with the crystallized Camphor. When the Chinese were using the old native stove, it was customary, whenever the retort was refilled with chips, to take off the distillery jar and spread the adulterant carefully over the crystallized Camphor, thus forming alternate layers of Camphor and sea-weed paste. If this was skilfully done, the resulting product might contain from 10 to 30% of the false stuff without being liable to detection at sight. Besides adding to the weight, Chai-yen is also valued by the user for preventing evaporation, as, by its sticky consistency, it binds together the Camphor crystals. The outer covering of the Formosan rattan is also frequently used. This, when crushed and then washed in water, yields a sticky fluid called by the Chinese "tien-sui," or rattan water, which is mixed with the Camphor. Rice flour, potato flour, a native-made vegetable gelatine, and powdered sandstone are also sometimes used. A well known Camphor merchant vouches for the following tale, which is not at all improbable. Very few are the Formosan Chinese who have seen snow at close quarters. In the winter time the highest peaks are often covered, and the snow on these hills can be seen even from Twa-tu-tia, but snow never reaches the plains. On one occasion, however, during the winter of 1892-3, during the coldest weather known in Formosa for many years, a little snow one bitter morning was found for the first time on the hills in the savage district not far from Tokoham. A wily Camphor worker saw in this gift from heaven possibilities of a great fortune. He ascended the hills, filled a few baskets, and, returning to his stove, mixed in a sufficient amount of Camphor to give an odor to the production, and then started off in a hurry to the nearest village to dispose of the stuff. The Camphor merchant looked at the clean, white crystals dumped down on the floor before him, deducted a trifle for water, which, in his wisdom he thought he detected, paid the anxious hill-man, who doubtless claimed a pressing engagement elsewhere which necessitated his prompt departure, and then packed the Camphor in a vat that it might drain while he enjoyed the pleasure of an opium pipe. The language which he used on the second inspection of his purchase has not been reported, but it was doubtless loud and voluminous; for it is told that, with the exception of a few catties of Camphor at the bottom, and a general appearance of moisture on the sides of the vessel there was no further trace of the several piculs of glittering crystals for which he had paid a considerable sum of good, hard Mexicans but an hour before. Fortunately, whatever adulterant is used, its presence can be easily detected. The presence of sea-weed paste and rattan water produces a product differing from the pure product slightly in color. Camphor crystals have a brilliant lustre, not unlike newly fallen snow. The presence of sea-weed paste gives a very slightly darker and duller color, while rattan water gives a darker shade still. When pure Camphor is burned, it remains white until entirely consumed, and leaves no residue. If sea-weed paste, rattan water, rice flour, potato flour, or powdered stone has been mixed with the drug, a considerable residue remains, and in the case of the first two adulterants, the flame sputters, and sparks fly out. Whether adulterants have been used or not can also be told by placing a little of the drug in benzine oil or even kerosene, when the pure Camphor and oil soon finds its way to the top, while the adulterant goes to the bottom.

For the first year following the occupation of the island by the Japanese the old Chinese imposts were remitted, and it was announced that there would be no taxes imposed for a year. October 31st 1895, official regulations were published which announced that only Camphor merchants who could produce permits granted by the Chinese government prior to the arrival of the Japanese would be permitted to engage in the industry. This caused much concern to some of the manufacturers, as the Chinese had not been at all uniform in the granting of permits, the mere willingness to pay the taxes and the tax receipt itself being considered in many instances sufficient evidence of the right to engage in the industry. The Japanese eventually gave way on this point, and if the Camphor man could give clear evidence to show that the Chinese had recognized his right to manufacture Camphor, this was accepted. This system, was, however, much complicated, as the Chinese authorities had sometimes made the very same concession to several different individuals. That is, when the original holder did not avail himself of the privilege granted, it was common, after a certain period, to give it to some one else who would work it; and if this second person likewise abandoned the forest, the permit would be passed on to even a third person, while the records of these transfers, Chinese fashion, were practically non-existent.

With the arrival of the Japanese and the likelihood of increased valuations of the Camphor districts, claimants to the same ground sprang up, each with some sort of evidence as to the genuineness of his representations, thereby causing much confusion in ascertaining the proper owners.

There were at first almost continual difficulties; misunderstandings arose, Camphor was seized, Camphor men arrested, while the savages raided and destroyed stoves, and rebels rendered the country so unsafe that money could not be carried up country, and eventually so unsatisfactory was the position that the foreigners both in the north and south gave up their stoves and withdrew from the trade, suffering considerable losses.

The industry in the north, which has always been the chief producing district, continued unabated under Chinese and Japanese control, but from the mid-Formosa districts, which since 1892 had sent varying amounts of Camphor to Anping for shipment, the output yearly became less, and from June 1897 some few hundred piculs only have been produced, and this went generally to Tamsui for shipment.

In 1896, the Japanese introduced a tax imposed in a manner which Camphor makers had long desired, viz., on the production rather than on the stoves, as was the case during the Chinese regime. This tax, which was officially put forward as representing the sale of the trees claimed as government property, amounted to ten yen a picul, and was collected at special tax offices established at central points in the most important districts, a check being kept on illicit manufacture by the requirement that the exporter at the port of shipment should present a certificate from the tax office showing that the impost had been paid.

This taxation at first applied only to Camphor in its crystallized state, and not to the oil, which, from the Japanese stoves, generally amounts to about fifty per cent. of the product. Certain Japanese merchants, soon after their arrival, discovered that the oil would dissolve large quantities of the Camphor crystals, the presence of which could not, without special tests, be detected. Therefore, as oil was free of duty, a profitable business was done in shipping Camphor in this way to Japan, where it was subjected to a distilling process, and the crystals separated from the oil. The government soon detected the artifice, however, and a tax of 3 yen, together with a careful inspection of the oil, nearly if not wholly put a stop to the practice.

As this chapter goes to press, the Formosan government declares its intention of placing Formosa Camphor under government control and monop- olizing its sale. The government appears to have two objects in view— increased revenue, and a more complete control over the Camphor forests. That both these quite praiseworthy objects might have been attained by the establishment of some more liberal system than a monopoly is most prob- able; but the government has given the Camphor problem considerable thought and study during the last four years; and the forests being claimed as the property of the Crown, the exclusive control of the sale of Camphor seemed to them to be the most satisfactory solution. The production of Camphor being practically confined to Japan and Formosa, no opposition from outside competing supply districts, at least for many years, is feared.

The difficulty, of obtaining revenue from the Chinese in the island by the institution of the usual forms of taxation existing in Japan and Occidental countries owing to the confused and complex family system and the com- plicated commercial methods in vogue among Chinese, has encouraged the Japanese to adopt other measures of raising revenue, such as the salt and opium monopolies, and now the Camphor monopoly.

The urgent need of some more efficient system of protection for the border residents against the attacks of the savages, and the institution of some system of afforestation to prevent the total destruction of the Camphor forests have long been apparent, and should the government be successful in these two aims, the new system will have much to recommend it.

The general plan of the new system of protection as outlined provides for two forces, one to give protection to villages on the savage border, and the other to guard the Camphor workers in the forests, and to secure the stills against molestation. The expenditure for this purpose is some 180,000 yen, and there will be employed in the work 1,500 armed men—Chinese and Japanese. The line of operations will extend from Polisia in south central Formosa to the northern districts, thence eastward to Gilan, a total distance of nearly 150 miles. There are at present in the island nearly a thousand Chinese who were, under the old regime, engaged as guards along the savage border ; and many of these will, doubtless, be brought into the new force. The work of organization and control will be entrusted to the police.

As regards afforestation, it has been stated that the government will set out young Camphor trees in Tokoham (Taikokan), Lamshun (Nansho), and other Camphor districts, an appropriation for this purpose having already been made. Young Camphor trees growing in the forests, which were formerly cut down for fuel by the Camphor workers, and shoots growing from Camphor stumps will be protected, and their destruction strictly forbidden.

The manufacture of Camphor by the regular manufacturers, i.e. those holding government permits, is not, within certain limits, to be interfered with ; but the entire production must be sold to the government at a certain fixed price, the maximum rate at present for the best grade being 30 yen per picul (133 lbs.)

The government names the maximum amount to be produced and agrees to take that quantity from the manufacturers. Since the establishment of the monopoly, the government has limited the annual production to an amount varying in different years from 30,000 piculs (4,000,000 lbs.) to 40,000 piculs (5,333,333 lbs.) This is with the object of insuring sufficient demand for the drug to support the high price which the government desires to obtain, and making it possible for the selling agent, who is obliged to take over the whole production, to pay the same. This will not probably require the direct interference of the government in closing stoves, as the price offered is so low that many plants will be voluntarily abandoned by their owners. For instance, during the summer of 1898, there existed some 14,000 stoves, though only about 4,000 were in constant operation. With the rise in the price of Camphor during the autumn, the number of stoves in operation increased to 7,000. But with the enforcement of the monopoly and the low price paid by the government, certain districts, Lin-ki-po (Rinkiho), Taichu, and Maoli (Bioritsu) especially, (they being far from the head Camphor office), have greatly decreased their output, thus reducing the present number of stoves in operation to some 2,000. It is stated that the government will endeavor to combine the manufacturers in different districts with the object of simplifying the purchase of camphor, and of obtaining a more effective control of the trade. The price, 30 yen, is paid for the drug at the Taipeh Camphor office. Camphor offices have also been established at Teckcham (Shinchiku), Maoli (Bioritsu), Taichu, Linkipo (Rinkiho), and Lotong (Rato), and the prices paid at these five offices are such as will, after meeting the cost of transportation and loss in weight, lay the Camphor down in Taipeh

(Taihoku) at 30 yen.[1] Kelung and Tamsui are named as the ports of shipment for Camphor and Camphor oil.

Formosan Camphor has in the past been notably dirty and oily. To raise the quality standard samples have been issued by the government to Camphor manufacturers with injunctions that their production must equal the sample in quality, in order to be classed as 1st grade. This has created some consternation among certain manufacturers, but it has been demonstrated by the government that it will require only a little closer attention to the stove and the application of perhaps a stronger and more steady heat, together with greater care in keeping the surroundings of the stove and crystallization boxes clean, to produce the desired grade. Camphor has been produced in Tansikak (Toseikaku), which has equalled and even excelled the sample, and the additional labor has been but trifling.

The procedure under which the monopoly is conducted is as follows : When Camphor is brought to the Camphor office it is inspected by an examiner, who declares its grade and weight. The examiner then issues a certificate which, on the Camphor being placed in the government godowns, is exchanged for a cheque on the Taiwan Bank, which the holder can cash without further endorsement. This closes the transaction so far as the manufacturer is concerned. The government receives the Camphor in bulk, and if the purchase has been made at one of the up-country posts, the government at its own expense packs the Camphor in canvas bags holding 50 or 100 kin, and transports the drug to Taipeh (Taikoku). Such of the drug as is destined for export as " Crude B " is subjected to a simple draining process to separate the oil. If the camphor is particularly oily some eight or even nine months is required before the drug is considered sufficiently dry. This grade runs 93 per cent. pure, and is largely in demand in the United States though considerable shipments are also made to Germany and other countries. At the capital (Taihoko) is erected a factory to clean the Camphor and press it ; and with the exception of such as is sold in its crude form, the Camphor is all treated here. The plant consists of six large distilling furnaces measuring some twelve feet wide by twenty-four feet long, and standing about 5 feet from the floor. Some thousand pounds of the crude Camphor are placed in the distilling oven, which is in the form of a large iron box. After the openings in the retort have been closed and sealed, air is forced in to hasten evaporation, and for the first forty-eight hours a slow fire is maintained, which drives off the water and oil, these passing through a pipe leading from the top of the retort into a tank cooled by water. The fire is now increased, and the above pipe having been shut off and a new one

1. Name of Office.	Government prices per picul (133⅓ lbs.) for Crystallized Camphor.			Government price per picul for Camphor oil.
	First Grade.	Second Grade.	Third Grade.	
Taipeh	30.00 yen	27.00 yen	24.30 yen	15.00 yen
Teckcham (Shinchiku)	29.00 ,,	26.10 ,,	23.56 ,,	14.50 ,,
Maoli (Bioritsu)	27.00 ,,	24.80 ,,	22.30 ,,	13.80 ,,
Taichu	26.00 ,,	23.40 ,,	21.10 ,,	13.00 ,,
Lin-ki-po	22.00 ,,	19.80 ,,	17.80 ,,	11.00 ,,
Lo-tong (Rato)	27.50 ,,	24.80 ,,	22.80 ,,	13.80 ,,

opened, the Camphor fumes pass through the latter into a large crystallization chamber, the roof of which is cooled by running water. Here it crystallizes as flowers of Camphor. This grade without further manipulation is sold as "Improved Crude," and is 97 per cent. pure.

For the block Camphor, the drug after having passed through the above operation, is first shaped in wooden forms; these blocks are then pressed by steam power to prepare them for final treatment, which is to subject them to very high hydraulic pressure. The resulting block is a hard, firm, slightly opaque brick weighing ten kin (13⅓ lbs.). These blocks are then packed in zinc lined boxes holding ten, and after receiving the government label are handed over to the selling agents. The last two grades represent in quantity about one half of the total output of government Camphor. Owing to their high quality they are frequently used in lieu of refined Camphor, and find a market in all countries except the United States, where the high duty practically prohibits their entrance. The Formosan Government also has on the market, a brand of "Refined Camphor" prepared for the retail trade.

The enforcement of the monopoly dates from August 5th (1899), but as there were large stocks of Camphor stored in Formosa owned by private firms, the disposal of which was not interfered with by the government, there was sufficient to supply the demand for the summer and fall. Thus, though the government purchased what Camphor was offered, they placed none on the market.

On March 24th (1900), tenders were called for from firms, Japanese and foreign, who were desirous of obtaining the sole selling agency for Formosan Camphor. In asking for bids the Formosan government named several conditions under which tenders would be accepted; the general tenor of the same being as follows :—The holder of the agency must conduct the sale of the Camphor at London, Hamburg, New York, and Hongkong, and must be prepared to accept from the government from 30,000 to 50,000 piculs of Camphor a year. The Camphor will be of two classes, "A" to be known as "Cleaned" or "Pressed," and "B," which is the Camphor in its ordinary crude form. When the amount of Camphor to be turned over to the selling agents exceeds 50,000 piculs a year, the selling price for the excess will be determined by the Formosan government in concert with the selling agents. The government will prepare and pack the Camphor ready for shipment; and the selling agents must not change the wrapping or package, nor place other materials among the contents. So far as in their power, the selling agents should send such quantities of Camphor to various leading markets, (London, Hamburg, New York, Hongkong, etc.,), as may be necessary to supply the demand. The term of the contract between the government and the selling agents will be three years. For the use of the government and also as raw material for the purpose of manufacture in the Japanese Empire, the Formosan government may sell to persons other than the selling agents. However, this extra-official sale will not affect the minimum limit of the quantity to be sold to the selling agents. The government requires of the selling agents a substantial guarantee, this security being permitted to take the form of a deposit of Formosan government bonds.

Government Camphor Works, Taihoku.
Taikokan (Tokoham) Village, Supply
Station for Leading Camphor District.
Kutsshaku (Kuchu) Village, on Border
of Savage District

Up-country Japanese Still.
Chinese Police on Savage Border.

Virgin Forest Land within the
Savage District, North Formosa

Although the government generally recommends the sale of the " Cleaned and Pressed " (semi-refined) grade owing to the saving in loss in weight, etc., still it has been announced that the crude form of the drug will be furnished to consumers specially applying for it through the regular channels.

An English firm was the fortunate recipient of the agency, their tender being the most favorable ; that is, they were prepared to conduct the business on the cheapest basis. The prices which will be asked for the drug abroad have been announced as follows :—For "A" Grade Camphor blocks for London, Hamburg, and New York 107,843 yen per picul (133 lbs.), (exclusive of import duties if any), and for Hongkong 102.378 yen. For crude Camphor 99.702 yen will be the price abroad. The government will receive from the selling agents 85.00 yen a picul for the crude and 94.323 yen for the "A" Camphor. It has been roughly estimated that the government expense in preparing the "A" grade Camphor, providing for loss in weight and other expenses in connection with the monopoly, will average over 25 yen a picul ; and, though it is at present somewhat premature to state figures as to the probable resulting profit, considering that the monopoly is so late a creation, still the figures appearing in the government budget are doubtless approximate, though some slight changes have been made in the monopoly system since the budget was framed. In the budget the total expenses, including cost of Camphor, are given as 2,127,611 yen, and the receipts as 3,455,035 yen. This leaves a profit of 1,327,424 yen, or about 34 yen a picul (133 lbs.). This is taking the probable production for the year at 39,000 piculs. The income to the government from the Camphor industry under the old system averaged about 400,000 yen a year.

Though Camphor has been monopolized at different times during the Chinese regime in the island, the system was quite different to the one the Japanese now intend to pursue, and the present monopoly may be considered somewhat in the light of an experiment.

While there appears to be at present no obstacle seriously to interfere with the working of the monopoly, the future may bring forth either some increase in the production from other lands, which may eventually require some important alterations in the present system, or perhaps the abandonment of a monopoly altogether. The Japan production which, in 1887, reached 8,615,740 lbs., has rapidly decreased until only some three hundred thousand pounds were produced in 1899. To what degree this lost trade in Japan can recover its former importance under the stimulus of steady high prices is not known. It is at least sure, however, that there are not sufficient available trees to permit of any lasting competition with Formosa. China, encouraged by the high prices ruling in 1895, produced throughout her dominions some 1,500,000 lbs., but it is doubtful if she could much exceed this in the future ; for, as previously mentioned in this chapter, although there are districts where Camphor trees abound, they are not sufficiently rich in the drug to pay for distillation. Still it will be well to watch the Chinese production, and in years to come new lands in which the tree is being introduced may need some attention.

Under the present monopoly regulations, the government controls the sale of Camphor oil as well as the crude Camphor. The trade in this article is in reality of only three years growth; yet to such proportions has it reached that, in 1898, over five million pounds were exported to Kobe.

This, even for Formosa, exceptional quantity, when separated yielded two and a half million pounds of true Camphor, being equal to the total output of Formosa crude Camphor shipped to Hongkong, India, and Europe, via Hongkong; though it must be explained that the crude Camphor export figures do not correctly represent the production for 1898, as large stocks of that year's Camphor were held over in Formosa over the calendar year.

Of course it must be noted that the government production of crude Camphor may not exceed 40,000 piculs (5,320,000 lbs). Still even with this amount, taking the proportionate yield of oil at 50 per cent., and allowing for loss in weight during transportation to place of manufacture, some million and a half pounds of oil will be produced, and this when distilled will yield some seven or eight hundred thousand pounds of true Camphor. Even this quantity might prove a disturbing factor. To provide against this, the government will probably arrange that the parties handling the oil shall dispose of it at a price which shall conform to the Formosa prices, and that the authorities shall be made acquainted with all sales.

The contract for the sale of the drug runs only for three years, which will give the authorities the opportunity of making alterations in the system if they find it necessary. Of course, the selling agents must be protected from outside competition, and it would not do to injure the market for Camphor by too high prices. Celluloid manufacturers may find some satisfactory substitute for Camphor, or celluloid consumers revert to the use of bone and other materials; while chemists, if driven to it, may even discover some article which may to a large extent replace Camphor as a drug.

NOTE.

(Regulations applying to the Monopoly of Formosa Camphor and Camphor Oil.)

NOTIFICATION No. 15, JUNE 22ND, 32ND YEAR MEIJI (1899).

Art. I.—By the term Camphor employed in this Regulation shall be understood the crude Camphor produced in this island, and by the term Camphor oil shall be understood Camphor oil which, with crude Camphor, forms the two products obtained by the distillation process.

Art. II.—Camphor and Camphor oil must be turned over by the manufacturers to the government, which holds a monopoly of them. With the exception of the Camphor or Camphor oil sold to the government, the possession, hypothecation, transfer, or export of all other [Camphor or Camphor oil is prohibited.

Art III.—The Government will make payment for Camphor or Camphor oil delivered to it, at a rate to be fixed by the Governor-General.

Art. IV.—Camphor or Camphor oil cannot be exported from the island except through the Ports named by the Governor-General.

Art. V.—The Camphor and Camphor oil manufacturers must render to the Government annually a report showing the anticipated amount of production for the ensuing year.

Art. VI.—All Camphor and Camphor oil will be sold by the government at a fixed rate, or, if desirable, will be offered to public tender.

Art. VII.—Officers will be despatched to inspect Camphor and Camphor oil manufactories and stores or any place where it is believed Camphor is stored and take suitable measures for control.

Art. VIII.—Persons who have violated clause 2 of Art. II and Art. IV will be fined a sum ranging from 50 to 500 yen, and the Camphor or Camphor oil concerned will be confiscated irrespective of its owners.

Art. IX.—Any persons who have refused or avoided or obstructed officers in the execution of their duty as laid down in Art. VII will be fined a sum ranging from 20 to 200 yen and if there is an aggravation of the offence which is covered by criminal law then the offending parties will be punished according to such law.

Art. X.—Those who make false declarations or neglect to make declarations to the government or to answer the interrogations of the authorized officers will be fined a sum ranging from 10 to 100 yen.

Art. XI.—Persons engaged in the Camphor and Camphor oil business who add any adulterant to Camphor or Camphor oil will be fined a sum ranging from 10 to 100 yen and the Camphor and Camphor oil concerned will be confiscated irrespective of its owners.

Art. XII.—To those who violate these Regulations the provisions of the Penal Code providing for cumulative punishment for second or several offences will not be applied.

Art. XIII.—When the family, lodgers, representatives, or employés of those engaged in the Camphor and Camphor oil business have offended against the foregoing provisions the manufacturer or his representative cannot escape from the penalties provided, though he had no cognisance of the offence.

SUPPLEMENTARY CLAUSES.

Art. XIV.—Any regulations which it may at later date be found necessary to add and the date for the enforcement of the present regulations will be announced in due time by the Governor-General.

Art. XV.—Notification No. 12 of the 29th year of Meiji providing for Camphor taxation, and Notification No. 9 of the 30th year of Meiji providing for Camphor oil taxation will be cancelled from the date of enforcement of this regulation.

Art. XVI.—These regulations will not be applied to Camphor and Camphor oil which has been manufactured prior to their enforcement, but to Camphor and Camphor oil on which the tax has not been paid these regulations will be applied and the owners must deliver the Camphor and Camphor oil to the Government.

Art. XVII.—To Camphor manufactured from Camphor oil these Regulations will not at present be applied.[1]

REGULATIONS APPLYING TO THE MANUFACTURE OF CAMPHOR AND CAMPHOR OIL IN FORMOSA.

NOTIFICATION No. 16.

Art. I.—A person desiring to manufacture Camphor or Camphor oil must obtain government permission.

Art. II.—Any person holding government permission to manufacture Camphor or Camphor oil who fails to commence work within the prescribed period, or who having commenced, discontinues the work, will forfeit his right, and his license may be cancelled by the government.

Art. III.—Should the manufacture of Camphor and Camphor oil (in any district) be found opposed to the public interest the Governor-General may suspend the manufacture and revoke the license.

Art. IV.—When a Camphor and Camphor oil manufacturer's license has been revoked by the government, or when the former discontinues work voluntarily, the trees remaining unused must be returned to the government. When work is discontinued voluntarily suitable compensation will be paid.

Art. V.—Persons manufacturing Camphor or Camphor oil without possessing government licenses will be punished by a fine ranging from 50 to 500 yen and the illicit Camphor and Camphor oil will be confiscated wherever found.

Art. VI.—Persons who utilize for some other purpose Camphor trees sold them by the Government for the express purpose of manufacturing Camphor and Camphor oil, or who transport them outside of the manufacturer's respective districts will be fined a sum ranging from 50 to 500 yen, and the trees found will be confiscated, and for such trees as are missing payment will be demanded.

Art. VII.—Articles IX. XII. and XIII. of the Camphor Monopoly Regulations will, in addition to the rules given herewith, apply to the manufacture of Camphor and Camphor oil.

SUPPLEMENTARY CLAUSES.

Art. VIII.—Any regulations which it may be found necessary at a later date to add, and the date for the enforcement of the present regulations will be announced in due time by the Governor-General.

Art. IX.—Such portions of Notification No. 26 of the 28th year of Meiji providing for the control of government forests and the manufacture of Camphor as apply to the manufacture of Camphor will be cancelled on the date of enforcement of the present regulations.

Art. X.—Persons who hold licenses to manufacture Camphor granted under Notification No. 26 of the 28th year of Meiji, providing for the control of Government Forests and the manufacture of Camphor, or under Notification No. 13 of the 29th year of Meiji providing for more complete control of the manufacture of Camphor will be registered as also possessing the permission indicated in the present Notification from the date these regulations are enforced and continuing till the natural term of the licenses expire.

---

1. Art. XVII, at first sight may appear to conflict with Art. II. This is not the case, however, as Art. XVII only refers to Camphor actually manufactured from the oil, which is quite a distinct process from the ordinary distilling done in the island at present. It is not a disturbing factor either, for while Camphor manufactured from Camphor oil will not be interfered with at present, the Government have virtually control over it for the reason that they hold all the Camphor oil, and if parties desire to purchase it for the purpose of converting it into ordinary Camphor, they must purchase it from the government, and the price asked for it will doubtless be sufficiently high to insure that the monopoly of Camphor will not be interfered with.

FORMOSA CAMPHOR STATISTICS.

Year.	Export from Tamsui in pounds.	Export from Anping and Takow in pounds	Shipped from Kelung (to Japan) in pounds. 1.	Total Export in pounds.	Average Formosa price Tamsui currency per picul, (133 lbs.) in local currency.
1856	—	1,330,000		1,330,000	$ 8.00
1864	1,171,464	Nil.		1,171,464	8.00
1865	1,035,405	,,		1,035,405	15.40
1866	1,123,474	,,		1,123,474	15.00
1867	674,310	,,		674,310	16.00 { official price under monopoly.
1868	1,485,477	107,996		1,593,473	9.00
1869	1,835,001	200,564		2,035,565	9.00
1870	1,925,973	314,279		2,240,272	9.49
1871	1,288,903	Nil.		1,288,903	8.22
1872	1,367,373	3,773		1,371,146	10.36
1873	1,430,415	Nil.		1,430,415	9.17
1874	1,606,507	,,		1,606,507	8.84
1875	949,487	,,		949,487	8.93
1876	1,169,602	,,		1,169,602	8.71
1877	1,752,408	,,		1,752,408	10.00
1878	1,795,766	41,629		1,837,395	9.50
1879	1,469,384	8,778		1,478,162	9.76
1880	1,640,555	Nil.		1,640,555	12.24
1881	1,239,028	,,		1,239,028	12.81
1882	656,089	36,841		692,930	12.33
1883	410,438	28,329		438,767	17.47
1884	58,919	2,394		61,313	11.95
1885	399	Nil.		399	13.89
1886	128,212	23,210		151,422	16.86
1887	335,160	31,388		336,548	13.56
1888	382,109	127,813		509,922	12.00 { official price under monopoly.
1889	476,273	79,268		555,541	13 and 20 { official price under monopoly.
1890	983,186	100,947		1,064,133	30 { official price under monopoly.
1891	2,511,173	282,093		2,793,266	36.50
1892	2,332,820	573,895		2,906,715	41.75
1893	4,431,560	889,903		5,321,463	44.85
1894	5,260,416	1,616,881		6,877,297	41.00
1895 ..	5,586,000	1,349,285		6,935,285	68.50
1896	4,702,348	1,064,133		5,766,481	57.00
1897	3,780,791	406,581	981,188	5,168,560	47.00
1898	2,920,680	121,121	1,761,452	4,803,253	42.00

1. The figures given in the column headed " Shipped from Kelung to Japan " represent only crystallized Camphor shipped to Japan since the occupation of the Island by the Japanese, and as this is trade with the home country, same are not given in the Japanese Custom Reports. They have been here included in the total export column in order that the reader may be able to arrive at the total Formosan production. Figures showing the export from Tamsui, Anping, and Takow are chiefly from Chinese and Japanese Custom Reports.

CAMPHOR OIL STATISTICS.

Year.	Export from Tamsui in pounds.	Export from Anping and Takow in pounds.	Shipped from Kelung to Japan in pounds.	Total Export in pounds.	Average Formosa price Tamsui currency per picul (133 lbs.)
1895	—	—	—	—	—
1896	7,581	665	800,000 (estimated.)	808,246	$ 20.00
1897	87,381	—	3,652,552	3,739,933	15.50
1898	20,216	977	5,633,614	5,653,830	16.50

The trade in Formosa Camphor Oil dates back only to 1895, the year of the arrival of the Japanese, who practically made the market for Camphor oil.

As with crystallized Camphor, Camphor oil shipped from Kelung to Japan is not included in the Custom Reports, and the figures, as well as the average price appearing in this table, are estimated. Figures showing the export from Tamsui and Anping and Takow are from the Japanese Custom Reports.

WORLD'S CAMPHOR PRODUCTION.

Year.	Export from Japan of Japanese Camphor. In pounds.	Total value of year's Export in Japanese yen.	Export from Formosa of Formosa Camphor including shipment to Japan. In pounds.	Total value of year's Export in Japanese yen.	Total Export Japan and Formosa Camphor in pounds.	Total value Japan and Formosa Camphor in Japanese yen.
1868	622,644	77,097	1,593,473	107,829	2,216,117	184,925
1873	592,750	68,437	1,430,415	98,623	2,023,165	167,060
1878	2,666,586	323,664	1,837,395	131,242	4,503,981	454,906
1883	6,456,274	707,992	438,767	57,528	6,895,041	765,520
1887	8,615,740	1,130,596	536 548	37,371	9,152,288	1,167,967
1889	6,612,559	1,391,371	555,541	68,920	7,168,100	1,460,291
1890	5,936,961	1,931,992	1,064,133	240,030	7,001,094	2,172,022
1891	5,800,637	1,629,104	2,793.266	766,573	8,688,903	2,395,677
1892	4,075,126	1,274,752	2,906,715	912,446	6,981,841	2,187,198
1893	3,308,355	1,308,610	5,321,463	1,794,493	8,629,818	3,103,103
1894	2,754,932	1,023,956	6,877,291	2,120,807	9,632,229	3,144,763
1895	2,976,939	1,226,831	6,935,285	2,877,000	9,912,224	4,103,831
1896	1,751,400	910,728	6,166,481	2,455,930	7,917,881	3,366,658
1897	1,661,442	290,000 estimated.	5,931,670	2,395,942	6,643,112	2,685,942
1898	600,000 estimated.	200,000 estimated.	6,868,688	2,163,636	7,468,688	2,363,636

The figures given in the above table for the year prior to 1896 are from the Japanese and Chinese Customs Returns, respectively, but the figures for the years 1896, 1897, and 1898 vary greatly from Customs statistics. For the three years mentioned the Customs figures are of trifling assistance in ascertaining the production of Japan and Formosa separately, and it has been accordingly necessary to calculate on a different basis.

The total export from Japan now consists almost wholly of Formosa crude Camphor or Camphor manufactured from Formosa Camphor oil. Therefore to arrive at the production for export of Camphor actually produced in Japan, I have given the Japanese Customs export minus the quantity of Formosa Camphor shipped to Japan. To obtain the value of the Japanese production, I have used the Japanese Customs figures as a basis.

The export from Formosa as stated in the Formosan Custom's returns, for the years mentioned provides only for shipments to Hongkong, India, Europe, and America direct; and naturally makes no mention of shipments to Japan. Therefore, to ascertain the true production of Formosa Camphor it has been necessary to add to the Customs figures, the amount of Camphor shipped to Japan, together with an amount equal to 50 per cent. of the exports to Japan of Camphor oil, for the reason that Camphor exists in Camphor oil, and when the latter reaches Japan, it is subjected to a distilling process, and made to yield roughly 50 per cent. of its weight in crude Camphor; therefore the latter should obviously be included in the total showing Formosa Camphor production. To arrive at the total value of the Formosan product, I have added to the Formosa Customs figures an amount based on the value of the Formosan Camphor in Japan and Camphor manufactured from the oil in Japan. For the year 1898, I have, to arrive at the Formosa production, included shipments to Japan and estimated their value by taking as a basis the value given by the Customs of the export to Hongkong, etc.

As absolutely exact statistics of the export to Japan of Formosa Camphor and oil are not obtainable, and as it is also difficult to ascertain what quantity of the Formosa drug is held in stock in Japan over the calendar year, or the amount, if any, of the Formosa drug consumed in Japan locally, the figures given above for the last three years can only be taken as approximately correct.

The so-called "Borneo" Camphor (Borneol) and other products which resemble Camphor are not included in the above table, as they are not classed as true Camphor; neither have the trifling exports of China Camphor been inserted.

LEADING CAMPHOR CONSUMING COUNTRIES.

This table gives the quantity of Camphor actually consumed in the countries named and not re-exported from them.

Average for the years from 1893 to 1897.

Germany	2,240,917 pounds.
United States ..	1,835,533 ,,
England	1,722,664 ,,
France	1,204,847 ,,
India	1,002,155 ,,

For the single year 1898.

Germany	2,915,000 pounds.
United States ..	2,017,000 ,,
England	394,000 ,,

During the year 1899, England imported 853,000 pounds.

CHAPTER XXV.

THE FORMOSAN SUGAR INDUSTRY.

Sugar.—Production regions—Northern and southern fields compared—Area under cultivation—History of cultivation—Sugar cultivation introduced during Dutch occupation—Cultivation and manufacture during Koxinga's reign—Rapid extension of cultivation—Trade in 1833—Robinet & Co. (1856) Export from Takow —Market figures for 1856—Sugar boom of 1870—Australia and the Formosa market—Shipment to London—Foreign markets for Formosa product—State legislation destroys American market—Sugar districts in North Formosa— Growth of plant and soil—Cultivation of the cane—Harvesting—Yield per acre —Native Sugar factory—Mill charges—Employés—Land tenure—Methods of financing—Bad debts and high interest—Japanese banks and the Sugar trade— Dr. Myers report on the Sugar industry—Soil—Description of cane—Absence of proper fertilizing and irrigation—Method of planting—Cane crushing mills— Description of machinery used—Process of extraction—Cost of mill—Capacity— Estimate of losses incurred through use of imperfect machinery—Advantages of foreign machines—Stupid conservatism—Absence of cleanliness—Clarification of juice—Boiling process described—Clayed or white Sugar—Use of sewer refuse —Grading of Sugar—Manufacture of " samshu "—Market relations—Yield of southern district—Takow brown Sugar—Gross adulteration—Grades of Sugar —Markets for same—Foreigners share in Sugar trade—Export to Japan— Opportunity for foreign enterprise doubtful—Government assistance—Funds devoted to improvement—School for Sugar experts—Demand in Japan—Introduction of Hawaiian seed cane—The Formosa Sugar Manufacturing Company —Japanese white Sugar factory—American Sugar mills—Climatical conditions —Dr. Nitobe's report—Improved cane required—Irrigation—Fertilizing—Extension of area under Sugar—Improved methods of manufacture—Table showing increase of production expected—Export statistics.

OF the several agricultural products exported from Formosa, Sugar, in respect to the area devoted to its growth and the number of employés engaged in its cultivation, occupies first place, while as regards the value of the output it is exceeded only by tea.

There are few cultivated tracts of any size in the island, in which some Sugar cannot be found; but the true producing region, where the plant finds its most congenial home, is in the mid and south Formosa districts.

Thus in the north, only occasional fields, covering each a few acres or so, and producing but a small quantity of the article, chiefly for local consumption, are met with; while in central and southern Formosa, near Kagi for instance, practically a continuous field exists stretching from the interior hills to the sea; a distance of perhaps twenty-five miles. In the north the cane is used for the manufacture of brown unclayed Sugar alone, whereas in the south both brown and white are produced.

It has been roughly estimated that some 35,000 acres of land are devoted to the production of Sugar, of which 28,771 are in the single district covered by the old prefecture of Tainan.

The cultivation of Sugar appears to have followed closely the settlement of Chinese in south Formosa. The Dutch on their arrival in 1624 found Sugar one of the principal articles of export, and the first difficulty which occurred between the Dutch and the Japanese and Chinese colonists in the island had its rise in an attempt on the part of the Dutch to impose an export duty on Sugar and rice.[1] In the trade which followed under the Dutch regime, the export of Sugar was an important item, the shipments to Japan being especially extensive. One authority states that as much as 80,000 piculs (10,640,000 lbs.) were shipped to Japan in a single year. This is difficult to believe, however, when we consider the comparatively small area under cultivation at that time.

The Koxinga family who followed the Dutch as the rulers of Formosa, gave a great impetus to Sugar cultivation by introducing from Fokien province, China, large quantities of seed plants. Chengching, the son of Koxinga, gave special attention to the industry during his reign, and taught the colonists new methods of cultivation and manufacture. With the encouragement received from the boy king the cultivation of the cane was greatly extended. Fifty years later the production had doubled, and in the middle of the 18th century Luchow, the famous Chinese statesman, called attention to the thousands engaged in the cultivation of the cane, and to the fact that a great part of the Sugar consumed in the northern provinces of China was produced in the island. In 1833, the Canton Register states that more than 20 junks arrived annually in Tientsin with Formosa Sugar.

In 1856, Robinet & Co., an American firm, the first foreign arrivals following the occupation of the island by the Chinese, established themselves at Takow, and exported, among other products of Formosa, the local Sugar. At this date a good trade in brown Sugar existed with Japan; while to North China there was annually shipped Sugar to the amount of about 160,000 piculs (21,280,000 lbs.), valued at some $470,000, one third being white, and the balance brown Sugar. The cost in those days was $2.00 (Mexican) a picul (133 lbs.) for brown, and $4.50 for white.

Prior to the year 1870, the total export of Sugar had never exceeded some 37 million pounds, but during this year the export doubled, and from that period the tendency was to increase. A growing demand in Australia

---

1. See page 14.

had much to do with this. In 1873, a representative of Melbourne Sugar houses visited Takow and gave large orders. This and other purchases were largely due to the existence of rival refineries in Australia, each desirous of obtaining for itself control of all the available raw stock. In 1875, in spite of high prices, further large purchases were made in Formosa ; but the bright prospects of those engaged in the Formosan industry, who anticipated the continued patronage of such a satisfactory customer, were blasted by the amalgamation of the rival concerns, and their withdrawal entirely from the Formosan field ; their usual supplies from the Mauritius being sufficient for their requirements.

In 1872, some 5,200,000 lbs. of Formosa Sugar was shipped to London, but this was exceptional business, and after the withdrawal of Australia, only two foreign markets remained—Japan and California. The next blow was caused by state legislation in America which placed a high duty on the Formosa product, practically preventing its importation ; and, though strenuous exertions were made to induce the authorities to deal with the product more kindly, the only result was an alteration in the wording of the law, granting exemption from duty only on Sugar arriving in cases, this being the form of packing utilized by Hawaiian shippers. Owing to the expense, cases could not be used for the Formosa product, and thus the once promising trade was stifled.

Though a temporary boom was experienced in 1876, owing to the partial failure of the cane crop in the Mauritius and West Indian Islands, and the beet-root crop in France, still the withdrawal of so much foreign custom was very dispiriting, and it was feared that the export business would gradually fall away. But fortunately, Japan, which had always been a stable customer, if not a large one, now began to feel the effects of the new order of things following her great political changes, and with the resulting growth of trade and prosperity, the consumption of Sugar increased. The Formosa product enjoyed great favor, and Japan was soon able to take a quantity largely in excess of its former share, with the amount previously consumed in the United States combined. The demand in China likewise increased, though this trade was generally looked upon as unremunerative ; and in later years, Hongkong became a small customer. This placed the industry on a more favorable basis, and in 1880, the total export reached over 141½ million pounds,—the largest known.

In the north of the island there are several districts, although small in comparison with those in the south, where considerable attention is given to the cultivation of the cane and the manufacture of brown Sugar, the quality of the product being said to be fully equal to the best brown Sugar produced in the south. The most extensive fields are to be found a few miles up the Tamsui river from Taihoku (Taipeh) the capital. On each side of the bank the growing of cane extends for several miles over the rich alluvial plain which spreads out on either side. There are Sugar mills in the neighborhood to handle the product. The cane grows well, is not often affected by climatical extremes, but does not equal in height and size the

Sugar cane which grows in the south, though even the latter is far inferior to the Sugar cane of the Hawaiian Islands.

In the north, there is only one large crop a year, the harvesting occurring in the winter months. In the early spring, the land is carefully plowed, furrows from 2½ to 4½ feet apart are made, and the stumps of the old plants inserted in an inclined position some 12 to 15 inches apart, to be replaced once in three or four years by cane cuttings. These are manured after the process of planting is completed, a second manuring being applied one or two months later. No further fertilizing is done, even the second manuring being sometimes dispensed with.

In some parts of Kagi, rice is planted in rotation with Sugar every two or three years. In the north, potatoes, peanuts, or beans are sometimes grown in alternate years, and sometimes these plants are grown between the furrows, without apparent injury to them or the Sugar. In harvesting, the lower leaves are first stripped or burned off, and the cane is then cut near the ground with a kind of sickle. Women and children are often engaged to strip off the leaves, but the cutting of the cane is done exclusively by men. It is estimated that the average yield in Formosa is from 160 to 320 piculs (20,000 to 42,000 lbs.) of cane per acre. In the north, the harvested product is carried to the crushing mills by coolies, but in the south much of the transportation is done by ox-carts.

The crushing-shed, the machinery of which is described in a special paper which follows, is a cone-shaped structure having a diameter of some fifty feet at the base, and is thirty feet in height. The supports are of bamboo, and the roof is thatched with straw. The boiling house, which adjoins the above shed, is provided with a tiled roof, and is usually more strongly built. Sometimes a third building for storing the Sugar is added. The establishment is not a very imposing one, and the crushing-sheds seldom get through the typhoon season without being almost, if not entirely, destroyed.

In the south, especially at Tainan, the buildings are generally of a more substantial nature; a white Sugar factory will have two or three large structures, will employ more men, and the whole plant is more in accordance with the idea a foreigner has of a factory as the term is used. In the north, a Sugar factory is often owned by one man, who, though he usually has a large quantity of his own cane to care for, still depends principally for his support on the other growers in the neighborhood. Sometimes such a manufacturer will undertake to do all the work, from cutting the cane to preparing and selling the finished product, the general remuneration for this service being half of the total receipts from the sale of the Sugar. Other contracts are made, by the terms of which the manufacturer advances to the farmer a certain sum to cover cost of cultivation, and then takes from the receipts of the sale of the Sugar a certain percentage as remuneration. A factory complete represents a first cost varying from 500 yen to perhaps 2,000 yen From ten to fourteen employés suffice for the factory, though each establishment usually keeps from eight to sixteen coolies to attend to the transportation of the cane and Sugar. In round numbers there are some 1,400 of these factories in the island.

The southern half of Formosa is, as above stated, the principal seat of the Sugar industry, and it is to this portion of the island, that the balance of this chapter refers.

The land in the south is almost wholly in the hands of large Chinese capitalists, who lease it out to farmers, and take as rent a share in the produce amounting in value to 15 or 20 per cent. of the market price of the land. Taxes and cost of collection are paid by the landlord, so that the rental is not so excessively high as it would at first sight appear. The farmer requires implements and stock to work the ground, and the where-with-all to live until the crop is harvested. If he is about to put the land under Sugar, and it is only with this class of cultivation that we are now concerned, he applies to one of the large Chinese Sugar merchants for an advance of say 50 yen, at interest varying from 14 to say 24 per cent. a year, according to the standing of the borrower, and as additional compensation, the farmer agrees to sell to the lender his whole Sugar crop at the regular market price. From time to time further advances are required. When the Sugar cane is nearly ripe and ready to cut, arrangements must be made for crushing. Sometimes a number of farmers combine together, and erect a sugar mill to handle their total crop. More often, however, the crushing is done by the money lenders or by a syndicate of brokers representing them. The farmers are expected to give their patronage to the mill controlled by the merchant to whom they are indebted. As payment for crushing the cane and extracting the Sugar, 7 per cent. of the produce is reserved, and there are other trifling charges to be paid. Frequently, the money lender will obtain the Sugar at a very favorable price by purchasing the standing cane for a lump sum. Men well up in the business visit a certain field and estimate the amount of juice to be obtained from the cane in sight. An offer is then made, and if the deal is closed, the mill sends laborers, who cut the cane, and transport it to the mill. While large gains frequently result from such deals, large losses also sometimes occur.

Not only is the farmer under moral obligations to dispose of his product to the merchant who has supplied him with funds, but it is customary to allow the money lender a small commission, amounting to about 5 cents on each picul (133⅓ lbs). If the price to be obtained, excluding this commission, is unfavorable, the farmer frequently seeks purchasers for his Sugar elsewhere. Outside merchants who do not care to run the risks attendant upon the making of advances indiscriminately to farmers, pay a higher price for their Sugar, sometimes as much as 10 or 15 cents a picul.

It has doubtless frequently occurred that certain farmers, through crop failure or other unavoidable trouble, have been unable during a certain year to meet their obligations. The high interest charged added to the principal and compounded, plus the advances for the year following, would comprise a sum so large that it would be very difficult for the farmer to discharge his liabilities.

Once behind in his payments, with his debt rapidly increasing, but a few years need intervene before the farmer's obligations reach to an amount which it is impossible for him ever to pay. If he is a compliant, tractable individual he may slave till his dying day for the money lender without the slightest hope of improving his position, but more often he becomes careless, repudiates his obligation, and sells his Sugar wherever he can. As the majority of the farmers possess no property which can be given as security, many of the loans are absolutely irrecoverable. The famous Tan family are said to have written off, during 25 years, more than one million yen of bad debts. To the great risk run in making advances is largely due the high rate of interest demanded. Thus the industrious and successful farmer suffers by the shiftlessness and incapacity of his neighbor. The Japanese Government has given the subject considerable attention with the object of remedying the evil, and the Japanese banks have placed a considerable amount of capital at the disposal of Chinese merchants at a rate of interest somewhat below that previously existing. The position of the farmers, however, is such that but little can be done for them, and the Sugar consumption tax, lately imposed throughout Japan and Formosa, has for the time at least doubled their burdens.

The cultivation of the cane, the practice of local Sugar manufactures, and the classification of the finished products, have been so well described by W. Wykeham Myers, M. B., late of Takow, that I take great pleasure in placing before my readers an essay which he has kindly contributed, and which is an extract from his original paper appearing in a British Consular Report.[1] It has by additions and alterations been brought up to date.

"The soil in the different districts, and indeed in various parts of the same divisions, differs considerably in its Sugar producing properties. Thus, although no more care in cultivation of the cane or treatment of the juice is shown in the 'Takow' district than in the 'Taiwanfu' (Tainanfu) Department, the products of the former are richer in crystallizable Sugar, and consequently, grade for grade, of higher commercial value.

"The species of plant grown is that known as the 'Chinese Cane,' which locally the growers distinguish into three varieties, based on the thickness and color of the skin. It has been stated that the Sorghum, or Sugar grass, is cultivated in Formosa, but so far as I know, that is not the case in the southern part of the island at least. Through negligence in cultivation, the cane here dwindles to a very small size, the joints only averaging from one to one and a half inches in circumference, and little or no attention seems to be devoted to the plant beyond putting it in the ground. Even for irrigation, which during the periods of small rain-fall or drought, would be of material advantage, no means whatever are provided. Plantings are made from cuttings about once in three years. These are first soaked in water for about twenty days, until the buds begin to sprout. They are then placed obliquely in the ground, more or less in a line, with one end protruding, the furrow for their reception being scraped with the hands. A little manure is placed over them, but beyond this, with perhaps an exceptional and occasional weeding by some of the more careful growers, nothing further is done. The crops for the intervening two years are raised from 'Ratoons,' and at the end of the third year the roots are dug out and burned. Cane crushing is effected by stone mills, worked by two, and sometimes three, buffaloes. These mills are generally set up and owned in the 'Takow' district by agents of the money-lenders.

"The producers who have received loans are expected to bring their cane to the money lender's mill, to which is also attached the boiling-house. Each participant must provide two buffaloes, if he wishes only to be charged 7 per cent. of the produce from his cane as the cost of manufacture. In the more southern parts of the island, the buffaloes are supplied by the mills, when the growers are subjected to a higher charge. These mills are erected at the beginning of each season, usually early in December, and are dismantled at its conclusion, the stones being buried in the earth for their preservation. The animals work in spells of from an hour to an hour and a half, according to the time taken to extract, say, about two piculs of juice. There are, as a rule, four boiler men and four attendants on the mill, working in day and night shifts, besides 'cowmen,' all of whom are chiefly paid by what they can squeeze from the Sugar, and sale of cane-trash.

"The following is a description of the mills in use in Formosa, which shows how very far short they come of fulfilling even ordinary requirements, a fact that leads to much loss of product. The granite

1. See 1890 British Consular Report for Tainan.

rollers, 25 inches in diameter by 30 inches in height, are placed in apposition. At the top of each roller a row of depressions is cut, into which are fitted hardwood cogs. By means of the latter, the motion is imparted to the right-hand stone from the left-hand one. Wooden spindles are let into the centre of each stone at top and bottom respectively. By the lower of these the stones fit into a granite, or sometimes wooden, bed-plate, while the top ones project through a transverse wooden binding-beam, the left-hand upper spindle being prolonged so as to afford attachment for the lever, at the farther end of which the buffaloes are yoked. The apposition of the rollers to each other is secured and judged according to the ability of the millwright; and as the wooden binding-beam is constantly wearing, and thus the distance between the rollers always varying, the pressure on the cane, only roughly set at first, is most irregular in its application all through. To modify the effects of this as far as possible, the natives pass the cane thrice through the mill, but as the following experiments show, the results obtained are by no means perfect. Then again, the frequent stoppages for readjustment and repairing the mills are also a constant trouble and drawback. The wooden cogs have also frequently to be replaced, as, indeed, is the case with all the other wooden parts of the machine; causing the millowner a never ceasing outlay.

"The minimum first cost of one of these mills, not counting the house, is $150, and besides that, at the commencement of each season, renewing the wooden fittings, erecting the shed, and setting up the mill amounts to at least $100; and then there is the ever recurring cost of repairs during the whole time the mill is running. By careful experiments made alongside several native mills with those of foreign manufacture, it was found that for every 100 lbs. of cane thrice pressed by the Chinese mill, 60 lbs. weight of juice was extracted from the cane, as against 68 lbs. got by passage once through the iron mills; showing a gain in favour of the foreign mill of 18 per cent. per weight of cane. The native boiler-men all admitted that the juice got either directly from the cane by the foreign mill, or from the begass that they discharged from their own mill, was as good as, if not better than, that obtained by their own methods. Calculating out what this means on even the limited crop from the Takow districts to which the usurers have of late years reduced it, say 300,000 piculs, it being further remembered that this only comprehends that which is shipped in foreign bottoms, we find that 37,600,000 lbs. of juice are burnt up every year in begass. This would give 108,000 piculs of Sugar if manufactured, which at only $2 50 per picul, shows a total loss of money, consequent on the imperfections of the mills, of $270,000, a sum which would leave an ample margin of profit if every cane-grower purchased a foreign machine, got his canes crushed in the ordinary way by the Chinese mills, merely contenting himself with using his machine for crushing the begass as it came out from the native establishment. In other words, the cost of their fuel is very nearly equal to one-third of the total amount realized on the whole crop of 300,000 piculs. To try and improve this condition amongst the people, the present writer drew up a simple 'Primer' on the cultivation of cane and manufacture of raw Sugar, which was translated into Chinese by the then Acting Commissioner of Customs; but even those whose interests would seem most likely to prompt them to study the question, and whose comparative educational advantages easily enabled them to read what had been written (i e. the dominating money lenders and their agents the mill-owners), could not be got to take much interest in the subject, and, indeed, seemed only to fear lest any innovations, either from instruction or mechanical aids, might interfere with the arrangements which they said were, 'as far as they were concerned, sufficiently remunerative to themselves.'

"The surroundings of these mills are dirty in the extreme, and the juice flows from the rollers by means of a leaky bamboo pipe, led under a filthy buffalo walk, until it arrives at the first pan, or what ought to be the clarifying receptacle. In the 'Takow' districts, the cane tops are ignited, and thus burnt off while the plants are still standing. More or less charred material thus adheres to the cane, discoloring the exposed juice until it is literally as black as ink. There is here also a complete absence of any attempt at cleanliness; the filthiest hands are dipped and even washed in the juice; and while large pieces of trash, saturated with the fluid they have absorbed, are roughly taken out and thrown away, no efforts are made to get rid of the smaller fragments ('cush-cush.')

"In the clarification of juice, beyond stating that lime is added according to the discretion of the boiler-men, exercised in very rough and ready fashion, there is little to be further described. The unslaked lime used is kept in a corner of a very dirty room, constantly exposed to the atmosphere, and is full of dirt and other extraneous matter. There is no attempt at filtration, as the juice is ladled from the receiving pan into the first 'tache.' The boiling 'battery' consists, as a rule, of from four to five 'taches,' and under each one is a furnace. As the boilerman, by some rule which it seems impossible to discover, thinks a sufficient amount of concentration has been arrived at in one 'tache,' he ladles the contents into another, and so on. It is quite possible at any given time that the fires beneath the lower pans are burning less briskly than those under the upper ones; and although the liquor thrown into the first pans shows a low percentage of 'invert,' by the time it has reached the 'striking tache,' this has probably been trebled. In the northern districts, where special efforts are made to 'grain large,' the result is accompanied by a very great loss from inversion. The object of this latter attempt is to get 'laotsai,' the raw material from which so-called 'white,' is produced by means of claying.

"With reference to the other brown varieties of Sugar made in Formosa, it has not been discovered that other than mere chance, perhaps regulated to some slight extent by rough experience, determined either the grain of the product or the amount of crystallisation which happens to survive the crude treatment the liquor has been subjected to all through.

"Clayed or 'White' Sugar, as before explained, is got from 'laotsai.' Each jar holds from 133½ lbs. to 200 lbs. The clay or mud placed at the top of the jars is that scraped from the bottom of sewers, canals, or ponds; and the natives about Taiwan-fu assert that that got from the bottom of the canal, just outside the city walls, which is in fact nothing but a gigantic sewer, produces Sugar with the best taste. This may be due to the fact that the canal, being connected with the sea, always contains more or less salt water, which latter may impart the improved taste. These jars, conical in shape, have a hole in the bottom, and as the moisture from the wet clay slowly trickles through, it washes the face of the crystals, removing the adhering molasses. and leaves the crystallizable material bereft of color in direct ratio to the amount of washing undergone. It thus comes about that so called whites of varying grades are formed in strata more or less deep as they lie from above downwards in the jar.

" The following are the proportions of different grades of white Sugar from one picul of 'laotsai.' The top layer of all, equal in amount to 5 per cent. of the whole, is known as 'No. 1' white; the second layer (15 per cent.) is known as 'No. 2' white; the third layer (25 per cent) is known as 'No. 3' white; the fourth layer (25 per cent.) is known as 'No. 4' white; while 30 per cent. of molasses drains out. The last is reboiled, and about 60 per cent. of Sugar procured from it. This is known as 'cha-soa,' and is in some demand in North China.

" From the foregoing brief description of the manufacturing methods, it is hoped that some idea may be conveyed as to the extremely backward condition of the industry, and it must distinctly be understood that all here stated only refers, and only can refer, to Formosa as it has been. Now that the Japanese have come as rulers, no doubt they will, by introducing machinery, and improving methods both of culti-vation and manufacture, very soon set up a different condition of affairs.

" A spirit ('samshu') is very roughly distilled from molasses that cannot be further utilized at the boiling houses; but the distillation is carried on indiscriminately over the country by any person who cares to buy the molasses. The skimmings at the mills and other saccharine refuse, are generally given to pigs, and the idea of using them for the ground seems to be unthought of.

" As to market relations with the Formosan Sugar trade, it is necessary to note that 'Taiwan-fu' is the name of the southern sugar district as known to trade, the comparatively new official designation of Tainan-fu as applied to the southern prefecture has as yet scarcely come into general use. As before stated, there are two Sugar districts known to the trade in South Formosa, namely:—'Takow' and 'Taiwanfu.' Takow used to produce in good years some 530,000 piculs (70,580,000 lbs.) and Taiwanfu some 310,000 piculs (41,230,000 lbs). In later years, however, the crops of the former have fallen off so that now the production of the Taiwanfu (Tainanfu) district usually surpasses that of Takow. Both in the 'Takow' and 'Taiwanfu' divisions raw Sugar is manufactured, this being the only description exported from Formosa.

" Takow Sugar is an ordinary brown variety, that is to say, it is the raw, undrained article, exported as it comes from the boiling pans. The only modifications in quality known to the trade are those either consequent on an excess of molasses (i.e. inversion, owing to deficiencies in the mode of manufacture), or on a superfluity of moisture, due to atmospheric conditions, varying with the period of the year at which the Sugar is exported. Technically speaking, and in spite of the numerous drawbacks which its crude method of preparation presents, so rich is the quality of the cane, and so suitable the soil, that 'Takow Brown' at any time contains a proportion of crystallizable Sugar which compares most satisfactorily with varieties produced elsewhere and under much more favorable conditions. Looking at this Sugar merely as a saccharine material, Western refineries would be glad to get it, but by reason of its gross adulteration with coarse extraneous matter, it is said not to be well adapted to the machinery in ordinary use, and this to some extent modifies the advantages its composition would seem at first sight to offer. For this reason, and the fact that the average cost price in Formosa has been much above that which might tempt foreign buyers, an outlet through Western and American markets has been practically closed for several years.

" Four kinds or grades of Sugar are produced in the 'Taiwanfu' district, one of which ('lao-tsai') is not exported, but is solely used for the production of so-called 'white' Sugar; while from the molasses drained therefrom in this process, a fifth variety is got by re-boiling, and known as 'Cha-soa., The other three kinds of brown Sugar produced in these districts are known respectively as 'Sheung-tao,' 'Tiong-tao,' and 'Kapan' or 'Ship.' They differ from each other by the care taken in manufacture, thus producing better graining with less amount of 'invert Sugar,' and are classed in order of merit and price as above given, from the clean, fine-grained, dry 'Sheung-tao' down to the irregularly crystallized 'Ka-pau' with its superabundance of molasses. Practically the sole markets to which the Taiwanfu Sugars, both white and brown, go are those supplied by the coast ports, beginning at or about Foochow, or Wenchow, in the south and extending up to Tientsin and Newchwang in the north. Shanghai, Chefoo, and Tientsin are the places through which the greatest bulk of the crop appears to be absorbed, although a certain and not inconsiderable amount is also carried away by native craft to places all along the coast line indicated. The native-borne cargoes from Takow are comparatively small, no doubt because of the very much greater demand for this Sugar in Japan, to which place it is carried entirely in merchant steamers.

" Owing to the determined action of the various Sugar guilds in China, and the pertinacity which they show in boycotting any foreign vendors who venture to engage in the trade, the latter have for several years, and after losing considerably by the attempt to overcome the opposition, completely refrained from attempting to enter the China trade; hence it comes about that the only chance they have of touching Sugar in Formosa is for the Japanese market, and from the Takow districts.

" It will be obvious from the above that the openings available to foreign enterprise, in the Takow Sugar districts, have been as limited as their tenure is uncertain, and there does not seem much reason for hope that, so long as matters remain as they are, foreign merchants can look for a fairer and more reliable share of the business."

Dr. Myers describes in his essay, given above, the processes of Sugar manufacture practised by the natives. A new factor in the industry has been introduced by the construction of a modern Sugar factory by Japanese, as described below.

The Formosan government has pledged itself to a vigorous campaign in behalf of the Sugar industry. After a thorough investigation, for a period of five years, of the various products of the island, the decision has been reached that Sugar has the greatest future, and that government assistance in building up this industry will be most fruitful in results. Accordingly, a special Sugar bureau has been established, and the services of a well known economist and scholar, Dr. Nitobe, Ph. D., requisitioned for its control. During the fiscal year 1902, it was intended to devote 289,769 yen to the development of the Sugar industry. A yearly appropriation will be expended in the purchase of seed cane and machinery, experiments in cultivation and manufacture, subsidy to the two Sugar plants at present in operation, and in other ways which may help the industry. The Sugar machines will be loaned to the farmers. The government is also prepared to grant leases of government land to Sugar cultivators, and to supply funds for the construction of irrigation works. Provision has been made for the education of 30 students desiring to become Sugar experts. Instruction in botany, physics, chemistry, agriculture, Sugar cultivation and Sugar manufacture will be givn. A monthly allowance of 8 yen will be made to each student during the term of study, and government employment given to all graduates. Applicants must pass an entrance examination, be of sound body and of good reputation, and over 23 and under 40 years of age.

Formosa is exceptionally fortunate in possessing in Japan a large market, to which it can gain entrance on more favorable terms than will probably ever be offered foreign Sugar producing lands. The consumption of Sugar in Japan is steadily on the increase, and during the past three years, importations from foreign lands have avaraged about 30,000,000 yen in value, which gives Sugar second place on the list of imports. Japan has proven unsuited for Sugar cultivation. Strenuous attempts have been made to build up the industry, and the government has from time to time given its assistance. Refineries exist in Japan, but they are dependent upon outside sources for their supplies, and have been unable to compete with foreign refineries. With the excess of imports over exports, Japanese economists looked hopefully towards Formosa to restore the balance, and it was hinted, directly after the occupation, that refineries in the island would soon supply Japan with all its Sugar requirements. Several projects for refineries were made public, but none materialized and five years passed without witnessing any attempt on the part of Japanese either to increase the local production or to improve the crude and extremely wasteful process of manufacture.

The agricultural section of the Formosan government turned its attention to Sugar in 1899, and during that year Hawaiian cane cuttings were brought into the island and planted in the experimental garden. The results were most encouraging, the Hawaiian cane, as compared with the local plant, giving a much larger yield of cane per acre, and a larger Sugar yield per pound of cane. The following year more seed cane was obtained from Hawaii, and the experimental station was able to supply the farmers with small quantities of seed cane. The next step was to encourage the adoption of more modern methods of manufacture. In 1900, two American crushing mills were purchased for the experimental garden, and proved to be far

Native Sugar Mill.   Boiling-room in Native Sugar Mill.

Modern Sugar Mill at Kyoshito, South Formosa.

Port of Anping.   Port of Takow.

superior to the native stone mills. Overtures were then made to Japanese capitalists to erect a modern Sugar factory in south Formosa. The first plan called for a capital of only a hundred thousand yen or so. The Government agreed to grant a yearly subsidy amounting to six per cent. of the capital invested, and the Mitsui Bussan Kwaisha undertook to organize a company to carry out the government designs.

The Sugar factory project was received with much favor in Japan, and after preliminary investigations had been made, it was decided to increase the capital to one million yen, divided into 20,000 shares at 50 yen each. Many well known names, such as Count Inouye, Prince Mori, Mr. Masuda, the Mitsui family, etc., were found among the promoters, and no difficulty was experienced in disposing of the stock. The heaviest share holders are the Imperial Household with 1,000 shares, the Mitsui family 2,000, the Mori family 1,000, a wealthy Formosan native interested in the sugar industry, 1,000, Mr. Yoshikawa, 550, and Messrs. Hayashi, Sumitomo, Hosokawa, Hara, Fujita, Tajima, Nagao, Uyeda, Masuda, Suzuki, and others, 500 each.

The site for the factory was selected at Kyoshito, a point 10 miles distant from Takow on the Tainan-Takow section of the Formosan railways. The plant was completed and commenced operations on December 11th, 1901. The factory building is double storied in part and covers over 25,000 square feet. The plant of the defunct Yayeyama factory was bought outright for 75,000 yen, and an English five-roller crushing mill, a French triple-effect apparatus and vacuum pan, and some other apparatus which was found in good condition—much of it had never been used—was removed for use in the Formosan factory. A new five-roller mill, 2 vacuum pans, 4 centrifugal separators, an engine and other machinery were purchased from England, 6 eliminators, 6 filters, boilers and other equipment from Japan, and an engine and electrical machinery from America. The total expenditure on the completion of the factory amounted to 850,000 yen, divided as follows :—Buildings, 230,000 yen; machinery, 360,000 yen; land 220,000 yen; miscellaneous expenditures for organization, surveys, etc., 40,000 yen. The expenditure for land represents, in addition to the factory site, 2,500 acres of cultivated land, which the company intends to devote eventually to the cultivation of Hawaiian cane. It is hoped in time to control sufficient land under cultivation to supply their entire requirements. The land will be rented to cultivators, who will be supplied with seed cane, implements, and capital to work their land, and the company will take the cane over at a fixed rate. The factory employs at present some 18 Japanese and 50 Chinese, and 500 families will be given employment on the company's land, when operations are well under way.

The original intention was to manufacture a brown Sugar ranging between Dutch 10 and Dutch 14, and to cater specially to the requirements of the Osaka and Tokyo refineries, but after the opening of the factory, it was decided to place on the market higher grades of Sugar as well, and experimental shipments of the latter have been made to Ningpo and Shanghai, where, it is reported, the product has been received with favor. The company also hopes to supply the local demand for such grades. The annual output of the factory at present is small, amounting to some 4,000 tons only, but it is expected gradually to increase it as circumstances permit. The Formosan railway has given assistance to the new Sugar company, first by constructing a spur from the main line to the factory buildings, and second by offering low freight rates for the transportation of Sugar from various points along the railway.

In addition to the government assistance given the Formosan Sugar Manufacturing Company, above described, a grant of 40,000 yen was made to Mr. M. Nakagawa, who undertook to construct a factory for the manufacture of a white Sugar, and furthermore to establish a model plantation of Hawaiian cane covering upwards of 50 acres, one tenth of the crop to become the property of the government for a period of five years. The factory must continue in operation for at least five years, and the suspension for more than one year, either of the cultivation or manufacture, will be considered by the government as an abandonment of the industry, and the government will in this case, confiscate the plant and land. Mr. Nakagawa erected his factory at Tainanfu, and commenced the manufacture of Sugar in May, 1902. It is expected that a market for the output will be found in Osaka, Japan.

The government is in possession of seven modern American crushing mills ; one of these machines has been set up at Mato and another at Daimokuko, and three have been sent to Tainan to be disposed of later. There are many large fields in the south, where mills of twenty ton capacity could with advantage be used. It is hoped to induce the natives to abolish their old stone crushers and adopt these modern machines, and also to utilize narrow gauge tramways for purposes of transportation. The saving by modern methods of handling the cane is so large that the first cost of the entire plant can be met in two or three seasons.

The future of the Sugar industry in Formosa is reported very promising by experts who have investigated the matter. Dr. Nitobe has made a very interesting report on the subject, and is personally confident that the production can be increased five times within the next ten years. The methods by which he would accomplish this seemingly great undertaking are described fully in his interesting report. First, we are informed that the climatic condition of central and southern Formosa is very favorable to the growing of the cane. The annual rainfall of the Formosan districts referred to is about 58 inches, which complies precisely with the conditions of humidity necessary for the best results. Furthermore, the rainy season comes during the heated term, which is a very great advantage. Hawaii, for instance, has no summer rains, and this necessitates irrigation at great expense. The Formosan soil contains the right admixture of lime and magnesia to give the best results. Altogether, local conditions are so favorable that cane which requires 18 months to ripen in Hawaii, reaches maturity in Formosa in 12 months. Again, Formosa possesses in its Chinese population a comparatively abundant supply of labor at a moderate price. This is a most valuable feature.

The unique advantages possessed by Formosa have not been fully utilized. The mode of cultivation is crude, and the methods of manufacture are ridiculously primitive and wasteful. Dr. Nitobe reports that these difficulties can be overcome. His recommendations are given under seven heads, briefly as follows :—

Variety of Cane.—A new Sugar cane must be introduced. At present the natives depend chiefly on the so-called Bamboo cane (Chikusho). The Lahaina cane introduced from Hawaii and grown under precisely similar conditions gave a yield of 96,000 lbs. per acre against 32,000 lbs. obtained with the native Bamboo. Not only is the yield per acre much larger, but Formosa grown Lahaina cane has given from 9 to 15 per cent. of Sugar against only 6 per cent. obtained from the native Bamboo cane. Thus the Lahaina cane yields some 2,880 lbs. of Sugar per acre against 1,920 lbs. from the native cane. Lahaina cane can be easily introduced. A second variety, known as Rose Bamboo, which has also been obtained from Hawaii, has likewise given very good results.

Irrigation.—In Hawaii the adoption of a system of irrigation increased the production four to five times. In Formosa no such results can be anticipated, but an increase of at least 30 per cent. can be expected. Experimental plantations should be established throughout the Sugar district to demonstrate this to the farmers. The growers should also be urged to co-operate in erecting irrigation works.

Fertilizing.—By the use of proper manures the production can be increased 50 per cent. Hawaii consumes 30,000 tons of fertilizers yearly, and the yield of cane per acre is about 30 tons. Java with the abundant use of fertilizers is rewarded with some 34 tons, but Formosa without aid to the soil obtains only about 12 tons an acre.

New Territory for Cultivation.—There are at present in mid-Formosa considerable districts not under cultivation. The government should arrange that this land be handed over to cane growers. There are 125,000 acres thus available, which would increase the production of Sugar by about 40,000,000 lbs. In Queensland the government gives the land to the cultivators and advances them money at 5 per cent. interest, which must be repaid in 15 years. This plan has worked well. There are considerable districts given over to rice culture, which owing to an insufficiency of water, are not profitable for that cereal. There are 25,000 acres of such land which should be put under Sugar, to which it is well suited, thus increasing the production by about 8,000,000 lbs.

Manufacturing.—The Chinese method of manufacture is undoubtedly the most crude and wasteful process in existence anywhere in the world. Their primitive appliances yield only half the Sugar that can be obtained by the most modern methods known. However, this means large and perfect factories, which we cannot expect to see introduced at once ; still, with the small modern steel mills, which are not expensive, 20 per cent. more juice is obtained than from the crude Chinese mills.

Summary.—The result to be obtained by the adoption of the above improvements is formulated in the following table (The present yearly production is taken at 93,000,000 lbs.) :—

Improvement recommended.	Increase possible.	Minimum increase of output in pounds.	Maximum increase of output in pounds.	Minimum total of output in pounds.	Maximum total of output in pounds.
Introduction of superior cane	30 to 90%	28,000,000	84,000,000	121,000,000	177,000,000
Improved cultivation, fertilizing, etc... ..	10 to 100%	9,300,000	93,000,000	102,300,000	186,000,000
Irrigation	10 to 50%	9,300,000	46,600,000	102,300,000	139,600,000
Improved crushing machinery	20 to 40%	18,600,000	35,300,000	111,600,000	128,300,000
Improved manufacturing methods	10 to 30%	9,300,000	28,000,000	102,300,000	121,000,000
New land to enlarge area under sugar	75,000 acres	36,000,000	72,000,000	129,000,000	165,000,000
Rice fields to be placed under sugar	25,000 acres	12,000,000	24,000,000	44,000,000 *(105)*	66,000,000 *(143)*
Total		122,500,000	382,900,000	215,500,000	475,000,500

NOTE.

FORMOSA SUGAR REGULATIONS.

The Sugar Consumption Tax Law shall be enforced in Formosa from the 1st of October, 1901.

Rules for the operation of the Sugar Consumption Tax Law.

Art. I.—Anyone wishing to manufacture sugar, molasses, or syrup, shall report in writing to the local office (cho) naming the article to be manufactured, and the name and the address of the manufacturer. In case any change modifies the report above mentioned, such modifications shall be reported.

Art. II.—Manufacturers desiring to discontinue operations shall report the matter to the proper local offices.

Art. III.—Manufacturers intending to transport their products from their factories must apply for a certificate of permission from the tax collectors, naming the article, quantity and destination of the same.

Art. IV.—Any person desiring to take delivery of sugar products from factories, custom houses, or bonded warehouses, shall designate the article intended for exportation, and report to the proper offices, naming the article and quantity.

Art. V.—Any person desiring to apply for postponement of payment of consumption tax as provided by Art. IV of the Sugar Consumption Tax Law, shall make application to the proper offices, presenting the report described in the Article next above.

Art. VI.—Upon receiving the reports provided for in Art. IV, the district offices shall classify the sugar products according to kind and quantity, and collect the tax from those who are not entitled to postponement, and notify those whose application for postponement has been received as to the amount of security they must give.

Art. VII.—The security required from persons availing themselves of the terms provided for by Articles IV. and V., of the Sugar Consumption Tax Law, is limited to treasure or bonds or stocks of companies either subsidized by the government or under their supervision.

Art. VIII.—The security above mentioned must be deposited in the Treasury, and a receipt for the same be presented to the proper district offices. If no office of the Treasury exists in the vicinity, the security may be deposited in a local office. The proper authorities of the local office shall give a receipt for the security, and deposit the security in the Treasury.

Art. IX.—In case the value of the securities given falls in value, the proper authorities may demand that further securities be added.

Art. X.—On receipt of payment of the tax, or the security as guarantee for the same, the proper authorities shall issue the delivery permit.

Art. XI.—The delivery permit shall be handed over by the parties holding same to the factory, custom house, or bonded warehouse at the time delivery is taken. Manufacturers, custom houses or bonded warehouses are not permitted to make delivery unless they are in possession of the delivery permit.

Art. XII.—Prior to shipment persons desiring to export sugar products for which the tax has been duly paid, or for which security has been deposited, shall apply to the proper offices for the issue of tax payment or security certificate, and these certificates shall be attached to the goods to be exported.

Art. XIII.—The certificates referred to in the preceding article shall be presented to the customs at the time of exportation or of shipment to Japan proper.

Art. XIV.—Persons desiring to obtain the release of security given in accordance with the provisions of Art. V., of the Sugar Consumption Tax Law, shall produce an application to the local office concerned within 6 months after receiving the delivery permit, presenting the export permit, and the import permit issued by the customs at the foreign port of arrival, or other documentary evidence of the landing at a foreign port.

Art. XV.—In the event of it becoming necessary to realize on the security held as provided by Articles IV. and V. it shall be disposed of by public auction, said auction to be advertised for 3 days.

Art. XVI.—In advertising the auction as provided by the preceding article the name and address of the party who deposited the security shall be given, together with the amount and kind of security, the place and time of auction and other points considered necessary.

Art. XVII.—In case the persons concerned shall prior to the auction sale of their security make payment of the consumption tax and auction expenses in full, the auction shall be annulled.

Art. XVIII.—Should there remain after the auction sale a balance in favour of the person on the behalf of whom the security has been sold, this balance shall be deposited in the Treasury.

Art. XIX.—Parties who are entitled to a return of the amount of tax paid as provided by Art. XI. of the Consumption Tax Law shall prior to the transport of the material to their factories, report to the proper office naming the kind and quantity of the material to be used, and obtain a certificate authorizing the transport. After manufacture the quality of the product obtained shall likewise be reported to the proper office.

Art. XX.—Persons desiring to avail themselves of the provisions of the preceding article shall apply to the local office at which payment of the tax was made for the issue of a certificate of payment, and this certificate shall be attached to the report described in the preceding Article.

Art. XXI.—Persons intending to apply for a return of the tax paid as provided for in Art XI. of the Sugar Consumption Tax Law shall produce an application for the same to the proper local office.

Art. XXII.—Manufacturers of sugar products shall keep complete records of the following transactions: Kind and quantity of material received and the names of persons from whom it has been obtained, and the date of receipt; the quantity of material used; the date of manufacture; and the kind and quantity of the resulting product. Also the kind, quantity and value of sugar product disposed of to other persons, date of delivery and name and address of person taking delivery.

Art. XXIII.—Sellers of sugar products shall keep complete records of the following transactions:—Kind, quantity and value of sugar product received for sale, and names and addresses of persons delivering same; kind, quantity and value of sugar product sold, date of sales and names and addresses of buyers. To retail sales the above does not apply.

SUGAR EXPORT STATISTICS.

Year.	Export of Brown Sugar from Takow and Anping in pounds	Export of White Sugar from Takow and Anping in pounds.	Total export from Takow and Anping in pounds.	Export of Brown Sugar from Tamsui in pounds.	Total Export from all Formosa in pounds.
1856	—	—	21,280,000	--	21,280,000
1865	--	—	19,403,636	—	19,403,636
1866	—	—	27,953,674	1,977,976	29,931,650
1867	—	—	32,891,166	855,722	33,746,888
1868	—	—	36,638,973	—	36,638,973
1869	—	—	35,921,837	—	35,921,837
1870	73,522,267	5,938,851	79,461,118	—	79,461,118
1871	74,122,230	3,530,352	77,652,582	—	77,652,582
1872	81,264,064	2,369,395	83,633,459	—	83,633,459
1873	65,213,092	1,666,756	66,879,848	613,396	67,493,244
1874	89,466,041	1,801,219	91,267,260	6,650	91,273,910
1675	64,098,552	681,359	64,779,911	243,257	65,023,168
1876	113,247,904	3,784,515	117,032,419	80,199	117,112,618
1877	75,488,406	4,279,142	79,767,548	1,104,432	80,871,980
1878	52,116,582	2,903,390	55,019,972	—	55,019,972
1879	93,323,972	8,460,662	101,784,634	8,113	101,792,747
1880	132,684,125	8,847,293	141,531,418	—	141,531,418
1881	95,571,805	4,805,689	100,377,494	26,866	100,404,360
1882	76,228,285	5,361,097	81,589,382	—	81,589,382
1883	97,708,849	5,359,634	103,068,433	103,740	103,172,223
1884	119,315,497	9,299,094	128,614,591	17,423	128,632,014
1885	66,616,508	7,648,032	74,264,540	79,800	74,344,340
1886	48,225,060	3,655,372	51,880,432	10,241	51,890,643
1887	69,684,419	4,058,761	73,743,180	3,724	73,746,904
1888	81,905,390	5,098,422	87,003,812	201,362	87,205,174
1889	72,381,925	3,435,656	75,817,581	10,374	75,827,955
1890	90,010,809	6,100,577	96,111,386	71,687	96,183,073
1891	72,531,151	3,268,741	75,799,892	8,778	75,808,670
1892	74,297,258	5,649,175	79,946,433	—	79,946,433
1893	63,910,357	3,908,870	67,819,227	—	67,919,227
1894	89,372,542	8,458,800	97,831,342	—	97,831,342
1895	85,070,790	9,143,484	94,214,274	--	94,214,274
1896	85,479,366	10,293,402	95,772,768	138,586	95,911,354
1897	76,781,166	9,182,852	85,964,018	44,555	86,008,573
1898	65,956,695	22,648,836	88,605,531	71,687	88,677,218
1899	58,640,500	9,721,700	68,362,200	177,600	68,539,800

DETAILED STATISTICS FOR YEARS 1896-1898.

EXPORT OF FORMOSA BROWN SUGAR.

Year.	Export from Anping to China and Hongkong in pounds and value in yen.	Export from Anping to Japan in pounds and value in yen.	Export from Takow to China and Hongkong in pounds and value in yen.	Export from Takow to Japan in pounds and value in yen.
1896	36,862,679 Y.1,017,082	14.574.938 Y. 386,855	168,910 Y. 4,565	33,872,839 Y. 876,740
1897	33,285,511 Y. 964,199	5,980,212 Y. 174,995	130,207 Y 2,946	37,464,770 Y. 905,330
1898	33,604,445 Y.1,165,413	353,115 Y. 21,713	208,278 Y. 6,077	31,777,557 Y. 989,400

EXPORT OF FORMOSA WHITE SUGAR.

Year.	Export from Anping to China and Hongkong in pounds and value in yen.	Export from Anping to Japan in pounds and value in yen.	Export from Takow to Japan in pounds and value in yen.	
1896	8,862,854 Y. 434,827	1,430,548 Y. 69,642		
1897	7,002,583 Y. 344,708	2,180,269 Y. 104,509	37,506 Y. 1,776	
1898	10,606,484 Y. 565,695	12,042,352 Y. 418,676		

CHAPTER XXVI.

GOLD IN FORMOSA.

Island's chief mining industry—Mineral possibilities little known—Gold discoveries on East Coast—General distribution of Gold fields—Lower Kelung river alluvial deposits—Upper Kelung river deposits—Kyufun, Dairin, Shosoko, and Daisoko river deposits—Kyufun, Kinkwaseki, etc., quartz fields—Gilan auriferous district—Buroko alluvial and reef Gold—Shinjio, Sansan, and Tokiri placer fields —Shukoran Gold district—Rich field practically unaccessible—Gold in Hongkong hills—East coast attractive field for prospectors—Historical description—Doubtful historical references—Benyowsky's tales of Formosan mineral wealth— Savages the probable first miners—Chinese adventurers, year 1430, seek Gold on east coast—Chinese colonists search for reported Gold deposits on east coast— Cruel slaughter of friendly savages—Savage warfare initiated—Savages' methods of mining described—Japanese reputed ancient discoveries—Gold sands rediscovered by Dutch and again by Koxinga's retainers—Chinese rediscover after two centuries—Rush to Gold fields—Futile attempt by officials to prevent mining —Illiberal policy abandoned—Gold offices established—System of control and revenue obtained—Gold washing attracts many mainland natives—Auriferous reefs discovered—Government Gold offices and their attendants—Chinese method of Quartz mining—Primitive process of extraction—Gold washers at Shinjio— Annihilated by savages—Reported richness of Hongkong deposits—Japanese occupation of Formosa—Mining regulations issued—Valuable claims granted— Mining operations Zuiho district—Advice to prospective visitors—Gold washing on Kelung river—Principal sources of Gold supply—Description of journey to Zuiho—Zuiho mining village and district—Method of excavation—Richness of deposits—Washing appliances used by Chinese—Description of cradle and native method of operating same—Wasteful processes—Retorting—Estimated annual production placer district—Journey to Quartz mines—Kyufun an unique settlement—The Fujita Mining Co.'s income—Value of daily production—Fujita Co.'s quartz mill—Foot power stamp batteries—Proposed development—Description of Fujita mines, output, etc.—Coal mines in convenient proximity—Road to Kinkwaseki — Kinkwaseki's rich deposits — Geological formation — Tanaka's modern mill and its machinery—Treatment of Formosan ore—Amalgamating process—Retorting—Convenient coal supplies—Tanaka's employés and system of labor—Formosan Gold deposits the richest in Japanese Empire—Opportunity for profitable operations on east coast—Gold and its promising future—Translation of Mining regulations.

OF the island's mineral products, Gold is the most important. Although but a small portion of the mountainous district of Formosa has been prospected, yet this valuable mineral has been discovered in several parts of the island, and the mining of it in the north is now an industry exceeding in importance the workings of coal and sulphur together. Gold thus takes a lead in the island's minerals, and promises a future development which may possibly make it the leading product of Formosa. Coal, while present throughout the island in considerable quantities, exists in numerous thin seams which do not justify the introduction of extensive mining plants; but Gold, both in alluvial gravels and quartz veins, is of sufficient richness to encourage investment. The Japanese have recognized this by introducing modern mining machinery at an expenditure exceeding that of private firms in any other of the island's industries.

With the exception of the north, researches by mining experts have been limited to few districts, where in most cases the presence of Gold had been previously reported, and, as the vast mountain range running through that portion of the island occupied by savages remains unexplored, it is somewhat premature to make any comparisons as to the relative richness of the island's various districts. It may be said, however, that of the limited area investigated, the north, particularly the region known as the Zuiho (Sui-hong) district, possesses the most valuable Gold deposits.

At several places along the inhospitable east coast, where mining engineers have landed, Gold has been discovered, which has led to the belief that auriferous rock is to be found along the whole east coast. That portion of the western half of the island under Japanese control is not generally of a geological formation favorable to reef Gold, although some alluvial deposits may be found.

Commencing with the north of the island, Gold is first found in the Kelung river. This stream rises in hills to the south-east of the port of Kelung, in the heart of the Zuiho Gold district, and flows in a general westerly direction, until it intersects the Tamsui river near Daitotei (Twatutia), thus affording an outlet to the sea. From the capital Taihoku (Taipeh), a trip of 12 to 15 miles up the Kelung river to a point near the village of Suihenkiaku (Sui-teng-ka) will bring one within the reach of Gold; for here the gravel in the river-bed will yield, after an hour's work with pan or cradle, a few grains of the glittering metal, which, if not very plentiful, will at least give evidence that the precious substance is about. The higher up the river we proceed the more plentiful the mineral becomes, and in some seasons of the year Gold-washing will be in progress from Suihenkiaku to the head waters at the foot of Sanshorei (Samtiao) hills, a distance of some 20 miles. From the Kyufun hills, some two miles south east of Zuiho run the Kyufun (Kau-hun), Daiurin (Twa-koa-la), Sho-soko (Sio-sha-kng), and Daisoko (Twa-sha-kng) rivers. The first two empty into the sea, and the last two unite with the Kelung river. Near their sources they are in contact with the auriferous rock of the Kyufun field, and the four yield more or less Gold by placer mining, though owing to their comparatively limited extent they do not equal the Kelung river in quantity produced.

Kyufun, Daisoko, Shosoko and Daiurin are also the names given to quartz fields in close proximity on either side of the Kyufun hills. Kinkwaseki (Kim-koe-tsio) is a high peak, capped with an overhanging rock, 1¼ miles further to the south-east, and is rich in auriferous rock. Kyufun and Kinkwaseki are at present being worked with modern mining appliances.

Across the mountains some 25 miles to the south on the border of the Kapsulan plain of the Gilan district, auriferous rock is reported; and it is said that, in ancient days, Gold deposits to the south-west of Gilan were profitably worked; but, owing to the attacks of the savages, operations were discontinued.

The Buroko (Bu-ro-kau) stream, which runs into the sea just to the north of Suao (So-o), a village on the coast some 12 miles south of Gilan city, has its source in auriferous rock lying in the savage district; and placer mining was once carried on along its bed; but, owing to savage raids, operations have been abandoned for many years.

On the east coast, 35 miles south of Suao (So-o), in the vicinity of Shinjio (Sin-sia), the Sansan (Sam-tsan), Tokiri (Tek-ki-leh), and other rivers have been worked and found rich in gold bearing sands. Here alluvial Gold is found over a wide area, the field being a strip along the sea shore 10 miles in length, and of varying width, running from Shinjio to Karenko (Ho-ling-kang). It is believed by mining experts that this district contains the largest quantity of placer Gold of any known field in the island.

Further to the south, along the east coast, some thirty miles from Karenko, is the Shukoran (Siu-kor-luan) Gold field. This is a district extending along the Taikoko (Twa-kang-kau) river for a distance of four miles from its mouth. Here not only alluvial deposits exist, but quartz veins are found in the neighboring cliffs. Though no very careful examination has been made, yet from a hasty survey it would appear that the auriferous rock field here is the most extensive so far known in the island. The river gravel is doubtless rich, but, owing to the depth and swiftness of the stream, it would be very difficult to work the bed. This attractive district remains unexploited owing to the practical inaccessibility of the place. Landing through the surf is difficult and unsafe; and the savages command the hills to the north, south, and west. The government has been urged to improve the mouth of the Taikoko river so as to permit small steamers to enter, and to establish a post in the district.

As regards the western half of the island, no valuable deposits have yet been found, though in the extreme south corner some Gold is reported to exist in one of the Fuko (Hongkong) hills near the savage border. The hill district has, however, been but roughly inspected, and it is quite within the bounds of possibility that more careful examination will result in some satisfactory discoveries.

The east coast, from its geological formation, presents the most attractive field for investigation, and the known deposits, as recorded above, in the

Zuiho, Gilan, Shinjio, and Shukoran districts, warrant the belief that the efforts of mining engineers in other parts of the eastern half of the island will be successful; and when government control is established and roads constructed in that at present wild and unsettled territory, the lack of agricultural land will doubtless be fully compensated for by the wealth obtained from its mineral treasures.

Having briefly dealt with the present known auriferous fields, it will be of interest to look at the historical side of the subject; for although the location of the Gold deposits has been known to the present inhabitants only during the last nine years, yet of the Formosan mineral products, Gold appears to have been the first that was worked, and furthermore the first that was carried away from the island, although it can not be said that its original owners parted with it willingly. It appears to be an incurable habit of early voyagers to attribute to unknown districts in every land visited by them rich deposits of this precious metal. Formosa was no exception; for of the many old books in which reference to the island is made, there is scarcely one that does not contain some fanciful tale of vast golden riches; to which some of the more audacious have added precious stones. It is not that these descriptions may not some day be appropriate, but it is certain that they were not so at the time the volumes referred to were written. For instance, Count Benyowsky, the Hungarian adventurer who spent some time on the east coast in 1771, writes in his memoirs, that the savage chief to whom he had given assistance presented his party with "some fine pearls, eight hundred pounds of silver, and twelve pounds of Gold." Besides this, the count received for his private use "a box containing 100 pieces of Gold which together weighed thirteen pounds and a quarter." It is quite possible that the count might have received some few Gold nuggets or a quantity of dust; but the Dutch, who were in the island a century before, had close relations with the savages and heard of no such quantities of Gold; while as to silver, no definite traces have been ever found: and the savages of the present day seem not aware of the presence of any precious metals within their territory. It is quite probable, therefore, that Benyowsky's tale of the gifts was largely imaginative.

It would not be safe, however, to assume that the savages did not in ancient days to some extent work Gold: in fact many of the old authorities are so unanimous on this point that any one who accepts their statements on other subjects would be scarcely justified in disregarding them on this point. It would not be extraordinary if savages, who had at one time worked the Gold deposits, should later have abandoned them, owing perhaps to some superstitious belief, or should have lost sight of them owing to the invasion of some unfriendly tribe, or that the presence of Gold, then of no special significance to them, as its value was probably not known, should be forgotten in a generation or so.

The earliest reference to the production of Gold in the island which is at all definite informs us that, in 1430, a party of Chinese adventurers landed on the east coast to investigate the reports that rich Gold mines existed there. They failed to discover the precious metal sought for, and it is said that so great was their anger that they attacked and slaughtered every living being they could lay hands on, before leaving the island in disgust.

The outrage was repeated on a more elaborate scale during the first few years following the Chinese occupation. Father de Mailla, one of the Jesuit priests who visited Formosa in 1715, and who gave the world much reliable information on the condition of the island in his days, tells us that the Chinese lost no time, after the subjection of the plain savages, in searching for the treasures which had been so frequently reported as existent in the savage districts on the east coast. They equipped a small vessel that they might make the voyage by sea, rather than attempt the dangerous journey over the mountains. Hospitality was then considered a virtue by the savages; and on the arrival of the strangers they were given a generous and friendly welcome. Houses were placed at their disposal, food provided, and every assistance rendered them during the week they remained. Diligent search and persistent questioning did not reveal to the Chinese the location of the Gold deposits. They did, however, unfortunately find in one of the huts of the savages a few ingots of Gold, which the aborigines regarded as of little value. This discovery aroused the baser instincts of the visitors, who, discontented with the result of their voyage, and determined to acquire possession of the Gold without payment, concocted a dastardly plan which, for refined treachery and cruelty, could hardly be exceeded. The Chinese feigned to be desirous of showing their gratitude to the savages, whom they praised as their loving friends and accordingly, after having prepared their vessel for the return voyage, they invited the hospitable and unsuspecting savages to a grand feast, given, the Chinese represented, in token of their affection. The unfortunate guests on arriving were plied plentifully with intoxicating liquor, and, when in a state of semi consciousness, were massacred to a man, and the Chinese, quickly possessing themselves of the Gold, set sail and returned to the west coast. The mandarin took no notice of the outrage, and the chief of the expedition was in no way interfered with. Still, as the good father noted, the Chinese of the island paid the penalty. The news of the crime spread throughout the savage districts, and a large band invaded the Chinese territory, slaughtering in cold blood men, women, and children, and burning to the ground many villages; and from that day warfare between the two peoples was unceasing.

In ancient papers two methods are described by which the savages obtained the Gold. One authority, writing in the early years of the eighteenth century in regard to "a great and rich Golden mine in Formosa" states, "In August the great rains sweep down an incredible store of this rich metal, which falls into pits made on purpose at the foot of the hill, which the inhabitants draining gather the ore from the bottom,"[1] while a second writer asserts that the savages "scooped" Gold out of certain creeks in the Gilan district (presumably sand washing), and that they melted the metal into bars. The Gold appeared to them to be an article of beauty rather than value,

1. Ogilby's Atlas Chinensis. London MDCLXXI.

and the dazzling metal was concealed in earthen jars and brought forth only for the gratification of some favored visitor. Among the strangers arriving in the island, the Japanese, who were for a short time settled in Kelung during the 16th century, are said to have been aware of the presence of Gold-bearing sands in North Formosa. But on their departure they carried the secret with them. A hundred years intervened; the Dutch occupied Formosa; and the Gold deposits were rediscovered by them only to be again lost on the departure of the foreigners. Koxinga's retainers likewise made what they doubtless considered a virgin find, and were apparently able to keep the fact secret from the Imperial Chinese who followed; for the latter settled throughout the Gold district, and yet two centuries elapsed before they became aware of the wealth about them. Their discovery was quite accidental. During the year 1890, at the time of the construction of the new Taipeh Kelung railway, some workmen, erecting a railway bridge across a branch of the upper Kelung river, near Hatto (Poe tau), observed some glittering flakes of metal in the gravel which they were handling. Some of the more intelligent of the men commenced panning, with encouraging results. Finally the news reached the China mainland. Chinese who had returned from California or Australia, and who were familiar with Gold washing, flocked across the channel in thousands. They introduced Gold washing cradles and "long toms," and carried on the work with great energy. Washers were soon busy all along the higher waters, and there was scarcely a shingle bed exposed without its quota of excited workmen. For living accommodation, little rude grass huts were hastily erected along the river banks, and some of the Gold seekers were provided with boats to shelter them at night. The mainland Chinese suffered much from sickness, however; not a few died, and during a great typhoon in 1892, the river rose suddenly in the night, sweeping away, and destroying numerous huts and boats, and causing considerable loss of life.

In September, 1891, a local proclamation was issued prohibiting Gold washing; but without effect, and the mandarins, taking a characteristically practical view of the subject, decided that, as the evil could not be cured, it should be endured—to their profit. Accordingly, in 1892, special offices were established at convenient stations, and persons desiring to engage in the washing were forced to provide themselves with licenses. Workers were divided into classes, of apparently the weak and strong, 15 Mexican cents being the daily license fee for full grown men, and 10 cents for women or children; while even prospectors were charged ten cents a day. The licensed workmen were provided with a wooden tag bearing the government seal. Collection of this impost was made every five days. There were some 3,000 washers then at work, and the returns to the officials from this tax averaged about 12,000 yen a month; but owing to the expense of keeping up the various offices, together with squeezes, which were reported as considerable, the actual net revenue to the Formosan treasury was slight. There was also evidence of secret workings; so to place the industry on a more satisfactory footing as concerned government revenues, the right to work the deposits was sold out to four wealthy Chinese for eighteen months from January 1893, for the sum of 75,000 yen. In that year a rich placer district was discovered in the Kyufun (Kau-hun) hills, and the fortunate monopolist who controlled that district is said to have obtained for a considerable period several thousand yen worth of Gold a day.

The number of Chinese employed in the industry depended somewhat on the general demand for labor, and during the months in the year when agricultural work was not pressing, many farm laborers took a hand at washing. It is said that the number engaged reached at one time to several thousands, and that a million yen worth of gold was produced in a single year.

Up to 1894, no auriferous reefs had been discovered; but during this year a Chinese expert who had engaged in Gold mining in California found Gold bearing quartz in the Kyu-fun (Kau-hun) hills. The industry was now more promising than ever, and to profit by it to the fullest extent possible, the government, at the expiration of the eighteen months private grant, again took charge, and re-established the gold offices, to which they added new ones.[1] Chinese official control continued until the next year (1895), when the island was ceded to Japan.

The quartz mining by the Chinese was carried on in a very primitive manner. The district above Zuiho was controlled by 13 Chinese. They divided the land among them, and each party sunk a narrow shaft to a depth of some 130 feet. Side tunnels were then put in, following the vein, to the approximate border of their respective districts. Experienced Japanese experts have stated that the Chinese were very skillful in working in small tunnels. The writer, while on a trip through the Gold district, inspected an old Chinese mine, and was struck with the size of the shaft and tunnels,—so small that it seemed impossible for a human being to work in them. In the shaft, as a substitute for a ladder, ran a spliced pole of sufficient length to reach from top to bottom, notches having been cut in it at intervals of 10 or 12 inches, offering slight but apparently sufficient footing for the Chinese miners. The drifts on the lode were so small that the workmen negotiated them on all fours, and were obliged to excavate while in a reclining position. The ore obtained was brought to the shaft in a bag or basket, and this was hoisted to the mouth at the end of a rope, moved by a roughly constructed windlass above. The Chinese controlling the mine took no part in the extraction of the Gold from the ore, which they sold as such, delivered at the mouth of the mine. From 30 cents upwards per 30 catties, according to the richness of the vein, was obtained for the Gold bearing rock, and the purchaser carried the ore away for treatment. If the ore was of

1. The Chinese Government offices with the number of attendants at each were as follows :

	officials	guards and inspectors	
Zuiho (Sui-hong) Head Office .. .. 6 officials	85	guards and inspectors.	
Shikiaku-tei (Si-kah-tieu) Branch Office .. .. .. 1 ,,	14	,,	,,
Dandan (Wan-wau) ,, ,, ... 1 ,,	14	,,	,,
Goto (Go-taw) .. ,, ... 1 ,,	14	,,	,,
Kyu-fun (Kau-hun) .. ,, ... 2 ,,	24	,,	,,
Shosoko (Sio-sha-kng) ,, ,, ... 2 ,,	14	,,	,,
Total 6 offices .. .. 13 ,,	164	,,	,,

a soft, clayey, or decomposed character, as much of it was, it was broken up by hand and then taken directly to the cradle, where it was washed, and panned, and the free Gold taken out. The hard quartz was broken with a hammer or stone and pulverized in a native stone mortar, and then washed. The iron pyrites were also ground to powder in a mortar, the Gold being extracted by washing. Both processes were, of course, very wasteful; still so rich was the ore handled that the Chinese found the work profitable.

The Chinese were almost solely interested in the northern Gold mines, the other deposits in the island, with two exceptions, not appearing to them to be of much importance. In 1894, some 30 native washers, learning of the Shinjio (Sin-sia) field, arrived there from the north, and commenced washing the gravel to the right of the Shinjio river. Water being difficult to obtain there, they moved the scene of their operations to the sea shore, but the high waves interfered with their work there also, and they again removed, locating on the right bank of the Tokiri (Tek-ki-le) river. Here they were meeting with some success when, during the winter of 1895, a band of savages on a head-hunting expedition swept down, and, it is reported, utterly exterminated them. In the extreme south of the island, in 1890, an extensive landslide, doubtless caused by heavy rains, carried away a large section of one of the Fuko (Hong-kong) hills, exposing, it is said, in the hillside a considerable quantity of free Gold. It is reported by natives that the place was worked quietly by the Chinese living in the vicinity, in hopes that news of its existence would not reach the ears of the mandarins. The field (presumably in limited sections) was so rich, the Chinese claim, that it was customary to exchange a measure of rice for a measure of the Gold bearing earth. These hills are between Pangliau (Borio) and Fuko villages.

On the arrival of the Japanese, the Gold districts, which had been held by the Chinese as government property, passed into the possession of the Japanese Government. For the first year no attempt was made to control the mining industry, and some two to three thousand Chinese engaged daily in gravel washing. In September 1896, mining regulations having been issued,[1] the government received applications for claims, a large number of washing permits were granted, and valuable alluvial and quartz districts passed into the hands of Japanese. Considerable care was exercised in granting valuable claims to provide that only responsible parties should obtain them; the right to do this being reserved by the government. The Kyufun and Kinkwaseki applicants were obliged to deposit 15,000 yen as a guarantee of good faith, and as an example of the success of this system, it may be noted that the parties obtaining the above mines, being men of capital and experience, extensive development of their properties was commenced at once. The government granted five claims for quartz and eighty-nine for placer mining. A report on the present condition of the Gold mining industry, both quartz and placer mining, is confined to a description of the works in the north Formosa district, frequently referred to as the Zuiho (Sui hong) fields; there being no other deposits worked at present.

---

1. For translation of mining regulations see note closing this chapter.

To persons who take pleasure in travel off "unbeaten tracks" and are interested in industrial investigation, a visit to the Gold district will be found enjoyable, though the traveller, owing to the fact that no comfortable inns exist, must be prepared to put up with more or less hardship.[1]

Though that section of the Kelung river which flows for a distance parallel with the Kelung-Taipeh railway is not rich in gold, there are usually a few washers at work, and a glimpse of the operation can be easily obtained from the train windows when running between Suikenkiaku (Sui-teng-ka) station and the tunnel under the Kelung hills. While Chinese at times wash for gold all along the upper Kelung river, the centre of this industry is in the Zuiho (Sui-hong) district, where have sprung up some three compact little villages inhabited entirely by gold miners.

As previously mentioned, Zuiho district is to the south-east of Kelung. The village of Zuiho, the first place of interest, is 9 miles from Kelung, and the trip can be easily made by Chinese chair, and in some seasons of the year even by bicycle. It is best to start early in the morning. The road runs from Kelung in an east and south-easterly direction, and then mounting the low ridge of hills which surrounds the harbor enters a coal mining district. The road passes within a few feet of the mouths of several Chinese worked coal tunnels, and a few moments may be spent with interest in observing the crude method of mining here practised. The rich soil of the hills, together with the abundant rain-fall, is conducive of a wealth of semi-tropical vegetation, in which ferns, from the little clinging species attached to banks of rock or earth to the large tree ferns, which in Formosa sometimes reach a height of 60 feet, are most abundant.

About 1½ miles from Kelung the road crosses the summit of the hills, 350 feet above sea-level, and then descends along a picturesque pathway which at Ryutanto (Liong-tam-tah) approaches the Kelung river, and following on the left bank leads over a level road to Zuiho village, the journey from Kelung by Chinese chair with three carriers taking some two hours. At Zuiho are stationed district officers and a few police. The population of the village, including the inhabitants in the immediate vicinity, who are all either engaged in Gold washing or in occupations largely dependent on the industry, numbers nearly four thousand.

The Gold bearing gravel in the Kelung river actively worked in the vicinity of Zuiho is distributed over a large area, and has resulted from the erosion and disintegration of the auriferous rock in the hills through which the higher reaches of the stream pass. The Kelung river is generally shallow, save in the rainy season, lasting usually from late October to early March, and in most places in the upper river it is possible by the construction of a small embankment to work the bed gravel. As is usually the case with

---

1. While the writer finds pleasure rather than discomfort in an up-country trip for a few days, and can for a short time put up comfortably with the rather limited food supplies which are to be obtained in every village, such as chicken, eggs, rice, sweet potatoes, and possibly fish, still visitors who would feel inconvenience in being deprived of the service afforded by foreign hotels had better, if they are desirous of making the trip to the gold district, take a cook with them, together with a store of food and drinkables. There is a small Japanese inn at Zuiho village, but none in the quartz district.

shallow hill streams, which are often flooded; the river bed is wide, and in the summer a large portion of it is dry.   It therefore provides a strip of considerable though varying width on either side, which for some seven months can be worked with the greatest ease.

Chinese washers have also added much to the area by gradually digging away the river banks; and as in some places these banks are natural levees, protecting by their height or formation adjoining low lands, no little consternation has been caused owing to the increasing damage done by floods.   In some sections an auriferous gravel stratum, covered with an upper soil of loam, extends from the river on either side for varying distances, but this has not been carefully examined as yet, and the native washers confine their operations almost wholly to the gravel along the river bank.   Although pits and holes with adjoining mounds of washed-out gravel, which are visible all along the upper Kelung river, give evidence of widely spread work, experts assert that the field has only been scratched over; and one government mining engineer estimates that there is over 1,275,000 tsubo of auriferous gravel in sight, which will yield on an average over four pennyweight of Gold per cubic tsubo (6 cubic feet).

In working the alluvial deposits the Chinese use only the more primitive washing appliances, such as the "cradle" and "Long Tom."   No large sluice-works or hydraulic mining appliances, which make an extensive mining of placer deposits possible, have yet been introduced.

The cradle used in the island varies but slightly from the implement of like name seen in the western states, from which in reality it was copied; the model having been introduced into the island by a Chinese who had worked in the placer diggings of California.   The present Formosan cradle consists of a wooden trough some 4 feet long and 1 foot wide.   One end is closed in, and the sides of the trough at this end are some six inches high, but slope down to an inch or so as they approach the opposite end, across which runs a slat.   The two sides and the end of the upper section form a support, on which is placed a square coverless box or hopper with a tin bottom perforated thickly with holes some half inch in diameter.   From the forward lower edge of the hopper, when in position, inclines downward towards the closed in end of the trough a board, the edge of which is but an inch or so from the floor and a like distance from the end of the trough.   On the bottom side of the trough to the front and rear are two wooden knobs, and from one side near the centre, but projecting vertically above the box, extends a wooden handle, by which the trough can be given a rocking motion.

Two Chinese ordinarily work together, one excavating the gravel and the other attending to the cradle.   The cradle is placed near some stream or other supply of water, and is fixed in a slightly sloping position.   The "pay dirt" is thrown in the hopper; and the operator, with the left hand, pours basin after basin of water on to the mass, while, with the right, he rocks the cradle.   The finer gravel is carried by the water through the perforated bottom down the inclined board, and, falling near the closed in end of the trough, proceeds slowly along the floor towards the open end, most of the lighter earth and sand passing out with it over the slat, while the heavy particles of Gold and iron pyrites, together with more or less gravel, remain in the bottom. The hopper containing such stones as were too large to pass through the perforated bottom is taken off, and then the cradle is rocked until most of the gravel is washed out, leaving little flakes of free Gold which are easily visible, and a more or less quantity of iron pyrites. The latter is crushed to powder in a Chinese mortar and washed again; but, as the reader may surmise, only a portion of the Gold contained is obtained by this crude process.

The yield of Gold naturally varies greatly; but it is estimated that the product of one cradle, divided between the washer and his assistant, will amount to some 70 cents (local currency) a man, though 15 or 20 cents of this had, in most districts, to be paid as rent money to the owner of the claim. Without doubt there is a considerable percentage of Gold that is not extracted, and complete and modern apparatus would quite likely show more profitable results.

The Gold obtained is either disposed of directly as dust, or made up into little ingots some $2\frac{1}{3}$ inches long. In preparing the latter, the dust is placed in a small clay crucible, together with about one tenth of its own weight of borax to promote fusion, which being subjected to strong heat, such as is obtained in a forge, melts in 15 or 20 minutes and is poured into an iron mould. Although the crucible is crushed to a powder and washed to obtain such Gold as may cling to it, still there remains a loss of upwards of 8%. The Gold ingots obtained contain from 8 to 25% of silver. The dust or bars are sold either to the Chinese Gold merchants, who are usually at hand, or to the two Japanese mining companies. Owing to the fact that the Gold washing is in the hands of small workers, many of whom give their attention to Gold when there is no pressing agricultural work at hand, and also that they probably conceal the larger part of their earnings, it is impossible to ascertain correctly the yearly output; but it doubtless exceeds a hundred thousand yen.

To reach the quartz mines it is necessary to ascend by a rough mountain path-way up the Kyu-fun mountain to a village of the same name $2\frac{1}{2}$ miles from Zuiho. The last stage of the journey is up a steep slope which the chair coolies find it very difficult to negotiate, and though the distance is comparatively short, nearly two hours are required for the trip. Kyu-fun is as odd looking a settlement as one could find. From the houses one would judge that worldly treasures were very evenly distributed among the inhabitants, for each little straw hut is a counterpart of every other structure in the place; and never before has the writer seen so many houses in such a small space. Some appear to be partially telescoped in adjoining buildings, others standing above as though unable to force their way to the ground, and each structure seems to be making a silent appeal to its neighbor to move over. Water is supplied from the Fujita mill, and runs in many small streams, directed so as to provide each building with a little rivulet, passing sometimes by the doorway or even over the floor of the building. Such is the settlement of Kyu-fun, and at each hut the work of Gold-washing with cradles and pans will be found progressing vigorously, so that the output of Gold must be considerable. The claim worked is the property of the Fujita Company, who mine the auriferous rock at this place, and the washers, of whom there are generally some 450 at work, pay 20 cents a day each for their placer mining privilege. The value of the daily output here averages some 70 cents per man, which, after payment of the company's fees, leaves a profit of say 50 cents, or 15 yen a month, not a bad income for a Chinese laborer. There are other washers in the vicinity, making a total in some seasons of as many as 700 persons paying tribute to the Fujita Company, giving an income from this source, in some months, of nearly 4,000 yen; this being clear profit to the Company.

The Fujita was the first of the Japanese companies to engage in quartz mining in Formosa. Their expert arrived in December 1896, and erected soon after a small experimental plant equipped with man-power stamps some four or five in number. These stamps, though crude, were sufficiently effective for testing purposes. They resembled, and were on the same principle as, the pounding apparatus used by Chinese in hulling rice. A stamp consisted of a large stone hammer-head, perhaps 2½ to 3 feet in length, to which was attached a strong piece of lumber, some 7 to 10 feet in length. This beam rested near the centre on an elevated structure forming a fulcrum. Power is given to the appliance by a laborer, who, resting against a bamboo rail which runs from side to side, alternately steps on and off the end of the beam, raising and letting fall the hammer-head. The hammer moved by this see-saw motion falls on a cup-like stone base, across which passes the ore to be crushed. In 1899, a 20 horse-power steam plant with a crusher and ten stamps was put in by this Company; and though now working the deposits on a commercial basis, the present works are only of a temporary nature, to be replaced shortly by a large and complete mill on the sea shore, at a place called Koshiryo (Kiah-liao), where convenient water communication will be afforded. The ore from the mines, which are several hundred feet above sea-level, will be delivered to the mill by a tram-way; a pier will be built, and electric plant and other industrial conveniences introduced. It is reported that the total investment in the new establishment will reach half a million yen. D. Fujita, the owner of the claim, is a wealthy mine-owner residing in Osaka, possessing an abundance of capital to erect a plant on a scale of any magnitude necessary, and the Formosa mine will have the largest gold extracting mill in the Empire erected by private enterprise.

The Fujita Company's claim covers about 2½ square miles. The strata have a general north and south direction, dipping towards the east, with an inclination reaching 40°. The veins are in rock of sandstone formation, and the pay streak is a soft clay quartz. Much of it is yellow in color, though the richest portion is a white streak against the foot wall, and some of it is so soft that it can be crumpled in the hand. Considerable quantities of the ore yield about 5 parts Gold in 10,000, but the average quartz runs 5 in 100,000, which is the equivalent of 1½ ozs. to the ton. The shafts and tunnels are roomy, well ventilated, and drained, and are being rapidly extended. The principal tunnel running in from the hill side is provided with a tramway; and rock is carried out in iron automatic dump cars. The mine being at present run on an experimental basis the output is not extensive. Upwards of three tons of rock are treated daily, yielding about 4 ozs. of gold. The miners and mill workmen employed number 230, of whom 150 are Japanese. They are divided into three gangs each working for eight hours. A rather interesting point in connection with the above field, is that there are two seams of coal below the Gold veins. The Gold stratum has a greater inclination than the coal layers, and the latter can be worked at a distance of only some sixty feet from the nearest Gold deposits. The coal seams are about three feet in thickness, and their presence is most convenient, affording as they do practically free fuel for the boilers of the milling plant. The Fujita Company pay a tax on their property amounting to 4,700 yen, which is at the government rate of 2 yen per thousand tsubo.

While the Fujita mine is, owing to its extent, perhaps the most valuable property, it is the opinion of some experts that the Kinkwaseki (Kim-koe-tsio) mine contains the richest ore yet found in the island. At all events, the Tanaka Company, who are the owners, appeared sufficiently pleased with it to commence operations on a comparatively large scale at once; and there exists on this property a complete mill equipped with modern machinery.

Kinkwaseki is an independent mountain peak 1¼ miles from Kyufun, and the mines are worked over a thousand feet above sea level. It can be reached by a rough mountain pathway leading from Kyufun, and an hour should be allowed for the up trip if the traveller is being carried in a Chinese chair. On approaching the summit, the attention of the visitor will be doubtless attracted to a large over-hanging rock which crowns the cliff. That this rock is quite as dangerous as it looks, may be understood when it is noted that while a party of Chinese were excavating beside it in 1898, a portion of the mass broke away, killing some thirty of the miners.

The Kinkwaseki mines differ from the Kyufun deposits in geological formation. While the latter consist of a more or less friable sandstone, Kinkwaseki is of hard igneous rock. The Gold is found in a reddish clayey rock of a harder nature than the Kyufun ore. There is an abundance of ore, giving one part Gold to 10,000, and several small pockets have been found in the pay shoots running as high as 1 in 100, but the average is about 2 in 10,000, which is the equivalent of 5¾ ozs. to the ton.

Although there are several shafts, the ore is carried out by a roomy tunnel which runs in from the side of the hill, and communicates with the five levels in which mining is now carried on and their connecting shafts. A tram-way is provided to transport the ore through the tunnel, and when at the entrance, an aerial tram carries it down to the mill located in the valley below, about one third of a mile distant.

The path-way leading down from the mine is steep and rocky, but as there is little to be transported save the ore handled by the aerial tram, a good road is not necessary. The mill is a series of large buildings, joined together, and the big smoke stack, the dust and steam, the noise and other signs of industrial activity, seem quite out of place in the quiet valley with its profusion of vegetation.

The mill is built on a slope, and the ore is received from a sorting platform at the highest point. The largest size quartz goes to the crusher. This machine, which is of the type known as Blake's ore crusher, is driven independently by a double cylinder engine of some 8 horse-power. The smaller pieces, together with the broken ore from the crusher, go to a battery of medium weight stamps, and the finer pieces into a circular mill, the crushing agency being two heavy, solid revolving wheels. The stamp and mill, together with some smaller machinery not necessary to mention here, are driven by an engine of 17 horse-power, and a Pelton water wheel of 30 horse-power. Water carries the pulverized ore from the stamps on to a series of connected troughs known as "tables," which contain sheets of copper amalgamated on the upper surface with mercury, alternating with sections, of which ordinary coarse woolen blanketing is the covering, the idea of utilizing the latter being that the heavier particles of the metal which do not adhere to the amalgamated plates will be caught in the fuzzy flocculent surface of the blanket. From the end of the last table the crushed stuff remaining runs off with the water into a pit, where the tailings are reserved for future attention. The amalgamating plates are cleaned down every three hours or so, and when a sufficient quantity has been gathered, the Gold is obtained by squeezing some of the mercury out through calico or chamois leather, and the amalgam remaining is retorted in an iron retort, the nozzle of which is kept under water, that the mercury vapor may be converted again into metallic form. The residue remaining is a spongy cake of Gold, containing some small percentage of silver, but no other metals. As with the Fujita mine, the Tanaka Company possess a coal mine a short distance from the mill, which provides an abundance of coal at no further cost than the expense of excavation. At present from 6 to 8½ tons of Gold ore are treated daily, yielding 18 or more ozs. of Gold, which brings to the company proceeds of over 12,000 yen a month.

There are 400 men, Japanese and Chinese, employed in the mine and mill. Work is continued day and night, and the men are divided into three gangs, each working eight hours. In the mine, where the least skill in excavating is required, the Japanese workmen are found superior to the Chinese. The Japanese in certain specified levels receives 3.00 yen per foot advance, and at this rate the average Japanese miner earns some 30 yen a month. The Chinese are paid from 40 to 60 yen cents per day. Some income is derived from Gold washing privileges disposed of to the Chinese, but in comparison with the neighboring mine this is very small. The Chinese excavate earth-like ore from crevices in the rocks, and carrying it down to a near by stream wash it in cradles.

It is stated that the limited section of the property now being worked has yielded some ore the richest yet found in the whole Empire. The

Kinkwaseki Gold Quartz Mill.   Kyufun Village and Gold Quartz Mill.

Chinese Family Gold Washing in Kelung River.   Chinese Female Gold Washer.

Entrance to a Formosa Coal Mine.   Chinese Children employed in Coal Mine.

Tanaka claim covers 2 square miles in area and will be steadily developed. The company are perfecting plans to increase the capacity of their plant, and are confident that their property is a very valuable one.

In closing the subject, it might be well to repeat that of the known Gold deposits only the northern fields are being worked, and that there is opportunity for profitable operations in the several districts on the east coast, which have been described. It is not at all impossible that investigations in the vast mountain district, occupied now by wild head-hunters, may reveal fields of Gold far more extensive and valuable than those yet known.

There is very little, if any, land in the island suitable for agriculture that is not already under cultivation; so that not much increase in the island's wealth can be looked for from that quarter, but in Formosa's Gold fields there is likelihood of great development, and if new deposits are found in the savage district, we may anticipate a considerable advancement in the island's prosperity.

NOTE.—As only a trifling portion of the Gold produced in Formosa is passed through the Customs on being exported from the island, the statistics issued by the Customs are not at all representative, and have accordingly not been inserted here.

FORMOSA MINING REGULATIONS, ISSUED ON SEPTEMBER 7TH, 1896.

Article I.—The term *Mining* as used in these Regulations refers to the obtaining of minerals by excavating or otherwise. Earth and stone used for building purposes is exempt.

Article II.—The occupation of mining shall be permitted to Japanese subjects only; and none but Japanese subjects can become members or shareholders of any mining corporation or association.

Article III.—A person desirous of engaging in mining may apply for a mining license to the Governor-General through the Prefectural offices, describing the location of the mine. The applicant may request the authorities to despatch a mining expert to make a survey of the desired claim; but in this case the authorities will collect the travelling expenses and other costs of the survey from the applicant.

A person on presentation of an application for a mining license must pay to the government a fixed fee to be determined by the Governor-General.

Article IV.—When circumstances warrant, the Governor-General can limit the area of any mineral field for which mining applications may be received.

Article V.—When two or more applications have been received for one field, the Governor-General may accept the application of the person best qualified for the undertaking.

Article VI.—In case a mining claim has been applied for and the area specified is considered too extensive, or its boundaries are too complicated, or are such as to be detrimental to the interests of adjoining claims, the Governor-General may order the applicant to make any necessary alterations in the application within a stated period.

Article VII.—Such mining fields as are considered necessary for government use will not be granted to applicants.

Article VIII.—On the Governor-General approving any application, the applicant will be instructed to deposit, within a stated period, a guarantee sum ranging from 100 yen to 30,000 yen, prior to the issuing of the license.

Bonds will be accepted as a substitute for money. The character and value of such bonds will be determined by the Governor-General.

Article IX.—The guarantee sum is to provide against non-payment of taxes, compensation for damages, and for expenses incurred in the execution of official measures. If the government find that the amount of the guarantee already paid is insufficient, the mine-holder may be ordered to increase the sum before the expiration of a stated period.

Article X.—Any mining license obtained by false representation or fraud is null and void.

Article XI.—The right to a mining claim can be inherited.

No mining right can be sold, transferred or hypothecated without first obtaining permission from the Governor-General.

Article XII.—Mineral fields within a distance of 300 ken of a fort, naval station, strategical port, powder mill, powder magazine, or ammunition stores can not be mined; but, as regards a naval station or strategical port, this rule may be dispensed with provided applicants obtain permission from the commandant of the place.

Article XIII.—The approval of the local authorities or consent of the land owner or persons concerned shall be necessary to commence mining operations in any place within a distance of 30 ken either above or below the surface from railway, public road, river or lake, water-works, canal, embankment, reservoir, religious structure, cemetery and its buildings.

When the land-owner or the persons concerned refuse the consent specified as necessary in the foregoing clause, and the mine is not a source of danger, the applicant may refer the case to the chief of local authorities for decision.

In case the party concerned is dissatisfied with the decision of the chief of local authorities he may refer the subject for final settlement to the Governor-General within 30 days from the date of the first decision.

Article XIV.—Persons desiring to combine, or divide, or make other alteration in their claims must apply to the Governor-General for permission.

When mining claims granted are found injurious to general mining interests, or when there is discovered an error in the grant, the Governor-General may issue instructions to make, within a stated period, such alterations as may be necessary.

Article XV.—Holders who desire to discontinue mining operations for more than 60 days must apply to the Governor-General for permission.

In case holders do not engage in proper mining operations, or do injury to the public interest, or cause their mine to become a source of danger, the Governor-General may order that immediate improvement be made where necessary, or may suspend operations entirely.

Article XVI.—The Governor-General may annul mining grants in the following cases:

a. Discontinuance of operations for more than one year, or failure to start work within one year from the date of grant.

b. When grant has been made through error.

c. Neglect to deposit the prescribed guarantee money within the period named in the second clause of Article IX.

d. Violation of second clause of Article XIV and second clause of Article XV.

Article XVII.—No claim for compensation can be entered for losses resulting from decisions rendered by the Governor-General.

Article XVIII.—A person desirous of surveying or making other investigation within the district of another, in order that information may be obtained for forming an application for a mining claim or of mining, may apply to the chief of local authorities for permission.

The owner of the land or persons concerned must recognize the official permission granted, and permit such action to be taken as is therein specified; but in case the property is in any way damaged while the surveys or investigations are being conducted, compensation must be paid by the applicant.

Article XIX.—Claim-holders have the right to demand of land owners or other persons concerned, a lease of any land which it is necessary they should possess for the successful working of their holdings.

In such case, the owner of the land or other persons concerned may lawfully demand a suitable rent for the land required, and may demand that payment shall be made in advance.

Article XX.—In case of a dispute arising between land-owners or persons concerned and persons who have applied for a survey or other investigation, or between the former and claim-holders regarding the lease of land or amount of rent or indemnity for damages or the price of land, either party may apply to the chief of local authorities for an adjustment of the dispute.

Either party not content with the adjustment made by the chief of local authorities may within 30 days appeal to the Governor-General for revision, where the dispute relates to the lease of land, and may bring action in the local court when the dispute relates to the recovery of damages or the amount of rent or price of land.

Article XXI.—No appeal can be entered against the action of the Governor-General in matters mentioned in the 3rd clause of Article XIII and the 2nd clause of Article XX.

Article XXII.—All costs incurred in bringing a case before the chief of local authorities or before the Governor-General shall be paid as provided for civil cases in court.

Article XXIII.—Parties are permitted to make use of land for mining purposes if the chief of local authorities has declared in their favor, even though the land-owners or persons concerned still withhold consent when the case refers to rent of land or damages to be recovered or price of land, provided that the miners have paid to the latter the remuneration required as fixed by the authorities, or in case of refusal to accept the said payment if the sum of money has been deposited with the authorities.

Article XXIV.—When the grant of a mining claim has expired, or it has been annulled by the government, or the claim holder abandons his work, no structure or material utilized which is considered by the authorities necessary in preventing injury to the mine, can be removed.

Article XXV.—Persons engaged in coal, kerosene oil, sulphur, tin and iron mining shall pay, as the mining claim tax, one yen per 1,000 tsubo (4,000 sq. yds.) per annum; and those engaged in gold quartz and placer mining and other precious minerals shall pay 2 yen per 1,000 tsubo (4,000 sq. yds.) per annum. The annual tax for each year shall be paid prior to the 15th of December of the preceding year; but for that year during which the claim has been first obtained the tax shall be paid within 60 days of the date when the claim was granted, and for that portion of the year remaining.

Taxes once collected will not be returned.

Article XXVI.—Claim holders shall make to the Governor-General, through a local office, a statement showing the amount of ore worked, the amount of mineral obtained, and the amount sold, and the price obtained, also a table showing working days and number of laborers engaged.

The reports mentioned in the foregoing clause must be made within thirty days after the mining grant has expired, or has been annulled, or the holders have abandoned the mine, or the claim has been sold or otherwise transferred.

Article XXVII.—Persons engaged in mining without possessing an official license or who have obtained the latter by fraud will be fined a sum of money ranging from 50 yen to 500 yen.

Article XXVIII.—Those who violate the provisions of Article XII and the 1st Clause of Article XIII will be fined a sum of money ranging from 20 yen to 200 yen.

SUPPLEMENTARY CLAUSES.

Article XXX.—Native miners who have obtained mining claims before the enforcement of these regulations shall be allowed to continue unrestricted their work until the 8th of May of the 30th year of Meiji (1897). On that date mining claims held by natives who have become Japanese subjects shall be considered as having been obtained in accordance with these regulations.

Article XXXI.—Rules and instructions for the placing in force of these regulations will be issued by the Governor-General.

Article XXXII.—These regulations will be enforced from the 10th of September of the 29th year of Meiji (1896).

AMENDMENTS ISSUED ON THE 5TH OF OCTOBER, 1898.

Article VIII and Article IX are cancelled.

Article XVI.—The Governor-General of Formosa may annul grants to mining claims in the following cases:—

a. Discontinuance of operations for more than one year or failure to commence work within one year from the date of grant.

b. When grant has been made through error.

c. Violation of the provisions of the 2nd clause of Article XIV and the 2nd clause of Article XV.

d. Non-payment of mining tax within the period prescribed.

CHAPTER XXVII.

COAL IN FORMOSA.

THE island possesses a supply of fuel almost unlimited. From Kimpauli (Kinpori) in the extreme north to the mountain range to the rear of Pangliao (Borio) in the far south, Coal abounds, and even in the flat barren isles of the Pescadores this useful mineral exists. A half hour's walk from Taipeh, the capital of Formosa, will bring one to Coal measures. Coal exists in the hills enclosing Kelung, and it is actually possible for a few fortunate farmers engaged in agricultural work along the foot hills to step out of the back door of their shanties, picks and baskets in hand, and to obtain sufficient fuel for the day's requirements, with but little more difficulty than a farmer at home would have in obtaining it from his own coal-bin. Coal also exists in the savage districts, and in one locality it is found so bituminous and inflammable that the savages use it for torches. This wide distribution of Coal in Formosa means very little, however, when the profitable working of the same is considered; for nature, in a seeming attempt to make a limited supply cover the whole island, has spread out innumerable thin seams abounding with faults and fissures, and ranging, so far as is at present known, from a foot to three feet in thickness, producing bituminous Coal of varying quality, and rendering work on a large scale, with modern machinery, a venture of doubtful practicability.

Still, the mining of Coal has been carried on with more or less energy for many years. The exports at one time provided Kelung with a flourishing trade, and supplied the Chinese southern squadron with a good portion of its requirements: Chinese so far overcame their dislike to foreign innovations as to establish a large mining plant with modern machinery in the Kelung Coal district; and even at present the matter is of much interest to the Japanese, and the possibility of discovering seams of suitable size, permitting the establishment of large works is a source of unceasing speculation and prophecy.

It is perhaps unsafe to make any definite statement in regard to the Coal deposits of the island; for so far only a small district has been prospected, and this superficially. Future investigation and the sinking of shafts may disclose a supply in the middle measures sufficient to encourage the use of modern machinery and make the Coal mining industry one of great importance; for the almost universal signs of this mineral throughout the island would make it appear not unreasonable to anticipate such valuable discoveries. Still even without extensive machinery, it may be hoped that, with improved means of transportation, the adoption of more perfect tools, and the institution of a more effective system of labor, the output, which at present barely reaches 36,000 tons a year, may be doubled and even trebled. At the present high prices obtainable, this would add considerably to the prosperity of the island, especially of the north, where the most extensive deposits exist.[1]

The early history of the industry is of interest. The practical Koxinga appreciated the value of the "black fire-nourishing rocks," and the Chinese mandarins who followed, half superstitious and half conservative, at first opposed the mining of Coal with much vigor; but later on permitted the industry, and, during the last years of Chinese occupation, encouraged it.

The first mining of Coal appears to have occurred in the vicinity of Kelung. Chinese history speaks of Kelung hill, which contained a number of caverns, as the abode of genii, and as the source of the "arterial current" for the whole of Formosa. To the "fengshui" wor-

---

[1]. For details of known Coal Fields see Note on page 489.

shipping literati, no more important place could exist. Yet the hill, owing to its many fissures, tempted numerous "unthinking" laborers to go to it for building material, which could be easily excavated. But the literati, during the reign of the Emperor Keelung (1735—1796), under the belief that the geomantic influence of the whole island was involved, became alarmed at the desecration; and as a result of their representations, a tablet was erected directing that the hill be not disturbed, and threatening dire punishment to "all unheeding children." The so-called caverns were in reality openings in the Coal measures; the presence of this useful mineral was not unknown to the villagers; and while apparently giving the instructions of the mandarins due attention, Kelung residents did not want for fuel. Furthermore, needy persons were inclined to visit the out-croppings in the neighboring hills and gather a few baskets of Coal for market. Other persons of low birth were likewise willing to risk the total destruction of the island by the angry genii, and joined in the lucrative occupation.

This was too much, and in 1835, the gentry and literati united in a petition to the Tamsui District officer, who reported on the subject to the provincial government. This resulted in a second tablet, the former having disappeared, (doubtless not without assistance). To insure its permanency, this tablet was of stone, and on its surface was engraved, in peremptory wording, the declaration that the mining of Coal was absolutely and for all eternity prohibited. But the foolish, unemployed country people still persisted in disturbing the geomantic influence, "inviting dire disaster on all the peoples," and in 1847, the gentry and others again petitioned, accompanying their document with a scapegoat in the shape of a wretched miner who had been selected for punishment that his fate might be a warning to others. A third prohibitory tablet was now set up.

The next year, 1849, the U. S. brig *Dolphin* visited Kelung. American officers in the East were taking a more than ordinary interest in the island, and the occupation of some portion of Formosa by the Americans was being strongly advocated in certain quarters. The officers made careful investigation of the Coal pits then in existence, and, in a report on the subject, stated that "the practicability of working the Coal appears not at all a difficult matter. Plenty of trees are growing on the spot and may be felled, the largest being about the size suitable for sleepers for a tram-road; the length of iron (rail) required is about a mile, and the ascent is one foot in fifteen. A canal or creek connects the road with the harbor, which is navigable for flat-bottomed boats of four or five tons, and the Coal would not have to be carried more than three miles and a half. The mine is 230 feet elevation by barometer. The Coal and land round about appears to be unclaimed, any one taking away as much as he likes. The inhabitants themselves offered to bring us forty or fifty tons at a day's notice, at less than a dollar a ton; probably a much larger quantity might be obtained with a little exertion."

In 1850, the British plenipotentiary addressed the Chinese government, requesting that the Kelung Coal deposits might be worked, and offering to co-operate with the authorities in opening the mines. The mandarins reported in answer, that they had given the minister's kind offer careful consideration; but that "upon examining the records," they were obliged to state, "that as the surrounding hills of the port contained the dragon's pulse for all Formosa, and the gentry and people of all Formosa had repeatedly and publicly prohibited interference therewith, it was obviously right to comply with the wishes of the people, and inexpedient to forcibly insist upon the opening of the mines, which might lead to trouble and furnish occasion for disaster."

In 1854, two foreign vessels anchored at Kelung, and men were sent on shore to the Coal fields, and there personally excavated a sufficient amount of Coal to supply their vessels. On learning of this, the Tamsui ting observed that the strangers had given no heed to the prohibition, and that the village headmen and constables should reprimand the offenders. This brought up the subject again, and Mr. Parkes, British consul at Amoy, represented that, "as British steamships came from afar, the conveyance of Coal from the home-land was very cumbersome, and that Formosa, possessing abundant supplies, the Chinese at Kelung should be permitted to supply foreign vessels calling in at that port with Coal for their requirements."

Furthermore, in 1864, a French engineer, M. Dupont, in the employ of the Fuchow arsenal, made a survey of the Kelung Coal districts; and the Fuchow and Tamsui Commissioners of Customs requested that foreigners should be allowed to mine there. To all such applications the mandarins turned a deaf ear. Meanwhile secret mining was carried on with increasing activity, and the gentry again petitioned in a body, that, as rumors were current to the effect that the mines would be opened on a large scale, and that the genial influence of "fengshui" would thus surely be destroyed, the intendant of the circuit should take steps to prevent it. This officer reported the matter to the governor of Fokien, who in turn referred it to the Tsung-li yamen. More proclamations resulted, but they, like the others, went unheeded. On the establishment of the Foochow arsenal, opposition practically ceased, and the Chinese in Kelung were able to supply this institution with no small part of its requirements; and the Kelung village officers imposed an export duty on the Coal shipped.

The high authorities, noting that it was no longer to their advantage to attempt further the enforcement of the prohibition, took a characteristical personal view of the affair, and decided that, if the mining of Coal in Formosa could not be prevented, it should at least be conducted for their benefit, and the governor-general of Fokien accordingly instructed the Formosan intendant to appoint a commission to visit Kelung and investigate the fields, and after conferring with the local gentry, to ascertain as to the feasibility of opening the mines. This was done, and in an official memorandum the commission stated that they had found that the villagers were working 44 Coal pits, and that 12 localities, which were specified, were "situated in hills apart from that which contains the spring of geomantic influence" and could therefore be worked without "in any wise interfering with the genial properties thereof nor, owing to their location, "can they exercise any baneful influence on either house, grave, garden, or enclosure." Following the opening of the island to foreign trade in 1860, numerous foreign vessels had called in at Kelung, and the annual yield of Coal for some years had ranged from 6,000 to 18,000 tons, varying with the demand. Likin equal to about one half the export tariff rate had been imposed on all the out-put, save the supplies forwarded to Foochow for the use of the government arsenal there. The commission recommended the abandonment of the government prohibition, but suggested the adoption of certain measures to prevent foreigners obtaining an interest in the industry.[1]

Now awakened to the possibility of an additional source of income, the Fokien higher authorities despatched, in 1873, a Chinese expert who, starting from Tainan, travelled north to Kelung, making a rough survey along the way. The result of his visit was a report advocating that, as Kelung residents were without sufficient means to establish modern mining plants, the Chinese government should erect machinery and other western appliances and commence the mining on a large scale; and after the utility of this system had been demonstrated, the miners might be advised to establish similar plants for themselves. The expert added the consoling information that as the principal Coal deposits existed only in the "side arteries," the mines could be worked without injury to the "main geomantic properties of the district."

With the construction of a modern navy, together with the requirements of the Foochow arsenal, the Chinese government found that the working of some of their Coal deposits was now necessary, and the Formosan fields were the most tempting. Accordingly, Shen Pao chan, who, during the Japanese expedition to Formosa in 1874, had held the post of Imperial Commissioner to the island, sought and obtained permission from the Peking authorities to erect a modern mining plant in the Kelung district. Mr. David Tyzack, a foreign mining expert, was engaged in 1874; and after having made a careful survey of the Kelung fields, this gentleman was despatched in 1875 to England, where he purchased the necessary machinery and engaged a party of mining experts. To prepare the way and disarm

---

1. The commission suggested the following measures for adoption in connection with the mines, viz.:

"1st.—That at Sheu-ao-kang and the other spots where mines are mentioned as existing, boundaries be fixed beyond which no mines be opened, whilst within the radius proposed no mine be rented to foreigners or mortgaged to others by original owners."

"2nd.— That in the district surveyed, and which may be put down as extending 20 li from north to south, and 5 or 6 li from east to west, the number of working mines be limited to 70 in all, and that no new ones be opened."

"3rd.—That master miners be all natives of the neighborhood having their ancestral tombs and their houses within easy distance. They must find security and take out licences, no individual being eligible for a licence who is in any way connected with a foreign hong."

"4th.—That the men employed as colliers be all natives of the region within 50 li of the coal mines, that not more than 20 be employed in one mine, and that all be secured by the master miners. There must, in fact, be a system of mutual bond and security."

"5th.—That all coal purchases must be transacted through the (appointed) hongs, which will be officially supervised. Direct dealings with the miners should be held to constitute an infraction of Treaty stipulation."

Translation as given in the I. M. Chinese Customs Report for Tamsui, 1871-2.

suspicion, the Formosa intendant issued a proclamation announcing to the headmen, traders, miners, and others of Kelung neighborhood that the proposal to work the mines on western principles emanated from the government alone, and that the foreign experts were engaged in order that native miners might learn from them the method of modern mining, and that Formosa might produce adequate supplies. It was intended that the Coal produced by the government mine should be purchasable by either foreign or native merchants. In closing, the intendant observed, that as an act of indulgence, the local imposts on Coal would be remitted in toto; and further, that operations in Coal-pits then under native direction, might continue, as heretofore, so long as the same did not interfere with the site intended for the erection of mining machinery.

Machinery sufficient to handle several hundred tons of Coal a day arrived in 1876, and was erected in the centre of the most promising district, at a point known as Pa-tou (Hatto), some three miles east of Kelung, and near an indentation in the coast, later known as "Coal Harbor."

Work was at once commenced on this site, a circular shaft $12\frac{1}{2}$ feet in diameter being sunk 295 feet. The main seam, with a thickness of 3 feet $5\frac{1}{2}$ inches, was encountered at a depth of 270 feet. It was necessary, owing to dislocated strata and much shattered rock, to line the shaft with stone, and the plant was not completed until the close of the year, when the output of Coal was from 30 to 40 tons a day. An abundance of the mineral was in sight, and according to a report made by the foreign engineer in charge, the quality was evidently very satisfactory.[1]

During the next year the mine was in complete working order. A Guibal fan had been put in to furnish ventilation to the pits, and a shaft 8 feet 6 inches in diameter and 88 feet in depth had been sunk for the same purpose. The underground workings had been greatly enlarged and were now capable of producing 200 tons a day, while the engineer estimated that 200,000 tons could be obtained without exhausting the pit.

The sea was a mile distant from the mine, and here, in the small bay known as "Coal Harbor," was erected a jetty and Coal chutes. From the mine to the jetty was laid a tramway, by means of which the Coal was transported in cars which ran down quickly and without power, owing to the

---

1. "The Coal in the winning heading and to the deep side was found to be of very excellent quality, working into large masses by the use of gun-powder, and giving off great heat when burned in a boiler fire; it is, therefore, very suitable for steaming purposes, indeed it was found too hot for ordinary purposes in our own tubular boiler in good round and screened pieces, and we are now obliged to use the slack, or dead small Coal, for firing, as too much steam is generated by the larger Coal for ordinary use. I have raised steam with this Coal in a nominal 40-horse-power boiler from cold water to 70 lbs. pressure in 70 minutes.

"The Coal to the deep continues of even better quality as we proceed, but that to the immediate rise is softer and more friable, but this is to be expected, as we are passing through a series of small faults, the greatest of which is 5 feet rise, but sufficient to disturb locally the normal condition of the Coal for the worse. We are now driving in a westerly direction from the shaft bottom, with several winnings to the rise and dip, with afore-mentioned results as regards quality, but we expect very early to meet with another fault which the native miners say is the last in this series (they having proved it in their Coal drifts to the rise in the hill sides), when I confidently look forward to a large tract of strong, good Coal before us, which is known by me, by the examination of all surrounding outcrops, to be of superior quality."—I. M. Chinese Customs Report for Tamsui, 1877.

favorable gradient ; making it possible to transport the Coal from the mine and to place it in the barges within 8 minutes after leaving the shaft.

Although the plant was now in every way complete, the machinery serviceable, and the mining experts competent, a great hindrance to the successful working of the mine was the difficulty of obtaining efficient labor. The district in the vicinity of the Coal mines is perhaps the most unhealthy in Formosa. Dense jungle abounds, and the rains, which are extremely heavy in these parts, are ordinarily followed by intense heat, causing evaporation, which fills the air with vaporous fumes. As a result, a large proportion of the workmen, the first gang of whom were chiefly from the mainland, were stricken down with fever, not a few succumbing to it. It was thus extremely difficult, especially in summer, to secure workmen, only about one half of the requisite number being forthcoming. Even those who were obtained were very unsatisfactory. The foreign chief reported that they were very slow to learn and not to be trusted with any task of importance ; that their capacity for work was small; and especially as coal-hewers, they accomplished surprisingly little, as compared with what coal-hewers in other countries can do. The foreigners engaged in the work also suffered greatly from fever, two deaths occurring among them. In three years there were 52 deaths among the Chinese staff, including an interpreter and several clerks ; and even the high Chinese official in charge was very ill and forced to give up his position. At last the doctor was stricken and died, and from that time on no high Chinese official could be induced to reside in the place ; the result being that the control over the Chinese engaged at the mine became very lax; great inconvenience was experienced owing to the delay in going to Kelung to confer with the chief authority on matters of every day occurrence ; and the successful working of the mine was thus threatened.

To make matters worse, the success obtained in the mechanical working of the mine was nullified by the inability of the mandarins to arrange for the transportation of Coal from Coal Harbor to Kelung. This apparently easy task they managed so poorly that the total annual Kelung export for some years scarcely exceeded the annual amount obtained during favorable years prior to the establishment of the foreign mine. Coal harbor is so unfavorably located that during some six months in the year, owing to the prevailing north-east wind, it was frequently impossible to ship coal. Furthermore, only sailing barges were utilized, which being dependent upon favorable winds, constituted a very unsatisfactory form of transport. The result was that, as the output of the mine increased, huge piles of coal accumulated near the shaft, and there remained for considerable periods, dusky monuments to the incapacity of the officials, and a source of danger from fire to the plant. It was stated by foreign experts that the only remedy required was a sufficient number of barges when the sea was not too rough and a steam launch to tow them around to Kelung, where the Coal could be stored until wanted. Steam launches had not been permitted to engage in the coasting trade, and the mandarins were resolute that none should be engaged in the present work. The fact that the business of Coal mining in which the mandarins were engaged had been by these same officers declared a crime only a few years before did not strike them as inconsistent with the position they now took in refusing to utilize steam launches.

Had the mandarins not interfered with the native miners, the total production of Coal during this period would have been considerable, and the local demand for Coal would have been satisfied. For several years preceding the opening of the foreign mine, supplies had been quite abundant, and, though the high authorities had repeatedly declared that the government had no intention of monopolizing Coal, and that the official establishment would not interfere with private mining in any way, no sooner was the new mine in operation, than the officials commenced to put the screw on independent miners. Restrictions of all kinds were imposed, and attempts made in other ways to close up the outside mines. The result was that in 1877, although but little Coal could be obtained from the new mine, the local native mines were permitted to supply only a portion of the demand. The Kelung junk trade was consequently much depressed, and foreign vessels which were wont to visit the port for Coal, went elsewhere for their requirements. In 1878, the decrease in production was still more marked, and great inconvenience was felt owing to the scarcity and the high cost of the supplies at hand. For the next few years the government mine continued in operation in spite of increasing difficulties ; but so intent were the officials on obtaining complete control of the whole product, and so persistent were they in persecuting outside producers, that had not complaint been made by foreigners, the trade in Coal would have resolved itself into a recognized government monopoly. Even as it was, virtual control of the output was obtained by the officials, who engaged all the cargo and Coal boats, and if a customer in Kelung desired to purchase Coal, the price was raised to such an extent as to be practically prohibitory, while the officials themselves retailed the product in Shanghai and other Chinese ports at current prices.

During the early eighties, some change for the better was made in the government mine, and a marked improvement introduced in the method of handling the product. In 1881, there were a thousand hands employed, and the export from Kelung that year reached 46,000 tons, being, with the exception of one year, the largest known. A tunnel 460 feet long was driven through the solid rock with the idea of obtaining an increased production; but, contrary to expectations, the output during the next two years dropped off.

Early in August 1884, the difficulties between China and France having reached a crisis, the French fleet arrived at Kelung and bombarded the forts. Liu Ming-chuan, the then governor-general of Formosa, feared the worst ; and having no intention of presenting the French with a well equipped mine and a large stock of Coal, gave orders that the works should be destroyed, the pits flooded, and the stock of Coal—some 15,000 tons—set fire to. His orders were carried out without loss of time, and thus was rendered useless a large plant on which much money had been spent and many lives sacrificed.

After the close of the war, some new machinery was obtained, and operations in the same district were resumed. But the work was not carried on with the energy and enthusiasm previously exhibited, the output, with the exception of one year, amounting to only about half of that turned out in former years ; and in 1891, it having been reported that the deposits were exhausted, all work was thenceforward abandoned. The mandarins obtained their Coal thereafter from private miners, and at one time financial assistance was given to an association of five companies, on the understanding that they should supply the government with all that was required.

In 1895, the writer, accompanied by a friend, made a trip to the Coal district. Shortly after leaving Kelung, we came to an abandoned Coal brick factory. This plant had been erected by private enterprise, was fully equipped with machinery, and at the time of our visit was in apparently good condition. From this place we followed up a picturesque valley, and after a walk of some two hours, encountered the old tramway which winds its way upwards toward the mines. Here and there we saw an overturned car and again one partially dismantled. At last, we reached the works, and a desolate scene it was. Not a person was in sight and the stillness was oppressive. We entered the building which had been partially destroyed, doubtless by storm, and there before us stood boilers, engines, and other expensive machinery ; so far as appearances were concerned only awaiting the opening of the throttle to start the whole plant in motion. The works had apparently suffered little at the hands of marauders, perhaps the would-be robbers were impressed as we were by the extreme silence of the place and the gloomy, if not weird aspect of the big machines, renounced by those who had once cared for them, and now as quiet and lifeless as the occupants of the graves on a neighboring plot, who had likewise met their end in the service of the Formosan government mines.

Having disposed of the historical part of the subject, we are brought down to the present occupation of the island by the Japanese. During 1894, the year prior to the arrival of the Japanese, the Coal export exceeded 24,000 tons ; but during the years 1895 and 1896, the confusion attending the change of administration, as well as the military operations in the north, reduced the Coal production greatly, and it was not until 1897 that the industry was again flourishing. During 1896, mining regulations were issued by the government and applications for the granting of mining claims received.[1]

K. Yamada, an energetic Japanese merchant who has been foremost in many commercial industries in North Formosa, was the first Japanese to engage in Coal mining in the island. In March 1896, he commenced working in a small way, a valuable Coal claim which he had obtained at Pangliao (Borio), a short distance up river from Twatutia. The first year the monthly output amounted to some 200 tons, the second year to 550 tons, and at present 625 tons are produced, or a total of 7,500 tons yearly. Although this is a trifling production, the coal from this mine is of the best

----

1. For translation of mining regulations see closing note of preceding chapter.

quality obtained in Formosa, and a scientific analysis made by the Government shows that it compares very favorably with the best bituminous Coal obtained in other lands.

Other Japanese mines in operation are the Mukoyama mine near Kelung, the Koshima mine near Shutingkiaku (Sui-teng-ka), the Aoyagi mine near Shakko (Sikkau), and the Tsumura mine at Gofunsho. The total output from both Japanese and Chinese mines has reached 5,000 tons a month; but, as the demand has not supported such a production, the output has been somewhat reduced, until at the present writing, the total remains steadily at about 4,000 tons monthly. This quantity slightly exceeds the production for the last few years of the Chinese regime, the average monthly production from 1890 to 1894 amounting to about 2,000 tons. Whereas in Chinese days the principal production was from the Kelung district, at present the Taipeh district provides almost half the total. This output for the whole island is not, at first sight, satisfactory. It was thought that on the arrival of the Japanese in the island, now freed from Chinese official restrictions, the large coal deposits would be worked extensively; that foreign methods and the employment of elaborate machinery would be utilized to the utmost. This has not been done; and, unless an exceptional demand is created establishing a higher basis of prices, or some very favorable deposits are discovered, it is doubtful if works on a large scale, or even a plant similar to the former Chinese government mines, will be seen in Formosa. This is not through lack of funds; for Japanese capitalists have established complete mills in the Gold district, but is simply due to the fact that government experts who have made careful investigations are of opinion that the Formosa deposits, such as are at present known, are distributed in beds too thin and yielding Coal of too low a value, to make large works at present profitable.

To appreciate the difficulties of mining in Formosa the character of the Coal beds must be taken into account. Coal in Formosa is generally found between strata of sand-stone. The seams range only from 1½ to 3 feet in thickness, with the rare exception of one or two beds where seams from four to five feet exist. The inclination of the strata is in some places so great, reaching even to 90 degrees and more, that mining is impracticable. The distance between the upper and middle measures is sometimes very great, ordinarily exceeding several hundred feet. This fact, combined with the simple system of mining in vogue in the island, renders the working of the lower measures, after upper beds have been exhausted, a difficult task.

Most of the seams have been discovered from the out croppings along the foot hills, and work is usually carried on at each seam proceeding into the hill for as great a distance as the inclination and surrounding formations will permit. A great distance is rarely attained, the seam is not of sufficient value to encourage expensive shaft construction, and where it is found inconvenient to proceed further, the old source is abandoned, a new out cropping attacked, and the process of merely scratching the surface continued as before. If a large supply is desired, work is carried on at many seams rather than at one.

Although some fourteen mines have Japanese engaged as overseers or laborers, the bulk of the labor, in not only Chinese, but in the Japanese controlled mines also, is carried on by Chinese. With the exception of the Japanese works, wherein many improvements have been introduced, the present Chinese system of mining is virtually the same as has existed in Formosa from the earliest days of the Kelung mines.

That Chinese are generally wasteful of labor has often been noted, and this characteristic is well exemplified in their methods of working Coal. Observers familiar with both systems have stated that Chinese miners in Formosa are even inferior in their methods to their fellow workmen in China. At all events, the work could scarcely be more crudely conducted.

Provided with a roughly made tool, half pick, half sledge hammer, possessing a handle some 2½ feet in length, a bowl of oil, with a rag inserted as a wick to afford light, and a basket to carry out the Coal, the Chinese miner is prepared to open and work a mine; and with no more extensive outfit or supplies than these, much of the Coal in Formosa is obtained.

The Chinese—occasionally he is proprietor, miner, carrier, and salesman all in one,—selects a site where the mineral is observed out cropping. Here the Coal, softened by exposure, is so friable, that only a small opening is made, for scarcely ever do the Chinese use any artificial supports. An entrance having been gained and the appearance of the seam being satisfactory the floor of the tunnel is made sufficiently wide and level to admit the basket, the preliminary operations are considered complete, and the mine is ready for business. The entrance is so small that the miner enters on his hands and knees; the height of the tunnel very little exceeds the thickness of the seam, being thus so small, that, in excavating, the miner must work on his knees, or in a half reclining position, resting partly in mud and water; and the writer has seen tunnels so low that the miner was obliged to lie at full length, and in this position handle his pick. In the absence of ventilation, the atmosphere in a few hours becomes so foul that the lamp flame is reduced to a sickly flicker, and the miner, with strength exhausted, is obliged to stop work and seek fresh air. No attempt is made to improve the ventilation, though, before a mine is abandoned on this account, the gods are appealed to, by burning a large quantity of joss paper in the offending pit, and the believing pagan is not infrequently rewarded by an improvement in the atmosphere; for the heat creates a current which brings a change of air, and the miner is able to renew his labors, convinced of the infallibility of the generous joss. Should success not result, however, failure is attributed to the wrath of the spirits, and the mine is accordingly abandoned.

It also frequently occurs that the inclination is such that water accumulates to an extent interfering with work; and, if there is too great a quantity to be carried out in buckets, the seam is given up. Furthermore, owing to the absence of artificial supports, a land slide sometimes occurs, not only obstructing work, but occasionally resulting in loss of life. Thus with these obstacles, all of which could be easily overcome, the Chinese often abandons a seam just when it is giving the best results. Fortunately, fire-damp is unknown in Formosa, otherwise the mines would become frequently untenable, and alarming accidents would occur.

The excavating in Chinese mines is done in a very unskillful way, being a mere wearing away of the seam by constant picking, no attempt being made to obtain the mineral in large pieces. Yet in the narrow tunnels, with the heat and foul air, it speaks well for their powers of endurance that the Chinese can work at all. The Coal as excavated is passed to the rear, and loaded into a basket some three feet in length, the bottom of which is pro-tected by wooden shoes. The workman drags this along the tunnel by a hauling rope. In time a groove is worn in the floor the exact size of the basket, and its surface becoming hard and firm, the task of hauling is not such a difficult one as might appear. If the tunnel bed is too rough, however, planks are laid, on which the baskets slide. Little stone wheels are also sometimes placed on the basket. From the entrance of the mine, coolies carry the Coal in baskets swung from the end of a shoulder pole, and by this wasteful and expensive system of transportation, the article reaches market; or, if the destination is far distant, the nearest navigable river, so that the Coal may make, if possible, a part of its journey by boat.

While, as stated above, no machinery is utilized in the Formosa Coal mines worked by Japanese, the method of operation varies considerably from the Chinese. The entrance is large, the tunnels are roomy and supported by wood-work wherever it is required. Drainage and ventilation are provided for by extra shafts or tunnels if necessary, improved tools are used, and in some cases easy transport from the mines established.

The best example of the present style of mining can be seen at Pangliao (Borio). There, mines are being worked by Chinese and Japanese almost side by side. The mines are only some three miles distant from Taipeh, and the trip can be very easily made by boat from Twatutia (Daitotei). Provided a clean river-boat is obtained, and if wind and tide are not unfavorable, an interesting and not unpleasant ride of an hour will bring one to the large brick and tile works of the Arima Company, and the site of the Japanese Ice Company's original plant. A little beyond the last mentioned establishment, a small creek runs in from the river shore, on which are the Coal storing yards. Here is the terminus of the small tramway owned by the Yamada Coal Company, which runs through the fields from the river to the base of the foot hills to the rear, where the mines are, just one mile up from the river. Here, if the stranger's curiosity overcomes his aversion to Coal dust, he can enter the tunnel of the Japanese works and see the miners excavating. Also, if possessed of exceptional powers of endurance and an extra suit of clothes, he might crawl into one of the Chinese tunnels, not far distant, and see the manner of carrying on work there.

In the Yamada mines, 30 Japanese and 60 Chinese are employed, though, owing to sickness, the actual number at work does not generally exceed 75. With the exception of the overseers, who receive a monthly salary, the miners are paid according to the amount excavated. Japanese receive nine sen and Chinese eight sen per picul (133 lbs). This rate is about two or three sen higher than is paid in other districts, such as the Kelung mines for instance, but the coal from Pangliao is harder, and therefore more difficult to excavate. The Japanese workmen receive higher pay than the Chinese, as the former are more careful and exhibit greater skill in their work than the latter, whose product contains too much small coal and dust. Before the Coal leaves the mine, it is screened until the dust is removed, and is again screened before loading into the boats. Thus the actual cost for excavation of lump Coal is higher than the figures given above. If it is desired that the Coal be taken out only in large pieces, as much as eighteen sen a picul must be paid. The miners work in couples, one man to excavate, while the other transports the coal to the entrance. The Japanese miner appears to have a greater capacity for work than the Chinese, for the former excavates on an average about 3,000 kin (3,990 lbs.) a day, thus earning for himself and assistant about yen 2.70 for a full day's work; while the Chinese average 1,500 kin (1,995 lbs.) a day, with earnings of some yen 1.20 for the two men engaged. Work can not be carried on steadily, however, day by day; and the total payments for the month show that the average daily earnings for the Japanese and his assistant amount to about yen 2.00 a day, and for the Chinese to about 80 sen. The Company possesses twenty tram cars, and the Coal is transported in these to the river, where it is loaded in the Chinese river-boats and carried by them to Twatutia or Tamsui (Hobe), in which places much of the Coal is sold.

The principal local consumers of Formosa Coal are the Osaka Shosen Kwaisha—both Tamsui and Kelung lines, the railway, the river and coastwise launches, and steamers; while establishments such as the opium factory, the arsenal, and the numerous brick and tile factories take a considerable quantity. From August to October, Chinese junks carry Coal dust to Amoy and Foochow; and some small shipments of lump Coal are occasionally made. Formosa Chinese also consume some Coal in the manufacture of a crude coke. The process is very simple; live coals are placed in the centre of a circular pile of Coal in the open air, and the smouldering glow is allowed to penetrate through the mass, while, by sprinkling with water, the right intensity of heat is obtained, and the flame is kept under.

With almost no assistance from machinery or other labor-saving devices, only a very small capital is required, and the price of Formosan Coal is therefore largely dependent upon the cost of labor. Formosan miners now find that some 5 to 6 yen a ton must be obtained in order to make the industry profitable, whereas in the old days they could afford to sell for half that sum. This becomes perfectly comprehensible when we note that the price of labor has doubled during the period. It also explains why the export trade in Formosan Coal has declined since the Chinese days. The increased price of labor has raised the price so high that, when the cost of freight is added, the Formosan product cannot generally compete with other Coals in foreign markets. Fortunately, however, the domestic demand has so increased that the total production is about the same as for the last years of the Chinese regime.

In closing, it may be well to point out that, while the present outlook for Coal as a leading industry of Formosa is not very promising, the Coal fields in the district under Japanese control are small as compared with the vast unexplored territory within the domain of the savages. Coal is known to exist there ; but as to the extent and character of the deposits, nothing is known. Still such geological information as has been obtained, makes it appear that not only Coal but more valuable minerals may be found there.

NOTE I.

KNOWN COAL FIELDS IN FORMOSA.

(Compiled from Japanese Official and other Reports.)

The Kinpori (Kimpau-li) measures, commencing 2½ miles west of the village of Kinpori, take a N. 30° E. direction extending through the Daitou (Twa-tun) mts., thence pass Hokuto (Pak-tau) and Kōtō (Kan-tau), and entering the district south-east of Toshien (Toa-hong) appear at Kiron (Ku-run), Seki-kwaiko (Chio-he-kng), and Hinau (Pi-lam), taking a direction in the latter district of nearly N. and S. The seams range in thickness from 7 inches to 2 feet.

Coal obtained from the Kinpori district can be transported by water to Kelung, that from Hokuto or Tamsui by water to Hobe or Taipeh, that from the Kiron district must be carried some three to five miles overland and then be transported by railway from Toshien.

At Maren (Ma-lien), 2½ miles east of Kinpori, Coal measures, consisting of two seams, are found ; the upper 1 foot and the lower 1½ feet in thickness. Inclination is 30° S.E. and direction N. 30° East, and the mineral should appear somewhere near Pat-chi-na.

The Kan-kiak (Kham-ka) measures lie about a mile east of the Maren measures, and have a similar direction. They show four seams, one above the other, with a thickness of ½ foot, 5 feet, 8 inches and 1 foot respectively, the distance from the top to the bottom seam being about 120 feet. These measures should be also found somewhere in the vicinity of Shakko (Sik-kau). No other known mines have a seam as great as 5 feet in thickness, and as the quality of the Coal is good, this is considered one of the most valuable coal-beds in Formosa. It is the property of the Navy, and is not in operation. Coal from these mines could be carried 2½ miles to the sea coast and thence be transported by water.

The Naigwai-Bokuzan (Lai-goa-bok-soa) measures lie about 2 miles south of the above, and extend in the same direction. They consist of two seams, the upper being 2 feet and the lower 1½ feet in thickness. Nai-bokuzan and Gwai-bokuzan are two mines 2½ miles N.W. of Kelung working the above deposits. These beds also appear at Maryoko (Ma-lui-kng), Yuzeisho (Yu la-tseng), Pachirenko (Pat-lien-kang). The inclination of the strata is 12°, thickness of seam 2 f-et, and the Coal is of good quality.

The Denryoko measures lie above the Nai-bokuzan and Gwai-bokuzan beds ; and, as they appear near Kelung, are mined extensively, and were formerly worked by the Chinese Government. Commencing at Hatto (Pa-tou) they cross the Kelung Zuiho (Sui-hong) road, pass through Denryoko and Sekikoko (Chio-gi-kang) to about ½ mile south of Kelung city, thence crossing the Kelung-Taipeh railway pass through Shikyugin (Sai kyu-niah), Suirenbi (Sui-lien-be), Maryosho (Ma-lui-kng), Pachirenko (Pat-lion-kang), Hokukokei (Pah-kang-koe) and extend as far south as Naikosho (Nai-a-tsung) a distance of some 25 miles in all. The strata dip to the south-east, 25° in the vicinity of Kelung, and 12° or 13° near Suikenkiaku (Sui-teng-ka) ; the deposits appear in one seam with a thickness of 3 feet. The Coal from the Hatto (Pa-tao) district can be transported to Kelung by water, and Coal from Denryoko and Sekikoko districts must be transported by land for a mile or two to the villages of the same name ; thence to Kelung by water.

The Shikiaktei (Si-ka-tien) deposits lie over the Denryoko beds, in fact are above all other known beds. The coal is found in three seams in the vicinity of Shikiaktei. Daisuikutsu the lowest seam, is 400 to 500 feet above the Denryoko beds, and some 200 feet higher still are the second and third seams. The three seams are 1½ feet, 4 feet, and 6 inches in thickness respectively. The inclination is generally 30° but ranges from 5° to 80°. One portion of the fields runs nearly parallel with the Denryoko deposits and terminates near Hatto on the N. E., in the vicinity of Dandangai (Ka-ton-chia) a village 2½ miles south of Kelung on the S. W. The Coal strata dipping towards the N. W. extend in a north-east direction to Zuiho, where the Koshiryo (Kin-a-liao) Ryutan to (Liong-tam-tao) mines are found : the seams worked here vary in thickness from 2 to 3 feet. The same measures extend southwards through Shikiaktei, 1½ miles south of Dandangai, and south of both Suihenkiaku and Shakko (near Shakko is the Namkoshiko mine) thence to the south of Taipeh, and appear on the banks of the Taikokan (Tokoham) river. Farther than this point, the measures have not been traced. As these deposits lie along the bank of the Kelung river and are near both Taipeh and Kelung, they are mined extensively, and the product can be easily transported to Taipeh by river-boats. The Coal mined in the vicinity of Zuiho (Sui-hong) is consumed in the gold quartz mills, but if the Kelung river rises sufficiently high to permit, the Coal is sent by boat to Taipeh. The Shikiaktei deposits, in number and thickness of seams, in ease of excavation and in the convenience for transportation rank first in the island, and are, like the Kaukiak (Ham-ka) mines, reserved for the use of the navy.

The Sanshorei (Sam-tiao) measures which lie to the south of the Shikiaktei field, dip towards the S.E., and extend in a direction N 60° E. Inclination is from 12° to 20°, and from Sanshorei the measures extend through the Happun (Poe-hun) Mts., and traversing a section of the Savage district, pass through Shinten (Sin-tiam), Saukakuyu (San-kak-eng), and Taikokan (To-ko-ham) and proceed as far as Shakumon. The principal seam is under 2 feet in thickness and the coal is of good quality near Sanshorei. At Shinten the strata dip 85° and the quality of the local is very bad. At Taikokan, the inclination is 30° and the quality is good. At Shakumon, outcroppings have been observed, but nothing is known definitely about the seams. The Coal from this field is mined chiefly by the tea farmers both at Taikokan and Shinten.

In addition to the above, Coal is reported as existing at Kutsushaku (Ku-chu) and in the district near the upper reaches of the Taikokan river, both in Taipeh district.

These coal measures lie mostly in Taipeh Prefecture.

TECKCHAM DISTRICT.

At Nankosho, 5 miles S.E. of Hokupo, Coal measures are encountered showing two seams 1 foot and 3 feet in thickness respectively. The direction taken is N. and S. Outcroppings of this field are visible along the road-side between Nansho and Hokupo.

Coal deposits appear at Sanwan 10 or 12 miles east of Chūkó (Tiong-kang) near the upper stream of the Tiong-kaug river. Direction is N. 30° E., the strata dip 50° to the north west, and the thickness of the principal seam is 5 feet.

Near Saukosho at the foot of the Daitotsu Mts 9 miles east of Bioritsu (Maoli) Coal deposits appear. Direction taken is N. 40° W., strata dip 50° to S. W., thickness of principal seam 6 feet. This field extends S. E. to the Seupitsu Mts and Kokwansho, but at these two places the largest seam found is only 1 foot thick.

At Taiko (Twa-o) Coal exists, a seam of 2 feet in thickness having been found.

The above deposits in the Teckcham district have not been mined, owing to the difficulty of access and the expense of transportation. With the completion of railway improvements in the island, however, there may be an opportunity for profitable operations.

In Toseikaku (Tang-si-kak) region, although no seams have been discovered, pockets of Coal have been found among the sandstone.

CENTRAL FORMOSA.

In the district adjacent to the upper reaches of the Hokkōkei (Pak-kang), Coal is known to exist.

Twelve miles west of Horisha (Pulisia) a Coal seam of 1 foot in thickness appears. Direction taken is N. and S. and strata dip about 70°.

SOUTH FORMOSA.

2½ miles N. of Pinan Pilam) on the Pinan river, near a savage village called Rikirikisha, Coal is found. It is very good for fuel, but the quantity seems small. Coal is found in several river-beds in Taito, (Taitong) district, but the true source of these specimens has not yet been determined. Coal deposits also exist in the Ariko (Ahlikang) district, east of Takow, and near Toko (Tangkang).

In the neighboring islands, dependencies of Formosa, coal is found only in the Pescadores. Near the sea shore of Seirago, 10 miles from the district city Makung, Coal is found. During the Chinese regime, the deposits were worked in a small way for a considerable period, until a bad accident occurred in the mines, killing several of the workmen. Then the superstitious natives, attributing the calamity to the wrath of spirits avenging the disturbance of the geomantic properties of the island, ceased work, and no Coal has been excavated there since. Expert examination has been made of the above and other deposits in the group, and they have been reported practically worthless.

NOTE II.
TABLE SHOWING EXPORT OF FORMOSA COAL.

Year.	Quantities in tons.	Year.	Quantities in tons.
1856	1,500	1884	30,933
1865	7,162	1885	5,767
1866	17,887	1886	16,659
1867	12,860	1887	12,301
1868	26,662	1888	26,639
1869	15,467	1889	43,419
1870	7,935	1890	25,518
1871	19,604	1891	27,950
1872	42,243	1892	14,503
1873	47,447	1893	21,748
1874	15,982	1894	24,243
1875	27,665	1895	10,004
1876	31,593	1896	{ Export 6,842 / Estimated production 14,000 }
1877	28,948	1897	{ Export 7,966 / Estimated production 20,000 }
1878	25,788	1898	{ Export 15,707 / Estimated production 60,000 }
1879	28,823	1899	{ Export 18,112 / Estimated production 50,100 }
1880	24,000		
1881	46,002		
1882	42,202		
1883	31,818		

The above figures are chiefly from Customs Reports. Figures for the years from 1896 to 1899, are given to show both export and production This is done that the reader may learn the total output; the figures prior to the year 1875 in reality show very nearly the output, as but little Coal was used locally; whereas at present the production is largely consumed in the island by steamers running from the ports of Keluug and Tamsui, of which no mention is made in the Japanese Customs returns.

For 1899, the two northern ports shared the export trade between them as follows:

Export from Tamsui .. .. 7,695 tons.
Export from Keluug .. .. 10,417 tons.

The above went chiefly to China ports.

CHAPTER XXVIII.

FORMOSAN PETROLEUM, NATURAL GAS, SULPHUR, AND SALT.

Petroleum.—Natural Gas—Districts in which these are found—Historical references—Burning springs—Gas at Koukan self-igniting—Oil and gas springs worshipped by savages—Hakka method of collecting Oil—First commercial deal in Oil—Foreign interest in Oil fields officially discouraged—Mandarins engage American experts—Oil fields surveyed—Foreign machinery introduced—Drilling described—Production of Oil—Disagreement with experts—Work under difficulties—Experts depart from Formosa—Oil wells abandoned—Oil fields remain undeveloped—Oil springs in savage district.

Sulphur.—Location of Formosa deposits—Chief solfataras—Hokuto district—Activity of springs—Hot streams—Effect on plant life—Numerous geysers—Sulphur vents—Hanreisho pit—Journey from Hokuto—Description of deposits—A Sulphur mine—Alum—Beautiful mineralogical formation—Sulphur in an extinct volcano—Sulphur geysers—Streams of fluid Sulphur—Kimpauli Sulphur pits described—Natural cauldron of semi-fluid Sulphur—Prohibitory proclamations—Imperial edict regarding suppression of Sulphur—Unique fight against nature—Obstinate Sulphur pits—Illicit manufacture—Proclamation against foreigners—Official prohibitory measures futile—A generous Sulphur manufacturer—Government policy of suppression abandoned—Sulphur a government monopoly—Sulphur bureau established—Japanese occupation—Baba's Sulphur experiments—Sulphur furnaces at Hokuto and Hanreisho—Methods of manufacture—Crude Chinese process—Japanese system of extraction—Hanreisho Sulphur plant—A picturesque location—The distilling furnaces—Detailed method of operation—Cost of stills—Production—Increased capacity proposed—Small Hokuto stoves—American Sulphur market and conditions necessary in supplying same—Export figures for eleven years.

Salt.—Its future as a Formosa industry—District favorable for manufacture—Location of present Salt farms—Present production—History of the industry—Salt industry introduced by Koxinga family—First government monopoly—Growth of the trade—Savages' method of manufacture—Special concession—Salt smuggling—

Procedure of government sale—Profits to the government—Japanese occupation— Free Salt—Process of manufacture described—The Takow Salt district—The evaporation plant—Cost of production and revenue from sale—Japanese Govern- ment monopoly—Japanese and Chinese systems compared—Local consumption— Financial results—Procedure of purchase and sale—Government encouragement to manufacturers—Formosa Salt monopoly regulations—Salt manufactory regulations.

PETROLEUM AND NATURAL GAS.

AT the present day, when the developed Petroleum fields of the world are bringing such large returns, it is interesting to note that this useful product exists in Formosa.

Indications of the presence of Petroleum and Natural Gas have been met with in several places, notably at Kwashozan some 10 miles south of Taipeh, near Ankō north west of Shinten (Sintian), in the vicinity of Bioritsu (Maoli), at Suiriko 5 miles east of Chip Chip, near Dakusuikei (Chiok-tsui river), near Onsuikei and Hokushokei to the south-east of Kagi, and in Tainan Prefecture at Konaisho 6 miles east of Shohanen, and at Rokkiri (Lakuli) 9 miles north of Banshoryo (Hanchuliao). There are also places reported within the savage district, where oil is seen as a heavy scum on the water of certain springs.

There is no mention of mineral oil in the early commercial history of Formosa. If the then authorities were aware of its presence, they evidently thought it not of sufficient value to demand recording. Chinese historians speak of "burning mountains" as phenomena witnessed in South Formosa; but it is now believed that the flames which they doubtless saw were not volcanic, but were natural gases issuing from springs or crevices along the hill sides, spontaneously ignited, and which had perhaps set fire to the adjacent forest.

Swinhoe writes in his *Notes on Formosa:* "Twenty miles south of Kagi city, there exists a fire hill whence water and fire burst out together. The fire emits no smoke except when wood or other combustibles are thrown upon it. In November, 1861, those on board ships lying off the port had a clear view of the central mountain chain, one peak of which was emitting smoke in large volumes. This is doubtless the volcano to which Chinese writers refer, and which is also marked upon the Chinese Govern- ment map." Near the village of Koukan, east of Koro (Aulang), in a district where several oil springs exist, crevices in the shale emit gas, sometimes accompanied with oil or water. The discharge at times ceases, but occurs again after a few months. This gas at Koukan frequently ignites of itself in the summer, and has been known to burn several years. The vicinity of such jets is often marked by the absence of vegetation for a distance of some 12 or 15 feet around the spring.

At Rokkiri (Lakuli) exists an oil spring which, when ignited, burns with a roar. The savages attribute to it supernatural qualities, and worship it as a god.

To John Dodd belongs the credit of having first called attention to the Formosan Petroleum deposits. In 1866, Dodd leased land on the savage border some 20 miles south-east of Koro (Aulang). In this land he had discovered oil, and purposed sinking wells and extracting Petroleum. The Hakkas were then utilizing the oil, collecting it in large wooden tubs six feet in diameter, as it flowed from crevices at the foot of a hill. The oil was used in its crude state for illuminating purposes and for medicine, it being considered a valuable remedy for wounds of various kinds. A Cantonese shroff in the employ of a foreigner had also collected a quantity of the oil and forwarded it to Koro for shipment.

In dealing with the matter, the mandarins took a course of action almost identical with their conduct in connection with coal mining : first con-demning, and later engaging in, the trade themselves. On learning the intentions of the foreigner, the officials became suddenly most interested in the merchant's safety, and sought to warn him in an official communication that the oil hills are visited from time to time by fierce and savage aborigines who have repeatedly come forth from their own wild country and done mischief to the Chinese people. " On this account, the place is seldom visited by traders. Moreover, the neighboring Chinese people are fierce and violent, and when they see profit, they forget what is right ; therefore I enjoin the foreign merchant to come away, for fear the neighboring people will attack him." This was but another way of expressing the intention of the mandarins to prevent the merchant from interesting himself to any degree in the oil fields, and the foreigner was therefore obliged to abandon his plans ; while the unfortunate Chinese head-man who had leased the ground to him was seized by the authorities and beheaded. For ten years following no steps were taken to obtain the oil.

In 1877, the high provincial authorities in Fokien, having thrown superstition and conservatism aside in establishing the Kelung coal mines, were able to muster sufficient courage to engage foreign experts to work the Formosan oil deposits. Accordingly, in 1878, two American engineers arrived, with complete oil-well machinery. On the arrival of the machinery in the East, the mandarins undertook to convey it to Formosa on board one of the their men-of-war. The craft was too large to get close to Koro (Aulang) harbor, and there were no cargo boats sufficiently large to handle the cargo. Eventually, however, after delay and with much difficulty, the machinery was placed on shore.

Although the experts were of opinion that the oil-bed extended from Koro to the savage border, they selected, as the most favorable site for ex-perimental operations, a spot on the slope of one of the foot hills inland. After having erected the derrick, and removed the earth down to the rock, drilling was commenced with a 7½ inch drill. A flow of salt water caused slight trouble, and at a depth of 100 feet, more water was encountered: but these difficulties were surmountable. Water with Oil was struck at a depth of 380 feet; but on proceeding deeper, the falling in of the earth interfered greatly with the work, and at last, after a month of hard labor at a depth of 394 feet, drilling was discontinued, the well was tubed, and pumping apparatus erected. Some 15 piculs (1995 lbs.) of Oil could now be obtained per day, but this not being considered satisfactory, the tubing was withdrawn and drilling commenced in a new place. Meanwhile, the two Americans had become very much dissatisfied with their treatment. No accommodation had been provided for them by the authorities, and they were obliged to live in the same quarters as the soldiers. Furthermore, the experts were not well supported in their work by the local authorities. Great difficulty had been encountered in obtaining the necessary lumber to carry on the work, no road existed, and absolutely no provision had been made for disposing of the Oil obtained. The two foreigners had only been engaged for a short term, and on the expiration of their contract, they refused all overtures to renew the same, and in November 1878, left the island. The total production so far had been 400 piculs. Of this, 100 piculs had been disposed of. With the departure of the foreign experts all work ceased, and a few days later the Chinese official in charge withdrew with the various native employés; the machinery was left uncared for, and no attempt has since been made to work the Formosa Oil fields.

The coal-oil claims are now held by the Japanese, and it is to be regretted that five years have been permitted to pass without witnessing any attempt by actual boring to ascertain the richness and value of the deposits. It is now announced, however, that the Asano Company, which holds the most promising fields, is making preparations to commence boring at once, and definite information will thus soon be forthcoming. If the deposits are found valuable, numerous wells will be sunk, and the production of Formosa Oil engaged in on a large scale. As with coal, the savage districts when opened may reveal richer Oil fields than the lowlands. There is an Oil spring at Shuhoisha, in the savage district south east of Taiko (Twao), and in other places across the boundary Oil is known to exist.

SULPHUR.

Although there are other districts in Formosa in which some Sulphur is found, Taipeh prefecture contains the principal deposits. Owing to the great abundance of this article in North Formosa, it has for years been pointed out by writers on the island as a resource which in time would prove of considerable value.

The chief solfataras lie within a radius of some 15 miles in the large promontory forming the extreme north of the island. This district is covered by the Daiton range of mountains, the highest peak of which reaches an altitude of over 4,000 feet. There is abundant evidence of volcanic action throughout, extinct craters are found in several of the hills, and in eight different pits on the range, various geysers, Sulphur springs, and other signs of volcanic life are in more or less violent action.[1]

Some seven miles to the east and south of Hobe and nine miles to the north of Taipeh, at an elevation of about 450 feet, are the Sulphur springs of Hokuto (Pok-tau). Owing to the hot springs, the salubrious atmosphere, and the novelty of the scenery, the place has sprung into prominence as a health resort. The Japanese have erected there numerous hospitals, and the picturesque slopes in the vicinity are dotted with cottages and bath-houses, while a very good Japanese hotel has been erected.

These Sulphur pits being but three miles from the right bank of the Kelung branch of the Tamsui river, whence a small creek leads much closer, the transportation of Sulphur by water is an easy task, and accordingly this district has been more in favor than some other superior producing ones more difficult of access.

The Sulphur pits are here found in a gulch which cuts through the foot hills. The Sulphur is obtained from the earth and rock which have been impregnated by the Sulphur fumes arising from the volcanic fires below.

On approaching the district along the well built road constructed by the Japanese, the site of the springs can be easily distinguished as a greyish bleached out patch in the foot hills, its ashy color accentuated by the rich green of the surrounding slopes and the lighter green of the mountain range in the back ground. The springs vary at different times in activity; but, if exceedingly lively, the vapor arising from the pits may be seen for a distance of several miles, and with a favoring wind the sulphurous odor is sometimes noticeable in travelling along the Tamsui river, some six miles distant.

On reaching the foot hills, the pathway mounts a gradual slope, beside a gulch, at the bottom of which tumbles along a mountain stream, in appearance quite innocent of unusual qualities; yet on actual examination the water is found to be hot and highly acidulated. As the Sulphur pits are neared, the steam arising from the stream gives evidence of a high temperature, and if the actual springs which feed it are reached, the water is found in a great state of agitation, as though the ordinary movement of boiling water was insufficient to release the heat generated by the vast furnace below. The Sulphur pit is a large circular cavity in the hills, one side being cut away as if by the action of water and at present furnishing a means of exit to the numerous boiling springs. There is a complete absence of plant life, which is apparently unable to survive the poisonous vapor. Geysers are found every few yards, some showing pools of boiling water, or semi-fluid Sulphur and boiling mud, while others are obscured from sight by large jets of steam escaping as though under great pressure and with a deafening hiss and roar, which, echoing through the gulch, may from certain directions sometimes be heard a mile away. The odor from the

---

1. The eight Sulphur producing districts in North Formosa are as follows: On the south side of the Daiton mts: Hokuto, Kwokeinai, Shichiseiton, and on the north side of the same range Daiyukwozan, Daikwoshizan, and Chikuko.

Sulphur Hill near Hokuto.   Sulphur Springs Hotel.

Hot Stream, and Government Bath House at Hokuto.

Roots of a single Banyan Tree.   A Chinese Country Hut.

sulphurous fumes is very strong, although not specially objectionable, and the heat arising from below is quite noticeable. The ground all about is perforated, and puffs of vapor escape from innumerable small vents, in and around which minute Sulphur crystals are visible. So numerous are the openings that the earth has become permeated with Sulphur; and by submitting a quantity of this soil to a certain degree of heat, the Sulphur, which melts and separates from the other matter, can be easily obtained. A second pit, much more extensive, though perhaps not so active, is to be found at Hanreisho (Poa na-tung) situated about one mile beyond the Hokuto (Pak-tan) Sulphur pit, and, from the hotel an interesting hour's tramp over the ridge and along the hillsides. Here the Sulphur deposits are very extensive, two slopes, rising from either bank of a rushing tumbling mountain stream, extending for perhaps half a mile in length, present that greyish burned out color, which gives evidence of volcanic origin, and the steaming jets, which are inactive at one end of the pit, show that the process of permeating the adjacent soil with Sulphur still continues. These deposits are the most valuable in the island, not only in extent but also in richness. A portion of the pit undoubtedly formed at one time a crater of a volcano, and here, amidst partially decomposed lava permeated with Sulphur, is found a perfect net-work of small seams of pure Sulphur varying in thickness from half an inch to 12 or more inches. This formation was beautifully exhibited in a cave-like crevice. The wall rock itself was nearly white, and this was crossed and traversed by numerous bright yellow streaks of pure crystallized Sulphur; while, in other parts, a heavy glistening coat of snow-white frost, formed of tiny crystals of pure alum, lies beside rich brown streaks of a semi-fluid paste of alum and Sulphur softened by acid. It was an example of mineralogical formation as brilliant and beautiful as one could wish to see. Here Sulphur extracting works, the most extensive in the island, are erected, as will be described later.

Large and important as are the above solfataras, they are less active than a pit in an extinct crater of one of the high hills some three hours' climb from the hotel up the mountains to the north east. In 1895, I visited this place with a friend. On approaching the hill we observed the summit partially obscured by clouds of vapor. Occasionally, a slight breeze would, for the moment, clear away the steam, revealing a large cavity, with floor and sides of an unbroken grey. This is undoubtedly an extinct crater with walls extending nearly round the entire circle, and broken only on the side approached. In the pit was found a mass of ragged, disjointed, burned rock, with frequent fire holes, through which rushed out currents of vapor under apparently intense pressure, and with a terrific roar. These at times appeared to be almost colorless, and again white with dense steam. The Sulphur vapor does not seem to be so overpowering as might be supposed, and it is possible to stand quite close to the vents. Moreover, the rock, although ash like and in places lying at irregular angles as though recently disturbed, seems fairly firm. In several crevices, were seen little trickling streams of molten Sulphur, showing varying shades of blue, red, and brown; while the sides of the openings were covered with bright yellow crystals. At one opening which we had enlarged with our sticks we could see through the darkness of the hole, at a distance which we could not judge, a bluish red stream which seemed to be a mass of tiny flames. But the supposed rivulet of fire may have been nothing more than a stream of molten Sulphur, which became apparent in the interior when our bodies overshadowed the opening, and a phosphorescent light combined with the moving mass of Sulphur may have presented the appearance of combustion. Though there are large quantities of Sulphur to be obtained here, no attempt has been made of late to work the deposits, and doubtless the expense of carriage would be too great to permit of the industry being carried on at a profit.

The most interesting, most extensive, and, were it not for the difficulties of transportation, perhaps the most valuable, Sulphur deposits in Formosa are in the vicinity of Kinpori (Kimpauli) near the sea coast, across country to the north-east of Taipeh. The writer has not visited them, but they are realistically described by Mr. William Hancock of the Chinese Customs Service as follows :—

"The place (Sulphur pit) is a mountain glen at some 1,400 feet above the sea, the bottom covered with heaps of stones, *débris*, and decomposed rocks of a greyish tint, with patches resembling silicified sinter, and in many places white from the bleaching action of the sulphurous acid. At various points are cracks and vents, from which jets of steam are expelled with considerable force, the edges of the cracks exhibiting a yellow surface of sulphur, whilst lower down, the place has the appearance as though it had been full of water—in fact, a lake. The floor is a level tract of boiling mud, small jets being thrown up at distances apart, and the whole place being in a perpetual state of agitation. In one corner, higher up, the steam escapes as from a high pressure boiler. The rocks surrounding the glen are blanched, and vegetation is destroyed. A river of hot water, overhung by clouds of steam, flows down through a gorge extending to the foot of the mountain ; this gorge was formed during the earthquake of 1867, when the mountain was split open on the west side. I endeavored to reach the edge of this mud lake, to ascertain the temperature, but found the surface of the ground so precarious and the heat so oppressive that I was compelled to desist.

"Continuing my journey on up into the mountains, I suddenly came upon a set of geysers at 1,800 feet above the sea, which entirely eclipsed those I had just examined. The place bore some resemblance to a lime quarry with precipitous sides, from which vast volumes of steam were being expelled into the air with a roar so great that I heard it reverberating in the mountains at several miles off, and such was the volume of steam that at the same distance I mistook it for a cloud arising on the side of the mountain. Into this place, then, I descended, and found a wonderfully interesting spectacle. The main vent from which the noise proceeded stands in a narrow chasm by itself, a branch of the ravine, and owing to the aperture being surrounded by other minor vents, I was unable to approach it. At another part of the ravine, however, there is a cavernous hole in the rock, in form resembling the entrance to a tunnel, and large enough to walk in at. From the mouth of this place, clouds of white smoke, like steam, continued to pour forth in slow rolling volumes, occasionally almost hiding the entrance. Having observed this for some time at a distance, I watched a favorable opportunity when a slight shift of the wind blew towards the mouth, and so carried the clouds of sulphurous steam over the top, and then I went up to the entrance and looked in. The bottom was a cauldron of semi-fluid sulphur, somewhat of the color and consistency of treacle, whilst the arched roof presented a scene of great beauty, being a mass of glistening yellow crystals of sublimated sulphur. From the interior proceeded deep subterranean rumbling sounds; but I was unable to remain more than a few seconds, the heat and smell were so overpowering. From the color and consistency of the contents, I was able to judge approximately of the temperature. Sulphur melts at 232 degrees Fahrenheit, and is then of an amber tint and as fluid as water, but if still further heated, it changes in form, assuming, between 430 degrees and 48J degrees, the color and consistency of that which I had just seen. All these geysers vary in activity and intensity, and I was told that during earthquakes they exhibited great violence, the boiling water being thrown as high as 50 feet."

The history of the Sulphur industry, so far as the Chinese mandarins were concerned, is but a repetition of the history of coal and oil, with the addition that, in the case of Sulphur, the authorities actually endeavored to destroy the deposits, wishing to rid the island of the stuff entirely.

Apparently, little attention was given to the island's Sulphur deposits during the days of the Dutch and Koxinga ; for the books of that period make no mention of the article. Soon after the establishment of the Chinese government, however, Sulphur became a source of anxiety, lest the colonists, who were wont to break out in rebellion on the least provocation, might obtain material from the Sulphur pits for the manufacture of gunpowder. At least, that was the story put forth by the officials; and, accordingly, the manufacture of Sulphur was strictly forbidden. Proclamations were issued by dozens, the peasants living in the vicinity of the Sulphur pits looked on these impressive documents with all due reverence, *kowtowed* to the official inspector on his periodical visits, but kept on making Sulphur. Klaproth, on his visit to the island in the early years of the present century, discovered that at that time considerable quantities were being shipped to China.

During the great rebellion of 1830 to 1833, when the capital of the island was captured and the Chinese officials driven out, considerable quantities of Sulphur from the northern pits were gathered by the insurgents presumably for other purposes than medical use. This fact seems to have been discovered by the authorities towards the end of 1833. After the disturbed people had been subjugated and Imperial control again established, the governor-general of Fokien memorialized the Emperor on the subject of the Formosa Sulphur deposits. This elicited an Imperial edict, directing the said governor-general to devise measures for effectually suppressing the production of Sulphur. This resulted in orders as unique as they were impracticable. The chief dignitary had doubtless learned that Sulphur was inflammable. Therefore he thought it ought not to be difficult to destroy all the deposits by fire. Officials were consequently instructed to visit the pits four times a year in the middle of each season to set fire to the Sulphur which oozed from the mouths of the geysers, and if there were any violent refractory vents noisily spitting forth clouds of steam and ill-smelling flames, simply to fill them up with earth.

On inspection, it was reported that there were 88 unruly vents of all kinds to be dealt with. The Chinese officials were persevering and not without hope, and for several years they continued making their quarterly calls, burning and filling in the vents, while in the intervals the peasants were as active as ever in the manufacture of Sulphur; for, as the local authorities were at last obliged with grief to declare, although the 88 vents were regularly destroyed, there were 88 new ones inviting attention at the time of their next visit; that "they never could tell, when they had burned out one vent, whether another would not break out in its place."

At last, the task was given up as impossible, and the officials directed their energies towards preventing the clandestine manufacture and the shipping of the production to China. In this they had varying success, dependent upon the number of soldiers and others they could detail to guard the pits.

In 1850, the Formosan authorities were either apprehensive of foreigners assisting the native manufacturers in smuggling the Sulphur, or they wished to appear so, for obvious reasons; for, during this year, an official proclamation reading as follows, was issued: "In the Tamsui sub-prefecture Sulphur exists. The question arises whether or not it is stealthily collected by disloyal Chinese and taken to foreign countries for sale. As regards the request made last year by the foreigners proposing to go to Kelung to get coal, it is not impossible that this would be made a deceptive pretext, and it ought to be sedulously forbidden and guarded against. Let the Commandant and Taotai be directed to investigate the matter and report for action. Also let a deputed officer be secretly sent to investigate as to whether or not the prohibition has been enforced, so that crime may be nipped in the bud. This is very important! Respect this."

To control the deposits at Hokuto (Pak-tau) was not a huge undertaking, but at the pits further inland, and in the vicinity of Kinpori (Kimpauli) the task was more difficult, and it is safe ·to say that at no time did the production entirely cease. ·If it was found expedient to abandon the work for a time in one pit, it was continued in another, and so on. Thus, in 1867, at one of the Kinpori pits, some thirty or ·forty furnaces were in operation, about one hundred workmen being employed. The product was all carried to the sea coast and thence smuggled in junks to be eventually disposed of in Hong-kong and China.

This same year, a wealthy Chinese endeavored to induce the govern-ment to farm out the manufacture of Sulphur, or to grant him permission to work the pits on behalf of the government, the latter paying for the product at a fixed rate. In this way the government would not only have a new source of income, but they would be able to exert a more effective control over the industry. The mandarins, however, refused the permission; and in absence of it, the merchant, with a spirit quite characteristic of the Formosan Chinese, worked the deposits without it. The enterprising celestial doubt-less thought that, having given the officials a chance to share in the profits, which they had not availed themselves of, he was quite justified in ignoring them altogether.

The Chinese officials at length began to appreciate the futility of their weak prohibitory measures, and in 1877, it was decided that they should legalize the industry and declare Sulphur a government monopoly. This decision was put into effect, and under the new arrangement three pits were opened; the work at Hokuto (Pak-tau) and Shamaoshan being placed in the hands of headmen who were to manufacture the Sulphur and pay all expenses connected with the same; and the product was to be turned over to the government, which agreed to take the total output at the rate of $1.00 a picul (133 lbs.). The pit at Yukeng was worked directly by the govern-ment. During 1877, 8,000 to 9,000 piculs were produced in the two first mentioned pits; but the quality was very low. The local officials desired to control the export and sale in foreign ports as well, but found that the demand for low grade Sulphur for legitimate uses was very slight; and, after accumulating a stock of about 10,000 piculs in the government godowns, the taotai gave orders to discontinue the manufacture in the two pits. Soldiers were then stationed at these two points to prevent illicit manufacture The output at the government pit at Yukeng was limited to the amount desired for local use, some 500 to 600 piculs a year.

No further attempt was made by the government to engage in the industry on any considerable scale until 1887, when the demand for Sulphur having increased, the officials established a Sulphur bureau, where the output of the Formosa pits was offered for sale to legitimate buyers. No independent local trade in the article was permitted, and with every purchase an official certificate was furnished establishing the buyer's right to the Sulphur. The price paid by the government was increased to $1.40 a picul, and the quality of the production was improved. The export under this new system commenced with 3,360 piculs in 1887, and had doubled in 1891. A powder mill had been constructed at Taipeh consuming a certain quantity of Sulphur; and this, combined with the sale for export, gave an estimated gross income to the officials amounting to some $30,000 a year.

In 1894, the year prior to the occupation of the island by the Japanese, the export of Sulphur amounted to 5,950 piculs (791,850 lbs.). The following year (1895), military operations put an end to the industry for the time. The deposits were left undisturbed till 1896, when they were worked in a small way; the production amounting to less than a thousand piculs for export.

In 1897, more interest was shown in the industry, and during this year a Japanese merchant, Baba by name, invested considerable money and started the manufacture of Sulphur on a comparatively large scale. The Sulphur produced was shipped to Hongkong, but the high freight rates then existing induced Baba to charter a steamer and place it on the Hongkong run in opposition to the Douglas Steamship Co., trusting to obtain sufficient outside support to make the venture profitable, and at the same time to afford him cheap transportation for his Sulphur. The shipping public, however, did not favor him with their cargo; and after having sunk all his earnings from Sulphur in the steamship line, Baba eventually gave up his Formosa interests and retired from the island.

During the following year, the Hokuto pit remained idle; but during 1899, new furnaces were erected at both the Hokuto and the adjoining Hanreisho pits.

There are three methods of manufacture, although an improved Japanese apparatus has practically driven the primitive Chinese stoves out of existence, and the natives, if they engage in the industry, use either the complete Japanese stove or a crude imitation of it.

The Chinese process was extremely simple, but very wasteful. The Sulphur stove consisted of a number of shallow iron pans, about two to three feet in diameter and sometimes lined with clay. It was placed over a narrow fireplace built of mud bricks. These rough furnaces were partially enclosed by rudely built sheds roofed with dry grass gathered from the neighboring slopes. The apparatus was not calculated to impress one as a wonder of mechanical ingenuity; in fact, the stranger at first sight of the operation might easily be deceived into believing that the soup for some adjacent settlement was in progress of preparation. To obtain the Sulphur, the rock or earth impregnated with the mineral was thrown into the pans, a strong fire built, and the stuff slowly melted down; the lighter impurities coming to the surface forming a frothy slag, while the heavy foreign properties sank to the bottom.   During the operation the slag was frequently skimmed off, and eventually when the mass appeared thoroughly fused, the fluid Sulphur was poured out into wooden buckets with movable staves, which were released when the Sulphur had cooled and solidified, producing a hard block in the form of a truncated cone weighing some 60 pounds. The residue was now thrown out, the pan filled with fresh ore, and work continued as before.   The preparation was then considered complete, and the blocks were carried away to market.

The crude method above described has now been replaced by the more economical Japanese system of extraction.   The extreme wastefulness of the Chinese stove may be understood when it is noted that at the present time large Japanese stills at Hanreisho are using largely the residue which had been thrown away in previous years by Chinese workers; and from this slag, which the Chinese looked upon as exhausted refuse, some 50 % of Sulphur is being obtained.   The Chinese used only the richest mineral, from which they obtained some 60 or 70 % of low grade Sulphur.

At Hokuto there are usually in operation some five or six small stills of three or four retorts each; but the industry is carried on most extensively, and the most complete apparatus is in use, at Hanreisho, a mile beyond.   In travelling to the works along the pathway crossing the ridge which divides the Hokuto and Hanreisho pits, four large iron smoke-stacks pouring forth a large volume of heavy smoke are noticeable for a considerable distance. The plant is located at a most picturesque spot in a valley.   On one side is a noisy cascade dashing down in a series of foam-crested falls, while to the back is a graceful waterfall, fed by a stream which runs along the top of the hill, some fifty to sixty feet above the works.

Whereas the Chinese obtained the Sulphur by merely melting the ore in an open pan, the Japanese use a distilling apparatus.   At Hanreisho there are eight furnaces, each containing three stills.   Each furnace consists of a brick fire-place, provided with flues, and so arranged as to heat evenly a space some 15 feet long, 3 feet wide, and 2½ feet high.   The top of the fire-place is provided with shields to prevent the flames from coming in direct contact with the cast-iron retorts in which the Sulphur is placed. Each retort consists of two longitudinal sections, forming, when connected, an iron cylinder five feet long and two feet in diameter.   One end is flush with the side of the furnace, and is provided with a circular iron-door.   The Sulphur is thrown in at this opening.   The other end of the cylinder, in its upper half, contains a circular hole, which has attached to it a cone-shaped pipe some three feet long, and with a diameter of 8 inches, decreasing to 4 inches at its opposite end.   This end projects through a few inches into the side, near the top, of a circular cast-iron receiver 2½ feet in height and 2 feet in diameter, thus connecting the latter with the retort. There are three of these stills to each furnace, the retorts lying crosswise of the fire-place, and the receiver with its flat top and bottom resting upright on a stone foundation. From one side of the receiver near the bottom is a spigot, through which flows the Sulphur in liquid form. The receiver is exposed, but all other parts of the still, with the exception of one end of the retort, are covered over with brickwork. The total structure is about 15 feet long, 5 feet high, and 11 feet wide. The cost of one set of stills complete, including a rough straw shed, which partially encloses them, is 900 yen.

The apparatus is built in the centre of the pit, so the supplies of rock and earth impregnated with Sulphur are literally at hand. A strong coal fire having been started, each retort is two-thirds filled with ore, the circular door is closed and sealed with clay or ashes. The Sulphur in the mass of rock and earth commences to melt almost instantly; and in an hour or so, converted into gas, it is passing through the connecting tube into the comparatively cool receiver, where the gas condenses, and the Sulphur, now in liquid form, drips through the spigot into a cast iron receptacle, which, when the Sulphur has cooled and hardened, can be separated into two parts, thus releasing a block of Sulphur about half a picul in weight, which is now ready for the market. In seven hours' time the Sulphur has all been separated; and, when the retort is opened, there only remain a few bucketsful of fine dustlike ashes, in place of the two piculs of hard rock and earth at first inserted. The retorts are filled three times during the 24 hours, and with the material at present used, which contains about 50 % of Sulphur, each separate still yields about 3 piculs of practically pure Sulphur a day, and each furnace consumes about 5 piculs of coal a day. For export, the Sulphur blocks are enclosed in straw bags; and the present (1901) price is upwards of 2.00 yen a picul (133 lbs.) on board steamer at Tamsui. The freight to Hongkong is about 10 sen a picul.

In addition to the stills above described, the plant has been added to by the construction of several furnaces, which, though on the same principle as the former ones, are provided with a circular retort with a head piece and tube, somewhat similar in form to the ordinary still used at home for chemical purposes. Better results are being obtained from this apparatus, it requiring less fuel, and distilling more rapidly. The life of the new stove, however, is not as long by two months as that of the old style, which with ordinary care lasts about six months.

The Japanese company at present have eight furnaces with twenty-four stills in operation, giving a total daily production, when working at full capacity, of over four tons. The labor demanded is slight; the stills, exclusive of carrying coolies and excavators, requiring the services of only thirty men, divided into night and day gangs. These men receive 55 sen a day, and the excavators, who are paid according to the work accomplished, earn from 60 to 70 sen a day. With the exception of the overseers, all workmen are Chinese.

The total production is as yet insignificant, but if there is sufficient demand for the Sulphur, it is intended to put in additional stills to permit of an output of eight tons a day, there being sufficient raw material in sight to run such a plant for years. Should the new stills be unable to supply the demand, extensive works would be erected at Kimpauli, where there exist vast deposits of comparatively rich ore.

The small stoves at Hokuto it is unnecessary to describe; they are smaller than the Hanreisho stoves, which, however, they resemble in form, except that the retort is a circular pan with an opening in the top, through which ore is dumped.

In closing this paper, it is perhaps well to note that, though the production is trifling as compared with some of the Sulphur pits in Sicily, there is still an abundance of Sulphur ore in Formosa, and it is to be hoped that the future will see the industry engaged in on a large scale. There is a fairly good market for Sulphur in the western United States, but under present conditions so trifling is the Formosa production that it would scarcely be worth while for merchants to attempt a shipment. With the present low prices, to ensure a profit it is essential to eliminate every cent of expenditure not absolutely necessary. Consequently, shipments are generally made in large quantities, and not infrequently by sailing vessels. It would require, however, at the present rate of production, the output for several months to obtain sufficient Sulphur to load one sailing vessel. It is also necessary, in supplying the American demand, to keep in view the fact that refined Sulphur, that is Sulphur of 100% fineness, is subject to a duty of $8.00 (gold) per ton. All Sulphur under 100% of fineness is permitted entry free ; but consumers do not wish for Sulphur under 94%, as it is considered of too poor a quality. Hence, the Sulphur, to be attractive to American purchasers, must run between 95% and 98% fineness. The maximum is placed at 98% in order to give purchasers a safe margin, that they may avoid the likelihood of dispute, as to quality, with the government examiners.

NOTE.

EXPORT OF SULPHUR FROM FORMOSA.

(Shipped from Tamsui.)

Year.	Export in pounds.	Value in Japanese yen.
1887	446,880	—
1888	573,230	—
1891	928,872	—
1892	375,060	—
1893	642,257	18,910
1894	791,350	11,121
1895	—	—
1896	110,656	1,798
1897	98,952	1,791
1898	1,889,132	41,117
1899	1,400,000 (estimated)	—

SALT.

That most necessary of commodities, Salt, is manufactured in the island in considerable quantities. It is, also, one of the industries believed by Japanese experts to have a promising future, and is worthy of investigation.

Along the whole western coast from Hsinchiku (Teckcham) in the north to within a few miles of Takow in the south, a distance of 140 miles, runs a strip of low lands of varying width, as shown in the industrial map, admirably suited for the production of Salt by the system of sea-water evaporation; and in the future, should the introduction of improved methods of manufacture make the industry profitable, there is every probability of the island becoming not only independent of foreign supplies, but being able to supply an outside demand as well.

Commencing with the north, the first Salt manufacturing district is a strip of land on the coast, a few miles to the west of Hsinchiku (Teckcham). In this district there are seven large Salt farms, employing 325 workmen, and with a maximum production of 10,374,000 lbs. a year. Further south along the coast at Guho (Gu-pa) a few miles to the north of Rokkō (Lo kiang), and near Seiko (Sei kang) some 18 miles south of Rokko, are Salt farms, worked, however, in a desultory manner, employing at certain seasons of the year 100 workmen and producing about 305,900 lbs. The next Salt district to the south is within Tainan prefecture, as are the other and chief producing fields in the island, which lie further south.

These farms, with their maximum output, are as follows:—Hoteishi (Pa-te-chui) on the west coast, employs some 300 persons and produces about 18,000,000 lbs. Hokumonsho (Pak-bin-su) 5 miles south of Hoteishi, employs some 600 persons and produces about 32,000,000 lbs. Seishikiaku (Chih-a-ka) adjoins Hokumonsho on the south, employs some 500 persons, and produces about 33,000,000 lbs. Genteisho (Am tai ching), a few miles to the south of Anping, employs some 200 persons and produces about 25,200,000 lbs. A second village near Takow, also called Genteisho, employs some 300 persons and produces about 10,800,000 lbs.

The production of the various farms given above is based on the annual capacity of each; but, as work is often suspended when agriculture demands much attention, such as at harvest time, etc., the actual output would be more correctly represented by a third less than the figures given. Furthermore, the production is so much dependent upon demand, that it is quite impossible to obtain figures more exact than the above. The Government Salt-office estimates that some 90,000,000 lbs. will be produced and placed at their disposal during the present year (1900), and that in 1901 there will be an output of 160,000,000 lbs.

No known attempt to supply the island's Salt requirements by local manufacture was made during the Dutch regime, the colonists satisfying their wants by importing the commodity from China and Batavia. The Koxinga family, most active in making the island self-supporting, gave this important subject attention, and the young ruler, Cheng ching, (1662-

1682), made a special study of the method of producing Salt by the evaporation of sea-water, and induced his subjects to engage in this industry. No attempt was made to exact government revenue from the sale of the Formosa Salt until the Chinese occupied the island.

During the first years of the Imperial regime, although Salt was taxed, its sale was left in the hands of private merchants. In 1727, however, during the 5th year of the reign of Yung Ching, all private transactions were forbidden, and a government monopoly was established under the superintendence of the prefect of Taiwan. As the island increased in population, the demand for Salt became likewise greater, and in 1759 the government sales exceeded 100,000 piculs (13,300,000 lbs.); while in 1824, they reached 147,000 piculs (19,550,000 lbs.), yielding the government a revenue the equivalent of 72,760 yen, besides 22,000 yen exacted from the trade as a likin tax. A few years later, the Salt trade was for a second time placed in the hands of private merchants; but in 1855, it was again taken over by the government, under the charge of the prefect as before, though for a few years the trade was temporarily under the superintendence of the intendant of the circuit. The importance of the monopoly kept pace with the rapid increase in population, and in the middle of the present (nineteenth) century was controlled with great rigor. The prefect had supreme command over the industry, and through his agents stationed at Salt offices established in every town of importance, he reaped a very substantial revenue. A large corps of couriers was kept constantly engaged in keeping up communication between the capital and the various Salt offices. Still, in spite of the exacting measures, much contraband stuff from China was smuggled into the island, especially at Kelung, where in the early days cargoes of Salt were openly offered in exchange for coal, camphor, or rice. The importation of the foreign manufactured product was forbidden as well, and on several occasions foreign ships were forced to throw their cargoes of Salt overboard before being granted entry to the ports.

Comprehensive as the government control was planned to be, there were some exceptions to the regulations. Some of the savages in the western part of the island are reported to have utilized a certain Salt spring as a source of supplies, the article being obtained by boiling the water in bamboo tubes which had been plastered with mud, while the plain savages in other districts, notably Gilan, manufactured small quantities from sea water, which they used to carry up from the shore to their huts with great labor, and evaporate it there over their fires. On these savages acknowledging allegiance to China, they were permitted, as the result of a memorial to the throne, to continue their manufacture for the time. Furthermore, there was much Salt made in the island, the manufacture of which the mandarins were unable to prevent. For instance, a few miles to the South of Hsinchiku (Teckcham), unruly natives manufactured Salt to the extent of 20,000 piculs (2,660,000 lbs.) yearly.

While the interior and western districts were supplied with locally manufactured Salt, the large ports, such as Tamsui and Anping, received much of their supplies from Quemoy, China. The procedure of sale, up to the occupation of the island by the Japanese, was as follows :—The mandarins purchased in Formosa the Salt arriving from Quemoy, at a price slightly in advance of its cost, say from 28 to 33 Mexican cents a picul (133 lbs, distributed it to the various Salt stations, from which official depots all consumers were obliged to purchase, even to the coolie whose requirements did not exceed a few cash worth. The price demanded ranged from 1.15 to 2.50 yen a picul according to the quality, thus giving the government, after paying the cost of the administration of the mono poly, a very handsome profit. This same Salt cost in Quemoy only 18 to 20 cents a picul, and was often brought as ballast by junks trading with Amoy. The Formosan-made Salt was taken over by the Chinese government at about the same prices paid for the Chinese mainland product, and not infrequently Chinese gunboats were utilized by the mandarins to transport the Salt from the coast villages where it was made, to Tamsui or Anping.

On the arrival of the Japanese, the Chinese government monopoly, of course, ceased, and transactions in Salt were permitted free of taxation or restriction. This caused some consternation among the local manufacturers, who in lieu of a steady single cash customer, were now offered thousands of unstable ones, whom to reach required a system of distribution and finance with which the Salt-makers were not familiar. This, combined with the rapid rise in the price of labor and the disturbed condition of the country, resulted in the closing up of a large number of farms. Without proper care and repair many of the plants were destroyed, until at one time, the total production, as compared with former years, decreased 60 per cent. Later the Japanese government decided to re establish the old monopoly with some alterations, and on May 15th, 1899 the new Salt monopoly regulations came into force throughout the island.[1] This move was followed by the opening

---

1.   FORMOSA SALT MONOPOLY REGULATIONS.

Revised to Contain Amendments issued to Date (December 1899.)

Article I.—Salt, as the term is used in these regulations, refers to crude salt used for purposes of food.

Article II.—Salt is purchased (locally) and imported by the government, and is sold at a fixed rate.

No salt, except that sold by the government, can be sold, received, or consumed.

No salt can be imported from Japan or abroad except by the government (this clause was added by " Salt Monopoly Revision Regulations" of September 13th, 1899).

Article III.—All salt manufactured in Formosa must be sold to the government.

Article IV.—Upon a salt manufacturer presenting his product to the government, the government will take delivery, paying a certain fixed price for it. The price will be determined by the government and published in due time.

Article V. - (Cancelled by " Revision Regulations " September 13th, 1899.)

Article VI.-- Salt manufacturers must, on a date to be determined by the government, report as to the probable production of their farms for the coming year.

In case of a manufacturer passing his salt farm on to another, the fact must be reported by his successor.

Article VII.—Salt farms, warehouses, or any place where salt is kept or supposed to be kept, may be inspected by officials connected with the administration of the monopoly.

Article VIII.—(Cancelled by " Revision Regulations " September 13th, 1899.)

Article IX.—Any person who violates the provisions of Clause 2 or Clause 3 of Art. II., will be fined a sum ranging from 10 to 1000 yen, but the salt, if existing, will be taken over by the government at the price provided for in Art. IV.

Article X.—To persons violating this regulation, the code laws providing for the punishment of second offences, etc., will not be applied.

Article XI.—When representatives, members of the family, lodgers, or employes of a manufacturer,

of the majority of the local Salt farms, and under the increased prices paid by the Formosa government, the industry soon recovered its former importance.

The method of Salt manufacture in Formosa is the simple form of evaporation of sea-water, which is led over a series of basins, and there exposed to the heat of the sun. To illustrate the process, the methods in vogue in the Takow district may be given, the establishments there being representative of the usual Salt farm as found in other parts of the island. The Reinanjo (Toa lam-tyou) farms are situated on the north-east side of Takow lagoon, about one mile east of Takow village. Notwithstanding the fact that a small fresh-water stream empties itself into the lagoon, the water appears to contain as large a quantity of Salt as the sea water along the coast. The location offers great advantages over farms directly on the sea-coast, in that the works are not exposed to the strong waves of the open sea in stormy times. The ground here utilized in the manufacture is some 100 acres in extent. Each so-called Salt farm, or evaporation plant, covers about 2½ acres, and contains a shallow basin independent of the others when need be, but supplied with water gates which, when opened, connect each basin with the one above or below it. Along the shore is erected an artificial barrier against the waters of the lagoon; provided, however, with a movable section in order that the water may be admitted when required. In operation, the salt-water of the lagoon is admitted to the first basin. In twenty-four hours it is led to the basin below, while water from the lagoon is run into the first basin again. This continues each day until the seventh or eighth basin has been reached, when the sea-water, now partially concentrated, is collected in a reservoir. From this it is raised to a series of the crystallization basins, and, after remaining there some eight or ten hours, the finished Salt appears, and is removed to the store-room. In favorable weather, the complete operation from lagoon to store-house requires but ten days, and Salt is produced daily. In constructing a Salt farm, an attempt is made to have each basin slightly below the one from which the water must be received. But if this can not be done, as is frequently the case, the water is raised over the intervening embankment by the Chinese foot-power pump. The cost of production in the Takow district by this process is estimated at from 9 to 14 cents (local currency) a picul (133 lbs.), and the salt was, during the former regime, purchased by the Chinese Government at varying prices, ranging from 12 to 28 cents a picul. During the first few years of Japanese occupation, when the Salt trade was free of restriction, 18 to 30 cents a picul was obtained, though the expenses of placing the same on the various markets consumed most of this additional profit. Salt manufacturing can be carried on in the Takow district during the whole year, with the exception of the months of July and August when the weather is unfavorable; but the

---

in course of their avocations, have violated the foregoing provisions, the manufacturers can not escape from the penalties provided, though they may have no cognizance of the offense.

Article XII.—The rules and instructions necessary for the putting in force of these regulations, and the date of their enforcement will be announced by the Governor-General.

Article XIII.—To salt manufactured prior to the date of enforcement these regulations will not apply.

period from September to April yields the largest results. The cost of production in Formosa is said to be about one fourth of that in Japan.

The present Japanese Salt monopoly differs in system from the former Chinese monopoly. Whereas, during the Chinese regime, the official Salt station sold direct to the consumer, with the Japanese the government disposes of the Salt at a fixed rate to an association of native contractors known as the "Jentai Shokuyen Urisabaki Kumiai" (Formosa Salt Selling Association) who supply the consumers. This body has established 20 principal offices and 80 branches to cover the island. It was first intended that the government should care for this department of the monopoly as well, but it was found preferable, from an economical standpoint, to place the distribution in the hands of private persons.

Government Salt-offices have been established at Kelung, Tamsui, Hsinchiku (Teck-cham), Koro (Aulang), Rokko (Lokiang), Hoteishi (Pa te-chui), Hokumonsho (Pak-bin su), Tainan, and Takow, and the salt association obtain their supplies from these points.

The selling price for each district is announced, and cannot be increased by the association. The prices are dependent upon the expense of transportation, and range from 1.76 to 2.26 yen per picul (133 lbs.). Though this sum is excessive as compared with the original cost of the product to the Government, still it is not a heavy burden when we note that, even at the high figures mentioned, the value of the total amount consumed annually is estimated at only 24 yen cents per head, and though the present selling price averages slightly higher than in the Chinese days, the increase amounts to only $1\frac{7}{10}$ yen cents a head. The amount consumed annually per head amounts to 15 kin (20$\frac{1}{5}$ lbs.) The bright side of the system, if a monopoly can have anything to its credit, is that the Salt manufacturers are paid a higher price for their product than they obtained under the Chinese regime.

The Government pays 33 yen cents per picul (133 lbs.) for the Hsinchiku (Teckcham) product, and 21 cents for the South Formosa Salt. There is also a second grade article, for which 2 or 3 cents less is paid. The prices paid during the last days of the Chinese monopoly were 28 and 12$\frac{1}{2}$ cents respectively for the first grade. The Government sells the Salt to the distributing association at 85 cents per picul, which leaves a gross profit of upwards of 52 cents a picul. The total profit to the local Government appears in the budget for 1900 as 231,300 yen.

The Government purchases for the year 1900, it is estimated, will reach 800,000 piculs (106,400,000 lbs.), of which 680,000 piculs (90,440,000 lbs.) will be Formosa made and 120,000 piculs (15,960,000 lbs.) imported.

As the local production is increasing rapidly, far exceeding the amount required for local consumption, it is reported to be the government's intention to make Salt one of the important exports to the home land. The market price in Japan at present ranges from 50 to 80 yen cents a picul, and at this price the Formosa product can be laid down at a slight profit. It is thus hoped to make Japan independent of outside sources for her Salt supply, and to make the manufacture of Salt one of the leading industries of the island.

The prevention of smuggling is one of the problems of the monopoly. Undoubtedly considerable quantities of Salt are illegally landed along the west coast by junks, though the amount has not been sufficient to interfere seriously with the successful working of the monopoly. The government has a special police service to assist in the prevention of smuggling, with police boats patrolling the coast, and as the sale is controlled by an influential native organization which has representatives in practically every village in the island and employs numerous private police officers, the illicit import will probably in time, largely if not wholly, be done away with.

The procedure of purchase and sale is as follows :—

Salt manufacturers, during December of each year, must make a report showing the estimated amount of Salt they will be able to produce during the following year. The government will take over the Salt from time to time, as it is delivered at the government Salt offices, to a quantity during one year equal to the amount named, provided the quality of the same is up to the standard, and at a price which will be from time to time announced by the government. On the arrival of a vessel in which Salt forms in part or whole the cargo, the Customs office must immediately report the fact to the Salt office, which will despatch an inspector to examine the cargo, and place the same under official seal. Proper application may then be made by the owner to the Salt office, and the sale of the cargo to the government is effected. The selling contractors, when desiring to replenish their supplies, must present an application to the civil bureau for a license, naming the Salt office from which they wish to obtain their supplies, and the quantity desired ; and after receiving payment for the Salt, the civil bureau will grant the contractors an order on the Salt office, which, on presentation there, will obtain the supplies.

The most important difference between the present and the former Chinese monopoly is that, under the latter, the export of Salt from Formosa was not permitted, so that there was not much encouragement held out to the natives to go into the industry on a large scale ; whereas at present, under the Japanese, the object is to supply not only the local requirements, but also to build up an export trade, especially with Japan.

The government have adopted a liberal policy in encouraging the local manufacture of Salt. During June 1899, regulations were published announcing that such government lands throughout the island as were suitable for the production of Salt would be loaned to parties desiring to engage in the manufacture.[1] This grant takes the form of a lease

---

1.   FORMOSA SALT MANUFACTURING REGULATIONS.

Article I.—Any person desiring to open a Salt-farm must apply to the government for official permission.

Article II.—None but Japanese subjects are permitted to engage in Salt-farming.

Article III.—Government land, if it is the intention to utilize it for Salt farms, can be obtained without restriction or remuneration ; and, on the completion of the Salt farms, it will be loaned to the holder free of rent.

Article IV.—The limit of the area granted and the term of the lease of the land mentioned in Article III. will be determined by the Governor-General.

Article V.—The land intended for the opening of Salt farms will be inspected from time to time as the work progresses, and if the evaporation plant is not completed within the prescribed period, a part

free of rent or other impost. The holder must, however, commence the construction of the Salt works within six months, and if the same are not completed within a certain specified time, the lease will be cancelled, and no compensation will be paid for expenses incurred. No land or local taxes will be imposed on the Salt farms, but the holder must not cease to utilize the ground for the manufacture of Salt.

This offer on the part of the Government has not been without result. A combined Japanese and native company, known as the Nozaki Salt Manufacturing Co., opened an extensive farm near Hoteishi (Pa-te chui), which is being worked on modern principles, and is the first plant of this kind to be established in the island. At present only a hundred workmen are engaged, but it is the intention to steadily increase the capacity. A much larger concern is the Formosa Salt Manufacturing Co. of Osaka, which has been organized with a capital of a million yen. It is the intention to lay out Salt fields along the west coast, increasing the company's holdings yearly until an aggregate area of 7,500 acres has been covered, to accomplish which it is estimated a period of 13 years will be required. One fourth of the capital is to be called in at once, and the balance as required. According to a government estimate, there are some 15,000 acres of land suitable for Salt farms still remaining undeveloped.

Salt experts state that the formation of the West Coast of Formosa is such that an exceptionally favorable location for Salt manufactories is presented. Japan and, with one or two exceptions, China present no such attractive field, while the comparatively large number of hot and sunny days with which this district is blessed provide the most necessary requisite for cheap manufacture. Furthermore, the quality of the Formosa Salt, as

---

or the entire grant will be cancelled; and if the said land has been obtained in accordance with the provision of Article III., a part of the entire grant will be revoked.

When the entire lease is cancelled as above, the expenditure so far incurred will not be returned by the government.

Article VI.– If a person does not commence work within 6 months after having obtained official permission, as provided by Article I., his permit will be cancelled, unless he has been prevented from work by some natural obstruction ; and if the land has been obtained from the government the same will revert to the government.

Article VII.—When land has been returned to the government as provided by Articles V. and VI. or by voluntary action on the part of the former holder, if there are buildings or structures on the land, the owner must remove them within a period fixed by the government ; and, if he does not remove them within this period, they become the property of the government.

Article VIII.—The holder of government land as provided by Article III. can not lease further land unless he has completed the proposed work on the first land. But capitalists who are considered in a position to complete their undertakings will be exempted from this rule.

Article IX.—The Salt-farms already existing on the government land will be granted to the person responsible for the improvement or his successor.

Article X.—No land tax or local taxes will be imposed on Salt-farms.

Article XI.—Any person who establishes Salt-farms on government land without obtaining permission as provided by Article I. will be fined a sum ranging from 100 to 500 yen ; and any persons who have established farms on private land will be forced to cease their operation.

SUPPLEMENTARY CLAUSES.

Article XII.—To land which had been leased by the government prior to the enforcement of these Regulations, these Regulations will be applied, and the term of lease mentioned in Article VI will be calculated from the date of enforcement of these Regulations.

Article XIII.—The rules and instructions necessary for the placing in force of these Regulations and the date of their enforcement will be announced by the Governor-General.

shown by analysis, is very superior.[1]   The bitter taste which is so pronounced in some newly made Salts, is absent in the Formosa product, and it can go into immediate consumption, whereas some Salts, the Japan article for instance, when intended for certain uses, such as the manufacture of *Shoyu*, *Miso*, etc., must first be stored for two or three years.

It is the belief of Government experts that the Salt industry in Formosa will attain such importance that the Japan consumption can be entirely supplied from this island. At present the Japan product finds, yearly, increasing difficulty in competing with imported foreign Salt, which arrives from Germany and other countries; but under the favorable conditions existing in Formosa, Japan as an Empire may recover the ground lost in supplying her own people with this commodity.

In closing, the favorable opinion held by Japanese Salt experts in regard to Formosa as the coming source of supply for Japan is shown in the following quotation from a very complete report on the subject:—

" Some people have visions of competing China and German rock Salts proving in time detrimental to the growth of our Formosa Salt trade, but it must be obvious to any one that the advantages our product possesses, both as to quality and low cost of transportation, assure for it a prosperity in the future which no outside competitors are liable to disturb."

---

1.   ANALYSIS OF FORMOSA SALT.

	Hsinchiku.	Anping.	Takow.
Sodium Chloride	95.779	90.180	97.100
Potassium Chlorate	traces	traces	traces
Magnesium Chloride	traces	1.452	1.205
Magnesium Sulphate	0.123	0.678	0.000
Calcium Sulphate	0.116	3.681	0.076
Calcium Chloride	0.000	0.000	0.357
Insoluble matter	4.600	3.490	0.794

CHAPTER XXIX.

FORMOSAN ECONOMICAL PLANTS.

Indigo and other Dye Plants—Early history of Indigo—Difficulties of cultivation—Import trade—Local production—Species of plants used—" Tree-Indigo "—" Mountain-Indigo "—Districts under cultivation—Method of cultivation—Apparatus used in manufacture—Method of Manufacture—Yield of dye obtained—A modern factory—Quality of Indigo obtained—Extensive cultivation proposed—Future of the Industry—Turmeric—Dye yam—Gardenia.

Fibre plants—China Grass (Ramie)—Confusion in nomenclature—True " China Grass " and " Ramie " compared—District of cultivation—Cultivated by savages—Conditions for successful growth—Method of cultivation—Hand decortication—Local " Grass cloth "—Wearing among savages—Export—Principal markets—Machine decortication—Conversion into filasse—China fibre arrives in Europe—Promising future—Taika rush—Conditions of cultivation—Manufacture of mats described—Quality and value of mats—Yearly output—The cultivation, conversion into fibre, value and yield of the Fan Palm, Local Hemp, Pine Apple, Alpinia, Paper Mulberry, Banana, Screw Pine, Bowstring Hemp, Cyperus, Hibiscus, Silk Cotton Tree, Sterculia, Mulberry, Pueraria and Scirpus plants—Twenty-eight miscellaneous fibre plants.

Paper plants—Rice-paper plant :—Description of plant and cultivation—Sheet cutting—Market and export of—Bamboo :—District of manufacturing—Process of paper making described—Production—Local paper trade—Paper mulberry—Source of material—Method of manufacture—Water-proof paper—" Broussonetia Kashinoki " and " Wikstroemia " paper plants described.

Oil plants—Ground nut :—Cultivation—Method of oil extraction described—Ground nut cake – Cultivation and production of—Oil from Sesame, Soja Bean, Persimmon, Tallow Tree, Castor-oil, Rape-oil, " Elaeococca " (Aleurites), " Jatropha " and " Perilla " plants described.

Soap plants—Soap-trees—" Gleditschia " Tea cake.

Miscellaneous plants—Tobacco :—District under cultivation—Manufacture in savage district—Experimental cultivation—Present trade and prospects—Method of cultivation and trade in products of Coffee, Cocoa nut, Tapioca, Cassia Blumea, Tree-bean, Ficus and Areca plants—Twenty-four medicinal plants.

Agriculture—Taihoku Government Agricultural Station—Experiments with miscellaneous cereals, Fibre plants, Sugar cane, Tobacco, Indigo, Fruit and Stock.

Forests—Twenty-four chief timber trees—Development of forests—Government afforestation bounty.

FORMOSA is famous throughout the East for the great fertility of its soil, and it would thus seem only in accordance with nature's design that the development of plant life should bring to the island its greatest prosperity.

Tea, Camphor, Sugar, (Formosa's three most valuable products), have already been described in detail. Rice, Sweet Potatoes, and other familiar food products are not dealt with. Important as these food plants are, there is but little to be gained from the extension of their cultivation, which is sufficient at present to supply local wants. The brightest prospects are offered by the large number of tropical and semi-tropical plants which the study of economical botany has brought to the fore, and for which there is an increasing demand in the markets of Europe and America.

Formosa possesses, I believe, her share of economical plants, and there are to describe, in addition to those dealt with in earlier chapters, the twenty-three fibre plants, eleven oil-producing plants, four dye plants, five paper plants, nine miscellaneous plants ; there are also twenty-three plants which, at least in the eyes of the Chinese, are considered of medical value, and twenty-four forest trees valuable as timber. I have tried to make this list complete, and if there are plants unmentioned, they are among those of minor importance. I refer, of course, chiefly to the plants of the plains and savage border districts. Botanical research in the interior savage districts will add greatly to our knowledge of the island's flora ; and judging from the work already accomplished in this wild territory by Japanese explorers, we shall not have long to wait.

Only some forty-four of the ninety-nine economic plants described, excluding timber-trees, are at present utilized in Formosa ; and some of these in but a small way. I have included the others, however, as it is of interest to know that these plants which, in other countries are a source of more or less wealth, are now growing here, and that some, at least, are only awaiting recognition by local planters and merchants to add their share to the island's wealth. Interesting and valuable papers on the island's economic botany have been written by Mr. Hosie,[1] Mr. Hancock,[2] Dr. Mackay,[3] and Dr. Henry.[4] The first three writers give special attention to the north of the island, Dr. Henry to the south, but no attempt has been made, I believe, to deal with the subject at any length. The first and only really valuable work on the general botany of the whole island is that of Dr. Henry. His List of Formosan Plants, published by the Asiatic Society of Japan, records 1428 plants, and in addition to brief references as to the locality in which they occur, he mentions, in the case of economic plants, the uses to which they are put. His work is, at present, indispensable to students of Formosan botany, and affords a good foundation upon which others may build.

---

1. See Chinese Customs Trade Report on Tamsui (1881) by Alex. Hosie.

2. See British Consular Report on Formosa (1893) by William Hancock.

3. See "From Far Formosa (1896) by George Leslie Mackay, D.D. See British Consular Report on Formosa (1895) by B. M. N. Perkins.

4. See "A List of Plants from Formosa" by Augustine Henry M. A., F. L. S., Vol. XXIV; supplement (1896) Transactions Asiatic Society of Japan.

I personally have found it of great assistance in ascertaining the nomenclature of the plants which I wished to describe. I must above all acknowledge
the kind assistance rendered by Mr. Yasusada Tashiro, the chief botanist in
the forestry section of the Formosa government. This gentleman was
despatched to Russia as the Government Commissioner to the International
Exhibition of Horticulture held in St. Petersburg, and completed his studies
in botany under the eminent Russian botanist Maximowicz. He has visited
several European countries and many of the South Sea Islands, in connection
with his work. He is author of many Japanese books on botanical subjects;
but unfortunately, with the exception of a valuable report on shade trees,
the results of his Formosa researches remain unknown. Mr. Tashiro
showed great kindness in answering my numerous inquiries, and also gave
me much valuable information which otherwise I could not have obtained. I
am indebted also to Mr. Sojiro Yokoyama, the able chief of the Agricultural
Section of Taihoku Prefecture, who has helped me in many ways.

INDIGO.

In importance, the manufacture of Indigo should follow the industries
described in previous chapters; and if experiments now being made are
successful, this useful dye will soon occupy a much more prominent position
among the island's products.

No information is obtainable as to the date of the first cultivation of
Indigo in Formosa. It is not mentioned by the Dutch as one of the island's
products, and the Koxinga family do not appear to have introduced it. We
are assured, however, that it was prominent in the island during the first
half of the nineteenth century, for we learn that it was growing over a
considerable area and was known as one of the stable products as early as
1850. Comparatively large quantities of the dye were shipped from the
island in those early days, the export for instance in 1856 amounting to
7,000 piculs (931,000 lbs.), valued, however, at the low figure of $21,000.

Formosa Indigo was at this period famous in the neighboring districts of
China, and for some years it was customary to send manufactured grass-
cloth and other cloths to Formosa to be dyed and then returned to China.
Apparently the brilliant blues obtainable here with the freshly made Indigo
were at that time more difficult to secure when the dye was exported and
used elsewhere. The Formosa Indigo was usually purchased as it stood in
the field, the merchant extracting the dye. It was shipped direct, chiefly
from Banka, and formed a not unimportant part of the junk cargoes of coal,
hemp, etc., for Chinchu, Foochow, Wenchow, Ningpo, and Tientsin, where it
was exchanged for Nankeens, ironware, medicine, etc. In 1880 and thereabouts, it occupied in tonnage the third place among junk export cargoes, rice
and coal alone exceeding it, and it was frequently first in value. The yearly
Indigo export by junk at this time averaged about 21,000 piculs, valued at
some 150,000 yen.

Indigo was largely cultivated in the border districts, and the production
was consequently much dependent on the temper of the savages. The

mountain Indigo, which grew mostly in the hilly district, was still more under the control of the savages, and not infrequently the production was so lessened owing to the border warfare that there was not sufficient to supply domestic demands. The usual local abundance of the dye had accustomed the people to its use, and in case of a small home production, Swatow Indigo was imported to make up the deficiency. Difficulties with the savages tended to increase, and with the introduction of a growing and profitable tea trade the agriculturalists gradually gave tea the preference, with the result that the production of Indigo decreased so rapidly that during the last few years it has been necessary to import some of the Swatow Indigo regularly.[1] These amounts, however, reaching but a few thousand piculs a year supply but a small portion of the total requirements. Formosa Indigo is still produced extensively, and with the increased purchasing power of the masses, it is quite likely that the local consumption is larger than formerly, thus taking up much of the surplus that was formerly exported. When it is noted that there are very few of the two million and a half Chinese in the island who do not possess one or more garments which owe their serviceable and attractive coloring to this useful plant, it is not difficult to realize how large the home production must be. It requires but a glance at the passing crowd in any town in Formosa, to note how widely the dye is used; and the effect, both in the light blue so much favored by the island's fair damsels, and in the serviceable blue black of the abbreviated coolie dress, is not displeasing.

The plants from which the dye is obtained in North Formosa have not as yet been definitely determined. The Chinese divide them into the so-called " Tree or small Indigo " (Chiia) and the " Mountain or big Indigo." The former, although an undisputed *Indigofera*, seems to differ slightly from both the *Tinctoria* and *Anil* varieties as found in India, and the latter which belongs to a different order has been declared by Japanese botanists to be *Strobianthes Flaccifolius, Nees*, which is also known as *Ruellia indigotica*, the name proposed by Fortune, who discovered the plant in China. *Indigofera Tinctoria* is indigenous to the tropical parts of Asia, Africa, and America, and is the species most widely cultivated in the Madras and Bengal Provinces of India, and is also grown in Madagascar, the Isle of France, and St. Domingo. *Indigofera Anil* is a wild species found in some parts of North and South America, the West Indies, and along the Gambia in Africa. In Punjaub province, India, it is under cultivation. According to Dr. Henry, *Indigofera Tinctoria* is found in both North and South Formosa, and *Indigofera Anil* is under cultivation in South Formosa. In this paper the translated Japanese nomenclature of " Tree Indigo " and " Mountain-Indigo " will be retained for convenience sake.

The Tree-Indigo, in both Formosa varieties, is a bush very woody at base, and supporting an abundance of small pinnate, oval leaflets. It is at

1.   IMPORT OF MUD INDIGO.
                      (ALMOST WHOLLY FROM SWATOW, CHINA.)

1896	..	..	..	..	2,036 piculs	(270,678 lbs.) valued at 7,886 yen.
1897	..	..	..	..	1,907 „	(253,631 lbs.) „ 6,168 „
1898	..	..	..	..	6,485 „	(862,505 lbs.) „ 24,217 „
1899	..	..	..	..	4,964 „	(660,212 lbs.) „ 22,006 „

present cultivated largely in the plains and grows to a height of some 4 feet, though separate stems growing semi-vertically sometimes reach 5 or more feet in length. The Mountain Indigo is frequently found wild in the hills. It has numerous green colored stems with large oval, slightly serrated leaves reaching frequently 7 inches in length. The plant grows to a height of from 3 to 4 feet. It is cultivated in the hilly districts.

Throughout the island, but especially in the North, fields easily watered are as a rule given up to rice, and the remaining ground is put to sugar cane, cereals, Indigo, vegetables, peanuts, etc. Thus the ground selected for Indigo is often unfertile, and insufficiently watered. Taihoku (Taipeh) Taichu and Tainan prefectures produce the most Tree Indigo.[1]

There are practically no exclusive plantations of Indigo in Formosa, such as those found in India and other countries. Unlike the sugar and rice fields of the island, which sometimes spread over a thousand acres, Indigo is accepted as a side product by the farmers, and as a rule is given but a portion of their available ground. It is, however, grown throughout the whole western half of the island from Kimpauli in the north to Toko (Tang Kang) in the south.

As a rule, Tree Indigo is cultivated by the natives on an independent basis, the system of advances and loans on prospective crops, such as exists with sugar cane, and to a lesser extent with tea and rice, not being applied to it. In preparing for Indigo cultivation, the ground is freely ploughed and harrowed and then manured, night-soil being the usual fertilizing agent. During April, the seed is planted by hand, some ten grains being placed slightly below the surface, at distances eight or nine inches apart. When seedlings make their appearance, the weaker are pulled out, two or three strong young plants being left. In July or August, a second manuring is given, for which purpose refuse Indigo leaves from the manufacture, are sometimes used. Weeding also occurs about this time, though frequently both weeding and artificial fertilizing receive no attention whatever.

In Taichu Prefecture, the crop is harvested once a year, but in the north three crops are usually gathered in two years, the new plant yielding its first crop in August, its second in June, and its third in September. After the second or third growth, a portion of the plants are allowed to run to seed ; and in about a month or six weeks the seeds have appeared and are gathered for use in the next season's planting. The Formosa Indigo seeds

---

1. The chief Tree-Indigo producing districts in the island are as follows : —

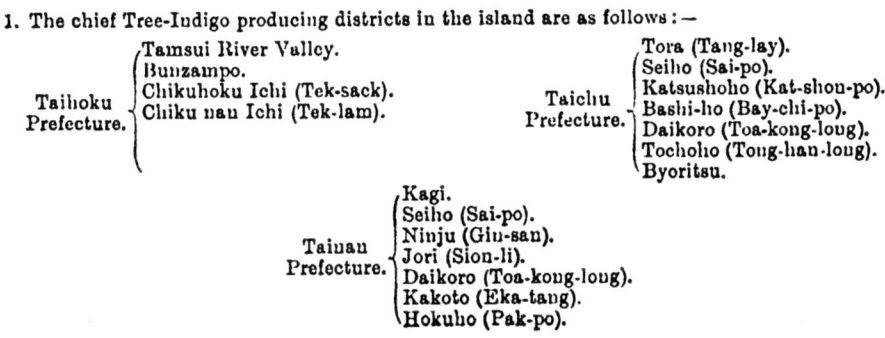

Taihoku Prefecture.
Tamsui River Valley.
Bunzampo.
Chikuhoku Ichi (Tek-sack).
Chiku nau Ichi (Tek-lam).

Taichu Prefecture.
Tora (Tang-lay).
Seiho (Sai-po).
Katsushoho (Kat-shou-po).
Bashi-ho (Bay-chi-po).
Daikoro (Toa-kong-loug).
Tochoho (Tong-han-loug).
Byoritsu.

Tainan Prefecture.
Kagi.
Seiho (Sai-po).
Ninju (Giu-san).
Jori (Sion-li).
Daikoro (Toa-kong-loug).
Kakoto (Eka-tang).
Hokuho (Pak-po).

have a good reputation in China, and are exported from the island (chiefly from Anping) to the extent of some 1000 piculs (133,000 lbs.) a year.[1]

In harvesting, a sickle is used, and the stems are cut so as to leave some five or six inches of the stalk above ground. The amount obtained is dependent upon the season and the quality and condition of the plant itself, but it is said to range from 15 to 30 piculs (1,995 to 3,990 lbs.) an acre. After the third harvest, the roots are ploughed up and the land prepared for seeding.

Mountain Indigo is grown under different conditions to Tree Indigo. As this plant does quite well in comparatively unfertile soil, it is customary to raise it on unattractive hilly land useless for other growths. A Japanese Company has taken up the cultivation of Mountain Indigo, centering their efforts in the vicinity of Tokoham (Taikokan); and it is this plant that furnishes the material for the manufacture of cake Indigo, lately instituted by the same company.

Mountain Indigo seems to grow best on the southern side of well shaded hills. In Gilan district, where a large quantity grows, it flourishes in rugged and almost barren mountain lands, and has a reputation among Chinese cultivators as being the most hardy and the easiest cultivated of all Formosa plants.

Propagation is by cuttings. Plants of good quality are selected and cut down some 6 inches from the ground, and the stems obtained are planted—four or more stems together—about one foot apart.

After the first harvest, refuse leaves are thrown on the fields as a fertilizer, and with the exception of a rough weeding three or four times a year, the plant receives no further attention. Under favorable circumstances, a plant will last four or five years. The heaviest yield is obtained the first harvest, and the yield decreases each harvest, until the plant is finally taken up to give place to new growths. The total yield is somewhat less than that of Tree Indigo.

The only Indigo dye manufactured in the island prior to the establishment of the Japanese factory was a very low grade semi-fluid stuff, to which the term "Mud Indigo" has generally been given. It is this preparation alone which the Chinese understand, and which for a hundred years they have made no attempt to improve. To manufacture the comparatively valuable cake Indigo would have required apparatus less complicated than the local Chinese at present use in the manufacture of sugar, but the ever-prevailing resolve "to do as father did" was not to be altered, and thus an industry which might have been of great value to the island received no encouragement, and was allowed to find a home in other lands where innovation and enterprise are not despised.

The method of manufacture practised in the island by the Chinese, even at the present day, requires as apparatus, a large steeping tub, an oxidizing

---

1. During 1897, 1,129 piculs (150,157 lbs.) of Indigo seed valued at 6,376 yen were exported. In 1898, however, the quantity exported reached only 356 piculs (47,318 lbs.) valued at 1,782 yen.

vat, a beating paddle, and a ladle. The tub is of wood, some 6 feet high, with a diameter of over 4 feet at the top decreasing to something over 3 feet at the bottom. It has two holes fitted with plugs, one being near the bottom and the other 1½ feet above. The vat, which is used in connection with, and sometimes in place of, a tub, is a rectangular cement tank sunk in the ground and provided with two outlets similar to those in the tub.

Now with the apparatus at hand for the manufacture, some four piculs (532 lbs.) of the freshly cut Tree Indigo stems, carrying their abundance of leaves, are placed in the tub and pressed down by large stones. Water is then poured into the tub till it covers the contents and is perhaps two inches above. After two or three hours, a kind of mucous fermentation sets in, bubbles of air are liberated, and the liquid rises slightly in the tub with the expansion of the mass below. After a short time, a thick froth will have formed on the surface. When this froth begins to subside, the attendant is aware that nearly all the leaves have been saturated, and as the coloring principle is freely soluble in water, it is readily extracted when the leaves are thus once thoroughly wetted. With the Formosa plant, about 24 hours is generally required before this action is effected. The fluid, which is now of a brownish color, is allowed to flow out from the bottom hole into the oxidizing vat provided for that purpose.[1] Some twenty catties (27 lbs.) of lime are now added to the liquid to incite oxidation. After the lime has been added the liquid is beaten for two hours or so, that the dye may become further oxidized, which when completely effected will cause the indigo to be precipitated to the bottom of the vat. After 24 hours, the precipitation is considered complete, and the upper plug is removed to permit the waste liquor to pass off. Now the semi-fluid dye, known as "Mud Indigo," at the bottom is dipped out with the ladle and is considered complete and ready for the market. The product is sometimes stored in cement vats sunk into the earth, and if any further precipitation should occur here the water on the surface is drawn off. The dye when marketed is placed in wooden tubs or baskets lined with paper, a package containing about a picul (133 lbs.) of the stuff.

For Mountain Indigo the process of manufacture is about the same as above, except that the stems must be kept in the steeping vat three days in the summer, and six days in winter, before the plant yields its dye material. Furthermore, after the lime has been thrown in, a small quantity of oil is added. After roughly straining the liquor to remove sticks, etc., the stuff is run into the oxidizing vat, and about 10 lbs. of alum is added. After two days, precipitation is effected and the dye is considered ready for the market. The refuse from the first manufacture is frequently put through the process a second time, for the purpose of extracting any Indigo which may remain. From the Tree Indigo plants, some .2 to .4 per cent., and from the Mountain Indigo some .3 to .4 per cent., of Mud-Indigo are obtained. From 4 to 8 yen a picul (133 lbs.) is obtained for this class of dye.

---

1. Sometimes the native manufacturer possesses but the one tub. In this case he withdraws the stems with the leaves attached and completes the process in the single receptacle.

A Japanese company is being organized to take up the manufacture of Indigo by modern processes. This company will establish a factory in Daitotei (Twatutia) with a capacity of some 40,000 lbs. of best cake Indigo a month. The method of manufacture will be similar to that in India, the Indigo being first steeped in artificially heated vats and then run into oxidizing tanks, where precipitation will be induced by the heating process. The stuff will then be filtered and pressed into cakes. From experiments made by the company with Mountain Indigo, a very high grade dye has been obtained, running in Indigotin (the essential coloring material of commercial Indigo) as high as 78 per cent. The government experimental station obtained with the same plant 75 per cent. of Indigotin. That this compares very favorably with the foreign product will be realized when we note that the average good marketable grades of foreign Indigo contain from 50 to 60 per cent. of Indigotin, good Bengal runs to 61 per cent., and the finest commercial Indigo very rarely reaches 75 per cent. The company will not only engage in the manufacture, but will undertake the cultivation as well. Large tracts of hill land have been obtained, and it is expected that 3,000 natives will be steadily engaged in cultivating the same.

Some three million yen worth of foreign Indigo is consumed yearly in Japan, and as the Formosa product will probably be able to enter duty free, it ought to have a prosperous future. The question of artificial Indigo is, of course, one of great importance, but it has not yet been satisfactorily determined that this product is equal to the natural dye for general purposes. It is asserted that many dye-houses in Europe, where artificial Indigo has been tried, have returned to the natural dye. Even should the artificial article eventually replace natural Indigo in western lands, the Formosa product would still have in Japan a great advantage in low freights and freedom from import duty, which would perhaps off-set the difference in original cost.

1.—TURMERIC ("CURCUMA LONGA, L").

JAPANESE : "UKON."   CHINESE : "CHIANG HUANG."

The cultivation of Turmeric is a very important industry in South Formosa, and the plant is second among the exports of the south and north, being exceeded only by sugar. Turmeric is one of the numerous plants of the Ginger tribe. It grows to a height of some 4 feet, has numerous large leaves, and possesses roots extremely grayish in color, but internally a deep yellow. From this root a yellow dye is obtained which is largely used by the Chinese. The root also affords material for a medicine, a condiment used in the manufacture of curry, and a chemical test. (See under miscellaneous plants). Over 3,500,000 pounds of Turmeric, valued at 125,587 Yen, were exported from Formosa, chiefly to China ports, during 1899. This was shipped almost wholly from Anping.

2.—DYE YAM ("Dioscorea Rhipogonoides, Oliver").

JAPANESE: "Shoro."   CHINESE: "Shulang."

This twining shrub is one of the important dye plants of Formosa, and grows wild in the mountainous savage territory throughout the island. The savage values it highly as his chief article of trade, and quantities of the tubers of the most common variety are seen in the savage border villages. The Dye Yam is dark brown in color with a rough surface. When scraped it reveals a fibrous interior of rich brownish red. In shape it is not unlike a double bulbed potato, and frequently reaches a very large size, say 15 or 16 inches long and 4 or 5 inches in diameter. The Chinese cultivate the plant but little, and obtain their supplies chiefly from the savages at some 70 or 80 Yen cents a picul (133 1/3 lbs.) The dye is obtained by cutting the tuber into small pieces. The latter are then added to a certain quantity of boiling water, and in this the articles to be dyed are placed. It is used by the savages in dyeing their cloth and by the Chinese in dyeing fishing nets, cloth, tea bags, etc. The color obtained is a reddish brown, not only permanent but also believed to render cloth, etc., proof, to some extent, against rot. The Dye Yam is largely cultivated in Tonking and in the Chinese provinces of Kwantung and Kwangsi. There is at present but a trifling export of these tubers from Formosa.

3.—GARDENIA ("G. Florida, L").

JAPANESE: CHINESE: "Huang-chi."

This plant, grown throughout China and Formosa for its beautiful flowers, which are used in scenting tea, is also of value as a dye plant. The fruit of this species yields a yellow dye well known in China and to some extent in Japan, but used very little in Formosa.

FIBRE PLANTS.

1.—CHINA GRASS ("Boehmeria Nivea, Hk. & Arn.")
OR SO-CALLED "RAMIE" OR "RHEA."

JAPANESE: "Karamushi or Ra-mi."   CHINESE: "Tui."

The popular names "China Grass," "Ramie" or "Rhea" have been generally applied indiscriminately to the produce of *Boehmeria nivea* and *B. tenacissima;* in fact, it was not generally known that any difference existed in the true Ramie or Rhea and China Grass. The plant common in China, and the Far East, and lately introduced into Algiers, Southern France, the United States, and some parts of India, is the true China Grass, the product of *Boehmeria nivea;* and it is this plant, often described as Ramie or Rhea, that has created so much interest in many parts of the world. According to Kew, the true Ramie or Rhea, (*B. tenacissima,*) which is a native of Assam, the Malay Peninsula, and adjacent islands, can be cultivated only in the tropics, attempts to introduce it within the temperate zone having met with failure. The two plants are easily distinguished, as· the leaves of China Grass (*Boehmeria nivea*) are silvery-white underneath, and the plant thrives in almost any of the temperate or subtropical portions of the world, while the under surfaces of the leaves of the Ramie or Rhea (*B. tenacissima*) are green, and successful growth of the plant is con· fined to the tropics.[1]

Ramie as a term for China Grass has been so widely used, even in scientific circles, and the error can now with such difficulty be corrected, that for practical purposes it might be advisable to adopt some modification of the term when referring to China Grass, such as China Ramie or "White Ramie,"[2] otherwise without a full explanation accompanying each essay on the plant, readers familiar with the term Ramie alone, may be of opinion that some other plant is the subject of discussion. China Grass in itself is a misleading term, inasmuch as the plant described belongs to the natural order *Urticaceae*, and is consequently a nettle rather than a grass.

In Formosa, no true Ramie has been found, though China Grass grows in abundance from North to South, both in the Savage territory and out of it. Perhaps nowhere in the East does the plant find a more congenial home. There is in North Formosa, at least, much land that affords just the soil, drainage, temperature, and rainfall that suits the plant. It grows here strong and big, whole fields with stems 9 and 10 feet high being no rare exception.

It is believed that China Grass is indigenous to China ; at all events its cultivation there extends back beyond all records. Botanist Tashiro is of opinion that the plant now found in the plains was probably brought over to Formosa by immigrants from China, but he is not so sure that the plant the savages now possess was not cultivated by them in the hill land prior to the arrival of the Chinese. China Grass is found growing wild in Formosa, but the stems possess so many branches and the bark of the plant is so thin and brittle that it is considered by both Chinese and savages of no value as a fibre plant. In connection with the China Grass found in the savage territory, Botanist Tashiro has put forward an interesting theory. The savages of Botel Tobago, near the south east coast of Formosa, who seem more closely related to some of the Philippine groups than the Formosa savages, utilize China Grass in the same way as do the tribes which they resemble in the Philippines. The short sleeveless tunic made from China Grass fibre is common to the savages of the three places mentioned, and taking these points into consideration, it is suggested that the plant which they cultivate may have been introduced into Formosa by the savages from some of the Malay islands, where it is probably indigenous.

1. In a letter addressed by Kew to the India Office, dated May 8th, 1890, the following opinion was expressed :—" Whether the fibre of Ramie is at its best really as good as the best China grass *(Boehmeria nivea)* is a point that appears not to have been definitely settled. It may turn out to be simply a question of soil and climate. China grass may give a larger and better supply of fibre under cool conditions, whereas Ramie or Rhea may do equally well under essentially tropical conditions." Page 84 Kew Bulletin on " Vegetable Fibres," London 1898.

2. The term " White Ramie " applied to China grass appears in an article entitled " Notice sur La Ramie " by Charles Roux.

In Formosa, China Grass appears to grow well either in sandy or in heavy soil rich with vegetable mold. A thin, clayey, or hard soil seems unattractive. The hill land from which the forests have been newly cleared gives the best results. We consequently find that the plants grown by the savages in their territory are superior to those found in the plains. The best fibre comes from Polisia, Taiko (Twao), Bioritsu (Maoli), all in Taichu prefecture. In Tainan prefecture such districts as Hozan and Banshoryo, which are adjacent to the savage territory, also produce considerable quantities, and the cultivation there is largely in the hands of the Chinese.

Along the south-east coast, in Taitong sub-prefecture, the Amis and others among the savages, produce a considerable quantity. Chinese in Gilan district likewise engage in the cultivation. In addition to the above districts, from which there is some export, many of the savages throughout the island, as well as many Chinese, grow small batches to supply their own domestic wants.

China Grass in Formosa seems to do best with plenty of sun, not too much wind, and a regularly watered, though not a wet, soil. To furnish these conditions we find many of the plantations in the North, sheltered by bamboo groves ; and unless the land is high and well drained, the ground is formed into long beds raised from 1 to 2 feet above the surrounding surface and highest in the center that water may pass off quickly. These beds are some 6 feet or so in width, and pathways perhaps 2 feet in width pass between them.

The plant is propagated by seeds, stem, or rhizoma cuttings, generally the latter in Formosa. If seeds are used it is customary to plant in some rich well-watered spot, and, when the nettle has appeared and is of sufficient size, to transplant to the field. When the supply of roots is limited, layering is sometimes resorted to. This consists of bending to the earth a stem, which is held down by covering the end of it with some few inches of earth. The tips soon form roots, and in a few weeks new stems will appear, which can be divided and transplanted. When rhizomas are used for planting, the roots are divided into cuttings some 4 or 5 inches in length, each showing one or more eyes, and during the month of December are set out, one every 7 or 8 inches, in rows about one foot apart. Several stems spring up from each rhizoma, with the result that when the plants are full grown the fields are very much crowded, and it is doubtful if better results would not be obtained were more space left between the plants.[1] The ground is well manured with night-soil prior to planting, and when the young stems have reached a height of some 6 or 7 inches, the field is again manured. Weeding then takes place, and in some few cases an additional manuring. No further attention is given to the plant until the first crop is ready for harvesting, which would occur in the North during the month of April.

---

1. According to a U. S. Government "Report (No. 7) on the Cultivation of Ramie in the United States" by Chas. Richards Dodge, planters are at wide variance as to the distance apart which the plants should be set to obtain the best results. In the United States the plants are generally set from 1 foot to 15 inches apart in rows from 4 to 4½ feet apart.

Three further crops, which mature more rapidly than the Spring one, are obtained during the year—in June, September, and December. In some districts where conditions are somewhat unfavorable, only three crops are obtained a year. After each harvest the soil is fertilized with night-soil and leaves from the stripped stems, and the old roots throw up new stems, though in some fields, the roots are first plowed under, and the ground newly levelled.

If the soil is fertile and other conditions favorable, no detèrioration will be observed in the plants for some three or four years, and when it does appear, the entire field is replanted. No definite information can be obtained as to the average yield per acre; but one field on the Tamsui river, which the writer visited, was reported by its owner to yield annually an acreage of over 10,800 lbs. of green stalks stripped of leaves, from which could be obtained some 980 to 1,100 lbs. of cleaned ribbon. The better grades grown in the hill districts would probably give different results.

When the plant has attained the height desired, the leaves are stripped off by hand, and left in the field for fertilizing purposes, and the stalks are cut down near to the ground, an easy operation with a sharp sickle.

The fibre forms the inner bark, and to extract it rapidly without damaging it is a problem which has interested inventors in several western countries for years. The Chinese decorticate by hand, and though it requires the services of perhaps 100 persons to do what one steam power machine with 4 attendants would accomplish, labor is so cheap and foreign machinery such a terrifying innovation, that even had the foreign appliances proved satisfactory for plantation work, which they have not entirely done, it is doubtful if the Chinese would have adopted them. The Chinese workmen, such as the writer has seen in North Formosa, show great agility in the work, and it is quite wonderful that their crude methods should give such satisfactory results. The tools used consist of a short hollow bamboo tube that it may be stuck over the right hand thumb, and a rounded wooden handle which has let into it, lengthwise, a brass blade and is likewise manipulated by the right hand.

The first step in the decortication of the plant is to peel off the bark. A sharp knife is run down lengthwise of the stem, cutting through the bark only; then the whole is doubled over, breaking the woody core, and causing the fractured ends to protrude through the side of the bark where cut. By pulling the fractured ends out from the bark, the inner part is quickly extracted, leaving the green bark in one long flat band, some five or more feet in length. The operation is quickness itself, each stem requiring but a few seconds. If the stripping has been done in the field, the bark is carried to some neighboring shelter where the fibre is to be extracted. The bark ribbons are first soaked for a few moments in water to make them soft and pliable. When sufficiently softened, a ribbon is picked up with the left hand and thrown over the scraping tool held in the palm of the right hand with the dull edge of the brass blade upwards. The bamboo tube inserted over the right hand thumb is now pressed against the scraping tool, thus holding the ribbon between the two. Now when the portion of the bark passing over the brass blade is pulled from the outside and below the scraper, the bark ribbon must form an acute angle in passing over the blade, and furthermore, owing to the pressure of the bamboo on the scraper, its surface must bear down strongly on the blade. The result is that the outer bark, which is more brittle than the fibre, cannot make the angle, but breaks and peels off, while soft or gummy portions are scraped off by the edge of the blade; the fibre, being the only part possessing strength as well as flexibility, passes over the blade safely and receives no injury. By lessening or increasing the pressure of the bamboo tube on the scraper, the workman can effectually control the varying scraping force which the different classes of ribbons may require. After having cleaned one end of the bark, this part is held and the other end thrown over, and after having been drawn entirely through, the ribbon is turned over and the reverse side cleaned. The fibre is now hung up to dry and bleach in the sun. This completes the operation, and leaves a narrow band of cleaned fibres held loosely together, reaching from 4 to 7 feet in length.[1]

I describe this minutely, as the treatment of China Grass by machinery is receiving much attention in western lands, and the wholly successful machine for plantation work, which we shall doubtless see ere long, will probably be that one which succeeds, to the greatest degree, in applying automatically, and on a large scale, the principles which now control the decortication by hand as practised by these Chinese laborers. The average operator (they are very often women) can easily extract some 16 to 20 lbs. of fibre in the form of cleaned ribbon in a Chinese working day of 12 hours. The writer has seen a skilled workman who could turn out 2½ lbs. of cleaned ribbons in one hour, and has been assured that this man can produce 30 lbs. in a Chinese working day (12 hours). Furthermore, it is stated that this is not an unusual result where the laborers are experienced men. This refers to wet ribbons. The weight of the dried material would be somewhat less.[2]

The China Grass grown by the savages is largely used by them for the manufacture of their so-called "savage cloth," from which their garments are chiefly made. This cloth is also an article of trade, and considerable quantities are purchased by the Chinese along the savage border. It is an extremely durable cloth, and though necessarily rough in texture, owing to the crude weaving appliances used, some of the work is distinctly ornamental. The savages introduce geometrical designs in color by weaving in dyed wool or cotton threads, which they obtain almost exclusively from unravelling colored blankets or other foreign textiles which they may have secured by barter. The designs are always original, and frequently striking, and should be very interesting to collectors of decorative and odd fabrics.

1. The writer has in his possession China Grass fibres measuring nearly 9 feet in length, but this is exceptional, the plants referred to having been specially selected on account of their size.

2. In Mr. Dodge's report on Ramie published by the U. S. Government, appears the statement "The Chinese strip the fibre by hand, producing, it has been stated, less than 2 lbs per day per laborer." In a British Consular Report by Mr. Hosie the weight of fibre that one man can extract in a day of ten hours is given as 8 lbs. Mr. Hosie may refer to the complete operation from peeling off the bark in the field to cleaning the ribbons, usually done at the planter's house.

Although formerly the Chinese women were expected to supply the cloth to meet the requirements of the family, of late the Formosa Chinese find that it is to their advantage to purchase cloth as they require it from professional weavers. Consequently, the fibre produced by the Chinese in Formosa, with the exception of a portion retained for the manufacture of twine, etc., is exported, chiefly to China. A portion of it returns later, made up into the so-called "Grass Cloth," for which there is a considerable local demand.

It is difficult to ascertain the exact export of China Grass fibre, as it does not appear as a separate item in the Customs returns. During the year 1898, 28,685 piculs (3,815,105 lbs.) of miscellaneous fibre, valued at 395,911 yen, were sent to China. China Grass fibre occupied the largest share, and probably reached in value to some 300,000 yen. Though this is not a large trade it is a growing one. In 1896, the export of this product did not reach 200,000 yen, and 10 years ago it was a small item in the tens of thousands. There is a considerable demand for China Grass ribbons in Japan, and a company has been lately formed in Osaka with, it is reported, 1,000,000 yen capital, to engage in the import and sale of the Formosa fibre.

Perhaps no plant during the last few years has attracted such wide attention as China Grass and Ramie. The fibre obtained from these plants stands at the head of all known vegetable fibres. In fineness it is excelled only by silk, in lustre silk is likewise its only opponent, and in strength, Russian Hemp, one of the strongest vegetable fibres, is surpassed by it three fold. It is not unnatural, therefore, that it should prove attractive both to the planter and the manufacturer.

Unfortunately, however, experts have not yet discovered a method of producing the finished fibre at a sufficiently low cost to permit of the product being placed on the market in competition with other fibres.

It is required that the fibre be first extracted by a cheap and practical process, preferably by machines which can be operated in the fields, on small plantations, as the threshing machine is used for wheat. Hand-labor, owing to its expense, is entirely out of the question. Then the fibre must be degummed and converted into filasse suitable for the textile manufacturers.

Inventors were first attracted to the so-called Ramie problem by the Indian Government, which offered a reward of 5,000 pounds sterling for the best process, mechanical or chemical, of preparing the fibre. None of the machines which were put forward to compete for the prize were successful, and the offer was eventually withdrawn. This action on the part of the Indian Government was not without result, however, for it aroused interest in other lands, and the attempts since then to solve the problem have been unceasing.

In decortication, partial success has been attained by several inventors. The Favier, de Sandtsheer, and Faure machines (all French), the Death (English), and the Allison, (American) have given comparatively good results.

The machines are not expected to accomplish more than the decortication of the plant and a rough cleaning of the resulting ribbons.[1]

The fibre, as it comes from the machines, is the marketable commodity known as " Machine cleaned China Grass," and it is not generally necessary for the planter to engage in the conversion of the ribbons into filasse, which is an operation best performed at the spinning mill.

The last process applied to China Grass, known as degumming, has scarcely emerged from the experimental stage. It is to eliminate from the ribbons an obstinate gummy substance, and to convert them into the fine white silky fibre known as filasse, ready for the spinning machine. It is generally recognized that this can only be accomplished by the use of chemicals. The Favier, Boyle, Gomess, Fleury-Moriceau, and other processes have been invented to accomplish this. For some uses, such as the manufacture of fish lines, nets, and coarse fabrics similar to the local Grass Cloth, the fibre need not be degummed chemically. It can be sufficiently cleaned, it is said, by running it through a cording machine.

The French have been perhaps more successful than any other nation in utilizing the fibre. The Favier process, both for decortication and degumming, is being used successfully both in France and Spain. The Favier Company spin the product of their own decorticating works, and have been carrying on a business for some years. There is a second successful spinning mill in Baden, Germany, and some five other factories in Europe are devoted to the spinning of imported China Grass or Ramie fibre. The product of these factories is utilized in the manufacture of lace, table damask, napkins, handkerchiefs, upholstery, curtains, etc., and general household linen. French hotels and railway companies are reported to have abolished ordinary linen in favor of the new product, owing to the latter's splendid wearing and washing qualities. The minister of war has adopted it for the cordage of balloons, ammunition bags, etc., and the army and navy use it for the dressing of wounds. It is in use as linen in some twenty city departments at Paris, and the Bank of France has adopted it exclusively in the manufacture of notes.[2]

This is a very creditable showing when we note that the manufacture of the fibre is a new industry, generally considered to be still in an experimental stage. That other countries will follow France in utilizing this valuable product there is scarcely a doubt. The most difficult problems in connection with the manufacture have been solved, and there remains only the more perfect application of known principles to produce appliances which can be easily and economically operated. When this is done, China Grass and Ramie will in a short time occupy a position well to the fore among vegetable fibres, and Formosa, which possesses above most lands the conditions required for the successful cultivation of the former, will find this fibre one of her most valued products.

1. In 1887, three small Death fibre machines were brought to Tamsui, Formosa, and the decortication of China Grass was commenced under the superintendance of Mr. F. Ashton. The venture, which was of an experimental nature, did not appear specially promising, however, and after a few months work was discontinued.

2. See the U.S. Gov. Report on Ramie by Mr. Chas. Richards Dodge.

TAIKA RUSH ("Scirpus.")

Of the very few productions which can be considered peculiar to the island, the Taika Mat, which is manufactured from an as yet unidentified rush grown in the centre of the island, is of most importance, and is believed by experts to be peculiar to Formosa. Locally, among both natives and Japanese, as well as in China, it is differentiated from all other mats ; and for want of a better appellation, has taken the name of its place of production, being known as the "Taika chio" (Taika Mat), in Japanese *Taiko Mushiro*. This mat, in beauty and softness, is equalled only by the famous Panama straw mats, and like the latter can be folded up in a small compass, like a piece of cloth, without injuring it in the least.

Mr. Hosie and other writers refer to the Taika Rush as *Cyperus tegetiformis*, but it is only necessary to compare certain China and Japan mats, which are definitely known to have been produced from *Cyperus tegetiformis*, with the Taika Mat, to see at a glance, that the material used in the latter is quite different from the others ; and this becomes a test of some importance, when we note that with some of the mats, the material is prepared in a manner similar to the Taika method, and therefore might be expected to resemble the latter when made up. Furthermore, the real *C. tegetiformis* is found in North Formosa, and while, when green, it somewhat resembles in appearance the Taika stem, it shows, when dry, several characteristics which differentiate it. The Taika stem is soft and pliable, and when dried is often of a light slate color. The *C. tegetiformis* is comparatively hard and brittle, shows considerable lustre, and when dried is of a yellowish color. Furthermore, the flowers of the plants are very different. Dr. Henry has intimated that the Taika plant may be *Scirpus*, and. Mr. Tashiro considers it as such. The *Scirpus* resembles the Taika rush in appearance, and like it is soft and pliable. Further investigations, however, will be necessary before the species can be definitely determined.

The Taika mat plant is a triangular rush, thriving in the low marshy ground of the Taika district, and cultivated only in fields where conditions permit of a bountiful supply of water. The original plants were found growing wild, but the material used at present is entirely from the cultivated plant, the latter being now superior to the wild rushes. The plant is propagated by seeds, and a light colored, clayey soil appears to give the best results. Planting occurs in January or February, and when the young plants have made their appearance, they are transplanted into a large well watered field. Oil cake and other fertilizers are applied, and the field is occasionally cleared of weeds. In June, the rushes are considered ripe, and are cut down as near the root as possible. A second crop is obtained in October, and this yield produces superior plants.

The manufacture of the famous mats from the above rush is not a new industry in Formosa. It is said that some two hundred years ago, a savage woman of a tribe living in the vicinity, while seeking for grasses which she might use in the making of mats, came across the present rush, then growing wild. She gave the plant a trial, and it was found to answer her purposes so admirably that she taught other savage women to use it, and through the latter, the Chinese, who were quick to appreciate the beauty and durability of the mats, picked up the method of manufacture.

As was often the case with the poor savages, they found themselves no match for the shrewd Chinese. Driven back into the hills, the fertile plain lands passed out of their possession for ever, and from that time the Taika mats were produced by the Chinese alone.

The mats are all hand-woven. The rushes when dry are split vertically into strips, the width of the latter being dependent upon the grade of mat it is desired to produce. The cheaper mats, which retail at 3 to 4 Yen, contain about 10 strips to an inch, and the better grades, retailing at 8 Yen or more, contain upwards of 20 to an inch. For the latter, a single rush would be divided into 6 or more strips. The work is done almost entirely by young women and girls, and it would shock Western opponents of child labor to see what a large share of it is in the hands of very little girls. At 8 or 9 years of age the children receive their first lessons in weaving, and as a rule they are fairly expert at 12, being then able to weave the better grades and introduce the geometrical designs which orna-ment these kinds.

Although some cheaper grades are made for local use, the export mats run in retail value from 3 Yen upwards. The very highest grade, such as the Chinese Mandarins frequently purchased in the old days, would cost as much as 60 or 70 Yen. The general high value may be understood when we note that for a full size mat, (5 × 6 feet), it takes the girl-weaver 20 to 40 days to make the lower grade, 60 to 70 days for the medium, and 120 days or more for the highest grade.

In the Taika (Taiko) district (Central Formosa), there are some 165 houses and over a thousand females steadily employed in the manufacture. Yenri (Wan-ni), Taika (Taiko), and Taiankang (Taianko) are the villages chiefly engaged in the industry.[1] In addition, there are many farm girls who give their spare time to the work. It is estimated that there are some 1,300 houses and 3,000 females engaged thus in irregular manufacture, and that the latters' earnings range from 5 to 20 Yen cents a day. The yearly output reaches some 10,000 full-size mats, valued at over 30,000 Yen, together with a considerable quantity of small mats, and a large number of foreign shaped hats. The manufacture of hats was commenced only some three years ago, and they are now much in favor among the Japanese in the island. They resemble in shape the so-called "Slouch hat" of Western lands, are light and durable, though not exactly ornamental. The hats can be purchased throughout the island, and they would without doubt, find a market in Japan, and in China among foreigners, and even abroad, were they made in shapes conforming more closely with western styles. They would be found an admirable substitute for the Panama hat, at a small part of its cost. The Japanese navy has taken into consideration the adoption of this material for the manufacture of sea-men's hats.

---

1. In the village of Nankan, in Toafuu district (North Formosa) a few houses are engaged in Taika mat making.

The mats are deservedly popular for the bed during the hot summer months. The well-to-do native rarely uses anything else. The better grades are as fine and soft as cloth, and by covering them with a sheet, foreigners find more comfort than could ever be obtained from the usual arrangement of bed-clothes. The Taika mat, unlike most mats, does not appear to have the sticky and clammy feeling, when moistened with perspiration. It is to be recommended to foreign residents in the tropics. The mat as made at present is not always even in color, running from a tan to a slate, but uniformity in color could be easily obtained if specially desired. No dye or chemical bleach of any kind is used, and the very attractive shading of slate and tan is but the natural color of the dried rush.

While there is no large export of Taika Mats through the Customs, large numbers are carried over to China by Chinese passengers. The avaricious Chinese always have an eye for business, and few leave the port of Tamsui without one or two of these mats, which they know that they can dispose of at a certain profit in China, thus paying their passage.

2.—JUTE PLANT ("Corchorus Capsularis, L.")

JAPANESE : "Tsunaso." LOCAL CHINESE : "Ma."

Among the island's fibre-producing growths, the Jute plant is next in importance to China Grass. It is the same plant as is extensively grown in Central and East Bengal and in China and Japan for its fibres, and finds a profitable and increasing market in England, where it is used in the manufacture of rugs, carpets, and other coarse fabrics.

It is a striking plant as seen in the field. The stems of the most common variety when young are a deep red, turning to a reddish green as the plant matures. Lanceolate leaves spring up from the upper third of the plant, and when the stems have reached their maximum length, say 10 or 12 feet, the whole presents, for an annual, quite an imposing appearance. There is a second variety, the stems of which are green, but it is little valued in Formosa. Like China Grass, the Jute plant is widely planted, and the ribbons obtained from it have appeared, under the misleading term of "Hemp-skin," as an export from Formosa since the year 1866, when the island's trade was first reported by the Chinese Customs.

Botanist Tashiro reports that the best quality of Jute plant is grown in South Formosa, in the vicinity of Tang kang (Toko). Gilan, in the north-eastern part of the island, also produces a good grade of fibre. The soil of these districts is chiefly soft and deep, contains much decomposed plant-matter, and is thus specially favorable for Corchorus. There is a considerable export from Tamsui of Jute produced in North Formosa and from Ku-kang (Kiuko) of the Teckcham (Hsin-chiku) district product. The South Formosa Jute is principally exported from Anping.[1]

---

1. The export of Jute fibre appears in the 1897 Japanese Customs Returns as follows —
"Hemp-skin" exported from Tamsui........ 1,908 Piculs valued at 6,028 yen.
      "   "   " Anping........ 377 "   "   " 1,298 "
      "   "   " Kukang ...... 946 "   "   " 4,694 "
      "   "   " Toseki .... 269 "   "   " 892 "
Total export—all Formosa—3,528 piculs (457,224 lbs.), valued at 13,008 yen.

Polishing local Dyed Cloth.

Cleaning China Grass.

Tamsui Jute Fields.

Jute Rope Making.

Tamsui China Grassfield.

Manufacture of Paper from "Paper Mulberry" Plant.

The cultivation of the plant is as follows :—

In April or May a small well-prepared bed is thickly grown to seed, and when the plants have made their appearance and are some 8 inches in height, they are transplanted to the fields. There is some direct planting, but it is the exception rather than the rule. When the stems are up some 3 or 4 feet, the fields are well manured with night-soil or bean cake dust, or both.

The Jute plant is able to bear excessive moisture to a greater extent than China Grass, and in the north, we find it growing on the Tamsui river lowlands—places subject to inundation. A day or two of submersion during the yearly typhoon freshets does not appear to damage it, unless the plant, or portions of it, are torn out entirely. The writer visited a field the second day after a freshet, and though the field was then covered by some 8 inches of water, the plants held their heads erect, were bright and vigorous, and apparently had received not the slightest injury.

In September, the stems are ready for harvesting. This operation is performed by the men. The plant is pulled out bodily from the ground, root and all. The stem is then placed between two rounded sticks, which are held tightly together by one of the men. A portion of the bark skin is loosened and thrown over one of the sticks, and the peeled end of the plant is pulled rapidly through by the second workman, thus separating the bark, in which the fibre is contained, from the inner stalk. It is this peel that forms the so-called " Hemp-skin " of commerce, and for the manufacture of rope and when split for the coarsest of bagging, no further preparation is required. When it is desired, however, to use it for a better grade of sacking or like material, the ribbons are soaked in water, and when softened the outer bark is scraped off by the following method :—From near the top of a post projecting some 2½ feet above ground, runs out at right angles a short block about 1 foot in length. The latter forms the bed for a knife-like tool, which is inserted, blade end in the post, and held by a single metal pin, the handle end being free, and the apparatus resembling somewhat the ordinary cake tobacco cutter. In cleaning the bark, two operators stand or sit facing each other, with the crude apparatus between them. The handle end being raised, a few stems are thrown in on the wooden block; the knife is then pressed down, and the stems pulled out. As the stems pass under the blade, sufficient pressure is applied to remove the outer bark without injuring the fibre, which operation is as a rule very satisfactorily effected. Some two piculs (266 lbs.) of fibre a day can be prepared by two workmen.

The fibre is bound together in picul (133 lbs.) bundles, worth in the local market some 5 yen.

As with China Grass, the introduction of practical machinery for the decortication of the Jute plant would probably place the industry on a more prosperous footing. Mr. Tashiro is of opinion that the Japanese should come forward and establish large plantations, improving the cultivation and producing the fibre on a large scale. There is a large district suited to the cultivation of the Jute plant; and with the comparatively cheap labour obtainable here, it should be possible to supply, at least Japan's requirements, from this island.

3.—FAN PALM ("Chamaerops excelsa, Thumb.")

JAPANESE: "Shuro."   CHINESE: "Tsang."

This species of the Fan Palm is widely cultivated throughout North Formosa for its strong and useful fibre. It is an ornamental tree as well, and an attractive addition to any garden. It is cultivated extensively in both China and Japan, where its fibre is greatly valued, and of all local palms it appears to be the most hardy.

It is propagated by seeds which are sown in a small bed, and after a few years' growth the young plant, which has reached a height of some 18 inches, is transplanted to a bed. The second year it is again transplanted, and the third year set out, the plants some 5 feet apart, in the field which is to be its final abode. The fourth year the young palm has reached a height of about six feet and yields its first crop of fibre; the eighth year it is some 10 feet high, and from then on to the fifteenth year the plant has its largest yield. Beyond this, the tree generally deteriorates in fibre-producing qualities, but not till it is some 50 years old does it cease to yield fibre which is worth collecting.

The base of each leaf stalk rests in a sheath, and as a large tree may possess from 8 to 10 of the fully grown leaves, there will be as many sheaths, and the latter possess in themselves the fibrous material desired. The fibre is generally gathered 4 times a year, and at each harvest some 4 or 5 sheaths will he found sufficiently developed. In large sheets the fibre is very light, a good grade sheet weighing scarcely 1½ ounces. Thus, the maximum yield of a tree will be some 30 ounces of fibre a year, worth at the market rate about 24 yen cents. One man can care for five hundred or more trees if need be, and can obtain from them an income which, for a China planter, is considered satisfactory. The fibre is obtained by cutting around the base of the sheath, which releases it. The sheet of fibrous material obtained is some 2 feet long by about 18 inches wide. It forms a completed fabric in itself, and to utilize it, the number of sheets required are sewn together like so many pieces of cloth.

The fibre must be first well dried in the sun, but no further preparation is required. The material is brown in color, resembles cocoanut fibre somewhat in appearance, is extremely durable, and will not rot with years of use. The fibre brings, in the local market, 15 to 16 yen a picul (133 lbs.) It is chiefly used for the manufacture of Chinese rain coats, several thicknesses of the big sheets being sewed with edges overlapping. The fibres when separated are also used extensively for the manufacture of large ropes for junks, etc. Several layers of the sheets are sewn together to form a mat which, when placed over a damp or muddy floor, provides the Chinese coolie with a dry bed. Chinese sun-hats are also manufactured out of the same material, and various kinds of brushes, in some of which the stiffer parts of the sheets form the handle.

That this interesting plant deserves more attention than it receives from the Formosan natives, there is scarcely a doubt. The ease with which it can be obtained, its strength and durability, combined with the fact that unlike many vegetable fibres, it is almost rot proof, should find for it a market in western lands where its good qualities can be taken full advan- tage of.

4.—SISAL HEMP PLANT ("Agave rigida, Mill.")

JAPANESE: "Ryujetsuso."   CHINESE: "Huan-qua" (?)

This very valuable fibre-plant though not plentiful, is met with in the vicinity of Tangkang (Toko), Takow, and Tainan ; and a second species of the Agave, the so called " American Aloe " (*A. americana*), is found in the north near Tamsui and Kelung and on Palm Island.[1] Although the inhabitants of Formosa seem unaware of the value of the Agave it has attracted in other lands great interest, and has become one of the most prominent and valuable of fibre-producing plants.

The Agave is one of the oldest fibre plants known, and has been culti- vated from time immemorial in certain parts of Mexico. In 1890, the species *A. rigida* was introduced into the Bahama Islands on a large scale. Foreign capital was interested, and the local government rendered assistance. It had been satisfactorily determined that the Sisal Hemp industry would bring profit to the islands, and almost unparalleled energy was shown in placing the industry on a substantial basis with as little loss of time as possible. Fibre is not obtained from the plant until the 4th or 5th year, and though some difficulties were encountered at first in obtaining suitable machinery for extracting the fibre, in 1897, over a million pounds of the fibre was produced, and it now holds third place among the exports of the Bahama group. According to the opinion of experts, the Sisal Hemp cultivation shows every indication of becoming in a few years the leading industry of the islands.

Mexico, the chief producing district, exported in 1897 over 155 million pounds, valued at 11,564,000 Mexican dollars. The market price of fibre in Mexico ranged during 1898 from about 7 to 9 U. S. Gold cents (14 to 18 Yen cents) per pound. The presence of the plant in Formosa, where it has flourished for years, though uncared for, renders it probable that it could be cultivated in this island to advantage.

Along the west coast of Formosa, long strips of sandy soil exist in many places. It is difficult to irrigate this ground, and as a result but little attempt is made to cultivate it. The Sisal Hemp plant would grow here without difficulty. It has been found in other lands to thrive in soil which

1. Dr. Henry reports the *Agave rigida* as introduced and naturalized about Takow. It has been reported by other writers that this species is also found at Tamsui (Hobe) and on Palm Island. *A americana* is found in abundance at Tamsui and Palm Island, and doubtless this species has been confused with *A rigida*. The first real Sisal Hemp plants (*Agave rigida* var. *Sisalana*) to be seen in North Formosa, so far as the writer has been able to ascertain, were introduced by Mr. A. E. Hodgins during the present year.

was generally supposed to be barren, and in Mexico, where it has proven very profitable, it is frequently grown on sandy or stony ground absolutely worthless for other plants. It is positively declared that the agaves grown on comparatively arid land, only a few feet above the sea, equal if they do not exceed in yield, the plants grown in soil apparently much more attractive.

Propagation is either by seeds or suckers, and the first plants are grown in a small bed and then transplanted. A plantation, started with plants about two feet in height, will give its first crop of fibre 3 years later, and continue to yield for from 10 to 20 years.

In Mexico some 400 plants are usually grown to the acre, and the average plant yields from 20 to 24 leaves annually. From this material from 450 to 500 lbs. or more of cleaned fibre is obtained, which would be worth at the present market rate upwards of 63 yen.

The cost of production is estimated at about 4 sen a pound, which leaves a profit to the planter of over 45 yen an acre.

Formosa is in a favorable position inasmuch as she possesses on the spot plants in sufficient number to start the cultivation on a small scale, while in some parts of the island the required conditions of soil and climate are so perfectly complied with that there seems scarcely a doubt that the cultivation of this plant would prove a profitable undertaking. With its introduction we may expect to see the now unproductive portions of the island yielding a return perhaps exceeding that obtained from some more attractive spots.

It is interesting to note that many of the Formosan Chinese look upon the agave with superstitious dread. They believe it is a bearer of disease, and not infrequently the plant is rooted up and destroyed.

5.—PINE-APPLE ("Ananas sativa, L.")

JAPANESE: "Ananasu."   CHINESE: "Huang-lai."

The Pine-apple plant grows throughout the island, but seems to thrive best in the southern half, where it grows to a large size and produces a luscious and refreshing fruit, which few other lands can excel. The southern pine is likewise superior to the northern as a fibre producer, and it is in South Formosa, chiefly, that the extracting of fibre is engaged in as a regular industry.

The fibre is obtained from the green leaves of the plant. Small leaves and the large reddish leaves which also surround the fruit, are inferior in fibre, and are consequently of little value.

The fibre is almost entirely extracted by women. The plant in placed on a bench, on one end of which the operator sits astraddle. The prickly edged leaves desired, which have been stripped off the plant by hand, are placed flat before her. Then with one hand the lower end of the leaf is held, and with the other, a small porcelain bowl,[1] inverted, is used as a scraper,

---

1. This is the ordinary small earthenware bowl used by the Chinese as a dish for rice at meal time.

the surfaces of the leaf being scraped until the fibre is exposed. As the fibre appears, it is picked out, the usual long finger-nails of the Chinese affording the operator an efficient tool for loosening the ends of the fibre. When a sufficient quantity has been extracted, the fibre is soaked in cold water and bleached in the sun, this latter operation being repeated six times when the finest quality is desired. The fibre is largely exported, though some quantity is locally used in the manufacture of a cool summer cloth.

For export, it is bound into bundles of 10 catties each, 10 of which form one package of a picul (133 lbs.) weight. It is shipped largely to Swatow, where it is made into a fine grade of grass cloth, and sells there for from 33 to 37 yen per picul.[1]

Pine apple is one of the fibres thought to have a bright future. In the Philippines, the production of this article is an important industry, and the " Pina cloth," which is manufactured from it, is a beautiful texture, the higher grades selling at a price equal to that paid in western lands. With the adoption of modern machinery it is thought the cost can be greatly reduced, and experts are consequently of opinion that this fibre is one of coming importance.

6.—ALPINIA FIBRE PLANT ("ALPINIA NUTANS, ROSC.")

JAPANESE: "SHANIN" OR "SHUKUSHA."   CHINESE: "YUE-TAO."

This plant grows wild throughout the island, though chiefly in the hill district. It is not cultivated, except as an ornamental plant in gardens, where it is valued for the beautiful blossoms which make their appearance in early summer. It yields a small round fruit, the surface of which is curiously striped. The fruit is used by Chinese for medical purposes. The stems average some 5 feet in height, though in favored localities they are frequently found to reach over 6 feet, and yield a strong though coarse fibre much used in some parts of the island, both by Chinese and savages.

Mr. Tashiro describes the fibre industry as follows :—

The Chinese pound the stems, which loosens the outer skin and exposes a fibrous strip. The latter is divided into very narrow ribbons, and is used for the manufacture of grass shoes and ropes. While the North Formosan tribes make little use of the plant, the savages in the south of the island, specially the Tsalisen and Paiwan groups and the Tamari tribe of Pinan (Pilam) district, appreciate it highly, and show no little skill in utilizing it. The methods used by the savages differ somewhat from those of the Chinese. The stems are cut near the root, and the sheaths which partially envelope them are carefully removed. .The stems are then rolled

---

1. The export of Pine-apple Fibre for the year 1899 is given in the Japanese Customs Returns as follows :—

From Anping	495 Picul (65,846 lbs.)	valued at 13,662 yen.
„ Rokko (Lokiang)	4 „ (630 „)	„ „ 94 „
„ Tokatsukutsu (Thow-kat-kut) ..	15 „ (2,080 „)	„ „ 313 „
„ Tamsui..	73 „ (9,752 „)	„ „ 1,882 „
Total export	588 Picul (78,308 lbs.)	valued at 15,451 yen.

up in cylindrical form and hung up to dry under the eaves of the huts. When the savages desire to utilize the product, the stems, now dry and stiff, are taken down and flattened out, and each is divided into narrow strips of the size desired. There is no attempt made to separate the filaments and utilize them for spinning, etc. The material obtained is very pliable, and is used almost exclusively for the manufacture of mats, baskets, etc., of a superior quality. The savages show great skill in weaving and shaping this material, and some of the mats are sufficiently ornamental to prove an attractive article in one's house. The baskets are of all sizes and shapes, varying from a cigarette case to a large travelling box. These articles are made for purposes of sale, as well as of domestic use, and form a considerable portion of the savage's stock in trade when he visits the border villages for purposes of barter.

7.—PAPER MULBERRY ("BROUSSONETIA PAPYRIFERA, VENT.")[1]

JAPANESE : " KOZO."   CHINESE : " LU-A SHU."

This plant grows throughout the plains and hills. It attains the dignity of a tree in Formosa, and is frequently found over one foot in diameter. Although known as the " Paper Mulberry" and used in several countries as material for paper making, it possesses a fibrous bark which in some lands is made into a sort of cloth. There are several methods of preparing this bark, but the one most common in the South Pacific Islands, where the tree is most largely utilized, is to soak small branches, one inch in diameter, in water until they become partly macerated. The epidermis is then scraped off, and the strips are pressed and beaten, while in a moist state, into a sheet of paper like cloth. The famous Pitcairn islanders were for many years dependent upon this plant, which was commonly known as the " Cloth tree," for their material for clothing. There is an interesting reference to the plant in " Beechey's Narrative," Capt. Beechey having visited the island in 1825. The author wrote, " If the cloth is required to be brown, the inner bark of which the cloth is made is wrapped in banana and put aside for about four days ; it is then beaten into a thick doughy substance, and again left till fermentation is about to take place, when it is taken out, and finally beat into a garment, both lengthwise and across. The color thus produced is of a deep reddish brown hue. The pieces are generally sufficiently large to wrap round the whole body."[2]

Taking into consideration the ease with which the cloth-like material could be obtained, and the value of it to primitive peoples out of touch with civilization, it is indeed strange that the savages of Formosa make no attempt to utilize this tree which grows in their territory. Hill savages wherever found are usually familiar with the trees which they can utilize to advantage, and the learned botanist has but little to teach them in this respect. In fact, the cleverness and true knowledge of the forests which

1. Also dealt with under " Paper Plants."
2. Page 131, Vol. I., " Beechey's Narrative," London, 1831.

they often exhibit in obtaining from plant-life, materials which by crude processes can be manufactured into something useful to them, are sometimes difficult to comprehend when we consider their general ignorance.

8.—BANANA OR PLANTAIN (" Musa sp.")

The Banana or Plantain family is represented in Formosa by several species. The Pepohoans in Gilan district manufacture cloth from fibre obtained from the Banana tree, but as yet the species they utilize has not been definitely determined. Mr. Tashiro, however, who has given some study to the subject, states that it is not the *Musa Textilis, Nees,* which is the source of the so-called Abaca or Manila Hemp, so widely cultivated in the Philippines. The cultivation of this last species, which as a fibre plant is the most important of the Banana family, might be introduced into the island, but the yield per plant is so small in comparison with the cost of cultivation that it is doubtful if it would be a profitable investment. The Banana fibre obtained in the island comes from the stem of a species of Musa locally known as the " Mountain Banana." The fruit of this species is not edible, and the plant is valued only for its fibre, which is white and of very fair quality. In Tainan prefecture a considerable quantity of Banana fibre is manufactured, and small quantities are sometimes exported to China. It is locally used in the manufacture of cloth, twine, etc. In Botel Tobago island, the savages grow the *Musa textilis* to obtain material for the manufacture of cloth. rope, etc. The stem of the ordinary Banana which supplies the edible fruit, yields a fairly strong fibre, which though coarse and unattractive, might be of some value for rope making. Run through a Death Fibre machine the stem yielded in weight about 1 per cent. of dry cleaned fibre. Chinese are above all economical, and one would expect to find them utilizing the ordinary banana for its fibre, after the stem has been cut down for its fruit. This is not the case, however; the stem is thrown aside and allowed to rot on the ground.

9.—SCREW-PINE (" Pandanus Odoratissimus, L.")

JAPANESE : "ADAN" OR " TAKONOKI." CHINESE : " NA-TAU."

This plant is found throughout the island, but most largely in the south. It is a large palm-like bush ranging from 8 to 15 feet in height. It thrives in sandy soil, and is frequently found along the sea coast. It yields a fruit which, at first sight, appears very much like the edible pine-apple. It is very widely grown in the Okinawa group of the Loochoo Islands, and its fibre is extensively used there. It is also a well-known plant in the South Sea Islands, where the fibrous leaves, when divided into strips, are used as a material for the manufacture of mats, baskets, etc.

In Formosa, Screw-Pines are frequently grown to form a hedge around a garden or farm house, and it is only in Taito (Taitong) and Koshun (Hengchun) districts that the fibre which is obtained from the aerial roots sent down from the stems is utilized to any extent. In the places mentioned, a very durable kind of straw shoe, valuable for hill climbing, is made. The plant is also used in several districts for rope-making. Very fair paint brushes are obtained from a piece of an aerial root, one end of which has been pounded out. Furthermore, the fruit itself presents in each of its strongly marked circular sections a Chinese pen ready for use. It has generally been cut to a point in taking it out, and the head is left on to form the handle. It is chiefly used for marking boxes, etc. When passed through a Death machine, a few fair grade rope fibres were obtained from the leaves of one species, which were sent up from Hongkong.

10.—BOWSTRING HEMP ("Sansevieria.")

JAPANESE: "Chitoseran." LOCAL POPULAR TERM: "Hokutomoto."
CHINESE: "Haw-be-lan."

This splendid fibre plant is represented by one species, as yet not definitely identified, which is found in the Pescadores, and has been introduced to Formosa as an ornamental garden plant. It thrives well and could be easily cultivated in South Formosa, where the rich moist soil and comparatively warm and humid climate of the lower hill-districts is eminently suited to its growth. A few leaves of this plant obtained from a Taihoku (Taipeh) garden were passed through a Death machine, and gave a fibre which appeared, at least to the writer's inexperienced eyes, the most beautiful of the many fibres of the island, with the single exception of China Grass when chemically prepared. It was quite white, of exceptional lustre, and when coiled up, very lively and elastic, resembling closely a ring of fine white hair; moreover, the fibre was firm and strong. In weight, 1.9 per cent. of clean dry fibre was obtained from the fresh leaves. There appeared to be no more difficulty in extracting the fibre by machinery than with the Agave, and if the plant can be easily grown, it would seem that it must have a bright future. Several species of *Sansevieria* are being cultivated by the Agricultural station at Taihoku (Taipeh).

11.—CYPERUS ("Cyperus Tegetiformis, Roxb.")

JAPANESE: "Shichito-i" OR "Sankaku-i." CHINESE: "Kiam-tsau."

This rush is cultivated to a considerable extent in North Formosa, and also to some degree in other parts of the island. It is perennial, grown in marshy or artificially watered fields, and reaches a height of 4 or 5 feet. It is the chief material the island affords for the manufacture of cheap matting. As mats are commonly used by the Chinese as an under covering for the bed, and sometimes as an outer coverlet as well, they have a large sale. Matting for packing purposes is also made from the plant, and single stems are used as twine for tying up packages, etc.

This plant is largely cultivated in Ningpo and Canton districts, China, and in Kyushu, Japan; being used in both countries for the manufacture of matting.

12.—ROSE MALLOW (" Hibiscus Esculentus, L.")

JAPANESE : " Tiioroaoi."   CHINESE : " Ng-sok-kwi."

This plant, sometimes called Okro or Okra, is well known throughout the tropics. It produces a seed which in some countries is used as an article of food, and its stout hairy stem is utilized. in the West Indies as a source of a long silky fibre of very fair quality, used in the manufacture of rope, twine, sacking, etc. Considerable interest has been taken in this plant in the Southern United States and Cuba, where it has been introduced for its fibre. This herb is found growing wild in the vicinity of Taihoku (Taipeh), and in other parts of Formosa. It is not utilized by the Chinese, and no attempt has been made to cultivate it.

13.—ROSE MALLOW (" Hibiscus Cannabinus, L.")

JAPANESE : " Koshokki."   CHINESE : " Ang-sok-kwi."

This herbaceous shrub is well known in Persia and India. It produces a soft, silky fibre, which is strong though elastic, and is a very satisfactory substitute for fibres like jute, etc., which are used for the manufacture of coarser textiles. This plant is not found wild in Formosa, but has been introduced as an ornamental garden plant. It grows well here, however, and if the high expectations of certain Russian enthusiasts are realized as respects the plant in Persia, it may become a profitable plant for the local farmers to take up.

14.—SILK COTTON TREE (" Bombax Malabaricum, D.C.")

JAPANESE : " Panya."   CHINESE : " Pan-ki."

This tree grows rather plentifully in South Formosa, especially in Hozan district. It is not often seen in the north, though in the mountains near Polisia in Taichu prefecture the tree is frequently met with. Though the plant is now growing wild, it is very probable that it was introduced to the island by Chinese and cultivated for a time. At present the Formosa natives rarely utilize the cotton-like material which is found in the capsules, which in China is used as a stuffing for pillows, mattresses, etc.

15.—STERCULIA FIBRE PLANT (" Sterculia Platanifolia, Linn.")

JAPANESE : " Aogiri."   CHINESE : "Ching-tung."

This tree is found growing wild, chiefly in the hill districts. It does not often reach a very large size in Formosa, nor is it very frequently met with. The fibre obtained from it is strong though rather rough and stiff, and the savages in Banshoryo (Han chu-liao) district utilize it for the manufacture of a so-called " savage cloth." The fibrous bark obtained from the young stems of the trees is sometimes used for making rough twine and rope.

16.—WHITE MULBERRY ("Morus alba, L.")

JAPANESE : "Shimaguwa."   CHINESE : "Son-su."

This tree thrives throughout the island. It is considered of no commercial value in the north, but Dr. Henry states that the savages in the neighborhood of Bankinshing, South Formosa, obtain a fibre from the root bark of the young trees, and utilize it in the manufacture of cloth, game bags, etc.[1]

17.—PUERARIA FIBRE PLANT ("Pueraria Thunbergiana, Benth.")

JAPANESE : "Kuzu" or "Kuzu-Kazura."   CHINESE : "Ko."

This vine grows wild throughout Formosa both in the mountains and low lands. Fibre obtained from the bark is utilized in some parts of China for the manufacture of a light cloth for summer wear of excellent quality. It is said that in ancient times the Japanese likewise made cloth of this fibre.

18.—ROSE MALLOW ("Hibiscus Tilaceus, L.")

JAPANESE : "Shimahamabo."   LOCAL CHINESE : "Ko-hio."

This is a small tree with numerous upright branches. From the latter the Paiwan savages of the extreme south of Formosa obtain a fibre which they use for twine, etc. The fibre is also used in the South Sea Islands in the making of fish-nets, etc. It is found growing wild in the Formosa hill districts. This fibre can be easily extracted by a fibre machine, such as the Death, but it is necessary first to peal off the bark, and not to run the heavy woody part through.

19.—ROSE MALLOW ("Hibiscus Mutabilis, L."

JAPANESE : "Fuyo."   CHINESE : "Bok-phu-yung."

This herb, from which a fibre of doubtful commercial value can be obtained, has been found growing wild near Toshien (Toahong) and in the vicinity of Takow. It grows locally to a height of some 6 feet and is not utilized by the Chinese.

20.—ALPINIA FIBRE PLANT ("Alpinia Chinensis, Rosc.")

JAPANESE : "Kumatakeran."   CHINESE : "Ko-lion-kion."

This plant grows wild in the hill districts throughout the island. A fibre can be obtained from its stems, and it is sometimes used as material for making the soles of straw shoes.

---

1. See Dr. Henry's "A List of Plants from Formosa" page 86, Vol. XXIV., Supplement. Transactions Japan Asiatic Society, Tokyo.

21 & 22.—SCIRPUS $\begin{cases} \text{(" Scirpus Triqueter, L.")} \\ \text{(" Scirpus Mucronatus, L.")} \end{cases}$

JAPANESE: "KANGAREI." JAPANESE: "SANKÀKU-I." CHINESE: "CHIA-CHO."

In addition to *Cyperus tegetiformis*, the above two plants of the Sedge Family are utilized in the manufacture of matting, though not on an extensive scale. The former is found throughout Formosa, but the latter is most frequently met with in the south of the island.

OTHER FIBRE PLANTS.

The fibre plants described above are those either used locally or of commercial value in other lands. There are many other fibre plants in Formosa, which though possessing little or no marketable value, are used by the native peoples of some countries in supplying their own personal wants. Without doubt some of these fibres will in time come into more general use, and may eventually be a source of wealth to the lands in which they grow.[1]

PAPER PLANTS.

I.— $\begin{cases} \text{RICE-PAPER PLANT} \\ \text{PITH-PAPER PLANT} \end{cases}$ (" Aralia [Fatsia] Papyrifera, Hook.")

JAPANESE: "Tsuso." CHINESE: Tung-tsao."

One of the most interesting of Formosa's vegetable products is the so-called Rice-Paper Plant. This deceptive title was given to the plant,

---

1. The following fibre plants, in addition to those described above, are found in Formosa :—

	WHERE UTILIZED.	FOR WHAT PURPOSES.
23. Abutilon indicum	Mauritius	Cordage.
24. Adiautum capillus-veneris	Hawaii	Stalks used for baskets, mats.
25. Anona squamosa	Guadaloupe	Cordage.
26. Areca catechu	India	Flower-sheath for cups, dishes, bags.
27. Carica papaya	Bernardin Commission reports it yielding fibre 5ft. long.	
28. Cordia myxa	India	Cordage, caulking material.
29. Cordyline terminalis	Australia	Has yielded good fibre for cordage.
30. Crotalaria striata	India	Cordage.
31. Curcuma longa	———	Mid rib of leaf stated to yield fibre.
32. Cyperis iria	India	Mats.
33. Desmodium latifolium	Ceylon, India	Cordage.
34. Dicksonia barometz (Tree Fern)	East Asia	Wool base of leaf stalk for stuffing.
35. Dolichos trilobus	China	Coarse cloth.
36. Dregea volubilis	India	Cordage.
37. Entada scandens	Ceylon	Bark as ropes, seeds for small boxes, spoons.
38. Hibiscus abelmoschus	India	Fibre found good for cordage.
39. Hibiscus surattensis	India	Fibre found good for cordage.
40. Kadzura Japonica	East Indies	Good white fibre obtained.
41. Kleinhovia hospita	Malay Archipelago	Cordage, fishing-nets.
42. Nelumbium speciosum	India	Wicks for sacred lamps.
43. Pachyrhizus angulatus	Fiji Islands	Fishing-nets.
44. Sesbania aegyptiaca	India	Cordage.
45. Sida rhombifolia	India	Cordage, coarse cloth.
46. Trachycarpus excelsus	China	Mats, coarse cloth, cordage.
47. Trema orientalis	Venezuela, India, Ceylon	Cordage, coarse cloth.
48. Urena lobata	Africa, India, Brazil	Cordage, paper manufacture.
49. Villebrunea integrifolia	India	Cordage, cloth.
50. Zizania aquatica	United States	Used by coopers as packing for barrel joints.

doubtless, owing to a slight similarity the finished product bears to the best Rice-Paper, but Pith-Paper is a far more accurate term and is coming into general use. The Pith-paper plant is indigenous to the island, and appears to thrive best on burned-off plots of ground in the savage border districts. Small forest fires on the savage border are frequent. Sometimes they are the work of the savage, who takes this method of clearing his ground; or of an adventurous Chinese farmer who possesses land on the border and wishes to extend his holdings, and again it is the Chinese peasant who adopts this means of avenging himself on his savage enemies, as well as increasing his safety by driving the savages further back into the hills. Among the new growths that spring up over these blackened areas, the Pith-plant is often prominent, and though generally found wild, the savages will, if the cleared spot is within their territory, often increase the production by putting out numerous cuttings. The plant grows rapidly and reaches a height of 10 and even 15 feet, and a diameter of from 2 to 5 inches at its base. In the centre of the stem and forming more than half of the whole is a cylindrical core of cellular pithy tissue. Towards the lower end of the tree the pithy centre is found divided into comparatively small hollow sections somewhat similar to the bamboo, though showing no outer rings. It is this pithy part of the tree that produces the material for the so-called Rice-paper. To extract it, the stem is cut into lengths of some 2 feet, the bark and woody covering is partly broken, and the pithy core loosened and then pushed out. If of marketable size these pith cylinders are an inch or more in diameter. In this state they are salable as pith, and some 30,000 lbs., valued at 5,000 yen, are exported yearly, the China ports and Hongkong being the chief markets. The greater portion of this product, however, goes forward in the form of the so-called Rice-paper, which in reality is merely parings of pith. To obtain it a very simple contrivance is used. A tile or hard wood plate, with two sides slightly elevated above its surface, affords support for a sharp straight-bladed knife, which can be drawn backwards and forwards at will, and the cutting edge of which is elevated above the bed a distance equal to the thickness of the sheet of paper it is desired to make. To perform the operation the pith cylinder is cut into such lengths as will give a section which can be rolled easily on the bed of the tile· With the knife at the extreme right of the plate and its edge facing inward, the pith cylinder is placed lengthwise against the blade, and is given with the left hand a rolling movement backwards, while the knife, guided by the right hand, follows, pressing closely, and thus paring off a long thin sheet. The operation requires considerable skill, and in the hands of an adept workman so quickly is it performed that it appears as though a roll of white ribbon was merely being unwound. The sheets obtained are now put under heavy pressure to remove all moisture and to flatten them. They are then cut into squares of some 3½ inches and packed up, 90 sheets to a package.

The Formosa pith-paper is exported largely to China and Hongkong (for transhipment to Canton) and is used by the Chinese in the manufacture of artificial flowers, and by Canton artists and others who find a considerable market for small fancy pictures painted on their truly beautiful paper. It is also used in the manufacture of sun-hats, for which, owing to its lightness, strength, and imperviousness to water, it is eminently suited. Artificial flowers are made from it locally, and in addition the pith is used as a drug. For export the paper is sold in three grades, the local price varying from 1.10 yen to 2.50 yen per hundred packages. Like Taika mats it is frequently carried to China by Chinese passengers, and thus much of it does not appear in the Customs Returns. For 1899, the Customs returns show an export of 28,514 lbs. valued at 15,388 yen, Tamsui being the chief port of shipment.[1]

2.—BAMBOO.

A small bamboo found in the hills is utilized in Formosa in the manufacture of a very coarse wrapping paper. The industry is carried on at several places in Taihoku (Taipeh) and Taichu Prefectures. Of these the village of Taikochosho, which is some 6 miles distant from the railway station Kironrei (Koo-loon-nia) on the Shinchiku (Tookcham) line, is perhaps the easiest to reach from Taihoku city. The village of Hachirifunpo, which lies at the foot of South Hill (Kan on-zan) where the industry is conducted on a small scale, can be easily reached from Hobe (Tamsui). In Formosa the production is not sufficient to supply even the local demand. As a rule the work is carried on only in the vicinity of the hills where the required variety of bamboo grows in abundance, and the chief method of manufacture is as follows:—

The young branchless bamboos which are used are cut during the months of May or June, when the plant has usually attained a height of 4 or 5 feet. The bamboos are first crushed with a wooden hammer, then placed in a cemented tank some 5 feet long, 3 feet wide, and 4 feet deep. Water to cover and a quantity of lime are added, and the material is left thus to decompose for about 45 days. The stuff is now removed, washed with fresh water, and placed in a second pit, similar in size to the above, and is soaked for a further 45 days or more. The fibrous matter, now much softened, is placed in a stone mortar, which is used with a stone pestle worked by feet, like the Chinese rice-cleaning mortar. Here the fibrous material is broken up and brushed until it has separated into short filaments, and has been reduced to a pulp. The stuff is now placed on a platform and trodden by foot, until the water has been partly driven out and the pulp becomes sticky. The pulp is then removed to a third cement vat, which has been previously partly filled with clean water slowly added, and is stirred until

1. VALUE OF EXPORT OF PITH AND PITH-PAPER DURING 1899.

PLACE OF SHIPMENT.		DESTINATION.	
From Tamsui	15,640 yen	To China..	9,534 yen
From Kukang (Kiuko)..	3,352 ,,	To Hongkong	10,455 ,,
From Lokiang (Rokko) .	488 ,,		——
From Auping	456 ,,		
From all Formosa	20,495 yen		——

the mixture has attained the right consistency. The pulp is now considered ready for the final operation. For this, a screen-like implement is brought into use. This consists of a frame 2 feet 4 inches by 9 inches supporting brass wires, crosswires, and lacquered bamboo strips lengthwise, forming a fine net-work. A second frame of thin wood fits closely upon the screen, and its outside rim is extended slightly to retain the quantity of pulp required for a single sheet. A third frame holds both the above together, and, by its projecting sides, furnishes a hold for the hands during its manipulation. The complete implement is now dipped in the vat in such a way that the screen becomes covered with the pulp. The implement is lifted out horizontally and shaken a bit to distribute the pulp evenly. Most of the water drains out quickly through the netting, and the outer frame being removed, the inner frame is placed in an inclined position to drain. When the water ceases to pass off by draining, the screen is inverted, and the soft sheet is allowed to fall out upon a board arranged for that purpose. Thus the operation proceeds, the sheets being placed one on another until the pile is some three or four inches high. A second board is now superimposed, and the lot placed under a long wooden lever near its attached end. By weights placed on the free end of the lever the sheets are subjected to considerable pressure, which removes the superfluous water, and gives compactness and firmness to them. On being released from the press, the sheets are taken out, four at a time, placed in a split bamboo, and hung out in the sun to dry. If the weather is unfavorable, the sheets are kept under cover until there is an opportunity to dry them. As might be expected, this extremely crude process is very wasteful of time, and not infrequently, owing perhaps to unfavorable weather, six months is required before the whole operation is complete. Sizing, glazing, hot pressing, and other methods of improving the grade of paper are unknown to the local Chinese, and the Formosa product is a thick rough coarse straw-colored paper, abounding in partly macerated bamboo fibres, which are often so slightly incorporated with the body of the paper that they can be shaken off. The sheets measure 12 × 29 inches, and are sold for 15 yen cents a hundred.

The chief centre of this industry is Kagi, and in that city and vicinity many million pounds of the paper are produced annually, valued at some 200,000 yen. There is practically no export. As common Chinese paper valued at over 350,000 yen was imported during the year 1899, in spite of a 15 per cent. Custom's import, it would appear that there is a considerable field open for the further development of the industry. With the water power obtainable in the higher reaches of the Tamsui river, and the abundance of raw material, it would also appear that a small modern paper-mill might be a profitable venture. Excluding the fine grade of paper imported by the Japanese, the comsumption among Chinese of all grades, excluding foreign glazed paper but including the local made paper, reaches an annual value of over 650,000 yen, and appears to be increasing. Raw material is more abundant in the island than in either China or Japan, and it would be quite possible to build up an export trade.

3.—PAPER MULBERRY (" BROUSSONETIA PAPYRIFERA, VENT.")

JAPANESE : " KOZO."   CHINESE : "LOK-A-CHU."

This tree, which is found growing wild throughout the island, is described in an earlier part of this chapter as a fibre plant. In several countries including China it is used in the manufacture of paper. It is likewise utilized in Formosa, but on a very small scale, the manufacture being confined to a few small establishments in North Formosa. There is not a large local demand for the paper, but it has been found very useful as material for paper umbrellas, lanterns, etc., the only use to which it is put locally. Keibi (Kingboi), North Formosa, a few miles south of Taihoku, is interested in the industry, and the method of manufacture described below is that practised there.

The bark is obtained from the hills to the east of Chureki (Tiong-lick) and Shinchiku (Teckcham), North Formosa, where the tree appears to be most abundant. Young trees 4 or 5 years old and those grown in shaded valleys appear to yield the best material. The bark of the whole trunk, from top to bottom, is stripped off, and its rough outer skin is removed by scraping. It is then dried in the sun, separated into strips an inch or so wide, and packed up into small bundles. The paper-maker purchases the latter at from 4 to 8 yen a picul (133½ lbs.), dependent upon quality, cost of transportation, etc. Eight sheets of the paper described below can be obtained from one pound of the bark. To prepare the bark for papermaking it is first soaked in cold water for 12 or 13 hours to clean and soften it. It is now placed in a large iron pan, covered with water, to which is added some 14 lbs. of Formosa lime to every 100 lbs. of bark, and boiled for 12 hours ; this operation removing all gummy matters. (If lime is not used, the bark must be soaked for a week.) The stuff is then vigorously washed for two hours to remove the lime, this being usually performed in the shallows of the river, a close picket bamboo fence being erected to prevent the fibre strips from floating away. The material is next removed to a flat stone, and receives a strong beating for a half hour or so with two wooden mallets, the workman holding one in each hand. The long fibres readily separate under this treatment. The fibres, now thoroughly softened, are immersed in water that they may be thoroughly wetted, and then with two knives are chopped up into very small pieces, some half hour being required for this operation. The stuff is then deposited in a vat on the river bank, water is added and the mixture is stirred for 15 or 20 minutes which sees its final conversion into a thin pulp requiring no further manipulation. While the mulberry pulp forms the fibrous material for the paper, a mucilaginous substance must be added, which is obtained from the leaves and small branches of young Wikstroemia trees. In preparing the latter the leaves and twigs are first well bruised with wooden mallets and, after water has been added, are vigorously kneaded by hand. The stuff is then transferred to a basket lined with coarse jute cloth, which is fastened over the vat, and the gummy liquor is permitted to strain through, adding itself to the pulp. In forming the sheet of paper is used an appliance consisting of a bamboo frame some 4 ft. long by 3½ ft. wide with inner cross pieces, over which is stretched a coarse sheet of jute cloth. A large number of these sieve-like utensils are required, and to operate them they are taken, one at a time, to the workman at the vat. Here the sieve is placed with one side of the frame resting on a post and the near side held by the vat-man's left hand. With his right hand the pulp is ladled out of the vat, poured on to the sieve, and the latter is then given a rocking motion until the pulp is spread over evenly, the surplus water finding its way through the coarse cloth. When partly thickened, the frame is removed and set up in an inclined position to dry. If the weather is suitable the pulp dries quickly, and on sunny summer days some four batches can be made a day, but in winter only three. When dried the paper can be stripped off the frame easily. It is of a light mouse colored grey, the sheets some 3 by 3½ ft. in size, and is light in weight, resembling in this respect a medium grade tissue. It is fairly smooth and soft, but owing to the coarse method of production, contains much half macerated matter, small pieces of bark, etc. It sells in the local market at from 1.00 to 1.80 yen per hundred sheets. It is used in the manufacture of paper umbrellas, Chinese lanterns, and rain coats. In the manufacture of these articles, the paper is first painted with persimmon liquor,[1] which hardens and renders it almost impervious to water. Two or more layers glued together are generally used, and the finished product is varnished, giving a strong, water-proof article. For these purposes, the Chinese manufacturer asserts that the local paper is superior to other available papers either domestic or foreign, not even excluding the uncommonly strong Japanese paper which, owing to its comparatively low cost, is sometimes used.

4.—BROUSSONETIA KASHINOKI, SIEB?

This shrub, it is pointed out by Mr. Tashiro, is valuable for its bark, which may be used in the manufacture of paper. It resembles the true B. Kashinoki of Japan, of which it will probably be found to be a variety.

As recorded above, the locally manufactured paper from *papyrifera* is used only for covering umbrellas, and it is interesting to note that another species of *Broussonetia* is found in Formosa. Mr. Tashiro reports having often met with it growing wild in the mountains, chiefly in the savage districts of Taikokan (Tokoham), Kusshaku (Kuchu), Heirimbi (Panebe), and Bunzampo, also in Taito and Tainan districts.

5.—WIKSTROEMIA.

Two species of this plant *W. indica, C. A. Mey* (Japanese: *Amami-gampi*; Chinese: *Pu-lun*; *W. retusa, A. G.* (Japanese: *Ryukyu-gampi*) are found in the island. The former is a small shrub growing wild in the hills and plains, and frequently met with near Kelung. Dr. Henry reports that in Kwangsi it is used for making paper and paper blankets.[2]

---

1. See Article Persimmon Oil under Oil Plants.
2. Page 80 " A list of plants from Formosa " by Augustine Henry, M. A., F. L. S.

W. retusa also grows wild throughout the whole island, especially in Taihoku (Taipeh), Pachina, Bunzampo in Kelung districts, and in the vicinity of South Hill. It is most plentiful on the coral reefs of extreme South Formosa.

A very beautiful soft paper resembling French tissue has been manufactured in Tokyo from plants sent there from Formosa for experimental purposes. The shrub is also abundant in Formosa, and it is to be hoped that further experiments will be conducted to ascertain definitely the practical value of the plant, if utilized in the island for paper-making. The plant is also found in certain islands of the Loochoos, and it is said that it was at one time utilized there for paper-making.

OIL PLANTS.

1.—PEANUT or GROUNDNUT ("Arachis hypogaea, L.")

JAPANESE: "Rakkwasho."   CHINESE: "Tu-tau."

This popular plant thrives throughout the island, and the nuts obtained from it are very highly esteemed by the Chinese as an article of food, as well as for the oil and fertilizing cake which can be obtained from it. It is most extensively cultivated in the south of the island, especially in Tainan and Kagi districts. There are two varieties grown, a large nut locally known as *toapan* and a small kind known as *wanyuntao*. The small variety contains the most oil, is most pleasant to the taste, and is largely exported. In the Pescadores also, the islanders are largely engaged in Peanut cultivation, in fact, it is the chief export of these islands. After harvest, the crop is usually sold to Formosa wholesale dealers, who are as a rule in close touch with the growers. There are several oil mills in the hands of the rich farmers. In Formosa the mills are usually situated in the large cities. Rokko (Lokiang), Koro (Aulan), Tainan, Toko (Tangkang), Shinchiku (Teckcham), and Daitotei (Twatutia) are important centres for the manufacture.

The mills are unpretentious establishments, and are in the hands of numerous small capitalists who employ each perhaps half a dozen men. The methods of manufacture are interesting, however, and as with many industries which the Chinese work on a small scale thought almost impossible in Western lands, it is astonishing to find what good results they obtain.

The green groundnuts in good condition are purchased by the manufacturers from the farmers, and stored until they can be used. To avoid heating, great care is taken to have the groundnuts thoroughly dry before storing. When ready for pressing, a considerable quantity of the nuts are placed over a drying oven, the surface of which is bamboo, for 12 hours, during which they have become partially roasted. They are then removed to the crusher, which consists of a stone wheel some 5 feet in diameter and 2 feet thick, revolving around a vertical centre pole to which it is attached by its axle, which projects on one side for that purpose. From the opposite and outer end of the axle run traces, to which is attached an ox; and this animal, blindfolded, walks slowly around on the circular pathway which is divided from an inner space on which the wheel revolves, by a low stone wall. The groundnuts are stacked up on the inner stone floor, over which the heavy wheel passes, and after an hour or so are sufficiently crushed. They are then run through a bamboo sieve of small mesh, which takes out much of the shell, a large portion of which is not very finely broken up by crushing. Could the shell material be wholly extracted, a better grade of oil could be made, but the Chinese have been unable to find an economical method of accomplishing this.

The groundnut powder is now placed, some 10 catties (13⅓ lbs.) at a time, in wooden buckets possessing perforated bottoms. The buckets are placed over steam holes, are tightly covered, and made steam-tight at the base by brushing earth and ashes about them. Here they are steamed for a few minutes, becoming soft and cakey. The stuff is not removed from the steaming furnace until the workmen are prepared to form the circular cake ready for the press. The latter operation brings into use for each cake five strong iron hoops half an inch thick and 17 inches in diameter. These hoops are laid one on top of another on a wooden base-board, forming thus a circular mold. A handful of straw is now placed over it, and on this the steaming ground-nut floor is placed until the mold is heaped full. A workman treads with bare feet the stuff into the mold firmly, keeping his balance by grasping a rope which is suspended above him. When the mass is hard and well packed in, the ends of the straw, which purposely project from the side of the mold, are deftly brought over by foot and pressed down on top, strengthening and binding the surface of the cake. The two lower and the two upper iron hoops and the bottom base-board are now removed, leaving a circular cake of considerable thickness unprotected, save by the straw that has been pressed into its surface and the single small hoop which encircles its centre. The last operation is the pressing, and this is accomplished in a crude wooden apparatus which, though slow, appears to be fairly effective. The body of the press consists of a huge log some 20 feet in height by 3 feet in diameter, which has a portion of its length hollowed out to form a circular shaft conforming in diameter to that of the cakes described above. A narrow opening runs lengthwise of the log; and this, as well as the centre shaft, is well protected and strengthened by iron bands. The log lies horizontally on a strong foundation raised some 2 feet above the ground, and the bottom is slightly inclined towards one end, where an opening connects with a large earthenware jar sunk in the ground. The molded cake is carefully inserted through the side opening, and then turned upright and moved along until it rests against the lower end of the shaft. Other cakes are inserted and placed one against another until the press contains 20. A heavy steel-protected base-board is then inserted to present a firm surface at the upper end, and against this are inserted several wooden or stone blocks, until the whole length of the shaft is apparently blocked up. The thin end of a 14 foot hardwood wedge is now inserted between the wooden or stone blocks at right angles with the longitudinal opening, and driven in by a stone hammer which swings from movable bars and is operated by two men. Later, as required, a second and third wedge are introduced, and are driven in for varying distances, until the cakes are so compressed that their thickness does not exceed that of the single narrow steel hoop which encircles them. This usually requires some 3 hours, and meanwhile the oil expressed has been running down slowly into the large jar below. After the oil has ceased to run, a stone block is knocked out, relieving the strain and making it possible to take out the contents. The cakes are now very hard and firm, and can be thrown about with but little danger of breaking them. From 15 to 18 per cent. of oil in weight is obtained by this process, valued at about 16 yen a picul (133 lbs.), and the cakes, which weigh nearly 7 catties (9⅓ lbs.) each, sell at yen 2.40 a dozen.

The groundnut cake is generally valued more highly as a fertilizing agent than bean cake, and is more expensive. It is largely used for fertilizing the young rice plant prior to transplanting, and is also highly valued for use on Jute, China grass, and Tobacco fields. In preparing it for agricultural use, it is pounded up and mixed with earth.

Formosa ground-nut cakes have been an important export from the island for a century or so. The present export of the nut and its products reaches in value to nearly 200,000 yen yearly. This is but a very small portion of the total production, however, as the products mentioned have a very large local sale.[1]

SESAME ("Sesamum indicum, L.")

JAPANESE : "Goma."   CHINESE : "Mua."

This very useful plant is extensively cultivated in South Formosa, and the seeds obtained from it have been one of the island's exports from the earliest days of foreign trade. It is grown to some extent throughout Formosa, the light sandy soil of which it appears to find specially congenial. Among the Chinese it is almost a household necessity. The oil extracted from the seed is highly valued for cooking purposes, and is also put to other uses. Both white and black seeded varieties are found in Formosa yielding white and black oils, the former being the most expensive. But little of the white oil is made locally, however, the black oil receiving the chief attention of local manufacturers.

The method of extraction is very simple. After the seeds have been well roasted in a large iron pan they are reduced to meal in the Chinese stone mortar ordinarily used for cleaning rice. The meal is then steamed until moist and cakey, and while still warm is placed in small jute bags which, after being supported by circular iron bands, are inserted in a vertical press similar in model to that used for expressing ground-nut oil, as described

---

1. The Customs returns give the export of Ground-nuts and Ground-nut products for 1898 as follows :—

Ground-nuts	..	..	..	8,402 piculs valued at 36,735 yen.
Ground-nut cakes	..	..	9,213 piculs valued at 140,957 „
Total	..	..	..	..	..	177,692 yen.

In addition to the above there is a small export of ground-nut oil.

above, though somewhat smaller. The product obtained is an oil and refuse meal in the form of circular cakes.

The savages near Pinam (South-eastern Formosa) understand the cultivation of this plant thoroughly, and have introduced it throughout Taito (Taitong) sub-prefecture. The Pepohoans are likewise engaged in its cultivation. Most of the Sesamum oil produced in Taito is used locally, but it is occasionally transported by water to the neighboring coast towns.

Sesamum is an annual. It is planted generally in May, and harvested in late September or October. In Formosa it reaches a height of some 4½ to 5 feet, and occasional plants are seen exceeding 5½ feet.

The Formosa seed is largely exported to China, and thence to France where the oil is extracted and used as an adulterant for olive oil. Some of the Formosa white seed is shipped to Foochow, where there are several native establishments devoted to the manufacture of the white oil.[1]

The best grade black sesamum seed will give nearly 5 % of oil, but the average seed runs a little below 4 %. The seed costs the oil maker from 6.00 yen upwards a picul (133 lbs.), and the black oil brings on the local market about 26 to 29 yen a picul, while the refuse meal cake realises 1.15 to 1.25 yen a picul. The meal cakes are specially valued as a fertilizer for young rice plants prior to transplantation.

4.—SOJA BEAN ("GLYCINE HISPIDA, MAX.")

JAPANESE: "DAIDSU."   CHINESE: "TAU."

There are several varieties of this plant grown in Formosa. One known as the "Yellow Bean" is very largely cultivated in the south of the island. The Soja Bean produces not only a very useful oil, but the refuse, known as "Bean Cake," is one of the most valuable of fertilizers used by the Chinese and a very important article of commerce throughout China. During the administration of the Chinese Governor Liu Ming Chan, the manufacture of the oil and cake was introduced in the island and given an extensive trial. The Chinese found it more profitable, however, to purchase the comparatively cheap imported cake, or the local ground-nut cake, and devote their time to other works, and consequently the industry was soon abandoned, and the writer cannot learn now of a single mill in Formosa manufacturing Bean Cake.[2]

5.—PERSIMMON ("DIOSPYROS KAKI, L.F."?)

JAPANESE: "KAKI."   CHINESE: "MOA."

A wild persimmon found in the hills of North Formosa, which appears to be D. Kaki, is valued by the Chinese for the highly astringent juice which is obtained from the fruit, and which is applied to paper, especially that made

---

1. The Customs Returns give the export of Sesamum seeds for the year 1898 as 26,703 piculs valued at 115,999 yen.

2. Bean cake to the value of 26,241 yen was imported into Formosa during the year 1898.

from the Paper mulberry (Broussonetia papyrifera), for the purpose of rendering the latter firm and durable and impervious to water. This paper thus prepared is used at Keibi (Kingbe) and other places in North Formosa as a covering for Chinese umbrellas, it being considered superior to any other paper available for the purpose.[1]

6.—TALLOW TREE ("STILLINGIA SEBIFERA, S. & N.")

JAPANESE : "TAHAZE."   CHINESE : "KIN-A-CHU."

This large and handsome tree is highly valued in China for the tallow and oil obtained from its seeds. This plant is found growing wild throughout the island, but only in a few places do the local people make use of it. In North Formosa, Kaizanko (Haisankau), and across the river from Kantau, the tree is specially abundant. At these two places the Chinese gather the seeds in considerable quantities. The tallow is found surrounding the berry, and is easily obtained by pounding and pressing. It is chiefly used in the manufacture of candles. An oil is also obtained from the kernel, likewise by pressing.

There is still a considerable import of material for candles, there being a large demand for a small candle used in religious ceremonies. There is a likelihood, therefore, that the sources of supply here will in time be more fully availed of.

7.—CASTOR OIL PLANT ("RICINUS COMMUNIS, L.")

JAPANESE : "TOGOMA."   CHINESE : "GA-POR-LO."

The Castor Oil Plant is another source of production yet undeveloped. The tree is found in a wild state throughout the plains of Formosa, and though it is widely cultivated in China for the valuable oil obtained from the seeds, no use whatsoever is made of the plant here. In addition to the medical value of the oil, it is used in cooking, and the juice of the leaves is taken internally by many females to increase their flow of milk, while in India it is frequently fed to cows for the same purpose. The leaves are valuable as a healing agent when applied externally to wounds and bruises, and the oil cake remaining after the oil has been extracted is a very superior fertilizer.

8.—RAPE OIL PLANT ("BRASSICA CHINENSIS, L.")

JAPANESE : "NATANE."   CHINESE : "TO-AH-TSAI."

This plant of the cabbage family is grown in Formosa chiefly as an edible vegetable. From its seeds are extracted an oil used by the Chinese for lighting purposes. While the industry is one of considerable importance in China, in Formosa, with the exception of a few families in Lokiang (Rokko) and Shimpu (Shimpo) who extract the oil on a very small scale only sufficient for their own domestic use, it is not manufactured. The oil is imported into the island from Wenchow, and is used locally as an adulterant for Sesamum oil.

---

1. See No. 3 under Paper Plants, pp. 545-6.

9.—"ELAEOCOCCA (ALEURITES) CORDATA, STEUD."

JAPANESE : "ABURA GIRI."   CHINESE : "TUNG-TZE-SHU."

This tree, locally known as the wood oil tree, is reported from both . North and South Formosa, and though not abundant is found in considerable numbers in the mountainous district near Taichu. The tree appears to grow well here, but no commercial use is made of it. In China, the oil expressed from the nuts of the *Elaeococca* is well known and is said to be the cheapest for lighting purposes. The oil is also employed as varnish and, when placed on fibre, for caulking ships.

10.—"JATROPHA CURCAS, L."

JAPANESE : "TAIWAN-YUTO."   CHINESE : "TUNG-YU-SHU."

This emphorbiaceous tree of American origin is reported by Dr. Henry as naturalized in South Formosa. The tree, which is small in stature, bears seeds from which an oil can be expressed, but no use of the plant is made here. In Hainam and Canton Province the oil is used for lighting purposes.

11.—"PERILLA OCYMOIDES, L."

JAPANESE : "NORA-E."

This representative of the mint family is found in Formosa, and from its seeds an oil of commercial value is extracted in China. It is not utilized in Formosa.

SOAP PLANTS.

SOAP TREE ("SAPINDUS MUKOROSSI, GAERTN."

JAPANESE : "MUKUROZI."   CHINESE : "HUANG MU-SHU."

This tree, which reaches a considerable size in the interior, is found throughout the island. The fruit, which is of a sapinaceous nature, is used by the Chinese and by the savages in the border districts as a substitute for soap. There is a growing demand abroad for this product known as "Saponin," which up to the present has been chiefly supplied by India. When the Formosa forests are freely opened it is quite possible that soap-trees may be found in sufficient number to make the export of the fruit a profitable venture. At present the production is slight, and only supplies the poorer up-country classes, who often personally gather the fruit sufficient for their own wants, or barter for their supplies some trifling object with the border peasants.

Gleditschia sp. a plant found in South Formosa, likewise supplies a soap-pod which can be put to the same use as the Sapindus.

Tea cake, the refuse material from tea seeds after the oil has been extracted, appears to be in almost universal use in the north as a saponaceous material for washing clothes. It is not a local product, however, being imported from China.

MISCELLANEOUS PLANTS.

TOBACCO.

Of all the products described above there is none with a future more bright than that of Tobacco. Large districts throughout the island possess the soil and climatic conditions favorable to the growth of Tobacco, and when the excessively high import duties are considered, it would appear that the local grower is offered a large premium over his China competitors in supplying the island's requirements. Furthermore, there are several varieties of the plant much in favor in Japan, which require for successful growth a warmer climate than the Japanese mainland affords. There is no reason why these kinds should not in time be supplied by Formosa. The Formosa Chinese have hitherto obtained most of their Tobacco from China. In the Formosa hill districts of Taichu, Kusshaku (Kuchu), and Wantan, and along the line of hills between Kelung and Gilan, Chinese have been engaged in the cultivation in a small way, but as the production of Tea and Camphor has in the past proved more profitable, Tobacco planting has not been much attended to. Consequently, the plants received but little care, and the leaf produced was naturally of inferior quality. The local Chinese government brought Manila seeds to the island, and endeavored to interest the hill planters; but with little success.

If the Chinese have neglected the cultivation, the savages can not be accused of similar remissness. Opposed as the savages are to general agricultural labor, they all exhibit a willingness to engage to some extent in the cultivation of tobacco. The northern tribes grow only sufficient for their own consumption, but the savages in Kagi, Arisan, Taito (Taitong), and Koshun (Heng-chun) districts supply not only their own wants but raise a quantity for barter with the Chinese. Mr. Tashiro reports that the plants in the savage districts generally appear to thrive well, and the leaves are large and attractive; but owing to the ignorance of the savages in curing and preparing the leaf, the resulting product is inferior. Of all the tribes, the 18 villages of Koshun (Heng-chun) produce the best tobacco. The leaf is rolled up in the form of a club, and is very tightly wrapped round with rattan and Broussonetia and other pliable wood barks weighing altogether from 7 to 13 lbs. The flavor of this tobacco is said to be not unlike that of the Manila leaf. The high mountain savages of Shinkaiyen (Shinkuihng) district of Taito-cho roll up their tobacco in the shape of a large radish about a pound in weight. The savages of Bokusekikaku in Taito-cho, Karenko (Hoshingkang) on the east coast, and the half civilized Pepohoans of Gilan make up their tobacco into the form of cheroots. These are intended primarily for their own consumption, but some is sold, it being possible to purchase a very fair grade article for some 40 yen cents a hundred. The writer has had some of these cheroots tested by foreign smokers, who have reported that, while lacking in attractive flavor, they are not inferior in any respect to the cheap cigars sold in Hongkong and other places. Men, women, and children among the savages smoke; and as they use only their own leaf, the total production in the savage districts must be considerable. It is lamentable that these wild people can not be induced to forego the existing occupation of hunting heads in order to devote their energy to the agricultural development of their hill lands. With tobacco alone, if grown and prepared according to modern methods, they could earn sufficient for their few wants.

Under the energetic control of Chief Yokoyama, the Agricultural Section of the Taihoku (Taipeh prefecture has given much attention to Tobacco. In the experimental garden attached to the Section, 3 varieties of Japanese and 5 varieties of American tobacco have been grown, and while the garden is not located in a district exactly suited to Tobacco, Mr. Yokoyama reports that of a great number of various economical plants grown there, Tobacco appears to give the best results. The small area under cultivation yielded leaf at the average rate of 1,200 lbs. an acre, valued from 160 to 200 yen. The two Japanese varieties were the most successful, and the best result was obtained with the crop which was planted in January and harvested in April. Seed is being obtained from the United States, and an attempt will be made to grow light colored leaf, so much in demand in Japan for the manufacture of cigarettes.

The yearly import of Chinese tobacco averaged in value during the years 1896 to 1898, 900,000 yen. In 1899, under very heavy duties, it fell to 480,000 yen. A large stock was imported in 1898, in anticipation of the increased duty ; and this, together with the considerable quantity smuggled into the island by native craft, would probably bring the consumption of Chinese tobacco during 1899 up to some 800,000 yen in value. At all events the amount may be safely taken as the average yearly demand under normal conditions for Chinese tobacco. Much of this will pay a duty of 40 per cent., and if this does not have a stimulating effect on Formosa planters there is but little hope for them. In addition to the above, over a half million yen worth of cut tobacco and cigarettes are imported yearly from Japan.

1.—COFFEE.

Some 12 years ago, a compradore of Messrs. Tait & Co., of Daitotei, supplied some young Coffee plants and seeds, which had been obtained from San Francisco, to a Tea planter in the vicinity of Sankakuyu (San-kak eng). A coffee plantation was set out, but soon after work had been commenced, a raid by savages was made on the place, and the enterprise was consequently abandoned. A few of the plants, however, had been set out near Pankyu ; and two brothers, Yu-ah-sung and Yu-ah-ku, undertook to grow the bean. The Chinese were not familiar, however, with the cultivation of coffee. The trees were grown in the open without the shelter they required, and the result was accordingly not satisfactory. One plantation was given up, but a second small field is still under coffee, a few hundred trees being at present found there. Since the arrival of the Japanese, interest has been awakened in the cultivation, and more trees are being set out in the Pankyu district, under conditions more favorable to success. There is much rich hill land in Formosa that might be devoted to coffee, and while owing to over production, the bean is not at present considered in other countries a very profitable crop, still there is sufficient demand in Japan alone, where coffee is finding increasing favor, to make a few thousand trees a paying venture, and should the Formosa bean be found to be of superior quality, there is a possibility of a larger market abroad.

2.—COCOANUT PALM.

The Cocoanut Palm flourishes in the island of Botel Tobago—a dependency of Formosa. Doubtless its cultivation could be greatly extended, Samasama island, also a Formosa dependency, and South Formosa offering attractive fields. This plant supplies the very primitive savages of Botel Tobago with cloth, rope, and food. The fresh nuts command a rather high price in China and Japan markets, and the foreign demand for Copra (the dried nut) is steadily increasing, being at present worth from 140 to 150 yen a ton. Copra is valuable for the oil (about 70 per cent.) which can be expressed from it. The refuse is made into cattle food, valued in foreign countries at some 70 yen per ton. There is also a demand for the fibre obtained from the husk, which is used for manufacturing ropes and matting.

3.—TAPIOCA PLANT ("Manihot Aipi, Pohl.")

From the long roots of this small shrub is obtained the well known food Tapioca. In Bokusekikaku district, south-east Formosa, the plant is widely cultivated, and the natives there understand the extraction from it of starch. The plant has also been seen in the Gilan district, at Horisha (Polisha), and at Maruyama near Taihoku (Taipeh). Mr. Tashiro notes that in Hawaii the yield per acre is worth some 172 dollars, and as the plant grows very luxuriantly in Formosa, he believes that its general cultivation in the island could be undertaken with profit.

4.—"Cinnamomum Cassia, Bl."

This tree is met with in the mountains throughout the island, and the bark is valued highly as a spice and medicine. Though not as fragrant as the real cinnamon, with which it has often been confused, it is a very good substitute, and is in fact often disposed of as cinnamon. Attempts have been made by foreigners (notably John Dodd) and others to add it to the island's exports, but as the tree was met with only in the mountains and was not specially abundant, and the cost of collection and transportation to the coast was very expensive, it was not found to be a profitable venture. The Chinese camphormen gather the bark in small quantities for domestic use, but I can learn of no Chinese undertaking its collection as a special business.

5.—"Blumea balsamifera, D.C."

This plant is found on the west coast and in South Formosa, but is not utilized. Dr. Henry writes " A peculiar kind of camphor of great value in the eyes of the Chinese is distilled in Hainan from the leaves of Blumea balsamifera, a shrubby plant about 2 or 3 feet in height, belonging to *Compositae*. This may be distinguished as Ai Camphor from the Chinese name of the product:—*ai fên* the crude state: *ai p'ien*, the purified form. The plant does not occur in the Chinese mainland; but is common enough in India, Burmah, and Formosa. The plant is worthy of attention from a commercial point of view."

6.—" CAJANUS INDICUS, SPR."

This plant, known as the "tree bean," is largely cultivated by the savages, especially the Ami, Tsalisen, and Pinam tribes. The bean like seeds obtained from it form an important part of their daily food. In Taichu, Tainan, and Hozan (Hengchun) districts it is cultivated by the Chinese, who grind the seeds into flour which they use in making cakes. Although a perennial, the plant becoming a tall shrub if left alone, both the savages and the Chinese replant yearly, cutting down the bush after each harvest and utilizing it as firewood.

7.—" FICUS PUMILA, L."

This vine is found in the savage territory of Kagi district and in the South Formosa hill district. It yields a fruit much valued by the Chinese for a jelly-like substance which is obtained by soaking the dried fruit in water, and, when softened, pressing by hand, thus forming out a viscous fluid which soon hardens; and, with the addition of a little sugar, is a favorite dish among Chinese.

8.—" ARECA CATECHU, L."

This handsome palm yields the well known Areca nut (frequently called "Betel nut,") which, with the addition of lime and the leaf of the Betel pepper, is a favorite chewing mixture in India and other countries. The South Formosa native is much addicted to its use. In Tainanfu, and also to some extent in Kagi and Shoka (Changwha), the leaf is utilized in the manufacture of a very unique fan.

Among other Formosa Plants, the following is a partial list of those valued by the Chinese for their medical qualities. Some are exported on a small scale, others while utilized in China, are not sufficiently abundant here to attract the attention of local drug merchants, and a few are known to the foreign medical world.[1]

1.	*Achyranthes aspera, L.*	13.	*Gymnema affine, Decne.*
2.	*Amarantus spinosus, L.*	14.	*Limacia sp.*
3.	*Aristolochia sp.*	15.	*Lysimachia sp.*
4.	*Atalantia buxifolia, Oliver.*	16.	*Lycium chinense, Miller.*
5.	*Alpinia galang, Saw.*	17.	*Pueraria Thunbergiava, Benth.*
6.	*Bombax malabaricum, D. C.*	18.	*Rhus semi alata, Murr.*
7.	*Breynia officinalis, Hemsley.*	19.	*Salaginella involvens, Spreng.*
8.	*Datura alba, Nees.*	20.	*Sterculia platanifolia, Linn.*
9.	*Dendrobium (two species.)*	21.	*Wikstroemia indica, C. A. Mey.*
10.	*Euphorbia pilulifera, L.*	22.	*Tribulus terrestris, L.*
11.	*Eupatorium japonicum, Thumb.*	23.	*Zingiber officinale, Rosc.*
12.	*Gnaphalium multiceps, Wall.*	24.	*Aloe chinensis, Baker.*

1. The list of medical plants is largely compiled from Dr. Henry's " A List of Plants from Formosa."

AGRICULTURE.

A description of the economical botany of Formosa would not be complete without reference to the several agricultural stations established in the island by the Japanese Government. I will confine my remarks here to the Agricultural Section of Taihoku (Taipeh) Prefecture, which I am most familiar with, though the station at Tainan is also doing much valuable work.

The Taihoku station is under the control of S. Yokoyama, a very intelligent, capable official. The mission of this department is to introduce to the island new plants of economic value and to improve the existing methods of cultivation. The Chinese, above all races, are not friendly to innovation. While other lands under intelligent rule find certain new plants add greatly to their prosperity, Formosa has for years remained content with its lot, and, with the exception of Tea, the practical introduction of which must be credited to foreigners, there is not on record a single attempt to add a new agricultural plant to the island. Furthermore, the methods of cultivation and the farming appliances are frequently crude and wasteful. For instance, actual field experiments with the foreign iron sugar-mill opposed to the native stone mill, the machine decortication of fibre plants opposed to native hand work, have given results so much in favor of the foreign methods, that the actual cash gains have been sufficient in some cases to pay the cost of the new appliances in a single season. It is the endeavor of this Department to demonstrate to the Chinese by actual work in the fields that there are new plants which can be profitably introduced to the islands, that admirable as the Chinese system of farming is, there is still much that they can learn as regards selection of seeds, fertilizing agents, use of modern agricultural implements, etc., etc. Blooded cattle and pigs have also been brought to the island in hopes of improving the local breed. The following plants, the majority of which are either entirely new to the island or are at least new species or varieties, are now under cultivation at the station; and that the test may be comprehensive, many varieties of each plant are grown; and under different soils, and with the assistance of different fertilizing agents:

Common and mountain Rice, Wheat, Barley, Oats, Rye, Millet, Teosinte Clover, Timothy, Orchard Grass, Red-tops, Beans, Sweet Potatoes, Indigo, Tobacco, Cotton, Coffee, Mulberry Trees, Tapioca Plants, Mountain Banana, Jute, China Grass, Sisal Hemp, Bowstring Hemp, Mauritius Hemp, Oranges, Persimmons, Figs, Grapes, Pine Apples, edible and fibre Bananas, and Sugar-Canes. So far the most notable successes have been with the following:— The Lahaina and Rose Bamboo varieties of Hawaian Sugar-cane yielded per acre in cane nearly double that of the local cane, while 8 per cent. of a superior sugar was obtained, against 4 to 5 per cent. from the local cane. As a result, the local Chinese planters in the vicinity are putting in these varieties. Japanese and American tobacco has done well, specially the Kokubu and Ibusuki varieties of the former; and their growth should be found profitable for local planters. Chinese in the vicinity of Keibi (King-boi) and Sintiam are putting in these kinds, and contracts have already been made for the produce.

The Natal (S. America) variety of indigo (I. tinctoria) grows magnificently, attaining a height of from 8 to 9 feet. The yield per acre is greater than that of the local plant, and more indigo of a better quality is obtained from the plant. Cotton has done fairly well; Teosinte thrives; but other fodder plants are only fair. Several new varieties of Beans and Sweet Potatoes show good results, the Mulberry Tree, Coffee, and the fruit trees are growing nicely, while American grapes of very good quality have been obtained. Among the stock are Ayrshire and Holstein cattle, Berkshire swine, and Andalusian chickens, which all appear to find the climate congenial.

FORESTS.

There is a large area in Formosa covered with virgin forests, and Timber-trees of great value abound. The chief of these, Camphor wood, has already been described, and the subject of forest trees is such a vast one and as yet so little is really known about the interior districts, that I will not attempt to deal with it in detail. I would mention, however, that among the Formosa woods which are at present utilized by the Chinese the following are considered of greatest value :—

		JAPANESE NAME.	CHINESE NAME.
1.	Machilus Thunbergii	Yabu-kusu	Lama
2.	Quercus sp.	Ichii-gashi	Cha-ko or chapi
3.	Pasania cuspidata	Shii	Tsui-ko
4.	Quercus sp.	Kashi	Ko-san
5.	Michelia champaca	Ogatama	Oshimcho
6.	Liquidambar formosana	Fu	Pung-a
7.	Melia Azedarach	Sendau	Ko-leu
8.	Bischoffia javanica	Akagi	Katan
9.	Thuya Formosana	———	Sho-lam
10.	Pinus sp.	Matsu	Cheug-pe
11.	Cryptomeria ?	Taiwan-sugi	Sam
12.	Cunninghamia sinensis	Koyosau	Chong-sam
13.	Podocarpus nageia	Nagi	Soau-sam
14.	Cinnamomum camphora	Kusu	Chiung
15.	Abies ?		Yu-sam
16.	Ulmus sp. (a)	Akinire ?	Ke-yu
17.	Zelkowa ? (b)	Taiwan-keyaki	Ke-yu
18.	Trema orientalis	Uraziro-muku	Soau-moa
19.	Lagerstroemia subcostata	Saru-suberi	Kiu-kiong
20.	Ficus retusa	Gadsu-maru	Cheng
21.	Ficus sp.	Inubiwa	
22.	Alnus sp.	Han-noki	Tsui-lau-koa
23.	Acacia Richii		Sau-sui
24.	Murraya exotica	Gets-kitsu (Loochoo)	Cho-liu

Unfortunately, with the exception of some comparatively small districts, there is but little immediate prospect of extensive development of these great resources. The Formosa trees of value are of hard wood varieties, the transportation of which is difficult and expensive. The mountains are steep, the savages are a constantly disturbing factor, and with but two or three exceptions there are no streams of sufficient depth to float full-sized logs. There are some few trees of value remaining on the border hills, which may supply a very limited local demand for a few years. At present it would appear most practical to replant the foot hills with timber trees. The Central Agricultural Department is convinced of the feasibility of this; and a wealthy Japanese planter has already invested considerable capital in the

Mount Morrison (Nitakayama). The Highest
Mountain in the Japanese Empire.

The Summit of Mount Morrison.

Half-way up Mount Morrison.

Jungle at the Base of Mount Morrison.

Kusshaku (Kuchu) district, with the intention of introducing the Japanese fir tree. When the railway line through the island is completed, it may be found possible to put out a few branch lines to the east. These, with the addition of tram lines into the hills, may make it possible to open up the interior forest district without financial loss, but there is at present no indication of such extensive enterprises being instituted.

Mention should be made, however, of the few districts which have received the attention of Japanese. The lower slopes of Mount Morrison (Niitaka-yama), covering several miles in area, are covered with valuable trees, and there are two streams which would afford, it is believed, a fairly effective means of transportation to the coast. Also a magnificent forest has been found in the Arisan range of mountains to the east of Kagi. A gov-ernment expert inspected the district and found a spacious valley called Hampokuku to be densely wooded with valuable trees, such as the *Chamaecyparis obtusa* and *C. pisifera*, the Japanese cedar (*Cryptomeria Japonica),* and *Pinus sp.* running from a foot to even 5 feet in diameter. Two streams, the Sobunkei (Tsan bun) and Seisuikei lead down into the plains, and the railway company have made arrangements to obtain a portion of their supplies from this district.

The Formosa government has already accomplished much in afforesta-tion, and with the idea of inducing the Chinese to plant trees in the plains a subsidy of 3.8 yen cents is offered by the Taihoku prefecture for each dozen of young trees set out, subject to conditions which provide that the trees shall not be cut down within 10 years without consent of the Prefect, and that young trees which die or have been accidentally destroyed, shall be replanted within 3 years. Planters possessing the most successful groves will be rewarded with a sum not exceeding 50 yen. Some 10,000 trees have been distributed by the Formosa Government. Forest Regulations have been issued to provide against the indiscriminating destruction of the existing forests and to afford protection to the young trees.

CHAPTER XXX.

THE INHABITANTS OF FORMOSA.

Arrival of Chinese and Japanese pirates—Hakka immigrants—Dutch occupation—
Chinese population prior to Japanese occupation—Three ethnological divisions.

Savage Population :—Mr. Ino's researches—Condition of savages prior to arrival of
Dutch—During Chinese occupation—Their origin—Their arrival—Eight savage
groups—Driven into the Hills—Pepohoans in early days—Ruins of a prosperous
State—Population statistics of various groups—Boundaries, Dwellings, Dress,
Ornaments, Tattooing, Marriage, Diseases, Burial, Head hunting, Religion, and
traditions of Atayal, Vonum, Tsou, Tsalisen, Paiwan, Puyuma, Ami, and Pepo
groups—Social state of above groups—Advancement along certain lines—
Domestic relationship—Restrictions among relatives—Rank of adult—Morality
—Social organization—Tribal government—Views regarding crime—Punishment
of offences—Savages of First Botel Tobago expedition—Origin of islanders—
Physical characteristics—Malayan and Papuan types—Their manners and
customs—Native boats—Fishing—Pottery making—Cultivation—Dwellings—
Garments—Ornaments—Food—Disease—Religion—Traditions—Plague of rats
—Miscellaneous notes.

Chinese Population :—Political divisions—Ethnical groups—Hakkas—Hoklos—Dis-
tinguishing features—Hakka's rough life—Hakka traders—Four Hoklo groups
—Distribution of same—Chinese life in Formosa and in China compared—
Their characteristics briefly reviewed.

Japanese Population :—First arrivals—Family life—Evolution of a Chinese house—
First habitations—Insanitary quarters—Large mortality—Construction of dormi-
tories—Mainland impressions—Improved conditions—Reconstruction of Taihoku
—A Japanese city—Its streets, buildings, and shops—Interior towns—Population
according to sex—Rapid increase in population—Employment of Japanese—
Difficulty of competition with Chinese—Village life.

COMPARED with the neighboring lands, China on the west and Japan on
the north, Formosa gained her industrial population at a comparatively
late day. This island has, however, been inhabited by savage peoples, the
so-called "aborigines," from the earliest days of which we possess authentic

record. Chinese and Japanese pirates made the island their headquarters during the latter part of the 15th century ; and following them came the first agriculturalists, the Hakkas. These people, practically outcasts in their own land, found the island much to their liking and immigrated in large numbers, forming the nucleus of the present Chinese population. The Dutch, numbering at the height of their influence over 2,000 in all, occupied a part of the island from 1624 to 1662. The Chinese population on the arrival of the Dutch numbered about 25,000, but the invasion of the Tartars induced many thousands more of Ming loyalists to emigrate to Formosa. The number of the Chinese population at the close of the Dutch occupation is indefinitely stated as many tens of thousands. Under Koxinga's rule which followed, Chinese, chiefly from Fokien province, flocked to the island in large numbers, the savages retiring before them towards the mountainous interior districts. In 1683, the Imperial Chinese Government obtained control, retaining the island until 1895, when it was ceded to Japan. During the Chinese regime immigration was encouraged, and thousands came yearly from the neighboring province of Fokien, until, in the middle of the 18th century, the population was over a million. Luchow, the famous Chinese statesman, computed the population to be 2,000,000 ; but taking into consideration the large increase which followed and the present population, it would appear that this estimate must have been a great exaggeration. Meanwhile, the savages had been gradually driven back into the hills, and the Chinese became the sole occupants of the plains. Immediately prior to the arrival of the Japanese, the Chinese population was generally stated as between two and three millions, and the savage population from 200,000 upwards. During the military troubles which followed the Japanese occupation, several thousands of Chinese left the island. Doubtless, however, this number did not exceed two or three hundred thousand, including soldiers and official employes.

The arrival of the Japanese added a third element to the population, making, at the present day, three broad divisions, savages (aborigines), Chinese, and Japanese, whom we will consider in the order named.

The account of the Formosa Savages which follows has been almost wholly constructed from new material kindly offered by an official friend, Mr. Y. Ino, for this work. Mr. Ino has devoted several years to the study of the Formosan Savages, has carried on investigations among every group, and to-day is, without doubt, the foremost authority on these wild people. With the exception of a very able essay by Mr. Taylor dealing with the South Formosa tribes, prior to the arrival of the Japanese, no valuable paper had been published regarding the island's savage population. The accounts of foreign travellers who have spent a day in the savage district, and who on their return to civilization have written descriptions of their journeys did not afford us much information regarding the inhabitants. With the single exception of Mr. Holst, a collector who confined his researches to South Formosa, no foreigner has made an extended stay in the savage territory, or has visited the east coast hill tribes. The Japanese, however, have crossed from east to west in several places, have spent months in close contact with the savages, and have carried on systematic investigations among their various groups from north to south continuously during the five years of their occupation. It is consequently to the Japanese that we must look for the most complete information regarding the savages, and to the Japanese friend above mentioned I must extend thanks for the opportunity afforded of presenting the first account placed before English readers of the savages of the whole island.

Prior to the arrival of the Dutch and Chinese, the savage tribes, or so-called aborigines, were spread over the whole island. Along the large fertile plain which forms the western half of the island, they were found everywhere. The Paiwan group, which retired before the advance of invaders to the mountainous region of the south and to one small part of the plain in the extreme south, occupied in the early days a large tract of land in the south-western part of the island. It is possible that the name of this tribe suggested to the first Chinese the name " Taiwan," which was later adopted for the whole island. The fact that the savages, in these early days, ·prospered and were at one time strong and powerful has been handed down to us by Chinese historians. One ancient Chinese geographer writes: " Their abodes, scattered everywhere, covered an area as large as a thousand *li*. The number of the tribes was very great; each of them forming a band consisting of five or six hundred or a thousand people. Each tribe had over it a chief whose command was absolute. They were a courageous people and gloried in warfare." Again from historical accounts of the Dutch we learn that there were two hundred and ninety-three tribes in the comparatively limited sphere of the foreigner's influence. From these and other writings we may safely infer that the tribes throughout the island were very numerous in early days.

Little is known as to the origin of these savage peoples. We may safely assume, however, that Formosa has been the home of some groups for at least two thousand years. Chinese historians report that, on the arrival of the first Chinese in the island (in 608 A. D.), they found different tribes existing, whose language was quite foreign to them. We also learn that they were of Malayan or Polynesian origin, their short stature, their yellowish brown color, their straight black hair and other physical characteristics, as well as their customs and language, bear sufficiently strong resemblance to the natives of the South Seas to confirm this. It seems also that these tribes did not all arrive in the island at the same time, or land at the same place, some trace their Formosa ancestors to a more ancient date than others ; some landed on the western coast, others on the eastern coast ; some established themselves in the south, others in the north. Though occupying limited areas, we find a more or less wide distinction between the tribes of one district and those of another. This distinction extends not only to dress, habits, and customs, but even to language ; there being in several instances groups of savages whose language is unintelligible to a second group. Taking note of these differences, recent investigations show that the savages of the island come under eight divisions. As many tribes, some showing minor charac-

Savage Head-Hunters of Formosa.

A GROUP OF NORTH FORMOSAN HILL SAVAGES. (MEN AND WOMEN.)

MALE TYPE OF NORTH FORMOSAN HILL SAVAGE, SHOWING THE TATTOOING ON FACE AND BREAST.

FEMALE TYPE OF NORTH FORMOSAN HILL SAVAGE, SHOWING THE TATTOOING ON FACE.

teristics peculiar to them, comprise a division, we will use the term group. The savages of the island may be classified as follows :—

1st.—Atayal group.	5th.—Paiwan group.
2nd.—Vonum group.	6th.—Puyuma group.
3rd.—Tsou group.	7th.—Ami group.
4th.—Tsalisen group.	8th.—Pepo group.

Of the above, the Pepo (Pepohoan), Puyuma, and Ami groups are known to the Japanese as " Jukuban " or domesticated savages. The Pepo live in the western plain, and the Puyuma and Ami groups in the eastern plain. The savages of these three groups have been despoiled of the greater part of their lands by the Chinese. Influenced by the superior strength and intelligence of the new comers they have abandoned many of their original customs, some of them even their language, and have adopted the customs and speech of the Chinese. It is this abandonment of ancient customs that has brought to them the designation of "domesticated savages." The other groups dwell in the central mountain range, some occupying districts of five or six thousand feet elevation. The traditions of all, however, agree that they did not occupy the rough mountainous districts prior to the arrival of the strangers. Then in undisputed possession, the vast and fertile plain of the western half was their home land, and here they enjoyed a life of ease and plenty. It was their defeat in the struggle for supremacy with the immigrants that drove them into the mountains.

The Pepo alone remained to compete with the strangers with a cruel result only too apparent; the Chinese proved the fittest and survived, while the savages decreased year after year in numbers and in influence, until now the population of the Pepo group is but one tenth of what it was a century ago, and is in a poor and miserable condition. Notwithstanding this, they at one time formed a prosperous and powerful state; occupying the most fertile districts of the extreme western plain, and possessing a geographical advantage over the other savages of the island. They even constructed boats and feeble rafts of timber with which they crossed the dangerous Formosa Channel, undertaking expeditions to other lands. Not only did some of the Pepo group invade the southern coast of China, but they crossed the Bashee Channel to the south, maintaining communication with Luzon island. These facts are known from their own traditions and from the works of Chinese historians. They seem to have reached the height of their influence during the twelfth and thirteenth centuries. It was only one hundred years ago, after they met defeat in their struggle for existence, that their prosperity was transferred to their opponents ; and, by the assimilating power of Chinese civilization and the oppression of the Chinese authorities, they retained but a minute portion of their former domains.

The other groups, unlike the once powerful Pepo, retired on the approach of strangers to the hill regions, where from the natural inhospitality of their position they were able to avoid the struggle for existence with the foreign people ; and as they have retained their warlike and primitive nature, they have been practically successful in preserving their original independence and status. Recent investigation shows the population of the Formosa savages, excluding the Pepohoans, to be as follows :—

Name of Group.	Number of Tribes.	Number of Houses.	Population.
Atayal - - - -	197	5,567	23,460
Vonum - - - -	144	2,072	16,610
Tsou - - - -	39	331	2,961
Tsalisen - - -	105	5,572	27,860
Paiwan - - - -	110	3,021	15,982
Puyuma - - - -	8	1,314	4,891
Ami - - - - -	84	3,183	21,775
Total - - -	687	21,060	113,539

The land occupied by these savage groups is about 7,500 square miles in area, or about one half the entire surface of the island.[1]

THE ATAYAL GROUP.

The Atayal group spreads itself over the mountainous region of the northern half of the island, or northward of a line drawn from east to west across the central mountain, and passing through Horisha (Polisia) ; and adjoins the territory of the Vonum group on the south. With the higher peaks of the middle range intersecting their land, this group may be divided into West Atayals and East Atayals, and these two sub-groups show some slight characteristics peculiar to each.

Dwellings.—The Atayals have their dwellings on the slopes of steep mountains. The West Atayals form several tribes, widely scattered, especially in the northern part, and have their huts from five or six hundred to a thousand feet apart. In the southern part, groups of huts, each consisting of from four or five to ten, are found. The East Atayals also form several villages, their huts being scattered, however, in an irregular way, some huts being but twenty or thirty feet apart, and others as far as five or six hundred feet. In building their huts they erect posts of wood and stone, with walls of bamboo interlaced with a kind of rush or grass and thatched with the same material. The dwellings of the East Atayals, however, are quite different from those of the West. They dig a cellar-like excavation some 3 to 6 feet deep, and with the earth thus obtained a wall is built around the mouth of the excavation, and the interior is paved with stone. Strong wooden pillars with cross poles are erected, and flat pieces of stone are used as roofing. These houses are unnoticeable at any distance, projecting as they do only some four feet above the surrounding ground. They have but a single entrance, and a ladder, consisting generally of a simple notched pole, is required to descend into their houses. Their store houses are erected on posts, and are raised some 3 or 5 feet above the ground. To provide against the ravages of rats a circular piece of board surmounts each post.

---

1. For a vocabulary of the different groups see Appendix.

Dress.—The garments of the Atayals consist, for the male, of a tunic and a square of native made cloth. The tunic is sleeveless, and reaches below the waist. It is open in front, and consequently provides covering for practically the back and shoulders of the body alone. The square cloth is considered as an extra garment, and when used is simply wrapped about the body above the waist. An abbreviated loin cloth completes the attire. The women wrap about the body, from left to right, a square of cloth, but those who live rear the border districts frequently add to this an under shirt-like jacket made of white cotton cloth obtained from the Chinese. They also tie about the lower leg a square of cloth which hangs down about the foot like a legging. The material for the sarong-like garment is woven by the savages on their crude looms, China grass being the fibre used. Woollen or other threads of red, blue, and black colors obtained by unravelling blankets originally procured from Chinese, are woven in with the local material in such a way as to present pleasing geometrical designs. The women who live near the Chinese district frequently wear Chinese coats, and they are fond of using as a head dress a length of colored cloth decorated with buttons and other ornaments. The men wear on the head a skull cap made of hide, obtained from the heads of young deer, with the small deer horns projecting. A cap made of rattan is also frequently worn.

Ornaments.—As ear ornaments, the Atayals favor bamboo sticks of ½ to ¾ of an inch in diameter and of varying length, but generally over 4 inches, which are placed through holes made in the ear lobes. These sticks are often nicely carved, chiefly with geometrical figures ; they are also sometimes wound with colored thread, or have tassels or other pendants, such as rectangular polished shell ornaments, attached to each end.

Tattooing.—This method of personal decoration is practised among both sexes. Not only do they consider it highly ornamental, but some designs are adopted as marks of maturity among both males and females, not being resorted to until the subject has reached the age of puberty. The designs follow well established patterns. The men tattoo their foreheads and chins with short heavy vertical lines, and on arriving at maturity and having been accepted by the tribe as recognized adults, tattoo short lines on their breasts, also sometimes on the legs and arms. The females on attaining womanhood add a rather complex pattern in pale blue leading from the mouth with an upward curve to the ears, and measuring nearly an inch in width. It is made up of three sets of three lines, each set being connected by a chevron line. The removal of certain teeth is also considered by the Atayals to improve their appearance. Both men and women remove from the upper jaw the two lateral incisors. In addition to the above, the Atayals are fond of necklaces, bracelets, and other similar ornaments. The teeth of animals, hard red berries obtained from a certain tree, and brass and other bright metals are used for these ornaments.

Food.—Their chief articles of food are millet, rice, sweet potatoes, and taros, together with the meat of deer and wild pig. They eat with their fingers, and the preparation of their food is limited to a hasty boiling or roasting. They also use salt to season their food. The Atayals of the high interior mountains, who are usually without salt, eat ginger root with their food.

Marriage.—The sexes appear to join in marriage on terms of equality. There is but one restriction,—the man must have fully reached manhood according to their own criterion and must have been duly recognized by the tribe as an adult. This means that the applicant must have attended the grand meeting of the braves, which is limited to those who have killed an outsider and brought forward the head of the victim. Thus the initial qualification of a would-be husband is to have engaged—and it must have been with success—in a head-hunting expedition. The east Atayals possess in their most populous district a hut elevated on piles some twenty feet above the ground. A newly married couple occupy this habitation five nights following the marriage.

Disease.—Disease is attributed to the anger of evil spirits. Every village possesses an old woman who undertakes to drive out the offending spirits. Squatting down near the sick one, she holds between her knees a bamboo tube which is permitted to project a few inches in front of her. On it she balances a sacred charm consisting of a small pierced stone. She waves her hand above it, imploring the spirits to withdraw their evil spell. If the stone falls she considers the spirits unwilling to release the victim ; if the ball remains balanced for a moment or so she believes a favorable answer has been received, and that consequently the patient will recover.

Burial.—On the death of one of the Atayals the family of the deceased mourn bitterly. New clothes are placed on the corpse, and it is further wrapped in a deer skin or large cloth. The West Atayals dig a grave under the sleeping room of the habitation occupied by the deceased during life, and the body is buried there. Mourning is continued by the family for from ten to thirty days, when the house is deserted for ever, it being in reality a tomb for the dead. The East Atayals bury the dead outside of the house and do not change their residence. They consider, however, the plot where the body lies as sacred property, and never visit it.

Head-Hunting.—Of all the savages in the island the Atayals are the most active and aggressive in head-hunting. This ferocious practice has entered into their life, and plays so prominent a part in their whole social system as to have become almost ineradicable so long as a remnant of their old life remains. The Atayals consider head-hunting justifiable, in fact obligatory, in the following cases :—

1. To be assured of a year of abundance, the heads of freshly killed human beings must be offered up to their ancestors.

2. To qualify for entrance into the councils as a recognized adult.

3. To gain favor with the unmarried female, making it possible to obtain as wife one of the most attractive damsels.

4. To obtain rank and influence. The degree of respect and admiration gained among fellow savages is dependent upon the number of heads secured.

5. To gain for the individual and his family, and even for the tribe, freedom from pestilence. For instance, small pox is sometimes prevalent; to drive out the pest the nearest relatives of the patient will engage in a head-hunting expedition.

6. To be considered victor in a dispute or to recover one's standing after having committed some offence against one's fellows. Thus, when two savages quarrel and cannot arrive at a settlement, both parties disappear; and the first to return with a head obtains a settlement of the dispute in his favor. Also one who is suspected of having offended against the established rules of Atayals may clear himself of reproach by bringing to his village a newly decapitated head.

Taking the above into consideration, it would appear that head-hunting enters into the religion of the Atayals. Furthermore, according to the moral standard of the people, it is positively obligatory on every male adult, unless such individual is prepared to incur the hatred and probably the hostility of his comrades. Head-hunting is a dangerous occupation, and the Atayal frequently meets his death. The event of a brave returning unharmed and bearing the much prized head of his victim is consequently an occasion for great rejoicing. On his approach being heralded, it is not uncommon for the members of his village,—men, women and children, to rush out and greet him. The story of his exploit is listened to with keen joy, the brave praised for his valor, and a celebration takes place in which dancing and the drinking of wines plays a most prominent part. Every village possesses a small narrow platform supported on wooden or bamboo poles some three or four feet high. It is out in the open air, and on it are placed the heads obtained by the braves of the village. This repository is under the charge of the village chief, and the heads are never removed. After exposure to the rain and ravages of insects and rats, the trophies are soon reduced to glistening skulls; and to the stranger, are the most striking objects to be seen in a savage village. Some villages possess several hundred heads, and the smallest habitation as a rule some ten. Tradition speaks of one brave who himself had captured 500 heads. The average at present for a recognized brave is about ten.

Religion.—After the rice or millet has been harvested, the Atayals select a day, during the period of a full-moon, and worship their ancestors. A similar ceremony occurs when seed is sown. The first is to express their gratitude for a bountiful harvest, which they attribute to the spirits of their dead ancestors; and the second is to beseech a continuance of favor in respect to the coming harvest. In such case the ceremony is as follows: Every family makes, from the rice or millet they have harvested, cakes, which they take during the darkness of night into the thick wood, and wrapping them in leaves, suspend them from the branches of trees. The spirits of their ancestors are expected to partake of their offerings. The day following, the whole village meet together, and mirth and gaiety prevails. At events where merriment prevails, the younger women frequently engage in very licentious dances consisting of twisting and squirming and suggestive muscle movements not unlike the Hawaiian dance. Time is kept by the music from jewsharp like instruments made of bamboo.

THE VONUM GROUP.

Boundaries.—The Vonum group spreads itself over the mountainous region of the centre of the island, joining the territory of the Atayals on the north, the district of Tsou group on the south east, and the Amis on the east. In addition, on the high plateau near Lake Candidius (Suishako) to the south of Horisha (Polisia), is a small settlement of Vonums who have adopted Chinese ways to some extent. To these semi-civilized aborigines the following does not apply.

Dwellings.—The Vonums live in villages, with their huts some 30 to 90 feet apart. Frequently they live at great elevations; with one or two exceptions the highest parts of the great central range are within their district. In erecting their houses a shallow pit one or two feet deep is dug, and over this the wood and stone work is constructed. The supporting posts are of wood and bamboo, and the walls are of interlaced rush and grass work. If the material is abundant, the pillars are sometimes of flat slabs of slate piled up evenly, but without mortar. The roof is thatched with grass or rushes, or covered with tree bark and frequently slate. The floor is paved with flat pieces of slate. The small yard in front of the entrance is also commonly paved with stone; and it is in this place that the savage family do most of their work.

Dress.—The men wear a sleeveless tunic similar to that of the Atayals, the material being either thin locally-made cloth, or leather. Women have short and tight-sleeved shirts reaching down to the belly, the material of which is usually light cotton cloth obtained from the Chinese, and the outer sarong-like garment reaching from their shoulders to the knees as worn by the Atayals. Besides the above, the males place about the breast, like a small apron, a square of cloth folded in triangular form and fastened about the body by strings attached to the corners of the cloth. A second apron similar to the above and fastened in like manner is placed about the lower part of the belly. The triangular front of the upper apron is embroidered.

Ornaments.—A hard red berry which has the appearance of a coral bead, a yellowish berry, animal teeth, bright transparent stones, or false jewels obtained from the Chinese are used for necklaces. Shells are also used. They root out the lateral incisors on the upper jaw.

Food.—Their chief food consists of millet, rice, sweet potatoes, taro, deer, wild pig, etc. A wooden spoon is used by some of the Vonums in eating their food, though the majority eat with their fingers. An intoxicating drink is made by this group from millet or rice. After the cereal has been bruised by pounding with a stone, a morsel at a time is taken into the mouth by the various people engaged in the work, and masticated until soft, being freely mixed with saliva. It is then thrown into an earthern jar where it ferments rapidly. Water is then added, and the stuff is ready for use.

East Atayals living near Polisia.
Arrangement of Skulls among Atayals.
Vonum Women as Burden Carriers.

Atayal House showing Rat Shields.
Savages of the Vonum Group.
Armed Vonum Savages visiting the Border to Trade

Marriage.—Perfect freedom exists as to marriage among both sexes. The custom of pretending to seize a bride by force is in existence among them. With a company of friends the bridegroom goes to the house of his intended, and in the face of pretended opposition seizes his bride and carries her off to his own habitation. After a few days, a feast is given to the friends of the couple. In some of the tribes, a sham-fight occurs between the relatives of the bride and bridegroom, and the drawing of blood on the part of one of them is considered of good omen.

Diseases.—Diseases are considered as a manifestation of the anger of evil spirits. An old female priestess is called in, who by waving the rushes which she carries, one in each hand, is supposed to induce the bad spirits to retire. Sometimes these sorceresses treat the patient by ruffling the afflicted part.

Burial.—On the death of a Vonum savage the surviving relatives make a great show of grief. The dead body is wrapped in a deer-skin and buried in a grave outside the house.

Head-hunting.—The Vonums do not at present engage in head-hunting to the extent that marks their more northern brothers. In some parts of their district, however, it is quite common. The practice does not enter into their religion. They regard the hunting of heads merely as evidence of one's courage and prowess, and the successful hunter who returns with a head is considered to have given abundant evidence that he is a brave warrior worthy of the tribe. Accordingly, the savage who has obtained the most heads is considered the chief warrior, the bravest man in the tribe. A savage who has refrained from head-hunting can obtain a wife among the less attractive girls, but a savage belle would look for a husband among the young braves who had proven their valor and intrepidity.

The Vonums have small straw-thatched receptacles built in the shape of houses near their habitations, and here are kept their collections of heads, not only human but those of animals as well, the latter being trophies of the hunt.

Religion.—The spirits of their departed ancestors are worshipped on a day following the harvest, and again before the sowing. With some of the Vonum tribes a bundle of green grass is placed in a certain part of a house as a symbol of the sacred day, and it is believed that the family's ancestral spirits will congregate about this emblem. Native wine is sprinkled on the floor about the sacred place, and prayers for good fortune are offered up to the spirits. Ordinarily fire is obtained with a flint and steel, but on these sacred days it is produced by rubbing together pieces of wood, which would appear to denote that the latter method was the one formerly in common use.

THE TSOU GROUP.

The Tsou group occupy the mountainous district to the immediate south-west of Nitakayama (Mt. Morrison). On the north, the Chimryuran river, a tributary of the Dakusuikei, separates them from the Vonum group.

To the south their district extends to the vicinity of Rokkiri (Lakuli), where it joins the territory of the Tsalisen group. On the east, the central mountain range marks their boundary, and on the west, their land ends with the boundary of the high hill district.

Dwellings.—The Tsou savages live in villages. Their habitations are situated in the dense jungle, and the houses are built from thirty to ninety feet apart. The construction of their houses is somewhat like that of the Dyaks of Borneo. The houses are oblong in shape. The supporting posts are unhewn logs or bamboo, and the wall is of rushes or grass interlaced. The roof is thatched with grass, and slopes down on four sides. Every tribe possesses in common a particularly large room called "Khuva" by the savages. The floor of this structure is elevated some 4 or 5 feet, and the knotched pole serves as a ladder to afford entrance. The building, which consists of one large room without walls, with a large open fire place on the floor in the centre, serves as a dormitory for the unmarried young men. The occupants are not permitted to enter a house where women reside; nor are they allowed to possess any article which was originally the property of the other sex, or which is specially intended for women's use. By these measures, premature intercourse with the girls of the village, as well as all effeminating influence, is provided against. Furthermore, cold and rain-laden winds find easy access to the sleeping room. Thus the young men are hardened, and become inured to the rough life of warriors. The special duty of the young men of the "Khuva" is to carry messages to other villages when required. It is while in the Khuva that the young men are trained in warfare; the manufacture and the use of various weapons is shown them, and they are taught such handicraft as their life requires.

"Khuva" is also used as the village meeting house, and when affairs of importance are to be discussed it is at this place the adult males assemble. The place is furthermore open to visiting savages from the neighboring villages.

Head-Hunting.—This practice is gradually falling into disuse among the Tsou savages. Every dwelling possesses a small elevated house-shaped structure, provided with shelves on which the heads are kept. Their views as to practice are similar to those held by the Vonums, but they regard the custom as one of the past glories of the tribe, and as one which has ceased to be profitable.

Dress.—The garments worn by this group resemble those of the Vonums, except that deer skins are more frequently used as the material for the dress of men. Like the Vonums, the men wear the triangular aprons on the chest and belly.

The women hang a piece of nicely embroidered white cloth about 5 × 12 inches in size about the chest by strings attached to the four corners.

Ornaments.—Pieces of brass and other bright metals are worn on the breast, and necklaces, consisting of bright colored berries strung like beads, are highly valued. Like the Vonums, they root out certain of the teeth.

Food.—The chief articles of food are rice, millet, sweet potatoes, taros, venison, wild pig meat, etc. They use a long flat trowel-like implement when eating, and they drink from a cup-like section of a particular gourd found in their forests. They brew an intoxicating liquor in the same manner as the Vonums.

Marriage.—There is the same freedom in marriage as characterizes other groups. The young Tsou brave presents to the young lady of his choice an ornamental hair-pin called "siisii," which is made of deer-horn. The acceptance of this gift signifies consent. The bridegroom now publicly announces his betrothal, and with several of his friends visits the home of the bride, and with a sham exhibition of force carries her away to his home. The following morning the bride runs away and returns to the home of her mother. Here she remains three days, when the friends of the bridegroom visit her house; and again, with a show of force, she is carried to the home of her lover, where a social meeting is held and the marriage ceremony is considered at an end.

Disease.—Disease is considered an expression of the wrath of a departed soul. Certain old men and women, who are considered to possess special powers as sorcerers, profess ability to pacify the angry spirits, and hence to cure disease. The sorcerer offers up two bamboo tubes, one with rice in it, the other with wine; and then, with a reed in each hand, he approaches the patient, waving the wands and praying for mercy. The rice and wine is thrown about in the vicinity of the house,

Burial.—Deep family mourning follows death. Near the entrance of the house a grave is dug, some 5 or 6 feet deep, and the dead is wrapped up in a deer skin and buried there. A stone of sufficient size to support the earth above is placed over this, at some little distance above the body; on this the earth is packed, and when the surface is reached, it is smoothed over, so as to resemble the ground about it: Contrary to the general custom among the savages, this plot of ground is put to ordinary use.

Head-Hunting.—The Tsous were at one time ardent head hunters, but the practice has now been given up. Their ancestors were great warriors, and frequently fought with other savages, often returning triumphantly with the heads of their enemies. In memory of these deeds, the group keep to this day the ancient shields and the trophies of war including a goodly array of skulls, all of which are preserved with great care in "Khuva," or the bachelor dormitory.

Religion.—A tree near the entrance to a village, usually selected on account of its large size, receives special homage from the various tribes of the Tsou group. It is thought that the spirits of their ancestors take their abode in these trees. Before sowing and after harvest, when they mow the grass, which is a ceremony performed once a year, and refil the bamboo water pipes, likewise an annual ceremony, the savages assemble under this tree, and sprinkling wine about the ground, they worship the spirits of their departed ancestors. A variety of orchid is also considered to be a sacred plant. The savages grow this flower at the foot of the holy tree and near the bachelors' dormitory. Traditions of the tribe are to the effect that their ancestors carried this flower into battle, and to it they attributed their victories. It is strictly forbidden to cut down or in any way injure these plants.

THE TSALISEN GROUP.

The Tsalisens occupy the southern portion of the central high range with Mount Kurayao as their centre. On the north, they join the Tsou group, and on the east the Puyuma and Paiwan groups, while the Paiwans are also on their southern border.

Dwellings.—The homes of this group are invariably built on the mountain slope. They cut into the hill-side to the depth they desire to give their house and wall up the front of the excavation,—a very simple method of obtaining a strong storm-proof habitation. The front and wall work, as well as the front roof supports, are of piled up slate, and the roof and floor are also made of the same material. As compared with the houses of other savages these structures are noticeable in that they are of stone and earth, while the rank of an occupant is denoted by the decorations of the eaves, a chief of a tribe possessing a house the eaves of which exhibit carvings of people, of snakes, etc. Some chiefs with large houses will have as many as 60 carved eaves. In the extreme south, the tribes sometimes erect boards standing some three or four feet high in front of their houses, each bearing on its face a crude engraving of a human-being.

Dress.—The Tsalisen savages commonly wear short, tight-sleeved tunics, open in front and reaching down to below the waist. About the lower part of the body they wind, from right to left, a length of cloth which is gathered in by many folds at the waist. The men wear these cloths down to the knees, but the women have them extended nearly to the feet.

Ornaments.—Like many of the South Sea islanders, the Tsalisens are fond of wearing grasses and flowers as a head dress. Both men and women tattoo, but among the former, tattooing is permitted only to chiefs and their families. It serves them both as an ornament and as a sign of high rank. The patterns are entirely unlike those of the northern savages. There is one geometrical design made up of parallel lines commencing at the elbow, covering the whole upper arm, and reaching to the shoulder, and a second pattern consists of a complicated geometrical figure leading from the breasts up over the shoulders and down the small of the back. The women tattoo only their hands, the design consisting of straight and accurately carved lines.

Food.—The chief articles of diet are millet, rice, sweet-potatoes, taros, venison, and wild pig meat. They eat with wooden spoons, and the dishes for food are made of closely woven rattan. An intoxicating drink is made by grinding millet or rice into a flour, adding water and the pollen of the flower of a variety of the goose foot plant (Chenopodium album) which incites fermentation. The Tsalisen group are inveterate chewers of betelnut. The meat of the nut is wrapped in a tobacco leaf, and when chewed has a slightly stimulating effect. This practice blackens the teeth and gives an unnatural reddish color to the gums, lips, and tongue.

Marriage.—Marriage among the group is not quite so free and unrestricted as with other Formosa savages. The consent of the parents on both sides must be obtained, and the preliminary arrangements must be placed in the care of a middleman. After matters have been definitely arranged, a month is allowed to intervene, and then on an appointed day the suitor visits the house of his intended and a simple ceremony sanctions the right of the couple to come together. The woman remains at the home of her mother until a child is born, when she removes to the home of her husband, and the marriage is then considered to have been effected. Should she be without issue, however, her suitor ceases to call, and all familiarity between the couple comes to an end. Both parties are now free to seek a mate elsewhere.

Disease.—As is general among the Formosa savages, this group attributes disease to the ill-will of the spirits of the departed, and a religious rite called "Parish" is resorted to, to drive away the offended ones.

Burial.—When a Tsalisen dies, all the village acquaintances of the departed visit the family to condole with them. The dead is dressed in new garments and is buried in a deep grave dug under the floor of the house. Until the day of the next full-moon following the death, the inmates refrain from removing from the house any article which may have been used by the departed. After this period "Parish" is held and the funeral observances are considered at an end.

Head-Hunting.—The Tsalisens consider head-hunting an honorable practice. Their method of slaughter is vividly expressed by a Chinese poet who wrote, "Like fierce tigers, they range the woods and pounce on human heads." Now, however, with many of the tribes of the group, head-hunting is gradually going out of fashion. The few who continue the practice celebrate the capture of a head with a great festival to which all are invited. The freshly decapitated head is boiled to remove all fleshy parts, and the cleaned skull is preserved with great care. The more civilized tribes preserve the skulls of animals as a substitute for the human head.

Religion.—The religious rites known as "Parish" are in full force among this group. The ceremony consists in arranging certain articles such as dishes, food, etc., in a certain form, mumbling over them certain incantations which the savages believe bring down the spirits of their ancestors, who are present so long as the ceremony lasts. Should one violate the rules of this ceremony or offend by entering the charmed circle over which the priestess alone presides, the spirits will visit on the offender their ill-will. In some respects this ceremony resembles that of "taboo" among certain South Sea islanders.

They worship the manes of their ancestors four times a year. Some Tsalisen tribes have a tradition that their ancestors came down from heaven with twelve earthen jars; and at the present day, in the house of a great chief a peculiar old earthen-ware jar is handed down from generation to generation; others have a tradition that the moon gave birth to their ancestors, and in the house of a chief a round stone, circular in form, intended to represent the moon, is preserved. Both the jar and the stone are considered as sacred objects, and strangers are not permitted to approach them. As with the Tsou group, they believe that the souls of their ancestors abide in a sacred tree near the entrance to their village.

THE PAIWAN GROUP.

The Paiwans live in the hilly plains of the extreme south of the island. On the east, their district extends nearly to the Chihon kei (River), where it joins the territory of the Puyumas; and on the north-west, the Tsalisen group are their neighbors. On the east, south, and west, their land extends to the sea-shore.

The Paiwans may be divided into three sub-groups as follows :—

1. Chakuvukuvum.   2. Pakurukal.   3. Parizarizao.

Dwellings.—The huts of the Paiwans show three stages of development in house building. The first is of primitive form. A large excavation is made in the mountain slope, and a strong back wall and support is thus obtained. Two posts are erected on each side, and extending across from their tops are placed large circular posts, which form arch-like supports for a rush-thatched roof. The walls are made of rushes or bamboo interlaced. A second style of structure resembles the ordinary form of hut such as the poorer Chinese classes construct, with thatched roof, bamboo or board wall, etc. The third consists of a series of houses just described, joined together so as to form a long building sometimes fifty feet or more in length.

The houses of chiefs in the Chakuvukuvum and Pakurukal sub-groups have, at the entrance door, posts decorated with carvings, showing human beings some four or five feet in height. In this way the residence of a chief is easily distinguished. The great chief of the Parizarizao group, possesses in his dwelling one room which is considered as a sacred chamber, and here certain religious ceremonies are held. The family of the chief rarely enter the chamber.

Dress.—The garments worn by this group resemble those of the Tsalisen savages. The Parizarizao savages have for many years been in close communication with the Chinese; and the influence of the latter has been sufficiently powerful to induce the aborigine to abandon his native dress for the clothes and queue of the stranger.

Ornaments.—The earring worn by the Paiwans is unique. It consists of a circular piece of wood about one inch in diameter, and the opening in the ear lap is accordingly very large. On account of this peculiarity, the Chinese have given the group the name of Toa-he-lan or " big ears."

Tattooing is not common. The men sometimes decorate themselves like the Tsalisen chiefs, but such marking has no special significance with them. The women, however, are permitted to tattoo only when belonging

Tsou Group, showing Head Dress worn by Chief.
Tsalisen Group House, showing Slate Roof.

Tsalisen Group Savage.
Savages of Parizarizao tribe of Paiwan Group.

to the family of a chief, and the design adopted is similar to that of the Tsalisen women.

Food.—The food and drink of the Paiwans is practically the same as that of the Tsalisens, with the exception of a few tribes in the more mountainous district, who refrain from eating rice, owing to a superstition which forbids it. Like others of the South Formosa savages, they are fond of Betel nuts.

Marriage.—The marriage ceremony is similar to that of many savage races. The young brave goes to the house of his beloved with fuel and water, which he places before the door. If the damsel puts them to the use for which they are intended, it signifies her acceptance. The young husband then takes up his residence among the wife's family for a few years, performing such duties as by custom fall to the men. He then removes the wife to his own house and holds there a festival to celebrate the event. The various relatives attend and offer presents of wine and betel-nuts.

Disease.—Disease, which they attribute to the ill-will of ghosts and spirits, is treated by a priestess who undertakes to appease the wrath of the spirits and obtain their favor. She judges as to her probable success by watching the movements of a berry, which she balances on the top of a gourd.

There is, however, a special and rational treatment for any one who has been bitten by a poisonous snake. A special snake-doctor is called, who sucks the bite, removing in this way as much of the poison as he can ; and the wound is then smeared over with the juice of a certain plant.

Burial.—On the death of one of the tribe the acquaintances of the deceased assemble to mourn. The near relatives call out the name of the dead repeatedly, and lament loudly that a great loss has been inflicted upon them. There are two ways of burial. The one most in vogue is to dig a deep grave under the floor of the house, and after burial to fill up the grave with stones. The second method is to bury in the thick wood, the body being deposited in a grave lined with stones. It is only the Parizarizao savages who practise this latter method.

Head-hunting.—The Paiwans were once great head-hunters, and those in the high hills still continue the practice to some extent. The Paiwans of the plain have Chinese ways, and have practically abandoned head-hunting. Heads possessed by the group are preserved with great care in stone boxes specially made for the purpose and put up outside the house.

Religion.—Some of the Paiwan group believe that the spirits of their ancestors abide in a thick wood ; others believe that the spirits are enshrined in swords handed down to them from ancient times. They worship the manes of their ancestors on the day when seeds are sown, and again at harvest time. Once in five years, on one of these sacred days, the savages join in a game called Mavayaiya. This amusement consists in endeavors on the part of the players to catch, on the point of a bamboo lance, a bundle of wood bark, rolled up so as to resemble in size a human head. The one who succeeds in impaling it is considered the victor. It is said that this is a survival of an ancient game in which a human head was tossed about and then offered up to the spirits.

In the village where the great chief of the Parizarizao savages lives, there is a rush-thatched hut near a thick wood. This building is considered a sacred temple in which the manes of their ancestors, which they worship as deities, are enshrined. The hut is never approached except on some fixed festival days. If a person draws near to it, save for religious reasons, it is believed misfortune will fall on the offender.

Traditions.—The Parizarizao tribe of the Paiwan group possess traditions that their ancestors came down from heaven, and that the descendants prospered and spread rapidly over the district. Also that, on one occasion when the district was visited by a great drought, and a dreadful famine seemed inevitable, the tribe held a grand meeting, and prayed that the spirits of their ancestors would bless them with rain. One night the spirits appeared to the people in their dreams, and announced that there lived in the mountain a great man called Terarok, and that if they would make him their chief the harvest would be plentiful. The tribe, therefore, searched for the great personage, and finally found a man named Kyakya, whom they believed to be the one described, and who was accordingly made their chief. Again they prayed for rain, and in fulfillment of the promise, a bountiful fall followed, and a rich harvest was obtained. These traditions, when compared with those of the other division of the group, would appear to show that the Parizarizao tribe are not pure Paiwans.

PUYUMA GROUP.

The Puyuma group occupy the greater part of the Pinan (Pilam) plain of south-east Formosa. On the north, they have the Amis and Vonums as neighbors, and on the west the Tsalisen group. To the south are the Paiwans. The Puyumas formed a very powerful state some 300 years ago. They expanded towards the north, and subdued and enslaved many of the tribes with which they came in contact. After some years, their power declined; and eventually the tribes whom they once controlled obtained their independence. There are now but eight tribes of Puyumas, and the territory held by them is the smallest of any of the groups.

Dwellings.—The Puyumas live only in the plains, the mountainous district in their vicinity remaining uninhabited. Their houses are built in close proximity with each other, and each village is surrounded by bamboo groves. The houses are primitive and badly built. Doubtless, the custom of deserting a house on the death of an inmate is the cause of the inferior type of architecture. There are two tribal buildings which the Puyumas possess in their villages. They are circular structures on piles ten feet above ground. A bamboo ladder affords entrance. One called "Takopan" is a dormitory, as well as a play-hall, for the boys. The second, known as "Parakowan," is a bachelor dormitory also, but is for youth nearer maturity,

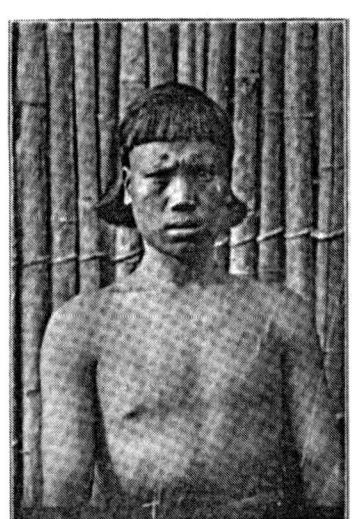
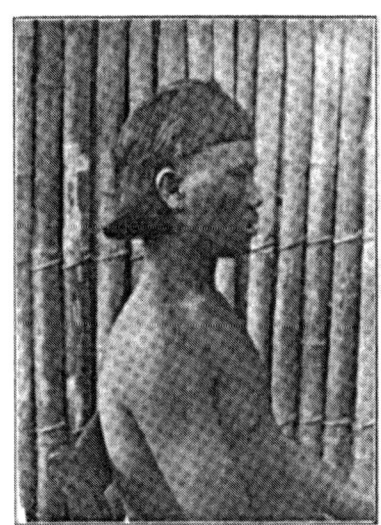
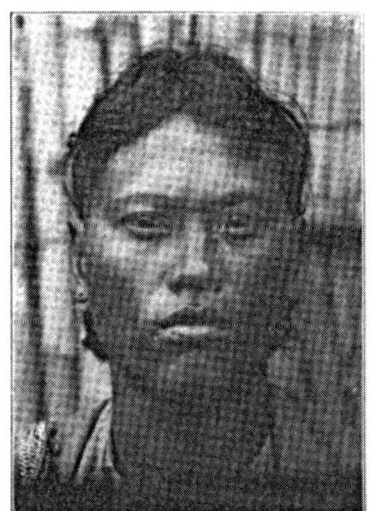

House of Chakuvukuvum Savage (Paiwan Group).   House of Parizarizao Savage (Paiwan Group).

Paiwan Chief's House, showing Totem Board.   Warrior of Puyuma Group, with Silver Yen as Ornaments.

Male Puyuma type (front view).   Male Puyuma type (side view).   Female Puyuma Type.

and is reserved for them during the day time as their workshop. On the young men who occupy these dormitories is imposed guard duty. While their elders sleep, the young men must keep careful watch from their elevated position, to give the alarm should an enemy approach. Women are strictly forbidden to approach these buildings.

Dress.—The native garments of this group resemble those of the Paiwans, but as the Puyumas have long had close association with the Chinese, many of them have adopted the dress of the latter.

Ornaments.—The Puyumas care little for ornaments, such as most savages delight in possessing. The women belonging to the family of a chief tattoo the back of the head with a design similar to that in vogue among those of their sex in the Tsalisen and the Paiwan groups.

Food.—The food of the Puyuma is almost identical with that of the Tsalisen and Paiwan, although. they appear comparatively advanced in preparing their meals.

Marriage.—The family system of the Puyuma group centres around the female. If a woman favors the attention of a certain suitor and marriage is decided upon, the man transfers himself to the house and family of the wife. The obtaining of a husband is thus chiefly under the control of the woman and her family. It is the wife's family that is responsible for the young husband. The latter's family have renounced all further claim to him. As a son he partakes of what the house offers, but possesses no authority over the family, nor is the house or property his, until the death of his wife's parents, when as the husband of the sole owner he comes into certain rights which custom grants him.

Disease.—Disease is a visitation of the wrath of angry spirits. A priestess is believed to possess the power of exorcism; she places a cup of wine before the patient; and waving aside the evil visitors with leaves of the banana plant, which she holds in each hand, she sprinkles the wine thrice about the ground, mumbling incantations all the while.

Burial.—On the death of one of the tribe, the family mourn bitterly. The body is wrapped in rattan matting, and is buried in a grave dug under the floor near where the deceased was wont to sleep. After the lapse of a certain number of days, the family permanently abandon the house, taking up their residence in an entirely new structure.

Religion.—Like the Tsalisens, the Puyumas practise the superstitious rites called Parisin. On the festival day, a monkey is captured and tied upon a tree in front of the boys' club, and is there killed with bows and arrows. The chief then throws wine three times skywards and three times to the ground. Then they all spit on the monkey, after which it is thrown away. They then join hands and dance. Puyuma traditions explain that, during the period when their people were all-powerful, one member of the subjugated tribes was offered up as a sacrifice each year. Now in their weakened condition, they explain, the Puyumas are obliged to substitute a monkey.

Traditions.—The Puyuma group account for their origin as follows :—
In very ancient days there existed a large stone at the foot of Mt. Aravanai
(southern extremity of Pinan plain). On an eventful day, however, this stone
burst and gave birth to a man and a woman, called Unai and Tanval respectively. The two marched northward as far as Chipun river, where they
settled, and founded a tribe called Chipun. The two now married and gave
birth to three boys and three girls, whose descendants became the ancestors
of the different tribes of the present Puyuma group. There were then eight
suns in heaven, and the heat from them was so excessively strong that people
suffered greatly from it. The first son of Unai, called Saieahao, made a
ladder of grass, ascended to heaven, and battling with the suns destroyed
six of them, leaving two—the present sun and moon.

THE AMI GROUP.

The Amis are spread over the greater part of the Taito region of south-
east Formosa. To the south are the Puyumas, and on the north their
border extends to the district of the Atayals. Much of their land is a fertile
plain : in fact, of all the territory occupied by the various groups, the Amis
possess the most attractive district. The group may be divided into the
southern Amis and the northern Amis, with the Shukorankei valley as the
boundary. The south Amis once occupied the large plain of Pinan (Pilam),
but the Puyuma group defeated them in warfare, seized their lands, and placed
the Amis in the position of a subject race bearing the title of Papiyan, " the
weaker." In later years when the Amis recovered their independence, the
Pinan still continued in the possession of the Puyumas, and now only a small
Ami village, called Varangao, remains there. The remainder of the group
spread themselves along the valley to the north. At the time of the invasion,
some Ami tribes escaped to the south, taking up their abode on the Koshun
plain in the district of the Paiwans. The Paiwans accepted their allegiance,
but imposed upon them certain degrading duties, some of which are required
of them even to this day. For instance, on the command of the great chief
of the Paiwan group, they are obliged to undertake the tilling of the fields.
At present they form six small villages, and lead an unhappy life.

Dwellings.—The hut of the south Amis has, as its supports, unhewn
logs. The walls are of bamboo and reeds, and the roof is heavily thatched
with rushes, and its ends are at a comparatively great inclination. The
north Amis build houses of bamboo and wood. The floor is comparatively
high above the ground, and is covered with matting of rattan work. It is
among these savages that we find the most perfect houses.

The various tribes possess each a bachelors' dormitory, which serves as
a meeting place for the tribal council as well. The young men who occupy
the dormitory are obliged to keep watch during the night hours.

Dress.—In dress the Amis imitate the savages of the outside groups
nearest them. For instance, the Amis living in the south dress similarly to
the Puyumas ; those further north copy the Vonum dress ; and those in the
far north adopt the costumes of the east Atayals. It should also be added

Bachelor's Dormitory, Puyuma Group.   Puyuma Savages trained for Military Purposes by Japanese.

Puyuma Students attending Japanese School at Pinam.   Savages of Ami Group.

Ami Savages Dancing.   Male Types, Ami Group.

that, on occasions when convenience or comfort is thus obtained, male Amis refrain from all dress whatsoever; even the customary loin-cloth being thought unnecessary.

While nearly all of the seven Formosa groups tattoo and root out certain teeth, the Amis do neither.

Food.—The Amis understand the manufacture of earthenware pots, useful for cooking food and as water jars. The north Amis are specially skillful in pottery making. No wheel is used; merely a round stone, which they place inside the well-kneaded clay; and by the aid of a small board, with which they pat the surface, they gradually mould the jar or dish, obtaining a very good shape. The ware thus made is dried in the sun and then burnt in a straw fire. The Amis understand the constructing of wells as a source of water supply. All other savages in this island obtain water from the mountain streams.

Marriage.—As with the Puyuma group, the husband is taken into the wife's family. It is the custom for the young brave to offer to his bride, prior to marriage, a ceremonial gift consisting of fuel from the Melia japonica tree. He sends four bundles on the first day, and one bundle each day thereafter, until the number reaches twenty. It is therefore customary for boys of ten years old to plant these trees, which on attaining a growth of 5 or 6 feet, are ready for use as fuel.

Burial.—On the death of one of the group, the family of the deceased show great grief. The corpse is wrapped in rattan matting and buried in a deep grave outside the former home of the deceased, with the head to the south and the face to the east. With the south Amis, it is customary for a member of the family to throw a handful of earth on the grave, and thereupon to exclaim, " You shall not return." Among the southern Amis, a pile of stones marks the grave; but with the northern Amis a wooden fence is erected.

Head-hunting.—As the majority of the Amis have become domesticated, head-hunting is no longer practised. The north Amis, however, while not engaging in expeditions for the sole purpose of obtaining heads, will, in their fights with the Atayal group on the neighboring mountains, decapitate those of the enemy who fall into their hands.

When such trophies have been obtained, they are preserved on a stand erected for that purpose, and a festival is held to celebrate the event. On some occasions, also, they eat the flesh stripped from the head.

Religion.—The Amis appear more advanced in their religious views than other groups. They believe in one supreme spirit who controls the universe. Like the Tsalisen and the Puyuma groups they practise the superstitious rites called Parisin. After harvest they hold a grand celebration, at which the spirits of their ancestors are worshipped. A similar celebration is held at the time of sowing. In the case of continued dry weather endangering the crops, they pray for rain.

Obedience to elders is enforced on the young of both sexes. This esteem for the old enters into their social system; and with the north Amis any disrespect shown to an elder makes the offender liable to expulsion from the tribe.

Disease.—As with the other groups, disease is attributed to the displeasure of the spirits of the dead, and a priestess is engaged to pray for their favor. This is common to all tribes of the group; but the north Amis also attribute certain pains to an offending substance in the flesh. A sorcerer is engaged, who undertakes to remove foreign matter. His method is to suck vigorously the flesh of the painful part, and then suddenly to produce various articles from his mouth, which he asserts were obtained from the body of the patient, and thus, he claims, recovery is made possible.

Traditions.—The Ami tribe account for their origin in two ways. One tradition resembles the Puyuma in that their ancestors were born from a stone which lay on a mountain near Chipun river. Tiruti and Tihongan being thus created, founded a village called Varangao. Four of their descendants, all brothers, proceeded to the north across the Pinan river, and became the ancestors of the tribe now there. Several of the tribes possess traditions describing the arrival of their ancestors from distant lands. According to the belief of the tribe occupying the Shukoran river valley, they originally occupied the neighboring island of Sanasanac and were called Sanasai. Later they came in boats, landed at the mouth of the Shukoran river, and established seven large villages there. Thus the name at present given to the island is perhaps a corruption of Sanasana. The Riru tribe of Kirai district of the northern Amis state that their forefathers originally lived in an island to the east of Formosa. One savage, called Tipots, and his family were out at sea in two canoes when a terrific gale arose, sweeping them away from their home-land, and wrecking them on the coast of Formosa, where they built houses and gave life to the present Riru tribe. This tribe possesses an old canoe, which they claim is the model of the one used by their forefathers. At present, the village people once a year put the canoe into the sea and mimic the landing of their ancestors. After this ceremony, the spirits of their departed ancestors are worshipped. A more fanciful tradition is to the effect that their ancestors came from over the sea on the back of a large tortoise.

Thus it would appear that the traditions of the north Amis describe comparatively recent occurrences, and are in the main very possible, if not probable.

THE PEPO GROUP.

The name "Pepo" was applied by Chinese originally to savages occupying the western plains of the island. It was thus a mere geographical classification, and was applied to any savages living in the plains, though certain villages might possess ethnological differences. Ethnologically considered, the Pepos are divided as follows:—

1. Makattao tribe, Hozan and vicinity.

2. Siraiya tribe, of Tainan and vicinity.
3. Loa tribe, of Kagi and vicinity.
4. Poavasa tribe, of Rokko (Lokiang) and vicinity.
5. Arikun tribe, of Shoka and vicinity.
6. Vupuran tribe, living north of Daitokei river.
7. Pazehhe tribe, scattered over the Taihoku plain, and in the Kelung and Tamsui districts.
10. Kuvarawan tribe, of Gilan district.

About three hundred years ago, the Pepos came under the influence of the Dutch, from whom they obtained some education; but after whose departure they were absorbed by the Chinese, as described in the first pages of this Chapter. At present so thoroughly have they adopted Chinese customs that they have abandoned even their own language, and in most cases the stranger can not distinguish the two races.[1]

To those tribes who had advanced further in adopting Chinese civilization the Chinese have applied the name of "Sakhoan" (Jukuban) or "domesticated savages." One familiar with the two peoples can, after careful observation, see the difference in the eyes; the Sakhoan possessing deep orbits. The women also do not bind their feet. Of the above, only two tribes, the Pazehhe and Kuvarawan, still preserve their native tongue, although they are also familiar with the Chinese language. As regards the other tribes, only a few old people, of perhaps 60 or 70 years of age, remember their native tongue. In fact, though there may be here and there slight traces of ancient manners and customs, still it would not be incorrect to state that their present day life is that of the Chinese. A brief account of their original customs, as given in ancient records and handed down by tradition, should, however, be recorded here.

Dwellings.—Their houses were generally built to resemble an overturned boat. The floor was elevated and was reached by the use of a ladder. Animal bones were hung about the outside of the house.

Dress.—Their principal article of dress was a short coat-like garment with sleeves, reaching to the belly. Over this sometimes was worn a second and longer coat reaching to the waist.

Ornaments.—They decorated their heads and breasts with bright colored stones. They generally perforated the lobe of the ear, and carried in the opening some ornament. They rarely rooted out their teeth, as some of the hill tribes did, and tattooing was not generally practised.

Their food was prepared by boiling or steaming. Native wine was brewed by two methods; in one saliva was used to incite fermentation, which action was in the other obtained by storing up the liquor.

Marriage.—There was generally freedom of marriage for both sexes. Among some of them, however, there was a custom of holding, on a certain

---

1. While there is much confusion in the Chinese terms "Pepohoan" and "Sakhoan," as a rule the former is applied to those savages of the plain who are easily distinguished from the Chinese, and the latter to those of savage origin who have so thoroughly adopted Chinese customs that there is practically no trace of their ancient life remaining.

day specially announced, a running race in which all young bachelors competed. The prize was the privilege of marrying the most beautiful girl of the tribe. Separate houses were also given to marriageable girls, who themselves possessed the right of selecting their husbands.

Disease.—They considered sickness as a manifestation of the anger of devils, and it was thought that certain female sorceresses possessed the power of driving the evil demons away. It was considered honorable to kill outsiders and to preserve the heads of the slain. The dead were buried within the houses by some, and outside by others. They were also wont, when agricultural work pressed heavily on them, to wrap corpses in grass cloth and place them near some stream or the sea.

SOCIAL CONDITION OF FORMOSA SAVAGES.

The social condition of the Formosa savages, taken as a whole, may be briefly described as follows :—

They have ceased to lead a nomadic life, and now live in villages, and are subject to certain social restrictions. They have emerged from a state of isolated individuality, and are now under the control of chiefs. They no longer make their homes in caves or trees, but have learned to build huts of wood and stone. They have more or less religious ideas, and worship the spirits of their ancestors. They have passed from the age of stone and bone as materials for their implements, and now utilize iron, though they do not yet understand the treatment of metals. Whereas formerly both sexes went naked, they now wear certain simple garments. They no longer make fire by rubbing together pieces of wood, but utilize flint and steel. They are not wanting in a sense of the artistic. The designs and color effects which are shown in their cloth give evidence of this, and some are very skillful in carving. They show fondness for music ; and, in addition to simple instruments such as bamboo jewsharps and one-string bows, both of which are incapable of rendering various tones, some of the tribes possess a kind of flute, with which they accompany their native songs.[1]

As regards domestic relationship, the Formosa savage recognises as near relations his descending line of offspring or ascending line of parentage for three generations, in the following order :—

Parents and brothers of parents ; parents, father and mother and sons and daughters of brothers of parents, and brothers and sons and daughters ; sons and daughters of brothers, and grandsons and granddaughters.

The above considered as near relatives are under the following restrictions :—

1. Marriage is not permitted between them.
2. Near relatives must protect and give special help to widowers, widows, and orphans, who require assistance.

---

1. With the exception of occasional bartering with the Chinese (when they trade chiefly the products of the forest for salt, blankets, gun-powder, etc.) they have not engaged in either industry or agriculture as a source of income.

3. The funeral of near relatives must be attended (Formosa savages avoid approaching the dead ; and, unless the deceased was a near relative, will never attend a funeral).

The strong distinction made between adults and youths is very striking· The savages do not count age by years, but rather by strength and ability, thus upholding the adage "Man is no older than he feels." They confer, by certain formal ceremonies, the status of adult on a youth whose physique gives evidence of maturity ; and, among some groups, on one who, lacking in strength, gives evidence of valor by bringing in the head of a stranger. The adult status is generally designated by tattooing some part of the body, or by extracting certain teeth. The privileges enjoyed by adults are :—

1. They are considered persons of capacity and responsibility.
2. They are permitted to marry.
3. They are permitted to chew betel-nut (chiefly among the Tsalisens).

Although marriage customs vary among the different groups, still there are no tribes that do not recognize marriage as an important event, or that do not endeavor to render it impressive by requiring the performance of certain formal ceremonies. The relationship between husband and wife continues until death ; and a woman is not permitted on the death or disappearance of her husband to remarry. Unfaithfulness on the part of a wife is unheard of, and prostitution and other immoral practices are practically non-existent. Some of the savages living on the border, corrupted by their contact with Chinese, have on rare occasions been found suffering from venereal disease, but no such cases have been reported among the savages of the interior. This, together with the strict observance of monogamy, the affection of parents for their children, the deep sorrow shown by members of a family on the death of one of their number, the respect shown to elders, gives evidence of a social state not only far superior to that of other savage tribes of the Pacific, but of a condition which, when compared with society under our much vaunted civilization, does not always reflect great credit on us.

The social organization of the Formosa savages is briefly as follows :—

A chief is appointed, either by inheritance or election, and the peace of the village is in his keeping.

Although there are two different forms of social organization,—that of self-government and that of despotism among the savages,—yet in general, the mere existence of a moral code, established by custom and tradition, keeps the savage in order. Each tribal member has such a deep respect for the opinion of his fellows, and considers his own interests and the interests of the community so inseparable, that he looks upon a crime against others as equally an injury to himself. True brotherhood is exemplified among savage tribes to a degree not found elsewhere. Consequently, a chief is but rarely called upon to severely discipline his followers. When his assistance is required it is usually to provide punishment for some petty offence.

The penalties are in keeping with the provocation and the views of the tribe on morality, and the chief endeavors to keep himself within precedent,

Crime is not regarded alike by the various groups. Frequently different tribes, perhaps living in close proximity, have different social standards. The following, however, are the principal crimes commonly recognized :—

1. Adultery.
2. An impolite or immoral act which is liable to disturb or endanger the existence of the whole tribe.
3. The stealing of any article the property of one of the tribe.
4. Disrespect towards elders (chiefly among the Amis).
5. Murder of one of the tribe (the killing an outsider is not considered a crime; but, on the contrary, receives high commendation).

For the above offences punishment is generally inflicted as follows :—

1. Capital punishment (chiefly inflicted for adultery).
2. Permanent or temporary banishment from the tribe.
3. Confiscation of property (there is no example of the confiscation of houses).
4. Whipping (beating on the back or thighs with bamboos or wooden sticks).
5. Censure (a chief will publicly censure an offender).

A description of the savage population of Formosa would not be complete without reference to the natives of Botel Tobago (Kotosho) island, which is a dependency of Formosa, and only some 35 miles from the south Formosa coast. Botel Tobago, which is only some 30 miles in circumference, consists of a single long hill, on the slopes of which the savages live. To the ethnologist the inhabitants of this little land are perhaps the most interesting of all the savages in the colony, and doubtless there are few tribes in the whole East who live in such a primitive manner, and who have had so little communication with the outside world, as the Botel Tobago savages.

There are but few historical references to the island. Captain Beechey, commanding the British government vessel " Blossom," visited Botel Tobago in 1826, determined its position, and constructed a plan of its northern and western sides. Beechey reports the lower slopes of the island as under cultivation, and that a large village was seen on the northern side. As this officer further reports that " The coast is rocky in almost every part, and probably dangerous to land upon, as needle rocks are seen in many parts of the island," it would appear that no landing was made. There is, however, a record of Chinese visitors. In a report on the Formosa savages made by a Chinese officer attached to the Formosa government, published in 1722, it is stated that the early Chinese of Formosa visited Botel Tobago in hopes of finding there some profitable trade. They found the island inhabited by a people with whom they could not converse, and who furthermore were unwilling to part with their little property. Disappointed at the failure of their trip they slaughtered many savages, and gathering together the scanty possessions of their victims, returned to Formosa. At a later date, other Chinese from South Formosa, adding to their party some savages from Koshun (Hengchun) district, who were expected to serve as interpreters, visited Botel Tobago. The natives, not forgetting the treachery of their former visitors, retaliated on this occasion; for it is recorded that not one of the party ever returned. The Chinese were content to look upon the island as a foreign land beyond their jurisdiction. The Japanese expedition of 1874, however, awakened in them the fear that some foreign power might occupy the island. Accordingly, in 1877, the Prefect of Koshun visited the place, and on his return drew up a voluminous report on the manners and customs of the inhabitants. From this date Botel Tobago was declared a dependency of Formosa, and two years later a new map of the Formosa district was published by the Fokien authorities, the island being marked as an Imperial possession. Although an occasional Chinese junk has anchored off the island and carried on some trifling trade with the natives, who brought out their wares by boat, there is no other record of any attempted exploration of the island until the Japanese occupation of Formosa. In 1896, the year following the arrival of the Japanese, a small expedition was despatched by the Formosa Government to explore the island. I was so fortunate as to be a member, and the following notes are largely the records of my observations made on that occasion.[1]

INHABITANTS: THEIR ORIGIN.

Several experienced Japanese anthropologists have, since the date of our expedition, visited Botel Tobago; and I believe it is their unanimous opinion that the inhabitants are of Malay origin. Undoubtedly these gentlemen are right in the main, the evidence even to an inexperienced layman appearing to show that the Malay element predominates. There are also, however, signs of outside influence in their life, sufficiently pronounced to demand some attention, and if this side of the question is carefully investigated, I believe evidence will be found sufficient to justify the announcement that the Botel Tobago savages, while approaching the pure Malay, are a mixed race.

The inhabitants of Botel Tobago, some 1,200 or 1,300 in all, occupy eight villages; Yakunawvmen, the largest settlement, being on the west coast and containing about 50 houses. The natives are small, averaging only five feet two inches in height. They are yellowish brown in color; and, with one individual exception, possess straight hair, black with a brownish tint. While thus conforming with the Malayan type in their straight hair and complexion, they appear, so far as face character is concerned, to be two types. We find the rather small nose and non-protruding lips of the Malay;

1. The first Botel Tobago expedition departed from Kelung aboard the naval transport "Fukui-maru" (2,928 tons) which was provided by the Navy Department, on March 10th, 1896, returning to Kelung on the 20th. One day was spent at Samasana island (Kwashoto), an interesting place occupied by Chinese fishermen, and five days at Botel Tobago. The expedition, which was under command of Major Tonoma Kikuchi, I.J.A., consisted of the following: T. Sano of the Formosa Civil Department, Lieutenant Yashiro I.J.N., Y. Narita, Mining Expert; S. Kayaba, Agricultural Expert, and K. Kumagui, M. Yokura, H. Inada, K. Fujimoto, K. Tokunaga, T. Ishikawa, T. Takahashi, G. Kurimura, and others. Also M. Nakahama, Japanese correspondent, and James W. Davidson, foreign correspondent. A guard of infantry under command of Lieutenant Okumoto, I.J.A., also accompanied the expedition.

and again a type with projecting eyebrows, deeply sunk orbits, short noses rather depressed at the root and with large nostrils,—in fact almost a Negrito nose,—together with the comparatively large mouth and thick lips of the pure Papuan type. One of the chief characteristics of the Papuan is his frizzled hair, of which no trace is found among the Botel Tobago natives, save in the case of one male adult who possesses hair distinctly curly. So much for their physical characteristics. In their usages and rites, their canoes and dwellings, they possess much in common with the Papuan, and in some instances opposed to the Malay. I do not refer to the Malayan type as seen in Formosa, (it is not unlikely that some of the groups of the latter island have also a strain of Papuan or other blood in their veins), but to the wild Malay of undoubted origin, regarding whom Wallace. Lubbock, Hickam, and others have written. The boat built by the Botel Tobago savages is almost an exact counterpart of the craft constructed by the Papuans in the Solomon islands, both as to form, method of construction and ornamentation, and is entirely unlike the boats built by any other peoples, including Malays, whose favorite model is a dug-out provided with an outrigger. It is a unique model, and it is almost inconceivable that a Malay savage should originate a boat agreeing so minutely with the rather complicated Papuan model. It would appear beyond dispute that the system of boat building referred to was introduced to the Botel Tobago natives by either a Papuan, or one familiar with Papuan life. There are several sizes of the truly splendid craft made in Botel Tobago, ranging from a small canoe with a capacity for two persons, up to a large boat which will hold twenty passengers. All appear to be of one model. They are beautifully rounded, and both stem and stern are shaped alike, being prolonged upwards in a graceful curve ending in a point from which, in time of festivity, is projected a bunch of feathers or some other decoration.

It is a built up boat; and, considering the crude tools used in its construction, is a remarkably creditable affair. The tribe possess no saws, and consequently each plank is adzed down, apparently from single trees. These planks, forming the sides of the boat, are so carefully shaped that they fit closely. Holes are bored near the seams, through which rattan lastings are passed and drawn tightly, literally tying the parts together. The bottom planks are fastened to the strong V shaped keel in the same manner. As in the Solomon islands, the principal tool used for this work is an adze. In Botel Tobago, this implement is so made that it can be converted into a chisel by altering the position of the blade, so that the edge will point to the front.

The native boats were found superior to the foreign-modeled ship boats for landing. The savages moved their craft about at will, the high bow cutting through the waves; and in landing they passed through a rather dangerous surf without the least difficulty, whereas we found landing with our boats, during at least one day, a rather exciting experience.

The Botel Tobago craft are nicely decorated; and with regard to the designs used, not only on their boats but on other articles as well, Papuan influence seems in evidence. Thus, the human figure nearly always appears in their decorations, whereas the wild Malay, as a rule, restricts his efforts to the production of geometrical designs.[1] It is well to note, however, that some of the Formosa groups also make use of the human figure for ornament, though not to the extent we find among Botel Tobago savages.

The natives erect grass huts for their boats on the shore, and these in shape and construction resemble very much the boat-huts of the Papuans of the Solomon islands.

Other points in which the Botel Tobago savage is in sympathy with Papuan customs are as follows :—The apparatus for fishing is complete and elaborate, including substantial seine nets for salt-water fishing, and much time is spent on this occasion. They also make fairly good pottery decorated with rough designs. The Malay generally depends upon wood or bamboo for bowls, dishes, etc. The Malay, except when taught by more experienced neighbors, does not, I believe, as a rule resort to irrigation to improve his fields. The Botel Tobago native, however, follows the Papuan and Negreto in arranging his taro fields in terraces, with a stream of water admitted at the top, which passes down from level to level, supplying just the quantity of water that will give the best results.

There would thus appear to be an element present among them that is not wholly Malayan.

This is probably due to the arrival at some ancient date of a few ship-wrecked Papuans, who in the course of time became absorbed by the Malay inhabitants, and from whom the improved methods of boat-building, cultivation, etc., were obtained ; or the strangers may have been from some of the Polynesian tribes, many of whom show close affinity with the Papuan. At all events, it is an interesting problem, for the solution of which we must look to Japanese anthropologists.

Dwellings.—The habitations of the Botel Tobago savages are very remarkable, not to say unique. Each family possesses a splendidly walled and stone-paved compound, wherein are three distinct houses, attesting the cleverness of the natives and their desire to obtain the maximum of comfort. One house, built half under ground, is their winter residence. For the warmer weather they have a comfortable building elevated some feet above ground, and for protection against the heat of summer they have a tower-like edifice sufficiently elevated to catch the cool breezes. These huts serve not only as habitations but also as workshops and storehouses. In construction, a considerable amount of wood is used as supports and cross-beams, and for the inner floor, ceiling, and walls, of the two large huts. The elevated structure is of wood, bamboo, and straw. A shelf projects level with the

---

1. Regarding Malay and Papuan decorations Hickam in his book " A Naturalist in North Celebes " writes : " If we compare the Malays throughout the Archipelago with their neighbors the Papuans we cannot fail to be impressed under the wide difference that exists between the two races in this respect. The Malay uses spears, shields, swords, canoes, and other weapons and implements, which are often entirely without ornament, and the colored designs on his clothes, his ceremonial shields, etc., are of the simplest geometrical patterns. The Papuan, on the other hand, covers everything he possesses with strange figures of men and animals, and fills up all the interstices between them with convenient designs of great regularity and beauty."

entrance ; and the inhabitants are obliged to mount this, and then crawl in on all fours, the door ways not being much larger than the entrance to a good sized dog kennel. The room is like a large flat box, some 7 by 8 feet, and is so low that one lying down can almost touch the ceiling with up-lifted hands. But the savages always squat ; so the place is high enough for them. Human figures and various rather pleasing geometrical designs are engraved on the interior woodwork, the only other decorations, (for such they are considered by the natives), are rows of animal jaw bones hung from side to side. The roof is thatched with a strong dried grass, and a similar material appears on the outer walls. The two buildings supported on piles have circular boards surmounting each post to keep off the large rats that literally overrun the island at night. During my first two nights in the island I was a guest in the tent of Major Kikuchi, but on the third night a terrific tropical downpour threatened to sweep us out into the sea, and we then removed to one of the native houses, which we found dry and, under the circumstances, comfortable.

Garments.—The dress of the islanders, even when they were so kind as to don any at all, can only be described as fragmentary. On occasions, the head was covered, when a conical shaped hat of rattan wood, or Areca fibre, evidently intended for hard service rather than for ornament or comfort, was alone in evidence. Again, the upper part of the body was enveloped in an abbreviated home-made tunic of China grass fibre, or reeds, or hard rough cocoanut fibre, the latter being apparently an indestructible affair which would dispose of the dress question for once and all. These tunics were sleeveless and open in front, thus really protecting only the shoulders and back. A very scanty breech cloth, resembling the Japanese *fundoshi*, and oddly enough tied in exactly the same manner, completed the attire. The legs were entirely bare, and no trace of any foot gear whatever was found by our party. Most surprising of all, perhaps, was to find the islanders in possession of hats actually made wholly of thin silver, which were used for ceremonial purposes. The women were more considerate ; an apron fastened at the waist hid, at times, the lower extremities; and on most occasions a square of cloth was wrapped about the body, one end being drawn over one shoulder and thence under the arm and around the back. The young women appeared well developed, and some were graceful and not unattractive, though like most savage races who suckle their children to a comparatively late age, the breasts of even young mothers scarcely out of their teens were long and flabby.

Ornaments.—The natives do not tattoo or otherwise disfigure them selves. The hair is shaved or closely cut about the neck and lower part of the head, in such a manner as to leave a circular mop of hair which is really quite ornamental. Necklaces of good wood, fish bones, shells, and berries are sometimes worn by both sexes, though they were not much in evidence at the time of my visit. The women also wear shell earrings, and they possess bamboo combs, which they frequently use. The islanders give great attention to the decoration of their canoes, weapons, implements, pottery,

Suspension Bridge of Rattan Built by Ami Savages.　　　Group of Botel Tobago Savages.

Two Types of Botel Tobago Savages.　　　　　Botel Tobago Boat.

Botel Tobago Natives handling Boat in the Surf.　View showing the Three Buildings constituting
a Botel Tobago Residence.

etc. Everything they construct, even down to some crude tool for use in the field, is brightened by skillfully carved designs. The boats, as before stated, are extensively ornamented, the human figure frequently appearing in their designs. Some of the pottery, though somewhat rough, was really very artistic, and the light geometrical designs which graced them gave, in most cases, a very happy effect. Dolls of most amusing forms are made of clay lightly burned. Metal bracelets were much in favor among the men, and one and all exhibited a most feverish desire to exchange their limited possessions for such silver coins as we possessed, which could be of no use to them except as ornaments or as material for the silver hats mentioned above. In fact, somewhat to our chagrin, we found that the various articles with which we had laden ourselves, such as tobacco, brightly colored cloth, buttons, bangles, cheap jewelry, etc., usually so highly prized by savages, excited not the least interest in the islanders, who wanted silver, or "pe lok" as they called it, and "pe lok" alone. There was just one exception; gold they gave us to understand was also acceptable, and of all the forms in which we possessed this precious metal, none was so attractive to them as the gold filled teeth of my interpreter. The prominence of these specially interested one most solemn individual who possessed as his sole treasure an English earthenware ale bottle, which he carried in a large box, where it had been gently deposited in a nest of worn out rags. He would carefully place the box on the ground, as carefully raise the lid, and with all the tenderness which a mother would bestow on her new born baby, produce the treasured bottle; then with pantomime which could not be misunderstood he would gravely point first to his bottle and then to my interpreter's gold teeth. He dogged the interpreter incessantly, repeating the amusing performance at every opportunity. The bottle had been doubtless obtained from some passing vessel, and the box looked like a ship's box though it had no name on it.

Food.—A considerable district on the hill slopes was under cultivation, and we found the water taro growing in terraced beds, with a perfect system of irrigation such as the Chinese possess. The dry taro, as well as the little millet, was also being grown,

Goats and peculiar long nosed pigs with long hair on the neck were found. Chickens also appeared abundant, so that the islands are well supplied with meat. Fishing is carried on industriously, the implements and nets used appearing to be very perfect. Shell fish also form an important article of food. Cocoanuts are very abundant, providing a luxurious food, while the milk is used as a beverage. Odd to relate, however, the natives have no intoxicating drink, and do not understand the use of tobacco. It is doubtful if there is another tribe in the whole Pacific that is not addicted to the use of tobacco.

Disease.—The islanders appeared remarkably free from disease. There was no sign of any venereal disease; and none of them were marked with small pox. Furthermore, there appeared to be no deformed, no blind, deaf, or dumb persons.

Religion.—No information could be obtained regarding their religious rites. They appear, however, to believe in a form of taboo. On the arrival of our party, the natives fled into the forest ; but projecting from the front of each hut had been placed a stick 5 or 6 feet long, and from the end of this hung a string to which was attached a piece of bone. This was doubtless intended as a taboo, protecting their place from the strangers. When friendly relations had been established, their taboos were all withdrawn, and we saw no more during our stay.

Traditions.—Their traditions tell of the arrival of strangers driven there by storm from the islands which they call "Ibatan" and "Ikubarat." They also declare that in ancient times a man and woman gave birth to many children. The father died in early life, and the mother was stolen by the natives of "Ibatan" island and carried away never to return. The children, however, grew up and prospered, and now inhabit the village of Irarai on the north west coast.

Miscellaneous.—Fire is obtained by friction, two pieces of wood being the agents. The only weapons appeared to be a few harmless looking spears. There are no dogs or cats on the island, which accounts for the great pest of rats. Immense rodents, as large as musk-rats, literally over-ran the villages at night. One could see them after dark running about without any signs of fear, just as hungry hogs would overrun a garden ; and it is no exaggeration to say we feared the rats more than we feared the natives. In addition to the pottery for domestic purposes, small vessels are made for melting silver. While their language appears to contain many Malay words, there is a large, if not a preponderating, number of words which appear to have no connection with the Malayan speech.

In closing my account of these simple people, living happy and peaceful lives, free from disease and strife, the doubt arises in my mind if civilization has anything to offer them. Would civilization make their burden lighter or their life happier? The records of the downfall of other savage races brought in contact with our so-called civilization suggest an answer.

Chinese Population of Formosa.—Politically, the Chinese population may be divided into those who have accepted Japanese nationality, (commonly called in government publications "Hontojin" (Islanders), and those who retain their own nationality. On the basis of language and customs, the Chinese population may be divided into two classes, Haklos, who speak the Amoy dialect, and who originally emigrated from Fokien province: and Hakkas, who speak a Cantonese dialect, and emigrated chiefly from Kwangtung province. In addition, there are a few true Cantonese traders, and here and there a north China man. The Hakkas, a hardy and warlike race (of whom I have treated in the first chapter), took up their residence in the savage border districts, where land could be had for the taking, and where a certain freedom from official oppression was ensured. To a stranger unacquainted with the language there is but little to distinguish the male Hakka boy or man from a Haklo, but with the women the case is different; their unbound feet and their complicated hair dress, somewhat resembling that of the Japanese, at once differentiating them from the Haklo women, who bind their feet and dress their hair with a single coil to the back. The barter trade carried on with the savages is often in the hands of the Hakkas, and the present agricultural development of the foot hills was partly inaugurated by them. Unlike their Haklo brethren they are generally fearless, and we thus find them, of all Chinese, most willing to undertake the making of camphor in dangerous districts. Their life in the Formosa hills is not one of ease and comfort. They live in rude huts, affording but little shelter from the elements ; and whether in the camphor forests or in their own homes, their fire arms must be always near them to repel an attack by the savages, who come when least expected and absolutely without warning. When in sufficient number and their occupation permits, they build their huts together on an elevation, if possible, with a clear outlook all round. If such a site is not available, a stockade is frequently built to enclose the settlement, and a high watch tower is erected, whereon watchmen are stationed to give warning should savages appear. But in spite of all precautions, scarcely a day passes without a Hakka in some district losing his life ; in fact, the daily average has of late been about two Chinese either killed or wounded, which is, however, exceptionally large. There are a few prosperous Hakka villages in the plain, but as a rule the Hakka prefers the hills. It is roughly estimated that there are in the island nearly 500,000 Hakkas, who are found in greatest numbers in the border district stretching from Bioritsu (Maoli) in the north to Nanto (Namtau) in central Formosa, while there are also some settlements south-east of Takow. There are also a few Hakkas to be found in Taito (Taitong) district on the south east coast.

During the Chinese regime, the Hakkas were considered by the authorities a turbulent lawless lot, and encounters between them and representatives of the government were frequent. After the occupation of the island by the Japanese, the Hakkas of south Formosa gave some trouble for a few weeks, but since then they have not shown any special opposition to the authorities.

The Haklos may be divided into four groups,—Amoy, Tswengchoo, Changchoo, and Changpoo,—according to their dialects and the districts in Fokien from which they come. Of these four groups, the Amoy and Tsweng choo people predominate in the north of the island and along the west coast, especially in the cities of Koro (Aulan), Taiko (!aika), Giubato (Gumatau), Gosei (Goche), Tokatsukutsu (Thawkakut), and Rokko (Lokiang). The Changchoo and Changpoo people are numerically greatest in the south, and are also in considerable numbers on the plains of central Formosa. The Haklos, who number over two million, are the predominant race throughout the island. There is little of interest to record about them. They have brought with them the customs of their home-land to such a degree that a country Chinese village in Formosa presents the same features as a village in their home province. The houses are of like materials and are crowded together in the same unsanitary way, the narrow ill smelling streets present the same filth and are as irregular, the street hawkers have the same calls and exhibit the same wares, and the people are alike in their dress and habits.

Like their brethren on the mainland they are industrious and economical, but unfortunately unclean and superstitious. If they possess any advantages over the great " masses " of the China mainland, it is that they are less conservative and more liberal in many ways. The parents of thousands of the Formosa Chinese arrived as strangers practically in a foreign land; they doubtless met with hardships and unfriendliness while obtaining a foothold: and it is perhaps this fact that has made them look with a more kindly spirit towards strangers in general. Without a doubt, the splendid work of the missionary bodies in the island, who lived down the disfavor with which they were at first regarded, accounts to a great degree for the absence of any strong anti-foreign spirit among the people at present.

In the Japanese census returns, the Chinese are all classed together irrespective of their home province; and, consequently, the numerical strength of Chinese, other than Haklos and Hakkas, cannot be ascertained. They number but a few thousands, however, at most; but owing to the fact that practically all the big merchants, wholesale and retail, are Cantonese, the latter class are an important element.

Japanese Population.—We will now deal with the new element, the Japanese population. The arrival of the Japanese dates from the occupation of the island by Japan in 1895. Prior to that event there was not in the whole island a single Japanese resident. The first civilian arrivals were not a very desirable class. They were chiefly adventurers following the army to pick up what they could by the wayside and return to Japan at the first opportunity. Thousands of military coolies were brought into the island to carry supplies for the army; and fortunately, at the expiration of their term of employment, they were returned to Japan by the Government. The camp followers led a horrible life, great numbers died from sickness; they found the island no Eldorado, and the survivors eventually drifted back to Japan. During the year 1896, after peace had been restored, a better element arrived. Merchants in Japan sent down representatives to look the field over from a commercial view; scholars and professional men visited the island in considerable numbers, and shopkeepers established themselves in the larger cities, carrying such goods as would appeal to the military, to travellers, etc. Towards the close of the year, the first Japanese women arrived, and carpenters were busy converting Chinese structures into habitations provided with the proverbial *tatami*, without which Japanese seem ill at ease. The evolution of a Chinese house in the hands of a Japanese was interesting. The typical Chinese house has the minimum of light and air, and the maximum of darkness and dampness! and the Japanese occupant endeavored to reverse this state of things. The first move was to punch holes through the long stretch of solid wall, so as to supply windows. Small regard was shown for the landlord's sensibilities; and frequently the openings were not plastered over, but were simply big jagged holes, which looked for all the world as though the building had been badly injured by a bombardment. An elevated wooden floor, two or three feet high, was then erected from end to end, with a passage down one side to the back. On the new floor were placed the Japanese mats, and in some instances Japanese sliding doors were added. While the converted house was superior to the original in cleanliness and much better lighted, it was far from healthy, even the elevated floor being too near the ground for this malarial climate; besides the vicinity was generally unsanitary, and the immediate drainage defective. The result may be imagined. Hundreds of Japanese died in the island, and hundreds returned to Japan invalided. During the last three months of 1896, an outbreak of plague carried away nearly a hundred in the north of the island. As a result of this state of affairs, the report spread throughout Japan that Formosa was a death hole; and at one period so universal was this belief that even Japanese servants could not be engaged for the island. This was unfortunate, as it discouraged the better class of Japanese from settling in the island. At this period, even the officials occupied Chinese quarters. The foreigners lived in the upper storeys of roomy well ventilated structures; and it was a great contrast to find a Japanese friend installed in a dirty, dark, ill-ventilated Chinese house with mud walls, set down in an ill-smelling disease breeding Chinese street. Under these circumstances, it was not so strange that pestilence should have broken out as that any should have escaped. That this sacrifice of life was unnecessary, and that, given good houses and sanitary streets, life would be quite as safe in Formosa as in other semi-tropical climes, was not known to people in Japan; they did know that their friends and relatives were dying in the island, and that was sufficient. In 1897, dormitories for some of the officials were erected, and work was commenced on others, with the idea of ultimately having all the government employés comfortably housed. The civilians also built a few new houses, while others improved the Chinese quarters they occupied; the attics of many of the single storeyed structures being re-modelled so that sleeping room could be obtained there. A notable decrease in mortality among Japanese followed these improvements. While the residents here began to regard the island in a more favorable light, it was difficult to erase impressions existing in the home land; and even now, when further innovations have made life more comfortable and secure, in Japan, (the country above all which one could expect to be well informed), there exists a general impression that Formosa is exceptionally unhealthy, an idea which is but little better than a libel on the beautiful Isle. Given a sanitary neighborhood, upper storeyed quarters, plenty of fresh air and light, good food, and protection for the head when exposed to the sun's rays, and life can be made quite as healthy as can be expected in a warm climate. The author's experience of six years in the island without a single day of sickness entitles him to speak with some authority on this point.

Excluding government works, the advent of the Japanese population has made little change in the outward appearance of things, except in the capital city, Taihoku (Taipeh). The change there, however, has been very striking to one who saw it under the Chinese regime. Even in 1896, it may be said to have been thoroughly Chinese. Probably not one in ten of the shops or other places of business was Japanese, and not a building was to be seen in other than Chinese style. During the summer of 1897, there were evidences of great changes, though the city still had a distinctly Chinese appearance. Now it is vastly different ; there is not one Chinese shop in twenty ; and all this has taken place without any pressure being brought to bear, but simply because the Chinese have gone down before the Japanese, who are willing to pay higher prices or higher rentals for land and houses. Taihoku is now a thoroughly Japanese city in every respect. In fact, with its fine macadamized streets, its imposing buildings, its well-stocked shops, it excels perhaps any city of its size in the whole empire of Japan. No other place in the island has witnessed like changes.[1] The streets are also generally cleaner and better cared for than under the Chinese regime, though there is much yet to be done before the Chinese town can be considered sanitary. The Japanese population, excluding the military, is at present some 40,000. With the exception of the official class who come chiefly from Tokyo, a large portion of the above are from the south of Japan. Many are from Kyushu, though the shopkeepers appear to have come chiefly from Osaka. During the early days of the Japanese occupation, wives and children were rarely brought to the island. Now family life is more in favor, and the number of Japanese females is consequently on the increase. At present the males outnumber the other sex by 3 to 1.[2] The Japanese population is steadily growing, however. Thus, during the year 1900, Japanese males arrived to the number of 13,316 and females 5,680, a total of 18,996. In 1899, there were 8,601 males, and 2,544 females, a total of 11,145. The island thus gained 7,851 in Japanese population during the year ; which, all things considered, would appear to show that the Japanese are finding life in Formosa worth living.

As yet, with the exception of some few wealthy firms who are interest· ing themselves in plantations, the Japanese do not take to agricultural employment; in fact, it would be difficult for them to compete with Chinese farmers, who grow nearly all they desire for food, and whose other require- ments are limited perhaps to one pair of cotton trousers a year. Again, it is doubtful whether, at least for some time, the Japanese can labor in the fields, in the hot Formosa sun, as many hours a day as the Chinese, who have greater powers of endurance. For artisans, coolie overseers, and shop assistants, and for general professional and skilled labor, there is, however, an opening. We consequently find the present Japanese population scat- tered throughout the cities and villages ; indeed there is hardly a village of any size in the island without at least half a dozen or so of Japanese, who get on so well with the villagers that many of them live in turbulent districts, where the natives, if so disposed, could attack them with perfect impunity.

---

1. Of course, it will be understood that portions of other cities also show signs of Japanese occupation.

2. For census statistics see following chapter.

Views at the Capital.

North End Taihoku City, the Day of Japanese Occupation (1895).
Taihoku City as viewed from Observatory.
Government Opium Factory, Taihoku.

North End of Taihoku City, under Japanese Rule in 1900, showing New Post-office on right.
Meteorological Observatory, Taihoku.
Appeal Court, Taihoku.

CHAPTER XXXI.

FORMOSA OF TO-DAY.

Administration :—Boundaries—Status of Formosan officials—Constitutional provisions —Formosan ordinances—Civil Administration Office—Administrative Divisions.

Population :—Census statistics—Twenty-three largest cities—Rate of Japanese increase —Births and deaths—Foreign residents.

Society :—Position of masses—Increased wages—Labor supply and demand—Improved condition of masses—Scale of wages—Inflow of capital.

Education :—Missions—Chinese schools—Present conditions—Difficulties encountered Paid students—System of government schools—Appropriation for education— Technical schools—Mission work—Success attained—Canadian Presbyterian Mission—English Presbyterian Mission—Mission statistics—First Formosan Newspaper—Roman Catholic Mission work.

Justice and Crime :—Status of Formosan courts—Application of Japanese laws— Distribution of courts—Prisons—Prison statistics—Police control—Native police —Gendarmes.

Sanitation :—Condition on arrival of Japanese—Hospitals established—Sanitary works —Water supply—Mission hospitals—The opium problem—Preventive policy adopted—Difficulties of control—Opium statistics.

Finance :—Revenue—Profit from monopolies—Tax statistics—Expenditures—Revenue items—Table of relative expenditures—Banking facilities—Currency problem— " Tamsui Dollars "—Exchange difficulties.

Defence : — Brigade headquarters — Permanent garrison — Fortifications — Military Transport—Arsenals.

Internal Communications :—Public highways—Japanese roadwork — City Paving —Narrow gauge tramways—Method of operation—Railways—Reconstruction of old line—Construction of main line—Tamsui line—Railway projected.

Posts and Telegraphs :—Telegraph and cable lines laid—Transportation of mails.

Shipping and Navigation :—Harbors—Steamship lines—Shipping subsidies—Harbor construction work—Kelung harbor improvement work—Tamsui and Takow harbors.

Foreign Trade .—Increase of imports—Increase of shipping —Trade via Hongkong and China—Trade of Formosa ports compared—Trade via Japan—Total trade— Foreign imports via Japan—Formosa government supplies—Trade with the United States and Great Britain compared.

ADMINISTRATION.

The administrative division of Formosa under Japanese control as defined by Imperial decree comprises all islands lying between the 119th and 120th degrees of Longitude (East from Greenwich) and the 23rd and 24th degrees of North Latitude.[1] The principal islands included are Formosa or "Taiwan" its official designation, Kwasho-to (Samasana Island), Kotosho (Botel Tobago Island), and Bokoto (Pescadores Group). Owing to the non completion of surveys the exact area of the division can not be stated, but it will probably be found to be over 15,000 square miles.

The government of the island is wholly under the control of the central government of Japan, there being no local representation. There is at present no office in the mainland devoted exclusively to Formosan affairs. The Governor-General of the Island is, however, nominally under the authority of the Home Minister. The supreme executive authority in Formosa, is vested in the Governor General.[2] This official under the present system must be of Shinnin rank, and possess the rank of Field Marshal, General, Lieutenant General, or Admiral. He has control of the Imperial military and naval forces and the civil administration within his jurisdiction. He may call out the military or naval forces to preserve order in the island when he deems it necessary; but must report such action to the proper authorities in Japan. He may also place military officers in control of civil officers when deemed advisable.

The Governor-General has the power to appoint or dismiss all officers of Hannin or lower rank, but officers above that rank cannot be appointed to, or dismissed from, office without the Emperor's sanction, obtained through the Home Minister. He can recommend these civil officers for promotion in rank, but the promotion is made by the Emperor through the Prime Minister. In obtaining the Emperor's sanction to any measure requiring the same by law, application is made through the Home Minister.

There having been issued no decree to the contrary, the provisions of the Constitution are generally considered in force in Formosa. The laws of Japan, however, do not apply to Formosa unless special provision to that effect has been entered in the law itself. The laws and regulations for Formosa which have been issued from time to time, have been drawn up

1. The boundary line to the south was in 1895 established by special convention between Japan and Spain to be as follows:—" A line parallel to a latitude passing through the middle of the navigable part of the Bashee Channel, shall, under the present declaration, mark the boundary between the territories of Japan and Spain in the western part of the Pacific.

The Government of Spain declares that it shall never lay claim to the islands lying to the north and north-east of the above mentioned boundary line.

The Government of Japan declares that it shall never lay claim to the islands lying to the south and south-east of the above mentioned boundary line.

2. The Governor-Generals during the Japanese occupation have been as follows :—

Admiral Kabayama appointed May 10th, 1895 . . . . . Retired June 2nd, 1896.
Lieut.-General Katsura appointed June 2nd, 1896. . . .   „   October 14th, 1896.
Lieut.-General Nogi appointed October 14th, 1896 . . .   „   February 26th, 1898.
Lieut.-General Kodama appointed February 26th, 1898.

with the peculiar condition and requirements of the island in view.[1] Formosa ordinances emanate from the Governor-General's office, bear his signature, and after obtaining the approval of the Formosa Council require the sanction of the Emperor. The Council of the Formosa Government consists of the Chief of Civil Administration, Chief of Financial Section, Chief of Military Staff, Chief of Naval Staff, and the official counsellors. The Governor-General may, if he deems it necessary, order other civil, military or naval officers connected or intimately acquainted with affairs under discussion, to attend the meetings, but they are excluded from voting. As his immediate advisers, the Governor-General has the Chief of Civil Administration, Chief of Military Staff, and the Chief Counsellor. Under the latter official, who must be of Chokunin rank, are two counsellors of Sonin rank. The counsellors receive orders from the Governor-General and Chief of Civil Administration, and their chief duties are in connection with legal questions. Under their control are sections in charge of the investigation of old customs, and official translation work.

Under the Department of Civil Administration are the Section of Police Affairs and the following Bureaux:—General Affairs (Somu kyoku), Finance, Communications, Agriculture and Industry, and Public Works. Under the General Affairs Bureau, which is in charge of the Chief Counsellor, are the Sections of Home Affairs, Foreign Affairs, Legislation, and Education. The Chief of Civil Administration and Chief Counsellor must be of Chokunin rank, the Inspector-General of Police and the five Chiefs of Bureaux must be either of Chokunin or Sonin rank; the four special Counsellors, 15 Secretaries (Jimukwan), 3 Chiefs of Police, 18 Experts (Gishi) and 5 Translators must be of Sonin rank, and the remaining officials, 320 in number, are to be of Hannin rank. The Railway Department, the Monopolies Bureau, and the Customs service are under the Civil Department. The Chief of Civil Administration acts as Chief of Railway Department and Chief of the Monopolies Bureau. There is also the temporary Bureau of Surveys which is likewise under the Civil Department.

· In place of the former system, which divided the island into 3 prefectures and 3 prefectures of second class, and which was abolished November 11th, 1901, local administrative offices known as " Cho " have been established at the following points :

Taihoku, Kelung, Giran (Gilan), Shinko (Chim-hua), Toshien (Tao-hong), Shinchiku (Teck-cham), Bioritsu (Maoli), Taichu, Shoka (Chang-wha), Nanto (Nam-tau), Toroku (Tau-lak), Kagi, Yensuiko (Kiam-tsui kang), Tainan, Banshorio (Han-chu liao), Hozan (Fang-shan), Ako (A-kau), Koshun (Heng-chun), Taito (Tai-tong), and Boko (Pang-hoo).

---

1. As respects privileges granted to foreigners in Japan and Formosa a proclamation issued on the 22nd of February 1896, by the Formosa Government contained the following reference ;
"Paragraph 2. Though special circumstances exist in Formosa, the Treaties of Commerce and Navigation, Tariff regulations, and other arrangements now existing between Japan and various nations having treaties with Japan, shall be applied, as far as possible, to the subjects of such nations who reside in or sail to and from Formosa."
"Those who enjoy the preceding privileges and conveniences must observe the laws and ordinances in operation in Formosa."

The Administrative or District Offices (Cho) are in charge of chiefs of Sonin rank, who are assisted by clerks, police inspectors, assistant experts, interpreters, and assistant police, all of Hannin rank. These officers of Hannin rank number 1230 for the whole island. The administration of Formosa, under the direction and superintendence of the Governor-General, is entrusted to these district offices.

POPULATION.

The following tables give the population of the island, excluding the military and the hill tribes of the interior mountainous district, which were dealt with in the preceding chapter:—

		JAPANESE.		Natives (CHINESE).		TOTAL
Taihoku prefecture	Male ..	12,198	Male .	391,883		
	Female..	6,335	Female..	325,506		
		18,533		717,389		735,922
Taichu ,, ...	Male ..	3,716	Male ..	441,477		
	Female..	1,303	Female..	369,583		
		5,019		811,060		816,079
Tainau ,, ...	Male ..	4,997	Male ..	526,621		
	Female..	2,407	Female..	443,958		
		7,404		970,579		977,983
Giran prefecture of 2nd class ..	Male ..	733	Male ..	53,549		
	Female..	285	Female..	44,975		
		1,023		98,524		99,547
Taito ,, ,, ..	Male ..	316	Male ..	25,376		
	Female..	155	Female..	23,331		
		471		48,707		49,178
Pescadores ,, ,, ..	Male ..	427	Male ..	25,870		
	Female..	243	Female .	25,716		
		670		51,586		52,256
Male Total		22,392		1,464,776		2,730,865 .
Female ,, ...		10,728		1,233,060		

The total population is divided up into 8,321 Japanese families, and 532,176 native families or 540,497 families in all, which gives an average among Japanese of near 4 to a family, and among Chinese of over 5.

THE TWENTY-THREE LARGEST CITIES.

Daitotei (Twatutia) ..	..	.. 31,533	Hokuto (Paktau)	5,581
Banka	..	.. 23,767	Taichu	4,014
Taihoku (Taipeh) ..	..	.. 5,921	Tainau	47,283
Shinchiku (Teckcham)	..	.. 18,528	Kagi	17,910
Kelung	..	.. 8,360	Toko (Tangkang)	7,624
Kobi (Hobe) ..	..	.. 6,150	Bokushikyaku (Boaka)	7,506
Shinsho (Shinching) ..	..	.. 5,148	Hozan (Pithau)	6,876
Taikoken (Tokoham) ..	..	.. 4,244	Yensuiko (Kiamtsuikang) ..	6,432
Rokko (Lokiang) ..	..	.. 18,414	Anping	4,385
Shoka (Changwha) ..	..	.. 13,988	Takow	3,702
Hokuko (Pakkang) ..	..	.. 6,314		

In Giran Prefecture of 2nd class Giran (Gilau), the capital city, has 15,637; and Haiuau (Pilam) the capital city of Taito, 2nd class prefecture, 1241.

North Formosa Views.

A View on the Kelung River at Maruyama.   The Tamsui as seen from Daitotei Twatutia.

The Upper Bund of Daitotei.

On the lower bund, Daitotei.   Market in a North Formosa Chinese town.

FORMOSA POPULATION ACCORDING TO OCCUPATION.

	Japanese Males.	Japanese Females.	Total.	Native (Chinese) Males.	Native Females	Total.	Grand Total.
Officials	5,214	697	5,911	569	285	854	6,765
Educationists including Missionaries	116	30	146	3,588	2,167	5,750	5,890
Agriculturists	54	11	65	735,217	635,141	1,370,358	1,370,423
Manufacturers	2,255	230	2,485	208,425	197,607	406,032	408,517
Merchants	4,458	3,597	8,055	122,910	99,422	222,332	230,387
Fishermen	--	--	—	4,938	3,827	8,765	8,765
Laborers..	1,260	146	1,460	89,111	66,858	155,969	156,429
Possessing no regular trade ..	165	84	249	40,800	48,381	89,181	89,430
Miscellaneous	3,912	2,832	6,743	162,269	156,420	318,689	324,432

Owing to the incompleteness of the early census records as respects the native (Chinese) population, we cannot determine the rate of increase or decrease of this class. The statistics for the Japanese population, however, are more exact, and the records for four years are as follows:—

											TOTAL.
1897..	..	..	Families	3,347	Consisting of Males	12,662	Females	3,659	16,321
1898..	..	..	,,	7,398	,,	,,	17,768	,,	7,817	25,585
1899..	..	..	,,	8,321	,,	,,	22,390	,,	10,728	33,120
1900 .	..	..	,,	——	,,	,,	27,105	,,	13,864	40,969

THE BIRTHS AND DEATHS FOR 1898.

BIRTHS.

			Japanese Males.	Japanese Females.	Native Males.	Native Females.	Total Males.	Total Females.	Total.
Taihoku-Ken	..	..	66	47	6,526	5,601	6,592	5,648	12,240
Taichu-Ken ..	..	..	6	9	4,429	3,365	4,435	3,374	7,809
Tainan-Ken ..	..	..	14	22	5,849	4,931	5,863	4,953	10,816
Pescadores ..	..	..	5	3	494	321	499	324	823
Total ..	..	..	91	81	17,298	14,218	17,389	14,299	31,688

DEATHS.

			Japanese Males	Japanese Females.	Native Males.	Native Females.	Total Males.	Total Females.	Total.
Taihoku-Ken	..	..	122	40	5,047	4,029	5,169	4,069	9.238
Taichu Ken ..	..	..	57	32	4,145	3,340	4,202	3,372	7,574
Tainan Ken ..	..	..	65	1	1,632	1,102	1,697	1,103	2,800
Pescadores ..	..	..	6	2	343	312	349	344	693
Total ..	..	..	250	75	11,167	8,813	11,417	8,888	20,305

As regards longevity, we find in Formosa 1418 natives (Chinese) from the age of 85 to 89, 125 from 90 to 94, 14 from 96 to 99, 1 at 100, and 1 who claims 106 years. Mortality appears to be greatest during the ages of 1 to 3, and from 48 onward.

But little space may be given to the representatives of western lands living in the island. They are so few and, if we except the missionaries, their influence, on existing institutions, is so slight that the desire for completeness is my only excuse for including them. The foreigners reside in practically but two places, Taihoku and Tainan. In the former place they live in Daitotei (Twatutia) a suburb of the capital, with the exception of the English Consular representatives and two missionary families who are in Tamsui (Hobe). Owing to the withdrawal of many of the merchants for the winter months, the population is greatest in the summer. Excluding the foreigners connected with the Customs, which have, of course, now been replaced by the Japanese service, the number has about doubled during the six years of Japanese occupation. This means little, however.

During the last of the Chinese days there were about a dozen, and now there are some 22 or more. During this period, 3 business houses have discontinued business, and 5 have been newly established. In Tainan the foreign missionaries reside in Tainan city, and the mercantile population, only half a dozen in all, live in the nearby port Anping. There has been no increase; in fact one firm has withdrawn from the place. The total foreign population of Tainan district numbers some 20. With the exception of tea, a part of the sugar export, and a small share in the import trade, the Chinese control the trade of the island. There is consequently but little for foreigners in Formosa, and while the numbers of westerners residing here may show some increase as years pass by, there is at present no evidence of a large foreign settlement ever coming into existence. Foreign trade will increase; but, with the exception of the exports, it will be handled as at present chiefly by Chinese and Japanese. The future, therefore, holds forth no specially bright prospect for the handful of foreigners here.

SOCIETY.

The Japanese occupation will improve the position of the masses throughout the island; of this there can be but little doubt. It will bring thousands within the reach of modern conveniences, the railway, improved shipping facilities, good roads, etc. It will afford them modern medical treatment, the advantages of modern education, and will offer encouragement to the development of the island's resources and the utilizing of machinery and other improved methods of manufacture.

The change in rulers is of too late a date, and affairs are in too much of a transitionary stage, to show marked results from the adoption of these principles at this day, though some changes, especially in the line of increased trade, are already noticeable. Development can not be rapid, owing to the conservatism of those who will profit by the innovations; but it will be sure and sound, and its effects will be increasingly apparent year by year.

That the occupation has already improved the material side of the life of the masses is evident. Prior to the arrival of the Japanese, the wages for unskilled labor ranged from 13 to 20 yen cents a day according to locality, supply, demand, etc. At present the coolie finds his wages doubled, and contractors who desire large forces of workmen frequently find it extremely difficult to obtain them even at the price mentioned.[1] The great demand

---

1. The present scale of day wages in yen for Japanese and native skilled labour in Formosa is given in the following :—

OCCUPATION.	JAPANESE.		NATIVES.	
	1st Class.	2nd Class.	1st Class.	2nd Class.
Carpenters, Cabinet makers, etc...	1.30	1.10	.70	.60
Stone and brick masons..	1.80	1.60	.70	.60
Tub-makers	1.00	.60	.60	.40
Boat-builders	1.30	1.10	.70	.60
Iron-workers	2.00	.80	.80	60
Tailors	35.00 per month	25.00 per month	20.00 per month	10.00 per month
Seal makers, engravers, etc... ..	.80	.60	.70	.45

The above prices will average nearly double the existing prices in either Japan or China.

for labor owing to the industrial and improvement works of the government, has increased the circulation of money, and the agricultural population find that they can obtain almost double the money for their products. True the laborer in paying more for his food does not find his increased wage clear gain, still with the proverbial economy of the coolie class, their wants under any circumstances are so few, that their cost can be easily doubled without deducting much from the increase they are receiving. Owing to improved methods of transportation, the use of steam launches to visit the coast ports which was forbidden under Chinese rule, and other factors, some staples are even cheaper in certain districts. That the purchasing power of the masses has increased is apparent when we note the great increase in the imports of certain articles which Chinese could easily do without if they wished. Flour, for instance, during the last year of the Chinese was imported into the island to the value of 82,680 yen. In 1900, under the Japanese, the island consumed 355,441 yen worth. Kerosene, which considering the abundance of cheap local vegetable oil, can be considered a luxury, had an increased demand during the same period of from 398,560 to 1,198,669 yen. Imports of foreign piece goods, yarns, etc., have likewise increased from 662,200 to considerably over a million yen in value. While the Japanese in the island are consumers of the staples mentioned, still their unmber is so small that the increase may be attributed almost wholly to the native population. More information on the increase in trade appears in the section on that subject given further on.

Furthermore, whereas the Chinese government invested practically nothing for the island's improvement, but remitted yearly varying sums to the Pekin government, the Japanese have not only spent all the island's revenue locally, but have, during the five years of their occupation, brought in from Japan fifty four million yen which has been utilized chiefly for public improvements; and this does not include the large expenditure for military and the no inconsiderable sum spent by the large number of Japanese travellers who are constantly visiting the island. This large sum has ultimately either found its way to the natives in cash or represents the value of machinery, building materials, etc., brought into the island to improve local conditions.

I should mention, however, that there is one class which has not profited by the arrival of the Japanese. It is the literati who, being without profession and unable to undertake manual labor, find no field open to them. They have left the island in large numbers, but there are still many left, and they are glad of employment at wages which an energetic jinrikisha man would look upon with disdain.

EDUCATION.

Prior to the arrival of the Japanese, education was, with the exception of two missionary schools, confined almost exclusively to the children of well-to-do parents who could afford to pay for it. Public and free schools were not in existence. Even the paid schools limited their instruction to the usual Chinese curriculum, which is devoted first to the study of the characters, and, if a higher education is desired, to the mastering of the Chinese classics; for the more familiar the student is with the latter the more advanced he is regarded by his friends. There were none of the studies which in western lands and in Japan are considered necessary for an educated man, and the general tendency of their training was to increase conservatism and love for ancient customs: the greatest stumbling block in the way of Chinese progress. The individual thus educated is conceited, superstitious, and illiberal, and regard less of the years of study, is still ignorant when judged by western standards.

A foreign friend well known in China, and who has perhaps as intimate a knowledge of the Chinese as any one in the East, after spending some weeks in the island, giving special attention to the work of the Japanese among the natives, expressed the opinion that the former would win their way with the people through school books and medicine.

The great mass of the population are unable to read and write, and thus the field for educational work is very vast. But the work laid out before the Japanese is not simple. If the Chinese would avail themselves of the opportunity of modern education when the same is within their reach, the problem would be a simple one. The proverbial conservatism of the race, however, is almost as strong as on the mainland, and the natives, at present, show a preference for their own educational methods.

We consequently find the Japanese actually obliged to employ at present young Chinese as scholars. This system has been adopted in several newly established government schools in the island, and not only are the total tuition and living expenses paid, but an allowance, liberal to Chinese, is made to supply them with clothes and a small balance for pocket money. All things considered, it is a wise procedure. It is the parents that require education; not that they must be themselves put through schools, but they must be taught by the younger men that modern education for the children is desirable, and that the Japanese schools should be availed of. The government schools in the island are of six classes, Normal Schools, National Language Schools, Native Language Schools, Primary Schools, Middle Schools, and Special Schools. There are at present three normal schools for Chinese, situated at Taihoku (Taipeh), Shoka (Changwha) and Tainan respectively. The curriculum includes moral science, Japanese, Chinese, mathematics, book-keeping, geography, history, natural philosophy and science, also music and gymnastics, and a general training in teaching. Board and tuition as well as an allowance for clothes, is made by the government to the Normal School students. It is the desire of the government that the Chinese teachers of private schools shall receive a training in the Normal School. There are at present attending the normal schools over 200 students. There is a so-called national language school, which is in reality a general high school, in Taipeh, and those branches which are intended for Japanese students attached to the same. Study is divided into several courses, and instruction in the following branches is given:—Japanese, Chinese, foreign language, moral science, reading, penmanship, arithmetic, general mathematics, book-keeping, history, geography, chemistry and drawing, and in the normal department the art of teaching. There is also a ladies school attached, at which are taught moral science, Japanese, reading, penmanship, needle-work, knitting, flower making, embroidery, and music. The term of study is 3 years. There are at present 199 students in the main school, and 172 in the branch school, including 40 girls. The normal department course covers 2 years, and all expenses of students there are paid by the government. There are 3 native language schools specially for Japanese students. The students at present attending the language school and its several branches number 511 Japanese, including 180 girls, and 471 natives including 183 girls. Students of the language course showing special ability can go to Japan and complete their education there at government expense. There are Primary schools in the following seven cities:—Taihoku, Tamsui (Hobe), Kelung, Gilan, Shinchiku (Teck-cham), Taichu and Tainan, and the course of instruction includes moral science, reading, composition, penmanship, mathematics, geography, history, natural philosophy, science, music, drawing and gymnastics.

There are 120 government public schools scattered throughout the island, many of them in new buildings specially built for the purpose. A general course of study, in which are included reading, writing, geography, arithmetic, history, Japanese, etc., affords a good primary education. The total number of native students attending the various schools is over 13,000 and Japanese over 1,000. The government teachers number 578 with salaries ranging from 600 to 2,400 yen a year. Whenever possible, preference is shown for graduates when there are government positions to fill. At present in the government service there are over 250 Japanese and 313 native (Chinese) graduates. The majority of them are given Hannin rank or receive treatment as of that rank. In addition, there are schools for teaching the savages at Pinan (Pilam), Barang (Karenko), Choroto, and Gilan, with about 260 students. The total amount appropriated for education in 1900 was 492,600 yen. The national treasury contributed 169,900 yen, local taxes provided 270,700 yen, and the villages and towns in which schools were established were assessed at 52,000 yen. This appropriation will be increased year by year until every village has its free public school. Excluding the salaries for teachers and other expenses of administration, there has been expended some 1,200,000 yen on schools. It is the intention to raise the language school gradually until it has the curriculum of a high school, and eventually it is intended to convert it into a university. Within two years it is expected there will be 300 public schools; additional primary schools for Japanese, and also middle schools will be established. There are also plans for 40 schools for savages to be erected in villages near the savage border. When educational facilities are in the reach of all, compulsory attendance at school will be enforced.

In addition to the above, the government supports a number of special schools. First in importance comes the Medical School attached to the splendidly equipped Central Hospital at Taihoku. The course is for 3 years, and all students are obliged to be familiar with Japanese, as that language only is used in the school. An allowance to cover tuition and board is made to each student by the government. A new building, provided with theater, etc., has been built for the school, and it is well provided with apparatus for the work. Criminals executed at the Taihoku prison who have no friends or relatives desiring the body for burial, are turned over to the school for postmortem examination. There are 70 students at present. A school for police and jailors has been established at the capital, and there are some 200 Japanese students obtaining the special training provided there. Fine buildings, which provide instruction rooms, drill hall, and dormitory, have been erected for the school outside the Taihoku south gate. At Tainan there exists a school for the training of native police. An agricultural school has been established in connection with the Taihoku Prefecture agricultural station. Applicants for tuition there must be over 20 years of age, and have control of a farm of over 4 acres in size. Lectures are given for two hours a day for one year, and if the student can remain during the day at the station and engage in the experimental work there conducted, he will receive from the government the sum of twenty-five yen cents a day. Graduates are expected to establish small classes for the young in the neighborhood of their homes. The course of study covers cultivation of plants, protection of plants from insects, care of cattle, agricultural manufactures, forestry, arithmetic, and rough surveying. In Taichu there is a school of silk culture. Students are taught the raising of silk worms and the preparation of raw silk. In the national language school is a department of railways and telegraphs. Instruction in the latter subjects is given to graduates of the main school, who wish to enter the railway service as telegraph operators, etc. Aside from the government schools, dealt with above, in which modern education is offered, nearly every village possesses one of the old style Chinese schools, with which the government does not interfere. There were in 1899, 1,496 instructors employed in these schools, and 27,568 students. There are numerous other private schools, at which Japanese, English, or the native language is taught. There is also a Colonial Administrative School organized by officials in their private capacity, which holds an evening session at which studies consistent with the title of the school are taken up.

MISSIONS.

This section would not be complete without reference to the admirable work of the missionaries in the island during the past thirty years. Frequent reference has been made to them in the historical part of the book, and the difficulties they encountered in establishing their missions have been recorded there. Although there appears to be a difference of opinion as to the value of the work accomplished by missionaries in China, an impartial observer who cares to investigate must admit that in Formosa the results have been highly successful. For the period under review, prior to the arrival of the Japanese, practically the only modern education available in the island was through the missionaries. There are two Protestant missions in the island, one under the auspices of the Canadian Presbyterian Mission, established by the late Dr. Mackay in 1872, the operations of which are confined to the northern part of Formosa, and that of the English Presbyterian Mission, first established by Dr. Maxwell in 1865, the field of which extends over the southern and remaining portion of the island.

Dr. Mackay's work and experiences have been fully set forth in his interesting volume, "From Far Formosa," to which we would refer those interested in the subject. The death of the worthy doctor, which occurred a few months ago, removed from the mission field one who could but ill be spared; and the great loss is, I am sure, fully appreciated, not only by his many thousand followers and his foreign friends, but by many Japanese officials stationed in the island. It can be truly said that the mission field has exhibited few workers who have accomplished as much in their time as Dr. Mackay. Nothing appears to have daunted this intrepid evangelist, who, from being one of the most persecuted and despised of men by the persons amongst whom he dwelt, came to be the trusted friend and counsellor of all, and the actual pastor of great numbers.[1] From 1872 to 1875, this gentleman labored alone, but in the latter year he was joined by the Rev. J. B. Fraser, M.D., who, after serving three years, returned to Canada in 1877. In 1878, the Rev. Kenneth F. Junor was sent out by the Canadian church; but he, too, retired in 1882. By this time the mission had established 20 chapels, each with a native preacher, attended by over 300 members in full communion with the church. In 1883, the Rev. John Jamieson came out, and in spite of repeated and prolonged periods of physical weakness, labored on until 1891, when death terminated his services. In May, 1892, the Rev. William Gauld joined Dr. Mackay and proved himself to be an able and zealous associate.

At Tamsui (Hobi), the headquarters of Dr. Mackay's mission, through the bounty of the Methodist church, Woodstock, Canada, from which was collected a considerable sum, a college or school was created, styled Oxford College, in which the youth of the church are trained in Biblical History, geography, and the systematic study of the doctrines of the Bible, besides which due prominence is given to the most important subjects in the curriculum of a western college. The students are Chinese and Pepohoans, and the whole work may be said to have been initiated and carried on by Dr. Mackay himself, with a result that is really no less surprising than interesting to the privileged spectator. Closely adjoining is the girls' school, where equally excellent educational work is in active operation.

We now pass on to describe the English Presbyterian Mission, established in the southern parts of the island. Dr. Maxwell, on behalf of this mission, commenced work in 1865, and his difficulties and trials were considerable. He was afterwards joined by the Rev. Hugh Ritchie, who died on the field in 1879. In 1871, the Rev. William Campbell, F. R. G. S.,

---

1. In a late report, the statistics of the mission showed two foreign and two native ordained missionaries, 60 unordained native preachers, 24 native Bible women, 1,738 native communicants in good and regular standing in the church, 2,633 baptized members, 60 chapels with medical dispensaries attached; one central hospital, at which, up to date, 10,736 patients have been treated; $2,375.74 contributed by natives for mission purposes, and $264.10 contributed by natives for the hospital during that year.

first came out, and his labors are, we are glad to say, still available for the mission. This gentleman is as favorably known in the south as was the late Dr. Mackay in the north, and in addition to his great work in the evangelistic field, his literary accomplishments have given him no little reputation abroad. His researches into the early history of the island have been very extensive, and he is without doubt the greatest authority on this subject living. In 1874, the Rev. Thomas Barclay, M.A., arrived, and in 1878 Dr. Peter Anderson, who came to take charge of the mission hospital. From this time on, several other gentlemen were sent out, but, unhappily, had either to be permanently invalided home, or, more sad still, succumbed to the climate. The latter were the Rev. William Thow, and Dr. Gavin Russell, whose work was localized in Mid Formosa. Both these gentlemen, by their untiring energy, kindly disposition, and noble Christian character, had earned the respect and admiration, not only of the natives amongst whom they labored, but of every one else privileged to come in contact with them.

In 1889, the Rev. Duncan Ferguson arrived, and though the period of his work has been limited, his success as a missionary has been very pronounced. In 1895, the Revs. A. B. Neilson, and C. N. Moody, together with Dr. Landsborough, entered the field. The two latter were specially set apart to carry on the work in Mid Formosa, so abruptly terminated a year or two previously by the death of Dr. Gavin Russell. These gentlemen have accomplished much during their short stay, and are men of education and ability. In 1900, James L. Maxwell, M.D. and F. R. Johnson joined the mission.

Working in cooperation with the English Presbyterian Mission is that of the Women's Missionary Association, the present members of which are Miss Joan Stuart, who arrived in 1885, Miss A. E. Butler, in 1885, and Miss M. Barnett, in 1888. These ladies have reason to be gratified at the success they have achieved. Further reference to their work will be found in the section of this chapter relating to sanitary works.

At present there are 77 places of worship attached to this mission. Many of these can hardly be honored with the title either of church or chapel, but every Sunday in 77 different places a number of people meet for Christian worship. It is the aim of the mission to make their churches self-supporting, and to such an extent has success been gained that some are able to contribute to other churches, while even the poorest are able to contribute at least a fourth or more towards their own support. Thus, for the year 1900, native churches contributed a total of $6,823, and $1,000 more was raised from the sale of Christian literature in the book shop at Tainanfu. One interesting feature of the work is the little foreign mission which is entirely supported by native contributions. The field selected is the Pescadores Islands, and native missionaries are there maintained.[1]

---

1. Late statistics give the number of communicants as 2,019, to which should be added baptized children, not yet admitted to communion, numbering 1,660, and 152 members under discipline, giving a total membership of adults and children of 3,837. Including adherents, that is, people who have renounced idolatry, and who attend Christian worship more or less regularly, the total is 10,758.

As to the work of the mission in the educational field, there are at most of the stations congregational schools, presided over by apt native teachers, and at some of these the pupils are undergoing a preliminary education to fit them for entrance into the middle school. This institution is at Tainanfu, and the lads attending there are given a liberal secular education, in addition to instruction in spiritual matters, which is, of course, not neglected. The students are housed in comfortable quarters, are well fed, and tenderly cared for. There is accommodation for forty boys, and the school is always full. Mr. Ede, a very competent man, had charge of this work up to a few years ago, when he was obliged to withdraw from the island owing to ill health. Picked boys are sent to the theological college, which exists solely for the training of native pastors and evangelists. This has been a very prominent feature of the mission work, and is being developed still more. Some forty students are accommodated here. Although several European and native instructors are engaged in the work, this institution owes much to the direction and instruction of the Rev. Thomas Barclay, a man whose scholarly and scientific attainments attracted some notice before he came to Formosa. Under the charge of the ladies attached to this mission is a girls' school, the members of which are carefully educated. Besides conducting this school, one or other of the ladies goes and resides at some country centre from time to time, forming reading classes for women and girls, while house to house visitation in the city is made a matter of almost daily routine. There is also, under the direction of the ladies, an establishment for the training of Bible women. The theological college and Bible women's school are free, but there is a nominal annual charge of $14 for the middle school, and $6 for the girls' school.

Out of sympathy for the large number of unfortunate blind in the island, Rev. Campbell some years ago established a school for this class, and personally devised a system of instruction which has been highly satisfactory. Rev. Campbell gave this school his personal attention until the arrival of the Japanese, when he was successful in inducing the Japanese government to take up and continue the work. Rev. Campbell obtained entrance for several of his most promising pupils to the government institution for the blind in Tokyo, and as evidence of the interest taken in his work, a charity concert was given under Imperial patronage and abundant funds were provided to cover the costs of their four or five years' residence in Tokyo.

An important factor in the diffusion of education among the natives interested in the mission, is the mission newspaper, entitled "The Tainanfu Church News." It has been in existence for fully sixteen years, and has a monthly circulation of about 800 copies. It is printed in Romanized Chinese, and is, therefore, read, almost exclusively, by Christians familiar with that system. This is the first newspaper published in the island, and owes its existence to Rev. Barclay, who, while on furlough in Scotland, some seventeen years ago, obtained instruction in type setting. He brought out with him a printing press, type, etc., and taught a few intelligent Chinese the printing trade. These, in turn, have taught others, so that at present there is an efficient force of Chinese printers. One of the European missionaries occupies the chair of editor in chief, Rev. Barclay at present holding that position. In addition to the newspaper, a great deal of Christian literature, chiefly in the Romanized Chinese, is issued. There are at present among the Christians more than 2,000 who can read fluently in Romanized Chinese.

In addition to the Protestant missionaries, the Spanish Catholics are doing evangelistic work in Formosa. As mentioned in the historical section of the book, the Spanish commenced mission work in the island as early as the year 1626, and in a few years they had flourishing stations on Palm Island, Samasana Island, and at Kimpauli (Kimpori), Chomong (Seimon), Tamsui (Hobe', villages in the north. After sixteen years of undisturbed possession, the Dutch in 1642 drove the Spanish from the island. Two hundred and seventeen years afterward, namely in 1859, Father Sainz was sent to Formosa, and arranged again for the establishment of their missions. He was followed by Fathers Chinchon, Herce, and Colomer. At present there are several priests at work, including the provincial vicar of Formosa, who has recently been made independent of Amoy. The island is divided into six central stations, at two of which there are large churches, and at the rest, chapels. Around each station is a circuit, extending several miles from the station as the centre. At each of these centres a Spanish priest presides, who keeps in constant touch with all parts of his circuit, and the various congregations connected with it.[1] The priests are assisted in proselytising work by native " Catechumens," specially trained at Takow. The mission consists entirely of brethren belonging to the Dominican order, the western headmasters of which are at Manila, where the Superior lives. They are each allowed one hundred dollars a year which has to do for every personal want, including traveling. The writer has found the Spanish fathers in the island genial, sympathetic, and courteous, and there can be no doubt that the mission is doing good work in the island.

JUSTICE AND CRIME.

Courts were first opened in the island during the summer of 1896. The system first instituted was a court of three instances. Later the higher court was abolished, and the present system of two instances adopted. The courts are constituted and governed by the " Formosa Government Court Regulations," which places them on a distinct basis from the courts of Japan proper. The wide difference in customs and manners of the inhabitants of Formosa as compared with the Japanese renders it impracticable to apply the laws of Japan in the island, although they are generally followed as closely as circumstances will permit. We may take for instance the murder of female infants or deformed children, which is of not uncommon occurrence with Chinese. While it is very evident that this horrible practice should be put

1. The six central stations are as follows: Takow (Chang-kim), Baukimtseng, Talibu (Tarimu), Lokliao, Lochutseng, and Taihoku. A late report gives the total number of accepted church members as 1,804; those undergoing preparation for baptism and admission, 600. The above includes only natives, as Japanese who are coming in increased numbers are not as yet formally placed on the church rolls.

down, still it would be obviously unjust to convict of murder a mother who might be found guilty of an act which, according to the customs of her people, was quite within her rights, and which in the case of deformed children is even considered praiseworthy. Moreover, many of the simple people in the hill districts are unfamiliar with commercial law, and it would be unjust to commit them for punishment for some offence which they in their ignorance did not know was opposed to the law. Judges in Formosa are consequently frequently obliged to use their own discretion, and their position is therefore a more arduous one than in Japan. Furthermore, owing to the difference in language, much of the court work must be done through interpreters, which causes delay and almost endless trouble.

All courts of justice in Formosa are under direct control of the Governor-General of Formosa, and he has full power to establish and abolish courts, and may suspend judges from service thus placing them on quarter pay, but he cannot dismiss or transfer judges against their will, unless they are guilty of crime. Formosa judges are qualified officials of the service in Japan, and thus, although transferred to Formosa, they still retain their position in the judicial service of Japan. There is but one court of appeal, which is established at the capital Taihoku, and there is no higher recourse. The court is divided into civil and criminal departments each in charge of three judges. In addition to the trial of appeal cases, this court passes on questions respecting the competency of district courts. District courts or their branches, the latter having the powers and functions of the former, are established at Taihoku, Shinchiku (Teckcham), Shoko (Changwha), Kagi, Tainan, Hozan, (Pithau) and Bako (Makung) of the Pescadores. In the district courts, cases are tried by a single judge. To each Formosa court of justice is attached the office of Public Procurator, this office being under direct control of the Governor-General and performing its functions independently of the court of justice. The district covered by the Procurators conforms with the district of the courts to which they are attached. Public Procurators, in addition to representing the state in civil and criminal cases, exercise control over such public offices as possess minor judicial power. At present, police inspectors may be appointed acting procurators for district courts and their branches. In Formosa, Bemmusho, the administrative office under the prefecture, now possesses the authority to settle disputes of small magnitude by inducing the parties concerned to come to an amicable arrangement. It is intended in the future to extend the power of the Bemmusho in this respect and to make it unlawful for cases thus disposed of to be later brought up before the courts. There are 32 judges and 20 procurators or acting procurators in the island service. The court buildings in Taihoku are pretentious structures, and other cities are being supplied with court buildings of a size and design worthy of the high use to which they are put. It should be added that the Chinese appear to have no little confidence in the courts. They are fond of litigation, and lose no time in bringing to court their fellowmen against whom they have some grievance, fancied or real. In fact, so eager were they to avail themselves of justice not based on the lines of Chinese official jurisprudence, that they brought up old cases dating back for many years, and literally overwhelmed the courts with them. It was consequently found necessary to issue a regulation forbidding the presentation of cases dating back beyond Japanese occupation.

Prisons of Formosa, unlike those of Japan, are under the direct control of the local Government, and the immediate supervision of the same in the different prefectures is imposed upon the Public Procurators of district courts. The main prisons are at Taihoku, Taichu, and Tainan, with branch prisons at Shinchiku (Teckcham), Shoka (Changwha), Kagi, Hozan (Pithau), and Gilan. In addition, every police station possesses its lock-up.

Soon after the arrival of the Japanese, the prisons were located in old yamens which were altered somewhat for that purpose. They were, however, unsanitary, and the mortality rate was large. Later, superior quarters were prepared for temporary use, and at present writing the several prisons in the island are in such buildings. Work has now commenced on model establishments, in which the best of modern prison architecture will be applied. The cost of these prisons are,—Taihoku 315,000 yen, Taichu 180,000 yen, Tainan 255,000 yen, besides the sum of 50,000 which represents the cost of plans, surveys, etc. In addition to this, Kagi, Hozan (Pithau), and Gilan are erecting with prefectural funds new prisons which, though not as large as those mentioned, will be built on modern principles. All prisons will be completed before 1903. In addition, as new police stations are erected, sanitary lock-ups will be constructed. When it is taken into consideration that much of the labor is performed by prisoners and without cost, the prisons even manufacturing their own brick, it will be seen that Formosa will possess very fine buildings in her prisons; in fact with two or three exceptions they will be the finest in the Empire.

The number of criminals in prison during 1899 averaged 2630, including 586 Japanese. According to prefectures, Taihoku cared for 175 Japanese, 944 natives; Taichu 46 Japanese, 407 natives; Tainan 64 Japanese, 672 natives; and the Pescadores 20 natives. The occupants on the accumulative principle numbered throughout the island 104,268 Japanese and 746,221 natives. These numbers include prisoners awaiting trial, the larger number of whom are in for but a few days or, at the most, weeks. As to sanitation, 2,044 prisoners were given medical treatment, and there were 266 deaths and 36 prison breakers. Every prison possesses its special doctor and nurses, and in Taihoku Prison, at least, a Japanese Christian evangelist spends much time with the prisoners. The classification of prisoners shows that thieves and robbers are in great preponderance, numbering 981, including 61 Japanese. Assault cases follow with 110; and then fraud with 84 including 41 Japanese. Murder in its different degrees numbers 55, including 11 Japanese. Forgery holds 11 natives and 9 Japanese, kidnapping 20, including 2 Japanese; and libel, perjury, and false accusation cause the detention of 21 natives; and transgressors against the opium laws number 20 natives. Prison breaking and the concealing of criminals accounts for 8 natives, and one bright youth attempted the private manufacture of imitation Taiwan Bank notes with the inevitable result. Miscellaneous offences, detention awaiting trial, etc., makes up the balance of :441 including 179 Japanese. The female prisoners included in the above number 10 Japanese and 73 Chinese. One peculiar feature as compared with foreign lands is the large number of robberies and the few cases of fraud.

Prison statistics give us an idea of the class of Japanese that visit the island, when we note that 14 in a thousand spend their time in prison; while native prisoners number but 1 in a thousand of population. It should be mentioned, however, that the majority of offences against the law committed by Chinese are never heard of by the authorities, and even many known criminals guilty of armed robbery are never apprehended, whereas there are probably very few Japanese who escape punishment for their misdemeanors. The total cost of prison administration, including repairs to buildings, is some 500,000 yen a year.

Each prefecture possesses its Police Department, which has control over the police affairs of the district; and each Bemmusho has its smaller police office. Branch offices follow, and lastly the village stations. There are at present 839 offices and branch offices; and 731 villages possess permanent police stations. In addition, there are very small villages in which the village head man is expected to keep order, and which are visited by police patrols daily. The force is made up as follows: Police inspectors 222, assistant police inspectors 307, police 4,381, or a total Japanese force of 4,919. Two years ago the experiment of utilizing native assistant police was tried, and it met with such success that at present no less than 569 natives are thus employed. The native police are supplied with board, clothes, and a salary varying from 6 to 14 yen according to length of service, together with a money gift to near relatives in case of a native meeting with death while in the performance of his duties; and furthermore he is pensioned in case of permanent injury. The men are well paid, appear to take pride in their position; and, in the up country districts especially, seem to be selected from the better class of residents. The writer personally has much admiration for this little band, and feels that they are a valuable agency towards ultimate peace and perfect protection in every part of the island. It is stated that the number of native police will be greatly increased.

The Japanese police, besides board and clothes, receive a monthly wage of from 9 to 15 yen according to the length of service. The pension laws for Formosa police are specially liberal. The term of service for police or jailors necessary to draw a pension is put at 7 years. Those who retire from active service at the age of 45, or those who are retired owing to sickness or disablements are granted a yearly pension equal to five months pay, and if in the service for a period exceeding 7 years, an additional allowance is made for each year equal to 10% of the salary. In case of officers dying in the service either from sickness or wounds, 5 months salary is presented to the family of the deceased. The whole force is armed with swords, and possesses for night use or in time of emergency Murata rifles. In addition, there is an artillery corps of 30 Japanese police who are trained in the use of mortar pieces, and are temporarily detailed for services on the savage border; being now stationed at Taikokan (Tokoham), the savages of this district being, at present

writing, in a disturbed state.   In addition to the ordinary police dealt with
above there is a corps of savage protection guards numbering 1,539 men
stationed on the savage border, and described fully in the chapter on
camphor.[1]   There are also 1,700 gendarmes in the island, and though this
corps is a branch of the army, it is frequently called upon in Formosa to
render police service.[2]   There are thus available for police duty a total of
8,727 men including the savage border guards.   The total cost of the
Formosa police service for 1900 was 2,228,125 yen.

SANITATION.

The Japanese, on their arrival in Formosa, found nothing more urgently
required than an immediate improvement of sanitary conditions.   Chinese
filth is proverbial, and the Japanese found the task of cleaning up the cities
a huge one.   With the exception of a few missionary institutions, which will
be referred to later, there were no hospitals in the island, and the sick were
cared for by ignorant Chinese doctors, who practised the most primitive forms
of superstitious quackery.   The first steps taken by the Japanese were to
clean the streets, and to improve, so far as they could, temporarily, the
sanitary conditions of the cities.   Hospitals were established by the central
government at Taihoku, Kelung, Shinchiku, Taichu, Kagi, Tainan, Hozen,
Pinan, Gilan, and the Pescadores.   Nearly a half million yen was expended
in the cost of hospital buildings, the Taihoku hospital, costing $262,000, being
the largest.   This is quite a commodious structure, the rooms provided
for first class patients being furnished in European style and quite luxurious.
There are fifteen specialists of different diseases and some forty trained
nurses employed in this hospital.   The number of cases treated in these
hospitals last year exceeded 60,000, nearly 14,000 being Formosa Chinese.
Destitute Chinese receive free treatment, and some 11,000 patients availed
themselves of this privilege during the year.   In addition to these hospitals,
there are institutions maintained in the smaller places by local funds.   Furthermore, there are some eighty-three physicians employed by the government,
who are stationed at various places in the island to give free treatment to
the needy.   There are also four hospitals for the examination and treatment
of prostitutes, and one special hospital for the treatment of plague, small-
pox, etc.   It is proposed to organize a special police force to be engaged in
sanitary work.   The above hospitals refer only to civil hospitals.   The
military maintain their own medical establishments throughout the island,
and some of these institutions, especially the Central hospital at Taihoku, and
the branch at Sulphur Springs, are well built, commodious, and have the best
of equipment.   There is also a government medical school for natives established at Taihoku.

Although sanitary improvement works have been carried on to some
extent throughout the island, only one city, Taihoku, the capital, has been

---

1. For description of system of defence against savage depredations see pages 430 and 436.
2. See section relating to defence.

Fort overlooking Kelung Harbor.
A View in the Pangkio Garden.
Japanese Bath Houses near Taihoku.

Japanese Police Station at Kinpori.
Christian Church at Sintiam.
Government Hospital at Taihoku.

thoroughly equipped with a modern system of sewerage. The system of open sewers, so satisfactory in Singapore, was adopted here, and some ten miles of drains were constructed at a cost, including road improvement, of 350,000 yen. Taihoku, and its surrounding suburbs, are very fortunate in possessing an abundant supply of fine water. By sinking a pipe from 140 to 200 feet, a fine artesian well is obtained, with a bountiful flow of water. As it costs from 35 to 40 yen to construct these wells, good water is within the reach of everyone. A number of public wells with large reservoirs have been constructed by the government. At Kelung and Tamsui, where water is not so abundant, water works have been constructed at a cost of 500,000 yen in the former, and 110,000 yen in the latter. It is intended to introduce sewerage and water works in all the principal cities in the island.

Reference should be made here to the hospitals established by the missionaries. In 1880, Dr. Mackay constructed a hospital at Tamsui, and a large number of patients have been treated there during its existence. Dr. Mackay in his travels was always provided with simple remedies to administer to the sick when called upon to do so. Medical work has been associated with the English Presbyterian mission in the south from the very first day of its existence. In 1878, Dr. Peter Anderson took charge of the mission hospital, and has since carried it on with the happiest results. A handsome and capacious building has been erected, which is the best private hospital in the island, and Dr. James L. Maxwell, M.D., arrived last year to associate himself with Dr. Anderson in medical work. There were some 9,000 cases treated at this hospital during last year. A branch hospital attached to the mission exists at Changwha (Shoka).

Owing to the large loss of life to women and children during child birth, there appeared to be a very pressing call for skilled ministrations during this period, and owing to the aversion of Chinese women to male medical aid, it became necessary that the attendants should be women. Appreciating the world of good to be accomplished in this work, two lady members of the mission made a careful study of the subject, under the direction of a regular medical practitioner. Thus equipped they have been practising in the south of Formosa with unprecedented success, I am informed, and case after case can be quoted, where but for their intervention, mother or child, often both, must have inevitably died.

Though not directly in the line of medical work, I wish to record here a very worthy service rendered by the Spanish priests in the rescue of Chinese children. Infanticide of female children is reported as very frequent in Formosa. I am informed by a medical friend that if not immediately killed, the general disgust at, and indifference to girl life, when this sex is thought to unduly predominate in a family, leads to such cruel neglect and bad treatment that fatal results are soon brought about. For some years the Catholic mission has been doing much to combat this evil. It is known that the priests are willing to receive all discarded children and take full charge of them, the parent having no further responsibility. Up to date, between 5,000 and 6,000 children have been thus rescued.

In addition to the hospital described above, there are nine private Japanese hospitals, and one charity hospital at Taihoku, supported by contributions from foreign and Chinese business establishments.

The Japanese on their arrival were confronted with a great problem in the opium question. The smoking of opium is very prevalent in Formosa, it being estimated that about 7 per cent of the total populace were addicted to the habit. The authorities were at first inclined to entirely prohibit the practice. It required but little examination into the condition of affairs, however, to find convincing evidence that any heroic measures would involve very serious results. A prohibitive policy would cause constant friction between the authorities and the Chinese, and as many of the smokers were among the better class, it would drive from the island just the element which the authorities wish to retain. Furthermore, it was very evident that it would be impossible to totally prevent the import of opium. Smugglers would swarm on the coast, prepared to risk arrest in view of the large profits to be obtained in the trade. It was then decided by the Formosan government to permit the smoking of opium by the Chinese under certain conditions. The smoking of opium is entirely prohibited to the Japanese, and offenders against this law are very severely dealt with. At first it was decided to determine by medical examination those smokers who were hopelessly addicted to the use of the drug, and to limit the supply of opium to such persons. It was thus hoped that the younger generation, being unable to obtain supplies of opium, and not having acquired the taste for the drug, would not practise the vice, and thus in fifty years or so, the practice could be entirely wiped out. This principle is still maintained, and only persons provided with certificates showing that they are habitual opium smokers are allowed the use of the drug. Further, the general sale of opium was limited to dealers who had complied with the law and obtained a certificate to that effect. Although this principle was a very perfect one in theory, there were found to be many obstacles when it was put into practice. Great difficulty was encountered in detecting a probable smoker when this individual resided in the same house with some one holding a certificate. Thus but one certificate would be obtained by a large household where there were many smokers, and the law was easily evaded. With this in consideration, and desiring to obtain a complete register of all smokers, the government relaxed the stringency of the regulations somewhat, and issued certificates to all adult applicants who declared themselves habitual smokers. The import of opium is reserved by the government as an official monopoly. The penalty for the import, or manufacture of opium, is very severe, the punishment being no less than imprisonment at hard labor for a term not exceeding eleven years, or a fine not exceeding 2,000 yen. There are over 30,000 licensed retailers in the island, and over 160,000 certificates have been granted to smokers, which is about 6 per cent of the population. Opium to the value of some 5,000,000 yen a year is consumed. The plant is not grown in the island, the supplies being imported from Persia, India, and China. There has been, however, some discussion as to the advisability of growing opium locally, and the government has purchased a small plat of land in the south of the island for the purpose of trial cultivation. The government obtains an annual profit from the monopoly of nearly 3,000,000 yen.

FINANCE.

The revenue of Formosa has shown a most satisfactory growth during the short period of Japanese occupation, and if the future brings a similar increase, it will not be many years before the island will, so far as ordinary expenditures are concerned, pay its own way. At present, of course, the island must be put in shape. Railways, harbors, roads, etc., must be constructed; and it is the expenses for these improvements that makes Formosa a drain on the imperial exchequer. The revenue and expenditures since 1895, excluding Army and Navy items which are included in the National expenditure of the Government, have been as follows :—

	Formosa Revenue. Yen.	Received from Japan. Yen.	Total Representing Expenditure. Yen.
Fiscal Year 1895	985,679	28,962,026	29,897,705
,, 1896	2,711,822	6,940,275	9,652,097
,, 1897	5,324,224	5,959,048	11,283,272
,, 1898	8,297,420	3,984,540	12,281,960
,, 1899	11,701,918	3,000,000	14,701,918
,, 1900	13,127,872	2,598,611	15,726,483
,, 1901 1.	14,401,979	2,386,689	16,788,668
Total	56,500,914	53,831,189	110,332,103

The chief items of Revenue, as appearing in the 1900 Budget, were as follows: Inland Taxes 1,652,000 yen, Customs Duties 1,840,000 yen, Tonnage dues 19,000 yen, Legal Stamps 73,000 yen, Licence fees 10,000 yen, Monopolies 4,049,722 yen.

The three Monopolies appear in the 1901 Budget as follows :—

	Revenue. Yen.	Expenditure. Yen.	Profit to Govt. Yen.
Camphor 2.	4,571,561	2,127,611	2,443,950
Salt.	723,708	474,698	249,010
Opium 3.	4,287,888	2,931,126	2,931,126
Total	9,583,157	5,533,435	4,049,722

Of the Inland Taxes the returns (1900 Budget) from the Land Tax were put at 824,000 yen, the Tea Tax at 411,000 yen, and the Sugar Tax at 230,000 yen. This gives a total for direct taxation of 1,465,000 yen.

Taking the population at 2,600,000, we find the impost on each individual as follows: Land Tax 34 yen cents, Tea Tax .15 yen cents, Sugar .09 yen cents. Total for each individual .58 yen cents. In addition to the above, there are small district and village imposts which persons owning property within city or village limits pay. The well-to-do resident is also expected,

---

1. Budget estimate.

2. In actual working during the years 1900 and 1901, the camphor monopoly has not yielded the revenue expected. This is due to a temporary spurt in the manufacture of camphor in Japan, the high prices ruling under the monopoly in Formosa, inducing the Japanese to search out every remaining tree and stump. This difficulty cannot be of long duration, however, as every available tree in Japan will soon be disposed of, there being no forests, save under government control, as exist in Formosa.

3. Owing to the difficulty of entirely preventing smuggling, and the sale of cheap inferior opium brought into the country in this manner, the income from this source has been lowered considerably.

though not required, to make some contribution toward the cost of schools, etc.

An idea of the local taxes and the share paid by natives and Japanese, may be gained from a review of the taxes of Taihoku prefecture, which are perhaps the highest of any of the Prefectures. The local Taxes are the land tax, house tax, business tax, and miscellaneous tax. Now the amount of land tax collected from Japanese in Taihoku-ken for the year 1899 was 248 yen, paid by 58 Japanese, and the amount collected from Natives was 167,986 yen paid by 58,831 natives; so the share of each Japanese is on an average 2.15 yen and that of the natives 2.16 yen.

The amount of house tax collected from Japanese was 1,256 yen paid by 997 Japanese, being 1.57 yen per head, on an average, and the amount collected from Natives was 153,926 yen, paid by 94,547 natives, being an average of 1.63 yen per head.

The total amount of business tax collected from Japanese was 44,940 yen, paid by 2,381 persons, which is an average of 18.87 yen per head, and the amount collected from natives was 95,096 yen, paid by 15,217 natives, an average of 3.25 per head.

In regard to miscellaneous taxes, the amount collected from Japanese was 4,292 yen, paid by 8,161 Japanese, an average of .56 yen cents per head, and the amount collected from natives was 59,340 yen, paid by 42,385 natives, an average of 1.44 yen per head.

The total amount of these various taxes levied on Japanese will therefore amount to 10,070 yen, which apportioned among the Japanese residing in the prefecture, gives 54 yen cents per head, and the total amount of taxes levied on the natives was 478,353 yen, or 66 yen cents per head.

The Formosa revenue is utilized for the ordinary expenses of the administration, which includes the cost of various local improvements, such as road and street work, sanitary measures, buildings, government agricultural work, schools, hospitals, etc., etc. In addition to this, a comparatively large sum is being expended for Railway and Harbor works, and the latter make up what is known as the Extraordinary Expenditures. To meet these, the Formosa Industrial loan, which was issued in 1900, provides 35,000,000 yen, and the Imperial Exchequer will be called upon for 15,006,284 yen, and this sum (50,006,284 yen) is to be extended over a period of ten years.

In addition to the funds expended by the Central Formosan Government for improvements, each prefecture has certain funds which it expends for similar purposes ; thus, the single prefecture of Taihoku expended 44,525 yen on country roads and 6,736 yen on bridges, during 1900. Important road and bridge work, however, is generally met by appropriations made by the Central Formosan Government. The total expenditures by prefectures on improvements, independent of the Central Formosan Government, may be placed at some 100,000 yen.

With the above statistics in view, we find that there has been the sum of 53,831,189 yen brought into the island from Japan, and if we include the money expended for the Army and Navy attached to the Formosan Government, and add the local revenue invested in the island, we obtain the sum of 144,673,182 yen, which represents the total expenditure for the island during the past years of Japanese occupation. A small portion of the above has doubtless gone out of the island in the form of savings from officers' wages and the profit to Japanese firms who have branches in Formosa. A larger sum represents the payments in Japan and foreign lands for the supplies, machinery, etc.; but by far the largest portion of the whole amount was expended in the island and reached the pockets of the inhabitants. It is the circulation of this large sum of money which has raised prices in Formosa and which has increased the purchasing power of the masses. To arrive at the total revenue for the single year 1901, we must take the following items as given in the Budget :—

Funds received from local revenue..	14,401,979 Yen
„ „ „ Imperial Exchequer	2,598,611 „
„ „ „ „ „ for Military and Naval expenses	8,130,000 „
Raised by Formosan Industrial loan	4,100,000 „
Total ..	29,230,590 Yen

Salaries and General Expenses Military Branch	5,596,000 Yen
„ „ „ Gendarme branch	606,000 „
Extraordinary expenditure for fortifications	1,357,000 „
New Barracks	519,000 „
Field Expenses	50,000 „
Total ..	8,130,000 Yen

The following table will show the relative cost of various branches of the administration taking 1,000 as a basis of calculation.

Government Laboratory (includes cost of opium)	238.27	Custom Houses..	18.90
Salt Bureau	173.30	Hospitals	18.66
Police	113.20	Educational expenses	13.83
Communications	62.50	Police and Jailors School	10.77
Civil Department	45.13	Marine Works	4.88
Prefectures and "Chos"	43.00	Relief Fund	4.02
Prisons	37.00	Public Physicians	3.08
Bemmusho..	36.08	Medical School..	2.08
Formosa Government Railways	33.77	Observatories	2.00
Repayment of Government Funds	28.38	Harbor Sanitary inspection	1.69
Court of Justice..	25.00	Miscellaneous repayments	.63
		Funds on deposit	24.27

The chief financial organ in Formosa is the Bank of Taiwan (Taiwan Ginko), which occupies in Formosa a position somewhat similar to that held by the Nippon Ginko in Japan. That is, while the stock is held chiefly by private parties, its connection with the government is very close, and its functions in some respects appear to be of an official, rather than private, nature. In March, 1899, a special law relating to the Formosa Bank was enacted, by which it was provided that the Government should subscribe for one fifth of the total amount of the Bank's capital, that it would allow the dividend on its shares to be included in the Bank's reserve for five years, and that it would loan to the bank for five years without interest, silver coins to the value of two million yen. In return for these special privileges, the Bank was to take up Formosan Government Bonds to the value of five million yen.

The Bank accepts deposits and does a general banking business. It has branches in the larger Formosan Cities, as well as in Amoy, China, Hongkong, and Kobe, Japan. The bank also issues silver certificates in several denominations.

Considerable confusion exists in Formosa owing to the presence of three currencies ; the Gold Yen of Japan, the local silver currency, and the so-called " Tamsui dollar." The Japanese Gold Yen circulate rather freely, but chiefly among Japanese. The old silver yen coin of Japan, the Mexican silver dollar, and the Taiwan Bank's silver notes are found throughout the island and are principal circulating mediums. The " Tamsui dollar " has practically become a fictitious coin, inasmuch as but few are ever seen. Most of the Chinese trade however, is conducted on a basis in which the Tamsui dollar is taken as a standard. When actual cash transfers, however, are required the equivalent in Silver Yen or Silver Notes is paid. Tamsui dollars owe their existence to the old custom of Chinese firms of mutilating with a metal punch, " Chopping " as it called, every dollar that passed through their hands. By constant chopping, the coin loses in weight, and eventually becomes a thin bowl shaped piece of junk, with little resemblance to a coin. It is now called a " Chopdollar " or a " Tamsui dollar." Before mutilation, the coin is known as a "clean dollar." Owing to the refusal of the Government as well as Japanese Banks to accept " chopped " coins of any kind, the custom has gradually fallen into disuse. The Tamsui dollar still remains, however, as a standard for calculation. It is generally some 3 to 4% below the clean silver yen in value, and mercantile houses, especially the tea merchants, believe, and not without reason, that they obtain as much in return for the Tamsui dollar as they would for the clean silver dollar, were the former abolished.

While Japan was under the silver standard, the difficulties of Formosan finance were not so great, but with the establishment of the gold standard, and the withdrawal of silver yen from circulation, there promised to be great inconvenience felt. This was owing to the unwillingness of the Chinese to accept Japanese paper money. Few of the masses read, and the national note to them was only a piece of paper of indefinite face value and without intrinsic worth. The first attempt to circulate paper yen was an expensive experiment. The Chinese refused to accept it save at a great discount over silver coins, amounting to as much as 10% in some cases. It consequently became absolutely necessary to issue for Formosan circulation, silver coins, and accordingly the Government brought from Japan silver coins to the value of several million, and made them legal tender in Formosa. This relieved the situation, the national note returned to its proper value as compared with silver, and the silver yen notes issued by the Bank of Taiwan were accepted by the Chinese because they found that they were convertible into silver.

DEFENCE.

The defence of the island is entrusted to three mixed brigades, each complete with cavalry, artillery, and infantry. Brigade headquarters are at

Taihoku, Taichu, and (Tainan).[1] No definite information is available as to the strength of this force; but it has been stated that each brigade consists of upwards of five thousand men. The only fortifications in this island are at Kelung, Tamsui, Takow, and the Pescadores, all of which were taken over from the Chinese, and some of which have been improved by the Japanese. A squadron of several men of war are on the Formosa station with a rendezvous at the Pescadores. The military are armed with the small calibre Murata rifle, and the artillery with breach-loading mountain guns, no field artillery being used in the island. The military have all their important posts connected by well built roads suitable for the moving of cavalry and artillery; and furthermore commissariat stations in districts not reached by rail are connected by narrow gauge tramways.[2]

The transport of troops to and from Japan is entrusted to the Nippon Yusen Kwaisha and Osaka Shosen Kwaisha, steamship companies running boats between the island and Japan. The nearest important port on the mainland is Nagasaki, and it is possible to land troops in north Formosa from that port in about 48 hours.

The maintenance of peace is generally entrusted to the police and it is only when the disturbance is beyond their power to control that the military are called out. Such occasions are decreasing yearly, the disturbances of late being limited to small skirmishes with banditti, in which usually but a dozen or so of men are engaged. Government arsenals are located at Taihoku, Tainan, and Taichu, for the repair of arms, etc.

INTERNAL COMMUNICATIONS.

Prior to the arrival of the Japanese, the means of communication were very limited. In the south there were a few stretches of heavy road passing through the sugar fields and suitable for buffalo carts; but these roads were for the convenience of the sugar growers, and could scarcely be called public highways. In other parts of the island, with few exceptions, roads were practically non existent. Rice fields are divided into small plots separated by an artificial earth ridge which presents a surface sometimes not over a foot in width. These ridges were frequently the only highways; and consequently travel, other than on foot or by chair, was impossible. On the arrival of the Japanese the military were at once set to road building, and a large number of men were engaged in the work. The roads built were wide, well graded, and the streams encountered were bridged with temporary wooden structures. Several hundred miles of road were thus constructed during the first few years of Japanese occupation. Later, squads of surrendered banditti were put to work on the roads and added many miles. In addition

---

1. Although the distribution of troops depends upon the state of the country, permanent garrisons are now to be found at Taihoku, Kelung, Shinchiku (Teckcham), in Taihoku prefecture; Girau (Gilan) in Giran sub-prefecture; Bioritsu (Miaoli), Shoka (Changwha), Unrin, Rinkiho (Limkipo) and Taichu in Taichu prefecture; Tainan, Kagi, Hozan (Pithau), and Takow in Taiuan prefecture; Boko in Bokoto (Pescadores) sub-prefecture, and Pinan (Pilam) in Taito prefecture.

2. See section on internal communications.

to this, the several prefectures have had a large force of men constantly engaged in road work, and thus by different means over eight hundred miles of road have been constructed during the six years of Japanese occupation.

Some of the roads, such as the mountain road leading from Taihoku to Gilan, have been of a very difficult nature. At present over a thousand miles of road are in process of construction at a very considerable cost.

The roads in and near Taihoku (Taipeh), the capital city, are the best in the island. Within the city walls, the roads are splendidly macadamized and possess open sewers built of stone and cement on either side. These roads are the best in the island, and are not excelled by any on the mainland itself. With the exception of mountain roads to Gilan, practically no road-work has been undertaken within the savage district. Owing to the very high hills and the hostility of the savages toward outsiders, the work is full of difficulties. The east coast of Formosa is being developed, however, and undoubtedly the Japanese will ultimately find roads across the mountain a necessity.

The Japanese have constructed over 200 miles of narrow gauge tramway in the island for the transport of military supplies, as well as general freight and passengers. The mainline runs from Shinchiku (Teckcham) in the north to Tainan in the south, a distance of some 140 miles. There are two branch lines, one from Kozitsu, a village south of Taichu, to Tokatsukutsu, and another from Tainan to Anping. Station houses have been erected at all important points, and passengers and freight are carried at fixed rates. The yearly expenditure on this account is some 250,000 yen The passenger cars are provided with seats for four, and are covered with a light awning. They are on a very miniature scale, and are pushed or pulled by relays of Chinese coolies. Young Hakka girls are frequently employed for this work, and fairly good time is made considering the method of operating. The average charge per passenger is some 4 yen cents a mile.

The first Formosa railway was built by the Chinese government and was completed in 1893. On the arrival of the Japanese, the line, some 62 miles in length, came into their possession. It was found to be in such wretched condition, however, that a satisfactory train service could not be maintained. The rolling stock was also limited and entirely unsuited to the requirements.

Accordingly work was commenced on the line at once. The Kelung-Taihoku branch was completely reconstructed as so to avoid the numerous short curves and the steep grades. The line leading from Taihoku to the south received also some attention, the total cost of these improvements reaching nearly two million yen. The railway was at this time under the direct control of the Military Department. In 1897, it came under the control of the Civil Department. It was the intention at one time to hand it over to the private railway company organized in Japan for the purpose of completing the Formosa railway system. The private railway company, however, failed to obtain public support, and in 1898 the Formosan government announced its intention of carrying on the work itself. Under the able direction of Chief Engineer Hasegawa the plans were soon formulated, and in 1899 work was commenced on the soutern line from Takow north to Tainan, a distance of 28 miles. This section was completed in November, 1900. The Kelung and Shinchiku (Teckcham), lines were repaired, much rolling stock was added, and in the fall of 1900 work was commenced on the short branch line from Taihoku, (Taipeh) to Tamsui, (Hobe), which was completed in June 1901. There is a great deal of traffic between the port Tamsui and Taihoku and its suburbs, Banka and Daitotei (Twatutia). The new line runs via Maruyama, Shirin, Hokuto, and Kantau. Maruyama is a picturesque park on the Kelung River, much frequented by Japanese merrymakers. Hokuto (Pak-tau) is a village at the entrance of the well known North Formosa sulphur district. There is an excellent Japanese inn here—perhaps the best in the island—and the sulphur springs provide hot mineral baths, healthy and delightful. The Japanese have recognized the value of the place as a sanitary resort, and extensive barracks and bath houses for the troops have been erected.

Beyond the springs lies a gorge reeking with sulphurous fumes. The ground appears to be but a thin, ashy crust, vegetation does not exist, the rocks are burnt out and ash like, and sulphur has permeated both rocks and earth. Numerous geysers, roaring and hissing like the escape valves of a hundred steam boilers, throw out quantities of hot sulphur and steam. The effect on entering the gorge is at first somewhat terrifying; but later, as confidence is regained, the scene becomes one of great interest, and numerous visitors are attracted to the place. Hokuto is the scenic resort of North Formosa, and with railway communication will doubtless grow greatly in popularity. From this district is shipped monthly some 200 tons of sulphur, the product of three Japanese extracting plants.

The sulphur-spring district, as well as Maruyama, present many attractive residential sites; and if the train service is convenient, it is quite possible that the city business men may elect to have their residences at one or the other of these interesting places.

The mainline when completed will run from Taihoku in the north to Takow in the south. In addition to the Kelung and Tamsui branches now constructed, it is the desire of the railway department to build a line on the east coast from Karenko to Pinan and connect it with the mainline by means of a branch running across the hills. Also to extend the line to the extreme southern point Garambi and to build from Taihoku to Suao via Gilan. Work on the mainline is now being carried on from both the Shinchiku and Tainan ends. In the south the section as far as Kagi will be completed, it is expected, during 1901, and in the north probably as far as Bioritsu (Miaoli). The central portion of the line will require numerous and expensive bridges and some thirteen tunnels. The improvements include a large railway bridge across the Tamsui river, 1,198 feet in length.

The cost of the mainline is estimated at 30,000,000 yen, and the Japanese Diet granted this sum in 1899, the expenditure to cover a period of ten years. It is expected, however, that this term will be greatly shortened and that cars will be running over the main line in about five years. Over 7,000,000 yen have already been expended on the Formosan railways by the Japanese. A splendid station is now being erected in Taihoku, where the general offices are located. There are large and well equipped repair shops; and the cars, with the exception of the iron work, will also be constructed here. It is the intention to have a foreign style hotel connected with the station, and when the railroad is completed more will be erected at other places on the line. The rolling stock consists of cars built on the English model, and American and English locomotives. The rails are American, and the bridges American and English.

Posts and Telegraphs.—Under the Chinese regime there was no postal service in the island. If it was desired to send a letter to an interior city, a special messenger was required, and the expense of this was naturally considerable. Under the Japanese every village has a post office, and mail matter is delivered to any city in the island at the regular rate existing in Japan proper. There are 109 post offices. The telegragh is under government control and is run in connection with the posts. Over 2,000 miles of telegraph and 600 miles of telephone wire, with cables between Formosa and the Japanese mainland and the Pescadores, have been laid. The cost of maintenance of the posts and telegraphs is about one million yen.

In addition to this, a large sum is being expended yearly in the construction of post offices. The central post office in Taihoku is a fine structure costing some 88,000 yen. The foreign mails are carried from Kelung, by the mail steamships of the Nippon Yusen Kwaisha, and Osaka Shosen Kwaisha, direct to Japan, and by the Douglas Steamship Company and Osaka Shosen Kwaisha from Tamsui and Anping to China ports.

SHIPPING AND NAVIGATION.

Formosa is unfortunate in possessing no really good, natural, harbors. Tamsui can be entered only by ships drawing less than fourteen feet of water, owing to a troublesome bar at the entrance. Takow is even less accessible, and the other ports, so far as sea going steamers are concerned, are merely open roadsteads, with the exception of So-o (Suao), which affords fairly safe shelter save from south east gales. Kelung, if not always safe, is at least commodious; and is by far the best, in fact, the only harbor for big ships, in the island. The large mail steamers running between the island and Japan have Kelung as their Formosa terminal. The steamers destined for Hongkong and other China ports sail from Tamsui and Anping. To encourage navigation and to provide frequent communication with Japan and China, the Japanese government grant the following subsidies :

Nippon Yusen Kwaisha 2 trips a month to Kobe, Japan, via Moji	..	..	..	..	50,000 yen
Osaka Shosen Kwaisha 2 trips a month to Kobe, via Moji	..	..	..	..	78,000 ,,
,,	.,	,,	3 trips a month to Kobe, via Moji and Ujina ..	..	..	170,000 ,,
,,	,,	,,	2 trips a month to Kobe, via Ishikawa, Naha and Kagoshima	..	75,000 ,,
,,	,,	,,	2 trips a month, East Coast Line }			
,,	,,	,,	2 trips a month, West Coast Line }	..	155,000 ,,
,,	,,	,,	2 trips a month, Kelung to Takow, via Pescadores	..	..	40,740 ,,
,,	,,	,,	2 to 4 trips a month, Tamsui to Tokatsukutsu..	..	..	5,000 ,,
,,	,,	,,	3 to 4 trips a month, Tamsui to Hongkong, via Amoy and Swatow..	123,000 ,,
,,	,,	,,	2 trips a month, Anping to Hongkong via Amoy and Swatow	..	60,000 ,,
,,	,,	,,	3 trips a month, Tamsui to Foochow, via Amoy	..	..	70,000 ,,

The total annual expenditure for navigation amounts thus to 826,740 yen, giving some 25 to 27 steamers a month. The Osaka Shosen Kwaisha's Japan lines are required to provide the military with free transportation for men and supplies.

Of the many improvements that the island requires, none is more important than the construction of harbors. The first necessity, from a Japanese point of new, is to obtain a harbor sufficiently commodious to shelter a naval fleet and transports; and, secondly, a harbor which will offer every facility to large merchant steamers. Kelung appears to be the only natural harbor that can be made, at any cost within reason, to yield these advantages. Consequently, the Japanese have given their first attention to the improving of Kelung harbor. A number of dredges have been purchased and are now at work, large work shops are being erected on shore, and the preliminary surveys have been completed. The first expenditure, 2,000,000 yen, is to be devoted to dredging, pier and quay work, that safe shelter for a limited number of merchant ships may be obtained as soon as possible. The inner lagoon, with at present but two or three feet of water, will be deepened to eight or nine, and will be the anchorage for junks and like craft. The remainder of the harbor will all be dredged to thirty-five feet, and be divided into the inner and outer harbors. Running parallel with the east shore of the inner harbor will be a landing pier, some 1,000 feet in length, which will accommodate several steamers, and is intended for domestic shipping—that is, coastwise and Japan steamers. Along the east shore of the outer harbor will be erected a quay with two piers, affording a total water line of 3,000 feet, which will accommodate seven or eight ocean-going steamers, the depth, thirty-five feet, being sufficient to accommodate the largest craft. The railway will be laid along both pier and quay, making it possible to handle cargo direct from car to steamer. A roofway will be erected to shelter cargo during the rainy season, and hydraulic and steam cranes will be provided that cargo may be handled quickly and safely. A large freight station will be erected near the pier and quay. This work, it is believed, will be completed within three years; later both piers and quay will be extended in length as required. Although these improvements will provide good shelter for steamers at the piers or quay, ships lying at anchor in the outer harbor would not obtain sufficient protection during northeast gales. Consequently, it is the intention to erect near the mouth of the harbor a breakwater over 4,000 feet in length. It will project from the northwestern point of Palm Island, across the low rocks known as Bush Island, and extend to a point nearly opposite Image (Imagi) Point, leaving an entrance of nearly 1,000 feet. The construction of the breakwater is a large undertaking, costing some 8,000,000 yen, and about six or seven years will be required for its construction. On the west side of the harbor will be erected docks and slips and piers for army and navy use. These improvements include the reclaiming of some 250 acres of land. The completion of the work will give Kelung a safe, commodious harbor, and will undoubtedly benefit trade.

While the Kelung harbor work is of first importance to the island, the improving of Tamsui harbor, is, from a local, commercial, point of view, urgently required. Tamsui, from its location, is the natural port of shipment for the products of North Formosa, and is also the most convenient for the import trade. It is at the mouth of the Tamsui river, and but nine miles by river from Daitotei (Twatutia) and Banka. These cities are the chief markets for the export and import trade of the northern half of the island. Thus the importance of possessing cheap and convenient means of shipment can be easily understood. Although some parts of the lower river have considerable depth, only steamers drawing thirteen feet or less can gain entrance to the anchorage, owing to a troublesome bar at the mouth, and only then at high tide. During stormy weather the bar is generally impassable, and it is always more or less dangerous. To remove this bar and erect such works as will prevent it from forming again are the principal requirements for this harbor. The Japanese have made careful surveys with these improvements in view, and while the plans have not as yet been definitely determined on, the engineers engaged are of the opinion that it will be necessary to lead the river out into deep water by constructing jetties, which will project seawards from each bank the required distance. The bar would then be removed and the present anchorage deepened by dredging. River works include considerable bunding; and the erection of a quay. The harbor if thus improved would give comfortable accommodation to steamers of from two to three thousand tons.

South Formosa is in even a more unfortunate state regarding harbors. Takow can be entered only by small steamers, and Anping is practically an open roadstead. Takow harbor is a shallow bay, or lagoon, several miles long. This bay is separated from the sea by a sand bank which, continuing below sea level opposite the entrance to the lagoon, constitutes the "bar." There is a depth of less than fifteen feet of water on this bar at high tide, and about the same depth in parts of the lagoon. The entrance is very narrow, and the Japanese contemplate widening this and dredging the bar and lagoon sufficiently to offer shelter to four or five large steamers. Ultimately it is intended to erect a breakwater to protect the entrance. Anping is a port of more or less importance, situated on a line of low flat coast, through which runs into the sea a small stream, the mouth of which is utilized for shelter by small cargo boats, launches, etc. Parallel with the coast line is a bar with but a few feet of water on it even at high tide. Only small cargo boats, launches, etc., can pass it in fair weather, and when the sea is somewhat rough only bamboo rafts are used, and in time of storm even this craft cannot venture across. A good harbor could, undoubtedly be made, but only at a cost out of all proportion to the advantages to be gained, and I cannot learn that the Japanese have ever taken the subject into consideration. On the east coast the ports, with the exception of So-o (Suao), are open roadsteads, and harbor improvements there have not as yet been discussed.

FOREIGN TRADE.

Since 1895, when Formosa was ceded to Japan, there has been but little increase in exports, though values have advanced in some lines; but the

Railway across Kelung River showing
Chinese Gold-Washers at work.

Temporary Bridge on the Narrow-
Gauge Line.

Railway Station at Taihoku (Taipeh).

Station on the Narrow-Gauge Line.

Passenger Push-Cars on the
Narrow-Gauge Line.

Japanese occupation has had a stimulating effect on imports. Of that statistics give abundant evidence, and of all nations, Japan, the United States, and Great Britain have reaped the most benefit from this. Under the Chinese regime imports were not generally classified as to place of origin, and, accordingly, statistics of the trade of the three countries mentioned are incomplete. As regards Great Britain and Japan, we can, however, by referring to the principal articles of import, note the great increase in these items. As the import of American goods during the Chinese regime was practically limited to the two staples, petroleum and flour, definite information is available regarding the trade of that country. In 1894, the last year of the Chinese regime, the total imports into Tamsui and Kelung (North Formosa) amounted in value to 5,736,060 yen. Of this 900,000 gallons of kerosene, valued at 161,177 yen, and 16,651 cwt. of flour, valued at 64,790 yen, a total in value of 225,967 yen, were goods from the United States. In South Formosa (through Anping and Takow) out of imports valued at 3,517,950 yen, the United States sent 603,710 gallons of kerosene, valued at 137,480 yen, and 3,567 cwt. of flour, valued at 17,890 yen, a total in value of 161,000 yen. Thus the whole island consumed American products to the value of only 386,967 yen. In 1899 under the Japanese regime, the United States sold to the island 2,315,855 gallons of oil, valued at 599,474 yen, and 83,400 cwt. of flour, valued at 334,491 yen, or a total of 933,965 yen for these two items alone. The total value of imports during this period more than doubled. In 1900, United States imports reached in value to over 2,000,000 yen. One striking feature, however, in the change of rulers was the opportunity offered for the introduction into the island of new products. Under the Chinese, the shipping (excluding native sailing craft) was limited to one English line, running four steamers between the island and Hongkong, and the foreign goods brought to the island, were, with the exception of oil and flour, chiefly of English or German origin, and obtained from Hongkong importers. Local contracts with the Chinese for government supplies were practically controlled by German and English firms, and the import of American goods, excluding the two staples mentioned, was absolutely nil. Now, eleven steamers connect Formosa with Japan. Four care for the trade with China, and Hongkong, and four run around the island visiting the various important coast ports and the Pescadores, and a dozen or so of large sea-going launches keep up communication with the smaller coast ports. Government experts now make their purchases where they believe best value can be obtained, and many countries are represented. The Japanese have, to some extent, introduced to the island the use of foreign goods, and the large amount of outside money, which, prior to 1900, was brought into the island by the Japanese administration, has increased the purchasing power of the masses. The benefit which might have been derived from all this, at least so far as concerned imports, was to some extent nullified by the imposition of a very largely increased customs tariff. This is specially apparent in the decreased imports of Chinese staples from the neighboring China ports; but this is doubtless satisfactory to the Japanese who were largely able to supply these wants from Japan, imports from the latter being free of duty. Still, regardless of the disadvantages of increased duties, the import trade has shown a large increase in many lines, and is in a generally flourishing condition.

VALUE (IN JAPANESE YEN) OF IMPORTS FROM VARIOUS COUNTRIES VIA HONGKONG AND CHINA.

Country.	1895.	1897.	1898.	1899.	1900.
Great Britain	1,146,328	1,975,777	1,617,656	1,093,638	1,398,014
United States	594,389	811,660	870,109	992,841	1,517,980
Germany	223,224	353,362	299,695	91,236	94,343
Australia	58,693	41,813	85,226	52,226	114,613
Russia	—	—	—	22,123	—
Austria	604	4,705	12,668	6,193	4,247
France	7,768	10,010	9,233	4,596	2,890
Denmark	19	120	245	4,291	—
Switzerland	3,271	2,365	974	3,103	5,995
China	4,094,390	7,363,550	10,103,053	6,296,713	5,997,236
Hongkong	290,613	411,101	954,197	415,200	608,870
Annam and other French Asiatic Possessions	442,535	105,565	509,357	2,405,390	102,346
Russian Asiatic	40,697	69,356	90,206	72,659	278,816
British India	604.957	439,098	489,006	37,957	464,036
Korea	42,420	43,140	24,011	19,643	12,820
Philippines	17,751	18,405	14,608	7,992	1,617
Siam	68,073	51,920	66,767	3,236	3,869
Other Countries	991,917	1,548,866	1,738,501	2,739,939	2,964,131
Total	8,631,001	12,659,298	16,879,190	14,270,588	13,571,223

Countries with a trade of less than 1,000 yen have not been inserted in the above. Owing to a partial failure of the Formosa rice crop in 1899, there was a large import of rice from the French Asiatic possessions, which explains the very large returns credited to the latter for the year mentioned. A portion of the imports from Hongkong should be credited to Great Britain, the United States, Germany, or other countries; as goods from these countries which may be purchased in or received via Hongkong by Chinese shippers, are frequently, through ignorance, declared as of Hongkong origin. It is necessary to explain here that, with the exception of a few of the staples, such as flour, oil, etc., which come to the island chiefly via Hongkong, many of the goods formerly arriving via that port, are now shipped to the island via Japan, and therefore do not appear in the customs returns. Consequently the decrease in imports shown by some countries in the above table is due to a transfer of the trade to Japan-importing houses rather than to a decrease in the consumption. The above table practically refers only to imports arriving from or via China and Hongkong.

The value in yen of the principal import items, and the chief countries supplying same excluding China and Japan for the year 1902, as given in the customs returns, are as follows:—

ARTICLES.	TOTAL IMPORT.	CHIEF PLACES OF ORIGIN.
Opium	Y.2,310 424	Persia,[1] 1,500,000; British India 468,849; Turkey,[2] 340,000.
Piece Goods (as follows)	1,743,961	
Cotton drills	3,104	Great Britain.
,, prints	6,883	Great Britain, 6,005.
,, satins	197,495	Great Britain, 189,553; Germany, 7,934.
,, velvets	4,253	Great Britain, 3,168; Germany, 1,052.

ARTICLES.	TOTAL IMPORT.	CHIEF PLACES OF ORIGIN.
Shirtings, grey ..	165,249	Great Britain, 163,067 ; Germany, 2,181.
„ white	278,103	Great Britain.
„ dyed	22,411	Great Britain, 7,901.
T-cloths ..	1,198	Great Britain.
Turkey-red cambrics ..	1,167	Great Britain.
Victoria lawns ..	2,553	Great Britain.
All other cotton tissues	818,570	Great Britain, 20,210 ; Hongkong, 17,766 ; Germany, 3,485.
Trimmings	18,875	Germany, 4,046.
Woollen and worsted yarns of all kinds	18,537	Germany, 9,739 ; Great Britain, 8,064.
Alpacas ..	1,266	Great Britain.
Camlets, lastings and crape lastings..	118,842	Great Britain, 117,178 ; Germany, 1,663.
Long ells..	12,523	Great Britain.
Spanish stripes ..	4,849	Great Britain.
Woollen and worsted cloths ..	38,513	Germany, 27,171 ; Great Britain, 11,342.
All other woollen and worsted tissues	29,522	Great Britain, 11,516 ; Germany, 5,446.
Oil, kerosene	841,069	U.S.A., 562,430 ; Dutch India, 242,880 ; Russian Asia, 33,430 ; Russia, 2,328.
Vessels, steam	688,913	Great Britain.
Rails and fittings thereof	571,326	U.S.A., 434,343 ; Great Britain, 74,773
Sugar (as follows) ..	453,842	
Sugar ..	34,227	Hongkong.
„ refined A...	179,692	Hongkong.
„ „ B...	221,551	Hongkong.
„ rock candy	18,372	Hongkong, 2,626.
Flour	339,728	U.S.A.
Rice ..	156,357	French India, 42,655 ; British India, 13,701.
Lead, pig, ingot and slab	102,680	Australia.
Unclassified machinery and parts thereof	94,863	Great Britain, 93,827.
Ginseng	70,471	U.S.A., 31,105.
Rails and fittings thereof	62,210	U.S.A., 434,343 ; Great Britain, 74,773.
Materials of bridges and buildings ..	57,285	U.S.A.
Locomotives, engines, and parts thereof	47,370	Great Britain.
Condensed milk	42,559	Great Britain.
Tinned plate or sheet	41,634	Great Britain.
Blankets ..	38,708	Great Britain, 32,385, Germany, 6,261.
Bar and rod, steel or iron	29,379	Great Britain.
Shrimps ..	24,281	Australia, 8,659 ; U.S.A , 6,978 ; French India, 1,416.
Gunny bags	21,039	Hongkong, 4,551 ; British India, 4,273.
Cotton threads	20,437	Great Britain, 9,420 ; Belgium, 6,080 ; Germany, 1,804.
Furnitures ..	20,062	Hongkong, 8,625 ; Austria, 2,143
Confectionary and sweetmeats ..	19,106	Hongkong, 3,832 ; Great Britain, 1,530.
Sandal wood	17,084	Philippines, 8,171 ; French India, 1,001.
Yarns and threads, unenumerated	16,145	Great Britain, 2,063.
Clothing and accessories..	14,957	
Mangrove ..	13,539	French India, 2,485 ; British India, 1,343.
Cement, Portland ..	12,619	Hongkong.
Plate and sheet metal	12,230	Great Britain, 6,314 ; U.S.A., 5,916.
Old iron or mild steel	11,257	Hongkong, 7,861.
Railway freight cars or parts thereof ..	11,025	Great Britain, 11,025.
Nails	9,545	Great Britain, 7,283 ; U.S.A., 1,460.
Tin, block, ingot and slab	9,369	Great Britain, 1,168.
Implements and tools of farmers and mechanics	8,374	U.S.A., 1,488.
Screws, bolts and nuts ..	7,874	Great Britain, 1,560 ; U.S.A., 2,713.
Lamps and parts thereof..	7,395	Germany, 3,213.
Steam engines, boilers and parts thereof	7,337	U S A , 3,731 ; Hongkong, 2,260 ; Great Britain 1,345.
Umbrellas (European style)	6,915	Hongkong.
Cutch and gambier	6,629	British India, 3,352.
Candles ..	6,158	Great Britain, 2,721 ; Germany, 1,927 ; Belgium, 1,152.
Smokers articles ..	6,012	Germany, 2,140.

1. and 2. estimated.

China, so far as imports are concerned, has a very large trade with Formosa, second only to that of Japan. Owing to the heavy duties imposed on foreign goods, China is rapidly losing her Formosa Trade, while Japan which enters her goods free of duty is the gainer.

The value in Yen for the year 1902 of the principal imports from China is given in the following table :—

ARTICLES.	VALUE.	ARTICLES.	VALUE.
Cotton tissues, Chinese	685,928	Bricks and tiles	48,133
Timber and boards	429,950	Salt, crude	41,554
Hogs	407,630	Lard, tallow and grease	35,263
Paper foils	384,277	Oil, bean	34,046
Paper (as follows):—	282,074	Oil, tea	33,343
Chinese	228,445	Flour, meal, and starches	32,973
Packing	19,925	Oils and waxes, unenumerated	31,083
Tea-box	19,049	Lily-flowers	28,410
All other stationery	14,655	Foils and powder of metal	25,400
Tobacco, leaf	212,683	Hemp-bags	22,856
Rice	173,475	Ginseng	21,553
Drugs and medicines, unclassified	161,529	Umbrellas, paper	20,561
Linen and cotton tissues	147,016	Linen tissues	18,946
Grass cloths	142,178	Mats and mattings	18,442
Porcelain and earthen-ware	132,088	Sugar	16,645
Silk goods (as follows):—	115,212	Tea	16,242
Silk threads	11,083	Wood, manufactures of	16,197
Silk satins	8,986	Sugar, rock candy	15,463
Silk satins figured	12,791	Trimmings	14,589
Other silk tissues	82,352	Eggs, fresh	14,561
Tobacco, cut	113,811	All other tissues, manufactures of	14,417
Fish, salted	113,043	Bone, animal	13,996
Pans	88,177	Beans, other than soja	13,642
Tea box boards	87,604	Shirtings, dyed	13,509
Vermicelli	86,646	Confectionery and sweetmeats	13,311
Beans, soja	76,805	Yarns and threads unenumerated	13,098
Oil-cake	74,797	All other clothings and accessories	12,744
Joss-stick	73,137	Gunny bags	12,713
Boots and shoes, Chinese	70,222	Lacquer, Chinese	12,670
Mats, packing	68,269	Indigo, liquid	12,236
Cotton raw, ginned	65,264	Vessels, sailing and boats	12,091
Fruits, fresh or dried, and nuts	57,847	Gypsum	11,691
Fire works of all kinds	56,589	Animals, other than hogs	11,160
Fungus	56,034	Chinese liquors	11,109
		Boots and shoes, unfinished	10,629

The above statistics cover only the imports received from or via China and Hongkong, and represent either the products of those places or foreign goods which have come in over that route.

To obtain a comprehensive view of the island's commerce, the large and rapidly growing trade with and via Japan must be included, and this is of special interest to us, as a considerable quantity of foreign goods arrive by this route. The trade with Japan has grown rapidly. In 1896, aside from supplies for the army, the import was trifling. In 1897, goods arrived to the value of about one million yen; in 1898 this trade had reached 4,599,311 yen; and in 1901, 8,782,258 yen, which is more than a third of the total imports.

That we may arrive at the total imports of leading goods, the following table gives both the foreign and Japanese trade, for the past three years, China being included among the foreign countries.

VALUE IN YEN OF THE PRINCIPAL IMPORTS FROM FOREIGN COUNTRIES AND JAPAN FOR THREE YEARS.

ARTICLES.		1899.	1900.	1901.
Piece goods, all kinds and raw material thereof ..	From foreign countries	2,028,024	2,157,068	2,264,527
	„ or via Japan	280,317	367,998	888,083
	Total	2,308,341	2,525,066	3,152,610
Opium	From foreign countries ..	2,775,809	3,392,602	2,310,424
Timber or boards	From foreign countries ..	525,312	538,182	430,281
	„ or via Japan	578,706	1,220,449	785,967
	Total	1,104,018	1,758,631	1,216,248
Kerosene Oil	From foreign countries ..	694,217	1,199,056	841,069
	„ or via Japan	—	37,480	49,860
	Total	694,217	1,236,536	890,929
Rice	From foreign countries ..	2,584,968	167,382	229,832
	„ or via Japan	836,713	545,410	506,502
	Total	3,453,681	712,792	736,334
Tobacco, cut and cigarettes ..	From foreign countries ..	449,981	87,755	113,931
	„ or via Japan	252,208	512,585	612,127
	Total	702,189	600,340	726,058
Sake (Rice wine)	From Japan	586,510	625,805	720,269
Vessels, steam	From foreign countries ..	47,667	256,126	688,913
Comestibles, unclassified ..	From foreign countries ..	391,129	393,825	284,811
	„ or via Japan	448,545	312,088	343,217
	Total	839,674	705,913	628,028
Paper and stationery	From foreign countries ..	374,110	356,971	302,113
	„ or via Japan	63,928	128,802	194,073
	Total	438,038	485,773	496,186
Sugar	From foreign countries ..	270,400	364,373	453,846
	„ or via Japan	1,696	8,541	11,976
	Total	272,096	372,914	465,822
Rails and fittings thereof ..	From foreign countries ..	—	211,410	571,326
	„ or via Japan	—	—	37,980
	Total	—	—	609,306
Fish, salted	From foreign countries ..	153,723	89,201	113,045
	„ or via Japan	98,522	195,276	341,547
	Total	252,245	284,477	454,592
Hogs	From foreign countries ..	660,549	562,126	408,170
	„ or via Japan	4,925	2,908	1,547
	Total	665,474	565,034	409,717
Paper foils	From China	207,724	337,070	384,277
Flour	From foreign countries ..	834,655	855,541	839,728

ARTICLES.				1899.	1900.	1901.
Drugs and medicines	From foreign countries	..		198,510	218,355	227,461
	„ or via Japan	..	..	283,832	100,340	111,474
	Total	..	..	482,342	318,695	338,935
Soy and Miso	From Japan	..		162,777	191,616	263,733
Tobacco leaf .. .. .. •	From foreign countries	..		26,259	116,891	242,683
	„ or via Japan	..	..	—	—	2,720
	Total	..	..	26,259	116,891	245,403
Machinery, unclassified and parts thereof.	From foreign countries	..		9,216	3,009	94,863
	„ or via Japan	..	..	114,558	144,104	130,023
	Total	..	..	123,774	147,113	224,886
Beer	From foreign countries	..		12,206	299	526
	„ or via Japan	..	..	165,212	212,470	213,755
	Total	..	..	177,418	212,769	214,281
Wines and other liquors ..	From foreign countries	..		15,111	12,410	20,034
	„ or via Japan	..	..	23,962	21.274	52,654
	Total	..	..	39,073	33,684	72,688
Matches..	From Japan	..		—	210,121	198,485
Oils and waxes other than kerosene	From foreign countries	..		196,641	211,029	125,968
	„ or via Japan	..	..	—	82,854	53,849
	Total	..	..	196,641	293,883	179,817
Porcelain and earthenware ..	From foreign countries	..		107,416	121,138	133,663
	„ or via Japan	..	..	22,103	40,867	44,602
	Total	..	..	129,519	162,005	178,265
Boots and shoes	From China	..		75,190	70,661	81,187
	„ Japan	..		21,347	40,553	66,671
	Total	..	..	97,537	111,214	147,858
Beans, peas and pulse.. ..	From foreign countries	..		153,961	153,877	90,447
	„ or via Japan	..	..	—	35,248	50,655
	Total	..	..	153,961	189,125	141,102
Clothing and accessories ..	From foreign countries	..		86,562	47,732	58,336
	„ or via Japan	..	..	—	4,074	68,436
	Total	..	..	86,562	51,806	126,772
Cement and lime	From foreign countries	..		7,951	109,530	12,619
	„ or via Japan	..	..	67,790	250,248	98,877
	Total	..	..	75,741	359,778	111,496
Lead	From foreign countries	..		104,603	117,023	106,801
Vermicelli	From foreign countries	..		113,577	95,678	86,646
	„ or via Japan	..	..	—	1,275	6,486
	Total	..	..	—	96,953	93,132

Articles.		1899.	1900.	1901.
Pans, iron	From China	71,792	69,636	88,537
Tea-box boards..	From China	84,218	84,462	87,604
Bricks and tiles ..	From foreign countries ..	58,115	68,647	52,212
	„ or via Japan	160,987	86,686	35,302
	Total	219,102	155,333	87,514
Glass, manufactures of ..	From foreign countries ..	18,291	12,945	8,710
	„ or via Japan	26,476	53,107	68,064
	Total	44,767	66,052	76,774
Mats, packing	From China	48,628	26,840	74,881
Joss sticks	From China	64,037	71,819	73,137
Ginseng	From foreign countries ..	58,088	53,436	70,471
Fruits, fresh and dry, and nuts	From foreign countries ..	70,506	60,440	59,019
	„ or via Japan	—	—	6,505
	Total	70,506	60,440	65,524
Coal and coke	.. ..	—	16,804	63,186
Furniture, trunks, etc. ..	From foreign countries ..	19,328	18,332	20,062
	„ or via Japan	—	1,765	39,542
	Total	—	20,097	59,604
Fireworks of all kinds.. ..	From foreign countries ..	37,272	54,406	56,589
Fungus of all kinds	From foreign countries ..	38,033	51,368	56,034
Tea	From foreign countries ..	19,406	20,526	16,759
	„ or via Japan	14,716	20,252	35,269
	Total	34,122	40,778	52,028
Condensed Milk	From foreign countries ..	41,263	39,711	42,559
Tinned plate or sheet.. ..	From foreign countries ..	10,853	22,073	41,634
Salt, crude	From foreign countries ..	51,602	110,136	41,554
Lard, tallow and grease ..	From foreign countries ..	56,011	38,517	35,263
Nails	From foreign countries ..	15,891	11,697	9,822
	„ or via Japan	—	20,032	19,710
	Total	—	31,729	29,532
Lacquered ware	From foreign countries ..	—	—	12,670
	„ or via Japan	4,154	21,306	24,918
	Total	4,154	21,306	37,588
Watches, clocks and accessories	From foreign countries ..	6,003	4,107	1,904
	„ or via Japan	1,450	2,420	18,495
	Total	7,453	6,527	20,399
Jinrikisha	From Japan	—	18,657	18,712
Earthen ware drain pipes ..	From Japan	—	20,646	18,292
Oil cake	From China	17,540	1,686	13,996
Gunpowder and explosive compounds	From Japan	—	27,156	13,882
Total import	From foreign countries ..	14,273,092	13,570,663	12,809,794
	„ or via Japan ..	8,011,826	3,439,032	8,782,258
	Total ..	22,284,918	22,009,695	21,592,042

On a previous page, the imports via Hongkong and China have been classified as to country of origin. It is impossible to give the same information for the above table, though such is required to ascertain the total of each country. In the case of goods imported via Japan, no declarations are required as to place of origin. The extent to which each country profits by this trade can be judged only by the material one sees used in government undertakings, the wares one may see exposed for sale in the shops, or being carted through the streets. The United States, Germany, Great Britain, of all countries seem by profit most largely by this trade.

Of American goods one finds the following :—Lumber, agricultural implements, sugar mills, telephones, watches including Waltham and other expensive movement, clocks, photographic supplies, acetylene apparatus, fire arms, ammunition, bicycles, condensed milk, patent medicines, groceries, tobacco, California wines, canned fruit and other canned goods, nails, hardware, soap, stationery, blankets, books of reference, lamps, confectionery, dental supplies, leather, hats and caps, lubricating oils, celluloid novelties, perfumes, sewing machines, oil stoves, rubber foot ware, railway material, locomotives, etc., etc. German chemicals have a large sale among the Japanese; and cutlery, cheap jewelry, and miscellaneous novelties bearing the familiar " Made in Germany " are also important among the foreign goods displayed. English photographic plates and papers imported via Japan are used almost exclusively throughout the island, and English books of reference have a considerable sale among the Government Departments. English toilet articles, patent medicines, scientific instruments, hats and caps, paints, condensed milk, hardware and chemicals, in addition to machinery, bridge material and locomotives are also found. France is represented by perfumes, soaps and wines; and France, Holland, and Denmark supply tinned butter. The above goods are purchased from wholesale merchants in Japan, and are usually imported together with miscellaneous Japanese supplies. With the exception of a very few items, the goods described are not imported in large quantities, but the trade is doubtless a growing one, and is of value in introducing to the large Chinese population many foreign lines with which they were formerly unfamiliar.

GOVERNMENT SUPPLIES.

Supplies for the government are purchased in Japan, and the articles generally enter one of the mainland ports and pay duty there, and are then transported to Formosa without passing through the local customs. We are thus without information from official sources as to the country of origin, value etc., of some of the most important items of import entering the island. From private sources, however, information has been obtained regarding the most important items. Regarding railway supplies the United States has supplied 4 locomotives, the bulk of the rails and bridge material for the new railway. England has supplied 6 locomotives, machinery for shops, a considerable quantity of bridge material, and the dredgers now at work in Kelung harbor. Up to the present no other foreign countries have been favored with any government orders.

FORMOSAN EXPORTS.

The principal exports from the island are tea, camphor, rice, gold, coal, fibres, and sulphur from North Formosa; and sugar, dyeplants, and fibres from the south. Six years ago this trade was conducted almost wholly via China and Hongkong. In 1896, excluding the old established trade in sugar, some 200,000 yen covered the value of exports to Japan, in 1897 this trade had increased threefold, and in 1898 it had reached to over 2,700,000 yen. This last large increase is accounted for by the very heavy and unusual export of rice to supply demand created by the failure of the rice crop in Japan. In 1899, Japan received Formosa commodities to the value of 3,650,475 yen including sugar to the value of 1,748,878 yen in 1900 to the value of 4,402,110 yen, and in 1901 to the high figure of 7,345,956 yen which nearly reaches the total export via Hongkong and China.

The following table gives for three years the value of the leading items of export to Japan and to foreign countries, in which China is included.

VALUE IN YEN OF THE PRINCIPAL EXPORTS TO FOREIGN COUNTRIES AND JAPAN AND TO FOREIGN COUNTRIES VIA JAPAN.

ARTICLES.			1899.	1900.	1901.
Tea	To foreign countries	..	5,308,327	4,831,812	3,517,300
	„ and via Japan ..	..	275,438	493,016	711,080
	Total ..	..	5,583,765	5,324,828	4,228,380
Camphor	To foreign countries	..	1,732,739	1,385,645	789,290
	„ and via Japan ..	..	292,261	945,383	1,571,496
	Total ..	..	2,025,000	2,331,028	2,360,786
Camphor oil	To foreign countries	..	1,328	—	—
	„ and via Japan ..	..	1,074,529	962,643	1,325,836
	Total ..	..	1,075,857	962,643	1,325,836
Brown sugar	To China	..	1,216,061	452,723	678,369
	„ Japan	..	1,748,878	1,537,837	2,243,452
	Total ..	..	2,964,939	1,990,560	2,921,821
White sugar	To China	..	370,884	216,521	352,944
	„ Japan	..	—	—	49,145
	Total ..	..	370,884	216,521	402,089
Rice	To China	..	1,265,727	2,276,359	1,132,419
	„ Japan	..	62,622	93,118	1,024,332
	Total ..	..	1,328,349	2,369,477	2,156,751
China Grass and other fibres..	To foreign countries	..	298,406	368,654	382,798
	„ Japan	..	—	1,176	640
	Total ..	..	298,406	369,830	383,438
Sesame	To foreign countries	..	31,179	61,341	213,883
	„ and via Japan ..	..	—	713	14,118
	Total ..	..	31,179	62,054	228,001
Coal	To foreign countries	..	97,489	134,706	184,687
Lungngans	To China	..	161,367	45,620	216,235
Oil cakes	To China	..	101,872	77,203	124,476
Hides	To Japan	..	22,333	57,058	60,869
	„ China	..	13,252	13,002	42,187
	Total ..	..	35,585	70,060	103,066

ARTICLES.		1899.	1900.	1901.
Turmeric	To China	125,587	128,732	91,186
	„ Japan	3,323	20,939	10,210
	Total	128,910	149,671	101,396
Salt	To Japan	—	49,958	87,447
Beans, peas, etc.	To China	41,547	47,241	45,364
Sekikasai	To China	2,080	14	4,151
	To Japan	25,997	32,866	37,193
	Total	31,077	32,880	41,344
Sulphur	To foreign countries	12,820	16,686	34,355
	To and via Japan	424	26,801	2,609
	Total	13,244	43,487	36,964
Fish	To China	5,558	1,497	27,910
Pine Apple fibre	To China	16,520	18,470	26,166
Timber and Lumber	To China	11,264	29,627	25,143
	„ Japan	166	1,448	800
	Total	11,430	31,075	25,943
Sundries free of duty	To foreign countries	7,293	47,070	25,364
Rattans	To foreign countries	15,672	17,372	23,184
Kerosene-oil	To China	—	12,521	19,088
Bamboo Sprouts	To China	21,578	22,795	18,627
Ground-nut Oil	To China	2,710	—	17,834
Pith-paper and Pith	To foreign countries	19,987	18,558	17,738
Jute ribbons and fibre	To China	7,393	14,530	22,989
Sundries for ships use	To China	21	318	14,669
Matches	To China	2,986	8,087	14,210
Wheat	To China	25,627	28,313	11,292
Glass manufactures	To China	511	4,068	7,340
Drugs	To China	1,654	3,043	6,251
Vegetables and Fruits	To China	2,200	1,319	3,613
Rape Seed	To China	2,833	6,146	2,350
Various unenumerated articles	To foreign countries	51,764	134,540	114,772
	„ and via Japan	119,034	17,434	18,424
	Total	170,794	151,974	133,196
Grand Total	To foreign countries	10,978,673	10,434,282	8,218,544
	„ and via Japan	3,631,125	4,248,594	7,163,178
	Total	14,609,798	14,682,876	15,381,722

Only a small portion of the gold production is declared at the customs, but for 1901 the export of this mineral may be taken as exceeding 1,500,000 yen in value.

It is interesting to note that the 34 exports given above show a considerable increase during the three years reviewed, with the exception only of tea, brown sugar, turmeric, bamboo sprouts, pith paper pith, wheat, and rape seed which show a decrease.

TOTAL TRADE OF FORMOSA.

With the above statistics before us we find the total import and export trade (values stated in yen) for the six years of Japanese occupation to be as follows:—

	Imports from or via Hongkong, China, etc. (Custom Returns.)	Imports from or via Japan. (Harbor Returns.)	Total Imports.	Exports to Hong- kong, China and foreign countries, via China (Custom Returns.)	Exports to Japan and to foreign countries via Japan (Harbor Returns.)	Total Exports.	Total Exports and Imports.
1896	8,631,001	500,000*	9,131,001	11,402,226	1,485,976	12,888,202	22,019,203
1897	12,659,298	1,000,000*	13,659,298	12,759,293	2,438,788	15,198,081	28,857,379
1898	16,875,404	4,599,311	21,474,715	12,827,189	4,198,215	17,025,404	38,500,119
1899	14,273,092	8,011,826	22,284,918	11,114,921	3,650,475	14,765,396	37,050,314
1900	13,570,663	8,439,032	22,009,695	10,571,285	4,402,110	14,973,395	36,983,090
1901	12,809,794	8,782,258	21,592,052	8,298,800	7,345,956	15,644,756	37,236,808

* Estimated.

The above tables show a steady increase in the total trade of Formosa for the period reviewed, this increase being equal to some 62 per cent.[1]

TOTAL TRADE WITH VARIOUS COUNTRIES COMPARED.

No exact statistics can be obtained to show the total annual trade between Formosa and the various western countries, but a rough estimate which can claim to be no more than an approximation is as follows:—

Countries.	Imports via Hongkong. Yen.	Exports of camphor to. Yen.	Exports of tea to. Yen.	Total Trade. Yen.
United States	1,515,507	517,000	5,800,000	7,832,507
Great Britain	2,109,443	460,203	600,000	3,169,646
Germany	126,634	684,000	—	710,634
France	4,923	316,000	—	320,923

There are small unrecorded exports reaching the various countries, and there is a large import of foreign articles from Japan, statistics for which are unobtainable. Excluding material for certain large government undertakings, which is a temporary trade at the most, the total of these items doubtless does not exceed some 2,600,000 yen in value. Without any accurate source of enquiry but estimating merely from information obtained from mercantile friends interested, I am led to believe that the United States has about 45 per cent of this trade, Germany 20 per cent, England 20 per cent, and other western countries 15 per cent. Adding this to the above figures we would obtain for the three countries chiefly interested a total trade in round numbers as follows:—United States, 8,740,000 yen; Great Britain, 3,600,000 yen; Germany, 1,110,000, yen.

FORMOSA PORTS.

Formosa now possesses twelve open ports, though only four—Kelung, Tamsui, Takow and Anping—are utilized by merchant steamers engaged in foreign trade. The remaining ports are visited by coasting vesssels, and by Chinese and native owned junks engaged in the China and Formosa trade.

The following tables cover the trade of these ports, excluding the coasting trade in Formosa produce, for the six years of Japanese occupation:—

1. In 1894, the last year of the Chinese regime, the entire import of piece goods including yarns, threads, raw material, &c., from foreign countries including China and Japan amounted in value to 988,759 yen, against 1,708,643 yen under the Japanese in 1900. Kerosene oil rose from 394,560 yen in 1894 to 1,209,056 yen in 1900, flour from 82,680 yen to 355,541 yen, and the total imports from 9,254,010 yen to 22,009,695 yen. It should be noted, however, in comparing the total trade, that much of the "junk" trade which did not, under the Chinese, pass through the Chinese Customs, is included in the present Japanese returns. The items given above, however, passed through the Chinese Customs, and can therefore be taken as fair examples of the general increase. Furthermore, comparing the first year of Japanese occupation with last year, thus obtaining for both years a like standard of calculation, we find the total imports for 1896 to be 9,131,001 yen, against 22,009,694 yen for 1900, which shows that the increase is real. Exports for the same period show an increase of nearly 3,000,000 yen. During the last five years of the Chinese occupation, we find imports increased from 7,127,534 yen to 9,254,010 yen, thus showing a nominal increase of less than 30 per cent., against over 140 per cent. for a similar period under Japanese rule.

VALUE IN YEN OF THE TOTAL TRADE OF FORMOSA PORTS WITH FOREIGN COUNTRIES (CHINA INCLUDED); AND WITH JAPAN, AND FOREIGN COUNTRIES VIA JAPAN, FOR SIX YEARS.

Year		Kelung.	Tamsui.	Anping.	Takow.	Rokko (Lokiang.)	Tokatsukuten (Goché.)	Toeki (Tangchio.)	Makung (Pescadores.)	Kakoko (Kh-akau.)	Kinko (Kukang.)	Toko (Tang-kanu.)	Koro (Auiang.)
1896.	Exports	16,681	7,821,419	2,315,619	251,643	860,504	—	—	—	—	136,358	—	—
	Imports	203,782	4,879,452	2,357,682	431,425	583,541	—	—	—	—	170,116	—	—
	Total	220,463	12,700,871	4,673,301	683,068	1,444,045					306,474		
1897.	Exports	50,578	8,315,766	1,888,049	208,392	878,036	705,141	396,173	52,163	—	146,998	35,843	82,214
	Imports	367,776	7,410,620	2,550,812	346,537	817,154	326,216	305,286	158,367	—	262,358	32,301	81,865
	Total	418,354	15,726,386	4,438,861	554,869	1,695,190	1,031,357	701,459	210,530	—	409,351	68,144	164,079
1898.	Exports	80,847	7,457,578	2,343,727	281,659	612,063	1,023,001	598,101	132,492	—	186,464	74,488	86,718
	Imports	764,340	9,871,538	3,230,921	380,411	817,314	514,039	519,494	249,177	—	329,189	74,745	123,984
	Total	845,187	17,329,116	5,574,648	662,070	1,429,377	1,537,040	1,117,595	381,669	—	465,653	149,233	210,702
1899.	Exports to foreign countries	83,449	7,293,415	2,015,594	225,326	239,940	604,969	192,443	88,227	101,827	93,320	97,192	69,213
	Exports to and via Japan	1,784,209	56,915	679,014	1,130,336								
	Total Exports	1,867,658	7,350,330	2,694,608	1,355,662	239,940	604,969	192,443	88,227	101,827	93,320	97,192	69,213
	Imports from foreign countries	408,007	9,668,733	2,236,658	274,097	376,274	398,395	200,534	210,888	101,642	213,498	101,829	82,647
	Imports from and via Japan	6,909,239	111,232	991,355									
	Total Imports	7,317,246	9,779,965	3,227,953	274,097	376,274	398,395	200,534	210,888	101,642	213,493	101,829	82,647
	Total Trade of Port	9,184,904	17,130,295	5,922,561	1,629,759	616,224	1,003,364	392,977	299,065	208,469	306,813	199,021	151,860
1900.	Exports to foreign countries	121,370	6,546,830	1,049,837	325,501	517,227	1,093,785	317,470	83,486	185,988	120,860	110,107	98,817
	Exports to and via Japan	2,586,297	112,786	653,777	1,044,028				5,221				
	Total Exports	2,707,667	6,659,616	1,703,614	1,369,529	517,227	1,093,785	317,470	88,707	185,988	120,860	110,107	98,817
	Imports from foreign countries	754,894	8,833,167	1,889,190	616,248	398,822	319,637	224,779	140,772	131,908	138,592	119,332	88,772
	Imports from and via Japan	6,516,646	203,757	967,069	479,971				135,401				
	Total Imports	7,271,440	9,036,824	2,857,259	1,096,219	398,822	319,637	224,779	286,173	131,908	138,592	119,332	88,772
	Total Trade of Port	9,979,107	15,696,440	4,560,873	1,712,448	797,049	1,413,422	542,249	974,880	317,896	259,452	229,439	187,589
1901.	Exports to foreign countries	202,023	4,665,399	1,422,451	147,161	375,305	545,967	273,174	137,716	214,645	98,209	115,551	101,183
	Exports to and via Japan	4,817,485		1,016,772	1,490,474				21,223				
	Total Exports	5,019,508	4,615,399	2,439,223	1,637,635	375,305	545,967	273,174	158,939	214,645	98,209	115,551	101,183
	Imports from foreign countries	1,587,666	7,220,198	1,788,084	479,971	474,067	254,280	215,878	187,358	140,889	152,750	130,075	85,664
	Imports from and via Japan	6,564,071	86,080	1,614,741					187,442				
	Total Imports	8,151,767	7,886,228	2,722,775	470,971	474,067	254,280	215,878	824,800	140,889	152,750	130,075	85,664
	Total Trade of Port	13,171,265	12,001,627	5,711,098	069,066	849,372	800,247	488,952	488,780	855,514	260,059	245,020	186,848

CARRYING TRADE.

The carrying trade, excluding junk traffic, is chiefly in the hands of the Japanese lines which receive a substantial subsidy from the Formosa government. The Douglas Company, an English line, which has since the year 1871 been closely associated with the trade of Formosa, has found competition with the subsidized lines to be unprofitable, and has consequently withdrawn several of its steamers. The shipping between Formosa and Japan is wholly controlled by the Japanese, and it is only on this Tamsui line which connects the north of the island with Amoy, Swatow and Hongkong, that the British Company is at present interested. Much of the Formosa tea is shipped over this route to Amoy, and the foreign merchants interested have in the past very wisely given sufficient support even at slightly advanced rates to justify the British Company in running one of its steamers. It is hoped that this support will continue, for although merchants have received very satisfactory service from the Japanese line, it is to the best interests of the shippers via Amoy that no single line be given a monopoly of the trade. The shipping trade of Formosa for 1901 was as follows:—[1]

	FOREIGN TRADE.										TRADE WITH JAPAN.		
	Japanese steamers.		British steamers.		Formosa junks.		China junks.		British sailing vessels.		Japanese steamers.		Total.
	No.	Ton.	No.	Ton.	No.	Ton.	No.	Ton.	No.	Ton.	No.	Ton.	Ton.
Kelung	6	9,986	1	2,961	19	765	233	10,038	—	—	130	208,996	232,746
Anping	26	21,034	8	7,787	29	647	66	2,427	3	1,513	84	116,880	149,788
Tamsui	51	43,449	45	33,140	57	2,746	463	13,835	—	—	2	1,349	94,519
Makung (Pescadores) ..	—	—	—	—	81	2,061	7	128	—	—	54	77,543	79,732
Takow	—	—	1	46	31	821	33	899	—	—	47	65,521	67,297
Tokatsukutsu (Goche)..	—	—	—	—	151	3,620	70	2,591	—	—	—	—	6,211
Rokko (Lokiang)	—	—	—	—	128	2,608	60	1,194	—	—	—	—	3,802
Toseki (Tangchio).. ..	—	—	—	—	44	1,218	49	1,315	—	—	—	—	2,533
Kakoko (Eh-akau) ..	—	—	—	—	20	915	40	1,480	—	—	—	—	2,395
Toko (Tangkang)	—	—	—	—	67	1,630	26	488	—	—	—	—	2,118
Kiuko (Kukang)	—	—	—	—	44	1,268	17	392	—	—	—	—	1,660
Koro (Aulang)	—	—	—	—	36	641	28	662	—	—	—	—	1,303
Total	83	74,469	55	43,934	707	18,940	1,097	35,449	3	1,513	317	469,789	644,104

TEA.

The arrival of a steamer in Kelung to load tea direct for the United States came somewhat sooner than was anticipated when the chapter on tea was written. On June 20th, 1902, the British steamer *Merionethshire*, engaged in the New York, China and Japan trade, entered Kelung and obtained a liberal cargo of tea and camphor. The *Merionethshire* is the first steamer to carry Formosa cargo from the island to an American port. Other steamers of the Shire line will call during the present tea season, and it is very probable that some vessels engaged in the Pacific trade will call during next season.

---

1. If we compare the shipping returns for 1901, with 1894 the last year of the Chinese occupation, we find a large increase. Thus in 1901 there were 455 steamers of 588,192 tons cleared from Formosan ports for Japan or foreign countries against 269 steamers of only 168,948 tons which cleared for China or foreign countries during 1894.

Whether the experiment, considering the present condition of Kelung harbor, will prove a success or not the present season will doubtless tell. At all events only some two or three of the tea firms are prepared at present to do their matting and marking here, which is necessary for direct shipments. The other firms with large vested interests in Amoy, China, will doubtless find it to their advantage, for the present at all events, to continue shipments via that port, as in the past. With the completion of the dredging at Kelung, some two or three years hence, a secure berth in the inner harbor will be obtainable, and the facilities offered for loading will be exceptionally good. The railway is increasing its rolling stock rapidly, and the authorities express their confidence in being able by that time to handle as much tea as will be offered.   When this time comes, Kelung will undoubtedly be a cheaper and, it is believed, a more convenient port of shipment than Amoy, and it is doubtless safe to prophecy that Kelung will ultimately be the port of shipment for practically the whole trade.

Since the chapter on tea was written there have been one or two developments of interest. The Japanese firm mentioned on page 389 has withdrawn from the island, and the tea trade is now in the hands of three American and three English houses. These firms have been long established in the East, have numerous connections in America, and are consequently thoroughly in touch with the trade in all its branches, and it is unlikely, so far as the American market is concerned, that Japanese export houses will again enter in competition.

As regards new markets, something may be done by the Japanese houses. Considerable interest has been taken, for instance, in the manufacture of Formosa tea dust into brick tea for shipment to Russia. The Agricultural Department of the Formosa Government sent a small shipment of tea dust to a Japanese brick-tea factory where it was manufactured, and the product was reported to be superior in some respects to Japanese brick tea. The adhesive quality of the Formosa dust made possible the production of a strong block, uniform in shape and dark in color, which are important requirements, I understand, though the liquor produced, was reported in some quarters to be rather too bitter to suit the Russian taste. As a result of these experiments a Japanese merchant undertook the manufacture of Brick tea in Daitotei (Twatutia) during the season of 1901, and shipped some 58,000 pounds of the product. Owing however to lack of capital he withdrew his establishment from the island at the close of the season. Although at present there is no brick-tea factory in the island, considerable quantities of dust, amounting to 363,088 pounds during 1901, were shipped to a brick tea factory in Nagasaki. What the result of these shipments will be it is difficult to foretell, but should they result in a demand for a large part of the Formosa dust, it would be a help to the trade in many ways.   Following the exhibit of Formosa tea at the Paris Exhibition, a few small orders were obtained from France, but it is not anticipated that a demand of any importance has been created. Another event of some interest to record is the shipment during 1900 and 1901, on Chinese account, of two small lots of tea to London.

The most notable development in the tea trade will be the construction, during the coming winter, of a model tea factory. Government experts have been studying the situation in Ceylon, and it is declared that the cost of production can be considerably reduced. While it is the intention of the government to introduce only such machines as will perform work of similar nature to that done at present by hand, the experts are not absolutely confident that the exact character of present tea so far as flavor and quality is concerned can be maintained. In this case the original plans will be abandoned, and only such of the machines retained as can with advantage be utilized. It is stated, however, that definite information on this subject cannot be actually obtained without establishing an experimental factory, and if it is later found that the favorable characteristics of Formosa Oolong have not been altered, the gain in the decreased cost of production will be so great that it is good policy to make the test even at a considerable expenditure ; and at the risk of failure. The total cost of production in Formosa for the entire crop for an average season is stated to be about 465,000 yen. By utilizing machinery the cost would be reduced to about 179,000 yen, which includes a liberal interest on the cost of the factory. The machinery necessary to accomplish this result is stated to be as follows :—

100 sets of dessicating machinery at 1,620 yen a set, requiring as labor. 250 men.

200 sets of assorting machinery at 455 yen a set, requiring 100 women.

200 sets of cutting machinery at 195 yen a set, requiring 100 girls.

200 sets of packing machinery at 455 yen, requiring 100 girls.

Steam power sufficient for the above at a total cost of 24,000 yen and requiring 20 men.

With the above machinery distributed in factories throughout the tea district and taking the tea season as lasting for 200 days a year, the total crop of Formosa tea could be handled at a cost of yen 1.77 a picul (133⅓ pounds) including interest, against the present cost of some yen 2.88 a picul.

The government model factory will be the smallest sized factory capable of making a practical test, and will contain according the present plans the following machines :—A Japanese machine similar to that at present used in Japan for performing the first firing. 1 set of withering machines of Japanese manufacture. 1 Jackson's Rapid Tea Roller. 1 Davidson's Desiccator. 1 Assorting machine. 1 Cutting machine. 1 Packing machine. Steam power for the above. Such a plant will have a capacity of about 300 pounds of Oolong tea a day, and the appropriation made by the government for the cost of the plant and its up keep and other expenses connected with the experiment for the first year is 46,000 yen. The location of the factory has not been definitely decided upon, but Anpeichin (Anpingching), a station in the tea district on the Shinchiku (Teckcham) line between Chureki (Tionglick) and Yobaireki (Yumoilick) will probably be selected. If the factory proves a success the Chinese planters will be encouraged to combine and establish similar or larger factories at convenient points. The government possess an experimental tea garden which is splendidly located in the hills near Toshien (Toahong). The garden covers some 10 acres, and is divided into various beds in which tea is being grown under various conditions, as to soil, fertilizer and pruning. Among the experiments made at the garden, has been the manufacture of green and black tea. The result in both instances was satisfactory, but it is not thought that it would be profitable to replace any part of the present Oolong production by such teas.

The tea trade is, at present, practically conducted wholly in Formosa, whereas but four years ago (1898) about half of the crop was purchased in Amoy, China. The settlements in Amoy for the past three years were as follows :—

Season 1899 - - 32% | Season 1900 - - 6% | Season 1901 - - 5%

Even the teas covered by the very small percentages for the last two years were nearly all tea which had been purchased on the Formosa market by Chinese holding definite orders from Amoy foreign firms. It may thus be said that Amoy has ceased to be a market for Formosa teas.

The following statistics of the tea export for the past three years are a continuation of statistics given on pages 395 and 396 :—

Season.	Export Formosa Oolong to the United States in pounds (Trade Returns).	Export Formosa Oolong to Europe in pounds (Trade Returns).	Average Invoice cost per picul (133⅓ pounds) in Tamsui currency (Consular Returns).	Total Export Formosa Pauchong in pounds (Custom Returns).	Total Export all kinds Formosa Tea in pounds for calendar year (Custom Returns).
1899 [1]	15,358,425	502,317	$40.83	2,911,636	19,837,331
1900	16,439,090	637,355	$37.89	3,341,059	19,913,549
1901	15,268,208	396,839	$34.74	2,927,600	20,085,038

The returns for the calendar year 1901 in detail as given by the Customs are as follows :—

			Shipped via Amoy.		Shipped via Japan.		Total Exports.	
			Quantity in lbs.	Value in yen.	Quantity in lbs.	Value in yen.	Quantity in lbs.	Value in yen.
Tea, Oolong ..	..	..	13,766,061	2,996,002	2,692,078	684,749	16,458,139	3,680,751
„ Pauchong	..	..	2,927,546	505,061	53	15	2,827,599	505,076
„ Bancha..	..	..	161,501	10,130	—	—	161,501	10,130
„ Dust	..	..	6,786	222	363,388	19,831	370,174	20,053
„ Stalk ..	..	..	108,473	5,718	—	—	108,473	5,718
„ Green ..	..	..	632	164	—	- -	632	164
„ Brick ..	..	..	—	—	58,520	6,485	58,520	6,485
Total ..	..	..	16,970,999	3,517,300	3,114,039	711,080	20,085,038	4,228,380

CAMPHOR.

The government monopoly of this article described on pages 397 to 443 has not proven the success that the authorities had anticipated. At the time the monopoly was first proposed (1898) the production of Camphor in Japan had decreased until it almost ceased to remain a factor in the trade, Formosa supplying at that time practically the world. This was due to the fact that the Camphor trees in Japan easily available had been almost

---

1. Some discrepancy will be noted between the 1899 figures given herewith and the figures given on page 395 for the same year, due to the latter being merely estimates as stated, whereas in the case of the present statistics it has been possible to obtain complete returns.

entirely consumed. The institution of the Formosa monopoly, however, with the greatly increased prices established, stimulated the production in Japan. Camphor workers found under the new conditions that it was well worth their while to seek out the remaining trees in the more inaccessible forests. They even went to the extreme of purchasing trees growing in private gardens and temple compounds, and also in digging up the stumps and roots of trees cut down years before. This increased the Japanese production to such an extent that merchants holding the Japanese supply found they could sell under the monopoly prices and still make a profit. This naturally interfered with the sale of Formosa Camphor and necessitated a change in the terms of sale held with the selling agents.

As the income from the Camphor monopoly had been depended upon as one of the chief sources of income for the support of the Formosa government, the Japanese cabinet gave its approval to a bill emanating from the Formosa government which was to give the latter control of both Japanese and Formosa Camphor. By the terms of the bill the Formosa government would not derive profit from the sale of Japanese Camphor. It simply provided for the regulation of the supply, and the maintenance of a price to be decided upon by the Formosa government. This would naturally put a stop to the competition existing between the Japanese and Formosa products. The bill passed the Lower House, but was thrown out without discussion by the Upper House owing to a technicality. It is understood that the same bill will in 1903 be placed again before the Parliament.

In regard to the Camphor production in Japan it is reported by a government expert that, without the present high monopoly prices, the industry in Japan could not be carried on. Although there are considerable forests of Camphor in Kagoshima, Miyazaki, Kumamoto, and Fukuoka prefectures of Kyushu, the trees are said to be generally small and the expense of production comparatively great. It is estimated that Kagoshima possesses 700,000 to 800,000 trees and Miyazaki 2,000,000 newly planted trees. There are also Camphor trees in Okinawa prefecture. It is estimated that if every Camphor tree in Japan were felled and utilized in the manufacture of the drug, the total production would be over 400,000 piculs (53,333,333 lbs.) which at the present rate of consumption would supply the world's requirements for some six years. It can thus be seen that even should legislation fail in granting to Formosa the control of Camphor production in Japan, the competition could not be of long duration.

Camphor trees are found in several forests in China, but owing to the comparatively small number of trees and the low yield of Camphor obtained from the wood, China has never been considered a competitor worthy of mention. The increased prices, however, following the establishment of the monopoly, heightened interest in the production of the drug, and it has been reported that a Japanese syndicate has entered into negotiations to obtain control of the sale of the product, the manufacture, however, to remain under Chinese control as before. It is also intimated that the Camphor and oil produced will be sent to Formosa for remanufacture and shipment. It is estimated that the maximum production of China Camphor will not exceed 200 piculs (26,600 lbs.) a month, and that the average will doubtless be much less.

Obstacles which the future may place in the way of an indefinite continuation of the monopoly on its present basis are the invention of artificial Camphor (German chemists have already achieved some success in this line), the production of Camphor in the United States, Ceylon, the Canary Islands and other countries where trees have lately been planted, and the discovery of other and cheaper chemicals which can replace Camphor in many of its uses. So far as the present is concerned the horizon is clear, and barring the production of a successful artificial Camphor, it is the opinion of the writer that the great resources of the Formosan forests and the cheap labor obtainable will give Formosa the practical control of the market for a great many years to come.

The following statistics are in continuation of those given on page 443.

THE WORLD'S CAMPHOR PRODUCTION.

Year.	Export of Japanese camphor in pound.	Export of Formosa camphor via Japanese in pound.	Total camphor Export from Japan.	Export of Formosa camphor direct.	Total Export of Formosa camphor.	Total Export of Japanese camphor.	Total Production for export from both Japan and Formosa.
1899.. ..	1,167,179	2,510,991	3,678,167	4,264,985	6,775,976	1,167,179	7,943,155
1900.. ..	1,933,544	2,440,743	4,374,287	2,094,933	4,535,676	1,933,544	6,469,220
1901.. ..	2,055,444	3,498,899	5,554,343	1,162,976	4,661,875	2,055,444	6,717,329

The following table gives the approximate shipments of Formosa Camphor to various countries during 1901, and does not necessarily represent consumption, owing to the fact that considerable quantities are reexported from Hongkong, Germany, England, Japan, etc.

Germany, 1,000,000 lbs.; United States, 737,000 lbs.; Great Britain, 569,000 lbs.; Hongkong (for shipment chiefly to India), 458,000 lbs.; France, 401,706; Japan, 504,530. A large portion, if not all, of the Japan shipments ultimately reached foreign markets.

SUGAR.

There is but little to add in regard to this product that is not dealt with in the special chapter devoted to the subject. It is of interest to record, however, that His Excellency Baron Kodama, the Governor-General, spent a few weeks in the southern sugar district during the present summer (1902), and on his return a very extensive plan of government irrigation works was announced. An immediate appropriation of 100,000 yen was made which is to cover the cost of investigations, as well as preliminary work at Soko in Hozan (Hengchun) district; Kotosan in Tainan district; Naikinai and Jurinto in Yensuiko (Kiamtsui) district; Rokuto in Kagi district; Rashi in Shoka (Changwha) district; and other places. A portion of this amount will also be devoted to embankment works near the mouth of the Toseki (Tangchio) river. The total cost of the complete works will reach several million yen, and the construction will be extended over a period of several years. When the works are completed the production of sugar will be largely increased.

Consistent with the government's intention to introduce modern machinery, Dr. Nitobe, the Chief of the Sugar Bureau, purchased in America a complete sugar mill of the most modern construction. This machine will crush 60 tons of sugar a day, and will be set up in the south during the coming spring. The machine laid down in Formosa represents an expenditure of 20,000 yen Other small crushing mills to replace the native stone mills will also be introduced next year.

The subsidized sugar mill at Koshito, South Formosa, was in successful operation during last season. The output ranged in value from 4.65 yen a picul to 9.35, the latter representing a white sugar of No. 18, Dutch standard. The bulk of the product was supplied to refineries in Japan.

In continuance of the statistics given on pages 457 and 458, I append a table showing the export of the various grades of sugar from the chief ports for the last three years.

FORMOSAN SUGAR EXPORTS.

	1899.	1900.	1901.
BROWN SUGAR.			
Export from Anping to China and Hongkong	lbs. 27,950,860 Yen 1,050,835	lbs. 7,372,643 Yen 287,521	lbs. 12,319,076 Yen 468,457
Export from Anping to Japan	lbs. 15,467,040 Yen 584,815	lbs. 12,942,205 Yen 502,922	lbs. 20,412,420 Yen 844,649
Export from Takow to China and Hongkong	Nil.	lbs. 2,400,309 Yen 81,013	lbs. 478,039 Yen 15,058
Export from Takow to Japan	lbs. 29,442,933 Yen 1,035,460	lbs. 24,632,533 Yen 966,073	lbs. 35,771,200 Yen 1,365,882
Export from other ports to China and Hongkong ..	lbs. 5,208,399 Yen 165,225	lbs. 658,653 Yen 84,189	lbs. 5,224,176 Yen 194,854
Export from other ports to Japan	Nil.	lbs. 131,621 Yen 4,839	lbs. 764,986 Yen 32,921
Total Export from all Formosa to China and Hongkong	lbs. 33,159,259 Yen 1,216,060	lbs. 10,431,605 Yen 452,723	lbs. 18,021,291 Yen 678,369
Total Export from all Formosa to Japan	lbs. 44,909,973 Yen 1,620,276	lbs. 37,706,360 Yen 1,473,834	lbs. 56,948,607 Yen 2,243,453
Total Export from all Formosa to all countries	lbs. 78,069,232 Yen 2,836,336	lbs. 48,137,965 Yen 1,936,557	lbs. 74,969,898 Yen 2,921,821
WHITE SUGAR.			
Export from Anping to China and Hongkong	lbs. 6,926,835 Yen 370,884	lbs. 3,710,531 Yen 215,980	lbs. 5,716,769 Yen 350,969
Export from Anping to Japan	lbs. 2,424,987 Yen 128,602	lbs. 1,137,753 Yen 63,004	lbs. 483,583 Yen 32,790
Export from Takow to China and Hongkong	Nil.	Nil	lbs. 32,592 Yen 1,707
Export from Takow to Japan	Nil.	Nil	Nil.
Export from other ports to China and Hongkong ..	Nil.	lbs. 9,707 Yen 541	lbs. 4,827 Yen 268
Export from other ports to Japan	Nil.	lbs. 13,333 Yen 1,000	lbs. 184,000 Yen 16,355
Total Export from all Formosa to China and Hongkong	lbs. 6,926,835 Yen 370,884	lbs. 3,721,238 Yen 216,521	lbs. 5,754,088 Yen 352,944
Total Export from all Formosa to Japan..	lbs. 2,424,987 Yen 128 602	lbs. 1,151,087 Yen 64,004	lbs. 667,587 Yen 49,145
Total Export from all Formosa to all countries	lbs. 9,351,822 Yen 499,486	lbs. 4,872,325 Yen 280,525	lbs. 6,421,671 Yen 602,089

FORMOSAN SUGAR EXPORTS.—*Continued.*

SUMMARY.			
Total Sugar Exports from Anping	lbs. 52,769,722	lbs. 25,163,132	lbs. 38,931,848
	Yen 2,135,136	Yen 1,069,427	Yen 1,896,865
Total Sugar Exports from Takow	lbs. 29,442,933	lbs. 27,032,842	lbs. 36,281,831
	Yen 1,035,460	Yen 1,047,086	Yen 1,382,617
Total Sugar Exports from other Ports[1]	lbs 5,209,399	lbs. 813,314	lbs. 6,177,959
	Yen 165,225	Yen 90,569	Yen 244,398
Total Sugar Exports from Japan	lbs. 47,334,960	lbs. 38,857,447	lbs. 57,616,194
	Yen 1,748,880	Yen 1,537,839	Yen 2,292,598
Total Sugar Exports from China and Hongkong[2] ..	lbs. 40,086,094	lbs. 14,152,643	lbs. 23,775,379
	Yen 1,586,945	Yen 669,245	Yen 1,031,313
Total Sugar Exports from to all Countries ..	lbs. 87,421,054	lbs. 53,010,090	lbs. 81,391,573
	Yen 3,335,825	Yen 2,207,084	Yen 3,323,912

COAL.

The first half of 1902 exhibited a considerable development in the export of Formosa Coal. During the first five months the export totalled 16,539 tons against 8,225 tons for the same period during 1901. A special steamer has been chartered by an English firm for trade, and makes regular trips between Tamsui, and Hongkong, and such China ports as provide a market for the Coal. It is expected that the export for the year 1902 will reach some 40,000 tons. The local consumption of Coal has increased steadily year by year, and the production in 1901 reached some 80,000 tons, the largest production known in the history of the island. To facilitate the transportation of coal the Formosa railway has opened a new station known as "Goto" near the Suihenkyaku (Suitengka) coal fields, and there has been constructed a short branch line connecting with a trolly line leading up to the mines, and at Tamsui there is in course of construction a jetty from the railway leading out into the stream. With these conveniences it is thought the Coal trade can be handled easily and economically, and the future of the industry which but a few years ago seemed very dark indeed, is now more promising. If the rate of increase for the past three years can be maintained for a few years longer, Coal will be one of the leading exports.

The following statistics are in continuation of those given on page 490.

Season.								Export in tons.	Purchased in port for ships' use in tons.	Estimated Total Production tons.
1900	..	..	..	..	..	..	..	24,001	6,458	52,435
1901	..	..	..	..	..	..	..	26,205	8,331	80,000

GOLD.

No product of Formosa has shown such rapid growth and has such a bright future as Gold. From an output of some 600,000 yen in value in 1876, the production reached in 1901 to over 1,500,000 yen, and with the

1. The ports, exclusive of Anping and Takow, interested in the Sugar export trade are as follow:— Kakoko (Ehakau), 118,040 yen ; Toseki (Tangchio), 70,936 ; Kelung, 32,921 ; value of Brown Sugar shipped in 1901 ; and Kalung, 16,355 yen representing White Sugar.

2. During 1901, Hongkong took 52,418 yen worth of white and 2,615 yen of Brown Sugar, or a total of 55,033 yen. China took 675,754 yen worth of Brown and 300,525 yen of White Sugar, or a total of 976,279 yen.

completion next year of the Kyufun plant described on page 470 which is now in course of construction, the annual production is expected to exceed 2,500,000 yen. During the present year (1902) Japanese have begun the development of the Shinjio deposits on the east coast (See industrial map) which are thought to be very rich. The number of gold washers in the Zuiho and Kelung river districts has greatly increased during the past three years. There are some 2,000 men under contract with the Fujita Company and there are several large Chinese gangs at work on the Kelung River, in addition to many private workers. It seems at present quite probable that within a half dozen years Gold will be exceeded in value only by tea among the island's exports.

SULPHUR.

The production of Sulphur has likewise shown considerable increase during the past three years. The producing field has been extended to Kinpori (Kimpauli) where the manufacture is now carried on, though the difficulties of transportation there are great.

The exports for three years given below is in continuation of the statistics given on page 504.

Year.			Export via China and Hongkong in pounds.	Value of China and Hongkong Shipments in yen.	Export via in Japan.	Value of Shipments via Japan in yen.	Total Export in pounds	Total value in yen
1899	..	..	2,436,752	34,356	21,200	425	820,792	13,245
1900	..	..	1,112,306	16,886	1,600,000	26,801	2,812,306	43,687
1901	..	..	2,436,752	34,356	141,206	2,609	2,577,958	36,965

FIBRES.

The last three years have shown considerable development in several lines of fibre manufacture. The Taika rush described on page 528 to 530, has come in favor locally and in Japan, as a material for hat making, and the local production during the year 1901 exceeded 50,000 piculs. Taika straw has been successfully bleached, and a hat made to conform with modern styles should prove a close competitor with the Panama hats now so much in demand. The screw pine (Pandanus) described on pages 537 and 538 has proven to be a most valuable material for the manufacture of hand cases, cigarette cases, and hats. Ribbons of pure color, soft, and nearly as flexible as Panama straw, are produced from the split fibre, and the Japan company which has taken up the development of this industry, believes that it has a very promising future. The company have established at Banka a factory employing over sixty hands to work the product. Looms have been introduced by the government in several places, and the weaving of cotton cloth is taught to native girls. Several private plants have as a result been established and furnish employment to quite a number of Chinese girls.

PAPER.

The Chinese method of paper manufacture as described on pages 543 and 544 is highly wasteful and expensive, and the product cannot but be inferior. The Formosan government have accordingly, at an expenditure exceeding 40,000 yen, established a model paper mill at Kagi which is run by water power and is engaged in the manufacture of all kinds of Japanese Paper. Bamboo, Paper mulberry (Broussonetia Papyrifera), Wikstroemia (See pages 543 to 547) and certain reeds are being experimented with as materials for paper making. It is the desire of the government to induce the native paper makers to adopt modern methods, the practicality of which will be exhibited to them at the government mill. A Japanese syndicate have also established at Kagi a small mill at an expenditure of some 20,000 yen, which is engaged in the manufacture of Japanese Paper.

MISCELLANEOUS INDUSTRIES.

In addition to the industries described in previous pages may be noted the establishment of modern factories in North Formosa for the manufacture of Indigo in Bunzampo district by the Wada Company, the establishment of a large plantation in Taito (Taitong) district, and a tobacco plantation in Tainan by the Kada Company, and the extensive nurseries, and the afforestation works carried on by the Dogura Company in Kusshaku (Kuchu) district, and a pineapple tinning factory which has commenced operations on a small scale in Tainan.

The Agricultural Department of the Formosa Government will give special attention to the development of sugar, tea, paper, rice, China grass, and other fibres, tobacco, stock raising, forestry, etc. To further the work the government have established a number of experimental gardens and nurseries throughout the island. At the Tainan station many tropical trees of commercial value are growing in the nursery, and will be distributed to applicants throughout southern Formosa. Perhaps the most important station of all is the tropical nursery established in Koshun district in the extreme south of the island. The garden covers an area of some 250 acres, and a large variety of tropical plants such as teak, mahogany, and sandal, ebony, rubber, cotton, various palms, etc. have been planted there. The work is under the control of Y. Tashiro, Botanist, perhaps the most capable man for work of this kind in Japan.

In conclusion, I would express my belief that the work the new administration is doing, will not be without beneficial result. The improved methods of transportation, the post and telegraph conveniences, the advantages of modern education, the scientific medical treatment, and enlightened jurisprudence, will make life for the masses more desirable than during the old days, and the strenuous efforts of the government to foster industry and commerce, can not but meet with some degree of success, thus adding to the general prosperity.

Mistakes will be made, that is inevitable, but as Japan has advanced, so may we expect improvement in Formosa.

"DEAR ISLAND, FARE THEE WELL."

THE END.

Palace of the Governor-General.

His Excellency, Lieut-General Baron Kodama,
Governor-General of Formosa.

Dr. Goto, Chief of Civil Government.

Residence of Chief of Civil Government.

APPENDIX.

COMPARATIVE VOCABULARY OF

	ATAIYAL.	VONUM.	TSO-O.	TSARISEN.
One	Koto	Tasi-a	Tsune	Ita
Two	Sajin	Rusya	Rusu	Rusa
Three	Tungal	Tao	Toru	Toru
Four...	Paiyat	Pä-ät	Siputo	Sipat
Five...	Mängal	Hima	Rimo	Rima
Six	Teyu	Noum	Nomu	Urum
Seven	Pitu	Pitu	Pitu	Pitu
Eight	Sipät	Vao	Woru	Waru
Nine...	Kairo	Siva	Siyo	Siwa
Ten	Mappo	Massan	Massok	Puru
Hair...	Sinonohu	Koruvo	Housu	Oval
Head	Tonnohu	Vongŏ	Ponngo	Uru
Eye	Raoyàk	Mata	Mutso	Matsa
Ear	Papàk	Tainga	Kŏru	Tsaringa
Nose...	nGaho	nGutos	nGutsu	nGodos
Mouth	Nokoàk	nGurus	nGaru	Angat
Tooth	Gennohu	Niepon	Hisi	Haresi
Beard	nGorus	nGisingisi	Maomao	nGisingisi
Hand	Kava	Ima	Mutsu	Rima
Nipple	Vovo	Tsitsi	Nunu	Tutu
Belly	Ruvoas	Tteyan	Vūro	Tteyat
Foot	Kàkai	Vantas	Tta-ango	Kūra
Blood	Rammo	Kaidan	Hampul	Damo
Father	Yava	Tama	Ammu	Kamma
Mother	Yaya	Tena	Ennu	Kinna
Son	Rakei	Uwa'a	Okku	Arra
Man...	Murekoi	Vananak	Hahutsun	Arai
Woman	Kunairin	Vennoa	Mamespinge	Vavayan
Child	Rakei	Uwa'a	Okku	Unu-unu
Chief	Taoki	Syatvina	Purongosi	Mazangeran
Village	Kàran	Vàu	Hŏsya *or* Noheu	Inaran
Heaven	Kàyal	Yakaneu	nGutsa	Karuruvan
Earth	Heyal	Darak	Tsoroa	Kadunangan
Sun	Wäge	Ware	Hire	Adao
Moon	Vuyatsin	Voan	Porohu	Iras
Star	Mintoyan	Mintokan	Tsongoha	Vituan
Cloud	Yurum	Ruhon	Tsumtsum	Arupus
Rain	Kwàrahu	Koranan	Vutsu	Udal
Wind	Vaihui	Heuhen	Porepe	Vare
Fire	Ponnyak	Sapos	Pujju	Sapui
Water	Kusiya	Ranum	Tsŏmo	Zarum
Mountain	Regyahu	Rivos	Purongo	Gàdo
River	Ririon	Haul	Tsoroha	Panna
Rice...	Voahu	Terras	Puressi	Vat
Dog	Hoyel	Atso	Avou	Vatū
Deer...	Wokannohu	Kannuwan	Uwa	Vunnan
Ox	Kàtsin	(?)	(?)	Roan
Monkey	Yungai	Hutton	nGohŏ	Karan
Clothing	Rukos	Hurus	Risi	Rikurao
Cap	Kovovo	Tamohon	Tsoropongo	Taropun

THE NINE SAVAGE GROUPS.

| PAIWAN. | PUYUMA. | AMIS. | PEI PO. | | BOTEL TOBAGO ISLANDERS. |
			PAZZEHE.	KUVARAWAN.	
Ita	Sa	Tsutsai	Ida	Isa	Asa
Rusa	Rua	Tusa	Dusa	Rusa	Roa
Tsru	Tero	Toro	Turu	Tusu	Atoro
Spat	Spat	Spat	Supat	Supat	Ap-pat
Rima	Rima	Rima	Hasuv	Rima	Rima
Unum	Unum	Unum	Hasuv-da	Unum	Anum
Pitu	Pitu	Pitu	Hasuve-dusa	Pitu	Pito
Aru	Waro	Waro	Hasuve-duro	Waru	Wao
Siva	Iwa	Siwa	Hasuve-supat	Siwa	Shiem
Purrok	Purru	Puro	Is'iit	Tahai	Po
Kovaji	Aruvo	Vūkos	Vukkus	Vokko	—
Kŏru	Taⁿgal	Woⁿgoho	Ponŏ	Uho	Voboya
Matsa	Mata	Mata	Daorek	Mata	Mata
Tsariⁿga	Raⁿgera	Tariⁿga	Saⁿgera	Kayal	Taregan
ⁿGurus	Ateⁿguran	ⁿGoso	Mujin	Unom	Momosa
Angai	Imdan	ⁿGoyos	Rahhal	ⁿGoyok	Bebe
Aris	Ware	Wares	Rupun	Wangan	—
ⁿGisⁿgis	ⁿGisiⁿgisi	ⁿGisⁿgis	Moddos	Mumus	Yanim (?)
Rima	Rima	Kayam	Rima	Rima	Tarere
Tutu	Susu	Tsutsu	Nunoho	Sisu	Soso
Tteyai	Tteyal	Teyas	Tyal	Tteyan	—
Kūra	Dapal	Saripa	Kärao	Rapal	—
Yamok	Modomok	Iran	Damo	Renan	—
Ama	Ama	Ama	Ava	Tama	—
Kina	Ina	Ina	Ina	Tena	—
Aryak	Wara	Wawa	Rakehal	Sones	—
Ohayai	Utu	Vainai	Mamarun	Riunanai	Shichi
Vavayan	Omos	Vavayan	Mamayus	Turuⁿgan	Yamits
K'kryan	Rarak	Kamaⁿgai	Rovarovan	Sunis	—
Mazaⁿgeran	Ayawan	Kokita-an	Huzumusao	Nakkeyan	—
(?)	Rukal	Mananyaro	Rutol	Ramu	Nahmen
K'junaⁿgan	Raⁿgèt	Kakarayan	Vavao-kawas	Rǎn	—
Ppepo	Däl	Sra	Rejik-ddahhu	Wanan	—
Kãdao	Kadao	Tsiral	Rezahu	Mata-no-kãn	—
Keras	Vuran	Urăt	Iras	Vūran	—
Vitukan	Teol	Uwes	Mintol	Waturan	—
Karupus	Kutum	Tounm	Ruron	Rãnum	—
Muyal	Mandal	Ulas	Udaru	Uran	—
Ware	Vare	Vare	Vare	Vare	—
Sapoi	Apoi	Ramal	Hapoi	Ramah	—
Zayon	Nnai	Nanom	Darūm	Rarum	—
Gãdu	Runan	Tukos	Vinayu	Ivavao	Woro
Pana	Inayan	Aru	Rahon	Vokahal	—
Vaᵗ	Vurras	Vurǎᵗ	Iyezaraha	Vokas	—
Vatu	Soan	Watso	Wazzo	Wasu	—
Vunnan	(?)	'Gavol	Ruhoᵗ	Apol	—
Agungan	Gun	Kurun	Noan	Waka	—
Putsawan	Ruton	Ruton	Rutʼpo	Hogoton	—
Itom	Kepen	Reko	Svato	Kurus	—
Tsarupun	Kavon	(?)	Kakomos	Kūvŏ	—

APPENDIX II.

THE LAND BIRDS OF FORMOSA

By J. D. DE LA TOUCHE.

Among recent continental islands there is probably none that surpasses in interest and
instructiveness the Chinese island named by the Portuguese Formosa or "The Beautiful."
—*Island Life.*

The Island of Formosa possesses a vertebrate fauna of the greatest interest, and the land
birds, especially, show a large proportion of peculiar species, many of them related to birds
living in far distant lands, rather than to those of the same tribe or family that reside on the
mountains of the neighboring mainland of S. E. China.   The relationship of Formosa
to China, her affinities with Japan in the North, and in the South with the Island of Hainan
and various parts of the Oriental Region, are treated in "Island Life" at some length by
Wallace, who devotes a considerable portion of the chapter on Formosa and Japan to the land
birds of Formosa which form the subject of this sketch.

The zoology of Formosa was in former days thoroughly gone into by Mr. R Swinhoe,
but since the death of that distinguished naturalist, scarcely anything has been done to
advance our knowledge of the bird life of the Beautiful Isle.   The late Mr. Seebohm had, it
is true, undertaken the collecting and study of Formosan birds; unfortunately his collector,
the late Mr. Holst, was unable to penetrate far into the interior, and died, leaving the work
far from accomplished.   Mr. Holst, during two or more years' stay on the Island, obtained two
new species, *Parus holsti*, and *Rallina formosana*, Seebohm Ibis 1895, and, a few years ago,
Mr. F. W. Styan procured some Formosan birds, one of which was described by him as new
under the name of *Pycnonotus taiwanus* (Styan, Ibis, 1893).

Up to the present time, 145 species of land birds have been met with in Formosa, of
which 34 are confined to the island.   These I will now endeavor to review briefly, together
with some of the more interesting of the non-peculiar species.

The first birds to be noticed are the Thrushes, a group of birds which, on account of their
shy and wary nature, will not often be noticed by travellers or by residents in the coast ports.
Five true thrushes and one ground thrush have up till now been known to occur in Formosa.
One of these, *Merula albiceps*, is peculiar to the island, and is conspicuously different in
plumage from its Chinese congeners.   The adult male has a pure white head and neck, black
upper parts and breast, and rich maroon underparts.   It was found by Swinhoe in Central
and North Formosa, and by Mr. Holst in the neighborhood of Mount Morrison.   I obtained
an immature specimen at Bangkimtsing in South-central Formosa.   The other Formosan
thrushes are: *Merula fuscata* or Dusky Thrush, *Merula chrysolaus*, a bird with warm brown
upper parts, brownish orange flanks and breast, and *no eyebrow*; *M. pallida*, which having
also brown upper parts and no white eyebrow, is distinguished by having the external tail
feathers largely marked with white at their tip.   The flanks and breast of this bird are of a
pale grey, or of a brownish tint.   The remaining thrush, *M. obscura*, is somewhat like the
two preceding birds, but it always has a white eyebrow.   The handsome ground thrush,
Geocichla varia, is not uncommon in North Formosa, and is probably found over the whole
island in winter.   It is a large bird, with light golden brown upper parts, each feather being
terminated by a black lunule.   The under parts are white, the breast and flanks being tinged
with yellow, and having each feather, as in the upper parts, edged with black.

Up country travellers will be sure to meet the handsome whistling Thrush of Formosa
(*Myiophoneus insularis*).   It is a large bird, blue black with metallic cobalt blue shoulders;
the feathers of the forehead, breast, flanks, and upper part of abdomen are dark blue-black

with a broad edging of brilliant ultramarine blue. Rocky torrent beds among the mountains are frequented by this bird, who lives in solitary style, feeding on water insects and small crustacea found in running waters. The call is a long drawn melancholy "tzeet" which will probably draw attention to the bird, as uttering its alarm note it quickly flashes down the stream, and in a second is lost behind some big boulder. The Formosa whistling Thrush is common on the mountain streams of North Formosa. I did not notice it in the south of the island.

The Eastern red-bellied blue Rock Thrush (*Monticola solitaria*) is too well known to need description. It is a sweet songster and is common about houses in the country and rocky hills.

We now come to a most interesting group of birds, the Timeliine Babblers, of which there are six known species in Formosa, all of them peculiar to the island. Five of these are allied to Chinese species mostly living in the Fokien province. Although no bird of the genus *Sibia* has as yet been discovered in South-Eastern China, one was described from South-west China (*Sibia desgodinsi*), and it is quite likely that a Sibia may yet be found in the mountains of South Fokien or Kwangtung. The best known among these babblers is the Huamei (*Trochalopteron taiwanum*). It is related to the Chinese Huamei (*Trochalopteron canorum*) and is somewhat like it in plumage, wanting, however, the white spectacles of the Chinese bird and being duller in color. Its habits seem to be precisely the same, and it is extremely abundant all over the lowlands and lower hills of Formosa. Not a village grove or bamboo copse in the valleys or plains but shelters some of these cheerful and interesting birds, wherever the cover affords them shade and good hunting grounds. They build a nest of bamboo leaves, twigs, and grasses, and lay from two to three lovely turquoise blue eggs. Another very common and at the same time handsome and interesting bird is the *Pomatorhinus musicus* or Lesser Scimitar Babbler of Formosa. Its stout curved bill, long white eyebrow, reddish hind neck, white throat, and white breast spotted with black will cause it to be easily recognized, as in active, restless bands it flits about the hedges by the roadside or explores the jungle on the mountain slopes, mingling its varied and melodious notes with the loud song of the Huamei, the call of the bamboo partridge, and the chattering of the smaller denizens of the jungle. The Large Scimitar Babbler of Formosa (*P. erythrocnemis*), is a much rarer bird and is only found in the hills of the interior. It has no eyebrow and is not so bright in plumage as its smaller relative; it is besides a very shy bird. The only place where I have met with it is Baksa in South Central Formosa; but it doubtless occurs among the mountains all over the interior. *Garrulax ruficeps* and *Yanthocincla pœcilorhyncha* would appear to be rare birds and confined to the interior of Formosa. The Sibia (*Sibia auricularis*) is abundant in the forests inland. It is a handsome bird with graduated tail and is remarkable for its very long white earcoverts. I found this bird to be common in the beautiful forest on Capiang hill near Bangkimtsing in South Formosa, where it may be seen flying among the tree tops in small parties.

The only Suthora hitherto found in Formosa is the pretty little *Suthora bulomachus*, a little pink brown and pink grey bird with rufous head and wings, which is met with in North Formosa, in the jungle among the lower hills, and about hedges near villages in the hills; but though probably a common bird, it is not often seen in the Tamsui district and would seem to be a hill species. It travels in more or less large flocks and is of a sociable noisy disposition.

About the rapids of the Tokoham river in the close vicinity of the mountains, the Dipper or Water Ouzel (*Cinclus pallasi?*)[1] occurs. I saw several there in February 1895. The Formosa bird resembles the Dipper found in Fokien in all but the bill, which is proportionately slighter and shorter. The general color of the plumage is perhaps paler.

Formosa from her position must be a great resting ground for all sorts of emigrants on their travels North and South, but the Yellow-browed Willow Warbler (*Phylloscopus superciliosus*) and the Northern Willow Warbler (*P. copusborealis*) are the only migratory warblers that I have come across in the north of the island. It is most likely that many of the Chinese and Japanese migrants touch at the South Cape or at the South-west Coast. The Bush warblers, the Fantail warblers, and the interesting long tailed Prinias and Suya are common enough. Of the Bush warblers the most abundant is undoubtedly *Cettia canturiens*. This bird frequents, like others of its tribe, thick brushwood; but at Hobe in North Formosa,

---

1. Originally described by Swinhoe as *Hydrobata marila*.

it was constantly to be seen on the banyans about the village. In April its loud note, sound-ing somewhat like "Koloko-wichit" or "Kolo-olo-olo-olo-wichit," was heard all over the place. It is, I expect, only a winter visitant to Formosa. Another Cettia, often found in its company is *Cettia minuta*, a miniature of the large bird. It is not nearly so abundant, however, although, at Tokoham, I found it very common during my short stay in that district. *Cettia cantans minuta*, a small edition of the Japanese bird, *Cettia cantans* seems plentiful in the south of the island where it is probably a resident species.

The charming little *Horornis squamiceps* is not at all rare. It might, however, be easily passed by, as it keeps itself well concealed, hunting among the thickets on or close to the ground.

The Fantail Warbler (*Cisticola cursitans*), is common everywhere in the open country, in the fields or on the mountains, where covered with grass. It is pleasant to hear its cheerful tinkling note as the little bird with outspread fan-like tail hovers up in the air to drop a few paces further into the long grass, flying up to repeat the performance if again disturbed by the inquisitive intruder. *C. exilis*, formerly re-described by Swinhoe as *C. volitans* is easily distinguished from *C. cursitans* in summer by its light yellow head. It is fairly common on the hills in North Formosa. That very fussy little bird, *Prinia inornata*, common all over South East China and also known from India and other places, is very abundant in Formosa. The nest of this species, bag shaped and sometimes domed, is composed of fine grasses closely knitted together, and is found among the high grass jungle fastened to the leaves and stems of the sword grass. It lays five or six pretty light greenish blue eggs with an ever varying pattern of reddish brown blotches, streaks and spots. The ground color of the eggs occasionally varies, being sometimes a dull yellowish pink or a light green. I obtained the former at Amoy and the latter at Foochow, but the Formosa eggs I collected are of the usual pale turquoise blue. Another *P. sonitans*, also a Chinese bird, builds a lovely nest with the back wall built up to form a perfect dome. The eggs are very glossy, bright orange red, heavily mottled with a darker shade of orange red which almost conceals the ground color. The remaining grass or jungle frequenting warbler is the Striped Warbler (*Suya crinigera*), brown above with darker stripes down the centre of the feathers. It is found on the North Hill near Tamsui at an elevation of about 1,000 feet, and also occurs in South and Central China and in India.

There are only three Tits known as yet from Formosa, and they are all peculiar to the island. The beautiful blue backed *Parus holsti*, with bright yellow underparts, was found two or three years ago by Mr Holst in the neighborhood of Mount Morrison. *Parus castaneiventris* is related to *Parus varius* of Japan, and *Parus insperatus* is a race of *Parus monticola* of China.

We now come to an interesting group of three birds *Stachyridopsis ruficeps*, *Alcippe brunnea*, and *Alcipa morrisonia*, which I will notice in succession as they associate with one another while ranging the jungle or undergrowth in the woods for food. They are more or less tit-like in their habits, but they have also affinities with the Babblers and are generally placed among the *Timeliidae*. The first of these, the pretty little *Stachyridopsis ruficeps*, is found commonly all over Formosa and is a common South China bird, being also known in India. It is olive green above with rufous head and greenish yellow underparts. It frequents the jungle and underwood on the lower hills, and when pursuing its way alone, its call, curiously strong for such a small bird, might be written "Tütütü-tütü." The bird, when solitary, is very shy, always keeping well hidden in the thickest jungle, its loud and melancholy whistle generally answered by the somewhat different note of its mate. Its feeding note or company call, so to speak, uttered when of a more sociable disposition, is a shrill sound like "Ti-chárr" or often like "Che-djeee."

I took a nest of *P. ruficeps* near Tamsui towards the end of June. It was placed in a high bush in a wooded ravine on the hills, and was made of bamboo leaves and shaped somewhat like an egg with part of the large end sliced off diagonally. It contained four young birds nearly fledged. After much difficulty I managed to bring over to China three of them; two died within the next month, but one was successfully reared and is a never ending source of amuse-ment. The Alcippe are gregarious birds, frequenting jungle or woods in mountainous districts. *A. brunnea*, olive brown above with long black eyebrows, and with greyish white underparts tinged with olive, is only found in the mountains of the interior. It seeks for its food under bushes in copses and woods; while *A. morrisonia*, a little bird with grey head and upper neck, white ring round the eye, light fawn color above and whitish below with sandy buff flanks and chest, is seen about the lower hills, and frequently explores trees and hedges in search of its food, which consists of insects and small seeds.

A charming bird, *Liocichla steerii*, occurs in the mountains of the South. In its general build and appearance it much resembles the *Liothrix* of China and the Himalayas, but the tail is not forked, being long and graduated.

Passing by the Wagtails and Pipits, which all occur on the mainland, we come to the Bulbuls, (*Pycnonotidae* and *Phyllornithidae*), of which there are four kinds in Formosa. One is the common Bulbul of China (*Pycnonotus sinensis*), abundant all over Western Formosa from Tamsui to Takow; and the other two are peculiar to Formosa, and one (*Spizixus cinereicapillus*) is confined to Formosa and Hainan. *P taivanus*, described by Mr. F. W. Styan in the Ibis of 1893, is the commonest bird about the South Cape, and strange to say, it has not been met with anywhere else. It much resembles *P sinensis*, but the head is wholly black above with white cheeks and black moustache, and it has a little red spot at the base of the lower mandible of the bill; there is a pale halter mark round the back of the neck, and the back and underparts show no tinge of greenish.

The Black Bulbul (*Hypsipetes nigerrimus*), with coral red bill and legs and grey edging to the quills of the wings and to the tail, is a very common species in the forests of South Formosa where I saw it in November flying in flocks, swiftly ranging the valleys and hill-sides, and settling in noisy bands on the forest trees. It also occurs at the South Cape and no doubt is found over the whole of the island; but I fancy that it is only a summer visitant to North Formosa, where it is quite common at that season. I believe that it nests in the taller banyans and other large trees about the country. The handsome green Mountain Bulbul, (*Spizixus cinereicapillus*), is distinguishable from its Chinese ally by its grey head, the crown of the head being black in the Chinese bird. It is a common enough bird in the mountains.

Of the two Orioles known on the island, one (*Oriolus diffusus*) is a common summer bird in China. It is very abundant in Formosa and appears to winter in the south of the island. It is, therefore, to be considered a resident Formosan species. I was never so lucky as to meet the beautiful crimson and black oriole, *Psaropholus ardens*. It is said to occur in the camphor districts, probably in Central Formosa.

Among the Shrikes, Drougos, and their allies, the most common about the west coast are a large Shrike (*Lanius schach*) and the Black Drougo or King Crow (*Buchanga atra*). The former is a somewhat showy bird with grey head and upper back, red lower back, and light underparts. It is a wonderful mimic, and one in Tamsui used to imitate the song or call of all the common birds of the locality in rapid succession, as he sat perched on the Light-house or on one of the taller trees in our compound. This shrike is one of the commonest birds of South China and is found as far north as the valley of the Huang-Ho. The Black Drougo abounds all over Western Formosa. Whether following the laborers in the fields to pick up the insects disturbed by the plough, or chattering in varied accents from the topmost twig of some waving bamboos, or again, dancing attendance on the buffaloes on their grazing grounds, this bird will be sure to attract the attention of any one out for a stroll in the country. It is a handsome bird, of slender build with a long forked tail; in color it is black shot with steel-blue, with a tinge of bronze on the wings and tail. The distribution of the Black Drougo is wide. It is common in India and on the great China plain, and is occasionally met on the South-east coast of China.

The forest-clad hills of the interior are the Formosan home of the charming grey throated Minivet, (*Pericrocotus griscigularis*). The brilliant coloring of the bird, bright red and greyish black in the male, and grey, yellow, and green in the female, with grey throat in both sexes, makes it a conspicuous object in the woods, as in twittering and screaming parties it travels through the forest and dots the tree tops with specks of crimson and bright yellow.

Among the flycatchers, there is a lovely little bird which is a very common resident species on the plains and among the lower hills. This is the Azure Flycatcher (*Hypothymis azurea*). It has bright cobalt blue upperparts, head, neck, and breast, with an occipital patch, and a chest band of black, and white underparts washed with blue.

The Swallows of Formosa number three species :—*Hirundo gutturalis*, the Eastern form of the European chimney swallow ; *Hirundo striolata*, a large race of the Red Rumped Swallow (*Hirundo alpestris*) and a resident species in Formosa ; and, the little Indian Sand Martin (*Cotyle sinensis*). All these are abundant in suitable localities.

Perhaps the most plentiful of all the Formosa birds seen about the West coast, is the little White Eye, the *Zosterops simplex* of Swinhoe—a near ally of the Indian *Z. palpebrosa*, from which it differs in being greener above. The nest is a tiny little cup of moss bound with spiders' webs and with a lining of fine vegetable fibre. In the country round about Tamsui, the bird builds on bamboos at a fair height from the ground. Swinhoe's White Eye is very abundant all over South East China. The Sparrows are the same as those found on the Chinese continent, namely the Tree Sparrow (*P montanus*), and the Ruddy Sparrow (*P rutilans*), which is no doubt confined to the hills of the interior. I never met with it. There are three Munias ; *Munia topela* and *Munia acuticauda*, abundant everywhere, and *Munia formosana*, until lately thought to be peculiar to the island. The latter is a bright red-brown bird with black head and neck and a black patch down the centre of the under-parts. It occurs in the hills of South Formosa, where I saw it on a grass and jungle covered hill in company with other Munias and various small birds.

Two Larks are resident in Formosa :—*Alauda sala* in the North, and *Alauda wattersi* (which also occurs in the Philippines and in Hainan) in the South and in the Pescadores Islands. They are races of the South China *Alauda coelivox* (or *gulgula*). The chief distinguishing character of the northern bird is its very large and thick bill resembling that of *Alauda coelivox*, while the southern species has a stout, and at the same time, rather short and conical bill, whose shape reminds one of that of the common Sky-lark (*Alauda arvensis*). The coloring in both species is much the same, but the Pescadores bird runs to ochreish red, due no doubt to the soil of the islands. *Alauda sala* is further distinguished by having occasionally a very long hind claw, and the spots on the breast are smaller than in *Alauda wattersi*.

We now come to the Starlings, a family poorly represented in Formosa. *Sturnus cineraceus*, the common Starling of China, is abundant in winter ; and in the plains of South Formosa, I found the Chinese Starlet (*Sturnia sinensis*), which is probably a resident down there. The Crested Mynah (*Acridotheres cristatellus*), so very common in China, is rare in Formosa (at least in the North and South) ; only here and there are a few met with, and they have none of the impudence and bold ways that render them such interesting birds, on the continent. In fact, they seem as if lost in a strange land and all their favorite avocations, such as following the plough, or attending cattle, are taken up by the Black Drougo. I feel sure that the species has been introduced by the Chinese settlers.

Among the birds of the crow tribe, no less than three out of five are peculiar to the island. The Jay, (*Garrulus taiwanus*), is a small ally of the Chinese Jay, (*Garrulus sinensis*). The Tree Pie (*Dendrocitta formosae*), common enough in the hills of the interior, is also closely related to the *D. sinensis* of South China ; but the Blue Magpie (*Urocissa coerulea*), is conspicuously different from the Chinese species. It is truly a magnificent bird, and when seen in its native haunts among the mountains of North Formosa, is one of the sights of its beautiful native country. The bill and legs are bright vermilion or coral red, the head and neck are deep black, and the rest of the body is of a beautiful violet blue, the quills of the wings being tipped (primaries), or edged towards the tips (secondaries) with white. The tail is tipped with white and has a subterminal black spot on all but the two central feathers, and the upper tail coverts have a terminal black bar with a pale violet subterminal band. The Formosa Crow is identical with *Corvus macrorhynchus* of China and Palæarctic Asia. It struck me as being rare in North Formosa, and I never saw one near Hobé. As for the Magpie, it is found in the south in the Taiwanfu district, but I did not see a single one in the north of the island.

Swifts—*Cypselus pacificus* and *Cypselus subfurcatus*—are found about the coast. I did not see the former, a large, white rumped species, but the latter which is a small bird, also with white rump, is common at Takow and I once saw a flock at Hobé in the spring of 1895.

The Goatsucker of Formosa, *Caprimulgus stictomus*, is another species confined to the island. I do not think that it is common. It is a near ally of *Caprimulgus monticola* of South China.

Of the three known Woodpeckers, one, *Picus insularis*, is peculiar to Formosa. It is an ally of *Picus leuconotus*. The handsome Ruddy Kingfisher, *Halcyon coromanda*, a somewhat rare bird though of wide distribution, was obtained by Swinhoe in Formosa. The only other kingfisher known on the island is the common *Alcedo bengalensis*.

In spring, the wooded hills of North Formosa echo the loud deep call of a Cuckoo (*Cuculus intermedius*). This bird resembles the common Cuckoo (*Cuculus canorus*) but is smaller, and its note is very different. "Hoohoo-hoohoo" repeated several times in succession might be given as rendering it, and when heard from a long distance it sounds strangely like the far away barking of some farmhouse dog. A ground Cuckoo, the Bengal Crow Pheasant (*Centropus bengalensis*) is a very common bird in the north of the island, though from its skulking habits it is but seldom seen.

The Formosan Barbet (*Cyanops nuchalis*), is found in the mountains of the south. This very handsome bird frequents the forests and would appear to be common among wooded hills. The general color of the male bird is bright green. The forehead is golden yellow, running into bright blue on the vertex. The chin and upper part of throat are orange yellow and the sides of the face and a band below the yellow throat are blue. The lores and eyebrows are black, and there is a bright red band on the lower neck. There is a crimson patch on the hind neck, and two small red spots appear at the base of the bill behind the nostrils.

Seven owls are known to occur in Formosa. Of these, *Scops glabripes*, occurs on the Chinese continent and *Scops japonicus* in Japan. *Scops hambroecki* and *Glaucidium pardalota* are confined to the island, *Ninox japonica* is a common migrant on the Eastern coast of China, breeding in Japan, and *Bulaca newarensis* and *Strix candida* (the Indian grass owl) are residents which also possibly occur in China.

Among the diurnal birds of prey, we find two harriers, *Circus spilonotus* and *Circus æruginosus*, both of them very common in South China and equally so in Formosa. There are three eagles; the Imperial Eagle (*Aquila heliaca*), seen by Swinhoe at Takow, *Spizaetus nipalensis*, and *Spilornis cheela* which occur in the mountains of the interior. The two latter birds are occasionally seen in China but are rare there, while in the Formosan mountains, one or both of them seem to be common. They are both possessed of a large occipital crest, but sportsmen will easily distinguish them by their legs, which in *Spilornis nipalensis* are feathered to the toes, while in *Spilornis cheela* the tarsi are bare. The Crested Goshawk, (*Lophospiza trivirgata*), a Malayan species, is in Formosa probably confined to the forests of the interior. It has not as yet been discovered in the Fokien or Canton Provinces.

We now come to the Pigeons, of which tribe Formosa possesses two peculiar species, *Treron formosae* and *Sphenocercus sororius*; but these birds together with *Palumbus pulchricollis*, a Himalayan species, are not seen near the ports. The beautiful Bronze Winged Dove (*Chalcophaps indica*), seems common at the South Cape. This is a charming bird; the deep and soft "coo" is, besides its pretty plumage, one of its great charms, and it appears to be easily tamed. The three common Chinese doves, *Turtur orientalis*, *Turtur chinensis*, and *Turtur humilis* are very common inland, and large flocks of the Chinese dove (*Turtur chinensis*) are of frequent occurrence.

The Pheasants and Partridges of Formosa that have as yet been described, are all peculiar to the island. The beautiful Swinhoe Pheasant, (*Euplocamus swinhoi*) is now well known in Europe as an aviary bird. It ranges from almost the extreme North to the extreme South of Formosa, but appears confined to the central chain of mountains and is said to be very common in Central Formosa. The common pheasant (*Phasianus formosanus*) is chiefly distinguished from *Phasianus torquatus* of China and Mongolia by its paler flanks. The two partridges are quite distinct from the Chinese members of that family, though the Bamboo Partridge (*Bambusicola sonorivox*), it is true, is allied to *Bambusicola thoracica* of South China.

Four Quails have been shot in Formosa; *Turnix rostrata* now united to *T. taigoor*, *T. dussumieri*, like the above, a common Indian species, and *Excalfactoria chinensis* also found in South China, the Philippines, Ceylon, and the Straits Settlements. The common quail (*Coturnix communis*) is a winter visitant to Formosa. During the winter 1895, I flushed on one occasion near Tamsui a bird which appeared to be this or the allied *Coturnix japonica*.

Before concluding these notes, a few words of explanation are necessary as regards the following list of Land Birds, which, I fear, appears incomplete and unsatisfactory. It will be noticed that out of 145 species appearing on the list, 101 are resident birds, 34 are winter visitants,[1] only eight are put down as occurring on migration, while we find only *two* summer visitants. There is, I believe, little doubt that many more migrants will have to be recorded when the island has been thoroughly worked, and that some summer visitants will be added to the list. For the present, as the results of Mr. Holst's collecting have not been published, and as Swinhoe's special papers on Formosa are not to be obtained out here,[2] I have had to make up the list from Swinhoe's "Revised Catalogue of the Birds of China and its Islands" (P.Z.S. 1871) and from David and Oustalet's "Oiseaux de la Chine," adding such birds as I have myself come across during my short stay on the Island.

The following birds will have in future to be omitted from the list of birds peculiar to Formosa :

Cettia cantans minuta	Chefoo (North China).
Cisticola volitans	*Cisticola exilis*; South China, Burmah, Assam, India, Australia, etc.
Graucalus sexpineti	Fokien Province (South China).
Cyornis vivida	Tenasserim.
Pitta oreas	*Pitta nympha*; China, Japan, etc.
Alauda wattersi	Philippine Islands (Whitehead), Hainan.
Munia formosana	Philippine Islands (Whitehead).
Chalcophaps formosana	*Chalcophaps indica*; South China, Straits, etc.
Areoturnix rostrata	*Turnix taigoor*; South China, India, Straits, etc.
Spizixus cinereicapillus	Hainan.
Alcippe brunnea	Fokien Province (South China).

The land birds peculiar to Formosa are as follows :

1. Merula albiceps.
2. Myiophoneus insularis.
3. Pomatorhinus musicus.
4. Pomatorhinus erythrocnemis.
5. Garrulax ruficeps.
6. Ianthocincla roecilorhyncha.
7. Trochalopteron taiwanum.
8. Sibia auricularis.
9. Alcippe morrisonia.
10. Suthora bulomachus.[3]
11. Notodela montium.
12. Parus insperatus.
13. Parus castaneiventris.
14. Parus holsti.
15. Liocichla steerii.
16. Pycnonotus taivanus.
17. Hypsipetes nigerrimus.
18. Psarolophus ardens.
19. Chapsia brauniana.
20. Alauda sala.
21. Garrulus taivanus.
22. Dendrocitta formosæ.
23. Urocissa cœrulea.
24. Caprimulgus stictomus.
25. Picus insularis.
26. Cyanops nuchalis.
27. Glaucidium pardalota.
28. Scops hambroecki.
29. Treron formosæ.
30. Sphenocercus sororius.
31. Phasianus formosanus.
32. Euplocamus swinhoi.
33. Arboricola crudigularis.
34. Bambusicola sonorivox.

---

1. Some of these will probably turn out to be residents.

2. See note at end of chapter.

3. *Suthora suffusa* of South China is I believe, fairly distinct from the Formosan bird, and *Suthora rilomachus* is, therefore, also retained here.

No.	List of Species.	Residents.	Summer visitants.	Winter visitants.	Occur on migration.	Peculiar to Formosa.	Occur in China.*	Occur in other countries.	Allies in China.	Allies in other countries.	Remarks.
1	Merula fuscata			x			x	x			
2	Merula pallida			x			x	x			
3	Merula chrysolaus				x		x	x			
4	Merula obscura				x		x	x			
5	Merula albiceps	x				x					
6	Geocichla varia			x			x	x			
7	Myiophoneus insularis	x					x		x	x	
8	Monticola solitaria	x					x	x			
9	Sibia auricularis	x					x		?x	x	
10	Pomatorhinus musicus	x					x		x	x	
11	Pomatorhinus erythrocnemis	x					x		x	x	
12	Trochalopteron taivanum	x					x		x	x	
13	Garrulax ruficeps	x					x		x	x	
14	Ianthocincla pacitorhyncha	x					x		x	x	
15	Stachyridopsis ruficeps	x					x	x			
16	Alcippe brunnea	x					x		x	x	
17	Alcippe morrisonia	x					x		x	x	
18	Suthora bulomachus	x					x		x		
19	Cinclus pallasi ?	x					x	x			May prove to be distinct from C. Pallasi.
20	Pratincola maura			x			x	x			
21	Ruticilla aurorea			x			x	x			
22	Rhyacornis fuliginosa	x					x	x			
23	Notodela montium	x				x				x	
24	Calliope camtschatkensis			x			x	x			
25	Suya crinigera	x					x	x			
26	Prinia inornata	x					x	x			
27	Prinia sonitans	x					x			x	
28	Cisticola cursitans	x					x	x			
29	Cisticola exilis	x					x	x			
30	Phylloscopus borealis			x	x		x	x			One shot in January out of a flock.
31	Phylloscopus superciliosus						x	x			
32	Cettia canturiens			x			x	x			Possibly resident.
33	Cettia minuta			x			x	x			Possibly resident.
34	Cettia cantans minuta	x					x			x	
35	Cettia fortipes			x			x	x			Possibly resident.
36	Horornis squamiceps			x			x	x			
37	Liocichla steerii	x				x					
38	Herpornis tyrannulus	x					x	x			Hainan and Fokien province.
39	Parus inspecatus	x				x			x	x	
40	Parus castaneiventris	x				x				x	
41	Parus holsti	x							x	x	
42	Motacilla leucopsis	x					x	x			
43	Motacilla ocularis			x			x	x			

* In this list the Island of Hainan is not included in China.

No.	LIST OF SPECIES.	Residents.	Summer visitants.	Winter visitants.	Occur on migration.	Peculiar to Formosa.	Occur in China.*	Occur in other countries.	Allies in China.	Allies in other countries.	REMARKS.
44	Motacilla lugens ?			x			x	x			Seen at Takow.
45	Motacilla taivana			x			x	x			
46	Motacilla melanope			x			x	x			
47	Anthus cervinus			x			x	x			
48	Anthus maculatus			x			x	x			
49	Anthus richardi			x			x	x			
50	Pycnonotus sinensis	x					x				
51	Pycnonotus taivanus	x				x			x		
52	Spizixus cinereicapillus	x				x			x	x	
53	Hypsipetes nigerrimus	x				x			x	x	
54	Oriolus diffusus	x					x	x			
55	Psaropholus ardens	x				x				x	
56	Buchanga atra	x					x	x			
57	Chapsia brauniana	x				x				x	
58	Graucalus rexpineti	x					x			x	
59	Pericrocotus griscigularis	x					x			x	Abundant in the high mountains in Western Fokien.
60	Lanius schach	x					x			x	
61	Lanius lucionensis			x			x	x			Would appear to winter occasionally in Formosa.
62	Hemichelidon sibirica				x		x	x			
63	Poliomyias luteola				x		x	x			
64	Cyornis vivida	x					x	x			
65	Niltava cyanomelaena				x		x	x			
66	Digenia superciliaris	x					x				
67	Tarsiger cyanurus			x			x	x			
68	Hypothymis azurea	x					x	x			
69	Ampelis japonicus			?x			x	x			
70	Hirundo gutturalis	x					x	x			
71	Hirundo striolata	x					x	x			
72	Cotyle sinensis	x					x				
73	Zosterops simplex	x					x	x			
74	Passer montanus	x					x	x			
75	Passer rutilans	x					x	x			
76	Chloris sinica	x					x	x			
77	Eophona melanura				x		x	x			One stray (?) bird seen at Tamsui in the spring.
78	Munia acuticauda	x					x	x			
79	Munia topela	x					x			x	
80	Munia formosana	x					x	x	x		
81	Emberiza spodocephala			x			x	x			
82	Emberiza fucata			x			x	x			
83	Emberiza cioides			x			x	x			
84	Emberiza sulphurata			x			x	x			
85	Emberiza aureola			x			x	x			

* In this list the Island of Hainan is not included in China.

No.	List of Species.	Residents.	Summer visitants.	Winter visitants.	Occur on migration.	Peculiar to Formosa.	Occur in China.*	Occur in other countries.	Allies in China.	Allies in other countries.	Remarks.
86	Alauda sala	x				x				x	
87	Alauda wattersi	x							x	x	
88	Acridotheres cristatellus	x					x	x			
89	Sturnia sinensis	x					x	x			
90	Spodiopsar cineraceus			x			x	x			
91	Corvus mactorhynchus	x					x	x			
92	Pica candata	x					x	x			
93	Urocissa cœrulea	x				x				x	No near ally in China.
94	Dendrocitta formosæ	x				x			x	x	
95	Garrulus taivanus	x				x			x	x	
96	Pitta nympha	x					x	x			
97	Cypselus pacificus	?x					x	x			Most probably is a resident.
98	Cypselus subfurcatus	x					x	x			
99	Caprimulgus stictomus	x				x			x	x	
100	Picus insularis	x				x			x	x	
101	Iyngipicus scintilliceps	x					x			x	
102	Gecinus guerini	x					x			x	
103	Alcedo bengalensis	x					x	x			
104	Halcyon coromandus	x					x	x			
105	Cuculus intermedius		x				x	x			
106	Cuculus poliocephalus		x				x	x			
107	Centropus bengalensis	x					x	x			
108	Centropus javanicus	x					x	x			
109	Cyanops nuchalis	x				x				x	
110	Bulaca newarensis	x						x			
111	Scops glabripes	?x					x				One specimen obtained on Thrasch probably a resident species.
112	Scops japonicus	?x					x	x			
113	Scops hambroecki	x				x			x	x	
114	Glaucidium pardalota	x				x			x	x	
115	Strix candida	x					?x	x			
116	Ninox japonica				x		x	x			
117	Pandion haliætus	?x					x	x			Probably a resident as it is found all the year round on the coast of China.
118	Circus spilonotus			x			x	x			
119	Circus æruginosus			x			x	x			
120	Buteo plumipes			x			x	x			
121	Aquila heliaca	?x					x	x			A resident on the Yangtze.
122	Spizætus nipalensis	x					x	x			
123	Spilornis cheela	x					x	x			
124	Accipiter virgatus	x					x	x			
125	Accipiter gularis	x					x	x			
126	Lophospiza trivirgata	x						x			A resident in South Japan.

* In this list the Island of Hainan is not included in China.

No.	List of Species.	Residents.	Summer visitants.	Winter visitants.	Occur on migration.	Peculiar to Formosa.	Occur in China.*	Occur in other countries.	Allies in China.	Allies in other countries.	Remarks.
127	Butastur indicus			?x			x	x			A resident on the Yangtze.
128	Falco communis			?x			x	x			
129	Falco tinnunculus			x			x	x			
130	Milvus melanotis	x					x	x			
131	Turtur orientalis	x					x	x			
132	Turtur chinensis	x					x	x			
133	Turtur humilis	x					x	x			
134	Chalcophaps indica	x					x	x			
135	Treron formosæ	x				x				x	
136	Sphenocercus sororius	x				x				x	
137	Palumbus pulchricollis	x							x		
138	Phasianus formosanus	x				x			x	x	
139	Euplocamus swinhoi	x				x				x	
140	Arboricola crudigularis	x				x				x	
141	Bambusicola sonorivox	x				x			x	x	
142	Coturnix communis			x			x	x			
143	Excalfactoria chinensis	x					x	x			
144	Turnix dussumieri	x						x			
145	Turnix taigoor	x					x	x			
	Total	100	2	34	8	36	...	...	...	...	

* In this list the Island of Hainan is not included in China.

NOTE.—Since the above was written, Mr. C. B. Rickett, F.Z.S., has most kindly lent me several of Swinhoe's papers, lately received by him, which have enabled me to make a few additions to the list of Formosan land birds.

I wish here to express my indebtedness to Mr. Rickett for his kindness in putting at my disposal his ornithological library, and also for his valuable help and advice while writing the foregoing pages.

Foochow, 24th November, 1896.

APPENDIX III.

MAMMALIA OF FORMOSA.

Our knowledge of the mammalia of Formosa is due wholly to the researches of that very versatile scientist, the late Mr. Robert Swinhoe. It is somewhat strange that Japanese Zoologists have not attempted study in a field which offers for them such unique opportunities.

While lamenting the absence of later observations, it is well to note that although Mr. Swinhoe's researches were conducted prior to 1872, so thorough was this eminent scientist in his work, that future labor will probably not reveal many important discoveries among the larger mammalia, though the practically unexplored mountainous district will undoubtedly yield much of value as respects the smaller and less obstrusive animals.

The list of the mammalia of Formosa which follows is constructed from Swinhoe's lists which were published originally by the Zoological Society, and reprinted by Alfred Russel Wallace in " Island Life "[1] with comments which are herewith reproduced.

List of the Mammalia of Formosa (The species peculiar to the island are printed in italics.)

1. *Macacus cyclopis.*—A rock monkey more allied to M. rhesus of India than to M. Sancti-johannis of South China.
2. *Pteropus formosus.*—A' fruit-bat closely allied to the Japanese species. None of the genus are found in China.
3. Vesperugo abramus.—China.
4. Vespertilio formosus.—Black and orange Bat. China.
5. Nyctinomus cestonii.—Large-eared Bat. China, S. Europe.
6. *Talpa insularis.*—A blind mole of a peculiar species.
7. Sorex murinus.—Musk Rat. China.
8. Sorex sp.—A shrew, undescribed.
9. Erinaceus sp.—A Hedgehog, undescribed.
10. Ursus tibetanus.—The Tibetan Bear. Himalayas and North China.
11. *Helictis subaurantiaca.*—The orange-tinted Tree Civet. Allied to H. nipalensis of the Himalayas more than to H. moschata of China
12. Martes flavigula, var.—The yellow-necked Marten, India, China.
13. Felis macroscelis.—The clouded Tiger of Siam and Malaya.
14. Felis viverrina.—The Asiatic wild Cat. Himalayas and Malacca.
15. Felis chinensis.—The Chinese Tiger Cat. China.
16. Viverricula malaccensis.—Spotted Civet China, India.
17. Paguma larvata.Gem-faced Civet. China.
18. *Sus taivanus.*—Allied to the wild Pig of Japan.
19. Cervulus reevesii.—Reeve's Muntjac. China.
20. *Cervus pseudaxis.*—Formosa Spotted Deer. Allied to C. sika of Japan.
21. *Cervus swinhoii.*—Swinhoe's Rusa Deer. Allied to Indian and Malayan species.
22. *Nemorhedus swinhoii* —Swinhoe's Goat-antelope. Allied to the species of Sumatra and Japan.

---

1. Pages 402 and 403 " Island Life " by Alfred Russel Wallace, Macmillan & Co., London and New York, 1895. This book has a chapter devoted to Japan and Formosa which will be found of great interest and value to those seeking information on the natural history of Formosa.

23. Bos Chinensis.—South China wild Cow.

24. Mus bandicota.—The Bandicoot Rat.   Perhaps introduced from India.

25. Mus indicus.—Indian Rat.

26. *Mus coxinga.*—Spinous Country-rat.

27. *Mus canna.*—Silken Country-rat.

28. *Mus losea.*—Brown Country-rat.

29. Sciurus castaneoventris—Chestnut-bellied Squirrel.   China and Hainan.

30. Sciurus m'clellandi.—M'Clelland's Squirrel.   Himalayas, China.

31. *Sciuropterus kaleensis.*—Small Formosan Flying Squirrel.   Allied to S. alboniger of Nepal.

32. *Pteromys grandis.*—Large Red Flying Squirrel.   Allied to Himalayan and Bornean species.   From North Formosa.

33. *Pteromys pectoralis.*—White-breasted Flying Squirrel.   From South Formosa.

34. Lepus sinensis.—Chinese Hare.   Inhabits South China.

35. Manis dalmanni.—Scaly Ant-eater.   China and the Himalayas.

Reviewing the above, Mr. Wallace comes to the following conclusion : " It is clear that before Formosa was separated from the mainland the above named animals or their ancestral types must have ranged over the intervening country as far as the Himalayas on the west, Japan on the north, and Borneo or the Philippines on the south ; and that after that event occurred, the conditions were so materially changed as to lead to the extinction of these species in what are now the coast provinces of China, while they or their modified descendants continued to exist in the dense forests of the Himalayas and the Malay Islands, and in such detached islands as Formosa and Japan.

The paper on the Land Birds of Formosa which is given in the appendix next preceding this, affords additional information confirming the observations of Mr. Wallace.

APPENDIX IV.

CLIMATE.

The climate of Formosa possesses some features which at first sight seem more than passing strange. It appears odd that one village may be bathed in brilliant sunshine day after day while another, at the same elevation and but ten miles distant, should be as continuously enveloped in clouds and rain. Again, we wonder that one third of the island should be blessed with a delightful summer with freedom from heavy rains; while another third, but a little over a hundred miles distant and practically at the same elevation, should be having its rainy season. Considering its very limited area, there are few lands that can show on one level such a variety of climatical conditions as exist on this one plain which extends, without break or obstruction, along the west coast of Formosa, from Tamsui in the north to Borio (Pangliao) in the far south.

The island also possesses varying climates to be found at the different elevations which increase in height until the great chain of mountains is reached with its Sylvia and Morrison (Niitakayama) peaks which share with Fujiyama of Japan the distinction of being the highest peaks in the Far East. On the lower levels we find plains of exuberant fertility with palms and tree ferns and the fruits of the tropics, the middle heights have a cooler atmosphere, and tropical plants gradually give way to those to those of hardier growth such as the camphor tree and small pines, while the summit of the range is clothed in heavy forests in which Chamaecyparis and Crytomerias predominate, and which in winter is frequently capped with snow. Unfortunately we are barred from an enjoyment of the invigorating climate of the mountains owing to the hostility of the savages who inhabit these regions.

There are three important factors in the climate of Formosa; namely, the south-west monsoon which blows from May until September, the north-east monsoon from November to April, and the Kurosiwo or Japan stream, which flows up the east coast of Formosa.

RAINFALL.

From May until November, during the south-west monsoon, the north of the island enjoys a pleasant climate with bright sunny days as a rule, and with refreshing showers which though frequent are generally, with the exception of typhoon storms, of but few hours duration. November is a month of contradictions. It is sometimes the most delightful month of the year, and again it is marked by cold cloudy days. December sees the north-east monsoon well under way, and as a result the weather is generally uncomfortable with cold drizzling rains broken now and then by a spell of pleasant weather. This condition continues until January or February, when it is not unusual to have fifteen or twenty days of unbroken mist and drizzle, a very unpleasant and depressing time for northern residents. April like November is a doubtful month; sometimes delightful with clear sunny days free from oppressive heat, and again a period of continuous rain fall.

Southern Formosa takes its pleasure while the north suffers. From November to April, during the north-east monsoon, the weather is mild, the air at times is even bracing, and showers are few, and of not long duration. This period is the most pleasant of the year, for in June with the south-west monsoon blowing the rains commence, and these are almost as constant and unpleasant, as those with which the north is assailed in winter. September generally witnesses a cessation of these rains, and the fall is, as in the north, the most pleasant time of the year. The railway when completed through the island, will afford, to those so fortunate as to be able to avail themselves of it, the means of enjoying a continual round of good weather. An establishment in Takow to which the northern resident could repair during the month or two of extremely disagreeable weather, would be a great boon.

The extreme north has a heavier rainfall than the south, due to the Kurosiwo or Japan stream. This current flows up along the east coast of Formosa, so close as to wash its shores and find an entrance into its harbors, and thence onwards towards Japan. The heated waters of this stream, which show a mean average temperature of some 80° Fah., load the air with a warm moisture which in winter is condensed by the action of the cold winds blowing down from the north-east, which come in contact with it in North Formosa or direct it towards the high hills where it is precipitated by their low temperatures. Frequently, when the humidity is not excessive and the monsoon winds are light, the hills landward from Kelung alone provoke condensation and this does not pass the range, with the result that Taihoku and even Suihen-kiaku (Suitengka) may enjoy a pleasant day while Kelung, but twenty miles distant from the former, and nine miles from the latter, is enveloped in rain.

Owing to this precipitation in Formosa, the wind passes over to the adjacent coast of China largely deprived of its moisture, with the result that the latter enjoys during the north-east monsoon comparatively bright and sunny weather. The China coast, however, has a lower winter temperature than Formosa districts in the same latitude, owing to the warmth which the latter receive from the Japan stream.

Kelung, Formosa, has the distinction of being one of the wettest places in the known world. There are stations in India, and one or two in central and south America, with a far heavier rainfall, but in the Far East it is not equalled. Kelung for the past five years has had a yearly average of 219 rainy days and over 150 inches of rain. The year 1901 was, however, an exceedingly dry year, and the average can be more correctly determined by including the records for the five years ending with 1900. This gives Kelung a yearly rainfall exceeding 158 inches.[1] In 1900 there were 242 rainy days and in 1898, 198 inches of rainfall. The wettest month recorded in Kelung for five years was November in 1898 with 26 rainy days out of 30, and a rainfall of 34.5 inches. The record for a day was September 30th, 1898, when 13.3 inches of rain fell. During January in 1900, rainy days were continuous for the whole month, the record standing at "31 days."

As regards Formosa, taken as a whole, there are very few places in the world with a greater average rainfall. Next to Kelung, Kosun (Hengchun) in the far south has the greatest rainfall, with a yearly average of 165 rainy days and over 91 inches of rainfall. Taihoku the capital follows with 188 rainy days and 88 inches of rain. Tainan is the driest spot, with but 104 rainy days and 58 inches of rainfall. This does not mean, however, that the latter city suffers from insufficient rainfall, as will be observed by comparing it with other places which are considered to possess ample rainfall.[1]

1. TABLE OF COMPARATIVE RAINFALL (INCHES) FOR THE WORLD.

(Formosan stations are printed in capital letters.)

Cherraponzee (India)	..	..	..	618
Maranhao (Brazil)	..	..	..	280
Vera Cruz (Mexico)	..	..	..	183
KELUNG	..	..	..	158
Caracas (Venezuela)	..	..	..	155
Solomon Islands (Coast station)		..	150
Buitenzorg (Java)	..	..	..	150
Cayenne (French Guiana)	..	..	108
Hongkong	..	..	..	96
Singapore	..	..	..	92
KOSHUN (HENGCHUN)	..	..	91
TAIHOKU	..	..	..	88
Sierra Leone	..	..	..	87
SOUTH CAPE	..	..	..	87
Naha (Loochoos)	..	..	..	85
Port Jackson (Australia)	..	..	82
Ceylon	..	..	..	77
Calcutta	..	..	..	76
Manila	..	..	..	76
TAKOW	..	..	..	74
TAICHU	..	..	..	73
Para	..	..	..	71
Swatow	..	..	..	65
Florida	..	..	..	62
San Juan (Porto Rico)	..	..	60
New Orleans	..	..	..	60
TAINAN	..	..	..	58

Bermuda	..	..	..	..	55
Kobe	..	..	..	..	55
Havana	..	..	..	..	52
Buenos Ayres	..	..	..	52
Fuchow	..	..	..	..	51
Sydney	..	..	..	..	49
Vancouver	..	..	..	47
Amoy	..	..	..	..	46
Shanghai	..	..	..	43
FISHER ISLAND (PESCADORES)	43
Canton	..	..	..	..	39
Honolulu	..	..	..	37
BOKOTO (PESCADORES)	..	..	36
Ayansk (Siberia)	..	..	35
Algiers	..	..	..	35
Pekin	..	..	..	..	27
London	..	..	..	..	25
Delhi	..	..	..	..	24
Berlin	..	..	..	..	24
Cape Town	..	..	..	23
Paris	..	..	..	..	22
San Francisco	..	..	..	22
Adelaide	..	..	..	..	21
Monterey (California)	..	..	12
Alexandria	..	..	..	10
Port Said	..	..	..	..	2

It is interesting to note that, although November is the wettest month in Kelung, averaging for the past five years 22 inches, Taihoku, but 20 miles distant, has during the same period found November the driest month but one in the year, the average rainfall being only 3 inches. The driest month in Kelung is July with 3 inches of rainfall. Taihoku has its heaviest rainfall during the month of August, when heavy summer down-pours, often preceding a typhoon, deluge the country. Tainan has its heaviest rains (18 inches) in August, and its lightest (0.6 inches) in January; Koshun its heaviest (28 inches) in June, and its lightest (0.4 inches) in December. In referring to the rainfall tables given below, it should be kept in mind, that though Kelung and Taihoku, especially the latter, show a rather steady monthly average of rainy days throughout the year, the nature of the rain varies much in winter and summer. The summer rains are as a rule very heavy but of short duration, frequently not exceeding an hour or so, and often scarcely obscuring the sun. They are as a rule refreshing showers cooling the air and are always welcome. In winter a rainy day is likely to mean 24 hours of drizzle, and this continues days at a time, while the actual rainfall is insignificant. Thus Taihoku with an average of 18 rainy days in November only recorded 3 inches of rain, or one inch every six days, whereas in August 16 rainy days resulted in 18 inches of rain, or more than an inch a day.

The heavy summer rainfalls of central and southern Formosa play havoc with communications. For the most of the year the mountain streams leading down from the great central range are with few exceptions but tiny rivulets almost lost in great dry river beds where water-washed boulders are so numerous that nearly every trace of soil is hidden. It requires but a few days of heavy rain, however, to transform these gentle rivulets into roaring, surging torrents which the rough bed over which they flow churns into spray and foam, and renders them even more wild and uncontrolable. In many places, when the stream is at its height, no boat is safe, and it is necessary to wait several days, or to make a long detour to reach a more favorable point, before travelers can cross and proceed on their way. These streams are generally without well formed channels and it is not uncommon for them during floods to seek new routes to the sea. The problem of controlling these waters and successfully bridging them without tremendous expenditure is one of the greatest problems which has been placed before the Japanese railway engineers.

GOVERNMENT RAINFALL TABLE FOR FORMOSA AVERAGE OF FIVE YEARS, 1897 TO 1901.

	Mean Depth of Rainfall (In Inches.)					Maximum Rainfall in a Day (In Inches.)					Rainy Days.					Monthly Rainfall at Kelung (In Inches.)						Rainy Days at Kelung.					
	Kelung	Taihoku	Taichu	Tainan	Koshun	Kelung	Taihoku	Taichu	Tainan	Koshun	Kelung	Taihoku	Taichu	Tainan	Koshun	1897	1898	1899	1900	1901	Mean	1897	1898	1899	1900	1901	Mean
Jan.	16.6	3.6	12.6	0.6	0.6	2.7	2.0	1.4	1.1	0.5	25.0	17.2	8.8	5.4	10.0		14.9	14.8	21.8	11.4	16.6		20	24	31	25	25.0
Feb.	10.8	6.4	4.2	2.7	2.2	2.0	2.2	2.2	3.9	3.7	18.5	17.6	12.6	6.2	9.2		13.0	10.6	10.0	9.7	10.8		14	18	22	20	18.5
Mar.	10.7	5.1	2.4	0.7	1.1	2.7	2.1	2.1	1.4	1.1	21.7	14.6	9.2	3.4	10.6		12.3	4.8	18.5	7.4	10.7		25	16	26	20	21.7
Apr.	8.8	6.0	4.6	2.4	1.2	3.1	3.6	4.2	4.0	2.2	18.2	16.6	10.4	6.4	6.6	8.15	7.9	14.7	6.0	7.3	8.8	14	19	21	20	17	18.2
May	6.9	7.2	9.3	4.5	6.3	2.8	5.3	4.9	2.3	1.4	16.2	13.6	10.6	9.4	11.0	6.72	5.7	9.3	6.6	6.2	6.9	15	13	18	16	19	16.2
June	9.8	10.1	14.9	14.9	28.1	4.0	6.2	6.8	6.2	10.7	17.2	16.0	17.6	16.6	19.2	6.69	14.9	10.5	11.9	5.4	9.8	17	18	17	20	14	17.2
July	3.3	9.1	9.5	9.2	11.4	6.7	4.1	5.3	6.0	5.9	7.4	12.6	14.4	13.8	21.4	1.41	0.7	1.9	9.1	3.6	3.3	8	2	6	10	11	7.4
Aug.	12.1	18.2	20.6	18.0	23.7	6.8	11.1	16.2	10.6	10.0	14.2	16.8	19.0	18.8	25.6	6.22	21.7	17.4	5.6	9.7	12.1	10	17	12	15	17	14.2
Sept.	14.4	10.9	5.0	2.8	5.7	13.1	8.2	11.5	4.1	5.0	13.4	13.1	6.4	7.6	13.6	12.44	16.2	17.4	16.1	9.9	14.4	16	6	13	17	15	13.4
Oct.	18.3	6.3	0.4	1.3	7.3	5.9	3.6	0.7	1.9	5.2	19.8	14.5	3.0	6.2	14.8	23.28	34.4	10.5	8.0	15.2	18.3	23	23	20	20	13	19.8
Nov.	22.7	3.4	0.8	1.0	3.7	5.2	2.2	1.5	1.2	3.0	24.8	18.1	6.8	6.4	13.6	20.07	34.5	31.7	19.5	7.8	22.7	25	26	26	22	25	24.8
Dec.	15.8	2.4	0.4	0.9	0.5	4.8	1.6	0.6	0.5	0.3	22.8	14.7	5.4	4.4	10.2	21.83	21.4	11.2	8.2	16.4	15.8	24	19	23	23	25	22.8
Total for year	150.8	88.3	73.5	58.6	91.9						219.2	188.4	124.2	104.6	165.8		197.9	158.8	141.7	110.4	150.8		202	214	242	221	219.2

In arriving at the number of rainy days at the various stations, all days on which more than one millimetre of rain fell are included. The average annual rainfall in Kelung for the five years ending with 1900 was 168 inches, which is considered more truly r-presentative than the rainfall for the past five years, which owing to an exceptionally dry year in 1901, brought the record down to a point below the usual average.

AIR TEMPERATURE.

In mean temperature the various stations in the Island do not show great difference. Koshun, the most southerly point, is 5° Fah. and Tainan 3° warmer than Taihoku in the north. In extremes of temperature the difference is more marked. Koshun experienced no cold greater than 49° and Tainan 37°, while Taihoku in the north witnessed a very few mornings when glistening crystals on the roof tiles denoted frost, with a minimum temperature of 31.6° recorded.

During these extreme cold spells, the "North Range" of hills in the vicinity of Tamsui, the highest peak of which is but 3638 feet above the sea, are occasionally capped with snow, and in February 1900, there were two days when the snow reached below the 2500 feet line. The highest hills of the interior are generally crested with snow on the coldest days.

The island is free from long periods of intense heat, though at certain times the humidity of the air makes even a moderately high temperature seem extreme. July is the hottest month with a mean temperature of 82.4° in both Taihoku and Tainan, and 81.7° in Koshun.

There are occasional days, however, excessively hot. The highest temperature recorded in the island in five years is 98.4° at Tainan, 97.7° at Taihoku, and only 92.10° in Koshun.[1] The mean maximum temperature has never, however, exceeded 91° for a month in the north, and 90.5° in the south. The nights are generally cool, and if one is so fortunate as to possess a well ventilated building with an upper storied bedroom, the heat will not generally disturb one's sleep. Even in the day time, if one possesses quarters which can be opened in all directions to the breeze, work can be carried on without feeling especial inconvenience from the heat.

Taihoku is slightly warmer than its neighboring city Kelung in summer, and a little colder in winter. It is also slightly warmer than Tamsui both in summer and winter by about 0.4°.

The range of temperature between the mean of the hottest month and that of the coldest month is as follows :—Taihoku from 82.4° to 56.7° or 25.7°; Taichu from 81.5° to 57.9° or 23.6°; Tainan from 82.4° to 60.6° or 21.8°, and Koshun in the extreme south 81.7 to 67.8° or only 13.9°. The figures given for Koshun appear to be almost identical with those of Havana, Cuba.

---

1. Shanghai, Ichang, Foochow, Amoy, and many other China points have recorded higher temperatures than any Formosa points.

GOVERNMENT TABLE OF AIR TEMPERATURE IN FORMOSA AVERAGE OF FIVE YEAR, 1897 TO 1901.

	Mean Temperature of Air. (Fahrenheit.)				Mean Maximum Temperature. (Fahrenheit.)				Mean Minimum Temperature. (Fahrenheit.)				Extremes of Maximum Temperature. (Fahrenheit.)				Extremes of Minimum Temperature (Fahrenheit.)			
	Taihoku.	Taichu.	Tainan.	Koshun.	Taihoku.	Taichu.	Tainan.	Koshun.	Taihoku.	Taichu.	Tainan.	Koshun.	Taihoku.	Taichu.	Tainan.	Koshun.	Taihoku.	Taichu.	Tainan.	Koshun.
January	60.4	61.5	63.9	68.0	66.6	70.7	75.6	76.6	56.3	55.2	56.7	64.8	83.3	82.0	84.0	85.1	43.7	39.1	42.3	51.0
February	56.7	57.9	60.6	67.8	62.4	66.2	72.5	74.7	51.8	52.0	53.4	62.4	81.0	81.7	85.3	83.8	31.6	30.2	37.4	49.0
March	62.6	64.8	67.3	72.5	69.4	73.4	79.0	79.5	57.7	58.6	59.5	67.1	85.5	87.1	89.6	89.1	46.9	48.6	46.8	56.1
April	68.9	71.8	74.5	76.6	75.7	80.1	84.7	83.8	63.7	65.7	66.7	71.6	94.6	92.9	92.7	89.6	48.4	54.1	54.7	62.2
May	76.1	77.7	79.7	80.2	83.5	85.6	88.5	87.3	70.0	71.4	72.7	74.7	97.7	94.3	93.2	91.8	54.3	59.9	50.9	65.8
June	79.0	79.5	80.8	80.4	86.7	87.1	88.5	85.8	73.2	73.9	73.0	76.1	96.4	93.7	94.6	91.9	62.2	62.2	67.8	65.5
July	82.4	81.5	82.4	81.7	81.0	89.4	90.5	87.3	75.6	75.2	76.1	76.6	97.2	93.7	94.4	94.1	67.1	70.0	71.8	69.6
August	81.5	80.8	81.5	80.4	89.1	88.3	89.1	86.0	75.9	76.0	76.7	76.1	93.5	94.3	97.9	91.4	71.4	71.4	71.4	70.3
September	78.4	79.3	81.0	80.1	83.5	88.0	90.6	86.9	62.9	73.2	74.1	75.0	96.3	95.0	97.0	90.5	62.4	65.1	65.8	65.7
October	78.6	75.0	76.6	77.5	80.4	84.2	86.0	83.8	68.0	68.5	69.8	73.2	93.8	92.1	94.5	89.6	54.7	54.8	61.0	65.8
November	67.6	68.9	66.9	73.8	73.4	78.8	81.0	70.2	63.8	62.4	63.5	60.8	87.8	89.0	95.4	87.6	45.0	44.4	47.5	54.0
December	61.9	63.1	69.1	70.8	68.7	73.9	77.2	76.1	56.8	55.8	57.7	65.4	83.7	84.7	90.7	80.5	41.2	39.9	48.0	55.4
Mean	70.7	71.8	73.6	75.0	77.7	80.4	83.7	82.2	65.5	66.7	71.1									

EARTHQUAKES.

Earthquakes are frequent in Formosa, but rarely severe. When we note that the island is of volcanic origin, and in the center of the volcanic chain, which includes Japan and the Philippines, two lands in which great earthquakes are frequent, the wonder is that Formosa is not more often disturbed. Signs of volcanic action are most apparent in the north of the island, and earthquakes have been responsible in comparatively late days for several rather extensive topographical changes. There are three craters in North Range between Tamsui and Kinpori (Kimpauli) of which North hill (Daitonzan) is the most extensive, ranging over 700 feet in diameter and some 400 feet in depth. This crater is sometimes filled with water, and is not as interesting as Mount Chikushi (Teck-ah-soan) (3,638 ft.) which is the highest peak of the North Range. The writer visited the latter in 1895, and found the crater abounding with sulphur springs, several of which were very active. There is also an interesting deposit of lava visible on the beach some twelve miles to the north east of Tamsui. It is reported on the authority of two foreigners who observed the phenomenon that, during the great earthquake of 1867, there was visible at sea, off Bush Island, Kelung, a column of water and steam which for a moment rose to a considerable height. The large quantity of pumice stone which has been washed upon the beach, and is sometimes seen floating at sea in the vicinity of Kelung, has given rise to the belief that there is possibly a submarine volcano off the port. Some 4 miles north of Toko (Tang-kang), South Formosa, a slight volcanic eruption occurred in September, 1902. From a newly formed crater only some thirty feet in diameter arose for several days dense smoke and hot mud was ejected, the latter doing some damage to the fields in the immediate vicinity. This is known as the Rigyo volcano. This is all evidence of the volcanic nature of the island, and it is a subject for congratulation that the more extensive convulsions are, evidently, of the past.

There are no records of any great destruction as the result of earthquakes. In 1867, during a severe earthquake, houses in Kelung, Kinpori (Kimpauli), Banka and other northern towns were destroyed, and some hundred persons were reported killed, and Kelung harbor was for a minute or so emptied of its water. It is difficult to account for this latter feature in any other way except as the result of some accompanying submarine convulsion.[1]

In 1881, a severe shock lasting 45 seconds caused some loss in life in Banka and destroyed several buildings. The late Dr. Mackay reports that at Kinpori some years ago a shock was felt and sulphurous water rose and covered certain rice fields which were found to have sunk three feet.

Of late years, though slight earthquakes have been frequently recorded, practically no damage has been done. The north with its volcanic hills seems most subject to these convulsions. During the past five years, 260 shocks have been recorded in Taihoku against 80 in Tainan and 11 at Koshun in the extreme south. This number includes many shocks which, though they do not escape the delicate instruments employed at the several government stations, are not otherwise perceptible.

NUMBER OF EARTHQUAKES IN FIVE YEARS.

Station.	Jan.	Feb.	Mar.	April.	May.	June.	July.	Aug.	Sept.	Oct.	Nov.	Dec.	Total.
Taihoku ..	19	17	19	27	25	16	16	26	29	21	18	27	260
Taichu ..	4	1	4	2	2	1	1	2	4	1	1	2	25
Tainan ..	8	2	4	12	7	5	12	9	6	2	8	5	80
Koshun ..	1	1	2	—	2	—	1	—	2	1	1	—	11
Total ..	32	21	29	41	36	22	30	37	41	25	28	34	376

WINDS.

The maximum records of wind velocity are interesting. Taihoku comes first with 97.3 miles an hour, Koshun second with 85.7, and Tainan and Taichu with 59.3 and 52.1 respectively. Bokoto, or the Pescadores Islands, which are dependencies of Formosa, have ex-

---

1. See page 187.

perienced a blow of 126.2 miles velocity or over 2 miles a minute, which as an official record is the highest but one ever obtained in the Far East, and is one of the highest in the world.[1]

These great winds are of course the records of destructive hurricanes. The Taihoku record is equal to a pressure of nearly 47 lbs. avoidupois on a square foot. In the case of the Bokoto record the pressure exceeded 60 lbs. These great storms, or typhoons as they are called, are one feature of the Formosan climate which is decidedly unpleasant. They never occur before May or later than November, and but rarely in May, June or November, while August and September seem to be the most likely months. There are generally four or sometimes five typhoons recorded in all Formosa a year, though generally only one storm is really severe. The storms seem to be most violent and destructive in the north of the island. With the exception of the damages to the fields, but little loss of life and property occurs in the south.[2]

Typhoons to northern residents seem much alike, and an account of the great typhoon of August, 1898, will suffice as a description of them all, though fortunately few of these great storms are as destructive of life and property as the one described.

The name Typhoon is generally believed to be a corruption of a Chinese word Ta-fung or "Great wind," and has come into general use as a term for the violent whirlwinds which are prevalent in the China seas.

A peculiar atmospheric condition which is generally noted by the skilled Chinese boatmen, and a falling barometer to the more scientific observers, give warning of the approach of a typhoon, and usually in sufficient time to permit foreign ships in harbor to make every thing fast, strengthen their moorings and effect other necessary preparations, and small Chinese boats to obtain perhaps more favorable anchorages, and larger native craft to alter their position or to run out lines to trees or other shore objects.

The great typhoon of 1898 was preceded by several days of steady rain as is frequently the case. The Tamsui river and tributary streams had risen considerably owing to the downpour, and on the sixth of August the barometer commenced to fall, the sky lowered and darkened, but at sunset lightened up slightly in the west with a few wierd yellow streaks which seemed to throw an unusual yellowish haze over the whole heavens. A dead oppressive stillness rudely broken at frequent intervals by strong gusts of wind completed an effect so peculiar that even an inexperienced observer like myself could not but feel that nature had for us some unusual event in store. The warning was not lost on the Chinese. They ran about with considerable show of consternation, crying out that the great wind was coming. All work along the river front came to a general stop. Even the shop keepers in the back streets put up their storm shutters and ceased business for the day. The large number of Chinese craft of various sizes which were tied up to the river front began to show much activity. The steam launches and smaller craft made for the several creeks in the neighborhood which offer typhoon shelter, large junks tried to improve matters by changing their

---

1. Other high wind velocities of which there is accurate record are as follows : —In Hongkong July 29th, 1895, during a typhoon there was recorded a velocity of 108 miles an hour. During the great storm which destroyed Galveston, Texas, a velocity of 86 miles was noted, and the observatory was then blown down. The wind was on the increase, however, and it is believed that it exceeded 100 miles an hour at the height of the storm. During the cyclone which visited St. Louis on May 27th., 1896, the wind velocity reached to 120 miles. The severest typhoon ever recorded in the East reached its greatest violence in the vicinity of Ishikakijima, of the Riukiu (Loochoo) group. For ten minutes a velocity at the rate of 156 miles was recorded, and then all further observations were put to an end by the destruction of the apparatus. This is the greatest velocity ever recorded in the East. With the exception of observations taken on high mountain peaks one of the highest records is 138 miles which was obtained at Cape Lookout, North Carolina, U.S.A., on August 18th., 1879. At this point the instruments were carried away by the gale, but it is believed that the wind reached to perhaps 160 or 165 miles. It should be noted that all Formosa observations are taken at stations on or near the sea level, whereas many foreign stations, notably some in the United States, are at a high elevation where the force of the wind is much greater than on the populated levels below. With this in consideration the Formosa velocity figures would need to be, in some instances, considerably increased to place them on an equal basis of comparison.

2. During the five years ending with 1901, the island was visited by 24 typhoons, as follows : —Twice in May, once in June, twice in July, eleven times in August, six times in September, twice in October and once in November. It is interesting to note that during these five years there has been yearly a typhoon during the first three days in August.

location, and making fast to any thing in the vicinity which promised a good hold. Some worked their way high up the river, others dropped down stream.

In an hour's time the river front was transformed from a scene of noisy activity to one of lonely quietude, with scarcely a boat to be seen. The gusts of wind were now more frequent, the velocity greater, and the river was gradually rising in height until at 8.30 p m. it had overflowed its banks. The Tamsui river flows in a north-westerly direction to the sea, and the wind which at this time was coming from the north-west was rapidly banking up the water and thus adding to the volume in the upper river. An hour later the winds were increasing in fury, and the water was now slowly entering the streets of Daitotei.

Formosa houses, in common with most Chinese buildings, are very badly constructed. Sun-dried mud brick is the favorite building material used, and even the more pretentious native establishments use these bricks for the main walls, with the addition of perhaps two or three brick pillars to help support the roof, or in the case of some houses which front on prominent streets, a facing of red brick or tile. A stone foundation extending up several feet above ground is expected to protect the buildings from ordinary floods, and such parts of the walls as are exposed are usually protected by flat tiles fastened with wooden pins, or by a covering of grass or plaster. If the terrific winds and rain tear down the tile facing or their coating of straw or plaster, the earth bricks are of course converted into mud again, with the natural result that the whole structure collapses. The use of so convenient and economical an article as mud seems to have appealed to Chinese builders in cases where substantial structures were desired and paid for, and the storm disclosed mud to the astonished owner where there should have been lime or cement, and mud where there should have been even brick or stone.

By midnight the flood had reached out over the low lands in every direction, and spread through the streets of Daitotei, entering the lower floor of the houses and stirring godown men and store keepers into activity that their goods might be removed to upper stories or piled up on hastily constructed staging, and thus temporarily at least out of danger from the water. Every building in the place trembles and creaks with the great wind, and the lighter frame structures may almost be said to rock. The storm continued to increase in volume until 4 in the morning when it appeared to be at its height. The situation then was alarming. The river had risen 22.4 feet above normal, and the wind was blowing with a velocity exceeding 71 miles an hour in Taihoku and over 97 miles in Kelung. The principal street in Daitotei was under 6 feet of water, and other places less favorably situated 10 to 14 feet. The water was up level with the roofs of most of the small Chinese structures, and in the larger upper storied structures there was from 4 to 8 feet on the ground floor. A half dozen or so houses situated on a narrow elevated strip which extends for a few blocks through the center of the city had but a foot or so of water in their compounds. The streets of Taihoku were nearly all under water ranging from 1 to 3 feet.

The most alarming feature of the storm at Daitotei was the great rapidity with which the water was running. The first street back from the river was a swift, noisy, torrent with a current so strong that one could not stand against it, while on the river front a terrific sea was running, and great waves were picked up bodily by the wind and thrown against the buildings with a force which would appear beyond the power of a mere flooded river. No boat could live in that sea, and many Chinese craft which broke from their fastenings were swamped, others driven up among the submerged houses, and many of the larger junks were carried far into the fields. The cries of the unfortunate sailors were sometimes heard above the storm, but assistance was impossible. The noise was a terrible feature itself, and subjected one to constant alarm. The rain was carried along by the gale with a force that sounded as though the house was being bombarded with pebbles, and each blast of wind seemed more fierce than the one that preceded it. Added to this, the rush of wild waters which one could not only hear but often feel as they dashed up against the building, and the occasional alarming crash as a neighboring structure was dashed to the ground, while one wondered if his own habitation would be the next to succumb; all tended to put one in a condition of mental torture not pleasant to anticipate.

After 4 a.m. the barometer began to rise slowly, and the wind which had veered around to the west, and later to the south, now commenced to blow from the south-east and with less force. Released from the pressure of a head wind, the water commenced to slowly recede, and by 6 a.m. it was evident that the typhoon had passed by, and that the strain was at an end. The river was still unfavorable for boats, and save for steam launches, remained so for much of the day, but the water in the streets was running quietly, and numerous boats were brought out and paddled here and there. At 7 o'clock the wind had quieted down into a light and steady blow, and the sun seemed striving to pierce the dense clouds which hung over the city. At noon nearly all the principal streets were cleared of water, though there was some one or two feet or more on the lower levels.

The great ruin and devastation, the work of the storm, was now fully apparent. The largest damage had been done in the lower levels of Daitotei. Many houses had been cut off by the high water during the night; and the shrieks of the occupants had been heard by those living on higher ground, but rescue was then impossible, and now that the water had receded it was in most cases too late, the unfortunates having been either carried out to sea or crushed under the heavy masses of mud-brick and tiles. Hundreds of Chinese who had fled from their houses and sought shelter in the higher districts returned to their houses only to find them totally destroyed. With no roof to shelter, one found them, men women and children prowling about the wreckage, sad and disheartened, and in many places they were gathered about the dead body of a relative or friend which had with difficulty been recovered from the ruins. Over 50 bodies were found buried in the wreckage the first day.

The buildings occupied by foreigners had with two exceptions all received some damage. One large foreign establishment on the bund had been deprived of its roof and rendered otherwise uninhabitable, and the building occupied by the writer was razed to the ground, though fortunately the collapse did not occur until the water had receded, and it had been possible for the occupants to remove by boat to a neighbor's house near by. Every sea wall along the river front had been destroyed, and foreigners had their verandas carried away, and some suffered considerable loss through damaged tea, etc. Many upper storied large Chinese buildings were destroyed, and the ordinary run of Chinese houses were down in some streets for blocks. Over 800 houses were destroyed and about half that number badly damaged. Within the walls of the capital Taihoku (Taipeh) the damage was not so great as the land is higher; still 71 houses were totally destroyed, 93 were badly damaged, and 10 Japanese lost their lives and 11 were badly injured. In Banka, out of 1,024 houses submerged, 529 were totally destroyed and 271 badly damaged while the number of bodies recovered from the ruins numbered 30 dead, and 130 persons received severe injuries. In upper Kelung harbor the water had risen over 6 feet and many buildings were partially submerged. There were 30 houses destroyed including Japanese barracks and government railway buildings, and 40 were badly damaged. The S. S. *Enoshima-maru* which had arrived in the harbor two days before, lost both anchors during the typhoon, and while running for the open sea, stranded on the rocks near the entrance and became a total wreck. Other towns in the vicinity of the capital suffered severely, and near Shinchiku (Teckcham) a steel railway bridge was swept from its piers and carried along the river bed for nearly one hundred feet, a striking example of the great force of the gale.

The total loss in Taihoku district was 2,075 houses totally destroyed, and 993 houses damaged and rendered temporarily uninhabitable. Bodies numbering more than 180 were recovered from the ruins, but as the largest number of dead were swept out to sea, the total will never be known, but was believed to have exceeded 400. The number of injured receiving medical treatment totalled some 160.

The losses in native shipping were very heavy. Many junks were destroyed, and others carried so far into the fields that they had to be abandoned and were eventually sold as old wood. Junks not far from the river were brought down into their element again, by digging canals leading from them to the channel. The crops of entire fields were in some places swept away, and in others buried under mud and sand.

No damage was on this occasion done to the shipping at Tamsui. As a rule steamers at anchor there during typhoons pass an extremely anxious time of it. The river frequently runs at a rate of over 10 knots, and steamers find it necessary to steam full speed against the current to avoid carrying away their moorings. Even in this they have not always been successful, and it has on a few occasions been necessary to beach a vessel in order to save her.

Some months were required to repair the streets, and remove the last signs of the damage done by this great storm. The total financial loss was a very large one. The recuperative power, however, of the Chinese is great, and in a few weeks new buildings exhibiting the same shoddy, ruinous construction were being erected, and with mud quite as strong a favorite as a substitute for lime as before. My present landlord has reconstructed his sea-wall four times in four successive years," and the "possibility of rebuilding it again the present year seems excellent. "Experience may be the best teacher," but it is apparently a very inefficient one when Chinese landlords are the scholars.

GOVERNMENT TABLE OF WIND VELOCITY AND ATMOSPHERIC PRESSURE IN FORMOSA, AVERAGE FOR FIVE YEARS, 1897 TO 1901.

	Mean Velocity of Wind (Miles per hour).				Extremes of Maximum Velocity of Wind (Miles per hour).			
	Taihoku.	Taichu.	Tainan.	Koshun.	Taihoku.	Taichu.	Tainan.	Koshun.
January	11.0	8.0	11.6	13.4	34.0	30.0	34.2	42.0
February	9.2	7.6	12.7	13.2	34.0	34.7	36.7	39.8
March	11.6	6.9	11.4	12.1	35.1	24.4	44.7	35.6
April	10.7	6.3	9.4	11.0	34.2	25.9	40.0	34.4
May	8.7	4.9	8.3	9.8	42.0	23.9	33.1	85.7
June	7.8	5.8	8.0	9.8	30.0	30.4	38.0	45.9
July	7.4	5.4	8.5	8.9	40.5	30.2	44.5	38.7
August	10.1	5.8	9.4	9.4	97.3	52.1	53.5	67.8
September	8.9	6.0	8.0	7.6	80.1	50.5	42.9	40.5
October	12.5	6.5	8.9	11.9	71.8	49.7	59.3	52.1
November	12.3	7.2	10.1	16.3	84.7	45.0	44.7	49.4
December	11.0	7.4	11.4	15.4	32.4	37.6	46.1	50.1
Mean	10.1	6.3	9.8	11.6	—	—	—	—

STRONGEST WIND, ITS DIRECTION AND DATE.

Station.	Velocity.	Direction.	Date.
Taihoku	97.3 miles	E.	5th August, 1899.
Taichu	52.1 miles	NNE.	23rd August, 1899.
Tainan	59.3 miles	SSW.	1st October, 1897.
Koshun	85.7 miles	S.	20th May, 1901.

ATMOSPHERIC PRESSURE.

	Mean Pressure of Atmosphere (In Inches.)				The Extreme of Minimum Pressure of Atmosphere recorded each month for five years.			
	Taihoku.	Taichu.	Tainan.	Koshun.	Taihoku.	Taichu.	Tainan.	Koshun.
January	30.13	30.05	30.06	30.04	29.76	29.56	29.78	29.77
February	30.12	30.04	30.03	30.02	29.56	29.54	29.52	29.56
March	30.05	29.99	29.99	29.98	29.74	29.61	29.72	29.76
April	29.95	29.90	29.90	29.90	29.68	29.57	29.69	29.61
May	29.83	29.80	29.81	29.82	29.44	29.40	29.52	29.38
June	29.72	29.71	29.72	29.74	29.27	29.25	29.28	28.82
July	29.72	29.72	29.72	29.74	29.23	29.98	29.33	29.33
August	29.67	29.65	29.67	29.69	28.75	28.45	28.59	28.76
September	29.82	29.77	29.77	29.79	29.92	28.66	28.75	28.93
October	29.96	29.87	29.87	29.88	29.15	29.11	29.12	29.35
November	30.05	29.95	29.95	29.94	29.58	29.43	29.44	29.73
December	30.15	30.04	30.04	30.03	29.84	29.71	29.78	29.78
Mean	29.93	29.87	29.88	29.88	28.75	28.45	28.59	28.76

METEOROLOGICAL STATISTICS OF THE GOVERNMENT STATION ON BOKOTO (PANGHOO)
ISLAND OF THE PESCADORE GROUPS FOR A PERIOD OF FIVE YEARS, 1897-1901.

Month.	Mean Depth of Rainfall (In Inches).	Maximum Rainfall in a Day (In Inches).	Mean Rainy Days.	Mean Temperature of Air (Fahrenheit).	Mean Maximum Temperature (Fahrenheit).	Mean Minimum Temperature (Fahrenheit).	Extremes of Maximum Temperature (Fahrenheit).	Extremes of Minimum Temperature (Fahrenheit).	Number of Earthquakes.	Mean Velocity of Wind (Miles per hour).	Extremes of Maximum Velocity of Wind.	Mean Pressure of Atmosphere (Inches).	The Extreme of Minimum Pressure of Atmosphere recorded each month for five years.
January ..	0.8	1.7	5 8	61.7	66.0	56.8	82.0	49.5	1	31.5	65.3	30.09	29.76
February ..	2.2	2.5	8.4	58.3	62 4	55.0	80.2	45.1	—	30.9	71.1	30.07	29 55
March	1.3	0.9	7.4	64.6	69.3	61.2	83.3	52.2	2	25.0	70.5	30.01	29.75
April	2.5	1.6	8.4	72.0	76.5	68.2	87.4	56.5	1	22.8	58 6	29.92	29.70
May	4.5	6.9	8.0	77.5	82.2	73.9	88.2	62 5	2	14.5	57.0	29.82	29.41
June	5.9	5.1	13.2	79.9	84.4	76.5	90.5	67.6	2	14.5	59.5	29.72	29.38
July	4.2	4.9	7.0	82 2	86.9	78.6	91.4	73.4	—	11.6	48.1	29.73	39.38
August.. ..	11.5	11.7	13.8	81.5	86.2	77.9	91.9	71.6	--	15.0	107.8	29.67	28 60
September ..	1.6	2.8	3.6	80.4	85 8	77.2	92.3	72.1	3	20 4	126.2	29.79	28.83
October ...	1.0	1.0	5.0	75.9	79.5	73.2	90.5	68.0	—	31.5	109.6	29.90	29.02
November ..	1.0	1.1	6.4	70.2	73.9	67.5	87.8	55.4	1	35 8	73.1	29.98	29.48
December ..	0.4	0.7	4.2	64.6	68.5	61.9	81.5	54.7	—	33.8	68.7	30.07	29.87
	Greatest.	Total.	Mean.	Mean.	Mean.	Highest.	Lowest.	Total.	Mean.	Strongest.	Mean.	Lowest in 5 years.	
	36.9	11.7	91.2	72.3	77.0	69.1	92.3	45.1	12	23.9	126.2	29.90	23.60

STRONGEST WIND, ITS DIRECTION AND DATE.

Station.	Velocity.	Direction.	Date.
Bokoto	126.2 miles.	N.	30th September, 1898.

INDEX.

8 INDEX.

明治參拾六年壹月二十二日印刷

明治參拾六年壹月二十五日發行

著作權所有

　　　　　　　　臺北廳大稻埕庄
著作權者　　　　北米合衆國領事
　　　　　　　　ビームス、ダブリユー、
　　　　　　　　　　　　デビッドソン

著作兼發行者　　神奈川縣横濱市山下町十番地
　　　　　　　　エス、エッチ、ソマルトン

印刷者

發行所　　　　　神奈川縣横濱市山下町十番地
　　　　　　　　ジヤパン、ガゼット新聞社

CPSIA information can be obtained at www.ICGtesting.com
Printed in the USA
BVOW05s0417310713

327426BV00004B/49/P

9 781432 640040